T0330975

Technology Transfer, Foreign Direct Investment, and the Protection of Intellectual Property in the Global Economy

World Scientific Studies in International Economics
(ISSN: 1793-3641)

World Scientific Studies in International Economics includes works dealing with the theory, empirical analysis, and evaluation of international economic policies and institutions, with topics covering international macroeconomics and finance, international trade theory and policy, as well as international legal and political economy. Monographs and edited volumes will comprise the core of the publications.

Vol. 82 *Technology Transfer, Foreign Direct Investment, and the Protection of Intellectual Property in the Global Economy*
edited by Kamal Saggi (Vanderbilt University, USA)

Vol. 81 *Globalization, Firms, and Workers*
edited by Ann E. Harrison (University of California, Berkeley, USA) & Keith E. Maskus (University of Colorado Boulder, USA)

Vol. 80 *Foundational Essays in Immigration Economics*
by George J. Borjas (Harvard University, USA)

Vol. 79 *Firms and Workers in a Globalised World: Larger Markets, Tougher Competition*
by Gianmarco I. P. Ottaviano (Bocconi University, Italy)

Vol. 78 *Broadening Trade Theory: Incorporating Market Realities into Traditional Models*
by James Markusen (University of Colorado, Boulder, USA)

Vol. 77 *Economic Effects of Antidumping*
edited by Thomas J. Prusa (Rutgers University, USA)

Vol. 76 *Policy Analysis and Modeling of the Global Economy: A Festschrift Celebrating Thomas Hertel*
edited by Peter Dixon (Victoria University, Australia),
Joseph Francois (University of Bern, Switzerland) &
Dominique van der Mensbrugghe (Purdue University, USA)

Vol. 75 *Competition, Innovation and Trade*
edited by Larry D. Qiu (Lingnan University, Hong Kong)

Vol. 74 *Understanding the Implications of Trade and Financial Market Integration for Business Cycles*
edited by Mario J. Crucini (Vanderbilt University, USA)

The complete list of the published volumes in the series can be found at
https://www.worldscientific.com/series/wssie

82 World Scientific Studies in International Economics

Technology Transfer, Foreign Direct Investment, and the Protection of Intellectual Property in the Global Economy

Editor

Kamal Saggi

Vanderbilt University, USA

World Scientific

NEW JERSEY • LONDON • SINGAPORE • BEIJING • SHANGHAI • HONG KONG • TAIPEI • CHENNAI • TOKYO

Published by

World Scientific Publishing Co. Pte. Ltd.
5 Toh Tuck Link, Singapore 596224
USA office: 27 Warren Street, Suite 401-402, Hackensack, NJ 07601
UK office: 57 Shelton Street, Covent Garden, London WC2H 9HE

Library of Congress Control Number: 2023028645

British Library Cataloguing-in-Publication Data
A catalogue record for this book is available from the British Library.

World Scientific Studies in International Economics — Vol. 82
TECHNOLOGY TRANSFER, FOREIGN DIRECT INVESTMENT, AND THE PROTECTION OF INTELLECTUAL PROPERTY IN THE GLOBAL ECONOMY

ISBN 978-981-3233-01-0 (hardcover)
ISBN 978-981-3233-02-7 (ebook for institutions)
ISBN 978-981-3233-03-4 (ebook for individuals)

For any available supplementary material, please visit
https://www.worldscientific.com/worldscibooks/10.1142/10789#t=suppl

Desk Editors: Nandha kumar/Kura Sunaina

Typeset by Stallion Press
Email: enquiries@stallionpress.com

Printed in Singapore

Dedicated to
Rupi, Neha, and Kunaal

About the Editor

Kamal Saggi is the Frances and John Downing Family Professor of Economics at Vanderbilt University. He has held visiting appointments at Stanford University, the University of New South Wales, and the World Bank. After receiving his Ph.D. in Economics in 1995 from the University of Pennsylvania, Dr. Saggi joined the faculty at Southern Methodist University where he was named the Dedman Distinguished Collegiate Professor of Economics in 2007. Since 2010, Dr. Saggi has been on the faculty of Vanderbilt University, where he currently also serves as Associate Provost for Faculty Affairs. Dr. Saggi has held several other major administrative appointments at Vanderbilt including the Chair of the Department of Economics and the Dean of Faculty in the College of Arts and Science. He has published extensively in the fields of international trade and economic development. Much of his research is centered on two major themes: (i) the inter-relationships between foreign direct investment, innovation, and the protection of intellectual property rights in the global economy and the (ii) legal and economic underpinnings of the multilateral trading system.

About the Editor

Acknowledgments

My interest in the topics covered in this volume goes back decades, if not more. Indeed, my senior undergraduate thesis at Ohio Wesleyan written over 30 years ago was focused on the complex and politically charged relationship between multinational companies and developing countries. My doctoral dissertation at Penn had two main themes. First, it studied the role technology licensing and foreign direct investment (FDI) play in the international transmission of knowledge. Second, it investigated the effects that the degree of protection provided by national governments to intellectual property rights (IPRs) has on FDI and innovation in the world economy. Due to differences in economic conditions and technological capabilities across countries, international tensions frequently arise during discussions of these issues at multilateral institutions and in the public domain at large. Having been born and raised in India—a country that has often been at the forefront of the international debate regarding IPRs—these contentious issues have always been of intense personal and intellectual interest to me.

During graduate school, three teachers played a formative role in shaping my thinking and skill set as a professional economist: my dissertation advisor Bill Ethier, and the two other equally indispensable members of my committee—Gene Grossman and Howard Pack. Never one to waste unnecessary energy on lengthy conversations, Bill taught me a great deal simply by being who he is: a man of great intellectual integrity, possessing a scathing wit and a uniquely original mind. From Gene, I learned that one must always strive to take on big questions and be prepared to make the intellectual investment necessary for addressing them adequately, a challenge that I am forever struggling to meet. Gene's astounding productivity, the elegance of his modeling and prose, and his remarkable work ethic continue to be a source of constant inspiration to many like myself. In his inimitable style, Howard taught me that it is not enough to have a mathematically rigorous modeling approach to an important question; an economist must always take empirical evidence seriously or risk being irrelevant. Howard's dry humor and his constant "so what?" refrain made our collaboration especially fun while also increasing the likely impact of our joint work.

While many co-authors have contributed to my work, my definitive collaboration in the domain covered by this volume has undoubtedly been with Amy Glass. Conversations that began in a cramped office in the physically dreary but intellectually vibrant McNeil building on Penn campus, continued for well over a decade. The work that resulted from these conversations ended up providing a firm foundation for both our academic careers. My good friend Ping Lin has been a valuable collaborator since my early days as an Assistant Professor at Southern Methodist University (SMU). Our joint work on multinational firms and market structure has deepened my understanding of the interface between international trade and industrial organization. Nikos Vettas, a friend and mentor from graduate school days, has taught me a great deal about economics and his unique brand of ultra-dry humor has been an added bonus. Lee Branstetter and I enjoyed a rather efficient collaboration on two papers exploring the effects of IPR protection on FDI. His energy and professional commitment were key drivers of our joint work. Santanu Roy and I started working on the economics of parallel import policies toward the end of my working years at SMU. The close friendship that developed between us due to this collaboration has enriched the lives of both our families. Since moving to Vanderbilt in 2010, I have had the pleasure of collaborating with Rick Bond on some fundamental questions related to the compulsory licensing of patents. Rick is well known in the profession for his insightful mind and thoughtfulness and I am fortunate to have him as a colleague. Former Vanderbilt graduate student and ongoing collaborator Difei Geng has played a key role in developing our joint research agenda on external reference pricing and IPRs.

As I noted in the previous collection of my papers titled *Economic Analysis of the Rules and Regulations of the World Trade Organization* published by World Scientific in 2018, decades of academic research have demanded sacrifices not just on my part but also on the part of my family. My professional success, such as it is, rests on the love and unwavering support of three irreplaceable individuals: my parents Yashpal and Chander Kanta Saggi and my wife Rupi Saggi. They have been there for me every step of the way, and I thank them whole-heartedly. I also owe a special thanks to my wonderfully good-natured twins Kunaal and Neha for generously putting up with their nerdy Dad and his lame attempts at humor all these years! My siblings—Sabodh, Naveen, and Meenakshi—have always been in my corner, adding joy and a deep sense of security to my life.

Finally, I would like to thank all my co-authors and the following publishers for granting the permissions necessary for re-producing the chapters in this book: American Economic Association, Blackwell Publishers, Cambridge University Press, Elsevier, John Wiley, Oxford University Press, Springer, and the World Bank.

Contents

Part 1

Channels of International Technology Transfer

Chapter 1

International technology transfer and the technology gap[#]

Amy Jocelyn Glass [a,*], Kamal Saggi [b,1]

[a] *Department of Economics, The Ohio State University, 1945 North High Street, Columbus, OH 43210-1172, USA*

[b] *Department of Economics, Southern Methodist University, Dallas, TX 75275-0496, USA*

Received 28 February 1996; accepted 30 November 1996

Abstract

We build a quality ladders product cycle model that explores how the quality of technology transferred through foreign direct investment (FDI) is linked to innovation and imitation when the absorptive capacity of LDCs is limited. Successful imitation of low quality levels makes FDI involving high quality levels possible through reduction of the technology gap. A subsidy to imitation or a tax on low quality FDI production encourages imitation relative to innovation, thus releasing the constraint faced by foreign firms seeking to produce in the South. These forces that stimulate high-quality FDI raise Southern welfare through lower prices, faster innovation and higher wages. © 1998 Elsevier Science B.V.

JEL classification: F12; F23; F43; O14; O19; O31; O38

Keywords: R&D; Innovation; Imitation; Foreign direct investment; Technology transfer; Technology gap; Appropriate technology

1. Introduction

Countries frequently rely on successful assimilation of foreign technology to achieve indigenous technological development. For example, in the initial phases

* Corresponding author. Tel.: +1-614-292-1149; fax: +1-614-292-3906; e-mail: glass.29@osu.edu.

[1] Tel.: +1-214-768-3274; fax: +1-214-768-1821; e-mail: ksaggi@mail.smu.edu.

This chapter was originally appeared in *Journal of Development Economics* **55**, 369–398. © 1998 Elsevier Science B.V.

of development, much of the R&D undertaken in Japan was absorptive, aimed at integrating foreign technologies (Blumenthal (1976)). [2] More recently, countries such as Mexico, Brazil, India, and China view foreign direct investment (FDI) by firms from technologically advanced countries as a vehicle of technology transfer. However, a common fear of many such developing countries is that local affiliates of foreign firms may not transfer the latest technologies from their parent firms. [3]

Empirical evidence indicates that such fears are not unfounded; multinational firms generally transfer technologies that, despite being more advanced than indigenous technologies, still lag behind the state-of-the-art (Mansfield and Romeo (1980)). What determines how much FDI from industrialized countries to developing countries transfers state-of-the-art technologies?

Multinationals often transfer older technologies to safeguard themselves against future competition. While strategic considerations play a role in determining the quality of technology transferred by multinationals in some situations, the limited absorptive capacity of such countries must act as a constraint on the ability of foreign firms to transfer state-of-the-art technologies in other situations. In a seminal work, Teece (1976) demonstrated that the costs of technology transfer are substantial and decline with the age of the technology being transferred (Kumar (1994) provides more recent evidence). In countries that lag significantly behind the technology frontier, difficulties inherent in transferring state-of-the-art technology likely outweigh strategic considerations. Countries that are too backward to host frontier technologies are plausibly also too backward to provide much threat of real competition.

In this paper, we build a general equilibrium model that accounts for the limited ability of developing countries to host FDI that transfers state-of-the-art technologies. Our model links the quality of technology transferred through FDI to the technology gap between the countries, as determined by the rate of imitation relative to innovation. Our paper is unique in determining the degree that technology transferred to LDCs through FDI from DCs lags behind the state-of-the-art in a setting where innovation and imitation respond to profit incentives and FDI from the advanced North to the lagging South occurs only slightly ahead of the Southern technology frontier. This limitation on FDI makes the quality of technology transferred through FDI for each product react to the size of the technology gap between the North and the South for that product.

Local R&D in the South (imitation), by shrinking the technology gap, permits FDI to transfer more advanced technologies while local R&D in the North (innovation), by expanding the technology gap, limits FDI to transferring more primitive technologies relative to the state-of-the-art. Thus the quality of technol-

[2] See Pack and Saggi (1997) for an overview of the relationship between imported technology and domestic technological development.

[3] See the United Nations' (1992) *World Investment Report*.

ogy transferred relative to the state-of-the-art depends upon the incentives for imitation relative to innovation. Specifically, the extent of high-quality FDI depends on such parameters influencing the incentives for imitation relative to innovation as the share of income spent on high quality levels, the cost disadvantage of multinationals relative to Southern firms, the resource requirement in innovation relative to imitation, and Northern resources relative to Southern resources.

What policies can the government of a potential host LDC implement to attract FDI from DCs that transfers state-of-the-art technologies? A host country can encourage high-quality FDI by encouraging domestic R&D activities that push forward the local technology frontier and thus make high-quality FDI more attractive to source country firms. This task can be accomplished either by a tax on low-quality multinational production or a subsidy to imitation. Are such policies welfare improving? Product market prices decline, the rate of innovation accelerates and the Southern wage rises with the extent of high-quality FDI in the South, so these policies do improve Southern welfare. Our welfare results show that the Southern government does indeed desire a higher quality mix of FDI, thus ruling out the possibility that policies promoting high-quality FDI might reduce Southern welfare through adversely affecting the rate of innovation.

Our work springs from the extended literature examining the relationship between international trade and the quality of products such as Segerstrom et al. (1990). We build on the quality ladders product cycle model of Grossman and Helpman (1991) to address the South's limited ability to host FDI. First, following Glass and Saggi (1995), Northern firms can locate production in the South through FDI. [4] Second, following Glass (1997), two different quality levels of each product sell in equilibrium due to consumer heterogeneity, so FDI can involve production of high or low quality levels, distinguishing whether the technology transferred through FDI lags behind the state-of-the-art. [5] Third, the South hosts high-quality FDI only if indigenous firms have the knowledge to produce the low quality level of that product. The setup of our model is appropriate for a country that lags sufficiently behind the technology frontier to have difficulty hosting state-of-the-art FDI. [6]

While Glass and Saggi (1995) and Glass (1997) do share some features with our current paper, the issues differ substantially. In Glass and Saggi (1995), we analyze how innovation responds to an increase in the flow of FDI from the North

[4] To simplify analysis, FDI occurs immediately after innovation, not after a lag.

[5] The South never catches up to the North for any product, as in the inefficient Southern followers equilibrium.

[6] For countries that slightly lag behind the technology frontier, a one quality level model such as Glass and Saggi (1995) would be more appropriate, as these countries should be able to host state-of-the-art FDI.

to the South when Southern firms can imitate both Northern firms and multinationals. In our current paper, we analyze how FDI promotes the ability of Southern firms to imitate, which in turn shrinks the technology gap and thus promotes the South's ability to host FDI that transfers superior technologies. Glass and Saggi (1995) is relevant to more advanced Southern countries, countries capable of imitating the state-of-the-art technology even in the absence of the knowledge spillovers from FDI. Our current paper is relevant to more backward Southern countries, countries incapable of imitating the state-of-the-art technology even in the presence of the knowledge spillovers from FDI. Glass (1997) analyzes how relative resources, relative R&D efficiency and R&D subsidies affect Southern market penetration, the quality mix of Southern production. In our current paper, we address how these forces, plus multinational cost disadvantage and multinational production taxes, affect the quality mix of FDI. Since FDI does not occur in Glass (1997) and only one quality level sells in Glass and Saggi (1995), neither of those papers determines the quality mix of FDI.

Our model generalizes the results of Flam and Helpman (1987), Stokey (1991) and Glass (1997), where Northern production involves a higher quality mix than Southern production, to determine the quality mix of multinational production. Like the existing models, we determine the size of the technology gap between the North and the South. Additionally, we link the quality of technology transferred through FDI to the magnitude of the technology gap. FDI transfers technology to the South that is on average below the Northern technology frontier but above the Southern technology frontier. Thus, multinational production occurs in a range of quality levels with an average quality level between pure Northern production and pure Southern production.

International technology transfer occurs through multiple channels in our model. First, innovation makes old technology obsolete—available as a knowledge base to attract low-quality FDI. As Northern firms innovate and push forward the quality frontier, the knowledge required for producing the previous low quality level becomes discarded technology, no longer capable of generating profits. [7] When innovation occurs in markets where a large technology gap limits FDI to low quality levels, the previous low quality level becomes discarded technology available to the South. [8] Consequently, the previous state-of-the-art becomes the

[7] That discarded technology acts as a form of technology transfer is argued in Glass (1997). Some very poorly developed countries may lack the ability to absorb even discarded technologies. For the purposes of this paper, we are interested in the group of LDCs that do attract FDI (and thus must be able to absorb discarded technologies), but FDI that transfers technology below the state-of-the-art.

[8] When innovation occurs in markets with high-quality FDI, the previous low-quality level becomes discarded technology but the technology was already produced by a Southern firm. No technology is transferred through FDI in that case as the new (relatively) low quality level produced through FDI is the same technology in absolute terms as the previous high quality level produced through FDI.

new low quality level and production in the South becomes attractive thanks to discarded technology providing the necessary knowledge foundation. Even though FDI remains limited to the low quality level (relative to the state-of-the-art), a better technology is transferred through FDI since the state-of-the-art has risen.

Second, imitation upgrades the knowledge base in the South and consequently expands the South's absorptive capacity so that FDI in high quality levels of products becomes feasible. Katrak (1989), Kokko (1994), and Siddharthan (1992) all provide empirical evidence showing technology transfer through FDI and domestic R&D investment are complementary activities. Shifting production to the South lowers production costs but not all the way down to the production costs of potential Southern rivals. The theory of FDI according to Markusen (1995) supports the idea that multinationals are disadvantaged relative to native firms due to operating in an unfamiliar environment. We link this cost disadvantage of multinationals to the difference between the technology to be transferred and the present technological ability of the host country. In situations where the Southern technology frontier is far behind the potential technology to be transferred through FDI, Northern firms find shifting their production to the South prohibitively expensive due to the magnitude of the technology gap. However, as the technology gap shrinks, multinational production using state-of-the-art technology in the South becomes attractive as production costs fall due to the lessened expenses from bridging the technology gap. In this manner, imitation investments by Southern firms promote technology transfer by providing the technological base needed to attract FDI.

Our model examines the dynamics of FDI and the interplay between FDI, imitation and technology transfer. We introduce dynamic links between imitation and technology transfer. In particular, our model specifies links between initial low quality FDI, low quality imitation, and subsequent high-quality FDI, thus capturing the dynamic externalities between multinationals and Southern firms. We explore the implications of FDI for Southern technological progress and the reverse implications of Southern technological progress for FDI. [9] Our paper adds significant value by modeling FDI as being more difficult when the technology gap is large and also modeling FDI as creating knowledge spillovers that enable the South to reduce the technology gap.

Keller (1996) argues that mere access to foreign technologies may not increase growth rates of LDCs. He makes the important point that if a country's absorptive capacity (stock of human capital) remains unchanged, a switch to an outward orientation will not lead to a higher growth rate. Our paper complements Keller's analysis by giving investment in imitation a role similar to human capital accumulation in Keller's model. In our model, imitation investments by host country firms generate the necessary knowledge (or skill) foundation for FDI, and

[9] Findlay (1978) emphasized the contagion effects of FDI for Southern technological progress.

thus factors that promote imitation can promote a higher quality mix of FDI. While Keller's model stresses that a country's limited stock of human capital effectively constrains its ability to take advantage of foreign technologies, our model stresses that indigenous technological capability in an industry effectively constrains its ability to host foreign technology. [10] FDI directly transfers technology from the North to the South, but such transfers are cost effective for Northern firms only if the South is sufficiently advanced.

Blomström and Kokko (1995) find empirical evidence that the technology imports of multinationals respond positively to the investments of local firms. While such increased technology transfer may stem from increased local competition, investments by local firms in an industry may enhance that industry's technological capability, thus enabling multinationals to transfer improved technologies. When local firms provide their workers with the training needed to handle base technologies, multinationals then find less training is required to bring local workers up to the level needed to handle the best technologies available. When local firms provide key technological background that closes the technology gap between the countries, the ideal setting for a multinational wanting to transfer advanced technologies is not a complete absence of local firms.

Rodríguez-Clare (1996) argues that multinationals are beneficial to the host country when they generate linkage effects beyond those generated by the local firms displaced. In that framework, FDI transferring advanced technologies may involve more complex production activities that generate stronger linkage effects for the local economy thereby enhancing its appeal relative to FDI transferring less advanced technologies. We provide further reasoning behind the appeal of high-quality FDI to Southern economies: lower prices, faster innovation, and higher Southern wages. We also argue that local production may provide the fundamental background knowledge needed to transfer more advanced technologies in a cost effective manner, thus placing emphasis on the need to build a local technological foundation to attract a better mix of FDI.

The paper is organized as follows. After establishing the behavior of consumers and firms (Section 2) and finding the steady-state equilibrium (Section 3), we show that when FDI is limited to appropriate technologies, forces that promote imitation relative to innovation generate a higher quality mix of multinational production by closing the technology gap (Section 4). We then examine Southern policies that encourage high-quality FDI. A subsidy to local R&D or a tax on multinational production of low quality levels increases the extent of FDI in high quality levels of products. Finally, we explore the welfare implications of these policies and conclude. Proofs of results appear in Appendix A.

[10] Therefore, we take a more disaggregated view of the constraints on technology transfer relative to Keller. For example, a country may have a fair amount of human capital in the aggregate but may lack the technological sophistication in a particular product to be able to host high-quality FDI.

2. The economy

The economy is composed of two countries containing two types of consumers and many firms. Consumers differ in their valuation of quality so that high-type consumers purchase higher quality levels of each product than low-type consumers. Firms differ in their R&D abilities so that Northern firms innovate while Southern firms imitate. Firms in the North may produce in the South, where costs are lower, but only for appropriate technologies. Appropriate technologies are technologies for producing quality levels no more than one step ahead of the Southern technology frontier. In equilibrium, expected profits from the product market just compensate firms for their R&D costs, and the labor supply is fully employed in either R&D or production in each country.

2.1. Consumers

Consumers are each one of two types, $\omega \in \{\mathrm{A, B}\}$ low and high, and live in one of two countries, $i \in \{\mathrm{N, S}\}$ North and South. Consumers choose from a continuum of products indexed by $j \in [0, 1]$, available in a discrete number of quality levels indexed by m. Taste for quality improvement, λ^m, differs across types. Let $\lambda^{\mathrm{B}} > \lambda^{\mathrm{A}} > 1$, so that high-type consumers (B) value quality improvement more than low-type consumers (A).

Consumers of each type ω in each country i maximize lifetime utility subject to an intertemporal budget constraint. Consumers have additively separable intertemporal preferences given by lifetime utility

$$U_i^{\omega} = \int_0^{\infty} e^{-\rho t} \log u_i^{\omega}(t)\mathrm{d}t, \tag{2.1}$$

where ρ is the common subjective discount factor. [11] Instantaneous utility is

$$\log u_i^{\omega}(t) = \int_0^1 \log\left[\sum_m (\lambda^{\omega})^m x_{im}^{\omega}(j,t)\right]\mathrm{d}j, \tag{2.2}$$

where $(\lambda^{\omega})^m$ is the assessment by type ω consumers of quality level m and $x_m^{\omega}(j,t)$ is consumption by type ω consumers of quality level m of product j at time t. Consumers maximize lifetime utility subject to an intertemporal budget constraint. Since preferences are homothetic, aggregate demands for each group of

[11] For simplicity, the discount rate is common across countries. A higher discount rate in the South relative to the North could create a separate force reducing the extent of high-quality FDI by discouraging imitation relative to innovation due to requiring a higher rate of return for imitation to be undertaken.

consumers are found by maximizing lifetime utility subject to the aggregate intertemporal budget constraint

$$\int_0^\infty e^{-R(t)} E^\omega(t) \mathrm{d}t \le A^\omega(0) + \int_0^\infty e^{-R(t)} Y^\omega(t) \mathrm{d}t, \tag{2.3}$$

where $R(t)$ is the cumulative interest rate up to time t and $A^\omega(0) = f(\omega) A(0)$ is the aggregate value of any initial asset holdings by type ω consumers. [12] Aggregate income of type ω consumers is

$$Y^\omega(t) = \sum_i f(\omega) L_i w_i(t) \tag{2.4}$$

where $w_i(t)$ is the wage in country i at time t and L_i is the labor supply in country i. Thus $L_i w_i(t)$ is total labor income in country i at time t and $f(\omega) L_i w_i(t)$ is the share that goes to type ω consumers. [13] Aggregate spending of type ω consumers is

$$E^\omega(t) = \int_0^1 \left[\sum_m p_m(j,t) x_m^\omega(j,t) \right] \mathrm{d}j, \tag{2.5}$$

where $p_m(j,t)$ is the price of quality level m of product j at time t. Define aggregate spending by all consumers as $E = E^{\mathrm{A}} + E^{\mathrm{B}}$.

The consumers problem can be broken into three stages: allocation of lifetime wealth across time, allocation of expenditure at each instant across products, and allocation of expenditure at each instant for each product across available quality levels. In the first stage, consumers evenly spread lifetime spending for each product across time; in the second stage, consumers evenly spread spending at each instant across products. In the final stage, consumers allocate spending for each product at each instant to the quality level with the lowest quality adjusted price.

Introducing differences in valuation of quality across consumers permits more than one quality level of each product to sell in equilibrium. Both the approach taken here and the alternative approach of assuming indivisibility in consumption and differences in income generate multiple quality levels selling in equilibrium. Here we fix the price premium paid for a quality increment and let the quantity consumed adjust to achieve budget balance; Flam and Helpman (1987) fix the

[12] Individuals hold assets in the form of ownership in firms, but with a diversified portfolio, any capital losses appear as capital gains elsewhere, so only the initial value of assets enters the intertemporal budget constraint. Lack of perfect capital mobility could provide an additional reason for the South to favor a larger extent of high-quality FDI due to the greater value of Southern firms.

[13] For simplicity, the distribution of income across consumer types is identical across countries, even though most LDCs have a higher income share of low-type consumers. Allowing the distribution of consumer types to vary across countries would not alter any of our results since the taxes considered here are based on the location of production, not consumption.

quantity consumed and let the price premium adjust instead. Assuming indivisibility in consumption might appear to limit relevance to goods consumed in a fixed quantity. Further, any fixity of consumption would preclude general equilibrium adjustments occurring through labor demand for production, an undesirable trait when analyzing the incentives of innovation and imitation. [14]

Because consumers differ in their valuation of quality, the price that makes a consumer indifferent between one quality level and the quality level below varies across types: high-type consumers view a specific quality level offered at a given price as being a better value than do low-type consumers. Thus, when offered a menu of a low quality level for a low price and a high quality level for a high price, the two types of consumers need not agree on which quality level offers the best deal: for a range of prices, low-type consumers pick the low quality level while high-type consumers pick the high quality level. Provided a sufficient percentage of income is in the hands of high-type consumers, firms choose prices that cause high-type consumers to self-select by buying the high quality level, whereas low-type consumers buy the low quality level (see Section A.1).

The model focuses on the separating equilibrium, where consumers with different valuations of quality buy different quality levels of products. More than one quality level of each product must sell so FDI can be ranked by the technology transferred relative to the state-of-the-art. Having multiple quality levels of each product sell in equilibrium generates markets where Northern firms have a large lead over Southern firms and markets where Northern firms have only a small lead. The measure of markets where Southern firms have not yet copied the low quality level provides a concrete measure of the degree that the technologies Northern firms can transfer to the South are limited due to the technological backwardness of the South.

2.2. Firms

The firms problem can be broken down into two stages. First, when undertaking R&D, a firm chooses its intensity of R&D to maximize its expected value, given the R&D intensities of other firms. Once successful in R&D, the firm then chooses the price of its product to maximize its value, given prices and R&D intensities of other firms. R&D for Northern firms is innovation, designing higher quality levels, while R&D for Southern firms is imitation, copying quality levels designed by Northern firms. The technology frontier for each country and each product is the highest quality level of the product that can be produced by any native firm in that country.

[14] Flam and Helpman (1987) construct a static model, so incentives for innovation and imitation are not an issue there.

2.2.1. Production

Normalize the unit labor requirement in production to 1; further normalize all prices by the Southern wage. Thus the marginal cost of production is 1 for Southern firms and $w \equiv w_N / w_S = w_N$ for Northern firms. Let the marginal cost of production for a multinational be ζ for quality levels one step above the Southern technology frontier. Assume multinationals have a cost disadvantage relative to Southern firms, $\zeta > 1$, stemming from their lack of familiarity with the Southern environment and from employing their technologies in a foreign environment.

By the assumptions of two types of consumers and a separating equilibrium, two quality levels of each product sell at any point in time. By the assumption that Southern firms have access to discarded technology (technologies that no longer yield profits from production), the Southern technology frontier is at most two quality levels below the Northern technology frontier for any product. By the assumption that Southern firms imitating the state-of-the-art is prohibitively costly, the Southern technology frontier never catches up to the Northern frontier for any product; that is, Southern firms can never imitate the high quality level of any product. [15] Therefore, for some products, the North has a two-quality level lead over the South, while for other products, the North has only a one-quality level lead over the South. These assumptions lead to a simple version of the model that contains the essential features: in some markets, the technology gap is large enough to prevent high-quality FDI.

By assumption, for products where the North has a two-quality level lead over the South, only the low quality level is produced through FDI; where the North has only a one-quality level lead over the South, the high quality level is produced through FDI in the South. Transferring technology through FDI involves prohibitive costs if the host country is extremely technologically backward relative to the technology to be transferred. The underlying assumption is that $\zeta < w$ (in equilibrium) is the marginal cost of production for FDI one-quality level above the Southern technology frontier, while a much higher marginal cost of production $Z > w$ (in equilibrium) applies for FDI more than one-quality level above the Southern technology frontier. Since cost savings provide the incentive for Northern firms to undertake FDI, FDI then occurs only one-quality level above the Southern technology frontier.

Consider first markets where the North has a two-quality level lead over the South. Southern firms are sufficiently disadvantaged by their low quality in these markets that they cannot offer a price that covers costs and still attract customers. Thus the two active firms for each product are the two Northern firms that invented the current two highest quality levels for that product, where the

[15] The desire to attract high-quality FDI is most relevant to scenarios where the South cannot fully catch up to the North. If the South can catch up to the North, it is less likely that a large enough technology gap persists for enough products to limit state-of-the-art FDI significantly.

low-quality firm becomes a multinational to produce in the South through FDI but the high-quality firm does not, as the South is too technologically backward to host the state-of-the-art. The high-quality Northern firm engages in limit pricing against the low-quality multinational, charging a premium reflecting a high-type consumer's valuation of quality; the low-quality multinational in turn engages in limit pricing against inactive Southern firms with discarded technology one quality level below, charging a premium reflecting a low-type consumer's valuation of quality. The high-quality Northern firm charges price $p_{\mathrm{N}}^{\mathrm{H}} = \lambda^{\mathrm{B}}\lambda^{\mathrm{A}}$ and the low quality multinational charges price $p_{\mathrm{M}}^{\mathrm{L}} = \lambda^{\mathrm{A}}$. The Northern firm has marginal cost of production w, while the multinational has marginal cost of production ζ. Instantaneous profits for the high-quality Northern firm are

$$\pi_{\mathrm{N}}^{\mathrm{H}} = E^{\mathrm{B}}\left(1 - \frac{w}{\lambda^{\mathrm{B}}\lambda^{\mathrm{A}}}\right) \tag{2.6}$$

and instantaneous profits for the low-quality multinational are

$$\pi_{\mathrm{M}}^{\mathrm{L}} = E^{\mathrm{A}}\left(1 - \frac{\zeta}{\lambda^{\mathrm{A}}}\right) \tag{2.7}$$

where $E^{\mathrm{B}} \equiv f(B)E$ and $E^{\mathrm{A}} \equiv f(A)E$ are the shares of aggregate spending by high- and low-type consumers, respectively. We call these markets *low-quality FDI* markets since the magnitude of the technology gap limits FDI to low quality levels.

Now consider markets where the North has only a one-quality level lead over the South. Southern firms are somewhat disadvantaged in these markets: the Southern firm that imitated the low quality level can charge a price that covers costs and attract low-type consumers; however, the Southern firm is limited to the low end of the market.[16] Thus the two active firms for each product are the Northern firm (which becomes a multinational) that invented the current highest quality level and the Southern firm that imitated the next highest quality level. The high-quality multinational engages in limit pricing against the low-quality Southern firm, which in turn engages in limit pricing against the multinational at the same low-quality level. The high-quality multinational charges price $p_{\mathrm{M}}^{\mathrm{H}} = \lambda^{\mathrm{B}}\zeta$ and the low-quality Southern firm charges price $p_{\mathrm{S}}^{\mathrm{L}} = \zeta$. The multinational has marginal cost of production ζ, while the Southern firm has marginal cost of production 1. Instantaneous profits for the high-quality multinational are

$$\pi_{\mathrm{M}}^{\mathrm{H}} = E^{\mathrm{B}}\left(1 - \frac{1}{\lambda^{\mathrm{B}}}\right) \tag{2.8}$$

[16] As in Glass (1997), the equilibrium concept is subgame perfection in the repeated-play game, where tit-for-tat strategies support market segmentation as value maximizing for both firms (when the share of income spent on high quality levels $f(B)$ is sufficiently large).

and instantaneous profits for a low-quality Southern firm are

$$\pi_{\mathrm{S}}^{\mathrm{L}} = E^{\mathrm{A}}\left(1 - \frac{1}{\zeta}\right) \tag{2.9}$$

We call these markets *high-quality FDI* markets since the technology gap is small enough for the South to host FDI at high quality levels.

Northern firms target all markets for innovation and Southern firms target only low-quality FDI markets (since targeting high quality levels is too difficult). A Northern firm successful at innovation gains the value of a high-quality Northern firm $v_{\mathrm{N}}^{\mathrm{H}}$; a Southern firm successful at imitation gains the value of a low-quality Southern firm $v_{\mathrm{S}}^{\mathrm{L}}$. Let $v_{\mathrm{M}}^{\mathrm{L}}$ denote the value of a low-quality multinational and $v_{\mathrm{M}}^{\mathrm{H}}$ denote the value of a high-quality multinational.

To find the value of producing firms, discount the flow of instantaneous profits for each type of producing firm to account for the chance that the profit stream will be terminated due to innovation or imitation. Low-quality FDI markets are targeted by both imitation and innovation. For a high-quality Northern firm, subsequent innovation (ι) makes the firm a low-quality multinational, while subsequent imitation (μ) makes the firm a high-quality multinational.

$$v_{\mathrm{N}}^{\mathrm{H}} = \frac{\pi_{\mathrm{N}}^{\mathrm{H}} + \iota v_{\mathrm{M}}^{\mathrm{L}} + \mu v_{\mathrm{M}}^{\mathrm{H}}}{\rho + \iota + \mu} \tag{2.10}$$

For a low-quality multinational, subsequent innovation or imitation pushes the firm out of the market.

$$v_{\mathrm{M}}^{\mathrm{L}} = \frac{\pi_{\mathrm{M}}^{\mathrm{L}}}{\rho + \iota + \mu} \tag{2.11}$$

High-quality FDI markets are targeted by innovation only. For a high-quality multinational, subsequent innovation makes the firm a low-quality multinational.

$$v_{\mathrm{M}}^{\mathrm{H}} = \frac{\pi_{\mathrm{M}}^{\mathrm{H}} + \iota v_{\mathrm{M}}^{L}}{\rho + \iota} \tag{2.12}$$

For the low-quality Southern firm, subsequent innovation pushes the firm out of the market.

$$v_{\mathrm{S}}^{\mathrm{L}} = \frac{\pi_{\mathrm{S}}^{\mathrm{L}}}{\rho + \iota} \tag{2.13}$$

By repeated substitution, the value terms can be eliminated from the right-hand side of Eqs. (2.10) and (2.12), leaving the value of a high-quality Northern firm and the value of a low-quality Southern firm as the discounted streams of expected instantaneous profits. These values indicate the reward to successful innovation and imitation. These rewards must offset the costs of innovation and imitation for innovation and imitation to occur in equilibrium.

2.2.2. Innovation and imitation

To produce a quality level of a product, a firm must first design it. Firms are willing to endure the costs of developing higher quality levels because they earn profits in the product market if successful. The potential for quality improvement is unbounded; however, both innovation and imitation must proceed one quality level at a time. While Northern firms push forward the quality frontier of existing products through innovation, Southern firms pursue the quality frontier through imitation.

R&D races occur simultaneously for all products. A Northern firm undertaking innovation intensity ι for a time interval dt requires $\gamma a \iota dt$ units of labor at cost $w \gamma a \iota dt$ and leads to success with probability ιdt; for a Southern firm, undertaking imitation intensity μ for a time interval dt requires $a \mu dt$ units of labor at cost $a \mu dt$ and leads to success with probability μdt. Innovation is more difficult than imitation, and thus requires relatively more resources: $\gamma > 1$.

Assume the South is at worst just out of each product market. Such a situation occurs if knowledge of the design of quality levels no longer produced (discarded technology) leaks out to Southern firms. A technology becomes discarded when any firm that invented or imitated that quality level no longer earns any profits from producing it; therefore, no firm would have any reason to protect its design. Otherwise, no Southern firm could ever imitate even the low-quality level once enough innovations occur uninterrupted by imitation because the South would lack the base technological knowledge needed to imitate even low quality levels.

The South is limited to imitating *appropriate technologies*, quality levels within one step of their present capabilities. The underlying assumption is that the unit labor requirement a applies to imitation one quality level above current capabilities but a substantially higher unit labor requirement $A > a$ applies to imitation of the state-of-the-art quality level, so that imitation costs exceed the expected reward to imitation of the state-of-the-art (in equilibrium): $A > v_S^H$. The South may lack infrastructure or other public investments necessary to make imitation of the state-of-the-art cost effective. Additionally, subsequent imitation would be undertaken by follower firms, firms that lack the background information of leader firms that imitate low quality levels. [17] Finally, multinationals may more actively protect state-of-the-art technologies than other inferior (less valuable) technologies, thus reducing the spillovers to potential imitators. [18]

Each firm chooses its intensity of R&D to maximize its expected value, given the R&D intensities of the other firms. To maximize their value, firms engage in

[17] See Grossman and Helpman (1991) for the distinction between leaders and followers and Glass (1997) for application of the leaders and followers distinction to imitation.

[18] If the South could catch up to the North for some products, Southern firms would push multinationals out of the market due to their lower costs. Assuming the South cannot completely catch up to the North for any product eliminates a market structure with no FDI. Since we focus on the quality of technology transferred through FDI, this simplification should not alter our results.

positive rates of innovation or imitation whenever the expected gains are no less than their costs. To generate finite rates of innovation and imitation, the expected gains must not exceed their cost. Northern firms target all markets at intensity ι, earning the reward v_N^H if successful.

$$v_N^H \leq w\gamma a, \iota > 0 \Leftrightarrow v_N^H = w\gamma a \tag{2.14}$$

Southern firms target low-quality FDI markets at intensity μ, earning the reward v_S^L if successful.

$$v_S^L \leq a, \mu > 0 \Leftrightarrow v_S^L = a \tag{2.15}$$

Resource constraints and steady-state conditions complete the model.

3. Steady-state equilibrium

Having established the purchasing decisions of consumers and the R&D and pricing decisions of firms, we now constrain R&D according to resource availability. Further, we impose conditions for a steady-state equilibrium and establish key linkages between variables of interest in a steady-state equilibrium.

3.1. Resource constraints

Let η be the extent of high-quality FDI (percentage of markets with high-quality multinational production), and thus $1-\eta$ the extent of low-quality FDI. In the labor markets, the fixed supply of labor is allocated between R&D and production. In the North, labor demand for innovation is $\gamma a \iota$, while labor demand for production is $(1-\eta)\ [(E^B)/(\lambda^B\lambda^A)]$; in the South, labor demand for imitation is $a\mu(1-\eta)$ while labor demand for production is $(1-\eta)(E^A/\lambda^A)+\eta[(E^B/(\lambda^B\zeta))+(E^A/\zeta)]$. For equilibrium in the labor market, the total demand for labor must equal the total supply of labor in each country:

$$\gamma a \iota + (1-\eta)\left[\frac{E^B}{\lambda^B\lambda^A}\right] = L_N \tag{3.1}$$

$$a\mu(1-\eta) + (1-\eta)\left[\frac{E^A}{\lambda^A}\right] + \eta\left[\frac{E^B}{\lambda^B\zeta} + \frac{E^A}{\zeta}\right] = L_S \tag{3.2}$$

The resource constraints limit the amount of R&D and production performed in each country.

3.2. Constant measures

For any product, whether FDI occurs at high or low quality levels changes over time as innovation or imitation occurs; however, the measure of products where FDI shifts from high quality to low quality due to innovation must equal the measure of products where FDI shifts from low quality to high quality due to imitation for the extent of high-quality FDI to remain constant at the aggregate level.

$$\iota\eta = \mu(1-\eta) \tag{3.3}$$

This condition is especially useful for deriving relationships between variables of interest in the steady-state equilibrium.

Since innovation targets all markets, the rate of innovation is the intensity of innovation ι (see Fig. 1). Since imitation targets only low-quality FDI markets, the rate of imitation is the intensity of imitation times the extent of low-quality FDI: $\mu(1-\eta)$. Using Eq. (3.3) the rate of imitation relative to the rate of innovation equals the extent of high-quality FDI.

$$I \equiv \frac{\mu(1-\eta)}{\iota} = \frac{\iota\eta}{\iota} = \eta \tag{3.4}$$

Thus, forces that increase the rate of imitation relative to innovation also increase the extent of high-quality FDI.

Technology is transferred between countries through FDI and between firms through imitation. Imitation of low quality levels allows the South to host high-quality FDI: technology for producing high quality levels flows into the South through FDI at the rate $\mu(1-\eta)$, equal to the rate of imitation. Innovation in markets with low-quality FDI brings a higher quality level produced in the South through FDI in absolute terms: technology for producing low quality levels

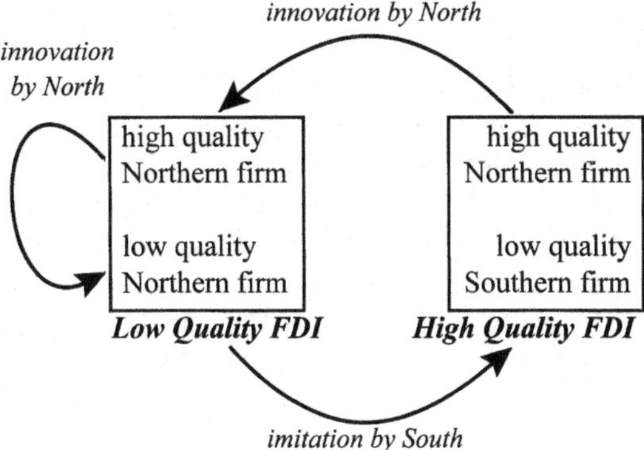

Fig. 1. Flow chart.

flows into the South through FDI at the rate $\iota(1-\eta)$. [19] Using Eq. (3.3), the aggregate flow of technology transferred to the South through FDI equals the rate of innovation.

$$F \equiv \iota(1-\eta) + \mu(1-\eta) = \iota(1-\eta) + \iota\eta = \iota \tag{3.5}$$

Thus, forces that increase the rate of innovation increase the aggregate flow of technology transferred to the South through FDI.

In low-quality FDI markets, the South is two quality levels below the Northern technology frontier, while in high-quality FDI markets, the South is only one quality level below the Northern technology frontier. Therefore, the average technology gap is negatively related to the extent of high-quality FDI, and using Eq. (3.4), the average technology gap is also negatively related to the rate of imitation relative to innovation.

$$G = 2(1-\eta) + \eta = 2 - \eta = 2 - I \tag{3.6}$$

Thus forces that increase the rate of imitation relative to innovation I shrink the technology gap G and expand the extent of high-quality FDI η. After collecting the key equations into a system, we find what forces have this effect.

3.3. Solution

The equations reduce to a system of four equations in four unknowns. The resource constraints (Eqs. (3.1) and (3.2)) form two equations. The return to R&D equations (Eqs. (2.14) and (2.15)), with producing firm values (Eqs. (2.10), (2.11), (2.12) and (2.13)) and profits (Eqs. (2.6), (2.7), (2.8) and (2.9)) included, form the remaining two equations. The system (see Section A.2) determines aggregate spending, the relative wage, the rate of innovation and the extent of high-quality FDI given the parameters. The solution is a combination of the endogenous variables such that resources are fully employed in each country and R&D yields no excess returns.

The relative wage is exclusively determined as the value of the marginal product of labor in producing innovations by the innovation valuation condition. The imitation valuation condition can be solved for aggregate spending E and inserted into the remaining resources constraints, leaving a system of two equations that determine the rate of innovation ι and the extent of high-quality FDI η, as in Fig. 2. The Northern resource constraint is upward sloping: a higher ι requires a higher η to free up resources from production for use in innovation. The Southern resource constraint is downward sloping: a higher ι requires a lower η.

[19] Innovation in a high-quality FDI market leads to low-quality FDI, which is the same technology in absolute terms (just at a larger lag relative to the state-of-the-art).

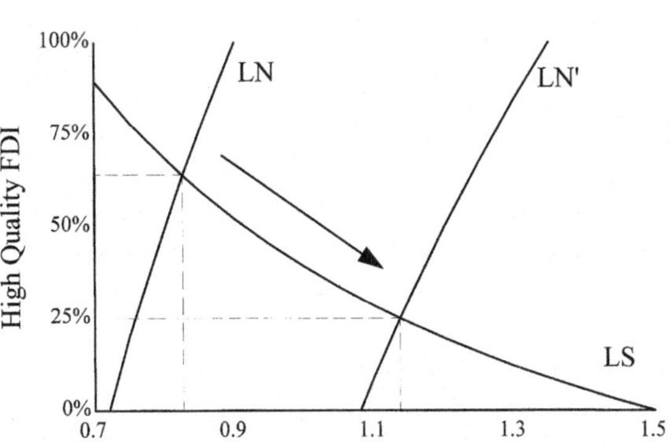

Fig. 2. Increase in relative resource supply.

Now we turn to determining the effects of various parameters on the endogenous variables to find what forces lead to a greater extent of high-quality FDI. While the extent of high-quality FDI remains constant in a steady-state equilibrium, different parameters lead to different steady-state solutions, with potentially different extent of high-quality FDI.

4. Technology transfer and the technology gap

In this section we explore how the extent of high-quality FDI, the rate of innovation and aggregate spending depend on the parameters of the model and draw some policy implications. Southern governments are often concerned with catching up to the North. What parameters decrease the technology gap between the North and the South? Southern governments are also often concerned with attracting FDI that transfers technologies closer to the technology frontier. What parameters increase the extent of high-quality FDI?

A smaller steady-state technology gap implies a larger extent of high-quality FDI (and vice versa), so these two questions share the same answer. By Eq. (3.6), the extent of high-quality FDI is tied to the rate of imitation relative to innovation, so any force increasing the rate of imitation relative to innovation increases the extent of high-quality FDI (by shrinking the technology gap). We start with parameters that contract the extent of high-quality FDI. Proofs for all propositions appear in Section A.2.

4.1. Relative resources

Define $\psi \equiv L_N / L_S$ as Northern resources relative to Southern resources. Larger Northern resources relative to Southern resources is a force pushing against imitation relative to innovation. Resources are needed to conduct R&D, so larger Northern relative to Southern resources supports a larger rate of innovation relative to imitation.

Proposition 1. *The extent of high-quality FDI decreases, the rate of innovation increases and aggregate spending increases with larger resources in the North relative to resources in the South* ψ.

Fig. 2 illustrates this effect. An increase in ψ means Northern firms can expand their innovative activity for a given η so the Northern resource constraint shifts right. The Southern resource constraint is unaffected. Thus the equilibrium shifts along the downward sloping Southern resource constraint to smaller η and larger ι.[20]

4.2. High-quality income share

Let $\phi \equiv f(B) = 1 - f(A)$ denote the share of income spent on high-quality levels. The model displays an interesting relationship between the size of the market for high-quality products and the extent of high-quality FDI. One might think that more extensive demand for high-quality products would increase the extent of high-quality FDI; however, such logic fails to account for the incentives for innovation relative to imitation. A larger market for high quality levels increases the rewards to innovation relative to imitation. With innovation occurring faster relative to imitation, the Southern technology frontier falls farther behind, and consequently FDI is limited to the lower quality levels for more products.

Proposition 2. *The extent of high-quality FDI decreases, the rate of innovation decreases and aggregate spending increases with a larger share of income spent on high quality levels* ϕ.

The South's ability to host FDI is limited to low quality levels when a large technology gap separates the Northern and Southern technology frontiers. The technology gap is larger when innovation is faster relative to imitation. Thus, a larger market for high quality levels of products implies a smaller extent of high-quality FDI due to the increase in incentives for innovation relative to imitation. Now we turn to forces that expand the extent of high-quality FDI.

[20] Graphical analysis of other forces that contract the extent of high-quality FDI markets is complicated by effects on E that shift both resource constraints.

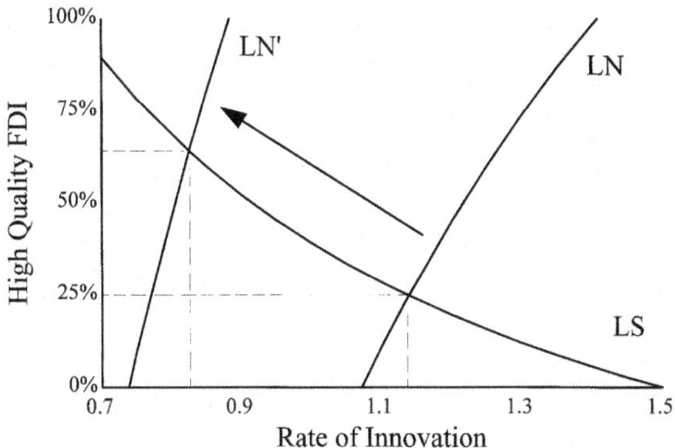

Fig. 3. Increase in relative innovation difficulty.

4.3. *Relative resource requirement in innovation*

A larger resource requirement in innovation relative to imitation is a force pushing towards imitation relative to innovation. Since the resource requirement in production is normalized to 1 in each country, the resource requirements in R&D indicate the opportunity costs of R&D, the number of units of output forgone to increase R&D activity. Intuitively, the higher the opportunity cost of innovation relative to imitation, the smaller the rate of innovation relative to imitation, and hence the smaller the technology gap and the larger the extent of high-quality FDI.

Proposition 3. *The extent of high-quality FDI increases, the rate of innovation decreases and aggregate spending decreases with a larger resource requirement in innovation relative to imitation* γ.

Fig. 3 illustrates this effect. An increase in γ means Northern firms must contract their innovative activity for a given η so the Northern resource constraint shifts left. The Southern resource constraint is unaffected. Thus the equilibrium shifts back up along the downward sloping Southern resource constraint to larger η and smaller ι. [21]

4.4. *Multinational cost disadvantage*

As the cost disadvantage of multinationals increases, the rate of imitation relative to innovation rises. The higher costs for a multinational decrease the profits during those phases where production in the South is possible and thus decrease the incentives for innovation relative to imitation.

[21] Graphical analysis of other forces that expand the extent of high-quality FDI markets is complicated by effects on E that shift both resource constraints.

Proposition 4. *The extent of high-quality FDI increases, the rate of innovation increases and aggregate spending decreases with a larger cost disadvantage of multinationals relative to Southern firms* ζ.

In addition, since Southern firms successful in imitation compete against multinationals at the same quality level, Southern firms price at the multinational's cost to keep the multinational out of the market. The higher price for successful imitators leads to higher profits that increased incentives for imitation. Further, the high-quality multinational then charges a premium over the low-quality Southern firm's price to reflect the extra willingness of high-type consumers to pay for quality. When the cost disadvantage of multinationals increases, the price of both quality levels in high-quality FDI markets rises, and thus production levels fall. The resources freed from production in the South are then available for imitation, adding another force in this direction. Together, the reduced relative innovation incentives, increased imitation incentives, and expanded resources for imitation lead to a faster rate of imitation relative to innovation, a smaller technology gap and thus a larger extent of high-quality FDI.

4.5. Tax on low-quality multinational production

What government policies might help close the technology gap and thus encourage high-quality FDI? The constraint facing Northern firms is the limited ability of the South to host FDI due to the technology gap between the North and the South. The technology gap reflects the rate of innovation relative to imitation. Thus to encourage high-quality FDI, policies must shrink the technology gap by raising the rate of imitation relative to innovation.

Let τ denote the (specific) production tax on low-quality FDI. A production tax on low-quality FDI effectively increases a multinational's production costs by τ, reducing profits for low-quality multinationals. A production tax on low-quality FDI also raises the price charged by low-quality Southern firms since successful imitators limit price against low-quality multinationals, thus raising profits for Southern firms and increasing the incentives for imitation. The tax also raises the price charged by high-quality multinationals since high-quality multinationals engage in limit pricing against low-quality Southern firms. The higher prices reduce consumption quantities, which frees up relatively more resources for imitation.

Proposition 5. *The extent of high-quality FDI increases, the rate of innovation increases and aggregate spending decreases with a larger low-quality multinational production tax* τ.

Imitation is profitable due to the production cost advantage of Southern firms relative to multinationals. A production tax acts like a greater cost disadvantage of multinationals in encouraging high-quality FDI by shrinking the technology gap through raising the rate of imitation relative to innovation.

4.6. Subsidy to Southern imitation

Similarly, a subsidy to Southern imitation also encourages high-quality FDI by shrinking the technology gap. Let σ denote the subsidy to Southern imitation. A subsidy to imitation places a term $(1-\sigma)$ on the cost of imitation in the imitation valuation condition (Eq. (2.15)), as the Southern government pays a portion of Southern firms' imitation costs.

Proposition 6. *The extent of high-quality FDI increases, the rate of innovation increases and aggregate spending decreases with a larger Southern imitation subsidy* σ.

The technological backwardness of the South limits its ability to host high-quality FDI; a subsidy to imitation spurs imitation relative to innovation and releases the constraint on Northern firms wanting to produce high quality levels in the South. The effect of a subsidy to imitation resembles the effect of increased relative resources requirement in innovation; however, a subsidy to R&D only affects the R&D valuation conditions, not the resource constraints, since no change in the resources demanded for a given R&D intensity occurs.

4.7. Welfare

Now that we have determined the Southern government can raise the extent of high-quality FDI, we determine whether the Southern government would want to do so, if its policy objective is to maximize Southern welfare. How is Southern welfare affected by changes in the extent of high-quality FDI, the rate of innovation, and aggregate spending?

By the law of large numbers, the expected number of innovations arriving in time period t is $\overline{m}=\iota t$. Instantaneous utility (2.2) is

$$\log u_i^{\omega}(t)=\log E_i-\log \overline{p}^{\omega}+\overline{m}^{\omega}\log \lambda^{\omega} \tag{4.1}$$

where the average price paid by low-type consumers is

$$\overline{p}^{\mathrm{A}}=(1-\eta)\lambda^{\mathrm{A}}+\eta\zeta=\lambda^{\mathrm{A}}-\eta(\lambda^{\mathrm{A}}-\zeta), \tag{4.2}$$

the average price paid by high-type consumers is

$$\overline{p}^{\mathrm{B}}=(1-\eta)\lambda^{\mathrm{B}}\lambda^{\mathrm{A}}+\eta\lambda^{\mathrm{B}}\zeta=\lambda^{\mathrm{B}}\left[\lambda^{\mathrm{A}}-\eta(\lambda^{\mathrm{A}}-\zeta)\right] \tag{4.3}$$

the average quality level consumed by low-type consumers is one level below the state-of-the-art, $\overline{m}^{\mathrm{A}}=\overline{m}-1$, and the average quality level consumed by high-type consumers is the state-of-the-art, $\overline{m}^{B} = \overline{m}$. An increased extent of high-quality FDI lowers the average price paid by low-type consumers $\partial\overline{p}^{A}/\partial\eta = -(\lambda^{A}-\zeta) < 0$, lowers the average price paid by high-type consumers $\partial\overline{p}^{B}/\partial\eta = -\lambda^{B}(\lambda^{A}-\zeta) < 0$ and does not affect the average quality level consumed by either type consumer (holding fixed the highest quality level available).

Lifetime utility (2.1) for type ω consumers is

$$U_i^{\omega} = \frac{\log E_i + \left(\frac{\iota}{\rho} - 1\right)\log \lambda^{\omega} - \log\left[\lambda^{A} - \eta(\lambda^{A} - \zeta)\right]}{\rho} \tag{4.4}$$

For both types of consumers, the first term indicates utility rises with aggregate spending due to the larger quantity consumed, the second term indicates utility rises with the rate of innovation due to the higher quality consumed (magnitude differs across types) and the third term indicates utility rises with the extent of high-quality FDI due to lower prices. The first term also indicates utility rises for Northern consumers with the relative wage and falls for Southern consumers with aggregate spending. [22] Any force that decreases E while concurrently increasing ι and η does increase Southern welfare. Accordingly, a reduction in the share of income spent on high quality levels ϕ, an increase in the cost disadvantage of multinationals relative to Southern firms ζ, an increase in the low-quality multinational production tax τ or an increase in the Southern imitation subsidy σ do increase Southern welfare. This welfare analysis supports the observation that Southern governments are actively seeking means of attracting FDI that transfers a better mix of technologies: their efforts, if successful, do raise Southern welfare.

5. Conclusion

This paper develops a model of FDI from DCs to LDCs, where multiple quality levels sell of each product. Firms from the developed country can shift their production to the less developed country where costs are lower, only for quality levels slightly above the current Southern technology frontier for that product. Where multiple quality levels sell, in some markets a large technology gap limits FDI to low quality levels, while in other markets a small technology gap permits FDI at high quality levels. The paper shows how the quality of technology transferred through FDI is linked (through the technology gap) to the rate of imitation relative to innovation by studying parameters that determine how much FDI occurs to produce using the best technology available.

[22] Aggregate spending is normalized by the Southern wage, so an increase in aggregate spending implies a reduction in the Southern wage.

The larger the market for high quality levels of products or the larger the resources in the North relative to the South, the smaller the extent of high-quality FDI. However, the larger the resources required for innovation relative to imitation or the larger the cost disadvantage of multinationals relative to Southern firms, the larger the extent of high-quality FDI. The host country can shrink the technology gap and thus encourage high-quality FDI by imposing a tax on low-quality FDI production or providing a subsidy to imitation. Encouraging domestic R&D activities that push forward the technology frontier releases the constraints faced by Northern firms wanting to produce using advanced technologies in the South. Such policies improve Southern welfare by raising Southern wages, lowering prices and accelerating innovation.

This paper provides a contrasting view to the common depiction of imitation as exclusively the foe of FDI. In situations where a substantial technology gap persists between source and host countries, imitation can provide the technological foundation needed to make state-of-the-art technology transfer through FDI more attractive from the viewpoint of Northern firms.

Acknowledgements

We thank Sean Durkin, Bill Ethier, Eric Fisher, Keith Head, Ed Ray, Paul Segerstrom, and participants at the Midwest and Southeast International Economics Conferences and AEA session of the ASSA meetings for comments. We especially thank Paul Segerstrom for the flow chart.

Appendix A

A.1. Condition for separation

Under pooling, all Northern firms become multinationals as the technology gap is exactly one quality level for all products due to only one quality level selling in equilibrium and discarded technology. Each firm would charge price $p^{\mathrm{P}} = \lambda$ and have marginal cost of production ζ and instantaneous profits

$$\pi^{\mathrm{P}} = E\left(1 - \frac{\zeta}{\lambda}\right)$$

which lead to a present discounted value

$$v^{\mathrm{P}} = \frac{\pi^{P}}{\rho + \iota}$$

For separation to emerge in low-quality FDI markets, by charging the price $p_N^H = \theta\lambda^2$ with marginal cost of production ζ, the firm must earn instantaneous profits π_N^H that lead to a present discounted value, taking as given the R&D intensities of other firms under pooling (only targeted by innovation)

$$v_N^S = \frac{\pi_N^H}{\rho + \iota}$$

that exceeds the reward to innovation under pooling. For $v_N^S > v^P$, must have enough income spent on high quality levels

$$\phi > \frac{\lambda - \zeta}{\lambda - \frac{1}{\theta}\left(\frac{w}{\lambda}\right)} < 1$$

as $\zeta > 1$ and $w < \theta\lambda$ in equilibrium (necessary for imitation to occur and Northern production to be profitable). Similarly, for separation to emerge in high-quality FDI markets, must also have enough income spent on high quality levels

$$\phi > \frac{\lambda - \zeta}{\lambda - \frac{1}{\theta}\left(\frac{w}{\lambda}\right)} < 1$$

since $\theta > 1$ by the definition of high-type consumers, so income shares spent on high quality do exist that generate a separating equilibrium. A separating equilibrium is more likely (occurs for a wider range of income shares spent on high quality levels) the larger the cost disadvantage of multinationals ζ and the larger the premium high-type consumers pay θ (heterogeneity in consumer types).

A.2. Proofs of results

Let $\lambda \equiv \lambda^A > 1$ represent the base quality increment and $\theta \equiv \lambda^B/\lambda^A > 1$ represent the quality premium in the view of high-type consumers. All consumers agree that new innovations are at least λ-times better than the previous innovation, but some consumers have an extra idiosyncratic taste for quality. The model reduces to three equations in the three unknowns $\{E, \iota, \eta\}$:

$$\gamma a\iota + \left[\frac{\phi(1-\eta)}{\theta\lambda^2}\right]E = \psi L$$

$$a\iota\eta + \left[\frac{\theta\zeta(1-\phi) + \eta[\phi + \theta(\lambda - \zeta)(1-\phi)]}{\theta\lambda\zeta}\right]E = L$$

$$(1-\phi)\left(1 - \frac{1}{\zeta}\right)E = a(\rho + \iota)$$

with w determined separately by the innovation valuation condition (using the solution from the reduced system). Then solve the imitation valuation condition for aggregate spending

$$E=\frac{a(\rho+\iota)}{(1-\phi)\left(1-\frac{1}{\zeta}\right)}$$

and substitute into the resource constraints, leaving a system of two equations in the two unknowns, $\{\eta,\iota\}$, as drawn in Fig. 2.

$$\gamma a\iota+\left(\frac{\phi(1-\eta)}{\theta\lambda^2}\right)\left[\frac{a(\rho+\iota)}{(1-\phi)\left(1-\frac{1}{\zeta}\right)}\right]=\psi L$$

$$a\iota\eta+\left(\frac{\theta\zeta(1-\phi)+\eta[\phi+\theta(\lambda-\zeta)(1-\phi)]}{\theta\lambda\zeta}\right)\left[\frac{a(\rho+\iota)}{(1-\phi)\left(1-\frac{1}{\zeta}\right)}\right]=L$$

An increase in ψ shifts the Northern resource constraint down so that η smaller for a given ι; an increase in γ shifts the Northern resource constraint up so that η larger for a given ι.

A.2.1. Proof of Proposition 1

The derivatives with respect to ψ are generated by

$$\begin{bmatrix} b_{11} & -b_{12} \\ b_{21} & b_{22} \end{bmatrix}\begin{bmatrix} \mathrm{d}\iota \\ \mathrm{d}\eta \end{bmatrix}=\begin{bmatrix} Ld\psi \\ 0 \end{bmatrix}$$

where

$$b_{11}\equiv\left[\frac{a}{\theta\lambda(1-\phi)(\zeta-1)}\right]\left[\frac{\gamma\theta\lambda^2(1-\phi)(\zeta-1)+\zeta\phi(1-\eta)}{\lambda}\right]>0$$

$$b_{12}\equiv\left[\frac{a}{\theta\lambda(1-\phi)(\zeta-1)}\right]\left[\frac{\zeta\phi(\rho+\iota)}{\lambda}\right]>0$$

$$b_{21}\equiv\left[\frac{a}{\theta\lambda(1-\phi)(\zeta-1)}\right][\theta\zeta(1-\phi)[\eta(\lambda-1)+1]+\eta\phi]>0$$

$$b_{22}\equiv\left[\frac{a}{\theta\lambda(1-\phi)(\zeta-1)}\right][\theta(1-\phi)[\zeta\iota(\lambda-1)+\rho(\lambda-\zeta)]$$
$$+\phi(\rho+\iota)]>0.$$

Consequently, the determinant of the matrix is positive

$$D \equiv b_{11} b_{22} - (-b_{12}) b_{21} = b_{11} b_{22} + b_{12} b_{21} > 0.$$

An increase in relative resources increases the rate of innovation

$$\frac{\partial \iota}{\partial \psi} = \frac{L b_{22}}{D} > 0$$

decreases the extent of high-quality FDI

$$\frac{\partial \eta}{\partial \psi} = -\frac{L b_{21}}{D} < 0$$

and increases aggregate spending

$$\frac{\partial E}{\partial \psi} = \frac{a \zeta L b_{22}}{(\zeta - 1)(1 - \phi) D} > 0.$$

To simplify expressions, L from the Southern resource constraint and ψ from the Northern resource constraint have been inserted after calculating the following derivatives.

A.2.2. Proof of Proposition 2

An increase in the share of income spent on high quality levels decreases the rate of innovation

$$\frac{\partial \iota}{\partial \phi} = -\frac{\left[\theta(1-\phi)(1-\eta)\left[\zeta\iota(\lambda-1) + \rho(\lambda-\zeta)\right] + \phi(\rho+\iota)\right] a b_{12}}{\phi\theta\lambda(1-\phi)^2(\zeta-1) D}$$

decreases the extent of high-quality FDI

$$\frac{\partial \eta}{\partial \phi} = -\frac{\left[\gamma\eta\lambda(\zeta-1) + \zeta^2(1-\eta)\left[\eta(\lambda-1)+1\right]\right] a b_{12}}{\zeta\theta\lambda(1-\phi)(\zeta-1) D}$$

and increases aggregate spending

$$\frac{\partial E}{\partial \phi} = \frac{\left[\theta(1-\phi)\left[\zeta\iota(\lambda-1) + \rho(\lambda-\zeta)\right]\left[\lambda^2\gamma\theta(\zeta-1) - \zeta(1-\eta)\right] + N_\phi\right] a^2 b_{12}}{\phi\theta\lambda(1-\phi)^2(\zeta-1)^2 D} > 0$$

where $N_\phi \equiv \phi(\rho+\iota)[\lambda^2\gamma\theta(\zeta-1) + \zeta[\theta\zeta\eta(\lambda-1) + \theta\zeta - 1]]0.$

A.2.3. Proof of Proposition 3

An increase in the relative resource requirement in innovation decreases the rate of innovation

$$\frac{\partial \iota}{\partial \gamma} = -\frac{a \iota b_{22}}{D} < 0$$

increases the extent of high-quality FDI

$$\frac{\partial\eta}{\partial\gamma}=\frac{a\iota b_{21}}{d}>0$$

and decreases aggregate spending

$$\frac{\partial E}{\partial\gamma}=-\frac{a^2\zeta\iota b_{22}}{(\zeta-1)(1-\phi)D}<0.$$

A.2.4. Proof of Proposition 4

An increase in the cost disadvantage of multinationals relative to Southern firms increases the rate of innovation

$$\frac{\partial\iota}{\partial\zeta}=\frac{[\phi(\rho+\iota)[\eta(\zeta-1)+1]+\theta\lambda(1-\phi)[\zeta\iota+\rho[\eta(\zeta-1)+1]]]ab_{12}}{\zeta\theta\lambda(1-\phi)(\zeta-1)^2D}$$

$$>0$$

increases the extent of high-quality FDI

$$\frac{\partial\eta}{\partial\zeta}=\frac{[\gamma\theta\lambda^2(1-\phi)[\eta\phi+\theta(1-\phi)[\eta(\lambda-1)+1]]+\phi^2\eta(1-\eta)]ab_{12}}{\zeta\phi\theta\lambda(1-\phi)(\zeta-1)D}$$

and decreases aggregate spending

$$\frac{\partial E}{\partial\zeta}=-\frac{[\gamma\theta^2\lambda^2(1-\phi)^2[\zeta\iota(\lambda-1)+\rho(\lambda-\zeta)]+N_\zeta]a^2b_{12}}{\zeta\phi\lambda(1-\phi)^2(\zeta-1)^2D}$$

where $N_\zeta\equiv\phi(\rho+\iota)[\gamma\theta\lambda^2(1-\phi)-\phi\zeta\eta]$.

A.2.5. Proof of Proposition 5

With a tax on low-quality multinational production, the three equations become

$$\gamma a\iota+\left[\frac{\phi(1-\eta)}{\theta\lambda^2}\right]E=\psi L$$

$$a\iota\eta+\left[\frac{\theta(\zeta+\tau)(1-\phi)+\eta[\phi+\theta(\lambda-\zeta-\tau)(1-\phi)]}{\theta\lambda(\zeta+\tau)}\right]E=L$$

$$(1-\phi)\left(1-\frac{1}{\zeta+\tau}\right)E=a(\rho+\iota)$$

with w determined as before. The expression for aggregate spending from the imitation valuation condition becomes

$$E=\frac{a(\rho+\iota)}{(1-\phi)\left(1-\frac{1}{\zeta+\tau}\right)}$$

The reduced system becomes

$$\gamma a\iota+\left(\frac{\phi(1-\eta)}{\theta\lambda^2}\right)\left[\frac{a(\rho+1)}{(1-\phi)\left(1-\frac{1}{\zeta+\tau}\right)}\right]=\psi L$$

$$a\iota\eta+\left(\frac{\theta(\zeta+\tau)(1-\phi)+\eta[\phi+\theta(\lambda-\zeta-\tau)(1-\phi)]}{\theta\lambda(\zeta+\tau)}\right)$$

$$\times\left[\frac{a(\rho+\iota)}{(1-\phi)\left(1-\frac{1}{\zeta+\tau}\right)}\right]=L$$

An increase in the tax on low-quality FDI increases the rate of innovation

$$\frac{\partial\iota}{\partial\tau}=\frac{[\phi(\rho+\iota)[1+\eta(\zeta+\tau-1)]+\theta\lambda(1-\phi)[\iota(\zeta+\tau)+\rho[1+\eta(\zeta+\tau-1)]]]ab_{12}^{\tau}}{\theta\lambda(1-\phi)(\zeta+\tau)(\zeta+\tau-1)^2D^{\tau}}>0$$

increases the extent of high-quality FDI

$$\frac{\partial\eta}{\partial\tau}=\frac{\left[\gamma\theta\lambda^2(1-\phi)[\theta(1-\phi)[\eta(\lambda-1)+1]+\phi\eta]+\phi^2\eta(1-\eta)\right]ab_{12}^{\tau}}{\theta\lambda\phi(1-\phi)(\zeta+\tau)(\zeta+\tau-1)D^{\tau}}>0$$

and increases aggregate spending

$$\frac{\partial E}{\partial\tau}=-\frac{\left[\gamma\theta^2\lambda^2(1-\phi)^2[(\zeta+\tau)\iota(\lambda-1)+\rho(\lambda-\zeta-\tau)]+N_{\tau}\right]a^2b_{12}^{\tau}}{(\zeta+\tau)\phi\theta\lambda(1-\phi)^2(\zeta+\tau-1)^2D^{\tau}}$$

where $N_{\tau}\equiv\phi(\rho+\iota)[\gamma\theta\lambda^2(1-\phi)-\phi(\zeta+\tau)\eta]>0$ and $b_{12}^{\tau}=[(\zeta+\tau)(\zeta\text{-}1)]/[\zeta(\zeta+\tau\text{-}1)]b_{12}$. In the limit as the tax rate goes to zero $\tau\to 0$, these effects approach the effects of an increase in multinational cost disadvantage.

A.2.6. Proof of Proposition 6

With a subsidy to imitation, the three equations become

$$\gamma a\iota + \left[\frac{\phi(1-\eta)}{\theta\lambda^2}\right]E = \psi L$$

$$a\iota\eta + \left[\frac{\theta\zeta(1-\phi) + \eta[\phi + \theta(\lambda-\zeta)(1-\phi)]}{\theta\lambda\zeta}\right]E = L$$

$$(1-\phi)\left(1-\frac{1}{\zeta}\right)E = a(\rho+\iota)(1-\sigma)$$

with w determined separately by the innovation valuation condition using the solution from the reduced system). The expression for aggregate spending from the imitation valuation condition becomes

$$E = \frac{a(\rho+\iota)(1-\sigma)}{(1-\phi)\left(1-\frac{1}{\zeta}\right)}$$

The reduced system becomes

$$\gamma a\iota + \left(\frac{\phi(1-\eta)}{\theta\lambda^2}\right)\left[\frac{a(\rho+\iota)(1-\sigma)}{(1-\phi)\left(1-\frac{1}{\zeta}\right)}\right] = \psi L$$

$$a\iota\eta + \left(\frac{\theta\zeta(1-\phi) + \eta[\phi + \theta(\lambda-\zeta)(1-\phi)]}{\theta\lambda\zeta}\right) \times \left[\frac{a(\rho+\iota)(1-\sigma)}{(1-\phi)\left(1-\frac{1}{\zeta}\right)}\right] = L$$

An increase in the subsidy to Southern imitation increases the rate of innovation

$$\frac{\partial\iota}{\partial\sigma} = \frac{[\iota\theta\lambda(1-\phi)(\zeta-1)(1-\eta) + (1-\sigma)(\rho+\iota)[\phi+\theta\lambda(1-\phi)]]ab_{12}^{\sigma}}{\theta\lambda(1-\phi)(\zeta-1)(1-\sigma)D^{\sigma}} > 0$$

increases the extent of high-quality FDI

$$\frac{\partial\eta}{\partial\sigma} = \frac{(\gamma\lambda[\theta(1-\phi)[\zeta(1-\eta)+\eta\lambda]] + \phi\eta^2\zeta + \eta(\gamma\lambda^2 - \phi\zeta))ab_{12}^{\sigma}}{\phi\zeta(1-\sigma)D\sigma} > 0$$

and decreases aggregate spending

$$\frac{\partial E}{\partial \sigma} = -\frac{\left[\gamma\theta\lambda(1-\phi)\left[\iota\lambda(\zeta-1)+(\rho+\iota)(\lambda-\zeta)(1-\sigma)\right]+N_\sigma\right]a^2 b_{12}^{\sigma}}{\phi(1-\phi)(\zeta-1)(1-\sigma)D^{\sigma}}$$

$$< 0.$$

where $N_\sigma \equiv \phi(1-\sigma)(\rho+\iota)(\gamma\lambda+\zeta\eta) > 0$ and $b_{12}^{\sigma} = (1-\sigma)b_{12}$.

References

Blomström, M., Kokko, A., 1995. Multinational corporations and spillovers: A review of the evidence. Mimeo.

Blumenthal, T., 1976. Japan's technological strategy. J. Dev. Econ. 3, 245–255.

Flam, H., Helpman, E., 1987. Vertical product differentiation and North–South trade. Am. Econ. Rev. 77, 810–822.

Findlay, R., 1978. Relative backwardness, direct foreign investment, and the transfer of technology: A simple dynamic model. Q. J. Econ. 92, 1–16.

Glass, A.J., 1997. Product cycles and market penetration. Int. Econ. Rev. 38, 865–891.

Glass, A.J., Saggi, K., 1995. Foreign direct investment and the nature of R&D, OSU w.p. 95-07, ISER d.p. 420, SMU w.p. 9515.

Grossman, G.M., Helpman, E., 1991. Quality ladders and product cycles. Q. J. Econ. 106, 557–586.

Katrak, H., 1989. Imported technologies and R&D in a newly industrializing country. J. Dev. Econ. 31, 123–139.

Keller, W., 1996. Absorptive capacity: Understanding the creation and acquisition of technology in development. J. Dev. Econ. 49, 199–227.

Kokko, A., 1994. Technology, market characteristics, and spillovers. J. Dev. Econ. 43, 279–293.

Kumar, N., 1994. Multinational Enterprises and Industrial Organization: The Case of India. Sage Publications, New Delhi.

Mansfield, E., Romeo, A., 1980. Technology transfer to overseas subsidiaries by U.S.-based firms. Q. J. Econ. 95, 737–750.

Markusen, J.R., 1995. The boundaries of multinational enterprises and the theory of international trade. J. Econ. Perspect. 9, 169–189.

Pack, H., Saggi, K., 1997. Inflows of foreign technology and indigenous technological development. Rev. Dev. Econ. 1, 81–98.

Rodríguez-Clare, A., 1996. Multinationals, linkages, and economic development. Am. Econ. Rev. 86, 852–874.

Segerstrom, P.S., Anant, T.C.A., Dinopoulos, E., 1990. A Schumpeterian model of the product life cycle. Am. Econ. Rev. 80, 1077–1091.

Siddharthan, N.S., 1992. Transaction costs, technology transfer, and in-house R&D. J. Econ. Behav. Organization 18, 265–271.

Stokey, N.L., 1991. The volume and composition of trade between rich and poor countries. Rev. Econ. Studies 58, 63–80.

Teece, D.J., 1976. The multinational corporation and resource cost of international technology transfer. Ballinger, Cambridge, Massachusetts.

United Nations, 1992. World investment report: Transnational corporations as engines of growth. United Nations, New York.

Chapter 2

Innovation and wage effects of international outsourcing[#]

Amy Jocelyn Glass[a,*], Kamal Saggi[b]

[a]*Department of Economics, Ohio State University, 1945 North High Street, Columbus, OH 43210-1172, USA*

[b]*Department of Economics, Southern Methodist University, Dallas, TX 75275-0496, USA*

Received 1 May 1997; accepted 1 December 1998

Abstract

We investigate the effects of increased outsourcing of production to a low wage country. Such international outsourcing lowers the marginal cost of production and thus increases profits, creating greater incentives for innovation. A reduction in the resource requirement in adapting technology relative to improving products or an expansion in the portion of production that can be outsourced generates a greater extent of international outsourcing, a lower relative wage and a faster rate of innovation. An increase in production taxes in the North, production subsidies in the South, or a subsidy to adapting technologies has similar effects. © 2001 Elsevier Science B.V. All rights reserved.

JEL classification: F21; F43; O31; O34

Keywords: International outsourcing; Innovation; Adaptation

1. Introduction

U.S. firms have increasingly been outsourcing their basic stages of production to countries such as Mexico and China, where production costs are much lower.

* Corresponding author. Tel.: + 1 614 292 1149; fax: + 1 614 292 3906.
E-mail address: glass.29@osu.edu (A. J. Glass)

This chapter was originally appeared in *European Economic Review* **45**, 67–86. © 2001 Elsevier Science B.V.

Due to the increased extent of international outsourcing of production, the effect of international outsourcing on wages has become an important policy issue.

For example, in March 1996, General Motors employees (at an Ohio plant) went on strike to protest increased outsourcing of production to low wage countries. In October 1995, Boeing employees (in Kansas, Washington, and Oregon) went on strike to protest Boeing's commitment to outsource half of the value of the average jet aircraft, mostly to China. The negative impact of increased international outsourcing on U.S. wages has helped fuel the political campaigns of such candidates as Ross Perot and Pat Buchanan, backed by workers whose livelihoods are threatened.[1]

We construct a North–South product cycle model to help identify the forces that can lead to increased outsourcing as well as a lowering of the Northern relative wage. An important goal of this paper is to determine the effect of these forces on the rate at which the technology frontier progresses. Thus, our analysis brings a dynamic approach to an issue that previously has been analyzed in static models.

We develop a product cycle model with international outsourcing of basic production to low wage countries. Northern firms import basic components from the South, assemble the components into finished products using Northern labor and then sell the finished products on world markets. Cheaper Southern labor substitutes for Northern labor in basic production. International outsourcing of production is viewed as detrimental to the welfare of workers in industrialized countries due to the resulting negative impact on wages. We explore what forces lead to a greater extent of international outsourcing along with a relative decline in Northern wages.

However, the emphasis on the detrimental effect of international outsourcing on Northern wages ignores potential benefits. Increased access to the work force in low wage countries increases the profitability of Northern firms through cost savings. Since profits provide the incentive for firms to improve products through costly innovations, international outsourcing logically should encourage innovation. By increasing the rate of innovation, international outsourcing can potentially create gains sufficient to offset the decline in Northern wages. Thus, ignoring the dynamic aspects of the problem can lead to overly pessimistic conclusions.

In existing papers such as Jensen and Thursby (1987), Segerstrom et al. (1990), and Grossman and Helpman (1991), production shifts to the low cost country through imitation by firms located there.[2] In contrast, here production shifts

[1] Workers may also object to outsourcing within a country if they are not able to follow production shifts. The features and results of our model also apply to separate labor markets within the same country.

[2] In Helpman (1993) and Glass and Saggi (1999), production shifts to the South through foreign direct investment by Northern firms.

through the original innovator outsourcing part of its production to the low wage country. Once firms have successfully innovated, they then may adapt their basic production techniques for production in the low wage country. Due to differences in the technology involved in the two stages of production, Northern firms find international outsourcing of only the basic stage attractive. Since international outsourcing requires firms to adapt production technologies, newly developed designs remain produced in the high wage country while older designs have basic production shifted to the low wage country, similar to Vernon (1966).

While empirical analysis of the impact of international outsourcing on wages in the United States is prevalent, only Feenstra and Hanson (1996a) model the effects of international outsourcing. In their model, a single manufactured good is produced from a continuum of intermediate goods that differ in their relative use of skilled and unskilled workers. Intermediate goods that require a range of inputs up to some critical ratio of skilled to unskilled labor are produced by the South, whereas the remaining goods are produced in the North. An increase in the relative capital stock of the South results in the South producing a greater range of intermediate goods. Total payments to labor in the North decline as the South produces goods that require a higher ratio of skilled to unskilled labor. However, an increase in international outsourcing benefits Northern workers by lowering the prices of goods and, if the South is small enough, this effect outweighs the negative wage effects, leading to an overall welfare gain.

Our approach differs from that of Feenstra and Hanson in the fundamental model of international trade in which outsourcing occurs. Their model is driven by differences in factor endowments, while ours is driven by differences in technology. An increase in international outsourcing results from changes in the South's capital stock in their model, while the increase results from reduced costs of adapting technologies for Southern production or a wider span of production that can be outsourced in our model. We also demonstrate that increases in production taxes in the North, production subsidies in the South, or subsidies to adapting technologies for Southern production lead to increased international outsourcing. Furthermore, international outsourcing can provide a welfare gain for the North by lowering prices in their model, while a welfare gain can occur through faster innovation in our model. Thus our analysis complements Feenstra and Hanson's results by determining the impact of international outsourcing on the rate of innovation.

Section 2 constructs the model and determines the equilibrium. Section 3 examines how the rate of innovation, extent of international outsourcing (fraction of all production that occurs in the South) and relative wage respond to outsourcing opportunities, labor supplies, production taxes or subsidies, and R&D subsidies. Section 4 concludes.

2. International outsourcing model

Each country is composed of a representative consumer and many firms. Consumers are willing to pay a premium for quality because they derive more utility from higher quality levels of products. This premium gives Northern firms an incentive to develop quality improvements. Once successful in inventing a higher quality level of a product, a Northern firm can then attempt to outsource production by adapting its basic production technology for the low cost country. If the firm is successful in adapting its technology, it then licenses a Southern firm to perform basic production at cost.

2.1. Consumers

Consumer preferences are as described in the quality ladders product cycle model of Grossman and Helpman (1991). Consumers live in one of two countries, North and South $i \in \{N, S\}$. Consumers choose from a continuum of products indexed by $j \in [0, 1]$, where products are available in a discrete number of quality levels indexed by m. A consumer in country i has additively separable intertemporal preferences given by lifetime utility

$$U_i = \int_0^\infty e^{-\rho t} \log u_i(t) \, dt, \tag{1}$$

where ρ is the common subjective discount factor, instantaneous utility is

$$\log u_i(t) = \int_0^1 \log \left[\sum_m \lambda^m x_{im}(j, t) \right] dj, \tag{2}$$

λ^m is the assessment of quality level m and $x_{im}(j, t)$ is consumption by consumers in country i of quality level m of product j at time t. Each quality level m is λ-times better than quality level $m - 1$, where λ denotes the size of the quality increment. By the definition of quality, higher quality levels are valued more: $\lambda > 1$.

Since preferences are homothetic, aggregate demand can be found by maximizing lifetime utility (1) subject to the aggregate intertemporal budget constraint

$$\int_0^\infty e^{-R(t)} E(t) \, dt \leq A(0) + \int_0^\infty e^{-R(t)} Y(t) \, dt, \tag{3}$$

where $R(t) = \int_0^t r(s) \, ds$ is the cumulative interest rate up to time t and $A(0)$ is the aggregate value of initial asset holdings. Aggregate income is

$$Y(t) = \sum_i L_i w_i(t), \tag{4}$$

where $w_i(t)$ is the wage in country i at time t and L_i is the labor supply in country i.[3] Thus $L_i w_i(t)$ is total labor income in country i at time t. Aggregate spending is

$$E(t) = \int_0^1 \left[\sum_m p_m(j,t) x_m(j,t) \right] \mathrm{d}j, \tag{5}$$

where $p_m(j,t)$ is the price of quality level m of product j at time t.

The consumer's maximization problem can be broken into three stages: the allocation of lifetime wealth across time, the allocation of expenditure at each instant across products, and the allocation of expenditure at each instant for each product across available quality levels. In the first stage, each consumer evenly spreads lifetime spending for each product across time; in the second stage, each consumer evenly spreads spending at each instant across products (see Grossman and Helpman, 1991 for details). In the final stage, each consumer allocates spending for each product at each instant to the quality level with the lowest quality adjusted price, p_m/λ^m. Thus, consumers are willing to pay a premium of λ for a one quality level improvement in a product.

2.2. Producers

To produce a given quality level of a product, a (Northern) firm must first design it. However, due to assumed differences in technological knowledge across countries, only Northern firms innovate. The innovation process is the same as in Grossman and Helpman (1991). Assume innovation races occur simultaneously for all products, with all Northern firms able to target the quality level above the current highest quality level for each product. Normalize the Southern wage to one, so $w \equiv w_N/w_S = w_N$ is the Northern wage relative to the Southern wage. Assume undertaking innovation intensity ι for a time interval $\mathrm{d}t$ requires $a_\iota \iota\, \mathrm{d}t$ units of labor at a cost of $w a_\iota \iota\, \mathrm{d}t$ and leads to success with probability $\iota \mathrm{d}t$.

We part from Grossman and Helpman's model by allowing Northern firms to purchase basic stages of production from Southern firms: outsourcing takes the place of imitation in shifting production to the South. Production occurs in two stages: a basic stage followed by an advanced stage. Normalize the unit labor requirement in production to one. Of the one unit of labor needed to produce one unit of the final product, α is used in the basic stage and the remaining $(1-\alpha)$ is combined with the output of the basic stage in the advanced stage to produce the final product. The output of the basic stage is a tradeable intermediate component; the output of the advanced stage is the tradeable final product. Hence, the two stages of production can be located in different countries.

[3] Throughout the paper, wages refer to wages per efficiency unit of labor.

To outsource basic production, a firm must first expend resources to adapt its production process for the Southern economic environment.[4] Like innovation, outsourcing involves certain costs with uncertain rewards: a firm might never find a feasible adaptation of its production process. Undertaking outsourcing intensity ϕ for a time interval dt requires $a_\phi \phi dt$ units of labor at a cost of $wa_\phi \phi dt$ and leads to success with probability ϕdt. If successful at its efforts, a firm outsources all basic production.

A firm's problem can be broken down into two stages. First, when undertaking innovation, the firm chooses its intensity of innovation to maximize its expected value, given the innovation intensities of other firms. Once successful in innovation, the firm then chooses the price of its product and intensity of adaptation to maximize its value, given the prices and innovation intensities of other firms. Current producers do not undertake any innovation due to the familiar profit destruction argument (Grossman and Helpman, 1991).

To generate a finite intensity of innovation, expected gains must not exceed cost, with equality when innovation occurs with positive intensity:

$$v_N \leq wa_\iota, \quad \iota > 0 \Leftrightarrow v_N = wa_\iota, \tag{6}$$

where v_N is the value a firm gains from successful innovation. Similarly, expected gains from international outsourcing must not exceed cost, with equality when outsourcing occurs with positive intensity

$$v_O - v_N \leq wa_\phi, \quad \phi > 0 \Leftrightarrow v_O - v_N = wa_\phi, \tag{7}$$

where $v_O - v_N$ is the capital gain from outsourcing basic production.[5] We focus on equilibria with both innovation and outsourcing, so both of these conditions hold with equality.

A Northern firm that successfully innovates earns the reward

$$v_N = \frac{\pi_N + \phi(v_O - wa_\phi)}{\rho + \phi + \iota}, \tag{8}$$

where upon successfully adapting its technology for Southern production the firm's value becomes

$$v_O = \frac{\pi_O}{\rho + \iota} \tag{9}$$

until rival innovation terminates its value. The reward to innovation is the discounted stream of profits from production.

---

[4] An alternative interpretation of the adaptation process is that Northern firms must spend resources locating a suitable licensee.

[5] Subscripts denote the type of market: N for Northern production and O for outsourcing basic production.

Under Bertrand competition, the most recent innovator for each product engages in limit pricing behavior by choosing a price that just keeps its closest rival from earning a positive profit from production. Each most recent innovator has a one quality level lead over the closest rival and so chooses a price equal to λ times the rival's marginal cost.

Assume all old technologies have full international outsourcing potential. Old technologies are designs that have already been improved. While Southern firms are never able to produce the advanced stage of production (of state-of-the-art technologies), once technologies no longer yield profits in equilibrium, these old technologies become fully available to Southern firms.[6] This assumption provides a common marginal cost of production of one for all technologies no longer produced in equilibrium.

Thus each producing firm charges price $p = \lambda$ and makes sales $x = E/\lambda$ regardless of whether the firm outsources basic production.[7] International outsourcing does affect costs and thus profits. Let $\delta = 1/\lambda$. Firms that do not outsource basic production have marginal cost w, yielding instantaneous profits

$$\pi_N = E(1 - w\delta). \tag{10}$$

Firms that do outsource basic production have marginal cost $c \equiv \alpha + (1 - \alpha)w$, where $0 < \alpha < 1$ represents the labor share in basic production, yielding instantaneous profits

$$\pi_O = E(1 - c\delta) = E[1 - w\delta + \alpha\delta(w - 1)]. \tag{11}$$

The cost savings of outsourcing increase profits, which provide an incentive for firms to endure the cost of adapting technologies.

Inserting profits (10), (11) into the producing firm valuations (8), (9) and inserting those values into the innovation and adaptation conditions (6), (7), under equality, yields the valuation conditions

$$E(1 - w\delta) = wa_\imath(\rho + \imath), \tag{12}$$

$$\alpha E\delta(w - 1) = wa_\phi(\rho + \imath), \tag{13}$$

which must hold for any equilibrium with both innovation and outsourcing.

The assumption that the advanced stage of production never occurs in the South is supported by more fundamental assumptions. Suppose that, while the

[6] Free access to old technologies may arise because the potential for opportunistic behavior keeps Northern firms from providing the knowledge of advanced stage production to Southern firms. Once a technology becomes obsolete, Northern firms have no incentive to protect knowledge of their technology (see also Glass, 1997).

[7] We purposely develop a model that keeps price independent of outsourcing so that innovation provides the sole positive consequence of outsourcing on Northern welfare. This isolation helps us better contrast with Feenstra and Hanson (1996a) the root of additional outsourcing benefits here.

unit labor requirement in basic production in the South is one (by normalization), the unit labor requirement in advanced production in the South is $\zeta > 1$. Provided the unit labor requirement in advanced production in the South is greater than the Northern wage in equilibrium $\zeta > w$, producing the basic stage will be cheaper in the South while producing the advanced stage will be cheaper in the North. Based on the expression for the equilibrium wage (to follow), this condition is satisfied if the size of the quality increment is not too large.[8]

Alternatively, suppose the cost of adapting the advanced stage for Southern production A_ϕ is larger than the cost of adapting the basic stage for Southern production a_ϕ relative to the share of production transferred:

$$\frac{A_\phi}{1-\alpha} > \frac{a_\phi}{\alpha} \rightarrow A_\phi > a_\phi\left(\frac{1-\alpha}{\alpha}\right). \tag{14}$$

The expected gain from adapting the advanced stage then would be less than the cost of adapting the advanced stage for Southern production:

$$E\delta(1-\alpha)(w-1) < wA_\phi(\rho + \iota), \tag{15}$$

even though the expected gains from adapting the basic stage cover costs, as indicated in (13). The lower level of development in the South ensures that adapting advanced stages of production is more difficult than adapting basic stages.

Finally, the limitation on how much of production can be shifted to the South could stem from concerns over opportunistic behavior. Northern firms possess an advantage due to their innovation success. International outsourcing involves purchasing some stages of production from outsiders. If a firm were to purchase all stages of production from outside the firm, its full knowledge advantage would be shared with outsiders. These outsiders could then exclude the innovator since the innovator no longer serves any necessary function. Keeping at least a small step of production (broadly defined) within the firm ensures that outsiders cannot fully replicate the production process.[9]

2.3. Market measures and resources

A product has basic production outsourced when adaptation occurs and reverts to Northern production with each new quality improvement. In a steady

[8] See Deardorff (1997) and Jones and Kierkowski (1997) for static models of fragmentation (also known as segmentation) of the production process.

[9] How the desire to minimize technology diffusion and associated opportunistic behavior affects a firm's choice of mode for serving a foreign market is discussed in Ethier and Markusen (1996) and Saggi (1996).

state, the flows in must equal flows out of basic outsourcing so that the fraction of products outsourced n_O remains constant. Let n_N similarly denote the fraction of products not outsourced (all production occurs in the North). The flows into outsourcing are ϕn_N while the flows out are ιn_O; therefore, $\phi n_N = \iota n_O$. Additionally, the product measures must sum to one: $n_N = 1 - n_O$.

The fixed supply of labor is allocated between innovation, adaptation and production in the North and to production in the South.[10]

$$a_\iota \iota + a_\phi \phi n_N + [n_N + (1-\alpha)n_O]E\delta = L_N\,, \tag{16}$$

$$\alpha n_O E\delta = L_S\,. \tag{17}$$

The North produces only the advanced stage in markets with outsourcing and both stages otherwise; the South produces only the basic stage in markets with outsourcing.[11]

Define the extent of international outsourcing as the fraction of all production outsourced to the South, $\chi \equiv \alpha n_O$, the fraction of products outsourced times the fraction of production outsourced for each product. Also, define the resource requirement in adaptation relative to innovation $a_R \equiv a_\phi/a_\iota$. The market measures and intensity of adaptation can be eliminated from the resource constraints, leaving

$$\left(1 + \frac{a_R \chi}{\alpha}\right) a_\iota \iota + (1-\chi)E\delta = L_N\,, \tag{18}$$

$$\chi E\delta = L_S \tag{19}$$

These two resource constraints (18), (19) combined with the two valuation conditions (12), (13) comprise the system.[12] The system of four equations (12), (13), (18) and (19) determines aggregate spending E, the relative wage w, the rate of innovation ι, and the extent of international outsourcing χ.

[10] Adaptation could be conducted in the South, which would resemble imitation except that only basic production would be imitated so ownership would remain exclusively with Northern firms.

[11] If adaptation instead occurs in the South, the labor demand for adaptation enters into the Southern rather than the Northern labor constraint. This modification only strengthens our results since more labor demand (both basic production and adaptation) is shifted to the South.

[12] The Northern resource constraint clearly indicates that less labor is involved in production in the North as the extent of international outsourcing increases. If unions organize only production workers, not workers employed in laboratories doing innovation and adaptation, this reduction in production employment reinforces their wage concerns.

2.4. Steady-state equilibrium with outsourcing

The valuation conditions (12), (13) exclusively determine the relative wage consistent with innovation and outsourcing both occurring in equilibrium:

$$w = \frac{\alpha + a_R \lambda}{\alpha + a_R} > 1. \tag{20}$$

A higher relative wage reduces the incentives for innovation (due to lower profits in the product market) and expands the incentives for international outsourcing of production (due to larger cost savings). The solution for the relative wage narrows the potential forces behind a reduced relative wage down to the labor share in basic production α, the resource requirement in adaptation relative to innovation a_R or the quality increment λ since only these parameters affect the relative wage.[13]

For various extents of international outsourcing $\chi \in (0, \alpha)$, Fig. 1 traces the rate of innovation ι that equates labor demand and labor supply in each country.[14] The innovation condition (12) is solved for real expenditure and substituted into the two resource constraints. The Northern resource constraint is represented by LN:

$$\left(1 + \frac{a_R \chi}{\alpha}\right) a_\iota \iota + (1 - \chi)\left[\frac{(\alpha + a_R \lambda)}{\alpha(\lambda - 1)} a_\iota(\rho + \iota)\right] = L_N \tag{21}$$

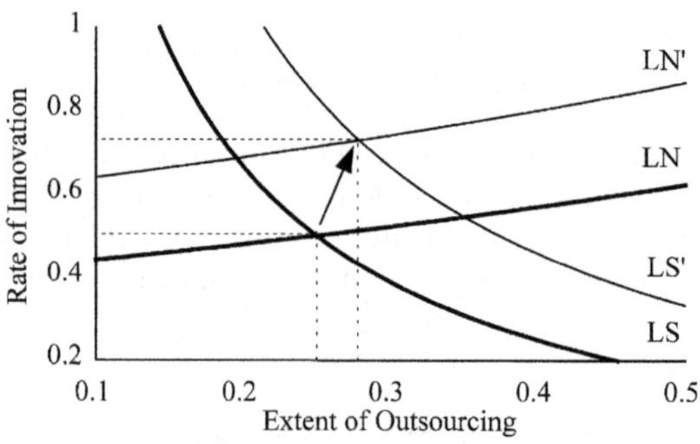

Fig. 1. Outsourcing and innovation.

[13] The labor supplies do not affect the relative wage due to constant returns in innovation and adaptation (recall that the relative wage is determined by the innovation and adaptation conditions).

[14] Figures are drawn for $\rho = \frac{1}{6}$, $\lambda = 2$, $a_\iota = 2$, $a_R = \frac{1}{2}$, $a'_R = \frac{1}{4}$, $\alpha = \frac{1}{2}$, $L_S = 1$, and $L_N = \frac{17}{4}$. The steady-state equilibrium is $E = 8$, $w = \frac{3}{2}$, $\iota = \frac{1}{2}$, and $\chi = \frac{1}{4}$.

and the Southern resource constraint by LS:

$$\chi\left[\frac{(\alpha + a_R\lambda)}{\alpha(\lambda - 1)} a_\iota(\rho + \iota)\right] = L_S. \tag{22}$$

The intersection of the two resource constraints indicates the equilibrium extent of international outsourcing and rate of innovation.

3. Outsourcing causes and effects

Recently, most industrialized countries have experienced an increased extent of international outsourcing χ with a decreased relative wage w. Feenstra and Hanson (1996b) document that international outsourcing by U.S. firms has expanded from 5.34% of material purchases in 1972 to 11.61% in 1990 (doubling over less than 20 years).

Meanwhile, wages in countries where basic production is shifted from have fallen relative to the wages of countries where basic production is shifted to. From 1970 to 1980, manufacturing earnings per employee rose by an average annual rate of 4.0% in the East Asian NICs (Korea, Singapore, Malaysia, Indonesia, Thailand) but only an average annual rate of 2.0% in the leading developed countries (Germany, U.S., Japan, U.K. and Canada) as reported in the World Bank's *World Development Report* (World Bank, 1975–1995, various issues). Similarly, from 1980 to 1991, these earnings rose by 5.3% for the NICs but only 1.3% for the DCs.[15] What forces could explain these trends? What effect do these forces have on the rate of innovation?

3.1. Outsourcing opportunities

The range of activities that can be undertaken in the South is a function of many factors. These many factors, in one way or another, represent an increased ability to outsource: Northern firms face a lower cost of adapting technologies or can outsource a greater share of production activities.

Therefore, an increased ability to outsource can be represented by two parameters in our model: a fall in the resource requirement in international outsourcing relative to innovation a_R or an increase in the share of production activities that can be outsourced for each product α. The first approach implies that the costs of international outsourcing fall as adapting production for the South becomes easier. The second approach implies that the benefits of

[15] The data does not control for other forces affecting wages. Data limitations make the wage coverage 1970–1991 slightly wider than the outsourcing coverage 1972–1990.

international outsourcing rise as production becomes cheaper due to outsourcing a larger proportion of production to the South. We show both these forces increase the extent of international outsourcing and reduce the relative wage. Additionally, both these forces increase the rate of innovation.

First consider the role of a_R. A smaller labor requirement in adaptation relative to innovation means fewer resources must be spent to achieve cost reduction. Fig. 1 shows that the Northern resource constraint LN′ supports a faster rate of innovation for any given extent of outsourcing, and similarly for the Southern resource constraint LS′ as a_R falls. Hence, the rate of innovation and extent of international outsourcing rise. However, the relative wage must fall to maintain the incentives for innovation in the presence of higher opportunity cost of innovation in terms of adaptation.

Next consider the role of α. An increase in the fraction of production outsourced leads to a direct decrease in costs of production when outsourcing occurs. Furthermore, an increase in α also has an indirect effect on costs of production: the relative wage decreases according to (20). This decrease in the relative wage reinforces the direct decline in costs of production. As with a fall in a_R, a rise in α requires the relative wage to fall to preserve the incentives for innovation.

Proposition 1. The smaller the resource requirement in adaptation relative to innovation or the larger the share of production activities that can be outsourced, the greater the extent of international outsourcing, the faster the rate of innovation and the lower the relative wage.

Both of these forces may occur as a natural consequence of development in the South. As the South develops, the Southern economic environment becomes more similar to the North. Thus, adapting technologies is not as difficult and more advanced production stages can be outsourced.

3.2. Labor supplies

Much attention has been drawn to the phenomenal rate of factor accumulation by the East Asian Tigers, which would be represented here by an increase in Southern resources. An increase in the Southern labor supply leads to a greater extent of international outsourcing of production and a faster rate of innovation, as international outsourcing relies on abundant Southern labor. While Southern resources affect the capacity of the South for hosting production, the Southern labor supply does not directly affect the incentives for innovation and international outsourcing, so the relative wage does not change. Thus, an increase in Southern resources does not appear to be (exclusively) behind the increased extent of international outsourcing since the relative wage is unaffected. Similarly, while a smaller Northern labor supply does lead to a greater extent of outsourcing, it does not affect the relative wage. Thus, a decrease in Northern resources does not appear to be (exclusively) behind the increased extent of international outsourcing.

Proposition 2. The smaller the Northern labor supply, the greater the extent of international outsourcing, and the slower the rate of innovation, with no effect on the relative wage. The larger the Southern labor supply, the greater the extent of international outsourcing, and the faster the rate of innovation, with no effect on the relative wage.

An increase in Southern resources could be encouraging outsourcing in the presence of other forces generating the reduction in the relative wage. If so, then the dynamic benefits of outsourcing would be more pronounced.[16]

3.3. Production taxes and subsidies

Having found two probable natural economic forces behind an increased extent of international outsourcing and a decline in the relative wage, we now explore the potential for government policies to induce similar effects. Discussions surrounding trade and investment agreements often center around not only lower wages attracting basic production but also lower taxes. How do differences in tax rates across countries affect international outsourcing?

Industrialized countries that provide the source of international outsourcing generally have stricter environmental protection regulations, labor safety, unemployment and social security provisions and higher overall tax rates that raise the cost of production in the North relative to the South beyond the level indicated by wages alone. Suppose the marginal cost of production in the North is $w(1 + \tau)$, the relative wage elevated by the tax rate τ.[17]

Not only do Northern governments tend to impose environmental and other regulations that raise production costs, but Southern governments adopt policies that lower production costs there. Southern governments may enforce wage ceilings, tolerate harsh work conditions, permit depletion of natural resources or directly subsidize exports.[18] Suppose the marginal cost of production in the

[16] An increase in the quality increment (or similar forces increasing product prices) leads to a greater extent of outsourcing and a faster rate of innovation, but causes the relative wage to rise. Thus, an increase in the quality increment does not appear to be (exclusively) behind the increase in the extent of outsourcing because the effect on the relative wage occurs in the wrong direction.

[17] We consider a production tax that applies to workers employed in producing output, not to workers employed in innovation or adaptation, since only production can be outsourced.

[18] Southern countries may also have poorly defined property rights, political risk, corruption or other factors that raise production costs. The effects for an increase in a Southern subsidy also apply to a reduction in a Southern tax (for a production tax, $\sigma < 0$).

South is $(1 - \sigma)$, the Southern wage (normalized to one) depressed by the subsidy rate σ. Recall $\delta \equiv 1/\lambda$.

The valuation condition for innovation then becomes

$$E[1 - w(1 + \tau)\delta] = wa_\iota(\rho + \iota) \tag{23}$$

and the valuation condition for adaptation becomes

$$E\alpha[w(1 + \tau) - (1 - \sigma)]\delta = wa_\phi(\rho + \iota). \tag{24}$$

These new valuation conditions determine the new relative wage

$$w = \frac{\alpha(1 - \sigma) + a_{\mathrm{R}}\lambda}{(1 + \tau)(\alpha + a_{\mathrm{R}})}. \tag{25}$$

The solution for the relative wage indicates that a reduction in the relative wage could stem from an increase in production taxes in the North or an increase in production subsidies in the South.

Higher production taxes in the North increase the incentives for international outsourcing (to escape the taxes), which in turn permits a faster rate of innovation due to the resources freed from production in the North. Similarly, higher production subsidies in the South increase the incentives for international outsourcing (to obtain the subsidy), which in turn permits a faster rate of innovation due to the resources freed from production in the North. In both cases, the relative wage must decline to maintain the incentive for innovation.

Proposition 3. The larger the Northern production tax or the larger the Southern production subsidy, the greater the extent of international outsourcing, the faster the rate of innovation and the lower the relative wage.

Thus increases in Northern production taxes and Southern production subsidies can also provide an explanation for the observed increase in the extent of international outsourcing and decline in the relative wage. Like the natural economic forces examined, these government interventions share the trait that the rate of innovation rises.

3.4. R&D subsidies

Governments distort not only production decisions, but investment decisions as well. Suppose the government offers a subsidy s_ι to innovation, so a potential innovator bears only an innovation expense of $1 - s_\iota$ of the true cost of innovation. Suppose also that the government offers a subsidy s_ϕ

to adaptation, so a firm bears only the share $1 - s_\phi$ of the true cost of adaptation.[19]

The valuation condition for innovation then becomes

$$E[1 - w\delta] = wa_\iota(1 - s_\iota)(\rho + \iota) \tag{26}$$

and the valuation condition for adaptation then becomes

$$E[\alpha(w - 1)\delta] = wa_\phi(1 - s_\phi)(\rho + \iota) \tag{27}$$

These valuation conditions determine the new relative wage

$$w = \frac{\alpha(1 - s_\iota) + a_R\lambda(1 - s_\phi)}{\alpha(1 - s_\iota) + a_R(1 - s_\phi)}. \tag{28}$$

The solution for the relative wage indicates that a tax on innovation would depress the relative wage. However, a subsidy to innovation (not a tax) yields a greater extent of outsourcing. Thus, a policy of either taxing or subsidizing innovation does not seem to be behind the greater extent of outsourcing with a lower relative wage.

The solution for the relative wage does indicate that a reduction in the relative wage could stem from an increase in the subsidy to adaptation. We confirm that subsidizing adaptation does indeed lead to a greater extent of outsourcing.

Proposition 4. The larger the innovation subsidy, the greater the extent of international outsourcing, the faster the rate of innovation and the higher the relative wage. The larger the adaptation subsidy, the greater the extent of international outsourcing, the faster the rate of innovation and the lower the relative wage.

The relative wage falls when adaptation is subsidized but rises when innovation is subsidized. When adaptation is encouraged by a subsidy, the relative wage must fall to ensure the same return to innovation (through lower costs of innovation and lower production costs). On the other hand, when innovation is encouraged by a subsidy, the relative wage must rise to ensure the same return to adaptation (through greater cost savings from outsourcing).

Similar to Northern production taxes or Southern production subsidies, subsidizing adaptation increases the incentives for firms to outsource basic production to the South.[20] Subsidizing investments in adapting technologies for

[19] Subsidies could be paid by a Southern government keen to attract Northern production to its market.

[20] Thus our model is well-behaved: it does not exhibit the peculiar features that concern Cheng and Tao (1999) and Davidson and Segerstrom (1998) in the closed economy quality ladder model (with innovation and imitation) by Segerstrom (1991). In particular, a subsidy targeted at a form of R&D succeeds in stimulating that form of R&D, while the effects on the other form of R&D follow economic intuition.

Southern production results in encouraging innovation as well. In addition to the incentive effect already described, the increased outsourcing frees Northern resources for innovation.

4. Conclusion

This paper examines the sources and impact of increased international outsourcing of production. As for sources, we find five forces with the potential to explain an increased extent of international outsourcing along with a decline in the relative wage. A reduction in the costs of adapting technologies for production in low wage countries or an increase in the portion of production sufficiently basic to be outsourced could play a role. An increase in production taxes in high wage countries, an increase in production subsidies (reduction in production tax) in low wage countries, or a subsidy to adapting technologies for the South could also play a role. Each of these forces, along with raising the extent of international outsourcing and lowering the relative wage, also leads to a faster rate of innovation. Product market profits provide the reward to costly improvements in products, and international outsourcing increases product market profits. Also, shifting production to the South frees Northern resources for innovation. Thus, forces that increase international outsourcing accelerate the progression of the technology frontier.

As for impact, increased international outsourcing affects the welfare of Northern citizens in two conflicting directions. First, increased international outsourcing fuels the rate of innovation leading to a faster arrival of product improvements, a positive growth effect. Second, increased international outsourcing lowers the relative wage (and aggregate spending), a negative level effect. Evaluating Northern welfare requires weighing the innovation benefits of international outsourcing against sacrificed purchasing power due to reduced wage earnings. Restricting attention to the wage damage from international outsourcing is overly pessimistic, since this negative effect can be offset by the positive effect from faster innovation.[21]

Acknowledgements

We thank Elias Dinopoulos, Paul Evans, Elhanan Helpman, participants in the OSU Macro Seminar, Midwest International Economics Meetings and Southeast International Trade Meetings, and an anonymous referee for their helpful comments.

[21] Details of welfare analysis can be found in an earlier version of this paper.

Appendix A

A.1. Proof of Proposition 1

Derivatives with respect to each parameter are generated by

$$\underbrace{\begin{bmatrix} (\alpha + a_R)(\lambda - \chi) & -[\alpha(\rho + \imath) + a_R(\lambda\rho + \imath)] \\ \chi(\alpha + a_R\lambda) & (\alpha + a_R\lambda)(\rho + \imath) \end{bmatrix}}_{B} \begin{bmatrix} \mathrm{d}\imath \\ \mathrm{d}\chi \end{bmatrix} = \begin{bmatrix} c_1 \\ c_2 \end{bmatrix},$$

where the determinant is clearly positive $|B| \equiv b_{11}b_{22} - b_{21}b_{12} > 0$, since $\lambda > 1$ and $\chi \equiv \alpha n_{\mathrm{O}} < 1$ as $\alpha < 1$ and $n_{\mathrm{O}} < 1$ so $\lambda > \chi$. The values of L_{S} and L_{N} that solve the resource constraints are applied in these derivatives to simplify the expressions. An increase in the resources required in adaptation relative to the resources required in innovation a_{R} decreases the rate of innovation, decreases the extent of international outsourcing and increases the relative wage:

$$\frac{\partial \imath}{\partial a_{\mathrm{R}}} = -\frac{(\rho + \imath)\,[\alpha\imath\chi(\lambda - 1) + \lambda(\alpha + \lambda a_{\mathrm{R}})\,(\rho + \imath)]}{|B|} < 0,$$

$$\frac{\partial \chi}{\partial a_{\mathrm{R}}} = -\frac{\chi(\lambda - 1)\,[\alpha\imath(\lambda - \chi) + \lambda\rho(\alpha + \chi a_{\mathrm{R}})]}{|B|} < 0,$$

$$\frac{\partial w}{\partial a_{\mathrm{R}}} = \frac{\alpha(\lambda - 1)}{(\alpha + a_{\mathrm{R}})^2} > 0.$$

An increase in the basic share of production α increases the rate of innovation, increases the extent of international outsourcing, and decreases the relative wage:

$$\frac{\partial \imath}{\partial \alpha} = \frac{a_{\mathrm{R}}}{\alpha}\frac{(\rho + \imath)\,[\alpha\imath\chi(\lambda - 1) + \lambda(\alpha + \lambda a_{\mathrm{R}})\,(\rho + \imath)]}{|B|} = -\frac{a_{\mathrm{R}}}{\alpha}\frac{\partial \imath}{\partial a_{\mathrm{R}}} > 0,$$

$$\frac{\partial \chi}{\partial \alpha} = \frac{a_{\mathrm{R}}}{\alpha}\frac{\chi(\lambda - 1)\,[\alpha\imath(\lambda - \chi) + \lambda\rho(\alpha + \chi a_{\mathrm{R}})]}{|B|} = -\frac{a_{\mathrm{R}}}{\alpha}\frac{\partial \chi}{\partial a_{\mathrm{R}}} > 0,$$

$$\frac{\partial w}{\partial \alpha} = -\frac{a_{\mathrm{R}}(\lambda - 1)}{(\alpha + a_{\mathrm{R}})^2} = -\frac{a_{\mathrm{R}}}{\alpha}\frac{\partial w}{\partial a_{\mathrm{R}}} < 0.$$

The link between the effects of a_{R} and α suggests that what matters is the share of production that can be outsourced once adaptation is successful per unit of labor devoted to adaptation.

A.2. Proof of Proposition 2

An increase in Northern L_N increases the rate of innovation, decreases the extent of international outsourcing and does not affect the relative wage:

$$\frac{\partial \imath}{\partial L_N} = \frac{\alpha(\lambda - 1)(\rho + \imath)(\alpha + \lambda a_R)}{a_N|B|} > 0,$$

$$\frac{\partial \chi}{\partial L_N} = -\frac{\alpha\chi(\lambda - 1)(\alpha + \lambda a_R)}{a_N|B|} < 0.$$

An increase in Southern resources L_S increases the rate of innovation, increases the extent of international outsourcing and does not affect the relative wage:

$$\frac{\partial \imath}{\partial L_S} = \frac{\alpha(\lambda - 1)[(\rho + \imath)\alpha + \rho\lambda a_R + \imath a_R]}{a_N|B|} > 0,$$

$$\frac{\partial \chi}{\partial L_S} = -\frac{\alpha(\lambda - \chi)(\lambda - 1)(\alpha + a_R)}{a_N|B|} > 0$$

A.3. Proof of Proposition 3

The condensed system with production taxes and subsidies is

$$\left(1 + \frac{a_R\chi}{\alpha}\right)a_\imath\imath + (1 - \chi)\left[\frac{\alpha(1 - \sigma) + a_R\lambda}{\alpha[\lambda - (1 - \sigma)](1 + \tau)}a_\imath(\rho + \imath)\right] = L_N,$$

$$\chi\left[\frac{\alpha(1 - \sigma) + a_R\lambda}{\alpha[\lambda - (1 - \sigma)](1 + \tau)}a_\imath(\rho + \imath)\right] = L_S.$$

An increase in the Northern production tax τ increases the rate of innovation, increases the extent of international outsourcing, and decreases the relative wage (evaluated at $\tau = 0$ and $\sigma = 0$):

$$\frac{\partial \imath}{\partial \tau} = \frac{a_\imath^2(\rho + \imath)(\alpha + \lambda a_R)[\alpha(\rho + \imath) + [\lambda\rho + \imath\chi + \imath\lambda(1 - \chi)]a_R]}{|B|} > 0,$$

$$\frac{\partial \chi}{\partial \tau} = \frac{\chi a_\imath^2(\lambda - 1)(\alpha + \lambda a_R)(\rho + \imath)(\alpha + \chi a_R)}{|B|} > 0,$$

$$\frac{\partial w}{\partial \tau} = -\frac{\alpha + a_R\lambda}{\alpha + a_R} < 0.$$

An increase in the Southern production subsidy σ increases the rate of innovation, increases the extent of international outsourcing, and decreases the relative wage (evaluated at $\tau = 0$ and $\sigma = 0$):

$$\frac{\partial \iota}{\partial \sigma} = \frac{\lambda a_\iota^2(\rho + \iota)(\alpha + a_\mathrm{R})[\alpha(\rho + \iota) + [\lambda\rho + \iota\chi + \iota\lambda(1 - \chi)]a_\mathrm{R}]}{(\lambda - 1)|B|} > 0,$$

$$\frac{\partial \chi}{\partial \sigma} = \frac{\chi\lambda a_\iota^2(\alpha + a_\mathrm{R})(\rho + \iota)(\alpha + \chi a_\mathrm{R})}{|B|} = \left(\frac{\lambda}{\lambda - 1}\right)\left(\frac{\alpha + a_\mathrm{R}}{\alpha + a_\mathrm{R}\lambda}\right)\frac{\partial \chi}{\partial \tau} > 0,$$

$$\frac{\partial w}{\partial \sigma} = -\frac{\alpha}{(\alpha + a_\mathrm{R})} < 0.$$

A.4. Proof of Proposition 4

The condensed system with innovation and adaptation subsidies is

$$\left(1 - s_\iota + \frac{a_\mathrm{R}\chi(1 - s_\phi)}{\alpha}\right)a_\iota\iota + (1 - \chi)$$

$$\left[\frac{\alpha(1 - s_\iota) + a_\mathrm{R}\lambda(1 - s_\phi)}{\alpha(\lambda - 1)}a_\iota(\rho + \iota)\right] = L_\mathrm{N},$$

$$\chi\left[\frac{\alpha(1 - s_\iota) + a_\mathrm{R}\lambda(1 - s_\phi)}{\alpha(\lambda - 1)}a_\iota(\rho + \iota)\right] = L_\mathrm{S}.$$

An increase in the innovation subsidy s_ι increases the rate of innovation, increases the extent of international outsourcing, and increases the relative wage (evaluated at $s_\iota = 0$ and $s_\phi = 0$):

$$\frac{\partial \iota}{\partial s_\iota} = \frac{\alpha a_\iota^2(\rho + \iota)[\alpha(\rho + \iota) + [\lambda\rho + \iota\chi + \iota\lambda(1 - \chi)]a_\mathrm{R}]}{|B|} > 0,$$

$$\frac{\partial \chi}{\partial s_\iota} = \frac{\chi\alpha a_\iota^2(\lambda - 1)(\alpha + \chi a_\mathrm{R})(\rho + \iota)}{|B|} > 0,$$

$$\frac{\partial w}{\partial s_\iota} = \frac{\alpha a_\mathrm{R}(\lambda - 1)}{(\alpha + a_\mathrm{R})^2} > 0.$$

An increase in the adaptation subsidy s_ϕ increases the rate of innovation, increases the extent of international outsourcing, and decreases the relative wage (evaluated at $s_2 = 0$ and $s_\phi = 0$):

$$\frac{\partial \iota}{\partial s_\phi} = \frac{\lambda a_\mathrm{R} a_\iota^2(\rho + \iota)[\alpha(\rho + \iota) + [\lambda\rho + \iota\chi + \iota\lambda(1 - \chi)]a_\mathrm{R}]}{|B|} = \frac{a_\mathrm{R}\lambda}{\alpha}\frac{\partial \iota}{\partial s_\iota} > 0,$$

$$\frac{\partial \chi}{\partial s_{\phi}} = \frac{\chi \lambda a_{\mathrm{R}} a_{\iota}^{2}(\lambda - 1)(\alpha + \chi a_{\mathrm{R}})(\rho + \iota)}{|B|} = \frac{a_{\mathrm{R}}\lambda}{\alpha}\frac{\partial \chi}{\partial s_{\iota}} > 0,$$

$$\frac{\partial w}{\partial s_{\phi}} = -\frac{\alpha a_{\mathrm{R}}(\lambda - 1)}{(\alpha + a_{\mathrm{R}})^{2}} = -\frac{\partial w}{\partial s_{\iota}} < 0.$$

References

Cheng, L.K., Tao, Z., 1999. The impact of public policies on innovation and imitation: The role of R&D technology in growth models. International Economic Review 40, 187–207.

Davidson, C., Segerstrom, P.S., 1998. R&D subsidies and economic growth. Rand Journal of Economics 29, 548–577.

Deardorff, A.V., 1997. Fragmentation in simple trade models. Mimeo.

Ethier, W.J., Markusen, J.R., 1996. Multinational firms, technology diffusion and trade. Journal of International Economics 41, 1–28.

Feenstra, R.C., Hanson, G.H., 1996a. Foreign investment, outsourcing, and relative wages. In: Feenstra, R.C., Grossman, G.M., Irwin, D.A. (Eds.), The political Economy of Trade Policy. M.I.T. Press, Cambridge, MA.

Feenstra, R.C., Hanson, G.H., 1996b. Globalization, outsourcing, and wage inequality. American Economic Review 86, 240–245.

Glass, A.J., 1997. Product cycles and market penetration. International Economic Review 38, 865–891.

Glass, A.J., Saggi, K., 1999. Foreign direct investment and the nature of R&D. Canadian Journal of Economics 32, 92–117.

Grossman, G.M., Helpman, E., 1991. Quality ladders and product cycles. Quarterly Journal of Economics 106, 557–586.

Helpman, E., 1993. Innovation, imitation, and intellectual property rights. Econometrica 61, 1247–1280.

Jensen, R., Thursby, M., 1987. A decision theoretic model of innovation, technology transfer, and trade. Review of Economic Studies 54, 631–647.

Jones, R.W., Kierkowski, H., 1997. Globalization and the consequences of international fragmentation. Mimeo.

Saggi, K., 1996. Entry into a foreign market: Foreign direct investment versus licensing. Review of International Economics 4, 99–104.

Segerstrom, P.S., 1991. Innovation, imitation, and economic growth. Journal of Political Economy 99, 807–827.

Segerstrom, P.S., Anant, T.C.A., Dinopoulos, E., 1990. A Schumpeterian model of the product life cycle. American Economic Review 80, 1077–1091.

Vernon, R., 1966. International investment and international trade in the product cycle. Quarterly Journal of Economics 80, 190–207.

World Bank, 1975–1995. World Development Report. Oxford University Press, Oxford.

Chapter 3

Vertical technology transfer via international outsourcing[#]

Howard Pack [a,1], Kamal Saggi [b,*]

[a] *Department of Public Policy and Management, The Wharton School, University of Pennsylvania, Philadelphia, PA 19104, USA*

[b] *Department of Economics, Southern Methodist University, Dallas, TX 75275-0496, USA*

Received 1 April 1999; accepted 1 January 2001

Abstract

To analyze the effect of vertical technology transfer on industrial development in lesser developed countries (LDCs), we develop a model in which the technology transferred to an LDC supplier by a developed country (DC) importer can diffuse to other LDC firms. Surprisingly, even if such diffusion in the LDC market leads to entry into the DC market, it can benefit *both* the initial DC importer and its initial LDC supplier by reducing the double marginalization problem. This effect does not depend upon whether firms compete in prices or quantities and exists even when the number of entrants into each market is endogenously determined.

JEL classification: O14; O19; O32; F23; L13

Keywords: International technology transfer; Diffusion; Vertical structure; Oligopolistic competition

1. Introduction

A substantial body of empirical evidence indicates that considerable vertical knowledge transfer from industrialized countries to the Asian newly industrializing countries (NICs) has occurred as firms from industrialized countries have bought part or all of the output of local firms and have sold it under the name of the purchaser (Hobday, 1995). For example, companies such as Radio Shack and

[*] Corresponding author. Tel.: +1-214-768-3274; fax: +1-214-768-1821.

E-mail addresses: packh@wharton.upenn.edu (H. Pack), ksaggi@mail.smu.edu (K. Saggi).

[1] Tel.: +1-215-898-0089; fax: +1-215-898-7635.

[#] This chapter was originally appeared in *Journal of Development Economics* **65**, 389–415. © 2001 Elsevier Science B.V.

Texas Instruments have commissioned firms from NICs to produce components or entire products, which are then sold under the retailer's name in world markets. Rhee et al. (1984), summarizing the results of extensive interviews in Korea in the late 1970s, report that:

> The relations between Korean firms and the foreign buyers went far beyond the negotiation and fulfillment of contracts. Almost half of the firms said they had directly benefited from the technical information foreign buyers provided: through visits to their plants by engineers or other technical staff of the foreign buyers, through visits by their engineering staff to the foreign buyers, through the provision of blueprints and specifications, through information on production techniques and on the technical specifications of competing products, and through feedback on the design, quality and technical performance of their products (p. 61).

A large survey of many firms in Korea and Taiwan in the late 1970s found that importers maintained very large staffs based in the countries who spent considerable time with their local manufacturers (Keesing, 1982). Studies in other countries such as Taiwan have confirmed such findings of significant technology transfer by developed country importers (Hou and Gee, 1993). Once mastered by local firms, such knowledge is useful to other potential importers in developed countries.[2]

There are several interesting aspects to the process of technology transfer undertaken by importers from developed countries (DCs). Most importantly, why does a DC importer provide such knowledge to a firm in a lesser developed country (LDC) given that it could diffuse to other local firms (say via worker mobility) who may then sell to rival DC importers? In the context of NICS, the types of knowledge transmitted include product designs, improvements in production technology including adjustments in machinery settings, and advice on packaging and instruction materials. When these transfers occurred in the 1960s and 1970s, property rights were very weak in all of the Asian countries and the types of knowledge transferred are, in any regime of intellectual property rights, difficult to protect. In such situations, the DC firms are providing a form of general training that is highly transferable to other firms (Becker, 1964). While it is possible that the recipients of knowledge transfers implicitly pay for them (say by receiving lower prices for their products), we develop an alternative view of why technology suppliers may offer their knowledge even when they are unable to extract the full benefits that accrue to LDC firms.

[2] Such knowledge transfers have also raised the issue of whether exporting indeed increases productivity of exporters or whether it is the case that the more productive firms self-select into exporting. See Clerides et al. (1998) for an empirical investigation of this issue.

We construct a simple model in which a DC firm may choose to engage in vertical technology transfer by outsourcing basic production to firm(s) in a LDC. Under exclusive outsourcing, the DC firm transfers technology to an LDC firm and markets its output in the DC market. A key feature of the model is that once the technology is transferred to an LDC firm, some of the knowledge may seep out to a non-affiliated firm within the LDC.[3] How does the possibility of such leakage affect the incentives for vertical technology transfer? If LDC firms lack the ability to successfully market their products in the DC market, technology leakage in the LDC market actually *benefits* the DC firm since it increases competition among the LDC suppliers.

However, there is a possibility that the decrease in price due to technology diffusion in the upstream LDC market may induce entry into the downstream DC market thereby making it more competitive.[4] Accordingly, we also analyze the case where such entry is indeed feasible. While increased competition in the DC market may erode profits of the original DC firm, this effect is not necessarily strong enough to dissuade it from transferring technology to the LDC market. In fact, our analysis shows that diffusion of technology among LDC suppliers accompanied by entry in the downstream DC market may actually *benefit* the two original firms engaged in technology transfer. In other words, Sears may benefit even if knowledge transferred to a Korean firm eventually helps Penney's.

The intuition for this surprising result is as follows. In the absence of diffusion upstream and entry downstream, the two original firms are in a bilateral monopoly and they impose a pecuniary vertical externality upon each other by charging a price above marginal cost (i.e. the double marginalization problem). Diffusion upstream brings the LDC price closer to marginal cost and benefits the DC firm. Entry downstream brings the downstream price closer to marginal cost and benefits the original LDC firm. As a result, as long as the competition resulting from diffusion upstream and entry downstream is not too severe, both firms gain from diffusion that leads to entry in the downstream market.[5] Note that if the DC firm and the LDC supplier were vertically integrated, diffusion would harm the

---

[3] This possibility has led to a concern in the U.S. that transfer of technology by American firms will eventually adversely affect U.S. income.

[4] Panasonic, to name one firm, is largely a marketing company that had remarkable success in penetrating the U.S. market after Japanese firms mastered technologies originally developed by American firms (for example, consider the case of tape recorders and VCRs). Similarly, there are numerous instances in the Asian NICs of the emergence of marketing firms that purchased local products and sold them in the developed countries. For example, by 1978, Korea had over 2000 trading companies (Keesing, 1982). Taiwan's experience has been similar.

[5] Of course, in the absence of downstream entry, diffusion hurts the original LDC firm, given that it has accepted an outsourcing contract. However, one must be careful here. Suppose diffusion does not lead to downstream entry. Does it necessarily hurt the original LDC firm? The answer is that given that the DC firm's decision to outsource is not affected, it does. But it is entirely possible that in the absence of the possibility of diffusion, the DC firm would be unwilling to transfer technology.

DC firm since, under vertical integration, the DC firm can source the upstream good at marginal cost in the first place. The implication of this result is that *fully integrated multinational firms may be more averse to technology diffusion* than firms that are involved in international arms length arrangements. This may explain, in retrospect, the gain that accrued to South Korea and Taiwan from licensing and other arms length arrangements of technology transfer.

Our model emphasizes technology transfers that are vertical, conforming to the growing amount of trade between DC wholesalers and retailers and LDC manufacturers. This contrasts with recent analyses of the horizontal aspects of technology transfers among firms that compete in the same product market (Ethier and Markusen, 1996; Saggi, 1996, 1999; Kabiraj and Marjit 1993; Glass and Saggi, 1999a,b).

This paper is also related to several strands of literature in industrial organization. Outsourcing in our model is akin to licensing of an innovation to another producer that has a lower cost of production. Unlike the literature on licensing (see, for example, Katz and Shapiro, 1985; Kamien and Tauman, 1986), we emphasize how such transfer of technology can diffuse to other firms and then have implications for competition at both stages of the market. Furthermore, the vertical aspect of technology transfer (i.e. from a buyer to a seller) is novel to our model.[6]

A second relevant strand of industrial organization literature deals with the issue of how vertical relations between an upstream and a downstream firm can be disadvantageous for competitors of the downstream firm. For example, such vertical relations between two firms may increase the price of an input(s) supplied by the upstream industry or completely eliminate a source of supply of an input for another downstream firm (the case of vertical foreclosure). A prominent example of this line of research is Ordover et al. (1990) who demonstrate that even if those threatened by vertical foreclosure can adopt some counter strategies, such foreclosure can indeed emerge in equilibrium. In another vein, in a model of a monopoly facing a competitive fringe, Salop and Scheffman (1987) argue that the monopolist may be able to benefit by undertaking costly actions that increase the cost of its rivals. One example of such behavior is where the dominant firm can affect the price of an input used by the entire industry. Clearly, our argument complements these two preceding lines of research: in our model, a firm can gain from technology transfer even if diffusion *lowers* the marginal cost of production

[6] The licensing literature does analyze situations where a patent holder (who itself does not produce the good) can license its technology to competing producers. This situation has a *vertical* aspect to it in that it involves technology transfer from a research lab to producers. But the important distinction is that, in our model, the DC downstream firm that transfers technology to LDC firm(s) also sources an intermediate good from them. Thus, the firms are in a vertical relationship in *both* the goods market and the market for technology where the *supplier of technology is the buyer of an intermediate good.*

of a potential rival. What is crucial for our result, as well as the results of the literature on vertical relations, is that actions of one firm can alter the market structure in both upstream and downstream markets. Our contribution to this literature is to show how a single downstream firm's decision to transfer technology can affect market structure at both the upstream and downstream level due to the feedback effects between the two markets.

The paper is organized as follows. Section 2 presents our basic model in which firms compete in prices. In this section, we examine two different scenarios: one in which entry is blocked and another in which potential entry disciplines the behavior of incumbent firm(s). In Section 3, we examine the case where firms compete in quantities so that actual entry takes place in equilibrium. In this section, the model is also extended to endogenize the number of entrants into each market. Section 4 offers conclusions. All supporting calculations not reported in the paper are contained in Appendix A.

2. Model

Our basic model is a three-stage game involving one incumbent DC firm, two LDC firms, and one potential entrant into the DC market. Since we wish to focus on the transfer of technology and not on its generation, we assume that the technology is patented by the incumbent DC firm. In the first stage, the incumbent DC firm (labelled by 0) chooses to outsource production to a subset of the LDC firms. The profits that the incumbent DC firm can earn by producing in the DC market are normalized to zero. The incumbent DC firm is willing to take a chance on transferring a technology over which it could conceivably lose control as it perceives itself to have a complementary asset (marketing skills) in the absence of which sales in the DC home market are not possible. Let ψ_0 denote the incumbent DC firm's marginal cost of marketing. The potential DC entrant can also provide marketing services skills but has a higher marginal cost of marketing than the incumbent DC firm. Let ψ_3 denote the potential entrant's marginal cost of marketing, where $\psi_3 \geq \psi_0$. When the potential entrant's marginal cost exceeds the optimal (monopoly) price charged by the incumbent DC firm, entry into the DC market is effectively blocked. In what follows, we will analyze two scenarios: one in which entry into marketing is blocked and another in which it is not. Before analyzing each of these scenarios, we describe those aspects of our model that are common to both scenarios.

Successful outsourcing requires transfer of technology to the LDC firm(s) and involves a per firm fixed cost of I that may be substantial (Teece, 1997). Let θ denote the share of this fixed cost that is borne by the incumbent DC firm. Technology transfer allows LDC firm(s) to produce a good that can be sold in the DC market by the incumbent DC firm.

After the DC firm makes its outsourcing offers, each LDC firm decides whether or not to accept the offer it faces. In the final stage, the incumbent DC firm obtains the basic product from its LDC supplier(s) and then markets the product in the DC market. The output of the LDC firm and the marketing effort of the incumbent firm are complements—one unit of output requires one unit of marketing.

Complicating the decision of both the incumbent DC firm and the LDC firms is the possibility of technology diffusion: once the technology is transferred to a LDC firm, it may leak out to the other firm. Suppose only one LDC firm were to receive the technology from the DC incumbent firm. Let us refer to this LDC firm as the incumbent LDC firm. Let p denote the probability that the technology leaks out to the other LDC firm.[7] All firms recognize the possibility of inter-firm technology diffusion and take this possibility into account while making their decisions. Technology diffusion within the LDC economy may be incomplete: post diffusion, the marginal cost of production of a firm which is not directly involved in outsourcing equals $c_2 \geq c_1$. The idea behind this assumption is that without the explicit involvement of the firm that owns the patented technology, LDC firms may achieve only a partial understanding of the technology as many of the elements are not codified but are part of the informal knowledge of the incumbent DC firm that remains within the firm's possession (Nelson and Sidney Winter, 1982). Upon technology adoption, the LDC firms compete in prices. As is well known, under Bertrand competition with homogenous products, in equilibrium, the higher cost firm is limit priced out of the market: the LDC incumbent firm supplies its output to the DC incumbent firm at price equal to the marginal cost of the higher cost firm (c_2).

As mentioned earlier, we analyze two different cases. In case one (blocked entry), successful technology diffusion in the LDC market does not pose any threat of potential entry in the DC market so that the incumbent DC firm is free to act as a monopolist. In this scenario, the second LDC firm must also hire the incumbent DC firm as its marketing agent.[8] The alternative case is where heightened competition in the LDC market lowers the upstream price sufficiently so that the potential entrant in the DC market becomes a disciplining force on the DC incumbent: if the incumbent DC firm were to charge its unconstrained monopoly price, the potential entrant into marketing finds it optimal to offer marketing

[7] This may occur as a result of labor movement or the informal interchange of knowledge between managers and workers. See Kauffman (1997) and Glass and Saggi (1999b) for formal models of this process and Schive (1990) for evidence of this phenomenon in Taiwan.

[8] We assume that the original recipient of knowledge (i.e. the LDC incumbent) is contractually bound to the provider of knowledge (i.e. the DC incumbent) and does not violate its contract. In the real world, even if a firm was tempted to violate its contract, the reputation effects would likely be severe. In markets where new blueprints or designs are needed on a regular basis, such a violation would not be in interest of the LDC incumbent.

services to the new LDC supplier by undercutting the DC incumbent firm.[9] In this scenario, potential competition prevails in both markets and disciplines the behavior of incumbents at both stages. We begin with the case where entry into the DC market is blocked.

2.1. Blocked entry

In order to obtain a sub-game perfect Nash equilibrium, we solve the game by backwards induction. In the final stage of the game, the incumbent DC firm markets the output of the upstream LDC supplier(s). At this stage, the number of LDC suppliers is given. Recall that if there are multiple LDC suppliers, they compete with each other in prices.

Let the demand curve facing the incumbent DC firm (labelled by 0) be given by $q(p)$. Let w denote the price of the good supplied by the LDC firm(s). Taking the upstream price w as given, the incumbent DC firm decides on what price to charge in the DC market. Therefore, the DC incumbent is a monopolist whose marginal cost of providing the good to DC consumers equals $w + \psi_0$. Facing the demand curve $q(p)$ in the DC market, the incumbent DC firm solves the following problem

$$\underset{p}{\text{Max}}\ \pi_0(p) \equiv (p - w - \psi_0)q(p)$$

The first order condition for profit maximization can be written as

$$q(p) + (p - w - \psi_0)\frac{\mathrm{d}q(p)}{\mathrm{d}p} = 0. \tag{1}$$

Let the optimal solution to the above problem as a function of the upstream price w be denoted by $p^{\mathrm{m}}(w)$ and let the equilibrium output of the DC incumbent be given by $q^{\mathrm{m}}(w) \equiv q(p^{\mathrm{m}}(w))$.[10]

Moving backwards, next consider the decision of those LDC firms that are approached by the incumbent DC firm for possible outsourcing. Due to price competition in the upstream LDC market, if both LDC firms accept the outsourcing contract, upstream equilibrium price equals marginal cost c_1. Since all firms foresee the nature of competition at the next stage, given that one LDC firm accepts the offer, the second LDC firm prefers to take its chances regarding costless technology diffusion rather than incur any part of the cost $(1 - \theta)I$. Thus, an outsourcing deal that does not compensate LDC firms for their share of the costs of technology transfer is not accepted by more than one firm. The question

[9] This additional marketing firm could even be an LDC firm. The crucial point is that a drop in LDC supply price makes downstream entry attractive.

[10] The dependence of p^m on ψ_0 is suppressed for expositional ease.

then becomes whether it is ever in the interest of the incumbent DC firm to outsource production to both LDC firms by bearing the entire (per firm) fixed cost I. In other words, if side-payments are possible among firms, by bearing the entire fixed cost I, the incumbent DC firm can create an alternative LDC supplier with probability one or it can choose to take the chance that the technology will leak out to the other LDC firm with probability p, where $0<p<1$.[11] To explore the trade-off between outsourcing a single versus multiple firms, we first need some notation.

Let the optimal price charged by the incumbent LDC firm (labelled by 1) in the absence of technology diffusion be given by w_1, where w_1 is obtained by solving the following problem

$$\operatorname*{Max}_{w} \pi_1(w) \equiv (w-c_1)q^{\mathrm{m}}(w)$$

where $q^{\mathrm{m}}(w)$ is the derived demand curve facing the LDC incumbent and is derived from Eq. (1). The first order condition for the above problem is given by

$$q^{\mathrm{m}}(w)+(w-c_1)\frac{\mathrm{d}q^{\mathrm{m}}(w)}{\mathrm{d}w}=0. \tag{2}$$

Clearly, in the absence of technology diffusion, the two original firms (0 and 1) are in a bilateral monopoly and impose a pecuniary vertical externality upon each other since both charge a price above their respective marginal costs (i.e. there exists a double marginalization problem). In this scenario, the incumbent DC firm's maximized profits (gross of fixed costs of technology transfer) as a function of the upstream price w can be written as

$$\pi_0^*(w) \equiv (p^{\mathrm{m}}(w)-\psi_0-w)q^{\mathrm{m}}(w). \tag{3}$$

In equilibrium, the LDC incumbent's profits equal

$$\pi_1^*(\psi_0) \equiv (w_1-c_1)q^{\mathrm{m}}(w_1) \tag{4}$$

and those of the DC incumbent equal

$$\pi_0^*(w_1) \equiv (p^{\mathrm{m}}(w_1)-\psi_0-w_1)q^{\mathrm{m}}(w_1).$$

If there is technology diffusion, the LDC supply price falls from w_1 to c_2: the LDC incumbent firm prices at the marginal cost of its competitor thereby limit pricing it out of the market. Of course, the incumbent DC firm can also create a second LDC supplier rather than depend upon the vagaries of diffusion. However,

---

[11] An alternative but equivalent interpretation is that technology diffuses over time and p is the discount factor which applies to profits earned post diffusion. Also note that the key assumption here is that while the transfer between the DC firm and a second LDC firm entails the cost I, the second LDC firm may learn from the first LDC firm at a lower cost once that technology has been successfully absorbed by that first LDC firm. Demonstration effects or movement of workers between the firms may contribute to such learning.

to do so, it must fully bear the full additional cost (I) of technology transfer. Thus, while making its outsourcing decision, the DC incumbent firm faces the following decision problem: incur the fixed cost $2I$ to outsource two LDC and buy their output at price c_1 or outsource to only one of them, pay a lower fixed cost of θI but pay a higher price for its output (w_1 if technology does not leak out to the second LDC firm and c_2 if it does). Let the net profits of the incumbent DC firm under outsourcing to both LDC firms be given by

$$v_0(2) = \pi_0^*(c_1) - 2I$$

where

$$\pi_0^*(c_1) \equiv (p^{\mathrm{m}}(c_1) - \psi_0 - c_1)q^{\mathrm{m}}(c_1)$$

denotes the incumbent DC firm's profits when it buys the upstream good at price c_1.

Under exclusive outsourcing, the incumbent DC firm's net expected profits are given by

$$\begin{aligned} v_0(1) &= (1-p)\pi_0^*(w_1) + p\pi_0^*(c_2) - \theta I \\ &= \pi_0^*(w_1) + p(\pi_0^*(c_2) - \pi_0^*(w_1)) - \theta I. \end{aligned}$$

Therefore, the incumbent DC firm chooses to outsource to only one LDC firm iff $v_0(1) > v_0(2) \Leftrightarrow I > I^*$ where

$$I^* \equiv \frac{[\pi_0^*(c_1) - \pi_0^*(w_1)] - p[\pi_0^*(c_2) - \pi_0^*(w_1)]}{2-\theta}.$$

Hence, a high enough fixed cost of outsourcing implies that only one of the LDC firms will be outsourced.[12] This completes the conditions required for outsourcing of a single LDC firm to be an equilibrium. Note that LDC firms always accept an outsourcing deal since they are assumed unable to sell in the DC market without technology and marketing skills of the incumbent DC firm.

Since $c_2 < w_1$, it must be that $\pi_0^*(c_2) > \pi_0^*(w_1)$. Consequently,

$$\frac{\partial v_0(1)}{\partial p} = \pi_0^*(c_2) - \pi_0^*(w_1) > 0.$$

Thus, our first main point is that $v_0(1)$ increases in p: technology diffusion between LDC manufacturers benefits the incumbent DC firm.[13] Note also that the

---

[12] Teece (1997) and others have shown that technology transfer costs are quite large, as much as 25% of total project costs for a multinational establishing a wholly owned subsidiary. For a subcontractor in which the technology supplying firm has no control over the staff, the initial fixed cost of transfer is likely to be considerably greater.

[13] There is an interesting if imperfect analogy between this and the Prebisch–Singer argument that technical diffusion within developing countries leads to a deterioration in their terms of trade relative to developed countries because of greater competition in the sectors undergoing such diffusion.

more incomplete is technology diffusion (i.e. higher is c_2 relative to c_1), the less attractive is exclusive outsourcing to the DC incumbent firm ($v_0(1)$ decreases in c_2 whereas $v_0(2)$ is independent of it). In other words, incurring the fixed cost of outsourcing twice is more worthwhile when technology diffusion does not create stiff competition between LDC suppliers whereas outsourcing to both of them does.

The analysis above indicates that so long as entry into the DC market is blocked, the decision to transfer knowledge by developed country importers is fully consistent with profit maximization even when it is understood that the benefits of the knowledge provided are not fully appropriated by the recipient in the LDC. We next extend the model to allow for the possibility of downstream entry to determine whether this insight is robust to the possibility of potential downstream competition.

2.2. Potential entry into marketing

As noted above, technology diffusion in the LDC market lowers the price of the good produced by LDC firms from w_1 to c_2. Consequently, the potential entrant (denoted by 3) may now find it profitable to provide marketing services if the incumbent DC firm continues to charge the monopoly price $p^m(c_2 + \psi_0)$. Such entry is profitable iff $p^m(c_2 + \psi_0) > \psi_3 + c_2$. When this condition holds, potential entry into marketing disciplines the incumbent DC firm. Nevertheless, due to its cost advantage, the incumbent DC firm can effectively limit price the potential entrant out of the market by lowering its price to the potential entrant's marginal cost (which equals $c_2 + \psi_3$).[14] In this scenario, the DC incumbent firm's markup falls from $p^m(c_2 + \psi_0) - (c_2 + \psi_0)$ to $\psi_3 - \psi_0$, the output sold increases to $q(c_2 + \psi_3)$, and its profits are given by

$$\pi_0^*(c_2, \psi_3) \equiv (\psi_3 - \psi_0) q(c_2 + \psi_3).$$

Since $\psi_3 < p^m(c_2 + \psi_0)$, the profits of the incumbent firm decline when it is unable to charge its optimal price due to threat of entry, i.e. $\pi_0^*(c_2, \psi_3) < \pi_0^*(c_2)$.

Next consider the profits of the incumbent LDC firm. When the price in the DC market drops to $c_2 + \psi_3$, the profits of the LDC incumbent firm equal

$$\pi_1^*(c_2, \psi_3) \equiv (c_2 - c_1) q(c_2 + \psi_3)$$

where $c_2 - c_1$ denotes its markup and $q(c_2 + \psi_3)$ the output supplied to the incumbent DC firm. Since its markup is unchanged relative to the case of blocked

[14] Note that a fixed cost of entry at the marketing stage is easily handled. Suppose F_d denotes the fixed entry cost for firm 3. In this context, we need to merely define a limit price p_L which makes entry unprofitable for firm 3. This price would exceed firm 3's marginal cost whenever $F_d > 0$ and is defined by $\pi_3(p_L) = F_d$, where $\pi_3(p_L)$ denotes firm 3's profits as a monopolist if it successfully undercuts firm 0's price and captures the entire downstream market by charging a price $p_L - \varepsilon$. In Section 3.2, we allow for actual entry and positive fixed costs of entry in both markets.

entry, whereas output sold is higher (i.e. $q(c_2+\psi_3) > q^m(c_1)$), the LDC incumbent is necessarily better off when entry is not blocked, i.e. $\pi_1^*(c_2, \psi_3) > \pi_1^*(c_2)$.

The above analysis informs us that, *given that technology diffusion has occurred*, the possibility of entry into marketing makes the DC incumbent firm worse off whereas the LDC incumbent firm better off. However, how does the possibility of technology diffusion affect the original participants in technology transfer (the two incumbent firms) when downstream entry is not blocked? This question is central to our analysis since it is technology diffusion in the LDC market that *creates* conditions for downstream entry.

First consider the fate of the LDC incumbent. When entry is not blocked, technology diffusion makes the LDC incumbent worse off iff

$$\pi_1^*(c_2,\psi_3) < \pi_1^*(w_1) \Leftrightarrow (c_2-c_1)q(c_2+\psi_3) < (w_1-c_1)q(p^m(w_1)).$$

The above equation says that technology diffusion has two conflicting effects on the fate of LDC incumbent firm. On one hand, it lowers the upstream price from w_1 to c_2, thereby making it worse off. On the other hand, downstream entry lowers the price in the DC market from $p^m(w_1)$ to $c_2+\psi_3$, thereby making the LDC incumbent better off by increasing the demand for its product. The aggregate effect depends upon the relative strength of these effects. The key parameters that determine whether the LDC incumbent firm gains or loses from technology diffusion are c_2 and ψ_3. When c_2 is close enough to w_1 and ψ_3 is close to ψ_0, the LDC incumbent firm experiences a large increase in sales and suffers only a small reduction in price as a result of technology diffusion. In this situation, its profits increase because of technology diffusion. In effect, it is as if the ex-post elasticity of demand faced by the firm in the non-competitive market is high.

This result can help explain in retrospect why some of the policies of the Japanese and Korean governments may have succeeded though the rationale provided here may not have been understood ex ante by policy-makers. In Japan, dissemination of knowledge to all firms who could benefit from it, without any additional fees, was a condition for the approval of foreign technology licensees (Ozawa 1974; Nagaoka 1989). In addition, in both countries cost reducing incentives were provided for domestic firms that became international marketing or trading companies. The potential private benefits of a low marginal cost of marketing to the first LDC firm that is outsourced may be thought of as an externality to be captured by precisely the type of interventions undertaken by MITI in Japan and the Economic Planning Board in Korea (Jones and Sakong, 1980; Nagaoka, 1989; Ozawa, 1974).

As was noted above, when the emergence of a new marketing agent is infeasible, the incumbent DC firm necessarily benefits from technology diffusion. What happens when downstream entry is not blocked? Just as for the incumbent LDC firm, technology diffusion also creates a trade-off for the incumbent DC firm when downstream entry is not blocked. On one hand, diffusion creates competition among suppliers thereby lowering price in the upstream LDC market. On the other hand, it invites entry into the downstream DC market thereby reducing the incumbent DC firm's mark up.[15] The incumbent DC firm *may still benefit* from technology diffusion if the demand in the final goods market is sufficiently elastic and the degree of competition downstream is weak.

When entry into marketing is blocked, the interests of the two incumbent firms *necessarily* clash. Surprisingly, however, downstream entry can tie the interests of the two together—they *both* could benefit from technology diffusion. As noted earlier, the intuition for this result is that diffusion upstream coupled with entry downstream reduces the extent of the pecuniary externality between the two incumbent firms by moving prices closer to marginal cost in both markets. The arms length nature of outsourcing is critical for this result. If the LDC incumbent firm were a fully owned subsidiary of incumbent DC firm, the vertically integrated firm would *necessarily lose* from diffusion since downstream entry reduces profits without reducing the price of the upstream good (which would be sourced at marginal cost under vertical integration). This suggests that multinational firms that operate wholly owned subsidiaries in LDCs would be more averse to technology diffusion than those firms that have arms length arrangements with LDC firms.[16]

Next, we explore the properties of the equilibrium with the help of a linear demand example.

2.3. Linear demand example

Suppose the demand curve in the downstream DC market is given by

$$q = A - p$$

where p denotes the price and q the output sold in the DC market.

2.3.1. Equilibrium in the absence of technology diffusion

In the absence of technology diffusion, the incumbent DC firm behaves as a monopolist to maximize its profits:

$$\underset{p}{\mathrm{Max}}(p - w - \psi_0)(A - p).$$

[15] Note that in the absence of diffusion, the potential entrant into the DC market has no source of supply since we assume that the incumbent LDC firm cannot supply its output to any competitors of the incumbent DC firm (who provides the incumbent LDC firm the critical technology and know-how needed for production).

[16] This result may help explain why many LDCs have preferred licensing and other arms length means of technology transfer to direct investment: technology may be more likely to diffuse in the host country under licensing.

This optimization yields the optimal price

$$p^{\mathrm{m}}(w) = \frac{A + w + \psi_0}{2}.$$

From the demand curve for the final product, derived demand for the incumbent LDC firm's output is given by

$$q^{\mathrm{m}}(w) = \frac{A - w - \psi_0}{2}.$$

Given the above demand curve, the incumbent LDC firm chooses its price w to maximize

$$\pi_1(w) \equiv (w - c_1)\left[\frac{A - w - \psi_0}{2}\right]$$

which yields

$$w_1 = \frac{A - \psi_0 + c_1}{2}. \tag{5}$$

Using the above we have

$$\pi_1^*(\psi_0) = (w_1 - c_1)q^{\mathrm{m}}(w_1) = \frac{[A - \psi_0 - c_1]^2}{8} \tag{6}$$

and

$$\pi_0^*(w_1) = (A - q^{\mathrm{m}}(w_1) - \psi_0 - w_1)q^{\mathrm{m}}(w_1) = \frac{[A - \psi_0 - c_1]^2}{16}. \tag{7}$$

In what follows, we only consider the case where potential entry is not blocked since in the other case, it is clear that the incumbent DC firm benefits from technology diffusion whereas the incumbent LDC firm does not.

2.3.2. Equilibrium under technology diffusion with downstream entry

After technology diffuses in the LDC market, and with potential entry in the DC market, prices equal c_2 and $\psi_3 + c_2$, respectively, in the two markets. This implies

$$\pi_0^*(c_2, \psi_3) \equiv (\psi_3 - \psi_0)(A - \psi_3 - c_2) \tag{8}$$

and

$$\pi_1^*(c_2, \psi_3) \equiv (c_2 - c_1)(A - \psi_3 - c_2). \tag{9}$$

Therefore, technology diffusion increases the incumbent LDC firm's profits iff

$$\pi_1^*(c_2, \psi_3) > \pi_1^*(\psi_0).$$

Using Eqs. (6) and (9), the above inequality can be written as

$$(c_2 - c_1)(A - \psi_3 - c_2) > \frac{[A - \psi_0 - c_1]^2}{8}.$$

Imposing the normalization $c_1 = \psi_0 = 0$, the preceding inequality simplifies to

$$A^2 < 8c_2(A - \psi_3 - c_2).$$

The above inequality is illustrated as Curve A in the (c_2, ψ_3) space in Fig. 1. Along Curve A, $\pi_1^*(c_2, \psi_3) = \pi_1^*(\psi_0)$ so that the incumbent LDC firm's profits are unaffected by technology diffusion. Above this curve, the LDC incumbent loses from diffusion whereas below it, it gains. As the marginal cost of the potential LDC entrant increases (c_2), the competition that results from technology diffusion does not affect the incumbent DC firm's profits much. On the other hand, if even a small drop in upstream price is sufficient to induce entry in the downstream market, the LDC incumbent firm gains from technology diffusion. Thus, for incumbent DC firm's fate to be unaffected by technology diffusion, it must be that ψ_3 increases with c_2, the reason Curve A is upward-sloping.

Similarly, diffusion benefits the incumbent DC firm iff $\pi_0^*(c_2, \psi_3) > \pi_0^*(w_1)$. Using Eqs. (7) and (8) and imposing the normalization $c_1 = \psi_0 = 0$, we can rewrite the preceding inequality as

$$A^2 < 16\psi_3(A - \psi_3 - c_2).$$

In Fig. 1, Curve B plots the locust of $\pi_0^*(c_2, \psi_3) = \pi_0^*(w_1)$. Along this curve, the incumbent DC firm's profits are unaffected by technology diffusion. Above

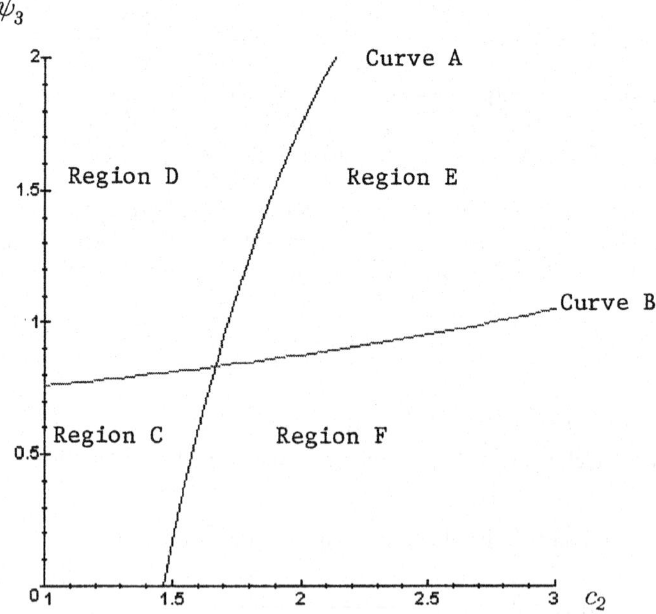

Fig. 1. Effect of technology diffusion under Bertrand competition.

this curve, diffusion benefits the DC incumbent, whereas below the curve, it hurts it. By logic similar to that used above, for the DC incumbent's profits to be unaffected by diffusion, ψ_3 must increase with c_2.

The two curves partition the space into four regions. In Region C, both firms lose from technology diffusion. In this region, both c_2 and ψ_3 are small so that drop in the price of the upstream (downstream) good hurts the LDC (DC) incumbent firm more than the reduction in the marginal cost in the downstream (upstream) market. In Region D, the incumbent DC firm gains from diffusion while the LDC incumbent firm loses: c_2 is low here and ψ_3 is high so that upstream price drops substantially, whereas downstream price is not affected much. In Region E, both ψ_3 and c_2 are high and *both* firms gain from technology diffusion: a small increase in competition at both stages helps reduce the vertical externality. Finally, in Region F, the incumbent DC firm loses from diffusion, whereas the LDC incumbent firm actually gains since a small reduction in upstream price results in a large reduction in downstream price (since ψ_3 is large relative to c_2).

3. Diffusion led entry

In the basic model, we assumed Bertrand competition in both the upstream and the downstream market. As a result, in equilibrium, potential entrants are limit priced out of the market. How do our results change if actual entry takes place? We next assume Cournot competition on both markets to allow actual entry to take place in equilibrium. The following section proceeds as follows. First, we show that our results do not change in any significant way if firms choose quantities instead of prices. Second, taking advantage of the properties of Cournot competition, we endogenize the number of entrants in each market.[17]

3.1. Equilibrium with one entrant in each market

Since equilibrium in the absence of diffusion and entry has already been derived under the assumption that firms choose prices, we now restrict attention to the case where entry takes place in both markets.[18]

Let the output marketed in the DC market by firm j be given by q_j where $j = 0, 3$. The demand curve in the downstream DC market is given by

$$p = A - q_0 - q_3.$$

[17] We thank an anonymous referee for suggesting this analysis.

[18] Note that when there is only one firm in each market, it makes no difference whether firms choose prices or quantities.

Profit function for downstream DC firm j is given by

$$\pi_j = (A - q_j - q_{-j} - \psi_0 - w) q_j$$

where $-j$ denotes the rival downstream firm and w denotes the price of the output supplied by upstream LDC firms. Standard calculations yield:

$$q_j = \frac{A - 2\psi_j - w + \psi_{-j}}{3}. \tag{10}$$

Adding the above two equations yields the demand curve facing the upstream LDC suppliers:

$$w = A - \frac{\psi_3 + \psi_0}{2} - \frac{3X}{2}$$

where X denotes the total quantity demanded by DC firms when LDC supply price equals w. The two LDC suppliers choose their outputs x_1 and x_2 non-cooperatively to maximize their respective profits, where in equilibrium we must have $x_1 + x_2 = X$. This optimization on the part of LDC suppliers yields the following equilibrium output levels:

$$x_i = \frac{A - \psi_3 - \psi_0 + 2c_{-i} - 4c_i}{9}$$

where c_{-i} denotes the marginal cost of the rival LDC firm. The equilibrium price in the LDC market equals

$$w^* = \frac{2A - \psi_3 - \psi_0 + 2c_2 + c_1}{6}.$$

This equilibrium price can be substituted back into the appropriate equations to derive equilibrium profits of all firms. We do not report these formulae to save space.

We are now in a position to consider the effect of technology diffusion and entry into marketing on the profits of the firms involved in the original outsourcing deal. Fig. 2 plots the change in profits of firms 0 and 1 before and after technology diffusion.

Just as in Fig. 1, the two curves in Fig. 2 divide the parameter space into four regions which are interpreted as before. Clearly, the two figures are very similar qualitatively. In particular, in both figures, there exists a region where diffusion upstream coupled with entry downstream makes both incumbent firms better off. Thus, the nature of market competition is not critical for our results. We now endogenize the number of firms in each market.

3.2. Endogenous number of entrants

To keep notation consistent throughout the paper, let the marginal cost of production of an entrant in the upstream LDC market equal c_2 while that of an

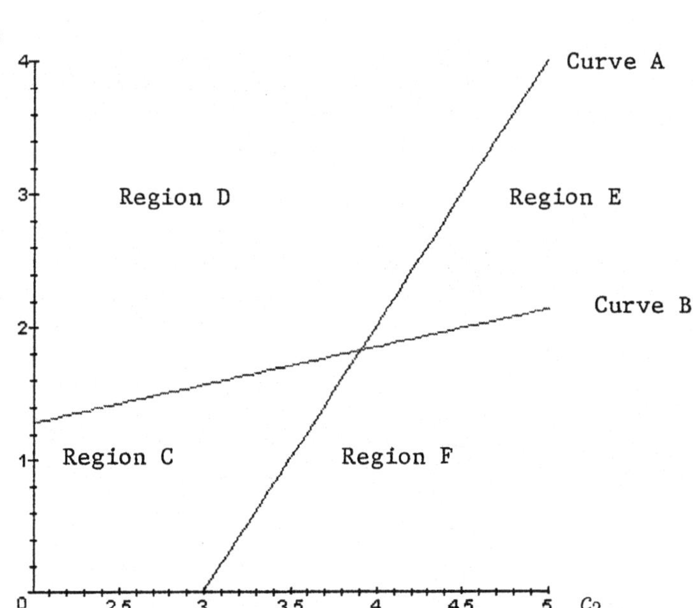

Fig. 2. Effect of technology diffusion under Cournot competition.

entrant into the downstream DC market equal ψ_3. Let the fixed cost of entry into the LDC market be given by F_u and that of entry into the DC market by F_d. We introduce these fixed costs to endogenize the number of entrants into both markets.[19]

As in the basic model, we assume that in the absence of diffusion, entry into the DC market is unprofitable (i.e. blocked). Thus, equilibrium in the absence of diffusion involves the DC incumbent sourcing its output from the LDC incumbent so that equilibrium profits for the two firms are described by Eqs. (6) and (7).

Now consider the equilibrium under technology diffusion with many potential entrants in both markets. As in the model with only one potential entrant at each stage, the timing of events is as follows. After the incumbent DC firm transfers its technology to the LDC incumbent, and in case technology diffuses throughout the LDC economy, other LDC firms decide whether or not to begin production. Each LDC entrant into production must pay the fixed cost F_u. After potential LDC

[19] Alternatively, if we allow marginal costs to differ across potential entrants, we could rank all potential entrants in each market in order of increasing marginal costs and find a marginal firm that is indifferent between entering and staying out, given the number of firms in the other market. Since price declines with entry, the indifferent firm in each market would be unique. However, introducing fixed costs is a cleaner method for endogenizing entry.

suppliers have made their entry decisions, potential entrants into marketing make their decisions. Each entrant into marketing must incur the fixed cost F_d. Next, all LDC suppliers simultaneously choose their production levels. Lastly, all marketing firms simultaneously choose their level of sales in the DC market. As before, we solve for a sub-game perfect equilibrium using backward induction.

3.2.1. Upstream and downstream cournot competition

The final stage involves competition in the downstream DC market, given the number of LDC suppliers, the number of downstream marketing firms, and the LDC supply price w. Let the number of entrants into marketing equal $n-1$ so that there are n firms in the DC market. Let the output sold by downstream entrant j be given by q_j where $j=0\dots n-1$.

Let the number of entrants into the LDC market equal $m-1$ so that there are m LDC suppliers who choose their output levels to maximize their respective profits. It is easy to show that

$$\pi_i^* = Bx_i^{*2} \quad \text{for } i=1\dots m \quad \text{and} \quad \pi_j^* = q_j^{*2} \quad \text{for } j=0\dots n-1 \tag{11}$$

where x_i^* denotes the equilibrium output of LDC supplier i and q_j^* that of DC marketing firm j. These quantities are given in Eqs. (20), (21) and (24) in Appendix A.

3.2.2. Equilibrium entry

Given the number of LDC suppliers, the equilibrium number of marketing firms in the DC market is found by setting post entry profits equal to the fixed cost of entry:

$$\pi_j^* = F_d, \quad j=1\dots n-1.$$

The above equation defines the number of downstream entrants $n-1$ as a function of the total number of LDC suppliers m. Denote this dependence by the function $n(m)$.

Finally, LDC suppliers correctly anticipate the number of DC marketing firms that operate in equilibrium so that entry into LDC market proceeds till post entry profits just cover the fixed cost of entry:

$$\pi_i^*(m,(n(m)) = F_u, \quad i=2\dots m.$$

Since the goal of this section is to endogenize the number of entrants and study the interaction between entry into the two markets, we simplify the analysis by assuming that entrants are as efficient as incumbents in respective markets:

$$\psi_3 = \psi_0 \text{ and that } c_3 = c_1.$$

Under these assumptions, we have $\pi_i^* = \pi_1^*$ and $\pi_j^* = \pi_0^*$. We show in Appendix A that

$$\frac{\partial \pi_i^*}{\partial n} > 0.$$

i.e. entry downstream benefits LDC suppliers by increasing the derived demand for their product. Unlike before, the degree of this competition is now determined by the number of entrants, as opposed to the marginal cost of a single potential entrant. Similarly, entry in the LDC market also benefits downstream DC firms:

$$\frac{\partial \pi_j^*}{\partial m} > 0.$$

Of course, given the number of LDC suppliers, equilibrium in the downstream market requires that:

$$\pi_j^* = F_{\mathrm{d}}.$$

After making appropriate substitutions, we can show that (see Appendix A):

$$n(m) = \frac{m}{m+1} \frac{(A - \psi_0 - c_1)}{\sqrt{F_{\mathrm{d}}}} - 1. \tag{12}$$

From Eq. (12), we have:

$$\frac{\partial n(m)}{\partial m} = \frac{(A - \psi_0 - c_1)\sqrt{F_{\mathrm{d}}}}{\left(A - \psi_0 - c_1 - \sqrt{F_{\mathrm{d}}}(m+1)\right)^2} > 0$$

i.e. the equilibrium number of downstream marketing firms increases with the number of LDC suppliers. In other words, increased competition in the LDC market makes entry in the DC market more attractive. Furthermore, we show in Appendix A that

$$\frac{\partial n(m)}{\partial A} > 0 \text{ and } \frac{\partial n(m)}{\partial F_{\mathrm{d}}} < 0$$

i.e. an increase in the DC market or a decrease in the fixed cost of entry into the DC market induces more entry into the DC market.

Similarly, given the number of marketing, equilibrium in the LDC market requires that

$$\pi_i^* = F_{\mathrm{u}} \tag{13}$$

which, after appropriate substitutions, implies that

$$m(n) = \sqrt{\frac{n}{n+1}} \frac{(A - \psi_0 - c_1)}{\sqrt{F_{\mathrm{u}}}} - 1. \tag{14}$$

From Eq. (29), we can show that

$$\frac{\partial m(n)}{\partial n} > 0$$

so that entry downstream induces entry upstream. Finally, it is also straightforward to show that

$$\frac{\partial m(n)}{\partial A} > 0 \text{ and } \frac{\partial m(n)}{\partial F_{\mathrm{u}}} < 0$$

i.e. an increase in the size of the DC market or a decrease in the fixed cost of entry into the LDC market induces entry into the LDC market.

Finally, for both markets to be in equilibrium, from Eqs. (13) and (14) we have that:

$$\left[m(A-\psi_0-c_1)-(m+1)\sqrt{F_{\mathrm{d}}}\right][A-\psi_0-c_1]=m(m+1)^2F_{\mathrm{u}}. \tag{15}$$

The relevant solution to the above equation defines the equilibrium number of LDC suppliers as a function of marginal costs of production and marketing as well as fixed costs of entry in both markets. Plugging back the equilibrium number of LDC suppliers into Eq. (27) delivers the equation determining the equilibrium number of downstream firms:

$$\left((A-\psi_0-c_1)\sqrt{n}-\sqrt{(n+1)F_{\mathrm{u}}}\right)^2=(n+1)^2nF_{\mathrm{d}}. \tag{16}$$

Clearly, Eqs. (15) and (16) are quite complicated. Nevertheless, the equilibrium exhibits sensible properties. For example, it is easy to show that an increase in the fixed cost of entry into the DC market not only lowers the number of firms in the DC market but also in the upstream LDC market: reduced downstream entry reduces profitability of upstream entry. Thus, an important insight that can be obtained from the above two equations is that the equilibrium number of entrants in *each* market is a function of downstream market size, marginal costs of production as well as marketing, and the fixed costs of entry in *both* markets.

4. Conclusion

Much empirical evidence indicates that downstream DC buyers transferred technology to LDC firms which helped them export to DC markets. In this paper, we provide a simple model that captures that process. Our results indicate that 'vertical' international technology transfer differs substantially from the horizontal technology transfer emphasized in the literature. In our model, a downstream incumbent DC firm actually benefits from the diffusion of the knowledge it transfers to an LDC firm since diffusion increases demand for its services. This argument survives, with qualification, a model in which additional upstream entry may invite downstream entry, which increases competition for the original supplier of technology. More surprisingly, the two firms involved in the original technology transfer may benefit from diffusion since it increases competition in both the upstream as well as the downstream market. This result is possible because of the original distortion that exists in the vertical relationship: a limited amount of increased competition at both stages moves the two firms closer to a vertically integrated firm. An immediate implication of this result is that DC firms that are vertically integrated with their LDC suppliers cannot benefit from technology diffusion. Thus, if they can help slow down diffusion to other LDC firms (say through restricting labor turnover), they are more likely to do so than firms that deal at arms length with their LDC suppliers.

Our results also suggest that, sometimes, a firm can benefit from undertaking actions that generate more competition for itself. In our particular model, such competition results from technology diffusion in the upstream market and the DC incumbent firm does not necessarily lose from competition in its market since its supplier is also forced to behave more competitively as a result of diffusion. Future research may describe additional scenarios in which such an effect arises due to different forces.

Our basic insights are robust to the nature of product market competition (Bertrand versus Cournot). This robustness is important since results in oligopoly models often hinge critically on the assumptions regarding firm behavior. Finally, we generalize the model with Cournot competition to allow for an arbitrary number of entrants in both markets. Such a model nicely highlights the interdependence between the two markets and its equilibrium has sensible properties.

Note, however, that even in this general model, we assume that only one DC firm can engage in technology transfer. What if multiple DC firms could transfer technology to LDC suppliers? Results will again depend upon whether further entry into the DC market is feasible or not. When such entry is blocked, competition among existing DC firms would imply that each DC firm would ignore the impact of technology diffusion on other DC firms. Since diffusion increases demand for the services of DC firms, one may expect that too few DC firms will engage in technology transfer since each DC firm will ignore the positive impact of its decision on other DC firms.

When further entry into the DC market is feasible and there exist multiple DC firms who can transfer technology, in addition to the positive externality described above, DC firms will now exert a negative externality on each other as well. Technology transfer followed by diffusion in the LDC market may induce further entry into the DC market thereby hurting all existing DC firms. Thus, when entry into the DC market is not blocked, the equilibrium amount of technology transfer will be determined by which of the preceding effects dominates. The analysis of such a scenario, while beyond the scope of our paper, deserves further research.

Our analysis has some implications for an argument often made that developed country importers can obtain all the rents that may accrue to LDC firms from mastering new technologies by offering lower prices to LDC manufacturers. The preceding analysis implies this is not necessary. The simplest model suggests that the LDC costs falls due to technology diffusion. However, when entry of an additional marketing firm is allowed, the profits of the original LDC firm may actually increase. Thus, the view that the potential rents from technology diffusion are all appropriated by DC firms depends on the response of local agents, particularly whether managers and workers supply other producing firms with relevant knowledge and whether domestic marketing firms arise, perhaps with government support. Case studies demonstrate that many marketing firms did emerge in both Korea and Taiwan (Levy, 1989). In the case analyzed here of vertical transfers (that were quantitatively important during the early period of industrialization in Korean and Taiwan), it is very likely that the LDC firms indeed benefited.

Acknowledgements

We thank Bernard Hoekman, Jim Tybout, and two anonymous referees for helpful comments. We also thank Research Foundation of the University of Pennsylvania, University Research Council of Southern Methodist University, and the World Bank's Development Research Group for financial support.

Appendix A

This appendix reports the derivations underlying the results discussed in Section 4. The demand curve in the downstream market is given by

$$p = A - \sum_{j=0}^{n-1} q_j. \tag{17}$$

Profit function for the incumbent DC firm is given by

$$\pi_0 = \left(A - \sum_{j=1}^{n-1} q_j - q_0 - \psi_0 - w \right) q_0.$$

The first order condition for profit maximization is given by

$$\frac{\partial \pi_0}{\partial q_0} = -2q_0 + A - \sum_{j=1}^{n-1} q_j - \psi_0 - w = 0. \tag{18}$$

Similarly, the profit function for a typical entrant into the DC market is given by

$$\pi_j = \left(A - \sum_{\substack{k \neq j \\ k=0}}^{n-1} q_k - q_j - \psi_3 - w \right) q_j,$$

and the associated first order condition for profit maximization is given by

$$\frac{\partial \pi_j}{\partial q_j} = -2q_j + \sum_{\substack{k \neq j \\ k=0}}^{n-1} q_k - \psi_3 - w = 0. \tag{19}$$

Solving the first order conditions (18) and (19) yields the equilibrium sales of the downstream DC entrants as a function of the price in the upstream market:

$$q_j = \frac{A - 2\psi_3 - w + \psi_0}{n+1}. \tag{20}$$

Similarly, sales of the incumbent DC firm equals

$$q_0 = \frac{A - n\psi_0 + (n-1)\psi_3 - w}{n+1}. \tag{21}$$

Adding sales over all DC firms yields the derived demand curve facing the upstream LDC suppliers:

$$w = A' - BX \tag{22}$$

where

$$A' = A - \frac{\psi_3(n-1) + \psi_0}{n} \text{ and } B = \frac{n+1}{n},$$

and X denotes the total quantity marketed by the downstream firms when upstream price equals w. The linear downstream curve in Eq. (17) translates into a derived demand curve for upstream LDC suppliers given in Eq. (22) that is also linear. Note that

$$\frac{\mathrm{d}B}{\mathrm{d}n} = -\frac{1}{n^2} < 0.$$

In other words, due to an increase in the number of marketing firms, the derived demand curve pivots outwards about its vertical intercept, thereby benefiting upstream LDC suppliers.[20]

Let the number of entrants into the LDC market equal $m-1$ so that there are m firms in the market. The upstream LDC suppliers choose their output levels to

[20] Since $(\mathrm{d}A'/\mathrm{d}n) = -((\psi_3 - \psi_0)/n) < 0$, the vertical intercept of the derived demand curve also shifts down as n increases. This negative effect arises because entrants are assumed to be less efficient than the incumbent. Note, however, that this effect is not large when the (common) marginal cost of entrants is close to that of the incumbent. Furthermore, as we show below, the shifting outward of the demand curve dominates this secondary effect so that upstream LDC suppliers benefit from increased entry downstream.

maximize their respective profits. Given the derived demand function in Eq. (22), the profit function of a typical entrant into the LDC market is given by

$$\pi_i = (A' - B(x_i + X_{-i}) - c_2)x_i, \tag{23}$$

where $i = 2, \dots m$, x_i denotes the output of LDC firm i, and X_{-i} the total output of its rival suppliers. The profit function of the LDC incumbent is found by replacing c_2 by c_1 in the above formula. As in the downstream market, we can easily calculate the output levels of upstream LDC suppliers. We have:

$$x_1^* = \frac{A' - mc_1 + (m-1)c_2}{B(m+1)} \text{ and } x_i^* = \frac{A' - 2c_1 + c_2}{B(m+1)} \text{ for } i = 2 \dots m. \tag{24}$$

Using the above output levels and the derived demand curve in Eq. (22), we obtain the equilibrium supply price of LDC firms:

$$w^* = \frac{A + c_2(m-1) + c_1}{m+1} - \frac{(n-1)\psi_3 + \psi_0}{n(m+1)}. \tag{25}$$

Finally, the equilibrium LDC supply price can be substituted back into the appropriate equations to derive equilibrium profits of LDC suppliers. We have:

$$\pi_i^* = Bx_i^{*2}, \quad \text{for } i = 1 \dots m. \tag{26}$$

Similarly, we can obtain the equilibrium sales levels and profits of DC marketing firms. We have:

$$\pi_j^* = q_j^{*2}, \quad \text{for } j = 0 \dots n-1$$

where the equilibrium quantities can be recovered from (Eqs. (20), (21) and (24). Given the number of LDC suppliers, the equilibrium number of marketing firms in the DC market is found by setting post entry profits equal to cost of entry:

$$\pi_j^* = F_d, \quad j = 1 \dots n-1.$$

The above equation defines the number of downstream entrants $n-1$ as a function of the total number of upstream firms m. Denote this dependence by the function $n(m)$.

Entry into LDC market proceeds till post entry profits just cover costs:

$$\pi_i^*(m, n(m)) = F_u, \quad i = 2 \dots m.$$

Assume

$$\psi_3 = \psi_0 \text{ and that } c_3 = c_1.$$

Under these assumptions, $\pi_i^* = \pi_1^*$ and $\pi_j^* = \pi_0^*$. Furthermore, after making appropriate substitutions, we have

$$\frac{\partial \pi_i^*}{\partial n} = \frac{(A - \psi_0 - 2c_1)^2}{(m+1)^2(n+1)^2} > 0.$$

Similarly, entry upstream also benefits downstream marketing firms:

$$\frac{\partial \pi_j^*}{\partial m} = \frac{2m(A - \psi_0 - c_1)^2}{(n+1)^2(m+1)^3} > 0.$$

Of course, given the number of LDC suppliers, equilibrium in the downstream market requires that:

$$\frac{m^2(A - \psi_0 - c_1)^2}{(n+1)^2(m+1)^2} = F_{\mathrm{d}}$$

which implies that

$$n(m) = \frac{m}{m+1}\frac{(A - \psi_0 - c_1)}{\sqrt{F_{\mathrm{d}}}} - 1 \tag{27}$$

where, for actual entry to take place, we need that the fixed costs be not too large relative to market size:

$$m(A - \psi_0 - c_1) > 2(m+1)\sqrt{F_{\mathrm{d}}}.$$

From Eq. (27), we have:

$$\frac{\partial n(m)}{\partial m} = \frac{(A - \psi_0 - c_1)\sqrt{F_{\mathrm{d}}}}{\left(A - \psi_0 - c_1 - \sqrt{F_{\mathrm{d}}}(m+1)\right)^2} > 0.$$

Furthermore,

$$\frac{\partial n(m)}{\partial A} = \frac{m}{(m+1)\sqrt{F_{\mathrm{d}}}} > 0 \text{ and } \frac{\partial n(m)}{\partial F_{\mathrm{d}}} = -\frac{m(A - \psi_0 - c_1)}{F_{\mathrm{d}}(m+1)} < 0.$$

Similarly, given the number of marketing, equilibrium in the LDC market requires that

$$\frac{n(A - \psi_0 - c_1)^2}{(n+1)(m+1)^2} = F_{\mathrm{u}} \tag{28}$$

which implies that

$$m(n) = \sqrt{\frac{n}{n+1}}\frac{(A - \psi_0 - c_1)}{\sqrt{F_{\mathrm{u}}}} - 1 \tag{29}$$

where, as in the downstream market, we require that

$$\sqrt{n}(A - \psi_0 - c_1) > 2\sqrt{F_{\mathrm{u}}(n+1)}.$$

From Eq. (29), we have

$$\frac{\partial m(n)}{\partial n} = \frac{A - \psi_0 - c_1}{2(n+1)F_u\sqrt{n(n+1)}} > 0$$

so that entry downstream induces entry upstream. Finally, it is also straightforward to show that

$$\frac{\partial m(n)}{\partial A} = \frac{n}{nF_u\sqrt{n(n+1)}} > 0 \text{ and } \frac{\partial m(n)}{\partial F_u} = -\frac{(n+1)F_u\sqrt{n(n+1)}}{F_u^2(n+1)} < 0.$$

Finally, for both markets to be in equilibrium, from Eqs. (28) and (29) we have:

$$\frac{m(A-\psi_0-c_1)-\sqrt{F_d}(m+1)}{\sqrt{F_d}(m+1)} \times \frac{(A-\psi_0-c_1)^2}{\left(\frac{m(A-\psi_0-c_1)-\sqrt{F_d}(m+1)}{\sqrt{F_d}(m+1)}+1\right)(m+1)^2} = F_u$$

which simplifies to:

$$\left[m(A-\psi_0-c_1)-(m+1)\sqrt{F_d}\right]\left[A-\psi_0-c_1\right] = m(m+1)^2F_u. \qquad (30)$$

Substituting back the equilibrium number of LDC firms into Eq. (27) gives:

$$\left((A-\psi_0-c_1)\sqrt{n}-\sqrt{(n+1)F_u}\right)^2 = (n+1)^2nF_d. \qquad (31)$$

References

Becker, G., 1964. Human Capital. University of Chicago Press, Chicago.

Clerides, S.K., Lach, S., Tybout, J.R., 1998. Is learning by exporting important? Micro-dynamic evidence from Colombia, Mexico, and Morocco. Quarterly Journal of Economics 113, 903–948.

Ethier, W.J., Markusen, J.R., 1996. Multinational firms, technology diffusion and trade. Journal of International Economics 41, 1–28.

Glass, A.J., Saggi, K., 1999a. Foreign direct investment and the nature of R&D. Canadian Journal of Economics 32 (5), 1275–1298.

Glass, A.J., Saggi, K., 1999b. Multinational firms and technology transfer, World Bank Policy Research Working Paper No. 2067.

Hobday, M., 1995. Innovation in East Asia: The Challenge to Japan. Edward Elgar, London.

Hou, C.M., Gee, S., 1993. National systems supporting technical advance in industry: the case of Taiwan. In: Nelson, R.R. (Ed.), National Innovation Systems: A Comparative Analysis. Oxford Univ. Press, New York, pp. 384–413.

Jones, L.P., Sakong, I., 1980. Government, Business, and Entrepreneurship in Economic Development: The Korean Case. Harvard Univ. Press, Cambridge.

Kabiraj, T., Marjit, S., 1993. International technology transfer under potential threat of entry. Journal of Development Economics 42, 75–88.

Kamien, M.I., Tauman, Y., 1986. Fees versus royalties and the private value of a patent. Quarterly Journal of Economics 101, 471–492.

Katz, M., Shapiro, C., 1985. On the licensing of innovations. Rand Journal of Economics 16, 504–520.

Kauffman, L., 1997. A model of spillovers through labor recruitment. International Economic Journal 11 (3), 13–33.

Keesing, D.B., 1982. Exporting Manufactured Consumer Goods from Developing to Developed Economies: Marketing by Local Firms and Effects of Developing Country Policies. World Bank, Washington, DC.

Levy, B., 1989. Export traders, market development, and industrial expansion. Williams College Center for Development Economics, research memorandum series, No. RM-114, pp. 1–24.

Nagaoka, S., 1989. Overview of Japanese industrial technological development. Industry Series paper 6. World Bank Industry and Energy Department, Washington, DC.

Nelson, R., Winter, S., 1982. An Evolutionary Theory of Economic Change. Harvard Univ. Press, Cambridge.

Ordover, J., Saloner, G., Salop, S., 1990. Equilibrium vertical foreclosures. American Economic Review 80, 127–142.

Ozawa, T., 1974. Japan's Technological Challenge to the West, 1950–74: Motivation and Accomplishment. MIT Press, Cambridge.

Rhee, Y., Ross-Larson, B., Pursell, G., 1984. Korea's Competitive Edge: Managing Entry into World Market. Johns Hopkins Univ. Press, Baltimore.

Saggi, K., 1996. Entry into a foreign market: foreign direct investment versus licensing. Review of International Economics 4, 99–104.

Saggi, K., 1999. Foreign direct investment, licensing, and incentives for innovation. Review of International Economics 7 (4), 699–714.

Salop, S., Scheffman, D.T., 1987. Cost raising strategies. Journal of Industrial Economics 36, 19–34.

Schive, C., 1990. The Foreign Factor: The Multinational Corporations Contribution to the Economic Modernization of the Republic of China. Stanford Univ. Press, California.

Teece, D.J., 1997. The Multinational Corporation and Resource Cost of International Technology Transfer. Ballinger, Cambridge.

Chapter 4

Trade, Foreign Direct Investment, and International Technology Transfer: A Survey*

Kamal Saggi

What role does trade play in international technology transfer? Do technologies introduced by multinational firms diffuse to local firms? What kinds of policies have proved successful in encouraging technology absorption from abroad and why? Using these questions as motivation, this article surveys the recent trade literature on international technology transfer, paying particular attention to the role of foreign direct investment. The literature argues that trade necessarily encourages growth only if knowledge spillovers are international in scope. Empirical evidence on the scope of knowledge spillovers (national versus international) is ambiguous. Several recent empirical plant-level studies have questioned earlier studies that argued that foreign direct investment has a positive impact on the productivity of local firms. Yet at the aggregate level, evidence supports the view that foreign direct investment has a positive effect on economic growth in the host country.

Economic growth results from accumulation of factors of production or from improvements in technology or both. To encourage the generation of new knowledge, industrial countries have elaborate systems of intellectual property rights (IPRS) in place and conduct the majority of the world's research and development (R&D). Technologies resulting from R&D spread throughout the world via a multitude of channels. On a fundamental level, international trade in technology differs from other indirect channels of international technology transfer, such as trade in goods and international movement of factors of production. This article critically surveys the literature that explores the roles of trade and foreign direct investment (FDI) as channels of international technology transfer. With respect to FDI, a distinction is made between wholly owned subsidiaries of multinational firms and international joint ventures. Furthermore, the role of FDI is contrasted with that of arm's-length channels of technology transfer, such as licensing.

Although the literature has done a decent job of outlining the various channels through which international technology transfer occurs, not enough is known, both

* This chapter was originally appeared in *The World Bank Research Observer* **17**, 191–235.

in theory and practice, about the relative importance of each of these channels. There is a limited understanding of the role that policy can play in facilitating international technology transfer. For example, the literature continues to debate whether increased openness to trade encourages economic growth. Although Dollar (1992) and Sachs and Werner (1995) find support for the view that open economies grow faster, Rodriguez and Rodrik (1999) are quite skeptical about this conclusion.

As a practical matter, few economists advocate the imposition of trade restrictions. In fact, the general feeling seems to be that traditional analyses may very well understate the true cost of protectionism because most utilize static models and do not capture the dynamic costs of trade protection. Underlying this view is the notion that, somehow, trade, FDI, and interaction among countries in various other forms all play roles not only in improving the global allocation of resources but also in transmitting technology globally. How exactly this transmission occurs is not fully understood, making international technology transfer an active area of research.

Dynamic trade models shed light on the complex relation between technology and trade. These models frequently lead to ambiguous welfare conclusions. The literature (both theoretical and empirical) does not provide a blanket endorsement of trade as an engine for growth because introducing dynamics in an interesting fashion often requires multiple departures from the neoclassical model of perfect markets. Imperfect competition and externalities are central to the new dynamic models of trade, and such distortions can easily lead to perverse results. Of course, the argument cuts both ways. Introducing such elements in the traditional static model also furnishes additional arguments in support of free trade. Nevertheless, it is difficult to make the unconditional case for free trade purely on the basis of logic. For example, see Krugman (1987) for a pragmatic argument for free trade even in the presence of market failures.

It is also not the case that anything can happen if a closed economy opens up to free trade. In fact, the theoretical literature suggests that the scope of knowledge spillovers is a crucial determinant of whether trade necessarily encourages growth (Grossman and Helpman 1995). However, the empirical evidence has been mixed: some studies discover that knowledge spillovers have a limited geographical scope, whereas others find the opposite. The ambiguous nature of this empirical evidence immediately raises the following question: What factors determine the scope of knowledge spillovers? Clearly the scope of knowledge spillovers must be determined in part by the interaction between innovators (potential suppliers of technology) and those firms and entrepreneurs that seek access to newer technologies through imitation, technology licensing, and other forms of collaboration with innovators. In other words, a fair bit of technology transfer may indeed be endogenous.

In a discussion of the special properties of knowledge as an economic good, Romer (1990) makes the important point that knowledge is a nonrival good: it can be used simultaneously by two different agents. However, this does not mean that knowledge can be transferred across agents at zero cost. If technology transfer entailed no costs, the room for fruitful policy intervention with respect to assimilation of foreign technology would be quite limited because any technology transfer that would yield even a minutely positive return to any agent would take place automatically. Pack (1992) provides an overview of what can be reasonably expected in terms of technology transfer to developing economies, given that the potential for transfers is large.

The nonrival nature of knowledge only implies that if two agents are willing to pay the cost of adopting a new technology, they can do so without interfering with each other's decisions. Much empirical evidence indicates that international technology transfer carries significant resource costs (Mansfield and Romeo 1980; Ramachandran 1993; Teece 1977). In his survey of 29 technology transfer projects, Teece (1977) found that on average such costs were approximately 20 percent of the total costs of the project, and in some cases, they were as high as 60 percent.

The fact that international technology transfer occurs through a multitude of channels makes it difficult to arrive at an aggregate measure of the activity and accurately assess its contribution to economic growth. Most research, theoretical as well as empirical, tends to focus on one or two channels of technology transfer. Of these, trade and FDI have received the most attention. If one could somehow rank the different channels of technology transfer in terms of their relative importance, empirical analysis could then proceed by ignoring the relatively unimportant channels. However, given that multiple options exist in theory, the dominance of any one channel in the data would itself require explanation. Indeed, the emergence and expansion of multinational firms, given the existence of alternative arrangements for transacting in technology, has been viewed as a phenomenon that requires explanation. Furthermore, the various channels of technology transfer, though independent to a certain degree, are linked to each other in important ways. For example, the extent to which inward FDI contributes to technology transfer (in addition to international trade) may very well be a function of a country's trade policy. An important challenge for both theoretical and empirical research is to isolate the marginal contribution of inward FDI to technology transfer and its relation to a country's trade and investment policies. I discuss the relevant research in this survey to the extent the literature has addressed these questions.

Once a technology has been introduced into a country (by a multinational firm, say), how does it subsequently diffuse throughout the rest of the economy? The presence of trade barriers across countries as well as international differences in market conditions and policy environments imply that technology diffusion within a country should be considerably easier than international transfer of technology. For example, the mobility of labor is severely constrained only at the international level (exceptions include contact with consultants and the return of foreign-educated nationals). Thus labor turnover across firms may be crucial for driving technology diffusion within a country and may not play any role in international technology transfer. This article discusses the role of technology licensing, imitation, and FDI in the process of international technology transfer and its subsequent diffusion in the host country.

One goal of this article is to help identify the role policy plays in facilitating international technology transfer. The range of relevant policies is clearly quite large. To limit the scope of the discussion, I address the role of trade, FDI, and IPR policies. Given the central questions of interest, I discuss the literature on FDI and IPRS in greater detail than that on trade policy.

Blomström and Kokko (1998) review the theory and evidence regarding spillovers from multinational firms. Unlike the present article, their survey is concerned exclusively with spillovers from FDI and does not deal with trade and the effects of policy on international technology transfer. Furthermore, they do not emphasize the endogeneity of international technology transfer. Blomström and Kokko focus on the internal diffusion of technologies introduced by multinational firms. By contrast, this article emphasizes the interaction between domestic diffusion and incentives for international technology transfer. Furthermore, at least in the context of tradable goods, a relevant issue (not addressed by the Blomström and Kokko survey) is that a complete definition of spillovers from FDI ought to account for technology diffusion that would result in the absence of FDI but in the presence of international trade.

Knowledge Spillovers through Trade

Figure 1 plots worldwide exports of goods and services as a percentage of gross domestic product (GDP) for 1970–96. During this period, the percentage of exports increased from approximately 14.1 to 21.4. An interesting consideration is whether this increase in world trade yielded primarily static efficiency gains or dynamic gains by facilitating international technology transfer. An extensive literature studies the dynamic effects of trade. Much of the relevant work emphasizes two intertwined aspects of the relationship between trade and technology: that trade alters the allocation of resources in an economy and plays a role in transmitting knowledge internationally.

Much of the literature on trade and international transmission of technology derives from closed-economy growth models. For this article, endogenous growth models are those in which economic growth results from the intentional actions of individuals who seek to profit from their investments in technological innovation. In traditional growth theory, capital accumulation is the major determinant of economic growth; a natural conclusion of this research was that unless the return to capital accumulation could stay bounded away from zero, growth would peter out or cease in the long run. A natural implication of this finding is that over time, poor countries eventually converge to the per capita income levels of the countries. However, the evidence on convergence is weak; although some areas—such as the Re-

Figure 1. Worldwide Exports over GDP, 1972–96

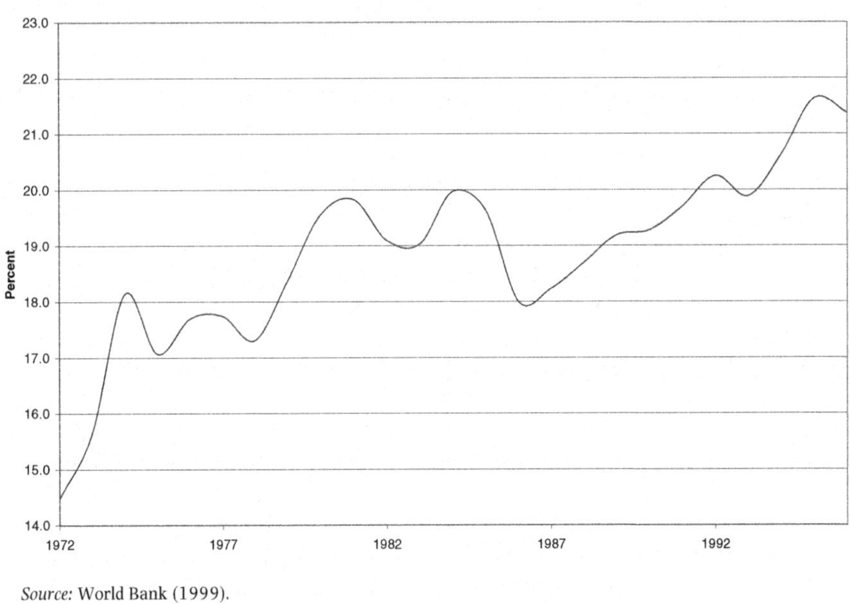

Source: World Bank (1999).

public of Korea; Taiwan, China; and Hong Kong, China—have achieved enviable rates of growth for sustained periods, most developing economies do not seem to be on a path of convergence toward rich countries (Pritchett 1997).

Standard neoclassical growth models assume costless technology transfer by positing a common production function across countries. The fact that chosen production techniques differ across countries is not evidence against the neoclassical view; when faced with different factor prices (due to differences in factor endowments), firms typically adopt different production techniques in different countries. Thus, the issue is whether all firms can access the global pool of technologies at the same cost. Parente and Prescott (1994) emphasize barriers to technology adoption as a key determinant of differences in per capita income across countries. In their model, although any firm can access the underlying stock of knowledge in the world economy, the cost of such access differs across countries due to differences in legal, regulatory, political, and social factors. Thus in their view, some countries make it inherently costlier for their firms to adopt modern technologies and thereby retard the development of the entire economy. In fact, Parente and Prescott (1994) go on to suggest that trade may affect growth by lowering the barriers to technology adoption.

In contrast to neoclassical models that stress capital accumulation, the new growth theory emphasizes technological change and the accumulation of human capital

(Lucas 1988). For the purposes of this survey, the literature on R&D-based growth models is clearly more relevant, and I restrict attention to this strand of growth theory. Romer (1990), Grossman and Helpman (1991), Aghion and Howitt (1990), and Segerstrom and others (1990) are among the pioneers of R&D-based models of economic growth. These models provide a coherent framework for the Schumpeterian notion of creative destruction. Although they differ from each other in important ways, the models all share the idea that entrepreneurs conduct R&D to gain temporary monopoly power made possible by patents and other IPRS.

Grossman and Helpman (1991) provide a unifying framework for two widely used strands of R&D-based endogenous growth models: the varieties model, which builds on foundations laid by Dixit and Stiglitz (1977), Ethier (1982), and Romer (1990), and the quality ladders model developed by Aghion and Howitt (1990), Segerstrom and others (1990), and Grossman and Helpman (1991). In a closed economy, growth is sustained in the varieties model through the assumption that the creation of new products expands the knowledge stock, which then lowers the cost of innovation. As more products are invented, both the costs of inventing new products and the profits of subsequent innovators are lower because of increased competition (no products disappear from the market in this model). By contrast, the quality ladders model assumes that consumers are willing to pay a premium for higher-quality products. As a result, firms always have an incentive to improve the quality of products. The important assumption that sustains growth in this model is that every successful innovation allows all firms to study the attributes of the newly invented product and then improve on it. Patent rights restrict a firm from producing a product invented by some other firm but not from using the knowledge (created due to R&D) that is embodied in that product. Thus, as soon as a product is created, the knowledge needed for its production becomes available to all; such knowledge spillovers ensure that anyone can try to invent a higher-quality version of the same product.

Although R&D-based endogenous growth theory is quite appealing theoretically, empirical evidence does not provide a strong endorsement (Pack 1994). In fact, Jones (1995a, 1995b) explicitly tests the empirical implications of R&D-based growth models and finds that the data reject these implications. However, rejecting a particular model of R&D-based economic growth does not imply that R&D is not an important determinant of growth. In fact, a reasonable conclusion may be that although R&D is crucial for the generation of new ideas (and economic growth), early variants of R&D-based growth models do not adequately capture the relationship between R&D and growth. The newer strand of growth theory has not abandoned R&D as a determinant of growth; instead, it has focused on creating models that do not have the "scale effects" that Jones demonstrates are not supported by the data. Roughly speaking, scale effects imply that large economies grow faster than small economies (see Dinopoulos and Thompson 1999 for a discussion of scale effects in endogenous growth models).

R&D-based models of growth argue that new products result from new ideas; therefore, trade in goods could help transmit knowledge internationally. This is the central insight of many open economy growth models. Of course, trade in ideas can take place without trade in goods. Rivera-Batiz and Romer (1991) analyze two different models (the lab equipment model and the knowledge-driven model) of endogenous growth to highlight the role of trade in goods versus trade in ideas. The general conclusion of their analysis is that trade in either goods or ideas can increase the global rate of growth if such trade allows a greater exploitation of increasing returns to scale (in the production of goods or ideas) by expanding market size.

Multicountry models of endogenous growth have two strands: those that study trade between identical countries and those that have a Northern Hemisphere–Southern Hemisphere structure. Although knowledge spillovers are central to both, technology transfer in the sense emphasized here is a central feature only of North–South models. Prominent early works include Krugman (1979), Rivera-Batiz and Romer (1991), and Grossman and Helpman (1991). The literature is now rather large and a complete discussion requires a survey of its own (see Grossman and Helpman 1995). North–South models that emphasize the product-cycle nature of trade have been particularly useful for understanding international technology transfer and merit some further discussion.

Product-cycle models assume that new products are invented in the North and, due to the lower relative Southern wage (endogenous in the model), Southern firms can successfully undercut Northern producers by succeeding in imitating Northern products. A typical good is initially produced in the North until either further innovation (in the quality ladders model) or successful Southern imitation (in both the varieties model and the quality ladders model) makes profitable production in the North infeasible. Consequently, either production ceases (due to innovation) or shifts to the South (due to imitation). Thus, prior to imitation, all products are exported by the North, whereas postimitation they are imported, thereby completing the cycle. These models capture technology-driven trade and have been generalized to consider technology transfer more explicitly. Neither FDI nor licensing (choices available to innovators for producing in the South) was considered in the early variants of these models.

What do R&D-based models of growth imply about the effect of trade on growth? An important conclusion of this line of research is that much importance hinges on whether knowledge spillovers are national or international in nature (Grossman and Helpman 1995). If the spillovers are international, these models endorse the view that trade is an engine of growth. However, when the spillovers are national, perverse possibilities can arise. Note that this perspective is more relevant for North–North models of trade because international knowledge spillovers (of one form or another) are assumed in North–South product-cycle models of trade, where the South is modeled as a pure imitator. In North–South models, the more interesting question is how Southern imitation affects incentives for innovation in the North.

What factors can help account for the explosive growth of economies like Hong Kong, Korea, and Taiwan? Some economists argue that the accumulation of resources has driven economic growth in these countries (Young 1995). Others argue that improvement in productivity (driven partly through trade) has played a large role (Nelson and Pack 1999). However, even if capital accumulation were the driving force, why did it take place at such a high rate? What kept the returns to capital accumulation so high? Perhaps technology transfer (again, partly through trade) kept the marginal product of capital from falling and kept investment rates high (Nelson and Pack 1999).

What does the empirical evidence say about the scope of knowledge spillovers? Should research focus primarily on determining their geographical scope? The frequent agglomeration of R&D-intensive industries (such as in Silicon Valley) suggests that spillovers may be primarily local. However, several studies find that R&D activity in a country is not strongly correlated with productivity growth, suggesting that the benefits of R&D in one country spill over substantially to other countries. Eaton and Kortum (1996) find that more than 50 percent of the growth in some Organisaton for Economic Co-operation and Development (OECD) countries derives from innovation in the United States, Germany, and Japan. Yet Eaton and Kortum also report that distance inhibits the flow of ideas between countries, whereas trade enhances it.

In their micro-level study of the semiconductor industry, Irwin and Klenow (1994) find that learning (resulting from production) spills over as much across national borders as it does between firms in the same country. Similarly, Coe and Helpman (1995) and Coe and others (1997) argue that international R&D spillovers are substantial and that trade is an important channel of such spillovers. Using estimates of international R&D spillovers from these two studies, Bayoumi and others (1999) simulate the impact of changes in R&D and in exposure to trade on productivity, capital, output, and consumption in a multicountry model (the International Monetary Fund [IMF]'s MULTIMOD model). Their simulations indicate that R&D can affect output not only directly but also indirectly by stimulating capital investment. Incidentally, this finding is also of interest for the debate regarding the Asian growth miracle.

Keller (1998) casts some doubt on the latter finding by generating results similar to those of Coe and Helpman (1995) for randomly generated trade weights. However, a recent paper by Coe and Hoffmaister (1999) argues that Keller's weights are not actually random. When alternative weights are used, estimated international R&D spillovers are nonexistent for the case of random weights.

In principle, trade in both consumption and capital goods can contribute to technology transfer, and the empirical studies discussed typically utilize a country's imports of all goods while attempting to measure knowledge spillovers through trade. For example, when Korea imports a manufactured consumption good, such as an automobile, local firms can absorb some technological know-how by simply studying the design and the engine of the imported automobile. Attempts at reverse-engineering may be important, but they probably contribute less to technology transfer than does trade in capital goods (such as machinery and equipment) that are used in the production of other consumption goods. Xu and Wang (1999) argue that trade in capital goods is more relevant than total trade for measuring knowledge spillovers because capital goods have higher technological content than consumption goods. Xu and Wang measure trade in capital goods by exports of machinery and transport equipment (SITC 7). They show that although the volume of such trade helps explain cross-country differences in total factor productivity (TFP), trade in all other goods does not. This result fits well with the finding by De Long and Summers (1991) that investment in machinery and equipment has a strong association with growth.

Capital goods trade is a prominent part of world trade, and its importance has increased over time. Table 1 reports worldwide exports of capital goods (as measured by trade in machinery and transport equipment) as a percentage of total exports. In 1975, approximately 23 percent of total trade in the world was trade in capital goods; this ratio was over 30 percent in 1996. During 1975–96, worldwide exports of machinery and transport equipment as a percentage of GDP increased from about 4.2 to approximately 7.0. In 1996, roughly 30 percent of capital goods exports were destined for developing economies. Although the developing economy share of imports of capital goods has increased over time, this increase has not been substantial (from 28.9 percent in 1980 to 30.8 percent in 1996). Within the OECD countries, there is significant cross-country variation in the magnitude of imports of capital goods. In 1983–90, more than 50 percent of U.S. imports from other OECD countries was made up of capital goods; this ratio was only 25 percent for Japan (Xu and Wang 1999). Such variation in the data suggests that using total trade to measure the degree of knowledge spillovers across countries might lead to erroneous conclusions.

Table 1. Global Exports of Capital Goods as a Percentage of Total Exports

Year	*Percent*	*Year*	*Percent*
1975	23.5	1986	27.9
1976	23.8	1987	28.3
1977	24.1	1988	28.5
1978	25.0	1989	28.0
1979	22.7	1990	28.4
1980	21.5	1991	28.6
1981	22.2	1992	27.8
1982	23.3	1993	28.8
1983	23.9	1994	30.2
1984	24.6	1995	30.6
1985	25.8	1996	30.7

Source: United Nations (1983–98).

Most theoretical models assume knowledge spillovers from R&D to be national or international in scope and then compare the predictions of the two scenarios. Following this line of argument, the goal of the empirical economist is simply to determine which assumption is appropriate. Yet this approach sits rather uncomfortably with the central tenets of the literature on trade and growth. A major theme of this literature is that technological change occurs due to intentional and costly investments undertaken by firms that seek to profit from monopoly power that results from successful innovation. If this is the case, arbitrage in knowledge, which is basically what the spread of know-how across countries amounts to, cannot be totally exogenous to economic activity. Those agents that invest heavily in creating new technologies face strong incentives to control the spread of their hard-earned successes. If such control were not possible, they would have little incentive to make those investments in the first place. For the theory of trade and innovation to be internally consistent almost requires that inventors partially control the rate at which their technologies spread internationally. Therefore it is misleading to focus on the geographical scope of knowledge spillovers without giving innovators some role in that process.

In addition to the incentives of innovators, other factors determine the scope of knowledge spillovers, including incentives facing potential buyers and imitators of technologies. The literature in this area has not paid adequate attention to the choices that both potential suppliers and buyers of technology face. However, the literature seeks to explain the emergence of multinational firms that play a central role in international technology transfer.

Explaining FDI: Location and Mode of Production

There are two distinct questions that a firm seeking to serve foreign markets must address. First, is it better to produce the good in the home country and export to foreign markets, or is production abroad more profitable? Second, for production abroad, how should technology be transferred overseas? Firms can choose from a variety of arrangements that differ in their relative use of markets and organizations. One extreme arrangement transfers technology to wholly owned subsidiaries; the other extreme transfers technology to unrelated parties through licensing.

Exports versus Production Abroad

When serving a foreign market, a firm can choose from a menu of options. The literature mainly focuses on the choice between exports and FDI, assuming that exports and FDI are substitutes for one another. However, empirical work usually uncovers a complementary relationship between exports and foreign affiliate sales. For example, Lipsey and Weiss (1981) find that sales of foreign affiliates are positively correlated with exports at the industry level. Firm-level studies, such as Lipsey and Weiss (1984), Grubert and Mutti (1991), and Blomström and others (1988) also uncover a complementary relationship between trade and FDI.

Does the evidence imply that most theoretical models are flawed? Perhaps not. Blonigen (1999) suggests that a reasonable interpretation of the evidence shows that such studies find net complementarity: aggregation bias in the data simply buries the substitution effects emphasized in theoretical models. Blonigen's major contribution lies in using product-level data because theory implies the substitution effect at this level. Blonigen uses data on Japanese production and exports to the United States for two types of products: automobile parts and automobiles. His study is particularly useful in the context of Japanese multinational firms located in the United States that import relatively large amounts of parts from Japan and seem quite unwilling to substitute between U.S. and Japanese parts.

Only a study of the type done by Blonigen (1999) can really sort out the complementary nature of trade between intermediate goods and affiliate sales on the one hand and the substitutability of exports of final goods and FDI on the other. Not surprisingly, Blonigen's results conform nicely to the theory: exports of intermediate goods and sales of affiliates are complements, whereas exports and sales of final goods are substitutes. The only unresolved issue is why aggregate studies find a net complementary relationship. The explanation probably lies in a fact that Ethier (1982) emphasizes: most intraindustry trade between industrial countries involves exchange of intermediate goods. The literature on intraindustry trade as derived from Dixit and Stiglitz's (1977) model may overemphasize the role of product differentiation and consumer emphasis on variety. As Ethier (1982) notes, actual trade is in intermediate goods needed for production. Thus, if such trade is indeed pervasive, there should be a strong complementary relationship between exports and FDI at the aggregate level.

The theoretical models have also argued that strategic considerations influence the choice between exports and FDI (see Horstmann and Markusen [1992] and Motta and Norman [1996]). The presence of trade barriers creates a tariff-jumping motive for FDI. Bhagwati and others (1987, 1992) argue that the mere threat of future trade restrictions may lead to anticipatory investment (called quid pro quo investment) by foreign firms. However, the preceding research emphasizes the interdependence of decisionmaking between multinational firms. For example, when two firms are exporting to a foreign market, a switch from exports to FDI by one creates an incentive for FDI on the part of the other firm, which finds itself at a competitive disadvantage (Lin and Saggi 1999 call this the competitive incentive for FDI). An old tradition in the management literature describes the interdependence between the decisionmaking of large multinationals as follow-the-leader behavior.

As far as the static choice between exports and production abroad, the theoretical models seem reasonably well developed. However, firms face a dynamic problem, not just a one-time choice between exports and FDI. Firms may (and indeed do) switch between the two activities over time. Unfortunately, there is scarce literature that explores the dynamics of optimal entry strategies into foreign markets. Roberts and Tybout (1997) highlight the role of sunk costs in determining the dynamic behavior of exporters. Using data for Colombian manufacturing plants, Roberts and Tybout show that prior exporting experience is an important determinant of the current tendency to export as well as the profitability of exporting. Their findings show that sunk costs are indeed relevant for export behavior and that learning is subject to strong depreciation. The entry costs of a plant that has never exported do not differ significantly from those of plants that have not exported for more than two years.

Although Roberts and Tybout (1997) do not consider other modes of serving foreign markets, their insight can be utilized in a more general context. Suppose firms also have the option of FDI. Building on the Roberts and Tybout approach, the choice between exports and FDI is a choice between two different technologies, where exports entail a higher marginal cost and a lower fixed (sunk) cost than FDI. Under uncertainty, if firms do face such a cost structure, an interesting dynamic relation between exports and FDI may emerge.

Saggi (1998) builds a two-period model to examine a firm's choice between exports and FDI in the face of demand uncertainty. First-period exports yield information about demand in the foreign market. As a result, first-period exports have an option value. That is, if a significant portion of the fixed cost of FDI is sunk, it is optimal for a firm to export in the first period and to choose FDI if and only if demand abroad is large enough.

Clearly, the preceding argument is not specific to demand uncertainty and can be generalized with respect to other types of uncertainty about which sales through exports can yield information. Similarly, exports and initial FDI may be strongly complementary because firms are not likely to shift the entire production process to a new location immediately. If initial investment is profitable, local sourcing may reduce the need for imported intermediates. Over time, such substitution effects may become stronger, and the complementarity between exports and FDI may become weaker (assuming local suppliers are indeed competitive or local production is consistent with comparative advantage considerations).

Of course, generalizing the preceding argument to the case of multiple firms also creates the possibility of information externalities among investors; that is, the experience of one firm may impart lessons to others. Such externalities may be particularly relevant for FDI in many developing and formerly closed economies (China and much of Eastern Europe) that have only recently opened their markets to foreign investors. Firms from industrial countries have little prior experience in operating in these new environments. This lack of experience coupled with the complexity surrounding the FDI decision implies that firms seeking to invest in these markets can learn valuable lessons from the successes and failures of others. FDI involves hiring foreign labor, setting up a new plant, meeting foreign regulations, and developing new marketing plans; these decisions require adequate information. In this context, decisions made by rival firms can lower a firm's fixed cost by helping avoid mistakes. For example, Lin and Saggi (1999) use a duopoly model in which the first firm to switch from exporting to FDI confers a positive externality on the subsequent investor by lowering its fixed cost of FDI.

In their survey of Japanese firms planning investments in Asia, Kinoshita and Mody (1997) find that both private and public information play important roles in determining investment decisions. They argue that information regarding many operational conditions (such as the functioning of labor markets, literacy, the productivity of the labor force, and timely availability and quality of inputs) may not be available publicly. Such information is either gathered through direct experience or through the experience of others. Indeed, Kinoshita and Mody's empirical analysis finds that a firm's current investment is strongly affected by its own past behavior as well as by the investments of its rivals.

Although the degree of fixed/sunk costs may play a role in determining the choice between licensing, joint ventures, and FDI, other considerations are probably more important. A new foreign plant is the primary contributing factor behind higher fixed/sunk costs of FDI relative to exports. This factor is unlikely to be of first-order importance in determining the choice between different entry modes that are distinguished primarily by the extent of foreign ownership.

Mode of Operation: Licensing, Joint Venture, or FDI?

A major question in the theory of the multinational firm is when and why firms choose to internalize technology transfer, thereby forgoing the option of utilizing market based alternatives such as technology licensing. Markusen (1995) and Caves (1996) discuss the relevant economics literature regarding internalization. A vast literature in the field of international business deals with some of the questions posed. By and large, this literature involves empirical tests of the ownership, location, and internalization paradigm developed by Dunning (1988). To limit the scope of this survey, I discuss this literature only to the extent that it offers new insights with respect to the economics of multinational firms (see Caves 1996 for a relatively recent survey of this literature). I focus on the central conclusions of this line of research, particularly those that relate to technology transfer.

Markusen and Maskus (1999) suggest that the literature that attempts to link the emergence of multinational firms with firm- and country-level characteristics can be understood as emerging from a common underlying model—the knowledge capital model. Research that deals directly with technology transfer includes Horstmann and

Markusen (1987, 1996) and Ethier and Markusen (1991). Markusen (1998) argues that the knowledge capital model rests on the fact that knowledge has a public good property, that is, it can be utilized in multiple locations simultaneously. Thus any innovation can then be fruitfully applied at multiple plants dispersed all over the world, giving rise to horizontal multinational firms. Markusen and Maskus (1999) show that there is indeed strong empirical support for this horizontal model of multinationals.

How does the knowledge capital model explain internalization? Once again, the public good nature of knowledge occupies a central role. If licensees (or local partners under a joint venture) can get access to the multinational's proprietary knowledge, the value of its knowledge based assets can be dissipated either because of increased competition (Ethier and Markusen 1991; Markusen 2000; Saggi 1996, 1999) or because the local partner has inadequate incentives to protect the multinational's reputation (Horstmann and Markusen 1987). The incentive to prevent the dissipation of knowledge-based assets is reflected in the fact that multinationals transfer technologies of new vintage through direct investment and license or transfer their older technologies through joint ventures (see Mansfield and Romeo 1980). Alternatively, it may be easier to trade older technologies through the market; potential buyers are likely to be better informed about well-established technologies compared with new ones.

In an empirical paper, Smarzynska (1999a) focuses on intraindustry differences in R&D intensity as a determinant of the mode of entry chosen by firms investing in Eastern European countries. Like past work, this study finds that a firm's R&D expenditure is negatively related to the probability of a joint venture and positively related to direct entry. Furthermore, a firm's R&D expenditure relative to the rest of the industry is positively correlated with the probability of greenfield entry in high-technology sectors. In low-technology sectors, higher relative R&D expenditure by a firm actually increases the likelihood of a joint venture rather than a greenfield entry. Thus, a firm's R&D expenditure relative to other firms in the industry and the aggregate R&D expenditure of the industry relative to other industries may interact in subtle ways to influence the choice between alternative entry modes. Smarzynska (1999a) argues that protecting technology is of greater concern in high-tech industries, thereby encouraging technological leaders to adopt direct entry. However it is also possible that in industries characterized by a fast pace of technological change, any technology leakage will hurt a firm for only a short period of time. Furthermore, the formation of joint ventures may be easier in relatively mature host industries because they can more easily find suitable local partners. Thus Smarzynska's results call for a careful interpretation but raise some interesting possibilities and questions.

Foreign firms may not be the only ones that have valuable information that is subject to the risk of dissipation. Horstmann and Markusen (1996) argue that a potential licensee in the host country may have better information about local demand and could use this information to extract rents from the licenser. Such agency costs can also be utilized to explain the dynamics of optimal entry modes. In his studies of British multinationals, Nicholas (1982, 1983) finds that 88 percent of the firms sold their products through a contract with a local agent before converting to directly owned sales or production branches. Furthermore, the decision to terminate the licensing arrangement was based on a desire to avoid agency costs. Once the multinational had acquired the information it needed through its alliance with the local partner, continuing the agency relationship was no longer attractive. Similarly, in their survey of Japanese multinationals in Australia, Nicholas and others (1994) find that 60 percent of the firms used a local agent before making a direct investment and 69 percent exported to Australia before making a direct investment of any sort. Such temporary licensing could be viewed as a method of information acquisition on the part of the foreign firm, as opposed to the local firm seeking superior production technology.

In Horstmann and Markusen's (1996) model, when the multinational firm's fixed costs of investment are high relative to the agent's and there is risk of large losses due to low demand, the multinational opts for an initial licensing contract that becomes permanent ex post in case of low demand. Their analysis can be applied to examine the choice between a joint venture and a wholly owned subsidiary, except that cost uncertainty may be more relevant than demand uncertainty for this scenario. For example, if the productivity of foreign labor is in doubt, forming a joint venture may present a low (fixed) cost option. If labor productivity turns out to be high, an acquisition of the foreign partner may be optimal ex post, resulting in the establishment of a wholly owned subsidiary.

However, dynamic issues remain underexplored in the literature. Although the comparative statics of the models provide some partial intuition about forces that are important for dynamic choice, such an approach is a poor substitute for explicit dynamic modeling. Several central questions deserve further research. For example, what determines the sequencing pattern of different activities? Do firms first form joint ventures and then proceed with direct investment? If so, why? To what extent do the dynamic choices of foreign firms result from their efforts at restricting diffusion of their own technology while at the same time maximizing the acquisition of valuable information from local firms? Do host country welfare and the rate of technology diffusion depend on the sequencing pattern?

FDI, Technology Transfer, and Spillovers

Although the increase in world trade has received significant attention, the role FDI has played in the explosion of world trade is not often appreciated. Today, intrafirm trade, that is, trade between subsidiaries and headquarters of multinational firms, may account for one-third of total world trade. The importance of FDI can also be gauged from the fact that sales of subsidiaries of multinational firms now exceed worldwide exports of goods and services. In 1998, the total estimated value of foreign affiliate sales was US$11 trillion, whereas the value of worldwide exports was $7 trillion (U.N. Conference on Trade and Development [UNCTAD] 1999). Thus, FDI is the dominant channel through which firms serve customers in foreign markets.

Historically much of the flows of FDI occurred between industrial countries (much like most intraindustry trade). For example, during 1987–92, industrial countries attracted $137 billion of FDI inflows a year on average; developing economies attracted only $35 billion, or slightly more than 20 percent of global FDI inflows. Yet developing economies have become increasingly important host countries for FDI, especially because of the large-scale liberalization undertaken by formerly closed economies, such as China. During 1996 and 1997, over 40 percent of global FDI flows went to developing economies (UNCTAD 1999).

Figure 2 plots net FDI inflows as a percentage of gross domestic investment for low- and middle-income countries (those countries with per capita income below $9,655) for 1975–96. During this period, FDI became an increasingly important source of capital for such countries. On average, FDI inflows now constitute approximately 10 percent of their annual gross domestic investment.

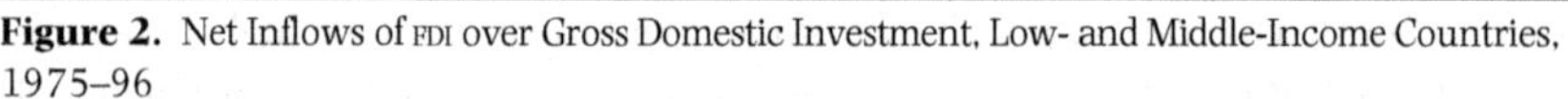

Figure 2. Net Inflows of FDI over Gross Domestic Investment, Low- and Middle-Income Countries, 1975–96

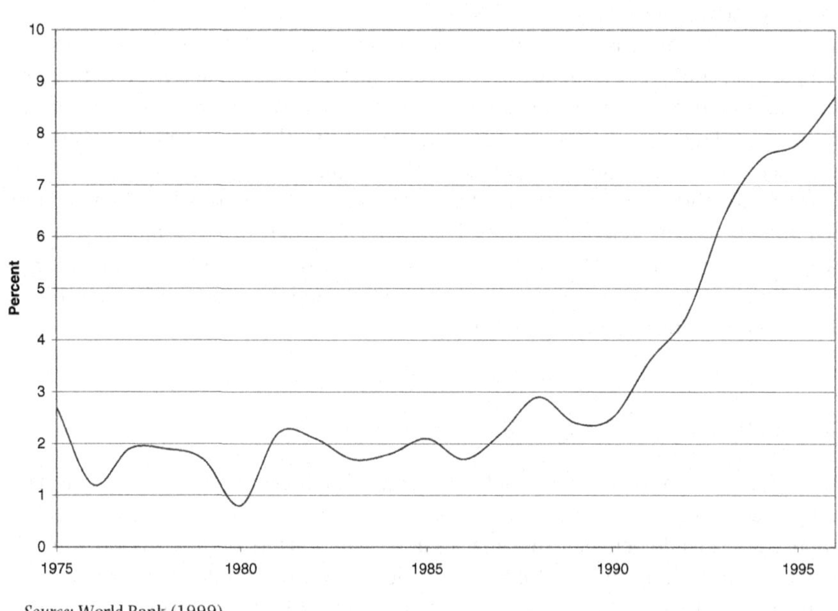

Source: World Bank (1999).

The recent surge in capital flows to developing economies, of which FDI has been a significant part, is also reflected in the fact that approximately 30 percent of the total stock of FDI is in developing economies (table 2). FDI is of relatively greater importance to developing economies because of their smaller size. In 1997, the total inward stock of FDI as a percentage of GDP was almost 17 percent in developing countries, compared with less than 12 percent in industrial countries (table 2).

For the purposes of this article, the role of FDI as a channel for transferring goods and services internationally is of secondary concern. Instead, the main issue is the role of FDI as a channel of technology transfer. It is difficult to find fully convincing evidence of the dominance of FDI as a channel of international technology transfer (among those channels that directly involve the owner of the technology being transferred). However, several facts hint in that direction. For example, in 1995 over 80 percent of global royalty payments for international transfers of technology were made from subsidiaries to their parent firms (UNCTAD 1997). In general, technology payments and receipts have risen steadily since the mid-1980s, reflecting the importance of technology for international production.

Table 3 reports data for Germany, Japan, and the United States. For example, from 1985 to 1997, Germany's receipts of royalties and license fees increased from approximately $0.5 billion to more than $2 billion. For the United States, the increase was even sharper, from $6 billion to more than $33 billion. The data also indicate the importance of FDI for international trade in technology. During 1985–97, between two-thirds and nine-tenths of technology flows were intrafirm in nature. Furthermore, as is evident from table 3, the intrafirm share of technology flows has increased over time. Of course, royalty payments only record the explicit sale of technology and do not capture the full magnitude of technology transfer through FDI relative to technology transfer via imitation, trade in goods, and other channels.

Yet another confirmation of the strong role FDI plays in transmitting technology internationally comes from the interindustry distribution of FDI. It is well known that multinational firms are concentrated in industries that exhibit a high ratio of R&D relative to sales and a large share of technical and professional workers (Markusen

Table 2. FDI Inward Stock, 1987–98

FDI inward stock	*1980*	*1985*	*1990*	*1995*	*1997*
Billions of dollars					
World	506	783	1769	2790	3437
Percent in industrial countries	73.8	69.7	78.9	71.1	67.3
Percentage of GDP					
World	5.0	6.9	8.7	9.9	11.7
Industrial countries	4.8	6.1	8.4	9.0	10.5
Developing economies	5.9	9.8	10.5	14.1	16.6

Source: UNCTAD (2000).

Table 3. Receipts of Royalties and License Fees, 1985–97
(millions of dollars)

	Germany			*United States*		
		Intrafirm			*Intrafirm*	
Year	*Total*	*German parent firms only*	*Foreign affiliates in Germany*	*Total*	*U.S. parent firms only*	*Foreign affiliates in the United States*
1985	546	464	83	6,680	—	—
1986	780	597	122	8,114	5,994	180
1987	997	698	146	10,183	7,668	229
1988	1,081	883	124	12,147	9,238	263
1989	1,122	899	106	13,818	10,612	349
1990	1,547	1,210	235	16,635	12,867	383
1991	1,515	—	345	17,819	13,523	583
1992	1,680	—	472	20,841	14,925	733
1993	1,596	—	498	21,694	14,936	752
1994	1,720	—	489	26,712	19,250	1,025
1995	2,174	1,486	642	30,289	21,399	1,460
1996	2,315	1,667	653	32,823	22,781	1,929
1997	2,282	1,659	509	33,676	23,457	2,058

— Not available.
Source: UNCTAD (1999).

1995). In fact, it is commonly argued that multinationals rely heavily on intangible assets, such as superior technology, for successfully competing with local firms that are better acquainted with the host country environment.

By encouraging FDI, developing economies hope not only to import more efficient foreign technologies but also to generate technological spillovers for local firms. Not surprisingly, a large body of literature tries to determine whether host countries enjoy spillovers from FDI. It is important to be clear about the meaning of the word *spillover*. A distinction can be made between pecuniary externalities (that result from the effects of FDI on market structure) and other pure externalities (such as the facilitation of technology adoption) that may accompany FDI. A strict definition of spillovers would count only the latter, and this is the definition employed here. In other words, if FDI spurs innovation in the domestic industry by increasing competition, I do not view that as a spillover from FDI because this effect works its way through the price mechanism. However, it is difficult to isolate empirically the pure externalities from FDI from its other effects that work through the market. Furthermore, policy ought to be based on the aggregate effect of FDI on welfare, not just on the extent of positive externalities from FDI.

The central difficulty is that spillovers, as defined here, do not leave a paper trail; they are externalities that the market fails to take into account. Nevertheless, several studies have attempted the difficult task of quantifying spillovers. But what are the potential channels through which such they may arise? A more difficult question is whether it is even reasonable to even expect spillovers to occur from FDI. Multinationals have much to gain from preventing the diffusion of their technologies to local firms (except when technologies diffuse vertically to potential suppliers of inputs or buyers of goods and services sold by multinationals).

Potential Channels of Spillovers

At a general level, the literature suggests the following potential channels of spillovers:

- *Demonstration effects.* Local firms may adopt technologies introduced by multinational firms through imitation or reverse engineering.
- *Labor turnover.* Workers trained or previously employed by the multinational may transfer important information to local firms by switching employers or may contribute to technology diffusion by starting their own firms.
- *Vertical linkages.* Multinationals may transfer technology to firms that are potential suppliers of intermediate goods or buyers of their own products.

Demonstration effects. In its simplest form, the demonstration effect argument states that exposure to the superior technology of multinational firms may lead local firms to update their own production methods. The argument derives from the assumption that it may simply be too costly for local firms to acquire the necessary information for adopting new technologies if they are not first introduced in the local economy by multinationals (and hence demonstrated to succeed in the local environment). Incidentally, the demonstration effect argument relates well to the point made by Parente and Prescott (1994) that trade may lower costs of technology adoption.

Clearly, geographical proximity is a vital part of the demonstration effect argument. As noted earlier, empirical evidence on the geographical scope of R&D spillovers is mixed. However, studies that reach optimistic conclusions with respect to the international nature of R&D spillovers typically involve data from industrial countries and therefore require qualification. Geographical proximity may indeed be crucial for developing economies that are not as well integrated into the world economy and that have fewer alternative channels for absorbing technologies.

The main insight of the demonstration effect argument is that FDI may expand the set of technologies available to local firms. If so, this is a potential positive externality. However, a mere expansion in choices need not imply faster technology adoption, especially if domestic incentives for adoption are also altered due to the impact of FDI on market structure. FDI may expand choices, but it also generally increases competition. The industrial organization literature on market structure and innovation does not provide an unambiguous answer to this question. A rough conclusion is that a monopolist has a stronger incentive to invest in R&D that yields innovations that complement existing technology, whereas competitive firms have a stronger incentive to invest in R&D that yields innovations that replace existing technology. The net effect on the incentives for adopting new technologies may indeed be ambiguous.

Suppose FDI does lower the cost of technology adoption and lead to faster adoption of new technologies by local firms. Does that imply that relative to trade (that is, a scenario in which foreign firms export to the domestic or world market), inward FDI necessarily generates spillovers for the local economy? A point to keep in mind is that technology diffusion may strengthen the competitors of the foreign firms. Foreseeing the consequences of such diffusion, foreign firms may alter the very terms of their original technology transfer. For example, a foreign firm may choose to transfer technologies of lower quality when there is a risk of leakage to local firms. It is conceivable, however, that due to their larger size and other advantages they enjoy in the product market, multinationals can alter the market outcome in their favor despite technology leakage. Thus, a multinational would not have to resort to such strategies.

For example, Das (1987) presents a model in which native firms may learn from the subsidiary of a multinational firm that acts as a dominant firm facing a local competitive fringe in the product market. Wang and Blomström (1992) present a related model. In their duopoly model with differentiated goods, a multinational transfers technology to its subsidiary so that the local firm can learn from the new technologies introduced. Learning occurs both through costless technology spillovers as in the contagion effects that Findlay (1978) first emphasized, as well as through the local firm's costly investments. The most interesting implication of Wang and Blomström's model is that technology transfer through FDI is positively related to the level of the local firm's investment in learning. This result suggests that multinationals respond to local competition by introducing newer technologies faster.

Assuming the rate of increase in efficiency of the local firms to be positively related to the scale of operation of the multinational firm's subsidiary, Das (1987) investigates the optimal time paths of the multinational's output and price. She shows that despite technology leakage, the multinational may find it profitable to transfer technology. Huizinga (1995) models a multinational's incentive for technology transfer where it faces risk of competition caused by expropriation by the government of the host country. The main result is that the multinational responds by lowering the quality of technology transfer even when such transfers are costless.

Because the demonstration effect argument is largely an industry-level argument, relating industry-level variation in R&D expenditures by local firms to the extent of FDI is one method of checking whether local adoption efforts are encouraged through FDI. Of course, such an exercise would have to control for the effect of FDI on market structure, and this seems rather difficult. To the best of my knowledge, a convincing empirical exercise of this type has not been performed. Instead, the existing literature has focused on the effects of FDI on TFP in local firms.

Labor turnover. Although researchers have extensively studied direct imitation and reverse engineering as channels of interfirm technology diffusion, they have tended to neglect the role of labor turnover. Labor turnover differs from the other channels because knowledge embodied in the labor force moves across firms only through the physical movement of workers. The relative importance of labor turnover is difficult to establish because it would require tracking individuals who have worked for multinationals, interviewing them regarding their future job choices, and then determining their impact on the productivity of new employers. Few empirical studies attempt to measure the magnitude of labor turnover from multinationals to local firms. To the best of my knowledge, there are no empirical studies that attempt to measure the role such turnover plays in improving productivity in local firms.

The available evidence on labor turnover itself is mixed. For example, although Gershenberg's (1987) study of Kenyan industries finds limited evidence of labor turnover from multinationals to local Kenyan firms, several other studies document substantial labor turnover from multinationals to local firms. UNCTAD (1992) discusses the case of the garment industry in Bangladesh (see also Rhee 1990). Korea's Daewoo supplied Desh (the first Bangladeshi firm to manufacture and export garments) with technology and credit. Thus, Desh was not a multinational firm in the strict sense; rather, it was a domestic firm that benefited substantially from its connection with Daewoo. Eventually, 115 of the 130 initial workers left Desh to set up their own firms or to join other newly established garment companies. The remarkable speed with which the former Desh workers transmitted their know-how to other factories clearly demonstrates the role labor turnover can play in technology diffusion.

Pack (1997) discusses evidence documenting the role of labor turnover in disseminating the technologies of multinationals to local firms. For example, in the mid-1980s, almost 50 percent of all engineers and approximately 63 percent of all skilled workers that left multinationals left to join local Taiwanese firms. By contrast, Gershenberg's (1987) study of Kenyan industry reports smaller figures: of the 91 job shifts studied, only 16 percent involved turnover from multinationals to local firms.

To synthesize these empirical findings, the cross-country variation in labor turnover rates itself requires an explanation. One possible generalization is that in areas such as Korea and Taiwan, local competitors are less disadvantaged relative to their counterparts in many African economies, thereby making labor turnover possible. Thus the ability of local firms to absorb technologies introduced by multinationals may be a key determinant of whether labor turnover occurs as a means of technology diffusion in equilibrium. Furthermore, the local investment climate may be such that workers looking to leave multinationals in search of new opportunities (or other local entrepreneurs) find it unprofitable to start their own companies, implying that the only alternative opportunity is to join existing local firms. The presence of weak local competitors probably goes hand in hand with the lack of entrepreneurial efforts because both may result from the underlying structure of the economic environment.

Glass and Saggi (forthcoming) argue that because superior technology is one of the key intangible assets that permit multinationals to successfully compete with local firms, multinationals may attempt to limit technology diffusion by offering higher wages to their workers relative to local firms. Thus, the wage premiums paid by a multinational can provide a rough estimate of the value it places on the knowledge it transfers to its workers. The more interesting point is that such a premium may either exceed or fall short of the benefit the local economy would enjoy if the multinational were to allow its workers to leave. Note that if the multinational must raise wages to restrict technology diffusion to local firms, the wage premium might not be related to the social value of the knowledge embodied in the workers. Thus, technology diffusion is not necessarily optimal for the local economy. Policies designed to encourage technology transfer do not always increase the welfare of the recipient country.

Local competition policy may also affect labor turnover. For example, Bulgaria's competition law does not permit an individual to join the management of a competing firm operating in the same line of business as the person's original employer for the first three years after leaving an enterprise (Hoekman and Djankov 1997). Of course, in many industrial countries, trade secrets laws protect firms against the loss of valuable information to their rival firms. But it is difficult to see how such laws could protect against the kind of basic technology diffusion that results from labor turnover from multinationals in developing economies.

Labor turnover rates may vary at the industry level as well. Casual observation suggests that industries with a fast pace of technological change (such as the computer industry in Silicon Valley) are characterized by very high turnover rates relative to more mature industries. Therefore, cross-country variation in labor turnover from multinationals could simply stem from the global composition of FDI: developing economies are unlikely to host FDI in sectors subject to rapid technological change.

Vertical linkages. For quite some time, analysts have recognized that multinationals may benefit the host economy through the backward and forward linkages they generate. However, merely documenting extensive linkages between multinationals and local suppliers or buyers is insufficient for arguing that net benefits accrue to the local economy as a result of FDI. Rodriguez Clare (1996) develops a formal model of linkages and shows that multinationals improve welfare only if they generate linkages over and beyond those generated by the local firms they displace. Yet the question of relevance here is whether the generation of linkages is expected to result in technology diffusion. Although analytical modeling of such issues is scarce, there is limited empirical evidence in support of the view that multinationals are involved in vertical technology transfers (Lall 1980).

Mexico's experience with FDI is illustrative of how such a process works. In Mexico, extensive backward linkages resulted from FDI in the automobile industry. Within five years of investments by major auto manufacturers there were 300 domestic producers of parts and accessories, of which 110 had annual sales of more than $1 million (Moran 1998). Foreign producers also transferred industry best practices, zero defect procedures, and production audits to domestic suppliers, thereby improving their productivity and the quality of their products. As a result of increased competition and efficiency, Mexican exports in the automobile industry boomed. Thus, although direct competitors of multinational firms may not realize technological benefits (as evidenced by Aitken and others 1996), suppliers of intermediate goods are likely to benefit substantially.

Even more interesting is the possibility that such vertical transfers when accompanied by spillovers may lead to interaction between upstream and downstream multinational firms that encourages industrial development. Markusen and Venables (1999) develop a model that abstracts from technology spillovers but focuses on the pecuniary externalities that accompany vertical linkages and result in industrial development. Pack and Saggi (2001) emphasize that downstream buyers in industrial country markets benefit from technology diffusion among potential suppliers in developing economies because such diffusion increases competition among suppliers. In their model, by increasing demand in the downstream market, competition caused by technology diffusion in the developing market may induce entry into marketing, thereby increasing competition in the downstream market. Their analysis implies that fully integrated multinational firms may be more averse to technology diffusion than are firms involved in international arm's-length arrangements. Although they do not model FDI, it is not hard to see how their model can be applied to understand the consequences of technology diffusion under FDI rather than exporting.

Empirical Evidence on Spillovers

Early efforts in search of spillovers from FDI proceeded by relating the interindustry variation in productivity to the extent of FDI (Blomström 1986; Blomström and Persson 1983; Caves 1974; Globerman 1979). These studies largely find that sectors with a higher level of foreign involvement (as measured by the share of the labor force in the industry employed by foreign firms or the extent of foreign ownership) tend to have higher productivity, higher productivity growth, or both. The fact that these studies involve data from different countries (Australia for the Caves study, Canada for Globerman, and Mexico for Blomström) lends a strong degree of robustness to this positive correlation between the level of foreign involvement and local productivity at the sector level.

Of course, correlation is not causation and, as noted by Aitken and Harrison (1999), this literature may overstate the positive impact of FDI on local productivity. Investment may have been attracted to the more productive sectors of the economy instead of being the cause of the high productivity in such sectors. In other words, the studies ignore an important self-selection problem. Both trade and FDI help ensure an efficient allocation of global resources by encouraging investment in those sectors in which an economy enjoys comparative advantage. In this sense, Aitken and Harrison's point is almost necessarily implied by traditional trade theory. However, if trade protection encourages investment in sectors in which a host economy does not enjoy comparative advantage, trade protection may be welfare-reducing. This possibility was relevant for countries that sought to industrialize by following a strategy of import substitution.

Nevertheless, only plant-level studies can control for the self-selection problem that may plague industry-level studies. Taking the argument a step further, the self-selection problem may also arise in plant-level studies: the more productive plants may be the ones that attract foreign investment. For example, Clerides and others (1998) find support in favor of the self-selection hypothesis in the context of exporting. They find that the more productive firms self select into exporting. However, if plant-level studies fail to find a significant relationship between foreign involvement and productivity, the self-selection problem might not be important. It might be important if foreign firms seek out plants with low productivity and bring them up to par with more efficient local plants. In this case, there might be no significant productivity differential between foreign and local firms. This argument seems far-fetched, but it could make sense. Suppose local plants with very low productivity are relatively undervalued by local agents because the skills (technology and modern management) needed to make them competitive are in short supply locally. In this scenario, such plants would be attractive to foreign investors who can, through their technology, generate productivity improvements that simply cannot be achieved by local agents.

What do empirical plant-level studies find with respect to spillovers from FDI? Haddad and Harrison's (1993) study was the first to employ a comprehensive data set at the level of the individual firm over several years. The data came from an annual survey of all manufacturing firms in Morocco. An important result was that foreign firms exhibited higher levels of TFP, but their rate of TFP growth was lower than that for domestic firms. As the authors note, at first glance, such a finding suggests that perhaps there was some sort of convergence between domestic and foreign firms. However, this was not the case. Although there was a level effect of foreign investment on the TFP of domestic firms, such an effect was missing for the growth rate of the TFP of domestic firms. In addition, when sectors were divided into high and low tech, the effect of FDI at the sector level was found to be more positive in low-tech sectors. The authors interpret this result as indicative of the lack of absorptive capacity on the part of local firms in the high-tech sector, where they may be further behind multinationals and unable to absorb foreign technology.

Aitken and others (1996) undertake a somewhat different approach to measuring spillovers from FDI. The idea behind their study is that technology spillovers should increase the marginal product of labor, and this increased productivity should show up in the wages for workers. The study employs data from manufacturing firms in Venezuela, Mexico, and the United States. For both Mexico and Venezuela, a higher share of foreign employment is associated with higher overall wages for both skilled and unskilled workers. Furthermore, royalty payments to foreign firms from local firms are highly correlated with wages. Most important, the study finds no positive impact of FDI on the wages of workers employed by domestic firms. In fact, the authors report a small negative effect for domestic firms, whereas the overall effect for the entire industry is positive. These findings differ from those for the United States, where a larger share of foreign firms in employment is associated with both a higher average wage as well as higher wages in domestic establishments.

Putting the Aitken and others (1996) findings into the context of previous work, it is clear that wage spillovers (from foreign to domestic firms) are associated with higher productivity in domestic plants. Conversely, the absence of wage spillovers appears to accompany the existence of productivity differentials between domestic and foreign firms. Why might this be so? Any serious explanation of this association requires studying the interaction of the market for labor and goods. Glass and Saggi (1999b) develop a model to capture this interaction (their findings are discussed in the section on labor turnover).

The most recent study on the issue of spillovers from FDI is Aitken and Harrison (1999). This study uses annual census data on more than 4,000 Venezuelan firms. Because each plant was observed over a period of time, the self-selection problem of previous sector-level studies (that is, FDI goes to the more productive sectors) could be avoided. The authors find a positive relationship between foreign equity participation and plant performance, implying that foreign participation does indeed benefit plants that receive such participation. However, this own-plant effect is robust for only small plants, that is, those plants that employ fewer than 50 employees. For larger plants, foreign participation results in no significant improvement in productivity relative to domestic plants.

More interestingly, productivity in domestic plants *declines* when foreign investment increases. In other words, the authors find evidence of negative spillovers from FDI and suggest that they could result from a market stealing effect. That is, foreign competition may have forced domestic firms to lower output and thereby forgo economies of scale. Note that if loss in output is large enough, local plants may have lower productivity despite enjoying some sort of technology spillovers. Nevertheless, on balance, Aitken and Harrison (1999) find that the effect of FDI on the productivity of the entire industry is weakly positive. They also note that similar results are obtained for Indonesia, except that the positive effect on its own plants is stronger, whereas the negative effect on domestic plants is weaker, suggesting a stronger overall positive effect.

Djankov and Hoekman (2000) also find a negative spillover effect of FDI on purely domestic firms in industry in the Czech Republic. Interestingly, however, when joint ventures are excluded from the sample and attention is restricted to the impact of majority-owned foreign affiliates (that is, FDI) on all other firms in an industry (including joint ventures), the negative effect loses statistical significance. The authors report that survey questionnaires reveal that joint-venture firms invest significantly more in new technologies than do purely domestic firms. The authors suggest that purely domestic firms might lack the ability to absorb the technologies introduced by foreign firms (due to their lower R&D efforts).

Overall, several studies have cast doubt on the view that FDI generates positive spillovers for local firms. But such findings need not imply that host countries have nothing significant to gain (or must lose) from FDI. The point is that the reallocation of resources that accompanies the entry of foreign firms may not be immediate. Domestic firms should be expected to suffer from an increase in competition; in fact, part of the benefit of inward FDI is that it can help weed out relatively inefficient domestic firms. Resources released in this process will be put to better use by foreign firms with superior technologies, efficient new entrants (domestic and foreign), or some other sectors of the economy. Existing studies of spillovers may not cover a long enough period to be able to accurately determine how FDI affects turnover rates (entry and exit). Furthermore, their design limits such horizontal studies because they cannot clarify linkages and spillovers that may result from FDI in industries other than the one in which FDI occurs.

Spillovers from FDI: A Recapitulation

A challenge facing the optimistic view regarding technology spillovers from FDI is to explain how such spillovers can ever be in the interest of the multinational firms. Clearly, under most circumstances, multinationals would rather limit diffusion in the local economy. In fact, the heart of the theory that seeks to explain the emergence of multinationals is that such firms are able to successfully compete with local firms precisely because they possess superior technologies, management, and marketing. Why, then, would multinationals not take actions to ensure that such advantages do not diffuse to local competitors?

Part of the answer must lie in the fact that such actions are costly and may even entail externalities between multinationals. Suppose a costly action (such as litigation in local courts to enforce protection of IPRS) can indeed help limit the loss of knowledge capital for a multinational. A difficulty arises if all potential multinationals benefit from the curtailment of technology diffusion, whereas the costs fall on only the one who takes legal action. Thus the public good nature of such actions suggests that developing economies hosting multinationals may expect the rivalry among such firms to result in some degree of technology diffusion. Of course, the preceding argument also overstates the case a bit: some loss of knowledge will result despite all precautions. Nevertheless, it is beyond dispute that multinationals can take actions to limit diffusion, and while they are making their decisions regarding where to set up subsidiaries, the expected costs of technology diffusion will enter their calculus of profit maximization.

That being said, the entry of multinationals may indeed benefit host countries even if it fails to result in spillovers for local firms. First, the preceding discussion suggests that spillovers to local firms that directly compete with the multinationals would be the most elusive of benefits that host countries may expect to enjoy from FDI. Second, local agents other than domestic competitors of multinationals (for example, local workers) may enjoy positive externalities from FDI. If so, the total effect of FDI on local welfare may be positive despite the lack of technology spillovers.

Third, spillovers may be of an entirely different nature: local firms may enjoy positive externalities from foreign firms that make it easier for them to export. Such externalities may come about because better infrastructure (transportation, storage facilities, and ports) emerges in regions with a high concentration of foreign exporters. Aitken and others (1997) provide direct evidence on this issue. They conducted a detailed study of 2,104 manufacturing plants in Mexico. In their sample, 28 percent of the firms had foreign ownership and 46 percent of the foreign plants exported. Their major finding is that the probability of a Mexican-owned plant exporting is positively correlated with its proximity to foreign-owned exporting plants. Such spillovers may result from informational externalities and are more likely to lower fixed costs rather than marginal costs of production.

FDI and Growth

Regardless of the channel through which technology spillovers occur, the fact that FDI often involves capital inflows along with technology transfer implies that one would expect a positive impact of FDI on growth in the host country. Yet there are several important caveats to this assertion. First, a positive correlation between the extent of FDI and economic growth in cross-country regressions may simply reflect the fact that countries that are expected to grow faster attract FDI because it yields higher returns there. Thus the causation could run from growth to FDI and estimation of a simultaneous equation system may be needed to resolve the issue. Second, multinationals often raise the required capital in the host country, and in such a scenario capital inflows associated with FDI may not be substantial. An optimistic view of FDI would then look to technology transfer and/or spillovers as the mechanism through which FDI may affect growth. Indeed, Romer (1993) argues that FDI can have a positive effect on growth in developing economies by helping them bridge the idea gap with respect to industrial countries.

Glass and Saggi (1999) examine the question of spillovers from FDI in a product-cycle model. In their North–South model, the demonstration/proximity argument is formalized as follows. Southern firms are assumed to be able to imitate multinationals located in the South at a lower cost than firms located in the North. However, multinational firms are also stronger competitors than firms that produce only in the North because multinationals produce in the same low-wage location as potential imitators. The model delivers the surprising result that a faster flow of FDI increases the aggregate rate of technology transfer to the South only if local firms lack the ability to imitate firms located in the North (that is, if geographical proximity is a prerequisite for imitation). If firms in the North can be imitated, FDI does not alter aggregate technology transfer because imitation focusing on firms located in the North slows down with a hastening of imitation targeting multinationals.

Although the internalization question is a central one in the theory of FDI, almost all theories of FDI and licensing have been developed in either static or partial equilibrium models. A few dynamic general equilibrium models explore the effect of FDI on growth, but these models have ignored the possibility of licensing. Glass and Saggi (2002b) develop a model of FDI that captures the internalization decision and its implications for both the rate and magnitude of innovation. They also examine how policy interventions (taxes or subsidies to FDI) that alter the incentive to internalize production within the firm affect economic growth. They find that the ability of firms to switch modes from licensing to FDI in response to policy changes is vital for ensuring that a subsidy to FDI leads to faster economic growth.

In a comprehensive paper, Borensztein and others (1998) utilize data on FDI flows from industrial countries to 69 developing economies to test the effect of FDI on growth in a cross-country regression framework. Their findings are as follows. First, FDI contributes *more* to domestic growth than domestic investment, suggesting that it is indeed a vehicle of technology transfer. Second, FDI is more productive than domestic investment only when the host country has a minimum threshold stock of human capital. The latter finding is especially interesting because it clarifies when exactly FDI should be expected to effect growth.

Using cross-section data from 46 developing economies, Balasubramanyam and others (1996) also investigate the effect of FDI on growth in developing economies. They report two main findings. First, the growth-enhancing effects of FDI are stronger in countries that pursue a policy of export promotion rather than import substitution, suggesting that the trade policy regime is an important determinant of the effects of FDI. Second, they find that, in countries with export-promoting trade regimes, FDI has a stronger effect on growth than domestic investment. Both findings relate well to the results of Borensztein and others (1998). The second finding may be viewed as a confirmation of the hypothesis that FDI results in technology transfer.

The findings of Borensztein and others (1998) relate well to Keller (1996), who argues that mere access to foreign technologies may not increase the growth rates of developing economies. In his model, if a country's absorptive capacity (stock of human capital) remains unchanged, a switch to an outward orientation does not lead to a higher growth rate. Using a model quite different from Keller's, Glass and Saggi (1998) focus on the issue of the quality of technology transferred through FDI. They argue that investment in imitation by host country firms generates the necessary knowledge (or skill) foundation for FDI, and thus factors that promote imitation can promote a higher-quality mix of FDI. Keller's (1996) model stresses that a country's stock of human capital effectively constrains its ability to take advantage of foreign technologies; Glass and Saggi (1998) emphasize that indigenous technological capability in an industry effectively constrains a country's ability to host foreign technology. Thus, they take a more micro-level view of the constraints on technology transfer relative to Keller (1996), although both studies make similar points. For example, a country may have a fair amount of human capital in the aggregate but may lack the technological sophistication to be able to host high-quality FDI in any particular industry.

Xu (2000) provides yet another confirmation of the argument that, in the absence of adequate human capital, technology transfer from FDI may fail to increase productivity growth in the host country. Using data on outward FDI from the United States to 40 countries, Xu finds that technology transfer from FDI contributes to productivity growth in more developed countries but not in less developed economies because the latter lack adequate human capital. Incidentally, as Xu notes, FDI may contribute to productivity growth due to reasons other than technology transfer. Thus a statistically significant coefficient on some measure of FDI in a productivity growth equation does not necessarily imply that technology transfer is the mechanism through which FDI contributes to productivity growth.

Xu (2000) measures the technology transfer intensity of multinational firms affiliates by their spending on royalties and license fees as a share of their gross output and estimates that, of the total effect of trade (through R&D spillovers) and FDI (through technology transfer) on productivity growth in industrial countries, 41 percent is due to technology transfer. These results for industrial countries confirm the findings of Barrell and Pain (1997), who find that FDI has a positive impact on technological change in Germany and the United Kingdom. Xu and Wang (2000) find that although capital goods trade serves as a channel of technology transfer among industrial countries, bilateral flows of FDI do not. However, Xu and Wang (2000) raise questions regarding these results because of the poor quality of the FDI data.

The Role of Policy

What does the literature say about the role policy plays in the process of international technology transfer? There is a large range of policies; this section focuses on policies on trade, FDI, and protection of IPRS.

Trade Policy

Although the literature on trade policy is voluminous, it does not pay significant attention to the interaction between protection and technology transfer. In fact, most models treat the process of technology transfer in a rather rudimentary way, focusing instead on other aspects of the problem. Here I discuss a few prominent examples of this line of research.

Miyagiwa and Ohno (1995) examine a domestic firm's incentives for technology adoption when a foreign rival has already adopted a superior technology. They assume that the cost of adoption decreases over time, and they examine how the nature (tariff versus quota) and the duration (temporary versus permanent) of trade protection influence the domestic firm's incentives for technology adoption. Their most interesting result is that temporary protection (that is, protection that is removed on successful adoption by the domestic firm) actually delays the date of technology adoption. In a related paper, Miyagiwa and Ohno (1999) show that if temporary protection is credible, it may indeed increase R&D relative to free trade. However, if the domestic firm expects that protection will be removed early should innovation occur before the preannounced terminal date of protection, the firm will invest less in R&D under protection relative to free trade. Similarly, as first emphasized by Matsuyama (1990), if the domestic firm expects protection to be extended in case of no innovation by the terminal date, its investment incentives are marred by protection.

The literature also investigates the effect of trade protection in R&D-based models of endogenous growth (see Grossman and Helpman 1991, 1995). As expected from models in which increasing returns, imperfect competition, and externalities play a central role, the results depend on the details of a particular model and require careful interpretation. To the extent that one can draw a general conclusion from such a complex body of literature, it would be that the literature does not provide an unconditional argument against trade protection. The conclusions hinge dramatically on the scope of knowledge spillovers: international knowledge spillovers strongly tilt the balance in favor of free trade, whereas national spillovers create a role for policy intervention that can combat path dependence resulting from a historical accident. For example, if productivity improvements depend only on a country's own R&D, a case can be made for policies that ensure that industries in which such improvements occur at a rapid rate are not all located elsewhere.

Dinopoulos and Segerstrom (1999) develop a specific-factor variant of the quality ladders model of endogenous growth without scale effects. They examine the consequences of contingent protection, that is, tariffs imposed on imports whenever domestic firms lose their technological leadership to foreign firms who successfully innovate over them. Their approach is interesting because protection in the real world is usually not marginal (for example, antidumping duties may be levied on foreign firms with the explicit goal of providing sufficient relief to domestic industry). Somewhat interestingly, Dinopoulos and Segerstrom find that tariffs that allow domestic firms to capture the domestic market are positively related to the global rate of technological change in the short run.

Grossman and Helpman (1991) also analyze the effects of tariff protection in a two-country quality ladders model. Unlike Dinopoulos and Segerstrom, Grossman and Helpman analyze only tariffs that are too small to allow domestic firms to capture the market. Both models assume Bertrand competition on the product market, so that a low-quality firm can monopolize the market only if a tariff of sufficient magnitude is imposed on higher-quality imports. A small tariff can extract rents from foreign firms but fails to protect domestic firms that have been innovated over by foreign firms. It should be noted that Dinopoulos and Segerstrom's (1999) analysis assumes that both countries adopt symmetric policies.

FDI Policy

There is no simple way of describing the policy environment that faces multinationals in developing economies. In countries that historically emphasized import substituting industrialization—such as most of Africa, Latin America, and Southeast Asia— FDI was either completely prohibited or multinational firms had to operate under severe restrictions. In fact, even where technology acquisition was a major policy objective, multinationals were rarely permitted to operate wholly owned subsidiaries; Japan, Korea, and Taiwan all imposed restrictions on FDI at various points in time. In other words, "outward-oriented" economies were not particularly keen on allowing multinational firms into their markets. Japan's Ministry of International Trade and Investment (MITI) played an active role in the country's acquisition of foreign technology. MITI limited competition between potential Japanese buyers, did not allow inward FDI until 1970, never greatly liberalized FDI, and even sometimes insisted that foreign firms share their technology with local firms as a precondition for doing business in Japan. Ozawa (1974) provides a rich description of the role imported technology and local R&D (aimed at facilitating absorption of foreign technology) played in Japan's economic development.

In contrast to the restrictive stance toward FDI, licensing of foreign technology was aggressively encouraged (Layton 1982). Korea's experience has been quite similar to that of Japan. For example, annual inflows of licensed technology increased steadily during the 1970s and 1980s. FDI inflows into Korea, which were always relatively low, stagnated during 1978–83, but annual inflows of licensed technology (as measured by royalty payments) increased steadily during the 1970s and 1980s (Sakong 1993). This slowdown of FDI into Korea was partially a result of restrictive FDI policies instituted by the Korean government during that period (see Hobday 1995 for further details on Korea's experience).

What is the rationale behind policies that discourage FDI? Pack and Saggi (1997) argue that by prohibiting FDI and placing other restrictions on the conduct of multinationals, government policies in many countries may have effectively weakened the bargaining position of foreign firms. They note that in Japan, MITI restricted many local firms from participating as potential buyers exactly for this reason.

Sometimes policy has also favored licensing and joint ventures relative to wholly owned subsidiaries of multinationals. For example, the Chinese government has been particularly interventionist in technology transactions and has encouraged FDI in the form of joint ventures. Although wholly owned subsidiaries are not prohibited, the policy environment favors joint ventures over such enterprises. Of course, an immediate reason for this might be that all such policies simply reflect protectionism. Large public firms or hitherto protected private firms may not be able to compete with multinationals and may secure protection through the political process. However, is it also possible that joint ventures (as well as technology licensing) lead to more local involvement and therefore greater technology spillovers to local agents.

Saggi (1999) develops a two-period model in which a foreign firm chooses between FDI and technology licensing. The key assumption is that licensing results in greater transfer of know-how to the local firm than does FDI, under which the local firm must compete with the subsidiary of the multinational firm. The main result is that the local firm would have the strongest incentive for innovation if the foreign firm were to follow initial licensing by direct investment. However, in equilibrium, the foreign firm never adopts such a course of action.

Using plant-level data for 1991 for all Indonesian establishments with more than 20 employees, Blomström and Sjoholm (1999) shed light on two important questions. First, do establishments with minority and majority ownership (that is, joint ventures versus wholly owned subsidiaries) differ in terms of their (labor) productivity levels? Second, does the degree of technology spillovers vary with the extent of foreign ownership? The second question is crucial for the purposes of the present study. Blomström and Sjoholm obtain several interesting results. First, as in many other previous studies, they find that labor productivity is higher in establishments with foreign equity than in purely domestic firms. Second, the extent of total foreign production is positively associated with the productivity of domestic firms, suggesting some sort of spillovers from FDI. Third, the degree of foreign ownership affects neither the productivity of firms that get foreign equity nor the extent of spillovers to the domestic sector.

These findings are puzzling. Clearly, the degree of foreign participation does matter in that plants with no foreign investment are less productive. Perhaps the results suggest some sort of threshold effects in which beyond a certain degree of foreign ownership additional foreign equity affects neither the productivity of those that receive the investment nor the degree of spillovers to local firms. The authors do not report the minimum level of foreign equity (for those plants that do get foreign equity) in their sample. It is important to keep in mind that the study only measures labor productivity and treats some important endogenous variables as exogenous. Overall, it seems fair to say that the question remains open. Several earlier studies document that technologies transferred to wholly owned subsidiaries are of a newer vintage than licensed technologies or those transferred to joint ventures (Kabiraj and Marjit 1993; Mansfield and Romeo 1980; Saggi 1996).

Djankov and Hoekman (1999) also uncover an interesting role for joint ventures and suggest that such enterprises may have greater ability to absorb foreign technologies than do purely domestic firms. Hoekman and Saggi (2000) suggest that although the motivation behind policies that discriminate between licensing, joint ventures, and establishment of wholly owned subsidiaries is not easy to decipher, a plausible interpretation may be that such policies seek to maximize technology transfer to local firms while limiting the rent erosion that results from the entry of multinational firms.

Another policy issue is that many Southeast Asian countries still do not allow free entry of multinational firms and often express preferences with regard to the type of FDI; that is, entry by Pepsi or Coke is viewed differently than entry by General Motors or Texas Instruments. Unfortunately, the literature provides little insight for understanding such policies. Other than the standard argument that certain industries are able to secure greater protection for themselves, perhaps it may also be the case that spillovers to the local economy are higher under certain types of FDI. For example, it might be that domestic content protection policies involve more local firms and therefore generate greater spillovers. However, there is no formal model or empirical evidence to support this position. In addition, this argument is closely related to the idea of industrial targeting in general, and the pitfalls of the government's ability to correctly identify high-spillover industries are well known.

Despite the subtle policy interventions outlined, when measured by a broad yardstick, overall government policy has become more liberal across the world. For example, as of 1997, there were 1,513 bilateral investment treaties among countries, compared with 400 seven years earlier (UNCTAD 1998). Economic reform in many formerly communist countries has added to the list of countries vying for FDI. Coupled with this rise in treaties, both industrial and developing economies have a proliferation of fiscal and financial incentives to lure in FDI. Such overly optimistic policies carry dangers of their own and may reduce welfare in host countries. Although a case for such policies can indeed be made on the basis of positive externalities from FDI, there is no convincing evidence on this front.

Barry and Bradley (1997) describe Ireland's experience with FDI. Both favorable policies (reduced taxes and trade barriers, and investment grants) as well as strong fundamentals (such as infrastructure and an educated labor force) seem to have played a role in attracting FDI to Ireland. The strong performance of the Irish economy since the mid-1980s is attributable to both strong fundamentals as well as significant FDI inflows.

An alternative case for the use of FDI incentives can be made on the basis of the oligopolistic nature of the markets within which FDI occurs. For example, consider Mexico's recent experience with FDI in its automobile industry. Initial investments by U.S. car manufacturers in Mexico were followed by investments not only by Japanese and European car manufacturers but also by firms that made automobile parts and components. As a result, competition in the automobile industry increased at multiple stages of production, thereby improving efficiency. Such a pattern of FDI behavior (that is, investment by one firm followed by investment by others) reflects strategic considerations involved in FDI decisions. Because multinational firms compete in concentrated markets, they are responsive to each other's decisions. An important implication of this interdependence between competing multinationals is that a host country may be able to unleash a sequence of investments by successfully inducing FDI from one or two major firms.

Protection of IPRS

Common sense suggests that if any policy variable should affect international technology transfer, it ought to be the host country's IPR regime. The theoretical literature has often investigated the effect of IPR enforcement on technology transfer and FDI in several endogenous growth models. Other approaches also exist. For example, in a strategic partial equilibrium model, Vishwasrao (1995) argues that the lack of adequate enforcement of technology transfer agreements may encourage FDI relative to licensing. In her screening model, depending on the type of licensee, licensing may or may not lead to imitation. The tradeoff between FDI and licensing is that FDI avoids the risk of imitation at the expense of higher production costs.

To limit the scope of the discussion, I omit models in which technology transfer does not play a central role. Several of the articles are linked through their use of the two models used intensively by Grossman and Helpman (1991). Before turning to these, I discuss Taylor's (1994) work because it differs from the other studies in that it employs a model of endogenous technological change with Ricardian features.

In a two-country model, Taylor examines two scenarios: one in which IPR enforcement is symmetric across the two countries (it applies to innovators regardless of country of origin) and one in which it is asymmetric (it protects only domestic innovators). Although Taylor conducts the analysis under the assumption of costless technology transfer and equal productivity in R&D in the two countries, his results hold even when these assumptions are dropped, making it possible to apply them to a North–South setting. A subtle qualification must be made: symmetric versus asymmetric treatment implies both countries adopting one policy as opposed to another. Taylor's model does not analyze incentives for unilateral adoption of a symmetric policy. His major result is that asymmetric protection of IPR distorts the pattern of world trade and lowers the global rate of growth.

Interpreting the exogenous rate of imitation as a proxy for the level of IPR enforcement in the south, Helpman (1993) shows that a decline in the intensity of imitation promotes FDI (with exogenous innovation). Krugman (1979) addresses the issue as well, although his model has a greater degree of exogeneity than does Helpman's. The major contribution of Helpman's work lies in providing the first detailed welfare analysis of IPR enforcement in the South (as measured by an exogenous decline in the rate of imitation) in a dynamic general equilibrium growth model. He shows that a strengthening of IPR protection is not in the interest of the South, and that a weak enforcement of IPR protection in the South may even benefit the North, provided the rate of imitation is not too fast. Lai (1998) extends the Helpman model to allow for FDI and shows that innovation is promoted along with FDI if the South strengthens its IPR protection. The common weakness of both models is that stronger IPR enforcement is modeled as an exogenous decline in the rate of imitation. Nevertheless, Helpman's model is a tour de force in that it clearly specifies the alternative channels through which a strengthening of Southern IPR protection affects Northern and Southern welfare.

Yang and Maskus (2001) study the effects of Southern IPR enforcement on the rate of innovation in the North as well as on the extent of technology licensing undertaken by Northern firms. A key assumption in their model is that increased IPR enforcement increases the licenser's share of rents and reduces the costs of enforcing licensing contracts, thereby making licensing more attractive. Consequently, both innovation and licensing increase with stronger IPR protection in the South.

Glass and Saggi (2002a) provide an analysis of Southern IPR protection in a comprehensive product-cycle model of trade and FDI. In their model, Southern imitation targets both multinationals producing in the South and purely Northern firms producing in the North. They treat stronger IPR protection as an increase in imitation cost stemming perhaps from stricter uniqueness requirements in the South. In their model, FDI actually *decreases* with a strengthening of Southern IPR protection because an increase in the cost of imitation crowds out FDI through tighter Southern resource scarcity. Although products like books, videos, and CDs receive a lot of press about conflicts over IPR protection, imitating most products is not so simple (see Pack and Westphal 1986). Empirical evidence indicates that imitation is indeed a costly activity for a wide range of high-tech goods, such as chemicals, drugs, electronics, and machinery. For example, Mansfield and others (1981) find that the costs of imitation average 65 percent of the costs of innovation (and very few products are below 20 percent).

Less efficient imitation absorbs more resources, although the rate of imitation declines with a strengthening of Southern IPR protection. In addition, the contraction in FDI tightens resource scarcity in the North: increased production leaves fewer resources for innovation, so the rate of innovation falls. It is worth emphasizing that if strengthening Southern IPR protection increases the cost of imitation, targeting both firms producing in the North as well as multinationals producing in the South, Northern incentives for FDI (at the firm level) are basically unaffected.

It should be clear from the discussion so far that the theoretical literature does not give an unambiguous prediction regarding the effects of stronger Southern IPR protection on the extent of FDI and the rate of growth. Does empirical evidence help resolve the issue? The literature largely has not explored the interaction between optimal policies in the two regions (for a recent exception, see Lai and Qiu 1999).

Consider the effect of Southern IPR enforcement on FDI. Surveys of U.S. multinational firms frequently find that such firms are more willing to invest in countries with stronger IPR protection (see Lee and Mansfield 1996). How does the researcher reconcile the ambiguous predictions of the theoretical models with this empirical finding? There are two ways out. First, increased IPR enforcement can be asymmetrical in that firms investing in a country may expect to have a greater influence in local courts relative to those that simply export. Second, imitation of firms located in the North may not be an option for local firms in some developing economies, as is assumed by some theoretical models. In such a scenario, any increase in IPR enforcement by the South will benefit multinational firms, thereby encouraging them to engage in FDI.

As Ferrantino (1993) notes, all of the proceeding models suffer from a fundamental problem: either FDI or licensing is the only channel through which Northern firms are allowed to produce in the South. A more complete treatment of FDI requires that Northern firms be given the option of transacting in technology through the market. What are the consequences of strengthening IPR protection in the South if Northern firms can choose between licensing and FDI? Does FDI increase with IPR enforcement, or does such a change in policy encourage licensing by lowering the risk of opportunism in market transactions? The latter scenario is equally likely, and studies that ignore the possibility of licensing (or joint ventures for that matter) are likely to overstate the effect of IPR enforcement on inward FDI. In fact, a more subtle analysis may be needed. Increased IPR enforcement by the South may indeed make it a more attractive location for production (thereby increasing FDI relative to exports). However, the technologies transferred for that purpose might flow through licensing rather than FDI, so that the net effect on technology transfer through FDI is ambiguous. Of course, aggregate technology transfer to the South may increase, although general equilibrium effects may also require qualifications of this conclusion (Glass and Saggi 2002a).

Using data for 1982 on U.S. exports and sales of overseas affiliates of U.S. firms, Ferrantino (1993) presents a detailed cross-country study that attempts to identify the determinants of both exports and sales of multinational affiliates of U.S. firms, as suggested by the gravity model. His analysis reveals many insights, but perhaps the most interesting finding is that the U.S. firms export more to their affiliates in countries that have weak IPR regimes. Ferrantino (1993) suggests that this result may reflect attempts by the U.S. firms to limit technology leakage to their rivals abroad by confining production within the United States. This interpretation fits well with a central theme of this survey: multinational firms will adjust their strategies to optimize against policies and market conditions they face in various host countries, casting doubt on the conclusions of empirical (or theoretical) work that treats FDI as given.

Empirical evidence indicates that the level of IPR protection in a country also affects the composition of FDI in two different ways (Lee and Mansfield 1996; Smarzynska 1999b). First, in industries for which IPRs are crucial (pharmaceuticals, for example), firms may refrain from investing in countries with weak IPR protection. Second, regardless of the industry in question, multinationals are less likely to set up manufacturing and R&D facilities in countries with weak IPR regimes and more likely to set up sales and marketing ventures because the latter run no risk of technology leakage.

These studies present useful findings but are unable to address perhaps the most central question of all: does a country's IPR regime affect its economic growth? Although there are several theoretical analyses of this question, empirical studies are scarce. One such study is Gould and Gruben (1996), who use cross-country data on patent protection, trade regime, and economic fundamentals. They find that IPR protection, as measured by the degree of patent protection, is an important determinant of economic growth. Somewhat more interestingly, they find that the effect of IPR protection is stronger for relatively open economies than it is for relatively closed economies. In other words, a strengthening of IPR protection is more conducive for growth when it is accompanied by a liberal trade policy.

A possible interpretation of this finding is that by increasing foreign competition trade liberalization not only curtails monopoly power granted by IPRs but also ensures that such monopoly power is obtained only if the innovation is truly global. If firms in other countries can export freely to the domestic market and have better products or technologies, a domestic patent is useless in granting monopoly power. Furthermore, note that trade liberalization alone can improve productivity. Using data from Mexican manufacturing firms, Tybout and Westbrook (1995) find that trade liberalization is associated with higher rates of productivity growth. The results of Gould and Gruben (1996) show that IPR enforcement matters over and above trade orientation and that both have mutually reinforcing effects.

Finally, what does the empirical literature tell us about the effect of IPR protection on trade? Theory informs us that asymmetric IPR protection across countries can distort the pattern of world trade; empirical evidence supports this result. Using bilateral trade data for manufactured goods from 22 exporting countries to 71 importing countries, Maskus and Penubarti (1995) find that within the group of large developing economies, the importing country's strength of IPR protection (as measured by patent rights) exerts a significantly positive effect on bilateral manufacturing imports in many product categories. In other words, in such countries, weak IPR protection is indeed a barrier to the manufacturing exports of most OECD countries. Maskus (2000) provides an up-to-date discussion of the empirical evidence on the effects of IPR protection on trade and FDI. Smith (1999) updates the study by Maskus and Penubarti (1995), using data on exports of U.S. states to 96 countries. She makes the interesting point that because countries with strong IPR protection also have sophisticated technological capabilities that facilitate local imitation of foreign technologies, within industrial countries there is an ambiguous relationship between strength of IPR protection and the volume of trade.

Conclusions

This article has covered a rather large terrain. This section highlights the eight main points.

First, the role of trade in encouraging growth hinges critically on the geographical scope (national versus international) of knowledge spillovers. As Grossman and Helpman (1995) note, knowledge spillovers are neither exclusively national nor international; they are probably both to some extent. However, spillovers are more likely to be national in scope for developing economies than for industrial ones. Consequently, whether R&D and high-technology production are carried out in close geographical proximity to such countries may indeed matter for their development.

Second, little is known about the relative role of trade and FDI (with licensing and joint ventures as special cases) as mechanisms of technology transfer. Given that foreign firms opt to produce in a developing economy, FDI seems to be the preferred route and is therefore a prominent channel of technology transfer.

Third, the existence of several channels of international technology transfer raises two important quantitative questions that merit further research. First, is it possible to arrive at an aggregate measure of international technology transfer and its contribution to economic growth in developing economies? Second, can one isolate the role of each channel? For example, how much does FDI contribute to growth in addition to trade? The marginal contribution of FDI has important policy implications and can only be settled through careful empirical studies.

Fourth, a well-developed paradigm (called the OLI paradigm, for ownership, location, and internalization) seeks to explain the emergence of multinational firms, given the existence of viable alternatives such as exports, licensing, and joint ventures. The OLI framework is useful for explaining a one-time choice between alternative modes of serving foreign markets but is virtually silent regarding the dynamics of entry strategies. Future research needs to explicitly consider the dynamic decision problem facing multinational firms.

Fifth, local policy often causes foreign firms to opt for licensing or joint ventures over FDI. There is little or no empirical evidence to support the idea that licensing or joint ventures are more likely than FDI to lead to increased learning. To be fair, few careful studies have attempted this difficult task. The jury may still be out on this issue.

Sixth, policies designed to lure in FDI have proliferated in recent years, but it is difficult to base the case in favor of these policies on the notion of positive spillovers from FDI to domestic firms. Several recent plant-level studies have failed to find positive spillovers from FDI to their direct competitors. However, these studies require careful interpretation because they treat FDI as exogenous. In addition, FDI spillovers may be vertical in nature rather than horizontal (as is assumed in such studies). Furthermore, all such studies find that the subsidiaries of multinationals are more productive than domestic firms. Thus, regardless of the evidence on the spillover issue, FDI does result in a more effective use of resources in host countries.

Seventh, several studies (both theoretical and empirical) indicate that absorptive capacity in the host country is crucial for obtaining significant benefits from FDI. Without adequate human capital or investments in R&D, spillovers from FDI may simply be infeasible. Thus, liberalization of trade and FDI policies needs to be complemented by appropriate policy measures with respect to education, R&D, and human capital accumulation if developing economies are to take full advantage of increased trade and FDI.

Eighth, empirical evidence supports the argument that IPRs are trade related and that asymmetric IPR protection across countries distorts the pattern of world trade. Furthermore, a country's IPR policy may alter the composition of FDI at both the industry and firm levels. In industries in which IPRs are crucial, firms may refrain from FDI if IPR protection is weak in the host country, or they may not invest in manufacturing and R&D activities. Last, IPR policy may also lead foreign firms to choose FDI over other arm's-length modes of technology transfer, such as licensing.

Note

Kamal Saggi is with the Department of Economics at Southern Methodist University. He can be reached via e-mail at ksaggi@mail.smu.edu. This article was written as a background paper for the World Bank's Microfoundations of International Technology Diffusion research project. The author thanks the World Bank's Development Research Group for financial support and Amy Glass, Bernard Hoekman, Aart Kraay, Aaditya Mattoo, Howard Pack, David Tarr, Jim Tybout, and three anonymous referees for helpful comments.

References

Aghion, Philippe, and Peter Howitt. 1990. "A Model of Growth through Creative Destruction." *Econometrica* 60:323–51.

Aitken, Brian, and Ann E. Harrison. 1999. "Do Domestic Firms Benefit from Direct Foreign Investment?" *American Economic Review* 89(3):605–18.

Aitken, Brian, Gordon H. Hanson, and Ann E. Harrison. 1997. "Spillovers, Foreign Investment, and Export Behavior." *Journal of International Economics* 43:103–32.

Aitken, Brian, Ann E. Harrison, and Robert E. Lipsey. 1996. "Wages and Foreign Ownership: A Comparative Study of Mexico, Venezuela, and the United States." *Journal of International Economics* 40:345–71.

Balasubramanyam, Venkataraman N., Mohammed A. Salisu, and David Sapsford. 1996. "Foreign Direct Investment and Growth in EP and IS Countries." *Economic Journal* 106:92–105.

Barrell, Ray, and Nigel Pain. 1997. "Foreign Direct Investment, Technological Change, and Economic Growth within Europe." *Economic Journal* 107:1770–86.

Barry, Frank, and John Bradley. 1997. "FDI and Trade: The Irish Host Country Experience." *Economic Journal* 107:1798–811.

Bayoumi, Tamim, David T. Coe, and Elhanan Helpman. 1999. "R&D Spillovers and Global Growth." *Journal of International Economics* 47:399–428.

Bhagwati, Jagdish N., Richard A. Brecher, Elias Dinopoulos, and T. N. Srinivasan. 1987. "Quid Pro Quo Foreign Investment and Welfare: A Political-Economy-Theoretic Model." *Journal of Development Economics* 27:127–38.

Bhagwati, Jagdish N., Elias Dinopoulos, and Kar-Yiu Wong. 1992. "Quid Pro Quo Foreign Investment." *American Economic Review* 82:186–90.

Blomström, Magnus. 1986. "Foreign Investment and Productive Efficiency: The Case of Mexico." *Journal of Industrial Economics* 15:97–110.

Blomström, Magnus, and Hakan Persson. 1983. "Foreign Investment and Spillover Efficiency in an Underdeveloped Economy: Evidence from the Mexican Manufacturing Industry." *World Development* 11(6):493–501.

Blomström, Magnus, and Ari Kokko. 1998. "Multinational Corporations and Spillovers." *Journal of Economic Surveys* 12:247–77.

Blomström, Magnus, and Fredrik Sjoholm. 1999. "Technology Transfer and Spillovers: Does Local Participation with Multinationals Matter?" *European Economic Review* 43:915–23.

Blomström, Magnus, Robert E. Lipsey, and Ksenia Kulchycky. 1988. "U.S. and Swedish Direct Investment and Exports." In R. E. Baldwin, ed., *Trade Policy and Empirical Analysis*. Chicago: University of Chicago Press.

Blonigen, Bruce A. 1999. "In Search of Substitution between Foreign Production and Exports." *Journal of International Economics* 53(1):81–104.

Borensztein, E., J. De Gregorio, and J.-W. Lee. 1998. "How Does Foreign Direct Investment Affect Economic Growth?" *Journal of International Economics* 45:115–35.

Caves, Richard E. 1974. "Multinational Firms, Competition, and Productivity in Host-Country Industries." *Economica* 41(May):176–93.

———. 1996. *Multinational Enterprise and Economic Analysis*. Cambridge: Cambridge University Press.

Clerides, S. K., Saul Lach, and James R. Tybout. 1998. "Is Learning by Exporting Important? Micro-Dynamic Evidence from Colombia, Mexico, and Morocco." *Quarterly Journal of Economics* 113:903–48.

Coe, David T., and Elhanan Helpman. 1995. "International R&D Spillovers." *European Economic Review* 39:859–87.

Coe, David T., Elhanan Helpman, and Alexander W. Hoffmaister. 1997. "North-South R&D Spillovers." *Economic Journal* 107:13–149.

Coe, David T., and Alexander W. Hoffmaister. 1999. "Are There International R&D Spillovers among Randomly Matched Trade Partners? A Response to Keller." IMF Working Paper No. WP/99/18. International Monetary Fund, Washington, D.C.

Das, Sanghmitra. 1987. "Externalities and Technology Transfer through Multinational Corporations: A Theoretical Analysis." *Journal of International Economics* 22:171–82.

De Long, Bradford J., and Lawrence H. Summers. 1991. "Equipment Investment and Economic Growth." *Quarterly Journal of Economics* 106:445–502.

Dinopoulos, Elias, and Paul Segerstrom. 1999. "The Dynamic Effects of Contingent Tariffs." *Journal of International Economics* 47:191–222

Dinopoulos, Elias, and Peter Thompson. 1999. "Scale Effects in Schumpeterian Models of Economic Growth." *Journal of Evolutionary Economics* 9:157–85.

Dixit, Avinash K., and Joseph E. Stiglitz. 1977. "Monopolistic Competition and Optimum Product Diversity." *American Economic Review* 67:297–308.

Djankov, Simeon, and Bernard Hoekman. 2000. "Foreign Investment and Productivity Growth in Czech Enterprises." *World Bank Economic Review* 14(1):49–64.

Dollar, David. 1992. "Outward Oriented Developing Economies Really Do Grow More Rapidly: Evidence from 95 LDCS, 1976–85." *Economic Development and Cultural Change* 523–44.

Dunning, John H. 1988. "The Eclectic Paradigm of International Production: A Restatement and Some Possible Extensions." *Journal of International Business Studies* 19(1):1–31.

Eaton, Jonathan, and Samuel Kortum. 1996. "Trade in Ideas: Patenting and Productivity in the OECD." *Journal of International Economics* 40:251–78.

Ethier, Wilfred J. 1982. "National and International Returns to Scale in the Modern Theory of International Trade." *American Economic Review* 72:389–405.

Ethier, Wilfred. J., and James R. Markusen. 1991. "Multinational Firms, Technology Diffusion and Trade." *Journal of International Economics* 41:1–28.

Ferrantino, Michael J. 1993. "The Effect of Intellectual Property Rights on International Trade and Investment." *WeltwirtschaftlichesArchive* 129:300–331.

Findlay, Ronald. 1978. "Relative Backwardness, Direct Foreign Investment, and the Transfer of Technology: A Simple Dynamic Model." *Quarterly Journal of Economics* 62:1–16.

Gershenberg, Irving. 1987. "The Training and Spread of Managerial Know-how: A Comparative Analysis of Multinational and Other Firms in Kenya." *World Development* 15:931–39.

Glass, Amy J., and Kamal Saggi. 1998. "International Technology Transfer and the Technology Gap." *Journal of Development Economics* 55:369–98.

———. 1999. "Foreign Direct Investment and the Nature of R&D." *Canadian Journal of Economics* 32:92–117.

———. 2002a. "Intellectual Property Rights and Foreign Direct Investment." *Journal of International Economics* 56:387–410.

———. 2002b. "Licensing versus Direct Investment: Implications for Economic Growth." *Journal of International Economics* 56:131–53.

———. Forthcoming. "Multinational Firms and Technology Transfer." *Scandinavian Journal of Economics.*

Globerman. 1979. "Foreign Direct Investment and 'Spillover' Efficiency Benefits in Canadian Manufacturing Industries." *Canadian Journal of Economics* 12(February):42–56.

Gould, David M., and William C. Gruben. 1996. "The Role of Intellectual Property Rights in Economic Growth." *Journal of Development Economics* 48:323–50.

Grossman, Gene M., and Elhanan Helpman. 1991. *Innovation and Growth in the Global Economy.* Cambridge, Mass.: MIT Press.

———. 1995. "Technology and Trade." In Gene Grossman and Kenneth Rogoff, eds., *Handbook of International Economics*, Vol. 3. Amsterdam: Elsevier Science.

Grubert, Harry, and John Mutti. 1991. "Taxes, Tariffs, and Transfer Pricing in Multinational Corporate Decision Making." *Review of Economics and Statistics* 73:285–93.

Haddad, Mona, and Ann Harrison. 1993. "Are there Positive Spillovers from Direct Foreign Investment? Evidence from Panel Data for Morocco." *Journal of Development Economics* 42:51–74.

Helpman, Elhanan. 1993. "Innovation, Imitation, and Intellectual Property Rights." *Econometrica* 61:1247–80.

Hobday, Michael. 1995. *Innovation in East Asia: The Challenge to Japan*. Cheltenham: Edward Elgar.

Hoekman, Bernard, and Simeon Djankov. 1997. "Competition Law in Post-Central Planning Bulgaria." Mimeo, World Bank, Washington, D.C.

Hoekman, Bernard, and Kamal Saggi. 2000. "Multilateral Disciplines for Investment-Related Polices?" In Paolo Guerrieri and Hans-Eckart Scharrer, eds., *Global Governance, Regionalism, and the International Economy*. Baden-Baden: Nomos-Verlagsgesellschaft.

Horstmann, Ignatius J., and J. R. Markusen. 1987. "Strategic Investments and the Development of Multinationals." *International Economic Review* 28:109–21.

———. 1992 "Endogenous Market Structures in International Trade (Natura Facit Seltum)." *Journal of International Economics* 32:109–29.

———. 1996. "Exploring New Markets: Direct Investment, Contractual Relations and the Multinational Enterprise." *International Economic Review* 37:1–20.

Huizinga, Harry. 1995. "Taxation and the Transfer of Technology by Multinational Firms." *Canadian Journal of Economics* 28:648–55.

Irwin, Douglas A., and P. J. Klenow. 1994. "Learning by Doing Spillovers in the Semiconductor Industry." *Journal of Political Economy* 102:1200–1227.

Jones, Charles. 1995a. "Time Series Tests of Endogenous Growth Models." *Quarterly Journal of Economics* 110:495–525.

———. 1995b. "R&D-Based Models of Economic Growth." *Journal of Political Economy* 103:759–84.

Kabiraj, Tarun, and Sugata Marjit. 1993. "International Technology Transfer under Potential Threat of Entry." *Journal of Development Economics* 42:75–88.

Keller, Wolfgang. 1996. "Absorptive Capacity: On the Creation and Acquisition of Technology in Development." *Journal of Development Economics* 49:199–227.

———. 1998. "Are International R&D Spillovers Trade-Related? Analyzing Spillovers among Randomly Matched Trade Partners." *European Economic Review* 42:1469–81.

Kinoshita, Yuko, and Ashoka Mody. 1997. "Private and Public Information for Foreign Investment Decision." World Bank Policy Research Working Paper No. 1733. World Bank, Washington, D.C.

Krugman, Paul R. 1979. "A Model of Innovation, Technology Transfer, and the World Distribution of Income." *Journal of Political Economy* 87:253–66.

———. 1987. "Is Free Trade Passe?" *Journal of Economic Perspectives* 1:131–44.

Lai, Edwin L. C. 1998. "International Intellectual Property Rights Protection and the Rate of Product Innovation." *Journal of Development Economics* 55:131–51.

Lai, Edwin L. C., and Larry D. Qiu. 1999. "Northern Intellectual Property Rights Standard for the South?" Mimeo, City University of Hong Kong and Hong Kong University of Science and Technology.

Lall, Sanjaya. 1980. "Vertical Inter-Firm Linkages in LDCs: An Empirical Study." *Oxford Bulletin of Economics and Statistics* 42:203–6.

Layton, Duane W. 1982. "Japan and the Introduction of Foreign Technology: A Blueprint for Lesser Developed Countries?" *Stanford Journal of International Law* 18:171–212.

Lee, Jeong Y., and Edwin Mansfield. 1996. "Intellectual Property Protection and U.S. Foreign Direct Investment." *Review of Economics and Statistics* 78:181–86.

Lin, Ping, and Kamal Saggi. 1999. "Incentives for FDI under Imitation." *Canadian Journal of Economics*, 32:1275–98.

Lipsey, Robert E., and Merle Yahr Weiss. 1981. "Foreign Production and Exports in Manufacturing Industries." *Review of Economics and Statistics* 63:488–94.

———. 1984. "Foreign Production and Exports of Individual Firms." *Review of Economics and Statistics* 66:304–7.

Lucas, Robert E. Jr. 1988. "On the Mechanics of Economic Development." *Journal of Monetary Economics* 22:3–42.

Mansfield, Edwin, and Anthony Romeo. 1980. "Technology Transfer to Overseas Subsidiaries by U.S. Based Firms." *Quarterly Journal of Economics* 95:737–49.

Mansfield, Edwin, Mark Schwartz, and Samuel Wagner. 1981. "Imitation Costs and Patents: An Empirical Study." *Economic Journal* 91:907–18.

Markusen, James R. 1995. "The Boundaries of Multinational Enterprises and the Theory of International Trade." *Journal of Economic Perspectives* 9:169–89.

———. 1998. "Multilateral Rules on Foreign Direct Investment: The Developing Countries' Stake." Mimeo, University of Colorado at Boulder, Boulder, Colo.

———. 2000. "Contracts, Intellectual Property Rights, and Multinational Investment in Developing Countries." *Journal of International Economics* 53(1):189–204.

Markusen, James R., and Keith E. Maskus. 1999. "Discriminating Among Alternative Theories of the Multinational Enterprise." NBER Working Paper No. 7164. National Bureau of Economic Research, Washington, D.C.

Markusen, James R., and Anthony Venables. 1999. "Foreign Direct Investment as a Catalyst for Industrial Development." *European Economic Review* 43:335–56.

Maskus, Keith E. 2000. *Intellectual Property Rights in the Global Economy*. Washington, D.C.: Institute of International Economics.

Maskus, Keith E., and Mohan Penubarti. 1995. "How Trade-related Are Intellectual Property Rights?" *Journal of International Economics* 39:227–48.

Matsuyama, Kiminori. 1990. "Perfect Equilibrium in a Trade Liberalization Game." *American Economic Review* 80:480–92.

Miyagiwa, Kaz, and Yuka Ohno. 1995. "Closing the Technology Gap under Protection." *American Economic Review* 85:755–70.

———. 1999. "Credibility of Protection and Incentives to Innovate." *International Economic Review* 40:143–64.

Moran, Theodore. 1998. *Foreign Direct Investment and Development*. Washington D.C.: Institute for International Economics.

Motta, Massimo, and George Norman. 1996. "Does Economic Integration Cause Foreign Direct Investment?" *International Economic Review* 37(4):757–84.

Nelson, Richard R., and Howard Pack. 1999. "The Asian Miracle and Modern Growth Theory." *Economic Journal* 109(July):416–36.

Nicholas, Stephen. 1982. "British Multinational Investment before 1939." *Journal of European Economic History* 11:605–30.

———. 1983. "Agency Costs, Institutional Modes, and the Transition to Foreign Direct Investment by British Manufacturing Multinationals before 1939." *Journal of Economic History* 43:675–86.

Nicholas, Stephen, W. Purcell, D. Merritt, and A. Whitewell. 1994. "Foreign Direct Investment in Australia in the 1990s." Mimeo, University of Melbourne.

Ozawa, Terutomo. 1974. *Japan's Technological Challenge to the West, 1950–1974: Motivation and Accomplishment*. Cambridge, Mass.: MIT Press.

Pack, Howard. 1992. "Technology Gaps between Industrial and Developing Countries: Are There Dividends for Late-comers?" In *Proceedings of the World Bank Annual Conference on Development Economics, Supplement to the* World Bank Economic Review *and* World Bank Research Observer. Washington, D.C.: World Bank, pp. 283–302.

———. 1994. "Endogenous Growth Theory: Intellectual Appeal and Empirical Shortcomings." *Journal of Economic Perspectives* 8(1):55–72.

———. 1997. "The Role of Exports in Asian Development." In Nancy Birdsall and Frederick Jaspersen, eds., *Pathways to Growth: Comparing East Asia and Latin America*. Washington, D.C.: Inter-American Development Bank.

Pack, Howard, and Kamal Saggi. 1997. "Inflows of Foreign Technology and Indigenous Technological Development." *Review of Development Economics* 1:81–98.

———. 2001. "Vertical Technology Transfer via International Outsourcing." *Journal of Development Economics* 65: 389–415.

Pack, Howard, and Larry E. Westphal. 1986. "Industrial Strategy and Technological Change: Theory versus Reality." *Journal of Development Economics* 22:87–128.

Parente, Stephen L., and Edward C. Prescott. 1994. "Barriers to Technology Adoption and Development." *Journal of Political Economy* 102:298–321.

Pritchett, Lant. 1997. "Divergence, Big Time." *Journal of Economic Perspectives* 11(3):3–17.

Ramachandran, Vijaya. 1993. "Technology Transfer, Firm Ownership, and Investment in Human Capital." *Review of Economics and Statistics* 75:664–70.

Rhee, Yung Whee. 1990. "The Catalyst Model of Development: Lessons from Bangladesh's Success with Garment Exports." *World Development* 18:333–46.

Rivera-Batiz, Louis A., and Paul Romer. 1991. "Economic Integration and Endogenous Growth." *Quarterly Journal of Economics* 106:531–56.

Roberts, Mark, and James Tybout. 1997. "The Decision to Export in Columbia: An Empirical Model of Entry with Sunk Costs." *American Economic Review* 87:545–64.

Rodriguez, Francisco, and Dani Rodrik. 1999. "Trade Policy and Economic Growth: A Skeptic's Guide to the Cross-country Evidence." NBER Working Paper no. 7081. National Bureau of Economic Research, Boston, Mass.

Rodriquez-Clare, Andrés. 1996. "Multinationals, Linkages, and Economic Development." *American Economic Review* 86(4):852–74.

Romer, Paul. 1990. "Endogenous Technological Change." *Journal of Political Economy* 98:S71–S102.

———. 1993. "Idea Gaps and Object Gaps in Economic Development." *Journal of Monetary Economics* 32:543–73.

Sachs, Jeffrey, and Andrew Werner. 1995. "Economic Reform and the Process of Global Integration." *Brookings Papers on Economic Activity* 1:1–118.

Saggi, Kamal. 1996. "Entry into a Foreign Market: Foreign Direct Investment versus Licensing." *Review of International Economics* 4:99–104.

———. 1998. "Optimal Timing of FDI under Demand Uncertainty." In Jean-Louis Mucchielli, Peter J. Buckley, and Victor V. Cordell, eds., *Globalization and Regionalization: Strategies, Policies, and Economic Environments*. Binghamton, N.Y.: Haworth Press.

———. 1999. "Foreign Direct Investment, Licensing, and Incentives for Innovation." *Review of International Economics* 7:699–714.

Sakong, Il. 1993. *Korea in the World Economy*. Washington, D.C.: Institute for International Economics.

Segerstrom, Paul S., T. C. A. Anant, and Elias Dinopoulos. 1990. "A Schumpeterian Model of the Product Life Cycle." *American Economic Review* 80:1077–91.

Smarzynska, Beata K. 1999a. "Technological Leadership and the Choice of Entry Mode by Foreign Investors: Evidence from Transition Economies." Mimeo, World Bank, Washington, D.C.

———. 1999b. "Composition of Foreign Direct Investment and Protection of Intellectual Property Rights in Transition Economies," Mimeo, World Bank, Washington, D.C.

Smith, Pamela. 1999. "Are Weak Patent Rights a Barrier to U.S. Exports?" *Journal of International Economics* 48:151–77.

Taylor, M. Scott. 1994. "TRIPS, Trade and Growth." *International Economic Review* 35:361–81.

Teece, David J. 1977. "Technology Transfer by Multinational Firms: The Resource Cost of Transferring Technological Know-how." *Economic Journal* 87:242–61.

Tybout, James, and M. Daniel Westbrook. 1995. "Trade Liberalization and Dimensions of Efficiency Change in Mexican Manufacturing Industries." *Journal of International Economics* 39:53–78.

UNCTAD. 1992. *World Investment Report: Transnational Corporations as Engines of Growth.* New York: United Nations.

———. 1997. *World Investment Report: Transnational Corporations, Market Structure, and Competition Policy.* New York: United Nations.

———. 1998. *World Investment Report: Trends and Determinants.* New York: United Nations.

———. 1999. *World Investment Report: Foreign Direct Investment and the Challenge of Development.* New York: United Nations.

———. 2000. *World Investment Report: Foreign Direct Investment and the Challenge of Development.* New York: United Nations.

United Nations. 1983–98. *International Trade Statistics Yearbook.* New York: United Nations.

Vishwasrao, Sharmila. 1995. "Intellectual Property Rights and the Mode of Technology Transfer." *Journal of Development Economics* 44:381–402.

Wang, Jian-Ye, and Magnus Blomström. 1992. "Foreign Investment and Technology Transfer." *European Economic Review* 36:137–55.

World Bank. 1999. *World Development Indicators.* Washington, D.C.: World Bank.

Xu, Bin. 2000. "Multinational Enterprises, Technology Diffusion, and Host Country Productivity Growth." *Journal of Development Economics* 62:477–93.

Xu, Bin, and Jianmao Wang. 1999. "Capital Goods Trade and R&D Spillovers in the OECD." *Canadian Journal of Economics* 32:1258–74.

———. 2000. "Trade, FDI, and International Technology Diffusion." *Journal of Economic Integration* 15(4):585–601.

Yang, Guifang, and Keith Maskus. 2001. "Intellectual Property Rights, Licensing, and Innovation in an Endogenous Product-Cycle Model." *Journal of International Economics* 53(1):169–88.

Young, Alwyn. 1995. "The Tyranny of Numbers: Confronting the Statistical Realities of the East Asian Growth Experience." *Quarterly Journal of Economics* 110(3):641–80.

Chapter 5

Transfer of Technology to Developing Countries: Unilateral and Multilateral Policy Options[#]

BERNARD M. HOEKMAN
World Bank, Washington, DC, USA

KEITH E. MASKUS
University of Colorado, Boulder, CO, USA

and

KAMAL SAGGI [*]
Southern Methodist University, Dallas, TX, USA

Summary. — This paper analyzes national and international policy options to encourage the international transfer of technology, distinguishing between four major channels of such transfer: trade in products, trade in knowledge and technology, foreign direct investment, and intranational and international movement of people. A typology of countries and appropriate policy rules of thumb are developed as a guide to both national policymakers and multilateral rule making in the WTO. We argue that the optimal policy mix varies across countries and that there is a need for differentiation in the design and application of rules in trade agreements as well as for a more explicit focus on evaluation of the impacts of policies.

Key words — technology transfer, multilateral trade negotiations, WTO

1. INTRODUCTION

The importance of international technology transfer (ITT) for economic development can hardly be overstated. Both the acquisition of technology and its diffusion foster productivity growth. Developing countries have long sought to use both national policies and international agreements to stimulate ITT. *National* policies range from the general, such as education and intellectual property rights (IPR) protection, to the specific, such as tax incentives for purchase of certain types of capital equipment. A prominent episode of *international* efforts to encourage ITT came in the late 1970s, when many developing countries sought a Code of Conduct to regulate technology transfer under United Nations (UN) auspices.

Given the incentives of owners not to transfer technology without an adequate return and the problem of monitoring compliance with international regulations, it is not surprising that ITT is predominately mediated by national policies. Existing multilateral rules on, for example, subsidies, trade policy, and IPR regimes, define limits on what is permissible. In contrast, agreements regarding actions that governments should pursue to encourage ITT are largely of a best-endeavor nature.

Starting in the mid-1990s, multilateral disciplines on ITT-related policies began to deepen. The WTO Agreement on Trade-Related Aspects of Intellectual Property Rights (TRIPS), adopted in 1995, calls on countries to enforce

[*] We are grateful to three anonymous referees for their comments. The views expressed are personal and should not be attributed to the World Bank. Final revision accepted: May 20, 2005.

[#] This chapter was originally appeared in *World Development* **33**, 1587–1602. © 2005 Elsevier Ltd.

comprehensive minimum standards of IPR protection on a nondiscriminatory basis. It also has provisions relating to ITT, as discussed later in this article. In 2001, WTO members established a Working Group on Trade and Technology Transfer to examine the relationship between trade and ITT and explore ways to increase technology flows to developing countries.

This paper discusses options that could be pursued by countries to promote ITT and the implications for international rule making and development assistance. Three dimensions are highlighted: safeguarding national "policy space" to address market failures; identifying actions by source countries to encourage ITT; and multilateral initiatives to address international externalities associated with technology markets or national policies. Section 2 reviews the major channels of technology transfer and the main policy instruments that could be used to enhance ITT. In Sections 3–5, our discussion turns to normative policy implications, focusing on policies of host (importing) countries, source (exporting) countries, and multilateral cooperation in the WTO, respectively. In Section 6, we summarize the discussion by means of suggested policy rules of thumb for countries at different stages of development. In Section 7, we conclude with a brief discussion of how trade agreements can help improve ITT policies.

2. CHANNELS OF TECHNOLOGY TRANSFER

We start with a brief discussion of the main avenues through which ITT occurs: trade in goods, direct investment and licensing, and movement of people.

(a) *Trade in goods*

Economic growth centrally relies on technological change through the creation of new products and processes (Grossman & Helpman, 1991). New products embody novel ideas and international trade can transmit knowledge across borders. Indeed, barriers to technology adoption are a key determinant of international differences in per-capita income (Parente & Prescott, 1994) and greater trade openness can increase growth by lowering such barriers. Trade contributes to ITT by allowing local reverse engineering and access to new machinery and equipment. Coe, Helpman, and Hoffmaister (1997) found that foreign R&D embodied in imported capital goods has a significantly positive impact on total factor productivity (TFP) of importing countries. [1] Later studies noted that this impact is greater, the more open the countries are, the more skilled is their labor force, and, in the case of developing countries, the more their trade is with developed countries (Schiff, Wang, & Olarreaga, 2002). Further, variations in capital-goods trade explain cross-country differences in productivity better than does overall trade (Eaton & Kortum, 1999).

These results suggest that open trade policies are crucial for developing countries to be able to attract technology. But openness alone is not sufficient, for strong absorptive capacity and the ability to adapt foreign technology are important for ITT to effect local technical change. In developing countries, technology acquisition often amounts to adapting existing methods to local circumstances (Evenson & Westphal, 1995). Gradual adoption of new techniques or inputs may be optimal for risk-averse producers in the face of costly investment and uncertain returns. Producers need to learn how to apply the new technology and improve it gradually over time (Tybout, 2000). Countries tend to acquire international technology more readily if domestic firms have R&D programs, there are domestic research laboratories and universities, and there exists a sound basis of technical skills and human capital (Maskus, 2000). These factors reduce the costs of imitation, adaptation, and follow-on innovation.

(b) *Foreign direct investment and licensing*

Investment by multinational enterprises (MNEs) may provide developing countries with more efficient foreign technologies and result in technological spillovers. In addition to demonstration effects, spillovers may arise because of labor turnover and vertical linkages. Case studies suggest that substantial technology diffusion occurs due to FDI (Blomstrom & Kokko, 1997). However, econometric studies support a more diverse set of conclusions. Some found that firms in sectors with a relatively high MNE presence tend to be more productive (Kokko, Tansini, & Zejan, 1997), while others noted that competing domestic firms do worse as the foreign presence in their industry increases (Aitken & Harrison, 1999). Such negative horizontal spillover effects may occur if MNEs siphon off domestic demand or bid away high-quality labor. Similarly, there is a risk that imports of technology may reduce R&D efforts of local firms, which may have happened in some sectors in China in the 1990s (OECD, 2002).

Moran (2004) argued that there is a substantial difference in operating characteristics between subsidiaries that are integrated into the international sourcing networks of the parent MNEs and those that are prevented from such integration by policy barriers such as mandatory joint venture and domestic content requirements. These different characteristics include size of the plant, proximity of technology and quality-control procedures to global best practices, speed with which production processes are brought to the frontier, and cost of output. Integrated subsidiaries have a more positive impact on the host country, often accompanied by vertical backward linkages and externalities. Isolated affiliates have a less positive, and sometimes negative, impact on the local economy.

Drawing upon case studies and econometric evidence, Moran claimed that this contrast in performance holds across different industries, countries, and time periods. He noted that failure to differentiate between export-oriented FDI and import-substitution FDI, or between foreign investors free to source from any location and those operating under domestic content requirements, or between foreign investors obliged to operate as minority shareholders and those with complete or majority ownership, accounts for the inability of earlier studies to isolate the influences of FDI on host-country welfare.

Studies focused on spillovers to local competitors of MNEs miss the fact that such firms typically transfer technology to local suppliers. Mexico's *maquiladora* sector is a recent example of vertical ITT. Most maquiladoras began as subsidiaries of US firms that shifted labor-intensive assembly operations to Mexico. However, over time, the maquiladoras adopted more sophisticated imported production techniques (Saggi, 2002). [2] A recent case study of the effects of Intel's investment in Costa Rica by Larrain, Lopez-Calva, and Rodriguez-Clare (2000) found that local suppliers benefited substantially from Intel's investment. Similar evidence exists for other sectors and countries (Moran, 1998, 2001). For example, in the electronics sector, foreign investors helped their local subcontractors keep pace with modern technologies by assigning technicians to the suppliers' plants to help set up and supervise automated production and testing procedures.

Javorcik (2004) examined backward linkages and technology spillovers using data from Lithuanian manufacturing firms over 1996–2000 and found that productivity is positively affected by a sector's contacts with multinational customers but not by the presence of MNEs in the same industry. Thus, her results supported the existence of vertical spillovers from FDI. Blalock (2001) used panel data from Indonesian manufacturing establishments to check for similar effects. He found a strong positive impact of FDI on productivity growth of local suppliers, suggesting that effective technology transfer does occur. He also plausibly suggested that, since MNEs tend to source inputs that require relatively simple technologies, local intermediate suppliers are in a good position to learn from affiliates.

Licensing is an important source of ITT for developing countries (Correa, forthcoming). Contracts typically involve the purchase of production or distribution rights and the underlying technical information and know-how. [3] The general determinants of decisions to license are similar to those involving FDI, including market size and policy certainty and transparency. An important additional factor is the confidence of licensor firms that proprietary technologies will not leak into the host economy through copying or defection of personnel. If this is likely, foreign firms may prefer FDI, may not engage in licensing at all, or may transfer lagging technologies (Maskus, 2000).

Successful transfer typically requires capacity to learn and investments to apply technologies into local production processes. This factor explains why countries with substantial engineering skills and R&D programs for adaptation and learning are greater recipients of licensing flows than others (Yang & Maskus, 2001).

(c) *Labor turnover and movement of people*

Little attention has been given to the role of labor flows as a channel for ITT. Some studies have found that domestic labor turnover from MNEs to local firms is limited, while others claimed the opposite (Rhee, 1990). An explanation is that in countries where local firms are not far behind MNEs in technical terms, labor turnover is more likely. Thus, the ability of local firms to absorb new technologies is a determinant of whether labor turnover is a means of diffusion.

International movement of people, associated with nationals studying or working abroad for a limited period, or the inward movement of foreign citizens, is another potential channel for ITT. The recent experience of India in developing a software and related services industry illustrates that payoffs from such movements may take time to materialize but can be large. A policy challenge for developing countries is to facilitate temporary movement abroad and encourage returnees to undertake local research and business development.

(d) *Market failures and the need for policy*

Markets within which ITTs take place are subject to at least three major problems. The first is asymmetric information (Arora, Fosfuri, & Gambardella, 2001; Horstmann & Markusen, 1987). Technology suppliers cannot fully reveal their knowledge without destroying the basis for trade, while buyers cannot fully determine the value of the information before buying it. This problem can lead to large transaction costs and stifle technology flows. In the international context, information and contract enforcement problems may be severe. A second problem is that owners of new technologies typically have substantial market power resulting from lead time and IPR (Maskus, 2000). Thus, the price of technology will exceed its marginal cost. While this exclusivity allows developers to profit from innovation, it reduces the static national welfare of those importing technologies. A third problem is that externalities arise if the costs and benefits of technology exchange are not internalized by participants (Saggi, 2004). A major share of benefits to recipient countries of ITT is likely to arise from uncompensated spillovers, wherein technological information is diffused into the wider economy and the technology provider cannot extract the associated economic value.

These market failures support the potential for policies to increase welfare by altering the incentives of private agents to engage in ITT. This task is complex, and it is difficult for policymakers to identify optimal policies or even to rank order them according to effectiveness. [4] However, the problematic characteristics of knowledge markets noted above suggest that policy should aim at three targets: First, increase access of local buyers to the international stock of knowledge and improve the ability of technology owners to signal the true value of their inventions to buyers. Second, reduce the costs of acquiring and absorbing existing technologies. Third, increase incentives for domestic innovation. We next turn to policy options for host countries, source countries, and international cooperation.

3. NATIONAL POLICIES

A basic challenge for host developing countries is to improve the local environment for ITT and its diffusion. Both FDI and licensing respond to such factors as an effective infrastructure, transparency and stability in government, and a reasonably open trade and investment regime (World Bank, 2004). Also important is an entrepreneurial environment that attracts skilled workers home from developed countries. Given that vertical spillovers are strongest in countries where MNEs work with competitive suppliers, reducing entry barriers in upstream industries can also assist ITT.

An important determinant of the ability to absorb and adapt technology is the return to investing in at least simple R&D capacity. If existing technology policies, capital market regulations, and taxes discourage such investments, they could be reformed to encourage innovation. Similarly, absorption and competitive deployment of ITT depend on an adequate supply of engineering and management skills, making domestic education and training policies important. Governments can reduce the technological distance between local and foreign firms by establishing innovation systems that encourage R&D, transfer knowledge from universities and public laboratories to domestic firms, and promote use of cost-saving technologies.

Host-country governments also need to recognize the risk taking involved in adopting foreign technologies. Suppose domestic firms are considering the costly adoption of some foreign technology, and that significant uncertainty exists regarding the degree to which it can be used effectively. Firms adopting the technology first generate positive spillovers for others who can watch and learn. In the presence of such informational externalities, it makes sense to subsidize the adoption of foreign technologies. Hausmann and Rodrik (2003) have emphasized that in many developing countries, the market undersupplies investment by firms in new activities because of appropriability problems. If so, a subsidy or similar incentive can expand innovation and risk taking. [5]

(a) *Trade and FDI policies*

Available evidence suggests that diffusion of knowledge is facilitated by an open trade regime (Saggi, 2002). Firms need access to capital equipment and imported inputs that embody foreign knowledge. At the same time, the existence of market failures makes questionable any unconditional arguments against trade protection.

An important question is the scope of knowledge spillovers. International spillovers, for which there is considerable evidence (Eaton & Kortum, 1996), tilt the balance in favor of free trade. In contrast, intranational spillovers create a role for policy intervention, though trade policies would be neither efficient nor effective. Instead, general policies encouraging agents to undertake activities that generate social benefits exceeding private returns, without simultaneously creating additional distortions, are more appropriate.

Historically, restrictive trade policies were complemented by restrictions on FDI. Thus, Japan, the Republic of Korea, and Taiwan imposed restrictions on FDI, whereas policies were more welcoming toward other modes of ITT. Moran (1998) summarized the approach taken by Korea and Japan as a combination of import barriers coupled with export promotion; fiscal subsidies to create national champions in certain sectors; and restrictions on FDI coupled with insistence upon licensing and other arrangements. More recently, national FDI policies have become more liberal, but policies may differentiate between joint ventures and majority-owned FDI. For example, the Chinese policy has encouraged joint ventures more than inward FDI. Whether this approach is beneficial depends on the incentives MNEs have to transfer technologies to recipient firms and there is evidence that joint ventures obtain less advanced technology (Mansfield & Romeo, 1980; Moran, 1998).

While the magnitude of ITT undertaken by MNEs may not be socially optimal, evidence exists that they are keen to transfer technology to local suppliers (Moran, 1998). Policies that facilitate this process, rather than insisting that MNEs engage in ITT to local competitors, are more likely to succeed. In practice, many countries seek to attract foreign investors through special economic zones, subsidies, tax holidays, and other grants. Such investment incentives can be justified only if host countries enjoy positive learning and productivity externalities from inward FDI.

The prevalence of "follow the leader" behavior among MNEs provides a potential case for FDI incentives. One new entrant may attract investments by both other firms and upstream suppliers. If so, competition at multiple stages of production may increase, thereby improving both efficiency and overall output. An implication is that a host country may be able to unleash a sequence of investments by successfully inducing FDI from one or two major firms.

If the local economy lacks a well-developed network of potential suppliers, however, MNEs might not invest and suppliers may not develop. In such cases, growth is constrained by coordination problems that can partially be resolved by initiating investments from key firms. Such problems cannot be tackled solely through investment incentives, however. Policy efforts need to improve the investment climate and reduce the costs of absorbing technology. The latter task is complex and involves improving property rights, expanding innovation systems, and investing in efficient infrastructure. Thus, for incentives to be effective, important preconditions relating to the investment climate and absorptive capacity must be satisfied. Once upstream capacity exists, there may be a case for programs that help potential suppliers meet the needs of MNEs as customers. Such programs have been successfully implemented in a number of middle-income countries.

One set of policies often justified on the basis of regulating ITT are trade-related investment measures (TRIMs), such as local content rules and technology transfer requirements. However, TRIMs are implicit taxes on intermediate goods imports because manufacturers are forced to use higher-cost local inputs. They provide little incentive for the protected producers of intermediate goods to acquire knowledge and improve productivity. If the constraints imposed by TRIMs are too strict, MNEs may refrain from investing.

(b) *General versus specific technology-related policies*

Many studies indicate that absorptive capacity is crucial for obtaining significant spillover benefits from trade or FDI. For example, Borensztein, De Gregorio, and Lee (1998) tested the effects of inward FDI on growth in 69 developing countries. They found that it contributes *more* to domestic growth than does domestic investment but only where the host country has a minimum threshold stock of human capital. Similarly, Keller (1996) argued that access to foreign technologies alone does not increase growth rates of developing countries.

Consider the role that subsidies can play in facilitating learning and technology acquisition when returns to such investments cannot be appropriated by private agents. Such commentators as Amsden (1989) argued that policy interventions, including implicit or explicit subsidies, lay behind the economic miracles in Korea and Taiwan. Their case is that carefully targeted subsidies allowed these governments to stimulate key sectors that became efficient and provided positive spillovers. It is important, however, to differentiate between sector-specific subsidies and general policies facilitating learning and enterprise development. In a recent retrospective on the East Asian development experience, Noland and Pack (2003) argued that sector-specific policies did not result in high rates of TFP growth for manufacturing. In Korea and Taiwan, TFP growth was not much higher than in OECD countries. In India, selective interventionist policies were associated with declining TFP growth rates, while the opening of the economy led to an increase in TFP growth (Krishna & Mitra, 1998).

The case for general policy supports for innovation, education, transport infrastructure, and similar public goods is uncontroversial. Regarding more commercial activities, however, the efficient use of support policies requires that governments can both identify cases that justify intervention and implement it appropriately. In practice, governments may fail to avoid potential problems, including subsidies that support inefficiency and strategic subsidy seeking by firms. Because these problems become difficult to control, credible exit strategies are needed to weed out successes from failures.

(c) *IPR and technology transfer*

IPR can support markets in technology, including ITT (Arora *et al.*, 2001). Patents and trade secrets provide a legal basis for revealing the proprietary characteristics of technologies to subsidiaries and licensees, supporting the formation of licensing contracts. [6] Patent protection both increases flows of ITT to countries with sufficient technological capacity and shifts incentives for investors between FDI and licensing.

The empirical literature supports several observations. First, patent applications from foreign firms are associated with productivity growth in recipient countries (Eaton & Kortum, 1996). Thus, "trade in ideas" is a significant factor in world economic growth. Second, information from patent citations suggests that the most significant patents are widely diffused, as is knowledge in highly technological sectors (Peri, 2003). Knowledge flows have a positive impact on international innovation.

Third, international trade flows, especially in patent-sensitive industries, respond positively to increases in patent rights among middle-income and large developing countries but not among poor countries (Smith, 2001). Next, the evidence on patent laws and inward FDI is mixed but recent studies find positive impacts among middle-income and large developing countries. However, in poor countries, patents do not expand FDI (Blyde & Acea, 2002; Smith, 2001). Fourth, strengthening IPR tends to shift ITT from exports and FDI toward licensing and also increases R&D expenditures undertaken on behalf of affiliates in recipient countries with strong imitative abilities (Smith, 2001). Fifth, the sophistication of technologies transferred rises with the strength of IPR protection and domestic capacities to absorb and improve technology.

A common finding is that the poorest countries are unlikely to benefit from strong IPR (McCalman, 2001). Stronger patent rights may be expected to raise monopoly rents earned by international firms as such rights become more valuable, obliging developing countries to pay more for protected technology. These are also countries where ITT-related spillovers are likely to be small. Thus, in poor countries policy should aim at lowering costs of imports of IPR-intensive goods and raising the capacity to absorb and adapt technologies.

(d) *Summary: Theory and experience*

Economic theory does not provide unambiguous guidance regarding the relative social payoff to alternative channels of ITT. Much depends on whether spillovers are international or intranational, the capacities to absorb and improve technologies, and other factors. A "one size fits all" approach to policy is inappropriate. Consider, for example, the choice between licensing and FDI from a host-country's viewpoint. If the relevant market is imperfectly competitive, the choice is not simple. The alternative to suffering market power at the hands of MNEs might be sustaining domestic incumbents with significant market power. While the profits of the latter add to national income, such incumbents will generally possess inferior technologies. If there exists a strong domestic incumbent, limiting FDI and encouraging technology licensing to that firm can increase its market power *vis-à-vis* weaker domestic rivals (Saggi, 1996). On the other hand, if FDI were restricted and open technology licensing encouraged, licensing would be preferable to FDI if the technology owner agreed to transfer the technology.

Given the limited guidance offered by theory, it is helpful to revisit briefly the history of successful efforts to move up the technology ladder. One reason for Japan's rapid growth and industrialization after World War II was that its patent system was designed for both small-scale innovation and diffusion. The system encouraged incremental innovation by Japanese firms and promoted the diffusion of knowledge into the economy (Maskus, 2000). Japan also encouraged foreign firms to license to Japanese firms, in part through restrictions on FDI.

Korea encouraged learning *via* "duplicative imitation" of mature technologies that were in the public domain or available cheaply (Kim, 2002). IPR protection was weak and encouraged imitation and adaptation. In the 1970s, Korea specialized in labor-intensive goods, with firms importing "off the shelf" technologies and adapting them to produce differentiated goods. Government promoted the development of technical skills through education and workplace training and significantly reduced antiexport bias. In the 1980s, Korean firms shifted to "creative imitation," involving more significant transformation of imported technologies. This shift required domestic R&D and in-house research capabilities. The government also became more welcoming to formal channels of ITT and strengthened the IPR regime.

Brazil, Mexico, Malaysia, and the export-intensive regions of China and India are other examples of movement from "pure" to "creative" imitation. In these cases, IPR protection was limited and firms took advantage of available foreign technologies. As the technological sophistication of production processes matured and the depth and complexity of knowledge for effective absorption grew, firms resorted more to formal means of ITT and governments strengthened the IPR regime.

These experiences suggest that the nature of ITT and appropriate policies follow a technology ladder. Many middle-income developing countries are at the duplicative imitation stage, hoping to absorb foreign technologies into labor-intensive export production and evolve into higher value-added strategies over time. The poorest countries have barely stepped onto this rung. Thus, a differentiated approach is needed for national policy and multilateral rulemaking. Specifically, the priority in poor countries with weak institutions and limited R&D capacity is to improve the business environment, with liberal trade policies to encourage imports of technology. Such countries should be exempt from strong IPR obligations and have access to mechanisms to reduce the cost of imports of IPR-protected goods. This could be achieved, for example, through either subsidies or differential pricing schemes.

Because absorptive capacity is weak in low-income countries, the emphasis should be on using trade to benefit from foreign knowledge and acquiring technology through FDI. Licensing is not a realistic option for least-developed countries (LDCs), given weak business environments and absorptive capacity. In poor countries, there is a greater need for FDI because the incentives for licensing or joint ventures are weaker. Indeed, this situation may provide a case for outward FDI investment incentives by high-income countries as part of their development assistance.

As countries move up the income and technology ladder, they gain more from IPR, which becomes important for licensing and benefits home entrepreneurs and innovators. Based on the experience of Asian economies, developing countries should adopt standards for patentability, novelty, and utility that are stricter (raising a higher bar to patenting) than those found in the United States and the European Union. This approach is consistent with WTO rules, which do not specify substantive criteria on the basis of which IPR grants are awarded. Upper-middle-income countries would benefit less from subsidy schemes to lower the price of technology.

4. SOURCE-COUNTRY POLICIES

Perhaps the most powerful indirect incentive for ITT that source countries could provide is to grant greater market access for products in which poor countries have a comparative advantage, including agricultural products and labor-intensive goods. The linkage is that better assurance of foreign market access would expand incentives to transfer new technologies to producers in developing countries.

Turning to specific measures aimed at ITT, fiscal incentives or subsidies are the most obvious candidates. Subcentral governments in OECD countries often offer tax incentives to induce firms to establish facilities or to remain in their own countries, especially in low-income areas. One option is for central governments to offer the same fiscal benefits to firms transferring technologies to developing countries as are available for domestic activities. Developed countries could also offer the same tax advantages for R&D performed abroad as for R&D done at home.

In designing such incentives, home countries could tailor interventions toward channels appropriate for countries at different stages of development. Given the foregoing arguments in favor of FDI over licensing in low-income countries, for example, policies that subsidize direct ITT through licensing may not be beneficial to poor countries. A better approach would be to ensure that incentives target (or minimally do not discriminate against) outward FDI. Source countries should also differentiate between countries in initiatives to lower the cost of technology-intensive imports through promotion of differential pricing schemes. Although not a direct ITT policy, such price segmentation would avoid undesirable reverse transfers from South to North through arbitrage. [7]

Several other options to increase ITT incentives exist. First, permit tax deductions for contributions of technology to nonprofit entities engaged in ITT, taking the form of grants, technical assistance, or mature patent rights. Second, offer fiscal incentives to encourage enterprises temporarily to employ recent graduates from developing countries. Here there are potential synergies with efforts to expand the temporary movement of natural service suppliers under mode 4 of the General Agreement on Trade and Services (GATS). Third, public resources, such as those from the US National Science Foundation, could be used to support research into the technology needs of developing countries. Technologies developed under such programs could be made publicly available.

Fourth, universities could be encouraged to recruit and train students from LDCs. Financial incentives that tap into development aid funding for setting up degree programs through distance learning or even foreign establishments may be particularly effective. Finally, additional initiatives could center on increasing information flows. For example, technical standards play a role in diffusing production and certification technologies. Thus, developed countries could finance participation by experts from developing countries in their standards-setting bodies.

Convincing OECD governments to offer incentives for transferring technology is a challenge, but could be part of their overall development assistance efforts.

5. INTERNATIONAL COOPERATION

Many of the suggestions in the previous section will come at a cost to source countries. Similarly, a number of the developing country policy options discussed in Section 3 will require financing. Moreover, their effectiveness will depend importantly on design, discipline, and monitoring. These considerations provide rationales for using international agreements as commitment devices and enforcement mechanisms to increase the credibility and impacts of ITT policies. Safeguarding the ability of countries to pursue beneficial policies is also important. Certain avenues that were used in the past to achieve industrialization have been narrowed as a result of the WTO, suggesting a need to ensure that policy space exists to encourage ITT.

Helleiner (2000), Finger (2002), and Sabel and Reddy (2002), among others, emphasized that countries need the freedom to experiment with regulatory policies. Thus, detailed international policy harmonization is inappropriate. As argued by Hoekman (2005), multilateral monitoring and information exchange mechanisms can play a useful role in preventing capture and identifying effective policies. Such institutions as the OECD, UNCTAD, and UNIDO have provided a forum for exchanging experiences and discussing appropriate policies. The WTO Working Group on Trade and Technology Transfer provides a forum for dialogue that could be used more effectively.

There is a close connection between ITT discussions in the WTO and the concept of special and differential treatment (SDT) of developing countries. The argument that needs (market failures) differ depending on the type of country suggests that ITT policies should be differentiated. The same is arguably true of SDT more generally, although differentiation is resisted by many developing countries. [8] Similar questions arise in regional trade and investment integration agreements. Most such agreements do not address technology transfer explicitly in the form of binding commitments, instead imposing disciplines on the ability to use specific instruments such as subsidies or TRIMs. However, some North–South agreements put substantial emphasis on financial and technical assistance to be granted by the high-income partner(s). The best example is the European Union, which has included such provisions in its partnership agreements with Mediterranean and other countries and has provided assistance for improving both absorptive and innovation capacity in its partners. To date, no such links have been made in the WTO and we now discuss areas where actions could be considered in that forum.

(a) *Subsidies*

The WTO Agreement on Subsidies and Countervailing Measures (ASCM) divides subsidies into three categories: prohibited, actionable, and nonactionable. R&D and related technology subsidies are nonactionable if they are not specific, or, if specific, satisfy certain conditions. These conditions cover "assistance for research activities conducted by firms or by higher education or research establishments on a contract basis with firms." Fundamental research, defined as "an enlargement of general scientific and technical knowledge not linked to industrial or commercial objectives" is not subject to disciplines. [9] However, the provisions on nonactionability of R&D subsidies lapsed in 1999 and should be reinstated to permit developing countries to use them. In defining what is permitted, scope should exist to adopt measures that can be justified on the basis of externalities of the type identified by Hausmann and Rodrik (2003), discussed above. This does not mean complete freedom, for there is an important role for multilateral disciplines to help governments control subsidy policies and prevent capture. One approach would be to develop monitoring and surveillance mechanisms in the WTO aimed at increasing information on the effectiveness of policies to encourage innovation.

The current focus of the WTO is disciplines on national use of subsidies. A complementary approach would seek commitments by high-income countries to provide financing for risk-reducing entrepreneurial programs that promote entry into new activities. Such funding should be nondiscriminatory, made available to both foreign and domestic firms, because the nationality of innovating firms does not matter for realizing knowledge spillovers. The possibility of funding foreign entry through FDI or joint ventures might also enhance the support for such aid programs by creating a constituency in its favor in source countries.

(b) *Temporary movement of people and labor turnover*

Learning by doing, and subsequent labor turnover, are important channels of ITT. While most of the literature has focused on within-country labor turnover associated with FDI, international movement of people has a potentially larger role to play in fostering ITT. In order to be most beneficial to developing countries, policies should encourage temporary movement of people. The classic problems with international migration are that it is often long-term and can give rise to a "brain drain" with potentially negative impacts on home-country welfare. Such problems would not arise if labor movements were temporary and returnees applied new skills and knowledge at home.

Negotiations over the temporary cross-border movement of people have been launched in the WTO. These discussions arise in the GATS, for one mode of supplying services is through the temporary movement of suppliers. While GATS is limited to people providing services, its approach could be extended to a category of personnel that relocate temporarily in order to increase their human capital and acquire new skills ("training services"). In effect, such movements could be regarded as a mechanism for host countries to export knowledge to developing countries. While it may not be feasible to incorporate this idea into the GATS, the mode 4 precedent might be used to negotiate a stand-alone arrangement under which developing countries would be granted additional temporary visa allocations for working in OECD countries, motivated by ITT objectives. This would also be a way to provide concrete SDT to developing countries. [10] The visa allocation mechanism could be similar to the "GATS visa" regime that has been suggested by a number of WTO members (Mattoo & Carzaniga, 2003).

Donor countries and organizations could also consider establishing special trust funds for training scientific and technical personnel, facilitating the transfer of technologies that are particularly sensitive for the provision of public goods, and encouraging research in developing countries (Roffe, 2002). To the extent that data and research results must be purchased, differential pricing schemes for governments and institutions in poor countries could be encouraged. At the margin, visa allocations could be aimed at students and researchers from poor countries. More generally, developed countries could help developing countries build capacity for improving education and science, including their ability to access international information and the Internet.

(c) *IPR and TRIPS*

TRIPS Article 66.2 imposes an obligation on developed economies to find means of increasing ITT to the LDCs. One option would be for governments in developed countries to increase technical and financial assistance for improving the ability of poor countries to absorb technology and engage in trade. Examples of such assistance include capacity building in IPR management and technical standards, establishing public and public–private research facilities, and facilitating trade in technology-related services. The terms of TRIPS Article 66.2 could also be expanded to include all developing countries without a significant domestic science and technology base. In addition, a special fee on international patent applications could be considered, through the Patent Cooperation Treaty, with revenues earmarked for improving IPR administrative systems in developing countries. Given different interests of developing countries regarding criteria for patentability, novelty, and utility, efforts toward harmonization of criteria or tests could be limited to the regional level, through, for example, cooperative examination offices that apply regional standards (Maskus, 2003).

Poor countries face major shortages in expertise for developing and enforcing antimonopoly laws. One way for their governments to gain confidence in the system would be for authorities in developed countries to undertake enforcement actions against firms headquartered or located in their jurisdictions. A committed effort on the part of rich countries to prevent market-power abuses in developing-country markets by their sellers of technology could help achieve the goals of TRIPS Article 66.

(d) *Protecting and expanding the global commons for knowledge*

Another proposal that has considerable potential to expand ITT to poor countries is to negotiate a WTO Agreement on Access to Basic Science and Technology (ABST) (Barton & Maskus, 2004). This would place into the public domain the results of publicly funded research. The idea is to preserve and enhance the global commons in science and technology without unduly restricting private rights in commercial technologies. The agreement could encourage researchers from other countries to participate in, or compete with, local research teams for grants and subsidies, possibly combined with increased opportunities for temporary migration. It could also give researchers in other countries access to nationally generated science and data. It may be necessary to adopt a GATS-like approach to the ABST, permitting governments to reserve sensitive areas of technology and to designate different levels of commitment to open access. Safeguards for security-related regulation would be required as well.

(e) *Information exchange and multilateral monitoring*

To reduce problems of asymmetric information, international organizations such as the WTO could serve as an intermediary conduit for knowledge about successful technology-acquisition programs of national and subnational governments. Firms in many developing countries may have little knowledge about the structure of international ITT contracts. What are reasonable royalty rates? What conditions have sellers of technology been willing to negotiate? Which contract clauses have proved helpful in encouraging local technological development? Answers to such questions exist but their dissemination requires efforts by both the private and public sectors of developed countries. Privacy concerns should not be a major obstacle, as summarizing expired licensing contracts would not reveal confidential data.

More emphasis on information exchange and multilateral monitoring would also be beneficial. This effort should focus on the success of various policies in achieving particular objectives. Rather than only seeking to regulate what countries may do to encourage ITT and innovation, a more productive approach could be to establish a broad framework that requires countries to engage in a regular exchange of information and policy assessments. Sabel and Reddy (2002) provided a conceptual sketch of such a "learning to learn" framework that could be applied to the ITT arena. The framework could also be devised to monitor the operation of subsidy programs supported by high-income countries.

6. RULES OF THUMB

Determining optimal policies to maximize ITT is difficult. ITT depends on many factors, including proximity to markets, size, growth, competition conditions, human capital basis, governance, and infrastructure. Significant uncertainty remains regarding the extent of market failures and spillovers, complicating the identification of good policies. Nonetheless, the foregoing analysis identified some rules of thumb for policy intervention as well as a number of specific proposals. We summarize the main policy implications in Table 1, distinguishing between low-income, lower-middle-income, and upper-middle-income countries. These categories are illustrative only and are useful primarily in distinguishing between the types of general policies that are most appropriate for countries at different levels of development. We also suggest a rank ordering of polices on the basis of likely social benefits.

A main priority in all types of developing countries is effective general technology policies, including improving basic education, building appropriate infrastructure, and reducing entry barriers for local firms that could be suppliers for MNEs. For local economies to gain productivity from ITT, such broader policy initiatives are important. This is a complex task that involves building human capital, expanding national innovation systems, and appropriately protecting IPR. Lower-income and middle-income economies could gain from investing in R&D support, especially as regards collaborations between public research entities and private enterprises, as part of their innovation systems. Source (donor) countries should support such investments.

Turning to specific policies, the evidence suggests that countries pursuing relatively closed trade policies fail to achieve the benefits from technology implicit in international trade. We therefore argue for liberal trade policies as a key priority, as important as sound general technology policies. As noted earlier, R&D-intensive capital-goods imports from high-income countries are associated with higher TFP in developing economies. Further, spillovers from technology-intensive imports can encourage exports because exporters need to deploy technologies that support international quality levels and standards.

Again, there is compelling evidence of vertical spillovers from FDI (Javorcik, 2004; Saggi, 2002). FDI is likely to be particularly important for low-income and lower-middle-income countries. The weak investment climates in many of these countries may justify a temporary case for encouraging FDI inflows, which we would rank second behind open trade policies. Such incentives should avoid discrimination across both sectors and foreign origins. Governments are not good at picking winners and should focus on encouragement of new activities. Given the possibility of coordination failures and learning externalities, any incentives for new "nontraditional" activities should apply to both domestic and foreign firms. Ideally, such support would be financed by development assistance.

A third specific priority for developing economies, especially poorer countries, is temporary international movement of technical workers abroad for education and training. Upper-middle-income countries could see growing two-way movements in skilled personnel. Such movements are an important source of learning, and will also lead to establishment of networks in foreign countries that are potential markets as well as sources of knowledge. China, India, and other emerging economies illustrate the importance of having a significant and sustained outflow of people who, upon their return, raise productivity. Even if they stay abroad for an extended period of time, they can be part of networks supporting trade and investment flows.

While licensing is an important source of technical transformation, successful transfer generally requires capacity to learn and adaptive investments by local firms. Poor countries are most likely to achieve these gains by taking advantage of mature technologies in the public domain or available cheaply. Thus, specific policies here are not as likely to be a high priority. They could aim at improving information flows about such technologies, as well as building skills and R&D capacity. Middle-income countries, in which firms have engineering skills and

Table 1. *A rule-of-thumb typology and examples of ITT policies*

	Trade in goods	FDI	Temporary movement of natural persons	Trade in knowledge (licensing)	IPR	General technology policies
Own policies						
Low-income countries	(1) Liberal access	(2) Nondiscriminatory investment promotion	(3) Incentives for education abroad and training-related movement	(4) Improve information flows about public domain and mature technologies	(5) Basic protection and minimum standards only	(1) Basic education; improve infrastructure; reduce entry barriers
Lower-middle-income countries	(1) Liberal access	(2) Nondiscriminatory investment promotion	(4) Incentives for education abroad and training-related movement	(3) Improve information; limited incentives for licensing	(5) Wider scope of IPR protection; employ flexibilities	(1) R&D support policies; improve infrastructure; reduce entry barriers
Upper-middle-income countries	(1) Liberal access	(3) Upstream supplier support programs	(2) Encourage two-way mobility	No active policy	(4) Apply full TRIPS	(1) R&D support policies; improve infrastructure; reduce entry barriers
OECD policies toward						
Low-income countries	(1) Subsidize public-good-type imports; free trade	(2) Incentives for outward flows exceeding those for FDI to LMICs (see below)	(3) Preferential access; subsidies for education; incentives for universities to accept DC students in STI disciplines and temporary employment	(5) Subsidize transfer of public domain and mature technologies	(4) Forbearance in disputes; differential pricing for exports of IPR products; assistance in competition policy	(1) Support for general DC technology policies (see above); public and public–private research facilities
Lower-middle-income countries	(1) Free trade; no controls	(2) Incentives equal to those granted for own disadvantaged regions	(3) Wider access for education and training; temporary employment of DC scientific personnel/engineers	(4) Assistance in establishment of joint venture partnerships; matching grants	(5) Differential pricing of public-good type IPR protected goods; assistance in competition policy	(1) Support for general DC technology policies (see above); fiscal incentives for R&D performed in DCs
Upper-middle-income countries	Free trade; no controls	No incentives	Encourage mode 4 type mobility	No active policy	No active policy	No active policy

Notes: Numbers in parentheses indicate authors' rank ordering of policy on basis of economic importance or anticipated payoff. DC: developing country; LMIC: lower-middle-income country.

active R&D programs, are more likely to be the recipients of significant licensing flows. To enhance these flows, policy efforts could focus on reducing the costs of absorbing technology. The upper-middle-income economies require no active intervention in licensing, where technology markets may be expected to operate effectively. Note that our analysis in no case supports extensive government involvement in selecting technologies or placing restrictions on the use of technical information.

Despite the intense focus on IPR in the literature, we would argue that this is a relatively less important area for policy, so long as IPR regimes are tailored to levels of development and technological capacities. In Table 1, we hint at the issues and far more detail could be added. [11] Thus, low-income countries would find it advantageous to enforce basic protection of trademarks, trade secrets, utility models, and industrial designs in order to encourage both local small-scale innovation and inward FDI in labor-intensive technologies. However, it is inadvisable to move beyond minimum TRIPS standards, while requirements for patents, plant variety rights, and copyrights should be as pro-competitive as possible. The LDCs may be expected to do relatively little in terms of enforcing foreign patent rights in any case. There is a strong case for forbearance by OECD governments in pursuing enforcement-related dispute settlement at the WTO. For their part, lower-middle-income countries should take advantage of TRIPS flexibilities while offering somewhat wider scope of protection.

The bottom half of Table 1 encapsulates policy recommendations for high-income source economies that desire to encourage ITT to poor countries. Here again, market access for goods and services produced in developing countries is a priority. Fiscal incentives may be an effective means for overcoming market failures in ITT. As mentioned, such financial support should be directed at the general technology policies that are a top priority in most developing countries.

In terms of specific support policies, FDI is most important for low-income countries as they have the most to gain from investments in "new" activities and from entry by efficient foreign firms. Such incentives should be at least equal to those offered for investments in OECD countries, and, as argued above, could extend to entry by local firms into new markets and activities, including as suppliers to MNEs.

Liberal policies toward, and explicit encouragement of, labor movement through improved access to educational establishments, scholarships, and temporary employment of graduates and professionals is a third priority area for source-country action. This idea is politically sensitive and thus may be less feasible than the other areas. Finally, OECD governments could improve flows of public-domain technologies with appropriate subsidies and support the establishment of extensive price differentiation for exports of IPR products to low-income developing economies.

7. LEVERAGING TRADE AGREEMENTS FOR ITT

Many of the suggestions made in this paper can be implemented unilaterally. However, some require action in the WTO and many can be made more credible by incorporating them as specific commitments. This idea could be achieved as part of a new approach to SDT in the WTO that provides greater scope for policy flexibility on the part of developing countries. Alternatively, various ITT-related policy initiatives could be embedded in a mix of existing and new WTO agreements.

Although binding disciplines help ensure policy certainty, there is a rationale for flexible government tools to encourage ITT and address externalities in information markets. Thus, a key option is to negotiate clear criteria that differentiate among beneficiary countries. Broad, transparent categories would minimize transaction costs and uncertainty, but would not do much to help countries achieve ITT objectives. An alternative suggested by Hoekman (2005) is to provide for greater flexibility in the enforcement of multilateral disciplines in specific areas, such as ITT-related policies, but to accompany this with multilateral monitoring and periodic discussions among WTO members about the incidence and effectiveness of the policies pursued.

A related issue is whether the proactive ITT measures we have suggested for source countries should take the form of binding and enforceable commitments in the WTO or regional trade agreements. In some cases, such as the suggested implicit exemption from enforcement of TRIPS for low-income countries, a change in the relevant WTO rules is needed. However, in areas that are not now covered by the WTO a "soft law" approach that establishes broad guidelines and relies on ensuring transparency and accountability *via* regular multilateral monitoring of performance is likely to be more effective at increasing cooperation and compliance. What matters most is that "demandeur" developing countries elucidate the need for specific policies and engage in a process of analysis to identify the most appropriate instruments. Insofar as these are subsidies, proposals should be put forward in development assistance allocation discussions. The extent to which such requests are met should be part of the proposed multilateral monitoring mechanism. The same is true with regard to allowing developing countries to pursue general technology-related policies and to encourage the use of specific channels of ITT.

NOTES

1. See Keller (1998) for a criticism of earlier work by Coe and Helpman (1995), the results of which may have been spurious. However, that trade embodies technical information is evident in numerous studies, including Eaton and Kortum (1996) and Keller (2002). Keller (2002) noted that information diffusion declines with distance but recognized that one channel must be trade.

2. Similar findings apply to transition economies; see, for example, Javorcik (2004).

3. With intrafirm ITT, the MNE retains proprietary control of the know-how, while in the arm's-length case, it must be provided the licensee.

4. In practice, the potential for beneficial policy may be frustrated by mistakes or rent seeking.

5. In such cases, IPRs may not be effective, for often the technology would already have been invented elsewhere. The objective is to encourage imitation of "revealed successes" through entry into what are new productive activities for the country concerned.

6. See Correa (forthcoming) for the counterargument that IPR stifle ITT as firms exploit market power.

7. A recent example was the August 2003 decision by WTO members to permit poor countries to issue compulsory import licenses for essential medicines, in return for effective means to prevent the backflow of medicines to higher-price countries.

8. Hoekman, Michalopoulos, and Winters (2004) offered an extensive discussion of the need for moving toward greater differentiation in SDT in the WTO.

9. A distinction is made between industrial research and pre-competitive development activity. For the former, the maximum amount of government participation is 75%; for the latter it is 50%.

10. A proposal by the LDC Group in the WTO, that they be given preferential access to a mode 4 "quota" as part of the GATS negotiations, goes in this direction.

11. World Bank (2001) offers extensive discussion.

REFERENCES

Aitken, B. J., & Harrison, A. E. (1999). Do domestic firms benefit from direct foreign investment? Evidence from Venezuela. *American Economic Review, 89*(3), 605–618.

Amsden, A. (1989). *Asia's next giant: South Korea and late industrialization.* New York, Oxford: Oxford University Press.

Arora, A., Fosfuri, A., & Gambardella, A. (2001). *Markets for technology: The economics of innovation and corporate strategy.* Cambridge: MIT Press.

Barton, J. H., & Maskus, K. E. (2004). *Economic perspectives on a multilateral agreement on open access to basic science and technology* (Manuscript). University of Colorado. Boulder.

Blalock, G. (2001). *Technology from foreign direct investment: Strategic transfer through supply chains* (Mimeo). Cornell University.

Blomstrom, M., & Kokko, A. (1997). *How foreign investment affects host countries.* World Bank PRD Working Paper No. 1745, Washington, DC.

Blyde, J. S., & Acea, C. (2002). *The effects of intellectual property rights on trade and FDI in Latin America* (Manuscript). Inter-American Development Bank, Washington, DC.

Borensztein, E., De Gregorio, J., & Lee, J.-W. (1998). How does foreign direct investment affect economic growth? *Journal of International Economics, 45*(1), 115–135.

Coe, D. T., & Helpman, E. (1995). International R&D spillovers. *European Economic Review, 86*(1), 859–887.

Coe, D. T., Helpman, E., & Hoffmaister, A. W. (1997). North–South R&D spillovers. *The Economic Journal, 107*(440), 131–149.

Correa, C. M. (forthcoming). Can the TRIPS agreement foster technology transfer to developing countries? In K. E. Maskus, & J. H. Reichman (Eds.), *International public goods and transfer of technology under a globalized intellectual property regime*. Cambridge: Cambridge University Press.

Eaton, J., & Kortum, S. J. (1996). Trade in ideas: Patenting and productivity in the OECD. *Journal of International Economics, 40*(3–4), 251–278.

Eaton, J., & Kortum, S. J. (1999). International technology diffusion: Theory and measurement. *International Economic Review, 40*(3), 537–570.

Evenson, R. E., & Westphal, L. E. (1995). Technological change and technology strategy. In J. Behrman & T. N. Srinivasan (Eds.). *Handbook of development economics* (Vol. 3A, pp. 2209–2300). Amsterdam: North-Holland.

Finger, J. M. (2002). *The Doha agenda and development: A view from the Uruguay round*. Manila: Asian Development Bank.

Grossman, G. M., & Helpman, E. (1991). *Innovation and growth in the world economy*. Cambridge: MIT Press.

Hausmann, R., & Rodrik, D. (2003). Economic development as self-discovery. *Journal of Development Economics, 72*(2), 603–633.

Helleiner, G. K. (2000). Markets, politics, and globalization: Can the global economy be civilized? In *10th Prebisch lecture*. UNCTAD, Geneva. Available from www.unctad.org.

Hoekman, B. M. (2005). Making the WTO more supportive of development. *Finance & Development, 42*(1), 14–18.

Hoekman, B. M., Michalopoulos, C., & Winters, L. A. (2004). Special and differential treatment in the WTO after Cancun. *The World Economy, 27*(3), 481–506.

Horstmann, I., & Markusen, J. R. (1987). Licensing versus direct investment: A model of internalization by the multinational enterprise. *Canadian Journal of Economics, 20*(3), 464–481.

Javorcik, B. S. (2004). Does foreign direct investment increase the productivity of domestic firms? In search of spillovers through backward linkages. *American Economic Review, 94*(3), 605–627.

Keller, W. (1996). Absorptive capacity: On the creation and acquisition of technology in development. *Journal of Development Economics, 49*(2), 199–227.

Keller, W. (1998). Are International R&D spillovers trade-related? Analyzing spillovers among randomly matched trade partner. *European Economic Review, 42*(8), 1469–1481.

Keller, W. (2002). Geographic localization of international technology diffusion. *American Economic Review, 92*(1), 120–142.

Kim, L. (2002). *Technology transfer and intellectual property rights: Lessons from Korea's experience*. UNCTAD/ICTSD Working paper, Geneva.

Kokko, A., Tansini, R., & Zejan, M. (1997). *Trade regimes and spillover effects of FDI: Evidence from Uruguay* (Manuscript). Stockholm School of Economics, Stockholm.

Krishna, P., & Mitra, D. (1998). Trade liberalization, market discipline, and productivity growth: India. *Journal of Development Economics, 56*(2), 447–462.

Larrain, B. F., Lopez-Calva, L. F., & Rodriguez-Clare, A. (2000). *Intel: A case study of FDI in Central America*. CID Working Paper No. 58, Harvard University.

Mansfield, E., & Romeo, A. (1980). Technology transfer to overseas subsidiaries by US-based firms. *Quarterly Journal of Economics, 95*(4), 737–749.

Maskus, K. E. (2000). *Intellectual property rights in the global economy*. Washington, DC: Institute for International Economics.

Maskus, K. E. (2003). *Encouraging international technology transfer*. UNCTAD/ICTSD Working Paper, Geneva.

Mattoo, A., & Carzaniga, A. (Eds.). (2003). *Moving people to deliver services*. Washington, DC: World Bank.

McCalman, P. (2001). Reaping what you sow: An empirical analysis of international patent harmonization. *Journal of International Economics, 55*(1), 161–186.

Moran, T. (1998). *Foreign direct investment and development*. Washington, DC: Institute for International Economics.

Moran, T. (2001). *Parental supervision: The new paradigm for foreign direct investment and development*. Washington, DC: Institute for International Economics.

Moran, T. (2004). How does foreign direct investment affect host country development: Do we already know the answer? Using industry case studies to make reliable generalizations. In M. Blomstrom, E. M. Graham, & T. Moran (Eds.), *The impact of foreign direct investment on development*. Washington, DC: Institute for International Economics.

Noland, M., & Pack, H. (2003). *Industrial policy in an era of globalization: Lessons from Asia*. Washington, DC: Institute of International Economics.

Organization for Economic Cooperation and Development (2002). *Science and technology industry outlook*. Paris: OECD.

Parente, S. L., & Prescott, E. C. (1994). Barriers to technology adoption and development. *Journal of Political Economy, 102*(2), 298–321.

Peri, G. (2003). *Knowledge flows, R&D spillovers, and innovation* (Manuscript). University of California at Davis, Davis, CA.

Rhee, Y. W. (1990). The catalyst model of development: Lessons from Bangladesh's success with garment exports. *World Development, 18*(2), 333–346.

Roffe, P. (2002). *Preliminary note on the WTO working group on trade and transfer of technology* (Manuscript). UNCTAD, Geneva.

Sabel, C., & Reddy, S. (2002). *Learning to learn: Undoing the Gordian knot of development today*. New York: Columbia University, Available from www.sopde.org/discussion.htm.

Saggi, K. (1996). Entry into a foreign market: Foreign direct investment versus licensing. *Review of International Economics, 4*(1), 99–104.

Saggi, K. (2002). Trade, foreign direct investment, and international technology transfer: A survey. *World Bank Research Observer, 17*(Fall), 191–235.

Saggi, K. (2004). *International technology transfer to developing countries*. Economic Paper 64, Commonwealth Secretariat, London, UK.

Schiff, M., Wang, Y., & Olarreaga, M. (2002). *North–south and south–south trade-related technology diffusion: An industry level analysis* (Manuscript). World Bank, Washington, DC.

Smith, P. J. (2001). How do foreign patent rights affect US exports, affiliate sales, and licenses? *Journal of International Economics, 55*(2), 411–440.

Tybout, J. R. (2000). Manufacturing firms in developing countries: How well do they do and why? *Journal of Economic Literature, 38*(1), 11–44.

World Bank (2001). *Global economic prospects and the developing countries 2002: Making trade work for the world's poor*. The World Bank, Washington, DC.

World Bank (2004). *World development report 2005: A better investment climate for everyone*. The World Bank, Washington, DC.

Yang, G., & Maskus, K. E. (2001). Intellectual property rights and licensing: An econometric investigation. *Weltwirtschaftliches Archiv, 137*(1), 58–79.

Part 2

Multinational Firms, Market Structure, and Welfare

Chapter 6

Incentives for foreign direct investment under imitation*

PING LIN Lingnan University
KAMAL SAGGI Southern Methodist University

Abstract. We study the symmetric mixed strategy equilibrium of a dynamic model where at each instant two exporting firms choose their probability of foreign direct investment (FDI). The first firm's FDI generates cost-lowering spillovers for the second and leads to local imitation, thereby intensifying competition. While an increase in imitation risk usually makes FDI less likely, there exist parameter values for which the converse holds. The key point is that by delaying the second firm's switch to FDI, an increase in imitation risk can increase the value of being first to invest, thereby increasing the equilibrium probability of FDI. JEL Classification: F23, F12, L13

Incitation à l'investissement direct à étranger quand il y a imitation. Les auteurs étudient l'équilibre de stratégies mixtes symétriques dans un modèle dynamique où à chaque instant deux firmes exportatrices choisissent leur probabilité d'investissement direct à étranger. L'investissement direct à l'étranger de la première firme engendre des effets de retombée qui réduisent le coûts pour la seconde et engendre un effet d'imitation au niveau local, ce qui a pour effet d'augmenter le degré de concurrence. Alors que l'accroissement du risque d'imitation réduit la probabilité d'investissement direct à l'étranger, il existe des valeurs des paramètres pour lesquels c'est l'inverse qui se produit. Le point central est que, en faisant en sorte de reporter le recours à l'investissement direct à l'étranger par la seconde firme, un accroissement du risque d'imitation peut accroître l'avantage d'avoir été le premier à investir à l'étranger et donc accroître la probabilité d'équilibre d'un investissement direct à l'étranger.

1. Introduction

During the early 1980s there began a worldwide trend of liberalization of national policies towards inward foreign direct investment (FDI). This trend accelerated

We thank Bill Ethier, Amy Glass, Hideo Konishi, Nikos Vettas, seminar participants at the Midwest International Trade Meetings at Northwestern University, spring 1997, and especially two anonymous referees of this journal for very helpful comments. All errors are our own. Email: plin@ln.edu.hk

* This chapter was originally appeared in *Canadian Journal of Economics* **32**, 1275–1298.

further in the 1990s and manifested itself most starkly in the policies adopted by formerly communist economies such as Russia and China.[1] This remarkable shift in the policy environment has created new profit opportunities for firms from industrialized countries that have gained access to hitherto closed markets and to many cheap locations of production for the first time. The virtual lack of enforcement of intellectual property rights (IPR) in many newly liberalizing countries, however, implies that FDI into such countries may increase the risk of imitation relative to exporting.[2]

Although initial investors will internalize their own losses from imitation that may result from FDI, they will ignore the adverse consequences of their FDI decision for subsequent investors. In other words, if FDI *facilitates* local imitation, there exists a negative externality between initial investors and subsequent ones. However, since firms from industrialized countries have little experience in operating in many newly liberalized countries and because FDI is a complex undertaking, firms investing abroad will learn from the successes and failures of other firms that have made similar decisions before them. Thus, the negative externality due to imitation is counterbalanced by a positive externality that originates from such learning effects. Our main goal in this paper is to explore how the presence of these two types of externalities (from early investors to subsequent ones) influences the incentives for FDI when investors are fully aware of their existence.

Building on a companion paper (Lin and Saggi 1998), we construct a dynamic model, in which at each instant two exporting firms non-cooperatively choose their probability of FDI into a foreign market.[3] Our basic model (in section 2) abstracts from the possibility of imitation and focuses on cost-lowering externalities that the first firm's FDI (called the leader) generates for the second firm (called the follower).[4] These externalities clearly generate an incentive to delay FDI. Each firm also faces two additional incentives, however, that, coupled with the preceding incentive, generate a trade-off between exporting and FDI. First, given that its rival exports, each firm's stand-alone incentive for FDI is the gain in value that accrues because of a lower marginal cost of production in the foreign market (much like the case in Horstmann and Markusen 1992).[5] Second, if its rival switches to FDI, each firm has an incentive to switch as well, in order to eliminate the competitive disadvantage it suffers because of the increased efficiency of its competitor; we call

1 Of the 102 new legislative measures adopted in 57 countries during 1993, as many as 101 were in the direction of greater liberalization towards inward FDI (see UNCTAD, 1995).

2 Mansfield (1994) reports findings from a survey of executives of multinational firms, who clearly state that the strength of local IPR protection has a significant impact on their decision to set up manufacturing units in a foreign country. More anecdotal evidence is also available. See the article in *Business Week* (1996), which provides details of the experience in China of Chrysler, whose executives were shocked to discover illegal clones of Jeep Cherokees being manufactured a few miles from their own plant.

3 We construct a model of oligopoly because, as is well known, multinational firms are found predominantly in oligopolistic industries (see Markusen 1995).

4 This section of the paper is based on a modified version of the model in Lin and Saggi (1998). In that paper, we focus solely on the positive externality between firms.

5 The existence of tariff/transportation costs or lower wages in the host country could be the source of this incentive.

this the competitive incentive for FDI. Clearly, the stand-alone incentive is what pushes the leader towards FDI, while the competitive incentive accomplishes the same task for the follower.

In section 3 we examine the more general model, in which, in addition to the cost-lowering spillovers present in the basic model, FDI also facilities imitation in the foreign economy. We explore two different formulations of imitation. In our first formulation, imitation is assumed to occur after a fixed lag following the leader's FDI. In our second formulation, we assume that imitation follows a Poisson process: at any time t, conditional on no imitation thus far, firms face a constant risk of imitation.[6] A natural presumption is that the later imitation takes place (in certain or expected time), the more likely is FDI. While this view is supported by our model, there also exist parameter values for which faster imitation may make FDI more likely. The intuition for this result is that by delaying FDI on the part of the follower, faster imitation can make FDI more attractive for the leader. Hence, both firms may find it in their interest to be the leader if the gain in value obtained due to a delay in FDI by the follower outweighs the direct loss incurred by stiffer competition generated by imitation.[7]

In past literature the only work in which the issue of optimal timing of FDI is considered is Buckley and Casson (1981), who examine a monopolist's switch from exporting to licensing to FDI.[8] While there is an extensive literature on the effect of imitation on innovation (see Grossman and Helpman 1994), the interaction of FDI and imitation has only recently begun to receive attention (Ethier and Markusen 1996; Glass and Saggi 1998, and 1999).[9] Typically, however, the issue has been examined under the assumption of monopoly (with free entry into R&D). To the best of our knowledge, ours is the only dynamic analysis of the incentives for FDI in a oligopoly when FDI spurs local imitation. Thus, our model highlights strategic considerations absent in past work.

The paper is organized as follows. In section 2 we present a benchmark model that studies incentives for FDI when only positive spillovers (the learning effect) are present. In section 3 we present the more general model in which FDI leads to imitation. In section 4 we conclude. All proofs are collected in the appendix.

2. Basic model

Time is continuous and is indexed by $t \in [0, \infty)$. There are two identical firms (currently exporting to a foreign market) who are faced with the decision of FDI

6 While our second formulation is the one more commonly adopted in the literature on imitation, the advantage of the first formulation is that it allows analytical results. Our strategy is to derive analytical results under the first formulation and demonstrate their robustness for the second formulation.

7 As a referee has pointed out, although we develop our results in the context of FDI, they would also be valid in a more general investment model.

8 Horstmann and Markusen (1987) also construct a dynamic model where multinational firms choose the timing of their FDI. In their model, however, FDI is undertaken to deter local entry.

9 An early paper by Findlay (1978) discusses 'contagion' effects from FDI, but they are exogenous in his model.

into that market. The marginal cost of supplying the foreign market is lower if production is undertaken abroad. This could be either because wages are lower abroad or because exporters must incur tariff and/or transportation costs. Let π_{jk} denote a firm's flow profits when it serves the foreign market by mode j, given that its rival adopts mode k, where j, $k = E$ (Exporting) or F (FDI). Since the firm that switches to FDI first enjoys a lower marginal cost of production, it immediately follows that $\pi_{FE} > \text{Max}\,\{\pi_{EE}, \pi_{FF}\}$ and $\text{Min}\,\{\pi_{FF}, \pi_{EE}\} > \pi_{EF}$.

Denote firm i's switching time by t_i, $0 \leqq t_i < \infty$, $i = 1, 2$. FDI involves a fixed cost I_i where

$$I_i = \left\{ \begin{matrix} I & \text{if } t_i \leqq t_j \\ Ie^{-\gamma(t_i - t_j)} & \text{if } t_i > t_j \end{matrix} \right\}. \tag{1}$$

That is, if firm i switches to FDI before firm j, then it pays a fixed cost I. If, however, it switches later than firm j then it pays a lower fixed cost $Ie^{-\gamma(t_i - t_j)}$, where $\gamma > 0$ captures the positive externalities enjoyed by the firm i if it switches to FDI later than firm j.[10]

Given that its rival continues to export, each firm has a stand-alone incentive to switch to FDI, since this switch increases flow profits by $\pi_{FE} - \pi_{EE}$. FDI by one firm, however, puts at a disadvantage the other (exporting) firm, which sees its rival's marginal cost decline. The desire to eliminate this disadvantage gives rise to what we call the competitive incentive for FDI (it equals $\Delta \equiv \pi_{FF} - \pi_{EF}$). The competitive incentive is counterbalanced, by the positive spillovers parametrized by γ: once one firm switches to FDI, the second firm's investment cost falls over time. These positive spillovers generate an incentive to delay FDI.

2.1. Preliminary analysis

At each point in time, the two firms simultaneously and independently decide whether or not to switch to FDI. If they both switch to FDI simultaneously, then neither enjoys any cost-lowering spillovers. If one firm switches to FDI at time t, whereas the other continues to export, then at time $t + dt$, the other firm faces a simple decision problem: it switches to FDI just when the marginal benefit of further delay is exactly offset by the corresponding marginal cost (see below). If both firms choose to export, they face the same decision at the next instant.

Let p_i denote the probability that firm i switches to FDI at time t, conditional on no FDI by either firm yet.[11] Since both firms are identical ex ante, we restrict attention to the symmetric mixed-strategy equilibrium where $p_i = p$.

10 A similar formulation can be found in the literature on technology adoption (Reinganum 1981a,b; Fudenberg and Tirole 1985). In that literature, however, the cost of adopting a new technology declines *exogenously* over time so that there are no positive externalities from the first adopter to subsequent one's.

11 Since the cost of switching to FDI for a firm starts to decline with time *only after its rival switches* to FDI, firms face a stationary environment in our model: as long as both firms continue to export, they both face the same decision problem at each instant. Therefore, we proceed by considering the stationary equilibrium in which p is constant over time.

Call the first firm to switch to FDI 'the leader' and the second to switch to FDI 'the follower.' First, consider the follower's problem, given that the leader switches to FDI at time $t = 0$. Let $V_F(0, t_F)$ denote lifetime profits of the follower if it switches to FDI at some t_F. Then,

$$V_F(0, t_F) = (1 - e^{-\rho t_F})\frac{\pi_{EF}}{\rho} + e^{-\rho t_F}\frac{\pi_{FF}}{\rho} - Ie^{-(\rho+\gamma)t_F}, \tag{2}$$

where ρ is the discount rate. It follows that

$$\frac{\partial V_F}{\partial t_F} = -e^{-\rho t_F}[\Delta - I(\rho+\gamma)e^{-\gamma t_F}], \tag{3}$$

where $\Delta \equiv \pi_{FF} - \pi_{EF}$ equals the follower's competitive incentive for FDI. We make the following assumption throughout the paper:

ASSUMPTION 1. $I\rho < \Delta < I(\rho+\gamma)$.

If $\Delta \geqq I(\rho+\gamma)$, the follower opts for FDI at time $t = 0$ because the spillovers (γ) are not strong enough relative to the competitive incentive (Δ) to justify any delay in FDI. The first part of the assumption ($I\rho < \Delta$) guarantees that simultaneous FDI in not unprofitable.

Setting $\partial V_F/\partial t_F = 0$ yields the follower's optimal switching time t^*,

$$t^* = \frac{1}{\gamma}\ln\left[\frac{(\rho+\gamma)I}{\Delta}\right]. \tag{4}$$

Given that the follower enters at time t^*, its payoff equals

$$V_F \equiv (1 - e^{-\rho t^*})\frac{\pi_{EF}}{\rho} + e^{-\rho t^*}\frac{\pi_{FF}}{\rho} - Ie^{-(\rho+\gamma)t^*}, \tag{5}$$

whereas the leader's payoff equals

$$V_L \equiv (1 - e^{-\rho t^*})\frac{\pi_{FE}}{\rho} + e^{-\rho t^*}\frac{\pi_{FF}}{\rho} - I. \tag{6}$$

If both firms switch to FDI at time $t = 0$, each firm receives

$$V \equiv \frac{\pi_{FF}}{\rho} - I. \tag{7}$$

PROPOSITION 1. *Under Assumption 1, the following hold:*

(i) The leader's payoff exceeds that of the follower ($V_L > V_F$);

(ii) The optimal switching time t^* increases with I, decreases with Δ. Furthermore, it increases with γ when γ is relatively small while it decreases with γ when it is relatively large; and

(iii) In the symmetric mixed-strategy equilibrium, the probability of FDI is given by

$$p^* = \frac{V_L - V_F}{V_L - V}. \quad (8)$$

Part (i) of proposition 1 tells us that although the leader incurs a bigger fixed cost than the follower, the higher flow profits received by the leader prior to the follower's switching are big enough for it to enjoy a higher payoff. The properties of the optimal switching time reported in part (ii) are also not hard to understand. The higher the fixed cost, or the weaker the competitive incentive, the later the follower switches to FDI. The effect of γ on t^* is understood as follows. As γ increases, delaying FDI becomes more attractive, since costs of FDI decline with γ. This effect is not obtained indefinitely, because a bigger γ also implies that the follower can achieve a given reduction in fixed cost in a shorter time period. When γ is large, the latter effect dominates, leading to faster FDI on the follower's part. The proof of proposition 1 is based on arguments presented in Lin and Saggi (1998); here, we simply present the derivation of part (iii) of the proposition.

Consider any time t. Recall that firm i's probability of FDI, conditional on no FDI by either firm yet, is given by $p_i = p$. With probability p^2, both firms switch to FDI at t. In this case, each firm's payoff seen from time t is given by V in equation (7). With probability $p(1-p)$ one firm becomes the leader, whereas the other becomes the follower, in which case the follower switches to FDI at time $t + t^*$, where t^* is given by equation (4). Along this path, the leader receives V_L and the follower receives V_F. With probability $(1-p)^2$, neither firm does FDI at t, in which event they face the same game at time $t + dt$. Let V_0 denote the value of playing this stationary game for each firm.

Given that the rival firm switches to FDI at time t with probability p, a firm collects $pV + (1-p)V_L$ if it, too, adopts FDI, whereas it collects $pV_F + (1-p)V_0$ if it continues to export. A firm is indifferent between the two options if and only if $pV + (1-p)V_L = pV_F + (1-p)V_0$. Solving this indifference equation for p, we get

$$p = \frac{V_L - V_0}{V_L - V_0 + V_F - V}. \quad (9)$$

Furthermore, if both firms switch to FDI with probability p, then V_0, by definition, must satisfy the following equation:

$$V_0 = p^2 V + (1-p)^2 V_0 + p(1-p)(V_L + V_F). \quad (10)$$

Solving equations (9) and (10) simultaneously yields the equilibrium probability p as given in proposition one.[12]

In addition to the symmetric equilibrium found above, there are also asymmetric equilibria in this model. In particular, there exist equilibria in which one firm

12 Since $V < V_F$ by the definition of V_F, it follows that $0 < p^* < 1$.

switches to FDI at time 0 (and collects V_L) with probability 1, while the other does so with probability 0. Of course, the second firm switches to FDI at time t^* and collects V_F.

Before turning to the general model with imitation, we present some comparative properties of the equilibrium, since they highlight an effect that plays an important role in the more general model. Consider the effect of a change in the fixed cost on the leader's payoff:

$$\frac{dV_L}{dI} = (\pi_{FE} - \pi_{FF})e^{-\rho t^*}\frac{dt^*}{dI} - 1. \tag{11}$$

The negative effect of an increase in I on V_L is obvious. A more subtle effect is that a higher I also implies a higher t^*: the follower chooses to export for a longer time period when faced with a bigger fixed cost ($dt^*/dI > 0$). This *delay effect* confers an indirect benefit upon the leader, since the follower suffers a higher marginal cost under exporting.[13]

In the next section, we study how the possibility of imitation affects incentives for FDI. We find that the main insight provided by the basic model – factors that delay FDI by the follower may benefit the leader, even though they impose a direct cost on the leader – proves robust in the two imitation models considered below.

3. FDI under imitation

In this section, we introduce imitation into our basic model by assuming that FDI by a firm makes imitation by local producers possible. Successful imitation reduces flow profits of the two foreign firms from π_{jk} to π'_{jk}, where $\pi'_{jk} < \pi_{jk}$ for all j and k. As in the basic model, we define the competitive incentive for FDI post imitation as follows

$$\Delta' \equiv \pi'_{FF} - \pi'_{EF}.$$

In what follows, we will consider only the case that $\Delta > \Delta'$, that is, successful imitation weakens the competitive incentive for FDI.[14]

We consider two different formulations of imitation, one in which imitation is a certain event and another in which it is uncertain. Both formulations share the assumption that so long as the two firms continue to export, imitation is infeasible; this is the simplest way to capture the idea that FDI increases the risk of imitation relative to exporting.[15]

13 A similar result applies with respect to γ: the value of being the leader increases with γ if and only if an increase in γ delays switching time by the follower ($dt^*/d\gamma > 0$).

14 An almost equivalent assumption is widely employed in the industrial organization literature: the gain to a firm from a reduction in its cost decreases if its rival becomes more efficient. See, for instance, Reinganum (1981b).

15 This treatment of imitation reflects the optimism with which many developing countries view FDI; they hope to encourage technology transfer to local firms by encouraging investment from technologically advanced multinational firms. Such technology spillovers may occur because FDI lowers costs of imitation by allowing local firms to spy on foreign technology more easily, or by providing them with the opportunity of hiring away workers trained by the multinationals.

Our first formulation posits that if the leader does FDI at time t, then imitation occurs with certainty at time $t+T$. In our second formulation, imitation is assumed to follow a memoryless Poisson process with the parameter $\mu > 0$. The advantage of the first formulation is that it is simple and allows us to analytically isolate the affect of imitation on incentives for FDI.

In both models, imitation reduces the competitive incentive for FDI and thus delays the follower's switch to FDI. An immediate implication of this delay is that the leader derives an indirect benefit from the presence of imitation. As a result, the benefit of being the first to conduct FDI may be greater in the presence of imitation than in its absence. In the following two sections, we show that due to the delay effect, for some parameter values imitation can increase both the payoff of the leader as well as the equilibrium probability of FDI.

Note that the derivations of the equilibrium probability of entry in the previous section do not depend on whether or not imitation is feasible. Thus, the formula obtained there, namely, $p = (V_L - V_F)/(V_L - V)$ continues to apply in the following sections.

3.1. Certain imitation

Suppose that, upon FDI by the leader at time t, imitation occurs with certainty at time $t + T$. When making their FDI decisions, both firms are fully aware that imitation follows the leader's FDI with surety after time lag T. While the formula for the equilibrium probability of FDI continues to apply in the presence of imitation, the payoffs V_L, V_F, and V are functions of the imitation lag T and need to be re-derived.

Suppose that the leader switches to FDI at time 0, and consider the follower's decision problem. Since imitation occurs with certainty at time T, the follower has two options: switch to FDI either before imitation occurs or after. If it switches before imitation occurs, namely, at any time $t \leqq T$, its payoff equals

$$V_F^-(t,T) \equiv (1 - e^{-\rho t})\frac{\pi_{EF}}{\rho} + (e^{-\rho t} - e^{-\rho T})\frac{\pi_{FF}}{\rho} + e^{-\rho T}\frac{\pi'_{FF}}{\rho} - Ie^{-(\rho+\gamma)t}. \tag{12}$$

If, instead, it switches at time $t > T$, its payoff equals

$$V_F^+(t,T) \equiv (1 - e^{-\rho tT})\frac{\pi_{EF}}{\rho} + (e^{-\rho T} - e^{-\rho t})\frac{\pi'_{EF}}{\rho} + e^{-\rho t}\frac{\pi'_{FF}}{\rho} - Ie^{-(\rho+\gamma)t}. \tag{13}$$

We know that in the absence of imitation the follower switches to FDI at time t^*, where t^* is given in equation (4). Suppose, for the moment, that imitation occurs as soon as the leader switches to FDI (i.e., $T = 0$). In this case, the follower's optimal switching time equals

$$t' = \frac{1}{\gamma}\ln\left[\frac{(\rho+\gamma)I}{\Delta'}\right]. \tag{14}$$

Note that, since $\Delta > \Delta'$, then $t' > t^*$.

What is the follower's optimal switching time when $T > 0$? According to the following lemma, if imitation occurs relatively late (T is large), then the follower ignores the presence of imitation and switches to FDI at time t^*, and if imitation occurs relatively early (T is small), then it behaves as if it occurs immediately after the leader's FDI and itself switches to FDI at time t'.

LEMMA 1. *Suppose that the leader switches to FDI at time* 0. *There exists* $\hat{T} \in (t^*, t')$ *such that the follower's optimal switching time is given by*

$$t_F(T) = \left\{ \begin{matrix} t' \text{ if } T \leqq \hat{T} \\ t^* \text{ if } T > \hat{T} \end{matrix} \right\}.$$

The intuition for this result is as follows. Suppose the leader does FDI at $t = 0$ and imitation were to happen quite soon in the future. Under this situation, the competitive incentive facing the follower equals Δ for only a short time (i.e., till imitation happens) and post imitation it drops to $\Delta' < \Delta$. Consequently, he acts as if the gain in flow profits that FDI brings equals only Δ'. A similar intuition applies to the case where imitation happens after a significant lag following the leader's FDI. This discontinuity in the follower's response arises because, whereas the existence of future imitation lowers the lifetime payoff of the follower, it does not affect the marginal trade-off facing the follower till it is actually realized.

Having characterized the follower's decision, we can easily derive the values of $V_L(T)$, $V_F(T)$ and $V(T)$ (see appendix A). We can now analyse the stationary equilibrium of the game under imitation. In the next proposition the way the probability of FDI depends on the imitation lag T is stated.

PROPOSITION 2. *The equilibrium probability of FDI $p(T)$ has the following properties:*

(i) $p(T)$ is continuous and strictly increases in the imitation lag T for $T \leqq \hat{T}$;
(ii) $p(T) = \bar{p}$ (a constant) for $T > \hat{T}$; and
(iii) $p(\hat{T}) > \bar{p}$

According to the above proposition, when T (the imitation lag) is below $\hat{T}$, the probability of FDI decreases as the imitation lag decreases. For $T > \hat{T}$, however, the equilibrium probability of FDI is unaffected by a change in T.[16] But when T drops just below $\hat{T}$, FDI is more likely to happen, that is, $p(T) > \bar{p}$, so that, for a range of T, a decrease in the imitation lag increases the likelihood of FDI. The intuition for this result follows from lemma 2. If $T \leqq \hat{T}$, that is, imitation happens relatively quickly, the follower postpones its FDI to t' while if $T > \hat{T}$ the follower essentially ignores the presence of imitation and switches to FDI at time t^*. Increased competition due to imitation directly lowers the payoff of both the follower and the leader. In addition to this direct loss, however, the leader

16 For $T > \hat{T}$, a change in T does affects the payoffs V_L, V_F, and V, though it does not affect the follower's FDI time. But these values change in such a way that the equilibrium probability is unaffected.

also enjoys an indirect benefit if imitation occurs before $\hat{T}$, since in this situation the follower delays FDI from t^* to t'. Consequently, if we compare two possible imitation times $\hat{T}-\epsilon$ and $\hat{T}+\epsilon$, then the direct loss that the leader suffers under $\hat{T}-\epsilon$ compared with $\hat{T}+\epsilon$ is small, whereas the indirect benefit that it enjoys because of the delay in the follower's FDI is large. Thus, there is a *discrete* increase in the payoff of the leader if the imitation lag is reduced from $\hat{T}+\epsilon$ to $\hat{T}-\epsilon$, whereas both payoffs V and V_L change by a small amount (for ϵ small enough, this change is inconsequential). Since $p(T) = (V_L(T) - V_F(T))/(V_L(T) - V(T))$ and the numerator increases to a greater extent than the denominator, the equilibrium probability ends up increasing when T falls slightly below $\hat{T}$.

Proposition 2 highlights the basic insight of the model we want to emphasize: while the occurrence of imitation reduces flow profits in the product market, the postponement of FDI by the follower may benefit the leader so much that each firm's preference to be the leader instead of the follower may become stronger. As both firms try to be the leader instead of the follower, the probability of FDI increases in equilibrium. In the next section, we show that a result in the spirit of proposition two can also be obtained under our second formulation of imitation.[17]

3.2. *Uncertain imitation*

Suppose imitation follows a memoryless Poisson process with the parameter $\mu > 0$ so that the probability that imitation occurs by time t is $1 - e^{-\mu t}$, given that FDI by some firm has already been undertaken at time $t = 0$. As usual, we first consider the problem facing the follower, given that the leader has already switched to FDI. We then derive the payoff of the leader, the payoff of the follower, and each firm's payoff under simultaneous FDI. Based on these calculations, the equilibrium probability of FDI can be derived as before.

3.2.1. The follower's switching decision

In contrast to the case where there is no risk of imitation, the follower's optimal switching time here is a random variable. If imitation occurs at time $t = 0$, the follower does FDI at time t' as defined in equation (14). As time passes, what should the follower do at any arbitrary time t if imitation has not occurred by then? Should it switch to FDI at time t or should it continue to wait? As we show next, the follower waits till some point in time, denoted as $t^*(\mu)$, which is smaller than t', and then switches to FDI at that time if imitation has not yet occurred. Thus, the follower's optimal switching time is either t' or $t^*(\mu)$, depending on whether or not imitation has occurred by time $t^*(\mu)$.

We next determine the value of $t^*(\mu)$, where $t^*(0)$ equals t^*, the follower's optimal switching time given by equation (4). First, note that since imitation reduces the competitive incentive for FDI (from Δ to Δ'), the follower will never do FDI prior to $t^*(0)$; that is, $t^*(\mu) \geqq t^*(0)$. Consider any time $t \geqq t^*(0)$. If imitation has not occurred by time t, the follower must balance the value of doing FDI against

17 We thank an anonymous referee for raising this issue and for suggesting the model considered next.

the value of waiting. Given that the leader has already switched to FDI, the value of doing FDI seen at time t equals

$$V_f(t,\mu) = \frac{\pi_{FF} + \mu\pi'_{FF}/\rho}{\rho + \mu} - Ie^{-\gamma t}.$$

The above equation is understood as follows. FDI at time t entails the fixed cost $Ie^{-\gamma t}$ and brings flow profits π_{FF}. If imitation occurs at that instant, the follower collects flow profits π'_{FF} forever.[18]

Next, we derive the value of waiting at time t. Define $H(t)$ as the follower's total payoff from time t conditional on the occurrence of imitation during the interval $(t, t+dt)$

$$H(t) = \frac{\pi'_{EF}}{\rho} + e^{-\rho(t'-t)}\frac{(\pi'_{FF} - \pi'_{EF})}{\rho} - Ie^{-\gamma t'}e^{-\rho(t'-t)}.$$

The payoff $H(t)$ is interpreted as follows. In the case of imitation, the follower's optimal FDI time equals t'. Till time t', the follower continues to export and it receives flow profits π'_{EF}. At time t', it switches to FDI by incurring the fixed cost $Ie^{-\gamma t'}e^{-\rho(t'-t)}$ and its flow profits jump to π'_{FF}.

Using $H(t)$, we next define $V_w(t,\mu)$ as the payoff from waiting. Since the flow payoff from waiting equals the flow profits π_{EF} plus the expected 'capital loss' suffered by the follower in case imitation occurs, $V_w(t,\mu)$ must satisfy the following equation

$$\rho V_w(t,\mu) = \pi_{EF} + \mu[H(t) - V_w(t,\mu)].$$

From the above equation, we have

$$V_w(t,\mu) = \frac{\pi_{EF} + \mu H(t)}{\rho + \mu},$$

which has a structure similar to the payoff of doing FDI, V_f, derived earlier, and it can be interpreted similarly.

In addition to the decline in the fixed cost of FDI, waiting here may also be beneficial for the follower, since it wants to avoid switching FDI at the wrong time: if imitation occurs during waiting, the follower will know with certainty that it should switch to FDI at time t'. On the other hand, by switching immediately to FDI at time t, and thus collecting V_f, the follower loses this option. Of course, the follower will not wait indefinitely. In particular, if $t > t'$, the follower has no incentive to wait any longer; Thus, it does FDI immediately, receiving the payoff $V_f(t,\mu)$. $V_w(t,\mu)$ therefore is meaningfully defined only for $t \in [t^*(0), t']$. For t in

18 As is standard in these models, the imitation parameter increases the effective discount rate (which becomes $\rho + \mu$ instead of ρ), since the flow profits prior to imitation accrue only till imitation arrives.

this range, the follower switches to FDI at time t iff $V_f(t,\mu) \geqq V_w(t,\mu)$. Let $t^*(\mu)$ be defined by $V_w(t^*,\mu) = V_f(t^*,\mu)$:

$$\pi_{EF} + \mu\left(\frac{\pi'_{EF}}{\rho} + \left[e^{-\rho t'}\frac{(\pi'_{FF} - \pi'_{EF})}{\rho} - Ie^{-(\rho+\gamma)t'}\right]e^{\rho t^*(\mu)}\right)$$
$$= \pi_{FF} + \mu\frac{\pi'_{FF}}{\rho} - (\rho+\mu)Ie^{-\gamma t^*(\mu)}. \tag{15}$$

Using the above definition of $t^*(\mu)$, we state the follower's optimal decision rule in the following proposition.

PROPOSITION 3. *There exists a threshold risk of imitation μ, $\bar{\mu} > 0$, such that*
(i) for $\mu \leqq \bar{\mu}$, the follower switches to FDI at $t^*(0)$ given that there is no imitation by this time; otherwise, it switches at t'; and
(ii) for $\mu > \bar{\mu}$, the follower switches to FDI at time $t^*(\mu)$ where $t^*(\mu)$ is defined uniquely by the equation $V_w(t^*,\mu) = V_f(t^*,\mu)$ given that there is no imitation by this time. Otherwise, it switches at time t'. Moreover, $t^*(\mu) \in (t^*(0), t')$ and increases with μ.

The above proposition says that for low levels of imitation risk ($\mu \leqq \bar{\mu}$), waiting is not yet attractive enough, so the firm never waits beyond $t^*(0)$, the optimal switching time in the absence of imitation.[19] When $\mu > \bar{\mu}$, the follower's optimal switching time, $t^*(\mu)$, conditional on no imitation yet, is illustrated in figure 1. For $t < t^*(\mu)$, waiting is more valuable than switching, so the follower continues to wait beyond $t^*(0)$. For $t > t^*(\mu)$, the value of waiting diminishes as time approaches t', beyond which waiting is no longer attractive. Therefore, the follower switches to FDI at exactly $t = t^*(\mu)$ if no imitation has occurred by then. The reason that $t^*(\mu)$ increases in μ is easy to understand. As the risk of imitation increases, the follower has a stronger incentive to avoid switching to FDI at the wrong time and, as a result, the value of waiting increases.

According to proposition 3, the follower's expected FDI time equals

$$(1 - e^{-\mu t^*(\mu)})t' + e^{-\mu t^*(\mu)}t^*(\mu) = t' - [t' - t^*(\mu)]e^{-\mu t^*(\mu)}. \tag{16}$$

In other words, with probability $(1 - e^{-\mu t^*(\mu)})$ imitation occurs before $t^*(\mu)$, in which case the follower switches to FDI at time t'; and with probability $e^{-\mu t^*(\mu)}$, imitation does not occur before $t^*(\mu)$, in which case it switches to FDI at $t^*(\mu)$. The remark below emphasizes the delay effect that stems from the properties of $t^*(\mu)$.

19 In fact, for $\mu < \bar{\mu}$, $V_f(t,\mu) > V_w(t,\mu)$ for all $t \in [t^*(0), t']$. The critical risk level $\bar{\mu}$ is defined by $V_f(t^*(0),\mu) = V_w(t^*(0),\mu)$.

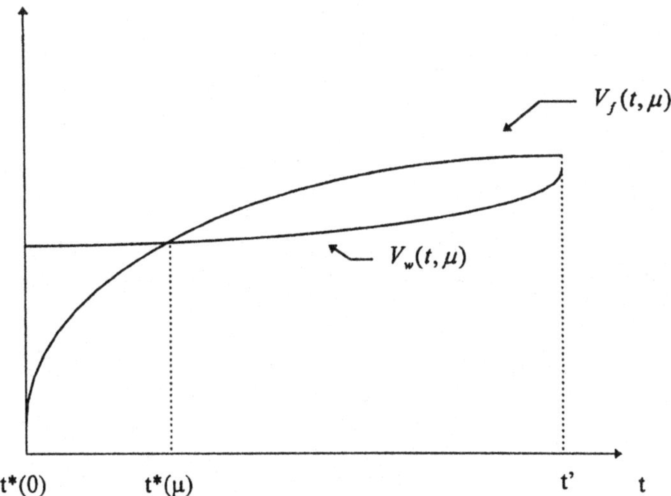

FIGURE 1 The follower's optimal switching time $t^*(\mu)$

Remark 1 (the delay effect).
(i) Since $t^*(\mu)$ increases with μ, the expected FDI time by the follower is an increasing function of μ. An increase in μ affects the follower's optimal FDI time through two different channels. First, $t^*(\mu)$ increases in μ. Second, a larger μ means that imitation is more likely to occur prior to $t^*(\mu)$, and thus it is more likely that the follower switches to FDI at t' instead of $t^*(\mu)$.[20]
(ii) Also note that from equation (16), the follower's expected FDI time is concave in the risk of imitation. Thus, a given increase in μ causes a larger delay by the follower for small values of μ than for large values of μ. (This feature is important in understanding the examples in section 3.2.3, below).

Given the follower's strategy, we are now in a position to describe equilibrium payoffs.

3.2.2. Equilibrium payoffs
Given that the leader switches to FDI at time 0 and the follower adopts the above optimal strategy, we can calculate the follower's expected payoff. Seen at time 0, the follower's expected switching time is given in equation (16). Thus, the follower's expected switching cost equals

$$EC(\mu) = (1 - e^{-\mu t^*(\mu)}) I e^{-(\gamma+\rho)t'} + e^{-\mu t^*(\mu)} I e^{-(\gamma+\rho)t^*(\mu)}. \tag{17}$$

20 Note that in the simpler imitation model the second channel is absent, since imitation is known to occur with certainty at a particular time.

The follower's payoff seen at time $t = 0$ under the optimal strategy equals

$$V_F(\mu) = \int_0^{t^*(\mu)} e^{-(\mu+\rho)t}[\pi_{EF} + \mu G(t)]dt + \int_{t^*(\mu)}^{\infty} e^{-(\mu+\rho)t}\left[\pi_{FF} + \mu \frac{\pi'_{FF}}{\rho}\right] dt - EC(\mu). \tag{18}$$

In the above formula, $G(t)$ equals the follower's discounted profit stream (gross of fixed cost I) if imitation occurs at time t (in which case it enters at time t'); that is,

$$G(t) = \frac{\pi'_{EF}}{\rho} + e^{-\rho(t'-t)}\frac{(\pi'_{FF} - \pi'_{EF})}{\rho}. \tag{19}$$

Substituting (19) into (18) and simplifying yields

$$V_F(\mu) = V_F^E + e^{-(\mu+\rho)t^*(\mu)}[V_F^F - V_F^E] + [1 - e^{-\mu t^*(\mu)}]\frac{\pi'_{FF} - \pi'_{EF}}{\rho} e^{-\rho t'} - EC(\mu), \tag{20}$$

where

$$V_F^E = \frac{\pi_{EF} + \mu\pi'_{EF}/\rho}{\rho + \mu} \text{ and } V_F^F = \frac{\pi_{FF} + \mu\pi'_{FF}/\rho}{\rho + \mu}$$

In the above expression V_F^E would be the follower's payoff were it to export forever, whereas V_F^F would be its payoff were it to switch to FDI at $t = 0$. The second and the third terms represent the jumps in the follower's payoff caused by the switch to FDI. With probability $e^{-\mu t^*(\mu)}$, imitation does not occur by time $t^*(\mu)$, in which case the follower switches to FDI at time $t^*(\mu)$ and its payoff increases by $V_F^F - V_F^E$. With probability $1 - e^{-\mu t^*(\mu)}$, imitation does occur by time $t^*(\mu)$, in which case it switches to FDI at time t', forgoing exporting profits π'_{EF}/ρ and collecting FDI profits π'_{FF}/ρ from time t' on.

The payoff of the leader seen at time $t = 0$, given the follower's optimal strategy, is given by

$$V_L(\mu) = V_L^E - e^{-(\mu+\rho)t^*(\mu)}[V_L^E - V_L^F] - [1 - e^{-\mu t^*(\mu)}]\frac{\pi'_{FE} - \pi'_{FF}}{\rho} e^{-\rho t'} - I \tag{21}$$

where

$$V_L^E = \frac{\pi_{FE} + \mu\pi'_{FE}/\rho}{\rho + \mu} \text{ and } V_L^F = \frac{\pi_{FF} + \mu\pi'_{FF}/\rho}{\rho + \mu}$$

The term V_L^E denotes the leader's payoff were the follower to export forever, and V_L^F denotes its payoff were the follower to switch to FDI at the same time as the leader. Given the follower's optimal strategy, with probability $e^{-\mu t^*(\mu)}$ the follower switches to FDI at time $t^*(\mu)$, and the leader's payoff drops by $V_L^E - V_L^F$. With probability $1 - e^{-\mu t^*(\mu)}$ imitation occurs by $t^*(\mu)$ and the follower switches to FDI at time t', in which case the payoff of the leader drops by $(\pi'_{FE} - \pi'_{FF})/\rho$ from time t' on.

Finally, if both firms do FDI at the same time, the payoff of each firm seen at that time equals

$$V(\mu) = \frac{\pi_{FF} + \mu\pi'_{FF}/\rho}{\rho + \mu} - I. \tag{22}$$

Along the mixed-strategy equilibrium described in our basic model, the equilibrium probability of FDI, as derived in section 2, equals

$$p(\mu) = \frac{V_L(\mu) - V_F(\mu)}{V_L(\mu) - V(\mu)}.$$

The question we are interested in is the following: how does an increase in μ affect the equilibrium probability of FDI? The answer clearly depends on how an increase in μ affects the values $V_L(\mu)$, $V_F(\mu)$, and $V(\mu)$. First, consider $V_F(\mu)$. An increase in μ effects V_F in three different ways. First, it has the direct effect of decreasing V_F, because flow profits prior to imitation must be discounted by the imitation risk, and flow profits post imitation are lower by assumption. The other two channels work through the effect of μ on the follower's FDI time: as μ increases not only does $t^*(\mu)$ increase, but it also becomes more likely that the follower switches to FDI at t' instead of $t^*(\mu)$. All three effects work in the same direction and the follower unambiguously suffers from an increase in imitation risk. Next consider $V(\mu)$. Since $\pi'_{FF} < \pi_{FF}$, we have $dV(\mu)/d\mu < 0$.

Finally, consider how an increase in μ affects $V_L(\mu)$. As in the previous model of certain imitation, the effect of an increase in μ on $V_L(\mu)$ is ambiguous. The intuition here is similar to that of the previous case: an increase in imitation risk has the direct effect of lowering the payoff of the leader but has the indirect effect of increasing its payoff, since the follower's switch to FDI gets delayed; and the higher μ is, the more likely it is that the follower switches at t' instead of t^*. Thus, the main driving force (the delay effect) behind proposition two operates also in this model. Thus, our earlier results regarding the payoff of the leader as well as the equilibrium probability of FDI (proposition 2) should go through, in principle, even in the case of uncertain imitation. As the preceding derivations indicate, however, the current model is significantly more complicated than the previous one, and further analytical results are virtually impossible.

Therefore, our strategy is to construct numerical examples that demonstrate that a result similar to proposition 2 can be obtained here as well. To that end we consider the special case where $\rho = \gamma$, in which case we can explicitly solve for the follower's switching time $t^*(\mu)$.

3.2.3. Numerical examples and discussion

Equation (15), which determines the value of $t^*(\mu)$, can be rewritten as follows:

$$(\rho+\mu)Ie^{-\gamma t^*(\mu)}+\mu\delta e^{\rho t^*(\mu)}=\Delta-\mu\Delta'/\rho, \tag{23}$$

where

$$\delta=\left[e^{-\rho t'}\frac{\Delta'}{\rho}-Ie^{-(\rho+\gamma)t'}\right].$$

For the special case of $\rho=\gamma$, equation (23) is quadratic and can be solved for $t^*(\mu)$. The relevant solution is given by[21]

$$t^*(\mu)=\frac{1}{\gamma}\ln\left(\frac{(\Delta+\mu\Delta'/\rho)-\sqrt{(\Delta+\mu\Delta'/\rho)^2-4\mu\delta(\mu+\rho)I}}{2\mu\delta}\right).$$

Using the above formula, we provide two numerical examples, below. In the first example, both the equilibrium probability of FDI and the payoff of the leader increase with the risk of imitation for some feasible range of parameter values. In the second example, an increase in the risk of imitation always lowers the equilibrium probability of FDI, though it may benefit the leader over some range.

We adopted the following procedure in constructing these examples. First, we assumed values of γ, ρ, π_{jk}, π'_{jk}, and I and calculated the threshold level of imitation risk $\bar{\mu}$ above which waiting at $t^*(0)$ is optimal for the follower. Next, we calculated the equilibrium values V_L, V_F, V_L, and then the probability of FDI $p(\mu)=(V_L-V_F)/(V_L-V)$. Finally, we plotted V_L and $p(\mu)$ as functions of μ for $\mu>\bar{\mu}$.

Example 1. The following parameter values are assumed: $\gamma=0.1$, $\rho=0.1$, $I=16$, $\pi_{FE}=20$, $\pi'_{FE}=15$, $\pi_{EF}=10$, $\pi'_{EF}=5$, $\pi_{FF}=12$, $\pi'_{FF}=5.2$. For these values, $\bar{\mu}=10/81$. Figure 2 plots V_L and figure 3 plots p. As is clear, V_L increases with μ utill μ reaches a value of about 0.32, and it decreases after. Similarly, p increases till μ increases to 0.18 and decreases after.

Example 2. All parameters are the same as in example 1 except π'_{FF}, which equals 6. So the competitive incentive for FDI (after imitation) equals 1 ($\pi'_{FF}-\pi'_{EF}=6-5$) rather than 0.2. In this case, $\bar{\mu}$ is calculated to be 0.4. Figure 4 plots V_L and figure 5 plots p. Although V_L is not monotonically decreasing in μ, p is strictly decreasing.

There are two driving forces that determine the effect of μ on V_L and p. The first is the direct effect of μ: imitation lowers the flow profits of both firms. The second is the indirect delay effect (see remark 1): imitation benefits the leader by delaying the follower's FDI and thereby causes firms to be more willing to switch to FDI first. The delay effect is weaker in the second example: while the payoff

21 The other solution is larger than t' and thus is irrelevant.

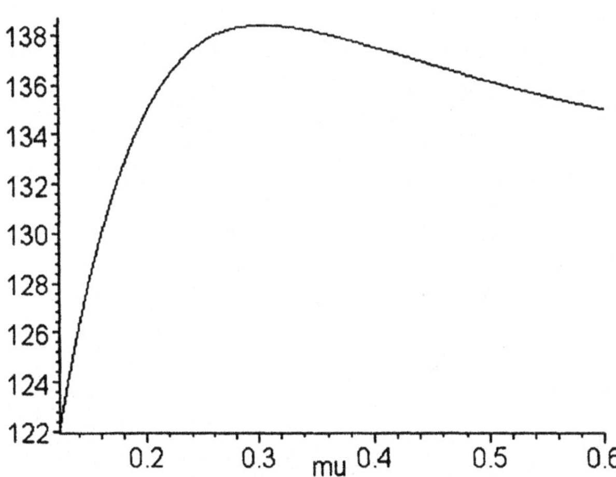

FIGURE 2 The leader's payoff in example 1

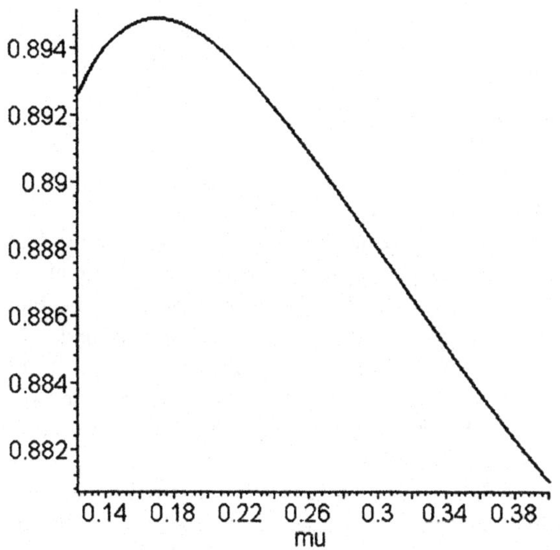

FIGURE 3 The probability of FDI in example 1

of the leader does increase with imitation risk over a small range, the equilibrium probability of FDI always declines for feasible values of μ.

To gain further insight behind the two examples, recall that the expected FDI time of the follower is increasing but concave in μ (remark 1). Thus, while an increase in μ always delays the follower, this delay effect is stronger when μ is

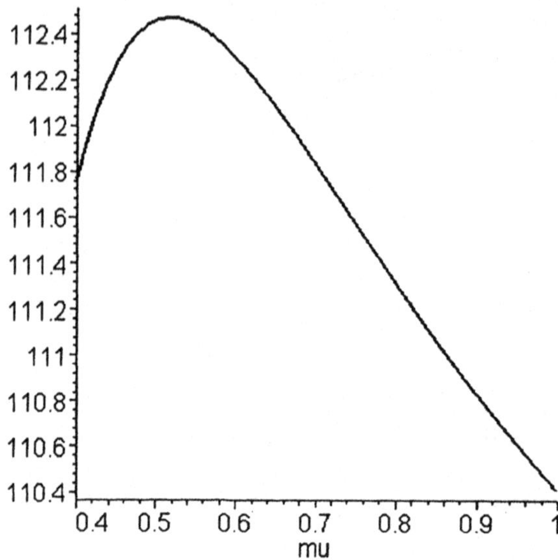

FIGURE 4 The leader's payoff in example 2

small. For higher values of μ, the delay effect is dominated by the direct effect of imitation, so that V_L and p decline with μ.

As we noted before, the competitive incentive for FDI (Δ') is much stronger in example 2 than in example 1. This stronger incentive has two implications. First, the resulting threshold of μ, $\bar{\mu}$, is 0.4 relative to $10/81$ in example 1. Imitation hurts the follower less in the second example, so that a higher level of imitation risk is needed to make waiting at $t^*(0)$ optimal. Thus, the delay effect is applicable to larger values of μ and is weaker in example 2 (owing its concavity). Second, the post-imitation FDI time, t', is much smaller in example 2 than in example 1 (11.6 versus 28). Thus, imitation causes less delay in example 2.[22] Because of these two effects, equilibrium probability of FDI in example 2 does not have the increasing portion it does in example 1, though V_L still does.[23]

Finally, we want to point out another common feature of the examples we have considered. This feature has to do with how imitation affects the flow profits of the follower (i.e., the gap between π_{FF} and π'_{FF}) relative to those of the leader (i.e., the gap between π_{FE} and π'_{FE}). In both examples, imitation hurts the follower more than the leader: $(\pi_{FF} - \pi'_{FF})/\pi_{FF}$ is greater than $(\pi_{FE} - \pi'_{FE})/\pi_{FE}$. Loosely speaking, in such situations imitation greatly discourages the follower's FDI, but it does not hurt the leader as much.

22 Note that $t^*(0)$ is the same in both examples. Also, simulations showed that the expected FDI time in example 2 is almost half that in example 1 for feasible values of μ.

23 If we increase π'_{FF} further, then both the value of the leader and the equilibrium probability of FDI always decline with an increase in imitation risk.

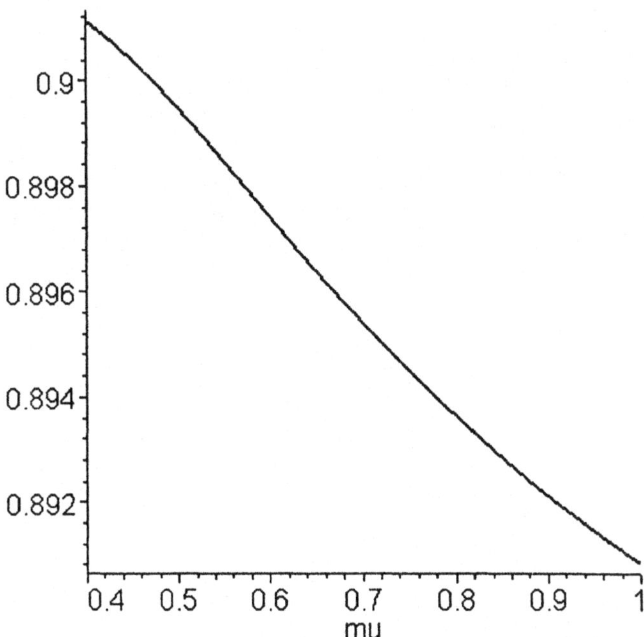

FIGURE 5 Probability of FDI in example 2

Under what circumstances in the real world should we expect imitation to make FDI more likely? In our view, this result is most appealing when the product market competition is such that the first firm to switch to FDI gets a strong foothold in the market, so that imitation in the future hurts it less than it hurts its exporting rival. Such a 'first-mover advantage' may arise if customers are less likely to switch to alternative sellers when the foreign firm is producing locally than when it is exporting to their market.

4. Conclusion

In this paper we explore the incentives for FDI in a duopoly when FDI by one firm generates cost-lowering externalities for the other firm while at the same time runs the risk of fostering local imitation. We argue that there are good reasons to believe that such a model well describes the situation facing firms from industrialized countries that are considering FDI into many newly liberalized economies.

We characterize the symmetric stationary equilibrium of this model and study how the likelihood of FDI varies with the basic parameters of the model. We consider two different formulations of imitation: one in which imitation is assumed to occur with certainty after a lag after the leader's FDI and another in which imitation is assumed to follow a Poisson process. We show that the model has sensible comparative statics and it provides a robust insight that leads to some unconventional results. This central insight is that, in a strategic setting, the faster arrival of imitation (in either of the two imitation models) may actually increase the leader's payoff by delaying the follower's FDI. This effect can be strong enough to lead to the result that, for some parameter values, the faster arrival of imitation actually increases the likelihood of FDI. Models that rely on monopolies or perfect competition in the product market are unable to capture this important element. Since multinationals exist, by and large, in oligopolistic industries, our model provides an insight that could be of value in understanding patterns of FDI in the real world.

Appendix

1. Proof of lemma 1

First, note that

$$\frac{\partial V_F^-(t,T)}{\partial t} = [-\Delta + I(\rho+\gamma)e^{-\gamma t}]e^{-\rho t} \tag{A1}$$

and

$$\frac{\partial V_F^+(t,T)}{\partial t} = [-\Delta' + I(\rho+\gamma)e^{-\gamma t}]e^{-\rho t}. \tag{A2}$$

Consider $T < t^*$. By the definition of t^*, $\Delta = I(\rho+\gamma)e^{-\gamma t^*}$. Thus, it follows that $\Delta < I(\rho+\gamma)e^{-\gamma T}$. This fact, along with equation (24), implies that $V_F^-(t,T)$ is increasing in t when $t \leqq T$ and that the follower's optimal switching time is the solution to $\partial V_F^+(t,T)/\partial t = 0$, which yields $t_F(T) = t'$. Similarly, for $T > t'$, we know by the definition of t' that $\Delta_2' > I(\rho+\gamma)e^{-\gamma T}$. This implies that $V_F^+(t,T)$ is decreasing in t when $t > T$. Thus, $t_F(T)$ is the solution to $\partial V_F^-(t_F,T)/\partial t = 0$, namely, $t_F(T) = t^*$.

Next consider the case $t^* < T < t'$. Since in this case $\Delta > I(\rho+\gamma)e^{-\gamma T} > \Delta'$, it follows that $\partial V^-(T,T)/\partial t < 0$ and $\partial V^+(T,T)/\partial t > 0$. Therefore, the follower's lifetime payoff has two local maxima: one at $t = t^*$ and the other at $t = t'$. Its optimal switching time then depends on the ranking of $V_F^-(t^*,T)$ and $V_F^+(t',T)$. Note that $V_F^-(t^*,T) < V_F^+(t',T)$ when $T = t^*$ (because $V_F^-(t,T)$ increases with t and thus $t = t'$ is the only maximum). Similarly, $V_F^-(t^*,T) > V_F^+(t',T)$ when $T = t'$ (because $V_F^+(t,T)$ decreases in t and thus $t = t^*$ is the only maximum). Therefore, there exists $\hat{T} \in (t^*, t')$ such that $V^-(t^*,\hat{T}) = V^+(t',\hat{T})$. Therefore, $V_F^-(t^*,T) < V_F^+(t',T)$ if $T < \hat{T}$, and $V_F^-(t^*,T) > V_F^+(t',T)$ if $T > \hat{T}$. It then follows that $t_F(T) = t'$ if $t^* < T < \hat{T}$ and $t_F(T) = t'$ if $\hat{T} \leqq T < t'$.[24] ■

24 At $T = \hat{T}$, the follower is indifferent between doing FDI at t^* or at t'. We assume it does so at t'.

2. Proof of proposition 2

We prove this proposition by considering each case separately. First, consider the case where $T \leqq \hat{T}$. In this case, the follower switches to FDI post imitation at time t'. Then,

$$V_F(T) = (1 - e^{-\rho T})\frac{\pi_{EF}}{\rho} + (e^{-\rho T} - e^{-\rho t'})\frac{\pi'_{EF}}{\rho} + e^{-\rho t'}\frac{\pi'_{FF}}{\rho} - Ie^{-(\rho+\gamma)t'}. \tag{A3}$$

Given the follower's optimal response, the leader's payoff, if it switches to FDI time $t = 0$, is given by

$$V_L(T) = (1 - e^{-\rho T})\frac{\pi_{FE}}{\rho} + (e^{-\rho T} - e^{-\rho t'})\frac{\pi'_{FE}}{\rho} + e^{-\rho t'}\frac{\pi'_{FF}}{\rho} - I. \tag{A4}$$

If both firms switch at time 0, each firm's payoff equals

$$V(T) = (1 - e^{-\rho T})\frac{\pi_{FF}}{\rho} + e^{-\rho T}\frac{\pi'_{FF}}{\rho} - I. \tag{A5}$$

Since V_L, V_F, and V all are continuous in T, so is $p(T)$. Next, we show that $p'(T) > 0$.

Simple algebra shows that $p'(T) > 0$ is equivalent to

$$(\pi_{FE} - \pi_{EF} - \pi'_{FE} + \pi'_{EF})(V_L - V) > (\pi_{FE} - \pi_{FF} - \pi'_{FE} + \pi'_{FF})(V_L - V_F).$$

Since $V_L > V_F > V$, the above condition holds if

$$\pi_{FE} - \pi_{EF} - \pi'_{FE} + \pi'_{EF} > \pi_{FE} - \pi_{FF} - \pi'_{FE} + \pi'_{FF},$$

which is nothing but $\Delta > \Delta'$ and therefore holds. Therefore, $p'(T) > 0$ for $T \leqq \hat{T}$. This proves part (i) of the proposition.

Next, consider the case where $T > \hat{T}$. In this case, the follower does FDI before imitation occurs (at time t^*) and its payoff equals

$$V_F(T) = V_F^-(0, t^*) = (1 - e^{-\rho t^*})\frac{\pi_{EF}}{\rho} + (e^{-\rho t^*} - e^{-\rho T})\frac{\pi_{FF}}{\rho} + e^{-\rho T}\frac{\pi'_{FF}}{\rho} - Ie^{-(\rho+\gamma)t^*},$$

whereas the leader's payoff equals

$$V_L(T) = (1 - e^{-\rho t^*})\frac{\pi_{FE}}{\rho} + (e^{-\rho t^*} - e^{-\rho T})\frac{\pi_{FF}}{\rho} + e^{-\rho T}\frac{\pi'_{FF}}{\rho} - I.$$

Finally, if both firms do FDI at time 0, each firm's payoff equals

$$V(T) = (1 - e^{-\rho tT})\frac{\pi_{FF}}{\rho} + e^{-\rho T}\frac{\pi'_{FF}}{\rho} - I.$$

It is obvious that neither $V_L - V_F$ nor $V_L - V$ depends upon T. Therefore, when $T > \hat{T}$, the equilibrium probability of FDI $p(T)$ is independent of T and we denote it by $\bar{p}$. This proves part (ii) of the proposition.

To prove part (iii), note that V is continuous in T for all T. Since $V_F^-(t^*, \hat{T}) = V_F^+(t', \hat{T})$ (see the proof of lemma 1), V_F is also continuous in T for all T. But when T increases from $\hat{T} - \epsilon$ to $\hat{T} + \epsilon$, there is a discrete downward jump in V_L because the follower's switching time changes from t' to t^*. Because $p(T)$ is an increasing function of V_L, a downward jump in V_L implies a downward jump in $p(T)$. This proves that $p(\hat{T}) > \bar{p}$. ■

3. Proof of proposition 3

We first prove a lemma that describes some useful properties of the functions $V_f(t, \mu)$ and $V_w(t, \mu)$.

LEMMA 2. *The functions $V_f(t, \mu)$ and $V_w(t, \mu)$ have the following properties:*

(i) Both $V_f(t, \mu)$ and $V_w(t, \mu)$ increase in t.

(ii) While $V_w(t, \mu)$ is convex in t, $V_f(t, \mu)$ is concave.

(iii) $V_f(t', \mu) > V_w(t', \mu)$ for all $\mu > 0$.

(iv) $V_w(t^*(0), 0) < V_f(t^*(0), 0)$.

Proof of lemma 2. (i) and (ii) Obvious.

(iii) By direct calculation, we have

$$V_f(t', \mu) - V_w(t', \mu) = \frac{\pi_{FF} - \pi_{EF} - \rho I e^{-\gamma t'}}{\rho + \mu},$$

which is positive because $\pi_{FF} - \pi_{EF} > \pi'_{FF} - \pi'_{EF} > \rho I e^{-\gamma t'}$.

(iv) If there is no risk of imitation ($\mu = 0$), then at $t = t^*(0)$,

$$V_w(t^*(0), 0) = \frac{\pi_{EF}}{\rho} \text{ and } V_f(t^*(0), 0) = \frac{\pi_{FF}}{\rho} - Ie^{-\gamma t^*(0)}.$$

By the expression for $t^*(0)$, it follows that $V_w(t^*(0), 0) < V_f(t^*(0), 0)$.

We now prove proposition 3. From part (iii) of lemma 2, we know that $V_f(t', \mu) > V_w(t', \mu)$ for all μ. On the other hand, as $\mu \to \infty$, $V_w(t^*(0), \mu)$ approaches $H(t^*(0))$, which is nothing but the firm's payoff from time $t^*(0)$ on, given that it switches to FDI at time t'. Similarly, as $\mu \to \infty$, $V_f(t^*(0), \mu)$ approaches $\pi'_{FF}/\rho - Ie^{-\gamma t^*(0)}$, which is the firm's payoff from switching to FDI at time $t^*(0)$. By the definition of t', $V_w(t^*(0), \mu)$ is necessarily greater than $V_f(t^*(0), \mu)$ for μ large enough. Thus, there exists a threshold level of imitation risk $\bar{\mu}$ such that for $\mu > \bar{\mu}$,

$$V_w(t^*, \mu) = V_f(t^*, \mu) \text{ and } V_w(t, \mu) > V_f(t, \mu) \text{ iff } t < t^*(\mu)$$

for some $t^*(\mu) \in (t^*(0), t')$. Moreover, since $V_f(t,\mu) - V_w(t,\mu)$ is concave, there are at most two roots to the equation $V_f(t,\mu) - V_w(t,\mu) = 0$. Given this, we know that $t^*(\mu)$ is unique by noticing that $V_f(t,\mu) - V_w(t,\mu) > 0$ at $t = t'$.

Differentiating both sides of the equation $V_w(t^*,\mu) = V_f(t^*,\mu)$ and rearranging terms gives us

$$\frac{dt^*(\mu)}{d\mu} = \frac{\dfrac{\partial V_f}{\partial \mu} - \dfrac{\partial V_w}{\partial \mu}}{\dfrac{\partial V_w}{\partial t} - \dfrac{\partial V_f}{\partial t}}.$$

Since both V_w and V_f are increasing in t and $V_w(t,\mu) > V_f(t,\mu)$ iff $t < t^*(\mu)$, it must be that $\partial V_w/\partial t < \partial V_f/\partial t$ at $t = t^*(\mu)$. Thus, $dt^*(\mu)/d\mu > 0$ iff $\partial V_w/\partial \mu > \partial V_f/\partial \mu$, which we show next.

By the definitions of V_w and V_f, we have

$$V_w - V_f = \frac{\pi_{EF} - \pi_{FF} + \mu(H(t) - \pi'_{FF}/\rho)}{\rho + \mu} + Ie^{-\gamma t}.$$

Therefore,

$$\frac{\partial(V_w - V_f)}{\partial \mu} = \frac{\Delta + \rho(H(t) - \pi'_{FF}/\rho)}{(\rho+\mu)^2}.$$

Since $H(t)$ by definition is the optimal payoff of the follower in the case of imitation, $H(t)$ is greater than the payoff the follower would receive if it does FDI at t, $\pi'_{FF}/\rho - Ie^{-\gamma t}$. Since $\Delta > \rho I$, we have $\Delta + \rho(H(t) - \pi'_{FF}/\rho) > 0$. This proves that $t^*(\mu)$ is an increasing function of μ. ■

References

Buckley, P.J., and M. Casson (1981) 'The optimal timing of foreign direct investment,' *Economic Journal* 91, 75–82

Business Week, (1996) 4 March, 56–64

Ethier, Wilfred J., and James R. Markusen (1996) 'Multinational firms, technology diffusion and trade,' *Journal of International Economics* 41, 1–28

Findlay, Ronald (1978) 'Relative backwardness, direct foreign investment, and the transfer of technology: a simple dynamic model,' *Quarterly Journal of Economics* 92, 1–16

Fudenberg, D., and J. Tirole (1985) 'Preemption and rent equalization in the adoption of new technology,' *Review of Economic Studies* 52, 383–401

Glass, Amy, and Kamal Saggi (1998) 'International technology transfer and the technology gap,' *Journal of Development Economics* 55, 369–98

— (1999) 'Foreign direct investment and the nature of R&D,' *Canadian Journal of Economics* 32, 92–117

Grossman, Gene M., and Elhanan Helpman (1994) 'Technology and trade,' in *The Handbook of International Economics*, Vol. 3, ed. G.M. Grossman and K. Rogoff (New York: Elsevier Science)

Horstmann, Ignatius J., and J.R. Markusen (1987) 'Strategic investments and the development of multinationals,' *International Economic Review* 28, 109–21

— (1992) 'Endogenous market structures in international trade,' *Journal of International Economics* 32, 109–29

Lin, P., and Kamal Saggi (1998) 'Timing of entry under externalities,' Southern Methodist University Working Paper No. 9612

Mansfield, Edwin (1994) 'Intellectual property protection, foreign direct investment, and technology transfer,' International Finance Corporation, Discussion Paper 19

Markusen, James R. (1995) 'The boundaries of multinational enterprises and the theory of international trade,' *Journal of Economic Perspectives* 9, 169–89

Reinganum, J. (1981a) 'On the diffusion of new technology: a game-theoretic approach,' *Review of Economic Studies* 48, 395–406

— (1981b) 'Market structure and the diffusion of new technology,' *Bell Journal of Economics* 12, 618–24

Tirole, J. (1988) *The Theory of Industrial Organization* (Cambridge, MA: MIT Press)

UNCTAD (1995) *World Investment Report* (New York: United Nations)

Chapter 7

Multinational Firms and Technology Transfer*,#

Amy Jocelyn Glass

Texas A&M University, College Station, TX 77843-4228, USA
aglass@econ.tamu.edu

Kamal Saggi

Southern Methodist University, Dallas, TX 75275-0496, USA
ksaggi@mail.smu.edu

Abstract

We construct an oligopoly model in which a multinational firm has a superior technology compared to local firms. Workers employed by the multinational acquire knowledge of its superior technology. The multinational may pay a wage premium to prevent local firms from hiring its workers and thus gaining access to their knowledge. In this setting, the host government has an incentive to attract FDI due to technology transfer to local firms or the wage premium earned by employees of the multinational firm. However, when FDI is particularly attractive to the multinational firm, the host government has an incentive to discourage FDI.

Keywords: Multinational firms; technology transfer; wages

JEL classification: *F*13; *F*23; *J*41; *L*13; *O*14; *O*33; *O*38

I. Introduction

Foreign direct investment (FDI) is one of the most important channels through which technology can be transferred across countries. In a typical year, transactions between parent firms and their subsidiaries in royalties and license fees account for over 80 percent of international technology transactions; see UNCTAD (1992). By encouraging multinationals to establish local production facilities, developing countries hope to generate technology transfer to local firms: the presence of multinational firms may facilitate

*We thank Nancy Chau, Michelle Connolly, Wilfred Ethier, Eric Fisher, Gene Grossman, Eckhard Janeba, Wolfgang Keller, Steve Magee, Jim Markusen, Howard Marvel, Howard Pack, Dann Millimet, Horst Raff, Anthony Venables, Bruce Weinberg, two anonymous referees and participants at the Midwest International Economics meetings, AEA/ASSA meetings, annual congress of the European Economic Association, Duke University, George Washington University, Indiana University, University of Miami, Miami University of Ohio, Southern Illinois University, University of Michigan, University of Texas, Texas A&M University, University of Minho at Braga, University of Paris Sorbonne, the USITC, and the World Bank, for advice and comments.

This chapter was originally appeared in *Scandinavian Journal of Economics* **104**, 495–513.

imitation, as in Glass and Saggi (1999a) or have more general contagion effects, as in Findlay (1978).[1]

However, the role of labor mobility as a channel of technology transfer across firms has not received adequate attention. This channel differs from others because technology moves across firms through the physical movement of workers who have been exposed to the technology. The goal of this paper is to capture the role of labor mobility as a mechanism of technology transfer and examine the implications of this transfer for host country policy toward FDI.

In our model, a source firm decides whether to establish a production facility in a host country (by engaging in FDI). If the source firm undertakes FDI, the host firm it competes with may gain access to the source firm's superior technology by hiring away its workers. Recognizing the attractiveness of its workers to the host firm, the source firm weighs the cost of paying higher wages against the benefit of limiting technology transfer to the host firm.

The source firm may instead choose to produce in a more expensive location where physical separation protects against the spread of its technology to its rivals. Both methods of preventing technology transfer—production elsewhere or paying a wage premium—raise the source firm's costs. Our model identifies the circumstances under which a multinational chooses to pay a wage premium or produce elsewhere to preserve its technological superiority.

We find that the choices made by the source firm commonly clash with the interests of host welfare, providing a motive for an active host government FDI policy. FDI-inducing policies can indeed raise host welfare, and can do so even if technology transfer does *not* result, due to the wage premium paid to prevent technology transfer.[2] On the other hand, banning FDI can raise host welfare if source firms would reap a significant cost reduction through FDI.

Evidence on the mobility of workers from multinationals to host firms is consistent with our model. Labor mobility from multinationals to host firms occurs predominantly in more developed countries, where multinationals do not have as substantial an advantage over host firms. Gershenberg (1987) finds evidence of only minor labor mobility from multinationals to Kenyan firms. Bloom (1992) finds substantial technological transfer in South Korea when production managers left multinationals to join host firms. Pack (1997) reports that in the chemical industry in Taiwan during the mid-1980s, almost

[1] See Pack and Saggi (1997) for further discussion of the role multinationals play in technology diffusion.

[2] Glass and Saggi (1999b) provide a related argument based on general equilibrium effects.

50 percent of all engineers and 63 percent of skilled workers that quit multinationals, left to join local firms.

Evidence documenting that multinationals pay higher wages than host firms is also consistent with our model. These wage differentials are usually larger in less developed countries, where multinationals are more advantaged relative to host firms. Using data from Mexico, Venezuela, and the United States, Aitken, Harrison, and Lipsey (1996) find that multinationals pay higher wages than host firms in the developing countries, but not in the United States.[3] Haddad and Harrison (1993) collected data on wage premiums paid by multinationals relative to local firms by industry in Morocco. In some industries such as textiles and metal products, multinationals pay roughly the same wages as local firms, and local firms share roughly the same technology. In other industries such as food products and chemicals, multinationals pay more than local firms and maintain their productivity advantage.[4] This is the pattern our model would predict. Of course, multinationals may pay wage premiums for many reasons. For example, multinationals may pay efficiency wages to control shirking. Multiple explanations could be behind the data—we isolate one previously neglected reason.

While the potential importance of technological transfer from multinationals is widely recognized, few rigorous models examine this process of technology transfer across firms. The main exception is Ethier and Markusen (1996).[5] Our paper differs from theirs in key areas. We examine the transfer of process (rather than product) technology so that the source firm always faces competition: the issue is the strength of competition. We explore the implications of partial technology transfer, where the host firm may remain disadvantaged relative to the multinational, even with access to the superior technology. In our model, workers decide *individually* whether to leave to work for the local firm and we analyze the implications of our model for host country policy toward FDI.[6]

Taylor (1993) allows firms to disguise their technology to limit technology

---

[3]Similarly, Globerman, Ries, and Vertinsky (1994) find no wage premium for foreign affiliates in Canada, after adjusting for size and capital intensity.

[4]Xu (2000) finds evidence that technology transfer from U.S. multinationals generates productivity growth in developed countries but not developing countries; see also Borensztein, De Gregorio, and Lee (1998) and Kokko (1994).

[5]See also Ethier (1986) and Horstmann and Markusen (1992) for the choice of entry mode between exporting, FDI, and licensing. Choi (2001) considers the choice between FDI and licensing under moral hazard; see also Saggi (1999). We assume the source firm keeps its operations within the firm.

[6]In Fosfuri, Motta, and Ronde (2001) and Markusen (2001), the local partner of a multinational becomes the competition.

transfer through imitation.[7] Taylor considers product technology, whereas we consider process technology, so the strategy used to control technology transfer differs. Our argument is related to the idea in Salop and Scheffman (1987) that firms may take actions to raise their rival's costs, but our analysis adds an active role for host firms in countering the cost increase.[8] The costs of host firms in equilibrium are always less than or equal to the costs in the absence of the source firm since host firms can choose not to hire the multinational's workers.

Section II develops our basic model of technology transfer through labor mobility across firms. Section III extends the model to allow for the possibility of production elsewhere and considers the welfare implications of FDI in the host country. Section IV explores whether the host government has an incentive to encourage or discourage FDI. Section V concludes. Proofs are provided in the Appendix.

II. A Model of Technology Transfer

A source (S) firm and a host (H) firm produce a homogeneous good and compete as Cournot oligopolists in a market outside the host country. Each firm has constant returns to scale production technology. The source firm's technology is superior: it requires less labor per unit of output than the host firm.[9]

Workers employed by the source firm acquire knowledge about some of its technology, and some of this knowledge can be transferred to the host firm if they switch employers. The exposure of workers to the superior technology occurs immediately upon arrival at the source firm. The assumption of instantaneous exposure captures the trait that the time required to observe a new technology is extremely short relative to the length of time during which the source firm has to protect its technological advantage. Instantaneous exposure also implies that wage premiums cannot be recovered by initially depressing wages.

It is worth emphasizing that exposure to technology differs from general training: firms have a choice whether or not to train their workers, training involves costs, and replacing trained workers with untrained workers affects productivity. If workers were costly to train, then the source firm would have an additional incentive to pay wage premiums to keep its workers from

[7]Siotis (1999) has emphasized that diffusion makes FDI less attractive for source firms and Petit and Sanna-Randaccio (2000) also consider the effect of spillovers on a firm's entry mode; see also Dinopoulos and Syropoulos (1998).

[8]Roy and Viaene (1998) also model cost-raising strategies of multinationals.

[9]Ownership advantages such as unique product designs and superior process technologies are a mainstay of the theory of the multinational firm; see Markusen (1995) and Brainard (1997).

leaving, even if they left for non-competing firms. Wage premiums due to training costs are already well understood. Our model is designed to determine whether any wage premiums are paid *purely* to control technology diffusion.

Workers are considered *informed* if they have knowledge of the superior technology and *uninformed* otherwise. Due to instantaneous exposure, all workers employed by the source firm are informed. To produce one unit of output, the source firm needs one unit of labor (by normalization). To produce one unit of output, the host firm needs θ units of informed labor or Θ units of uninformed labor. Technology transfer enhances a host firm's productivity $\theta \leqslant \Theta$. Define the relative labor requirement for the host firm as $\Gamma \equiv \Theta/\theta \geqslant 1$.

Technology transfer may remain incomplete ($\theta \geqslant 1$) for numerous reasons. First, workers may only know about the portion of the technology they worked with at the source firm. Second, the source firm may be able to maintain an advantage because the host firm lacks the superior management and organization made available to the source firm by its headquarters. Third, the technology may not be as well suited for the host firm. Other economic fundamentals such as the level of a country's development, the education level of its workers, and perhaps its protection of intellectual property may also play a role.

Workers are identical except for whether they are initially employed by the source firm. If not employed by this industry, all workers can earn a wage equal to one (by normalization) elsewhere in the economy. Thus, firms face a perfectly elastic supply of uninformed labor at the given host wage.

Our model proceeds as follows. The firms compete for informed workers, and then they compete in the product market. Once the source firm chooses the wage it offers to its workers, the host firm chooses the wage it offers the source firm's workers (given the wage offered by the source firm). We analyze the subgame-perfect equilibrium of this model through backward induction, beginning with the output stage.

Output Stage

Let the output of firm i be given by q_i, where $i \in \{S, H\}$ represents source or host, and let total output be $Q = q_H + q_S$. The demand function is given by $p(Q)$, with $p' < 0$ and $p'' < 0$. Each firm i picks its quantity q_i to maximize its profits $\pi_i = [p(Q) - c_i]q_i$, given the quantity chosen by the other firm, where the marginal cost c_i of each firm i depends on whether technology transfer occurs. The equilibrium outputs of the firms solve the standard first-order conditions: $\partial\pi_i/\partial q_i = p(Q) + q_i p'(Q) - c_i = 0$. The second-order conditions are $\partial^2\pi_i/\partial q_i^2 = 2p'(Q) + q_i p''(Q) < 0$.

Wages and Technology Transfer

Consider the wage decision of the host firm. Denote the wage offered by the source firm by w_S. By offering a wage arbitrarily above w_S, the host firm can lure away workers from the source firm. The host firm's optimal response is to match the source firm's wage for informed workers unless uninformed workers are a better value.

Lemma 1. *The host firm matches the source firm's wage* $w_H = w_S + \varepsilon$ *for informed workers if the source firm's wage is sufficiently low* $w_S < \Gamma$ *or offers the market wage* $w_H = 1$ *to uninformed workers otherwise.*

For the host firm, producing a unit of output costs Θ using uninformed workers or θw_S using informed workers.[10] For any wage the source firm offers, the host firm hires informed or uninformed workers, depending on which is the cheaper method of production. When $w_S = \Gamma \equiv \Theta/\theta$, the two methods of production are equally expensive, and the host firm hires only uninformed workers by convention. Our assumptions regarding the perfectly elastic supply of *uninformed* workers and instantaneous knowledge transfer to workers imply that if the host firm decides to match the wage of the source firm, the host firm faces a perfectly elastic supply of *informed* workers at the source firm's wage.

Next consider whether paying a wage premium to prevent technology transfer raises the source firm's profits, which depends on the extent that technology transfer to the host firm remains incomplete (magnitude of θ). In the *no technology transfer* (N) equilibrium, the source firm's marginal cost equals $c_S^N = \Gamma > 1$ and the host firm's marginal cost equals $c_H^N = \Theta > \theta$. In the *technology transfer* (T) equilibrium, the source firm's marginal cost equals $c_S^T = 1$ and the host firm's marginal cost equals $c_H^T = \theta$. The source firm can either produce at marginal cost 1 and have its rival's marginal cost be θ or produce at marginal cost Γ and have its rival's marginal cost be Θ. Thus, the no technology transfer equilibrium involves higher costs of production for both firms. We denote each profit function π_i^j by $\pi_i^j(c_S^j, c_H^j)$ to highlight the marginal cost of each firm under each equilibrium j, with $j \in \{N, T\}$ representing no technology transfer or technology transfer.

We first examine the behavior of $\pi_S^T(1, \theta)$ and $\pi_S^N(\Gamma \equiv \Theta/\theta, \Theta)$ to determine parameter conditions under which the two equilibria arise. Both profits are strictly increasing in θ. The more incomplete is technology transfer, the higher are source profits under the technology transfer equilibrium due to the larger marginal cost of the host firm:

[10] Since ε is arbitrarily close to zero, we drop it from further expressions.

$$\frac{\partial \pi_S^T(1, \theta)}{\partial \theta} = p'\left(\frac{\partial q_H^T}{\partial \theta}\right) q_S^T > 0. \tag{1}$$

Source profits under no technology transfer also increase in θ due to the lower marginal cost ($\Gamma \equiv \Theta/\theta$) of the source firm:

$$\frac{\partial \pi_S^N(\Theta/\theta, \Theta)}{\partial \theta} = \left[p' \frac{\partial q_H^T}{\partial \theta} + \frac{\Theta}{\theta^2}\right] q_S^N > 0. \tag{2}$$

When $\theta = 1$, source profits under technology transfer exceed source profits under no technology transfer: $\pi_S^T(1, 1) > \pi_S^N(\Theta, \Theta)$. In a Cournot equilibrium where firms have constant marginal costs, a uniform increase in the cost of all firms lowers profits of each firm. Furthermore, at the upper boundary where $\theta = \Theta$, both firms have the same marginal cost under technology transfer and no technology transfer, so source profits do not depend on whether technology transfer occurs: $\pi_S^T(1, \Theta) = \pi_S^N(1, \Theta)$. For both technology transfer and no technology transfer to arise under different parameter values, there needs to be an intersection of the two profit functions at some threshold θ_S where $1 < \theta_S < \Theta$.

Definition 1. *The source firm threshold θ_S is the level of θ such that source profits under technology transfer equal source profits under no technology transfer: $\pi_S^T(1, \theta_S) = \pi_S^N(\Theta/\theta_S, \Theta)$.*

We are assured of at least one intersection between the two profit functions if $\pi_S^T(1, \theta)$ (plotted against θ) meets $\pi_S^N(\Theta/\theta_S, \Theta)$ from below at the upper boundary $\theta = \Theta$:

$$\left.\frac{\partial \pi_S^T}{\partial \theta}\right|_{\theta=\Theta} > \left.\frac{\partial \pi_S^N}{\partial \theta}\right|_{\theta=\Theta}. \tag{3}$$

We assume the above condition is satisfied (as it is if Θ is sufficiently large) so that the source firm curtails technology transfer for sufficiently high values of θ.[11] The case where the profit functions do not intersect (due to Θ being very small) is uninteresting because then the source firm always

[11]Using the first-order conditions and noting that $q_S^T = q_S^N$ when $\theta = \Theta$, condition (3) is equivalent to $p'\partial q_H^T/\partial\theta > p'\partial q_H^N/\partial\theta + 1/\Theta$. When Θ is large, the second term on the RHS is small and the above condition essentially implies that an increase in the host firm's own cost θ must have a larger negative impact on its output than a decrease in its rival's cost (recall that $p' < 0$). Condition (3) is satisfied for linear demand.

prefers technology transfer. Figure 1 illustrates the two equilibria for the case of linear demand: S^T depicts π_S^T and S^N depicts π_S^N.[12]

Proposition 1. *When $\theta \geqslant \theta_S$, the source firm offers the wage $w_S^N = \Gamma$ and the no technology transfer equilibrium occurs, whereas when $\theta < \theta_S$, the source firm offers the wage $w_S^T = 1$ and the technology transfer equilibrium occurs.*

It might be conjectured that a source firm's desire to limit the diffusion of its technology should be largest when diffusion would be most complete, but such logic tells only half of the story. Diffusion is more costly to prevent—the wage premium required would be larger—when it would be more complete. In fact, the *source firm curtails technology transfer when technology transfer to the host firm is highly incomplete* (θ is large). In curtailing technology transfer, the source firm's marginal cost increases by $(\Theta - \theta)/\theta$ whereas the host firm's marginal cost increases by $\Theta - \theta$. Clearly, the bigger is θ, the bigger the increase in the marginal cost of the host firm *relative* to the source firm, making the no technology transfer equilibrium more attractive for the source firm. An increase in its own costs is more attractive to the source firm when accompanied by a larger relative increase in the costs of its rival (which happens when θ is large).

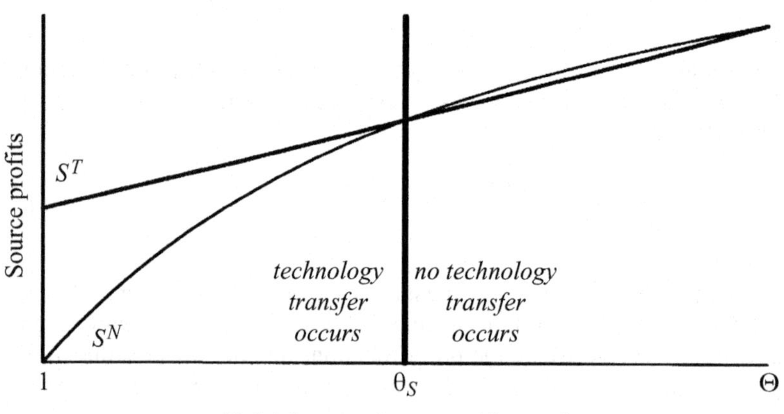

Fig. 1. Source profits and technology transfer

[12]For linear demand $\theta_S = 2$ so that there exists a range over which the source firm prevents technology transfer if $\Theta > 2$.

How does the host firm fare under the two equilibria? The host firm enjoys higher profits in the technology transfer equilibrium than in the no technology transfer equilibrium $\pi_H^T \geqslant \pi_H^N$. Total industry profits are lower in the no technology transfer equilibrium and the source firm's profits must be higher relative to technology transfer. As a result, the host firm must have lower profits under the no technology transfer equilibrium.

Thus, a clear conflict emerges between the interests of the source firm and the host firm: the source firm prefers no technology transfer when its advantage remains substantial (for $\theta \geqslant \theta_S$), while the *host firm prefers technology transfer.* More surprising is that the interests of the workers fall in line with those of the source firm, not the host firm, since they earn a wage premium only in the no technology transfer equilibrium.

Multiple Host or Source Firms

How do our results change if there are multiple host or source firms? Let n be the number of symmetric host firms and m the number of symmetric source firms. To ease exposition for this extension, let the demand function be given by $p = A - Q$. Our main interest is in determining the source firm threshold θ_S.

First, all source firms simultaneously choose the wages they offer to the informed workers. Next, all host firms simultaneously choose whether to hire informed or uninformed workers. Consider a host firm's decision of whether or not to hire informed workers. All host firms seek to hire workers away from the source firm that pays the lowest wage, denoted by $\underline{w}$. A host firm's choice is independent of the wage offered by other host firms because, given the marginal cost of production of its rivals, a host firm always seeks to minimize its own cost. Thus, Lemma 1 applies to any host firm (with w_s replaced by $\underline{w}$), regardless of the wage offered by all other host firms. Recall that due to our assumption of instantaneous technology transfer, host firms seeking to hire informed workers do not face a binding constraint regarding the supply of such workers. Consequently, cost minimization dictates the choices of host firms and given the wages offered by source firms, either all host firms offer the wage $\underline{w}$ or none.

Suppose $m - 1$ source firms decide to retain their workers by paying the wage Γ. The mth source firm can prevent technology spillovers to all host firms by offering the wage Γ or allow technology spillovers by offering the wage 1.[13] When is it advantageous to prevent technology spillovers?

[13]Clearly, no source firm seeking to retain informed workers would offer a wage other than Γ: a higher wage increases own cost without offering any benefit whereas a lower wage cannot prevent technology spillovers.

Proposition 2. *For linear demand, the source firm threshold is $\theta_S(m, n) = (m + n)/n$: if $\theta > \theta_S(m, n)$, then all source firms offer the wage Γ and no technology transfer occurs.*

The threshold θ_S is increasing in the number of source firms m and decreasing in the number of host firms n. If there is only one source firm ($m = 1$), then $\theta_S(1, n) = (1 + n)/n$ and as the number of host firms n becomes very large, the source firm *always* prevents technology transfer: $\lim_{n\to\infty} \theta_S = 1$. With many host competitors, the benefit of restricting technology transfer is large since the source firm can increase the costs of all host competitors by paying the wage premium.

If instead there is only one host firm ($n = 1$), then $\theta_S(m, 1) = m + 1$ and as the number of source firms m becomes very large, the source firm always allows technology transfer: $\lim_{m\to\infty} \theta_S = \infty$. The incentive to curtail technology transfer is dampened when there are several source firms: each is tempted *not* to offer a wage premium given that all of its source rivals are doing so.

In summary, the presence of multiple host firms decreases the likelihood of technology transfer whereas the presence of multiple source firms increases it relative to duopoly. An interesting property is that the threshold $\theta_S(m, n)$ equals 2 *whenever* $m = n$. Under linear demand, moving from the duopoly case where $m = n = 1$ to say $m = n = 2$ does not affect the range of parameters over which technology transfer occurs. The effect of an increase in the number of host firms n exactly offsets the effect of an increase in the number of source firms m.

III. Production Location

We now consider a preliminary stage in which the source firm chooses between locating its production facilities in the host country or some alternative location. If the source firm chooses the alternative location, its marginal cost is $\omega \geqslant 1$ and the possibility of technology transfer to the host firm is eliminated, as host firms cannot hire away the source firm's workers in other countries.

FDI Decision

The host country offers potential cost savings to the source firm, but with greater potential for technology transfer to rival firms. When making its decision regarding production location, the source firm realizes that its own cost of production, as well as the cost of its rivals, depends on whether or not it finds preventing technology transfer attractive. The implied costs are summarized in Table 1 (recall that $\Theta \geqslant \theta \geqslant 1$, $\Gamma \equiv \Theta/\theta \geqslant 1$, and $\omega \geqslant 1$).

Table 1. *Marginal costs under different regimes*

Regime	Source firm's cost	Host firm's cost
Production elsewhere	ω	Θ
FDI with no technology transfer	Γ	Θ
FDI with technology transfer	1	θ

Begin by defining the change in profits $\Delta\pi_i^{jk} \equiv \pi_i^j - \pi_i^k$, for firm $i \in \{H, S\}$ due to switching equilibrium regimes between j, $k \in \{E, N, T\}$. $\Delta\pi_S^{EN} = 0$ depicts the boundary between production elsewhere and FDI with no technology transfer; $\Delta\pi_S^{ET} = 0$ depicts the boundary between production elsewhere and FDI with technology transfer; $\Delta\pi_S^{TN} = 0$ depicts the boundary $\theta = \theta_S$ between FDI with and without technology transfer.

Lemma 2. *The locus of $\Delta\pi_S^{ET} = 0$ is downward sloping in θ and intersects the ω-axis below the locus of $\Delta\pi_S^{EN} = 0$. The locus of $\Delta\pi_S^{TN} = 0$ is a vertical line at $\theta = \theta_S$. These loci all intersect each other at (θ_S, ω_S) where $\omega_S \equiv \Theta/\theta_S$.*

These three source firm profit loci divide the (θ, ω) space into three regions: production elsewhere (when ω is low), FDI with technology transfer (when ω is high and θ is low), and FDI with no technology transfer (when ω is high and θ is high), as in Figure 2.

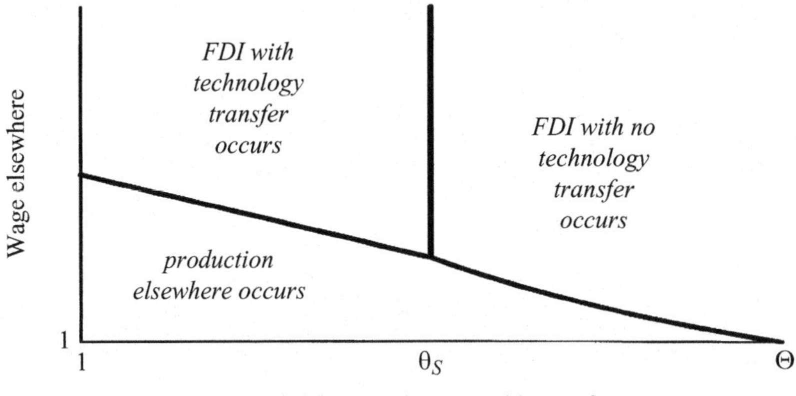

Fig. 2. Source firm chosen entry mode

Proposition 3. *When $\theta \geqslant \theta_S$, the source firm produces elsewhere iff the cost elsewhere is sufficiently low $\omega \leqslant \Gamma$ or else engages in FDI and prevents technology transfer. When $\theta < \theta_S$, the source firm produces elsewhere iff the cost elsewhere is sufficiently low $\omega \leqslant \Omega$ or else engages in FDI and allows technology transfer.*

Welfare Implications of FDI

How does welfare in the host country depend on the regime chosen by the source firm? Define host welfare in equilibrium j as the host firm's profits and any wage premium $W^j \equiv \pi_H^j + B^j$, where the total wage premium is $B^j \equiv (w_S^j - 1)q_S^j$. No wage premium is paid in the technology transfer equilibrium $B^T = 0$, while the wage premium in the no technology transfer equilibrium is $B^N \equiv (\Gamma - 1)q_S^N > 0$. Consumption is assumed to occur outside the host country for simplicity, so no consumer surplus need be measured.

Begin by constructing the boundaries where host welfare is the same across regimes in the (θ, ω) plane. $\Delta W^{ET} \equiv W^E - W^T = \pi_H^E - \pi_H^T = 0$ forms the boundary between where production elsewhere or FDI with technology transfer are best for host welfare in Figure 3. Similarly, $\Delta W^{EN} \equiv W^E - W^N = 0$ forms the boundary between where production elsewhere or FDI with no technology transfer are best for host welfare. Host

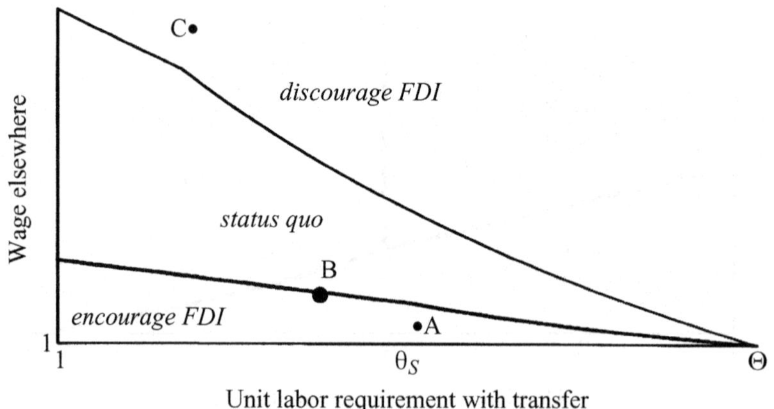

Fig. 3. Host policy toward foreign investment

welfare favors production elsewhere when costs are higher elsewhere, as high costs for the source firm shift profits toward the host firm.

Lemma 3. *The locus of* $\Delta W^{ET} = 0$ *is downward sloping in* θ *and intersects the* ω*-axis above the locus of* $\Delta W^{EN} = 0$.

IV. Policy Analysis

Technology transfer is one of the dominant reasons why developing countries are interested in attracting FDI. We examine whether host countries can benefit from attracting FDI through a lump-sum subsidy conditional on FDI.

Inducing FDI with No Technology Transfer

Figure 3 compares the source firm's choice of entry mode (FDI or production elsewhere) to the mode that maximizes host welfare. Suppose the parameter values are such that the source firm opts for production elsewhere. In addition, suppose $\theta > \theta_S$ so that, if the source firm engages in FDI, it will not allow technology transfer (such as at point **A** in Figure 3). Would the host country want to *induce* FDI by the source firm? Even absent technology transfer, the host country's welfare can be improved by inducing FDI.

When $\omega = \Gamma$, an arbitrarily small payment to the source firm conditional on producing in the host economy will improve host welfare. Since FDI with no technology transfer involves a wage premium, host welfare is strictly higher under FDI with no technology transfer than under production elsewhere. The interests of the host workers tip the balance in favor of FDI (with no technology transfer) over production elsewhere, even though technology transfer is absent. The first rationale for attracting FDI suggested by our model is *increased wages for host workers*.

In general, when $\omega < \Gamma$, the source firm must be offered a subsidy of at least $(\Gamma - \omega)q_S^N$ so that its profits are unaffected. The profits of the host firm are unaffected. Host workers, however, gain the amount $(\Gamma - 1)q_S^N$. Thus, such a policy of inducing FDI improves welfare because $\omega > 1$. Host welfare improves since some part of the source firm's cost savings from FDI are transferred to host workers as higher wages.

Inducing FDI with Technology Transfer

Again, suppose the parameter values are such that the source firm opts for production elsewhere. But now suppose $\theta < \theta_S$ so that, if the source firm engages in FDI, it will allow technology transfer (such as at point **B** in Figure 3). Would the host country then want to *induce* FDI by the source firm? Here, too, there exists a potential rationale for attracting FDI: the host firm enjoys technology transfer from the source firm. To attract FDI, the host government can induce FDI by compensating the source firm for the loss in profits that FDI entails relative to production elsewhere. Are there circumstances under which such a policy improves welfare? Yes.

Suppose parameters lie on the boundary between production elsewhere and FDI with technology transfer with $\theta < \theta_S$. Then, the source firm is exactly indifferent between production elsewhere and FDI with technology transfer, but the host country *strictly prefers FDI* with technology transfer. A small incentive to FDI can yield an improvement in host welfare, net of the subsidy payment. Here, the improvement in host welfare results from *higher profits of the host firm.*

In general, the host government can benefit from attracting FDI that generates technology transfer if industry profits rise.[14] Moving below the boundary where the source firm is indifferent, the subsidy required rises, but there remains a region where the gain in host profits still warrants the subsidy required. The host government must offer a subsidy of at least $\Delta\pi_S^{ET}$ to keep source profits unaffected. Host profits increase by $\Delta\pi_H^{TE}$, so provided $\Delta\pi_H^{TE} > \Delta\pi_S^{ET}$, the host profit gains are sufficient to offset source profits losses.

Preventing FDI

Does FDI with technology transfer always dominate production elsewhere in terms of host welfare? Not necessarily. In a region (including point **C** in Figure 3), the source firm chooses FDI with technology transfer but host welfare is highest under production elsewhere. Here, *FDI with technology transfer actually lowers host welfare relative to production elsewhere*. Since the wage elsewhere ω is high in this region, the source firm enjoys a substantial decline in its marginal cost if it switches from production elsewhere to FDI, thereby harming the host firm's profits, despite the host firm enjoying lower costs due to technology transfer.

Similar adverse consequences from FDI can result even when the source firm pays a wage premium to curtail technology transfer. The harm to host firms can dominate the benefit to workers, causing a net reduction in host welfare. Therefore, host welfare can be raised by restricting FDI when the source firm finds FDI highly attractive.

[14]Host consumption would add more benefits under technology transfer due to lower price and larger output.

Policy Contrast

If both ω and θ are high, as for countries at low levels of development, the host government *discourages* FDI; whereas if both ω and θ are low, as for countries at higher levels of development, the host government *encourages* FDI. A shift in policy toward encouraging FDI may occur as a country develops: the potential for technology transfer becomes less partial in nature due to enhanced absorptive capacity, and the cost reduction from FDI for source firms is reduced when host wages become closer to wages elsewhere.

Proposition 4. *The host government has an incentive to induce FDI (if FDI would not otherwise occur) when the cost elsewhere ω is sufficiently low and prevent FDI if the wage elsewhere ω is sufficiently high.*

V. Conclusion

We examine a market where a source firm possesses a superior technology relative to a host firm. If the source firm opts for FDI, technology may diffuse to the host firm if it hires workers who have been exposed to the superior technology by working for the source firm. We show that the source firm may be able to increase its profits by raising the wage it pays its workers by enough to prevent them from switching employers. Such a wage premium can raise the source firm's profits by preventing the cost reduction for the host firm that would otherwise occur.

Our model implies that there could be two possible rationale for attracting FDI: technology transfer which increases the host firm's profits or wage premiums that benefit workers. Yet the realization of one of these benefits is insufficient to make FDI always more attractive relative to production elsewhere for the host country. Nevertheless, there do exist circumstances under which the host country can improve its welfare by making the source firm switch to FDI through policy intervention.

Appendix

Proof of Lemma 1

The host firm matches the source firm's wage if $\pi_H^T(w_S, \theta w_S) > \pi_H^N(w_S, \Theta)$. $\pi_H^T(w_S, \Theta)$ is strictly increasing in w_S. When $w_S = \Gamma$, $\pi_H^T(w_S, \theta w_S) = \pi_H^N(w_S, \Theta)$. Furthermore, at $w_S = 1$, $\pi_H^T(w_S, \theta w_S) > \pi_H^N(w_S, \Theta)$. For all $w_S < \Gamma$, $\pi_H^T(w_S, \theta w_S) > \pi_H^N(w_S, \Theta)$, whereas for all $w_S > \Gamma$, $\pi_H^T(w_S, \theta w_S) < \pi_H^N(w_S, \Theta)$. Thus, the unique intersection $\pi_H^T(w_S, \theta w_S) = \pi_H^N(w_S, \Theta)$ occurs at $w_S = \Gamma$.

Proof of Proposition 2

Suppose $m-1$ source firms offer the wage premium Γ and consider the decision of the mth source firm. The source firm m's profits under technology transfer equal

$$\pi_m^T = \left[\frac{A-(m+n)+(m-1)\Gamma+n\theta}{m+n+1}\right]^2, \tag{A1}$$

whereas its profits under no technology transfer equal

$$\pi_m^N = \left[\frac{A-(n+m)\Gamma+(m-1)\Gamma+n\Theta}{m+n+1}\right]^2. \tag{A2}$$

Then, $\pi_m^N - \pi_m^T > 0$ and no technology transfer is the Nash equilibrium if

$$-(m+n)\left(\frac{\Theta-\theta}{\theta}\right)+n(\Theta-\theta)>0 \rightarrow \theta>\theta_s(m,n)\equiv\frac{m+n}{n}. \tag{A3}$$

Proof of Lemma 2

Consider first the derivation of the locus $\Delta\pi_S^{EN} \equiv \pi_S^E - \pi_S^N = 0$, along which the source firm is indifferent between production elsewhere and FDI with no technology transfer. Since under both regimes the host firm's marginal cost equals Θ, the source firm prefers FDI with no technology transfer over production elsewhere iff the wage elsewhere exceeds the wage required to prevent technology transfer $\omega > \Gamma$. The equation $\omega = \Gamma \equiv \Theta/\theta$ traces a downward sloping curve: above the curve the source firm prefers FDI with no technology transfer and below the curve production elsewhere.

Next consider the derivation of the locus $\Delta\pi_S^{ET} \equiv \pi_S^E - \pi_S^T = 0$ along which the source firm is indifferent between production elsewhere and FDI with technology transfer. The *maximum cost elsewhere* Ω (such that production elsewhere dominates FDI with technology transfer) is defined as a function of θ by [15]

$$\pi_S^E(\Omega,\Theta) = \pi_S^T(1,\theta) \leftrightarrow \Delta\pi_S^{ET} = 0. \tag{A4}$$

The equation $\omega = \Omega$ also traces a downward sloping curve: above the curve, the source firm prefers FDI with technology transfer while below the curve production elsewhere.

Next, consider the derivation of the locus $\Delta\pi_S^{TN} \equiv \pi_S^T - \pi_S^N = 0$ along which the source firm is indifferent between FDI with technology transfer and FDI with no technology transfer. Proposition 1 indicates that $\Delta\pi_S^{TN} = 0$ is a vertical line at $\theta = \theta_S$. To the left of this line, the source firm prefers FDI with technology transfer, while to the right FDI with no technology transfer. Since neither equilibrium under

[15]Since the RHS is increasing in θ, the LHS must also be increasing in θ, so Ω is decreasing in θ.

comparison involves production elsewhere, the difference in profits is independent of the cost of production elsewhere.

First, we show that the $\Delta\pi_S^{ET} = 0$ locus is downward sloping in the (θ, ω) space. Along the $\Delta\pi_S^{ET} = 0$ locus, $\pi_S^E(\omega, \Theta) = \pi_S^T(1, \theta)$. The RHS is increasing in θ while the LHS is unaffected. Thus, for the two to stay equal, as θ increases, ω must decrease. Second, we show that the $\Delta\pi_S^{ET} = 0$ locus intersects the ω-axis below the $\Delta\pi_S^{EN} = 0$ locus. The $\Delta\pi_S^{EN} = 0$ locus intersects the ω-axis at Θ. Let the $\Delta\pi_S^{ET} = 0$ locus intersect the ω-axis at some $\bar{\omega}$. At $\theta = 1$, $\pi_S^N(\Theta, \Theta) < \pi_S^T(1, 1)$ and $\pi_S^E(1, \Theta) > \pi_S^T(1, 1)$, so $\pi_S^E(\bar{\omega}, \Theta) = \pi_S^T(1, 1)$ at $1 < \bar{\omega} < \Theta$, since $\pi_S^E(\omega, \Theta)$ is decreasing in ω. Third, we show that the $\Delta\pi_S^{EN} = 0$ locus and the $\Delta\pi_S^{ET} = 0$ locus intersect at (θ_S, ω_S), where $\omega_S \equiv \Theta/\theta_S$. At $\theta = \theta_S$, $\pi_S^N(\Theta/\theta_S, \Theta) = \pi_S^E(\omega_S, \Theta)$ if $\omega_S \equiv \Theta/\theta_S$, so $\Delta\pi_S^{EN}(\Theta/\theta_S, \Theta) = 0$. Also, at $\theta = \theta_S$, by definition $\pi_S^N(\Theta/\theta_S, \Theta) = \pi_S^T(1, \theta_S)$. Subtracting $\pi_S^E(\omega_S, \Theta)$ from both sides implies that at $\theta = \theta_S$, we must have $\Delta\pi_S^{EN}$ $(\Theta/\theta_S, \Theta) = \Delta\pi_S^{ET}(1, \theta_S)$. By transitivity, all three loci must intersect at (θ_S, ω_S).

Proof of Lemma 3

First, we show that the $\Delta W^{ET} = 0$ locus is downward sloping in the (θ, ω) space. Along the $\Delta W^{ET} = 0$ locus, $W^E = W^T$, which requires $\pi_H^E(\omega, \Theta) = \pi_H^T(1, \theta)$, as no wage premiums are paid in either case. The RHS is decreasing in θ while the LHS is unaffected. Thus, for the two to stay equal, as θ increases, ω must decrease to lower host profits when the source firm produces elsewhere. Second, we show that the $\Delta W^{ET} = 0$ locus intersects the ω-axis above the $\Delta W^{EN} = 0$ locus. Let the $\Delta W^{ET} = 0$ locus intersect the ω-axis at some $\bar{\omega}$ such that $\pi_H^E(\bar{\omega}, \Theta) = W^T$ and the $\Delta W^{EN} = 0$ locus intersect the ω-axis at some $\hat{\omega}$ such that $\pi_H^E(\hat{\omega}, \Theta) = W^N$. At $\theta = 1$, $W^N > W^T$ as $1 = \theta < \theta_W$, which implies $\pi_H^E(\hat{\omega}, \Theta) > \pi_H^E(\hat{\omega}, \Theta)$, where θ_W is the host welfare threshold such that $\Delta W^{NT} = 0$. Since increasing ω raises $W^E = \pi_H^E(\omega, \Theta)$, $\bar{\omega}$ must exceed $\bar{\omega}$. Third, we show that the $\Delta W^{EN} = 0$ locus and the $\Delta W^{ET} = 0$ locus intersect at (θ_W, ω_W). At θ_W, by definition $W^N = W^T$, neither of which depend on ω. Define ω_W such that $\pi_H^E(\omega_W, \Theta) = \pi_H^T(1, \theta_W)$, which implies $W^E = W^T$. Thus, by transitivity, all three loci intersect at (θ_W, ω_W), and $\omega_W > \omega_S$ follows from $\theta_W < \theta_S$ (and $\hat{\omega} > \Theta\tilde{\omega}$).

References

Aitken, B., Harrison, A. E. and Lipsey, R. E., (1996), Wages and Foreign Ownership: A Comparative Study of Mexico, Venezuela, and the United States, *Journal of International Economics 40*, 345–371.

Bloom, M. (1992), *Technological Change in the Korean Electronics Industry*, OECD, Paris.

Borensztein, E., De Gregorio, J., and Lee, J. W. (1998), How Does Foreign Direct Investment Affect Economic Growth? *Journal of International Economics 45*, 115–135.

Brainard, S. L. (1997), An Empirical Assessment of the Proximity–Concentration Trade-off between Multinational Sales and Trade, *American Economic Review 87*, 520–544.

Choi, J. P. (2001), Technology Transfer with Moral Hazard, *International Journal of Industrial Organization 19*, 249–266.

Dinopoulos, E. and Syropoulos, C. (1998), International Diffusion and Appropriability of Technological Expertise, in M. R. Baye (ed.), *Advances in Applied Microeconomics*, Vol. 7, JAI Press, Greenwich, CT.

Ethier, W. J. (1986), The Multinational Firm, *Quarterly Journal of Economics 101*, 805–833.

Ethier, W. J. and Markusen, J. R. (1996), Multinational Firms, Technology Diffusion and Trade, *Journal of International Economics 41*, 1–28.

Findlay, R. (1978), Relative Backwardness, Direct Foreign Investment, and the Transfer of Technology, A Simple Dynamic Model, *Quarterly Journal of Economics 62*, 1–16.

Fosfuri, A., Motta, M., and Ronde, T. (2001), Foreign Direct Investment and Spillovers through Workers' Mobility, *Journal of International Economics 53*, 205–222.

Gershenberg, I. (1987), The Training and Spread of Managerial Know-how: A Comparative Analysis of Multinational and Other Firms in Kenya, *World Development 15*, 931–939.

Glass, A. J. and Saggi, K. (1999a), Foreign Direct Investment and the Nature of R&D, *Canadian Journal of Economics 32*, 92–117.

Glass, A. J. and Saggi, K. (1999b), FDI Policies under Shared Factor Markets, *Journal of International Economics 49*, 309–332.

Globerman, S., Ries, J. C., and Vertinsky, I. (1994), The Economic Performance of Foreign Affiliates in Canada, *Canadian Journal of Economics 27*, 143–156.

Haddad, M. and Harrison, A. (1993), Are There Positive Spillovers from Direct Foreign Investment? Evidence from Panel Data from Morocco, *Journal of Development Economics 42*, 51–74.

Horstmann, I. J. and Markusen, J. R. (1992), Endogenous Market Structures in International Trade (Natura facit saltum), *Journal of International Economics 32*, 109–129.

Kokko, A. (1994), Technology, Market Characteristics, and Spillovers, *Journal of Development Economics 43*, 279–293.

Markusen, J. R. (1995), The Boundaries of Multinational Enterprises and the Theory of International Trade, *Journal of Economic Perspectives 9*, 169–189.

Markusen, J. R. (2001), Contracts, Intellectual Property Rights, and Multinational Investment in Developing Countries, *Journal of International Economics 53*, 189–204.

Pack, H. (1997), The Role of Exports in Asian Development, in N. Birdsall and F. Jaspersen (eds.), *Pathways to Growth: Comparing East Asia and Latin America*, Inter-American Development Bank, Washington, DC.

Pack, H. and Saggi, K. (1997), Inflows of Foreign Technology and Indigenous Technological Development, *Review of Development Economics 1*, 81–98.

Petit, M.-L. and Sanna-Randaccio, F. (2000), Endogenous R&D and Foreign Direct Investment in International Oligopolies, *International Journal of Industrial Organization 18*, 339–367.

Roy, S. and Viaene, J.-M. (1998), On Strategic Vertical Foreign Investment, *Journal of International Economics 46*, 253–279.

Saggi, K. (1999), Foreign Direct Investment, Licensing, and Incentives for Innovation, *Review of International Economics 7*, 699–714.

Salop, S. C. and Scheffman, D. T. (1987), Cost Raising Strategies, *Journal of Industrial Economics 36*, 19–34.

Siotis, G. (1999), Foreign Direct Investment Strategies and Firm's Capabilities, *Journal of Economics and Management Strategy 8*, 251–270.

Taylor, M. S. (1993), TRIPS, Trade and Technology Transfer, *Canadian Journal of Economics 26*, 625–637.

UNCTAD (1992), *World Investment Report*, United Nations, New York.
Xu, B. (2000), Multinational Enterprises, Technology Diffusion, and Host Country Productivity Growth, *Journal of Development Economics 62*, 477–493.

First version submitted February 2001;
final version received January 2002.

Chapter 8

Multinational firms, exclusivity, and backward linkages[#]

Ping Lin [a,1], Kamal Saggi [b,*]

[a] *Department of Economics, Lingnan University, Hong Kong*
[b] *Department of Economics, Southern Methodist University, Dallas, TX 75275-0496, USA*

Received 4 August 2004; received in revised form 5 August 2005; accepted 6 February 2006

Abstract

How does the nature of contractual relationships between a multinational and its local suppliers affect backward linkages and welfare in the local industry? We address this question in a two-tier oligopoly model where a multinational transfers technology to its suppliers if they accept an exclusive contract that precludes them from serving its local rivals. Invited suppliers balance the benefits of gaining access to new technology and the derived demand of the multinational against the opportunity of selling to other local firms. Exclusivity reduces competition among local suppliers and can lower backward linkages and local welfare relative to autarky.

Keywords: Multinational firms; Backward linkages; Vertical technology transfer; Exclusivity

JEL classification: F23; F12; O19; O14; L13

1. Introduction

Two important channels through which the entry of multinational firms can affect a host country are technology transfer and the generation of backward linkages. While these two channels have been studied extensively in isolation, no existing model allows them to operate simultaneously. What is the relationship between vertical technology transfer (VTT) from a multinational to its local suppliers and the degree of backward linkages?[2] Second, and perhaps more importantly, how

* Corresponding author. Tel.: +1 214 768 3274; fax: +1 214 768 1821.
E-mail addresses: plin@ln.edu.hk (P. Lin), ksaggi@smu.edu (K. Saggi).
[1] Tel.: +852 2616 7203; fax: +852 2891 7940.

[2] In his empirical study of VTT in the Indian trucking industry, Lall (1980) notes that VTT can occur in several ways. A multinational might (1) help prospective suppliers set up production capacities; (2) provide technical assistance/information to raise the quality of suppliers' products and/or to facilitate innovations; or (3) provide training and help in management and organization.

[#] This chapter was originally appeared in *Journal of International Economics* **71**, 206–220. © 2006 Elsevier B.V.

does the nature of vertical contracts between a multinational and its local suppliers affect welfare in the host industry? We address these questions in a two-tier oligopoly model that focuses on the entry decision of a single multinational firm. Upon entry, the multinational sources a required intermediate good locally and provides VTT to its suppliers if they agree to abide by an exclusivity condition that precludes them from serving its local rivals.

Exclusivity requirements in the context of international technology transfer are empirically relevant. In a recent survey of 413 companies in the automobile sector in Central and Eastern Europe, Lorentzen and Mollgaard (2000) found that 61% of the automobile parts manufacturers had received technology from their customers (automobile assemblers, which are mostly multinational companies), and 36% of the customers imposed an exclusivity condition on their suppliers. Similarly, according to Mizuno (1995), car component suppliers in South Korea can be classified into three categories: (1) the exclusive type that supplies over 75% of their total production to their principal car manufacturers; (2) the semi-exclusive type for whom this measure lies in the 50–70% range; and (3) the dispersed/independent type for whom this measure falls below 50%.

In our model, exclusivity delinks local rivals of the multinational from (some of) their suppliers. Such delinking makes the intermediate good market less competitive and can cause local welfare to decline due to the multinational's entry. The delinking effect is reminiscent of an astute observation made by Rodriguez-Clare (1996): multinationals do not just create new linkages—they also displace pre-existing linkages between local firms and suppliers. In our context, such displacement occurs contractually, whereas in Rodriguez-Clare (1996), it occurs if the multinational chooses to source intermediates from its headquarters.

We argue that exclusivity confers two strategic advantages upon the multinational. First, VTT under exclusivity lowers the production cost of only those suppliers that serve the multinational. Second, exclusivity limits the number of suppliers that sell to local producers—i.e., it can act as a strategy via which the multinational can foreclose competition in the intermediate market (Salop and Scheffman, 1987). On the other hand, since an exclusive contract with the multinational requires local suppliers to forego the opportunity of serving local firms, only a limited number of them are interested in accepting such a contract. In fact, in equilibrium, the multinational is able to implement exclusivity if and only if the extent of VTT exceeds a critical level.

The analytical literature on multinationals and technology transfer is vast, but with the exception of Pack and Saggi (2001), much of this literature has ignored technology transfer between multinationals and their suppliers. This is unfortunate since empirical evidence indicates that VTT is quite pervasive—see Lall (1980), Moran (1998), Javorcik (2004), and Blalock and Gertler (2005). To the best of our knowledge, there exist only two analytical models that explore the relationship between multinationals and backward linkages in the host country: Markusen and Venables (1999) and Rodriguez-Clare (1996).[3] In both models, the intermediate goods sector is monopolistically competitive and foreign investment induces entry into such markets by generating derived demand for intermediates. These models emphasize demand creation effects of multinationals whereas our paper focuses more on supply-side effects.[4]

The rest of the paper is organized as follows. Section 2 contains the basic model, including the benchmark case prior to the entry of the multinational. Section 3 highlights the demand creation

[3] See Lin and Saggi (2005) for a critical survey of the existing analytical literature on the linkage effects of FDI.

[4] The Markusen and Venables model also allows for a competition effect wherein the entry of a multinational hurts its local rivals. In Rodriguez-Clare (1996), the host country is assumed to be in a 'bad' equilibrium where the final good is produced only by multinationals. As a result, the competition effect is absent in his model (which has substantial richness along other dimensions).

Table 1
Autarkic equilibrium

$Q_i^A = \dfrac{n\alpha}{(m+1)(n+1)}$	$\Pi_i^A = \dfrac{n\alpha^2}{(m+1)^2(n+1)}$
$w^A = \dfrac{\alpha}{m+1} + c_I$	$\pi_j^A = \dfrac{\alpha^2 m^2}{(m+1)^2(n+1)^2}$

effect of the multinational's entry, while Section 4 derives the market equilibrium under exclusivity. In Section 5, the equilibrium of the entry game is studied and conditions under which exclusivity occurs are derived. Section 6 focuses on the effects of exclusivity on backward linkages and local welfare for the case of two local suppliers. Section 7 extends the basic model to the case where the multinational is able to contract on the price of the intermediate good. Section 8 concludes.

2. Basic model

There are $n \geq 1$ local firms (denoted by $j=1\ldots n$) that produce a (final) good the demand for which is given by $Q=a-p$. One unit of the final good requires one unit of an intermediate good that is produced at unit cost c_I by $m \geq 2$ firms (denoted by $i=1\ldots m$). From hereon, intermediate good producers are called 'suppliers' while final good producers are called just 'producers.' The marginal cost of a producer equals the sum of the price of the intermediate good and the unit cost of transforming the input into the final product (given by c).

Our benchmark model is a variant of the successive Cournot model developed in Salinger (1988). In this model, each stage of production is characterized by Cournot competition between firms, with the downstream firms taking the price of the intermediate as given, and the suppliers taking the demand curve for the intermediate generated by downstream Cournot competition as given.

We examine the effects of the entry of a single multinational firm (who produces the final good) on domestic industry. The multinational's marginal cost of transforming the intermediate good is $(1-\delta)c$, where $\delta \in [0,1]$ measures the degree of its cost-advantage over local producers. As a benchmark, we first describe market equilibrium in the absence of the multinational.

2.1. Autarky

Prior to the entry of the multinational (referred to as autarky), all producers buy the intermediate good in the open market. Given the price of the intermediate (denoted by w), Cournot competition downstream yields the derived demand for the intermediate. Facing this derived demand, suppliers compete in Cournot fashion, leading to the equilibrium of the entire industry. The equilibrium output (Q_i^A) and profit of each supplier (Π_i^A), price of the intermediate (w^A), and the profit of each downstream producer (π_j^A) are given in Table 1.

An obvious way to measure the degree of backward linkages (BL) in this two-tier industry is to use the aggregate output level of the intermediate good:

$$BL^A \equiv mQ_i^A = \frac{mn\alpha}{(m+1)(n+1)} \tag{1}$$

where $\alpha \equiv a-c_I-c>0$. Clearly, backward linkages increase with the number of firms at each level of the industry as well as with market size.

We now study an entry game that endogenizes the multinational's mode of interaction with its local suppliers.

2.2. Entry by the multinational firm

Upon entry, the multinational sources the intermediate good locally and competes with local producers in supplying the final good.[5] The sequence of moves is as follows:

- First, the multinational chooses between two alternatives: (i) an arm's length arrangement with its suppliers (i.e., market interaction) wherein it simply buys the intermediate from the market as an anonymous buyer and (ii) a contractual relationship that involves vertical technology transfer (VTT) from the multinational to its suppliers. In exchange for VTT, the selected suppliers agree to serve the multinational exclusively (EX). We assume that VTT reduces the marginal cost of producing the intermediate from c_I to $c_I - d$, where d captures the degree of VTT.[6]
- If a contractual relationship is chosen, the multinational approaches k suppliers (called invited suppliers) with the offer (VTT, EX) and invited suppliers simultaneously decide whether or not to accept the multinational's offer.
- Next, the multinational carries out VTT to those suppliers that accept its offer. The other suppliers serve local producers with their old technologies. Given market structure, payoffs of all parties equal their respective profits in the successive Cournot model. If no supplier accepts the multinational's offer, market interaction prevails.

It is worth noting here that our basic model assumes that the multinational cannot specify a price for the intermediate while contracting with its suppliers. Following Antrás (2003) and Antrás and Helpman (2004), such an assumption can be justified on the basis of contract incompleteness (the source of which is not considered in our basic model). In any case, in Section 7, we examine how our main results change if the multinational can contract over the price of the intermediate good. This analysis considers two frequently used vertical contracts: a two-part contract and a bundling contract.

3. Market interaction and demand creation

Under market interaction, the multinational buys the intermediate good in the open market, as do all local final good producers.[7] As under autarky, firm behavior at both levels of the industry is described by the successive Cournot model. The only difference with respect to autarky is that the multinational's entry increases the number of final goods producers by one. Equilibrium expressions

[5] Local sourcing might arise because of technological reasons (such as high transportation costs or the costs of relying on far away suppliers) or due to policy restrictions such as local content requirements imposed by the host country government—see Qiu and Tao (2001).

[6] Alternatively, we can interpret VTT as an improvement in the quality of the intermediate good. Specifically, due to the multinational's help, the product quality of local suppliers improves so that one unit of the intermediate becomes equivalent to λ units where $\lambda \geq 1$. This is equivalent to a typical supplier's marginal cost becoming c_I/λ with the reduction in cost equalling $d = (1 - 1/\lambda)c_I$.

[7] This case is standard in the literature and it allows a comparison of our results with those of Markusen and Venables (1999) and Rodriguez-Clare (1996).

Table 2
Equilibrium under market interaction

$Q_i^M = \frac{(n+1)\alpha+\delta c}{(m+1)(n+2)}$	$\Pi_i^M = \frac{(n+2)}{n+1}\left(Q_i^M\right)^2$
$\pi_f^M = \left[\frac{m(n+1)\alpha+\delta c(n(m+1)(n+2)+m)}{(n+2)(n+1)(m+1)}\right]^2$	$\pi_j^M = \left[\frac{m(n+1)\alpha-\delta c((m+1)(n+1)+1)}{(n+2)(n+1)(m+1)}\right]^2$

for the output (Q_i^M) and profit of each supplier (Π_i^M), and the profit of each producer (π_j^M) and that of the multinational (π_j^M) are reported in Table 2.Using Table 2, we have

$$BL^M \equiv mQ_i^M = m\frac{(n+1)\alpha+\delta c}{(m+1)(n+2)} \tag{2}$$

Comparing with autarky, it is easy to show that BL^M always exceeds BL^A (see Table 1): when the multinational buys the intermediate in the open market, its entry always raises the degree of backward linkages in the local industry. The multinational's entry provides a boost to the upstream sector through two channels. First, the demand for the intermediate increases because of greater competition in the final good (the number of producers increases from n to $n+1$). Second, since the multinational enjoys a cost-advantage over its rivals ($\delta>0$), it generates greater derived demand than a typical local producer.

4. Exclusive contract

Under exclusivity, local suppliers are divided into two groups: those that serve only the multinational and receive VTT from it and those that supply only local producers. Suppose (without loss of generality) that suppliers 1... k serve the multinational while suppliers $k+1$... m cater to local producers. Below, we derive market equilibrium for a given k and then explore the multinational's optimal k. Let w_f and w_h denote the unit prices of the intermediate paid by the multinational and local producers, respectively, where the price within each group is determined as in the successive Cournot model. Given these prices, the multinational's marginal cost of production equals $w_f+(1-\delta)c$ while that of local producers equals w_h+c. Using the derived demands of the multinational and local producers, it is easy to solve for the equilibrium output level of a supplier that caters to the multinational (Q_f^{EX}) and that of a supplier that serves local producers (Q_h^{EX}):

$$Q_f^{EX}(k) = \frac{(m+n-k+1)\alpha+(n+1)(m-k+1)(\delta c+d)}{2(n+1)(k+1)(m-k+1)-k(m-k)n} \tag{3}$$

and

$$Q_h^{EX}(k) = \frac{n(k+2)\alpha-nk(\delta c+d)}{2(n+1)(k+1)(m-k+1)-k(m-k)n} \tag{4}$$

while the prices of the intermediate paid by the multinational and the local producers are

$$w_f^{EX}(k) = 2Q_f^{EX}(k)+c_I-d \quad \text{and} \quad w_h^{EX}(k) = \frac{n+1}{n}Q_h^{EX}(k)+c_I \tag{5}$$

respectively. Using the above expressions, the equilibrium profit of a typical supplier to the multinational equals

$$\Pi_f^{\mathrm{EX}}(k) = 2[Q_f^{\mathrm{EX}}(k)]^2 \tag{6}$$

while that of a supplier serving local producers is

$$\Pi_h^{\mathrm{EX}}(k) = \frac{n+1}{n}[Q_h^{\mathrm{EX}}(k)]^2 \tag{7}$$

Finally, the profit of each local producer equals

$$\pi_j^{\mathrm{EX}}(k) = \left[\frac{(m-k)Q_h^{\mathrm{EX}}(k)}{n}\right]^2 \tag{8}$$

whereas that of the multinational equals

$$\pi_f^{\mathrm{EX}}(k) = [kQ_f^{\mathrm{EX}}(k)]^2 \tag{9}$$

which increases with k, d and δ. As before, backward linkages under exclusivity are defined as

$$BL^{\mathrm{EX}} \equiv kQ_f^{\mathrm{EX}}(k) + (m-k)Q_h^{\mathrm{EX}}(k) \tag{10}$$

We are now in a position to consider the trade-off facing each invited supplier. On the one hand, by serving the multinational a supplier captures a share of the multinational's demand for the intermediate while also receiving VTT from it. On the other hand, it must forego the option of serving local producers. Whether or not it is profitable for a supplier to serve the multinational depends on (i) how many other suppliers accept the multinational's offer; (ii) the extent of VTT; and (iii) the magnitude of derived demand for the intermediate generated by local producers.

To make exclusivity an attractive option for suppliers, the following assumption is necessary (it ensures that at least one invited supplier accepts the multinational's offer):

Assumption 1. $\Pi_f^{\mathrm{EX}}(1) \geq \Pi_h^{\mathrm{EX}}(0)$.

The right-hand-side of the inequality $\Pi_h^{\mathrm{EX}}(0)$ is the profit of a typical supplier under market interaction (i.e., when no supplier accepts the multinational's offer), whereas $\Pi_f^{\mathrm{EX}}(1)$ is the profit of a supplier when it is the only one serving the multinational. Assumption 1 holds if d is not too small.

To preclude the uninteresting case where all local suppliers become the multinational's exclusive suppliers (thereby driving all local producers out of the market), we make the following assumption.

Assumption 2. $\Pi_h^{\mathrm{EX}}(m-1) \geq \Pi_f^{\mathrm{EX}}(m)$

This assumption says that a supplier prefers to be the sole supplier to all local producers than to serve only the multinational (together with all other $m-1$ suppliers). Assumption 2 requires that $(d+\delta c)/\alpha$ be not too big—in other words, the technological advantage of the multinational over its local rivals and the degree of VTT be not too large relative to the local market size.

Given that $k-1$ suppliers accept the multinational's offer, the kth supplier is willing to serve the multinational if and only if

$$\Pi_f^{\mathrm{EX}}(k) \geq \Pi_h^{\mathrm{EX}}(k-1) \tag{11}$$

Remark 1. *The profit of a supplier that accepts the multinational's offer decreases with k, whereas the profit of a supplier that rejects the multinational's offer increases with k.*

The intuition behind Remark 1 is simple: As more suppliers switch to serving the multinational exclusively, competition among them intensifies, whereas competition among those that supply local producers declines. Let $\bar{k}$ be the largest integer that satisfies (11). From Remark 1 we know that $\bar{k}$ is unique. Clearly, the multinational announces $k=\bar{k}$ and all invited suppliers accept its offer. Although $\bar{k}$ cannot be solved for analytically, it is easy to see that it increases with the degree of VTT (d), as well as the technological gap between the multinational and its local rivals (δ). As d or δ rises, the function $\Pi_f^{\mathrm{EX}}(k)$ shifts upwards and the function $\Pi_h^{\mathrm{EX}}(k-1)$ shifts downwards, implying that $\bar{k}$ goes up. Intuitively, for larger d or δ, the option of becoming an exclusive supplier to the multinational becomes more attractive, leading a larger number of suppliers to accept the multinational's offer. Since $\pi_f^{\mathrm{EX}}(k)$ is an increasing function of k, the optimal strategy for the multinational, given that it chooses exclusivity, is to set $k=\bar{k}$ and its equilibrium profit equals $\pi_f^{\mathrm{EX}}(\bar{k})$.

5. Equilibrium mode of entry

From the multinational's perspective, exclusivity is attractive for two reasons. First, exclusivity prevents the multinational's local rivals from being able to enjoy the benefits of VTT provided by the multinational to its suppliers. Second, exclusivity limits the number of suppliers that serve the multinational's local rivals. Both of these advantages raise the production costs of the multinational's rivals. The disadvantage of exclusivity is that the multinational is served by only $\bar{k}$ ($< m$) suppliers while if it buys the intermediate in the open market, it is served by m competing suppliers. One thus naturally expects that either exclusivity or market interaction can be optimal for the multinational firm depending on parameter values. Exclusivity occurs in equilibrium if and only if $\Delta\pi_{\mathrm{f}} \equiv \pi_f^{\mathrm{EX}}(\bar{k}) - \pi_f^M \geq 0$.

Since $\pi_f^{\mathrm{EX}}(k)$ increases with d and k and the number of equilibrium suppliers of the multinational ($\bar{k}$) also rises with d, the profit differential $\Delta\pi_f$ definitely increases with d. It follows that $\Delta\pi_f > 0$ if and only if d exceeds a critical threshold d^*.[8]

Proposition 1. *Exclusivity occurs in equilibrium if and only if the extent of VTT undertaken by the multinational firm is sufficiently large (i.e., $d > d^*$).*

The multinational's entry under exclusivity impacts local industry in three ways: (i) it increases competition downstream and, all else equal, this raises the level of backward linkages (and thus consumer surplus); (ii) delinking reduces the degree of competition among suppliers and this tends to lower the aggregate output level of the intermediate good (as well as consumer surplus); and (iii) local suppliers benefit from VTT and this tends to raise the level of backward linkages. The net effect of these three forces can be either negative or positive.

[8] We assume that there exists a d^* such that $\Delta\pi_f|_{d=d^*} = 0$. If d^* does not exist, $\Delta\pi_f$ is either always negative or positive and such cases are of limited interest.

Local producers are affected in two separate ways by the multinational's entry under exclusivity. First, their market shares decline due to increased competition from a more efficient producer. Second, local producers suffer from the decline in the number of suppliers that sell to them. The delinking of $\bar{k}$ producers changes market structure of the two-tier industry and raises the market power of the $m-\bar{k}$ suppliers that serve local producers.

How do suppliers fare under exclusivity relative to autarky? Since the equilibrium number of suppliers serving the multinational ($\bar{k}$) cannot be solved for analytically, we are unable to derive general analytical results regarding the effects on suppliers. However, in the special case of upstream duopoly (considered in the next section), we show that, relative to autarky, if the extent of VTT is large then the supplier that serves the multinational is always better off while the other supplier is worse off. Nevertheless, the average profit across the two types of suppliers goes up.

6. Two local suppliers

To further explore the choice between exclusivity and market interaction, this section considers the case of upstream duopoly (i.e., $m=2$). Assumptions 1 and 2 imply that the equilibrium number of exclusive suppliers equals one (i.e., $\bar{k}=1$). Thus, exclusivity obtains in this case if and only if $\pi_f^{EX}(1)\geq\pi_f^M$, which is equivalent to

$$H\equiv\frac{(n+2)\alpha+2(n+1)(d+\delta c)}{7n+8}-\frac{2(n+1)\alpha+(3n^2+6n+2)\delta c}{3(n+2)(n+1)}\geq 0 \tag{12}$$

As per Proposition 1, the above inequality holds if and only if $d>d^*$. Furthermore, we can show the following:

Lemma 1. *Suppose Assumptions 1 and 2 hold and* $m=2$. *Then, the larger the cost-advantage of the multinational over its local competitors (i.e., the larger is* δ*), the weaker its incentive to choose an exclusive contract over market interaction* ($\frac{\partial H}{\partial \delta}<0$).

This result can be understood as follows. If the multinational has a large cost-advantage in transforming the intermediate good into the final product, then it is less worried about lowering the production cost of the intermediate and is more concerned about creating competition among its suppliers. As a result, when δ is big, the multinational is more likely to prefer market interaction to exclusivity with technology transfer.

To explore the effects of exclusivity on backward linkages and local welfare, we next confine our attention to the case where $\delta=0$. Based on (12), we can show the following result:

Proposition 2. *Suppose Assumptions 1 and 2 hold,* $m=2$, *and* $\delta=0$. *Then, (i) if* $n\geq 2$ *exclusivity always occurs in equilibrium; and (ii) if* $n=1$ *exclusivity arises iff* $d/\alpha>1/12$.

When the final good market is a duopoly (i.e., $n=1$) and the extent of VTT is large ($d/\alpha>1/12$), the benefit to the multinational of improving its supplier's technology dominates the cost of having only a single supplier. By contrast, when the final good market is relatively competitive ($n\geq 2$), delinking drives the multinational's choice: the multinational's strategic benefit of reducing the number of suppliers that serve its (many) local competitors is so significant that it prefers exclusivity regardless of the degree of VTT.[9]

[9] It is useful to note that Assumption 1 is less likely to hold when n is large: supplier 1's opportunity cost of becoming an exclusive supplier to the multinational is high when the number of local producers (n) is large.

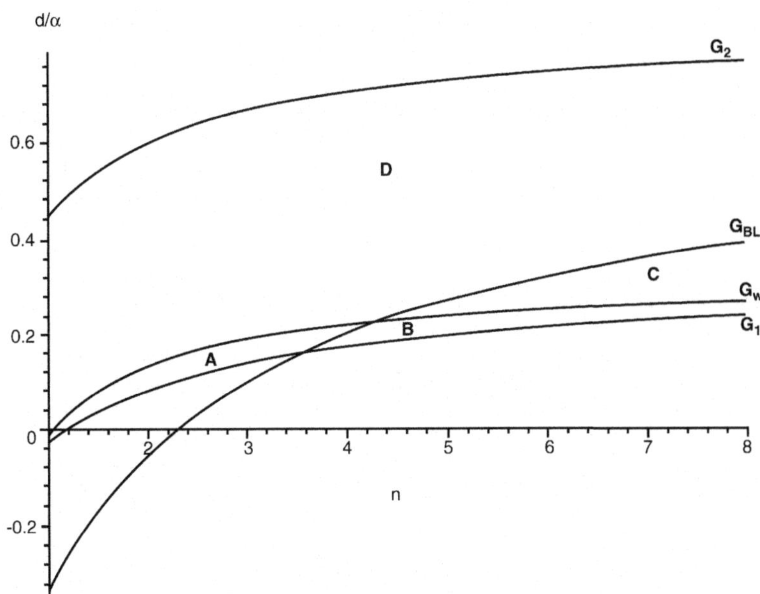

Fig. 1. Backward linkages and welfare under exclusivity ($m=2$).

How does exclusivity affect the two local suppliers? Assumption 1 guarantees that supplier 1 is better off relative to market interaction (and thus also relative to autarky). Straightforward calculations show that supplier 2 is better off under exclusivity if and only if $d/\alpha<(2n+1)/(3n+3)$. Thus, if VTT to supplier 1 is not significant, supplier 2 also gains from the multinational's entry under exclusivity. This is because exclusivity reduces the competition facing supplier 2 (in fact eliminates it in the case of upstream duopoly). But if VTT is substantial, then the multinational commands too large a market share, leading to a sharp decline in the derived demand facing supplier 2. In such a case, supplier 2 is worse off relative to autarky. Recall that at the contracting stage of the game where the multinational selects suppliers, the equilibrium probability of a supplier being invited to become an exclusive supplier to the multinational equals $\bar{k}/m$ (1/2 in the present case). It is easy to show that the average profit across the two suppliers is higher under exclusivity relative to autarky.

Turning to effect on the degree of backward linkages, we have that $BL^{EX}>BL^{A}$ if and only if

$$\frac{d}{\alpha}>\frac{2(n^2-n-3)}{3(n+1)(n+2)}=G_{BL}(n) \tag{13}$$

That is, for a given n, exclusivity increases the level of backward linkages if and only if the extent of VTT exceeds a certain threshold level: i.e., $\frac{d}{\alpha}>G_{BL}(n)$. Furthermore, this critical threshold $G_{BL}(n)$ increases with n: i.e., as the number of local rivals of the multinational increases, exclusivity is less likely to raise the degree of backward linkages in the host industry. The intuition for this is that if n is small, the increase in the derived demand for the intermediate caused by the multinational's entry is relatively large. As a result, the level of backward linkages rises despite the delinking effect of exclusivity. However, when n is big, the extra demand for the intermediate generated by the multinational's entry is too small to offset the negative effect of exclusivity on the degree of backward linkages in the local industry.

The entry of the multinational certainly hurts downstream producers. For the host economy, aggregate local welfare equals $W^{EX} = \Pi_f^{EX} + \Pi_h^{EX} + n\pi_j^{EX} + 0.5[BL^{EX}]^2$. Prior to the entry of the multinational, the level of local welfare is $W^A = 2\Pi_i^A + n\pi_j^A + 0.5[BL^A]^2$. It is tedious but straightforward to show that $W^{EX} > W^A$ if and only if the extent of VTT is above a certain threshold level: $\frac{d}{\alpha} > G_W(n)$.

Fig. 1 illustrates the effects of the multinational's entry on backward linkages and local welfare in the $(n, \frac{d}{\alpha})$ space. Assumptions 1 and 2 require that the feasible parameter values lie above curve $G_1(n)$ and below $G_2(n)$. Within the feasible region, Fig. 1 can be divided into four regions: A, B, C, and D. In region D, the multinational's entry raises both the level of backward linkages and local welfare. In region B, however, the multinational's entry lowers both the level of backward linkages and local welfare. For the other two areas, the degree of backward linkages and welfare do not move in the same direction: in region C, the multinational's entry raises local welfare even as it lowers the degree of backward linkages, whereas the opposite is true in region A.

The intuition for why the multinational's entry enhances both backward linkages and local welfare in region D is simple: If VTT is substantial, the multinational's entry is beneficial to the host country despite the negative effects of exclusivity. Likewise, if the extent of VTT is small and the local final good market is relatively competitive (i.e., n is big), such as in region B, the negative effect of exclusivity dominates the positive effects of demand creation and VTT and both local welfare and the level of backward linkages decline due to the multinational's entry.

For the other two areas (A and C), the multinational's entry increases either local welfare or the level of backward linkages (but not both), depending on the value of n. If n is small and VTT is not very substantial (region A), backward linkages increase but welfare declines. This is because when n is small, the multinational's entry leads to a substantial increase in the output of the intermediate good which translates into higher consumer surplus and greater profits for suppliers. However, for small n, the erosion of the profits of local producers that results from the multinational's entry is large and this negative effect on local producers leads to a reduction in local welfare. Area C can be similarly understood: If n is large and VTT is moderate, backward linkages decrease but local welfare increases with entry. The negative effect on backward linkages stems from the fact that the demand–creation effect of entry is weak when n is large. Local welfare increases despite the reduction in backward linkages because the benefits of VTT dominate the losses of local producers.

The following proposition highlights the possible negative effect of exclusivity on backward linkages:

Proposition 3. *Suppose Assumptions 1 and 2 hold, $m=2$, and $\delta=0$. Then, there exist parameter values (regions B and C in Fig. 1) for which the multinational firm enters with an exclusive contract and its entry lowers the level of backward linkages.*

7. Extensions of the basic model

We now consider several extensions of our basic model. First, we discuss the implications of entry and exit for our main results. Next, we establish that exclusivity can obtain in equilibrium even if the multinational transfers technology under market interaction. Finally, we examine exclusive contracts that, in addition to forbidding the multinational's suppliers from serving local producers, can also specify the price and/or quantity of the intermediate input. Throughout these extensions, we focus on the case of two local suppliers (i.e., $m=2$) in order to highlight the main forces at work.

7.1. Possibility of induced entry

In the basic model, the numbers of local producers and suppliers are assumed to be fixed. We now consider a situation where entry into each level of production is feasible and it involves a fixed (sunk) cost. Let free entry under autarky yield m suppliers and n producers. Also, assume that the multinational's cost advantage (δ) over local producers is such that it finds entry profitable whereas local producers do not. Under market interaction, the increase in derived demand generated by the multinational's entry can induce further entry into the intermediate market even in the absence of VTT (as in Markusen and Venables, 1999). If such induced entry does occur, the positive effect of the multinational's entry on the degree of backward linkages relative to autarky is even stronger.

Now consider exclusivity under free local entry. When (VTT, EX) is offered to local suppliers, the possibility of further entry affects their decisions regarding whether or not to accept the multinational's offer. Suppose $m=2$ and let supplier 1 be the invited supplier. If supplier 1 accepts the multinational's offer, supplier 2 becomes the sole supplier to local producers and competition in the intermediate market is softened due to exclusivity. Such reduction in competition may lead to further entry in the intermediate market where all new suppliers compete with supplier 2 in serving local producers. However, as was shown in the basic model, if the extent of VTT is large, supplier 2 is worse off under exclusivity despite that fact that it becomes the sole supplier to local producers: the multinational's entry significantly lowers the market share of local producers thereby lowering the derived demand facing supplier 2. Therefore, when VTT is large, further entry into the intermediate market does not occur. As a result, supplier 1's profit if it accepts the multinational's offer (VTT, EX) is the same as that in the basic model. If supplier 1 rejects the multinational's offer, market interaction takes place and the expansion in derived demand for the intermediate can encourage the entry of new suppliers (thereby lowering supplier 1's profit). Therefore, the possibility of further entry makes it more likely that the multinational's exclusivity offer is accepted by supplier 1 (i.e., Assumption 1 is more likely to hold).

One can also show that Assumption 2 is also more likely to hold when further entry into the intermediate market is feasible. Recall that Assumption 2 guarantees that if both suppliers are invited by the multinational, then at least one of them rejects its offer. Consider supplier 2's decision regarding the multinational's offer given that supplier 1 has accepted an exclusive contract. If supplier 2 also accepts the multinational's offer and further entry occurs, then new suppliers serve local producers and this causes supplier 2's profits to decline. On the other hand, if supplier 2 rejects the multinational's offer (given that supplier 1 accepts) then, as said before, no further entry takes place. Thus, compared to the basic model, the possibility of entry reduces supplier 2's payoff from accepting the multinational's offer while leaving its payoff from rejecting it unchanged.

In sum, we have argued that even when further entry into the intermediate market is feasible, no new suppliers enter the market when the extent of VTT is sufficiently large. While softening competition in the intermediate market, delinking also lowers the demand for local suppliers that are not invited by the multinational by creating a 'squeezing out' effect on local producers. In fact, if this squeezing out effect is strong enough, delinking may actually drive out some suppliers, further hurting local producers and lowering the degree of backward linkages in the local industry.

7.2. VTT under market interaction

In the model studied so far, only those suppliers that agree to exclusively serve the multinational receive VTT from it. Would the multinational find it profitable to transfer technology to local suppliers without restricting them from serving local producers (i.e., under market interaction)? The trade-off from the multinational's perspective is that VTT to both local suppliers reduces the market price of the intermediate relatively more compared to that under exclusivity but this price reduction also benefits its local competitors. Straightforward derivations show that the multinational's profit under market interaction with VTT equals

$$\pi_f^M(d) = \left[\frac{2(n+1)(\alpha+d)+(3n(n+2)+2)\delta c}{3(n+2)(n+1)}\right]^2 \tag{14}$$

while the profit of each supplier equals

$$\Pi_i^M(d) = \frac{n+2}{n+1}\left[\frac{(n+1)(\alpha+d)+\delta c}{3(n+2)}\right]^2 \quad \text{for } i=1,2, \tag{15}$$

where the dependence of both profit levels on d has been noted to emphasize that market interaction now involves VTT.

Since VTT incurs no direct costs in our model, it is easy to see that the multinational always prefers market interaction with VTT than without it: the own cost reduction effect of VTT dominates the indirect loss resulting from the decline in rivals' costs. Thus, if VTT is possible under market interaction, the entry decision of the multinational depends on the comparison between $\pi_f^{EX}(1)$ (i.e., its profit under (VTT, EX)) and $\pi_f^M(d)$ above. This comparison yields the following result:

Proposition 2B. *Suppose Assumptions 1 and 2 hold, $m=2$, and $\delta=0$. Then, (i) if $n\geq 2$ exclusivity always occurs in equilibrium; and (ii) if $n=1$ exclusivity arises iff $d/\alpha>1/2$.*

Thus, when the local final good market is a duopoly (i.e., $n=1$), exclusivity is less likely to occur if VTT occurs under market interaction. However, if $n\geq 2$, once again, the multinational prefers exclusivity because of the delinking it creates, i.e., the strategic incentive of raising rivals' costs proves dominant when the number of such rivals is large.

7.3. Exclusivity under input price contracting

Here we consider the case where the multinational can not only impose exclusivity in return for VTT but can also specify the price at which its (exclusive) suppliers provide the intermediate good. Such a contract is realistic if the multinational has substantial bargaining power over its suppliers and can use that power to implement contracts that local producers cannot. We consider two possible contracts under exclusivity: one in which the multinational adopts a two-part pricing scheme and the other in which the contract is a quantity–price package. As in the case of other extensions, we limit our attention to the case of two local suppliers (i.e., $m=2$). The contract proposed by the multinational is carried out if the approached supplier accepts its offer and market interaction with VTT prevails otherwise. Thus, $\Pi_i^M(d)$ in equation (15) is the reservation payoff of the approached supplier.[10]

[10] We assume throughout that the multinational's entry does not change the nature of interaction between local firms and their suppliers. That is, the local industry continues to interact via the market after the multinational's entry. See Conclusions for further discussion of this issue.

7.3.1. Two-part pricing

Under two-part pricing, the contract offered by the multinational is of the form (VTT, EX, $F+(c_I-d)q$). That is, the multinational provides VTT to supplier 1 and secures the intermediate at marginal cost (c_I-d) for a lump sum fee F. The intermediate price w paid by local producers to supplier 2 is determined by the successive Cournot model and the marginal cost of a typical local firm equals $w+c$. The resulting Cournot quantities determine their derived demand for the intermediate input. Facing this derived demand, supplier 2 chooses its output (which in turn determines w). Straightforward derivations yield the multinational's profit under the two-part pricing contract:

$$\pi_f^{TP} = \left[\frac{(n+4)\alpha + (3n+4)(d+\delta c)}{4(n+2)}\right]^2 - F \tag{16}$$

The multinational prefers a two-part pricing contract if and only if it leads to greater joint profits for it and its supplier relative to market interaction with VTT:

$$\pi_f^{TP} + F > \pi_f^M(d) + \Pi_1^M(d) \tag{17}$$

Assuming $\delta=0$, it is easy to show that, as in the basic model, exclusivity occurs under two-part pricing if and only if $n<n^{TP}(d)$.[11] The intuition for this is that as n increases, the multinational has to compensate supplier 1 more for agreeing to be its exclusive supplier because its reservation profit, $\Pi_I^M(d)$, increases with n.

With regard to the effect on the backward linkages, it can be shown that the multinational's entry under an exclusive two-part pricing contract always raises the degree of backward linkages relative to autarky. This is because a two-part pricing contract eliminates the double markup problem that exists under linear contracts and market interaction. However, the effect on local welfare is ambiguous: While a larger output enhances consumer welfare, local producers and their suppliers get hurt under two-part pricing since such a contract allows the multinational to obtain the intermediate good at marginal cost thereby giving it a sharp cost advantage over its local rivals.

7.3.2. A bundling contract

Suppose now that the multinational proposes a bundling (or price–quantity package) contract of the form (q_f,T), where q_f is the amount of intermediate input delivered by supplier 1 in exchange for total payment T. As before, the multinational makes a take-it-or-leave-it offer and market interaction with VTT occurs if there is disagreement between the multinational and the approached supplier (i.e., supplier 1). If the multinational's offer is accepted by supplier 1, then local producers compete in a Cournot fashion observing the contract (q_f,T). Therefore, under a bundling contract,

[11] It is easy to show using Maple that $n^{TP}(d)$ is given by

$$n^{TP}(d) = \frac{4(\alpha+d)(3\alpha+21d+\sqrt{30\alpha^2+60\alpha d+246d^2})}{(7\alpha+13d)(\alpha-5d)}$$

and that $n^{TP}(d)$ increases with d, i.e., the likelihood of a two-part pricing contract being chosen over market interaction increases with the degree of VTT.

the multinational effectively becomes a Stackelberg leader (as in Milliou et al., 2003). It can be shown that the joint profits of the multinational and its exclusive supplier equal:

$$\pi_f^B + \Pi_1^B = \frac{[(n+2)\alpha + 2(n+1)(d+\delta c)]^2}{8(n+1)(n+2)} \tag{18}$$

and that $\pi_f^B + \Pi_l^B > \pi_f^M(d) + \Pi_l^M(d)$ for all parameter values. In other words, exclusivity always occurs under bundling. Furthermore, $\pi_f^B + \Pi_l^B > \pi_f^{TP} + F$, i.e., a bundling contract always dominates a two-part pricing contract.

Similar to the case of two-part pricing, the multinational's entry under a bundling contract always raises the level of backward linkages in the local industry. However, as under two-part pricing, the welfare effects of such entry on the local industry can be negative.

8. Concluding remarks

This paper adds value to the literature on backward linkages and FDI in two main respects. First, while existing literature focuses primarily on the demand-creating effects of the entry of multinationals on local industry (e.g., Markusen and Venables, 1999), we analyze the supply-side effects of such entry. In particular, the possibility of VTT from a multinational to its suppliers coupled with an exclusivity condition is a novel feature of our analysis. Second, our model considers oligopolistic competition at both stages of production. Such a setting enables us to examine how the contractual relationship between the multinational and its local suppliers affects strategic interaction in the local industry.

We show that, in addition to the competition effect identified in Markusen and Venables (1999), the multinational's entry can also create a delinking effect: When exclusivity arises in equilibrium, local producers lose some of their old suppliers to the multinational. Put differently, while the entry of the multinational creates additional demand for the intermediate good, it can also reduce the number of suppliers available to local producers. This negative supply-side effect can dominate the positive demand-side effect so that the total output of the intermediate good (as well as the final good) can shrink due to the multinational's entry.

In the present model, under an exclusive contract, the multinational buys the intermediate good only from its exclusive suppliers. In reality, an exclusive contract may entail a commitment only from the suppliers' side. Under such an exclusive contract, the multinational would be free to source the intermediate from all available suppliers (i.e., it can 'mix' between exclusive and non-exclusive suppliers). The benefit to the multinational of such a mixing strategy is that it can put competitive pressure on its exclusive suppliers. But such pressure, if effective, will make exclusivity less attractive to local suppliers. Furthermore, mixing on the part of the multinational will increase the profitability of those suppliers that do not commit to serving the multinational exclusively. We believe that an exclusive contract that leaves the multinational free to source from all suppliers can still emerge in equilibrium. However, the number of local suppliers that accept such a contract is likely to be smaller relative to the case where the multinational commits to sourcing only from its exclusive suppliers.

Our model assumes that local producers cannot engage in exclusive relationships with their suppliers. This assumption is made for tractability and to capture the idea that the ability to transfer technology gives the multinational leverage over its suppliers that is not available to local producers. Finally, the model does not consider competition amongst multinational firms. Further research is needed to determine how the possibility of such competition will alter the main results of this paper.

Acknowledgement

We thank two anonymous referees, Jonathan Eaton, Taiji Furusawa, Jörn Kleinert, Jim Markusen, Larry Qiu, Santanu Roy, and participants at Kiel Institute's Conference on Multinationals and International Integration (Oct. 2004), at Kobe University's Conference on New Dimensions in International Trade: Outsourcing, Cross-border Merger and Culture (Dec. 2004), and at SMU's Economics Department's Faculty Symposium (Dec. 2004) for helpful comments.

References

Antrás, P., 2003. Firms, contracts, and trade structure. Quarterly Journal of Economics 118, 1375–1418.

Antrás, P., Helpman, E., 2004. Global sourcing. Journal of Political Economy 112, 552–580.

Blalock, G., Gertler, G., 2005. Welfare gains from foreign direct investment through technology transfer to local suppliers. Cornell University and University Of California, Berkeley, Mimeo.

Javorcik, B.S., 2004. Does foreign direct investment increase the productivity of domestic firms? In search of spillovers through backward linkages. American Economic Review 94, 605–627.

Lall, S., 1980. Vertical inter-firm linkages in LDCs: an empirical study. Oxford Bulletin of Economics and Statistics 42, 203–206.

Lin, P., Saggi, K., 2005. Multinational firms and backward linkages: a critical survey and a simple model. In: Blomstrom, M., Graham, E., Moran, T. (Eds.), Does Foreign Direct Investment Promote Development? Institute for International Economics, Washington, DC.

Lorentzen, J., Mollgaard, P.H., 2000. Vertical restraints and technology transfer: inter-firm agreements in Eastern Europe's car component industry. Copenhagen Business School, Mimeo.

Markusen, J.R., Venables, A., 1999. Foreign direct investment as a catalyst for industrial development. European Economic Review 43, 335–356.

Milliou, C., Petrakis, E., Vettas, N., 2003. Endogenous Contracts Under Bargaining in Competing Vertical Chains. CEPR Discussion Papers Series, vol. 3976.

Mizuno, J., 1995. The present condition and problems of the automobile industry in the Republic of Korea. Institute of Developing Economics, Mimeo.

Moran, T., 1998. Foreign Direct Investment and Development. Institute For International Economics, Washington, DC.

Pack, H., Saggi, K., 2001. Vertical technology transfer via international outsourcing. Journal of Development Economics 65, 389–415.

Qiu, L.D., Tao, Z., 2001. Export, foreign direct investment, and local content requirement. Journal of Development Economics 66, 101–125.

Rodriguez-Clare, A., 1996. Multinationals, linkages, and economic development. American Economic Review 86, 852–873.

Salinger, M., 1988. Vertical mergers and market foreclosure. Quarterly Journal of Economics 103, 345–356.

Salop, S.C., Scheffman, D.T., 1987. Cost raising strategies. Journal of Industrial Economics 36, 19–34.

Chapter 9

FOREIGN DIRECT INVESTMENT IN A TWO-TIER OLIGOPOLY: COORDINATION, VERTICAL INTEGRATION, AND WELFARE*,#

BY PING LIN AND KAMAL SAGGI[1]

Lingnan University, Hong Kong; Vanderbilt University, U.S.A.

We study foreign direct investment (FDI) by two independent investors/entrants into a two-tiered oligopolistic industry. An FDI subsidy at a single stage of production can be sufficient to resolve the coordination problem facing investors thereby inducing entry at both stages. However, due to *linkage offsetting*, FDI at both stages may yield lower domestic welfare than FDI at a single stage. Vertical integration not only solves the coordination problem, it also eliminates double marginalization. But since the integrated multinational does not sell the intermediate to local firms, its entry generates *no* vertical linkages and can yield lower welfare than FDI by independent firms.

1. INTRODUCTION

In this article, we study foreign direct investment (FDI) via direct entry into a two-tiered vertically related industry and derive the welfare effects of such FDI from the host country's perspective. Given the *complementarity* of production in vertically related industries, it stands to reason that decisions regarding FDI into such industries are likely to be *interdependent*. For example, FDI by an intermediate good supplier can enhance the FDI incentive of a final good producer by ensuring steady local supply of the intermediate, helping lower its local price due to increased competition in the intermediate market or providing a higher-quality version of the intermediate relative to local suppliers. Similarly, an upstream/intermediate good producer may find it more attractive to undertake FDI into a country if prior (or simultaneous) FDI into the downstream sector increases derived demand for the intermediate good. Thus, FDI into one type of production activity may induce additional FDI into related upstream and/or downstream activities. Casual observation suggests that the aspects of FDI we model in this article are highly relevant in the real world. For example, the investment of Japanese automakers in Southeast Asian countries in the 1970s and 1980s was accompanied by investment by producers of auto parts and subsystems.[2] More generally, FDI flows occur in virtually all interrelated sectors of the world economy, including resource sectors, manufacturing, distribution, and services.

In our two-tiered oligopoly model, two foreign investors—one that produces an intermediate good and another that produces a final good—decide independently whether or not to enter a host country. FDI by either firm incurs a fixed cost and potentially generates technological

*Manuscript received June 2009; revised May 2010.

[1] We thank the co-editor Charles Horioka and three anonymous referees for extremely helpful comments on an earlier draft of this article. All errors are our own. Please address correspondence to: Ping Lin, Department of Economics, Lingnan University of Hong Kong, Tuen Mun, Hong Kong. Telephone (852)-2616-7203. E-mail: *plin@ln.edu.hk*.

[2] A more specific example of the considerations captured by our model is provided by PepsiCo's recent experience in China. PepsiCo's entry into the potato chip business in China has involved both coordinated entry with an upstream supplier as well as vertical integration (after the initial supplier pulled out shortly after entering the Chinese market). PepsiCo entered China in the early 1980s. In 2001, due to rising local demand for potato chips, PepsiCo started to plant potatoes in the country and even brought one of its biggest suppliers in the United States, Black Gold Potato Sales of North Dakota, to China. One year later, however, Black Gold Potato Sales pulled out of China, partly due to a lack of understanding of the local environment. Subsequently, PepsiCo continued its potato production in China as a vertically integrated firm utilizing imported proprietary potato seeds. See *The Wall Street Journal*, December 19, 2005, for further details.

This chapter was originally appeared in *International Economic Review* **52**, 1271–1290.

spillovers for local firms in that sector that reduce their marginal cost of production. The interdependence between the decision making of the two investors manifests itself in the form of multiple Nash equilibria. More specifically, if fixed entry costs are large, there exist two Nash equilibria—one in which both firms enter and another in which neither does. The no-entry equilibrium can exist even when entry at each level is profitable provided both firms choose to invest. Under such circumstances, a *coordination problem* characterizes the decision making of firms.[3] Our model fits well with Rodrik's (1996) argument that in the absence of scale economies in production, for coordination failures to exist between upstream and downstream industries some type of imperfect tradability for some of the goods, services, or technologies associated with manufacturing was necessary. In our stylized model, such imperfect tradability arises because both goods need to produced locally in the host country.

The existence of the coordination problem implies that an appropriately designed government subsidy to FDI at one level of the two-tiered industry can induce FDI at both levels. For example, an FDI subsidy upstream can make entry a dominant strategy for the foreign firm producing the intermediate good. Realizing this, the foreign firm producing the final good, which otherwise would not have entered the local market, will choose to enter as well.[4] However, our model clarifies that, from the host country's viewpoint, FDI at both stages of production is not necessarily preferable to FDI at a single stage. The novel insight underlying this result is that FDI at both levels of the industry involves a partial *offsetting of vertical linkages* relative to FDI at only one level of the industry. To see this more clearly, suppose FDI occurs at only the final good stage. Such FDI increases *backward linkages* in the local industry by increasing total demand for the intermediate good. Now imagine that FDI into the final good market is accompanied by FDI into the intermediate market. If so, the backward linkages generated by FDI in the final good market are partially captured by the foreign entrant into the intermediate market, something that is detrimental for domestic welfare. Similarly, FDI at both stages involves a partial offsetting of *forward linkages* between local suppliers and downstream producers relative to FDI at (only) the intermediate stage. The welfare cost imposed on the local economy by such offsetting of vertical linkages can make single stage FDI more attractive than FDI at multiple stages.

Unlike much of the existing literature on coordination failures, we also consider vertical integration as a solution to the coordination problem. This is important because foreign investors with intertwined profitabilities have a strong incentive to coordinate their decisions, and vertical integration is one such method of doing so.[5] If vertically integrated, the two foreign investors no longer face a coordination problem since the integrated unit can always choose to enter at both levels of the industry. However, the vertically integrated firm is subject to an important incentive constraint: It must take into account the fact that supplying the intermediate good to rival downstream producers hurts the profitability of its downstream business. As a result, one would expect that, relative to an independent intermediate good supplier, the vertically integrated firm may be less willing to sell the intermediate good to local final good producers. This intuition is borne out rather sharply in our model: The negative effect of supplying the intermediate good turns out to be so strong for the vertically integrated firm that it chooses to not supply its downstream rivals at all. This naturally implies that the vertically integrated firm forgoes profit that could be earned by supplying the intermediate to local final good producers. As a result, there exist circumstances where a vertically integrated firm is *less likely* to undertake

[3] See Pack and Westphal (1986) and Okuno-Fujiwara (1988) for early analyses of how coordination failures can arise during industralization and the types of policies government can use to address such failures.

[4] Coordination problems arising from production and investment complementarities are not the only reason why FDI sometimes fail to occur. For example, Gordon and Bovenberg (1996) have shown that the informational disadvantage faced by foreign investors relative to domestic ones can also make capital internationally immobile. They also show that subsidies to capital inflows by capital importing countries can sometimes be optimal in order to address the "lemons" problem created by the presence of such type of asymmetric information.

[5] Clearly, coordination can, in principle, be achieved without vertical integration. However, in the context of a vertically linked industry, it is natural to focus on vertical integration since it helps avoid the double markup problem (or double marginalization).

FDI than two independent firms. For example, we find that the joint profit of two independent firms is higher than that of a vertically integrated unit when the local final good market is highly competitive (i.e., the number of downstream local producers is large). Furthermore, even though the vertical integrated unit avoids the double marginalization problem that characterizes oligopolistic market interaction between independent upstream and downstream firms, the decision of such a firm to not supply the intermediate good to local final good producers has adverse welfare consequences for the host country. Indeed, we show that the entry of a vertically integrated firm is preferable to that of two independent firms only if the downstream market is sufficiently competitive; otherwise, the host country is better off with independent entry at both stages. Interestingly, the decision of foreign firms regarding vertical integration turns out to be in harmony with local welfare considerations only when market structure at both levels is moderately competitive.

Our two-tier model also shows that greater technological spillovers from FDI to local competitors can actually *encourage* FDI under certain conditions. This occurs because higher spillovers at one level of the industry intensify post-FDI competition at that stage, which makes FDI into the *other* stage more attractive, and due to complementarity in production this indirectly enhances the incentive for FDI into the first stage. For instance, an increase in FDI spillovers in the final good market increases derived demand for the intermediate good, making FDI into the intermediate stage more attractive. And FDI into the intermediate good makes FDI into the final good relatively more profitable.[6] To the best of our knowledge, this positive relationship between incentives for FDI and the degree of technological spillovers has not been identified in the existing literature.[7] Indeed, in models with only one stage of production, greater spillovers from FDI to local firms generally make FDI less likely.

In the existing literature on FDI, two questions in particular have received a great deal of attention. The first question is locational: when and why firms opt for FDI over exporting. The second question pertains to the organizational form of foreign entry: Given that production is to be shifted abroad, what is the optimal entry mode of FDI? The typical menu of organizational choices considered includes technology licensing, the formation of a joint venture, or the establishment of a wholly owned subsidiary.[8] The two strands of literature analyzing these questions have enriched our understanding of real-world patterns of FDI and its effects on host countries, but they have had little to say about FDI into vertically related activities. Indeed, to the best of our knowledge, only a handful of papers study FDI at multiple levels of a vertically related industry. Markusen and Venables (1999) model the effects of FDI on the host economy in a two-tier industry, but they consider FDI only into the downstream market. In addition, their monopolistic model abstracts from strategic interaction among foreign investors that are central to our oligopoly model. Lin and Saggi (2007) consider the effects of downstream FDI in a two-tier oligopolistic model, but they focus on the effects of an exclusivity condition that a multinational might impose on local suppliers in return from transferring technology to them. In particular, they abstract from FDI into the intermediate market and do not study vertical integration and its effects.

The remainder of the article is organized as follows. Section 2 presents our basic model of FDI in a two-tier industry, and it highlights the coordination problem affecting the entry decisions of foreign firms. Section 3 derives and compares the welfare effects of various patterns of FDI. Section 4 examines how technology spillovers at both levels of the vertical industry affect incentives for FDI. Section 5 compares the FDI incentive of a vertically integrated firm with that of two independent firms. Section 6 discusses the case of export-oriented FDI and Section 7 concludes.

[6] Obviously, a similar logic implies that an increase in technological spillovers in the intermediate market can increase the incentives for FDI at both stages of production.

[7] See Saggi (2002) for a detailed critical survey of this literature.

[8] See, for example, Saggi (1996), Buckley and Casson (1998), Markusen and Venables (1999), Helpman et al. (2004), Eicher and Kang (2005), and Nocke and Yeaple (2007). For an in-depth discussion of the basic considerations at play, see Markusen (1995).

2. MODEL

We consider a host economy that produces two final goods (x and y) and an intermediate good (z). Good x serves as the numeraire and is produced by a perfectly competitive sector. Labor is the only factor of production. One unit of labor produces one unit of good x so that the price of good x equals the wage rate in the economy that is normalized to 1.

Consumer preferences over the final two goods are as follows: $U(x, y) = x + u(y)$. Since preferences are quasi-linear, the inverse demand function for good y can be written as $p(y)$. To facilitate analytical derivations, we assume that $u(y)$ is quadratic so that demand for good y is linear: $p(y) = a - y$.

One unit of good y requires one unit of good z. From here on, we refer to good y as simply "the final good" and good z as "the intermediate good." There exist $n \geq 1$ downstream firms that produce the final good and $m \geq 1$ upstream firms (called local suppliers) that produce the intermediate. Each local supplier's unit cost of production equals $c_I > 0$. The marginal cost of a final good producer equals the sum of the price of the intermediate, denoted by w, and the unit cost of transforming the intermediate into final good, denoted by $c > 0$.

A foreign producer of the intermediate good, called firm A, and a foreign producer of the final good, called firm B, are contemplating entry via greenfield FDI into the host country industry. The fixed cost of FDI entry at the intermediate stage equals $F \geq 0$ while that at the final good stage equals $G \geq 0$. Each foreign firm possesses a cost advantage over its local competitors. Specifically, the unit cost of production for firm A equals c_A, where $c_A \leq c_I$, whereas that of firm B is c_B, where $c_B \leq c$.[9]

We assume that incoming FDI has the potential to generate technology spillovers to local firms, and we model such spillovers as follows. Upon FDI by firm A, the unit cost of each local supplier i becomes

$$c_i = c_I - s_A(c_I - c_A) = c_A + (1 - s_A)\Delta_A, \quad i = 1, 2, \ldots, m,$$

where $s_A \in [0, 1]$ measures the degree of technological spillover at the intermediate stage, and $\Delta_A \equiv c_I - c_A$ represents the cost differential between local suppliers and firm A (in the absence of any spillovers). Similarly, FDI by firm B at the final good stage reduces the cost of production of each domestic producer j to

$$c_j = c - s_B(c_I - c_A) = c_B + (1 - s_B)\Delta_B, \quad j = 1, 2, \ldots, n,$$

where $s_B \in [0, 1]$ is the spillover parameter in the downstream market and $\Delta_B \equiv c - c_B$ equals the cost advantage of the firm B over its local competitors (in the absence of any spillovers).

The timing of the game is as follows. First, the two foreign firms simultaneously decide whether or not to enter the host country. Then, as in Salinger (1988), interaction between suppliers of the intermediate good and producers of the final good occurs as follows. Taking the unit price of the intermediate as given, all final good producers compete in quantities (i.e., Cournot fashion). And given the derived demand generated by downstream competition, intermediate good suppliers compete in quantities, which establishes the equilibrium price of the intermediate. It is straightforward to show that the equilibrium price of the intermediate good under autarky (or no FDI entry) denoted by $\langle N \rangle$ equals

$$w^N = \frac{a - c + mc_I}{m + 1}. \tag{1}$$

[9] In what follows, we assume that the cost advantages of the foreign firms are not so large that foreign entry leads to exit of local firms.

2.1. *FDI at the Intermediate Stage.* Let $\pi_A^A(s_A, m, n)$ denote the equilibrium profit of firm A (gross of entry cost) if it enters the host country but firm B does not. Under this market structure, denoted by $\langle A \rangle$, derived demand for the intermediate good is as the same as that under autarky. If firm A enters the local market, the number of suppliers of the intermediate good increases relative to autarky, and the cost configurations of these suppliers may also change because of technological spillovers from firm A.

Increased competition upstream and the possible cost reduction implied by such spillovers lowers the equilibrium price of the intermediate good, which in turn benefits downstream final goods producers—that is, FDI upstream creates additional *forward linkages* in the local industry. Furthermore, it also lowers the price of the final good and increases consumer surplus relative to autarky. At the same time, however, FDI entry by firm A hurts local suppliers of the intermediate good by increasing competition in that market. The equilibrium price of the intermediate good under $\langle A \rangle$ is easily calculated:

$$w^A = \frac{a - c + m(c_I - s_A\Delta_A) + c_A}{m+2}, \tag{2}$$

where it is straightforward that $w^A < w^N$.

2.2. *FDI into the Final Good.* Let $\pi_B^B(s_B, m, n)$ denote the equilibrium profit of firm B under the market structure $\langle B \rangle$ where it enters but firm A does not. FDI entry by firm B intensifies competition in the final good market by increasing the number of firms and by generating FDI spillovers to local downstream firms. Increased competition downstream raises derived demand for the intermediate good and the sales of upstream suppliers increase—that is, FDI downstream creates additional *backward linkages* in the local industry. Increased competition in the downstream sector also enhances consumer welfare. The negative effect of firm B's entry on the host country is that it increases competition in the final good market so that market shares and profits of local final good producers tend to decline due to firm B's entry (unless the spillover effects are sufficiently strong). The equilibrium price of the intermediate good under the FDI entry pattern $\langle B \rangle$ equals

$$w^B = \frac{a - (c_B + n(c - s_B\Delta_B)/(n+1)) + mc_I}{m+1}, \tag{3}$$

where $w^B \geq w^N$ and $w^B > w^N$ if $c_B < c$.

2.3. *FDI at Both Levels.* Denote the FDI entry pattern where both firms A and B enter the local industry by $\langle AB \rangle$. As is clear, under $\langle AB \rangle$ the degree of competition in the local industry increases at both stages of production, and this lowers prices of both the intermediate good and the final good. Furthermore, local firms at both levels of the industry may enjoy the benefits of spillovers from FDI.

Let $\pi_A^{AB}(s_A, s_B, m, n)$ and $\pi_B^{AB}(s_A, s_B, m, n)$ denote the equilibrium profits of firm A and firm B, respectively, under the FDI entry pattern $\langle AB \rangle$. It is obvious that

- $\pi_A^{AB}(s_A, s_B, m, n) > \pi_A^A(s_A, m, n)$; and
- $\pi_B^{AB}(s_A, s_B, m, n) > \pi_B^B(s_A, m, n)$.

In other words, each foreign firm earns greater profit from entering the host market if the other foreign firm also enters the other tier of the vertically related industry than if it does not. For example, firm A's profit is greater if both firms A and B enter the local market relative to when firm A enters alone. This is due to two reasons. First, firm B's entry intensifies competition in the downstream sector, and this increases demand for the intermediate good. Second, technological spillovers generated by firm B also benefit firm A: Such spillovers in the final good market enable local firms to produce a larger quantity of the final good, thereby creating more demand for the intermediate good.

It is straightforward to derive the equilibrium price of the intermediate good under $\langle AB \rangle$:

$$w^{AB} = \frac{1}{m+2}\left[a - \frac{c_B + n(c - s_B\Delta_B)}{n+1} + m(c_I - s_A\Delta_A) + c_A\right]. \tag{4}$$

2.4. *The FDI Entry Game.* Firms A and B simultaneously and independently decide whether or not to enter the host country. The payoff matrix of this FDI entry game is as follows:

		Firm B	
		Enter (E)	Not Enter (N)
Firm A	Enter (E)	$\pi_A^{AB} - F,\ \pi_B^{AB} - G$	$\pi_A^A - F,\ 0$
	Not Enter (N)	$0,\ \pi_B^B - G$	$0,\ 0$

Depending on parameter values, each of the four cells can arise as an equilibrium outcome: $\langle A \rangle$ obtains if $\pi_A^A > F$ but $\pi_B^{AB} \leq G$; $\langle B \rangle$ obtains if $\pi_B^B > G$ but $\pi_A^{AB} \leq F$; $\langle AB \rangle$ results if $\pi_A^{AB} > F$ and $\pi_B^{BB} > G$; and the autarkic market structure $\langle N \rangle$ persists if $\pi_A^A \leq F$ and $\pi_B^B \leq G$. The equilibrium pattern of the FDI entry game is depicted in Figure 1.

For parameter values in Region I of Figure 1, entry costs are so low that it is a dominant strategy for both firms A and B to enter. In Region II, entry is the dominant strategy for B but not for firm A; it is worthwhile for firm A to enter only if firm B enters as well. Similarly, in Region IV, entry is the dominant strategy for firm A but not for firm B, and firm B enters only if firm A does so as well. In Region III, two Nash equilibria coexist. In one equilibrium both firms enter whereas in the other neither firm does. Obviously, the two firms are better off under

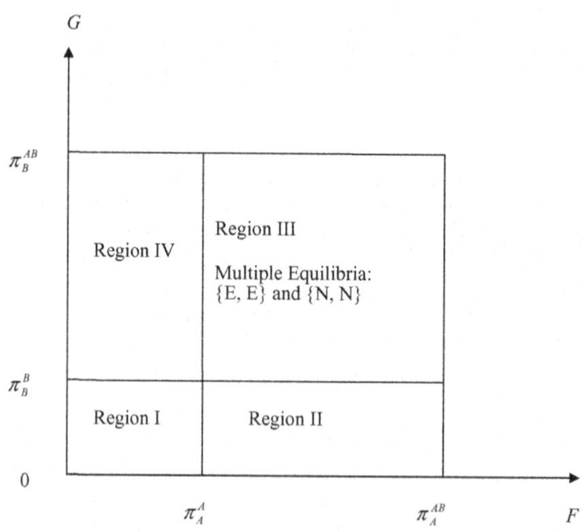

FIGURE 1

EQUILIBRIUM PATTERNS OF FDI

the first Nash equilibrium. The coexistence of $\{N, N\}$ in Region III highlights the coordination problem faced by the two firms while making independent decisions regarding entry at the two stages of the vertically linked industry in the host country.

PROPOSITION 1 (COORDINATION PROBLEM OF VERTICALLY RELATED FDI). *If* $\pi_A^A(s_A, m, n) < F < \pi_A^{AB}(s_A, s_B, m, n)$ *and* $\pi_B^B(s_B, m, n) < G < \pi_B^{AB}(s_A, s_B, m, n)$, *then both* $\{E, E\}$ *and* $\{N, N\}$ *are Nash equilibria of the FDI entry game.*

Perhaps the purest illustration of the coordination problem characterizing FDI into the vertically related industry can be provided by the case where $m = n = 0$. When local industry is nonexistent at both levels, the absence of FDI implies that the final good is not supplied to the local economy at all. Under such a scenario, the coordination problem manifests itself in two starkly different Nash equilibria: one in which domestic welfare is zero and another in which it is strictly positive. In general, it is easy to show that the degree of the coordination problem declines with the degree of local industrial development: That is, an increase in industry scale either upstream (as measured by m) or downstream (as measured by n) reduces the parameter space over which $\{N, N\}$ obtains as a Nash equilibrium. We can show that

$$\frac{\partial(\pi_B^{AB} - \pi_B^B)}{\partial m} < 0 \quad \text{and} \quad \frac{\partial(\pi_A^{AB} - \pi_A^A)}{\partial n} < 0,$$

that is an increase in the number of domestic suppliers reduces the dependence of firm B on firm A's entry decision while an increase in the number of domestic final good producers reduces the dependence of firm A's entry decision on that of firm B.

The coordination problem facing the two firms can be overcome in at least two separate ways. First, the host country could subsidize FDI, thereby making entry a dominant strategy for one of them, which in turn induces the other firm to enter even if it is not subsidized.[10] The other way to solve the coordination problem is for firms A and B to enter as a *vertically integrated* entity—a strategy we consider in Section 5. To examine the desirability of an FDI subsidy policy, in the following section, we first study the welfare effects of FDI on the host industry. An interesting insight of this analysis is that the host country is not necessarily better off with FDI at both levels of the industry.

3. PATTERNS OF FDI AND DOMESTIC WELFARE

In this section we examine two important questions from the viewpoint of the host country. First, how do the different patterns of FDI rank in terms of domestic welfare? Second, do the various patterns of FDI necessarily yield higher welfare than autarky?

The existing literature on FDI has emphasized two types of benefits of FDI to the host country: technological spillovers to domestic firms at the level of the industry at which FDI occurs (see Saggi, 2002, for an in-depth discussion) and the vertical linkages generated within the domestic industry—see Rodriguez-Clare (1996), Markusen and Venables (1999), and Lin and Saggi (2007).

As was already noted, when market structure is oligopolistic, FDI also generates a competition effect since multinationals gain market share at the expense of competing local firms. However, besides this usual horizontal competition effect of FDI, in our model, FDI has an additional negative effect on local firms that arises due to the two-tier production structure we consider. For example, consider the FDI entry pattern $\langle B \rangle$ relative to autarky. The entry of firm B increases derived demand for the intermediate good, which in turn raises its price—an outcome that is

[10] It is worth noting that fiscal and financial incentives designed to attract FDI are widespread in the global economy (UNCTAD, 2003). It is conceivable that in economies with a severely limited degree of industrial development, such incentives to FDI, if properly designed, can help overcome coordination problems affecting the decisions of independent foreign investors.

detrimental to local final good producers. This indirect price effect of firm B's entry, together with increased competition in the downstream market, makes such entry doubly problematic for local competitors of firm B. It is easy to see that the same argument applies with respect to a comparison of FDI entry patterns $\langle AB \rangle$ and $\langle A \rangle$. In fact, using (1), (2), and (3) we can show the following lemma:

LEMMA 1. *If $c_B < c$, then $w^B > w^N$ and $w^{AB} > w^A$, for all s_A and s_B. That is, FDI entry by firm B raises costs of its local competitors by increasing the price of the intermediate good.*[11]

Let $\pi_z^k(s_A, s_B, m, n)$ denote the equilibrium profit of a typical local supplier in the intermediate sector and $\pi_y^k(s_A, s_B, m, n)$ that of a local final good producer under FDI entry pattern k, where $k = \langle N \rangle, \langle A \rangle, \langle B \rangle$, or $\langle AB \rangle$. Aggregate domestic welfare is then given by

$$W^k \equiv m\pi_z^k(s_A, s_B, m, n) + n\pi_y^k(s_A, s_B, m, n) + CS^k(s_A, s_B, m, n),$$

where CS^k denotes domestic consumer surplus under FDI entry pattern k.

We are now ready to study the welfare properties of different FDI entry patterns. We initially ignore technology spillovers and concentrate on the effects of FDI on market structure and vertical linkages in the domestic industry. Once these effects are clearly understood, we then discuss the impact of technology spillovers.

3.1. *Is More FDI Necessarily Better?* To concentrate on the trade-off between the beneficial linkage effects of FDI and its negative competition effects, in this section we abstract from technology spillovers from FDI and set $s_A = 0$ and $s_B = 0$. For simplicity, we assume that firms A and B do not have any cost advantages over their counterparts in the host country. In fact, as we shall see in the next section, the competition effects of FDI almost dominate the linkage effects even when foreign firms do not possess any cost advantages over their local competitors.

Our first welfare result is rather surprising in that it shows that in an economy that has production capabilities at both stages, opening up to FDI at only the level of the local industry can sometimes be *more* desirable than opening up at both levels.

PROPOSITION 2. *Suppose $c_A = c_I$ and $c_B = c$ so that technological spillovers from FDI are irrelevant. Then,*

(i) $W^A \geqslant W^{AB}$ *for all m and n and $W^A = W^{AB}$ holds only if $m = n = 1$*
(ii) $W^B > W^{AB}$ *for all m and n.*

In other words, given that there are no spillovers from FDI, the host country is strictly better off with FDI at just one level of the market as opposed to both, except for the case where the domestic market is a successive monopoly. This result places an important qualification on the intuitive notion that the complementarity of FDI into two stages of production of a vertically related industry necessarily implies that FDI at both stages is necessarily more beneficial to the host country than FDI at a single stage. The logic for this surprising result is as follows. Given that FDI has occurred at one level, FDI at the second level partially *offsets the vertical linkages* created by the initial FDI while at the same time creating additional competition for local firms. For example, entry by firm B into the final good market increases backward linkages by increasing demand for the intermediate good and thereby benefits local suppliers. Now imagine that firm B's entry is accompanied by firm A's entry into the intermediate market. As a result of firm A's entry, part of the backward linkages created by firm B accrue to firm A, and its profits do not count as a part of domestic welfare.

[11] If $c_B = c$, then firm B's entry changes the slope but not the vertical intercept of the derived demand for the intermediate good. In this case, we have $w^B = w^N$ and $w^{AB} = w^A$.

Similarly, compare entry patterns $\langle AB\rangle$ and $\langle A\rangle$. If firm A enters, it creates forward linkages that benefit local final good producers. However, if firm B also enters, a portion of the forward linkages created by firm A's entry accrue to firm B. In sum, while complementary to one another, FDI at both stages of production involves a partial offsetting of the linkage benefits conferred on the host industry by FDI at only one stage of production. Finally, note that when the domestic market is heavily lacking in competition, as is the case under successive local monopoly, the benefits of increased competition implied by FDI at both stages of production exactly cancel the offsetting of linkages caused by such FDI relative to FDI at only one stage of the local industry.[12]

Our results above regarding the offsetting affects of FDI on vertical linkages are reminiscent of an insightful point made by Rodriguez-Clare (1996), who observed that incoming FDI does not just create new linkages, it also *displaces* existing linkages between local firms at different stages of the production chain. Such displacement also occurs in our model since FDI reduces the output levels of firms that compete with the multinational(s). By considering the impact of FDI at two vertically related stages of production, our model further extends this insight of Rodriguez-Clare (1996): Given that a multinational has entered the local industry, the entry of a multinational at another, vertically linked stage of production ends up severing some vertical links between the first multinational entrant and the local industry, something that can be detrimental for local welfare.

3.2. *Comparison with Autarky.* Given the relative welfare ranking of various FDI entry patterns, it is natural to ask: Under what conditions does each FDI entry pattern make the host country better off relative to autarky? The result here is analogous to Proposition 2: In the absence of FDI spillovers, FDI into one or both levels of the domestic industry increases domestic welfare if and only if the domestic industry is (almost) a successive monopoly under autarky.

PROPOSITION 3. *Suppose $c_A = c_I$ and $c_B = c$. Then, the following hold:*

(i) $W^A > W^N$ *if* $m = n = 1$ *and* $W^A < W^N$ *otherwise*
(ii) $W^B > W^N$ *if* $(m, n) \in \{(1, 1), (2, 1), (1, 2), (2, 2)\}$ *and* $W^B < W^N$ *otherwise*
(iii) $W^{AB} > W^N$ *if* $m = n = 1$ *and* $W^{AB} < W^N$ *otherwise.*

This result can be understood in terms of the competition effect of FDI on local firms. As the host country opens up to FDI, the resulting intensification of competition lowers profits of those firms that directly compete with the foreign entrant(s). When spillovers from FDI are absent, the competition effect is so strong that it dominates the vertical linkage effects of FDI as well as the beneficial effects on consumers so that domestic welfare declines (except for the cases where m and n are both close to 1). In other words, unless there is very little domestic competition at each level of the domestic industry, increasing competition in the local industry is not sufficient justification for further opening up to FDI since the increase in competition also transfers rents to foreign firms. In this context, it is worth noting that if the domestic industry is comprised of a single stage of production with Cournot competition, under the assumptions of our model, foreign entry into the industry would *necessarily* reduce domestic welfare if it is not accompanied by any technological spillovers to the local industry. By contrast, in our two-tiered oligopoly model, FDI has the potential to enhance welfare even when there are no technology spillovers provided that market concentration in the domestic industry is rather high (i.e., m and n are small).

[12] It can be shown that whether or not FDI entry pattern $\langle A\rangle$ leads to higher domestic welfare than FDI entry pattern $\langle B\rangle$ depends on values of m and n. Loosely speaking, FDI into the intermediate market is preferable to FDI into the final good market if the number of final good producers (n) is sufficiently large relative to the number of intermediate good suppliers (m). Furthermore, it is worth noting that if market structure at the two stages of production is symmetric (i.e., $m = n$), then FDI into the final good market is preferable: $W^B > W^A$.

Proposition 3 suggests that the usual backward linkage effects that economists have long recognized may not be significant enough to justify policies aimed at attracting FDI. This raises the question of whether a case for proactive FDI policies in oligopolistic markets could be made on the basis of technological spillovers to local firms. We examine this possibility next.

4. EFFECTS OF FDI SPILLOVERS

Proposition 3 informs us that in the absence of spillovers, FDI into the local industry increases domestic welfare only when the industry is either a successive monopoly (in case FDI occurs in the intermediate market) or at most a successive duopoly (in case FDI occurs in the final good market). We show below that the presence of FDI spillovers increases the parameter range for which FDI increases domestic welfare relative to autarky. We use the FDI pattern $\langle AB \rangle$ to illustrate this argument. The analysis below also provides a rationale for the FDI subsidization policies that are considered at the end of this section.

4.1. *Spillovers and the Desirability of FDI.* Now consider the case where the FDI entry of firms A and B generates technological spillovers to the local economy—the spillover parameters s_A and s_B are strictly positive. We show that in the presence of spillovers, entry by firms A and B can enhance domestic welfare, even when the domestic market is not highly concentrated at both levels. For simplicity, consider the symmetric case where $c_A = c_B = 0$, $c_I = c = \Delta$, and $s_A = s_B = s$. The parameter Δ then represents the cost advantage each foreign firm enjoys over its local competitors. As might be expected, domestic welfare W^{AB} depends on the level of spillovers as well as on the cost differential parameter: $W^{AB} = W^{AB}(s, \Delta)$ where W^{AB} increases with the level of FDI spillovers s whereas it decreases with the cost advantage Δ of foreign firms.

An example: successive duopoly. For the special case where $m = n = 2$, $c_A = c_B = 0$, $c_I = c = \Delta$, and $s_A = s_B = s$, we have

$$W^{AB}(s, \Delta) = \frac{1}{96}(3a - 8(1-s)\Delta)^2 + \frac{1}{1152}(9a - 28(1-s)\Delta)^2 + \frac{1}{2}\left(\frac{9}{16}a - \frac{3}{4}(1-s)\Delta\right)^2.$$

Let Δ_{min} be defined by $W^{AB}(0, \Delta_{min}) = W^N$. It can be shown that the following holds:

PROPOSITION 4. *Assume $c_A = c_B = 0$, $c_I = c = \Delta$, $m = n = 2$, and $\Delta \geq \Delta_{\min} > 0$; then there exists a threshold level of spillovers $s^*(\Delta)$ such that $W^{AB}(s, \Delta) > W^N$ if and only if $s > s^*(\Delta)$. Furthermore, $s^*(\Delta)$ decreases with Δ.*

This result is easy to understand. For the extreme case where spillovers are complete (i.e., $s = 1$) domestic welfare under $\langle AB \rangle$ exceeds that under autarky because FDI by both firms lowers the cost of all domestic firms by the amount Δ and this cost reduction dominates the negative effects of increased competition on the profitability of local firms. Given that domestic welfare is an increasing function of the spillover parameter s, there exists a threshold level $s^*(\Delta)$ that exhibits the above property. For example, for $a = 10$, it is easy to calculate that $\Delta_{\min} = 0.2$, $s^* = 0.36$ if $\Delta = 0.5$, and $s^* = 0.06$ if $\Delta = 2$.

Proposition 4 suggests that possibility of technology spillovers is the second potential rationale for the use of fiscal and financial incentives designed to induce multinational firms to invest locally (UNCTAD, 2003), the first being the coordination problem noted in Proposition 1. We discuss this in greater detail in Section 4.3.

4.2. *How Spillovers May Encourage FDI.* The conventional belief is that technology spillovers tend to discourage FDI since multinationals have an incentive to preserve their technological superiority over local firms. In this section, we show that this argument may be incomplete since it ignores vertical linkage effects that lie at the heart of our model. We argue

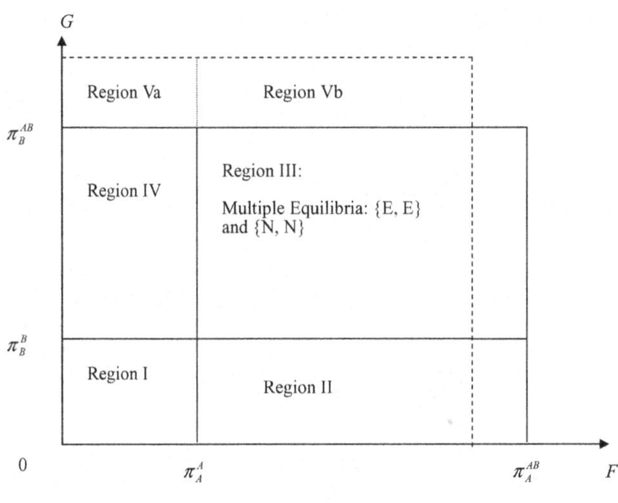

FIGURE 2

EFFECTS OF AN INCREASE IN SPILLOVERS UPSTREAM (s_A)

below that an increase in the degree of spillover may actually *increase* the incentive for FDI on the part of foreign firms.

Suppose that the level of upstream spillover (s_A) rises. Following this, π_A^{AB} decreases but π_B^{AB} increases since the price of the intermediate good falls. The new equilibrium entry pattern as a function of the entry costs is depicted in Figure 2.

For the parameter values in Region Vb, entry was profitable for neither firm before the rise in s_A. However, at a higher level of upstream spillover, it is a Nash equilibrium for both firms A and B to enter. A higher level of upstream spillover increases the incentive for downstream entry by firm B, and, anticipating this, firm A chooses to enter as well. Therefore, an increase in the level of technological spillovers upstream (s_A) induces additional entry at *both* stages of production. Of course, a similar logic applies to changes in the level of downstream spillover s_B. A rise in s_B enhances downstream competition and raises the demand for the intermediate good, thereby encouraging upstream entry. Additional upstream entry in turn leads to additional downstream entry, which would not otherwise have occurred. To emphasize this, we state the following result:[13]

PROPOSITION 5. *An increase in the degree of technological spillovers at either the intermediate or the final stage may encourage FDI into both tiers of the domestic industry.*

4.3. *Attracting FDI via Subsidies.* In many situations, multinational companies may lack the incentive to enter a host country because of the entry costs involved or because technology spillovers benefit their local competitors too much.[14] Suppose parameters are such that entry by both multinationals is indeed desirable from a welfare perspective but firms do not find it profitable. We argue below that a properly designed FDI subsidy at one stage of the industry has the potential to encourage entry at both levels of the industry.

[13] Of course, an increase in spillovers also has the usual effect of discouraging entry. For example, an increase in s_A reduces π_A^{AB} so that the vertical boundary defining Region III in Figure 3 shifts leftward.

[14] Furthermore, multinational firms will typically not take into account the beneficial effects of their entry on domestic consumers.

For purposes of illustration, suppose that $F > \pi_A^{AB}$ and $\pi_B^{AB} > G > \pi_B{}^B$, that is, no entry is firm A's dominant strategy (it would not enter even if firm B enters: $F > \pi_A^{AB}$) and no entry is firm B's best response to firm A's choice of no entry but it prefers to enter if firm A were to enter. Clearly, in such a situation, no entry occurs in the absence of an FDI subsidy and the host country remains in autarky.

Consider two different FDI subsidy policies on the part of the host country: (i) Subsidize the entry cost of firm A by the amount just over $F - \pi_A^A$ or (ii) subsidize the entry cost of firm B by the amount just over $G - \pi_B^B$. It is easy to see that policy (i) can make entry a dominant strategy for firm A, which in turn induces firm B's entry even though it does not receive any subsidy: Firm A's entry increases the supply of the intermediate good, which in turn makes it profitable for firm B to enter as well. The net benefit of to the host country in this case is the increase in domestic welfare minus the costs of FDI subsidy: $W^{AB} - W^N - (F - \pi_A^A)$. Policy (ii), if implemented, would attract firm B, but firm B's entry would not be accompanied by firm A 's entry because $F > \pi_A^{AB}$. Unlike policy (i), policy (ii) attracts FDI into just one level of the vertical industry. The net benefit of this policy to the host country is $W^B - W^N - (G - \pi_B^B)$. Therefore, policy (i) is more desirable than policy (ii) if and only if $W^{AB} - (F - \pi_A^A) > W^B - (G - \pi_B{}^B)$.

From Proposition 2 we know that, in the absence of FDI spillovers, simultaneous entry by both firms yields lower domestic welfare relative to FDI at just one level of the industry because the entry of one foreign firm partially cancels out the vertical linkage effects generated by the entry of the other firm. However, if FDI spillovers are present and substantial, the host country can enjoy spillover effects at both stages of production only if both firms choose to enter. In this case, policy (i) can be preferable to policy (ii). For example, consider the case where $c_A = c_B = 0$, $c_I = c = \Delta$, $s_A = s_B = s$, $m = n = 2$, and $\Delta \geq \Delta_{\min} > 0$. To make the point in the clearest way and without loss of generality, assume that $s = 1$ (complete spillovers). Then, we have $W^{AB} = 0.32a^2$, $W^B = 0.35(a - \Delta)^2$, $W^N = 0.35(a - 2\Delta)^2$, $\pi_A^A = (a - \Delta)^2/24$, and $\pi_B^B = (a - \Delta)^2/36$. Hence, simultaneous entry by firms A and B enhances domestic welfare, and indeed domestic welfare is the highest under this entry pattern if Δ is not too small. Therefore, policy (i) is more desirable than policy (ii) if $W^{AB} - W^B > (F - \pi_A^A) - (G - \pi_B^B)$, that is, if $0.32a^2 - 0.28(a - \Delta)^2 > F - G$.[15]

A general point can be made here. Due to the presence of complementarities in production, FDI subsidization at certain stages of an industry (in particular those with high entry costs relative to post-entry profits) may generate multiple benefits to the host country by encouraging FDI inflows into other related production stages of the same industry or into other vertically linked industries.

It was shown earlier in this article that FDI into different levels of a vertically industry of the host industry may suffer from a coordination problem, namely, it may be a Nash equilibrium for both firms A and B to not enter the host country, even when each firm responds by entering if the other firm chooses to enter (Proposition 1). It can easily be seen that for the parameter region over which $\{E, E\}$ and $\{N, N\}$ are both Nash equilibria, the host country can induce both firms to enter by subsidizing only one of them just enough to make entry a dominant strategy for it.

Of course, FDI subsidies by the host country are only an indirect solution to the coordination problem faced by firms A and B. In the next section, we consider vertical integration between the two firms as a possible solution to the coordination problem and examine its desirability relative to independent entry. This analysis also allows us to shed light on the welfare implications of the different *organizational forms* of FDI.

[15] Similarly, if $G > \pi_B^{AB}$ and $\pi_A^{AB} > F > \pi_A{}^A$ the dominant strategy for firm B is to not enter, and firm A enters only if firm B does. This implies that an FDI subsidy granted to firm B can induce both firms to enter, whereas an FDI subsidy to firm A does not induce entry by firm B. Finally, note that if $F > \pi_A^{AB}$ and $G > \pi_B^{AB}$, the host country must subsidize both firms in order to induce them to enter.

5. VERTICAL INTEGRATION AND COORDINATION

Suppose that firms A and B enter the host country as a vertically integrated firm, denoted as firm VI, which makes the intermediate good in house and then transforms it into the final good. Upon entry, the integrated firm competes in the final good market with local firms and has the option to supply the intermediate good to them. If it chooses to supply the intermediate to local final good competitors, it also ends up competing with local intermediate good suppliers.

Vertical integration offers two main advantages to firms A and B. First, since the intermediate good can be secured at marginal cost by the vertically integrated firm, the integrated firm does not suffer from the standard double marginalization problem faced by independent firms. Second, the vertically integrated firm can coordinate its upstream and downstream entry decisions, thereby overcoming the no-entry equilibrium that can arise in the case of entry by independent firms.

However, there is a subtle trade-off that the vertically integrated firm must also consider. After entry, such a firm needs to choose the extent to which it will supply the intermediate good to its downstream competitors. On the one hand, demand for the intermediate good from such local competitors represents a lucrative business opportunity. On the other hand, supplying the intermediate good to its competitors hurts the integrated firm's downstream business since increased competition in the intermediate market reduces the price of the intermediate and therefore the costs of its downstream rivals. Thus, it is not immediately obvious whether, after entry, it is optimal for the integrated firm to supply the intermediate good to its rival producers or not.

We next consider this incentive constraint in more detail and show that under the assumptions of our model, the vertically integrated firm chooses *not* to supply the intermediate good to its competitors in order to protect its downstream business.

5.1. *The VI Firm's Incentive Constraint.* Let q_{VI} denote the quantity of intermediate good that firm VI produces for its own use and Q_{VI} the quantity it produces for sale to other downstream firms. In what follows, we show that it is optimal for the integrated firm to set $Q_{VI} = 0$.

Given the intermediate price w determined by the competition among suppliers of the intermediate good z, all downstream firms compete in Cournot fashion. The marginal cost of production for the VI firm equals $c_A + c_B$ whereas that for all other downstream firms equals $w + c - s_B(c - c_B)$ since they purchase the intermediate good from upstream suppliers. The derived demand for the intermediate good is $Q_d(w) \equiv q_1(w) + \cdots + q_n(w)$, where $q_j(w)$ is the Cournot quantity of the other firms in the downstream sector, $1 \leq j \leq n$.

As an integrated unit, firm VI maximizes the sum of its upstream and downstream profits $\pi_z^{VI}(Q_{VI}, Q_{-VI}) + \pi_y^{VI}(w)$, where Q_{-VI} denotes the aggregate output level of other upstream firms. Obviously, $\pi_y^{VI}(w)$ increases in w. Given Q_{-VI}, the best response of firm VI in the upstream sector is determined by the following first order condition:

$$\frac{\partial \pi_z^{VI}(Q_{VI}, Q_{-VI})}{\partial Q_{VI}} + \frac{\partial \pi_y^{VI}(w)}{\partial w}\frac{\partial w}{\partial Q_{VI}} = 0. \tag{5}$$

If Q_{VI} increases, the equilibrium price w of the intermediate good z goes down, which lowers the costs of local downstream firms and thus hurts firm VI's profit in the downstream market. Hence the second term on the left-hand side of the equation captures the "*helping the rivals effect*" created by the integrated firm's decision to supply the intermediate to them: $\frac{\partial \pi_y^{VI}(w)}{\partial w} \cdot \frac{\partial w}{\partial Q_{VI}} < 0$. The following result, proved in the Appendix, informs us that for linear demand this negative effect is so strong that the vertically integrated multinational chooses to not sell the intermediate good it produces in house to rival downstream producers:

LEMMA 2. *It is optimal for the vertically integrated multinational to not supply the intermediate good to its downstream rivals:* $\frac{\partial \pi_z^{VI}(Q_{VI}, Q_{-Vi})}{\partial Q_{VI}} + \frac{\partial \pi_y^{VI}(w)}{\partial w} < 0$, *for all* Q_{-VI}.

Thus, FDI by a vertically integrated multinational firm does not create *any* forward linkage effects for local final good producers.[16] Nor does it generate any backward linkage effects for local intermediate suppliers, since it produces the intermediate good by itself. Rather, the derived demand for the intermediate good declines after the entry of the vertically integrated firm by reducing the output of other downstream producers for any given w. However, relative to the case of FDI by two independent firms (A and B), entry under vertical integration avoids the double markup problem since the downstream unit of the integrated FDI firm buys the intermediate good from the upstream unit at marginal cost; this tends to lower the price of the final good and partly benefits the host country.

It is straightforward to derive the price of the intermediate good under vertical integration. We have

$$w^{VI} = \frac{\widetilde{a} + m\left[c_I - s_A \Delta_A\right]}{m+1}, \tag{6}$$

where $\widetilde{a} \equiv [a - 2(c - s_B\Delta_B) + c_A + c_B]/2$. The equilibrium output and profit of firm VI are

$$q^{VI} = \frac{(2m+n+2)(a - c_A - c_B) + 2mn\left((1-s_A)\Delta_A + (1-s_B)\Delta_B\right)}{2(m+1)(n+2)} \tag{7}$$

and

$$\pi^{VI}(s_A, s_B, m, n) = \left[q^{VI}\right]^2, \tag{8}$$

respectively.

Having described the behavior of the vertically integrated unit, we now turn to two central questions. First, under what circumstances do the two firms find it beneficial to vertically integrate? Second, how does domestic welfare under entry by the vertically integrated firm compare with entry by independent firm A and B?

5.2. *Vertical Integration versus Uncoordinated FDI.* Although vertical integration overcomes the coordination problem faced by independent firms A and B and also helps avoid double marginalization, it is not always more profitable for them to vertically integrate since the vertically integrated firm VI forgoes profit that can be earned by supplying the intermediate good to other downstream firms. This trade-off delivers the following result:[17]

PROPOSITION 6. *Suppose* $c_A = c_I$ *and* $c_B = c$. *Then, for any given* m, *there exists an* $n^{VI}(m)$ *such that (i)* $\pi^{VI} > \pi^{AB} \equiv \pi_A^{AB} + \pi_B^{AB}$ *if and only if* $n < n^{VI}(m)$ *and (ii)* $\frac{dn^{VI}(m)}{dm} > 0$.

The proof of this proposition involves a straightforward comparison of the relevant profit functions that can be solved for n^{VI}—the analytical expression for which is somewhat tedious and therefore not reported (we plot $n^{VI}(m)$ in Figure 3). The intuition for part (*i*) of Proposition 6 is easy to grasp. Part (*i*) basically says that the incentive for a vertically integrated firm to enter the host industry is stronger than that of two independent firms if and only if the number of local final good producers is sufficiently small—that is, $n < n^{VI}(m)$. This is because a reduction in the degree of downstream competition (i.e., a fall in n) lowers the opportunity cost of not supplying the intermediate good to rival downstream firms, making vertical integration relatively more attractive to the firms.

[16] Note that this result need not obtain when demand is nonlinear.

[17] For simplicity, we focus on the case without spillovers.

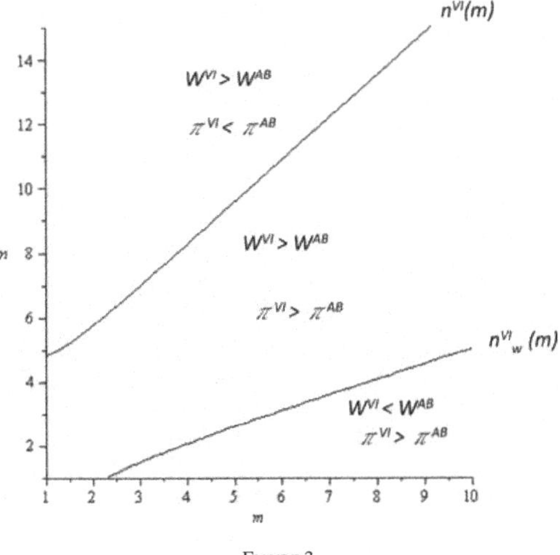

FIGURE 3

VERTICAL INTEGRATION VERSUS INDEPENDENT ENTRY

Consider part (*ii*) of Proposition 6, which says that $n^{VI}(m)$ increases in m. The intuition for this result is as follows: As the intermediate market becomes relatively more competitive, the profit earned from selling the intermediate to local final good producers declines under independent entry, which in turn increases the incentive to vertically integrate.

Taken together, the two parts of Proposition 6 point out that the incentive for vertical integration depends upon the degree of market competition at both stages of production. Holding n constant, an increase in m makes vertical integration more attractive by reducing the profitability of selling the intermediate to local producers. On the other hand, holding m constant, an increase in n makes vertical integration less desirable by increasing the opportunity cost of not selling the intermediate to local final good producers.

Consider now the choice between the entry of a vertically integrated firm and that of two independent firms from the viewpoint of the host country. We can show the following:

PROPOSITION 7. *Suppose $c_A = c_I$ and $c_B = c$. Then, there exists a threshold degree of downstream competition $n_w^{VI}(m)$ such that*

$$W^{VI} > W^{AB} \textit{ if and only if } n > n_w^{VI}(m) \textit{ where } \frac{dn_w^{VI}(m)}{dm} > 0.$$

Although the analytical expression for $n_w^{VI}(m)$ is tedious, we can plot it using Maple (Figure 3) from where we observe that $n_w^{VI}(m) < n^{VI}(m)$. To understand the intuition behind Proposition 7 it is useful to first consider a comparison of $\langle VI \rangle$ and the FDI entry pattern $\langle B \rangle$. Note that since the vertically integrated firm does not supply local downstream competitors, under both $\langle VI \rangle$ and $\langle B \rangle$ competition increases (only) in the final good market. However, there is a crucial difference between the two entry patterns: Whereas the entry pattern $\langle B \rangle$ creates additional backward linkages in the local industry by raising the derived demand for the intermediate good, no such effect arises under $\langle VI \rangle$ since the vertically integrated firm does not buy the intermediate locally but rather produces it in house. But this beneficial backward linkage effect of entry pattern $\langle B \rangle$ relative to $\langle VI \rangle$ has to be weighed against the fact that the degree of double marginalization problem in the local industry is worse under $\langle B \rangle$ relative to

$\langle VI \rangle$—under $\langle B \rangle$ all downstream firms purchase the intermediate at a markup whereas under $\langle VI \rangle$ only local firms do so. Intuition suggests that when the number of downstream firms (n) is large relative to the number of upstream firms (m), the increase in the derived demand or the backward linkage effect of entry pattern $\langle B \rangle$ would be minor whereas the degree of double marginalization problem in the local industry would be significant due to the relative lack of competition in the intermediate market. As a result, under such circumstances we would expect domestic welfare to be higher under the entry pattern $\langle VI \rangle$ relative to that under $\langle B \rangle$. Indeed, it is straightforward to show that $W^{VI} > W^B$ if and only if $n > 4m - 2$.

Once the welfare comparison of $\langle VI \rangle$ and $\langle B \rangle$ is understood, it is relatively easy to contrast $\langle VI \rangle$ and $\langle AB \rangle$. As we noted earlier in Proposition 2, the FDI entry pattern $\langle AB \rangle$ yields lower domestic welfare than the FDI entry pattern $\langle B \rangle$ for all m and n, due to the linkage-offsetting effect inherent to $\langle AB \rangle$. Furthermore, it is straightforward to show that $n_w^{VI}(m) < 4m - 2$. Proposition 7 and the preceding inequality together imply that a weaker parameter restriction needs to be satisfied for domestic welfare under $\langle VI \rangle$ to be higher than that under $\langle AB \rangle$.

Note the *contrast* between what foreign firms prefer and the welfare ranking of the host country implied by Propositions 6 and 7. In particular, note that although vertical integration obtains whenever $n < n^{VI}(m)$, the domestic economy is better off under such integration whenever $n > n_w^{VI}(m)$. This implies the following corollary:

COROLLARY 1. *If $n > n^{VI}(m)$, firms A and B choose not to vertically integrate whereas domestic welfare is higher under vertical integration. If $n_w^{VI}(m) \leq n \leq n^{VI}(m)$, vertical integration is preferred both by firms as well as the host country. Finally, if $n < n_w^{VI}(m)$, firms A and B prefer to enter as a vertically integrated firm whereas host country welfare is strictly higher under independent entry.*

Figure 3 shows that there is harmony between choices of foreign firms and domestic welfare only when both stages of production are relatively competitive. When the final good market is relatively competitive and the intermediate good market less so, the firms choose not to vertically integrate whereas the host country would be better off if they were to do so. By contrast, when the intermediate market is quite competitive whereas the final good market is not, the two firms prefer to vertically integrate whereas the domestic economy is better off under separate entry.

6. EXPORT-ORIENTED FDI

Thus far, our analysis assumes that foreign firms sell all their output in the domestic market, where they compete with local firms. In this section, we briefly discuss how our results are modified if FDI is export oriented rather than geared towards the domestic market. For simplicity, we consider exporting of the final product only and assume that domestic firms do not export, perhaps due to product quality considerations and/or lack of overseas distribution channels, etc.

If firm B exports all of its output to a foreign market, the competition effect of its entry on local final good producers is no longer present. However, the indirect effect on local competitors still exists: Firm B's entry raises the price of the intermediate good and this hurts local final good producers. Clearly, the larger the magnitude of firm B's exports, the stronger this negative effect on its local competitors.[18] Thus, even in this case of export-oriented FDI, firm B's entry may lower domestic welfare relative to autarky (unless it generates significant spillovers to local firms).

[18] For example, if the demand for the final product in the foreign market is given by $p_{EX} = \beta - y_{EX}$ and firm B is the monopoly supplier in that market, then the quantity of the intermediate good it buys from the host country is $y_{EX}^B = (\beta - c_B - t)/2$, where t is the transportation cost associated with exporting. It is straightforward to show that the increase in the price of the intermediate good that results from firm B's entry is increasing in the demand intercept β.

Note also that this indirect effect of firm B's entry on the intermediate good market exists regardless of whether firm A enters or not. If firm A also enters, the degree of competition in the intermediate market increases and the indirect effect of firm B's entry is softened. However, under the entry pattern $\langle AB \rangle$, the linkage-offsetting effect identified in Proposition 2 comes into play. Hence, the result that domestic welfare may be lower if both firms A and B enter relative to when only one of them enters can still obtain.

A key question of interest in the context of export oriented FDI is whether the vertically integrated firm would still find it optimal to not sell its intermediate good to competing local firms. Let q_{Ex}^{VI} denote that optimal quantity of the final product that the vertically integrated firm VI chooses to export, given its marginal cost of production $c_A + c_B$, the demand conditions in the foreign market, and any per unit transportation cost t incurred from exporting.

It is useful to consider two separate scenarios: one where the vertically integrated firm exports all of its output (perhaps due to a "must-export" policy restriction imposed by the host country) and another where it serves both markets. In the first case, FDI in the local economy is purely export oriented, and such FDI indeed occurs in many countries in especially designated areas called export processing zones. When FDI is intended only for exports, the vertically integrated firm does not compete with local final good producers (given that they do not export).[19] If so, there is no reason for the vertically integrated firm to not supply the intermediate good to local producers (so that Lemma 2 no longer holds).[20] The profit of the vertically integrated firm then equals its profit from selling the intermediate good in the local market, which is essentially the same as π_A^A, plus its profit from exporting the final good to the foreign market, π_{Ex}^{VI}.

Now consider the second scenario where the vertically integrated firm sells the final good at home as well as abroad. In this case, whether the firm chooses to supply the intermediate to local final good producers depends on cost conditions. If, as is assumed in the model here, the marginal cost of producing the final good is constant, then regardless of the level of its exports, the vertically integrated always sells the final good in the domestic market. In this case, it competes with local firms in the final good market and will therefore choose not to supply the intermediate good to them because of the "helping the rivals" effect of such supply. However, if the vertically integrated firm's marginal cost of producing the final good is not constant but increasing, and the foreign market is sufficiently large, then a rather large volume of exports can make it profitable for the firm to not sell its final good in the domestic market. If this is the case, local competition in the final goods market is no longer a concern and the vertically integrated firm will choose to sell the intermediate good to domestic final good producers.

How does the possibility of exporting affect the vertical integration decision? We argue below that this choice can be affected in either direction. To see this, consider the entry pattern $\langle AB \rangle$ where firms A and B enter the host country as separate firms. It suffices to consider the case where firm B exports all its output. In this case, unlike the vertically integrated firm, the entry of firm B generates backward linkages in the host country, as its exports add to the derived demand for the intermediate good. These linkages benefit local suppliers as well as firm A. Relative to the case of vertical integration, firm A's profit is higher than π_A^A because of the increase in derived demand, whereas firm B's profit, denoted as $\pi_{Ex}^B(w)$, is lower because firm B must buy the needed intermediate good in the domestic intermediate market as opposed to being able to access it at marginal cost. As a result, the aggregate profits of firms A and B may be higher or lower than that of the vertically integrated firm, depending on such factors as the demand condition in the foreign market, the size of the transportation cost, as well as the nature of market structure (i.e., m and n) at both stages of production.

[19] Interestingly, this suggests that a "must export" policy of the host country not only shields local producers from having to compete with the vertically integrated firm, it also ensures that they have access to the intermediate good produced by that firm. Of course, the local suppliers of the intermediate good are likely to lose from having to compete with the vertically integrated firm when it chooses to serve local final goods producers.

[20] We thank an anonymous referee for pointing out this difference between market-oriented FDI and export-oriented FDI.

7. CONCLUSION

In this article, we construct a two-tier oligopoly model of FDI. The model is motivated by the simple observation that although real world FDI flows occur at various production stages of almost all manufacturing and services industries, quite a few of which tend to be oligopolistic in nature, existing literature has tended to focus mostly on FDI in final goods markets. The model is built on the insight that the complementarity underlying various stages of the production chain creates an interdependence between the FDI entry decisions of multinationals. Such interdependence can in turn lead to a coordination problem: In our two-tier model, FDI at both stages can fail to occur even though entry at each level is profitable provided both firms choose to invest. We argue that a local subsidy to FDI at one level of the domestic industry can sometimes be sufficient to induce FDI at both stages.

The two-tier structure of our model allows us to address some novel welfare questions. For example, is FDI at both stages necessarily better than FDI at a single stage? We provide conditions under which more FDI is better for the local economy as well as when it is not. An important insight underlying this analysis is that if FDI occurs at both stages, part of the vertical linkages created by FDI at any one stage are captured by FDI at the *other* stage. As a result of such offsetting of linkages, the local benefits of FDI at one stage of the local industry can be muted by FDI at the other stage. We show that only when the local industry is highly concentrated (or simply nonexistent) is FDI at both stages of production necessarily preferable for the host country.

We also consider firm incentives for vertical integration and the impact such integration has on local welfare. This analysis provides fresh insights regarding the choice between various organizational modes of FDI and the impact it has on welfare. We show that from the viewpoint of foreign entrants, vertical integration is not necessarily the optimal arrangement. On the one hand, vertical integration helps coordinate entry decisions and eliminates the double marginalization problem. On the other hand, the vertically integrated firm forgoes profit that can be earned by supplying the intermediate good to other downstream firms—something the vertically integrated firm does not find optimal to do. As a result, if the final good market is sufficiently competitive, the two foreign firms are better off entering as independent firms as opposed to as a vertically integrated one. For related reasons, from the viewpoint of the local economy as well, vertical integration does not necessarily dominate entry by two independent foreign firms.

Although our model is rather stylized, it captures some novel and potentially important considerations that arise under a two-tiered production structure with market power at each stage. For example, we find that technology spillovers from FDI to a foreign firm's local rivals can actually encourage it to enter the local market. The intuition is central to the working of our model: If technology diffuses in the final goods market, it increases derived demand for the intermediate good, making entry into that market more attractive, which in turn makes FDI into the final good market more attractive as well. Nevertheless, our model is only a first step in the analysis of FDI at multiple stages of production of an oligopolistic industry since it focuses largely on the host country. Future research could analyze whether our insights extend to a multicountry environment.

APPENDIX

Here we collect proofs and calculations omitted from the main text.

PROOF OF PROPOSITION 2.

(i) It can be shown that $W^A \geq W^{AB}$ is equivalent to $(2n^2 + 2n - 1)m^2 + 2mn^2 + 2n^2 + 2n - 2mn - 6m - 1 \geq 0$, which holds if and only if $m = n = 1$.

(ii) It is straightforward to show that $W^B > W^{AB}$ is equivalent to $(2m^2 + 2m - 1)n^2 + (4m^2 + 2m - 4)n + (6m^2 + 8m - 1) > 0$, which holds for all $m \geq 1$ and $n \geq 1$. ■

PROOF OF PROPOSITION 3. It is straightforward to show that

$$W^A - W^N = \frac{n(2+n+2m-2mn-m^2n)(a-c_I-c)^2}{(n+2)^2(n+1)^2(m+1)^2},$$

which is positive if $m = n = 1$ and negative otherwise. This proves part (i). Similarly,

$$W^B - W^N = \frac{m\,(n^2+3n+2-mn^2-mn+5m)\,(a-c_I-c)^2}{(n+2)^2(n+1)^2(m+1)^2},$$

which implies that (ii) holds.

If $m = n = 1$, $W^{AB} - W^N = (\frac{6}{27} - \frac{7}{32})(a-c_I-c)^2 > 0$. For all other $(m, n) \neq (1, 1)$, since $W^A < W^N$ by part (i) of this proposition and $W^{AB} < W^A$ by Proposition 2, we have $W^{AB} < W^N$. ∎

PROOF OF LEMMA 2. Given the price of the intermediate good, w, all downstream downstream firms compete in quantities, yielding the following equilibrium quantities

$$q_{VI}(w) = \frac{a-(n+1)(c_A+c_B)+n(w+c-s_B\Delta_B)}{n+2}, \tag{A.1}$$

for firm VI and

$$q_1(w) = \cdots = q_n(w) = \frac{a-2(w+c-s_B\Delta_B)+c_A+c_B}{n+2},$$

for local downstream producers. The derived demand for the intermediate good is thus

$$Q_d(w) = q_1(w)+\cdots+q_n(w) = n\frac{a-2(w+c-s_B\Delta_B)+c_A+c_B}{n+2},$$

or equivalently

$$w = \tilde{a} - \frac{n+2}{2n}Q_d = \tilde{a} - \frac{n+2}{2n}\left[Q_{VI}+Q_{-VI}\right], \tag{A.2}$$

where $\tilde{a} \equiv [a-2(c-s_B\Delta_B)+c_A+c_B]/2$.

The total profit of VI is

$$\begin{aligned}\pi_z^{VI}+\pi_y^{VI} &= (w-c_A)Q_{VI}+(p-c_A-c_B)q_{VI}\\ &= \left[\tilde{a}-c_A-\frac{n+2}{2n}(Q_{VI}+Q_{-VI})\right]Q_{VI}\\ &\quad+[a-c_A-c_B-(Q_{VI}+Q_{-VI}+q_{VI})]\,q_{VI}.\end{aligned}$$

Straightforward algebraic simplifications yield

$$\frac{\partial(\pi_z^{VI}+\pi_y^{VI})}{\partial Q_{VI}} = \frac{-2n(c-c_B)(1-s_B)-(n+4)Q_{VI}-2Q_{-VI}}{2n} < 0.$$

This completes the proof. ∎

REFERENCES

BUCKLEY, P. J., AND M. CASSON, "Analyzing Foreign Market Entry Strategies: Extending the Internationalization Approach," *Journal of International Business Studies* 29 (1998), 539–61.

EICHER, T., AND J. W. KANG, "Trade, Foreign Direct Investment or Acquisition: Optimal Entry Modes for Multinationals," *Journal of Development Economics* 77 (2005), 207–28.

GORDON, R. H., AND A. L. BOVENBERG, "Why Is Capital So Immobile Internationally? Possible Explanations and Implications for Capital Income Taxation," *American Economic Review* 86 (1996), 1057–75.

HELPMAN, E., M. J. MELITZ, AND S. R. YEAPLE, "Export versus FDI with Heterogeneous Firms," *American Economic Review* 94 (2004), 300–16.

LIN, P., AND K. SAGGI, "Multinational Firms, Exclusivity, and the Degree of Backward Linkages," *Journal of International Economics* 71 (2007), 206–20.

MARKUSEN, J., "The Boundaries of Multinational Enterprises and the Theory of International Trade," *Journal of Economic Perspectives* 9 (1995), 169–89.

——, AND A. VENABLES, "Foreign Direct Investment as a Catalyst for Industrial Development," *European Economic Review* 43 (1999), 335–56.

NOCKE, V., AND S. R. YEAPLE, "Cross-Border Mergers and Acquisitions versus Greenfield Foreign Direct Investment: The Role of Firm Heterogeneity," *Journal of International Economics* 72 (2007), 336–65.

OKUNO-FUJIWARA, M., "Interdependence of Industries, Coordination Failure, and Strategic Promotion of an Industry," *Journal of International Economics* 25 (1988), 25–43.

PACK, H., AND L. WESTPHAL, "Industrial Strategy and Technological Change: Theory versus Reality," *Journal of Development Economics* 22 (1986), 87–128.

RODRIGUEZ-CLARE, A., "Multinationals, Linkages, and Economic Development," *American Economic Review* 86 (1996), 852–73.

RODRIK, D., "Coordination Failures and Government Policy: A Model with Applications to East Asia and Eastern Europe," *Journal of International Economics* 40 (1996), 1–22.

SAGGI, K., "Entry into a Foreign Market: Foreign Direct Investment versus Licensing," *Review of International Economics* 4 (1996), 99–104.

——, "Trade, Foreign Direct Investment, and International Technology Transfer: A Survey," *World Bank Research Observer* 17 (2002), 191–235.

SALINGER, M., "Vertical Mergers and Market Foreclosure," *Quarterly Journal of Economics* 103 (1988), 345–56.

UNCTAD, *World Investment Report 2003: FDI Policies for Development* (New York: United Nations, 2003).

Part 3

Intellectual Property Rights, Foreign Direct Investment, and Innovation

Chapter 10

Licensing versus direct investment: implications for economic growth[#]

Amy Jocelyn Glass[a,]*, Kamal Saggi[b]

[a]*Department of Economics, Ohio State University, Columbus, OH 43210, USA*
[b]*Department of Economics, Southern Methodist University, Dallas, TX 75275, USA*

Abstract

We develop a symmetric two country model of foreign direct investment (FDI) that captures the internalization decision and its implications for both the *rate* and *magnitude* of innovations. When mode choice (licensing versus FDI) is fixed, a subsidy to multinational production increases the rate but decreases the size of innovations. When mode can switch, the rate and size of innovations both increase, provided the subsidy is not too large. Although innovation size decreases for industries where firms already were choosing FDI, innovation size increases for industries where firms switch from licensing to FDI because multinationals choose larger innovations than licensors.

Keywords: Innovation; Licensing; Foreign direct investment; Multinational firms

JEL classification: F21; F43; O31; O34

1. Introduction

For several decades, foreign direct investment (FDI) flows have been growing much faster than world trade, and worldwide sales of foreign affiliates of multinationals now exceed exports (UNCTAD, 1997). Part of this expansion in FDI can be attributed to the policy shift of many governments toward attracting FDI or restricting it less. Between 1991 and 1998, some 58 countries began to take

*Corresponding author. Tel.: +1-614-292-1149; fax: +1-614-292-3906.
E-mail address: glass.29@osu.edu (A. J. Glass).

[#] This chapter was originally appeared in *Journal of International Economics* **56**, 131–153.

a proactive approach toward attracting FDI, roughly doubling the number of such countries from 60 to 118 (Moran, 1998).

Despite the growing importance of FDI and the increased desire of many countries to attract FDI, the consequences of FDI for economic growth have received scant attention in the theoretical literature – a void noted by Grossman and Helpman (1995). Empirical evidence on the effects of FDI on growth does suggest that, on balance, FDI has a positive impact on growth: recent studies include Borensztein et al. (1998) and Balasubramanyam et al. (1996).

Almost all existing theories of FDI and licensing have been developed in either static or partial equilibrium models.[1] A few dynamic general equilibrium models do explore the effect of FDI on growth but these models have ignored the possibility of licensing.[2] This omission is significant: as Ethier (1986) notes, the study of FDI must be foremost a study of internalization – the decision to keep activities within the firm. Historically (and even today), some countries have not allowed foreign firms to choose their mode of supply, preferring technology licensing (or joint ventures) over fully owned subsidiaries of foreign firms.[3] How do such policy interventions affect economic growth?

We build a symmetric two – country model of FDI that captures the internalization decision and its implications for both the rate and magnitude of innovation. We examine how policy interventions (taxes or subsidies to FDI) that alter the incentive to internalize production within the firm affect economic growth.[4] To our knowledge, ours is the first work to analyze these issues in a setting where firms can choose between FDI and licensing.[5] We find that the ability of firms to switch modes from licensing to FDI in response to policy changes is vital for ensuring that a subsidy to FDI leads to faster economic growth.[6]

Markusen (1995) provides several stylized facts about FDI that are central to our model. First, FDI is mostly horizontal, where multinationals create local

[1]See Markusen (1984, 1989); Ethier (1986); Horstmann and Markusen (1987, 1992, 1996); Saggi (1996, 1999); Markusen and Venables (1998); Wright (1993) and Vishwasrao (1994).

[2]See Wang and Blomström (1992); Helpman (1993); Walz (1997); Glass and Saggi (1998, 1999), and Petit and Sanna-Randaccio (2000). The main exception is Ethier and Markusen (1996) but their focus is on mode choice rather than innovation.

[3]Licensing can also be interpreted as a joint venture between a local firm and a foreign firm. The crucial distinction is that, unlike FDI, arms length arrangements such as licensing force foreign firms to share rents with local firms.

[4]In our model, a subsidy to FDI can also be interpreted as a decline in the cost disadvantage suffered by multinationals due to some other factors such as improvements in communications technology that facilitate coordination across countries.

[5]Horstmann and Markusen (1992) consider shifts in the mode firms choose of serving markets abroad, but in a setting without growth. Aghion and Howitt (1990) determine the innovation magnitude, but in a model without FDI or licensing.

[6]Our model also shares a feature similar to the inefficient entry in Horstmann and Markusen (1986): parameter changes that lead to more FDI do so by drawing in (from licensing) firms with higher production costs than existing multinationals.

production facilities within each country or region. Second, multinationals have substantial intangible assets and arise in industries with large R&D expenditures relative to sales – see also Brainard (1997) and Caves (1996). Third, multinationals suffer cost disadvantages relative to their local rivals due to operating in unfamiliar environments or logistical difficulties of coordination.

As Davies (1977) noted, foreign firms typically suffer a cost disadvantage relative to local firms due to lack of familiarity with local conditions. As a result, local firms will enjoy greater present value in a given project than foreign firms as long as they employ the same technology. If a foreign firm with a superior technology could appropriate the entire rent using technology licensing, it would always prefer licensing to FDI. However, empirical evidence indicates that, on average, licensors can appropriate less than half of the surplus associated with the license transaction (Caves, 1996; Caves et al., 1983). This aspect of technology licensing serves as an important assumption in our analysis.

Since our interest is in aggregate implications, we abstract from the details of why licensors are forced to share rents.[7] We assume that the share of rents captured by licensees is the same in the two countries. If rent sharing is primarily due to information asymmetries, then roughly the same rent shares should apply everywhere. Legal systems and protection of intellectual property rights may also affect the share of rents that licensees retain – see Markusen (2001); Vishwasrao (1994) and Yang and Maskus (2001) for models that capture such effects.

Our model is based on the familiar ownership, location and internalization (OLI) paradigm where exports, licensing, or multinational production can arise as the chosen method of serving markets abroad. In our model, ownership advantage results from investments in innovation. There is a continuum of industries and firms may attempt to improve the product in any industry – they pick an innovation intensity and an innovation size as well as which industry to target with their innovation.

Once a firm is successful in innovation, it chooses its market *mode*: whether to serve the market abroad by establishing a local production subsidiary or by licensing its technology to a local firm (a location advantage such as transportation costs rules out exports). Our model uses two parameters to capture the tradeoff between incomplete extraction of rents as a licensor and greater costs as a multinational. An increase in the *share of profits retained by licensees* or a decrease in the *cost disadvantage suffered by multinationals* strengthen the incentives for internalization, thus making FDI more attractive relative to licensing.

While our primary interest is in understanding how adjustments in the market mode between licensing and multinational production contribute to changes in the speed and size of innovation, we begin with a base case where the mode and size

[7]See Gallini and Wright (1990); Rockett (1990); Horstmann and Markusen (1987, 1996) and Wright (1993) for models generating this outcome based on informational considerations.

of innovations are fixed. In this benchmark, a decrease in licensee profit retention or in the cost disadvantage of multinationals increases the rate of innovation.

Next, we examine how internalization advantage affects the size and speed of innovation when firms can choose their modes of serving markets abroad. We assume that industries inherently differ with respect to their multinational cost disadvantage because technologies in some industries are harder to adapt to different economic environments or to coordinate across geographically separated locations. As a consequence, some industries serve markets abroad through multinational production while others choose licensing. In this general model, a subsidy to multinational production causes *multinationals to reduce the magnitude of their innovations* by reducing their need to generate ownership advantage.

However, the subsidy also makes FDI more attractive relative to licensing thereby increasing the extent of FDI, the fraction of all industries that choose to serve markets abroad through multinational production. Since multinationals choose larger innovations than firms that license their technologies, *firms switching from licensing to FDI raise the magnitude of their innovations*. Provided the subsidy is not too large, the average innovation magnitude (across both multinationals and licensors) rises. Thus, host country policies that attract FDI through financial incentives *increase both the rate and average magnitude of innovations*, clearly increasing economic growth.

Mode switching also has the potential to alter the effect of licensee rent retention on economic growth. Policy, either directly or indirectly, can affect the allocation of rents between the licensor and the licensee. With mode fixed, an increase in the licensee's share of rents reduces the speed of innovations without altering their size, so economic growth necessarily declines. However, when some industries switch their mode from licensing to multinational production, the average innovation size increases due to multinationals choosing larger innovations than licensors. The larger size of innovations can dominate their less frequent occurrence, leading to an increase in economic growth.

Section 2 establishes the behavior of firms. Section 3 characterizes how the parameters central to the internalization decision influence the rate of innovation for the base case where innovation size and the mode of serving markets abroad are fixed. Section 4 examines the effect of internalization advantage on the magnitude as well as the rate of innovation when firms may switch market modes between FDI and licensing and contrasts these findings with the base case. Section 5 concludes. All proofs appear in Appendix A.

2. Dynamic OLI model

We build a dynamic OLI model based on the quality ladders model of innovation by Grossman and Helpman (1991a,b), but with two symmetric innovating countries. Assuming symmetric countries greatly simplifies our analysis and may not be too far from reality for similarly developed countries. Our model formalizes the view that ownership, location and internalization advantages dictate whether firms serve markets abroad through export, FDI (establishing a production subsidiary abroad), or licensing their technology to local firms.

Ownership advantage refers to some aspect, such as a unique product design, that a firm does better than others.[8] Location advantage refers to some aspect, such as tariffs or transportation costs, that makes producing in the same location as consumption preferable to producing in one place and shipping to wherever demand is located. Internalization advantage refers to some aspect, such as incomplete contracts, that makes keeping transactions within the firm preferable to arms-length transactions between firms.[9]

We are primarily interested in FDI and licensing, so we assume that tariffs or transportation costs are sufficiently high that FDI and licensing are the only relevant options remaining for serving markets abroad. Initially, we assume that an exogenous fraction η of all industries use multinational production to serve markets abroad, while the remaining $1-\eta$ use licensing. We will refer to η as the *extent of FDI* and $1-\eta$ as the *extent of licensing*. In this base case of exogenous internalization, we explore how parameters that affect the profitability of licensing and FDI alter the rate of innovation. Later, we will allow the extent of FDI η and the innovation magnitude λ to vary, but for now they are fixed.

2.1. Product market

A continuum of products $j \in [0,1]$ are each available in different quality levels. Assume consumers are willing to pay a premium λ for a one-quality-level improvement in a product, where λ is the innovation size or magnitude. Consumer preferences giving rise to these properties are the same as in Grossman and Helpman (1991a,b) – details are provided in Appendix A. Let E be aggregate expenditure, the amount consumers that spend on each product. Consumers live in either the domestic or the foreign country. Of the total spending, $E_D = f_D E$ is spent by domestic consumers and $E_F = f_F E$ is spent by foreign consumers, where the expenditure shares sum to one $f_D + f_F = 1$.

Normalize the unit labor requirement in production of any quality level of any product to one in each country. Let the labor requirement in innovation be given by a in both countries. Further, let L denote the total world labor supply so that each country's labor supply equals $L/2$. As a result, the countries have the same wage, and the expenditure shares both equal one-half $f_D = f_F = 1/2$. Altogether, these assumptions make the two countries exactly identical.

Also, normalize the common wage to one. Thus, the marginal cost of producing

[8]See Horstmann and Markusen (1989) and Markusen (1984).

[9]See Markusen (1995); Saggi (1996, 1999); Ethier and Markusen (1996) and Horstmann and Markusen (1996).

one unit of output (of any quality) is 1 in either country. Assuming Bertrand behavior, suppose in each industry, one firm can produce the highest quality level and another firm can produce the quality level one below.[10] Firms maximize profits by engaging in limit pricing. Each firm that invented the highest quality level available of a product charges the highest price that keeps its rival (the firm able to produce the next highest quality level of that product) out of the market.

Thus, prices will be $p = \lambda$, a mark-up of the quality increment relative to marginal costs. A rival could sell the lower quality level at no less than its marginal cost of one and make non-negative profits. Consumers view the higher quality level sold at price λ to be equivalent to the lower quality level sold at a price of one, so λ is the limit price. With these prices, sales are $x = E\delta$, where define the inverse innovation magnitude as $\delta \equiv 1/\lambda$. A firm's instantaneous profit takes the form $\pi = (p - c)x$ (where c is marginal cost), which depends on how the market abroad is served.

Let $\zeta > 0$ be the cost disadvantage of multinationals operating abroad. A multinational has marginal cost $c^{\mathrm{M}} = 1 + \zeta/2$ and thus earns instantaneous profits.

$$\pi^{\mathrm{M}} = E\left[1 - \left(1 + \frac{\zeta}{2}\right)\delta\right] \tag{1}$$

The downside of FDI is the additional costs ζ of operating in an unfamiliar location.[11]

While multinationals face a cost disadvantage, licensors do not capture the full rents created by an ownership advantage. Let $\theta > 0$ be the fraction of profits collected by licensees, with the remaining $1 - \theta$ collected by the licensor. A licensor has marginal cost $c^{\mathrm{L}} = 1$ and thus earns instantaneous profits.

$$\pi^{\mathrm{L}} = E(1 - \delta)\left(1 - \frac{\theta}{2}\right) \tag{2}$$

The two countries have the same θ and ζ to keep them symmetric. We do not permit θ to be a function of the innovation size λ because we will develop an alternative explanation of why larger innovations are kept within the firm; we will show that multinationals develop larger innovations than licensors.

2.2. Ownership advantage through innovation

Firms must have some ownership advantage to offset the difficulty of serving foreign markets. Ownership advantage here takes the form of the unique knowledge of how to produce a higher quality level of a product relative to any other firm.

Innovation resembles a lottery: costs are born up front with an uncertain payoff.

[10] A description of the innovation process yielding these properties follows in Section 2.2.

[11] A subsidy to multinational production is a reduction in multinational cost disadvantage.

The innovation process is the same as in Grossman and Helpman (1991a,b). Assume innovation races occur simultaneously for all products, with all firms able to attempt to invent the quality level above the current highest quality level.[12] Further assume undertaking innovation intensity ι^k for a time interval dt requires $a\iota^k$ dt units of labor and leads to success with probability ι^k dt, where $k \in \{M,L\}$ denotes industries whose market mode is multinational production or licensing. Since price competition yields no profits when firms have the same technology, no quality level is ever invented twice.

Each non-producing firm chooses its intensity of innovation to maximize its expected value, given the innovation intensities of other firms.[13] To generate finite rates of innovation, expected gains must not exceed their cost, with equality when innovation occurs with positive intensity

$$v^k \leq a,\ \iota^k > 0 \Leftrightarrow v^k = a, \tag{3}$$

where v^k is the value a firm gains from successful innovation if it serves the market abroad using mode k. This reward to innovation is the discounted stream of profits from production. We focus on equilibria with positive innovation intensities for both modes: innovation targets industries that serve markets abroad through multinational production as well as those that use licensing.

All producing firms are exposed to further innovation that ultimately ends the stream of profits earned from an innovation. Firms that successfully innovate earn the reward

$$v^k = \frac{\pi^k}{\rho + \iota^k}, \tag{4}$$

where π^k denotes instantaneous profits defined in Eqs. (1) and (2), ρ the discount rate, and ι^k the innovation intensity targeting industries that engage in market mode k.

The aggregate (or average) rate of innovation ι is the extent of FDI η times the innovation intensity targeting industries that engage in multinational production ι^M plus the extent of licensing $1 - \eta$ times the innovation intensity targeting industries that engage in licensing ι^L.

$$\iota \equiv \eta\iota^M + (1 - \eta)\iota^L \tag{5}$$

Once we characterize the labor constraints, we can describe the general equilibrium in the next section.

[12] See also Segerstrom (1991); Segerstrom et al. (1990); and Taylor (1993).

[13] Innovation is done by followers – see Grossman and Helpman (1991b).

3. Rate of innovation for the base case

Initially, we assume that the innovation magnitude λ and the extent of FDI η are exogenous.[14] To hold mode fixed, we assume that the fraction η of industries engage in multinational production, while the others engage in licensing. We determine the equilibrium aggregate expenditure E and rate of innovation ι, as well the composition of innovation between targeting industries that conduct FDI and those that conduct licensing.

3.1. Labor constraint

By the assumed symmetry, each country performs half of the world's innovation, does half of the world's spending and provides half of the world's labor force. Each country's labor constraint is therefore equivalent to the world labor constraint. In the world, $a\iota = a[\eta\iota^{M} + (1-\eta)\iota^{L}]$ units of labor are needed for innovation, and $x = E\delta$ units of labor are needed for production. The world labor constraint requires world labor demand for innovation and production to equal the world labor supply.

$$a[\eta\iota^{M} + (1-\eta)\iota^{L}] + E\delta = L \tag{6}$$

The labor constraints, together with innovation conditions for multinationals and licensors derived next, provide the three key equations in our model, which will determine the variables ι^{M}, ι^{L}, and E.

3.2. Innovation conditions

In industries that conduct FDI, the valuation condition for firms is given by Eq. (3). Substituting the producing firm valuation Eq. (4) and multinational profits Eq. (1) into Eq. (3) yields the valuation condition for multinationals.

$$E\left[1 - \left(1 + \frac{\zeta}{2}\right)\delta\right] = a(\rho + \iota^{M}) \tag{7}$$

Decreases in multinational cost disadvantage ζ increase profits and thus the reward to innovation.

Substituting the producing firm valuation Eq. (4) and licensor profits Eq. (2) into Eq. (3) yields the valuation condition for licensors.

$$E\left(1 - \frac{\theta}{2}\right)(1-\delta) = a(\rho + \iota^{L}) \tag{8}$$

[14]The proof of Proposition 1 allows the exogenous innovation magnitude for multinationals to exceed that for licensors, for later use.

Decreases in licensee profit retention θ also increase profits and thus the reward to innovation.

3.3. Solution

The system of equations is the labor constraint Eq. (6), the innovation condition for FDI Eq. (7), and the innovation condition for licensing Eq. (8). The system determines the equilibrium level of aggregate expenditure

$$E = (L + a\rho)\left[\frac{2}{2 - \theta(1-\eta)(1-\delta) - \eta\delta\zeta}\right], \tag{9}$$

the equilibrium innovation intensity targeting the products of multinationals

$$\iota^{\mathrm{M}} = \frac{LN - (L + a\rho)[2\delta + (1-\eta)\zeta\delta\theta(1-\delta)]}{aN}, \tag{10}$$

and the equilibrium innovation intensity targeting the products of licensors

$$\iota^{\mathrm{L}} = \frac{LN + (L + a\rho)[2\delta + \eta(\theta(1-\delta) - \zeta\delta)]}{aN}, \tag{11}$$

where $N \equiv 2 - \theta(1-\eta)(1-\delta) - \eta\delta\zeta$.

Using the innovation intensities Eqs. (10) and (11), we find the equilibrium rate of innovation Eq. (5) to be

$$\iota = \frac{LN - 2(L + a\rho)\delta}{aN} \tag{12}$$

If we set the multinational cost disadvantage to be zero $\zeta = 0$ and licensee's rent share to zero $\theta = 0$, the equilibrium of the model replicates the aggregate expenditure and rate of innovation of the closed economy quality ladders model by Grossman and Helpman (1991a). In the absence of any friction between them, the two countries are just like one country split in half.

3.4. Comparative statics

Our first result reports the impact of various parameters that alter the profitability of licensors and multinationals. Reducing the multinational cost disadvantage ζ or reducing licensee profit retention θ increases the reward to innovation and hence leads to faster innovations. The composition of innovation between targeting licensors and targeting multinationals responds to the relative incentives for innovation: the first change favors innovation targeting multinationals while the latter favors innovation targeting licensors. Aggregate expenditure falls to free up labor from production to be used for innovation.

The intuition for why an increase in ζ lowers innovation targeting multinationals but increases innovation targeting licensors comes from the general equilibrium nature of our model. An increase in ζ makes multinationals less attractive candidates as innovation targets so that resources shift into innovation targeting licensors. Alternatively, for both licensing and FDI to occur in equilibrium both licensors and multinationals must earn the same rate of return: if multinationals become less profitable, they must face a lower risk of being innovated over relative to licensors. Of course, innovators face reduced profitability overall when either mode becomes less desirable (due to an increase in θ or ζ) so that the aggregate rate of innovation must fall.

Proposition 1. (Fixed mode and innovation size) *A decrease in the cost disadvantage of multinationals ζ increases the aggregate rate of innovation and the innovation intensity targeting multinationals, while decreasing the innovation intensity targeting licensors and aggregate expenditure. Similarly, an increase in the share of profits retained by licensees θ decreases the aggregate rate of innovation, increases aggregate expenditure, and also shifts innovation toward targeting multinationals and away from targeting licensors.*

Empirical evidence supports this result. A survey by Mansfield et al. (1979) found that large US companies drew 29 to 34% of the returns from their R&D projects from foreign markets. Furthermore, the firms indicated that if they were to collect no returns from abroad, they would reduce their R&D anywhere from 16 to 26%, and if they were forced to use other methods than foreign subsidiaries, they would reduce their R&D anywhere from 12 to 15%.

4. Endogenous mode and innovation size

Now we allow the multinational cost disadvantage ζ to vary across industries and examine how the extent of FDI as well as the magnitude of innovations chosen by multinationals responds to incentives to FDI. Then we describe how the innovation conditions and resource constraint can accommodate this general case and show that the effects on the rate of innovation resemble those for the base case.

4.1. Mode choice

Now suppose the continuum of industries differ in the degree of cost disadvantage suffered by multinationals. Industries may differ in the difficulties of coordinating decisions over considerable distances; also, the technology involved in some industries may be less perfectly adaptable to different economic environments. For simplicity, assume the multinational cost disadvantage is uniformly distributed $\zeta(j) \in [\underline{\zeta}, \overline{\zeta}]$.

A firm serves the market abroad through multinational production rather than licensing if its profits as a multinational Eq. (1) exceed those as a licensor Eq. (2).

This condition holds if licensee profit retention is larger than the reduction in profits due to the multinational cost disadvantage.

$$\theta > \tilde{\theta} \equiv \frac{\zeta}{\lambda - 1} \Leftrightarrow \zeta < \tilde{\zeta} \equiv \theta(\lambda - 1) \tag{13}$$

The measure of industries conducting FDI is the *extent of FDI*

$$\eta = \frac{\tilde{\zeta} - \underline{\zeta}}{\bar{\zeta} - \underline{\zeta}}, \tag{14}$$

with the remaining $1 - \eta$ conducting licensing.[15] We focus on parameters such that $0 < \eta < 1$ so that both FDI and licensing occur (for different industries): $\underline{\zeta} < \tilde{\zeta} < \bar{\zeta}$.

Fig. 1 depicts the maximum licensee profit retention $\tilde{\theta}$ that leads to licensing for a range of multinational cost disadvantages ζ, given the innovation magnitude λ. The boundary (13) is an upward-sloping line through the origin with slope $1/(\lambda - 1)$: above the line, FDI arises and below it licensing. Drawing a horizontal line to represent a given level of licensee profit retention θ, the intersection with the boundary line (13) indicates the threshold $\tilde{\zeta}$ for that value of θ. Industries with a low value of multinational cost disadvantage $\zeta \leq \tilde{\zeta}$ choose multinational production, while those with high values $\zeta > \tilde{\zeta}$ choose licensing.

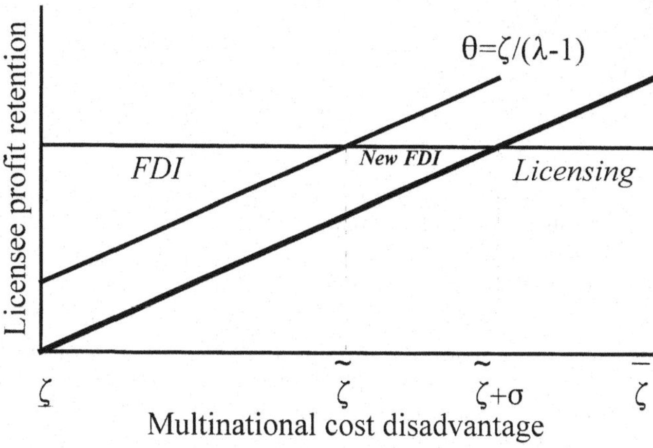

Fig. 1. Licensing versus direct investment decision.

[15] If FDI dominates licensing based on the innovation size chosen under licensing, then FDI will also dominate for any larger λ. Hence the expression for η is a lower bound when λ can be chosen.

4.2. Innovation size for multinationals versus licensors

Following the technique of Aghion and Howitt (1990) and Grossman and Helpman (1991a), suppose the resource requirement in innovation $a(\lambda)$ depends on the magnitude of the innovation attempted. We assume that the resource requirement in innovation increases with the size of the quality improvement $a'(\lambda)>0$ at an increasing rate $a''(\lambda)>0$.

The optimal quality increment equates the increase in the value of the innovation with the increase in the cost of the innovation.

$$v'(\lambda)=a'(\lambda) \tag{15}$$

Multiply each side of Eq. (15) by λ and, using the equilibrium condition (3), divide each side by v and a, respectively.

$$\frac{\lambda v'(\lambda)}{v(\lambda)}=\frac{\lambda a'(\lambda)}{a(\lambda)} \tag{16}$$

The left-hand side is the elasticity of the reward to innovation with respect to the magnitude of the innovation attempted, which depends on how a firm serves the market abroad. The right-hand side is the elasticity of the resource requirement in innovation with respect to the magnitude of the innovation attempted.

Calculate $\partial v^{\mathrm{M}}/\partial\lambda^{\mathrm{M}}$ and similarly $\partial v^{\mathrm{L}}/\partial\lambda^{\mathrm{L}}$ and then multiply each by the quality increment divided by the reward to innovation λ/v^{M} or λ/v^{L} to find the condition for determining the quality increment for multinationals

$$\frac{1+\zeta/2}{\lambda-1-\zeta/2}=\frac{\lambda a'(\lambda)}{a(\lambda)} \tag{17}$$

and for licensors

$$\frac{1}{\lambda-1}=\frac{\lambda a'(\lambda)}{a(\lambda)}. \tag{18}$$

The condition for licensors is identical to the condition found by Grossman and Helpman (1991a) in their single country model.

The profits dissipated by the licensee act like a tax on profits earned in the foreign market: licensee profit retention does not distort the quality level chosen by a licensor.[16] In contrast, for any $\zeta>0$, the quality increment chosen by a multinational exceeds the quality increment chosen by a licensor: $\lambda^{\mathrm{M}}>\lambda^{\mathrm{L}}$. Multinationals choose larger innovations because larger innovations shrink the importance of their cost disadvantage and because they collect the entire increase in profits that results from an improvement in the quality of their products. If

[16] If θ were to increase in λ, the quality increment under licensing would be depressed: this property would reinforce our result that multinationals choose larger innovations than licensors. An increase in profit taxes abroad would act like an increase in θ.

licensing will occur, firms pick the innovation magnitude λ^{L}. If multinational production will occur, firms picks an innovation magnitude $\lambda^{M}(\zeta)$ that increases in the multinational cost disadvantage $\partial\lambda^{M}/\partial\zeta > 0$.

Fig. 2 illustrates the equilibrium quality increments chosen by multinationals and licensors. The upward-sloping curve **A** represents the increase in cost $\lambda a'/a$, while the downward sloping curves **L** and **M** represent the increase in reward $\lambda v'/v$ for licensors and multinationals. The **M** curve lies above the **L** curve provided $\zeta > 0$. Licensors choose quality increment λ^{L} while multinationals choose $\lambda^{M} > \lambda^{L}$. The larger the cost disadvantage faced by multinationals, the larger the magnitude of ownership advantage they create through innovation. When the multinational cost disadvantage is reduced (such as if multinational production is subsidized), the reward line shifts down to **M′** and multinationals decrease their quality increment to $\lambda^{M'} < \lambda^{M}$.[17]

Proposition 2. *Multinationals choose larger innovations than licensors. A decrease in multinational cost disadvantage reduces the magnitude of innovations chosen by multinationals. An increase in the share of profits retained by licensees does not affect the magnitude of innovation chosen by licensors.*

The trait that multinationals invent larger improvements than licensors matches

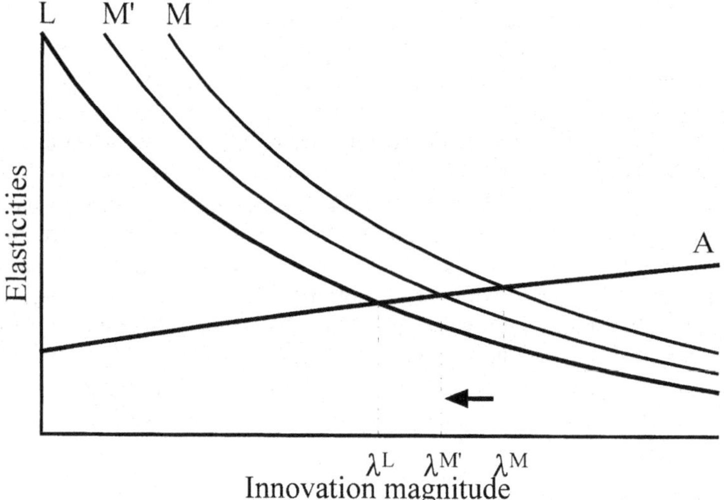

Fig. 2. Subsidy shrinks innovations when mode fixed.

[17] A reduction in the fixed costs of multinational production, or equivalently a lump-sum subsidy to FDI, would increase ι but not affect λ.

empirical evidence (see Mansfield and Romeo, 1980). We relate this property to the disadvantages faced by multinationals due to operating in unfamiliar economic environments and having to coordinate production over larger distances (see Markusen, 1995).

4.3. Composition effects with mode shifts

What happens if production by multinationals is subsidized so that the multinational cost disadvantage falls? Let $-\Delta\zeta(j) = \sigma$ so that the multinational cost disadvantage for each industry (net of any subsidy) falls by the amount of the subsidy to multinational production. Industries with multinational cost disadvantage in the range $(\tilde{\zeta}, \tilde{\zeta}']$ will switch from licensing to FDI, where $\tilde{\zeta}' \equiv \tilde{\zeta} + \sigma$, as the subsidy is sufficient to make FDI attractive relative to licensing. This switch from licensing to FDI is depicted in Fig. 1 by the segment labeled **New FDI** between the old boundary line and the new one. Thus the extent of FDI rises and the extent of licensing falls: $\partial\eta/\partial\sigma = \sigma/(\bar{\zeta} - \underline{\zeta})$.

Industries that continue to license still pick the same innovation magnitude λ^{L}. Industries that continue with FDI reduce their chosen innovation magnitude $\lambda^{M'}(j) < \lambda^{M}(j)$: an industry with multinational cost disadvantage $\zeta(j)$ picks the innovation magnitude based on $\zeta'(j) \equiv \zeta(j) - \sigma$. But the industries that *newly serve* the market abroad through FDI (that originally licensed local firms) *increase* their innovation magnitude as the innovation magnitude for multinationals exceeds that for firms that license $\lambda^{M'}(j) > \lambda^{L}$. We additionally require $\tilde{\zeta} + \sigma \leq \bar{\zeta}$ so that there are enough industries that were licensing to switch to FDI. Table 1 captures the effects on innovation size.

Fig. 3 helps visualize that the average innovation magnitude must rise. The area under **ML** indicates the average innovation size chosen initially, and the area under **M′L** is that with the subsidy. Thus, comparing areas amounts to comparing the average innovation size. The shaded triangle indicates the degree that the average innovation size increases due to the subsidy. The innovation magnitude chosen over $[\underline{\zeta} + \sigma, \tilde{\zeta} + \sigma]$ with the subsidy matches that chosen over $[\underline{\zeta}, \tilde{\zeta}]$ in the absence of the subsidy. Provided $\sigma < \underline{\zeta}$ so that some multinational cost disadvantage remains net of the subsidy, the smallest innovation magnitude $\underline{\lambda}^{M}$ must still exceed the innovation magnitude under licensing λ^{L}. Thus, the degree that innovation magnitude for the range $[\underline{\zeta}, \underline{\zeta} + \sigma]$ exceeds the innovation magnitude

Table 1
Adjustment in innovation size

FDI	$[\underline{\zeta}, \tilde{\zeta}]$	$\Delta\lambda < 0$
Switch	$(\tilde{\zeta}, \tilde{\zeta}']$	$\Delta\lambda > 0$
License	$(\tilde{\zeta}', \bar{\zeta}]$	$\Delta\lambda = 0$

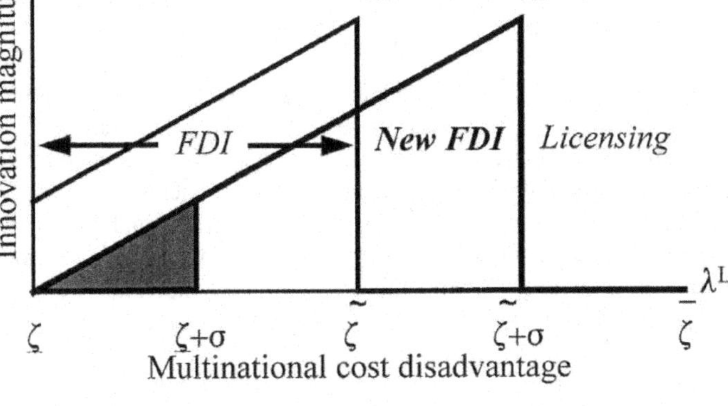

Fig. 3. Subsidy expands innovations when mode adjusts.

under licensing (the shaded area) is positive and represents the degree that the overall innovation magnitude increases due to the FDI subsidy.[18]

Proposition 3. *A subsidy to multinational production expands the extent of FDI and contracts the extent of licensing. Each industry conducting FDI shrinks its innovation magnitude, but some industries switch from licensing to FDI and these industries increase their innovation magnitude. The average innovation magnitude under FDI falls but the overall average innovation magnitude (under FDI and licensing) rises, provided the subsidy is not too large.*

Similar analysis can be performed for the case of an increase in licensee profit retention θ. An increase in θ increases the extent of FDI as the threshold $\tilde{\zeta}$ defined in Eq. (13) increases. Firms in industries that switch from licensing to FDI pick larger innovations than before. In fact, they have larger multinational cost disadvantages ζ than firms in industries that were already engaged in FDI; consequently, the firms that switch pick larger innovations than existing multinationals. Thus, the average innovation size for multinationals increases, as does the overall average innovation size. In this case, the increase in innovation size is generated entirely by firms that switch mode from licensing to multinational production.

Proposition 4. *An increase in the share of profits retained by licensees expands*

[18]In effect, we shift the innovation magnitude curve **M′L** with the subsidy to the left by the amount of the subsidy to overlap the innovation magnitude curve **ML** without the subsidy, wrapping the range from $\underline{\zeta}$ to $\underline{\zeta} + \sigma$ around to the right.

the extent of FDI and contracts the extent of licensing. Industries that switch from licensing to FDI increase their innovation magnitude. The average innovation magnitude under FDI and the overall average innovation magnitude (under FDI and licensing) both rise.

When the mode (licensing versus FDI) is exogenous, subsidizing multinational production leads to smaller innovations and increasing licensee profit retention leaves innovation size unchanged. However, allowing firms to choose their mode of serving foreign markets drastically alters those conclusions: *any* force that increases internalization advantage (subsidies to multinational production or an increase in the licensee's share of profits) necessarily increases the average size of innovations. Yet allowing for the mode to shift does not alter the sign of our comparative static results for the speed of innovation.

4.4. *Rate of innovation for the general case*

Our key equations for determining the rate of innovation can be adapted to allow for differences in the magnitude of innovations across industry types. In the innovation valuation condition for multinationals (7), the inverse innovation magnitude $\delta^{M}(j) \equiv 1/\lambda^{M}(j)$ and the resource requirement in innovation $a^{M}(j)$ vary by industry j due to differences in the multinational cost disadvantage $\zeta^{M}(j)$ – based on the choice of the optimal innovation size discussed above. We then solve this innovation condition for the innovation intensity $\iota^{M}(j)$.

Define the average inverse of the innovation magnitude for multinationals as $\hat{\delta}^{M} \equiv \int_0^{\eta} \delta^{M}(j)\ \mathrm{d}j/\eta$ and the average inverse of the innovation magnitude over all industries as the extent of FDI times the inverse magnitude for FDI plus the extent of licensing times the inverse magnitude for licensing $\hat{\delta} \equiv \eta\hat{\delta}^{M} + (1-\eta)\delta^{L}$. In the world, production requires $x^{M} = E\hat{\delta}^{M}$ units of labor for each industry characterized by multinational production and $x^{L} = E\delta^{L}$ for each industry that licenses. World labor demand for production is then $x = \eta E\hat{\delta}^{M} + (1-\eta)E\delta^{L} = E\hat{\delta}$. Similarly, for the labor demand in innovation, calculate the average for multinationals $\hat{a\iota}^{M} \equiv \int_0^{\eta} a^{M}(j)\iota^{M}(j)\ \mathrm{d}j/\eta$ and for all industries $a\iota \equiv \eta\hat{a\iota}^{M} + (1-\eta)\iota^{L}$. The world labor constraint Eq. (6) is essentially unchanged but stated in terms of averages over industries.

Then we are ready to solve the world labor constraint and the innovation valuation conditions for licensors Eq. (8) for aggregate expenditure E and the innovation intensity for licensors ι^{L}. The average innovation intensity targeting multinationals is $\hat{\iota}^{M} \equiv \int_0^{\eta} \iota^{M}(j)\ \mathrm{d}j/\eta$ and the aggregate rate of innovation becomes $\iota \equiv \eta\hat{\iota}^{M} + (1-\eta)\iota^{L}$. Economic growth, which was $g \equiv \iota \log \lambda$ in the base case, now becomes

$$g \equiv \int_0^{\eta} \iota^{M}(j) \log \lambda^{M}(j)\ \mathrm{d}j + (1-\eta)\iota^{L} \log \lambda^{L}. \tag{19}$$

Parameter changes can affect economic growth through effects on the innovation intensities $\iota^{M}(j)$ and ι^{L}, the innovation magnitudes $\lambda^{M}(j)$ and λ^{L}, or on the composition of them based on the extent of FDI η.

With the mode adjusting, a subsidy to multinational production, by reducing the effective cost disadvantage of multinationals, will necessarily increase economic growth by increasing both the size and the rate of innovations.[19] The negative effect of licensee profit retention on the speed of innovations can be more than offset by innovations becoming larger due to the mode shift.[20]

Proposition 5. *When firms can shift their mode of serving markets abroad, if multinational cost disadvantage falls (such as due to a subsidy to multinational production), innovations occur faster and are larger. If the licensee's share of profits rises, innovations occur slower but are larger.*

5. Conclusion

In this paper, we constructed a model that combines the dynamic aspects of endogenous innovation with the OLI paradigm to determine the impact of variations in internalization advantage on technological progress. Our model is consistent with a set of stylized facts emphasizing the significance of two-way FDI between similar developed countries in high-technology industries.

In our model, FDI occurs if profit retention by licensees is more destructive than the cost disadvantage of multinationals. A decrease in the profits retained by licensees or a decrease in the cost disadvantage of multinationals (such as due to a subsidy to multinational production) increases the aggregate rate of innovation.

A subsidy to multinational production acts like a reduction in multinational cost disadvantage and thus increases the extent of FDI relative to licensing. Multinationals choose larger innovations than licensors because ownership advantage helps to offset the additional costs of conducting operations within a firm across multiple countries. A subsidy to multinational production decreases the magnitude of innovations under FDI by lessening the net cost disadvantage of multinational production. Thus, when the mode of serving foreign markets is held fixed, a subsidy to multinational production leads to smaller innovations so economic growth need not increase.

[19]We confirm the effect of a subsidy for a numerical example: $L=4$, $\rho=1/30$, $\theta=3/10$, $\underline{\zeta}=1/10$, $\bar{\zeta}=1/2$, and $a=1+\lambda/2+\lambda^2/4$. Increasing the subsidy from $\sigma=0$ to $\sigma'=1/10$ increases $\eta=1/2$ to $\eta'=3/4$, decreases E by 1.6%, decreases ι^{L} by 1.7%, increases $\hat{\iota}^{M}$ by 0.87%, increases ι by 2%, decreases $\hat{\lambda}^{M}$ by 1.8% but increases λ by 0.48%. Economic growth increases by 2.4%.

[20]Using the same parameters, we increase licensee profit retention from $\theta=3/10$ to $\theta'=2/5$ (with $\sigma=0$), which also increases $\eta=1/2$ to $\eta'=3/4$. E increases 0.8%, ι^{L} decreases 5.4%, $\hat{\iota}^{M}$ decreases 1.6%. ι decreases 0.8%. $\hat{\lambda}^{M}$ increases 1.7%. and λ increases 3.1%. Economic growth increases 3.3%!

Nevertheless, when firms can shift their mode, a subsidy to multinational production increases the average innovation magnitude over all industries, since innovations are larger under FDI than licensing and the extent of FDI rises in response to the subsidy. So when the mode is endogenous, a subsidy to multinational production leads to faster and larger innovations, and thus clearly faster economic growth.

Adjustment in mode also has key implications for the effects of licensee profit retention on economic growth. If mode were fixed, an increase in licensee profit retention makes innovations slower but has no effect on their size, so economic growth must necessarily decline. However, the shift in mode from licensing to multinational production leads to bigger innovations (since multinationals pick larger innovations than licensors). The impact of larger innovations can more than offset their reduced frequency, leading to the possibility of increased economic growth. We confirm through a numerical example that the size effect can indeed dominate the frequency effect, and thereby reverse the effect on economic growth compared to holding mode fixed.

While we pose our questions in terms of the choice between multinational production and licensing, our results apply more broadly to the decision whether to keep production within the firm. Any innovator might face a tradeoff between higher production costs if produce by itself or profit sharing if license production to a firm with better production abilities. The production cost disadvantage is apt to be less severe when operating abroad is not involved. Yet, some firms may be better suited for innovating than for producing, and thus license their technologies rather than produce in-house.

Acknowledgements

We thank Rick Bond, Bill Ethier, Eric Fisher, Peter Howitt, Jane Ihrig, Ron Jones, Jim Markusen, Jim Melvin, Usha Nair, Peter Neary, Francesca Sanna-Randaccio, Pam Smith, Diana Weinhold, two anonymous referees, and participants at Ohio State University, Southern Methodist University, the Midwest International Economics Meetings, the Canadian Economic Association Meetings, the Taipei International Conference on Economic Growth, an IEFS Session of the ASSA meetings, and the Dynamics of International Trade and Economic Growth for their comments.

Appendix A

A.1. Consumer's problem

Quality level m of product j provides quality $q_m(j) \equiv \lambda^m$. All products start at time $t = 0$ at quality level $m = 0$, so the base quality is $q_0(j) = \lambda^0 = 1$. All consumers value quality: $\lambda > 1$. For quality level m to provide higher quality than the previous quality level $m-1$, $q_m(j) > q_{m-1}(j) \rightarrow \lambda^m > \lambda^{m-1} \rightarrow \lambda > 1$. A representative consumer in country $i \in \{D,F\}$ has additively separable intertemporal preferences given by lifetime utility

$$U_i = \int_0^\infty e^{-\rho t} \log u_i(t)\, dt \tag{A.1}$$

where ρ is the common subjective discount factor. Instantaneous utility is

$$\log u_i(t) = \int_0^1 \log \sum_m \lambda^m x_{im}(j,t)\, dj \tag{A.2}$$

where λ^m is the assessment of quality level m and $x_{im}(j,t)$ is consumption of quality level m of product j at time t by consumers in country i.

The representative consumer maximizes lifetime utility subject to an intertemporal budget constraint. Since preferences are homothetic, aggregate demand is found by maximizing lifetime utility subject to the aggregate intertemporal budget constraint

$$\int_0^\infty e^{-R(t)} E_i(t)\, dt \leq A_i(0) + \int_0^\infty e^{-R(t)} Y_i(t)\, dt \tag{A.3}$$

where $R(t) = \int_0^t r(s)\, ds$ is the cumulative interest rate up to time t and $A_i(0) = f_i A(0)$ is the aggregate value of initial asset holdings. Individuals hold assets in the form of ownership in firms, but with a diversified portfolio, any capital losses appear as capital gains elsewhere so only initial asset holdings remain. Aggregate labor income is $Y_i(t) = L_i$, where L_i is the labor supply in country i. Aggregate spending is

$$E_i(t) = \int_0^1 \Big[\sum_m p_m(j,t) x_{im}(j,t) \Big]\, dj. \tag{A.4}$$

where $p_m(j,t)$ is the price of quality level m of product j at time t.

The representative consumer's maximization problem can be broken into three stages: the allocation of lifetime wealth across time, the allocation of expenditure at each instant across products, and the allocation of expenditure at each instant for each product across available quality levels. In the final stage, the representative consumer allocates spending for each product at each instant to the quality level $\tilde{m}(j,t)$ offering the lowest quality-adjusted price, $p_m(j,t)/\lambda^m$. Settle indifference in favor of the higher quality level so the quality level selected is unique.

In the second stage, the representative consumer then evenly spreads spending across the unit measure of all products, $E_i(j,t) = E_i(t)$, as the elasticity of substitution is constant at unity. Consumers demand $x_{\tilde{m}}(j,t) = E_i(t)/p_{\tilde{m}}(j,t)$ units of quality level $\tilde{m}(j,t)$ of product j and no units of other quality levels of that product. Thus lifetime utility (A.1) becomes

$$U_i = \int_0^\infty e^{-\rho t} \left[\log E_i(t) + \int_0^1 [\tilde{m}(j,t) \log \lambda - \log p_{\tilde{m}}(j,t)] \, dj \right] dt \tag{A.5}$$

by substituting for instantaneous utility (and demand).

In the first stage, the representative consumer evenly spreads lifetime spending across time, $E_i(t) = E_i$, as the utility function is time separable and the aggregate price level does not vary across time $\log p_{\tilde{m}}(j,t) = \log p_{\tilde{m}}(j)$. Since aggregate spending is constant across time, the interest rate at each point in time reflects the discount rate $r(t) = \rho$, so $R(t) = \rho t$ in the intertemporal budget constraint.

A.2. Proof of Proposition 1

After taking the derivatives, we evaluate them at $\zeta = 0$ and $\theta = 0$ for simplicity (we permit $\delta^M < \delta^L$ for use in the more general case below). Let $\partial\sigma \equiv -\partial\zeta$ represent a reduction in multinational cost disadvantage due to a subsidy to multinational production. A decrease in multinational cost disadvantage (or increase in the subsidy to multinational production) increases the aggregate rate of innovation

$$\frac{\partial \iota}{\partial \sigma} = \frac{1}{2} \eta \delta^M \delta \left(\frac{L}{a} + \rho \right) > 0 \tag{A.6}$$

increases the innovation intensity targeting multinationals

$$\frac{\partial \iota^M}{\partial \sigma} = \frac{1}{2} \delta^M (1 - \eta + \eta \delta^M) \left(\frac{L}{a} + \rho \right) > 0 \tag{A.7}$$

decreases the innovation intensity targeting licensors

$$\frac{\partial \iota^L}{\partial \sigma} = -\frac{1}{2} \eta \delta^M (1 - \delta^L) \left(\frac{L}{a} + \rho \right) < 0 \tag{A.8}$$

and decreases aggregate expenditure.

$$\frac{\partial E}{\partial \sigma} = -\frac{1}{2} \eta \delta^M \left(\frac{L}{a} + \rho \right) < 0 \tag{A.9}$$

An increase in licensee profit retention decreases the aggregate rate of innovation

$$\frac{\partial \iota}{\partial \theta} = -\frac{1}{2} \delta (1 - \eta)(1 - \delta^L) \left(\frac{L}{a} + \rho \right) < 0 \tag{A.10}$$

increases the innovation intensity targeting multinationals

$$\frac{\partial \iota^{M}}{\partial \theta}=\frac{1}{2}(1-\eta)(1-\delta^{L})(1-\delta^{M})\left(\frac{L}{a}+\rho\right)>0 \tag{A.11}$$

decreases the innovation intensity targeting licensors

$$\frac{\partial \iota^{L}}{\partial \theta}=-\frac{1}{2}\delta(1-\delta^{L})\left(\frac{L}{a}+\rho\right)<0 \tag{A.12}$$

and increases aggregate expenditure.

$$\frac{\partial E}{\partial \theta}=\frac{1}{2}(1-\eta)(1-\delta^{L})\left(\frac{L}{a}+\rho\right)>0 \tag{A.13}$$

A.3. Proof of Proposition 2

Define $M\equiv(1+\zeta/2)/(\lambda-1-\zeta/2)$ and $A\equiv\lambda a'/a$. Note that

$$\frac{\partial M}{\partial \sigma}=-\frac{\lambda/2}{(\lambda-1-\zeta/2)^{2}},\quad \frac{\partial M}{\partial \lambda}=-\frac{1+\zeta/2}{(\lambda-1-\zeta/2)^{2}},$$
$$\frac{\partial A}{\partial \lambda}=\frac{a'}{a}\left(1-\frac{\lambda a'}{a}\right) \tag{A.14}$$

and $\partial A/\partial\zeta=0$, when totally differentiating the condition (17), so a decrease in λ is required to restore the equality when σ increases (ζ decreases).

$$\frac{\partial \lambda}{\partial \sigma}=-\frac{1}{2}\left(\frac{\lambda a'}{a}\right)^{2}(1+\zeta/2)^{2}<0 \tag{A.15}$$

A.4. Proof of Proposition 3

The extent of FDI rises and industries that conduct FDI pick smaller innovations with an decrease in the multinational cost disadvantage, but the mode effect dominates so the average innovation size rises. A decrease in multinational cost disadvantage still unambiguously raises the rate of innovation

$$\frac{d\iota}{d\sigma}=\underbrace{\frac{\partial \iota}{\partial \sigma}}_{+}+\underbrace{\underbrace{\frac{\partial \iota}{\partial \eta}}_{+}\underbrace{\frac{\partial \eta}{\partial \sigma}}_{+}+\underbrace{\frac{\partial \iota}{\partial \hat{\delta}^{M}}}_{-}\underbrace{\frac{\partial \hat{\delta}^{M}}{\partial \sigma}}_{+}}_{+}>0 \tag{A.16}$$

where $\partial\iota/\partial\eta=(\delta^{L}-\delta^{M})(L/a+\rho)>0$ and $\partial\eta/\partial\sigma=\sigma/(\bar{\zeta}-\underline{\zeta})$.

A.5. Proof of Proposition 4

The negative effect of an increase in licensee profit retention on the rate of innovation is in part mitigated by the ability of firms to switch to FDI and the larger average innovation size.

$$\frac{d\iota}{d\theta} = \underbrace{\frac{\partial \iota}{\partial \theta}}_{-} + \underbrace{\underbrace{\frac{\partial \iota}{\partial \eta}}_{+}\underbrace{\frac{\partial \eta}{\partial \theta}}_{+}}_{+} + \underbrace{\underbrace{\frac{\partial \iota}{\partial \hat{\delta}^{M}}}_{-}\underbrace{\frac{\partial \hat{\delta}^{M}}{\partial \theta}}_{-}}_{+} < 0 \tag{A.17}$$

References

Aghion, P., Howitt, P., 1990. A model of growth through creative destruction. Econometrica 60, 323–351.

Balasubramanyam, V.N., Salisu, M.A., Sapsford, D., 1996. Foreign direct investment and growth in EP and IS countries. Economic Journal 106, 92–105.

Borensztein, E., De Gregorio, J., Lee, J.-W., 1998. How does foreign direct investment affect economic growth? Journal of International Economics 45, 115–135.

Brainard, S.L., 1997. An empirical assessment of the proximity-concentration trade-off between multinational sales and trade. American Economic Review 87, 520–544.

Caves, R.E., 1996. Multinational Enterprise and Economic Analysis. Cambridge University Press, Cambridge.

Caves, R.E., Crookell, H., Killing, J.P., 1983. The imperfect market for technology licenses. Oxford Bulletin of Economics and Statistics 45, 249–267.

Davies, H., 1977. Technology transfer through commercial transactions. Journal of Industrial Economics 26, 161–175.

Ethier, W.J., 1986. The multinational firm. Quarterly Journal of Economics 101, 805–833.

Ethier, W.J., Markusen, J.R., 1996. Multinational firms, technology diffusion and trade. Journal of International Economics 41, 1–28.

Gallini, N.T., Wright, B.D., 1990. Technology transfer under asymmetric information. Rand Journal of Economics 21, 147–160.

Glass, A.J., Saggi, K., 1999. Foreign direct investment and the nature of R&D. Canadian Journal of Economics 32, 92–117.

Glass, A.J., Saggi, K., 1998. International technology transfer and the technology gap. Journal of Development Economics 55, 369–398.

Grossman, G.M., Helpman, E., 1995. In: Grossman, G.M., Rogoff, K. (Eds.), Handbook of International Economics. Technology and Trade, Vol. 3. North Holland, Amsterdam, pp. 1279–1337.

Grossman, G.M., Helpman, E., 1991a. Quality ladders in the theory of growth. Review of Economic Studies 58, 43–61.

Grossman, G.M., Helpman, E., 1991b. Quality ladders and product cycles. Quarterly Journal of Economics 106, 557–586.

Helpman, E., 1993. Innovation, imitation, and intellectual property rights. Econometrica 61, 1247–1280.

Horstmann, I.J., Markusen, J.R., 1996. Exploring new markets: direct investment, contractual relations and the multinational enterprise. International Economic Review 3, 1–19.

Horstmann, I.J., Markusen, J.R., 1992. Endogenous market structures in international trade (natura facit saltum). Journal of International Economics 32, 109–129.

Horstmann, I.J., Markusen, J.R., 1987. Licensing versus direct investment: a model of internationalization by the multinational enterprise. Canadian Journal of Economics 20, 464–481.

Horstmann, I.J., Markusen, J.R., 1986. Up the average cost curve: inefficient entry and the new protectionism. Journal of International Economics 20, 225–247.

Mansfield, E., Romeo, A., 1980. Technology transfer to overseas subsidiaries by US-based firms. Quarterly Journal of Economics 95, 737–750.

Mansfield, E., Romeo, A., Wagner, S., 1979. Foreign trade and US research and development. Review of Economics and Statistics 61, 49–57.

Markusen, J.R., 2001, Contracts, intellectual property rights, and multinational investment in developing countries, Journal of International Economics, 53, 189–204.

Markusen, J.R., 1995. The boundaries of multinational enterprises and the theory of international trade. Journal of Economic Perspectives 9, 169–189.

Markusen, J.R., 1984. Multinationals, multi-plant economies, and the gains from trade. Journal of International Economics 16, 205–226.

Markusen, J.R., Venables, A.J., 1998. Multinational firms and the new trade theory. Journal of International Economics 46, 183–203.

Moran, T.H., 1998. Foreign Direct Investment and Development: The New Policy Agenda For Developing Countries and Economies in Transition. Institute for International Economics, Washington DC.

Petit, M.-L., Sanna-Randaccio, F., 2000. Endogenous R&D and foreign direct investment in international oligopolies. International Journal of Industrial Organization 18, 339–367.

Rockett, K., 1990. The quality of licensed technology. International Journal of Industrial Organization 8, 559–574.

Saggi, K., 1999. Foreign direct investment, licensing, and incentives for innovation. Review of International Economics 7, 699–714.

Saggi, K., 1996. Entry into a foreign market: foreign direct investment versus licensing. Review of International Economics 4, 99–104.

Segerstrom, P.S., 1991. Innovation, imitation, and economic growth. Journal of Political Economy 99, 807–827.

Segerstrom, P.S., Anant, T.C.A., Dinopoulos, E., 1990. A Schumpeterian model of the product life cycle. American Economic Review 80, 1077–1091.

Taylor, M.S., 1993. Quality ladders and Ricardian trade. Journal of International Economics 34, 225–243.

UNCTAD, 1997. World Investment Report: Transnational Corporations, Market Structure, And Competition Policy. United Nations, New York.

Vishwasrao, S., 1994. Intellectual property rights and the mode of technology transfer. Journal of Development Economics 44, 381–402.

Walz, U., 1997. Innovation, foreign direct investment and growth. Economica 64, 63–79.

Wang, J.-Y., Blomström, M., 1992. Foreign investment and technology transfer: a simple model. European Economic Review 36, 137–155.

Wright, D.J., 1993. International technology transfer with an information asymmetry and endogenous research and development. Journal of International Economics 35, 47–67.

Yang, G., Maskus, K.E., 2001. Intellectual property rights, licensing and innovation in an endogenous product–cycle model, Journal of International Economics, 53, 169–187.

Chapter 11

Intellectual property rights and foreign direct investment[#]

Amy Jocelyn Glass[a,*], Kamal Saggi[b]

[a]*Department of Economics, Texas A&M University, College Station, TX 77843, USA*
[b]*Department of Economics, Southern Methodist University, Dallas, TX 75275, USA*

Received 25 June 1999; received in revised form 5 September 2000; accepted 9 January 2001

Abstract

This paper develops a product cycle model with endogenous innovation, imitation, and foreign direct investment (FDI). We use this model to determine how stronger intellectual property rights (IPR) protection in the South affects innovation, imitation and FDI. We find that stronger IPR protection keeps multinationals safer from imitation, but no more so than Northern firms. Instead, the increased difficulty of imitation generates resource wasting and imitation disincentive effects that reduce both FDI and innovation. The greater resources absorbed in imitation crowd out FDI. Reduced FDI then transmits resource scarcity in the South back to the North and consequently contracts innovation.

Keywords: Innovation; Imitation; Intellectual property rights; Foreign direct investment; Product cycles

JEL classification: F21; F43; O31; O34

---

1. Introduction

In recent years, the literature on product cycle models has made some important strides. Yet while Vernon's (1966) original vision of the product cycle assigns a central role to foreign direct investment (FDI), most models capturing his ideas cast imitation as the only channel of international technology transfer from an innovating region (the North) to an imitating region (the South) — see Krugman

*Corresponding author. Tel.: +1-979-845-8507; fax: +1-979-857-8757.
E-mail address: aglass@econ.tamu.edu (A.J. Glass).

[#] This chapter was originally appeared in *Journal of International Economics* **56**, 387–410.

(1979), Grossman and Helpman (1991) and Segerstrom et al. (1990). Two recent exceptions are Helpman (1993) and Lai (1998); however, imitation is exogenous in these models.

An important contribution of our paper is to provide a product cycle model in which innovation, imitation, and FDI are all endogenous.[1] Starting from the quality ladders model of Grossman and Helpman (1991), we determine the composition of international technology transfer between imitation and FDI. A common perception is that due to local knowledge spillovers, Southern firms can more easily imitate the products of multinationals producing in the South relative to firms producing in the North. We formalize this idea by assuming that the costs of imitating a multinational's product are lower than costs of imitating a Northern firm's product. By distinguishing between imitation that targets the products of Northern firms and imitation that targets the products of multinationals, we are able to determine the effects of parameter changes on the imitation exposure of multinationals relative to Northern firms.

We apply our model to determine the effects of increased intellectual property rights (IPR) protection in the South, which we assume increases the cost of imitation due to stricter uniqueness requirements. This increased cost results in an *endogenous* decline in imitation. While products like books, videos and compact disks receive much press about conflicts over IPR protection, imitating most products is not so simple. Empirical evidence indicates that imitation is a costly activity for a wide range of high technology goods, such as chemicals, drugs, electronics and machinery. For example, Mansfield et al. (1981) finds that the costs of imitation average 65% of the costs of innovation, and very few products were below 20%. Since Southern firms must devote substantial effort to backward engineering products prior to producing imitations, IPR protection may affect the effort required by specifying how similar an imitation can be to the original.

We find that stronger Southern IPR protection makes multinationals more secure from imitation in absolute terms but no more secure from imitation relative to successful innovators still producing in the North. Consequently, stronger Southern IPR protection does not alter the expected profit stream from becoming a multinational *relative* to remaining a Northern firm and hence does not encourage FDI. The past literature could not address relative imitation exposure because imitation was exogenous.

An interesting result of our model is that FDI decreases with a strengthening of Southern IPR protection. This result arises because an increase in the cost of imitation crowds out FDI through tighter Southern resource scarcity. Less efficient imitation absorbs more Southern resources despite the reduction in the rate of imitation stemming from the reduced profitability of imitation. Additionally, the

---

[1]Here, FDI is endogenously determined through costly adaptation of technologies, unlike in Glass and Saggi (1999) where FDI opportunities arrived exogenously.

contraction in FDI tightens Northern resource scarcity. Increased Northern production leaves fewer resources for innovation, so the rate of innovation falls.

To highlight the forces behind our results, we show that an increased cost of imitation has both an *imitation disincentive effect* similar to a tax on imitation and a *resource wasting effect* similar to a reduction in the Southern labor supply. These two effects reinforce each other in reducing FDI and innovation. This decomposition demonstrates that even if the resource wasting consequences of stronger IPR protection were not present, the reduced incentive for imitation would still generate a reduction in FDI and innovation.

2. Product cycles with endogenous FDI

We begin with a description of the model. Consumers live in either the North or the South, and choose from a continuum of products available at different quality levels. Due to assumed differences in the technological capabilities of the two countries, Northern firms push forward the quality frontier of existing products through innovation, while Southern firms pursue the quality frontier through imitation. The increased utility from higher quality levels of products will be shown to drive innovation, while cost savings will drive imitation and FDI. Northern firms, by becoming multinationals, can shift their production to the South.

2.1. Consumers

The specification of the consumer's problem follows Grossman and Helpman (1991). Consumers choose from a continuum of products $j \in [0, 1]$. Quality level m of product j provides quality $q_m(j) \equiv \lambda^m$. By the definition of quality improvement, new generations are better than the old: $q_m(j) > q_{m-1}(j) \rightarrow \lambda^m > \lambda^{m-1} \rightarrow \lambda > 1$. All products start at time $t = 0$ at quality level $m = 0$, so the base quality is $q_0(j) = \lambda^0 = 1$.

A consumer from country $i \in \{N, S\}$ has additively separable intertemporal preferences given by lifetime utility

$$U_i = \int_0^\infty e^{-\rho t} \log u_i(t) dt, \tag{1}$$

where ρ is the common subjective discount factor. Instantaneous utility is

$$\log u_i(t) = \int_0^1 \log \sum_m (\lambda)^m x_{im}(j, t) dj, \tag{2}$$

where $x_{im}(j, t)$ is consumption by consumers from country i of quality level m of product j at time t.

Consumers maximize lifetime utility subject to an intertemporal budget constraint. Since preferences are homothetic, aggregate demand is found by maximizing lifetime utility subject to the aggregate intertemporal budget constraint

$$\int_0^\infty e^{-R(t)} E_i(t)dt \leq A_i(0) + \int_0^\infty e^{-R(t)} Y_i(t)dt, \tag{3}$$

where $R(t) = \int_0^t r(s)\, ds$ is the cumulative interest rate up to time t and $A_i(0)$ is the aggregate value of initial asset holdings by consumers from country i. Individuals hold assets in the form of ownership in firms, but with a diversified portfolio, any capital losses appear as capital gains elsewhere so only initial asset holdings remain. Aggregate labor income of all consumers from country i is $Y_i(t) = L_i w_i(t)$, where $w_i(t)$ is the wage in country i at time t and L_i is the labor supply there, so $L_i w_i(t)$ is total labor income in country i at time t. Aggregate expenditure of all consumers in country i is

$$E_i(t) = \int_0^1 \Big[\sum_m p_m(j, t) x_{im}(j, t)\Big] dj, \tag{4}$$

where $p_m(j, t)$ is the price of quality level m of product j at time t, and $E_i(t)$ is aggregate expenditure of consumers in country i, where overall aggregate expenditure is $E(t) = E_N(t) + E_S(t)$. Due to assumed free trade, price levels do not vary across countries.

A consumer's maximization problem can be broken into three stages: the allocation of lifetime wealth across time, the allocation of expenditure at each instant across products, and the allocation of expenditure at each instant for each product across available quality levels. In the final stage, consumers allocate expenditure for each product at each instant to the quality level $\tilde{m}(j, t)$ offering the lowest quality-adjusted price, $p_m(j, t)/\lambda^m$. Consumers are indifferent between quality level m and quality level $m-1$ if the relative price equals the quality difference $p_m(j, t)/p_{m-1}(j, t) = \lambda$. Settle indifference in favor of the higher quality level so the quality level selected is unique. Only the highest quality level available will sell in equilibrium.

In the second stage, consumers then evenly spread expenditure across the unit measure of all products, $E_i(j, t) = E_i(t)$, as the elasticity of substitution between any two products is constant at unity. Consumers demand $x_{i\tilde{m}}(j, t) = E_i(t)/p_{\tilde{m}}(j, t)$ units of quality level $\tilde{m}(j, t)$ of product j and no units of other quality levels of that product. In the first stage, consumers evenly spread lifetime expenditure across time, $E_i(t) = E_i$, as the utility function for each consumer is time separable and the aggregate price level will be shown to not vary across time $\log p_{\tilde{m}}(j, t) = \log p_{\tilde{m}}(j)$. Since aggregate expenditure is constant across time, the interest rate at each point in time reflects the discount rate $r(t) = \rho$, so $R(t) = \rho t$ in the intertemporal budget constraint.

2.2. Research and development

The premium consumers are willing to pay for quality gives firms an incentive to improve the quality of existing products. Our model shares the properties of endogenous and costly R&D with Grossman and Helpman (1991), but we introduce several unique features to capture the role of multinational firms. Firstly, we allow Northern firms to adapt technologies so that they can produce in the South. Secondly, we allow imitation targeting a multinational's product to be easier than imitation targeting a Northern firm's product.

To produce a quality level of a product, a firm must first devote resources to designing it. We model innovation success as a continuous Poisson process so that innovation resembles a lottery: at each point in time, firms pay a cost for a chance at winning a payoff. Assume undertaking R&D intensity ι for a time interval dt requires $a\iota dt$ units of labor at cost $wa\iota dt$ and leads to success with probability ιdt (subscripts suppressed). A higher investment in innovation yields a higher probability of success, but no level of investment in innovation can guarantee success.

Only the current level of innovation activity determines the chance of innovation success, since innovation is memory-less for simplicity. The potential for quality improvement is unbounded. Assume R&D races occur simultaneously for all products, with all innovating firms able to target the quality level $m + 1$ above the current highest quality level m and all imitating firms able to target the current highest quality level m for each product. Finally, assume free entry into R&D, with an endless pool of potential innovators and imitators.

In our model, the process of adapting techniques for Southern production resembles the process of conducting R&D. The resource requirements are a_N in innovation, a_F in adaptation, $(1 + \kappa)a_S$ in imitation targeting a Northern firm's product, and $(1 + \kappa)\gamma a_S$ in imitation targeting a multinational's product.[2] The corresponding R&D intensities are ι_N, ι_F, ι_{SN}, and ι_{SF}.

Higher levels of κ can be viewed as representing a strengthening of IPR protection: Southern firms must spend more resources for a given imitation intensity.[3] Stronger IPR protection can reduce imitation efficiency through various channels. Firms may need to add traits to the product that distinguish the imitation

[2] Subscripts denote the type of firms (Northern, FDI/multinational or Southern) that can produce the highest quality level available of a product if R&D is successful.

[3] We distinguish imitation from copying (or pirating), which is illegal duplication of a protected product design.

in the view of legal authorities.[4] Prolonged legal battles may be required to prove that a product is sufficiently unique. As IPR protection is strengthened, aspects of the design that would have been copied may have to be innovated anew. Thus, κ can be thought of as measuring how much of the design must be unique to satisfy the standard.

In our model, due to Bertrand behavior in product markets, once a quality level of a product has been invented, another Northern firm never invents the same quality level. Similarly, once a quality level has been imitated, another Southern firm never imitates the same quality level. For simplicity, we do not allow Northern innovation to target other Northern firms by making the necessary assumptions for such innovation to fail to earn the market rate of return.

Innovators can be separated into two groups: leaders and followers. Leaders are firms who developed the most recent quality improvement; followers are all other firms. Leaders are likely to enjoy a cost advantage in designing the next highest quality level due to their experience in having successfully designed the current highest quality level, as spillovers are apt to be incomplete. Assume the resource requirement in innovation for followers is sufficiently large relative to the resource requirement in innovation for leaders so that innovation is undertaken only by the firm that made the previous innovation for that product.

Also assume the quality increment λ is sufficiently large that Northern leaders do not undertake further innovation until their most recent innovation has been imitated. Thus, innovation targets products produced by Southern firms while imitation targets products produced by Northern firms and multinationals.

Our model distinguishes between imitation that targets multinationals and imitation that targets Northern firms. We assume that *the resource requirement in imitation is lower when targeting multinationals compared to Northern firms*: $\gamma < 1$. This assumption reflects the idea that Southern imitation of brands produced through FDI in the South may be easier than imitation of brands produced in the North due to larger knowledge spillovers. Moving production in close proximity to Southern firms trying to imitate a product may lower the cost of imitation, since Southern firms can more easily learn about the production techniques of multinationals than those of Northern firms. A Southern firm targeting a multinational's product can hire away some of the multinational's workers, spy on the multinational's production facilities or use similar means of acquiring information more feasible with proximity. Also, multinationals have already made adaptations for the Southern economic environment that have the side effect of making successful imitation easier to accomplish for Southern firms.

When undertaking R&D, a firm endures costs $wa\tilde{\iota}dt$ and gains an expected

[4] A legal imitation must be sufficiently distinct from the original innovation according to an $ABC \neq ABD \Leftrightarrow C \neq D$ rule, where at least one significant aspect of the production process or design must differ.

reward $v\tilde{\iota}dt$ (subscripts suppressed). Each firm chooses its intensity of innovation $\tilde{\iota}$ to maximize its expected gain from R&D

$$\max_{\tilde{\iota}\geq 0}\int_0^\infty e^{-(\rho+\iota)t}(v-wa)\tilde{\iota}dt=\max_{\tilde{\iota}\geq 0}\left(\frac{v-wa}{\rho+\iota}\right)\tilde{\iota}\leftrightarrow\max_{\tilde{\iota}\geq 0}(v-wa)\tilde{\iota}, \tag{5}$$

where v denotes the reward to successful R&D, the value of a firm in the appropriate product market where the firm produces if successful in R&D. The term $e^{-\iota t}$ captures the probability that no other firm will have succeeded in R&D in the same industry prior to time t, and ι is the R&D intensity of other firms (taken as given). Each nonproducing firm chooses its R&D intensity to maximize the difference between the expected reward and the costs of R&D.

Firms engage in innovation with nonnegative intensity whenever the expected gains are no less than their costs. To generate finite rates of innovation, expected gains must not exceed their cost, with equality when innovation occurs with positive intensity

$$v_N \leq wa_N,\ \iota_N > 0 \Leftrightarrow v_N = wa_N \tag{6}$$

and similarly for imitation of Northern firms

$$v_{SN} \leq (1+\kappa)a_S,\ \iota_{SN} > 0 \Leftrightarrow v_{SN} = (1+\kappa)a_S \tag{7}$$

and imitation of multinationals

$$v_{SF} \leq (1+\kappa)\gamma a_S,\ \iota_{SF} > 0 \Leftrightarrow v_{SF} = (1+\kappa)\gamma a_S, \tag{8}$$

where we have normalized the Southern wage to one $w_S = 1$, so that $w = w_N$ is the relative wage.

Northern firms also optimally choose how hard to attempt to adapt their production techniques for use in the South, so by similar logic, the cost of adaptation must equal the expected reward when the adaptation intensity is positive

$$v_F - v_N \leq a_F,\ \iota_F > 0 \Leftrightarrow v_F - v_N = a_F. \tag{9}$$

When successful at adapting its technology for Southern production, a firm experiences the capital gain $v_F - v_N \geq 0$, the difference between the value of a multinational and the value of a Northern firm. The adaptation process required to achieve lower costs through FDI resembles process R&D: expenses are incurred to achieve a lower marginal cost of production.

2.3. Production

Southern firms are exposed to only innovation since further imitation is not immediately possible, while Northern firms and multinationals are exposed to only imitation since further innovation has been assumed prohibitively costly.

A Northern firm successful in innovating over a product produced by a Southern firm earns the reward

$$v_N = \frac{\pi_N + \iota_F(v_F - v_N - a_F)}{\rho + \iota_{SN}} = \frac{\pi_N}{\rho + \iota_{SN}}, \tag{10}$$

where π_N is instantaneous profits for a Northern firm and the simplification imposes (9) assuming $\iota_F > 0$. Once successful in adaptation, its value becomes

$$v_F = \frac{\pi_F}{\rho + \iota_{SF}}, \tag{11}$$

where π_F is instantaneous profits for a multinational. Meanwhile, a Southern firm successful in imitating a brand produced by a Northern firm earns the reward

$$v_{SN} = \frac{\pi_{SN}}{\rho + \iota_N}, \tag{12}$$

while a Southern firm successful in imitating a brand produced by a multinational earns the reward

$$v_{SF} = \frac{\pi_{SF}}{\rho + \iota_N}, \tag{13}$$

where π_{SN} and π_{SF} are similarly defined. The effective discount rate is the subjective discount rate ρ plus the probability that the profit stream will end due to imitation or innovation.

Labor is the only factor of production, and production is assumed to exhibit constant returns to scale. Normalize the unit labor requirement in production to 1 in each country. However, we assume that the unit labor requirement for multinationals is greater than one ($\zeta > 1$), so that *multinationals face higher production costs relative to Southern firms*. Multinationals experience logistical difficulties when coordinating decisions over large distances and suffer from their lack of familiarity with the Southern economic environment. The theory of the multinational firm emphasizes that multinationals need advantages based on superior product design, advertising, or reputation to offset operating cost disadvantages relative to native firms: see Markusen (1995).

Once successful in R&D, each firm chooses its price p to maximize its profits $\pi = (p - c)x$, where c is marginal cost and x is sales. Under Bertrand competition, the market outcomes depend on the extent of competition from rivals priced out of the market. Each producing firm chooses a limit price that just keeps its rival from earning a positive profit from production (this price equals the second highest marginal cost in quality-adjusted terms). Firms that have just succeeded in innovation have a one-quality level lead over the former producer; they choose a price equal to the quality increment times their rival's marginal cost. When competing against a Southern firm, a Northern firm charges price $p_N = \lambda$ and makes sales $x_N = E/\lambda$ with marginal cost $c_N = w$, yielding instantaneous profits

$$\pi_N = E\left(1 - \frac{w}{\lambda}\right). \tag{14}$$

When competing against a Southern firm, a multinational charges price $p_F = \lambda$ and makes sales $x_F = E/\lambda$ with marginal cost $c_F = \zeta$, yielding instantaneous profits

$$\pi_F = E\left(1 - \frac{\zeta}{\lambda}\right). \tag{15}$$

For Northern production to be profitable ($\pi_N > 0$), the quality increment must be large enough to exceed the relative wage in equilibrium ($\lambda > w$), which will imply $\lambda > \zeta$, as needed for $\pi_F > 0$. The equilibrium value of the relative wage (24) will be derived shortly.

Firms that have just succeeded in imitation have no quality lead over the former producer; they choose a price equal to their rival's marginal cost. When competing against a Northern firm, a Southern firm charges price $p_{SN} = w$ and makes sales $x_{SN} = E/w$ with marginal cost $c_{SN} = 1$, yielding instantaneous profits

$$\pi_{SN} = E\left(1 - \frac{1}{w}\right). \tag{16}$$

When competing against a multinational, a Southern firm charges price $p_{SF} = \zeta$ and makes sales $x_{SF} = E/\zeta$ with marginal cost $c_{SF} = 1$, yielding instantaneous profits

$$\pi_{SF} = E\left(1 - \frac{1}{\zeta}\right). \tag{17}$$

Southern production with multinational rivals is profitable ($\pi_{SF} > 0$) because Southern firms are assumed to have a cost advantage relative to multinationals ($\zeta > 1$). We will show that $\zeta > 1$ also implies that the relative wage will exceed one ($w > 1$), which ensures that $\pi_{SN} > 0$.

2.4. Resource constraints

Let n_N denote the measure of Northern production, n_F the measure of multinational production, n_{SN} the measure of Southern production with Northern rivals, and n_{SF} the measure of Southern production with multinational rivals (each as a fraction of all production so the measures sum to one). Define the measure of Southern production as $n_S \equiv n_{SN} + n_{SF}$.

In each country, the fixed supply of labor is allocated between R&D and production. For equilibrium in each labor market, the demand for labor must equal the supply of labor in each country. In the North, labor demand for innovation is $a_N \iota_N n_S$ and for production is $n_N E/\lambda$

$$a_N \iota_N n_S + n_N \frac{E}{\lambda} = L_N. \tag{18}$$

In the South, labor demand for imitation is $(1+\kappa)a_S[\iota_{SN}n_N + \gamma\iota_{SF}n_F]$, for adaptation is $\iota_F a_F n_N$ and for production is $n_F E/\lambda + n_{SN}E/w + n_{SF}E/\zeta$

$$(1+\kappa)a_S[\iota_{SN}n_N + \gamma\iota_{SF}n_F] + a_F\iota_F n_N + \left[\frac{n_{SN}}{w} + \frac{n_{SF}}{\zeta} + \frac{n_F}{\lambda}\right]E = L_S. \tag{19}$$

The usual steady-state conditions for market measures to remain constant (that flows in equal flows out) $\iota_F n_N = \iota_{SF}n_F$, $\iota_{SF}n_F = \iota_N n_{SF}$, $\iota_{SN}n_N = \iota_N n_{SN}$ and sum to one $n_S + n_F + n_N = 1$ complete the model.

2.5. Steady-state system

We focus on steady-state equilibria and begin with the case where all four R&D activities occur so that international technology transfer occurs through both imitation and FDI. In Section 3 we establish results for this equilibrium and in Section 4 we show that they also hold for equilibria with only FDI or only imitation as the channel of international technology transfer.

If all four R&D activities occur $\iota_F > 0$, $\iota_N > 0$, $\iota_{SF} > 0$, and $\iota_{SN} > 0$, our model is a system of six equations. The four valuation conditions are gathered below from the appropriate profits and values of producing firms: innovation valuation condition from (6), (10) and (14)

$$E\left(1 - \frac{w}{\lambda}\right) = wa_N(\rho + \iota_{SN}) \tag{20}$$

adaptation valuation condition from (6), (9), (11) and (15)

$$E\left(1 - \frac{\zeta}{\lambda}\right) = (a_F + wa_N)(\rho + \iota_{SF}) \tag{21}$$

imitation of Northern firms valuation condition from (7), (12) and (16)

$$E\left(1 - \frac{1}{w}\right) = (1+\kappa)a_S(\rho + \iota_N) \tag{22}$$

and imitation of multinationals valuation condition from (8), (13) and (17)

$$E\left(1 - \frac{1}{\zeta}\right) = (1+\kappa)\gamma a_S(\rho + \iota_N). \tag{23}$$

The other two equations are the resource constraints (18) and (19).

The two imitation valuation conditions (22) and (23) are solved for the relative wage

$$w = \frac{\gamma\zeta}{\gamma\zeta - (\zeta - 1)}. \tag{24}$$

The lower cost of imitation targeting multinationals relative to Northern firms $(\gamma < 1)$ implies production costs are higher for Northern firms than for multinationals ($w > \zeta$). Also, wages are higher in the North than the South ($w > 1$) since $\zeta > 1$ by assumption. In the limit as $\zeta \to 1$, the relative wage goes to one, $w \to 1$. From (24), Southern IPR protection does not affect the relative wage and neither does a tax on imitation or a reduction in Southern resources.[5]

Define the cost of adaptation relative to innovation as $\theta \equiv a_F / wa_N$. Next solve the innovation and adaptation valuation conditions (20) and (21) for the relative effective discount rate

$$\xi \equiv \frac{\rho + \iota_{SF}}{\rho + \iota_{SN}} = \left(\frac{1}{1+\theta}\right)\left(\frac{\lambda - \zeta}{\lambda - w}\right). \tag{25}$$

The relative effective discount rate is the degree that multinational profits are deflated relative to the profits of Northern firms due to differences in exposure to imitation. In the limit as $\zeta \to 1$, $\gamma \to 1$ and $\theta \to 1$, the relative effective discount rate goes to one, $\xi \to 1$.

Our model conforms to the perception that multinationals face greater exposure to imitation than Northern firms (Mansfield, 1994; Helpman, 1993) when Northern firms face sufficiently slight adaptation costs

$$\xi > 1 \Leftrightarrow \theta < \tilde{\theta} \equiv \frac{w - \zeta}{\lambda - w}. \tag{26}$$

The threshold level $\tilde{\theta}$ for $\xi = 1$ stipulates that adaptation relative to innovation costs equals the cost reduction margin from adaptation ($w - \zeta$) relative to the profit margin from innovation ($\lambda - w$).[6] While the greater exposure of multinationals to imitation does in part reflect our assumption that their products are easier to imitate, it is nonetheless a result (provided $\theta < \tilde{\theta}$).

By encompassing both the Grossman and Helpman (1991) imitation product cycle and the Vernon (1966) FDI product cycle (see Fig. 1), our model determines the fraction of technology transferred to the South through imitation rather than FDI. To explore the consequences of Southern IPR protection on the rate of innovation and flows of FDI to the South, we first define these measures of interest and translate the system into these variables.

Let η be the fraction of all product cycles, and hence the fraction of international technology transfer, that occurs through imitation of Northern firms. Define the rate of innovation as the intensity of innovation times the measure of Southern production $\iota \equiv \iota_N n_S$, which captures the frequency of product cycles. Similarly, define the rate of imitation as the sum of imitation targeting Northern firms and multinationals $\mu \equiv \iota_{SN} n_N + \iota_{SF} n_F$. In the steady-state equilibrium, the rate of innovation must equal the rate of imitation, $\iota = \mu$, so that production shifts to the South at the same rate as production returns to the North.

Define the flow of FDI as the adaptation intensity times the measure of Northern

[5]This invariance likely depends on the assumed constant returns to scale in R&D.

[6]For $\zeta = 6/5$, $\lambda = 4$, and $w = 3/2$, the threshold is $\tilde{\theta} = 3/25 = 12\%$.

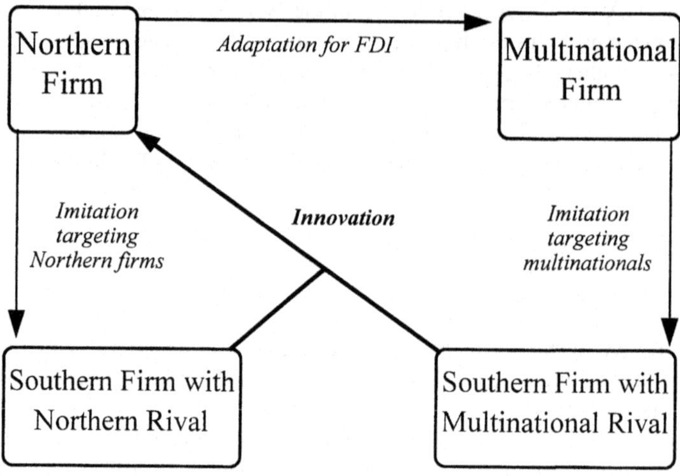

Fig. 1. Product cycle composition.

production $\phi \equiv \iota_F n_N$. Of all the $\iota = \mu$ flows in the product cycle, $\mu_N \equiv \iota_{SN} n_N = \eta\iota$ occur through imitation of Northern firms and $\phi = (1-\eta)\iota = \iota_{SF} n_F \equiv \mu_F$ occur through FDI (and then imitation of multinationals). In addition to the flow of FDI ϕ, the measure of multinational production n_F can also be used as a gauge of the extent of FDI.

The solutions for the relative wage (24) and the relative effective discount rate (25) take the place of the valuation conditions for adaptation (21) and imitation of multinationals (23), leaving *four remaining equations*: the Northern resource constraint (18), Southern resource constraint (19), innovation valuation condition (20) and imitation valuation condition (22). Making substitutions for $\{\iota_N, \iota_F, \iota_{SN}, n_F, n_S, n_{SN}, n_{SF}\}$ into the four remaining equations achieves a system in the *four remaining endogenous variables*: aggregate expenditure E, the measure of Northern production n_N, the rate of innovation ι, and the fraction of all product cycles that occur through imitation η.

The equilibrium can be seen graphically by solving the innovation and imitation valuation equations for E and n_N and then inserting these expressions into the Northern and Southern resource constraints. The two resource constraints then determine the rate of innovation ι and the fraction of international technology transfer that occurs through imitation of Northern firms η as in Fig. 2. The Northern resource constraint LN is downward sloping (larger η requires slower ι) while the Southern resource constraint LS is upward sloping (larger η permits faster ι). A larger η dictates that a smaller fraction of products that have not yet been imitated are produced in the South (through FDI) relative to the North

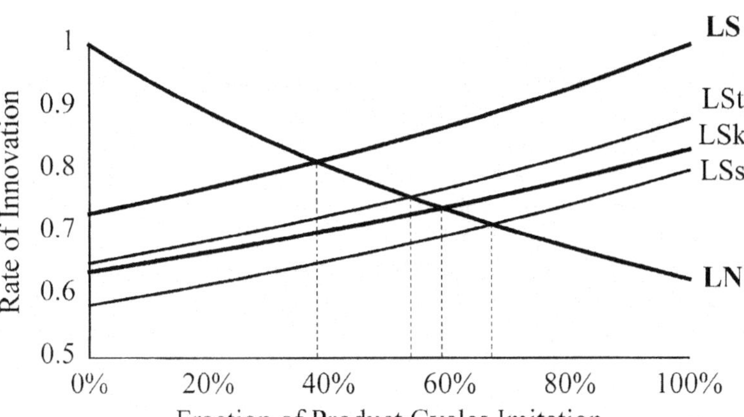

Fig. 2. Resource constraint shifts.

($n_R \equiv n_F / n_N$ falls). With more labor demand for production in the North and less in the South, Northern resources support a smaller rate of innovation, while Southern resources support a larger one. The equilibrium values of ι and η occur at the intersection of LN and LS.

Introduce a multiplicative term $(1+\tau)$ on the right-hand (cost) side of the imitation valuation conditions (22) and (23) to represent a tax on imitation and introduce a multiplicative term $(1-\psi)$ on the right-hand (supply) side of the Southern resource constraint (19) to represent a reduction in Southern resources. In the next section, we will relate the effects of changes in κ to those of changes in τ and ψ.

3. Intellectual property rights protection

We now determine how strengthening IPR protection in the South, through increasing the costs of imitation, affects the imitation exposure of multinationals relative to Northern firms, the composition of international technology transfer, FDI, imitation and innovation.[7] We also show that the reduced efficiency of imitation due to stronger Southern IPR protection is equivalent to a tax on imitation combined with a reduction in Southern resources.

[7]Additional details on the derivation of our results appear in an Appendix available on the web at http://economics.sbs.ohio-state.edu/pdf/glass/iprsup.pdf.

3.1. Relative imitation exposure

First note that stronger Southern IPR protection increases the profit incentive for Northern firms to undertake FDI in the South only if imitation of multinationals falls relative to imitation of Northern firms as a result. Our model is the first to determine the intensities of imitation targeting the products of multinationals and Northern firms in order to establish whether stronger Southern IPRs will increase the relative return to conducting FDI.

From (25), it is obvious that the relative effective discount rate is invariant to the strength of Southern IPR protection κ.[8] The value of a multinational relative to a Northern firm reflects relative profits deflated by the relative effective discount rate

$$v_R \equiv \frac{v_F}{v_N} = \frac{\pi_F/(\rho + \iota_{SF})}{\pi_N/(\rho + \iota_{SN})} = \frac{\pi_R}{\xi}. \tag{27}$$

Since the instantaneous profits of a multinational relative to a Northern firm are not affected

$$\pi_R \equiv \frac{\pi_F}{\pi_N} = \frac{E\left[1 - \dfrac{\zeta}{\lambda}\right]}{E\left[1 - \dfrac{w}{\lambda}\right]} = \frac{\lambda - \zeta}{\lambda - w}, \tag{28}$$

a strengthening of Southern IPR protection does not affect the relative imitation exposure faced by multinationals.[9]

Proposition 1. *The imitation exposure of multinationals relative to Northern firms is independent of a strengthening of Southern IPR protection, a tax on imitation, or a reduction in Southern resources.*

While multinationals become safer from imitation with a strengthening of Southern IPR protection, so do Northern firms. The intensity of imitation targeting the products of Northern firms decreases

$$\frac{\partial \iota_{SN}}{\partial \kappa} = \left(\frac{\zeta - 1}{w\xi}\right)\frac{\partial \iota}{\partial \kappa} = -\left(\frac{\zeta - 1}{w\xi}\right)\frac{\iota}{D} < 0, \tag{29}$$

as $\partial \iota / \partial \kappa = -\iota / D < 0$ (see Proposition 4).

[8] This invariance likely depends on stronger Southern IPR protection raising the costs of imitation to the same degree when targeting the product of a Northern firm as when targeting the product of a multinational.

[9] Applying the equilibrium relative effective discount rate (25) to the relative multinational to Northern profits (28), the higher profits of multinationals relative to Northern firms reflect the additional costs of adaptation and any greater exposure to imitation $\pi_R = \xi(1 + \theta) > 1$.

3.2. Composition of international technology transfer

Since multiple channels of international technology transfer are active in this equilibrium of our model, we can study the effect of a strengthening of IPR protection on the composition of international technology transfer between imitation and FDI. We find that the fraction of technology flowing to the South through imitation expands with stronger Southern IPR protection

$$\frac{\partial \eta}{\partial \kappa} = \frac{\frac{\lambda}{w} - (1-\eta)}{D} > 0, \tag{30}$$

where the denominator is

$$D \equiv 1 + \frac{En_N\left(1 - \frac{1}{\zeta}\right)\left[1 + \theta\xi\left(\frac{\lambda}{w} - 1\right)\right]}{\gamma a_S \xi \eta \iota} > 1. \tag{31}$$

For future reference, note that, in addition to other factors, the extent that the denominator D exceeds one is related to the extent that: adaptation costs exist ($\theta > 0$), multinationals are easier to imitate than Northern firms ($\gamma < 1$), and multinationals suffer a cost disadvantage relative to Southern firms ($\zeta > 1$).

Proposition 2. *The fraction of international technology transfer that occurs through imitation of Northern firms increases with a strengthening of Southern IPR protection, a tax on imitation, or a reduction in Southern resources.*

Southern imitation absorbs more resources when Southern IPRs are strengthened due to imitation becoming more difficult. Southern resource demand in imitation is

$$L_S^R \equiv (1+\kappa) a_S \iota[\eta + \gamma(1-\eta)]. \tag{32}$$

Differentiating with respect to κ yields:

$$\frac{\partial L_S^R}{\partial \kappa} = a_S\left\{[\eta + \gamma(1-\eta)]\left(\iota + \frac{\partial \iota}{\partial \kappa}\right) + \iota(1-\gamma)\frac{\partial \eta}{\partial \kappa}\right\} > 0. \tag{33}$$

The second term is clearly positive and represents the shift toward more difficult imitation of Northern firms. The first term is positive: innovation falls by less than the rate of innovation $|\partial \iota / \partial \kappa| = -\iota / D < \iota$ because $D > 1$ in (31) — see Proposition 4. Within the first term, the portion involving ι represents each unit of imitation using more resources and the term involving $\partial \iota / \partial \kappa$ represents the reduction in the overall level of imitation (therefore using fewer resources).

With greater Southern resources demanded for imitation, labor demand for production must be shifted from the South to the North to restore equilibrium. When products cycle through imitation, they generate more labor demand for production in the North relative to the South than when products cycle through FDI: $n_R \equiv n_F / n_N$ declines in η. With FDI, production occurs in the South that would have occurred in the North in the absence of FDI.

3.3. Foreign direct investment

We find that stronger Southern IPR protection discourages FDI. FDI flows are the fraction of all product cycles that occur through imitation times the frequency of product cycles $\phi = (1-\eta)\iota$. Since the rate of innovation ι falls (Proposition 4) and a larger fraction of international technology transfer occurs through imitation η (Proposition 2), the flows of FDI to the South doubly fall

$$\frac{\partial \phi}{\partial \kappa} = -\left[\frac{\iota}{1-\frac{w}{\lambda}(1-\eta)}\right]\frac{\partial \eta}{\partial \kappa} = \frac{\lambda}{w}\frac{\partial \iota}{\partial \kappa} = -\left(\frac{\lambda}{w}\right)\frac{\iota}{D} < 0. \tag{34}$$

The measure of multinational production n_F, an alternative measure of FDI, also decreases

$$\frac{\partial n_F}{\partial \kappa} = -\eta\xi[\lambda(1-n_F) + n_F(\lambda - \zeta) + 1]\frac{\partial \eta}{\partial \kappa} < 0. \tag{35}$$

Thus, FDI declines with stronger Southern IPR protection.

We further find that the rate of imitation of Northern firms $\mu_N \equiv \iota_{SN} n_N = \eta\iota$ actually increases

$$\frac{\partial \mu_N}{\partial \kappa} = -\left(\frac{\lambda}{w} - 1\right)\frac{\partial \iota}{\partial \kappa} = \left(\frac{\lambda}{w} - 1\right)\frac{\iota}{D} > 0. \tag{36}$$

While product cycles occur more slowly due to the slower rate of innovation, more of them occur through imitation, and this positive effect dominates.[10]

Proposition 3. *FDI flows to the South decrease while flows of production to the South through imitation of Northern firms increase with a strengthening of Southern IPR protection, a tax on imitation, or a reduction in Southern resources.*

3.4. Innovation and imitation

We find that stronger Southern IPR protection discourages innovation in our model. Stronger Southern IPR protection shifts international technology transfer toward imitation of Northern firms, which shifts labor demand for production from the South to the North. Resource scarcity in the South is transmitted back to the North and impinges on innovation

[10] While imitation substitutes for FDI in transferring technology to the South, the substitution is incomplete as the total flows of technology to the South $\mu_N + \phi = \iota$ fall (Proposition 4).

$$\frac{\partial \iota}{\partial \kappa} = -\left[\frac{\iota}{\frac{\lambda}{w} - (1-\eta)}\right]\frac{\partial \eta}{\partial \kappa} = -\frac{\iota}{D} < 0. \tag{37}$$

Proposition 4. *The rates of innovation and imitation decrease with a strengthening of Southern IPR protection, a tax on imitation, or a reduction in Southern resources.*

The positive effect on the fraction of product cycles that occur through imitation η and negative effect on the rate of innovation ι can be seen graphically in Fig. 2. Stronger IPR protection in the South (increase in κ) shifts the Southern resource constraint down to LSk (smaller ι for a given η) due to the larger resource requirements in imitation. The Northern resource constraint is unaffected. Thus the equilibrium shifts down along the downward-sloping Northern resource constraint to larger η and smaller ι. While the increased cost of imitation does reduce incentives for imitation, the total resources devoted to imitation increase, increasing resource scarcity in the South.

The parameters used to construct Fig. 2 are Northern labor supply $L_N = 3$, Southern labor supply $L_S = 6$, resource requirement in innovation $a_N = 3$, resource requirement in imitation $a_S = 2$, resource requirement in imitation of multinationals relative to Northern firms $\gamma = 1/2 = 50\%$, resource requirement in adaptation relative to imitation $\theta = 1/10 = 10\%$, cost disadvantage of multinationals relative to Southern firms $\zeta = 6/5$, subjective discount rate $\rho = 1/20$, and quality increment $\lambda = 4$. The initial equilibrium is for $\kappa = 0$, $\psi = 0$ and $\tau = 0$. In the subsequent equilibrium Southern IPRs are strengthened to $\kappa' = 1/5$ in LSk.[11] Table 1 shows how the equilibrium values are affected: for all cases in Table 1, multinationals are exposed to slightly more imitation than are Northern firms $\xi = 1.02$. These calculations confirm that there is indeed an equilibrium with all four types of R&D active, and that κ can be shifted without disturbing the type of equilibrium, provided that the shift is not too large. For these parameters, we can increase κ to $\overline{\kappa} = 143/250 = 0.572$ or decrease κ to $\underline{\kappa} = -97/250 = -0.388$

Table 1
Both FDI and imitation product cycles

κ	ι	η	E	w	n_N	n_S	n_F	ϕ
−0.388	1.000	0%	11.0	1.5	0%	33.8%	66.2%	1.000
−0.2	0.893	19.4%	10.9	1.5	11.8%	40.1%	48.1%	0.720
0	0.801	40.1%	10.8	1.5	22.1%	45.6%	32.3%	0.480
0.2	0.725	61.0%	10.8	1.5	30.6%	50.2%	19.2%	0.283
0.4	0.663	81.9%	10.7	1.5	37.7%	54.0%	8.2%	0.120
0.572	0.617	100%	10.7	1.5	43.0%	57.0%	0%	0

[11] The other shifts depicted are $\psi' = 1/5$ for LSs and $\tau' = 1/5$ for LSt.

and still achieve an interior solution.[12] Further numerical examples illustrating the equilibria for other values of κ are provided in Section 4.

3.5. Decomposition

Fig. 2 also illustrates that when κ, τ or ψ (depicted by LSk, LSt and LSs) are increased to the same degree, the effects of κ are in the same direction but between the smaller effects of a tax on imitation τ

$$\frac{\partial\eta/\partial\tau}{\partial\eta/\partial\kappa}=\frac{\partial\phi/\partial\tau}{\partial\phi/\partial\kappa}=\frac{\partial\mu_N/\partial\tau}{\partial\mu_N/\partial\kappa}=\frac{\partial\iota/\partial\tau}{\partial\iota/\partial\kappa}=\frac{\eta}{w}+\frac{1-\eta}{\zeta}<1 \tag{38}$$

and the larger effects of a reduction in Southern resources ψ in magnitude

$$\frac{\partial\eta/\partial\psi}{\partial\eta/\partial\kappa}=\frac{\partial\phi/\partial\psi}{\partial\phi/\partial\kappa}=\frac{\partial\mu_N/\partial\psi}{\partial\mu_N/\partial\kappa}=\frac{\partial\iota/\partial\psi}{\partial\iota/\partial\kappa}=\frac{L_S}{\iota a_S\gamma}\left(1-\frac{1}{\zeta}\right)>1. \tag{39}$$

The effect of ψ is a proportionate reduction in the entire Southern labor supply, while κ involves an expansion in labor demand of only the labor engaged in imitation. An increase in κ combines resource wasting and imitation disincentive effects, which reinforce each other in lowering ι and raising η.

A reduction in Southern resources (an increase in ψ) captures the *resource wasting effect.* When Southern resources contract, more product cycles must occur through imitation of Northern firms. A higher fraction of product cycles occurring through imitation η reduces labor demand in Southern production by keeping more production back in the North (n_F/n_N falls) and shifting Southern production toward higher priced products with lower sales (n_{SF}/n_{SN} falls). Also, a lower rate of innovation ι reduces labor demand in R&D in both countries to restore equilibrium. Thus, the composition of international technology transfer η adjusts the distribution of labor demand across countries, while the speed of the product cycles ι adjusts the overall level of labor demand.

A tax on imitation (an increase in τ) captures the *imitation disincentive effect.* The reduction in the rate of innovation helps both conserve Southern resources in imitation and restore the equality between the expected benefits of imitation and the greater costs of imitation. When the rate of innovation falls, a successful imitation earns a longer expected duration of profits due to the reduced probability of innovation terminating the profit stream. The increase in the reward to imitation needed to offset its increased cost due to the tax is also accomplished through an increase in aggregate spending, which increases profits. However, the increase in aggregate spending increases labor demand primarily in the South due to more lower priced production occurring there, implying larger sales. The extent that the

[12]Imitation costs at the upper bound are $(1+\overline{\kappa})/(1+\underline{\kappa})=256\%$ of imitation costs at the lower bound.

increase in labor demand occurs disproportionately in the South must be offset by increasing the importance of imitation of Northern firms in the product cycle, as η serves the function of reallocating labor demand across the two countries.

4. Other equilibria

Now we turn to considering equilibria for parameters such that one form of imitation or the other does not occur in equilibrium. As a result, in these equilibria, only one of the two types of product cycles occurs, either FDI or imitation. We find, however, that our results do not depend on the type of equilibrium that emerges.

4.1. Imitation cycle only

Here we consider the equilibrium of the model in which only innovation and imitation of Northern firms occur (with no FDI and no imitation of multinationals). The Northern labor constraint is

$$a_N \iota + n_N \frac{E}{\lambda} = L_N. \tag{40}$$

The Southern labor constraint is

$$(1+\kappa)a_S \iota w + (1-n_N)E = L_S w. \tag{41}$$

The valuation condition for innovation is

$$En_N\left(1-\frac{w}{\lambda}\right) = wa_N(\rho n_N + \iota). \tag{42}$$

The valuation condition for imitation targeting a Northern firm's product is

$$E(1-n_N)(w-1) = (1+\kappa)a_S[\rho(1-n_N)+\iota], \tag{43}$$

where $\iota = \iota_N n_S = \iota_S n_N = \mu$ is the rate of innovation, which equals the rate of imitation and $n_{SN} = n_S$ for notational ease. The system determines $\{E, w, \iota, n_N\}$. The valuation condition for adaptation (21) must be an inequality, with *rewards less than costs*.[13]

Using comparative statics techniques, we find that an increase in Southern IPR protection decreases the rate of innovation

$$\frac{\partial \iota}{\partial \kappa} = -\frac{\iota}{1+\dfrac{\lambda - w}{w(w-1)}} < 0, \tag{44}$$

[13]The model here is essentially the same as Glass (1997) but with only one quality level of each product selling in equilibrium.

decreases the relative wage

$$\frac{\partial w}{\partial \kappa}=\left(\frac{\lambda-w}{\iota}\right)\frac{\partial \iota}{\partial \kappa}<0, \tag{45}$$

increases the measure of Northern production

$$\frac{\partial n_N}{\partial \kappa}=-n_N(1-n_N)\left(\frac{\lambda-w}{w\iota}\right)\frac{\partial \iota}{\partial \kappa}>0, \tag{46}$$

and increases aggregate expenditure. In this equilibrium, any force that reduces the rate of imitation also reduces the rate of innovation, since the two rates are equal. These results mirror those of Grossman and Helpman's (1991) inefficient Northern followers equilibrium, if the effect of decreasing the Southern labor supply is combined with taxing imitation in the spirit of our decomposition result. Similarly, Helpman (1993) and Lai (1998) find that a reduction in the intensity of imitation leads to a slower rate of innovation.[14]

Table 2 shows equilibria with only the imitation product cycle that arise for large values of $\kappa>\bar{\kappa}$. For $\kappa=\bar{\kappa}$, the reward to adaptation exceeds its costs according to the valuation condition (21), so lower levels of $\kappa\leq\bar{\kappa}$ do not support an equilibrium with only the imitation product cycle — the FDI cycle also emerges.[15]

4.2. FDI cycle only

Now we consider the equilibrium of the model in which only innovation, FDI, and imitation of multinationals occur (with no imitation of Northern firms). The Northern labor constraint is

$$a_N\iota+(1-n_F-n_S)\frac{E}{\lambda}=L_N. \tag{47}$$

Table 2
Only imitation product cycle

κ	ι	η	E	w	n_N	n_S	n_F	ϕ
0.572	0.617	100%	10.7	1.50	43.0%	57.0%	0%	0
1	0.577	100%	11.2	1.65	45.4%	54.6%	0%	0
1.4	0.540	100%	11.6	1.80	47.4%	52.6%	0%	0
1.8	0.522	100%	11.9	1.87	48.3%	51.7%	0%	0

[14]In similar spirit, Taylor (1994) shows that failure to protect foreign patents reduces R&D by causing innovators to use inferior technologies. Aoki and Prusa (1993) find that discriminatory protection based on where a firm is located may decrease R&D.

[15]Rewards exceed costs by 144 for these parameters (at $\kappa=\bar{\kappa}=0.572$).

The Southern labor constraint is

$$[(1+\kappa)\gamma a_S + a_F]\iota + \left(\frac{n_F}{\lambda} + \frac{n_S}{\zeta}\right)E = L_S. \tag{48}$$

The valuation condition for innovation is

$$E\left(1 - \frac{w}{\lambda}\right) = w a_N \rho. \tag{49}$$

The valuation condition for imitation of multinationals is

$$En_S\left(1 - \frac{1}{\zeta}\right) = (1+\kappa)\gamma a_S(\rho n_S + \iota). \tag{50}$$

The valuation condition for adaptation is

$$En_F\left(1 - \frac{\zeta}{\lambda}\right) = (a_F + w a_N)(\rho n_F + \iota), \tag{51}$$

where $\iota = \iota_N n_S = \phi = \iota_F n_N = \mu = \iota_S n_F$ is the rate of innovation, which equals the flow of FDI and the rate of imitation, and $n_{SF} = n_S$ for notational ease. The valuation condition for imitation targeting a Northern firm's product (22) must be an inequality, with *rewards less than costs*.[16] We solve the innovation valuation condition for the relative wage, so the remaining system determines $\{E, \iota, n_F, n_S\}$.

Using comparative statics techniques, we find that an increase in Southern IPR protection decreases the rate of innovation

$$\frac{\partial \iota}{\partial \kappa} = \frac{\partial \phi}{\partial \kappa} = \frac{\partial \mu}{\partial \kappa} = -\frac{\iota n_S(1+\theta)}{\left(n_S + \frac{n_F}{\lambda}\right)(1+\theta) + \theta n_F\left(1 - \frac{\zeta}{\lambda}\right)} < 0. \tag{52}$$

Since the rate of innovation and the flow of FDI are one in the same, FDI flows decrease as well. Using the measure of multinational production as the extent of FDI yields the same result: the extent of FDI declines

$$\frac{\partial n_F}{\partial \kappa} = \frac{n_F}{\iota}\left(1 - n_F\frac{\zeta}{\lambda} + \frac{n_F}{\lambda}\right)\frac{\partial \iota}{\partial \kappa} < 0. \tag{53}$$

Again, here any force that reduces the rate of imitation also reduces the rate of innovation because they are equal. Now, the flows of FDI also equal these rates and thus also decline.[17] So regardless of the equilibrium considered, stronger Southern IPR protection reduces FDI (if it is present) and innovation.[18]

Table 3 shows equilibria with only the FDI product cycle that arise for low values of $\kappa < \underline{\kappa}$. For $\kappa = \underline{\kappa}$, the reward to imitation targeting the product of a

[16] Rewards exceed costs by 10.7 for these parameters (at $\kappa = \underline{\kappa} = -0.388$).

[17] Markusen (2001) examines the effects of Southern IPRs on FDI, but does not model R&D.

[18] The numerical solutions do indicate that an increase in κ may increase ι at the boundary $\kappa = \underline{\kappa}$ which switch equilibria from FDI only to having both product cycles.

Table 3
Only FDI product cycle

κ	ι	η	E	w	n_N	n_S	n_F	ϕ
−1	1.000	0%	19.2	3.88	0%	0%	100%	1.000
−0.8	0.716	0%	18.9	3.88	18.0%	9.1%	72.8%	0.716
−0.6	0.555	0%	18.7	3.88	28.6%	14.4%	57.0%	0.555
−0.388	0.452	0%	18.6	3.88	35.4%	17.9%	49.7%	0.452

Northern firm exceeds its costs according to the valuation condition (22), so higher levels of $\kappa \geq \underline{\kappa}$ do not support an equilibrium with only the FDI product cycle — the imitation cycle also emerges. When Southern IPR protection is the weakest ($\kappa = -1$), all products are produced by multinationals in the South.

5. Conclusion

This paper examines the effect of strengthening Southern IPR protection on the imitation exposure of multinationals relative to Northern firms, the composition of international technology transfer, FDI, innovation and imitation. Given the lively policy debate on these issues (see Maskus, 2000), our analysis has more than theoretical interest.

We focus on the case where FDI and imitation both serve as channels of international technology transfer, but Southern IPR protection crowds out FDI and innovation even when only one channel is present. In our model, stronger IPR protection in the South makes multinationals no more secure from imitation relative to Northern firms. Furthermore, by making imitation more costly, stronger Southern IPR protection forces the South to spend more resources for a given probability of imitation success. The scarce resources drawn into imitation in the South leave fewer resources for production, causing FDI to contract — a *resource wasting effect* that acts like a reduction in the Southern labor supply. The resources drawn into production in the North due to less FDI then leave fewer resources for innovation, causing innovation to contract as well. There is also an *imitation disincentive effect* that acts like a tax on imitation by making imitation more costly.

Past work by Helpman (1993) and Lai (1998) assumed stronger Southern IPR protection caused an exogenous reduction in the intensity of imitation. Since imitation was assumed to be costless, no resource wasting effects resulted — no labor was absorbed into imitation because no labor was needed for imitation. In contrast, we assume stronger Southern IPR protection raises the cost of imitation, which then causes the intensities of imitation to fall. However, we show that more labor is used in imitation, which crowds out FDI and consequently reduces innovation. Our model has the property that the effect of strengthening Southern

IPR protection on the rate of innovation does *not* depend on whether FDI or imitation is the channel of international technology transfer.

Several related topics beg for further research. Firstly, a varieties product cycle model with endogenous innovation, imitation, and FDI would be useful for determining which, if any, of our results depend on the quality ladders framework. Secondly, a product cycle model with FDI should be modified to remove the scale effect (innovation increasing with the labor supply) to see how the results change. Thirdly, trade restrictions should be added to consider how they affect the transfer of technology across countries. Fourthly, more work could be done to capture the full complexity of a country's IPR policy and thus derive further insights regarding policy alternatives. Finally, how Southern IPR protection affects internalization — whether Northern firms choose to license their technologies or opt for FDI — should be addressed.[19] Nevertheless, the model constructed here sheds new light on the complex inter-relationships between innovation, imitation, and FDI.

Acknowledgements

We thank Emily Cremers, Michael Devereux, Paul Evans, Eric Fisher, Gene Grossman, Peter Howitt, Edwin Lai, Ed Ray, Scott Taylor, participants at the Midwest International Economics, North American and South-East Asian Econometric Society, Western Economic Association, and Dynamics, Economic Growth and International Trade Conferences for helpful comments.

References

Aoki, R., Prusa, T.J., 1993. International standards for intellectual property protection and R&D incentives. Journal of International Economics 35, 251–273.

Glass, A.J., 1997. Product cycles and market penetration. International Economic Review 38, 865–891.

Glass, A.J., Saggi, K., 2001. Licensing versus direct investment: implications for economic growth. Journal of International Economics, in press.

Glass, A.J., Saggi, K., 1999. Foreign direct investment and the nature of R&D. Canadian Journal of Economics 32, 92–117.

Grossman, G.M., Helpman, E., 1991. Quality ladders and product cycles. Quarterly Journal of Economics 106, 557–586.

Helpman, E., 1993. Innovation, imitation, and intellectual property rights. Econometrica 61, 1247–1280.

Krugman, P.R., 1979. A model of innovation, technology transfer, and the world distribution of income. Journal of Political Economy 87, 253–266.

[19]For an analysis of how IPR protection affects economic growth when licensing serves as the channel of technology transfer, see Yang and Maskus (2001). Glass and Saggi (2001) model policy toward FDI when licensing is an alternative.

Lai, E.L.C., 1998. International intellectual property rights protection and the rate of product innovation. Journal of Development Economics 55, 133–153.

Mansfield, E., 1994. Intellectual property protection, foreign direct investment, and technology transfer. International Finance Corporation, Washington, DC, Discussion paper 19.

Mansfield, E., Schwartz, M., Wagner, S., 1981. Imitation costs and patents: an empirical study. Economic Journal 91, 907–918.

Markusen, J.R., 2001. Contracts, intellectual property rights, and multinational investment in developing countries. Journal of International Economics 53, 189–204.

Markusen, J.R., 1995. The boundaries of multinational enterprises and the theory of international trade. Journal of Economic Perspectives 9, 169–190.

Maskus, K.E., 2000. Intellectual Property Rights in the Global Economy. Institute for International Economics, Washington, DC.

Segerstrom, P.S., Anant, T.C.A., Dinopoulos, E., 1990. A Schumpeterian model of the product life cycle. American Economic Review 80, 1077–1091.

Taylor, M.S., 1994. TRIPS, trade and growth. International Economic Review 35, 361–381.

Vernon, R., 1966. International investment and international trade in the product cycle. Quarterly Journal of Economics 80, 190–207.

Yang, G., Maskus, K.E., 2001. Intellectual property rights, licensing, and innovation in an endogenous product-cycle model. Journal of International Economics 53, 169–187.

Chapter 12

INTELLECTUAL PROPERTY RIGHTS, FOREIGN DIRECT INVESTMENT AND INDUSTRIAL DEVELOPMENT*,#

Lee Branstetter and Kamal Saggi

This article develops a North–South product cycle model in which innovation, imitation and the flow of foreign direct investment (FDI) are all endogenously determined. In the model, a strengthening of intellectual property right (IPR) protection in the South reduces the rate of imitation and it increases the flow of FDI. Indeed, the increase in FDI more than offsets the decline in the extent of production undertaken by Southern imitators so that the South's share of the global basket of goods increases. Furthermore, while multinationals charge higher prices than Southern imitators, *real* wages of Southern workers increase while those of Northern workers fall.

How does the strengthening of intellectual property right (IPR) protection by developing countries impact their industrial development? How does it affect their ability to attract foreign direct investment (FDI)? Does it increase the rate of innovation in the global economy? These and related questions have been at the heart of an ongoing debate that was brought into sharp relief during the negotiations preceding the ratification of the WTO's Agreement on Trade Related Aspects of Intellectual Property Rights (TRIPS) in 1995. Opposition to stronger IPR regimes in developing countries rests on two general arguments. First, there is concern that consumer welfare may be adversely impacted by enhancing the monopoly powers of innovators. Second, there is fear that stronger IPR protection in developing countries will hamper their ability to absorb foreign technologies without having any appreciable effect on Northern innovation.[1] On the other side, TRIPS supporters argue that stronger IPRs world-wide will not only increase incentives for innovation but also foster industrial development in developing countries by encouraging multinationals

* Corresponding author: Kamal Saggi, Department of Economics, Vanderbilt University, PMB 351828, 2301 Vanderbilt Place, Nashville, TN 37235, USA. Email: k.saggi@vanderbilt.edu.

The model developed in this study builds upon and extends the theoretical work presented in Branstetter *et al.*, (2007). We are grateful to Ray Fisman and Fritz Foley for their contributions to that earlier work and for useful comments on this research. For helpful suggestions, we also thank two anonymous referees, the editor, seminar audiences at Stanford University's Center for International Development (SCID), University of Adelaide, University of Melbourne, University of New South Wales, University of Sydney, University of Wollongong and Vanderbilt University. Some of the initial ideas underlying this study were developed while Lee Branstetter was an Abe Fellow and visiting researcher at Hitotsubashi University as well as at the Research Institute of International Trade and Industry in Japan, and he thanks these institutions and the Abe Fellowship Program for hospitality and support. Parts of this study were written during Kamal Saggi's visit to SCID and he thanks SCID's Director Nick Hope, its affiliated researchers and the associated administrative staff for providing him with an excellent research environment. Finally, we acknowledge financial support from the National Science Foundation (SES grant no. 0241781) and the World Bank.

[1] For example, a critic of stronger IPR enforcement in developing countries may argue that the rapid postwar industrialisation in East Asian countries such as Japan and South Korea was achieved under relatively weak IPR regimes and that a premature imposition of a strong IPR regime could retard the industrial development of today's developing countries. See Maskus (2000), who notes these arguments, and the overview and evidence presented in Ordover (1991) and Maskus and McDaniel (1999). On South Korea, see Westphal *et al.*, (1985). For criticisms of stronger IPRs which stress static welfare losses, see McCalman (2001) and Chaudhuri *et al.* (2006).

This chapter was originally appeared in *The Economic Journal* **121**, 1161–1191.

to shift production there.[2] In this study, we seek to illuminate this important debate by developing a North–South product cycle model in which Northern innovation, Southern imitation and the North–South flow of FDI respond endogenously to changes in the degree of Southern IPR protection available to Northern firms. Building on Grossman and Helpman (1991*b*), the model provides a unified framework for assessing some of the key arguments for and against stronger IPR regimes in developing countries.

The theoretical product cycle literature on the effects of Southern IPR protection has been built on two types of growth models analysed in great detail in Grossman and Helpman (1991*a*) – the variety expansion model and the quality ladders model. Important contributions to this literature were subsequently made by Helpman (1993) and Lai (1998) both of which utilised the variety expansion model and Glass and Saggi (2002) who adopted the quality ladders approach. This research established that the effects of increased IPR protection in the South on the Northern rate of innovation depend very much on whether production shifts to the South via imitation of Northern firms or via North–South FDI. Furthermore, Helpman (1993) forcefully drove home the point that while stronger Southern IPR protection can indeed increase the pace of Northern innovation, such a policy change does not necessarily benefit the South since it reallocates production in favour of Northern firms whose prices tend to be higher than those of Southern ones. Thus, international production shifting matters not just for the nature and the extent of innovation but also welfare. Two important features of our model help to shed further light on these arguments. First, Like Lai (1998), the rate of innovation and the flow of North–South FDI respond endogenously to changes in the degree of Southern IPR protection. Second, like Grossman and Helpman (1991*b*), imitation is treated as a costly activity and the Southern rate of imitation is endogenously determined.[3]

Making both imitation and FDI endogenous helps to push forward the literature on North–South product cycle models of international trade. Furthermore, since imitation *is* a costly activity in the real world, analyses that treat it as exogenous fail to capture how changes in the Southern IPR regime alter the allocation of Southern resources among imitation and production. In addition to realism, an important reason for treating imitation as an endogenous activity is that North–South product cycle models with exogenous imitation have yielded remarkably different conclusions regarding the relationship between imitation and innovation from those that have treated it as endogenous. In a model with endogenous imitation and innovation, Grossman and Helpman (1991*b*) uncovered a positive relationship between the two activities while Lai (1998) found that when the rate of imitation is exogenously given and Northern firms can undertake FDI in the South, the relationship between them is negative.[4]

[2] See Paul Romer (1993) for an insightful discussion of how and why FDI can contribute to the economic development of poor countries by helping bridge the 'idea gap' that they face with respect to developed countries.

[3] Helpman (1993) noted that '...imitation is an economic activity much the same as innovation; it requires resources and it responds to economic incentives...'.

[4] It is worth noting here that results also depend upon the type of innovation being considered: the quality ladders model of Glass and Saggi (2002) and Glass and Wu (2007) behave rather differently from the variety expansion models analysed in our article.

In our model, a strengthening of IPR protection in the South reduces the incentive of Southern firms to imitate Northern multinationals. This decline in imitation risk has two important consequences for production and innovation. First, the South becomes a more attractive production location for Northern firms. Second, since all Northern firms have the option to shift production to the South, an increase in the value of multinational firms increases Northern incentives for innovation. Furthermore, we find that the *intra-regional reallocation of Southern production* (from Southern imitators to Northern multinationals) that results from a strengthening of Southern IPR protection is dominated by the accompanying *inter-regional reallocation of production*: in other words, the South's share of the global basket of goods increases with a strengthening of Southern IPR protection.

Our analysis also provides some interesting insights with respect to the effects of Southern IPR protection on prices and wages in the two regions. First, by making the South a more attractive location for production and thereby shifting aggregate labour demand from the North to the South, a strengthening of Southern IPR protection lowers the North's relative wage.[5] Second, since Northern multinationals charge lower prices relative to firms that produce in the North, the increase in FDI helps to lower prices. However, this beneficial effect on prices is partially offset by the intra-regional reallocation of Southern production from local imitators to multinationals since a typical multinational charges a higher price than a Southern imitator. Due to the nature of pricing behaviour under Dixit and Stiglitz (1977) preferences (prices are mark-ups over marginal costs), these changes in prices and nominal wages translate into clear-cut effects on real wages in the two regions: while Northern real wages decline due to stronger Southern IPR protection, Southern real wages increase. More specifically, the purchasing power of Southern workers in terms of Northern goods increases whereas their ability to purchase goods produced by Southern imitators and multinationals remains unaffected.

As noted earlier, a key argument in favour of weak IPR protection in the South is that Southern imitation lowers prices. Since Southern imitators price below Northern multinationals, this channel is also operative in our model. However, this argument ignores the labour market effects that accompany the increase in international production shifting induced by stronger IPR protection in the South. By contrast, in our model, a strengthening of Southern IPR protection raises real wages of Southern workers.[6]

Our model abstracts from Southern innovation. While this assumption is a good approximation for the case of many small developing countries, it is on weaker grounds insofar as the some of the larger developing countries are concerned. If the South has the ability to innovate, Southern IPR reform has the potential to increase local incentives for innovation. Chen and Puttitanum (2005) provide a two-sector oligopolistic model in which the optimal level of IPR protection in the

[5] This result contrasts with those of Krugman (1979) and Grossman and Helpman (1991*b*) who found a negative relationship between Southern imitation and the North's relative wage. Our result differs because imitation targets multinationals in our model whereas it targets Northern producers in theirs.

[6] The real wage effects captured by our model would not arise in partial equilibrium models that ignore the labour market effects of IPR reforms. Furthermore, such effects should only be expected to arise when IPR reforms are undertaken on an economy-wide basis as opposed to being focused on a few sectors.

South balances the trade-off between encouraging imitation of advanced Northern technologies and providing incentives for local innovation. While introducing Southern innovation is beyond the scope of the present study, it is worth noting that the considerations highlighted by Chen and Puttitanum (2005) are likely to strengthen the argument in favour of Southern IPR reform – in our model, such reform confers some benefits on the South even though it is assumed to lack the ability to innovate.[7]

While we endogenise the production location decision of a Northern firm, we do not consider the question of internalisation – that is, in our model, all technology transfer to the South occurs via FDI and arms length arrangements such as licensing are not considered. Antràs (2005) develops a North–South product cycle model in which the incompleteness of international contracts determines the choice between arms length technology transfer and FDI. His analysis shows that the effects of changes in the rate of technological standardisation on the North–South relative wage are quite different from those of changes in the rate at which new goods appear. This suggests that the effects of Southern IPR protection on wages in the two regions might also vary with the type of technological change being considered.[8]

The relationship between FDI and IPR protection has received significant empirical scrutiny in the literature.[9] As the survey by Park (2008) notes, as far as US data is concerned, there appears to be a clear positive relationship between the degree of IPR enforcement in developing countries and investment by US firms – see, for example, Lee and Mansfield (1996) and Nunnenkamp and Spatz (2004). Results derived from non-US data portray a more mixed picture: while Mayer and Pfister (2001) find a negative effect of stronger patent rights on location decisions of French multinationals, Javorcik (2004*a*) finds that stronger patent rights in Eastern Europe and former Soviet Union states have a positive effect on FDI in high-technology sectors. The most recent and perhaps the most relevant empirical study for our purposes is that by Branstetter *et al.* (2011). They investigate the impact of IPR reform on multinational production by analysing the responses of US multinationals to a series of well-documented IPR reforms by 16 countries in the 1980s and 1990s. Consistent with our model, they find that US-based multinationals expand the scale of their activities in reforming countries after IPR reform. They also analyse UN industry-level data from reforming countries and show that industry-level value added increases after reforms, particularly in technology-intensive industries.[10]

[7] He and Maskus (forthcoming) have shown that when the South invests in innovation and there exists a 'backward' spillover from the South to the North, there can be a U-shaped relationship between North–South FDI and the risk of imitation. When Southern innovation is not possible and the risk of imitation is exogenously given, like us, He and Maskus (forthcoming) find a negative relationship between FDI and imitation.

[8] Since we do not model internalisation, our model does not include the process of ongoing standardisation that plays a crucial role in the incomplete contracts framework of Antràs (2005).

[9] For a nuanced and detailed discussion of this literature, see Maskus (2000).

[10] Following Feenstra and Rose (2000), they also construct for each reforming country an annual count of 'initial export episodes' – the number of 10-digit commodities for which recorded US imports from a given country exceed zero for the first time. This serves as a rough indicator of the net rate at which production shifts to the reforming countries, capturing changes in multinational production as well as indigenous imitation. This net rate of production shifting increases sharply after IPR reform, suggesting that any decline in indigenous imitation is more than offset by the increase in the range of goods produced by multinational affiliates.

The rest of the article is organised as follows. Section 1 presents the model. Sections 2 describes the effects of a strengthening of Southern IPR protection. In Section 3, we provide an extensive discussion of the robustness of our main results. Section 4 concludes. There is also a Mathematical Appendix.

1. Model

Consider a world comprised of two regions: North and South. Labour is the only factor of production and region *i*'s labour endowment equals L^i, $i = N,S$. As in Grossman and Helpman (1991*b*) preferences are identical in the two regions and a representative consumer chooses instantaneous expenditure $E(\tau)$ to maximise utility at time *t*:

$$U = \int_t^{\infty} \mathrm{e}^{-\rho(\tau-t)} \log D(\tau)\mathrm{d}\tau \tag{1}$$

subject to the intertemporal budget constraint

$$\int_t^{\infty} \mathrm{e}^{-r(\tau-t)} E(\tau)\mathrm{d}\tau = \int_t^{\infty} \mathrm{e}^{-r(\tau-t)} I(\tau)\mathrm{d}\tau + A(t) \text{ for all } t, \tag{2}$$

where ρ denotes the rate of time preference; r the nominal interest rate; $I(\tau)$ instantaneous income and $A(t)$ the current value of assets. The instantaneous utility $D(\tau)$ is given by

$$D = \left[\int_0^n x(j)^{\alpha}\mathrm{d}j\right]^{\frac{1}{\alpha}}, \tag{3}$$

where $x(j)$ denotes the consumption of good j; n the number of goods available and $0 < \alpha < 1$.

As is well known, under the above assumptions, the consumer's optimisation problem can be broken down into two stages. First, he chooses how to allocate a given spending level across all available goods. Second, he chooses the optimal time path of spending. The instantaneous utility function D implies that the elasticity of substitution between any two goods is constant and equals $\varepsilon = 1/(1-\alpha)$ and demand for good j (given expenditure E) is given by

$$x(j) = \frac{Ep(j)^{-\varepsilon}}{P^{1-\varepsilon}}, \tag{4}$$

where $p(j)$ denotes the price of good j and P a price index such that

$$P = \left[\int_0^n p(j)^{1-\varepsilon}\mathrm{d}j\right]^{\frac{1}{1-\varepsilon}}. \tag{5}$$

Furthermore, as is well known, under the two-stage procedure the optimal spending rule is given by

$$\frac{\dot{E}}{E} = r - \rho, \tag{6}$$

that is, nominal consumption spending grows at a rate equal to the difference between the interest rate and the subjective rate of time preference.

1.1. *Product Market*

Three types of firms produce goods: Northern firms (N), Northern multinationals (M) and Southern imitators (S). Denote firms by J where $J = N$, M, or S. Northern firms can either produce in the North or the South. A Northern firm needs one worker to produce a unit of output in the North, whereas $\theta \geq 1$ workers per unit of output are needed in the South. Intuitively, this is due to the costs of coordinating decisions over large distances and operating in unfamiliar foreign environments. Indeed, the theory of the multinational enterprise argues that such firms rely on 'ownership' advantages derived from technological assets and/or brand names in order to offset the disadvantages they face relative to local firms (Markusen, 1995).

Given the constant elasticity demand functions, it is straightforward to show that prices of Northern firms are mark-ups over their marginal costs:

$$p^{\mathrm{N}} = \frac{w^{\mathrm{N}}}{\alpha} \quad \text{and} \quad p^{\mathrm{M}} = \frac{\theta w^{\mathrm{S}}}{\alpha}.$$

Southern firms can produce only those goods that they have successfully imitated and they need one worker to produce one unit of output. If successful in imitating a multinational, a Southern firm charges its optimal monopoly price

$$p^{\mathrm{S}} = \frac{w^{\mathrm{S}}}{\alpha}.$$

Note that this price can be sustained if and only if it lies below the multinational's marginal cost θw^{S}:

$$\frac{w^{\mathrm{S}}}{\alpha} < \theta w^{\mathrm{S}} \Leftrightarrow \theta\alpha > 1.$$

In what follows, we assume $\theta\alpha > 1$.[11]

Let x^{J} denote the output level of firm J where $J = N, M$, or S. We know from the demand functions that

$$\frac{x(i)}{x(j)} = \frac{p_i^{-\varepsilon}}{p_j^{-\varepsilon}}. \tag{7}$$

Using the pricing equations for the three types of products, we have

$$\frac{x^{\mathrm{S}}}{x^{\mathrm{M}}} = \theta^{\varepsilon}, \tag{8}$$

and

[11] When $\theta\alpha < 1$, a Southern imitator limit prices the Northern firm whose product it has copied by setting its price equal to the Northern firm's marginal cost θw^{S}. An earlier version of the article also analysed the case where Southern firms limit price. The analysis of this limit pricing case yields no additional insights regarding the main questions of interest and we omit its discussion in order to conserve space.

$$\frac{x^M}{x^N} = \left(\frac{\theta w^S/\alpha}{w^N/\alpha}\right)^{-\varepsilon} = \left(\frac{\theta w^S}{w^N}\right)^{-\varepsilon} \quad \text{and} \quad \frac{x^S}{x^N} = \left(\frac{w^S}{w^N}\right)^{-\varepsilon}. \tag{9}$$

Flow profit of a Northern producer is given by

$$\pi^N = (p^N - w^N)x^N = \frac{(1-\alpha)w^N x^N}{\alpha}. \tag{10}$$

Similarly, a multinational's flow profit equals

$$\pi^M = (p^M - \theta w^S)x^M = \frac{\theta(1-\alpha)w^S x^M}{\alpha}, \tag{11}$$

while that of a Southern firm equals

$$\pi^S = (p^S - w^S)x^S = \frac{(1-\alpha)w^S x^S}{\alpha}. \tag{12}$$

1.2. *FDI and Imitation*

Of the n goods that exist, n_N are produced in the North, n_M are produced in the South by Northern multinationals and n_I are produced by Southern imitators. Let $n_S \equiv n_I + n_M$ denote all goods produced in the South. In what follows, we think of the level of Southern industrial development as the Southern share of global manufacturing; that is, the ratio of goods produced in the South to the number of goods that exist at a point in time. Since this measure of industrial development explicitly includes the activities of affiliates of Northern multinationals, the advance of Southern industrial development in our model depends on the rate of FDI.

Let the rate of imitation μ be defined by

$$\mu \equiv \frac{\dot{n}_I}{n_M}, \tag{13}$$

that is, μ denotes the rate of increase of the stock of imitated goods relative to the total number of goods produced by Northern multinationals. Since both multinationals and Southern imitators produce in the South, imitation simply transfers ownership of a good (and the associated flow of profits) from the hands of a multinational to a Southern imitator.

The rate of North–South FDI is defined by

$$\phi \equiv \frac{\dot{n}_S}{n_N}, \tag{14}$$

where n_N denotes the number of goods produced in the North. In other words, at each instant, the the total stock of goods produced in the South increases by ϕn_N. Note that this measures the inflow of North–South FDI because imitation only targets Northern multinationals and does not, by itself, lead to North–South production shifting.

Like Grossman and Helpman (1991*b*) and Lai (1998), we study a steady state equilibrium in which prices, nominal spending, and all product categories grow at the same rate g:

$$g \equiv \frac{\dot{n}}{n} = \frac{\dot{n}_{\mathrm{N}}}{n_{\mathrm{N}}} = \frac{\dot{n}_{\mathrm{I}}}{n_{\mathrm{I}}} = \frac{\dot{n}_{\mathrm{M}}}{n_{\mathrm{M}}} = \frac{\dot{n}_{\mathrm{S}}}{n_{\mathrm{S}}} = \frac{\dot{E}}{E}. \tag{15}$$

Equations (6), (14) and (15) imply that in steady state the interest rate equals the sum of the subjective discount rate and the growth rate:

$$r = \rho + g.$$

Furthermore, the steady state allocation of products across the two regions satisfies

$$\frac{n_{\mathrm{N}}}{n} = \frac{g}{g+\phi} \quad \text{and} \quad \frac{n_{\mathrm{S}}}{n_{\mathrm{N}}} = \frac{\phi}{g}. \tag{16}$$

Similarly, the ratio of multinationals to their two types of competitors equals

$$\frac{n_{\mathrm{M}}}{n_{\mathrm{N}}} = \frac{\phi}{g+\mu} \quad \text{and} \quad \frac{n_{\mathrm{M}}}{n_{\mathrm{I}}} = \frac{g}{\mu}. \tag{17}$$

As in Grossman and Helpman (1991*b*), the lifetime value of a Southern producer (i.e. the reward earned by a successful imitator) equals

$$v^{\mathrm{S}} = \frac{\pi^{\mathrm{S}}}{\rho + g}. \tag{18}$$

Note from above that since future products creates competition for existing products, an increase in the rate of innovation (g) reduces the life-time value of a Southern firm. Similarly, the lifetime steady-state value of a Northern firm that opts to produce in the North equals:

$$v^{\mathrm{N}} = \frac{\pi^{\mathrm{N}}}{\rho + g}. \tag{19}$$

While it is cheaper to produce in the South (as we show below, the Southern relative wage is lower in equilibrium), shifting production to the South invites the risk of imitation and the value of a Northern multinational firm equals

$$v^{\mathrm{M}} = \frac{\pi^{\mathrm{M}}}{\rho + \mu + g}. \tag{20}$$

As is clear, in calculating the value of a multinational firm, the flow profit π^{M} is discounted not just by the effective interest rate (which equals $\rho + g$) but also by the rate of imitation μ. In our model, imitation targets only Northern multinationals and the risk faced by Northern firms that refrain from shifting production to the South has been normalised to zero.[12] In reality, Northern firms that do not undertake FDI can also have their technologies imitated but the risk of imitation they face is probably

[12] In Section 3.1, we discuss in detail why such a formulation of Southern imitation is sensible in the context of our model.

lower than that of multinational firms that produce in the South. As is known from the work of Mansfield (1994), Lee and Mansfield (1996) and Maskus (2000), multinational firms indeed internalise the risk of imitation that they face due to weak IPR protection in host countries.

As is clear, our modelling of the FDI decision is rather simple: it abstracts from the usually studied trade-off between exporting at a higher marginal cost to the Southern market versus bearing the fixed cost of building another plant there to serve the local market. We abstract from these considerations mainly for tractability and for focusing on the aggregate response of international production shifting to changes in imitation risk induced by IPR reform. In the real world, one observes 'horizontal' multinationals producing the same good in different locations. By design, such multinationals do not arise in our model.[13] To see briefly why we adopt this route, note that if a multinational were to split output across countries the question of imitation risk becomes more complicated. Should the risk of imitation depend positively upon the share of output produced by a multinational in the South? Or should it be independent of it in that any level of production shifting leads to the same risk? The underlying logic of our model would be more consistent with the former approach but adopting it complicates the model substantially since the risk of imitation faced by a firm would then depend on its allocation of production across the two regions. On the other hand, if the second formulation is adopted, our model does not have much to add to the already rich literature explaining the existence of horizontal multinationals. As a result, we have chosen the simpler formulation that allows us to focus on the main questions motivating our analysis.

1.3. *North–South Relative Wage*

Since all Northern firms have the option of becoming multinationals, we must have $v^{N} = v^{M}$ which implies

$$\frac{\pi^{M}}{\pi^{N}} = 1 + \frac{\mu}{\rho + g}.$$

Note immediately from above that if the risk of imitation is positive (i.e. $\mu > 0$) then we must have $\pi^{M} > \pi^{N}$. This is intuitive: since any Northern firm is free to become a multinational, the flow profit earned by a multinational must be higher in order to compensate for the risk of imitation faced (only) by multinationals.[14]

From the definition of profit we have

$$\frac{\pi^{M}}{\pi^{N}} = \frac{\theta w^{S} x^{M}}{w^{N} x^{N}} = \left(\frac{\theta w^{S}}{w^{N}}\right)^{1-\varepsilon}$$

[13] Note that the transfer of technology from the parent firm that undertakes the R&D in the North to its affiliate in the South can be viewed as giving rise to a 'vertical multinational' and all the multinationals in our model are of this type. We thank an anonymous referee for drawing our attention to the fact that our model abstracts from horizontal FDI, an important type of FDI in the real world. See Markusen (1995) for an insightful survey of theories explaining the emergence of such multinationals.

[14] Indeed, since prices of Northern firms and multinationals are marked up over their respective marginal costs by the same amount (i.e. $1/\alpha$) the relative value of sales of a typical multinational must exceed that of a Northern firm: $(p^{M}x^{M})/(p^{N}x^{N}) = 1 + \mu/(\rho + g)$.

The last two equations allow us to write the Northern relative wage (w^{R}) as a function of the rate of innovation and imitation as well as some of the exogenous parameters of the model:

$$w^{R} \equiv \frac{w^{N}}{w^{S}} = \theta\left(1 + \frac{\mu}{\rho + g}\right)^{\frac{1}{\varepsilon - 1}} \tag{21}$$

As is clear, the relative wage in the North increases with the production disadvantage faced by Northern multinationals (θ) as well as with the Southern rate of imitation (μ) since both of these factors discourage Northern firms from relocating production to the South. This reluctance to shift production to the South increases the relative demand for Northern labour and therefore North's relative wage.

As we noted earlier, this result differs from that of Grossman and Helpman (1991*b*) and is line with Lai (1998). Why do these models yield such different results regarding the determinants of the North–South relative wage? In Grossman and Helpman (1991*b*), Southern imitation of firms producing in the North serves as the channel through which international reallocation of production (and therefore labour demand) occurs. By contrast, in our model as well as in Lai (1998) Southern imitation targets multinational firms and North–South FDI is the channel of international reallocation of production. In our model, by lowering the risk of imitation, a strengthening of Southern IPR protection increases the incentive for FDI and the demand for Southern labour while it reduces demand for Northern labour. In Grossman and Helpman (1991*b*), the opposite happens: as imitation declines, more production stays in the North and less of it occurs in the South. Hence the North–South relative wage behaves rather differently across these models.

1.4. *Free Entry*

Free entry into innovation implies that the value of a Northern firm must exactly equal the cost of innovation:

$$v^{N} = \frac{w^{N} a_{N}}{n} \Leftrightarrow \frac{\pi^{N}}{\rho + g} = \frac{w^{N} a_{N}}{n}, \tag{22}$$

where a_{N} is the unit labour requirement in innovation and $(w^{N} a_{N})/n$ measures the up-front cost of product development. This formulation assumes that the cost of designing new products falls with the number of products (n) that have been invented. In other words, knowledge spillovers from innovation sustain further innovation. This assumption is standard in the literature (Romer, 1990; Grossman and Helpman, 1991*a,b*) and in its absence growth cannot be sustained in our variety expansion model with fixed resources. This is because the flow profit of a successful innovator declines with the number of products invented and incentives for innovation disappear in the long run if the cost of innovation does not also fall with an increase in the number of products.

Substituting from (19) into (22) gives the output level of a Northern firm

$$x^{N} = \frac{a_{N}\alpha(\rho + g)}{n(1 - \alpha)}. \tag{23}$$

Let the unit labour requirement in imitation be a_I and the cost function for imitation be given by

$$c_I = \frac{ka_I w^S}{n_S}, \tag{24}$$

where $n_S = n_I + n_M$ denotes the number of products produced in the South and $k \geq 1$ is an index of the degree of IPR protection in the South. The idea underlying this formulation is that as IPR protection is strengthened in the South (i.e. as k increases), imitation becomes a more costly activity for Southern firms because evading local enforcement of IPRs becomes more difficult.[15] Note also that the above cost function for imitation assumes that the cost of imitation declines with the number of goods produced in the South (n_S). Since both multinationals and local imitators produce in the South, the idea underlying this formulation is that both local imitation and Northern FDI generate knowledge spillovers for the South.[16] As is the case of innovation, the cost of imitation must decline over time in order to sustain imitation in the long run because as the number of products in the world economy expand, the flow profit of a successful imitator falls. In Section 3.2, we discuss a scenario where spillovers from past innovations are incomplete.

Free entry into imitation implies that the reward from imitation should equal its cost:

$$v^S = \frac{ka_I w^S}{n_S} \Leftrightarrow \frac{\pi^S}{\rho + g} = \frac{ka_I w^S}{n_S}. \tag{25}$$

Substituting from (18) into the above equation and using (8) gives the sales levels of a Southern imitator and a Northern multinational:

$$x^S = \frac{\alpha}{1-\alpha} \frac{ka_I(\rho + g)}{n_S(\theta - 1)} \quad \text{and} \quad x^M = \frac{ka_I(\rho + g)}{n_S(\theta - 1)\theta^{\varepsilon}}. \tag{26}$$

Finally, from (22) and (25) we have

$$\frac{n}{n_S} \frac{ka_I}{a_N} \frac{v^N}{v^S} \frac{w^S}{w^N} = 1 \Leftrightarrow \frac{n}{n_S} \frac{ka_I}{a_N} \frac{x^N}{x^S} = 1. \tag{27}$$

Using (9) and (21) the above equation becomes

$$\frac{n_S}{n} \frac{a_N}{ka_I} \frac{\theta^{\varepsilon}}{1-\alpha} \left(1 + \frac{\mu}{\rho + g}\right)^{\frac{\varepsilon}{\varepsilon - 1}} = 1. \tag{28}$$

Substituting from (16) and (17) into the above equation gives us the 'first equilibrium condition' in terms of three endogenous variables g, ϕ and μ and exogenous parameters of the model:

$$\frac{\phi}{\phi + g} \frac{a_N}{ka_I} \frac{\theta^{\varepsilon}}{1-\alpha} \left(1 + \frac{\mu}{\rho + g}\right)^{\frac{\varepsilon}{\varepsilon - 1}} = 1. \tag{29}$$

[15] Later in the article we briefly discuss the case where Southern IPR protection determines the degree to which Southern imitators can capture their product market profits post-imitation.

[16] This formulation of localised knowledge spillovers for the South is consistent with our modelling of FDI wherein we posit that only Northern firms producing in the South face the risk of imitation by local firms.

Intuitively, this condition follows from the assumption of free entry into imitation and innovation and it ensures that neither activity leads to excess profits for firms that are successful in such activities.

1.5. *Resource Constraints*

The other two equilibrium conditions are derived from the resource constraints in the two regions. In the North, labour is allocated between innovation and production:

$$\frac{a_N}{n}\dot{n} + n_N x^N = L^N. \tag{30}$$

Substituting into the above resource constraint from the market measure (16), (17) and (23) yields the 'second equilibrium condition':

$$L_d^N \equiv a_N g + \frac{g}{g+\phi}\frac{a_N \alpha(\rho+g)}{1-\alpha} = L^N. \tag{31}$$

Southern labour is allocated to imitation and production by multinationals and local firms:

$$\frac{ka_I}{n_S}\dot{n}_I + \theta n_M x^M + n_I x^S = L^S. \tag{32}$$

Substituting into the above resource constraint from (16), (17) and (26) gives the 'third equilibrium condition':

$$L_d^S \equiv \frac{ka_I g\mu}{g+\mu} + \frac{\theta\alpha k a_I(\rho+g)}{\theta^{\varepsilon}(1-\alpha)}\frac{g}{g+\mu} + \frac{\alpha k a_I(\rho+g)}{1-\alpha}\frac{\mu}{g+\mu} = L^S. \tag{33}$$

Observe immediately that the above equation can also be written as

$$\frac{a_I g\mu}{g+\mu} + \frac{\theta\alpha a_I(\rho+g)}{\theta^{\varepsilon}(1-\alpha)}\frac{g}{g+\mu} + \frac{\alpha a_I(\rho+g)}{1-\alpha}\frac{\mu}{g+\mu} = \frac{L^S}{k}. \tag{34}$$

In other words, from the viewpoint of the South, holding constant the rates of imitation (μ) and innovation (g), an increase in the degree of IPR protection (k) is an effective reduction in the real resources available since all three activities that the South is engaged in – imitation, production by multinational firms and production by local imitators – require more resources as k increases. It is intuitively obvious why an increase in the cost of imitation increases the resources required to sustain a given level of imitation. But why do the two production activities undertaken in the South also become more resource intensive with an increase in the IPR index k? The intuition for this comes from the free entry condition in imitation: as the cost of imitation increases, the sales of a firm that is successful in imitation also must increase in order to maintain the zero profit condition in imitation. Finally, the sales of a multinational (x^M) are proportional to the sales of a Southern imitator (x^M) and if x^S increases, so must x^M. We are now in a position to study the effects of a strengthening of Southern IPR protection.

2. Equilibrium Effects of Southern IPR Protection

We begin by establishing some crucial properties of the North–South flow of FDI.

2.1. *Flow of North–South FDI*

To do so, we first solve (29) for FDI flow ϕ in terms of the other two endogenous variables (g and μ). From (29) we have

$$\phi = \frac{g}{\frac{\theta^{\varepsilon} a_N}{A(\mu, g) k a_I} - 1}, \tag{35}$$

where

$$A(\mu, g) = \left(\frac{\rho + g}{\rho + g + \mu}\right)^{\frac{1}{\alpha}} < 1.$$

Lemma 1. *$A(\mu,g)<1$ and $\partial A(\mu, g)/\partial \mu < 0 < \partial A(\mu, g)/\partial g$.*

Observe immediately from (35) that holding μ constant the denominator of the right-hand side increases with g: this is because μ/g falls with g whereas $A(\mu,g)$ increases (Lemma 1). This implies the following result:

Remark 1. *Holding constant the rate of imitation (μ), factors that increase the North–South flow of FDI (ϕ) must also increase the rate of Northern innovation (g).*

Since both innovation and FDI are endogenous, Remark 1 simply notes that the flow of FDI and the rate of innovation are positively related in our model. In this context, it is worth noting that a large number of empirical studies have demonstrated that there is indeed a positive correlation between innovation and FDI; as Markusen (1995) notes, this finding is so pervasive that it has become a cornerstone of the modern theory of the multinational firm. Furthermore, since $A(\mu,g)$ decreases with μ, we have:

Remark 2. *Holding constant the rate of innovation (g), factors that decrease the Southern rate of imitation (μ) must also increase the North–South flow of FDI (ϕ).*

Since our model exhibits a negative feedback between FDI and imitation and a positive feedback between FDI and innovation, *it necessarily implies a negative feedback between innovation and imitation.* This is an important property of the model which differentiates it from the results of Grossman and Helpman (1991*b*) and aligns it with those of Lai (1998).

Consider now the direct effect of Southern IPR protection on the North–South flow of FDI. From (35) directly observe that the denominator in the formula of $\phi(\mu,g)$ decreases with k so that we have:

Remark 3. *Holding constant the rates of imitation (μ) and innovation (g), the flow of FDI (ϕ) to the South increases with a strengthening of Southern IPR protection (i.e. an increase in k).*

The intuition for this result comes from (28) which requires the rate of return on innovation and imitation to equal each other. Since the right-hand side of this equation always equals 1, an increase in the IPR index k must be counterbalanced by an increase in the ratio of production $(n_S)/n = \phi/(\phi+g)$ that occurs in the South for the cost of imitation to *not* increase relative to the cost of innovation which in turn requires the flow of FDI ϕ to increase with the degree of Southern IPR protection k.

It is well known that multinational firms conduct a large share of global research and development (R&D). Indeed, a generation of empirical studies have documented the positive correlation between FDI flows and R&D investment (Markusen, 1995). Given this, it is worth noting from (35) that, holding constant the rate of innovation and imitation, an increase in the R&D productivity of Northern firms (as measured by an decrease in a_N) implies a faster North–South flow of FDI. We later discuss the general equilibrium response of FDI to an increase in Northern R&D productivity taking into account its effects on the rates of imitation and innovation.

2.2. *Impact on Innovation and Imitation*

Equations (29), (31) and (33) define the steady-state equilibrium of the model in terms of the three endogenous variables: the rate of innovation g, the rate of imitation μ and the rate of FDI ϕ. All of the effects of increased IPR protection in the South (i.e. an increase in k) are derived from the effects on these endogenous variables.

Assuming the rate of imitation is exogenously given, Lai (1998) has shown that a decline in this rate increases Northern innovation and the rate of production shifting to the South. A crucial question is whether this important result holds when both imitation and innovation are endogenous and the underlying exogenous variable is the degree of IPR protection (i.e. parameter k). Using the equation for the equilibrium flow of FDI and the two resource constraints, we can derive a system of two equations in two unknowns that helps to provide a graphical illustration of the consequences of stronger IPR protection in the South.

First note from (33) that the Southern labour market constraint is *independent* of the flow of FDI ϕ. Also, recall that L_d^S measures aggregate labour demand in the South (given by the LHS of (33)). Direct calculations yield

$$\frac{\partial L_d^S}{\partial \mu} = \frac{ka_I[\theta^\varepsilon(g+\alpha\rho) - \alpha\theta(\rho+g)]}{(\mu+g)^2(1-\alpha)\theta^\varepsilon} > 0,$$

because $\theta^\varepsilon > \theta$ and $\alpha < 1$ – that is, holding constant the rate of innovation g, aggregate labour demand in the South increases with the rate of imitation μ. Similarly, holding constant the rate of imitation, demand for Southern labour increases with the rate of innovation:

$$\frac{\partial L_d^S}{\partial g} = \frac{ka_I[\mu(\mu-\alpha\rho)\theta^\varepsilon + \alpha\theta\rho\mu + 2\theta g\mu + \alpha\theta g^2]}{(\mu+g)^2(1-\alpha)\theta^\varepsilon} > 0,$$

where we have assumed that $\mu > \alpha\rho$.

Thus, the Southern labour market constraint (i.e. the *SS* curve) is downward sloping in the (g,μ) space:

$$\sigma^{S}(g,\mu) \equiv \left.\frac{d\mu}{dg}\right|_{L_d^S=L^S} = -\frac{\partial L^S(\mu,g)}{\partial g}\bigg/\frac{\partial L^S(\mu,g)}{\partial \mu} < 0.$$

In other words, since the South has only a fixed amount of labour resources, an increase in the Southern rate of imitation μ implies that the rate of innovation g that can be supported by the global economy must be lower.

Also, we have

$$\frac{\partial L_d^N}{\partial \mu} = \frac{ka_I(\rho+g)A(\mu,g)}{(\rho+\mu+g)(1-\alpha)\theta^{\varepsilon}} > 0,$$

that is, the higher the rate of imitation μ, the higher the demand for Northern labour. The logic for this is as follows. Since FDI is endogenously determined, a higher rate of imitation makes FDI less attractive to Northern firms. For a fixed rate of innovation, the demand for Northern workers is inversely related to the flow of FDI.

Next consider how an increase in the rate of innovation effects aggregate labour demand in the North. Recall that demand for Northern labour comes from innovation ($L_n^N \equiv a_N g$) and from production ($L_p^N \equiv n_N x^N$). It is obvious that an increase in g raises labour demand in innovation (L_n^N). On the production side, labour demand can be written as

$$L_p^N \equiv \frac{n_N}{n}\frac{a_N\alpha(\rho+g)}{(1-\alpha)} \quad \text{where} \quad \frac{n_N}{n} = \frac{g}{\phi+g}$$

which immediately implies that if n_N/n were to increase in g, then it must be that L_p^N (and therefore aggregate labour demand) in the North increases in g. Further note from above that if ϕ were independent of g, it would immediately follow that n_N/n increases in g. This thought experiment is useful for highlighting the role of the flow of FDI in our model: if the flow of FDI flow were invariant to the rate of innovation, labour demand in the North would necessarily increase with the rate of innovation. However, Remark 1 notes that the flow of FDI and the rate of innovation are positively related. This raises the possibility that n_N/n might decrease with g. Intuitively, such a situation could arise since the elasticity of the flow of FDI with respect to the rate of innovation exceeds unity in our model. Despite this, we show in the Appendix that labour demand in the North necessarily increases with the rate of innovation:

$$\frac{\partial L_d^N}{\partial g} > 0.$$

As a result, like the Southern labour market constraint, the Northern labour market constraint (i.e. the *NN* curve) is also downward sloping in the (g, μ) space:

$$\sigma^{N}(g,\mu) \equiv \left.\frac{d\mu}{dg}\right|_{L_d^N=L^N} = -\frac{\partial L_d^N}{\partial g}\bigg/\frac{\partial L_d^N}{\partial \mu} < 0.$$

It is worth emphasising the role FDI plays in this context: in the absence of FDI, in a variety expansion product cycle model such as Grossman and Helpman (1991*b*), the Northern market labour constraint is actually *upward* sloping in the (g, μ) space. This is because when imitation is the only channel via which production is reallocated internationally, an increase in the rate of imitation frees up Northern labour for use in innovation thereby generating a positive feedback between imitation and innovation.

By contrast, in our model imitation targets production by multinationals and by slowing down FDI, an increase in the rate of imitation actually pulls Northern resources out of innovation and into production.

For a unique steady-state equilibrium to exist, the *SS* curve and the *NN* curve must have a unique intersection in the (g, μ) space. We have already noted that both curves are downward sloping. Neither curve intersects the vertical axis and we show in the appendix that under minor conditions, the horizontal intercept (g^s) of the *SS* curve is larger than that (g^n) of the *NN* curve.

Given these properties of the two curves, any intersection of the two curves will be unique if the *NN* curve is steeper than the *SS* curve: i.e. $\sigma^r \equiv |\sigma^N|/|\sigma^S| > 1$. We can show that $\sigma^r > 1$ iff $a_R \equiv a_N/a_I$ exceeds some threshold a_R^*, where a_R^* is a function of exogenous parameters and the rates of imitation and innovation. Furthermore, as ρ approaches zero, a_R^* can be shown to be decreasing in the rate of imitation μ. In other words, for ρ close to zero, the required threshold a_R^* is the highest (and therefore the most difficult to meet) at $\mu = 0$. Next, it can be shown that at $\mu = \rho = 0$, a_R^* decreases in θ and at the lowest feasible value of θ (which is $1/\alpha$), the condition $a_R > a_R^*$ is necessarily satisfied for all feasible α. Thus, we proceed with the scenario where the *NN* curve is steeper than the *SS* curve and the two curves have a unique intersection that pins down the steady-state equilibrium of the global economy.

Intuitively, in the (g, μ) space the *NN* curve ought to be relatively steeper than the *SS* curve because the rate of innovation is determined primarily by the size of the Northern economy (since only the North innovates) while the rate of imitation is determined primarily by the size of the Southern one (since only the South imitates). Of course, the North–South flow of FDI is what links the two economies and their resource constraints to each other.

As was already noted, holding constant the rates of imitation (μ) and innovation (g), an increase in the degree of Southern IPR protection (k) increases labour demand in the South in all three activities (i.e. local imitation, production by Southern firms and production by multinationals).[17] This is equivalent to an inward shift in the Southern labour market constraint in the (g, μ) space. Further note that holding constant g and μ, an increase in k effects the Northern labour market constraint via its effect on the flow of FDI ϕ. Given that the flow of FDI increases in the Southern IPR index k, it follows that labour demand in the North $L^N(\mu, g)$ (i.e. the left-hand side of (31)) decreases with k. The effect of a strengthening of IPR protection in the South on equilibrium rates of imitation and innovation can now be derived. As IPR protection in the South increases, the Southern labour market constraint (i.e. the *SS* curve) shifts down while the Northern constraint (i.e. the *NN* curve) shifts up. These shifts in the two constraints deliver one of our key results:

PROPOSITION 1. *A strengthening of IPR protection in the South decreases the Southern rate of imitation (μ) while it increases the Northern rate of innovation (g):* $(d\mu/dk) < 0 < (dg/dk)$.

[17] It is worth noting here that since preferences are of the Dixit–Stiglitz type, the output of a typical multinational relative to a typical imitation is fixed and this ratio is given in equation (8). Furthermore, all else equal, the stronger the degree of IPR protection, the higher must be the equilibrium output level of a typical imitator for there to be equality between cost of imitation and the value of an imitating firm. Finally, by assumption, the degree of IPR protection directly affects the cost of imitation and therefore the aggregate resource requirement in imitation.

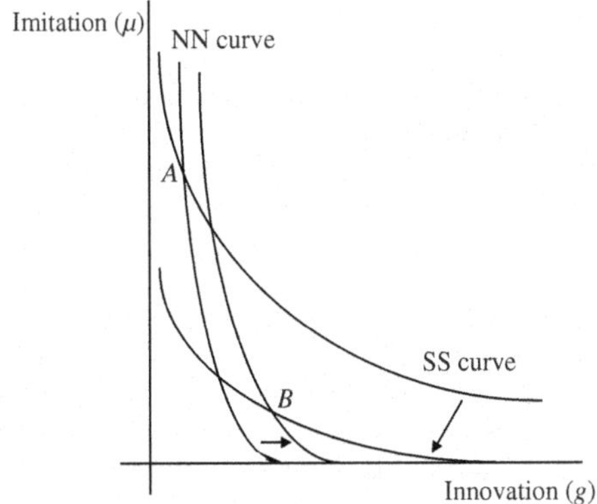

Fig. 1. *Effects of an Increase in Southern Intellectual Property Right Protection*

Since Proposition 1 is our central result, it is worth noting that it applies to *marginal* changes in the degree of Southern IPR protection k as opposed to large, discrete reforms that were called for by the TRIPS agreement. However, in the real world, any IPR reform is only as good as the degree of local enforcement. Since IPR enforcement is likely to improve gradually, it is reasonable to focus on the effects of marginal changes in k.[18]

Figure 1 drawn in the (g,μ) space illustrates Proposition 1.

In Figure 1, point A denotes the initial steady-state equilibrium. Now suppose that Southern IPR protection is strengthened (i.e. k increases). This policy change implies an inward shift in the Southern resource constraint and an outward shift in the Northern constraint. Why the Southern constraint shifts has already been explained: all three activities in the South become more resource intensive and this effectively reduces the resource base. The Northern constraint shifts out because of the FDI response: as the flow of North–South FDI increases, more Northern resources become available for innovation. The outward shift in the Northern constraint is relatively smaller because the North is affected via a single, indirect channel (i.e. through the response of North–South flow of FDI) whereas the effect on the South is a more direct one and it occurs via all three activities that take place there. As shown in Figure 1, these shifts in the two resource constraints caused by a strengthening of IPR protection in the South imply that in the new steady state equilibrium B the Southern rate of imitation is significantly lower than that at A while the Northern rate of innovation is higher.[19] We should emphasise that the properties of the model noted in Remarks 1 and 2 are quite crucial since these

[18] It is worth noting that the estimated response of US multinationals to IPR reform documented in Branstetter *et al.* (2006) and Branstetter *et al.* (2011) suggests a gradual shift in their investment, technology transfer and R&D in reforming countries. These studies found that there was no sharp change in the year of reform but, rather, a gradual change that was phased in over many years.

[19] In a two-country model where both countries invest in labour saving innovation, Taylor (1994) finds that the global innovation and technology transfer are both higher when countries offer the same degree of IPR protection to innovating firms regardless of their national origin relative to when they offer such protection to only their own firms.

establish a positive feedback between FDI and innovation and a negative feedback between these two variables and the rate of imitation. As long as a strengthening of Southern IPR protection discourages imitation, its positive effects on innovation and FDI are implied by Remarks 1 and 2.

Now briefly consider the case where a Southern imitator's flow profit from imitation equal $\pi_k^S = (1-k)\pi^S = (1-k)(\theta-1)w^S x^S$ where k determined the degree of IPR protection and $0 \leq k \leq 1$. Under such a formulation, the Northern labour market equilibrium condition is unaltered whereas the other two equilibrium conditions are slightly modified. In equation (29) we simply need to replace $1/k$ by $(1-k)$ whereas in equation (33) the same substitution is needed in the second and third terms of the LHS; in the first term of the same equation, k needs to be simply replaced by 1. It is straightforward to show that results obtained under our cost-based formulation of IPR protection continue to hold under this profit–tax formulation.

Finally, we note how an improvement in R&D productivity (i.e. a decrease in a_N) affects the North–South flow of FDI as well as the global allocation of production, once the effects on innovation and imitation are taken into account. First note that a decrease in a_N has no direct effect on the *SS* constraint whereas the effect on the *NN* constraint is essentially the same as that an increase in the Northern labour supply – that is in Figure 1, the *NN* curve shifts out. This immediately implies that with an increase in Northern R&D productivity, the rate of imitation decreases whereas the rate of innovation increases. Relying on arguments similar to those used to derive the effects of Southern IPR protection, we directly state the following:

PROPOSITION 2. *With an increase in the R&D productivity of Northern firms (i.e. a decrease in a_N), the rate of innovation, the North–South flow of FDI, the share of Southern production in the hands of Northern multinationals and the sales of multinationals relative to other firms, all increase whereas the rate of imitation decreases.*

2.3. *Allocation of Global Production*

An important objective of this article was to understand how a strengthening of IPR protection in the South alters the distribution of production across the two regions as well as between Northern multinationals and Southern imitators. How Southern IPR protection affects the global allocation of production depends on its effects on Southern imitation, Northern innovation, and the North–South flow of FDI. To see the effect of an increase in k on the international allocation of production, note that equation (28) can be written as

$$\frac{\theta_\alpha a_N}{k a_I}\left(1+\frac{\mu}{\rho+g}\right)^{\frac{\varepsilon}{\varepsilon-1}}\frac{n_S}{n}=1,$$

where $\theta_\alpha=[\alpha^{1-\varepsilon}(\theta-1)]/(1-\alpha)$ does not depend upon the degree of Southern IPR protection (k). As k increases, $(\theta_\alpha a_N)/(k a_I)$ decreases as does the term in the square parentheses (since the rate of imitation μ falls while the rate of innovation g increases). Since the right-hand side always equals 1, this implies that n_S/n must increase with an increase in the degree of Southern IPR protection k.

PROPOSITION 3 (INTERNATIONAL ALLOCATION OF PRODUCTION). *A strengthening of Southern IPR protection increases the South's share of the total basket of goods produced in the global economy:* $\mathrm{d}(n_{\mathrm{S}}/n)/\mathrm{d}k > 0$.[20]

Another way of restating Proposition 3 is that the North's share of the global basket of goods (n_{N}/n) must decrease with k:

$$\frac{\mathrm{d}(n_{\mathrm{N}}/n)}{\mathrm{d}k} < 0 \quad \text{where} \quad \frac{n_{\mathrm{N}}}{n} = \frac{1}{1+x} \quad \text{and} \quad x = \frac{\phi}{g}\left(1 + \frac{\mu}{g}\right).$$

Since μ/g falls with k, it must be that ϕ/g rises with k or else n_{N}/n cannot decrease with k. This finding sheds light on the relative impact of a strengthening of Southern IPR protection on the Northern rate of innovation and the North–South flow of FDI since it says that while both the flow of FDI and the rate of innovation increase with a strengthening of Southern IPR protection, the positive effect on the flow of FDI is relatively stronger:

$$\mathrm{d}\left(\frac{\phi}{g}\right)\Big/\mathrm{d}k > 0.$$

Given that $n_{\mathrm{I}}/n_{\mathrm{M}}=\mu/g$ decreases with k, we can state the following result regarding the allocation of production within the South between multinationals and Southern firms:

PROPOSITION 4 (INTRA-REGIONAL ALLOCATION OF PRODUCTION). *A strengthening of Southern IPR protection increases the share of Southern production undertaken by Northern multinational firms:* $\mathrm{d}(n_{\mathrm{M}}/n_{\mathrm{S}})/\mathrm{d}k > 0$.

It is straightforward to show that the total value of multinational sales relative to those of Southern imitators has the following simple expression:

$$\frac{n_{\mathrm{M}} p^{\mathrm{M}} x^{\mathrm{M}}}{n_{\mathrm{I}} p^{\mathrm{S}} x^{\mathrm{S}}} = \alpha^{\varepsilon - 1} \frac{g}{\mu}.$$

Since the rate of innovation (g) increases while the rate of imitation (μ) falls with an increase in the degree of Southern IPR protection, we can state the following result:

COROLLARY 1. *A strengthening of Southern IPR protection leads to an increase in the aggregate sales of multinational firms relative to those of Southern imitators.*

Now consider a comparison of multinational sales relative to those of firms producing in the North:

$$\frac{n_{\mathrm{M}} p^{\mathrm{M}} x^{\mathrm{M}}}{n_{\mathrm{N}} p^{\mathrm{N}} x^{\mathrm{N}}} = \frac{\phi}{g}\left(\frac{\theta w^{\mathrm{S}}}{w^{\mathrm{N}}}\right)^{1-\varepsilon} = \frac{\phi}{g}\left(1 + \frac{\mu}{\rho + g}\right). \tag{36}$$

[20] Recall that international production shifting occurs only via FDI in our model. In this sense, a strengthening of Southern IPR protection acts very much like a pro-FDI policy. Indeed, it can be shown that if multinational profits are taxed then a reduction in that tax rate has qualitatively the same effects as a strengthening of Southern IPR protection.

Since $n_M/n_N = \phi/g$, (36) implies that a typical multinational must have higher relative sales compared to a Northern firm (i.e. the ratio $p^M x^M/p^N x^N$ must exceed 1). Intuitively, since imitation only targets multinational firms, for a typical multinational to earn the same rate of return as a Northern firm producing in the North, the multinational must have a higher relative profit flow. However, with a decline in the rate of imitation, this relative profit flow actually has to shrink in order to ensure multinationals and Northern firms earn the same rate of return. This yields:

COROLLARY 2. *A strengthening of Southern IPR protection decreases the sales of a typical multinational firm relative to those of a Northern firm.*

In this context, one further subtlety that arises from general equilibrium considerations is worth noting: an decrease in the rate of imitation μ increases the relative Southern wage and therefore the cost of production of multinationals relative to Northern firms. However, since prices of both types of firms are mark-ups over their respective marginal costs, this cost increase has a proportional effect on prices of multinationals relative to those of Northern firms. In other words, by increasing the South's relative wage, IPR reform increases the prices charged by multinationals relative to those of Northern firms and this translates into lower relative sales for a typical multinational.

2.4. *Real Wages and the Price Index*

What are the effects of a strengthening of IPR protection in the South on real wages in the two regions? By definition, the real wage effects of such a policy change depends upon nominal wages in the two regions and the prices of goods produced by three types of firm: firms located in the North, multinationals producing in the South and Southern imitators. Recall that

$$p^N = \frac{w^N}{\alpha}; \quad p^M = \frac{\theta w^S}{\alpha}; \quad \text{and} \quad p^S = \theta w^S,$$

which allows us to write Northern real wages in terms of the three types of goods:

$$\frac{w^N}{p^N} = \alpha; \quad \frac{w^N}{p^M} = \frac{\alpha}{\theta} w^R; \quad \frac{w^N}{p^S} = \frac{1}{\theta} w^R.$$

In other words, the Northern real wage in terms of goods produced by Northern firms is unaffected by Southern IPR protection whereas in terms of the other two goods, it moves in the same direction as the Northern relative wage w^R. We already know that Northern relative wage w^R decreases as a result a strengthening of Southern IPR protection since the rate of imitation μ falls while the rate of innovation g increases with such a policy change. This decline in the Northern relative wage w^R implies the following:

PROPOSITION 5. *A strengthening of Southern IPR protection decreases real wages in the North.*

An important implication of Propositions 1 and 5 is that from the perspective of the North, stronger Southern IPR enforcement in our model generates a classic trade-off between a static welfare loss and a dynamic welfare gain: the static loss being the decrease in real wages (or in its terms of trade since the relative price of Northern exports is determined by the relative wage) and the dynamic gain being the increase in the rate of innovation. What is noteworthy, however, is that the trade-off in the North results from changes in the IPR policy of the South.

Consider now the effect on Southern real wages. We have

$$\frac{w^S}{p^S}=\frac{1}{\theta};\quad \frac{w^S}{p^N}=\frac{\alpha}{w^R};\quad \text{and}\quad \frac{w^S}{p^M}=\frac{\alpha}{\theta}.$$

In other words, the only effect on Southern real wages of a change in its IPR policy is in terms of goods produced in the North. However, since w^R decreases with an increase in g and a decrease in μ, we can now state the following:

PROPOSITION 6. *A strengthening of Southern IPR protection increases real wages in the South.*[21]

The general equilibrium nature of the above result deserves emphasis. The typical argument in favour of weaker IPR protection in the South is that Southern imitation lowers prices and therefore benefits consumers. Since prices of Southern imitators are lower than those of Northern multinationals, this channel is operative in our model as well. However, the standard argument ignores the labour market effects of international production shifting that results from a reduction in the rate of imitation. In our model, a strengthening of Southern IPR protection leads to a higher Southern relative wage since the resulting decline in imitation risk makes the South a more attractive location for Northern multinationals. Indeed, changes in prices are dominated by the change in the Southern relative wage so that the purchasing power of Southern workers in terms of goods produced in the North increases whereas there is no change in their ability to purchase goods produced in the South. Thus, somewhat surprisingly and perhaps controversially, we find that a strengthening of IPR protection confers both a static benefit and a dynamic benefit on the South: real wages of its workers increase, as does the Northern rate of innovation.

As is clear from the discussion above, the real wage effects captured here would not arise in partial equilibrium models that ignore the labour market effects of IPRs. However, this point should not be over-emphasised. In our model, IPR reform in the South affects *all* goods produced in the world economy. In the real world, this is unlikely. A multi-sector model in which IPR reform affects only those sectors that invest in imitation may not necessarily yield the same results as Propositions 5 and 6. In particular, if Southern IPR reform only affects a few of the sectors, it may not necessarily allocate aggregate labour demand in favour of the South thereby increasing its relative wage.[22]

[21] As we discuss in greater detail below, it bears keeping in mind that despite an increase in real wages, Southern welfare does not necessarily increase because the flow of utility equals the log of real spending ($\log u = \log E - \log P$) and a reduction in profits of Southern imitators lowers Southern income and can adversely impact Southern spending.

[22] We should note, however, that the conflict created by technology transfer between the welfare of Northern and Southern workers that is a feature of our model also appears to arise in Cheng *et al.*'s (2005) North–South Ricardian model of trade and FDI where the global economy produces a continuum of goods.

Another qualification of our wage results deserves mention. Suppose both the North and the South have a multi-sector economy where one of the sectors is perfectly competitive in both the labour market and the product market (call it 'traditional') with no ongoing innovation while the other sector comprises of differentiated goods of the type considered here. Then, if under free trade both countries are diversified (i.e. produce the traditional good as well as some of the differentiated goods) the North–South relative wage would be pinned down by the North–South relative productivity in the traditional sector, much like in a classical Ricardian model. Under such a situation, IPR reform in the multi-sector model will fail to have an impact on the North–South relative wage so long as both regions remain diversified in production.

An important assumption underlying the wage results reported in Propositions 5 and 6 is that Northern firms that do not shift production to the South are immune from the risk of imitation. As we show in Section 4.1, when Northern firms can be imitated regardless of their location of production, whether or not these results continue to hold depends on how the imitation risk facing multinationals responds *relative* to that facing Northern producers when Southern IPR protection is strengthened.

It is useful to consider how a strengthening of Southern IPR protection affects the aggregate price index P. By definition,

$$P = \left[\int_0^n p(j)^{1-\varepsilon} \mathrm{d}j\right]^{\frac{1}{1-\varepsilon}},$$

which can be rewritten as

$$P = \left[n_{\mathrm{M}}(p^{\mathrm{M}})^{1-\varepsilon} + n_{\mathrm{I}}(p^{\mathrm{S}})^{1-\varepsilon} + n_{\mathrm{N}}(p^{\mathrm{N}})^{1-\varepsilon}\right]^{\frac{1}{1-\varepsilon}},$$

which is the same as

$$P = n^{\frac{1}{1-\varepsilon}}\left[\frac{n_{\mathrm{M}}}{n}(p^{\mathrm{M}})^{1-\varepsilon} + \frac{n_{\mathrm{I}}}{n}(p^{\mathrm{S}})^{1-\varepsilon} + \frac{n_{\mathrm{N}}}{n}(p^{\mathrm{N}})^{1-\varepsilon}\right]^{\frac{1}{1-\varepsilon}}.$$

While goods produced by multinationals are cheaper than those produced by Northern firms ($p^{\mathrm{M}} < p^{\mathrm{N}}$), it is the Southern imitators that produce the cheapest goods ($p^{\mathrm{S}} < p^{\mathrm{M}}$). Recall that $n_{\mathrm{I}}/n_{\mathrm{M}}=\mu/g$ decreases with the degree of Southern IPR protection (k) since imitation slows down while innovation increases. This implies that $n_{\mathrm{I}}/n/n_{\mathrm{M}}/n=\mu/g$ decreases with k, that is the share of global production that is in the hands of multinational firms increases. Furthermore, recall from Proposition 3 that a strengthening of Southern IPR protection shifts production away from the North and towards the South (*international reallocation*). Since $p^{\mathrm{M}} < p^{\mathrm{S}} < p^{\mathrm{N}}$, the international reallocation of production from North to the South helps lower prices. However, since $p^{\mathrm{M}} > p^{\mathrm{S}}$, the intra-regional reallocation of Southern production in favour of Northern multinationals and away from Southern imitators tends to increase prices. This implies that if the international reallocation of production is substantial, Southern imitation has the potential to partially benefit Northern consumers by lowering the aggregate price index P. Indeed, this is the key reason why Helpman (1993) finds that some amount of imitation is in the interest of the North.

However, in our model, since FDI also offers the potential for lowering prices, imitation is not as crucial for welfare purposes. This is worth explaining in some detail. Unlike us, Helpman (1993) assumes that the risk of imitation applies equally to Northern firms and multinationals. As a result, multinationals and Northern producers can coexist in equilibrium only if the two regions have equal wages.[23] Under such wage equalisation, FDI offers no reduction in costs of production and therefore has no price effects. By contrast, in our model, both FDI and imitation imply cost savings and the allocation of production across regions as well as within the South have implications for the aggregate price index.

A complete welfare analysis along the lines of Helpman (1993) is beyond the scope of this article due to the model's underlying complexity. To see why, consider the viewpoint of the South. First, as has already been noted, changes in Southern IPR protection have conflicting price effects in our model and the overall price index can move in either direction: international production shifting lowers prices while interregional production shifting raises them. Second, since Southern imitation yields profits, aggregate income (and therefore expenditure) in the South depends both on wages as well as profits, which moves in opposite directions due to a strengthening of Southern IPR protection. In particular, the decline in imitation reduces Southern profit income while it increases Northern profit income. Similarly, from the North's viewpoint, Southern IPR reform unleashes countervailing effects. Firm profitability clearly increases: not only does a typical multinational enjoy its profit stream for a longer duration, a greater share of Southern production comes to lie in the hands of multinationals. These forces tend to increase Northern income. However, this beneficial profit effect for the North is offset by the decrease in real wages of its workers. These complex set of interactions imply that our results regarding real wages are only one component of the calculus determining the global welfare impact of Southern IPR reform and should be interpreted as such.

3. Further Discussion of Results and Robustness

In this Section, we examine whether our results are robust to three important assumptions underlying our model.[24] This discussion also helps to shed further light on the real wage results reported in Propositions 4 and 5.

3.1. *Imitation of Northern Production*

Our model assumes that Southern imitation targets Northern multinationals so that any Northern firm that chooses not to shift production to the South is *immune* from the risk of imitation. This is a strong assumption, and it contrasts sharply with the assumption made in Grossman and Helpman (1991*b*), where *all* international technology transfer occurs via imitation of Northern goods and *none* via FDI. Our

[23] Our model would yield the same result if the rate of imitation facing multinationals and Northern producers were the same (i.e. $\mu = 0$) and multinationals did not face any frictions that hamper their ability to be as effective in production as local Southern firms (i.e. $\theta = 1$).

[24] We thank the editor and two anonymous referees for comments and suggestions that led to the analysis presented in this Section.

assumption reflects the influence of recent theoretical and empirical work stressing the importance of multinationals as a conduit for international knowledge flows.[25]

However, our theoretical results do not require that Southern firms be incapable of imitating Northern firms. The structure of our model implies that so long as imitating multinationals is even slightly cheaper than imitating firms producing in the North – a highly plausible scenario – no Southern imitator would choose to imitate a Northern firm. To see why, consider the profit flow earned by a firm that successfully imitates a Northern firm. Given the nature of consumer preferences, such an imitator would charge the same price as one that is successful in imitating a multinational, that is, the optimal price p^S. Given that both types of imitators produce in the South, the cost of production for both would be same and so would be the profit flow. This immediately implies that the lifetime discounted flow of profits of both types of imitators (post-imitation) would be equal. But if copying multinationals is even marginally cheaper, no rational Southern entrepreneur would choose to imitate a firm producing in the North since the rate of return on targeting a multinational would be higher.

Recent empirical evidence strongly supports the view that imitating multinationals ought to be easier than imitating firms located in the North. In surveying this evidence, we start with the point that multinational managers perceive themselves to be more vulnerable to imitation when they set up facilities abroad. This is shown in the work of Mansfield (1994) and Lee and Mansfield (1996), which uses survey evidence to measure US multinational managers' concerns about investing in countries with weak intellectual property rights. These perceptions are fully consistent with two decades of empirical research on international knowledge flows, nearly all of which shows that knowledge flows much more easily within countries than across national borders. This result was convincingly documented by Jaffe *et al.* (1993) and recently reaffirmed by Thomson and Fox-Kean (2005).

Precisely because knowledge flows are limited by geographical, cultural and linguistic distance, multinationals can play an important role in facilitating technology diffusion, both intentionally and unintentionally. Branstetter *et al.* (2006), Keller and Yeaple (2009) and Griffith *et al.* (2006) present evidence in favour of this view for advanced industrial economies, while Javorcik (2004*b*) and Blalock and Gertler (2008) present evidence from developing economies. Researchers have long suspected that the movement of workers from multinationals to local firms is an important channel of knowledge diffusion, and Gorg and Strobl (2005) and Hale and Long (2006) provide some early direct evidence in favor of this view. More recent evidence drawn from fairly rich data-sets that track the movement of individual workers across firms in developing countries also strongly supports this view; see Poole (2009) for a particularly intriguing example. Obviously, movement of workers is easier within than across countries, and this mechanism alone makes multinationals an easier target for would-be imitators.

[25] In this context, it is worth noting that Antràs (2005) has argued that primary factor behind the technological development of the electronics industry in some of the East Asian countries such as Taiwan and Korea was production shifting and technology transfer by multinationals as opposed to imitation by local companies of firms producing in other countries. In particular, he notes that 'the bulk of technology transfer is driven by the *voluntary* decisions of Northern firms, which choose to undertake offshore production within firm boundaries or transact with independent contractors or licensees'.

If multinationals really are more susceptible to imitation than Northern firms, then a significant strengthening of the Southern IPR protection is likely to induce more FDI, as foreign managers' concerns about imitation are assuaged. This implication is supported by recent empirical work. Branstetter *et al.* (2011) find evidence of an increase in FDI by US-based multinationals after the IPR regime is strengthened in 16 countries, most of which would be considered developing countries at the time of IPR reform. Ito and Wakasugi (2009) find evidence that Japanese multinationals respond to stronger IPR by increasing measured technology transfer and investment.

The strength of this evidence notwithstanding, for theoretical completeness, we can consider here what impact imitation of Northern firms might have on our model. Since there might be products for which imitating multinationals is not necessarily cheaper than imitating Northern firms, suppose the unit labour requirement in imitating Northern firms is the same as that for imitating multinationals (i.e. is given by a_I).[26] Under such a scenario, both types of imitation would occur in the South. Let μ^N denote the imitation risk facing Northern firms producing in the North and μ that facing Northern multinationals. This implies that the life-time value of a Northern firm would equal $v^N = \pi^N/(\rho+g+\mu^N)$ while that of a typical multinational would be the same as before: $v^M = \pi^M/(\rho+g+\mu)$. Since all Northern firms are free to become multinationals if they wish, we must have

$$v^N = v^M \Leftrightarrow \frac{\pi^N}{\rho+g+\mu^N} = \frac{\pi^M}{\rho+g+\mu}.$$

Using the definition of flow profits for each type of firm and cancelling terms, we can write

$$\frac{w^N x^N}{\rho+g+\mu^N} = \frac{\theta w^S x^M}{\rho+g+\mu},$$

which immediately gives

$$w^R = \theta\left(\frac{\rho+g+\mu}{\rho+g+\mu^N}\right)^{\frac{1}{\varepsilon-1}}. \tag{37}$$

Observe from the above equation that in the unlikely event where the risks of imitation facing multinationals and Northern producers are exactly equal, that is $\mu = \mu^N$, the Northern relative wage equals the relative productivity of Northern labour in production *vis-à-vis* Southern labour employed by multinationals (i.e. $w^R = \theta$). Under such a scenario, the North–South relative wage becomes unresponsive to Southern IPR protection. This, of course, implies that our results regarding the impact of Southern IPR protection on real wages in the two regions reported in Propositions 4 and 5 would not hold for the boundary case of $\mu = \mu^N$.

[26] Of course, if copying Northern firms were cheaper than copying Northern multinationals and all successful imitators charge the optimal price p^S, no imitation of multinationals would occur since all imitative activity in the South would target firms producing in the North. But, as we noted above, this is not a plausible scenario for a variety of reasons.

However, when $\mu \neq \mu^{\mathrm{N}}$, using the above formula for w^{R} we have,

$$\frac{\mathrm{d}\ln w^{\mathrm{R}}}{\mathrm{d}k} = \frac{1}{\varepsilon - 1}\left[\frac{1}{\rho + g + \mu}\frac{\mathrm{d}(\rho + g + \mu)}{\mathrm{d}k} - \frac{1}{\rho + g + \mu^{\mathrm{N}}}\frac{\mathrm{d}(\rho + g + \mu^{\mathrm{N}})}{\mathrm{d}k}\right],$$

which implies that

$$\frac{\mathrm{d}\ln w^{\mathrm{R}}}{\mathrm{d}k} < 0 \quad \text{iff} \quad g_k(\mu^{\mathrm{N}} - \mu) + \mu_k(\rho + g + \mu^{\mathrm{N}}) < \mu_k^{\mathrm{N}}(\rho + g + \mu),$$

where

$$g_k \equiv \frac{\mathrm{d}g}{\mathrm{d}k}; \quad \mu_k \equiv \frac{\mathrm{d}\mu}{\mathrm{d}k}; \quad \text{and} \quad \mu_k^{\mathrm{N}} \equiv \frac{\mathrm{d}\mu^{\mathrm{N}}}{\mathrm{d}k}.$$

Suppose both types of imitation decline with IPR protection (i.e. $\mu_k^{\mathrm{N}} < 0$ and $\mu_k < 0$) whereas innovation increases with it ($g_k > 0$). Then, if the risk faced by multinationals is no lower than that faced by Northern producers (i.e. $\mu^{\mathrm{N}} \leq \mu$), the relative Northern wage necessarily decreases with Southern IPR protection if

$$\mu_k < \mu_k^{\mathrm{N}}\frac{\rho + g + \mu}{\rho + g + \mu^{\mathrm{N}}} \quad \text{or} \quad |\mu_k| > |\mu_k^{\mathrm{N}}|\frac{\rho + g + \mu}{\rho + g + \mu^{\mathrm{N}}},$$

a condition which requires that the decline in the rate of imitation targeting multinationals ($|\mu_k|$) be sufficiently larger than that targeting firms producing in the North ($|\mu_k|$).

3.2. *Incomplete Knowledge Spillovers*

As in Grossman and Helpman (1991*b*) and Romer (1990), growth is driven in our model by the assumption that past innovations lower the cost of future innovations. Recall that the cost of product development is given by $(w^{\mathrm{N}}a_{\mathrm{N}})/n$ and it declines at the rate at which n increases. What if such knowledge spillovers are incomplete? To address this question, let the cost of product development be given by $(w^{\mathrm{N}}a_{\mathrm{N}})/(\lambda^{\mathrm{N}}n)$ where $0 < \lambda^{\mathrm{N}} \leq 1$ measures the degree to which the stock of knowledge created by past innovations helps lower the cost of current innovation. Similarly, let the cost of imitation be given by $(ka_{\mathrm{I}}w^{\mathrm{S}})/(\lambda^{\mathrm{S}}n_{\mathrm{S}})$ where $0 < \lambda^{\mathrm{S}} \leq 1$.

Does the dampening of spillovers effect the qualitative nature of our results? We argue below that it does not. Solving the model under these alternative assumptions modifies our three equilibrium conditions as follows. The flow of FDI is now given by

$$\phi = \frac{g}{\dfrac{\lambda^{\mathrm{S}}\theta^{\varepsilon}a_{\mathrm{N}}}{\lambda^{\mathrm{N}}A(\mu, g)ka_{\mathrm{I}}} - 1}, \tag{38}$$

while the Northern labour market equilibrium condition becomes

$$\frac{a_{\mathrm{N}}}{\lambda^{\mathrm{N}}}g + \frac{g}{g + \phi}\frac{a_{\mathrm{N}}\alpha(\rho + g)}{\lambda^{\mathrm{N}}(1 - \alpha)} = L^{\mathrm{N}}. \tag{39}$$

Finally, in the South we have

$$\frac{ka_I}{\lambda^S}\frac{g\mu}{g+\mu}+\frac{ka_I}{\lambda^S}\frac{\theta\alpha(\rho+g)}{\theta^{\varepsilon}(1-\alpha)}\frac{g}{g+\mu}+\frac{ka_I}{\lambda^S}\frac{\alpha(\rho+g)}{1-\alpha}\frac{\mu}{g+\mu}=L^S. \tag{40}$$

A few points are worth noting. First, note from (38) that if the degree of spillovers is equally incomplete in both regions (i.e. $\lambda^S = \lambda^N$), the North–South flow of FDI is the same as that our core model. Second, as expected, the dampening of spillovers reduces the productivity of the two types of investment activities in our model (i.e. imitation and innovation). Indeed, this can be observed immediately from the modified labour market equilibrium conditions (39) and (40): a decrease in λ^S is akin to a shrinkage of the Southern resource base L^S while a decrease in λ^N has the same effect on the Northern resource base L^N. This in turn implies that the *level* of imitative activity that can go on in the South and the *level* of innovation that can be supported in the North would be lower when spillovers are incomplete. However, it is worth noting that all of our Propositions would continue to hold since these do not depend on the absolute levels of g and μ but rather on how these variables respond to changes in the underlying degree of Southern IPR protection.

3.3. *If Imitated Goods are Sold Only in the South*

For simplicity, our model assumes that all goods are sold in both markets. However, it be more realistic to assume that imitated goods are sold only in the South. How do our results change if we adopt this alternative formulation? Suppose the share of product market profits that a typical imitator collects from its sales in the Southern market is given by β where $0 < \beta < 1$. Then, the reward to a successful imitator $\pi^S(\beta) = (p^S - w^S)\beta x^S = [(1-\alpha)\beta w^S x^S]/\alpha$. Note that $\pi^S(\beta) = \beta\pi^S$ and since profits are linear in sales, such an export restriction scales down the reward from imitation. As might be expected, its basic effect is to reduce the incentive to imitate. However, since the mechanics of our model depend on how imitation and innovation respond to IPR protection and not on their absolute levels, the qualitative nature of our results remains unchanged. To see this clearly, first note that the relative wage equation (21) as well as equation (35) which determines the North–South flow of FDI remain unchanged. However, the equality between cost of imitation and the value of a successful imitator implies that we must have

$$x^S(\beta)=\frac{\alpha}{1-\alpha}\frac{ka_I(\rho+g)}{\beta n_S}=\frac{x^S}{\beta}.$$

Since $\beta < 1$, the above implies that, all else equal, Southern imitators must have higher sales in the South to cover their costs of imitation if they are unable to export to the Northern market. Similarly, we have $x^M(\beta) = (x^M)/\beta$. As a result, the Southern labour market equilibrium condition now becomes

$$\frac{ka_I g\mu}{g+\mu}+\frac{ka_I}{\beta}\frac{\theta\alpha(\rho+g)}{\theta^{\varepsilon}(1-\alpha)}\frac{g}{g+\mu}+\frac{ka_I}{\beta}\frac{\alpha(\rho+g)}{1-\alpha}\frac{\mu}{g+\mu}=L^S.$$

Intuitively, since sales levels are now higher in the South, more of the Southern labour gets allocated to production by Southern imitators and Northern multinationals, leaving less of it available for allocation to imitation which reduces the rate of imitation relative to before. However, as is evident from the above discussion, the basic mechanics determining the effects of Southern IPR reform remain unaltered when Southern firms cannot export their imitated goods to the North.

4. Conclusion

Opinions regarding the strengthening of IPR regimes in developing countries required under the TRIPS agreement of the WTO vary remarkably across individuals and nations. While the issue is multi-faceted and complex, the following statement broadly captures the disparity in views regarding TRIPs: developing countries have tended to argue that stronger IPR regimes in their markets will have adverse effects on prices without having much of a positive impact on innovation whereas developed countries have stressed that not only innovation but also FDI flows would respond strongly to such reforms. In principle, an increase in FDI has the potential to offer two major sources of welfare gains. One, it can lower prices by shifting production to lower cost locations. Two, FDI has the potential to encourage Southern industrial development by introducing new technologies into the South. In this article, we present a general equilibrium North–South product cycle model with a degree of endogenity that allows us to assess these arguments in a unified framework.

Our major results are as follows. First, we find that a strengthening of IPR protection in the South fosters innovation whereas it discourages imitation. Second, it increases FDI to a degree that the Southern production base actually expands – that is, the decline in Southern imitative activity is more than offset by the increase in the production activity of Northern multinationals who are drawn to the South because local IPR reform renders it a more attractive production location by reducing the risk of imitation. Third, while prices of those goods that are reallocated from firms producing in the North to multinationals fall, prices of goods that are reallocated from potential imitators to Northern multinationals increase. In other words, IPR reform in the South has conflicting effects on consumer welfare when viewed solely through the price channel. However, what actually matters for consumer welfare is purchasing power. And from this viewpoint, Southern IPR reform benefits the South since it increases not only the South's wage relative to the North but also the purchasing power of Southern consumers. By contrast, not only does the Northern relative wage decline, the real income of Northern workers also falters. It is worth emphasising that only a general equilibrium model such as ours can help to assess the full impact of the price changes that result from IPR reform since these can be offset (or be dominated) by the accompanying changes in wages. Finally, we should note that while the model's richness makes it difficult to provide a full-fledged welfare analysis along the lines of Helpman (1993), we hope that the clarity with which the various channels that affect welfare emerge in the model sheds new light on a rather complex set of issues.

Appendix A. Mathematical Appendix

A.1. *Slope of NN Curve*

We already noted in the main text that $\partial L^{N}(\mu,g)/\partial\mu > 0$. Direct calculations yield

$$\frac{\partial L^{N}(\mu,g)}{\partial g}=\frac{\theta^{\varepsilon}(\rho+\mu+g)a_{N}-a_{I}A(\mu,g)[\alpha(\rho+\mu+g)-\mu]}{(\rho+\mu+g)(1-\alpha)\theta^{\varepsilon}}.$$

From where it follows that a sufficient condition for $\partial L^{N}(\mu,g)/\partial g > 0$ is that $a_{N}/a_{I} > 1+\alpha/\theta^{\varepsilon}$. This is because $(\rho + g)[\theta^{\varepsilon}a_{N}-\alpha a_{I}A(\mu,g)] > 0$ due to the fact that $A(\mu,g) < 1$, $\alpha < 1$, $a_{N} \geq a_{I}$ and $\theta^{\varepsilon} > 1$. Next note that the condition $a_{N}/a_{I} > 1+\alpha/\theta^{\varepsilon}$ is satisfied for all feasible parameter values: since $a_{N} \geq a_{I}$, at the lowest feasible value of a_{N} this condition becomes $\theta^{\varepsilon} > 1 + \alpha$ which necessarily holds since $\theta > 1/\alpha$.

A.2. *Horizontal Intercepts*

It is trivial to observe that neither curve can intersect the vertical axis since labour demand in each country approaches zero as the growth rate approaches zero. The *NN* curve intersects the horizontal axes at g^{n} where

$$g^{n}\equiv\frac{\theta^{\varepsilon}L^{N}(1-\alpha)-\alpha\rho(a_{N}\theta^{\varepsilon}-a_{I})}{a_{N}\theta^{\varepsilon}-\alpha a_{I}}.$$

Similarly, the *SS* curve intersects the horizontal axis at g^{s} where

$$g^{s}\equiv\frac{L^{S}(1-\alpha)\theta^{\varepsilon}-\alpha\theta a_{I}\rho}{\theta a_{I}\rho}.$$

From where it follows that

$$g^{s} > g^{n} \quad \text{iff} \quad L^{S} > \overline{L^{S}} \quad \text{where} \quad \overline{L^{S}}\equiv\frac{(L^{N}+\rho a_{N})\alpha\theta a_{I}}{\theta^{\varepsilon}a_{N}-\alpha a_{I}}$$

We assume that $L^{S} > \overline{L^{S}}$.

Carnegie Mellon University
Columbia University
Harvard University
Vanderbilt University

Submitted: 13 July 2009
Accepted: 12 November 2010

References

Antràs, P. (2005). 'Incomplete contracts and the product cycle', *American Economic Review*, vol. 95(4), pp. 1054–73.

Blalock, G. and Gertler, P. (2008). 'Welfare gains from foreign direct investment through technology transfer to local suppliers', *Journal of International Economics*, vol. 74(2), pp. 402–21.

Branstetter, L., Fisman, R. and Foley, F. (2006). 'Does stronger intellectual property rights increase international technology transfer? Empirical evidence from U.S. firm-level data', *Quarterly Journal of Economics*, vol. 121(1), pp. 321–49.

Branstetter, L., Fisman, R., Foley, F. and Saggi, K. (2007). 'Intellectual property rights, imitation, and foreign direct investment: theory and evidence', NBER Working Paper No. 13033.

Branstetter, L., Fisman, R., Foley, F. and Saggi, K. (2011). 'Does intellectual property rights reform sp industrial development?', *Journal of International Economics*, vol. 38, pp. 27–36.

Chaudhuri, S., Goldberg, P. and Jia, P. (2006). 'Estimating the effects of global patent protection in ph maceuticals: a case study of quinolones in India'. American Economic Review, .vol. 96(5), pp. 1477–5

Chen, Y. and Puttitanun, T. (2005). 'Intellectual property rights and innovation in developing countri *Journal of Development Economics*, vol. 78(2), pp. 474–93.

Cheng, L.K, Qiu, L. and Tan, G. (2005). 'Foreign direct investment and international trade in a continu Ricardian model', *Journal of Development Economics*, vol. 77(2), pp. 477–501.

Dixit, A. and Stiglitz, J. (1977). 'Monopolistic competition and optimum product diversity', *American Econo Review*, vol. 67(3), pp. 297–308.

Feenstra, R. and Rose, A. (2000). 'Putting things in order', *Review of Economics and Statistics*, vol. 82(3), pp. 36 82.

Glass, A.J. and Saggi, K. (2002). 'Intellectual property rights and foreign direct investment', *Journal of In national Economics*, vol. 56(2), pp. 387–410.

Glass, A.J. and Wu, X. (2007). 'Intellectual property rights and quality improvement', *Journal of Developm Economics*, vol. 82(2), pp. 393–415.

Gorg, H. and Strobl, E. (2005). 'Spillovers from foreign firms through worker mobility', *Scandinavian Journa Economics*, vol. 107(4), pp. 693–709.

Griffith, R., Harrison, R. and Van Reenen, J. (2006). 'How special is the special relationship? Using the imp of U.S. R&D spillovers on British firms as a test of technology sourcing', *American Economic Review*, v 96(5), pp. 1859–75.

Grossman, G.M. and Helpman, E. (1991*a*). *Innovation and Growth in the Global Economy*, Cambridge: MIT pre

Grossman, G.M. and Helpman, E. (1991*b*). 'Endogenous product cycles', ECONOMIC JOURNAL, vol. 101(pp. 1214–29.

Hale, G. and Long, C. (2006). 'What determines technological spillovers of foreign direct investment: e dence from China', Discussion Paper no. 934, Economic Growth Center, Yale University.

He, Y. and Maskus, K. (forthcoming). 'Southern innovation and backward knowledge spillovers: a dynan model', *International Economic Review*.

Helpman, E. (1993). 'Innovation, imitation, and intellectual property rights', *Econometrica*, vol. 61(6), p 1247–80.

Ito, B. and Wakasugi, R. (2009). 'The effects of stronger intellectual property rights on technology transf evidence from Japanese firm-level data', *Journal of Technology Transfer*, vol. 34(2), pp. 145–58.

Jaffe, A., Trajtenberg, M. and Henderson, R. (1993). 'Geographic localization of knowledge spillovers evidenced by patent citations', *Quarterly Journal of Economics*, vol. 434, pp. 578–98.

Javorcik, B. (2004*a*). 'The composition of foreign direct investment and protection of intellectual prope rights in transition economies', *European Economic Review*, vol. 48(1), pp. 39–62.

Javorcik, B. (2004*b*). 'Does foreign direct investment increase the productivity of domestic firms? In search spillovers through backward linkages', *American Economic Review*, vol. 94(3), pp. 605–27.

Keller, W. and Yeaple, S. (2009). 'Multinational enterprises, international trade, and technology differences firm-level analysis of the productivity effects of foreign competition in the United States', *Review Economics and Statistics*, vol. 91(4), pp. 821–31.

Krugman, P.R. (1979). 'A model of innovation, technology transfer and the world distribution of incom *Journal of Political Economy*, vol. 87(2), pp. 253–66.

Lai, E. (1998). 'International intellectual property rights protection and the rate of product innovatio *Journal of Development Economics*, vol. 55(1), pp. 133–53.

Lee, J.-Y. and Mansfield, E. (1996). 'Intellectual property protection and U.S. foreign direct investme *Review of Economics and Statistics*, vol. 78(2), pp. 181–86.

Mansfield, E. (1994). 'Intellectual property protection, foreign direct investment, and technology transf Discussion Paper 19, International Finance Corporation, Washington, DC.

Markusen, J.R. (1995). 'The boundaries of multinational enterprises and the theory of international trad *Journal of Economic Perspectives*, vol. 9(2), pp. 169–90.

Maskus, K.E. (2000). *Intellectual property rights in the global economy*, Washington, DC: Institute for Internatio Economics.

Maskus, K.E. and McDaniel, C. (1999). 'Impacts of the Japanese patent system on productivity growth', *Jap and the World Economy*, vol. 11(4), pp. 557–74.

Mayer, T. and Pfister, E. (2001). 'Do stronger patent rights attract foreign direct investment? Evidence fr French multinationals' location', *Région et Développment*, vol. 13, pp. 99–122.

McCalman, P. (2001). 'Reaping what you sow: an empirical analysis of international patent harmonizatio *Journal of International Economics*, vol. 55(1), pp. 161–86.

Nunnenkamp, P. and Spatz, J. (2004). 'Intellectual property rights and foreign direct investment: a dis gregated analysis', *Weltwirtschaftliches Archiv (Review of World Economics)*, vol. 140(3), pp. 393–414.

Ordover, J. (1991). 'Patent system for both diffusion and exclusion', *Journal of Economic Perspectives*, vol. 5(pp. 43–60.

Park, W. (2008). 'Intellectual property rights and international innovation', in (K. Maskus, ed.), *Frontiers of Economics and Globalization: Intellectual Property Rights and Globalization*, pp. 289–327, Amsterdam: Elsevier.

Poole, J. (2009). 'Knowledge transfers from multinationals to domestic firms: evidence from worker mobility', Working Paper, UC-Santa Cruz.

Romer, P. (1990). 'Endogenous technical change', *Journal of Political Economy*, vol. 98(5), pp. S71–S102.

Romer, P. (1993). 'Idea gaps and object gaps in economic Development', *Journal of Monetary Economics*, vol. 32(3), pp. 543–73.

Taylor, S. M. (1994). 'TRIPS, trade, and growth', *International Economic Review*, vol. 35, pp. 361–81.

Thompson, P. and Fox-Kean, M. (2005). 'Patent citations and the geography of knowledge spillovers: a reassessment', *American Economic Review*, vol. 95(1), pp. 450–60.

Westphal, L.E., Kim, L. and Dahlman, C.J. (1985). 'Reflections on the Republic of Korea's acquisition of technological capability', in (N. Rosenberg and C. Frischtak, eds.), *International Transfer of Technology: Concepts, Measures, and Comparisons*, pp. 167–221, New York: Praeger Press.

Chapter 13

Does intellectual property rights reform spur industrial development?[☆,#]

Lee Branstetter[a,e,*], Ray Fisman[b,e,1], C. Fritz Foley[c,e,2], Kamal Saggi[d,3]

[a] Carnegie Mellon University, H. John Heinz III College, School of Public Policy and Management, and Department of Social and Decision Sciences, 5000 Forbes Avenue, Pittsburgh, PA 15213, United States
[b] Columbia University, Columbia Business School, 3022 Broadway, Uris Hall 622, New York, NY 10027, United States
[c] Harvard University, Harvard Business School, Soldiers Field Road, Boston, MA 02163, United States
[d] Vanderbilt University, VU Station B #351828, 2301 Vanderbilt Place, Nashville, TN 37235, United States
[e] NBER, United States

ARTICLE INFO

Article history:
Received 2 September 2008
Received in revised form 1 September 2010
Accepted 2 September 2010
Available online 15 September 2010

JEL classification:
F2
F1
K11
O3

Keywords:
Intellectual property rights
Multinational enterprises
Foreign direct investment
Industrial development
Production shifting

ABSTRACT

An extensive theoretical literature generates ambiguous predictions concerning the effects of intellectual property rights (IPR) reform on industrial development. The impact depends on whether multinational enterprises (MNEs) expand production in reforming countries and the extent of decline in imitative activity. We examine the responses of U.S.-based MNEs and domestic industrial production to a set of intellectual property rights reforms in the 1980s and 1990s. Following reform, MNEs expand the scale of their activities. MNEs that make extensive use of intellectual property disproportionately increase their use of inputs. There is an overall expansion of industrial activity after reform, and highly disaggregated trade data indicate higher exports of new goods. These results suggest that the expansion of multinational activity more than offsets any decline in imitative activity.

1. Introduction

Do stronger intellectual property rights (IPR) spur industrial development? Over the last two and a half decades, policy makers have debated the benefits of IPR reform.[4] One of the central concerns raised in these debates is that stronger IPR would curtail the ability of local firms to imitate and build on the advanced technologies of foreign firms, potentially slowing economic progress. This was a common concern in the discussions of the 1995 Agreement on Trade Related Aspects of Intellectual Property Rights (TRIPS) that required members of the World Trade Organization to comply with a set of minimum standards of IPR.[5] However, these costs could be partially offset by benefits that arise from increased investment and production by multinational enterprises (MNEs). Stronger IPR could induce MNEs to expand their scale of operations, manufacture technologically sophisticated goods, and quicken the rate of shifting production of existing goods to IPR-reforming countries. In this paper, we empirically assess the effects of stronger IPR on industrial development.

Our work is motivated by a rich theoretical literature on the global effects of IPR reform. Helpman (1993) develops several variants of a North–South general equilibrium product cycle model in which Northern innovation expands the range of differentiated goods produced in the world while Southern imitation leads to North–South production shifting. A robust finding of this analysis is that stronger IPR protection is never in the interest of the South. If stronger IPR in the

☆ The statistical analysis of firm-level data on U.S. multinational enterprises was conducted at the Bureau of Economic Analysis, U.S. Department of Commerce, under arrangements that maintain legal confidentiality arrangements. The views expressed herein are those of the authors and do not reflect the official positions of the U.S. Department of Commerce.

* Corresponding author. Tel.: +1 412 268 4649.
E-mail addresses: branstet@andrew.cmu.edu (L. Branstetter), rf250@columbia.edu (R. Fisman), ffoley@hbs.edu (C.F. Foley), k.saggi@Vanderbilt.edu (K. Saggi).
[1] Tel.: +1 212 854 9157.
[2] Tel.: +1 617 495 6375.
[3] Tel.: +1 615 322 3237.

[4] An excellent overview of the debate is provided in Maskus (2000).

[5] Another major area of concern focused on the high prices firms might be able to charge for patent-protected goods under strong IPR. The impact of IPR reform on prices and consumer welfare has been the focus of an extensive literature. See, for example, Maskus (2000), McCalman (2001), and Chaudhuri et al. (2006). In contrast, relatively little empirical work has focused on the potential impact of IPR reform on industrial development.

[#] This chapter was originally appeared in *Journal of International Economics* **83**, 27–36. © 2010 Elsevier B.V.

South is treated as a reduction in the rate of Southern imitation and Northern firms are assumed to not shift production to the South through foreign direct investment (FDI), Southern IPR reform lowers the rate of Northern innovation and thereby limits the portfolio of products available globally. [6] If North–South FDI is permitted, a reduction in Southern imitation leads to more FDI but hurts the South because Northern multinationals charge higher prices than Southern imitators.

Lai (1998) extends Helpman (1993) to allow both the level of FDI and Northern innovation to respond endogenously to changes in the strength of Southern IPR protection, and this model is further extended in Branstetter et al. (2007), to the case where innovation, FDI, and imitation are all endogenously determined. In these extensions, unlike Helpman (1993), in any equilibrium with a positive rate of imitation, North–South FDI does not lead to factor price equalization. A lower wage in the South creates an incentive to move production of existing varieties there, but multinationals seeking to benefit from this incur a higher risk of imitation when they move production to the South. In Branstetter et al. (2007), as in Grossman and Helpman (1991a), imitation is a costly activity that requires a deliberate investment on the part of Southern firms seeking to copy Northern products. Stronger IPR protection in the South increases these costs, reducing imitation and lowering the risks faced by multinationals. Multinationals that move to the South employ the labor resources freed up by the decline in imitative activity. Production shifting allows for a reallocation of Northern resources towards innovative activity. Under certain parameter assumptions, a strengthening of Southern IPR protection enhances Southern industrial development because the increase in North–South FDI more than offsets the decrease in Southern imitation.

We test three hypotheses that follow from this theory. First, using detailed data on U.S. MNE activity, we seek to determine whether multinational firms respond to reforms by increasing production in reforming countries. Second, we use industry-level data to test whether growth in production by MNEs and local firms that are not engaging in imitation exceeds the decline in imitative activity. Finally, we look for evidence that the production of new goods shifts to reforming countries by analyzing initial export episodes that are identified in disaggregated U.S. trade statistics.

In our analyses, we focus on the effects of well-documented discrete changes in patent regimes over the 1980s and 1990s. We follow Branstetter et al. (2006), which assemble a set of substantive IPR reforms based on a number of primary and secondary sources. These are listed in Table 1.[7] Our approach of analyzing responses to well-defined IPR changes has the advantage that we may use fixed effects to control for features of the business environment in a country that are constant, that are hard to measure, that are correlated with the strength of IPR in the country cross-section, and that may affect firm behavior and industrial development in a manner similar to IPR.[8] We provide a more detailed discussion of these reforms below.

While we employ some of the same data as Branstetter et al. (2006), in this paper our goal is to formulate a broader assessment of the impact of IPR reform on the level and nature of industrial development in reforming countries, whereas this earlier work focused solely on technology transfers within U.S. multinationals. We find that U.S.-based multinationals expand the scale of their activities in reforming countries after IPR reform along multiple dimensions. Affiliates increase their assets, net property, plant and equipment (net PPE), employment compensation, transfer of technology from abroad, and research and development (R&D) expenditures. These increases are particularly large for firms that are especially likely to value reforms in the sense that they, prior to reforms, deploy high levels of technology abroad.[9] This evidence is consistent with U.S. multinationals shifting production of more technologically intensive goods to affiliates in response to reforms.

We further assess the impact of IPR reform on overall industrial activity. Our results indicate that industry-level value added increases after reforms and that this effect is concentrated in technology-intensive industries and in industries where MNE activity is concentrated. These findings suggest that declines in imitative local activity are offset by increases in the activity of multinationals and other firms that are not engaging in imitative activity. Although the theory described above stresses the direct role of changes in MNE activity, a large body of empirical work indicates that MNE expansion could generate indirect benefits for the host country by fostering the growth of local input suppliers, as in Javorcik (2004a), and by transferring advanced knowledge and skills to the local workforce, as in Poole (2009). IPR reform appears to lead to an overall enhancement of Southern industrial development.

We obtain further suggestive evidence on the rate at which production is transferred to reforming countries by analyzing disaggregated U.S. trade statistics. Following Feenstra and Rose (2000), we construct for each reforming country an annual count of initial export episodes, defined as the number of 10-digit commodities for which recorded U.S. imports from a given country exceed zero for the first time in our data. This measure increases sharply after IPR reform, suggesting that any decline in indigenous innovation is more than offset by an expanded range of goods being produced by MNEs and other firms. Again, the evidence suggests that IPR reform enhances, rather than retards, Southern industrial development.

The rest of the paper is organized as follows. Section 2 briefly discusses the sample of IPR reforms we study. Section 3 describes our data on U.S. multinational affiliates and parents and presents

Table 1
Timing of major patent reforms.

Country	Year of reform
Argentina	1996
Brazil	1997
Chile	1991
China	1993
Colombia	1994
Indonesia	1991
Japan	1987
Mexico	1991
Philippines	1997
Portugal	1992
South Korea	1987
Spain	1986
Taiwan	1986
Thailand	1992
Turkey	1995
Venezuela	1994

Notes: this table provides information about the timing of reforms in the countries that strengthen their intellectual property rights and are included in the sample.

[6] Glass and Saggi (2002) obtain a result similar to that of Helpman (1993). See also Markusen (2001).

[7] We include patent reforms in Japan in our sample even though it is a high income country, and it may not therefore be relevant to the models in which a Southern country reforms its IPR. Many students of the Japanese economy have pointed to the existence of a dual economy in Japan, with some industries achieving extremely high levels of productivity relative to the U.S. and other lagging far behind the U.S. productivity frontier. Given the substantial relative productivity lags that existed in some sectors, particularly at the beginning of our sample, we incorporate data from Japan in the empirical analyses described below. See McKinsey Global Institute (2000) and Porter et al. (2000) for discussions of these issues.

[8] While the 16 countries in our sample are quite heterogeneous in terms of their income, location, and industrial development at the time of reform, we recognize the need to exercise caution in extrapolating these results to countries outside the sample.

[9] The results on technology transfer and research and development expenditure are similar to those presented in Branstetter et al. (2006). We report them here to illustrate that, as the scale of MNE activity expands in IPR-reforming countries, it also becomes more technology-intensive.

empirical tests and results based on these data. Section 4 characterizes data from United Nations Industrial Development Organization databases and presents empirical tests and results based on these data. Section 5 describes the disaggregated U.S. import statistics and presents tests and results based on these data. Section 6 concludes.

2. Patent reforms

Our sample of IPR reforms includes the 16 patent reform episodes identified in Branstetter et al. (2006) and listed in Table 1. These include changes in IPR that occurred between 1982 and 1999 and that occurred in countries where there was a substantial amount of U.S. MNE affiliate activity prior to reform.[10] Each reform can be classified according to whether or not it expanded or strengthened patent rights along five dimensions: 1) an expansion in the range of goods eligible for patent protection, 2) an expansion in the effective scope of patent protection, 3) an increase in the length of patent protection, 4) an improvement in the enforcement of patent rights, and 5) an improvement in the administration of the patent system. There is a surprising degree of similarity in these reforms, with 15 out of 16 exhibiting expansion of patent rights along at least 4 of these 5 dimensions. These substantive reforms could have a material impact on industrial development and are therefore well-suited to our empirical approach. A detailed discussion of the individual patent reform episodes, their distinctive characteristics, and their common features, is provided in the Appendix to Branstetter et al. (2006), particularly Sections A.2 and A.3.

This sample of 16 patent reform episodes does not include all episodes that take place over our sample period. To address the concern that our results depend on the reforms in the sample, we conduct robustness tests in which we augment our sample of reforms to include data on reforms in Austria (1984), Canada (1987), Denmark (1983), Ecuador (1996), Finland (1995), Greece (1992), Norway (1992), and Panama (1996). These reform episodes and dates are taken from Qian (2007), but they seem to be less substantive than the reforms we study. The reforms in Austria, Canada, Finland, Greece, and Norway consisted primarily of changes in the patent law's treatment of pharmaceutical products, and changes occurred in a context where national health insurance systems effectively set drug prices at the national level and limited the impact of intellectual property rights protection in this industry.[11] The *National Trade Estimate Reports on Foreign Trade Barriers* published by the United States Trade Representative after the patent reforms in Panama and Ecuador calls into question the effectiveness of enforcement of the legal changes and provides an interpretation of the timing of reform in Ecuador that differs from Qian (2007). Finally, direct communication with the Danish Patent Office suggested that the reforms of 1983 were quite minor and narrow in focus.[12] Nevertheless, in robustness checks below, we expand our set of reforms to include these countries, and their inclusion does not qualitatively affect our results.

In assigning dates to patent reform, we followed prior research like Maskus (2000) and Qian (2007), who have identified a key stage in the patent reform process that marked a clear shift in the trajectory of policy. We went to the original source documents consulted by Maskus (2000), discussed these reforms with multinational managers, and also sought the input of country-based experts in the details of local intellectual property law. This process led us to choose a date of reform that varied from the date identified in prior research like Maskus (2000) for Japan, Taiwan, and Brazil, and we checked the robustness of our results by using the alternative dates identified in prior research. Our main empirical results are not sensitive to these changes.

3. Multinational firm responses

3.1. Empirical specification

In assessing whether stronger IPR induces an expansion of multinational activity, we take a difference-in-differences approach. Individual affiliates are followed through time, and the basic specification tests how MNE activity changes around the time of reform, controlling for country, parent firm, and affiliate characteristics that might impact the variables of interest. The basic specification takes the form:

$$S_{ilt} = \alpha_0 + \alpha_{il} + \alpha_t + \beta_0 y_{jt} + \beta_1 P_{it} + \beta_2 H_{jt} + \beta_3 R_{jt} + \beta_4 R_{jt}{}^* \text{Tech}_{il} + \varepsilon_{it} \quad (1)$$

where l indexes the individual affiliate, i the affiliate's parent firm, j the affiliate's host country, and t the year.

Several measures of the scale of multinational activity serve as dependent variables. Taken literally, the theoretical models discussed in Section 1 define the scale of multinational activity as the number of distinct products for which production has shifted to the South. While our data on multinational activity are at the affiliate level, they do not include product-level data. Hence, our data are not sufficiently disaggregated to measure production so defined. However, by measuring the response of multinational affiliates to IPR reform along a number of dimensions, we look for evidence of a change in the scale of affiliate production, which is likely correlated with the notion of production shifting that is analyzed in theoretical work.

Using sales to measure changes in the scale of multinational operations after IPR reform creates serious problems of inference. Affiliate sales increase by about 18% following reform, but this increase could reflect an increase in market power resulting from IPR reform rather than production shifting. The extensive literature on the imperfect correspondence between accounting measures of profit and economic concepts of profit suggests that there is little we can do to get around this. We tracked the ratio of sales to employee compensation as one rough measure of markups and found no evidence that this measure increases after reform.[13] While reassuring, this does not conclusively prove the absence of any contamination of our sales data by changes in profitability.[14] As a consequence, we focus on measures of affiliate inputs rather than measures of sales.

We use measures of an affiliate's assets and net PPE as proxies for the scale of physical capital. In the theoretical literature discussed in Section 1, labor is the only factor of production, so it would naturally increase as a result of reform. In practice, production shifting of more technologically sophisticated goods might have a relatively modest effect on the overall size of the workforce and much more of an impact on its composition; the firm might change the skill mix of its affiliate

[10] These time constraints imply that we do not evaluate Indian patent reform. While it ratified the TRIPs Agreement in 1995, India delayed the final approval of a TRIPs-consistent patent law until 2005 and put off even the first major step toward patent reform until 1999, the final year of our sample period.

[11] Canada's reform, reviewed in detail by McFetridge (1997), also applied to foodstuffs, and we account for this in our robustness checks.

[12] We thank Annette Zerrahn of the Danish Patent Office for providing her insights. Ms. Zerrahn explained that the changes amounted to an adjustment of the fee structure in Danish patent law and the ratification of the Budapest Treaty regarding deposit of micro-organisms for examination.

[13] We thank an anonymous referee for suggesting this test.

[14] This is only one of the many concerns around the use of sales data. Short run fluctuations in sales could also be driven by demand shocks that are temporally correlated with the IPR regime change but conceptually distinct from it. In our input data, we see evidence consistent with the view that firms gradually expand their capital stock and increase the technological intensity of their activities in IPR-reforming countries. Sales changes driven by this response to IPR reform would likely emerge with a lag. Given the paucity of post reform observations for many of our reforming countries, our ability to quantify these shifts convincingly is limited.

workforce, hiring more managers and engineers. We therefore analyze data on total employment compensation. This variable should capture changes in the size of the workforce as well as shifts in its skill composition.

The production of more sophisticated products in reforming countries would likely require an increase in the use of the parent firm's technology. Following Branstetter et al. (2006), we use affiliate level data on the volume of intrafirm royalty payments for intangible assets to track changes in the licensing of technology from the parent.[15] If IPR reform induces firms to shift production of more technologically intensive products to affiliates in reforming countries, we would expect to see those payments increase relative to affiliate sales.[16]

Finally, the inception of production of more technologically intensive products should be associated with an increase in affiliate level R&D spending. While U.S. MNEs undertake basic and applied research abroad, the R&D conducted by affiliates in developing countries, which account for most of the countries in our sample, is focused on the modification of parent firm technology for local markets, as explained in Kuemmerle (1999) and other work. Thus, affiliate R&D and technology transfers from the parent should be considered complements, implying that R&D spending should increase as a result of IPR reform. Branstetter et al. (2006) also present results of tests analyzing the impact of IPR regime changes on affiliate R&D.

The key variables of interest are the Post Reform Dummy variable R_{jt}, and the interaction $R_{jt}*Tech_{il}$ that allows estimates of an affiliate's response to patent reform to differ for firms that extensively deploy intellectual property in non-reforming countries around the world prior to reforms. The High Technology Transfer Dummy, $Tech_{il}$, is generated as follows: affiliates of parents that, over the four years prior to a particular reform, receive at least as much technology licensing income from affiliates outside the reforming countries as the parent of the median affiliate in the reforming country over the same period are assigned a dummy equal to one. For the other half of the sample, $Tech_{il}$ equals zero. This dummy variable thus captures the relative propensity of different parent firms to both create intellectual property and deploy it outside the home country.[17] By comparing the responsiveness of this subset of firms where we expect a disproportionate impact of IPR reforms, we can better discriminate between the view that IPR reform leads to greater production shifting and alternative interpretations of our results.[18]

We include a number of controls. α_{il} are time-invariant fixed effects for the affiliate, α_t are year fixed effects for the entire sample, and y_{jt} are country-specific linear time trends. P_{it} and H_{jt} are vectors of time-varying parent and host country characteristics respectively. We control for the total sales of the parent system as well as the level of parent firm R&D spending. Host country characteristic controls include measures of median corporate tax rates, inward FDI restrictions, capital controls, dividend withholding tax rates applying to U.S. multinational firms, trade openness, the log of per capita GDP, the log of GDP, and the log of the real exchange rate. As such, our specification controls for the determinants of FDI that are captured by gravity equations. Each of the MNEs we analyze is a U.S. MNE so the affiliate fixed effect controls for the distance between the U.S. and the affiliate's host country. The time dummies absorb variation in the size of the U.S. economy, and, as indicated above, the specifications explicitly control for the log of GDP of the host country. We do not view this basic specification as a structural estimating equation in any sense, nor do we impute structural interpretations to any of the regression parameters generated by it.

3.2. Data

Data on U.S. multinational firms comes from the U.S. Bureau of Economic Analysis (BEA) annual Survey of U.S. Direct Investment Abroad and the quarterly Balance of Payments Survey, and our data covers the years 1982–1999. The survey forms concerning MNE activity capture extensive information on measures of parent and affiliate operating activity like levels of assets, net PPE, employment compensation, and R&D expenditures.[19] MNEs must also report the value of royalties paid by affiliates to parents for the sale or use of intangible property. American tax law requires that foreign affiliates make these payments. The reported figures on the value of intangible property transferred include an amalgam of technology licensing fees, franchise fees, and fees for the use of trademarks. However, the aggregate data indicate that intangible property transfers are overwhelmingly dominated by licensing of technology for industrial products and processes. R&D data were not reported annually in the early years of our sample period. Regular reporting began only in 1989. This means that pre reform R&D data are limited for a number of the reforms we investigate. As a consequence, we must interpret results based on R&D data with an extra measure of caution.

3.3. Results

Fig. 1 indicates the changes in the scale of affiliate activity across affiliates of firms that do and do not extensively deploy technology abroad. It illustrates median assets for affiliates in the Low and High Technology Transfer samples in the pre reform period and the post reform period. The clear bars present medians for the pre reform years, and the shaded bars present medians for the post reform years. There are large increases in the scale of activity for both kinds of affiliates, but the increases are larger for those affiliates that have parents that transfer technology abroad prior to the reform more aggressively.

To study these patterns more rigorously, Table 2 presents results based on Eq. (1) that test whether affiliates expand their operations at the time of reform. As noted above, our tests focus on measures of inputs to affiliate production. All variables are available annually for the period 1982–1999, except affiliate R&D which is only available from 1989 onwards. The statistical significance of coefficients in all tables is denoted by two asterisks to indicate significance at the 1% level and a single asterisk to indicate significance at the 5% level.

The dependent variable in column 1 is the log of affiliate assets. The positive coefficient on the Post Reform Dummy indicates that affiliates of U.S. MNEs expand their assets at the time of reform. Because the dependent variable is measured in logs, this coefficient has a semi-elasticity interpretation, implying an increase of about 16% following reforms. In column 2, we include the interaction term, allowing the impact of reform to vary for affiliates that are connected to parents that tend to extensively deploy technology abroad. The 0.1114 coefficient on the Post Reform Dummy indicates that even affiliates of U.S. MNEs with below median levels of technology transfer

[15] Our earlier paper describes at length the nature of these data and the issues that arise in using them as indicators of technology transfer.

[16] Rather than using payments for technology, Eaton and Kortum (1996, 1999) have used measures of patenting by inventors outside their home countries as an indicator of technology transfer. Lerner (2002) and Branstetter et al. (2006) find strong evidence that patenting by foreign inventors increases in developing countries after IPR reform.

[17] This approach has some advantages over the approach taken in Branstetter et al. (2006), where firms were differentiated on the basis of the patents generated by their parents. This relied on the incomplete mapping of firms to U.S. patent assignees developed in the NBER Patent Citation Database (Hall et al. (2001)) and did not adjust for the different propensities to patent observed across different industries (Cohen et al. (2002)).

[18] See, for example, Javorcik (2004b).

[19] In order to obtain information on parent firm R&D expenditures in years in which this item was not captured in BEA surveys, the BEA data on publicly traded parents is linked to COMPUSTAT using employee identification numbers.

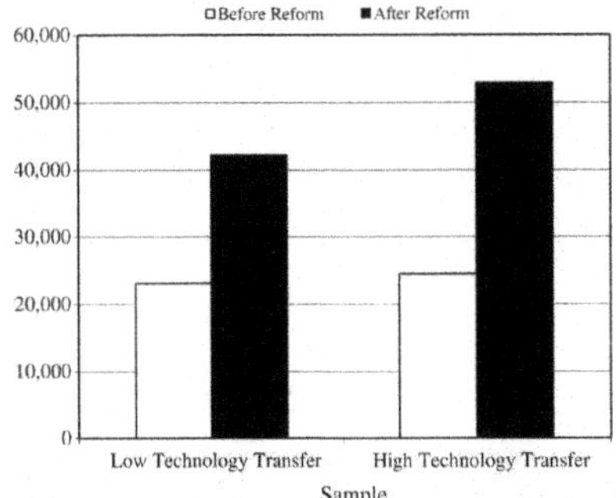

Fig. 1. The clear bars indicate median assets (in thousands) for affiliates in the Low and High Technology Transfer samples over all years in the pre reform period. The shaded bars depict medians following reform. The High Technology Transfer sample includes affiliates of parents that over the four years prior to a reform average total royalty payment receipts from all affiliates that are at least as large as the receipts of the parent of the median affiliate in the reforming country.

abroad expand their capital stock at the time of reform. The Post Reform Dummy interacted with the High Technology Transfer Dummy is also positive and statistically significant, indicating an additional 9% expansion among affiliates with a High Technology Transfer Dummy equal to one. Thus, IPR reforms trigger increases in affiliate assets, and these increases are larger among the firms most likely to benefit from reform.

Columns 3 and 4 present results of the same specification using the log of net PPE as the dependent variable. In the third column, the coefficient on the Post Reform Dummy is 0.1248, and it is significant at the 1% level. In column 4, we incorporate both this dummy and an interaction term. The coefficient on the Post Reform Dummy is now small and statistically insignificant at conventional levels, while the coefficient on this dummy interacted with the High Technology Transfer Dummy has a coefficient of 0.1882, significant at the 1% level.

The fifth and sixth columns present estimates of the impact of reform on employment compensation. In the fifth column, the estimated impact of reform on employment compensation is 0.1634. The sixth column also includes the interaction term. The results in this column imply that affiliates of firms with low transfers of technology abroad increase employment compensation by about 12%. Affiliates of firms that extensively transfer technology abroad increase employment compensation by an additional 8%, implying a total expansion of around 20% for affiliates of firms that make extensive use of intellectual property abroad.

While the results of the first six columns all imply an expansion of multinational activity in the wake of patent reform, they do not

Table 2
U.S. multinational affiliate responses to reform.

Dependent variable:	Log of affiliate assets		Log of affiliate net PPE		Log of affiliate employment compensation		100 × log of intrafirm royalty payments/affiliate sales		100 × log of R&D expenditures/affiliate sales	
	(1)	(2)	(3)	(4)	(5)	(6)	(7)	(8)	(9)	(10)
Post reform dummy	0.1590	0.1114	0.1248	0.0245	0.1634	0.1210	0.0787	−0.1311	0.0151	−0.0129
	(0.0140)**	(0.0173)**	(0.0328)**	(0.0430)	(0.0157)**	(0.0205)**	(0.0268)**	(0.0274)**	(0.0232)	(0.0252)
Post reform dummy*high		0.0912		0.1882		0.0790		0.3985		0.0546
Technology transfer dummy		(0.0181)**		(0.0443)**		(0.0217)**		(0.0323)**		(0.0275)*
Host country corporate tax rate	0.1315	0.1361	0.4965	0.5099	0.4701	0.4746	−0.0567	−0.0286	0.2946	0.2966
	(0.0985)	(0.0985)	(0.2371)*	(0.2370)*	(0.1104)**	(0.1104)**	(0.1690)	(0.1680)	(0.1433)*	(0.1432)*
Host country inward FDI restrictions	−0.0610	−0.0601	−0.0993	−0.0971	−0.0488	−0.0483	0.0373	0.0407	−0.0737	−0.0735
	(0.0386)	(0.0386)	(0.0749)	(0.0748)	(0.0328)	(0.0327)	(0.0512)	(0.0512)	(0.0480)	(0.0480)
Host Country Capital Controls	−0.0675	−0.0664	−0.0825	−0.0819	−0.0382	−0.0376	−0.0957	−0.0926	−0.0369	−0.0368
	(0.0235)**	(0.0235)**	(0.0556)	(0.0555)	(0.0244)	(0.0244)	(0.0436)*	(0.0431)*	(0.0299)	(0.0299)
Host Country Withholding Tax Rate	0.3340	0.3365	0.4333	0.4473	−0.4594	−0.4565	−0.5805	−0.5657	0.3824	0.3879
	(0.1387)*	(0.1386)*	(0.3137)	(0.3135)	(0.1646)**	(0.1646)**	(0.2342)*	(0.2324)*	(0.1784)*	(0.1783)*
Host Country Trade Openness	0.0063	0.0062	0.0072	0.0071	0.0001	0.0001	−0.0072	−0.0074	0.0016	0.0016
	(0.0016)**	(0.0016)**	(0.0035)*	(0.0035)*	(0.0016)	(0.0016)	(0.0029)*	(0.0029)*	(0.0020)	(0.0020)
Log of Host Country GDP per	0.3335	0.3406	0.6986	0.7166	0.4639	0.4713	0.6684	0.6963	0.0129	0.0196
Capita	(0.1522)*	(0.1518)*	(0.2916)*	(0.2908)*	(0.1904)*	(0.1900)*	(0.3208)*	(0.3193)*	(0.4142)	(0.4135)
Log of Host Country GDP	0.9086	0.9037	−0.1305	−0.1374	0.6229	0.6179	0.0196	−0.0007	−0.0512	−0.0537
	(0.1635)**	(0.1632)**	(0.3234)	(0.3226)	(0.1928)**	(0.1924)**	(0.3357)	(0.3339)	(0.4115)	(0.4109)
Log of Real Exchange Rate	−0.3179	−0.3161	−0.3280	−0.3231	−0.3673	−0.3657	−0.1181	−0.1097	0.0566	0.0578
	(0.0198)**	(0.0198)**	(0.0483)**	(0.0483)**	(0.0238)**	(0.0238)**	(0.0403)**	(0.0401)**	(0.0373)	(0.0373)
Log of Parent R&D Expenditures	0.0079	0.0076	0.0322	0.0315	0.0056	0.0054	0.0079	0.0072	0.0074	0.0072
	(0.0036)*	(0.0035)*	(0.0089)**	(0.0089)**	(0.0040)	(0.0040)	(0.0041)	(0.0040)	(0.0027)**	(0.0027)**
Log of Parent System Sales	0.0461	0.0467	0.0544	0.0555	0.0596	0.0601	0.0087	0.0058	−0.0019	−0.0015
	(0.0089)**	(0.0088)**	(0.0143)**	(0.0143)**	(0.0093)**	(0.0093)**	(0.0091)	(0.0092)	(0.0039)	(0.0039)
No. of obs.	26,184	26,184	22,342	22,342	24,844	24,844	25,600	25,600	16,143	16,143
R-squared	0.8882	0.8884	0.8375	0.8377	0.8788	0.8789	0.6625	0.6651	0.6644	0.6645

The dependent variables are the log of affiliate assets in columns (1) and (2), the log of affiliate net property plant and equipment in columns (3) and (4), the log of affiliate employment compensation in columns (5) and (6), 100 times the log of one plus the ratio of intrafirm royalty payments to affiliate sales in columns (7) and (8), and 100 times the log of the ratio of one plus the ratio of affiliate research and development expenditures to affiliate sales in columns (9) and (10). The Post Reform Dummy is a dummy equal to one in the year of reform and in the years following the reforms identified in Table 1. The High Technology Transfer Dummy is a dummy that is equal to one for affiliates of parents that over the four years prior to a reform average total royalty payment receipts from all affiliates that are at least as large as the receipts of the parent of the median affiliate in the reforming country. Host Country Corporate Tax Rate and Host Country Withholding Tax Rate are annual median tax rates paid by affiliates in a host country. Host Country Inward FDI Restrictions and Host Country Capital Controls are dummies equal to one when inward FDI restrictions and capital controls exist, and they are drawn from Brune (2004) and Shatz (2000). Host Country Trade Openness is the index of constant price openness taken from Heston et al. (2002). The Log of Host Country GDP per capita and Log of Host Country GDP are derived from data provided in the World Bank World Development Indicators. Log of Real Exchange Rate is computed using nominal exchange rates and measures of inflation are from the IMF's IFS database. The Log of Parent System Sales is the log of total sales of the parent and its affiliates. All specifications include affiliate and year fixed effects as well as country-specific time trends. Heteroskedasticity-consistent standard errors appear in parentheses. ** and * denote significance at the 1% and 5% levels.

necessarily imply a change in the rate at which the production of new goods is transferred to the South. Further evidence of production shifting is obtained by analyzing the transfer of technology from the parent firm and R&D performed by affiliates. These measures of affiliate activity were analyzed in Branstetter et al. (2006) in empirical work that focused specifically on these components of firms' reactions to IPR reforms. We measure transfers of technology using royalties paid by affiliates to parents for the sale or use of intangible assets. Because larger affiliate sales volumes may automatically result in higher levels of royalty payments to the parent and because many affiliates do not make royalty payments, we use the log of one plus the ratio of royalty to sales. For expositional purposes, we multiply this value by 100 in our reported results.

Specifications explaining this variable appear in columns 7 and 8 of Table 2. As indicated in column 7, the overall impact of reform on technology transfer is positive and statistically significant. When we include the interaction term as in column 8, the coefficient on the Post Reform Dummy is now negative and statistically significant. However, the 0.3985 coefficient on the interaction term is positive, highly significant, and its magnitude is very large. For the affiliates of firms that are more likely to value IPR reform because they make more extensive use of parent technology abroad, royalty payments increase substantially in response to reforms.

While most R&D spending by U.S. MNEs is concentrated in the U.S., some foreign affiliates have substantial R&D expenditures. As noted above, the vast majority of this R&D spending is designed to modify the parent firm's technology to local circumstances and conditions. It can thus be seen as a complement to technology transfers from the parent. If the post reform increase in technology licensing payments identified in columns 7 and 8 truly represents the deployment of new technology rather than simply an increase in the price of technology, then we would expect that increase to be mirrored by an increase in affiliate R&D spending. In columns 9 and 10 of Table 2, we show results of a specification using the log of one plus the ratio of affiliate R&D expenditures to affiliate sales as the dependent variable. As in columns 7 and 8, we multiply this value by 100 for expositional purposes. As indicated in column 9, the overall impact of reform on affiliate R&D is positive but not statistically significant at conventional levels. When we include the interaction term, as in column 10, the coefficient on the Post Reform Dummy is small and statistically indistinguishable from zero at conventional levels. However, the coefficient on the interaction of the Post Reform Dummy and High Technology Transfer Dummy is positive and statistically significant. Thus, for affiliates of parents that are likely to especially value strong IPR, there is a significant post reform increase in R&D.

Fig. 2 illustrates the dynamics of the increase in affiliate activity. To create this figure, we regress the log of affiliate assets on affiliate fixed effects, country–year fixed effects, the controls that are not collinear with the fixed effects (namely the log of total parent system sales and the log of parent R&D) and a set of indicator variables for the years that lead and lag IPR reform for affiliates that have a High Technology Transfer Dummy equal to one. As such, the coefficients on these time-specific dummies illustrate how the stock of assets changes for affiliates of firms that extensively deploy technology abroad. We plot these coefficients in Fig. 2, along with 95% confidence interval bounds. The coefficients show variation around zero before reform and an upward trend following reform. Thus, the changes in affiliate scale appear to begin at the time of reform.[20] Uncertainty concerning the effective enforcement of reforms could account for the lag in response. Managers might gradually update their beliefs on the efficacy of reforms, leading to an increase in the scale and scope of production.

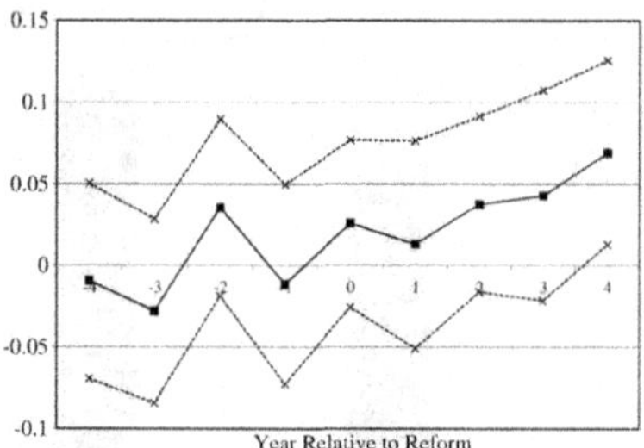

Fig. 2. This figure displays the dynamics of changes in affiliate size around the time of reform. The points are generated by regressing the log of affiliate assets on affiliate fixed effects, country–year fixed effects, the controls from the specifications in Table 2 that are not collinear with the fixed effects (namely the log of total parent system sales and the log of parent R&D), and a set of dummies that are equal to one in years relative to the IPR reform for affiliates that have a High Technology Transfer Dummy equal to one. The points are the coefficient estimates on these time-specific dummies for affiliates in the High Technology Transfer sample.

This general pattern of a gradual response that builds over several years is similar to the timing of increases in R&D spending, technology transfer, and multinational patenting reported in Branstetter et al. (2006).[21]

The results in Table 2 are robust to a number of considerations. As noted in Branstetter et al. (2006), while IPR-strengthening legislation was enacted in Argentina and China in the 1990s, multinational managers have called into question the effectiveness of enforcement of reform in these two countries. We therefore repeated the specifications shown in Table 2 with a restricted sample that excluded Argentina and China. We obtained results qualitatively similar to those shown here.[22] Because Japan differs in important ways from the other countries that undertook significant IPR reforms, we also repeated our analyses with Japan omitted from the sample. Our results are not qualitatively affected by this change. Our results are also robust to the inclusion of region–year fixed effects. Concerns that measurement of the High Technology Transfer Dummy might cause it to proxy for firm size led us to incorporate an interaction term of a measure of firm size and the Post Reform Dummy.[23] This also does not affect our results. Expanding the sample of reforms to include all affiliates in Austria, Denmark, Ecuador, Finland, Greece, Norway, and Panama and Canadian affiliates in the pharmaceutical and foodstuffs industries does not qualitatively affect our results, nor does substituting the reform dates for Japan, Taiwan, and Brazil from Maskus (2000) for our own.

While the specifications in Table 2 pool observations across countries and industries, we also ran the one in column 2 country by country. Although the sizes of the subsamples used in these tests are much smaller than those used to generate the results in Table 2, the coefficients on the interaction of the Post Reform Dummy and the High Technology Transfer Dummy is positive in 13 out of 16 cases, and it is at least marginally significant in 7 out of 16 cases.

We also ran industry by industry tests based on the specifications presented in columns 1 and 2 of Table 2 using the industry groups

[20] The coefficients on the dummies for the 4, 3, and 2 years before reform have an average that is close to zero, and they are not significantly different from zero in an F-test of joint significance. However, the coefficients on the dummies for the 4, 3, and 2 years after reform are positive and significant at the 10% level in an F-test of joint significance.

[21] The gradual increase could also reflect the fact that we are examining the stock of capital rather than the flow.

[22] These results are available from the authors upon request. The only specifications that were sensitive to the exclusion of Argentina and China were those that employed the log of the R&D to sales ratio as the dependent variable.

[23] We have also checked the robustness of the results to including the High Technology Transfer Dummy with other policy variables.

provided in the BEA data. The results indicate that activity in nearly all industry groupings increases, with the largest estimated increase occurring for affiliates in the chemical manufacturing industry.[24] The coefficient on the interaction of the Post Reform Dummy and the High Technology Transfer Dummy in specifications like the one in column 2 of Table 2 is positive for 6 of the 10 industry groupings, and it is significant for Chemical Manufacturing, Industry Machinery and Equipment, and an "Other Manufacturing" aggregate that includes the manufacturing of medical instruments and scientific equipment. In each of these industry domains, intellectual property protection is likely to be especially important.

Taken together, these results strongly suggest that multinationals respond to IPR reform by shifting production to reforming countries. To examine whether this positive impact is sufficient to have a positive effect on overall levels of industrial development, we turn to an analysis of industry-level data in reforming countries.

4. Industry-level output responses

The preceding analysis documents the positive effect of IPR reform on U.S. multinational activity. However, the overall impact on output also depends on whether the growth in production by U.S. MNEs, MNEs from other countries, and domestic firms not engaging in imitation is sufficient to offset any decline among local imitators. While we do not have firm-level data to examine these effects, we can use industry-wide measures of production in reforming countries to analyze broad economic changes. One important caveat to this analysis is that our data do not capture changes in imitative activity in the informal sector, so our estimates could understate the negative impact of stronger IPR on imitative firms.[25]

4.1. Empirical approach and data

We examine the impact of IPR reform on industrial output using a specification similar to that employed in the previous section:

$$VA_{jt} = \alpha_0 + \alpha_{ij} + \alpha_t + \beta_0 y_{jt} + \beta_1 H_{jt} + \beta_2 R_{jt} + \beta_3 R_{jt}{}^{*}IndTech_i + \varepsilon_{it} \quad (2)$$

VA measures the log of value added in industry *i* in country *j* in year *t*. The controls include country–industry pair fixed effects, time fixed effects, country-specific linear time trends, and a vector of time-varying characteristics of country *j*, including measures of the corporate tax rate, inward FDI restrictions, capital controls, trade openness, the log of GDP per capita, and the log of the real exchange rate. The main coefficients of interest are on R_{jt}, the Post Reform Dummy, and its interaction with industry-level attributes that indicate the extent of potential benefits from IPR reform. We consider two such industry characteristics. The first is a measure of the importance of technological innovation to firms in an industry, which we measure using a Technology-Intensive Dummy that is equal to one for the following industries: electrical machinery, industrial chemicals, other chemicals, professional and scientific equipment, and transportation equipment. As an alternative approach, we also generate an industry-level measure of FDI intensity by looking at the cross-industry distribution of U.S. FDI in countries where intellectual property is well protected throughout our sample. The intuition is that these are the sectors where multinationals would naturally choose to invest abroad if unconstrained by IPR concerns. We generate a High FDI Dummy equal to one for industries that had above median levels of affiliate sales activity in countries with a 1980 total patent protection index above 3.57 in Ginarte and Park (1997).

Data on industry value added are drawn from the United Nations Industrial Development Organization (UNIDO) database, which provides measures of value added at the ISIC 3-digit level in a common format for a large number of member states. This variable captures the activity of both multinational affiliates and domestic firms. While there are some gaps in the data, there is reasonably complete coverage for most countries in most years. To ensure comparability between these results and our earlier results on U.S. MNE activity, we limit our sample to the years 1982–1999.

4.2. Results

Table 3 reports results of estimating Eq. (2). The positive coefficient on the Post Reform Dummy in the first column suggests that value added increases after patent reform, and this effect is statistically significant at conventional levels.[26] This finding is inconsistent with the view that IPR reform induces a collapse of indigenous industrial activity that more than offsets MNE expansion. Column 2 reports a specification that includes the interaction of the Post Reform Dummy and the Technology-Intensive Dummy. The coefficient on this interaction term is positive and statistically significant at the 1% level, implying that output expansion is particularly pronounced in technology-intensive industries. The point estimate implies an expansion of industry-level value added of nearly 20% for these industries. Column 3 presents results of a specification in which the Post Reform Dummy is interacted with the High FDI Dummy. The coefficient on this interaction term is positive and statistically significant. Expansion in industry value added is also especially large in industries where MNEs are active.

These results are robust to a number of checks. As in our other analyses, we repeat our tests dropping China and Argentina from the sample and obtain qualitatively similar results, as indicated in columns 4–6. We consider an alternative specification incorporating country–year fixed effects. The country–year fixed effects absorb the impact of all variables that are the same for all industries in a given country at a given time, so in this specification it is no longer possible to estimate the impact of country controls or the direct effect of the Post Reform Dummy because these are the same for all industries in a given country at a given time. However, it is still possible to estimate the differential impact of IPR reform on technology-intensive and FDI-intensive sectors. These effects remain strongly positive and highly significant, even in this more demanding specification.[27] We have also expanded the sample of reforms to include those in Austria, Canada, Denmark, Ecuador, Finland, Greece, Norway, and Panama and changed the reform dates for Japan, Taiwan, and Brazil to conform to those of Maskus (2000). Neither of these adjustments has substantive effects on our results. Our use of country–industry fixed effects controls for time-invariant measures of factor endowments interacted with time-invariant measures of factor demands, but we also have included time-varying measures of human capital interacted with the human capital intensity of individual industries and time-varying measures of physical capital interacted with the physical capital intensity of individual industries. Including these controls does not qualitatively alter our results.

5. Initial export episodes

Interpreted literally, the models that motivate our empirical exercise focus on the initiation of production of new goods in

[24] The coefficient on the Post Reform Dummy is positive and significant for all industry groupings except Primary and Fabricated Metal Manufacturing and Wholesale Trade.

[25] We thank an anonymous referee for this observation.

[26] These results need to be interpreted with caution. A systematic expansion in markups in IPR-sensitive industries could be observationally equivalent to an expansion of output.

[27] We thank Nick Bloom for suggesting this additional specification.

Table 3
Impact of reform on industry value added in reforming countries.

Dependent variable:	Log of industry value added					
Sample:	All reforms			Drop China and Argentina		
	(1)	(2)	(3)	(4)	(5)	(6)
Post Reform Dummy	0.0956 (0.0167)**	0.0731 (0.0173)**	0.0501 (0.0203)*	0.0605 (0.0188)**	0.0383 (0.0194)*	0.0226 (0.0226)
Post Reform Dummy* Technology-Intensive Dummy		0.1252 (0.0252)**			0.1222 (0.0275)**	
Post Reform Dummy*High FDI Dummy			0.0924 (0.0211)**			0.0888 (0.0234)**
Host Country Corporate Tax Rate	−0.1503 (0.1107)	−0.1506 (0.1106)	−0.1140 (0.1147)	−0.0937 (0.1291)	−0.0933 (0.1290)	−0.0748 (0.1342)
Host Country Inward FDI Restrictions	−0.2450 (0.1012)*	−0.2448 (0.1016)*	−0.2350 (0.1098)*	−0.2381 (0.1012)*	−0.2375 (0.1016)*	−0.2320 (0.1097)*
Host Country Capital Controls	0.0851 (0.0329)**	0.0853 (0.0328)**	0.0602 (0.0336)	0.2097 (0.0336)**	0.2097 (0.0334)**	0.1819 (0.0338)**
Host Country Trade Openness	0.0008 (0.0023)	0.0008 (0.0023)	−0.0001 (0.0023)	0.0002 (0.0028)	0.0002 (0.0028)	−0.0012 (0.0029)
Log of Host Country GDP per Capita	2.1138 (0.1488)**	2.1157 (0.1485)**	2.0320 (0.1551)**	2.4143 (0.2007)**	2.4141 (0.2001)**	2.3596 (0.2130)**
Log of Real Exchange Rate	−0.3417 (0.0318)**	−0.3420 (0.0316)**	−0.3253 (0.0309)**	−0.4025 (0.0413)**	−0.4029 (0.0411)**	−0.3798 (0.0399)**
No. of obs.	6884	6884	6183	6069	6069	5427
R-squared	0.9595	0.9596	0.9582	0.9584	0.9586	0.9570

The dependent variable is the log of industry value added. Columns (4)–(6) report results obtained when China and Argentina are dropped from the sample. The Post Reform Dummy is a dummy equal to one in the year of reform and in the years following the reforms identified in Table 1. The Technology-Intensive Dummy is equal to one for ISIC codes 351, 352, 383, 384, and 385. The High FDI Dummy is equal to one in industries that had above median levels of affiliate sales activity in countries with a 1980 total patent protection index above 3.57 in Ginarte and Park (1997). Host Country Corporate Tax Rate is the annual median tax rates paid by affiliates in a host country. Host Country Inward FDI Restrictions and Host Country Capital Controls are dummies equal to one when inward FDI restrictions and capital controls exist, and they are drawn from Brune (2004) and Shatz (2000), respectively. Host Country Trade Openness is the index of constant price openness taken from Heston et al. (2002). The Log of Host Country GDP per capita is derived from data provided in the World Bank World Development Indicators. Log of Real Exchange Rate is computed using nominal exchange rates and measures of inflation are from the IMF's IFS database. All specifications include country-industry and year fixed effects as well as country-specific time trends. Heteroskedasticity-consistent standard errors appear in parentheses. ** and * denote significance at the 1% and 5% levels.

reforming countries following IPR reform. The measures of affiliate and industry activity analyzed above are not sufficiently disaggregated to permit the tracking of affiliate activity at the individual product level. Therefore, to capture more directly the extent of new production in reforming countries, we build on the method of Feenstra and Rose (2000).

This approach requires the use of disaggregated U.S. import statistics to obtain counts of initial export episodes. For each country-year observation, our measure of new goods production is the number of 10-digit commodities in U.S. imports from a given country that are recorded as exceeding zero for the first time in a given year. Because the U.S. is the world's single biggest market for many commodities, looking at the date at which a particular reforming country starts exporting a particular good to the U.S. may be a reasonable indicator of production shifting for that good.

This measure is imperfect in that domestic production may precede exports by several years. Furthermore, the notion of production shifting implies the initiation of production in one location and the cessation of production in another. However, it is very difficult to identify the termination of production of particular goods in countries that do not undertake reform. Because of these data constraints, we are only able to examine one side of production shifting.[28]

5.1. *Empirical approach and data*

In order to study the initiation of the production of new goods, we use this specification:

$$P_{jt} = \alpha_0 + \alpha_j + \alpha_t + \beta_0 H_{jt} + \beta_1 R_{jt} + \varepsilon_{it} \quad (3)$$

Our dependent variable P is a count measure that, for country j in year t, gives the number of 10-digit commodities where recorded U.S. imports exceeded zero for the first time. Intuitively, this is a proxy for the arrival rate of new products. This count is regressed on country–year variables that control for a country's changing export capabilities, including country dummy variables, time dummy variables, a vector of time-varying characteristics of country j, and the Post Reform Dummy. The country characteristics included in the vector H_{jt} are the same as those used in the specifications presented in Table 3. Because the data cover only an 11 year time frame, as explained below, country-specific time trends are not included.

For data, we utilize the U.S. trade database created by Feenstra et al. (2001). Annual data on U.S. imports from nearly all countries worldwide are available at the HS 10-digit level of disaggregation, which is very close to the level of individual products. One difficulty in using these data is that the 10-digit commodity classification system was extensively revised in 1989. As a consequence, data before and after the revision are not comparable at the most disaggregated level. We therefore focus on the post-1988 period, where the data are measured consistently. To maintain comparability with our earlier results, we do not extend the data past 1999, so that the results in this section draw upon data from 1989 to 1999.[29]

[28] Note, however, there is evidence that the expected cessation of production of certain goods in the U.S. is taking place. A recent study by Bernard et al. (2010) uses confidential plant-level data to show that cessation of production of certain goods is occurring at a fairly rapid rate within U.S.-based manufacturing plants. These authors document a shift to the production of more capital- and skill-intensive goods for surviving plants, consistent with the evolving comparative advantage of U.S. manufacturers. Plants that do not shift their product mix in this way are less likely to survive. These patterns are broadly consistent with the view of production shifting presented in Section 2.

[29] These data contain some observations that record extremely small trade flows, often followed by no activity. We are concerned that these anomalous observations might bias upward the counts of initial export episodes, so we report results obtained when we drop these questionable observations, though we obtain qualitatively similar results with the full data set.

As in our earlier specifications, we examine whether the estimated impact of IPR reform is stronger in technology-intensive product categories. In such tests, we analyze initial export episodes in HS 10-digit product categories that are associated with the industry codes identified in the previous section as being technology-intensive: electrical machinery, industrial chemicals, other chemicals, professional and scientific equipment, and transportation equipment. For all country–year observations, we create separate counts of initial export episodes arising in only these product categories. We refer to these product categories as Tech Goods.

5.2. Results

Table 4 provides results from regressions based on Eq. (3). The dependent variable measures the count of initial export episodes at the 10-digit level. In column 1 we provide results using the Poisson fixed effects regression model derived by Hausman et al. (1984) that takes into consideration the count nature of the dependent variable. In this specification, we use data on initial export episodes in all product categories and all reforming countries. The coefficient on the Post Reform Dummy is positive, significant at the 1% level, and has a semi-elasticity interpretation; the coefficient implies an increase in the production of new goods after IPR reform of about 28%. In column 2, we limit the sample to Tech Goods. For this subsample, the point estimate of the coefficient on the Post Reform Dummy is slightly larger in magnitude than that in column 1, and it is significant at the 1% level.

These results are also robust to several checks. As indicated in columns 3 and 4, the coefficients on the Post Reform Dummy are little changed by dropping Argentina and China from the sample. As an alternative specification, we employ the fixed effects negative binomial model of Hausman et al. (1984), and we obtain similar results, as shown in columns 5–8. Including a dummy variable measuring the onset of a free trade agreement with the U.S. does not alter the results, and our results are qualitatively unchanged when we substitute dates for the IPR reforms of Japan, Brazil, and Taiwan from Maskus (2000) for our own. Expanding the set of reforming countries to include Austria, Canada, Denmark, Ecuador, Finland, Greece, Norway, and Panama produces results qualitatively very similar to those shown here. Finally, if we restrict our counts to include only those in commodity categories that existed at the beginning of our data, thereby excluding counts of new export episodes emerging in new commodity categories, we obtain results very similar to those employed here.

6. Conclusion

Building on the work of Grossman and Helpman (1991a) and Helpman (1993), the theoretical literature on North–South product cycle models of international trade and investment shows that the effect of Southern IPR reform on the global economy hinge critically on the responses of multinational firms. In particular, this literature shows that if multinational firms based in the North are sufficiently responsive to the change in the Southern IPR regime, the expansion of their Southern affiliates could more than offset a decline in indigenous Southern imitation, thus spurring industrial development in the South. In this paper, we empirically confront hypotheses derived from these theories with a mix of evidence drawn from data on the activities of U.S. multinational affiliates, industry-level data from reforming countries, and disaggregated U.S. import data. We analyze changes in measures of affiliate activity, industry activity, and the introduction of new products in response to IPR reforms in 16 countries. All of the evidence indicates that stronger IPR in the South accelerates the transfer of production to reforming countries.

We find that U.S. MNE affiliate activity increases following reform and that increases are most pronounced among affiliates of firms that tend to deploy more technology abroad and that are therefore more likely to benefit from reform. These findings are consistent with parents sharing new technology with their affiliates so that these affiliates can begin the manufacture of new, more sophisticated goods.

The increase in production shifting through multinational firms could be smaller than the decrease in imitative activity by indigenous

Table 4
Impact of reform on initial export episodes.

Dependent variable:	Count of initial export episodes							
Specification type:	Poisson				Negative binomial			
Sample	All reforms		Drop Argentina and China		All reforms		Drop Argentina and China	
Goods categories	All goods	Tech goods	All goods	Tech goods	All goods	Tech goods	All goods	Tech goods
	(1)	(2)	(3)	(4)	(5)	(6)	(7)	(8)
Post Reform Dummy	0.2772	0.3182	0.2902	0.3866	0.2340	0.3420	0.2488	0.4165
	(0.0129)**	(0.0309)**	(0.0148)**	(0.0359)**	(0.0635)**	(0.1040)**	(0.0716)**	(0.1198)**
Host Country Corporate Tax Rate	0.0588	0.0949	−0.0363	0.1055	−0.2282	−1.2256	−0.1762	−0.8890
	(0.0794)	(0.1916)	(0.0961)	(0.2315)	(0.3653)	(0.5526)*	(0.4604)	(0.6793)
Host Country Inward FDI Restrictions	−0.0673	0.1598	−0.0338	0.1074	−0.1260	−0.1055	−0.1344	−0.1380
	(0.0248)**	(0.0508)**	(0.0268)	(0.0540)	(0.1187)	(0.1805)	(0.1246)	(0.1859)
Host Country Capital Controls	−0.1123	−0.1948	−0.0237	−0.0725	−0.1287	−0.1201	−0.1249	−0.1310
	(0.0198)**	(0.0559)**	(0.0226)	(0.0646)	(0.0831)	(0.1420)	(0.0970)	(0.1731)
Host Country Trade Openness	0.0110	0.0115	0.0114	0.0096	0.0057	0.0059	0.0081	0.0082
	(0.0008)**	(0.0018)**	(0.0008)**	(0.0018)**	(0.0034)	(0.0043)	(0.0038)*	(0.0047)
Log of Host Country GDP per Capita	0.0173	−0.1301	−0.1746	0.0964	−0.1582	0.0788	−0.1071	0.2670
	(0.0422)	(0.0944)	(0.0571)**	(0.1272)	(0.1571)	(0.2023)	(0.1915)	(0.2155)
Log of Real Exchange Rate	0.3140	0.2788	0.4101	0.2597	0.4106	0.2402	0.4748	0.3065
	(0.0268)**	(0.0634)**	(0.0302)**	(0.0740)**	(0.1282)**	(0.2009)	(0.1528)**	(0.1344)
No. of obs.	176	176	154	154	176	176	154	154
Log likelihood	−2342	−1162	−2147	−1061	−912	−691	−801	−606

The dependent variable is the annual count of HS 10 digit product categories in which a reforming country reports exports to the U.S. for the first time. Data are taken from the trade data base documented in Feenstra et al. (2001). The Tech Goods sample includes the set of 10-digit commodity categories that is associated with ISIC codes 351, 352, 383, 384, and 385. Columns (3), (4), (7) and (8) display results generated after removing Argentina and China from the sample. The Post Reform Dummy is equal to one in the year of reform and in the years following the reforms listed in Table 1. Host Country Corporate Tax Rate is the annual median tax rate paid by U.S. MNE affiliates in a country. Host Country Inward FDI Restrictions and Host Country Capital Controls are dummy variables drawn from Brune (2004) and Shatz (2000), respectively. Host Country Trade Openness is the index of constant price openness taken from Heston et al. (2002). The Log of Host Country GDP per Capital is derived from data provided in the World Bank World Development Indicators. Log of Real Exchange Rate is computed using nominal exchange rates and measures of inflation are from the IMF's IFS database. All specifications include country and year fixed effects. ** and * denote significance at the 1% and 5% levels.

Southern producers. Evidence from industry-level value-added data suggests that this is not the case. Rather, the estimated effect of reform on industry activity implies that the increase in activity by MNEs and other firms that are not engaging in imitative activity more than compensates for any decline in imitation. Furthermore, evidence from highly disaggregated U.S. import data indicates that initial export episodes increase following reform. Analyses of changes in industrial activity after reform point out that activity in technology-intensive industries responds particularly strongly to reform. Stronger IPR in the South appears to lead to an acceleration of production shifting, enhancing Southern industrial development.

Over the long run, production shifting should free up Northern resources for investment in innovative activity. In this paper, we do not attempt to estimate the magnitude or timing of this longer run, general equilibrium effect. However, other researchers have noted a robust expansion of U.S. innovative activity in the 1990s, even as manufacturing jobs have continued to move offshore. The rate of growth of real R&D spending in the U.S. accelerated significantly in the 1980s and 1990s as the IPR reforms we study unfolded. Relative to inventors based in other countries, those in the U.S. appear to have increased their generation of new ideas.[30] Along with this surge in innovative outcomes has come an acceleration in total factor productivity growth, which has persisted in recent years.[31] These developments are consistent with the kind of general equilibrium resource reallocation stressed in product cycle models like the one in Grossman and Helpman (1991b). However, these are complex phenomena with multiple causes; exploring the potential link between production shifting and the apparent acceleration of innovation in the U.S. is a focus of ongoing research.

Acknowledgements

We wish to thank Pol Antràs, Nicholas Bloom, Paul David, Jonathan Eaton (the Editor), Amy Glass, Gene Grossman, Bronwyn Hall, Elhanan Helpman, Fuat Sener, two anonymous reviewers, and seminar participants at Columbia University, Keio University, LSE, Stanford University, the University of Adelaide, UC-Berkeley, the University of Pittsburgh, and the NBER ITI and Productivity meetings for helpful comments. We are grateful to Matej Drev, Sergei Koulayev, and Yoshiaki Ogura for excellent research assistance and to the National Science Foundation (SES grant no. 0241781) for financial support. Foley also thanks the Division of Research at Harvard Business School for providing generous funding.

References

Bernard, A., Redding, S., Schott, P., 2010. Multi-product firms and product switching. The American Economic Review 100 (1), 70–97.

Branstetter, L., Fisman, R., Foley, F., 2006. Does stronger intellectual property rights increase international technology transfer? Empirical evidence from U.S. firm-level data. Quarterly Journal of Economics 121 (1), 321–349.

Branstetter, L., Fisman, R., Foley, F., Saggi, K., 2007. Intellectual Property Rights, Imitation, and Foreign Direct Investment: Theory and Evidence. NBER WP No. 13033.

Brune, N., 2004. In Search of Credible Commitments: The IMF and Capital Account Liberalization in the Developing World. Working paper. Yale University.

Chaudhuri, S., Goldberg, P., Jia, P., 2006. Estimating the effects of global patent protection in pharmaceuticals: a case study of quinolones in India. The American Economic Review 96 (5), 1477–1514.

Cohen, W., Goto, A., Nagata, A., Nelson, R., Walsh, J., 2002. R&D spillovers, patents, and the incentives to innovate in Japan and the United States. Research Policy 31 (8–9), 1349–1367.

Eaton, J., Kortum, S., 1996. Trade in ideas: patenting and productivity in the OECD. Journal of International Economics 40 (3–4), 251–278.

Eaton, J., Kortum, S., 1999. International technology diffusion: theory and measurement. International Economic Review 40 (3), 537–570.

Feenstra, R., Rose, A., 2000. Putting things in order. The Review of Economics and Statistics 82 (3), 369–382.

Feenstra, R., Romalis, J., Schott, P., 2001. U.S. Imports, Exports, and Tariff Data, 1989–2001. NBER WP No. 9387.

Ginarte, J., Park, W., 1997. Determinants of patent rights: a cross-national study. Research Policy 26 (3), 283–301.

Glass, A.J., Saggi, K., 2002. Intellectual property rights and foreign direct investment. Journal of International Economics 56 (2), 387–410.

Gordon, R.J., 2003. Exploding productivity growth: context, causes, implications. Brookings Papers on Economic Activity 2, 207–298.

Grossman, G.M., Helpman, E., 1991a. Innovation and Growth in the Global Economy. MIT Press, Cambridge.

Grossman, G.M., Helpman, E., 1991b. Endogenous product cycles. The Economic Journal 101 (408), 1214–1229.

Hall, B., Jaffe, A., Trajtenberg, M., 2001. The NBER Patent Citation Data File: Lessons, Insights, and Methodological Tools. NBER WP No. 8498.

Hausman, J., Hall, B., Griliches, Z., 1984. Econometric models for count data with an application to the patents-R&D relationship. Econometrica 52 (4), 909–938.

Helpman, E., 1993. Innovation, imitation, and intellectual property rights. Econometrica 61 (6), 1247–1280.

Heston, A., Summers, R., Aten, B., 2002. Penn World Table Version 6.1. Center for International Comparisons at the University of Pennsylvania (CICUP).

Javorcik, B., 2004a. Does foreign direct investment increase the productivity of domestic firms? In search of spillovers through backward linkages. The American Economic Review 94 (3), 605–627.

Javorcik, B., 2004b. The composition of foreign direct investment and the protection of intellectual property rights in transition economies. European Economic Review 48 (1), 39–62.

Kortum, S., Lerner, J., 1999. Stronger protection or technological revolution: what is behind the recent surge in patenting? Research Policy 28 (1), 1–22.

Kuemmerle, W., 1999. The drivers of foreign direct investment into research and development: an empirical investigation. Journal of International Business Studies 30, 1–24.

Lai, E.L.C., 1998. International intellectual property rights protection and the rate of product innovation. Journal of Development Economics 55 (1), 133–153.

Lerner, J., 2002. 150 years of patent protection. The American Economic Review 92 (2), 221–225.

Markusen, J.R., 2001. Contracts, intellectual property rights, and multinational investment in developing countries. Journal of International Economics 53 (1), 189–204.

Maskus, K.E., 2000. Intellectual Property Rights in the Global Economy. Institute for International Economics, Washington DC.

McCalman, P., 2001. Reaping what you sow: an empirical analysis of international patent harmonization. Journal of International Economics 55 (1), 161–186.

McFetridge, D., 1997. Intellectual property rights and the location of innovative activity: the Canadian experience with compulsory licensing of patented pharmaceuticals. Working Paper. Carleton University.

McKinsey Global Institute, 2000. Why the Japanese Economy is not Growing: Micro Barriers to Productivity Growth. McKinsey & Company, Inc.

Poole, J., 2009. Knowledge transfers from multinational to domestic firms: evidence from worker mobility. Working Paper. University of California at Santa Cruz.

Porter, M., Takeuchi, H., Sakakibara, M., 2000. Can Japan Compete? Perseus, Cambridge, MA.

Qian, Y., 2007. Do national patent laws stimulate innovation in a global patenting environment? A cross-country analysis of pharmaceutical patent protection, 1978–2002. The Review of Economics and Statistics 89 (3), 436–453.

Shatz, H., 2000. The location of U.S. multinational affiliates. Ph.D. dissertation, Harvard University.

United States Trade Representative, Executive Office of the President, Various Issues. National Trade Estimate Report on Foreign Trade Barriers.

[30] See Kortum and Lerner (1999) for a discussion of evidence based on patent data.

[31] See Gordon (2003) and the studies cited therein.

Chapter 14

Patent protection and the composition of multinational activity: Evidence from US multinational firms*

Olena Ivus[1], Walter G Park[2] and Kamal Saggi[3]

[1]Smith School of Business, Queen's University, Goodes Hall, 143 Union Street, Kingston, ON K7L 3N6, Canada; [2]Department of Economics, American University, Washington, DC 20016, USA; [3]Department of Economics, Vanderbilt University, PMB 351828, 2301 Vanderbilt Place, Nashville, TN 37235, USA

Correspondence:
K Saggi, Department of Economics, Vanderbilt University, PMB 351828, 2301 Vanderbilt Place, Nashville, TN 37235, USA.
e-mail: k.saggi@vanderbilt.edu

Abstract
This article examines how patent protection in developing countries affects the technology licensing strategy of US multinational firms and the associated technology transfer flows. Strengthening patent rights lowers appropriability hazards and so reduces the firms' reliance on affiliated licensing as the more secure means of transfer (the internalization effect). However lower appropriability hazards also encourage the firms to increase the volume of technology transfer via licensing both within and outside the firm (the appropriability effect). Which effect prevails depends on the underlying technological complexity of the firms' product. We find that a strengthening of patent protection in the host country increases the incentive to license innovations to unaffiliated parties. While unaffiliated licensing rises among all firms, the volume of affiliated licensing falls among complex-technology firms but rises among simple-technology firms. The positive appropriability effect on affiliated licensing is strong enough among simple-technology firms that the entire composition of their licensing further shifts towards affiliated parties. The results are significant for recent work on the internalization theories of multinational firms and the interaction between firm strategy and the institutional environment, as well as for patent policy in the developing world, where access to knowledge is critical.

Journal of International Business Studies (2017) **48,** 808–836.
doi:10.1057/s41267-017-0100-1

Keywords: international technology; transfer; licensing; internalization; appropriability; intellectual property rights; technological complexity; and imitation risk

Received: 16 February 2016
Revised: 2 June 2017
Accepted: 16 July 2017
Online publication date: 8 September 2017

INTRODUCTION

Multinational firms seeking to exploit their knowledge assets may do so either internally, within company boundaries, or externally by contracting with independent entities. Key questions in the theory of internalization are when and why multinational firms opt to transfer technology internally (where it is potentially more secure) instead of via arms-length market transactions (see Contractor, 1984). For developing economies, transfers of technology from foreign multinational companies, whether internal or external, can be important inputs for their development. Alliances, partnerships, ventures, or licensing contracts may provide

*This chapter was originally appeared in *Journal of International Business Studies* **48**, 808–836.

unaffiliated, local agents access to knowledge, technology, and marketing experience (see UNCTAD, 2001), and create prospects for wide technology spillovers locally (see Saggi, 2002).[1] The transfer of technology is an express objective of the Agreement on Trade-Related Intellectual Property Rights (TRIPS), the foremost trade agreement governing intellectual property.[2] Thus for both theoretical and practical purposes, it is important to understand the market and policy determinants driving firms' international technology licensing decisions in developing countries.

This article examines how the strengthening of patent protection in developing countries affects international technology licensing. We focus on US multinational firms' technology transfer via the licensing of intangible assets, distinguishing between affiliated and unaffiliated licensing flows, and examine the composition of licensing to study the effects of patent protection on the licensing strategy of US multinational firms. The paper shows that the impact of stronger developing countries' patent rights (PRs) on US firms' volume and nature of licensing is non-monotonic and depends critically on the strength of the appropriability regime as determined by the underlying technological complexity of the firms' products.

To the extent that appropriability hazards are high when knowledge is less complex because such knowledge is easy to misappropriate and imitate, one would expect a negative relationship between the strength of host's PRs and the prevalence of affiliated licensing. Stronger PRs lower appropriability hazards and so reduce the firms' reliance on affiliated licensing as the more secure means of transfer (i.e., the internalization effect). However, lower appropriability hazards also encourage the firms to increase the volume of technology transfer via licensing both within and outside the firm (i.e., the appropriability effect). Which effect prevails is theoretically ambiguous and depends on the underlying technological complexity of the firms' products. In order to evaluate the relative size of the two effects empirically, the two forms of licensing – affiliated and unaffiliated – have to be studied in an integrated framework, where firms decide on both the volume of licensing and the preferred mode of control. Previous literature has greatly increased our understanding of the role of patent protection and transaction characteristics in impacting firm strategy, but has not studied the interplay between the internalization and appropriability effects in the intergraded framework that this article provides.

We develop hypotheses linking the underlying technological complexity of firms' products to the volume and nature of licensing activity in the context of a simple model of a foreign market entry strategy, which draws on concepts and extends insights of the economics and international business literature. In the model, the firm owns proprietary technology generated by R&D activity and would like to exploit it through foreign production. International exploitation of knowledge is difficult and carries the risk of technology misappropriation and product imitation by rivals, even when technology is transferred within organizations (e.g., Zander & Kogut, 1995; Poole, 2013; Berry, 2014).[3] The firm's strategy involves two interdependent decisions: the volume of licensing (i.e., how much technology to transfer via licensing into a country) and the mode of control (i.e., whether to license its technology to an affiliated or unaffiliated party, with unaffiliated licensing carrying the higher risk of product imitation). The model predicts that the firm's response to the strength of host's PRs largely depends on the underlying technological complexity of the firm's products, which we interpret as the technological complexity of tasks involved in the manufacture of products. Technological complexity is an important conditioning factor in the impact of host's PRs because it increases the time to product imitation (or more precisely, decreases the hazard rate by which innovations are imitated), strengthens the appropriability regime and with that, reduces the firm's reliance on host's PRs.

We test our hypotheses using data from the US Bureau of Economic Analysis (BEA) on affiliated and unaffiliated technology licensing by US multinational companies to local agents in 44 developing countries over the 1993–2009 period. To explore the role of technological complexity we employ the task-based measure of Naghavi, Spies, and Toubal (2015), which distinguishes products by the average intensity of complex problem-solving "tasks" involved in the products' manufacturing. This important distinction and its role in determining the licensing impact of PRs has been largely overlooked in the multinational licensing strategy literature, and is emphasized in this article.[4] The measure of technological complexity is obtained from occupational data, where 809 occupations are ranked based on the level and importance of complex problem-solving skills. Occupations are interpreted as "tasks" that are embodied in products, and average task intensity in solving problems is interpreted as a measure of the underlying

technological complexity of products.[5] The measure is at the product category level and we focus on 15 high-tech manufacturing product categories, for which patent protection is expected to matter most.

We find that a strengthening of patent protection in the host country increases the incentive to license innovations to unaffiliated parties. While unaffiliated licensing flows rise among all firms, the change in the volume of affiliated licensing is non-monotonic: affiliated licensing falls among complex-technology firms but rises among simple-technology firms. This striking result is driven by the appropriability effect, which overtakes the internalization effect among simple-technology firms. Furthermore, the positive appropriability effect on affiliated licensing is strong enough among simple-technology firms that the entire composition of their licensing further shifts towards affiliated parties. These findings underscore the importance for simple-technology firms of carefully considering appropriability regimes when transferring their technology to developing countries.

RELATION TO PREVIOUS LITERATURE

The study is significant for existing work on the internalization theories of multinational firms (Buckley & Casson, 1976, 1998, 2009; Buckley & Pearce, 1979). A growing body of work in the international management literature has emphasized the high cost of sharing and managing knowledge across countries (e.g., Berry, 2006, 2014; Di Minin & Bianchi, 2011) and investigated the role of the local institutional environment (such as intellectual property protection) in impacting firm strategy (e.g., Hagedoorn, Cloodt, & Van Kranenburg, 2005; Allred & Park, 2007; Zhao, 2006; Coeurderoy & Murray, 2008; Hennart, 2009; Wang, Hong, Kafouros, & Wright, 2012). A well-established finding is that imperfections in contracting (e.g., due to weak PRs) can impede transfers of proprietary knowledge between independent entities, as multinational firms choose largely to internalize the market for technology within firm boundaries, or even to concentrate their critical R&D in their headquarters.

International transaction cost theory highlighted several transaction or project characteristics, such as asset specificity, the difficulty of contracting, the hazard of technological leakage, and the hazard of free-riding on brand name and reputation, which increase the appropriability hazards in contracting for the transfer of the technological innovation between independent entities. The empirical literature has further shown that these contractual hazards determine the impact of the institutional environment on multinational market entry mode. Oxley (1997, 1999), for example, focused on the difficulty of contracting, which encompasses the difficulty of specifying property or usage rights associated with the technology in a contract and the difficulty of monitoring and enforcing contractual terms.

A related strand of the literature studied the ability of innovating firms to profit from technological innovation and highlighted "appropriability hazards" which are distinct from contractual hazards discussed above and result from the technological leakage of information, leading to imitation by rivals (Mansfield, Schwartz, & Wagner, 1981; Levin, Klevorick, Nelson, Winter, Gilbert, & Griliches, 1987; Anand & Khanna, 2000; Cohen, Nelson, & Walsh, 2000). An important contribution to the literature is Teece (1986), which emphasized that an innovator's ability to capture the profits generated by an innovation depends critically on a regime of appropriability. Where the appropriability regime is weak, technology is very hard to protect and innovators must turn to business strategy in order to limit imitation. Two key dimensions of the appropriability regime are the efficacy of legal mechanisms of protection (such as patents) and the nature of technology. Teece (1986) argued that appropriability hazards are high when knowledge is less complex, because such knowledge is easy to misappropriate and imitate; and that the complex, tacit nature of knowledge, which is difficult to articulate and so imitate, reduces appropriability hazards.

The international trade literature highlighted the importance of the risk of imitation in determining the technology transfer impact of PRs.[6] Smith (1999), for example, showed that weak foreign PRs are a barrier to US exports, but only to countries that pose a strong threat of imitation. Ivus (2011) emphasized industry differences in the impact of PRs and showed that stronger foreign PRs expand exports more in industries with higher imitation risk. More recently, Bilir (2014) examined how the impact of PRs on multinationals' manufacturing location decisions depends on product life-cycle lengths, arguing that firms with short life-cycle products are less sensitive to patent protection because their technologies may become obsolete before imitation can occur. Naghavi et al. (2015)

argued that technological complexity of products acts as a barrier to imitation and distinguished products by the complexity level of the tasks involved in their production to study the impact of foreign PRs on the firms' product sourcing decisions.

Building upon these important factors – appropriability hazards and imitation risks – we study how patent protection affects two forms of international licensing: affiliated and unaffiliated. We provide an integrated, empirical framework, where firms decide on both the volume of licensing and the preferred mode of control. Previous studies have often worked with discrete choice indicators, allowing only for the observation of technology transfers at the external margin (i.e., whether or not a transfer takes place). This will not capture whether firms choose a different mode of transfer or adjust the levels of technology activities under each mode as the institutional regime shifts. In our framework, stronger foreign PRs could potentially expand both affiliated and unaffiliated licensing, shifting the composition of licensing in either direction, depending the strength of the appropriability and internalization effects of PRs. The findings provide a more nuanced understanding of how PRs affect technology transfers via licensing. The impact of PRs on the composition of licensing has significant policy implications since the two forms of licensing promote developing countries' access to new technologies to a different degree.[7]

Studies that are closest to our work include Aulakh, Jiang, and Sali (2010, 2013). Their focus is on whether or not the licensing contract will be *exclusive*. IPRs can affect this choice in two opposing ways. First, if IPRs are secure, firms spend less time and effort monitoring the actions of the licensee; hence, stronger IPRs reduce transactions costs and can encourage multiple, non-exclusive, licensing. Second, stronger IPRs enhance the ability of the licensee to earn monopoly rents, and those rents will be higher if the licensee faces fewer competitors (from other licensees and form the licensor itself); hence, stronger IPRs can motivate exclusive licensing. Aulakh et al. (2010) find that IPRs have an insignificant effect on the exclusivity of licensing, suggesting that the two opposing effects may cancel.[8] Importantly, these studies focus on arms-length licensing and do not incorporate affiliated licensing, which a firm may choose to do if it possesses the necessary complementary assets to develop technologies in-house (see Arora & Ceccagnoli, 2006). Moreover, the studies do not examine the volume of arms-length licensing but consider instead a binary decision of whether to grant exclusive rights. IPRs may affect the volume of such licensing without affecting the external margin.

Another related study is Anand and Khanna (2000), which analyzes licensing by industry, Chemicals, Computers, and Electronics in particular. The study points out that there are industry-specific technological and product characteristics that affect the profitability and nature of licensing. The study focuses on unaffiliated licensing and examines the different features that such contracts can contain.[9] Again, their outcome variables are discrete choice variables of licensing, rather than the volume of licensing fees and royalties. Most importantly, their study does not contain an analysis of the impact of changes in foreign IPRs.[10]

Zhao (2006) helps to resolve a puzzle regarding why MNCs conduct R&D in weak IP countries, like China and India. Zhao (2006) demonstrates that it is largely because multinational companies are able to substitute internal organizations for external IPRs in countries with weak institutional environments. The multinational firm is in essence a mechanism for *arbitraging* institutional gaps around the world using, where available, its close internal global knowledge network so as to exploit underutilized human capital in areas with relatively weak IPR protections. As its dependent variable, Zhao (2006) uses the ratio of patent self-citations to total (patent) citations of a firm. It is intended to measure the degree of internalization, as a multinational affiliate that conducts R&D in a weak IP country would be more reliant on internal resources for technological development. Consistent with its hypotheses, Zhao (2006) finds that the self-citation ratio of MNCs that conduct R&D is indeed higher in weak IP countries and that such firms have greater cross-border collaborations, indicating that they also have stronger internal linkages. But the Zhao (2006) study focuses on affiliate activity, and does not analyze the arms-length technology transfers, which firms sampled also have the option to engage in. Indeed, it is just as puzzling that some MNCs not only conduct R&D in weak IP countries but they also license to unaffiliated parties in places like China and India.[11]

Studies that do integrate arms-length and affiliate governance structures include Oxley (1999) and Hagedoorn et al. (2005). Oxley (1999) examines the impact of IPRs on whether a US firm chooses to engage in an equity joint venture or contractual (arms-length) alliance. The study finds that firms choose a hierarchical alliance, like an equity venture, when they partner with firms in weak IP countries. Hagedoorn et al. (2005) further confirms this by focusing on R&D ventures in a wider range of industries. Again, both focus on the (yes/no) decisions to engage in different hierarchical modes. Changes in IPR may not necessarily have drastic effects at the external margin, causing firms to abandon one structure for another, but rather may induce firms to adjust their levels of participation in either structure. Moreover, neither study controls for sectoral maybe use differences in IP dependence, due say to technological complexity.

Empirical studies that analyze licensing at the intensive margin include Branstetter, Fisman, and Foley (2006) and Park and Lippoldt (2005). Branstetter et al. (2006) analyze the impact of foreign patent reforms on the affiliated licensing of US multinational firms, while Park and Lippoldt (2005) examine the impact of various types of IPR protection abroad (patent, trademark, and copyright) on unaffiliated licensing of US firms. Neither study integrates both affiliated and unaffiliated licensing, and therefore do not address issues of internalization. Papageorgiadis, Cross, and Alexiou (2013) examine the share of affiliated licensing in total licensing, but do not study the effects of IPRs on the levels of affiliate and unaffiliated licensing separately. It is possible that IPRs raise the volume of both types of licensing, while favoring one type more than the other. Examining only the share does not reveal that possibility. Yang and Maskus (2001) examine the levels of affiliate and unaffiliated licensing jointly; however, this study uses aggregate national data, which aggregate firms that may only engage in one type of licensing over another, and so would not properly capture switching or adjusting between modes. Country-level data are also not suitable for studying the effects of technological differences in the impact of foreign IPR. We use firm-level data which have the advantage of capturing both the volume and substitution effect at the micro level, and also enable us to account for the parents' decision to enter or not enter a given country. This is important since the location decision is interdependent with the choice of the mode of control and volume of licensing.[12]

Thus this article expands upon the existing literature on IPRs and foreign licensing by going beyond discrete choice analysis and examining internal and external licensing jointly. Furthermore, we capture the differential responses to IPRs across sectors, specifically across product categories.

The paper emphasizes the importance of studying the interaction between transaction characteristics and the institutional environment and so is related to Oxley (1997, 1999) and Henisz (2000), but the type of characteristics considered is different. Oxley (1997, 1999) and Henisz (2000) focused on the appropriability hazards in contracting for the transfer of the technological innovation. We instead focus on the appropriability hazards which result from the technological leakage of information that leads to imitation by rivals. These hazards are of great concern when transferring technology to developing countries even if the transfer is within firm boundaries. The two types of hazards are also fundamentally different in how they relate to the degree of tacitness of know-how: the hazard in contracting rises while the hazard of technological leakage and imitation falls as the degree of tacitness of know-how rises.[13] The analysis reveals that stronger PRs in the host country increase affiliated licensing among simple-technology firms, strongly enough that the composition of their licensing further shifts towards affiliates. These findings hold even after we control for the firm's R&D intensity (as a percentage of sales), in order to proxy for contractual hazards as in Henisz (2000).

As the article studies the interaction between firm strategy and the institutional environment, it is also related to Zhao (2006). In our article, the firms take the imitation risk in a host country as given but the extent of their exposure to this risk varies: it is low among complex-technology firms and high among simple-technology firms. An explanation is that the more complex technologies could be fragmented to discourage imitation as in Zhao (2006), whereas the more simple ones have limited alternative methods of protection. Firms with more simple technologies choose the more secure means of transfer via affiliates and subsidiaries and also rely on a host's PRs to further limit the risk of imitation. This explains why the volume of their affiliated licensing rises in response to stronger host's PRs (in spite of the negative influence of the internalization effect), while it falls among complex-technology firms. This distinction is key to understanding the licensing impact of developing countries' PRs, and has not been highlighted previously.

Lastly, this article contributes to the international development literature by examining the consequences of patent protection on multinational firms' licensing strategy. Development scholars have stressed the fundamental role of technology for economic growth and development, but remain divided on the role and relevance of patent rights in facilitating technology transfer from developed to developing countries. The policy debate, moreover, largely abstracts from firm strategies, such as how global companies manage and choose their entry modes, and how their decisions interact with the policy environment. Our work underscores the importance of IPR policy taking into account firm decision-making processes and thus helps advance public policy debate using insights from international business research. The article focuses on host countries in the developing world, where patent systems are generally weaker and concerns about technological leakage of information and subsequent imitation by rivals are most prominent. The relative ease of imitation compels multinational firms to carefully consider appropriability regimes in their licensing strategies. The appropriability effect of stronger PRs is particularly important among simple-technology firms licensing to developing countries, and it overtakes the internalization effect.

The next section provides a conceptual framework for thinking about how appropriability and internalization motives condition the effects of PRs on a multinational firm's licensing strategies.

THEORY AND HYPOTHESES

Central to our analysis is the argument that the impact of stronger foreign PRs on the volume of licensing and the mode of control depends critically on the underlying technological complexity of the firms' products. To formalize this argument and develop testable hypotheses, we propose a simple model of the foreign market entry strategy, endogenous technological composition of licensing activity, and asymmetries in the impact of PRs.[14]

Let $z \in [0, 1]$ index the underlying technological complexity of a firms' products, with simple-technology firms having a lower z. Firms take the technological complexity of their products as given and decide on the volume of licensing (i.e., how much technology to transfer via licensing into a country) and the mode of control (i.e., whether to license its technology to an affiliate or unaffiliated party). Technological complexity determines the strength of the appropriability regime and so, influences the firm's ability to capture the profits generated by licensing technology. Teece (1986) argued that the complex, tacit nature of knowledge reduces appropriability hazards which result from technological leakage of information leading to imitation by rivals. Building on this insight, we assume that technological complexity z is negatively related to the hazard rate by which innovations are imitated. For simplicity, we assume that $m(z) \equiv \mu(1-z)$.[15] The imitation rate falls from its maximum of μ to its minimum of zero as technological complexity z rises from its minimum of zero to its maximum of one. The parameter μ measures the strength of foreign patent rights which according to Teece (1986) is the second key dimension of the appropriability regime.

Let $V^k(z)$ represent the expected present discounted value of the stream of profits for a firm which engages in affiliated ($k = A$) or unaffiliated ($k = U$) licensing. At every point in time, the firm with each z chooses the strategy with the maximum of the two options given by $V(z) \equiv \max[V^A(z), V^U(z)]$. Appropriability hazards are high when the firm transfers proprietary technical information to its subsidiaries in foreign countries with weak PRs (Zander & Kogut, 1995; Poole, 2013; Berry, 2014). Poole (2013), for example, finds that the firm's technology may be misappropriated by the subsidiary's employees and used to start up imitative production. Greater still are the appropriability hazards when technology is transferred to unaffiliated parties. Unaffiliated licensing involves sharing technology with arm's length firms which are generally independent of control. The inability of the firm to control the actions of a licensee creates an incentive to internalize transactions through affiliated licensing. We account for the greater appropriability hazards under unaffiliated licensing by assuming that unaffiliated licensing entails the imitation risk premium, $\imath > 1$, and that the terms of the licensing contract fail to limit this extra risk. Consequently, the imitation rate equals $m_A(z) = \mu(1-z)$ when the firm engages in affiliated licensing and $m_U(z) = \imath\mu(1-z)$ when the firm engages in unaffiliated licensing. The existence of $\imath > 1$ provides an internalization motive for affiliated licensing.

Once imitation occurs, the firm's future profits are driven to zero. Hence the expected present discounted value of the stream of profits from licensing is risk-adjusted $V^k(z) = \pi^k(z)/[r + m_k(z)]$, where $\pi^k(z)$ denotes instantaneous profits and r is the discount rate. The firm with a given z will choose unaffiliated licensing over affiliated licensing if profits from unaffiliated licensing, adjusted for higher risk, are sufficiently large

$$\frac{\pi^U(z)}{r+m_U(z)} > \frac{\pi^A(z)}{r+m_A(z)}. \quad (1)$$

A licensing contract stipulates rent sharing between the licensor and the licensee. With Cobb–Douglas preferences as in Ivus, Park, and Saggi (2015), the ratio of instantaneous profits $\pi^U(z)/\pi^A(z)$ is simply equal to λ_U/λ_A, where λ_U and λ_A are the shares of profits retained by the firm from unaffiliated and affiliated licensing, respectively. We can now rewrite inequality (1), as follows:

$$\frac{\lambda_U}{\lambda_A} > \frac{r+m_U(z)}{r+m_A(z)}. \quad (2)$$

The market for technology licensing is imperfect (e.g., due to limited information and uncertainty in the outcomes of licensing transactions) and these imperfections limit the licensor's ability to extract rents from the licensee. Hazards in contracting and information, bargaining and enforcement costs discourage technology transfer to unrelated parties and encourage affiliated licensing instead. Costly renegotiation, for example, increases transaction costs for arm's length technology transfer, while exercise of command and control within the firm avoids renegotiation costs. Unaffiliated licensing is difficult to manage effectively but at the same time, it could be a more attractive model of control. One reason is that little or no equity need be granted. Another reason is that licensing an independent local firm to produce and distribute the product allows the licensor to lower the cost of training foreign workers and coordinating foreign manufacturing activities, which could be significant under affiliated licensing. Contracting out also yields a cost advantage to the firm if the firm lacks specialized complementary assets such as manufacturing and marketing (Teece, 1986; Arora & Ceccagnoli, 2006). As such, λ_U could exceed λ_A when the risk of imitation is zero. But the key question for us is how the relative profitability of unaffiliated licensing varies with the rate of imitation, as determined by the underlying technological complexity of a firms' products, z. We consider this next.

Technological Complexity Differences in the Nature of Licensing

It is easy to show that the term on the right hand side of the inequality (2) is higher when z is lower. This is because low-z firms face high appropriability hazards due to imitation and unaffiliated licensing entails the imitation risk premium (i.e., $\iota > 1$ and so $m_U(z) > m_A(z)$).

The relationship between z and the term on the left hand side of (2) is less clear. To the extent that greater technological complexity implies lower appropriability hazards which result from technological leakage and imitation by rivals, λ_U/λ_A should be positively related to z. If for example, the firms share rents with their licensees to deter imitation, then the licensors' profit share will be low among low-z firms with high imitation risk. Such profit sharing is optimal in the presence of asymmetric information (Gallini & Wright, 1990) and is most relevant for unaffiliated licensing, which carries the imitation risk premium.

At the same time, greater technological complexity could also imply greater appropriability hazards in contracting for the transfer of the technological innovation (Oxley, 1997, 1999; Henisz, 2000). Concerns over contractual hazards are expected to be particularly important when licensing technology to unrelated parties – for example, because an unrelated party is more likely to renege on the terms of a licensing agreement (Anand & Khanna, 2000) – but arm's length contracts can also overcome the problems in contracting for complex know-how – if for example, know-how is bundled with other complementary inputs with the superior enforceability of contracts in a technology package (Arora 1996).

The relationship between λ_U/λ_A and z is ambiguous but we can still establish the result that the inequality (2) is more likely to hold for high-z firms provided the imitation risk premium under unaffiliated licensing, ι, is high enough. If we further assume that $\lambda_U > \lambda_A$ (so that unaffiliated licensing is the preferred mode of control for the $z=1$ firm with highly complex technology and zero imitation risk), we find that there exists a unique and interior cut-off level of technological complexity $\bar{z}$ such that the simple-technology firms with $z<\bar{z}$ choose the more secure means of transfer via affiliates and subsidiaries while the complex-technology firms with $z>\bar{z}$ choose unaffiliated licensing. We summarize the endogenous technological composition of licensing activity for a given strength of host's PRs in Hypothesis 1.[16]

Hypothesis 1: Compared to firms producing technologically complex products, firms producing technologically simple products prefer affiliated over unaffiliated licensing, all else equal. The composition of licensing is thus relatively more skewed towards affiliated parties among firms with more simple technology, holding the strength of host's PRs constant.

The licensing impact of strengthening PRs

Strengthening host's PRs limits imitation as measured by the parameter μ_k (i.e., $d\mu_k/\text{dPRs}<0$) and as a result, has two effects on the firm's licensing strategy: the appropriability effect and the internalization effect. First, production reallocates from imitators to multinational firms, and the volume of unaffiliated and affiliated licensing rises within each firm as a result. This is the appropriability effect of stronger foreign PRs. Second, the relative attractiveness of licensing to unaffiliated parties rises, motivating some firms to switch from affiliated towards unaffiliated licensing (as the cut-off level of technological complexity $\bar{z}$ falls). This is the internalization effect. Unaffiliated licensing benefits from limited imitation under strong PRs the most because it carries the imitation risk premium. Stronger PRs protection also reduces the costs of achieving mutually agreeable licensing contracts and strengthens the licensor's bargaining power (Yang & Maskus, 2001). The relative share of profits from unaffiliated licensing λ_U/λ_A could rise as a result, which would reinforce the internalization effect. Hypothesis 2 summarizes the two effects.

Hypothesis 2: Strengthening foreign PRs has two effects on the licensing strategy of a firm: (i) it increases the volume of technology licensing to both affiliated and unaffiliated parties, all else equal (i.e., the appropriability effect) and (ii) it reduces the firm's reliance on affiliated licensing as the more secure means of transfer and could motivate the firm to switch towards unaffiliated licensing (i.e., the internalization effect).

The appropriability effect of stronger foreign PRs acts to increase the volume of technology transfer via licensing both within and outside the firm. This increase could be the result of firms switching from keeping a technology secret to marketing/licensing their technology as appropriability hazards fall. The internalization effect, on the other hand, acts to increase the firms' reliance on unaffiliated licensing while at the same time, reducing the firms' reliance on affiliated licensing as the more secure means of transfer. The underlying decision here concerns the preferred mode of control – whether to license the technology to an affiliate or unaffiliated party.

The internalization effect of stronger foreign PRs is to reduce affiliated licensing and shift the composition of licensing towards unaffiliated parties, but the appropriability effect has an opposing impact. If the appropriability effect on affiliated licensing is relatively strong, the composition of licensing could shift further towards affiliates. The overall impact of stronger PRs on licensing strategy is ambiguous and depends on the endogenous technological composition of licensing activity, as summarized by H1. The technological composition of licensing is critical for determining the overall impact of PRs because (i) the average technological complexity of the firms' products varies among firms which choose to engage in unaffiliated or affiliated licensing when the host's PRs are weak and (ii) the effectiveness of patents varies with the degree of the underlying technological complexity of the firms' products. We discuss how the licensing impact of stronger host's PR varies with technological complexity of the firm's products next.

Technological Complexity Differences in the Licensing Impact of Strengthening PRs

Stronger PRs reduce the risk of imitation across all firms but the impact is strongest among low-z firms: $\text{d}m_k(z)/\text{dPRs} = (1-z)\text{d}\mu_k/\text{dPRs}$. The technologies of low-z firms are simple enough that they can be easily communicated, misappropriated, and imitated. Consequently, low-z firms rely relatively more on strong PRs in the host country to protect their inventions and lower appropriability hazards.[17] Furthermore, patents are perceived as relatively effective means of appropriating rents from simple technological innovations, because simple technologies can be easily described in a patent and inventing around such a patent is hard. Anand and Khanna (2000), for example, argue that a pharmaceutical patent is hard to invent around "since a slight change in the underlying gene sequence of a protein can result in very different functions."

The high-z complex-technology firms, by contrast, are less reliant on strong patent protection in the host country. The technologies of high-z firms are complex enough that they can be separated and recombined to discourage imitation and to devise alternative methods of protection in countries with weak PRs (Zhao, 2006). Moreover, patents are perceived as a relatively ineffective tool for preventing the imitation of complex technological innovations. A typical complex technological innovation has a large number of components each protected by a separate patent. The legal requirements for upholding the validity of such patents are high (Teece, 1986). Patents for one complex innovation are often owned by different firms, and the risk of patent infringement in complex-technology markets is high (Grindley & Teece, 1997). Complex-technology firms primarily use patents as a bargaining chip in cross-licensing negotiations, but their foreign market entry strategies are not as sensitive to country differences in the strength of PRs.

Taken together, the above arguments form the basis for hypotheses H3a–H3c:

Hypothesis 3a: Strengthening foreign PRs increases the flow of unaffiliated licensing across all firms, but cross-product differences in the impact are relatively weak.

The flow of unaffiliated licensing rises across all firms with stronger foreign PRs due to the combined impact of the appropriability and the internalization effects. The cross-product differences in the impact are expected to be relatively weak. This follows since from H1, unaffiliated licensing is primarily composed of complex-technology products, which have a low reliance on PRs as a means of limiting imitation and lowering appropriability hazards.

Hypothesis 3b: Strengthening foreign PRs increases the flow of affiliated licensing relatively more among simple-technology firms, as compared to complex-technology firms.

From H1, affiliated licensing is primarily composed of simple-technology products, which face higher risk of imitation and rely relatively more on strong host's PRs to lower appropriability hazards. The appropriability effect, which increases the flow of affiliated licensing, is expected to be relatively strong among these firms (compared to complex-technology firms). As technological complexity of firms' products rises, the appropriability effect becomes weaker, making it more likely that the internalization effect would dominate, in which case the flow of affiliated licensing will fall with strengthening host's PRs.

Hypothesis 3c: Strengthening foreign PRs shifts the composition of licensing towards affiliated parties relatively more among simple-technology firms, as compared to complex-technology firms.

METHODS

The unit of analysis is the US parent firm i which may transfer its proprietary technology to a foreign affiliate or unaffiliated party located in host country j in year t. The basic model of technology transfer is as follows:

$$T_{ijt} = \alpha + \beta_1 P_{jt} + \beta_2 X_{jt} + \beta_3 R_{it} + \beta_4 A_{it} + \beta_5 A_{it} \times P_{jt} + \alpha_j + \alpha_t + \tau_{jt} + \varepsilon_{ijt}, \quad (3)$$

where T_{ijt} is the technology transfer via the licensing of intangible assets. We consider three outcome variables (in logs): unaffiliated licensing fees and royalty receipts (T^U), affiliated licensing fees and royalty receipts (T^A), and the ratio of unaffiliated to affiliated receipts (T^U/T^A) to study the composition of licensing. The independent variable P_{jt} is the strength of PRs in host country j at time t. X_{jt} is the vector of time-varying host country controls, including the level of real gross domestic product (GDP), wages relative to the US, corporate income tax rates, and a measure of inward capital restrictions. R_{it} is the parent firm R&D intensity, measured by the ratio of the parent's R&D spending to its sales. A_{it} is the number of US patents granted to firm i at time t, and $A_{it} \times P_{jt}$ is the interaction of A_{it} with the host's strength of PRs. Similar to Branstetter et al. (2006), we include $A_{it} \times P_{jt}$ to allow the impact of PRs to vary with the extent to which firms utilize PRs. Next, α_j and α_t are the country and year fixed effects, and τ_{jt} the vector of country-specific linear time trends. Last, α is the constant term and ε_{ijt} the stochastic error term.

In order to examine the role of technological complexity, we augment the model (3) as follows:

$$T_{ijt} = \alpha + \beta_1 P_{jt} + \beta_2 X_{jt} + \beta_3 R_{it} + \beta_4 A_{it} + \beta_5 A_{it} \times P_{jt} + \beta_6 Z_p + \beta_7 Z_p \times P_{jt} + \alpha_j + \alpha_t + \tau_{jt} + \varepsilon_{ijt}, \quad (4)$$

where Z_p is the level of technological complexity of product p and $Z_p \times P_{jt}$ the interaction between the technological complexity measure and the host's PRs. By separately controlling for Z_p, we allow T_{ijt} to differ among the products for reasons other than the strength of PRs.[18]

The models (2) and (3) are estimated using the random effects estimator which treats the firm-by-country-specific effects as a random time-invariant component of the error. We do this to allow the estimation of time-invariant factors of interest, such as technological complexity. Importantly, our choice of the estimator is not critical to our results. We also considered the OLS estimator with firm-by-country fixed effects, which permits regressors to be endogenous provided that they are correlated with only a time-invariant component of the error. We found that this form of endogeneity does not explain our results and the firm-by-country-specific effects could be treated as random. We also employed Heckman's two-stage estimation procedure, to allow for the selection of firms into licensing, and confirmed that a selection bias does not explain our results. Last, we implemented the instrumental variable estimator using colonial origin to isolate exogenous variations in PRs, and concluded that the endogeneity of the strength of countries' PRs does not drive our results.

H1 implies a positive coefficient on Z_p in (4) when T^U or T^U/T^A is the outcome variable, and a negative coefficient on Z_p when T^A is the outcome variable. H2 further implies a positive coefficient on P_{jt} when T^U is the outcome variable. When T^A is the outcome variable, H2 implies a positive coefficient on P_{jt} if the appropriability effect is strong and a negative coefficient on P_{jt} if the internalization effect is strong. H3 discusses how the impact of PRs depends on the level of technological complexity of a firm's products. From (4), this dependence is given by $dT_{ijt}/dPR_{jt} = \beta_1 + \beta_7 Z_p$. H3a implies that the coefficient β_7 is relatively small or statistically insignificant when T^U is the outcome variable. We also expect $\beta_1 > 0$ and $\beta_7 < 0$ when T^A is the outcome variable (H3b) and $\beta_1 < 0$ and $\beta_7 > 0$ when T^U/T^A is the outcome variable provided the appropriability effect is strong (H3c).

DATA

Our data come primarily from a micro database of US parent companies with foreign direct investments and operations around the world.[19] The data are collected by the BEA in its benchmark and annual surveys of the operations of US multinational companies, its quarterly balance of payments survey of US direct investment abroad, and its annual and quarterly surveys of US international services transactions. The BEA surveys cover both direct investment activities abroad and service transactions, such as the licensing of intangible assets. We focus on technologies transferred by US parent companies to 44 developing countries, where concerns about weak IP protection have been the most prominent and where access to new technologies is crucial.[20,21] Together, these countries account for over 96% of affiliated, and over 98% of unaffiliated, licensing fees and royalties received by US multinational firms from the developing world. The data are annual from 1993 to 2009.[22] Only large US parent companies are required to complete a detailed survey form that includes the reporting of parent company R&D and so the sample is skewed towards large US parent companies that engage in R&D and patenting.[23] In total, 1,185 US firms operated across these 44 developing countries – some operated in only one country, while others in multiple countries – giving us 5,309 unique firm-by-host country pairs. Some of these pairs are observed in our data for a short period, while others exist for a longer period.

Outcome Variables

The level of unaffiliated licensing is the sum of all licensing fees and royalties received by the parent firm from unaffiliated parties in host country *j* at year *t*. Likewise, the level of affiliated licensing is the sum of all the licensing fees and royalties received by the parent firm from its foreign affiliate(s) in host country *j* at year *t*. The data are in real 2005 PPP-adjusted dollars.

The analysis is performed on the flow of licensing, but we also used the stock of licensing capital as an alternative measure and confirmed that our results are not driven by our choice of the measure of licensing. We constructed the stock measure using the perpetual inventory method with a depreciation rate of 20%.[24] This measure serves to account for any cumulative effects of technology transfer. Due to the characteristics of "knowledge" assets, a licensing transaction that gives access to knowledge could create some persistence in benefits. Unlike with physical rental properties, the licensee does not "return" the intangible asset or know-how upon the conclusion of the terms of a technology transfer agreement. Some of the knowledge assets acquired with the flow of licensing are retained by the licensee and continue to benefit the licensee until they are fully depreciated. The effects of technology transfer can therefore persist beyond the transaction period, even if the licensing agreement prohibits future use or exploitation of the intellectual property without the appropriate fees or royalties. The strength of PRs in a host country could affect the formation of this type of technology capital as well as impact the flow of technology transfer.

Independent Variables

We measure the strength of patent protection by an index of PRs (see Park, 2008). The index varies across countries and over time. It is based on legislation and case laws which establish how such legislative provisions are interpreted and enforced. The components which comprise the PRs index include membership in international agreements, duration of protection, the patentability of certain types of inventions such as software, enforcement mechanisms, and the presence of any restrictions on PRs such as compulsory licensing and working requirements. To avoid contemporaneous influence from foreign technology transfers to the setting of domestic patent protection, we lag the index 4 years.[25] We also consider a patent reform dummy variable as an alternative measure of patent protection. This dummy equals one for the year of major patent reform(s) and all years thereafter. When selecting the year of major patent reform(s), we considered only the most significant shifts in the patent system during our sample period and ignored minor revisions to countries' patent laws and practices.[26]

To explore the role of technological complexity, we employ the task-based measure from Naghavi et al. (2015). The measure is obtained at the product category level (two-digit *Nomenclature of Economic Activity*, or NACE, codes), based on the factor content of tasks that require complex problem-solving skills. It is constructed as the interaction of three variables. First is the complexity score for 809 (eight-digit) occupations as defined in the Standard Occupational Classification. The score is derived using expert information on the level and importance of complex problem-solving skills provided in the O*NET data.[27] Second is the industry occupational intensity, using information on the employment of labor across different occupations by 3-digit *Standard Industrial Classification* (SIC) industries from the US Bureau of Labor Statistics' Occupational Employment Statistics. Third is the share of industry in the production of each product. The overall measure indexes each product category according to the average intensity of complex problem-solving tasks involved in the product's manufacturing. In our analysis, we focus on 15 high-tech manufacturing product categories, for which patent protection is expected to matter most. To match the measure of technological complexity to our data, we sort the 4-digit NAICS codes associated with each firm into the corresponding product categories. Appendix III summarizes these data.

Control Variables

Data on US patents granted by firm (utility patent counts) are from the National Bureau of Economic Research's Patent Data Project. Starting with the firms in the BEA parent firm sample, we matched the firm employer-identification-numbers (EINs) to the Committee on Uniform Securities Identification Procedures (CUSIP) codes of firms in Compustat, since the NBER database uses CUSIP codes. This allowed us to find the US patents granted to a partial sample of the parent firms in our data. We match the rest of the data manually by comparing firm names and/or company initials.[28] To mitigate the concern that a firm's patenting strategies may depend on its licensing and commercialization decisions, we lag the number of parent patents 3 years.[29]

The parent firm R&D intensity is defined as the ratio of the parent firm R&D spending to its sales. Several studies have shown that firms that heavily use research inputs and proprietary technology in their production process have strong incentives to internalize technology markets (see for example, Buckley & Pearce, 1979). The corporate income tax rate faced by the foreign affiliates of the parent firm in the host country is defined as the ratio of income taxes paid to the firms' pre-tax net income.[30] Both of these measures come from the BEA data. The measure of inward capital restrictions is a dummy variable which equals one if a host country placed capital controls on inward foreign direct investment in a given year. These data are from the International Monetary Fund. To control for the market size of host countries, we use real GDP levels (in constant 2005 PPP dollars) from the World Development Indicators. We also use data on relative hourly wages (in US dollars) in the manufacturing industry to control for the relatively low cost of labor in developing countries, which motivates parent firms to establish foreign affiliates in these countries. The relative wage variable is constructed as the ratio of the host's hourly wage to the US hourly wage. The hourly wage data are compiled by the Occupational Wages around the World (OWW) Database.[31]

In our sensitivity analysis, we use eight additional variables: parent's capital–labor ratio (in logs); parent's assets; the share of a parent's foreign

Table 1 US parent firm sample statistics by technological complexity

		Unaffil. licensing flows	Affil. licensing flows	Ratio of unaff. to aff. lic.
All US parent firms	Mean	329.4	578.5	0.569
	Std dev	5311.6	3841.2	
Above median complexity	Mean	536.8	486.2	1.104
	Std dev	7939.2	4049.3	
Below median complexity	Mean	180.3	644.9	0.280
	Std dev	1774.8	3683.1	
Difference in means		356.5***	−158.7***	0.824***

Notes: The licensing figures are in thousands of real 2005 US dollars.
*** Statistical significance at the 1% level.

sales in its world sales; the share of a parent's unaffiliated exports in its total exports; the quality of legal institutions; the industry measure of product life-cycle length; affiliate R&D intensity; and the cost of patenting abroad per market size. The parent's capital–labor ratio is the ratio of its net property, plant, and equipment (PPE) to its employment.[32] Following Hall and Ziedonis (2001), we use the capital–labor ratio to capture the effects of sunk costs which can create patent holdup problems and so, provide incentives for firms to patent and cross-license. The parent's assets can proxy for firm size. Large firms have the resources to invest abroad and source globally.[33] The share of a parent's world sales that is foreign and the share of its exports that are unaffiliated are used to measure its foreign experience. A number of previous studies have used a company's international experience as a control variable.[34] Firms with greater foreign experience can build on existing trading relations and may therefore face lower fixed costs of foreign licensing. The data on institutional quality are from Kunčič (2014).[35] We add the measure of the quality of legal institution since our measure of PRs could be picking up the effects of broader institutional changes correlated with patent protection. Our measure of the industry product life-cycle length is binary and created using the data in Bilir (2014). Specifically, we calculated the median product life-cycle length and then constructed a dummy variable which takes the value of one if an industry's product life-cycle length is above the median and zero if it is below the median. We include this measure (by itself and interacted with PRs), since product life-cycle length matters for multinational activity (Bilir, 2014) and could be correlated with technological complexity. The R&D-to-sales ratio of the (aggregate) affiliates of the parent company enables us to see, if only tentatively, whether R&D transferred to affiliates reduces or obviates the need to transfer technologies to them via licensing. Given the potential for simultaneity between affiliate licensing and affiliate R&D, we lag this measure 3 years. The cost of patenting is from Park (2010). The measure covers both the cost of procurement (filing, attorney, translation, search and examination fees) and maintenance (renewal fees), and varies by host country and year. We divided the cost of patenting by GDP to obtain the cost of patenting per market size.

Table 1 summarizes data on the three outcome variables: the flow of unaffiliated licensing, the flow of affiliated licensing, and the ratio of unaffiliated to affiliated licensing flows across all parent firms and across firms by technological complexity (below and above median). Compared to firms with a more simple technology, firms with a more complex technology receive on average a greater flow of licensing income from unaffiliated parties and a lower flow of licensing income from foreign affiliates. The respective differences in means are 356.5 and −158.7. When unaffiliated licensing flow is evaluated relative to its affiliated counterpart, we see that this ratio is 0.824 points higher for firms with more complex technology. All the differences in means are highly statistically significant. Overall, these results support H1 and suggest that the technological complexity of products influences the licensing impact of PRs.

The results in Table 1 are not driven by the aggregation of product categories into two groups but also hold at the level of individual industries. Table 2 summarizes the results for eight industries. It shows that technological complexity is highest in *Machinery and equipment, Electronics and components*, and *Transportation*. These complex-technology industries together account for as much as 89.4% of the total unaffiliated licensing by US multinational firms in the 44 developing countries. At the same time, these industries' combined share of the

Table 2 Licensing and technological complexity by industry

	Unaffil. lic., % share of manufacturing	Affil. lic., % share of manufacturing	Ratio of Unaffil. to affil. lic.	Mean value of technological complexity
Electronics and components	36.1	13.1	1.56	0.381
Machinery and equipment	32.0	13.6	1.33	0.351
Transportation	21.3	18.1	0.63	0.283
Metals	0.1	1.0	0.06	0.280
Pharmaceuticals	0.9	8.3	0.06	0.258
Energy	2.7	0.6	2.61	0.254
Non-pharm chemicals	6.7	41.0	0.09	0.258
Other manufacturing	0.2	4.3	0.02	0.204
Total	100	100	0.57	0.298

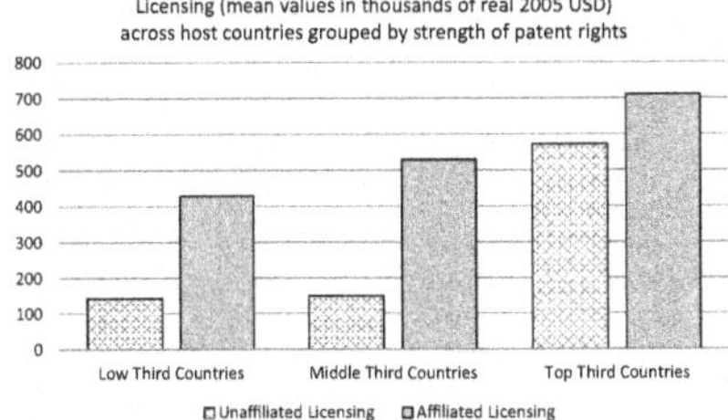

Figure 1 US licensing by destination.

total affiliated licensing is only 44.8%. Across industries with a more simple technology, by contrast, affiliated licensing is generally more common than its unaffiliated counterpart. The share of affiliated licensing is relatively high in all simple-technology industries, except *Energy*. Two industries (i.e., *Pharmaceuticals* and *Non-pharmaceutical chemicals*) account for 49.3% of all affiliated licensing in manufacturing.

Figure 1 further plots licensing flows (in thousands of real 2005 US dollars) across host countries grouped by the strength of their PRs. Here, the US parent firms' royalty fees and licensing receipts are pooled across all firms during the sample period. It is apparent that affiliated licensing is the most common. This is true for all three country groups, regardless of the strength of PRs, but the gap between affiliated and unaffiliated licensing is narrowest in countries with the strongest PRs. These country-level comparisons further reveal that countries with weak PRs (compared to the top third countries) obtain less affiliated and unaffiliated licensing from US parent companies. The difference is particularly striking for unaffiliated licensing.

RESULTS

Table 3 shows the results of estimating the basic model (3) in columns (1)–(3) and the augmented model (4) in columns (4)–(6). In columns (1)–(3), the outcome variables are T^U, T^A, and T^U/T^A. It is apparent that the coefficient on the PRs index is positive and statistically significant at the 5% level in columns (1) and (2). Stronger host's PRs promote the licensing of innovations to both affiliated and unaffiliated parties, all else equal. These results confirm H2 and suggest that the appropriability effect is strong. We further see that the coefficient on PRs is not statistically different from zero in column (3), where T^U/T^A is the outcome variable. Thus when technological complexity is not taken into account, stronger PRs promote unaffiliated and affiliated licensing to a similar degree, leaving the composition of licensing unchanged.

In columns (4)–(6), we add the measure of technological complexity (Z_p) and its interaction with PRs ($Z_p \times P_{jt}$) to our controls. It is apparent that the coefficient on Z_p is positive and highly statistically significant in column (6). Thus all else being equal, firms producing technologically simple products (relative to those producing technologically complex products) have a lower ratio of unaffiliated to affiliated licensing. That is, the composition of licensing is relatively more skewed towards affiliated parties among firms with more simple technology, which confirms H1. The results further show that the product difference in the composition of licensing is particularly pronounced in countries with strong PRs. The coefficient on $Z_p \times P_{jt}$ is positive and highly statistically significant in column (6). Simple-technology firms choose the more secure means of transfer via affiliates and subsidiaries, and also rely on a host's PRs to further limit the risk of imitation. Thus

Table 3 Aggregate and complexity results

	Unaff. Lic. (1)	Affil. Lic. (2)	Unaff./Aff. (3)	Unaff. Lic. (4)	Affil. Lic. (5)	Unaff./Aff. (6)
Log(host PRs)	0.118**	0.194**	−0.070	0.311***	1.389***	−1.068***
	(0.052)	(0.088)	(0.093)	(0.102)	(0.214)	(0.231)
Technological complexity				0.889**	−1.549**	2.498***
				(0.384)	(0.763)	(0.784)
Techn. complexity × log(host PRs)				−0.648*	−4.162***	3.500***
				(0.353)	(0.679)	(0.756)
Log(parent R&D/sales)	0.010***	0.039***	−0.031***	0.010***	0.046***	−0.038***
	(0.002)	(0.007)	(0.007)	(0.002)	(0.007)	(0.007)
Log(host GDP)	0.500***	1.447***	−0.943***	0.522***	1.549***	−1.023***
	(0.163)	(0.292)	(0.342)	(0.164)	(0.294)	(0.343)
Log(host/US wages)	−0.081	0.012	−0.095	−0.097	−0.021	−0.080
	(0.201)	(0.350)	(0.360)	(0.202)	(0.347)	(0.360)
Capital restrictions dummy	0.063**	−0.007	0.070	0.065**	−0.008	0.072
	(0.030)	(0.057)	(0.061)	(0.030)	(0.057)	(0.060)
Host corporate income tax	−0.013	−0.043	0.030	−0.014	−0.041	0.026
	(0.047)	(0.067)	(0.070)	(0.048)	(0.064)	(0.068)
Log(parent patents)	0.035**	0.034	0.003	0.036**	0.035	0.001
	(0.014)	(0.022)	(0.027)	(0.014)	(0.022)	(0.027)
Log(host PRs) × log(parent patents)	−0.023*	−0.015	−0.010	−0.023*	−0.012	−0.013
	(0.013)	(0.020)	(0.024)	(0.013)	(0.021)	(0.025)
Constant	−8.415***	−22.633***	14.128**	−9.019***	−23.889***	14.756***
	(2.704)	(4.838)	(5.635)	(2.724)	(4.872)	(5.655)
Observations	29,940	29,940	29,940	29,533	29,533	29,533
R^2	0.0910	0.0242	0.0470	0.0917	0.0475	0.0663

Notes: Random effects estimator. *** $p < 0.01$, ** $p < 0.05$, * $p < 0.1$. All outcome variables are in natural logarithms. Robust standard errors in parentheses are clustered by country × year. All regressions include year fixed effects, country fixed effects, and host-country-specific time trends.

technological complexity, by itself and together with patent protection, plays a key role in determining the composition of licensing.

The results in columns (4) and (5) further our understanding. In column (4), where T^U is the outcome variable, the coefficient on Z_p is positive and statistically significant at the 5% level and the coefficient on $Z_p \times P_{jt}$ is negative but not statistically significant at the 5% level. Thus across all firms, firms with a more simple technology engage in unaffiliated licensing less, and the product difference in unaffiliated licensing is similar across developing countries, regardless of the level of their PRs. In column (5), where T^A is the outcome variable, the coefficients on Z_p and $Z_p \times P_{jt}$ are both negative and statistically significant at the 5% and 1% level, respectively. Thus simple-technology firms engage in affiliated licensing relatively more, and this is especially true in countries with strong PRs.

We now consider the effects of PRs and test H3a. From column (4), the elasticity of unaffiliated licensing with respect to PRs is $d \ln T^U / d \ln PRs = 0.311$, which does not depend on Z_p.[36] This result implies that strengthening PRs in developing countries makes the licensing of innovations to unaffiliated parties more attractive, and that this effect is equally strong across all firms, regardless of the level of technological complexity of their products. This result confirms H3a.

H3b requires a positive coefficient on P_{jt} ($\beta_1 > 0$) and a negative coefficient on $Z_p \times P_{jt}$ ($\beta_7 < 0$) in column (5), which is what we see. The results imply that the impact of stronger PRs on affiliated licensing (given by $d \ln T^A / d \ln \text{PRs} = 1.389 - 4.162 Z_p$) is positive for any $Z_p < 0.333$. In our sample, the variable Z_p ranges from a minimum of 0.1839178 to a maximum of 0.4221271. Thus it follows that when PRs are strengthened, the attractiveness of affiliated licensing rises among simple-technology firms and falls among complex-technology firms. The results in column (6) further indicate that the increase in affiliated licensing among simple-technology firms is strong enough that the entire composition of their licensing shifts towards affiliated parties, since $d \ln(T^U/T^A)/d \ln PRs = -1.068 + 3.5 Z_p < 0$ for any $Z_p < 0.305$. For complex-technology firms, by contrast, strengthening PRs reduces the attractiveness of affiliated licensing and shifts the composition of licensing further towards unaffiliated parties. These results are consistent with H3c and suggest that the appropriability effect is strong.

The coefficients on the number of US patents of parent firms A_{it} and the interaction of A_{it} with the host's PRs are not statistically significant at the 5% level in columns (3) and (6). Thus we find no evidence that the composition of licensing differs with the extent to which firms utilize PRs. The coefficient on A_{it} is positive and statistically significant at the 5% level in columns (1) and (4). This result suggests that firms which utilize PRs more engage in more unaffiliated licensing, as they have more technologies, inventions, and other intangible assets to license to unrelated parties. At the same time, the coefficient on $A_{it} \times P_{jt}$ is not statistically significant at the 5% level. This result suggests that the licensing impact of stronger PRs does not vary with the number of parent patents. The coefficients on the host's relative wage and corporate income tax rate are statistically insignificant in all columns. Inward capital restrictions abroad encourage firms to access foreign markets by transacting with unaffiliated parties, as suggested by the positive and significant coefficient on capital restrictions in columns (1) and (4). Importantly, all of these factors appear to have a balanced or neutral effect on the licensing volumes so that the composition of licensing is left unchanged. The host's level of GDP and parent's R&D intensity are the only exceptions. These two variables are positively associated with both types of licensing but negatively associated with the ratio of unaffiliated to affiliated licensing. Thus consistent with the internalization literature, we find that R&D-intensive or knowledge-intensive parent firms favor affiliated over unaffiliated licensing (Henisz, 2003; Buckley & Casson, 2009). To the extent that firms invest more heavily in their research inputs and proprietary technology, they have a greater incentive to internalize international markets.

Sensitivity Analysis

Sensitivity to Additional Controls

Our results in Table 3 could be driven by cross-product differences in the licensing strategies of firms, independent of PRs. Technological differences in firms' modularization strategies, for example, could influence firm licensing decisions. Complex-technology products are easier to modularize, which could explain a positive coefficient on Z_p when unaffiliated licensing is the outcome variable.[37] To check that such cross-product differences are not driving our results, we re-estimate the model (3) with product fixed effects. Column (1) in Table 4 reports the results when T^U/T^A is the outcome variable. The coefficient on Z_p is not identified in this model (since all cross-product variation is consumed by the product fixed effects), but the coefficients on P_{jt} and $Z_p \times P_{jt}$ remain of the same sign and statistical significance. The coefficient on $Z_p \times P_{jt}$ rises in magnitude. In column (2), we also include eight interactions of industry indicators with the strength of PRs, since the impact of PRs could vary across industries for reasons other than differences in technological complexity. For example, we observe a lot of unaffiliated licensing in the *Electronics and components* industry because of its specific input–output structure. Components and intermediate inputs produced in this industry are used in other products or designed to work with other pieces. Often, multiple-patented inventions comprise a single product (e.g., smartphone), each owned by different parties from within and outside the firm network. Consequently, cross-licensing and outsourcing of production, assembly, or marketing tasks to agents external to the firm – which necessitate authorizing and giving access to know-how and technology to unaffiliated parties – are predominant in this industry. The modular, fragmentable nature of electronics products and technologies likely facilitates the external sourcing of components to countries where factor costs and access to raw materials are more advantageous (Ernst, 2005; Ziedonis, 2004). The industry-PRs interactions absorb cross-industry variation in the impact of PRs, leaving within-industry cross-product variation in complexity (as well as within-country over time variation in the strength of PRs) to identify the coefficient on $Z_p \times P_{jt}$. The coefficient on $Z_p \times P_{jt}$ is still positive and highly statistically significant, but larger in magnitude.

Our results are also robust to having additional controls: the parent's capital–labor ratio; the parent's assets; the share of a parent's foreign sales in its world sales; the share of a parent's unaffiliated exports in its total exports; the quality of legal institutions; the industry measure of product life-cycle length; and affiliate R&D intensity. Table 5 shows the results. The coefficients on P_{jt}, $Z_p \times P_{jt}$ and Z_p are of the same sign and all but the coefficient on P_{jt} in column (4) are statistically

Table 4 Complexity results, with product fixed effects

	Unaff./aff. lic. ratio (1)	Unaff./aff. lic. ratio (2)
Log(host PRs)	−0.997***	
	(0.227)	
Techn. complexity × log(host PRs)	3.281***	3.778***
	(0.746)	(1.030)
Log(parent R&D/sales)	−0.020***	−0.024***
	(0.007)	(0.007)
Log(host GDP)	−1.042***	−0.987***
	(0.337)	(0.332)
Log(host/US wages)	−0.078	−0.047
	(0.363)	(0.362)
Capital restrictions dummy	0.072	0.074
	(0.060)	(0.060)
Host corporate income tax	0.026	0.026
	(0.068)	(0.067)
Log(parent patents)	−0.000	−0.008
	(0.027)	(0.028)
Log(host PRs) × log(parent patents)	−0.019	−0.010
	(0.025)	(0.026)
Pharmaceuticals × log(host PRs)		−0.435
		(0.288)
Non-pharmac. chemicals × log(host PRs)		−1.227***
		(0.289)
Energy × log(host PRs)		−0.697**
		(0.306)
Metals × log(host PRs)		−1.303***
		(0.319)
Transportation × log(host PRs)		−1.702***
		(0.343)
Machinery and equipment × log(host PRs)		−0.985***
		(0.362)
Electronics and components × log(host PRs)		−1.366***
		(0.378)
Other manufacturing × log(host PRs)		−1.165***
		(0.248)
Product fixed effects	Yes	Yes
Constant	15.675***	14.744***
	(5.551)	(5.473)
Observations	29,533	29,533
R^2	0.123	0.134

Notes: Random effects estimator. *** $p < 0.01$, ** $p < 0.05$, * $p < 0.1$. All outcome variables are in natural logarithms. Robust standard errors in parentheses are clustered by country × year.
All regressions include year fixed effects, country fixed effects, and host-country-specific time trends.

significant at the 5% level. We further find that parents with a higher capital–labor ratio engage in more unaffiliated licensing (say via cross-licensing) when the host's PRs are strong. Parents with more assets also engage in unaffiliated licensing relatively more, regardless of the level of PRs. The unaffiliated licensing ratio is also high across firms with more foreign experience. We also observe more unaffiliated licensing in industries with a shorter product life-cycle. This could be because if product life-cycle is short, obsolescence is more likely to occur before imitation (Bilir, 2014). Patent protection is more effective in industries with a longer product life-cycle, where the impact of PRs is to shift the composition of licensing towards unaffiliated parties. Finally, affiliate R&D intensity is not a statistically significant factor in affiliated or unaffiliated licensing.[38]

Table 5 Additional controls

	Unaff./aff. (1)	Unaff./aff. (2)	Unaff./aff. (3)	Unaff./aff. (4)	Unaff./aff. (5)
Log(host PRs)	−1.063***	−1.278**	−1.596**	−1.222*	−2.394***
	(0.231)	(0.635)	(0.630)	(0.728)	(0.823)
Technological complexity	2.903***	3.166***	3.924***	4.423***	4.680***
	(0.776)	(0.978)	(0.965)	(1.001)	(1.207)
Techn. complexity × log(host PRs)	3.502***	3.858***	3.597***	3.574***	4.497***
	(0.755)	(0.903)	(0.924)	(0.977)	(1.286)
Log(parent R&D/sales)	−0.044***	−0.048***	−0.046***	−0.042***	−0.040***
	(0.007)	(0.008)	(0.008)	(0.010)	(0.012)
Log(host GDP)	−1.031***	−1.206***	−1.353***	−1.676***	−1.705***
	(0.345)	(0.398)	(0.443)	(0.445)	(0.477)
Log(host/US wages)	−0.081	−0.290	−0.465	0.553	0.884
	(0.362)	(0.416)	(0.495)	(0.539)	(0.607)
Capital restrictions dummy	0.072	0.035	0.043	0.090	0.118
	(0.061)	(0.074)	(0.074)	(0.085)	(0.094)
Host corporate income tax	0.028	0.096	0.099	0.129	0.204**
	(0.068)	(0.080)	(0.080)	(0.087)	(0.088)
Log(parent patents)	−0.001	−0.043	−0.040	−0.012	0.009
	(0.027)	(0.028)	(0.028)	(0.030)	(0.036)
Log(host PRs) × log(parent patents)	−0.015	0.013	0.009	−0.013	−0.024
	(0.025)	(0.027)	(0.027)	(0.029)	(0.034)
log(parent assets)	0.092***	0.161***	0.154***	0.236***	0.222***
	(0.021)	(0.051)	(0.051)	(0.049)	(0.056)
Log(host PRs) × log(parent assets)		−0.040	−0.037	−0.068	−0.035
		(0.042)	(0.042)	(0.042)	(0.046)
Log(parent K/L)		−0.175***	−0.245***	−0.285***	−0.337***
		(0.057)	(0.060)	(0.074)	(0.092)
Log(host PRs) × log(parent K/L)		0.164***	0.200***	0.208***	0.260***
		(0.050)	(0.052)	(0.065)	(0.080)
Product life-cycle length			−0.367***	−0.494***	−0.530***
			(0.066)	(0.083)	(0.106)
Product life-cycle l. × log(host PRs)			0.135**	0.205***	0.257***
			(0.066)	(0.075)	(0.093)
Quality of legal institutions			−0.056	0.151	0.429**
			(0.143)	(0.175)	(0.207)
Share of foreign in world sales				0.539***	0.460***
				(0.135)	(0.167)
Share of unaff. exports in total exports				0.506***	0.317***
				(0.075)	(0.088)
Log(affil. R&D intensity)					0.020
					(0.013)
Constant	13.134**	15.725**	19.335**	20.745***	20.257**
	(5.753)	(6.562)	(7.540)	(7.624)	(8.314)
Observations	29,530	23,491	22,576	19,831	15,361
R^2	0.0764	0.0723	0.0750	0.0850	0.0798

Notes: Random effects estimator. *** $p < 0.01$, ** $p < 0.05$, * $p < 0.1$. All outcome variables are in natural logarithms. Robust standard errors in parentheses are clustered by country × year. All regressions include year fixed effects, country fixed effects, and host-country-specific time trends.

Sensitivity to Model Specification

The results in Table 3 were obtained using the random effects estimator which treats the firm-by-country-specific effects as a random time-invariant component of the error. This estimator is inconsistent if the firm-by-country-specific effects are in fact correlated with the regressors. To allow for this form of endogeneity, we re-estimate (3) using the OLS estimator with firm-by-country fixed effects. These fixed effects wipe out all cross-sectional variation in our data, leaving variation within firm-country pairs over time to identify the coefficients of interest. Since the technological complexity measure does not vary over time, the coefficient on Z_p cannot be estimated here. Table 6 shows the results, which are very similar to those in columns (4)–(6) in Table 3. The coefficients on P_{jt} and $Z_p \times P_{jt}$ have the same sign, are close in magnitude, and have similar statistical significance. The coefficient on P_{jt} is statistically significant at the 5% level in all columns, and that on $Z_p \times P_{jt}$ is statistically significant at the 5% level in columns (2) and (3).

Not all firms license to all countries, and so some of the licensing flows are recorded as zero in our data. We disregarded these zeros thus far but if their occurrence is non-random, our results may be biased as they do not account for the selection of firms into licensing. To address this concern, we use Heckman's two-stage estimation procedure (Heckman, 1979). Stage 1 is the selection equation which models the probability of a firm selecting into licensing. Stage 2 is a linear regression equation which models the flow of licensing correcting for selection bias. We use the cost of patenting relative to a country's market size as the exclusion restriction. Firms that license abroad typically file for patent protection first in order to protect what they are licensing to others. The cost of filing may affect the decision to patent and then license, but it should not affect the flow of licensing directly. In other words, patenting cost affects firms' *decisions* to protect and market an asset, but not the extent of their activity with the asset once they acquire the protection. Table 7 reports the results of Stage 1 in columns (1)–(2) and Stage 2 in column (3). The outcome variable is equal to one if the flow of unaffiliated licensing is non-zero in column (1) and if the flow of affiliated licensing is non-zero in column (2). The coefficient on the cost of patenting is highly statistically significant, indicating that the cost of patenting is an appropriate exclusion restriction. The coefficients on the inverse Mills ratios λ_1 and λ_2 are not statistically different from zero. Thus no evidence of selection bias is detected.[39]

A wide range of domestic factors may influence countries' inflows of innovative products and technologies and their implementation of patent laws.[40] Moreover, the decision to strengthen PRs could be driven by foreign technology transfers themselves and the desire of a country to build and

Table 6 OLS with firm-by-country fixed effects

	Unaff. lic. (1)	Affil. lic. (2)	Unaff./aff. (3)
Log(host PRs)	0.298**	1.498***	−1.200***
	(0.141)	(0.236)	(0.277)
Techn. complexity × log(host PRs)	−0.539	−4.431***	3.892***
	(0.480)	(0.810)	(0.960)
Log(parent R&D/sales)	−0.001	0.031***	−0.033***
	(0.003)	(0.008)	(0.009)
Log(host GDP)	0.508***	1.593***	−1.085***
	(0.161)	(0.292)	(0.340)
Log(host/US wages)	−0.029	−0.100	0.071
	(0.226)	(0.338)	(0.374)
Capital restrictions dummy	0.057*	−0.011	0.067
	(0.031)	(0.053)	(0.061)
Host corporate income tax	−0.015	−0.037	0.022
	(0.046)	(0.063)	(0.072)
Log(parent patents)	0.052***	0.020	0.031
	(0.016)	(0.028)	(0.032)
Log(host PRs) × log(parent patents)	−0.036**	−0.016	−0.021
	(0.014)	(0.024)	(0.028)
Constant	−9.227***	−25.799***	16.571***
	(2.903)	(5.470)	(6.277)
Observations	29,533	29,533	29,533
R^2	0.667	0.659	0.643

Notes: OLS estimator. *** $p < 0.01$, ** $p < 0.05$, * $p < 0.1$. All outcome variables are in natural logarithms. Robust standard errors in parentheses are clustered by country × year.
All regressions include year fixed effects, firm-by-country fixed effects, and host-country-specific time trends.

Table 7 Two-stage selection model

	Stage 1		Stage 2
	Unaff. licen. (1)	Aff. licen. (2)	Unaff./aff. ratio (3)
Log(host PRs)	0.486**	1.278***	−2.500**
	(0.219)	(0.171)	(1.243)
Technological complexity	0.750	−1.379**	3.101**
	(0.865)	(0.692)	(1.448)
Techn. complexity × log(host PRs)	−1.363*	−3.547***	7.449**
	(0.730)	(0.577)	(3.334)
Log(parent R&D/sales)	0.014	0.027***	−0.070**
	(0.010)	(0.007)	(0.029)
Log(host GDP)	0.170***	−0.117**	−1.387*
	(0.063)	(0.049)	(0.744)
Log(host/US wages)	−1.630***	−1.655***	0.869
	(0.463)	(0.365)	(1.524)
Capital restrictions dummy	0.119*	0.086*	−0.059
	(0.066)	(0.051)	(0.133)
Host corporate income tax	−0.003	−0.001	0.003
	(0.078)	(0.057)	(0.091)
Log(parent patents)	0.065**	0.012	−0.032
	(0.028)	(0.022)	(0.053)
Log(host PRs) × log(parent patents)	−0.047*	0.003	−0.002
	(0.026)	(0.021)	(0.036)
Patenting cost per market size	0.177***	−0.157***	
	(0.068)	(0.053)	
The log of the variance $ln(\sigma_v^2)$	0.992***	0.780***	
	(0.055)	(0.040)	
Mills ratio λ_1			−1.135
			(2.175)
Mills ratio λ_2			−1.157
			(0.956)
Constant	−3.203***	2.525***	22.622
	(1.139)	(0.899)	(13.982)
Observations	32,238	32,238	29,408

Notes: 32,238 observations. Stage 1: Probit model. Stage 2: OLS. *** $p < 0.01$, ** $p < 0.05$, * $p < 0.1$. Robust standard errors in parentheses are clustered by country × year.
All regressions include year fixed effects, country fixed effects, and host-country-specific time trends.

protect its own innovative capacity. Techniques employed so far mitigate these concerns, but do not necessarily correct for this form of endogeneity. To estimate the causal effect of PRs, we adapt the IV approach from Ivus (2010) in which colonial origin is used to isolate exogenous variation in PRs. Specifically, Ivus (2010) argues that the imposition of TRIPS provided an exogenous shock to the PRs protection offered in a subset of developing countries. To isolate this exogenous variation, Ivus (2010) distinguishes developing countries by their colonial origin: countries which were not colonized by Britain or France (Non-colonies) are classified as treated, while those formerly colonized by Britain or France (Colonies) are classified as non-treated. The data show that over the 1990–2005 period, Non-colonies increased their PRs relatively more than Colonies, and colonial origin is relevant for explaining variation in changes of PRs over time.

To implement the IV approach, we difference the data over 15-year periods and relate changes in licensing between 1993–1994 and 2008–2009 to changes in PRs between 1990 and 2005.[41] The resulting data are a cross-section of firms. Among 44 countries in our sample, 25 are Non-colonies and 19 are Colonies. We use three variables – a Non-colony dummy variable (NC_j) and the interactions of NC_j with Z_p and A_{it} – as excluded instruments for the three endogenous variables – the changes in PRs (ΔP_{jt}) and the interactions of ΔP_{jt} with Z_p and A_{it}. Our IV approach is valid under the assumption that colonial origin has no effect on the outcome of interest, other than its effect through changes in PRs. This assumption might be too strong when growth in licensing flows is the outcome variable. It requires colonial origin to be unrelated to unobserved measures of licensing growth, which we cannot rule out. The assumption is, however, far less restrictive when the growth in the ratio of unaffiliated to affiliated licensing, $\Delta(T^U/T^A)$, is the outcome variable, as it requires the colonial origin of a developing country to have no direct impact on the growth in the *composition* of licensing.

Table 8 is as follows. Stage 1 results are in columns (1)–(3), where each of the three endogenous variables are the outcome variables. Stage 2 results are in column (4), where $\Delta(T^U/T^A)$ is the outcome variable. The test of underidentification rejects the null hypothesis of underidentification at the 0.001% level and indicates that the instruments are relevant. The Weak Identification test suggests that the instruments are not weak.[42] Also, the endogeneity test of endogenous regressors does not reject the null hypothesis that the PRs changes regressor and its interactions are exogenous variables, suggesting that the results reported so far do not suffer from endogeneity bias. Indeed, the IV estimates are in line with those in Table 3. From column (4), the coefficient on the PRs changes is negative and the coefficient on the interaction of PRs changes with Z_p is positive. Both coefficients are highly statistically significant.

Sensitivity to Measures of Licensing and PRs

Our results remain qualitatively unchanged when we adopt alternative definitions of the composition of licensing, use different measures of intangible assets, or employ a different measure of patent protection. To show this, we first re-estimate (4) using the patent reform dummy variable as an alternative measure of patent protection. The

Table 8 IV estimation

	Stage 1			Stage 2
	PRs changes (1)	PRs changes × techn. complexity (2)	PRs changes × parent patents (3)	T^U/T^A changes (4)
Non-colony dummy	0.027***	−0.009***	−0.438**	
	0.005)	(0.002)	(0.175)	
Techn. complexity × non-colony	−0.019	0.051***	−0.344	
	(0.016)	(0.006)	(0.410)	
Parent patents × non-colony	−0.000	−0.000	0.0506***	
	(0.000)	(0.000)	(0.005)	
PRs changes				−1.251***
				(0.269)
Techn. complexity × PRs changes				3.449***
				(0.640)
Parent patents × PRs changes				0.002
				(0.001)
Parent R&D/sales changes	−0.008	−0.001	0.351	−0.163***
	(0.008)	(0.002)	(0.424)	(0.042)
Host GDP changes	−0.015	0.020	8.005	0.449
	(0.160)	(0.053)	(7.865)	(0.455)
Host/US wage changes	1.550***	0.447***	25.97	1.679**
	(0.361)	(0.123)	(29.813)	(0.803)
Capital restrictions changes	−0.225***	−0.056**	−1.948	−0.269
	(0.071)	(0.022)	(4.353)	(0.160)
Host corporate income tax changes	0.556***	0.175***	8.911	−0.573
	(0.144)	(0.044)	(4.608)	(0.295)
Constant	0.043***	0.013***	0.713***	−0.008
	(0.002)	(0.001)	(0.175)	(0.012)

Notes: 2,567 observations. 2SLS estimator. *** $p < 0.01$, ** $p < 0.05$, * $p < 0.1$. Changes are measured as differences in natural logarithms. Robust standard errors in parentheses are clustered by country × product.
Underidentification test (Kleibergen–Paap *rk* LM statistic): $\chi^2 = 66.47$, *p* value = 0.000.
Weak identification test (Kleibergen–Paap Wald *rk F* statistic): 26.60.
Endogeneity test of endogenous regressors: $\chi^2 = 3.127$, *p* value = 0.373.

Table 9 Sensitivity test: measure of PRs

	Unaff. lic. (1)	Affil. lic. (2)	Unaff./aff. (3)	Unaff. lic. (4)	Affil. lic. (5)	Unaff./aff. (6)
Patent reform dummy	0.335***	1.065***	−0.735***	0.353***	0.999***	−0.646***
	(0.080)	(0.142)	(0.162)	(0.097)	(0.154)	(0.181)
Technological complexity	0.732***	−3.814***	4.577***			
	(0.247)	(0.483)	(0.506)			
Techn. complexity × log(patent reform)	−0.763***	−2.793***	2.052***	−0.783***	−2.577***	1.794***
	(0.260)	(0.450)	(0.515)	(0.302)	(0.502)	(0.594)
Log(parent R&D/sales)	0.010***	0.045***	−0.037***	−0.001	0.030***	−0.030***
	(0.002)	(0.007)	(0.007)	(0.003)	(0.008)	(0.009)
Log(host GDP)	0.525***	1.370***	−0.841***	0.509***	1.422***	−0.913***
	(0.152)	(0.270)	(0.325)	(0.146)	(0.272)	(0.326)
Log(host/US wages)	−0.007	0.111	−0.122	0.068	0.035	0.033
	(0.191)	(0.343)	(0.367)	(0.211)	(0.332)	(0.382)
Capital restrictions dummy	0.060**	−0.011	0.071	0.052*	−0.009	0.061
	(0.027)	(0.056)	(0.059)	(0.029)	(0.053)	(0.060)
Host corporate income tax	−0.003	0.002	−0.005	−0.001	0.006	−0.007
	(0.038)	(0.059)	(0.069)	(0.037)	(0.059)	(0.072)
Log(parent patents)	0.022**	0.035**	−0.014	0.029**	0.021	0.008
	(0.010)	(0.016)	(0.019)	(0.012)	(0.021)	(0.024)
Patent reform × log(parent patents)	−0.011	−0.013	0.001	−0.016	−0.015	−0.001
	(0.011)	(0.015)	(0.019)	(0.012)	(0.017)	(0.021)
Firm-by-country fixed effects				Yes	Yes	Yes
Constant	−9.148***	−20.518***	11.275**	−9.355***	−22.847***	13.493**
	(2.504)	(4.447)	(5.353)	(2.619)	(5.101)	(6.023)
Observations	30,001	30,001	30,001	30,001	30,001	30,001
R^2				0.665	0.658	0.642

Notes: Random effects estimator in columns (1)–(3) and OLS estimator in columns (4)–(6).
*** $p < 0.01$, ** $p < 0.05$, * $p < 0.1$. All outcome variables are in natural logarithms.
Robust standard errors in parentheses are clustered by country × year.
All regressions include year fixed effects, country fixed effects, and host-country-specific time trends.

patent reform dummy allows us to study changes in technology transfer that occur around the time of reform, while the PRs index allows us to study the relationship between licensing and the intensity of patent protection. Table 9 shows the results, with and without firm-by-country fixed effects. Our results are qualitatively unchanged.

We then re-estimate (4) using the stock measure of licensing. Columns (1)–(3) in Table 10 show the results. In the last two columns, we redefine our measure of the composition of licensing as the share of unaffiliated licensing in total licensing. The results in column (4) are for licensing stocks and those in column (5) are for licensing flows. Again, our results are qualitatively the same.

CONCLUSION

This article examined the impact of foreign patent protection on US multinational firms' technology licensing strategy and technology transfer flows to developing countries, where the security of PRs protection has been (and still remains) a major concern. It moves beyond previous work by studying affiliated and unaffiliated licensing flows in an integrated framework, where firms decide on both the volume of licensing and the preferred mode of control, and underscoring the role of the technological complexity of firms' products in determining the impact of foreign PRs. Using a detailed firm-level dataset on US multinational companies, we measured how the *volumes* and the composition of licensing respond to a strengthening of foreign PRs, and how their responses vary with the underlying technological complexity of the firms' products. Previous empirical work on multinational licensing has largely focused on one particular mode of licensing or worked with discrete dependent variables. The role of technological complexity, which plays a key role in determining the licensing impact of PRs, has also not been examined to date.

Our results show that strengthening PRs in developing countries provides all firms with a stronger incentive to increase their unaffiliated

Table 10 Sensitivity test: measure of licensing

	Stock of unaff. licen. (1)	Stock of affil. licen. (2)	Unaff./aff lic. stocks ratio (3)	Share of unaff. in total stock (4)	Share of unaff. in total flow (5)
Log(host PRs)	0.594***	2.013***	−1.419***	−1.149***	−0.830***
	(0.090)	(0.219)	(0.234)	(0.208)	(0.199)
Technological complexity	0.685*	−2.389**	3.102***	4.256***	3.313***
	(0.390)	(0.952)	(0.975)	(0.837)	(0.651)
Techn. complexity × log(host PRs)	−1.528***	−6..491***	4.964***	3.695***	2.177***
	(0.300)	(0.623)	(0.715)	(0.619)	(0.620)
Log(parent R&D/sales)	0.007***	0.036***	−0.030***	−0.031***	−0.045***
	(0.002)	(0.006)	(0.006)	(0.006)	(0.006)
Log(host GDP)	0.030	0.490	−0.460*	−0.545**	−1.421***
	(0.121)	(0.310)	(0.265)	(0.275)	(0.279)
Log(host/US wages)	0.051	−0.455	0.507	0.374	−0.068
	(0.162)	(0.361)	(0.313)	(0.311)	(0.310)
Capital restrictions dummy	0.056***	0.069	−0.013	−0.036	−0.003
	(0.021)	(0.062)	(0.057)	(0.057)	(0.055)
Host corporate income tax	−0.029	0.001	−0.030	−0.010	0.033
	(0.038)	(0.081)	(0.064)	(0.063)	(0.055)
Log(parent patents)	0.051***	0.079***	−0.029	−0.070***	−0.046**
	(0.012)	(0.021)	(0.023)	(0.020)	(0.022)
Log(host PRs) × log(parent patents)	−0.039***	−0.020	−0.019	0.008	0.033
	(0.010)	(0.016)	(0.018)	(0.015)	(0.020)
Constant	−0.900	−2.508	1.599	2.958	21.374***
	(2.028)	(5.306)	(4.542)	(4.732)	(4.639)
Observations	33,784	33,784	33,784	33,784	29,533
R^2	0.0393	0.0669	0.0542	0.0617	0.0449

Notes: Random effects estimator. *** $p < 0.01$, ** $p < 0.05$, * $p < 0.1$. All outcome variables are in natural logarithms. Robust standard errors in parentheses are clustered by country × year.
All regressions include year fixed effects, country fixed effects, and host-country-specific time trends.

licensing (i.e., the internalization effect). The attractiveness of affiliated licensing also rises among simple-technology firms (i.e., the appropriability effect), strongly enough that the composition of their licensing shifts towards affiliated parties. For firms producing complex products, by contrast, the appropriability effect is weak and so, the composition of licensing further shifts towards unaffiliated parties. Our regression analysis picks up these compositional shifts, once we allow for variations in technological complexity.

This research has significant policy implications. One of the objectives of global IPR reforms is to provide developing countries with greater access to new technologies. This is an explicit principle embodied in the TRIPS agreement. By specifically targeting incentives for *unaffiliated* licensing, policymakers can push technological knowledge beyond the multinational firm network. Although beneficial in its own right, greater flows of intra-firm technology transfers may not promote widespread access to new technologies in developing countries. One reason is that local (arms-length) firms may not obtain crucial know-how merely by relying upon knowledge externalities from foreign affiliates. Formal licensing contracts between unaffiliated parties might be needed to convey such tacit knowledge. Policy proposals to facilitate technology diffusion in the South often call for increased industry clusters or joint ventures with local partners. These are activities where arms-length licensing may be especially necessary. We find that patent protection facilitates unaffiliated licensing, but it is primarily complex-product firms that choose to switch from intra-firm to external contracting. Among simple-product firms (e.g., in the pharmaceutical industry), even greater internal transfers and control of technology are to be expected.

For future research, it would be useful to examine how strengthening PRs impacts prices. The prices of goods and services are critical in determining whether local access to new knowledge is enhanced. Another possible direction would be to examine how other forms of IPRs, such as copyrights and trade secrecy laws, affect international knowledge transfer (see Lippoldt & Schultz, 2014). One could also incorporate R&D location decisions jointly with licensing decisions and study the strategic implications. For example, do R&D investments by local subsidiaries substitute or complement parent-affiliate technology transfers? We touched upon this issue in our article, but clearly a more in-depth treatment is desirable. Finally, future research could measure the complexity of a technology using information from the specifications of a patent. Those specifications must be detailed enough to enable persons skilled in the art to replicate the invention, and could potentially be used to glean the types of production tasks and skills associated with the underlying product or process.

ACKNOWLEDGEMENTS

The authors thank seminar participants at Florida Atlantic University, Keio University, University of Bologna, University of International Business and Economics, US Bureau of Economic Analysis, Industry Canada, the 7th Asia-Pacific Innovation Conference (2016), Eastern Economic Association conference (2016), Asian Development Bank Conference on Economic Development (2016), Rocky Mountain Empirical Trade Conference (2016), Canadian Economics Association conference (2015), and Western Economics Association International conference (2015) for their helpful comments.

NOTES

[1]Providing greater local access to foreign knowledge may have been the major motivating factor behind China's controversial indigenous innovation policy, which required multinationals to share their technologies with local companies as a precondition for market entry.

[2]The Agreement on TRIPS was ratified by the World Trade Organization (WTO) in 1995. It expressly declares as its objective that the "protection and enforcement of intellectual property rights should contribute to the promotion of technological innovation and to the transfer and dissemination of technology." The text of this agreement is at www.wto.org/english/docs_e/legal_e/27-trips_01_e.htm.

[3]Poole (2013), for example, argues that transferring technology within organizations to countries with weak PRs carries the risk of imitation because local employees can misappropriate the firm's technology to start up imitative production.

[4]There can be differences in technological complexity between the manufacturing stage and innovation stage. A pharmaceutical product, for example, may require tremendous knowledge and skills to discover (i.e., the innovation stage is complex), but once the breakthrough is made, it is easy/simple enough to manufacture. What is important for the ability to recoup the fixed costs of R&D is the ability to sell products based on the technology, and this depends critically on the ease of imitating the innovated product at the manufacturing stage. It is this ease of imitation that we intend to pick up with our (production) measure of technological complexity. We thank an anonymous reviewer for drawing our attention to this important distinction.

[5]A similar measure was used in Keller and Yeaple (2008). Zander and Kogut (1977) note that "[t]echnology...consists of the principles by which individual skill and competence are gained and used, and by which work among people is organized and coordinated and measure technological complexity as the degree of distinct and multiple kinds of competencies used to manufacture a product, arguing that "the more complex a manufacturing capability, the more difficult it should be to imitate."

[6]Maskus and Penubarti (1995), Smith (1999), Javorcik (2004), and Ivus (2010).

[7]Local agents in low-income developing countries especially seek licenses to sell or distribute such products as drugs, medicines, new plant varieties, or pesticides.

[8]In a follow-up study, Aulakh et al. (2013) analyze the effects of IPR on the exclusivity of unaffiliated licensing, controlling for the technological potential of a foreign licensee. A tradeoff exists here because, on one hand, a formidable licensee with much technological potential has the capacity to raise the transactional value of an exclusive license, but on the other hand, such a licensee may be in a position to appropriate the technology and become a competitor. Stronger IPRs help to raise the transactional value and minimize appropriation risks.

[9]For example, exclusivity, restrictions, a related-party license (in the sense that the contracting parties had a prior relationship), or a cross-licensing agreement.

[10]Anand and Khanna (2000) argue that cross-industry variations in licensing can be explained by differences in the strength of IPRs across industries. However, IPR laws generally do not vary across industries – other than whether or not particular

inventions are patentable – but vary largely at the country level. Rather, different industries have different sensitivities to IP protection, due say to the complexity of their products or to the length of their product cycles.

[11]In 2014, China accounted for about 6% of all US firm's global unaffiliated licensing, while India accounted for about 1%. Consistent with internalization theories, affiliated licensing was more common (in volume). Specifically in 2014, the ratio of US unaffiliated to affiliated licensing was about 0.7 in China and 0.73 in India. Data source: www.bea.gov.

[12]We isolate the location decision in the Sensitivity Analysis section, where we model the probability of a parent firm licensing into a country, and show that our results remain robust.

[13]This distinction is underscored in Oxley (1997).

[14]This model is a modified version of that developed in Ivus et al. (2015).

[15]One reason the risk of imitation is lower among complex-technology firms is that their product domain does not coincide with their technological domain (which is why patent classifications differ from industrial classifications). The same invention can usually be in multiple industrial products, and one industrial product can be the result of multiple inventions. Parties cannot produce a good or innovation without access to the multiple necessary technologies. For pharmaceuticals, by contrast, there is a greater mapping between product and invention.

[16]This is not to preclude other compounding effects at work. Complex products involving multiple actors (i.e., IP owners) and long supply chains may give rise to the prevalence of arms-length (unaffiliated) contracting. We thank an anonymous reviewer for this insightful comment.

[17]Mansfield et al. (1981) and Levin et al. (1987) found that patents raise imitation costs by 30–40 percentage points in drugs and 7–15 points in electronics.

[18]In our data, each firm i produces within a single product category p over time.

[19]Our data sources are summarized in Appendix I.

[20]The countries are listed in Appendix II. Our classification of developing countries is based on that of the United Nations (see UNCTAD, 2009). Though some of these countries (e.g., South Korea and Singapore) have exhibited rapid growth during the sample period, there had been major concerns with their IP provision and enforcement, imitative activities, and piracy during that period (see Business Software Alliance, 2002).

[21]The data show significant differences in the strength of PRs across developing countries. From Table A.1 in Appendix IV, the coefficient of variation in the index of PRs is 0.39 for the sample of 44 developing countries and only 0.14 for the sample of 23 developed (OECD) countries. Table A.2 further reports the average ratio of unaffiliated to affiliated licensing and shows that compared to developed countries, the ratio for developing countries is higher across complex-technology firms but lower across simple-technology firms. These patterns are consistent with the developing countries having weaker patent regimes and with simpler technologies having higher imitation risks.

[22]Although our sample ends in 2009, the BEA data collection continues beyond.

[23]As for the foreign affiliates of US parents, the affiliates must be above a certain threshold level of assets or sales in order to be reported on the BEA surveys. The threshold amounts are usually lower in benchmark years (every 5 years) and as a result, the sample of foreign affiliates surveyed is not universal across years. In non-benchmark years, smaller affiliates under the threshold are not surveyed and data for them are extrapolated forward from benchmark years in order to generate a steady universal coverage.

[24]The stock of licensing in year t is $\text{Stock}_{ijt} = T_{ijt} - \delta\text{Stock}_{ijt-1}$ and the initial stock is $\text{Stock}_{ij0} = T_{ij0}/(g+\delta)$, where T_{ij0} is the initial flow, g the sample average growth rate of licensing flows, and δ the depreciation rate. We set $\delta = 0.2$. Alternative depreciation rates (e.g., 0.05, 0.1, and 0.15) yield similar results.

[25]The sample period goes up to 2009, and the PRs index goes up to 2005. The index values follow a step function, shifting approximately every 5 years during the sample period.

[26]This is comparable to a change of at least a half standard deviation in the PR index. The year of a major reform(s) in each country is listed in Appendix II.

[27]Complex problem-solving skills fall into the following eight categories: (1) problem identification, (2) information gathering, (3) information organization, (4) synthesis/reorganization, (5) idea generation, (6) idea evaluation, (7) implementation planning, and (8) solution appraisal.

[28]About 56% of our sample of firms (i.e., US parent firms engaging in FDI in the 44 developing countries) were matched to NBER's Patent Database using CUSIP codes. The rest of the data was matched manually.

[29]Since patenting is costly, a firm may choose not to acquire or maintain patents if it does not see much profit potential from licensing.

[30]Specifically for each host country, the income taxes of the parent's affiliates were aggregated and then divided by the aggregate pre-tax net incomes of these affiliates. The median ratio is used to represent the corporate income tax rate for that country. Net income is defined as gross income minus total costs and expenses. The tax base uses net, rather than gross, income to obtain a measure of taxable income. Countries vary in terms of their statutory tax rates and regulations on tax deductions, so that gross income would not consistently measure what is taxable.

[31]The OWW database offers several options. We chose the country-specific calibration method, which refers to how the wage dataset was cleaned up (for example, by making the wage figures consistent with country-specific figures on GDP per capita). We also selected the lexicographic method of treating differences in the reporting of data on hours worked and wages. This method assigns hours worked first by city, then by gender, then by pay concept, and so forth. These options are recommended for providing the largest sample. Details are discussed in Oostendorp (2012).

[32]Data on the stock of net PPE are available during the BEA's benchmark years (for example, 1989, 1994, 1999, 2004, and 2009). For the non-benchmark years, we used net expenditures on PPE to fill in the gaps.

[33]See Arora and Fosfuri (2000), Motohashi (2008), and Berry and Kaul (2015).

[34]See Oxley (1999), Hagedoorn et al. (2005), Aulakh et al. (2010, 2013), and Berry and Kaul (2015).

[35]The measure combines the information of several institutional indices from the Heritage Foundation, the Wall Street Journal, Freedom House, Fraser Institute, World Bank World Governance Indicators, and so forth.

[36]The coefficients on $Z_p \times P_{jt}$ and $A_{it} \times P_{jt}$ are not statistically significant at the 5% level in column (4) and so are not taken into account.

[37]We thank an anonymous referee for bringing this to our attention.

[38]While we do not find that affiliate R&D crowds out parent company licensing to affiliates or detracts from a parent's licensing to unaffiliated parties, we cannot preclude the possibility of a more nuanced firm strategy at work in licensing decisions.

[39]Results are similar when the cost of patenting not scaled by GDP is used as the exclusion restriction.

[40]For example, competition policy, innovative capacity, openness to trade, economic integration, and the level of development.

[41]The sample period goes up to 2009, but up to 2005 for the PRs index. The licensing data are averaged over two consecutive years (e.g., 1993 and 1994) before changes are calculated.

[42]The robust Kleibergen–Paap Wald *rk F* statistic equals 65.29.

The statistical analysis of firm-level data on US multinational companies and their foreign affiliates was conducted at the Bureau of Economic Analysis, United States (US) Department of Commerce, under arrangements that maintain legal confidentiality requirements. Views expressed in this article are those of the authors and do not necessarily reflect those of the US Department of Commerce.

REFERENCES

Allred, B. B., & Park, W. G. 2007. Patent rights and innovative activity: Evidence from national and firm-level data. *Journal of International Business Studies*, 38(6): 878–900.

Anand, B. N., & Khanna, T. 2000. The structure of licensing contracts. *Journal of Industrial Economics*, 48(1): 103–135.

Arora, A. 1996. Contracting for tacit knowledge: The provision of technical services in technology licensing contracts. *Journal of Development Economics*, 50(2): 233–256.

Arora, A., & Ceccagnoli, M. 2006. Patent protection, complementary assets, and firms' incentives for technology licensing. *Management Science*, 52(2): 293–308.

Arora, A., & Fosfuri, A. 2000. Wholly owned subsidiary versus technology licensing in the worldwide chemical industry. *Journal of International Business Studies*, 31(4): 555–572.

Aulakh, P., Jiang, M., & Sali, L. 2010. International technology licensing: Monopoly rents, transactions costs, and exclusive rights. *Journal of International Business Studies*, 41(4): 587–605.

Aulakh, P., Jiang, M., & Sali, L. 2013. Licensing technological potential and exclusive rights in international licensing: A multilevel model. *Journal of International Business Studies*, 44(7): 699–718.

Berry, H. 2006. Leaders, laggards, and the pursuit of foreign knowledge. *Strategic Management Journal*, 27(2): 151–168.

Berry, H. 2014. Global integration and innovation: Multicountry knowledge generation within MNCs. *Strategic Management Journal*, 35(6): 869–890.

Berry, H., & Kaul, A. 2015. Global sourcing and foreign knowledge seeking. *Management Science*, 61(5): 1052–1071.

Bilir, K. L. 2014. Patent laws, product lifecycle lengths, and multinational activity. *American Economic Review*, 104(7): 1979–2013.

Branstetter, L., Fisman, R., & Foley, C. F. 2006. Do stronger intellectual property rights increase international technology transfer? Empirical evidence from US firm-level panel data. *Quarterly Journal of Economics*, 121(1): 321–349.

Buckley, P. J., & Casson, M. C. 1976. *Future of the multinational enterprise*. Macmillan: London (2nd edn 1991; Anniversary Edition 2002).

Buckley, P. J., & Casson, M. C. 1998. Analyzing foreign market entry strategies: Extending the internalization approach. *Journal of International Business Studies*, 29(3): 539–561.

Buckley, P. J., & Casson, M. 2009. The internalization theory of the multinational enterprise: A review of the progress of a research agenda after 30 years. *Journal of International Business Studies*, 40(9): 1563–1580.

Buckley, P. J., & Pearce, R. D. 1979. Overseas production and exporting by the world's largest enterprises: A study in sourcing policy. *Journal of International Business Studies*, 10(1): 9–20.

Business Software Alliance, 2002. *Global Software Piracy Study*. Washington, DC: Business Software Alliance.

Coeurderoy, R., & Murray, G. 2008. Regulatory environments and the location decision: Evidence from the early foreign market entries of new-technology-based firms. *Journal of International Business Studies*, 39(4): 670–687.

Cohen, W., Nelson, R., & Walsh, J. 2000. Protecting their intellectual assets: Appropriability conditions and why us manufacturing firms patent (or not). *NBER Working Paper 7552*.

Contractor, F. 1984. Choosing between direct investment and licensing: Theoretical considerations and empirical tests. *Journal of International Business Studies*, 15(3): 167–188.

Di Minin, A., & Bianchi, M. 2011. Safe nests in global nets: Internalization and appropriability of R&D in wireless telecom. *Journal of International Business Studies*, 42(7): 910–934.

Ernst, D. 2005. Complexity and internalization of innovation – Why is chip design moving to Asia? *International Journal of Innovation Management*, 9(1): 47–73.

Gallini, N. T., & Wright, B. D. 1990. Technology transfer under asymmetric information. *Rand Journal of Economics*, 21: 14760.

Grindley, P. C., & Teece, D. J. 1997. Managing intellectual capital: Licensing and cross-licensing in semiconductors and electronics. *California Management Review*, 39(2): 1–34.

Hagedoorn, J., Cloodt, D., & Van Kranenburg, H. 2005. Intellectual property rights and the governance of international R&D partnerships. *Journal of International Business Studies*, 36(2): 175–186.

Hall, B., & Ziedonis, R. 2001. The patent paradox revisited: An empirical study of patenting in the US semiconductor industry, 1979–1995. *Rand Journal of Economics*, 32(1): 101–128.

Heckman, J. J. 1979. Sample selection bias as a specification error. *Econometrica*, 47(1): 153–161.

Henisz, W. 2000. The institutional environment for economic growth. *Economics and Politics*, 12(1): 1–31.

Henisz, W. 2003. The power of the Buckley and Casson thesis: The ability to manage institutional idiosyncrasies. *Journal of International Business Studies*, 34(2): 173–184.

Hennart, J. F. 2009. Down with MNE-centric theories! Market entry and expansion as the bundling of MNE and local assets. *Journal of International Business Studies*, 40(9): 1432–1454.

Ivus, O. 2010. Do stronger patent rights raise high-tech exports to the developing world? *Journal of International Economics*, 81(1): 38–47.

Ivus, O. 2011. Trade-related intellectual property rights: Industry variation and technology diffusion. *Canadian Journal of Economics*, 44(1): 201–226.

Ivus, O., Park, W., & Saggi, K. 2015. Intellectual property protection and the industrial composition of multinational activity. *Economic Inquiry*, 54(2): 1068–1085.

Javorcik, B. 2004. The composition of Foreign Direct Investment and Protection of Intellectual Property Rights: Evidence from Transition Economies. *European Economic Review*, 48: 39–62.

Keller, W., & Yeaple, S. 2008. Global production and trade in the knowledge economy. *National Bureau of Economic Research Working Paper* No. 14626.

Kunčič, A. 2014. Institutional quality dataset. *Journal of Institutional Economics*, 10(01): 135–161.

Levin, R. C., Klevorick, A. K., Nelson, R. R., Winter, S. G., Gilbert, R., & Griliches, Z. 1987. Appropriating the returns from industrial research and development. *Brookings Papers on Economic Activity*, 1987(3): 783–831.

Lippoldt, D., & Schultz, M. 2014. Uncovering trade secrets – An empirical assessment of economic implications of protection for undisclosed data. *OECD Trade Policy Papers*, No. 167. Paris: OECD Publishing.

Mansfield, E., Schwartz, M., & Wagner, S. 1981. Imitation costs and patents: An empirical study. *The Economic Journal*, 91(364): 907–918.

Maskus, K., & Penubarti, M. 1995. How trade-related are intellectual property rights? *Journal of International Economics*, 39: 227–28.

Motohashi, K. 2008. Licensing or not licensing? An empirical analysis of the strategic use of patents by Japanese firms. *Research Policy*, 37(9): 1548–1555.

Naghavi, A., Spies, J., & Toubal, F. 2015. Intellectual property rights, technological complexity, and the organization of multinational firms. *Canadian Journal of Economics*, 48(3): 881–902.

Oostendorp, R. 2012. The Occupational Wages around the world (OWW) database: Update for 1983–2008. www.nber.org/oww.

Oxley, J. E. 1997. Appropriability hazards and governance in strategic alliances: A transaction cost approach. *Journal of Law, Economics, and Organization*, 13(2): 387–409.

Oxley, J. 1999. Institutional environment and the mechanisms of governance: The impact of intellectual property protection on the structure of inter-firm alliances. *Journal of Economic Behavior and Organization*, 38(3): 283–309.

Papageorgiadis, N., Cross, A., & Alexiou, C. 2013. The impact of the institution of patent protection and enforcement on entry mode strategy: A panel data investigation of US firms. *International Business Review*, 22: 278–292.

Park, W. G. 2008. International patent protection: 1960–2005. *Research Policy*, 37(4): 761–766.

Park, W. G. 2010. On patenting costs. *The WIPO Journal: Analysis of Intellectual Property Issues*, 2(1): 38–48.

Park, W. G., & Lippoldt, D. 2005. International licensing and the strengthening of intellectual property rights in developing countries during the 1990s. *OECD Economic Studies*, 40: 7–48.

Poole, J. P. 2013. Knowledge transfers from multinational to domestic firms: Evidence from worker mobility. *Review of Economics and Statistics*, 95(2): 393–406.

Saggi, K. 2002. Trade, foreign direct investment, and international technology transfer: A survey. *World Bank Research Observer*, 17: 191–235.

Smith, P. 1999. Are weak patent rights a barrier to US exports? *Journal of International Economics*, 48: 151–177.

Teece, D. J. 1986. Profiting from technological innovation: Implications for integration, collaboration, licensing and public Policy. *Research Policy*, 15(6): 285–305.

UNCTAD. 2001. *World Investment Report: Promoting Linkages*. Geneva: United Nations.

UNCTAD. 2009. *Handbook of Statistics*. Geneva: United Nations.

Wang, C., Hong, J., Kafouros, M., & Wright, M. 2012. Exploring the role of government involvement in outward FDI from emerging economies. *Journal of International Business Studies*, 43(7): 655–676.

Yang, G., & Maskus, K. E. 2001. Intellectual property rights and licensing: An econometric investigation. *Review of World Economics*, 137(1): 58–79.

Zander, U., & Kogut, B. 1995. Knowledge and the speed of the transfer and imitation of organizational capabilities: An empirical test. *Organization Science*, 6(1): 76–92.

Zhao, M. 2006. Conducting R&D in countries with weak intellectual property rights protection. *Management Science*, 52(8): 1185–1199.

Ziedonis, R. 2004. Don't fence me in: Fragmented markets for technology and the patent acquisition strategies of firms. *Management Science*, 50(6): 804–820.

APPENDIX

I. Data Description

Variable	Description	Source
Affiliated licensing	Royalties and licensing receipts from foreign affiliates (firm level)	BEA *Benchmark Surveys of US Direct Investment Abroad (USDIA)* (BE-10 surveys); *Quarterly Balance of Payment Surveys of USDIA* (BE-577 surveys)
Unaffiliated licensing	Royalties and licensing receipts from unaffiliated parties (firm level)	BEA *Quarterly Survey of Transactions in Selected Services and Intellectual Property with Foreign Persons* (BE-125 surveys); *Annual Survey of Royalties, Licensing Fees, and Other Receipts and Payments for Intangible Rights between US and Unaffiliated Foreign Persons* (BE-93 survey)
Parent R&D, sales, assets, capital employment, exports	R&D performed by parent and data on these for the parent company (firm level)	BEA *Annual Surveys of USDIA* (BE-11 surveys) and *Benchmark Surveys of USDIA* (BE-10)
Affiliate R&D, sales	R&D performed by affiliates and total sales of affiliates (firm level)	BEA *Annual Surveys of USDIA* (BE-11 surveys) and *Benchmark Surveys of USDIA* (BE-10)
Income taxes, net income	Income taxes and net income of foreign affiliates (firm level)	BEA *Annual Surveys of USDIA* (BE-11 surveys); *Benchmark Surveys of USDIA* (BE-10)
US patents granted	Utility patent counts (firm level)	NBER *Patent Data Project*
Patent rights, patent reform	Index of the strength of patent protection (country level)	Park (2008)
Technological complexity	Complexity level of the tasks involved in the product's manufacturing (Product category level)	Naghavi et al. (2015)
Patent cost	The cost of procurement (filing, attorney, translation, search, and examination fees) and maintenance (renewal fees) (country level)	Park (2010)
GDP, PPP conversion factor	GDP in constant 2005 dollars and PPP conversion factor-to-market exchange rate ratio (country Level)	World Bank *World Development Indicators*
Inward capital restrictions	Presence of capital controls on inward foreign direct investment (country level)	IMF *Annual Report on Exchange Arrangements and Exchange Restrictions* (various years)
Hourly wages	Hourly wages (in USD) in manufacturing–country-specific calibration and lexicographic weighting (country level)	Occupational Wages Around the World (OWW) Database www.nber.org/oww

II. Developing Countries and Their Year of Major Patent Reform

Algeria 2000	Dominican Rep. 2000	Mexico 1995	Singapore 1995
Angola 2000	Ecuador 2000	Morocco 2000	Slovakia 1995
Argentina 1996	El Salvador 1996	Nicaragua 2000	South Africa 1996
Brazil 1995	Ghana 2000	Nigeria 2005	South Korea 1994
Bulgaria 2000	Guatemala 2005	Panama 2000	Sri Lanka 2000
Chad 2000	Hong Kong 2000	Peru 1995	Taiwan 1995
Chile 1995	Hungary 1996	Philippines 2000	Thailand 2000
China 1996	India 1999	Poland 1996	Trinidad Tobago 2000
Cote D'Ivoire 2000	Jamaica 2000	Romania 1996	Venezuela 1995
Cyprus 2000	Kenya 1995	Russia 1996	Vietnam 1995
Czech Rep. 2000	Malaysia 1995	Saudi Arabia 2005	Zimbabwe 2000

III. Technological Complexity Data

Complexity	Product category description	NAICS codes
.4221271	Computers and related	3341, 3343–3346
.3798102	Radio, television, and communic. equipment and apparatus	3342
.3790194	Commercial Machinery	3333
.3113132	Machinery and equipment n.e.c.	3331–3332, 3334–3336, 3339
.3073564	Electrical machinery and apparatus n.e.c.	3351–3353, 3359
.3033172	Trade, maint. and repair services of motor vehicles and motorcycles; retail sale of auto fuel	3362–3363
.3031925	Medical, precision and optical instruments, watches and clocks	3391
.2878633	Fabricated metal products, exc. machinery and equipment	3329
.2786216	Basic metals	3311–3315, 3321–3327
.2748125	Other transport equipment	3364–3366, 3369
.2596836	Motor vehicles, trailers, and semi-trailers	3361
.2580898	Chemicals, chemical products, and man-made fibers	3251, 3253–3256, 3259
.2537238	Coke, refined petroleum products, and nuclear fuels	3242–3244
.2058220	Rubber and plastic products	3252, 3261–3262, 3271–3273
.1839178	Other non-metallic mineral products	3279
N/A	Other miscellaneous manufacturing	3399

IV. Additional Tables

Table A.1 Patent rights by country group

	Mean	Median	Min	Max	Coefficient of Variation
Developed countries	4.12	4.33	1.67	4.67	0.14
Developing countries	2.65	2.78	0.00	4.54	0.39

Table A.2 Unaffiliated-to-affiliated licensing ratio by country group

	Developed countries	Developing countries
All US parent firms	0.408	0.569
Complex-technology firms (above median complexity)	0.708	1.104
Simple-technology firms (below median complexity)	0.321	0.280

Notes: The table shows mean ratios per group.

ABOUT THE AUTHORS

Olena Ivus is an Associate Professor and E. Marie Shantz Fellow of Business Economics at Smith School of Business, Queen's University. Her research employs both theory and empirical work to study aspects of international trade law and regulation, foreign direct investment, and intellectual property protection.

Walter G Park is a Professor of Economics at American University. He holds a PhD from Yale University. His field of research is on various aspects of intellectual property rights, focusing on patents, copyrights, and open innovation.

Kamal Saggi (Ph.D., University of Pennsylvania) is the Frances and John Downing Family Professor of Economics and the Dean of Social Sciences in the College of Arts and Science at Vanderbilt University. His two main research fields are: (i) the economics of intellectual property rights protection in the global economy and (ii) the economic underpinnings of the world trading system.

Accepted by Mariko Sakakibara, Area Editor, 16 July 2017. This article has been with the authors for three revisions.

Part 4

Parallel Imports and External Reference Pricing

Chapter 15

Equilibrium parallel import policies and international market structure[☆,#]

Santanu Roy[a,1], Kamal Saggi[b,*]

[a] Southern Methodist University, Dallas, TX, USA
[b] Vanderbilt University, Nashville, TN, USA

ARTICLE INFO

Article history:
Received 24 January 2011
Received in revised form 3 January 2012
Accepted 19 January 2012
Available online 27 January 2012

JEL classification:
F13
F10
F15

Keywords:
Parallel imports
Oligopoly
Quality
Product differentiation
Market structure
Welfare

ABSTRACT

In a North–South vertically differentiated duopoly we analyze (*i*) the effects of parallel import (PI) policies on price competition and (*ii*) the interdependence of national PI policies. Prices can be higher in the North if both countries permit PIs relative to when only the South does. If governments maximize national welfare and demand asymmetry across countries is sufficiently large, the North forbids PIs to ensure its firm sells in the South and international price discrimination – the South's most preferred market outcome – obtains. When demand structures are relatively similar across countries, the North permits PIs and uniform pricing – its most preferred outcome – results.

1. Introduction

Parallel trade is said to occur when a product protected by some form of intellectual property right (IPR) offered for sale by the rights holder in one country is re-sold in another country without the right holder's consent. As is clear, the incentive to engage in such trade naturally arises in the presence of significant international price differences, which in turn often reflect the underlying market power of sellers (Scherer and Watal, 2002).

The possibility of parallel trade affects firm behavior and pricing in many markets, perhaps the most important of which is the market for pharmaceuticals.[2] A recent article published in the *Financial Times* noted that several billion dollars of parallel trade in pharmaceuticals occurs within the European Union (EU) annually and that such trade accounts for roughly 10% of Europe's medicine trade.[3] The biggest destination markets tend to be Germany, UK, Netherlands, Denmark, Sweden, Ireland, and Norway – some of the richest countries in Europe where prices generally tend to be the highest. As one might expect, the important parallel exporters are Greece and Spain – countries where prices of medicines are lower than the EU average. Kanavos et al. (2004) document the increased importance of PIs in the EU pharmaceutical market. They find that from 1997 to 2002, the share of PIs as a percentage of the total pharmaceutical market increased from under 2% to 10.1% in Sweden and from 1.7% to about 7% in Germany. On the export side, Greece's share of parallel exports increased from under 1% to 21.6% over the same time period. Impressive as these figures are, it is worth emphasizing that the observed flows of parallel trade need not be large for *PI policies to matter*

☆ For helpful comments and discussions, we thank two anonymous referees, editor Bob Staiger, Kyle Bagwell, Rick Bond, Petros Mavroidis, Hodaka Morita, Nathan Nunn, Abhijit Sengupta, seminar audiences at Princeton, Syracuse, St. Louis Fed, Stanford, UC-Santa Cruz, the University of Sydney, the University of New South Wales, Vanderbilt, the Spring 2010 Midwest International Economics Meeting, and the Stony Brook 2011 Workshop on the Applications of Game Theory to Trade and Development. Parts of this paper were written during Kamal Saggi's visits to the Stanford Center for International Development (SCID) and the World Bank's Development Economics Research Group in Trade and Integration (DECTI); he is grateful to the affiliated researchers and the administrative staff of SCID and DECTI for their hospitality and support.

* Corresponding author at: Department of Economics, Vanderbilt University, Box 1819-Station B, Nashville, TN 37235-1819, USA. Tel.: +1 615 322 3237.
E-mail addresses: sroy@smu.edu (S. Roy), k.saggi@Vanderbilt.Edu (K. Saggi).
[1] Department of Economics, Southern Methodist University, 3300 Dyer Street, Dallas, TX 75275-0496, USA. Tel.: +1 214 768 2714.

[2] Parallel trade occurs in footwear and leather goods, musical recordings, cars, consumer electronics, domestic appliances, cosmetics, clothing, soft drinks, and several other consumer products (NERA, 1999).
[3] See "European drug groups fear parallel trade" *Financial Times*, June 7, 2010.

[#] This chapter was originally appeared in *Journal of International Economics* **87**, 262–276. © 2012 Elsevier B.V.

because firms will tend to make different pricing decisions when such trade is permitted relative to when it is not.[4]

Discussions regarding PI policies tend to be quite charged in the context of pharmaceuticals and perhaps for a good reason. The issue has often been heavily politicized in most countries, including the United States where it has been debated repeatedly over the years in Congress. For example, an article published in the *Wall Street Journal* on Dec 16, 2009 reported that a measure to allow importation of prescription drugs from abroad fell short in the US Senate by just 9 votes. The bill was sponsored by Senator Byron Dorgan of North Dakota who argued that his motivation was to protect consumer interests since "...the American people are charged the highest prices in the World". The pharmaceutical industry opposed the bill questioning the safety of imported drugs. While safety maybe a legitimate concern, there is little doubt that the primary issue for firms is the ability to maintain high prices in the United States.

Goldberg (2010) has argued that the practice of "global reference pricing" on the part of some rich countries and the possibility of PIs can induce pharmaceutical multinationals to not serve low income countries and/or raise their prices (even above their optimal monopoly prices) in such markets – outcomes that emerge quite sharply in our model. For example, multinational firms frequently refrain from introducing new drugs in India because the foregone profits in the Indian market are trivial relative to the profits that would be lost in Canada and many European countries if Indian prices were used as a reference point by these countries while determining local prices (Goldberg, 2010). More generally, using data regarding drug launches in 68 countries between 1982 and 2002, Lanjouw (2005) shows that the presence of price regulations and global reference pricing in the industrialized world contributes to launch delay in developing countries. In a similar vein, Danzon and Epstein (2008) find that the delay effect of a prior launch in a high-price EU country on a subsequent launch in a low price EU country is substantially stronger than the corresponding effect of a prior launch in a low price EU country.

Whether or not PIs can flow into a country is a matter of national policy. A country can choose to permit PIs by adopting the legal doctrine of *international exhaustion* of IPRs under which such rights are deemed to expire globally with the first sale of the relevant product, regardless of the geographical incidence of the sale. On the other hand, a country can effectively ban PIs by adopting *national exhaustion* of IPRs wherein rights are held to expire only in the market of first sale thereby leaving the right holder free to prevent its resale in other markets. While national laws pertaining to parallel trade are complex and multi-faceted, the following characterization broadly captures the global policy spectrum: the two largest markets in the world – i.e. United States and the EU – forbid PIs of patented and copyrighted goods from most other countries whereas developing countries tend to vary widely in their restraints on such imports (Maskus, 2000).[5] This variation in national PI policies reflects unilateral policy decisions since presently there is no multilateral cooperation or consensus over policies pertaining to parallel trade. Indeed, the key multilateral agreement on IPRs – i.e. the WTO's Agreement on Trade Related Aspects of Intellectual Property Rights (TRIPS) – leaves member countries free to implement PI policies of their choice.

Given the lack of any multilateral consensus regarding the desirability of parallel trade, two important questions arise. First, how do national PI policies affect oligopolistic competition in global markets? Second, what is the nature of strategic interdependence between PI policies of individual countries? We address these questions in a North–South model in which the two regions differ with respect to their domestic demand structure and the quality of goods produced by their respective firms. In particular, the Northern firm's product is of high quality whereas that of the Southern firm is of low quality and market size as well as the relative preference for high quality is larger in the North. Not only do these stylized asymmetries capture empirically relevant differences between Northern and Southern markets, we show that they shed new light on the causes and consequence of parallel trade. Indeed, without properly accounting for such asymmetries, it is difficult to explain the observed variation in PI policies across countries.

The timing of decisions in our model is as follows. First, governments simultaneously decide whether or not to permit PIs. Next, each firm chooses whether or not to offer its product for sale in the foreign market. Finally, given policies and market structure, firms compete in prices and international trade and consumption occur. To the best of our knowledge, ours is the first paper to provide an analysis of PI policies in a model that incorporates strategic interaction not only in the product market but also at the policy-setting stage.

The existing literature on PIs has extensively explored uniform global pricing and international price discrimination by firms with market power. In addition to these symmetric market outcomes, an asymmetric scenario where the low quality sells in both markets while the high quality firm sells only in the North plays a crucial role in our analysis. Such an asymmetric market structure can arise in our model because the two firms have uneven export incentives: the lure of the lucrative Northern market is stronger than that of the Southern market. We find that the strategic price competition under such a market structure tends to be rather subtle. To gain further insight, suppose the North permits PIs while the South does not. Under such a policy configuration, if demand is relatively similar across countries the low quality firm charges its optimal monopoly price in the South while both firms charge their optimal discriminatory prices in the Northern market. However, if demand structure is sufficiently asymmetric across countries, the low quality firm's optimal monopoly price in the South is lower than its optimal discriminatory price for the Northern market. Under such a scenario, the North's openness to PIs induces the low quality firm to set a common international price that actually *exceeds* its optimal monopoly price for the Southern market: i.e. it tolerates a sub-optimally high price in the Southern market to charge a more attractive price in the Northern market (Lemma 2). The resulting softening of price competition in the North, in turn, makes forsaking the Southern market more attractive for the Northern firm, because local demand for its product is relatively large. Indeed, we show that such an asymmetric market structure can arise not only when only one country permits PIs but also when both countries do so (Propositions 2 and 3).

Our policy analysis sheds new light on how heterogeneity in demand structure across countries determines national preferences for PI policies. We show that if governments maximize national welfare the North is more likely to permit PIs (i.e. it prefers to permit PIs over a larger parameter space) when the South does *not* do so. With its smaller market, the Southern government's influence on market structure tends to be weaker, something that is reflected in the nature of the policy equilibrium: if the North is open to PIs, the South also (weakly) prefers to be open to PIs whereas a Northern ban on PIs makes the South indifferent between its two policy options since it renders the Southern policy inconsequential for market structure.

The subgame perfect equilibrium of our model (stated in Proposition 6) is as follows: when the degree of asymmetry between the two markets is high and each government maximizes its national welfare, the North forbids PIs and international price discrimination

[4] In this regard, it is noteworthy that Gansland and Maskus (2004) found that after Sweden joined the EU and opened its pharmaceutical market to PIs, prices of drugs subject to competition from PI declined 12–19%.

[5] The US policy with respect to PIs of trademarked goods is relatively more open: it allows PIs of trademarked goods (such as cars) when the entities holding the US and the foreign trademark are the same or are in a parent-subsidiary relationship.

prevails; otherwise, it permits PIs and uniform pricing obtains.[6] This policy result is noteworthy for several reasons. First, it is surprising since North's welfare under uniform pricing is strictly higher than that under price discrimination. Therefore, only when the degree of asymmetry across markets is small can the North implement a policy that yields its most preferred market outcome. Why doesn't the North simply permit PIs? As was noted earlier, if the North permits PIs and markets are sufficiently asymmetric, uniform pricing does not emerge as an equilibrium outcome. Rather, under such circumstances, the high quality firm abstains from serving the Southern market in order to charge a high price in the Northern market, an outcome that is detrimental for Northern consumers and overall Northern welfare. To avoid this outcome, the North is better off prohibiting PIs: while international price discrimination is not as desirable to the North as uniform pricing, it is preferable to an asymmetric market structure under which its firm does not sell in the South. This policy result accords quite well with the type of PI policies that are observed in the world: recall that the two largest markets in the world – the EU and the US – prohibit PIs from most of the rest of the world.[7] Our explanation for these observed policy outcomes is that by inducing international market segmentation and shielding their respective firms from the threat of arbitrage-induced PIs from rest of the world, the prohibition of PIs by the EU and the US ensures that their firms choose to serve markets in other parts of the world. Furthermore, our model suggests that the adoption of these policies on the part of the EU and the US makes smaller developing countries indifferent between their policy options since what they do does not affect market outcomes. Such indifference on their part is consistent with the fact that we do not observe a common exhaustion regime across the developing world.[8]

The EU's stance on exhaustion of IPRs has been clarified over the years in a series of cases decided by the European Court of Justice (ECJ). A prominent recent example is *Silhouette International Schmied Gesellschaft mbH & Co. v. Hartlauer Handelsgesellschaft mbH*, a case involving the parallel imports of some spectacle frames into Austria from Bulgaria and Soviet Union against the wishes of the trademark owner (Silhoutette). In its 1998 ruling over this case, the ECJ held that national rules allowing for international exhaustion of trademark rights were incompatible with the functioning of the common internal market in the EU. The court ruled clearly in favor of community or regional exhaustion – i.e. parallel imports could flow freely within the EU but not from outside. This directive of the ECJ was in contrast to the historical policies of several major EU members: Austria, Germany, Netherlands, Finland, and the UK all followed international exhaustion provided parallel imports were essentially identical in quality to locally sold goods with the standard for what constituted "material difference" between the two sets of goods differing somewhat across countries.[9] One interpretation of this change in the exhaustion policy of these European nations is that with the formation of the EU, the combined market size of the region came to dictate the exhaustion policy of the region as opposed to the individual market size of each country. If so, the observed outcome is quite in line with what is predicted by our model: all else equal, a sufficiently large increase in the market size of the North makes it optimal for it to switch from allowing PIs from the rest of the world to forbidding them.

Our analysis contributes to, and to some extent unifies, two strands of the literature on PIs: one that studies interaction between firms taking government policies as given and another that analyzes the impact of alternative government policies but abstracts from strategic interaction between firms.[10] In the latter tradition, the seminal paper is by Malueg and Schwartz (1994) who show that the possibility of PIs can induce a monopolist to not serve markets with higher elasticities of demand and thereby lower world welfare.[11] The central question addressed by Malueg and Schwartz is a normative one: should firms be allowed to establish exclusive sales territories internationally? In our view, it is important to also identify the incentives that individual governments have to allow or restrict PIs from a national welfare perspective.

One of the few papers that analyzes the choice of PI policies in a multi-country setting is Richardson (2002). However, our analysis differs from his along several important dimensions. First, in our model each firm decides whether or not to sell its product in the foreign market, while Richardson (2002) considers a scenario where all countries import a common good from a foreign monopolist who necessarily sells in all markets. Second, by incorporating oligopolistic competition, our model captures strategic considerations absent from his analysis. Third, because each country is an importer as well as an exporter in our model, government policies must consider both consumer and producer interests, as opposed to only consumer interests. Indeed, firm profitability turns out to be an important determinant of PI policies in our model.

A commonly advanced argument against parallel trade is that it reduces innovation incentives by undermining the ability of IPR holders to profit from their investments in research and development (R&D) – see, for instance, Li and Maskus (2006).[12] In a North–South model of endogenous innovation, Grossman and Lai (2008) analyze strategic policy choice when the South determines its price control policy in response to the PI policy of the North and show that the incentives for product innovation in the North (as well as its aggregate welfare) can be higher when the North permits PIs relative to when it does not. While we focus on different questions, some of the international policy externalities identified in Grossman and Lai (2008) also appear in our analysis; in particular, Northern openness to PIs may induce the Northern firm to eschew the Southern market in order to avoid indirect competition, and this, in turn, can hurt the South.

2. Model

We consider a vertically differentiated industry in a world comprised of two countries: North (N) and South (S). The industry produces good x that comes in two quality levels where s_h denotes the high quality and s_l the low quality ($s_h > s_l = 1$). Assume that the Northern firm produces the high quality and the Southern firm the low quality and that the cost of production for both qualities equals

[6] A noteworthy aspect of this result is that a unilateral prohibition on PIs by the North generates a substantial *positive spillover* for the South: not only do Southern consumers enjoy lower prices for both goods under international price discrimination, the low quality firm also benefits from being able to charge a higher price in the Northern market.

[7] Furthermore, in several recent bilateral trade agreements that have been dubbed "TRIPS-Plus" – such as the one with Jordan – the US has insisted that the partner country not allow PIs from abroad, a policy that goes beyond TRIPS since it takes away the partner country's freedom to pick the exhaustion regime of its choosing but is consistent with safeguarding the profits of US industries in its market.

[8] Indeed, even within Africa, there is a significant variation in exhaustion policies: while Ghana, Namibia, South Africa, and Zimbabwe follow international exhaustion, Botswana, Madagascar, Mozambique, and Nigeria have opted for national exhaustion (Biadgleng, 2009).

[9] To be sure, not every EU member followed international exhaustion of trademarks: for example, Italy, France, and Greece did not follow this doctrine. See Baudenbacher (1998).

[10] It should be noted here that the literature on economic integration contains analyses of international oligopoly where integration or segmentation is exogenously given. See, among others, Smith and Venables (1988) and Venables (1990). Markusen and Venables (1988) examine optimal trade and industrial policy in this context. In our paper, national policies *endogenously* determine whether markets are segmented or integrated.

[11] Valletti and Szymanski (2006) build on Malueg and Schwartz (1994) by endogenizing product quality and show that international exhaustion yields lower welfare relative to national exhaustion.

[12] However, Valleti (2006) shows that parallel trade can actually encourage cost reducing R&D when differential pricing is cost based.

zero. Each consumer buys at most one unit of good x. If a consumer in country i buys quality j at price p_{ji}, its utility is given by

$$U_i = \theta s_j - p_{ji} \text{ where } j = h, l. \quad (1)$$

Utility under no purchase is normalized to zero and $\theta \geq 0$ is a taste parameter that captures the willingness to pay for higher quality. All consumers prefer high quality for a given price but those with a higher θ are willing to pay more for both qualities and, in addition, value high quality relatively more.

The high quality product produced by the Northern firm as well as the low quality product produced by the Southern firm are both protected by an IPR such as a patent or a trade-mark. In particular, it is perfectly legal for the Southern firm to sell its low quality product in both countries; the low quality product is not per se a counterfeit or illegal version of the high quality product. One can think of the two products as belonging to different generations – an existing drug and a more effective drug that is recently introduced after new scientific advances (with non-overlapping patent protection between the products); alternatively, one can think of the quality difference as reflecting country bias or perceived differences in regulatory conditions (such as monitoring of product safety), technology and input quality between the North and the South. The role of PI policy of each country is to determine whether or not the IPR enjoyed by a firm over its product is exhausted once it is sold abroad which, in turn, determines whether or not the firm can legally prevent PIs of units (of its own product) that it sells abroad.[13]

To capture demand asymmetry between the North and the South, we assume that market size is larger in the North than in the South; in particular, we set the number of consumers in the South equal to 1 and in the North to $\mu \geq 1$. Further, we assume that the preference parameter θ is uniformly distributed over the interval $[0,\mu_i]$ in country $i = N,S$ where $\mu_N = \mu \geq \mu_S = 1$. This formulation allows us to capture asymmetry in size as well as in the distribution of preferences by a single parameter μ. In what follows, we refer to μ as the extent of demand heterogeneity or asymmetry between the two markets.[14] Since $\mu \geq 1$, not only is the market demand for both qualities higher in the North, but in fact Northern consumers exhibit higher *relative* preference for high quality over low quality in the sense that the distribution of θ, the marginal willingness to pay for better quality, in the population of consumers in the North dominates that in the South (in a first order stochastic sense). As a result, the Northern market is more lucrative than the South for both products and relatively more so for the high quality product. Furthermore, when both products are offered for sale, demand for high quality is less price elastic in the North than in the South.

When trade is possible, the interaction between firms and governments occurs as follows. The PI policy of each government is either one of allowing (denoted by P) or forbidding PIs (denoted by N). Thus, there exist four possible global policy regimes: (P,P), (P,N), (N,P), and (N,N), where the policy of the North is listed first. In the next four sections, we treat the policy regimes as being exogenously given and focus on the resulting trade and market outcomes. Later, we analyze the problem of endogenous determination of PI policies through strategic interaction between governments.

[13] Note that in our framework, if PIs are permitted, consumers do not differentiate between units of the product sold directly by the manufacturing firm and those sold by an importer. This kind of differentiation may be important when the product comes with warranties and other services that are only provided by the manufacturer or its authorized dealers. See, for instance, Ahmadi and Yang (2000).

[14] It should be mentioned here that the assumption that the support of θ in each market has zero as lower bound ensures that if both firms set prices without bothering about the effect of their pricing on their profit in other markets, then both sell in equilibrium. In other words, if firms choose not to serve a market in our model it is not because of the "natural monopoly" effect that can arise in models of price competition in a vertically differentiated duopoly (see, Shaked and Sutton, 1983).

Given national PI policies, each firm decides whether or not to offer its product for sale in the foreign market. Our implicit assumption is that each firm has the option of offering its product for sale abroad via a retail sector that is perfectly competitive in each country.[15] Firms' decisions regarding the authorization of sales territories determine global market structure. In the final stage, given market structure and government policies, firms compete in prices and consumption (and trade) occur.

In our model, each firm decides whether or not to allow the sale of its product in the foreign market *prior* to setting prices. An important implication of this formulation is that if the high quality (Northern) firm decides not to serve the Southern market, then in the next stage, its pricing strategy in no way affects the demand for the low quality (Southern) firm's product in the South since there is no price competition between firms in the South. An alternative specification would be one where both products are always offered for sale in both markets and each firm simply chooses a pair of prices – one for each market. Under such a formulation, the high quality firm can effectively eliminate sales in the South by charging a price that is sufficiently higher than the price charged by the low quality firm. While equilibrium policy outcomes under this alternative approach are likely to be similar to ours, the price competition stage is more tractable under our formulation. The two approaches differ at the price competition stage because under the alternative specification an outcome where the high quality firm finds it profitable to abandon the Southern market – for instance, when PI policies prevent price discrimination and the Southern market is too small or the degree of market competition is too severe or both – could be consistent with a continuum of pricing equilibria where the high quality firm's foreign price (at which it sells zero in the South) still affects the demand curve facing the low quality firm and places a ceiling on its market power. Furthermore, these equilibria will differ with respect to the price at which Southern consumers buy the low quality good and therefore in terms of the welfare that they generate. By allowing firms to abandon foreign markets prior to price competition, our approach simplifies the price competition stage and avoids this kind of indeterminacy.

Under trade, if both qualities are available for purchase at prices p_{hi} and p_{li}, country i's consumers can be partitioned into three groups on the basis of two threshold parameters θ_{li} and θ_{hi}: those in the range of $[0,\theta_{li})$ buy neither high nor low quality; those in $[\theta_{li},\theta_{hi})$ buy low quality; and those in $[\theta_{hi},\mu_i]$ buy high quality where

$$\theta_{li} = \frac{p_{li}}{s_l} \text{ and } \theta_{hi} = \frac{p_{hi}-p_{li}}{\Delta s} \quad (2)$$

where $\Delta s \equiv s_h - s_l > 0$. Using these threshold parameters, demand functions in country i for the two qualities are as follows:

$$x_{ji}(p_{li},p_{hi}) = \begin{cases} \theta_{hi}-\theta_{li} = \dfrac{p_{hi}-p_{li}}{\Delta s} - \dfrac{p_{li}}{s_l} & \text{if } j = l \\ \mu_i - \theta_{hi} = \mu_i - \dfrac{p_{hi}-p_{li}}{\Delta s} & \text{if } j = h \end{cases}. \quad (3)$$

The demand functions in Eq. (3) can be used to calculate consumer surplus in country i over the two qualities:

$$cs_i(p_{li},p_{hi}) = \sum_j cs_{ji}(p_{li},p_{hi}) = \int_{\theta_{li}}^{\theta_{hi}} (s_l\theta - p_{li})d\theta + \int_{\theta_{hi}}^{\mu_i} (s_h\theta - p_{hi})d\theta \quad (4)$$

[15] Thus, firms do not have to share rents with retailers and the vertical pricing issues that are central to the analysis of Maskus and Chen (2002) and Maskus and Chen (2004) do not arise in our model. In a related context, Raff and Schmitt (2007) have shown that when competitive retailers order inventories before observing market demand, a manufacturer can actually benefit from parallel trade.

which simplifies to

$$cs_{li}(p_{li},p_{hi}) = (\theta_{hi}-\theta_{li})\left[\frac{s_l(\theta_{hi}+\theta_{li})}{2}-p_{li}\right] \quad (5)$$

$$\text{and } cs_{hi} = (\mu_i-\theta_{hi})\left[\frac{s_h(\mu_i+\theta_{hi})}{2}-p_{hi}\right].$$

In what follows, let $r \equiv \frac{s_h}{s_l} \geq 1$ denote the quality gap between goods and normalize $s_l = 1$.

3. Alternative market outcomes

In our model, PI policies influence global market outcomes through two channels. First, they determine whether a firm engaged in international trade can charge differential prices at home and abroad. Second, they affect a firm's incentive to authorize or not authorize sales of its product in the foreign market i.e., the decision of a firm to export or not. In this section, we briefly discuss the various market outcomes that can arise in our model. As we show later, the degree of demand asymmetry across countries (μ), the quality gap between goods (r), and the PI policies of the two governments jointly determine which of these outcomes emerges in equilibrium in any given situation.

The various market outcomes can be classified as follows:

(i) Autarky $\{A\}$: Neither firm exports so that each charges its optimal monopoly price in its home market.
(ii) International price discrimination $\{D\}$: Both firms export and charge discriminatory prices across markets.
(iii) Uniform pricing $\{U\}$: Both firms export and charge uniform prices at home and abroad.
(iv) Asymmetric market coverage $\{\Lambda\}$: only the low quality firm exports and it charges the same price in both countries.
(v) Asymmetric market coverage $\{\Lambda^m\}$: only the low quality firm exports but it price discriminates across countries. The superscript m indicates that the low quality firm exercises full monopoly power at home (South).
(vi) Asymmetric market coverage H: only the high quality firm exports and it charges the same price in both markets.
(vii) Asymmetric market coverage $\{H^m\}$: only the high quality firm exports but it charges different prices at home and abroad. The superscript m indicates that the high quality firm exercises full monopoly power at home (North).

For ease of reference, the classification of market outcomes (given that at least one firm exports) is given in Table 1 below:

As we will show below, market outcomes $\{H\}$ and $\{H^m\}$ do not arise in equilibrium. Therefore, we do not discuss these outcomes any further and refer the reader to Roy and Saggi (2011) for the relevant details. Under autarky, the local firm in each country acts as a monopolist and the autarkic equilibrium price in the North equals $p_h^m = \frac{\mu s_h}{2}$ while that in the South equals $p_l^m = \frac{1}{2}$.

Under price discrimination $\{D\}$, in country i the low quality firm chooses p_{li} to solve

$$\underset{p_{li}}{Max}\, \pi_{li}(p_{li},p_{hi}) = p_{li}x_{li}(p_{li},p_{hi}) = p_{li}\left(\frac{p_{hi}-p_{li}}{\Delta s}-\frac{p_{li}}{s_l}\right) \quad (6)$$

Table 1
Alternate market outcomes and pricing behavior.

	Differential international prices	Common international prices
Both firms export	$\{D\}$	$\{U\}$
Only low quality exports	$\{\Lambda^m\}$	$\{\Lambda\}$
Only high quality exports	$\{H^m\}$	$\{H\}$

whereas the high quality firm choose p_{hi} to solve

$$\underset{p_{hi}}{Max}\, \pi_{hi}(p_{li},p_{hi}) = p_{hi}x_{hi}(p_{li},p_{hi}) = p_{hi}\left(\mu_i-\frac{p_{hi}-p_{li}}{\Delta s}\right). \quad (7)$$

The reaction functions in market i under price discrimination are given by

$$p_{li} = \frac{p_{hi}}{2r} \text{ and } p_{hi} = \frac{\mu_i(r-1)}{2}+\frac{p_{li}}{2}.$$

Under uniform pricing $\{U\}$, the low quality firm chooses p_l to solve

$$\underset{p_l}{Max} \sum_i \pi_{li}(p_l,p_h) = 2p_lx_l(p_l,p_h) = 2p_l\left(\frac{p_h-p_l}{\Delta s}-\frac{p_l}{s_l}\right) \quad (8)$$

whereas the high quality firm chooses p_h to solve:

$$\underset{p_h}{Max} \sum_i \pi_{hi}(p_l,p_h) = \sum_i p_hx_{hi}(p_l,p_h) = \sum_i p_h\left(\mu_i-\frac{p_h-p_l}{\Delta s}\right). \quad (9)$$

The reaction functions under uniform pricing are as follows

$$p_l = \frac{p_h}{2r} \text{ and } p_h = \frac{(\mu+1)(r-1)}{4}+\frac{p_l}{2}.$$

The reaction functions for the low quality firm are the same under discrimination and uniform pricing because the demand asymmetry parameter μ directly affects demand for only the high quality good and it does not appear in the low quality firm's first order condition for profit maximization. In other words, an increase in μ leads to an increase in the low quality firm's price only because the high quality firm finds it optimal to raise its price due to an expansion in the set of Northern consumers that value quality relatively more. A comparison of the solutions to the pricing problems under $\{D\}$ and $\{U\}$ yields:

Lemma 1. *Under price discrimination, each firm charges a higher price in the North: $p_{jN}(D) > p_{jS}(D)$. Furthermore, each firm's price under uniform pricing is the average of its optimal discriminatory prices in the two markets: $p_j(U) = \sum_i p_{ji}(D)/2$.*

Lemma 1 highlights an important aspect of price discrimination and uniform pricing from the viewpoint of consumer welfare. While prices are strictly lower in the North under uniform pricing relative to price discrimination, the opposite is true in the South. As we will show later, this clash between consumer welfare in the two countries over these market structures plays an important role in determining the welfare implications of different policy regimes.

When both products are offered for sale in both markets and firms are constrained to charge uniform prices, if there is too much asymmetry in demand across markets then the equilibrium outcome could be one where there are no sales of the high quality good in the South. To ensure that positive quantities are sold in both markets under uniform pricing, we need $\mu < \bar{\mu} \equiv \frac{6r-1}{2r-1}$. Furthermore, as well shall show below, to avoid a scenario where price competition is so stiff that the low quality firm refrains from selling in the North when the high quality firm serves both markets, we need $r \geq r^* = 1+\frac{3\sqrt{2}}{8}$. For convenience, we collect these parameter restrictions in Assumption 1, which is assumed to hold through-out the paper:

Assumption 1. (i) $\mu < \bar{\mu} \equiv \frac{6r-1}{2r-1}$ and (ii) $r \geq r^* = 1+\frac{3\sqrt{2}}{8}$.

In the asymmetric market outcome $\{\Lambda^m\}$, the low quality firm charges its optimal monopoly price $p_l^m = 1/2$ in the South and the two firms charge their optimal discriminatory prices $p_{lN}(D)$ and $p_{hN}(D)$ in the North so that the outcome in the Northern market is identical to that under $\{D\}$.

Under $\{\Lambda\}$, the low quality firm chooses its common international price p_l to solve

$$\max_{p_l} p_l\left(\frac{p_h-p_l}{\Delta s}-\frac{p_l}{s_l}\right)+p_l\left(1-\frac{p_l}{s_l}\right) \tag{10}$$

where the first term denotes its profits in the North and the second in the South, where it is the sole seller. The high quality firm serves only the North and solves

$$\max_{p_h} p_h\left(\mu-\frac{p_h-p_l}{\Delta s}\right). \tag{11}$$

The first order conditions for these problems yield the following reaction functions under $\{\Lambda\}$:

$$p_l=\frac{r-1}{2(2r-1)}+\frac{p_h}{2(2r-1)} \text{ and } p_h=\frac{\mu(r-1)+p_l}{2}.$$

Using these reaction functions it is easy to show that the prices charged by both firms lie between their corresponding prices under $\{U\}$ and $\{D\}$; further, the low quality firm's price is *higher* than its monopoly price in the South.

Lemma 2. (i) *Under the asymmetric market outcome $\{\Lambda\}$ where (only) the low quality firm serves both markets at the common international price $p_l(\Lambda)$, the price $p_j(\Lambda)$ charged by firm of quality $j, j=h,l$, lies in between its prices under $\{U\}$ and $\{D\}$: $p_j(U)<p_j(\Lambda)<p_{jN}(D), j=h,l$. Furthermore, the low quality firm's price $p_l(\Lambda)$ exceeds its optimal monopoly price in the South.*

(ii) *In the asymmetric market outcome $\{\Lambda^m\}$ where (only) the low quality firm serves both markets, it charges its optimal monopoly price $p_l^m=1/2$ in the South while both firms charge their optimal discriminatory prices $p_{lN}(D)$ and $p_{hN}(D)$ in the North.*

Having discussed the candidate market outcomes, we next consider how PI policies of individual countries influence equilibrium market outcomes. Since PIs are induced by the possibility of arbitrage between national markets, it is useful to begin with the case where PIs are permitted by the North but not by the South.

4. If only the North permits PIs

In this section, we derive the equilibrium market outcome under the mixed policy regime (P,N) where the North permits parallel imports but the South does not. Under this policy configuration, the low quality (Southern) firm is free to compete in the Northern market at a price lower than its domestic price; however, the same is not true for the high quality (Northern) firm. We will show that this creates an incentive for the low quality firm to export i.e., serve both markets. Furthermore, if the asymmetry in demand structure between North and South is high so that the demand for high quality in the South is significantly lower than in the North, the high quality firm prefers to forsake the South and simply not export; in that case the asymmetric outcome $\{\Lambda\}$ or $\{\Lambda^m\}$ obtains. On the other hand, if the demand structures are not too different, the high quality firm serves both markets and we show that in that case, the North's openness to PIs is sufficient to ensure that both firms charge uniform prices i.e., market outcome $\{U\}$ obtains. In what follows, we develop the main arguments leading to these results (summarized in Proposition 2 toward the end of this section).

First suppose that the high quality firm chooses to not serve the Southern market while the low quality firm serves both markets. Under such a scenario, the low quality firm's pricing behavior depends upon the extent of disparity in demand for high quality between the two countries. While the North's openness toward PIs undoes any attempt on its part to charge a lower price in the South, it is free to charge a *higher* price there since PIs are forbidden by it. Furthermore, such pricing can indeed arise when the low quality firm enjoys monopoly status in the South. To see this, suppose that the low quality firm charges its optimal monopoly price $p_l^m=1/2$ in the South and the two firms charge their optimal discriminatory prices $p_{lN}(D)$ and $p_{hN}(D)$ in the North. Given that only the North permits PIs, such a configuration of prices can be sustained iff

$$p_{lS}^m \geq p_{lN}(D) \Leftrightarrow \frac{1}{2} \geq \frac{\mu(r-1)}{4r-1} \Leftrightarrow \mu \leq \mu_l^m \equiv \frac{4r-1}{2(r-1)}. \tag{12}$$

In other words, if $\mu\leq\mu_l^m$ the two markets in effect become perfectly segmented and despite the North's openness to PIs, the low quality firm is free to act as an *unconstrained monopolist* in the South. Note also that, under such a scenario, the market equilibrium in the North *coincides* with international price discrimination; in other words, we obtain the market outcome $\{\Lambda^m\}$. On the other hand, when $\mu>\mu_l^m$ the low quality firm must charge a common international price if it chooses to sell in both markets under (P,N) and therefore, the asymmetric market outcome $\{\Lambda\}$ obtains. As noted in Lemma 2, under the outcome $\{\Lambda\}$, the uniform price charged by the low quality firm actually exceeds its optimal monopoly price $p_l^m=1/2$ in the South while it falls short of its optimal discriminatory price for the North. The inequality $p_l^m<p_l(\Lambda)$ holds because Northern openness to PIs induces the low quality firm to tolerate a reduction in its Southern profit in order to get closer to its preferred Northern price $p_{lN}(D)$.

Whenever the optimal monopoly price in the South $p_l^m=1/2$ cannot be sustained by the low quality firm (which happens when $\mu>\mu_l^m$) its reaction function $R_l(\Lambda)$ under $\{\Lambda\}$ lies strictly above its reaction function $R_l(D)$ under $\{D\}$ – i.e. when $\mu>\mu_l^m$, relative to price discrimination, the low quality is relatively *more* aggressive in price competition. This is because $p_l(\Lambda)>p_l^m$ and the low quality firm is quite eager to reduce its price in response to a price cut by its rival. As a result, the equilibrium pair of prices under $\{\Lambda\}$ are lower relative to $\{D\}$ whereas they are higher relative to $\{U\}$.

It is straightforward to show that there exists μ_l^* where $\mu_l^*<\mu_l^m$ such that over the parameter range $\mu_l^*<\mu<\mu_l^m$ the low quality firm would be better off charging the common price $p_l(\Lambda)$ even though over this parameter range it can sustain its optimal monopoly price p_l^m in the South while charging its optimal discriminatory price $p_{lN}(D)$ in the North. This is because $p_l(\Lambda)>p_{lN}(D)$ whenever $\mu<\mu_l^m$: while the low quality firm would lose profit in its domestic market by charging the common international price $p_l(\Lambda)$, when $\mu>\mu_l^*$ this loss is more than compensated by the increase in profit that results from the softening of price competition in the Northern market. Of course, the high quality firm would necessarily benefit if the low quality firm were to charge a higher price. However, since the low quality firm cannot commit to charging a common price in both markets, when the policy regime is (P,N) and $\mu\leq\mu_l^m$, in Nash equilibrium it charges different prices in the two markets: $p_{lN}(D)$ in the North and p_l^m in the South.

Let $\pi_i(m)$ denote firm i's equilibrium profit under the market outcome m and define

$$\Delta\pi_l \equiv \left\{\begin{array}{l}\pi_l(\Lambda^m)-\pi_l(A) \text{for } \mu\leq\mu_l^m\\ \pi_l(\Lambda)-\pi_l(A) \text{for } \mu>\mu_l^m\end{array}\right\}$$

as the *low quality firm's unilateral incentive* to serve the North – i.e. $\Delta\pi_l$ is the incremental profit earned by the low quality firm from serving the North given that the high quality firm does not serve the Southern market.

Our first result is as follows:

Proposition 1. *If the North permits PIs whereas the South does not, the autarkic market outcome $\{A\}$ cannot arise in equilibrium since the low* *quality firm's unilateral incentive to serve the Northern market is strictly positive:* i.e. $\Delta\pi_l > 0$ *for all feasible* μ *and* r.

To see why this is true, suppose the policy regime is (P,N). When $\mu \le \mu_l^m$, if the low quality firm serves the North the market outcome $\{\Lambda^m\}$ obtains i.e., it earns optimal monopoly profit at home and additional profit $\pi_{lN}(D)$ abroad. Even though $p_l^m \ge p_{lS}(D)$, PIs cannot flow to the South due to its policy stance. Thus, if $\mu \le \mu_l^m$ then $\Delta\pi_l = \pi_{lN}(D) > 0$.

Now suppose $\mu > \mu_l^m$. Under this scenario, the pricing behavior described in part (*i*) of Lemma 2 applies and in Appendix A we show that $\Delta\pi_l = \pi_l(\Lambda) - \pi_l(A) > 0$. The intuition is as follows: when $\mu > \mu_l^m$, preserving its monopoly status in the much smaller Southern market is not particularly attractive to the low quality firm. Indeed, as noted earlier, for $\mu > \mu_l^m$ the low quality firm is willing to charge a price above its optimal monopoly price in the South so as to serve the North at a more desirable price.

Suppose now that the high quality firm chooses to serve the South and consider the low quality firm's best response. The *low quality firm's reciprocal incentive* for serving the North when it must charge a common price in both markets (due to the North's openness to PIs) is defined by

$$\Delta\pi_l(U) \equiv \pi_l(U) - \pi_l(H).$$

It is straightforward to show that $\Delta\pi_l(U) \ge 0$ iff $r \ge r^* = 1 + \frac{3\sqrt{2}}{8}$, which is guaranteed by part (ii) of Assumption 1.

Proposition 1 and part (ii) of Assumption 1 imply that to derive equilibrium outcomes under (P,N), we need to only consider the high quality firm's best response to the low quality firm serving the Northern market. Given that the low quality good is sold in both markets, if the high quality firm chooses to serve both markets uniform pricing obtains under (P,N). On the other hand, if the high quality firm decides to not serve the Southern market then the market outcome depends upon the degree of demand asymmetry: when $\mu \le \mu_l^m$ we obtain $\{\Lambda^m\}$ whereas for $\mu > \mu_l^m$, we get $\{\Lambda\}$.

Given this, the *high quality firm's reciprocal incentive* is defined as follows:

$$\Delta\pi_h(U) \equiv \left\{ \begin{array}{l} \pi_h(U) - \pi_{hN}(D) \text{ for } \mu \le \mu_l^m \\ \pi_h(U) - \pi_h(\Lambda) \text{ for } \mu > \mu_l^m \end{array} \right\}.$$

It is straightforward to show that for $\mu \le \mu_l^m$

$$\Delta\pi_h(U) \ge 0 \Leftrightarrow \mu \le \mu^* \equiv 1 + \sqrt{2}$$

whereas for $\mu > \mu_l^m$ we have

$$\Delta\pi_h(U) \ge 0 \Leftrightarrow \mu \le \mu^u$$

where $\mu^u \le \mu^*$ iff $\mu \le \mu_l^m$ and $\lim_{r \to \infty} \mu^u = \mu^*$. The fact that the high quality firm's reciprocal incentive is positive only when the Northern demand for high quality is not too large relative to the South is quite intuitive: given that the North permits PIs, the larger the Northern demand for high quality relative to the South, the more constrained is the high quality firm's pricing behavior in the North.

We can now derive market outcomes under the policy pair (P,N). These outcomes are illustrated in Fig. 1 drawn in the (r,μ) space.

The downward sloping curve μ_l^m in Fig. 1 defines the boundary below which the low quality firm is able to charge its optimal monopoly price p_l^m in the South so that the market outcome $\{\Lambda^m\}$ is relevant whereas above μ_l^m, the low quality firm charges the price $p_l(\Lambda)$ in both markets and the market outcome $\{\Lambda\}$ is relevant.

The horizontal line plots $\mu = \mu^*$: below this curve the high quality firm has a reciprocal incentive to serve the South when the low quality firm is able to sustain its optimal monopoly price (i.e. it plots $\Delta\pi_h(U) \ge 0$ for $\mu \le \mu_l^m$). Above μ^*, the high quality firm lacks such an incentive and prefers the market outcome $\{\Lambda^m\}$ to uniform pricing $\{U\}$. The upward sloping curve μ^u in Fig. 1 plots the locus of $\Delta\pi_h(U) = 0$ below which the high quality firm has a reciprocal incentive to serve the South when the low quality firm charges the common international price $p_l(\Lambda)$ (i.e. for $\mu > \mu_l^m$).

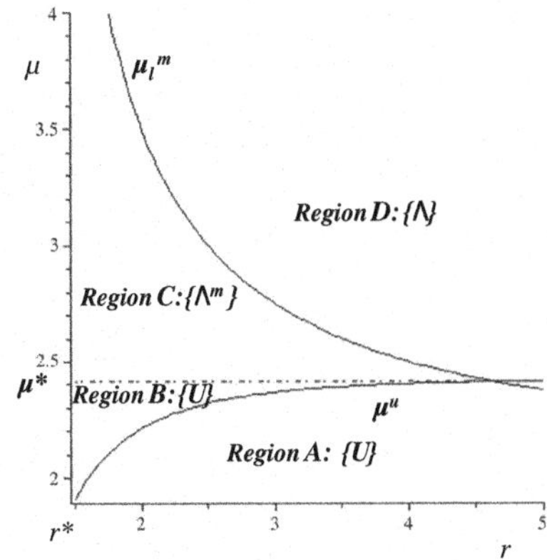

Fig. 1. Equilibrium market structure under (P, N).

When the demand asymmetry between the two countries exceeds the outer boundary defined by μ^u and μ^* – i.e. in region *C* where $\mu^* < \mu \le \mu_l^m$ and in region *D* where $\mu > \max\{\mu_l^m, \mu^u\}$ – the high quality firm prefers to *not* serve the South and the equilibrium market outcome is determined by the low quality firm's pricing behavior: in region *C* the equilibrium outcome is $\{\Lambda^m\}$ whereas in region *D* it is $\{\Lambda\}$. It is worth emphasizing that the decision to not serve the South on the part of the high quality firm reflects considerations that come into play solely due to the North's policy of permitting PIs since, by assumption, selling abroad imposes no additional costs on firms. On the other hand, below the outer boundary defined by μ^u and μ^* (i.e. over region *A* where $\mu \le \mu^u$ and region *B* where $\mu^u \le \mu \le \mu^*$), markets are fairly similar in demand structure and the market outcome is uniform pricing.

We close this section by summarizing the main results in Proposition 2:

Proposition 2. *If the North permits PIs and the South does not, the equilibrium market outcomes are as follows:*

(i) *uniform pricing obtains when* $\mu \le \max\{\mu^u, \mu^*\}$ *(regions A and B in Fig. 1);*

(ii) *the asymmetric outcome* $\{\Lambda^m\}$ *obtains when* $\mu^* < \mu \le \mu_l^m$ *(region C in Fig. 1); and*

(iii) *the asymmetric outcome* $\{\Lambda\}$ *obtains when* $\mu > \max\{\mu_l^m, \mu^u\}$ *(region D in Fig. 1).*

5. If both countries permit

In this section, we derive the equilibrium market outcome under the policy pair (P,P) i.e. when both countries permit PIs. We begin by observing that under (P,P), regardless of the degree of market asymmetry, if a firm serves both markets it must do so at a common international price. More specifically, this implies that market outcomes $\{\Lambda^m\}$ and $\{D\}$ cannot arise.

Next, we argue that Proposition 1 does *not* hold under (*P,P*): i.e., when both countries permit PIs, the low quality firm does *not* necessarily have a unilateral incentive to serve the North. Intuitively, when products are not highly differentiated, the decision to serve the North is not attractive to the low quality firm because price competition in the North is fierce. And since the low quality firm must charge a common price in both markets under (*P,P*), stringent competition in the North also undermines its profit in the Southern market.[16] Under (*P,P*), direct calculations show that

$$\Delta\pi_l \geq 0 \Longleftrightarrow \mu \geq \mu_l^{\Lambda}.$$

Uniform pricing is an equilibrium under (*P,P*) iff each firm has a reciprocal incentive to serve the foreign market: i.e. $\Delta\pi_j(U) \geq 0$ for $j = h, l$. Using the incentive functions $\Delta\pi_j(U)$ along with $\Delta\pi_h$ and $\Delta\pi_l$ allows us to fully describe equilibrium market outcomes under (*P,P*). Fig. 2 illustrates equilibrium market structures under (*P,P*).

Above the downward sloping curve $\Delta\pi_l = 0$ or $(\mu = \mu_l^{\Lambda})$ the low quality firm has a unilateral incentive to serve the foreign market. The negative slope of the curve is intuitive: as the intensity of product market competition decreases (i.e. *r* increases), the critical level of Northern demand required to induce the low quality firm to sell in the North declines. Below the upward sloping curve μ_h, the high quality firm has a unilateral incentive to serve the South.

It is useful to compare Figs. 1 and 2. The first point to note is that in region *D* (i.e. when $\mu > \max\{\mu_l^m, \mu^u\}$), the equilibrium outcome under both (*P,P*) and (*P,N*) is $\{\Lambda\}$. When the low quality firm cannot sustain its optimal monopoly price in the South under (*P,N*), the North's permissive policy toward PIs is the main determinant of market outcome since the high quality firm chooses not to serve the South in order to stay close to its preferred price for the Northern market.

Second, in region *C* (where $\mu^* < \mu \leq \mu_l^m$) while $\{\Lambda\}$ obtains when both countries permit PIs, $\{\Lambda^m\}$ obtains when only the North does so. Recall from Lemma 2 that under $\{\Lambda^m\}$ prices in the North equal $p_{jN}(D)$ while in the South the low quality firm charges its optimal monopoly price $p_l^m = 1/2$. Thus, given that the North permits PIs and the South does not, when $\mu \leq \mu_l^m$ the Southern firm is less aggressive during price competition under the asymmetric outcome $\{\Lambda\}$ relative to that under $\{\Lambda^m\}$: $p_l(\Lambda) > p_l^m$ and $p_{jN}(D) > p_j(\Lambda)$. Thus, as we emphasize in Proposition 3 below, over region *C* prices are *higher* in the North when both countries permit PIs relative to when only the North does so while the opposite is true of prices in the South. As a result, given that the North permits PIs and the Northern firm does serve the South, the firm's profit is higher in region *C* if the South permits PIs relative to when it does not. Thus, the presence of strategic competition implies that, holding the Northern PI policy constant, a unilateral reversal of Southern policy (from banning PIs to allowing them) can *increase* the Northern firm's profit by softening price competition in the Northern market.

Third, while rough intuition suggests that uniform pricing might be more likely to obtain when both countries permit PIs relative to when only the North does, a comparison of Figs. 1 and 2 shows that this is *not* the case. More specifically, note from these figures that over region *A* uniform pricing obtains under both (*P,P*) and (*P,N*) whereas over region *B* uniform pricing obtains only under (*P,N*). Over region *B*, the high quality firm's preference between alternative

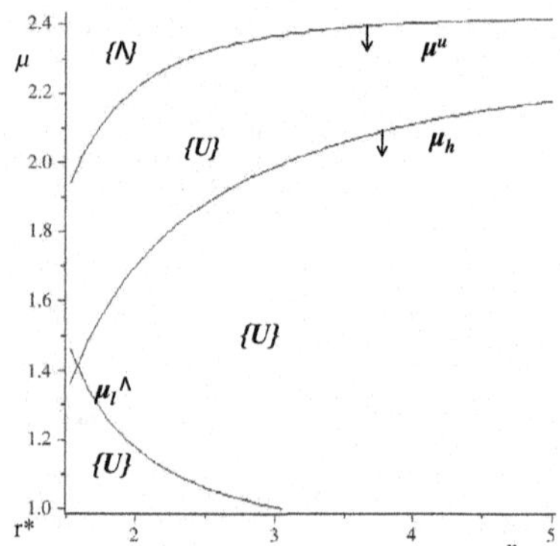

Fig. 2. Equilibrium market structure under (*P, P*).

markets outcomes is as follows: $\{\Lambda\} \succ \{U\} \succ \{\Lambda^m\}$. Over this region, when only the North permit PIs, the high quality firm ends up serving the South since it prefers uniform pricing $\{U\}$ to $\{\Lambda^m\}$. However, when both countries permit PIs $\{\Lambda^m\}$ is not feasible since the low quality firm must charge a common international price that exceeds its optimal discriminatory price for the North. The softening of price competition in the Northern market over region *B* under $\{\Lambda\}$ makes it worthwhile for the high quality firm to not serve the South under (*P,P*). It is noteworthy that it is the inability of its rival to price discriminate internationally under the regime (*P,P*) relative to (*P,N*) that makes the high quality firm opt for the asymmetric outcome $\{\Lambda\}$ over uniform pricing.

We collect the main results of this section below:

Proposition 3. *Suppose both countries permit PIs. Then, uniform pricing obtains when $\mu \leq \mu^u$ (region A in* Fig. 1*) and the asymmetric market outcome $\{\Lambda\}$ obtains otherwise.*[17] *For a subset of the parameter space where the degree of asymmetry between markets is in an intermediate range (i.e. over region C in* Fig. 1 *where $\mu^* < \mu \leq \mu_l^m$), prices are actually higher in the North when both countries permit PIs compared to the policy regime (P,N) where only the North permits PIs.*

6. If North forbids

In this section, we discuss the equilibrium market outcomes when the North forbids parallel imports. We begin by deriving the equilibrium market outcome under the policy regime (*N,P*) where the South permits PIs.

We first argue that the autarkic outcome cannot be an equilibrium when the North prohibits PIs since *the high quality firm has a unilateral incentive to serve the South*. To see why, suppose the low quality firm does not serve the North. Then, the high quality firm charges its optimal monopoly price in the North so long as the South's permissive policy toward PIs does not prevent it from doing so. But since $\mu \geq 1$, it follows that the high quality can *always* sustain its optimal monopoly price in the North when the Northern government forbids PIs and

[16] By contrast, under (*P,N*) the low quality firm's profit in the Southern market is relatively better protected due to the Southern prohibition on PIs and it therefore necessarily has a unilateral incentive to serve the North. Recall that when $\mu \leq \mu_l^m$, the low quality firm actually earns monopoly profit in its market under (*P,N*) if the high quality firm chooses to not sell its goods there.

[17] For completeness, we should note that there is a tiny area over which both autarky and uniform pricing are equilibria. This area is defined by $\mu_h \leq \mu \leq \mu_l^{\Lambda}$. In this area, each firm has a reciprocal incentive to serve the foreign market but no unilateral incentive to do so. For the remainder of the paper, we will take uniform pricing to be the equilibrium over this tiny region.

firms compete (only) in the South. This implies that beginning at autarky, under (N,P) the high quality firm will necessarily choose to serve the South. Doing so brings an incremental gain of $\pi_{hS}(D)$ while protecting its monopoly profit in the North: PIs are prohibited by the North and no PIs occur to the South since the price of the high quality goods is lower there $(p_h^m \geq p_{hS}(D))$.

We now argue that *the low quality firm necessarily has a reciprocal incentive to serve the North when it forbids PIs*. To see this simply note that, given that it does not serve the North, the low quality firm secures an incremental gain of $\pi_{lN}(D)$ by choosing to sell abroad without having any detrimental effect on its monopoly profit in the South.

Next, observe that when the North forbids PIs, the Northern policy makes it possible for the high quality firm to price discriminate internationally. This observation rules out uniform pricing as an equilibrium outcome. Thus, there remain only three candidates for equilibrium under (N,P): $\{\Lambda\}$, $\{\Lambda^m\}$, and $\{D\}$.

As before, the choice between two of three remaining candidates for equilibrium outcomes — $\{\Lambda\}$ and $\{\Lambda^m\}$ — is determined by the degree of demand asymmetry. When the South is open to PIs and the North is not, the low quality firm can charge its optimal monopoly price in the South only when that price is lower than its discriminatory price in the North: i.e. $p_{lS}^m \leq p_{lN}(D) \Leftrightarrow \mu \geq \mu_l^m$. Thus, over $\mu \geq \mu_l^m$, the equilibrium has to be either $\{\Lambda^m\}$ or $\{D\}$. However, $\{\Lambda^m\}$ fails to be an equilibrium because the high quality firm necessarily has a reciprocal incentive to serve the South when $\mu \geq \mu_l^m$: by serving the South it secures an incremental gain of $\pi_{hS}(D)$ in the South without lowering its profit $\pi_{hN}(D)$ in the North. Thus, we have shown that when $\mu \geq \mu_l^m$, both firms have a reciprocal incentive to serve the foreign market and international price discrimination $\{D\}$ is the equilibrium outcome.

Now consider the case $\mu < \mu_l^m$. Consider $\{\Lambda\}$ as a candidate for equilibrium over this parameter range. Starting at $\{\Lambda\}$ if the high quality firm chooses to serve the South, we move to market outcome $\{D\}$ whereas if the low quality firm chooses to withdraw from the North we revert to autarky $\{A\}$. This implies that $\{\Lambda\}$ is an equilibrium iff (*i*) $\pi_h(D) < \pi_h(\Lambda) \Leftrightarrow \mu > \mu_h^d$ and (*ii*) $\pi_l(\Lambda) > \pi_l(A) \Leftrightarrow \mu > \mu_l^\Lambda$. It is easy to show that the curve μ_h^d lies strictly to the left of r^* so that part (ii) of Assumption 1 rules out the parameter range $\mu_l^\Lambda \leq \mu < \mu_h^d$. In other words, since $r > r^*$ it must be that $\Delta\pi_h(D) > 0$.

Thus, we have argued that both types of incentives — unilateral as well as reciprocal — are positive for both firms under the policy pair (N,P). This necessarily implies that international price discrimination is the unique equilibrium outcome under (N,P).

Finally, it is transparent that if the policy pair is (N,N) and PIs cannot flow in either direction, it is a dominant strategy for each firm to serve the foreign market. Furthermore, absent the threat of PIs, firms will charge their optimal discriminatory prices in each market.

We have:

Proposition 4. *If the North forbids PIs, the Southern policy is inconsequential and international price discrimination obtains as the equilibrium outcome.*

It is worth noting that Proposition 4 does not imply that both firms are better off under international price discrimination relative to autarky. In fact, it is easy to see that both can be worse off relative to autarky when the degree of product differentiation (r) is relatively low: under such circumstances severe price competition lowers their respective profits below autarkic levels. This is shown in Fig. 3 which plots the zero-profit contours for $\Delta\pi_j(D) \equiv \pi_j(D) - \pi_j(A)$. The downward sloping contour is that of the low quality firm while the upward sloping one is for the high quality firm.

Fig. 3 can be divided into four regions. In region δ, the degree of demand asymmetry (μ) is moderate and products are highly differentiated (r is large) and both firms are better off relative to autarky: each firm gets access to another market that is comparable in

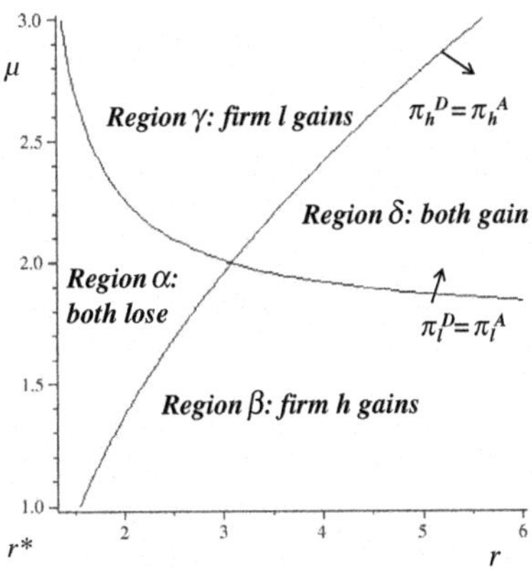

Fig. 3. Autarky versus price discrimination.

demand to its local market where such access is accompanied by price competition that is relatively weak. By contrast, in region α, the severity of price competition under international price discrimination tips the balance in favor of autarky for both firms. In region β, only the high quality firm is better off under international price discrimination while in region γ only the low quality firm is better off. The intuition is as follows. In region γ, the North–South demand asymmetry is large and the low quality firm benefits substantially from being able to sell its goods in the North whereas the high quality firm has to share its large domestic market with a competitor and therefore loses relative to autarky. Finally, in region β, demand asymmetry is small and product differentiation is moderately large: under such a scenario, sharing its local market in return for access to the comparably sized Southern market is not as costly for the high quality firm since its competitor is at a substantial quality disadvantage. For analogous reasons, in region β the low quality firm is better off under autarky relative to international price discrimination.

7. Equilibrium government policies

We are now ready to derive equilibrium policies. Each country's objective is to maximize its welfare. Country i's welfare under market outcome $\{M\}$ is a weighted sum of consumer surplus and firm profits:

$$w_i(M) = \lambda \sum_j cs_{ji}(m) + (1-\lambda)(\pi_{di}(M) + \pi_{ei}(M)) \tag{13}$$

where $M = D, \Lambda, \Lambda^m$ or U and $0 \leq \lambda \leq 1$. In the above welfare function, $\pi_{di}(M)$ denotes profit of country i's firm in its domestic market whereas $\pi_{ei}(M)$ denotes its export profit. Also, let world welfare under market outcome $\{M\}$ be given by $ww(M) = w_N(M) + w_S(M)$.

In what follows, we focus primarily on the case where government's maximize aggregate welfare (i.e. $\lambda = 1/2$) and then comment briefly on the two polar cases where governments care only about firms or consumers.

7.1. Welfare maximizing governments ($\lambda = 1/2$)

Our first welfare result reports a comparison of the different market outcomes from the viewpoint of each country:

Proposition 5. *Suppose governments seek to maximize national welfare (i.e. $\lambda = 1/2$). Then, each country's welfare ranking of the various market outcomes that can arise in equilibrium is as follows:*

(i) *For the North:* $w_N(U) > w_N(D) > w_N(\Lambda) > w_N(\Lambda^m)$ *whereas*
(ii) *for the South:* $w_S(D) > \max\{w_S(U), w_S(\Lambda), w_S(\Lambda^m)\}$.

Note in particular that the welfare of the North under uniform pricing is strictly higher than that under international price discrimination whereas the welfare of the South is strictly lower. From the South's perspective, price discrimination is preferred to uniform pricing due to two reasons. First, its firm enjoys strictly higher export profits under discrimination since price competition in the North is softer relative to uniform pricing. Second, recall from Lemma 2 that relative to uniform pricing, prices are lower in the South under price discrimination. As a result, both firm profitability and consumer welfare considerations work in the same direction for the South. However, as Proposition 4 notes, whether or not price discrimination obtains in equilibrium depends on North's PI policy and not on that of the South.

For the North, consumer welfare and firm profitability work against each other: while consumers are better off under uniform pricing, the high quality firm prefers discrimination. Since higher prices under discrimination transfer part of the Northern consumer surplus over to the low quality firm in terms of profits, the North's aggregate welfare is higher under uniform pricing relative to international price discrimination.

We are now in a position to consider each country's optimal PI policy in response to the other. Suppose South permits PIs. What is North's optimal PI policy? We can answer this question using Fig. 1 and Proposition 5. First note from Proposition 5 that the North will permit PIs so long as parameters are such that its firm exports to the South when both markets allow PIs. Using Fig. 1, we conclude that, given that the South permits PI, the North adopts the same PI policy iff $\mu \le \mu^u$ i.e. over region *A* where the Northern firm's reciprocal incentive is positive. Now suppose the South bans PIs. Then, Fig. 1 implies that the North will permit PIs over both regions *A* and *B* (i.e. iff $\mu \le \max\{\mu^*, \mu^u\}$) since the high quality firm's reciprocal incentive to export is positive over these regions under policy pair (*P,N*). Thus, over region *B* the North permits PIs *only when* the South forbids them implying that *Southern openness to PIs reduces North's willingness to permit PIs.*

Now consider the South's best response to the North's policy choice. Recall that a ban on PIs by the North makes the South indifferent between its policy options since the ban is sufficient to induce international price discrimination. But what if the North permits PIs? Then, Figs. 1 and 2 indicate that Southern policy matters only over region *B* ($\mu^u \le \mu \le \mu^*$) and region *C* ($\mu^* < \mu^* \le \mu_l^m$). Over the rest of the parameter space, Northern openness to PIs determines the market outcome and the South is indifferent between its two policy options.

Over region *B*, given that North permits PIs, South prefers to permit PIs in order to obtain the asymmetric market outcome $\{\Lambda\}$ as opposed to uniform pricing while over region *C*, it prefers to permit PIs to obtain $\{\Lambda\}$ as opposed to $\{\Lambda^m\}$ since $w_S(\Lambda) \ge w_S(\Lambda^m)$ iff $\mu \le \mu_l^m$. Thus, given that the North allows PI, the South strictly prefers to allow PIs over regions *B* and *C* whereas it is indifferent between its two policy options otherwise.

To derive equilibrium policies, suppose we are in region *A* (i.e. $\mu \le \mu^u$) so that the high quality firm's reciprocal incentive is positive when the low quality firm charges a common international price in both markets. It is easy to see that both (*P,N*) and (*P,P*) are Nash equilibria over region *A*: the North has no incentive to deviate since uniform pricing is its most preferred regime whereas the South's PI policy is inconsequential for the market outcome.

Now consider region *B* (i.e. when $\mu^u \le \mu \le \mu^*$). Here the market equilibrium under (*P,P*) is $\{\Lambda\}$ whereas under (*N,P*) it is international price discrimination. Since $w_N(D) \ge w_N(\Lambda)$ the North bans PIs in region *B* to ensure that international price discrimination obtains thereby making Southern policy inconsequential. Thus, in region *B*, both (*N, P*) and (*N,N*) are Nash equilibria. Similarly, in region *C* (i.e. when $\mu^* < \mu^* \le \mu_l^m$) and region *D*, i.e. for $\mu > \max\{\mu^u, \mu_l^m\}$, it is optimal for the North to forbid PIs to induce international price discrimination and avoid the asymmetric outcome $\{\Lambda\}$ while the Southern policy is inconsequential.

We can now state:

Proposition 6. *When governments maximize national welfare* (i.e. $\lambda = 1/2$) *the equilibrium market outcome is determined by the North's PI policy:*

(i) *For $\mu \le \mu^u$ (region A in Fig. 1) i.e., when the degree of asymmetry between demand structures of the two countries is not too large, permitting PIs is a dominant policy choice for the North and uniform pricing obtains independent of the South's PI policy.*[18] *In particular, (P,P) and (P,N) are both Nash equilibria.*
(ii) *For $\mu > \mu^u$ (regions B, C, and D in Fig. 1) i.e., when the degree of asymmetry between demand structures of the two markets is large, prohibiting PIs is a strictly dominant policy choice for the North and international price discrimination obtains, independent of the PI policy of the South. In particular, policy pairs (N, P) and (N,N) are both Nash equilibria.*
(iii) *The PI policy of the South is always inconsequential in equilibrium.*

When markets are sufficiently asymmetric in their demand structure, the North forbids PIs to rule out asymmetric market outcomes $\{\Lambda^m\}$ and $\{\Lambda\}$ under which its own firm chooses to *not* serve the South so as to charge a high price in the North, which is detrimental for Northern consumers and overall Northern welfare. Note also that the nature of the North's equilibrium policy is such that the Southern policy has no effect on market outcomes, and therefore, welfare. This policy outcome is quite consistent with the observed variation of PI policies across the world. As we noted earlier, the two largest markets in the world – EU and the USA – restrict PIs from the rest of the world while there is substantial variation among developing countries with respect to their PI policies, an outcome that might be indicative of the fact that no one type of PI policy is strictly preferable from their viewpoint.

To gain further insight into the welfare calculus underlying North's decision to ban PIs over all regions except region *A*, suppose the policy pair is (*P,N*) and the Northern firm chooses to not export. Now consider a reversal in North's policy from permitting PIs to banning them. The first point to note is that in region *C*, this unilateral change in Northern policy has *no effect* on prices in the Northern market since under the asymmetric outcome $\{\Lambda^m\}$, market prices in the North coincides with price discrimination (see Lemma 2). Thus, over region *C*, forbidding PIs increases Northern welfare because it yields additional export profits without having *any* adverse effect on local consumer surplus.

Over region *D*, if the North chooses to ban PIs in order to induce its firm to export, there are two conflicting effects on Northern welfare. On the positive side, the export profit earned by the high quality firm contributes to Northern welfare. On the negative side, prices in the North are higher under $\{D\}$ relative to $\{\Lambda\}$. However, since prices of both firms increase and it is the change in the reaction function of the Southern firm that causes equilibrium prices to change, it turns

[18] *If the inequality is strict – i.e. $\mu < \mu^u$ – then it is a strictly dominant strategy for the North to permit PIs.*

out that the share of Northern consumers buying the high quality actually increases. To see this, note that under international price discrimination we have

$$\theta_{lN}(D)=\frac{\mu(r-1)}{4r-1} \text{ and } \theta_{hN}(D)=\frac{\mu(2r-1)}{4r-1}$$

whereas under the asymmetric outcome $\{\Lambda\}$ we have

$$\theta_{lN}(\Lambda)=\frac{(\mu+2)(r-1)}{8r-5} \text{ and } \theta_{hN}(\Lambda)=\frac{4\mu r-3\mu-1}{8r-5}.$$

It is straightforward to calculate that

$$\theta_{lN}(D)<\theta_{lN}(\Lambda) \text{ iff } \mu>\mu_l^m \text{ and } \theta_{hN}(D)>\theta_{hN}(\Lambda) \text{ iff } \mu>\mu_l^m.$$

In other words, since $\mu>\mu_l^m$ in region D while market coverage (i.e. the total number of consumers buying either good) is lower in the North under price discrimination relative to the asymmetric outcome $\{\Lambda\}$, a higher proportion of them buy the high quality goods. This switching by consumers from low to high quality dampens the adverse effect of the price increases that result when the North changes its policy from allowing PIs to banning them thereby altering the market outcome from $\{\Lambda\}$ to $\{D\}$.[19]

Finally, note that in region B, the North has no unilateral incentive deviate from (P,N) to (N,N) since uniform pricing obtains under (P,N) whereas price discrimination obtains under (N,N). However, in region B, if the North were to permit PIs, the South also prefers to permit PIs to induce the outcome $\{\Lambda\}$. But since $w_N(D)>w_N(\Lambda)$ and a Northern ban on PIs is sufficient to yield international price discrimination, in equilibrium, the North ends up banning PIs to avoid $\{\Lambda\}$.

It is also noteworthy that when the North does ban PIs, its PI policy generates a substantial *positive spillover for the South*: not only do Southern consumers enjoy low prices under discrimination, the low quality firm also benefits from being able to charge a more attractive price in the North.

It is easy to show that aggregate world welfare is strictly higher under uniform pricing relative to price discrimination: $ww(U)>ww(D)>\max\{ww(\Lambda),ww(\Lambda^m)\}$.[20] Intuitively, by yielding price differentials across countries, international price discrimination creates an inefficiency relative to uniform pricing. The two symmetric market outcomes dominate the asymmetric ones because the latter involve less competition in the Southern market. Proposition 6 shows that when countries are not too different in demand structure (as is the case over region A), even though each is guided purely by its own interest, equilibrium policies are efficient in that they maximize aggregate welfare.

What if government policies were chosen not to maximize aggregate welfare? We turn to this next.

7.2. If $\lambda\neq 1/2$

Consider the case where $\lambda=0$ i.e. governments care only about firm profits. To derive equilibrium policies, simply recall that a unilateral prohibition of PIs by the North is sufficient to ensure price discrimination, the most preferred market structure of its firm. As a result, when $\lambda=0$ the policy outcome is as described by part (*ii*) of Proposition 6.

Now consider the situation where governments care only about consumers (i.e. $\lambda=1$). First consider South's best response to alternative Northern policies. As before, a Northern ban on PIs delivers South's most preferred outcome and its policy becomes irrelevant. If the North is open to PIs, Southern policy matters only when the high quality firm's reciprocal incentive is negative (i.e. it matters in all regions other than region A where $\mu^*\leq\mu^u$). Over region B, given that the North permits PI, it is optimal for South to ban PIs because doing so leads to uniform pricing under which prices are lower in the South relative to the market outcome $\{\Lambda\}$. Over region C, the South prefers to allow PIs because doing so yields the market outcome $\{\Lambda\}$ which is preferable to $\{\Lambda^m\}$ since $CS_S(\Lambda)\geq CS_S(\Lambda^m)$ whenever $\mu\leq\mu_l^m$. Finally, for $\mu>\max\{\mu_l^m,\mu^u\}$, the Southern policy is irrelevant since the equilibrium outcome $\{\Lambda\}$ is invariant to its policy. Thus, if the North permits PIs, the South prefers to ban PIs over regions B, permit them over region C, and it is indifferent otherwise whereas if the North forbids PI, the South is indifferent between its two policy options.

Recall that the prices in the North under $\{\Lambda^m\}$ is the same as that international price discrimination so that we have $CS_N(D)=CS_N(\Lambda^m)$. Part (*i*) of Lemma 2 implies that $CS_N(U)>max\{CS_N(D),CS_N(\Lambda)\}$. Furthermore, $CS_N(D)\geq CS_N(\Lambda)$ iff $\mu\leq\mu_l^m$ since the low quality firm's common international price $p_l(\Lambda)$ is higher than its optimal discriminatory price $p_{lN}(D)$ in the Northern market iff $\mu\leq\mu_l^m$.

Suppose the South permits PI and consider the North's best response. It is clear that in region A (i.e. for $\mu\leq\mu^u$) it is optimal for the North to permit PIs in order to induce uniform pricing. However, over other regions uniform pricing is not an equilibrium under (P,P) and the best the North can do is to induce the market outcome it prefers between $\{D\}$ and $\{\Lambda\}$. Since $CS_N(D)\geq CS_N(\Lambda)$ iff $\mu\leq\mu_l^m$, if the South permits PIs, the North forbids them in regions B and C to induce international price discrimination whereas it permits them in region D to induce the outcome $\{\Lambda\}$.

Consider now the scenario where South forbids PI. What is North's best response? As before, in region A it is optimal for the North to permit PIs to induce uniform pricing. In addition, the North permits PIs also over region B (i.e. when $\mu^u\leq\mu\leq\mu^*$) since doing so results in uniform pricing (see Fig. 1). In region C (i.e. when $\mu^*\leq\mu^*\leq\mu_l^m$) the North is indifferent between permitting and not permitting PIs since $CS_N(D)=CS_N(\Lambda^m)$. Finally, in region D i.e. when $\mu>\max\{\mu_l^m,\mu^u\}$ Northern consumer welfare is higher if it permits PIs since doing so yields the market outcome $\{\Lambda\}$ and $CS_N(\Lambda)\geq CS_N(D)$ when $\mu\geq\mu_l^m$. Thus, when $\lambda=1$, given that the South forbids PIs, the North (weakly) prefers to allow PIs: over region C it is indifferent between its policy options whereas everywhere else it strictly prefers to allow PIs.

We can now state the following result:

Proposition 7. *If governments care only about consumer surplus (i.e. $\lambda=1$), the following hold in equilibrium:*

(i) *Over region A and D i.e., when demand asymmetry is relatively small or very large, permitting PIs is a dominant strategy for the North and the policy choice of the South is inconsequential; both (P,N) and (P,P) are Nash equilibria. Uniform pricing is the resulting market outcome in region A while the asymmetric market outcome $\{\Lambda\}$ obtains in region D.*

(ii) *Over region B, the policy Nash equilibrium is (P,N) and uniform pricing obtains.*

(iii) *Over region C, prohibiting PIs is a dominant strategy for the North and the policy choice of the South is inconsequential; both (N,P) and (N,N) are Nash equilibria with international price discrimination as the market outcome.*

Two things are worth noting about Proposition 7. First, when governments care only about consumer welfare, equilibrium PI policies

[19] An analogous logic explains why the North finds it optimal to ban PIs over all regions other than A when the South permits PIs and its firm decides not to export. As is clear, Southern policy is irrelevant for explaining why the North forbids PIs over region D since the outcome $\{\Lambda\}$ obtains regardless. However, over regions B and C the PI policy of the South does matter since the outcome $\{\Lambda^m\}$ cannot arise when the South is open to PIs. To understand why the North deviates from (P,P) to (N,P) over regions B and C where $\mu\leq\mu_l^m$, note that this change in Northern policy causes local consumers to switch from high to low quality but this switching is offset by the fact that total market coverage *expands* – i.e. fewer consumers abstain from buying either good.

[20] Indeed, we can show that $ww(\Lambda)\geq ww(\Lambda^m)$ iff $\mu\leq\mu_l^m$.

are such that international price discrimination is *less likely* to arise as an equilibrium outcome since the North has a strong incentive to keep local prices low by keeping its market open to PI. Second, in region *D*, North chooses to open its market to PIs to induce the asymmetric outcome $\{\Lambda\}$ under which prices are lower in the North relative to international price discrimination. By contrast, recall from Proposition 6 that only symmetric market outcomes obtain when governments weigh consumer and firm interests equally.

8. Discussion of the model

Since the existing literature on PIs has tended to focus almost exclusively on monopoly, in what follows we highlight the conceptual value-added of allowing for oligopolistic competition in the product market. Furthermore, in order to make the study of strategic interaction at two different stages (policy setting and the product market) tractable, we made two key simplifying assumptions – i.e. exporting involves no additional costs and quality is exogenously given. In this section, we also briefly discuss the robustness of our results to changes in these assumptions.

8.1. Role of competition

Broadly speaking, incorporating strategic interaction in the product market provides two main types of new insights. First, we find that the effects of PI policies on prices and firm profitability under oligopoly differ substantially from those under monopoly.[21] Second, the equilibrium policy choices of the North also differ across the two types of market structures. Below, we discuss each set of insights in turn.

As was noted in Section 5, in our oligopoly model prices can be *higher* in the North when both countries permit PIs relative to when only the North does so (see the discussion below Fig. 2). This happens over region *C* in Fig. 1. As a result, given that the North permits PIs and its firm does not export, in region *C* the Northern firm's profit is higher if the South permits PIs relative to when it does not. By contrast, if there were no Southern firm, the pricing behavior of the Northern firm (as well as its profits) would be *independent* of Southern PI policy.[22] This result points to a new channel via which Southern policies affect Northern welfare.

Our oligopoly analysis also uncovers the interesting result that uniform pricing is actually *more likely* to obtain when only the North permits PIs relative to when both countries permit PIs – this happens over region *B* in Fig. 1. This implies that, given that the North permits PIs, the Northern firm's decision to serve the Southern market can also depend upon the Southern PI policy due to its effect on the pricing behavior of the Southern firm. By contrast, if the Northern firm were a monopolist, whether or not the Northern firm chooses to export as well as whether uniform pricing obtains or not depends only on the North's PI policy.

Consider now how the presence of the Southern firm affects strategic interaction at the policy setting stage as well as the nature of equilibrium policies. There are three key points here. First, a model without the Southern firm would be incapable of shedding any light on the interdependence of PI policies across countries since Northern policy would be totally independent of Southern policy. By contrast, in our oligopoly model if governments maximize aggregate welfare the (*i*) North is more likely to permit PIs when the South does not and (*ii*) if the North is open to PIs, the South (weakly) prefers to be open to PIs whereas a Northern ban on PIs makes the South indifferent between its two policy options.

Second, it is straightforward to show that if there were no Southern firm, in equilibrium, the North permits PIs in regions *A* and *B* whereas the South is indifferent between its policy options. By contrast, under oligopoly the North permits PIs in only region *A* (see Proposition 6). Thus, competition from the Southern firm makes it *less likely* that the North permits PIs. This result not only differentiates equilibrium policies across the two types of market structures, it also has an important empirical implication: it suggests that we should observe more restrictions on PIs in markets where foreign competition is more potent.

Third, the presence of oligopolistic competition has an even stronger effect on equilibrium policies when governments care only about consumer surplus (i.e. $\lambda = 1$). It is easy to see that absent the Southern firm, if the North cared only about consumer surplus it would always permit PIs: if its firm were to export, the North would enjoy a lower price by virtue of uniform pricing; if not, the firm's local price would be unaffected by its PI policy. By contrast, as we show in Proposition 7, under oligopolistic competition the North can actually generate greater consumer surplus by *forbidding* PIs (this happens over region *C*). The critical point is that this happens entirely due to the effect of the Northern PI policy on the Southern firm's reaction function: Northern openness to PIs makes the Southern firm less aggressive in price competition which in turn lowers prices of both firms in the North. It is noteworthy that in this scenario the Northern firm's price in its own market depends upon Northern PI policy *even though it does not sell in the South.* By contrast, if the Northern firm were a global monopolist, Northern PI policy affects its pricing behavior only if it sells in the South. Proposition 7 also shows that when $\lambda = 1$, over region *B*, the unique policy equilibrium is (*P,N*), i.e., Southern policy is consequential over region *B* since, over this region, it is optimal for the North to permit PIs only if the South forbids them.

8.2. Positive costs

For simplicity, like the existing literature on PI, we assume that authorizing products for sale in foreign markets does not impose any additional costs (marginal or fixed) on firms. An important advantage of this approach is that it allows us to highlight the interaction between PI policies, pricing behavior, and the strategic incentives firms have for selling or not selling in each other's markets even when such sales do not involve additional costs relative to domestic sales. In particular, in our model, whenever the Northern firm chooses to not serve the South it does so not to economize on costs but rather to increase profits by being able to charge a high price in the North.

We expect the qualitative nature of our results to continue to hold if firms face additional fixed costs for accessing foreign markets so long as these costs are small relative to product market profits. To see why, suppose firms incurred a fixed cost for selling abroad. If so, each of incentive functions plotted in Figs. 1 and 2 would shift so as to reduce the parameter space over which the two types of incentives (unilateral and reciprocal) are positive. For example, in Fig. 1 both the μ_h and μ^u curves shift downward when firms incur a fixed cost for selling abroad. While these shifts in the two curves would alter the parameter space over which each of the market structures is an equilibrium, it would not change the range of outcomes described in Figs. 1 and 2 provided that the costs of selling abroad are not so large so as to completely eliminate the incentive to do so under some (or all) of the policy regimes. As is clear, the key welfare rankings from the perspective of the two regions also would not be affected by the presence of such costs. For example, the North would still prefer uniform pricing to price discrimination while the South would have the opposite preferences. Of course, the existence of these costs would reduce each firm's export profit which in turn would imply that the Northern government would be less concerned

[21] In two-country Hotelling type duopoly model, Roy and Saggi (forthcoming) show that PI policy can act as an instrument of strategic trade policy regardless of whether firms compete in prices or quantities.

[22] Incidentally, if the degree of product differentiation (r) becomes arbitrarily large, our oligopoly model essentially converges to a monopoly model since product market competition disappears.

about inducing its firm to export. Note, however, that in our model the firm's incentive to export is always weaker than that what is socially optimal for its home economy. Thus, it would still be the case that the firm would choose not to export even when it is better for its home economy that it does so. This implies that the nature of the policy equilibrium would be similar to that in our model.[23]

8.3. Endogenous quality

Our model takes product quality to be exogenously given. While endogenizing quality is beyond the scope of this paper, it is worth discussing how we expect our analysis to be modified when quality is endogenously determined. Since what matters in the model is the relative quality level of the two firms, fix the Southern firm's quality at 1 and suppose the Northern firm's quality is determined by its investment in quality improvement. Following Valleti (2006), one would expect that the firm's incentive to improve quality would be stronger when it can price discriminate internationally relative to when it cannot. This implies that the Northern government's preference for uniform pricing could be reduced if the Northern firm's incentive to improve quality is substantially higher under international price discrimination. If so, our key policy result (i.e. Proposition 6) would need to be modified in the sense that uniform pricing would likely be preferred by the North over a smaller parameter space in order to increase its firm's incentive to improve quality. In our view, further research is necessary to formally verify this intuitive conjecture, particularly if both firms can invest in quality improvement as opposed to just the Northern firm. Indeed, given that the existing literature on the impact of PI policies on R&D has tended to focus almost exclusively on monopoly, our model could serve as a foundation for further research in the area.

9. Concluding remarks

A sizeable literature analyzes the pros and cons of parallel trade (see Maskus, 2000 for a comprehensive overview). However, this literature has shed only limited light on factors that determine national PI policies. In this paper, we endogenize PI policies in a North–South duopoly model where the Northern firm produces the high quality and the Southern firm the low quality. A crucial feature of the model is that, given government policies, each firm decides whether or not to offer its product for the sale in the foreign market. Incorporating this feature into the model allows us to endogenously derive asymmetric market structures of the type where both qualities are sold in the North while only the low quality is sold in the South. Not only are such market structures interesting with respect to the pricing behavior of firms, the possibility that they can arise under certain North–South policy configurations plays a crucial role in determining equilibrium policies.

Intuition suggests that the Northern policy stance ought to play a key role in determining international market structure. This intuition finds support in our model, but we show that heterogeneity in demand structure across countries can matter in rather unexpected ways. In this regard, our key result – and one that matches quite well with the observed nature of real world national PI policies – is that if the Northern demand and, more particularly, preference for high quality is sufficiently higher than that of the South, the North forbids PIs and international price discrimination obtains as the equilibrium outcome. An especially noteworthy aspect of this result is that international price discrimination is the South's most preferred market structure; the North's welfare is actually higher under uniform pricing. Of course, in choosing to forbid PIs, the North is motivated not by altruism but rather its own interests: a ban on PIs by the North prevents a scenario where its own (high quality) firm abstains from serving the Southern market in order to shore up its profit at home. Thus, when demand heterogeneity across markets is high, by preventing indirect competition from arbitrage-induced PIs, the Northern prohibition on PIs induces direct competition in both markets. Only when markets are relatively similar in demand structure does the North choose to permit PIs and obtain its most preferred market outcome – i.e. uniform pricing – as an equilibrium outcome.

Our analysis of PI policies is novel in that it allows for oligopolistic competition in the product market. In our view, this is important in the context of parallel trade: while market power is pervasive when firms are protected by patents or other IPRs, true monopolies are rather rare. For example, even in the context of pharmaceuticals several competing firms often supply drugs and medicines that help treat any given illness or disease. Secondly, in our model, government policy takes into account both consumer and firm interests. As noted above, while setting its PI policy, the North must account for the possibility that its own firm might forsake the Southern market in order to sustain a more attractive price in its local market. By contrast, in the existing literature, PI policies have been studied primarily from the viewpoint of importing countries.

While the model provides some new insights, it abstracts from several important aspects of parallel trade that deserve further research. For example, it remains to be seen what additional considerations arise under oligopoly when one explicitly takes into account the role of intermediaries in parallel trade and the problems of vertical control or contracting as analyzed by Maskus and Chen (2002 and 2004). It would also be worthwhile to study the two-way relationship between parallel trade and strategic R&D competition, particularly in terms of investments in quality improvement. Finally, our analysis considers PI policies in isolation, ignoring conventional instruments of trade policy such as tariffs and quotas. It would be useful to analyze a model in which PI policies are determined jointly with such trade policy instruments in order to obtain a better understanding of any potential linkages between these types of policies. We hope future research will address some of these topics.

Appendix A

Proof of Lemma 1. Under international price discrimination, equilibrium prices in country i are:

$$p_{li}(D) = \frac{\mu_i(r-1)}{4r-1} \text{ and } p_{hi}(D) = 2rp_{li}(D). \tag{14}$$

Equilibrium prices under uniform pricing are

$$p_l(U) = \frac{(r-1)(\mu+1)}{2(4r-1)} \text{ and } p_h(U) = 2rp_l(U). \tag{15}$$

Note from Eqs. (14) and (15) that under uniform pricing each firm charges the average of its optimal discriminatory prices:

$$2p_j(U) = \sum_i p_{ji}(D). \tag{16}$$

[23] Note also that a similar argument applies to the case where firms incur higher marginal costs for exporting, say due to the existence of tariffs or trade costs: under such a scenario each firm's export profit would shrink, but the Northern government would still be interested in inducing its firm to export.

Proof of Lemma 2. Using the reaction functions reported in the text, prices under uniform pricing are given by

$$p_h(U) = \frac{(\mu+1)(r-1)r}{4r-1} \text{ and } p_l(U) = \frac{p_l(U)}{2r}. \tag{17}$$

Firm reaction functions under $\{\Lambda\}$ are given by

$$p_l = \frac{p_h + (r-1)}{2(2r-1)} \text{ and } p_h = \frac{\mu(r-1) + p_l}{2} \tag{18}$$

which yield the following equilibrium prices

$$p_l(\Lambda) = \frac{(\mu+2)(r-1)}{(8r-5)} \text{ and } p_h(\Lambda) = \frac{(r-1)(2\mu(2r-1)+1)}{(8r-5)} \tag{19}$$

with associated profits $\pi_j(\Lambda)$. Since $r \geq 1$ it is straightforward that the low quality firm's common price in both markets under $\{\Lambda\}$ is higher than its price under uniform pricing:

$$p_l(\Lambda) - p_l(U) = \frac{(r-1)}{2} \frac{8r+3\mu+1}{(4r-1)(8r-5)} > 0. \tag{20}$$

Proof of Proposition 1. The proof proceeds in a straightforward way. Directly calculations show that $\Delta_l(\Lambda) \equiv \pi_l(\Lambda) - \pi_l(A)$ is increasing in μ and that $\Delta_l(\Lambda) > 0$ at $\mu = \mu_l^m$. This implies that $\Delta_l(\Lambda) > 0$ for all $\mu > \mu_l^m$. As argued in the paper, when $\mu \leq \mu_l^m$, the low quality firm faces no trade-off in its local market and serving the North yields a strictly positive gain.

Other supporting calculations

Equilibrium firm profits under uniform pricing equal

$$\pi_l(U) = \frac{r(r-1)(\mu+1)^2}{2(4r-1)^2} \text{ and } \pi_h(U) = 4r\pi_l(U)$$

whereas under international price discrimination we have

$$\pi_{lS}(D) = \frac{(r-1)r}{(4r-1)^2} \text{ whereas } \pi_{lN}(D) = \frac{\mu^2(r-1)r}{(4r-1)^2} \tag{21}$$

which implies

$$\pi_l(D) \equiv \sum_i \pi_{li}(D) = \frac{\left(\mu^2+1\right)(r-1)r}{(4r-1)^2}.$$

Similarly,

$$\pi_h(D) \equiv \sum_i \pi_{hi}(D) = 4r\pi_l(D).$$

Proof of Proposition 5. Let $\lambda = 1/2$. Directly calculating aggregate Northern welfare under uniform pricing and price discrimination and subtracting yields

$$w_N(U) - w_N(D) = \frac{r(4r+1)(r-1)(\mu+3)(\mu-1)}{16(4r-1)^2} \geq 0.$$

Furthermore, note that

$$w_N(D) - w_N(\Lambda^m) = \frac{\pi_{hN}(D)}{2} = \frac{2r^2\mu^2(r-1)}{(4r-1)^2} > 0$$

which implies

$$w_N(U) > w_N(D) > w_N(\Lambda^m).$$

The inequality $w_N(D) > w_N(\Lambda)$ can be shown as follows. First, we have

$$\frac{d(w_N(D) - w_N(\Lambda))}{d\mu} = -\frac{2(r-1)^3(\mu - \mu_l^m)}{(4r-1)(8r-5)^2} > 0 \text{ iff } \mu \leq \mu_l^m.$$

Furthermore, direct calculations show that at $\mu = 1$ we have $w_N(D) > w_N(\Lambda)$. Thus, it must be that $w_N(D) > w_N(\Lambda)$ whenever $\mu \leq \mu_l^m$. Now consider the case when $\mu > \mu_l^m$ so that the welfare difference $w_N(D) - w_N(\Lambda)$ is decreasing in North–South demand asymmetry μ. Direct calculations show that at the maximum permissible value of μ, i.e. at $\mu = \overline{\mu}$, we have $w_N(D) > w_N(\Lambda)$. Thus, it must be that $w_N(D) > w_N(\Lambda)$ for all μ.

Now consider Southern welfare. We have

$$w_S(D) - w_S(U) = \frac{r(r-1)(7\mu - 4\mu r + 20r - 3)(\mu - 1)}{16(4r-1)^2} \geq 0 \text{ since } \mu \leq \overline{\mu}.$$

Next, we have

$$w_S(D) - w_S(\Lambda^m) = \frac{4r(r-1)+3}{16(4r-1)} > 0.$$

Thus, we have

$$w_S(D) > w_S(U) > w_S(\Lambda^m).$$

The inequality $w_S(D) > w_S(\Lambda)$ can be shown as follows. We have

$$\left.\frac{\partial(w_S(D) - w_S(\Lambda))}{\partial\mu}\right|_{\mu = \mu_l^m} = \frac{(4r+1)(r-1)}{4(4r-1)(8r-5)} > 0$$

i.e. at the lowest value of μ that is relevant for comparing $w_S(D)$ and $w_S(\Lambda)$, the welfare difference $w_S(D) - w_S(\Lambda)$ is increasing in μ. Furthermore, we have

$$\frac{\partial^2(w_S(D) - w_S(\Lambda))}{\partial^2\mu} = \frac{3(r-1)^2\left(16r^2 - 8r - 1\right)}{2(4r-1)^2(8r-5)^2} > 0$$

which implies that $\frac{\partial(w_S(D) - w_S(\Lambda))}{\partial\mu} > 0$ for all $\mu \geq \mu_l^m$. Since we know that at $\mu = \mu_l^m$ we have

$$w_S(D) - w_S(\Lambda) = w_S(D) - w_S(\Lambda^m) = \frac{4r(r-1)+3}{16(4r-1)} > 0$$

it must be that $w_S(D) > w_S(\Lambda)$ for all $\mu \geq \mu_l^m$.

References

Ahmadi, R., Yang, B.R., 2000. Parallel imports: challenges from unauthorized distribution channels. Marketing Science 19, 279–294.

Associates National Economic Research, 1999. The economic consequences of the choice of regime of exhaustion in the area of trademarks. Final Report for DG XV of the European Commission.

Baudenbacher, C., 1998. Trademark law and parallel imports in a globalized world – recent developments in Europe with special regard to the legal situation in the United States. Fordham International Law Journal 22, 645–695.

Biadgleng, E.T., 2009. TRIPS Post-grant Flexibilities. Presentation at the UNCTAD Workshop on Flexibilities in International Intellectual Property Rules and Local Production of Pharmaceuticals for the Southern Central and West African Region 7–9 December 2009, Cape Town, South Africa.

Danzon, P., Epstein, A., 2008. Effects of regulation on drug launch and pricing in interdependent markets. National Bureau of Economic Research Working Paper No. 14041.

Gansland, Mattias, Maskus, Keith E., 2004. Parallel imports and the pricing of pharmaceutical products: evidence from the European Union. Journal of Health Economics 23, 1035–1057.

Goldberg, P.K., 2010. Intellectual property rights protection in developing countries: the case of pharmaceuticals. Journal of the European Economic Association 8, 326–353.
Grossman, G.M., Lai, E., 2008. Parallel imports and price controls. The Rand Journal of Economics 39, 378–402.
Kanavos, P., Costa-i-Font, J., Merkur, S., Gemmill, M., 2004. The economic impact of pharmaceutical parallel trade in European member states: a stakeholder analysis. Special Research Paper. LSE Health and Social Care, London School of Economics and Political Science.
Lanjouw, J. O., 2005. Patents, price controls and access to new drugs: how policy affects global market entry. National Bureau of Economic Research Working Paper No. 11321.
Li, C., Maskus, K.E., 2006. The impact of parallel imports on investment in cost-reducing research and development. Journal of International Economics 68, 443–455.
Malueg, D.A., Schwartz, M., 1994. Parallel imports, demand dispersion, and international price discrimination. Journal of International Economics 37, 167–195.
Markusen, J.R., Venables, A.J., 1988. Trade policy with increasing returns and imperfect competition. Journal of International Economics 24, 299–316.
Maskus, K.E., 2000. Parallel imports. World Economy 23, 1269–1284.
Maskus, K.E., Chen, Y., 2002. Parallel imports in a model of vertical distribution: theory, evidence, and policy. Pacific Economic Review 7, 319–334.
Maskus, K.E., Chen, Y., 2004. Vertical price control and parallel imports: theory and evidence. Review of International Economics 12, 551–570.
Raff, H., Schmitt, N., 2007. Why parallel trade may raise producers' profits. Journal of International Economics 71, 434–447.
Richardson, M., 2002. An elementary proposition concerning parallel imports. Journal of International Economics 56, 233–245.
Roy, S., Saggi, K., 2011. Equilibrium parallel import policies and international market structure. Vanderbilt University Economics Department Working Paper 11-W13 and World Bank Policy Research Working Paper No. 5802.
Roy, S., Saggi, K., forthcoming. Strategic competition and optimal parallel import policy. Canadian Journal of Economics.
Scherer, F., Watal, J., 2002. Post-TRIPS options for access to patented medicines in developing nations. Journal of International Economic Law 5, 913–939.
Shaked, A., Sutton, J., 1983. Natural oligopolies. Econometrica 51, 1469–1484.
Smith, A., Venables, A.J., 1988. Completing the internal market in the European Community: some industry simulations. European Economic Review 32, 1501–1525.
Valleti, T.M., 2006. Differential pricing, parallel trade, and the incentive to invest. Journal of International Economics 70, 314–324.
Valletti, T.M., Szymanski, S., 2006. Parallel trade, international exhaustion and intellectual property rights: a welfare analysis. The Journal of Industrial Economics 54, 499–526.
Venables, A.J., 1990. The economic integration of oligopolistic markets. European Economic Review 34, 753–773.

Chapter 16

MARKET POWER IN THE GLOBAL ECONOMY: THE EXHAUSTION AND PROTECTION OF INTELLECTUAL PROPERTY[*,#]

Kamal Saggi

We develop a North–South model in which a Northern monopolist can fully exercise its market power globally only if the North practises national exhaustion of intellectual property rights (IPR) and the South prohibits imitation. The firm's export incentive turns out to be a major determinant of equilibrium policy choices and their welfare effects. The North has a stronger preference for international exhaustion if the South forbids imitation, something the South is actually more willing to do under national exhaustion. Shutting down Southern imitation increases global welfare if and only if it is necessary for inducing the firm to export.

The extent to which the holders of intellectual property rights (IPR) can freely exercise their market power in the global economy depends upon (*i*) the amount of protection available to them against potential imitators (*ii*) the degree to which they can price discriminate across national markets. The objective of this article is to understand the linkages between policies that determine these two facets of the market power possessed by IPR holders. To achieve this objective, the article develops a stylised two-country model that is motivated by two simple observations. First, due to fundamental differences in the pattern of demand across countries, firms have an incentive to charge higher prices in developed countries relative to developing ones but they can engage in such international price discrimination only if policy restrictions in developed countries prevent *parallel imports.*[1] A country's stance towards parallel imports is determined by its policy regarding the territorial exhaustion of IPR: parallel imports are permitted under *international exhaustion* (IE) whereas they are restricted under *national exhaustion* (NE). The second key observation motivating the model is that while holders of IPR enjoy fairly strong protection in developed countries, such is generally not the case in developing countries. In fact, up until the ratification of the Agreement on Trade Related Aspects of Intellectual Property (TRIPS) in 1995, IPR protection in most developing countries was quite weak or simply non-existent and the widespread imitation of foreign technologies and products by firms in developing countries was a major reason why developed countries pushed strongly for a multilateral agreement on IPR at the World Trade Organization (WTO).

* Corresponding author: Kamal Saggi, Department of Economics, Vanderbilt University, VU Station PMB #351828, 2301 Vanderbilt Place, Nashville, TN 37235-1828, USA. Email: k.saggi@vanderbilt.edu.

I thank two anonymous referees and editor Rachel Griffith for detailed and insightful comments on an earlier version of this article. I also thank Rick Bond, Tannous Hanna Kass Hanna, Olena Ivus, Yan Ma, Jayashree Watal and seminar audiences at the 7th Annual Conference on Economic Growth and Development at ISI (New Delhi), the Geneva Trade and Development Workshop held at the Graduate Institute and at Queen's University School of Business (Kingston) for helpful comments.

[1] Following Maskus (2000), parallel trade is said to occur when a product (such as a patented medicine or software) offered for sale in one country by the holder of the relevant intellectual property right is re-sold in another country without the right holder's permission. As one might expect, such trade usually occurs when retailers attempt to arbitrage away international price differences.

[#] This chapter was originally appeared in *The Economic Journal* **123**, 131–161.

Given these observations, we consider a North–South model where a firm that enjoys monopoly status in the North by virtue of an IPR (such as a patent or a trademark) has the incentive to price discriminate internationally because Northern consumers value its product more than Southern ones. The firm's market power fully extends to the South only if the South protects its technology from being copied by local imitators. Thus, while Northern policy regarding the territorial exhaustion of IPR determines whether the firm can price discriminate internationally and therefore exercise its market power *across* regions, Southern policy regarding the protection of IPR determines its monopoly power *within* the Southern market. In the model, policy interaction between the two regions occurs as follows. In the first stage, both regions choose their respective policies: the North chooses between NE and IE while the South decides whether or not to protect IPR. If the South does not protect IPR, a competitive Southern industry that produces an imitated (lower quality) version of the firm's product comes into existence. Next, the firm decides whether to incur the fixed (sunk) cost necessary to export to the South. Finally, the firm chooses its price(s) and consumption and trade occur. After deriving the subgame perfect equilibrium of the model, we ask how an exogenously imposed prohibition on Southern imitation, say due to the implementation of an international agreement such as TRIPS, affects equilibrium market outcomes and welfare.

By design, the model aims to capture those markets where the degree of IPR protection and the nature of exhaustion policies both have a significant effect on firm behaviour. While IPR protection is relevant for many industries in which firms invest in innovation and in establishing brand names, exhaustion policies affect firm behaviour primarily in those markets in which trading costs are low relative to the value of the product. This is because parallel trade is motivated by the existence of price differentials across markets and the margins earned by those engaging in parallel trade are likely to be small (at least relative to monopoly mark-ups). Parallel trade occurs most frequently between geographically proximate countries (such as US–Canada, member countries of the EU, Australia–Southeast Asia) in products such as footwear and leather goods, musical recordings, consumer electronics, domestic appliances, cosmetics, clothing, pharmaceuticals, soft drinks and some other consumer products (National Economic Research Associates (NERA), 1999). Among these products, parallel trade is perhaps quantitatively most important in the market for pharmaceuticals. By some estimates, several billion dollars of such trade occurs annually within the EU and it currently accounts for roughly 10% of EU's total medicine trade.[2]

Interestingly enough, even with respect to IPR protection the pharmaceutical industry is of special relevance. It is widely recognised that the global pharmaceutical industry was a major proponent of the TRIPS agreement, largely because of the fact that costs of imitation in this industry tend to be very low relative to the costs of

[2] See 'European drug groups fear parallel trade', *Financial Times*, June 7, 2010. See also Kanavos *et al.* (2004) for a detailed discussion of parallel trade in the EU's pharmaceutical market. They report that from 1997 to 2002, the share of parallel imports as a percentage of the total pharmaceutical market increased from under 2% to 10.1% in Sweden and from 1.7% to about 7% in Germany. On the export side, Greece's share of parallel exports increased from under 1% to 21.6% over the same time period. Of course, the volume of parallel trade is likely to understate the consequences of openness to parallel trade since the pricing behaviour of firms is quite different when parallel imports are permitted relative to when they are not.

innovation. This makes protection against infringement of IPR crucial for patent holders in this industry. For example, a major reason the local pharmaceutical industry in India came into existence was that prior to 1995 Indian patent law only recognised process patents; virtually no protection was offered to product patents (Goldberg, 2010). As a result, local firms were free to imitate and reverse-engineer pharmaceuticals invented by foreign firms. As long as a local Indian firm could manufacture a patented drug via a production process that was not identical to the one used by a (foreign) patent holder, it could freely ignore the product patent and manufacture the drug in India. Thus, the two key policies analysed in this article – exhaustion policies and IPR protection – are both highly relevant for at least one major industry, i.e. the pharmaceutical industry. As patents create substantial monopoly power in this industry (indeed that is their very purpose), a monopoly model with a partial equilibrium framework is the most natural set-up within which to analyse the joint interaction of these policies.[3]

In our model, the most attractive global policy environment from the firm's viewpoint is one where the North adopts NE and the South forbids imitation while the worst scenario is one where these policies are reversed. Given this, an interesting question arises. What does the firm value more: protection of intellectual property or the freedom to price discriminate internationally? It turns out that the firm values IPR protection relatively more if and only if the North–South quality gap (γ) falls below a certain threshold (γ^f) as a smaller quality gap implies stiffer price competition. Furthermore, the threshold quality gap γ^f is decreasing in the relative size of the Northern market (η) as well as in the degree to which Northern consumer tastes are skewed in favour of high quality (μ). Intuitively, an increase in either demand parameter (η or μ) makes the two markets more asymmetric thereby making international price discrimination more valuable to the firm while simultaneously reducing the relative importance of the Southern market in determining its global profit.

Conditional on the South protecting intellectual property, IE of IPR is preferred by the North so long as it does not eliminate its firm's incentive to export: provided the firm serves both markets, the threat of arbitrage-induced parallel imports under IE forces the firm to set a uniform world price that is lower than the price it charges in the North under NE. However, as the firm's Southern price is lower under NE, the North's choice of its exhaustion regime ignores the *international price externality* generated by its decision. The North finds NE of IPR optimal when circumstances are such that the firm exports *only if* it can price discriminate internationally: while uniform pricing is attractive to the North, it is less desirable than a scenario where the firm refrains from exporting to safeguard its profit at home.[4] How does Southern IPR policy affect this trade-off? We show that the lack of Southern IPR protection not only shrinks the parameter range over which the North's exhaustion policy affects the firm's decision

[3] While market power also exists in models of oligopoly or monopolistic competition, policy analysis is substantially more complicated in such models. Furthermore, as was noted above, existing estimates of the amount of parallel trade that occurs in the world suggest that such trade is not large enough in magnitude for exhaustion policies to have significant general equilibrium effects.

[4] Malueg and Schwartz (1994) were the first to show that when parallel trade is possible a monopolist may choose to not serve markets with higher elasticities of demand. Goldberg (2010) provides an extensive discussion of the empirical literature that shows how the practice of 'global reference pricing' on the part of some rich countries and the possibility of parallel imports can induce pharmaceutical companies to not serve low income countries and/or raise their prices in such markets.

but it also makes it more likely that the North chooses NE as the adverse effect of imitation on the firm's export profit has to be offset by the freedom to price discriminate internationally to preserve its incentive to export.

Consider now the viewpoint of the South. Imitation is attractive to the South because it increases competition as well as variety by providing consumers access to a lower quality version of the Northern good. By lowering the profit of the Northern firm, Southern imitation inflicts a *negative rent externality* on the North. More interestingly, even though imitated goods cannot be sold in the North, the lack of IPR protection in the South also generates a *positive price externality* for Northern consumers when the Northern policy is IE and the firm sells in the South: as the firm sets a common international price under IE, competition from imitators in the Southern market is transmitted to the North in the form of a lower price.

We find that the South finds it optimal to protect intellectual property voluntarily only if such protection is necessary to induce the firm to sell in the South *and* the Northern good is sufficiently superior in quality to the local imitation. Furthermore, the minimum quality gap above which the South is willing to protect intellectual property is relatively lower under NE. This is because uniform pricing on the part of the firm raises the price of the high quality original in the South relative to price discrimination thereby making it less attractive for the South to protect intellectual property under IE.

In the subgame perfect equilibrium of the model, each region's optimal policy takes into account the firm's pricing strategy, its incentive to export and the other region's policy stance. If the firm exports to the South regardless of the global policy environment, then each region implements its preferred policy: the North chooses IE while the South does not protect intellectual property. However, when the export decision of the firm is policy dependent, the two regions find themselves in a policy stand-off: each region takes into account whether or not the other would be willing to induce the firm to export by choosing to implement its less preferred policy. While the firm views NE and protection from imitation as *substitutes* in the sense that both policies increase its market power, the two governments view them quite differently since, holding the firm's export decision constant, NE lowers Northern welfare while protecting intellectual property harms the South.

The interdependence of the two regions' policy decisions implies that a change in one region's policy can induce a change in the other's policy. Together with the endogeneity of the firm's export decision, the presence of such strategic interdependence at the policy setting stage allows the model to shed new light on the effects of the TRIPS agreement that required developing country members of the WTO to strengthen their protection of intellectual property while leaving the scope of exhaustion of IPR completely at the discretion of member countries. To be precise, TRIPS called for harmonisation of IPR laws and regulations across countries but as such laws were generally weaker (or sometimes simply non-existent) in developing countries, its main practical effect was to strengthen IPR protection in the developing world without calling for any significant changes in the developed world. With regard to exhaustion of IPR, TRIPS essentially left member countries free to implement policies of their choice: Article 6 of TRIPS says that 'nothing in this Agreement shall be used to address the issue of the exhaustion of intellectual property rights'.

A major result of the article is that the shutting down of Southern imitation increases global welfare if and only if it is necessary for *inducing* the firm to export to the South (Proposition 7). In other words, if the firm sells in the South despite the competition created by imitation or if it does not sell there even when such competition is absent (because the profit earned from such sales is too small relative to the fixed cost of exporting), TRIPS enforcement lowers world welfare. This is a strong result as it is independent of the magnitude of the North–South technology gap. An important practical implication of this welfare result is that the case for strengthening IPR protection in developing countries hinges critically on how such a change affects the *extensive margin* of exports from developed to developing countries – i.e. what matters is whether or not firms from developed countries are induced to sell new products in developing countries as a result of a strengthening of IPR protection on their part. In Section 3 of the article, we discuss empirical evidence which shows that TRIPS induced reforms in developing countries have already started to have a significant positive effect on developed country exports to their markets, particularly in sectors that are sensitive to IPR protection.

We also isolate conditions under which the TRIPS mandated change in Southern IPR policy leads to a reversal in the Northern policy from NE to IE. When this *policy reversal* occurs, Southern welfare takes an even harder hit due to TRIPS: variety is reduced as the low quality imitation is no longer produced and the price of the high quality good increases due to two separate reasons. First, shutting down imitation eliminates competition from the Southern industry. Second, the reversal in the North's policy causes the firm to switch to a single uniform price that exceeds its optimal discriminatory price for the South. However, on the flip side, the North gains on two separate counts: not only does the firm's total profit increase but Northern consumers also benefit as the firm's uniform price lies below its optimal discriminatory price for the North.

While the present article is unique in its focus on the interaction between imitation and exhaustion policies, several articles have explored parallel import policies in a multi-country setting. Richardson (2002) considers a setting where all countries import a common good from a foreign monopolist and shows that, in equilibrium, all importing countries choose to permit parallel imports. Roy and Saggi (forthcoming, *a,b*) explore how the presence of strategic competition in the product market affects incentives to export and the nature of equilibrium parallel import policies. Grossman and Lai (2008) consider a monopolistic competition model of endogenous innovation in which the South chooses its price control in response to the North's parallel import policy and show that, in contrast to conventional wisdom, the incentives for product innovation can be higher under IE as openness to parallel imports induces the South to loosen its price control to avoid its market from not being served by innovating Northern firms.[5]

The rest of the article is organised as follows. Section 1 presents the model while Section 2 describes North's optimal policy in the benchmark case where the South protects IPR. Section 3 describes how Southern imitation affects the North's optimal

[5] Valletti and Szymanski (2006) endogenise product quality in a monopoly model where demand differs across countries and show that the monopolist has a stronger incentive to invest in quality improvement when parallel trade is possible. However, Valetti (2006) shows that this incentive is reversed when differential pricing arises due to cost differences across markets as opposed to demand differences.

policy. Section 4 considers the South's decision regarding the protection of IPR. Section 5 presents the subgame perfect equilibrium of the model as well as the effects of TRIPS enforcement for the case where the firm values protection of IPR more than the freedom to price discriminate (i.e. when $\gamma \leq \gamma^f$) while Section 6 contains the case where $\gamma > \gamma^f$. In Section 7, we comment on some of the assumptions underlying the model and also analyse an extension where Southern IPR policy is treated as a continuous variable as opposed to a discrete one. Section 8 offers some concluding remarks while the online Technical Appendix contains supporting calculations and proofs.

1. Model

We consider a world comprised of two regions: North (N) and South (S). There is a single firm that produces good x whose quality is denoted by $q \geq 1$ and whose marginal cost of production is normalised to zero. The firm enjoys monopoly status in the North by virtue of an IPR such as a patent or a trade-mark that is protected in the Northern market.

Each consumer buys at most one unit of good x. If a consumer in country i buys good x at price p, its utility is given by $U_i = \theta q - p$. Utility under no purchase is normalised to zero and $\theta \geq 0$ is a taste parameter that captures the willingness to pay for higher quality.

The two regions are asymmetric in two fundamental respects. First, the Northern market is larger: there are η_i consumers in region i where where $\eta_N = \eta \geq 1 = \eta_S$. Second, and more importantly, Northern consumers value quality relatively more than Southern ones in that the preference parameter θ is uniformly distributed over the interval $[0, \mu_i]$ in region $i = N, S$ where $\mu_N = \mu \geq \mu_S = 1$.[6]

The interaction between the two governments and the firm occurs as follows:

Stage 1: In the first stage, the South decides whether or not to protect the (Northern) firm's intellectual property while the North simultaneously chooses between NE and IE of IPR: parallel imports into the North are prohibited under the former regime whereas they are permitted under the latter.

If the South does not protect intellectual property, imitation occurs in the South leading to the emergence of a competitive Southern industry that produces a lower quality version of the Northern good. Post-imitation, competition among Southern producers ensures that the equilibrium price of the low quality imitation equals its marginal cost (set to zero). Under such a scenario, the firm acts as a high quality producer facing competition from a low quality competitive industry in (only) the Southern market. If intellectual property is protected by the South, imitation does not occur and the firm acts as a global monopolist.[7]

[6] Note that if there exists a numeraire good, the assumption that $\mu \geq 1$ can also be seen as the North having a lower marginal utility of income than the South.

[7] This formulation of local imitation – i.e. it leads to the availability of a low-quality version of the patented good – is quite in line with the approach taken by Chaudhuri *et al.* (2006). In a counterfactual analysis based on a structural model of the antibiotic sub-segment of the pharmaceutical market in India, they showed that elimination of local brands in 2000 (something that would have resulted if India's patent regime had enforced product patents) would have generated significant welfare losses for Indian consumers by reducing variety and increasing prices due to the elimination of competition from local brands.

The global policy environment determined by each region's independent policy choice is denoted by the pair (X, Y) where X = IE or NE and Y = P or N where P denotes Southern policy decision to protect Northern intellectual property and N to not do so (i.e. to allow imitation).

Stage 2: After governments have chosen policies, the firm chooses whether or not to export to the Southern market. To be able to export, the firm must incur the fixed (sunk) cost $\varphi \geq 0$. If it exports to the South, the firm sells its product there via a competitive retail sector whose unit cost is normalised to zero. When the North chooses NE (i.e. prohibits parallel imports), Southern retailers can only sell locally. However, when the North chooses IE, Southern retailers have an incentive to engage in parallel trade if the Northern price exceeds the Southern one.

Stage 3: The firm chooses price(s) and consumption and trade occur.

We solve this game by backward induction. Before deriving the sub-game perfect equilibrium of this game, it is useful to describe the market outcome under autarky quickly (i.e. the complete absence of international trade).

Under autarky, the firm's optimal monopoly price p_N^d is found by solving

$$\max_p \eta p x(p) = \eta \frac{p}{\mu}\left(\mu - \frac{p}{q}\right) \Rightarrow p_N^d = \frac{\mu q}{2}.$$

At the price p_N^d, all Northern consumers for whom $\theta > \theta^d \equiv p_N^d/q = \mu/2$ buy the good so that half the Northern market is covered under autarky. The firm's autarkic equilibrium profit equals $\pi_N^d = p_N^d x_N^d$ where $x_N^d = (\eta/\mu)(\mu - p_N^d/q)$. Consumer surplus in the North under autarky and aggregate Northern welfare equal

$$cs_N^d = \frac{\eta}{\mu}\int_{\frac{p_N^d}{q}}^{\mu}(q\theta - p_N^d)\mathrm{d}\theta \text{ and } w_N^a = cs_N^d + \pi_N^d.$$

As might be expected, the nature of the North's optimal policy with respect to the exhaustion of IPR depends upon the South's policy regarding the protection of IPR. We first derive North's optimal exhaustion policy for the case where the South protects intellectual property. This case is a natural benchmark as it has been extensively analysed in the literature.

2. Optimal Northern Policy in the Benchmark Case

Suppose that imitation is prohibited by the South and consider the firm's pricing strategy as a function of Northern exhaustion policy assuming the fixed cost (φ) of exporting has been incurred. Under IE, the firm sets a common price in both markets to avoid losing profit to arbitrage induced parallel imports and the resulting market outcome is referred to as *uniform pricing*. By contrast, under NE, the firm is free to price discriminate internationally (i.e. charge a lower price in the South) and the resulting market outcome is called *price discrimination*. As the retail sector is assumed to be competitive with unit cost equal to zero, the final price in each market is effectively determined by the firm.

Under price discrimination the firm sets a separate price p_i for each region to solve

$$\max_{p_i} \frac{\eta_i}{\mu_i} p_i \left(\mu_i - \frac{p_i}{q} \right) \Rightarrow p_i^d = \frac{\mu_i q}{2}. \tag{1}$$

Since $\mu_N = \mu$ and $\mu_S = 1$, the firm's aggregate profit under price discrimination equals

$$\pi^d = \sum_i \frac{\eta_i}{\mu_i} p_i^d (\mu_i - p_i^d) = \pi_N^d + \pi_S^d = \frac{\eta \mu q}{4} + \frac{q}{4}. \tag{2}$$

Under uniform pricing the firm chooses a single price p for both markets to solve:

$$\max_p \sum_i \frac{\eta_i}{\mu_i} p \left(\mu_i - \frac{p}{q} \right). \tag{3}$$

Solving the above problem gives the optimal uniform price and the associated profits under uniform pricing:

$$p^u = \frac{q\mu(\eta + 1)}{2(\eta + \mu)} \text{ and } \pi^u = \frac{q\mu}{4} \frac{(\eta + 1)^2}{\eta + \mu}. \tag{4}$$

The optimal uniform price p^u has intuitive properties: it is increasing in the quality level of the firm (q), the extent to which Northern consumers tastes are skewed in favour of quality (μ), and the size of the Northern market (η). Furthermore, as might be expected, the optimal uniform price is bound by the optimal discriminatory prices for the two regions: $p_S^d \le p^u \le p_N^d$.[8] In fact, we have

$$p^u = \omega p_N^d + (1 - \omega) p_S^d \text{ where } \omega = \frac{\eta}{\eta + \mu} \text{ and } 0 < \omega < 1,$$

i.e. the firm's optimal price under uniform pricing is a weighted average of its optimal discriminatory prices where the weight (ω) on the Northern price (p_N^d) is increasing in the relative size of the Northern market (η).

We next note an important property of the model that follows from the assumption that θ is uniformly distributed over the interval $[0,\mu_i]$:

LEMMA 1. *Total global sales of the firm under uniform pricing and price discrimination are equal:* $\Sigma_i x_i^u = \Sigma_i x_i^d = (\eta + 1)/2$ *where* $i = N, S$.

Lemma 1 is important because it implies that relative welfare under price discrimination and uniform pricing does not depend upon the total output produced under the two types of pricing. This makes uniform pricing more attractive from an aggregate

[8] It is worth pointing out that there is positive demand in the South at the price p^u iff $\mu \le \overline{\mu} = 2n/(n-1)$. Observe that $\overline{\mu} \ge 2$ for all $n > 0$ and it approaches 2 when n approaches infinity. When $\mu > \overline{\mu}$, under IE the firm does not serve the South even if the fixed cost of exporting equals zero. Intuitively, if the two markets are highly asymmetric, under IE the firm is always better off serving only the Northern market at the optimal price p_N^d. Under such a scenario, Northern policy has no effect on the local price (and consumer surplus) since under both NE and IE, Northern price equals p_N^d. To rule out this uninteresting scenario, we assume that $\mu \le \overline{\mu}$.

welfare perspective (since it eliminates price differentials across markets) and provides an argument in favour of IE so long as the Northern firm exports. As we shall see below, this feature of the model turns out to play an important role in determining the welfare implications of the TRIPS agreement (analysed in Section 6 below).[9]

Next, we determine the firm's optimal export decision under the policy pairs (IE,P) and (NE,P). Under (IE,P), the firm chooses to export to the South if its global profit under uniform pricing exceeds its monopoly profit in the North:

$$\pi^u - \varphi \geq \pi_N^d \Leftrightarrow \varphi \leq \varphi^u = \frac{q\mu}{4}\frac{2\eta + 1 - \eta\mu}{\eta + \mu}. \tag{5}$$

Since $\varphi^u \geq 0$ iff $\mu \leq \mu^d = 2 + 1/\eta$, a sufficient condition for the firm to *forego* the Southern market is $\mu > \mu^d$.[10] Note also that $\partial\varphi^u/\partial\mu < 0$ and $\partial\varphi^u/\partial\eta < 0$ – i.e. as demand asymmetry increases across the two markets, entry into the Southern market under uniform pricing becomes less attractive to the firm. As one might expect $\overline{\mu} \geq \mu^d$ i.e. it is optimal for the firm to drop the Southern market well before its Southern sales hit zero under uniform pricing.

Similarly, the firm exports under NE if its Southern profit at the optimal discriminatory price p_S^d exceeds the fixed cost of exporting:

$$\pi_S^d \geq \varphi \Leftrightarrow \varphi \leq \varphi^d = \frac{q}{4}. \tag{6}$$

Thus, given that the South does not permit imitation, the firm's net profits under alternative policy choices by the North are as follows:

$$\pi(\text{IE},\text{P}) = \begin{Bmatrix} \pi^u - \varphi \text{ if } \varphi \leq \varphi^u \\ \pi_N^d \text{ if } \varphi > \varphi^u \end{Bmatrix} \text{ and } \pi(\text{NE},\text{P}) = \begin{Bmatrix} \pi^d - \varphi \text{ if } \varphi \leq \varphi^d \\ \pi_N^d \text{ if } \varphi > \varphi^d \end{Bmatrix}. \tag{7}$$

Note that $\varphi^d - \varphi^u = \pi^d - \pi^u \geq 0$: i.e. serving the Southern market is less attractive to the firm under IE as doing so requires it to lower price in the larger, more lucrative Northern market. We have:

LEMMA 2. *In the absence of imitation, the firm is more likely to export under NE:* $\varphi^d > \varphi^u$.

Now the North's optimal policy in the benchmark case can be derived. Given that the South protects IPR, Northern welfare under IE and IE is given by

$$w_N(\text{IE},\text{P}) = \begin{Bmatrix} w_N^u \text{ if } \varphi \leq \varphi^u \\ w_N^a \text{ if } \varphi > \varphi^u \end{Bmatrix} \text{ and } w_N(\text{NE},\text{P}) = \begin{Bmatrix} w_N^d \text{ if } \varphi \leq \varphi^d \\ w_N^a \text{ if } \varphi > \varphi^d \end{Bmatrix},$$

where $w_N^u = cs_N^u + \pi^u - \varphi$; $w_N^a = cs_N^d + \pi_N^d$; and $w_N^d = cs_N^d + \pi^d - \varphi$.

[9] Under alternative assumptions regarding the distribution of the taste parameter θ, it is possible for price discrimination to welfare dominate uniform pricing if it leads to an expansion in total output: see Schmalensee (1981) and Varian (1985). If so, some of the welfare implications of TRIPS that we discuss below would need to be modified. However, the equilibrium outcomes of our model would remain qualitatively unchanged if, all else constant, Northern welfare were to remain higher under uniform pricing by virtue of the fact that the price in its market is higher under discrimination (even though aggregate world output is also higher).

[10] Note that $\pi_N^d > \pi^u \Leftrightarrow \mu > \mu^d$. Thus, the firm's optimal pricing behaviour (post-entry) under the policy pair (IE,P) is to charge the price p^u if $\mu \leq \mu^d$ and p_N^d otherwise. Of course, when $\mu > \mu^d$, the firm would not incur the fixed cost of exporting under IE since Southern sales are zero at the price p_N^d.

Direct calculations (contained in the online Appendix) show that $w_N^u \geq w_N^d$ and $w_N^d \geq w_N^a$ with the inequality binding for $\varphi < \varphi^d$. These inequalities imply the following: for $\varphi \in [0, \varphi^u]$ we have w_N(IE, P) $\geq w_N$ (NE, P); for $\varphi \in (\varphi^u, \varphi^d]$ we have w_N (IE, P) $\leq w_N$ (NE, P); and for $\varphi > \varphi^d$ we have w_N (IE, P) $= w_N$ (NE, P) $= w_N^a$. Our first major result can now be stated:

PROPOSITION 1. *In the benchmark case of no imitation, for all* $\varphi \in [0, \varphi^d]$, *the optimal exhaustion policy of the North is such that its firm necessarily exports to the South. More specifically, the North's optimal policy varies with the fixed cost of exporting in the following manner:*

Exporting Cost	Optimal Policy
(*i*) $\varphi \in [0, \varphi^u]$	*IE*
(*ii*) $\varphi \in (\varphi^u, \varphi^d]$	*NE*
(*iii*) $\varphi > \varphi^d$	*IE or NE*

Part (*i*) of Proposition 1 informs us that when the North can implement IE without compromising its firm's incentive to export, it chooses to do so. However, part (*ii*) says that if the firm exports only when it can earn its optimal discriminatory profit, the North ends up implementing NE. Thus, an outcome where the firm does not sell in the Southern market is *not* in the interest of the North. It is worth emphasising that under NE, the firm's incentive to export is perfectly aligned with Northern government's preferences: when there is no link between Northern and Southern prices, exporting increases Northern welfare iff it increases the firm's total profit. However, under IE, the firm's incentive to export is *weaker* than that of the welfare-maximising Northern government as exporting lowers the firm's Northern profit by forcing it to charge a common price in both markets. From the viewpoint of aggregate Northern welfare, the benefit of this price reduction to local consumers is not taken into account by the firm when it is choosing whether or not to export.

Even though Northern policy is such that its firm always exports, it does not mean that Southern welfare is unaffected by the North's policy. In fact, conditional on the firm exporting, there is a direct clash between the preferences of the two regions: market coverage as well as welfare in the South are lower under uniform pricing relative to discrimination whereas the opposite is true in the North due to the fact that $p_S^d < p^u < p_N^d$. Thus, conditional on the firm exporting, we have w_S(NE, P) $\geq w_S$(IE, P).

We now consider the scenario where the South does not protect intellectual property.

3. Effects of Southern Imitation

As noted before, imitation in the South results in the emergence of a competitive industry that produces a lower quality version of the Northern good. By assumption, the enforcement of IPR in the North prevents the imitated good from being sold there so that competition occurs only in the South. Let the quality level of Southern imitation be given by q_S where $q_S \leq q$ and let its marginal cost of production equal zero. Define $\gamma = q/q_S \geq 1$ as the North–South quality gap.

Competition within the Southern industry ensures that the imitated good is sold at marginal cost (normalised to zero). As is well known, when both qualities are available for purchase at prices p (high quality) and 0 (low quality), Southern consumers can be partitioned into two groups: those in the range $[0, \theta_S)$ buy the low quality whereas those in $[\theta_S, 1]$ buy the high quality where $\theta_S = p/q_S(\gamma - 1)$.

As before, Northern exhaustion policy determines the pricing behaviour of the firm. Under IE, the firm must charge the same price in both markets (if it serves both of them) and taking the price of the low quality imitation as zero it solves:

$$\max_p \pi(0,p) = \frac{\eta}{\mu} p\left(\mu - \frac{p}{q}\right) + p\left[1 - \frac{p-0}{q_S(\gamma-1)}\right],$$

which gives the optimal uniform price post-imitation and the associated profit

$$p^{ui} = \frac{q\mu(\gamma-1)(\eta+1)}{2[\eta(\gamma-1)+\gamma\mu]} \text{ and } \pi^{ui} = \frac{\eta}{\mu} p^{ui}\left(\mu - \frac{p^{ui}}{q}\right) + p^{ui}\left[1 - \frac{p^{ui}}{q_S(\gamma-1)}\right].$$

As is obvious, we have $p^{ui} < p^u$ and $\pi^{ui} < \pi^u$ – i.e. competition from Southern imitation lowers the firm's optimal uniform price and reduces its global profit.

Consider now the firm's export decision under imitation. If the firm does not export to the South, it earns optimal monopoly profit π_N^d in the North as the imitated good cannot be sold in the North. Under IE, the firm does not export if[11]

$$\pi_N^d > \pi^{ui} - \varphi \Leftrightarrow \varphi > \varphi^{ui} = \frac{q\mu}{4}\frac{[(2\eta+1)(\gamma-1) - \gamma\eta\mu]}{\eta(\gamma-1)+\gamma\mu}.$$

If Northern policy is NE, the firm's optimal Southern price equals:

$$p_S^{di} = \frac{q_S(\gamma-1)}{2},$$

which implies that under the policy regime (NE,N) the threshold level of fixed cost φ^{di} is given by:

$$\varphi^{di} = \pi_S^{di} = \frac{q_S(\gamma-1)}{4}.$$

We thus have:

$$\pi(\text{IE}, \text{N}) = \begin{Bmatrix} \pi^{ui} - \varphi \text{ if } \varphi \leq \varphi^{ui} \\ \pi_N^d \text{ if } \varphi > \varphi^{ui} \end{Bmatrix} \text{ and } \pi(\text{NE}, \text{N}) = \begin{Bmatrix} \pi_N^d + \pi_S^{di} - \varphi \text{ if } \varphi \leq \varphi^{di} \\ \pi_N^d \text{ if } \varphi > \varphi^{di} \end{Bmatrix}.$$

The firm's incentive to export is summarised in the following Lemma:

LEMMA 3. *The following hold with respect to the firm's incentive to export: (i)* $\varphi^{ui} < \max\{\varphi^u, \varphi^{di}\} < \varphi^d$; *(ii)* $\varphi^{di} \leq \varphi^u$ *iff* $\gamma \leq \gamma^f$ *where* $\partial\gamma^f/\partial\mu < 0$ *and* $\partial\gamma^f/\partial\eta < 0$; *and (iii)* $\varphi^{di} - \varphi^{ui} > \varphi^d - \varphi^u$.

[11] Note that $\varphi^{ui} > 0$ iff $\mu < \frac{(\gamma-1)\mu^d}{\gamma} < \mu^d$.

Part (*i*) of Lemma 3 ranks the firm's incentive to export under the different policy configurations and highlights some crucial mechanisms of the model. It informs us that the Southern market is most attractive to the firm when the North chooses NE and the South forbids imitation whereas its the least attractive when the policies of the two regions are reversed. All else equal, the firm's incentive to export is stronger when the North implements NE.[12] Similarly, the firm is more likely to export when the South forbids imitation.

Available evidence indicates that the mechanisms captured by Lemma 3 are very much empirically relevant. Consider first the impact of exhaustion policies on the decision of Northern firms to sell in the South. In a recent article, Goldberg (2010) provides a detailed discussion of a variety of empirical studies, all of which find that the inability to price discriminate internationally either causes firms in the global pharmaceutical industry to drop developing country markets altogether or to introduce new products into such markets with significant delay (i.e. much after their initial launch in developed country markets).[13] For example, she notes that many antibiotic drugs were not introduced in India as foreign firms were concerned about the international repercussions of charging prices in India that were much lower than their prices in Europe and Canada. Of course, prior to the TRIPS induced patent reforms in India, high prices could not be sustained in India precisely because of competition from the local industry (that came into existence due to inadequate patent protection) and due to demand conditions in India *vis- à-vis* developed country markets, two factors that are at the heart of our model. Goldberg (2010) also notes that prior to the implementation of TRIPS, the retail coverage of foreign firms in the Indian pharmaceutical industry tended to be quite low because of their thin marketing and distribution networks, a situation that reflects the relatively weak incentives that foreign firms have for establishing their products in markets with inadequate IPR protection.

Regarding the effect of imitation on exports, it is now a well-established fact in the literature that IPR are 'trade-related' and that the lack of IPR protection can distort trade. Maskus and Penubarti (1995) showed that weak IPR protection in large developing countries was a significant barrier for manufacturing exports of OECD countries. Furthermore, they found that the pharmaceutical industry was particularly sensitive to the degree of patent protection in developing countries.[14] They also found that trade in goods that were difficult to imitate – such as machinery – was less sensitive to variations in IPR protection across countries. In the context of our model, this implies

[12] In this regard, note that any Northern policy that prevents the local firm from being able to price discriminate internationally would deter exporting on its part. In addition to exhaustion policies, the practice of *global reference pricing* by industrialised countries – under which the price a pharmaceutical company is allowed to charge in a particular market is determined, in part, on the basis of prices that it charges in other parts of the world – would also work very similarly to an open exhaustion regime.

[13] Lanjouw (2005) studied drug launches in 68 countries between 1982 and 2002 and found that firms usually launch new drugs in developed countries and that launch delay increased with a decline in *per capita* income. As Goldberg (2010) notes, her findings are consistent with the argument that the presence of price regulations and global reference pricing in the industrialised world contribute to launch delay in developing countries. Danzon *et al.* (2005) found similar effects in their study of drug launches within the EU: their results show that the likelihood of a drug being launched in a low-price EU country decreases with the risk of spillover to higher price EU countries through global reference pricing.

[14] The results of Maskus and Penubarti (1995) were updated and confirmed by Smith (1999) using more disaggregated data for US manufacturing exports.

that if the North–South technology gap is large, the effect of imitation on the Northern firm's export decision is weaker.

More recently, Ivus (2010) has shown that the TRIPS-induced increase in IPR protection in 18 developing countries increased the annual value of developed country exports to these countries by about \$25 million, an 8.6% increased in the imports of patent sensitive goods by developing countries in her sample. In a follow up article, Ivus (2011) further investigates the effects of stronger IPR protection using highly detailed data (at the 10-digit Harmonised System level) on US exports to 64 developing countries. The data used allow her to assess the effects of stronger IPR protection in developing countries on quantities, prices and the variety of US exports. She finds that TRIPS induced changes in the IPR regimes of developing countries increased the annual value of US exports in industries that rely heavily on patent protection (such as pharmaceuticals) by roughly 8% and that US exports to a typical developing country increased by \$317 million (1990 US dollars). Equally important are her findings that about 75% of the increase in US exports reflected an increase in product variety, something that is consistent with our result that stronger IPR protection can induce the firm to export to the South thereby introducing a high-quality good to the local market.[15] Finally, she also finds that IPR strengthening increased unit prices, a result that is also in line with our argument that imitation lowers prices by creating competition.

Part (*ii*) of Lemma 3 says that starting from the firm's most preferred policy regime (NE, P), whether a reversal in Northern or Southern policy lowers its export incentive more depends upon the magnitude of the North–South quality gap: when this gap is small (i.e. $\gamma \leq \gamma^f$) the removal of IPR protection in the South hurts the firm's export incentive more than a reversal in the exhaustion policy of the North. The quality gap threshold γ^f is decreasing in the size of the Northern market (η) and the degree to which Northern tastes are skewed in favour of quality (μ) because the firm's incentive to export under uniform pricing relative to that under price discrimination (post-imitation) decreases as the two markets become more asymmetric.

Part (*iii*) implies that *Southern imitation makes* NE *more attractive to the North.* As imitation cuts into the firm's export profits by creating competition in the South, it reduces the range of fixed costs over which the firm chooses to export.

The North's optimal policy under imitation can now be stated (proof is in the online Appendix):

PROPOSITION 2. *Even when the South does not protect IPR, for all $\varphi \in (0, \varphi^d)$ the optimal exhaustion policy of the North is such that its firm necessarily exports to the South. We have:*

[15] Of course, exporting is not the only way in which firms introduce their products in developing countries. Foreign direct investment (FDI) is also a commonly used strategy for entering foreign markets. In this sense, exporting in our model should be viewed as a general proxy for the various modes via which the firm can sell to Southern consumers. Existing empirical evidence indicates that FDI responds positively to IPR protection in developing countries. For example, Branstetter *et al.* (2011) investigate the impact of IPR protection on multinational production by analysing the responses of US multinationals to IPR reforms by sixteen countries during the 1980s and 1990s. They find that US based multinationals expanded their activities in reforming countries. Similar results were found by Mansfield (1994), Lee and Mansfield (1996), Nunnenkamp and Spatz (2004) and Javorcik (2004).

Exporting Cost	Optimal Policy
(*i*) $\varphi \in [0, \varphi^{ui}]$	*IE*
(*ii*) $\varphi \in (\varphi^{ui}, \varphi^{di}]$	*NE*
(*iii*) $\varphi > \varphi^{di}$	*IE or NE*

The interpretation of Proposition 2 is analogous to that of Proposition 1. If the fixed cost of exporting is low, the North is able to keep its market open to parallel imports without compromising its firm's incentive to export; otherwise, it has to shut down parallel imports to induce the firm to export. From the North's viewpoint, while uniform pricing (which can arise only under IE) is attractive, it is not more desirable than autarky which is what obtains if its firm chooses to not export to the South in order to safeguard its profit at home. A comparison of Propositions 1 and 2 provides two insights. First, as $\varphi^{di} < \varphi^{d}$, Southern imitation shrinks the parameter range over which the North's exhaustion policy affects the firm's incentive to export: without imitation, the firm does not export when $\varphi > \varphi^{d}$ whereas with imitation it makes the same choice whenever $\varphi > \varphi^{di}$. Second, if Northern policy affects the firm's export decision both with and without imitation (i.e. $\varphi \leq \varphi^{di}$), the North is more prone to choosing NE when the South allows imitation relative to when it does not: over $(\varphi^{ui}, \varphi^{u}]$ imitation causes the North to switch its policy from IE to NE. Intuitively, to sustain the firm's export incentive, the reduction in market power (and profits) suffered by the firm because of imitation needs to be offset by providing it the ability to price discriminate across markets.

Proposition 2 suggests that due to the TRIPS induced enforcement of IPR in developing countries, one should expect developed countries to be less opposed to parallel imports.[16] While widespread changes in exhaustion regimes among industrialised countries have not been observed since the ratification of TRIPS (at least not yet), it is worth noting that the EU's policy of community exhaustion – under which parallel imports flow freely within the EU but are forbidden from outside – is consistent with the basic message of Proposition 2 in the sense that IPR protection within the EU is stronger than developing countries from where parallel imports into the EU are likely to occur (if permitted). Similarly, at several points in time the US Congress has come close to opening its markets to pharmaceutical imports from Canada, a country where IPR protection is strong. By contrast, there is little support among US policy-makers for opening up the market to parallel imports from Mexico and other developing countries where IPR protection is much weaker. Our model suggests that the calculus underlying this policy stance of the EU and the US reflects the export incentives of their respective pharmaceutical industries.

4. South's Decision: to Protect or Not?

Propositions 1 and 2 describe the best response of the North to alternative policy choices of the South. We now consider the South's policy decision regarding protection of

[16] I thank an anonymous referee for pointing out that the recent opening up of its market to parallel imports in digital products by Australia is consistent with this result.

intellectual property. First note that, regardless of Northern policy, if the firm does not export, the South's payoff from imitation equals the consumer surplus obtained when the high quality is unavailable locally and the low quality is sold at zero price:

$$w_S^{ai} = cs_S^{ai} = \int_0^1 (\theta q_S - 0)\mathrm{d}\theta = \frac{q_S}{2}.$$

The careful reader will note that the South is assumed to have the ability to imitate the firm's technology imperfectly even when it does not export to the South.[17] This formulation is based on the idea that North–South technology transfer occurs through a variety of channels (exogenous to the model) and the only decision the South has to make is whether to allow imitation to occur or not; what is not at stake is the South's ability to imitate. Furthermore, this feature of the model makes it impossible for the firm to prevent imitation and helps to focus the analysis on policy issues by resting the entire control in the hands of the Southern government via its decision regarding the enforcement of IPR.[18]

Suppose the North chooses NE. The South's optimal IPR policy depends on the firm's export decision. If $\varphi \leq \varphi^{di}$, the firm exports regardless of the South's IPR policy. In such a situation, it is optimal for the South to not protect IPR. To see this, first note that if imitation occurs, Southern welfare equals the consumer surplus obtained when the high quality good is sold at $p_S^{di} = q_S(\gamma - 1)/2$ and the low quality good at zero price. At these prices, consumers in the range $(0, p_S^{di}/q_S(\gamma - 1)) = (0, \frac{1}{2}]$ buy the low quality good whereas those in the range $(\frac{1}{2}, 1]$ buy the high quality good. Therefore, we have:

$$w_S^{di} = cs_S^{di} = \int_0^{1/2} (\theta q_S - 0)\mathrm{d}\theta + \int_{1/2}^1 (q\theta - p_S^{di})\mathrm{d}\theta = \frac{q_S(\gamma + 3)}{8}.$$

Note that w_S^{di} increases in γ: i.e. the larger the North–South quality gap, the stronger the Southern desire to permit imitation to help lower the price of the high quality good.

If the South forbids imitation, its welfare equals

$$w_S^d = cs_S^d = \int_{1/2}^1 (q\theta - p_S^d)\mathrm{d}\theta = \frac{q}{8} = \frac{\gamma q_S}{8}.$$

Clearly, $w_S^{di} > w_S^d$: if the firm necessarily exports to the South, local imitation is desirable for the South because it increases competition as well as variety (by making a lower quality version of the Northern good available to consumers). The increase in competition brings down the price of the high quality good from p_S^d to p_S^{di} and the increase in variety ensures that those consumers that do not wish to purchase the high quality good have access to the low quality imitation.

Now consider the range $(\varphi^{di}, \varphi^d]$. Over this range of fixed costs, the firm chooses to export to the South only if the South protects IPR. Thus, *now the South faces a trade-off between price and quality*: if it permits imitation, the low quality is available to local

[17] I thank an anonymous referee for drawing attention to this aspect of the model.

[18] An alternative model would be one where exporting affects/increases the likelihood of imitation. Such a model should yield conclusions that are qualitatively similar to ours except that the firm would be more reluctant to export.

consumers at zero price; if it forbids it, the high quality is available at the (high) price p_S^d. Southern welfare in the absence of IPR protection is $w_S^{ai} = qs/2$ whereas that under IPR protection is $w_S^d = \gamma qs/8$. Thus, over $[\varphi^{di}, \varphi^d]$, it is optimal for the South to protect IPR iff $\gamma qs/8 \geq qs/2$ or $\gamma \geq \gamma^d = 4$. Intuitively, when the North–South quality gap is large (i.e. $\gamma > \gamma^d$), it is optimal for the South to protect IPR to ensure that the high quality good is sold in its market. When such is not the case (i.e. $\gamma \leq \gamma^d$), the South is better off eschewing consumption of the high quality good and permitting imitation. An alternative way of understanding this result is that for the South to prefer a high quality (foreign) monopolist to a low quality competitive industry that sells the good at cost, the quality advantage of the monopolist over the competitive industry has to be sufficiently large.[19]

Finally, let $\varphi > \varphi^d$. Over this parameter range, the firm does not export to the South regardless of whether the South protects IPR or not. Given that, it is optimal for the South not to protect IPR to ensure that local consumers at least have access to the low quality which ensures a welfare level of w_S^{ai}.

We summarise this discussion below:

PROPOSITION 3. *Suppose the North implements NE of IPR. Then, it is optimal for the South to protect voluntarily IPR if and only if*

(*i*) such protection is necessary for inducing the firm to export to the South (i.e. $\varphi \in (\varphi^{di}, \varphi^d])$ and
(*ii*) the North–South quality gap is sufficiently high (i.e. $\gamma > \gamma^d$).

Following the above discussion, it is clear that under IE, if $\varphi \leq \varphi^{ui}$ or $\varphi > \varphi^u$ it is optimal for the South to not protect IPR – in the former case, the firm sells in the South even when imitation occurs whereas in the latter case, it does not even in the absence of imitation. Thus, for these two cases, the South is better off permitting imitation: when $\varphi \leq \varphi^{ui}$ imitation increases *competition as well as variety* whereas when $\varphi > \varphi^u$ imitation ensures that at least a low quality version of Northern good is available locally.

It remains to be verified under what conditions, if any, it is optimal for the South to protect IPR when $\varphi \in (\varphi^{ui}, \varphi^u]$. Over this range, protecting IPR is *necessary* to induce the firm to sell in the South. If the South protects IPR its welfare equals

$$w_S^u = cs_S^u = \int_{p^u/q}^{1} (q\theta - p^u)\mathrm{d}\theta = \frac{(q - p^u)^2}{2q},$$

where p^u is given in (4). If the South does not protect IPR, its welfare is $w_S^{ai} = qs/2$. Thus, over $\varphi \in (\varphi^{ui}, \varphi^u]$, protecting IPR is optimal for the South iff

$$w_S^u > w_S^{ai} \Leftrightarrow \gamma > \gamma^u = \frac{4(\eta + \mu)^2}{(2\eta + \mu - \eta\mu)^2},$$

i.e. over this range of fixed costs, IPR protection is optimal for the South only if the North–South quality gap lies above the minimum threshold γ^u. The minimum threshold

[19] If the monopolist were domestic as opposed to foreign, the required quality threshold would be significantly lower (i.e. $3q/8 \geq qs/2 \Leftrightarrow \gamma \geq 4/3$) since its profit would be part of domestic surplus.

γ^u is increasing in both η and μ: as the two markets become more asymmetric, Southern willingness to prevent local imitation declines because an increase in the number of Northern consumers (η) or in their willingness to pay for higher quality (μ) leads to a higher price of the high quality good in the South. In other words, the larger the degree of market asymmetry, the larger must be the North–South quality gap to compensate the South for the welfare loss it suffers under the policy regime (IE,P) relative to (IE,N) with the firm choosing not to export. By contrast, prices in the two markets under NE are independent and the North–South quality gap threshold γ^d that determines the Southern willingness to prevent imitation does not depend on parameters that capture demand asymmetry between the two regions (i.e. μ and η).

We can now state a result analogous to Proposition 3:

PROPOSITION 4. *(i) If the North implements IE it is optimal for the South to voluntarily protect IPR if (i) such enforcement is necessary to induce the firm to serve the Southern market (i.e.* $\varphi \in (\varphi^{ui}, \varphi^u])$ *and (ii) the North–South quality gap exceeds the threshold* γ^u. *(iii) Furthermore, the minimum quality gap required for the South to be willing to protect IPR is higher under IE relative to NE (i.e.* $\gamma^u \geq \gamma^d$*).*

The intuition for part (*i*) of Proposition 4 is clear – if the firm chooses to serve the South even when if it is imitated or if the North–South quality gap is small, the South has no incentive to protect intellectual property. Part (*ii*) holds because Northern openness to parallel imports leads to a relatively higher price in the South that must be offset by a larger quality gap for Southern government to be willing to shut down local imitation.

Having described each region's best response to the policy choice of the other region, we are now ready to derive the equilibrium of the policy game and examine its welfare properties. Equilibrium outcomes depend upon whether or not the firm values protection from imitation more than the freedom to price discriminate internationally, i.e. whether or not $\gamma \leq \gamma^f \Leftrightarrow \varphi^{di} \leq \varphi^u$. As exhaustion policies remain completely unconstrained by the WTO while IPR policies are subject to strict disciplines, it seems reasonable to deduce that during TRIPS negotiations, holders of IPR must have put more pressure (via their governments) on shutting down imitation than on implementing NE as a harmonised exhaustion policy of all WTO members. As a result, we take $\gamma \leq \gamma^f$ as the benchmark case and then briefly discuss the scenario where $\gamma > \gamma^f$.

5. Equilibrium and Welfare When Firm Values IPR Protection More

In what follows, assuming $\gamma \leq \gamma^f \Leftrightarrow \varphi^{di} \leq \varphi^u$ we first derive equilibrium policies, then compare them to first-best policies and finally draw out the implications of the TRIPS agreement.

5.1. *Policy Equilibrium and Welfare*

Putting together the best responses of the two regions summarised in Propositions 1–4 allows us to state:

PROPOSITION 5. *Given that the firm values IPR protection more than the freedom to price discriminate internationally (i.e.* $\varphi^{di} \leq \varphi^u \Leftrightarrow \gamma \leq \gamma^f$*), equilibrium policies of the two regions are as follows:* [20]

Exporting Cost	Equilibrium policies
(*i*) $\varphi \in [0, \varphi^{ui}]$	*(IE, N)*
(*ii*) $\varphi \in (\varphi^{ui}, \varphi^{di}]$	*(NE, N) if* $\gamma < \gamma^u$*; both (NE, N) and (IE, P) otherwise*
(*iii*) $\varphi \in (\varphi^{di}, \varphi^u]$	*(IE, P) if* $\gamma > \gamma^u$*; (NE, N) or (IE, N) otherwise*
(*iv*) $\varphi \in (\varphi^u, \varphi^d]$	*(NE, P)if* $\gamma > \gamma^d$*; (NE, N) or (IE, N) otherwise*

Part (*i*) of Proposition 5 says that if the fixed costs of exporting are so small that the firm exports to the South regardless of the global policy environment, then each region ends up implementing its preferred policy: the North chooses IE and the South does not protect intellectual property. In this policy equilibrium, the high quality Northern good is sold in both markets at a uniform price while the low quality Southern imitation is sold locally at a price equal to its marginal cost. Interestingly, as $p^{ui} < p^u$ Northern consumers benefit from Southern imitation even though the imitated good is *not* sold in the North: Northern openness to parallel imports ensures that the competition created by imitation in the Southern market is indirectly passed on to the North. Thus, even though the imitated good is not sold in the North, under IE Southern imitation generates a *positive price externality* for Northern consumers just as it imposes a *negative rent externality* on the firm.

From the firm's viewpoint, NE on the North's part and a prohibition of imitation on the South's part are *substitutes* in the sense that both policies give it greater room for exercising its monopoly power. However, the costs of implementing these two types of policies fall on different regions: conditional on the firm exporting, implementing NE of IPR imposes a welfare cost on the North while protecting intellectual property imposes a welfare cost on the South except when local imitation delivers a good that is much lower in quality than the Northern good. Except for the parameters referred to in part (*i*) of Proposition 5, the two regions find themselves in a policy stand-off: each region chooses its policy recognising whether or not the other is willing to bear the welfare cost of inducing the firm to export. Over $(\varphi^{ui}, \varphi^{di}]$ *either* IPR protection in the South *or* NE in the North is sufficient to induce the firm to export. In such a situation, equilibrium policies depend upon whether the South prefers the high quality Northern good to the local imitation, i.e. whether or not $\gamma > \gamma^u$. When $\gamma < \gamma^u$, recognising that the South does not have an incentive to protect IPR, the North implements NE to allow the firm to price discriminate internationally and thereby earn sufficient profit to offset the fixed cost of exporting. On the other hand, when $\gamma > \gamma^u$, both (NE, N) *and* (IE, P) are Nash equilibria as each region is willing to bear the welfare cost of inducing exporting *only if* the other region's policy is not favourable to the firm. Of course, each region would rather that the other adopt the policy that suffices to induce exporting: while the

[20] If $\varphi^d \leq \varphi$, South does not protect IPR while North's policy is irrelevant since its firm chooses not to export.

North strictly prefers (IE, P), Southern welfare is strictly higher under (NE, N). It is worth noting that under (NE, N), the South benefits from more competition and greater variety because two quality levels are sold locally as opposed to one.[21]

If $\varphi \in (\varphi^{di}, \varphi^{u}]$ and $\gamma > \gamma^{u}$, the South chooses to not permit local imitation as the North–South quality gap is large and the North ends up choosing IE knowing that the Southern protection is sufficient to induce the firm to export. However, when the quality gap lies below γ^{u} the South has no incentive to offer IPR protection and the lack of such protection eliminates the firm's incentive to export, making Northern exhaustion policy irrelevant as the firm does not export if imitation occurs. Thus, if $\varphi \in (\varphi^{di}, \varphi^{u}]$ and $\gamma < \gamma^{u}$ both (NE, N) and (IE, N) are Nash equilibria. Over the range $(\varphi^{u}, \varphi^{d}]$, Northern exhaustion policy matters only if the South protects intellectual property (regardless of the North's exhaustion policy). The Southern decision, in turn, is determined once again by the North–South quality gap. When this gap is not too large (i.e. $\gamma \leq \gamma^{d}$), the South permits imitation and the firm refrains from exporting rendering Northern policy irrelevant. However, when $\gamma > \gamma^{d}$, the South protects intellectual property and it is optimal for the North to implement NE to ensure that its firm exports.

5.2. *Global Welfare*

In this Section, we discuss global welfare and provide a comparison of equilibrium outcomes with the first-best. Next, we draw out the implications of requiring the South to prohibit imitation. The goal of this exercise is to shed light on the effects of a strengthening of IPR protection in developing countries that was mandated by the WTO's TRIPS agreement.

Global welfare is defined as the sum of each country's welfare:

$$ww^{r} = w_{N}^{r} + w_{S}^{r} \text{ where } r = a, ai, d, di, u, \text{or } ui.$$

We begin with two preliminary but important observations regarding welfare. First, as imitation creates competition in the South while also increasing variety, *holding constant the firm's export decision*, imitation necessarily increases global welfare: $ww^{ri} > ww^{r}$ for $r = a$, d, or u. Thus, the only scenario where imitation can lower global welfare is when it causes the firm to not sell in the South. Second, as was noted earlier, in the absence of imitation, uniform pricing is preferable to price discrimination as aggregate output under both regimes is the same (Lemma 1) but the latter regime leads to unexploited price differentials across countries. Furthermore, both regimes necessarily dominate autarky under which the Southern market is not served by the firm and imitation is prohibited. Therefore we have: $ww^{u} > ww^{d} > ww^{a}$. For analogous reasons, this welfare ranking continues to hold under imitation: $ww^{ui} > ww^{di} > ww^{ai}$.

Given that the firm exports, which outcome is preferable for the world: uniform pricing without imitation or price discrimination with imitation? We can show the following:

[21] As we shall show below, aggregate world welfare is also strictly higher under (NE,N).

PROPOSITION 6. *From a global welfare perspective, price discrimination coupled with imitation is preferable to uniform pricing in the absence of imitation if the North–South quality gap falls below the threshold* γ^f: $ww^{di} \geq ww^u$ *iff* $\gamma \leq \gamma^f$.[22]

A secondary question is whether price discrimination in the absence of imitation is preferable to autarky is coupled with imitation. In this regard we can show that $ww^d \geq ww^{ai}$ if $\gamma \geq \gamma^w$ where $\gamma^w = 4/3$. In other words, so long as the Northern good is even mildly superior in quality to its Southern imitation, price discrimination is preferable from a social welfare perspective. For the remainder of the article, we assume that this is the case (i.e. $\gamma \geq \gamma^w$). This assumption just says that the North–South technology gap is not so small that autarky (coupled with imitation) is preferable to trade under price discrimination.

We are now in a position to compare equilibrium policy outcomes reported in Proposition 5 (which assumes $\varphi^{di} \leq \varphi^u \Leftrightarrow \gamma \leq \gamma^f$) with the first-best outcome reported in Proposition 6. Figure 1 illustrates equilibrium policies when $\gamma \leq \gamma^f$.

When fixed costs of exporting are so small (i.e. $\varphi \leq \varphi^{ui}$) that the firm exports even under its least preferred policy environment, i.e. (IE, P), the equilibrium policy outcome is (IE, P) and it is first-best. As noted before, in such a policy equilibrium, the benefits of imitation induced competition also accrue to Northern consumers due to the North's openness to parallel imports. Once the fixed cost is above φ^{ui}, the harmony between equilibrium policies and global welfare is no longer guaranteed. Consider the range $(\varphi^{ui}, \varphi^{di}]$. Over this range, the policy equilibrium (NE, N) is efficient when $\gamma \leq \gamma^f$: since the firm exports under both (NE, N) and (IE, P) over this range, from Proposition 6 we know that it is better to induce exporting by allowing price discrimination as opposed to forbidding imitation because the competition induced by imitation is intense when the quality gap is below γ^f. However, as Proposition 5 notes and Figure 1 shows, when $\gamma > \gamma^u$ both (NE, N) and (IE, P) are Nash equilibria so that the equilibrium outcome can be inefficient.

Now consider the range $(\varphi^{di}, \varphi^u]$. Figure 1 shows that over $(\varphi^{di}, \varphi^u]$, the policy pair (IE, P) is globally optimal but it emerges as an equilibrium if $\gamma \geq \gamma^u$; when $\gamma < \gamma^u$, the lack of Southern IPR protection ensures that the firm does not export so that Northern exhaustion policy is inconsequential and both (NE, N) and (IE, N) are equilibria. Finally, over the range $(\varphi^u, \varphi^d]$ the policy pair (NE, P) is socially optimal but it emerges as an equilibrium only if $\gamma \geq \gamma^d$; when $\gamma < \gamma^d$ the South chooses not to protect IPR and the firm refrains from exporting, making the North indifferent between its policy options.

It is worth noting from Figure 1 that if the South could reduce the fixed cost φ through some policy actions, it has an incentive to do so.[23] First, all else equal, a lower fixed cost is more likely to induce the firm to export. Second, as Figure 1 shows, if the fixed cost is very low the South can get away with no IPR enforcement without

[22] Together with Lemma 3, this result implies that the firm values protection from imitation more than the freedom to price discriminate precisely when world welfare considerations argue in the opposite direction, i.e., when $\gamma \leq \gamma^f$. Note also that if total output under discrimination were to exceed that under uniform pricing (as it could if θ were not distributed uniformly) then imitation would make discrimination even more desirable by increasing output as well as variety in the South while having no effect on Northern consumers.

[23] This issue is interesting since part of the fixed cost of exporting might reflect policy restrictions, bureaucratic hurdles and red tape etc. As a result, a reduction in φ could partly be thought of as economic reforms in the South that improve market access for foreign firms.

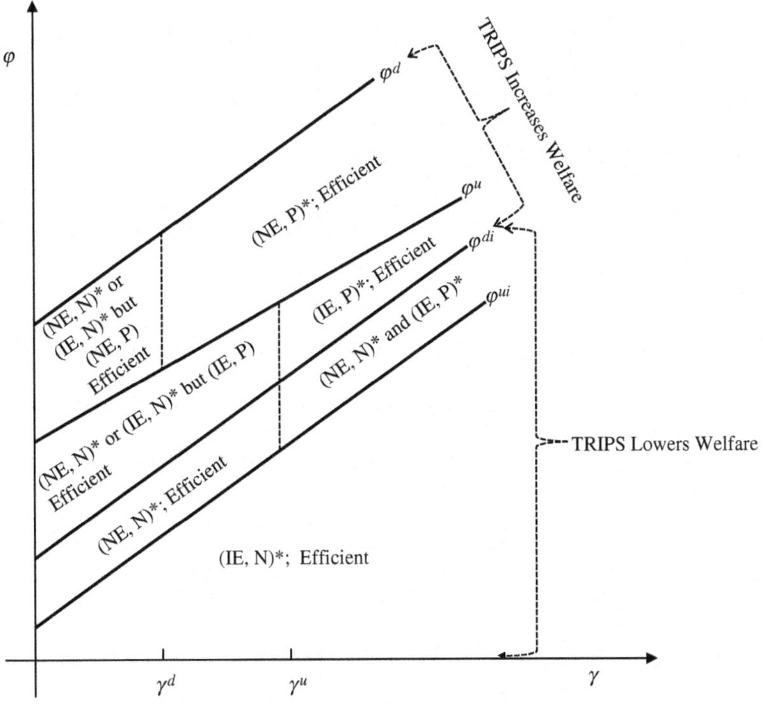

Fig. 1. *Policy Equilibrium and Welfare Effects of TRIPS* $\gamma \leq \gamma^f$

compromising the firm's incentive to export. However, a slight subtlety is worth noting: the South would not necessarily want to lower the fixed cost so much that it falls below φ^{ui}. This is because when $\varphi \leq \varphi^{ui}$, the equilibrium is (IE, N) whereas over the range $(\varphi^{ui}, \varphi^{di}]$ it is (NE, N) which is not only the South's most preferred policy combination but also the globally efficient outcome over this parameter range.[24] Intuitively, if the South can influence the North to pick NE to induce the firm to export, it would want to do so.

We can now use the model to evaluate the effects of the TRIPS agreement which required developing country members of the WTO to strengthen their protection of intellectual property but imposed no restrictions on national policies pertaining to the exhaustion of IPR.

5.3. *Effects of TRIPS*

Suppose the South no longer has the option of permitting imitation while the North is free to pick its preferred exhaustion regime. From Proposition 5 we know that if the South protects intellectual property, the North chooses IE if $\varphi \leq \varphi^u$; otherwise it opts

[24] To be precise, (NE,N) is the unique equilibrium over $(\varphi^{ui}, \varphi^{di}]$ only when $\gamma < \gamma^u$.

for NE. Thus, in a TRIPS constrained world, the equilibrium policy vector is (IE, P) when $\varphi \leq \varphi^u$ with uniform pricing as the market outcome and (NE, P) otherwise, with price discrimination as the market outcome.

The effects of shutting down Southern imitation when $\gamma \leq \gamma^f$ are as follows. Suppose $\varphi > \varphi^d$ so that the firm does not export to the South under any policy configuration. If so, enforcement of Northern IPR in the South confers a pure welfare loss on the South while having no effect on the Northern economy.[25] This is because Southern imitation ensures that at least a lower quality version of the Northern good is locally available and as the fixed costs of exporting are so large that the firm does not export to the South even if imitation is prohibited, shutting down imitation has no effect on its global profit.

Now suppose $\varphi \in (\varphi^u, \varphi^d]$. Over this range, whether or not a prohibition on Southern imitation has any consequences depends upon the North–South quality gap. We know that when $\gamma > \gamma^d$, the South finds it optimal to shut down imitation voluntarily in order to ensure that the high quality Northern good is sold locally and the North chooses NE. Thus, the policy outcome under TRIPS is the same as that without it implying that TRIPS has no effects on the world economy when $\gamma > \gamma^d$. However, when $\gamma \leq \gamma^d$, in the absence of TRIPS, the South permits imitation while the North is indifferent between its policy options as its firm does not export. Thus, when $\gamma \leq \gamma^d$, by forcing the South to prohibit imitation, TRIPS makes NE the preferred policy for the North as its firm exports under NE but not under IE. These policy changes reduce Southern welfare because the Northern good is not sufficiently superior in quality relative to its Southern imitation to justify its higher price; have no effect on Northern consumers since the price remains at p_N^d in the North; increase the firm's profit; and also increase global welfare because the rent externality generated by the Southern decision to permit imitation (in the absence of TRIPS) is eliminated. Thus, when $\varphi \in (\varphi^u, \varphi^d]$, TRIPS enforcement (weakly) increases global welfare: when $\gamma < \gamma^d$ it has no effect whereas when $\gamma > \gamma^d$ it strictly increases welfare. TRIPS is welfare enhancing over this range since prohibiting imitation induces the firm to export and the North–South quality gap is not high enough for the South to want to do so voluntarily.

Consider now the effect on Northern consumers of TRIPS over $\varphi \in (\varphi^{di}, \varphi^u]$. As Figure 1 notes, over this range TRIPS enforcement has no effect on world welfare when $\gamma > \gamma^u$ since the policy equilibrium remains unchanged at (IE, P). However, when $\gamma \leq \gamma^u$, firm does not export in the absence of TRIPS so that both (IE,N) to (NE, N) are equilibria. In such a situation, TRIPS increases world welfare by delivering the globally efficient outcome (IE, P). The South loses because TRIPS enforcement replaces the cheap low quality good by the expensive high quality good but the price–quality ratio is not favourable as the quality gap is small (i.e. $\gamma \leq \gamma^u$). But since the Southern decision to allow imitation imposes a rent externality on the

[25] One could alternatively interpret this result as saying that if the Southern market is so small that the Northern firm does not sell there even if its intellectual property is protected by the South then it is welfare reducing to offer such protection to the firm. This result is in line with the argument made by TRIPS opponents that enforcing IPR protection in poor developing countries reduces their welfare without generating any compensating benefits.

North (which the South ignores), TRIPS enforcement (weakly) increases global welfare over $(\varphi^{di}, \varphi^{u}]$.

TRIPS enforcement causes the sharpest change in the global policy environment when $\varphi \in (\varphi^{ui}, \varphi^{di}]$ and $\gamma < \gamma^{u}$: over this range, the policy equilibrium completely reverses due to TRIPS from (NE, N) to (IE, P).[26] Recognising that the TRIPS mandated change in Southern IPR policy (from N to P) is sufficient to sustain the firm's incentive to export, the North reverses its policy regarding the exhaustion of IPR from NE to IE. Southern welfare takes a sharp hit because of these policy changes: variety is reduced since the low quality imitated good is no longer sold and the price of the high quality good increases from p_S^{di} to p^u. The overall increase in the price of the high quality good (Δp^T) suffered by the South due to TRIPS enforcement can be broken down into two components (Δp_S^{N} and Δp_S^{IE}):

$$\Delta p^T = \Delta p_S^{\mathrm{N}} + \Delta p_S^{\mathrm{IE}} \text{ where } \Delta p_S^{\mathrm{N}} = p_S^d - p_S^{di} \text{ and } \Delta p_S^{\mathrm{IE}} = p^u - p_S^d.$$

Holding Northern policy constant at NE, the first component (Δp_S^{N}) measures the price increase that results from the elimination of competition from the imitation based Southern industry. The second component (Δp_S^{IE}) captures the price externality generated by the reversal in the North's policy from NE to IE: Northern openness to parallel imports induces the firm to raise its price in the South from p_S^d to p^u.

When $\varphi \in (\varphi^{ui}, \varphi^{di}]$ and $\gamma < \gamma^{u}$, the overall effect of the TRIPS induced policy reversal on the firm's profit can also be broken down into two components:

$$\Delta \pi^T \equiv \pi^u - \pi^{di} = \Delta \pi^{\mathrm{N}} + \Delta \pi^{\mathrm{IE}} \text{ where } \Delta \pi^{\mathrm{N}} = \pi_S^d - \pi_S^{di} > 0 \text{ and } \Delta \pi^{\mathrm{IE}} = \pi^u - \pi^d < 0,$$

i.e. while shutting down imitation makes the firm better off, the reversal in the Northern policy makes it worse off since it loses the ability to price discriminate internationally. Since $\Delta \pi^T \geq 0$ if $\gamma \leq \gamma^f$, the firm benefits from the TRIPS induced global policy reversal over the parameter range being considered. Further note that consumer welfare in the North is strictly higher under (IE, P) relative to (NE, N) – indeed this is the primary reason as to why the North reverses its policy. Thus, the TRIPS-induced policy reversal makes the North better off on two counts: it increases the firm's profits while also lowering price in the North. However, from Proposition 6 we know that, given that the firm exports, from a global welfare perspective (NE, N) welfare dominates (IE, P) when $\gamma \leq \gamma^f$, so that TRIPS induced policy reversal lowers world welfare when $\varphi \in (\varphi^{ui}, \varphi^{di}]$ and $\gamma < \gamma^u$ even as it benefits the North.

Finally, consider the scenario where the fixed costs of exporting are so small that the firm exports regardless of the policy environment: i.e. $\varphi \leq \varphi^{ui}$. Here, TRIPS enforcement increases prices worldwide and therefore hurts consumers in both regions. The firm's aggregate profit increases while Southern welfare declines, as does global welfare since the mark-up of the firm increases globally.

[26] Of course, such reversal can also occur when $\gamma > \gamma^u$ provided that the Nash equilibrium is (NE,N) and not (IE,P).

The key conclusion regarding TRIPS can now be stated:

PROPOSITION 7. *Requiring the South to protect IPR increases global welfare if and only if it is necessary for inducing the firm to export.*[27]

The most important practical implication of this result is that for TRIPS enforcement to increase global welfare, it is imperative that Northern firms respond to such enforcement by selling more products in the South, i.e. the *extensive margin* of Northern exports to the South needs to increase due to TRIPS. This result fits quite well with the existing empirical literature on this issue: as was discussed in Section 4, this literature finds that Northern exports to the South generally do respond in a manner that is consistent with increased IPR enforcement in the South being welfare improving in the aggregate.

6. When Firm Values Price Discrimination More

When $\gamma \geq \gamma^f \Leftrightarrow \varphi^{di} \geq \varphi^u$, the equilibrium outcome is as follows:

PROPOSITION 8. *Given that the firm values the freedom to price discriminate internationally more than IPR protection (i.e. $\gamma \geq \gamma^f \Leftrightarrow \varphi^{di} \geq \varphi^u$), equilibrium policies of the two regions are as follows:*

Exporting Cost	Equilibrium Policies
$(i)\ \varphi \in [0, \varphi^{ui}]$	*(IE, N)*
$(ii)\ \varphi \in (\varphi^{ui}, \varphi^u]$	*(IE, P) if* $\gamma > \gamma^u$ *and (NE, N) otherwise*
$(iii)\ \varphi \in (\varphi^u, \varphi^{di}]$	*(NE, N)*
$(iv)\ \varphi \in (\varphi^{di}, \varphi^d]$	*(NE, P) if* $\gamma > \gamma^d$ *and (IE, N) or (NE, N) otherwise*

The interpretation of Proposition 6 is completely analogous to that of Proposition 5 and we skip a detailed discussion of this result to avoid redundancy.

Figure 2 illustrates Proposition 8 as well as the welfare effects of TRIPS for the case $\gamma > \gamma^f$.

As before, when $\varphi \leq \varphi^{ui}$, TRIPS-induced protection of intellectual property lowers world welfare by altering the policy environment from (IE, N) to (IE, P). When $\varphi \in (\varphi^{ui}, \varphi^u]$, TRIPS enforcement causes a reversal in the global policy environment from (NE, N) to (IE, P) when $\gamma < \gamma^u$ whereas it has no effect when $\gamma > \gamma^u$. From Proposition 6 we know that such a policy reversal increases world welfare when $\gamma > \gamma^f$. Over $(\varphi^u, \varphi^{di}]$, TRIPS lowers world welfare by changing the policy environment from (NE, N) to (IE, P) and raising mark-ups in the South. Finally, over $(\varphi^{di}, \varphi^d]$, TRIPS increases world welfare when $\gamma \leq \gamma^d$ because it induces the firm to export whereas for $\gamma > \gamma^d$ it has no effect on welfare as the policy outcome remains unchanged at (NE, P) – the South protects IPR anyway and the North retains its policy of NE to ensure that its firm exports to the South.

[27] While the analysis in this Section assumes $\gamma \leq \gamma^f$, we show below that this result holds even when $\gamma > \gamma^f$.

Equilibrium W/O TRIPS:		(IE, N)*		(IE, P)* if $\gamma > \gamma^u$; (NE, N)* Otherwise		(NE, N)*		(NE, P)* if $\gamma > \gamma^d$; (NE, N)* or (IE, N)* Otherwise	
Efficient Policies:	0	(IE, N)	ϕ^{ui}	(IE, P)	ϕ^u	(NE, N)	ϕ^{di}	(NE, P)	ϕ^d

Outcome Under TRIPS:		(IE, P)		(IE, P)		(NE, P)		(NE, P)	
Effects of TRIPS:	0	ww ↓	ϕ^{ui}	ww ↑	ϕ^u	ww ↓	ϕ^{di}	ww ↑	ϕ^d

Fig. 2. *Policy Equilibrium and Effects of TRIPS* $\gamma \geq \gamma^f$

7. Discussion of Model and Robustness of Results

In what follows, we discuss three important aspects of the model and its results. First, we ask how our results would change if parallel importers incurred fixed costs and discuss why it is reasonable to assume that they do not. Second, we provide an extension of the model where Southern IPR enforcement is modelled as a continuous policy variable and show that our main results continue to hold under this more general formulation. Third, we provide some justification for the model's assumption that IPR are perfectly enforced in the North.

7.1. *Costly Parallel Imports*

The model assumes that parallel imports flow costlessly from the South to the North whenever prices in the two markets differ. This assumption is commonly used in the literature to make the analysis of alternative exhaustion regimes more tractable as it implies that Northern openness to parallel imports is sufficient to equalise prices across markets (provided the firm exports). In the real world, parallel imports are likely to be hampered by several types of frictions such as transportation costs and other costs of accessing foreign markets.[28] In the presence of such frictions, arbitrage would be imperfect and some amount of international price discrimination can arise even under international exhaustion. However, the assumption of costless parallel imports is reasonable in one important sense: while parallel imports are likely to be costly in the real world, they are unlikely to involve all of the costs that are incurred by firms when they export to foreign markets for the first time. In our model, the firm must incur the fixed cost φ *prior to being able to export* to the South. This fixed cost should be interpreted to include all the expenditures that the firm has to incur before selling its product in the Southern market, such as expenditures on establishing a retail presence, advertising and other promotional efforts. By contrast, from the viewpoint of parallel traders, Northern consumers are likely to be well aware of the product as the firm's entry into its home market (i.e. the North) is assumed to have already occurred and any associated costs with that already incurred. As a result, the fixed costs that parallel importers would need to incur before reimporting the good from the South would likely be much smaller than the fixed cost of initial exporting incurred by the firm.[29]

[28] For example, parallel importers might need to obtain a licence as is the case for parallel trade in pharmaceuticals in some European countries.

[29] Of course, as was noted earlier, the margins available to parallel importers are likely to be smaller relative to the mark-ups enjoyed by patent holders.

Nevertheless, it is useful to ask how our policy analysis is affected if parallel importers must incur a fixed cost like the one incurred by the firm prior to exporting. The main implication of incorporating such a fixed cost is that when the North's policy is IE, parallel imports would flow to the North only if the North–South price differential is sufficiently high. In turn, this implies that there would be scenarios where the North would be indifferent between its policy choices: if the international price differential is small relative to the fixed cost of parallel importing, Northern exhaustion policy would be inconsequential as there would be no incentive for parallel trading. This implies that the likelihood of a TRIPS induced policy reversal would be lower in the presence of such a fixed cost. The intuition becomes transparent if engaging in parallel importing becomes prohibitively costly: in such a situation, Northern exhaustion policy would be totally irrelevant and therefore unresponsive to Southern IPR protection. Furthermore, it is also clear that even if parallel imports were subject to only variable costs, the firm would have greater freedom to engage in international price discrimination and Northern exhaustion policy would be once again less potent and therefore less responsive to changes in Southern IPR protection.

7.2. *A Continuous Formulation of Southern IPR Protection*

In the model, the Southern policy decision is a binary choice: to protect or not protect IPR. This assumption is made for convenience and because it adds a degree of symmetry to the model in the sense that the policy choice of each region is discrete in nature. A more general formulation of the South's policy decision would be to treat it as the degree of IPR enforcement that determines the probability with which local imitation is detected and shut down. Below, it is shown that the results of the basic model extend quite naturally to such a setting.

Consider the following game. In the first stage, North determines its exhaustion policy while the South chooses the degree of IPR enforcement that determines the probability (x) that local imitation is detected and shut down by local authorities. Next, knowing the degree of IPR enforcement x and the exhaustion policy of the North, the Northern firm decides whether to incur the fixed cost (φ) of exporting. The final stage involves pricing, trade and consumption.

Suppose the North chooses NE and consider the firm's export decision. If it decides to export, its expected profit in the Southern market equals

$$\pi_S^d(x) = x\pi_S^d + (1 - x)\pi_S^{di}.$$

This implies that the firm chooses to export if

$$\pi_S^d(x) - \varphi \geq 0 \Leftrightarrow \varphi \leq \varphi^d(x) = \pi_S^d(x).$$

Note that $\varphi^d(0) = \varphi^{di}$, $\varphi^d(1) = \varphi^d$ and $\partial\varphi^d(x)/\partial x = \pi_S^d > 0$. Thus, this formulation naturally extends the basic model to a setting where the South's IPR policy is a continuous choice variable.

Consider the South's optimal IPR policy given that the North chooses NE. First observe that when $\varphi \leq \varphi^d(0) = \varphi^{di}$, the firm exports to the South even when $x = 0$ (i.e. the South offers no IPR protection). This in turn makes it optimal for the South to set $x = 0$ when $\varphi \in (0, \varphi^{di}]$ since allowing imitation creates competition and expands consumer choice. Similarly, when $\varphi \geq \varphi^d(1) = \varphi^d$, the firm does not export even if the South offers complete IPR protection (i.e. sets $x = 1$). This implies that for $\varphi \geq \varphi^d$, it is once again optimal for the South to choose $x = 0$: allowing imitation ensures that at least a low quality version of the Northern good is available locally.

Over the range $(\varphi^{di}, \varphi^d)$ if the North–South quality gap is sufficiently high (i.e. $\gamma > \gamma^d$) it is optimal for the South to choose a level of IPR protection that is just sufficient to induce the firm to export and this is found by solving the following equation for x:

$$\varphi = x\pi_S^d + (1 - x)\pi_S^{di},$$

which gives

$$x^d = \frac{\varphi - \pi_S^{di}}{\pi_S^d - \pi_S^{di}}.$$

Observe that x^d is defined only when $\varphi \in (\varphi^{di}, \varphi^d)$ and over this range we have $0 < x^d < 1$. This implies that the South's optimal IPR policy when the North's exhaustion policy is NE is given by

$$x^*(\text{NE}) = \begin{pmatrix} 0 \text{ if } \varphi \in (0, \varphi^{di}] \\ x^d \text{ if } \varphi \in (\varphi^{di}, \varphi^d) \text{ and } \gamma > \gamma^d \\ 0 \text{ if } \varphi \geq \varphi^d \end{pmatrix}.$$

In Figure 3, the thick dark line plots the South's optimal IPR policy $x^*(\text{NE})$ under NE given that $\gamma > \gamma^d$.

Outside $\varphi^{di} < \varphi < \varphi^d$, we have $x^*(\text{NE}) = 0$ – exactly what we obtained in the core model. The key difference arises over the range $\varphi^{di} < \varphi < \varphi^d$. Here, given that $\gamma > \gamma^d$, optimal IPR protection in the South $x^*(\text{NE})$ increases with the fixed cost φ to ensure that the firm continues to make sufficient profits to cover this cost.[30] By contrast, when the South's decision is discrete (i.e. $x = 0$ or 1), the level of IPR protection over this

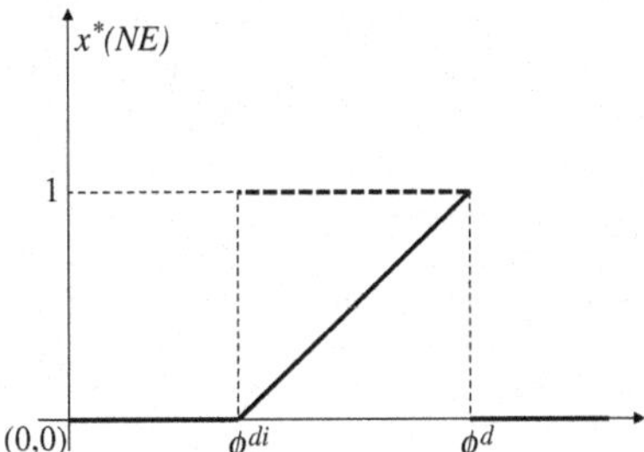

Fig. 3. *Optimal IPR Policy of the South Under NE*

[30] It is straightforward to show that x^d decreases with the quality gap γ. Intuitively, as the firm's quality advantage over imitators increases, a weaker level of IPR protection is needed to ensure that it makes enough profit to cover its fixed cost φ.

range of fixed costs is set at the maximum level (i.e. $x^* = 1$). This is shown by the thick dashed line in Figure 3. Intuitively, when the South picks only between two discrete policies (zero or full protection), it ends up offering too much protection to the Northern firm (i.e. $x^* = 1 > x^d$ when $\gamma > \gamma^d$). By contrast, under the more general model, the South can fine tune its IPR policy and offer 'just enough' protection to induce the Northern firm to sell locally.

Using corresponding logic, we can state the optimal Southern policy when the North picks IE:

$$x^*(\text{IE}) = \begin{pmatrix} 0 \text{ if } \varphi \in (0, \varphi^{ui}] \\ x^u \text{ if } \varphi \in (\varphi^{ui}, \varphi^u] \text{ and } \gamma > \gamma^u \\ 0 \text{if } \varphi \geq \varphi^u \end{pmatrix} \text{ where } x^u = \frac{\varphi - \pi^{ui} + \pi_N^d}{\pi^u - \pi^{ui}}.$$

Indeed, under this continuous formulation of Southern IPR protection, Propositions 3 and 4 need to be modified only slightly. The two statements of Proposition 3 remain intact. In addition, we need to add a third statement that specifies the level of IPR protection offered by the South to be x^*(NE). Similarly, Proposition 4 needs to be expanded by specifying the level of Southern IPR protection under IE to be x^*(IE). Finally, the key equilibrium result reported in Proposition 5 also needs a minor modification. We can state:

PROPOSITION 5A. *Suppose the level of Southern IPR protection x is endogenously chosen. Then, given that $\gamma \leq \gamma^f \Leftrightarrow \varphi^{di} \leq \varphi^u$, equilibrium policies of the two regions are as follows:*

Exporting Cost	Equilibrium policies
(*i*) $\varphi \in [0, \varphi^{ui}]$	(*IE*, $x^* = 0$)
(*ii*) $\varphi \in (\varphi^{ui}, \varphi^{di}]$	(*NE*, $x^* = 0$) *if* $\gamma < \gamma^u$; *both* (*NE*, $x^* = 0$) *and* (*IE*, $x^* = x^u$) *otherwise*
(*iii*) $\varphi \in (\varphi^{di}, \varphi^u]$	(*IE*, $x^* = x^u$) *if* $\gamma > \gamma^u$ *and* (*IE*, $x^* = 0$) *or* (*NE*, $x^* = 0$) *otherwise*
(*iv*) $\varphi \in (\varphi^u, \varphi^d]$	(*NE*, $x^* = x^d$) *if* $\gamma > \gamma^d$ *and* (*IE*, $x^* = 0$) *or* (*NE*, $x^* = 0$) *otherwise*

Given this result, it is clear that this alternative formulation of Southern IPR protection yields conclusions regarding the effects of TRIPS on equilibrium outcomes and welfare that are very similar to those yielded by the basic model.

7.3. *Role of Northern IPR Protection*

The model assumes that the North offers complete IPR protection to its firm, which allows the firm to act as a monopolist in the Northern market. In other words, why the North offers IPR protection is exogenous to the model. This is a reasonable way to proceed for several reasons. First, the objective of the article is to understand the North's choice between alternative exhaustion regimes and the relationship of that choice to the South's decision regarding IPR protection. Abstracting from Northern IPR protection allows us to focus on this interaction. Furthermore, when TRIPS came into existence, the industrialised countries already offered strong IPR protection so there was no real change in the Northern IPR protection as a result of TRIPS.

At a more general level, the decision to protect IPR is a deeper, more fundamental decision than the choice of an exhaustion regime. One reflection of this difference between the two policy decisions is the fact that exhaustion regimes can be changed relatively quickly and can actually even be fine tuned at the level of the industry as well as to the nature of the IPR in question (i.e. exhaustion policies for patents, copyrights and trademarks can be different). Indeed, one of the key motivating facts of this article is that TRIPS left WTO member countries completely free to implement exhaustion regimes of their choice while requiring complete harmonisation of virtually all other aspects of IPR. This stance implies that it is possible for two countries to implement the exhaustion regimes of their choice even if they have to offer the same level of protection to IPR holders. Indeed, exhaustion policies vary widely across member countries of the WTO. Even countries that offer strong IPR protection do not necessarily follow the same types of exhaustion policies. For example, the US practises NE with respect to patented goods, while the EU's chosen regime is community exhaustion under which parallel imports can flow freely within the community but are prohibited from the rest of the world. Thus, it is reasonable to focus on the interaction between exhaustion policies and protection of IPR in the South while abstracting from the North's decision to protect IPR.

8. Conclusion

Issues related to intellectual property have always been contentious in the context of North–South trade. This article provides a North–South model that focuses on the linkages between Northern policy regarding the exhaustion of IPR and Southern policy regarding the protection of intellectual property.

The model is built on the insight that while Southern IPR protection determines the firm's market power within the Southern market, Northern policy regarding the exhaustion of IPR determines its market power across regions. Which of these aspects of market power is more valuable to the firm depends upon the intensity of competition generated by imitation and the degree of asymmetry between markets. If the quality gap between the Northern original and the Southern imitation is quite small, IPR protection is more valuable to the firm as it helps avoid vigorous market competition. On the other hand, the larger the Northern market and the more skewed Northern consumer tastes are in favour of quality, the higher the premium the firm puts on the ability to price discriminate internationally. As a result, the threshold quality gap below which the firm values IPR protection relatively more than the ability to price discriminate internationally is decreasing in parameters that determine the degree of asymmetry across markets.

In the model, while choosing its policy each region takes into account not only the other region's policy but also the firm's decisions regarding pricing and exporting under alternative policy configurations. In this regard, we find that the North has a stronger incentive to adopt IE when the South protects IPR relative to when it does not. On the other side, the South is less likely to protect IPR if the North chooses IE. The nature of this interaction implies that, in equilibrium, the two regions can find themselves in a policy-standoff wherein each region takes into account whether or not the other would be willing to implement its less preferred policy to induce the firm to export. While from the firm's viewpoint, protection from imitation and the freedom to price discriminate internationally both serve to enhance its monopoly power on the world market, the two policies differ substantially with respect to their distributional burden. Conditional on the firm exporting, the North is better off under IE while the South is better off not protecting IPR, policies that are beggar-thy-neighbour in nature.

The interdependence of policy decisions implies that a change in one region's policy can induce a change in the other region's policy. For example, if the South is forced to shut down local imitation – say due to the enforcement of an international trade agreement such as TRIPS – there are circumstances where the North responds to the change in Southern policy by reversing its policy from NE to IE. When such a TRIPS induced policy reversal occurs, Southern welfare losses multiply. First, variety is reduced as the low-quality imitation is no longer sold locally. Second, the price of the high quality increases due to the elimination of Southern competition. Third, the reversal in the Northern policy induces the firm to switch to a uniform price that exceeds its Southern price under price discrimination. However, on the flip side, Northern consumers benefit from these changes, as does the Northern firm.

It is worth noting that as the model abstracts from innovation, its conclusions regarding the effects of increased IPR enforcement in the South on global welfare do not account for dynamic benefits that might accrue to the global economy from such a policy change. Ignoring these dynamic effects is quite reasonable insofar as increased IPR enforcement in small developing countries is concerned but less so when evaluating the consequences of IPR reforms in large countries such as Brazil, China and India. In the model's defence, however, it should be noted that the entry of the Northern firm into the South affects Southern welfare much like innovation: it introduces a new good to the local economy that is higher in quality than the one that is produced locally. Similarly, the result that TRIPS enforcement increases global welfare if it induces the firm to export is quite analogous to the idea that a sufficiently large innovation response by the North can make TRIPS enforcement by the South to be in its interest. What is not captured by the model, however, is that innovation can expand the set of products in the North or increase their quality (or both). If the model was extended to include such types of innovation, one would expect the case for enforcement of IPR in the South to be stronger. While exporting by Northern firms would continue to play a crucial role in terms of how Southern IPR enforcement affects local welfare, its role with respect to global welfare would be weaker, particularly if innovation was to be sufficiently elastic with respect to Southern IPR enforcement. Under such a situation, Northern welfare (and perhaps even global welfare) could increase with TRIPS enforcement even if the export response of Northern firms to Southern IPR reforms were not particularly strong.

Vanderbilt University

Submitted: 20 September 2011
Accepted: 20 April 2012

Additional Supporting information may be found in the online version of this article:

Appendix A. Mathematical Appendix Proofs.

Please note: The RES and Wiley-Blackwell are not responsible for the content or functionality of any supporting materials supplied by the authors. Any queries (other than missing material) should be directed to the authors of the article.

References

Branstetter, L., Fisman, R., Foley, F. and Saggi, K. (2011). 'Does intellectual property rights reform spur industrial development?', *Journal of International Economics*, vol. 83, pp. 27–36.

Chaudhuri, S., Goldberg, P. and Jia, P. (2006). 'Estimating the effects of global patent protection in pharmaceuticals: a case study of quinolones in India', *American Economic Review*, vol. 96(5), pp. 1477–514.

Danzon, P., Wang, Y.R. and Wang, L. (2005). 'The impact of price regulation on the launch delay of new drugs - evidence from twenty-five major markets in the 1990s', *Health Economics*, vol. 14, pp. 269–92.

Goldberg, P.K. (2010). 'Intellectual property rights protection in developing countries: the case of pharmaceuticals', *Journal of the European Economic Association*, vol. 8, pp. 326–53.

Grossman, G.M. and Lai, E. (2008). 'Parallel imports and price controls', *Rand Journal of Economics*, vol. 39, pp. 378–402.

Ivus, O. (2010). 'Do stronger patent rights raise high-tech exports to the developing world?', *Journal of International Economics*, vol. 81, pp. 38–47.

Ivus, O. (2011). 'The quantity, price, and variety response of U.S. exports to stronger IPR protection', mimeo, Queen's University.

Javorcik, B. (2004). 'The composition of foreign direct investment and protection of intellectual property rights in transition economies', *European Economic Review*, vol. 48(1), pp. 39–62.

Kanavos, P., Costa-i-Font, J., Merkur, S. and Gemmill, M. (2004). 'The economic impact of pharmaceutical parallel trade in European member states: a stakeholder analysis', Special Research Paper, LSE Health and Social Care, London School of Economics and Political Science.

Lanjouw, J.O. (2005). 'Patents, price controls and access to new drugs: how policy affects global market entry', Working Paper No. 11321, National Bureau of Economic Research.

Lee, J.-Y. and Mansfield, E. (1996). 'Intellectual property protection and U.S. foreign direct investment', *Review of Economics and Statistics*, vol. 78(2), pp. 181–6.

Malueg, D.A. and Schwartz, M. (1994). 'Parallel imports, demand dispersion, and international price discrimination', *Journal of International Economics*, vol. 37, pp. 167–95.

Mansfield, E. (1994). 'Intellectual property protection, foreign direct investment, and technology transfer', Discussion Paper 19, International Finance Corporation, Washington DC.

Maskus, K.E. (2000). 'Parallel imports', *World Economy*, vol. 23, pp. 1269–84.

Maskus, K.E. and Penubarti, M. (1995). 'How trade-related are intellectual property rights?', *Journal of International Economics*, vol. 39, pp. 227–48.

National Economic Research Associates (NERA) (1999). 'The economic consequences of the choice of regime of exhaustion in the area of trademarks', Final Report for DG XV of the European Commission.

Nunnenkamp, P. and Spatz, J. (2004). 'Intellectual property rights and foreign direct investment: a disaggregated analysis', *Weltwirtschaftliches Archiv (Review of World Economics)*, vol. 140(3), pp. 393–414.

Richardson, M. (2002). 'An elementary proposition concerning parallel imports', *Journal of International Economics*, vol. 56, pp. 233–45.

Roy, S. and Saggi, K. (forthcoming, *a*). 'Equilibrium parallel import policies and international market structure', *Journal of International Economics*.

Roy, S. and Saggi, K. (forthcoming, *b*). 'Strategic competition and optimal parallel import policy', *Canadian Journal of Economics*.

Schmalensee, R. (1981). 'Output and welfare implications of monopolistic third-degree price discrimination', *American Economic Review*, vol. 71, pp. 242–7.

Smith, P. (1999). 'Are weak patent rights a barrier to US exports?', *Journal of International Economics*, vol. 48, pp. 151–77.

Valleti, T.M. (2006). 'Differential pricing, parallel trade, and the incentive to invest', *Journal of International Economics*, vol. 70, pp. 314–24.

Valletti, T.M. and Szymanski, S. (2006). 'Parallel trade, international exhaustion and intellectual property rights: a welfare analysis', *Journal of Industrial Economics*, vol. 54, pp. 499–526.

Varian, H. (1985). 'Price discrimination and social welfare', *American Economic Review*, vol. 75, pp. 870–5.

Chapter 17

International effects of national regulations: External reference pricing and price controls[☆,#]

Difei Geng[a], Kamal Saggi[b,*]

[a] Department of Economics, Sam M. Walton College of Business, University of Arkansas, Fayetteville, AR 72701, United States
[b] Department of Economics, Vanderbilt University, VU Station B #351819, 2301 Vanderbilt Place, Nashville, TN 37235, United States

ARTICLE INFO

Article history:
Received 18 May 2016
Received in revised form 15 August 2017
Accepted 28 August 2017
Available online 5 September 2017

JEL classification:
F10
F12
D42
L51

Keywords:
External reference pricing policies
Price controls
Patented products
Welfare

ABSTRACT

Under external reference pricing (ERP) the price that a government permits a firm to charge in its market depends upon the firm's prices in other countries. In a two-country (home and foreign) model where demand is asymmetric across countries, we show that home's unilaterally optimal ERP policy permits the home firm to engage in a threshold level of international price discrimination above which it is (just) willing to export. If the firm faces a price control abroad or bargains over price with the foreign government, an ERP policy can even yield higher home welfare than a direct price control.

1. Introduction

Governments across the world rely on a variety of price regulations to combat the market power of firms selling patented pharmaceutical products. Two such commonly used regulations are external reference pricing (ERP) and price controls. Under a typical ERP policy, the price that a country permits a firm to charge in its market for a particular product depends upon the firm's prices for the same product in a well-defined set of foreign countries, commonly called the country's *reference basket*.[1] For example, Canada's ERP reference basket includes France, Germany, Italy, Sweden, Switzerland, the UK and the USA while that of France includes Germany, Italy, Spain, and the UK. Furthermore, while some countries – such as France and Spain – permit a seller to charge only the lowest price in its reference basket, others – such as Canada and Netherlands – are willing to accept either the average or the median price in their reference baskets. In a recent report, the World Health Organization (WHO) notes that 24 of 30 OECD countries and approximately 20 of 27 European Union countries use ERP, with the use being mostly restricted to on-patent medicines (World Health Organization, 2013).

While ERP policies affect prices by restricting the degree of international price discrimination practised by firms, governments can also directly control prices via a variety of other measures: for example, governments can control the ex-manufacturer price, the wholesale markup, the pharmacy margin, the retail price, or use some combination of these measures. Though few countries, if any,

☆ For helpful comments and discussions, we thank two anonymous referees, the editor, and the seminar audiences at Dartmouth College, Midwest International Economics Spring 2015 Meeting (Ohio State), Oregon State University, the Southern Economics Association 2015 Meeting, Florida International University, University of Arkansas-Fayetteville, the 3rd insTED workshop at the University of Indiana at Bloomington, and the 9th Annual Conference of the International Economics and Finance Society at the University of International Business and Economics (Beijing). All errors are our own.

* Corresponding author.
E-mail addresses: DGeng@walton.uark.edu (D. Geng), k.saggi@vanderbilt.edu (K. Saggi).

[1] Thus the use of an ERP policy by a country can help lower the domestic price of a product only if the price that would have prevailed in its market in the absence of its ERP policy were to exceed prices in the set of reference countries.

This chapter was originally appeared in *Journal of International Economics* **109**, 68–84. © 2017 Elsevier B.V.

use all such measures, many use at least some of them. For example, Kyle (2007) notes that price controls in the pharmaceutical market are common in most major European countries where governments are fairly involved in the health-care sector. Similarly, many developing countries have a long history of imposing price controls on patented pharmaceuticals, many of which tend to be supplied by foreign multinationals. For example, India has been imposing price controls on pharmaceuticals since 1962 and, despite the existence of a robust domestic pharmaceutical industry, it recently chose to significantly expand the list of drugs subject to price controls.[2]

This paper addresses several inter-related questions pertaining to ERP policies that have not been tackled by existing literature: What are the underlying economic determinants of such policies? What type of international spillovers do they generate? What are their overall welfare effects? Does their use by one country reduce or increase the effectiveness of price controls in *other* countries? Under what circumstances does an ERP policy dominate a direct price control?

We address these questions in a simple model with two countries (home and foreign) where a single home firm produces a patented product, that it potentially sells in both markets. The firm enjoys monopoly status in both markets by virtue of its patent. The home market is assumed to have more consumers and a greater willingness to pay for the product, which in turn creates an incentive for the firm to price discriminate in favor of foreign consumers. Home's ERP policy δ (where $\delta \geq 1$) is defined as the ratio of the firm's domestic price to its foreign price and it is chosen by the home government to maximize national welfare, which equals the sum of the firm's global profit and domestic consumer surplus. Under this formulation, if the firm sells in both markets when facing the ERP policy δ at home then its equilibrium home price is simply δ times its foreign price.

From the firm's perspective, home's ERP policy is a constraint on the degree of international price discrimination that it can practice while from the domestic government's perspective it is a tool for lowering the price at home (while simultaneously raising it abroad).[3] Since the domestic market is more lucrative for the firm, too tight an ERP policy at home creates an incentive on its part to not sell abroad in order to sustain its optimal monopoly price at home. This is an important mechanism in our model and there is substantial empirical support for the idea that the use of ERP policies on the part of rich countries can deter firms from serving low-price markets. For example, using data from drug launches in 68 countries between 1982 and 2002, Lanjouw (2005) shows that price regulations and the use of ERP by industrialized countries contribute to launch delay in developing countries. Similarly, in their analysis of drug launches in 15 European countries over 12 different therapeutic classes during 1992–2003, Danzon and Epstein (2012) find that the delay effect of a prior launch in a high-price EU country on a subsequent launch in a low-price EU country is stronger than the corresponding effect of a prior launch in a low-price EU country.[4]

While the firm only cares about its total global profit, home welfare also depends on the *source* of those profits, i.e., it matters whether profits come at the expense of domestic or foreign consumers. We find that the home country's unilaterally optimal ERP policy permits the firm to engage in the minimum level of price discrimination at which the firm just prefers selling in both markets to selling only at home. An important feature of this nationally optimal ERP policy is that the less lucrative the foreign market, the greater the room that the firm is given to price discriminate internationally. Such an ERP policy is optimal from the perspective of home welfare because of the following trade-off. On the one hand, given that the firm exports, home has an incentive to tighten its ERP policy to lower domestic price. On the other hand, tightening the ERP policy below the threshold level induces the firm to drop the foreign market and home consumers end up facing the firm's optimal monopoly price p_H^m. The outcome under which the firm sells only at home is decidedly worse for the home country than one in which the firm faces no ERP constraint whatsoever (and therefore necessarily sells in both markets) – while domestic consumers pay p_H^m under both scenarios, the firm collects monopoly profits abroad only in the latter scenario.

Though we model home's ERP policy as the extent to which the firm is free to price discriminate in favor of foreign consumers, as we noted earlier, in the real world countries often implement ERP policies by requiring the local price charged by a firm to be no higher than its prices in the set of countries that constitute its reference basket. Thus, the extent to which a firm is constrained by a country's ERP policy is a function of the *composition* of its reference basket. Our simpler two-country formulation allows us to capture the essence of ERP policies in a manner that is not only tractable but also useful for understanding the structure of real-world ERP policies. Casual empiricism suggests that when defining their reference baskets, countries typically tend to include foreign countries with similar market sizes and per capita incomes. For example, we do not observe EU countries setting ERP policies on the basis of prices in low income developing countries. If lowering local prices were the sole motivation of ERP policies, European governments would have an incentive to use the lowest available foreign prices while setting their ERP policies. The insight provided by our model is that they choose not to do so because casting too wide a net while setting ERP policies can backfire by causing firms to forsake foreign markets just so that they can sustain monopoly prices in their domestic markets.

We show that under home's unilaterally optimal ERP policy the equilibrium foreign price (p_F^*) ends up *exceeding* the firm's optimal monopoly price p_F^m for that market (*i.e.* $p_F^* > p_F^m$). Given this outcome, we build on our benchmark ERP model by allowing the foreign government to impose a local price control $\bar{p}_F$ on the firm in order to curtail the international spillover generated by home's ERP policy. When both countries are policy active, home sets its ERP policy taking into account the incentives of not just the firm but also the foreign country. We show that the tighter the home's ERP policy, the looser the foreign price control needs to be for the firm to be willing to sell there. Indeed, home's ERP policy undermines the effectiveness of the foreign price control since the minimum price at which the firm is willing to sell abroad is higher when home has an ERP policy in place relative to when it does not.

An interesting insight delivered by our analysis is that a tightening of the foreign price control $\bar{p}_F$ can raise welfare in both countries (i.e. it can be Pareto-improving). This surprising result arises whenever $\bar{p}_F \in [p_F^m, p_F^*]$ and the intuition for it is as follows. Whenever $\bar{p}_F \geq p_F^m$ a tightening of the foreign price control *increases* the firm's foreign profit even as it reduces its domestic profit due to the foreign price control spilling over to the home market via its ERP policy. However, since the firm's foreign profit is decreasing in $\bar{p}_F$ for all $\bar{p}_F \in [p_F^m, p_F^*]$, only a moderate relaxation of home's ERP policy is required to ensure that the firm continues to export if the foreign price control is tightened. As a result, whenever $\bar{p}_F \in [p_F^m, p_F^*]$ a tightening of the foreign price control $\bar{p}_F$ also lowers home price (which equals $\delta\bar{p}_F$). Thus, the existence of an ERP policy at home not only

[2] See "India Widens Price Control over Medicines" in *Wall Street Journal*, May 17, 2013 and "Government Notifies New Drug Price Control Order" in the *Indian Express*, May 17, 2013.

[3] In this sense, ERP policies are similar to exhaustion policies that determine whether or not holders of intellectual property rights (IPRs) are subject to competition from parallel imports when they choose to engage in international price discrimination. Unlike ERP policies, the economics of exhaustion policies has been investigated widely in the literature: see Malueg and Schwartz (1994), Maskus (2000), Richardson (2002), Li and Maskus (2006), Valletti (2006), Grossman and Lai (2008), and Roy and Saggi (2012).

[4] Further evidence consistent with launch delay spurred by the presence of price regulations is provided by Kyle (2007) who uses data on 1444 drugs produced by 278 firms in 134 therapeutic classes from 1980 to 1999 to study the pattern of drug launches in 21 countries.

causes the foreign price control to spill over to the home market, the nature of the spillover is such that a tightening of the foreign price control can make both countries better off.

A central result of the paper is that when both countries are policy active, the equilibrium ERP policy of the home country is Pareto-efficient and it results in the foreign country having to allow the firm to charge its optimal monopoly price p_F^m in its market (which is lower than p_F^* – the price that obtains abroad in the absence of the price control). In addition, we show that the jointly-optimal ERP policy – i.e. the policy that maximizes the sum of home and foreign welfare – is more stringent than the ERP policy implemented by the home government (who does not take into account the adverse effect of its ERP policy on foreign consumers).

In Sub-section 4.1, we expand the menu of policies available to the home country by allowing it to choose between a domestic price control and an ERP policy. This analysis shows when and why an ERP policy dominates a price control. The key difference between the two instruments is that, unlike an ERP policy, a domestic price control does *not* affect the foreign price control facing the firm and therefore has no bearing on its decision to export. Therefore, if home uses a price control as opposed to an ERP policy, foreign simply chooses the lowest price at which the firm is willing to sell in its market (i.e. it sets its price control at the firm's marginal cost thereby maximizing local consumer surplus and eliminating the firm's foreign profit). On the other hand, if home institutes an ERP policy, a stricter foreign price control also leads to a lower home price (holding constant home's ERP policy) – something that tends to make exporting less attractive to the firm. Recognizing the link between prices in the two markets created by home's ERP policy and its impact on the firm's incentives, the foreign government is unable to push down its price control all the way to the firm's marginal cost when home's price regulation takes the form of an ERP policy as opposed to a price control. As a result, from the perspective of home welfare, the trade-off between an ERP policy and a local price control boils down to the following: while a price control yields greater domestic surplus (defined as the sum of consumer surplus and firm's home profit), an ERP policy helps the firm earn greater profit abroad. Therefore, an ERP policy dominates a price control when maintaining the monopoly mark-up in the foreign market is important or, equivalently, when the profit earned from the foreign market accounts for a significant component of the firm's total profit – something that happens when demand in the foreign market is relatively similar in magnitude to that at home.

Since firms selling patented products (such as in the pharmaceutical industry) often bargain with governments over prices of their products, in Section 4.2 we consider Nash bargaining (both with and without side-payments) between the firm and the foreign government over price. We derive optimal ERP policies under both scenarios and investigate their properties. A major result of this analysis is that the weaker the bargaining position of the firm vis-à-vis the foreign government, the more likely it is that the home country prefers an ERP policy to a price control. This result can be viewed as a generalization of the core model since, after all, a foreign price control simply represents a scenario where all of the bargaining power resides with the foreign government.

By explicitly bringing in international pricing considerations and policy interaction between national governments, our paper makes an important contribution to the rapidly developing literature on the economics of *internal* reference pricing policies, i.e. policies under which drugs are clustered according to some equivalence criteria (such as chemical, pharmacological, or therapeutic) and a reference price within the same market is established for each cluster. Brekke et al. (2007) analyze three different types of internal reference pricing in a model of horizontal differentiation where two firms sell brand-name drugs while the third firm sells a generic version, that like in our model, is perceived to be of lower quality. They compare generic and therapeutic reference pricing – with each other and with the complete lack of reference pricing.[5] One of their important findings is that therapeutic reference pricing generates stronger competition and lower prices than generic reference pricing.[6]

Motivated by the Norwegian experience, Brekke et al. (2011) provide a comparison of domestic price caps and reference pricing on competition and welfare and show that whether or not reference pricing is endogenous – in the sense of being based on market prices as opposed to an exogenous benchmark price – matters a great deal since the behavior of generic producers is markedly different in the two scenarios; in particular, generic producers have an incentive to lower their prices when facing an endogenous reference pricing policy in order to lower the reference price, which in turn makes the policy preferable from the viewpoint of consumers.[7] Using a panel data set covering the 24 best selling off-patent molecules, they also empirically examine the consequences of a 2003 policy experiment where a sub-sample of off-patent molecules was subjected to reference pricing, with the rest remaining under price caps. They find that prices of both brand names and generics fell due to the introduction of reference pricing while the market shares of generics increased.

The rest of this paper is structured as follows. We first introduce our two-country framework and analyze home's optimal ERP policy as well as its welfare implications. Next, in Section 3, we allow the foreign country to utilize a price control and study its interaction with home's ERP policy. Section 4 extends the main analysis in two important directions. First, we endogenize the home country's choice between an ERP policy and a domestic price control. Next, we study the role of ERP policy when the firm and the foreign government bargain over price. We consider bargaining both with and without side-payments. Section 5 concludes while Appendix A presents all of the supporting calculations and contains two important extensions of our analysis: in Appendix A.2, we describe equilibrium outcomes when the two countries pick their respective policies simultaneously as well as when the foreign country moves first while in Appendix A.3 we consider a three-country model to derive one country's optimal ERP policy when it takes the form of a reference basket.

2. A benchmark model of ERP

We consider a world comprising two countries: home (H) and foreign (F).[8] A single home firm sells a patented product (x) with a quality level s. Each consumer in country i ($i = H, F$) buys at most 1 unit of the good at the local price p_i. The number of consumers in country i equals n_i. If a consumer buys the good, her utility is given by $u_i = st - p_i$, where t measures the consumer's taste for quality. Utility

[5] Therapeutic clusters upon which reference pricing is based can be defined in several ways. As per Brekke et al. (2007), under generic reference pricing the cluster includes products that have the same active chemical ingredients whereas under therapeutic reference pricing the cluster includes products with chemically related active ingredients that are pharmacologically equivalent or have similar therapeutic effects. While the cluster includes only off-patent brand-name drugs and generic substitutes under generic reference pricing, such is not necessarily the case under therapeutic reference pricing under which it may include on-patent drugs.

[6] In similar spirit, Miraldo (2009) compares two different reference pricing policies in a two-period model of horizontal differentiation: one where reference price is the minimum of the observed prices in the market and another where it is a linear combination of those prices. In the model, the reference pricing policy of the regulator responds to the first period prices set by firms (which, in turn, the firms take into account while setting their prices). The key result is that consumer surplus and firm profits are lower under the 'linear policy' since the first period price competition between firms is less aggressive under this policy.

[7] The Norwegian price cap regulation is an ERP policy where the reference basket is the following set of 'comparable' countries: Austria, Belgium, Denmark, Finland, Germany, Ireland, the Netherlands, Sweden, and the UK. Unlike us, Brekke et al. (2011) focus on the domestic market and take foreign prices to be exogenously determined.

[8] In the appendix, we derive home's optimal reference basket for the case of three countries.

under no purchase equals zero and the quality parameter s is normalized to 1. For simplicity, t is assumed to be uniformly distributed over the interval $[0,\mu_i]$ where $\mu_i \geq 1$.

From the firm's viewpoint, the two markets differ from each other in two ways. First, home consumers value quality relatively more, that is, $\mu_H = \mu \geq 1 = \mu_F$. Second, the home market is larger: $n_H = n \geq 1 = n_F$. As one might expect, since $\mu \geq 1$ the firm has an incentive to price discriminate internationally.[9]

The home government sets an external reference pricing (ERP) policy that stipulates the maximum price ratio that its firm can set across countries. In particular, let p_H and p_F be prices in the home and foreign markets respectively *given* that the firm sells in both countries. Then, home's ERP policy requires that the firm's pricing abide by the following constraint:

$$p_H \leq \delta p_F$$

where $\delta \geq 1$ reflects the rigor of home's ERP policy. A more stringent ERP policy corresponds to a lower δ which gives the firm less room for international price discrimination. Due to differences in the structure of demand across two countries, the firm has no incentive to discriminate in favor of home consumers so there is no loss of generality in assuming $\delta \geq 1$. Note also that when $\delta = 1$ home's ERP policy leaves the firm no room to price discriminate across markets.

2.1. Pricing under the ERP constraint

If the ERP constraint is absent, the firm necessarily sells in both markets since doing so yields higher total profit than selling only at home. In particular, when the firm can freely choose prices across countries, it sets a market specific price in each country to maximize its global profit as follows

$$\max_{p_H,\, p_F} \pi_G(p_H,p_F) \equiv \frac{n}{\mu}p_H(\mu - p_H) + p_F(1-p_F) \tag{1}$$

It is straightforward to show that the firm's optimal monopoly prices in the two markets are: $p_H^m = \mu/2$ and $p_F^m = 1/2$. The associated sales in each market equal $x_H^m = n/2$ and $x_F^m = 1/2$. Global sales under price discrimination equal $x_G^m = x_H^m + x_F^m = (n+1)/2$. Observe that

$$p_H^m/p_F^m = \mu \geq 1$$

i.e. from the firm's viewpoint, the optimal degree of international price discrimination equals μ. Let the firm's global profit under optimal monopoly pricing be denoted by $\pi^m \equiv \pi_G(p_H^m, p_F^m)$.

Now consider the firm's pricing problem under the ERP constraint $p_H \leq \delta p_F$. Since μ is the maximum price differential the firm charges across markets, in the core model we can restrict attention to $\delta \leq \mu$ without loss of generality.[10] Of course, we implicitly assume that the government has the ability to sustain its preferred degree of international price discrimination (i.e. any price differentials that arise cannot be undercut via arbitrage by third parties).

When faced with the ERP constraint, the firm can either choose to sell only at home thereby evading it or sell in both markets at prices that abide by the constraint, in which case it solves:[11]

$$\max \pi_G(p_H,p_F) \text{ subject to } p_H \leq \delta p_F$$

It is straightforward to show that the ERP constraint binds (i.e. $p_H = \delta p_F$) and the firm's optimal prices in the two markets are

$$p_H^\delta = \frac{\mu\delta(n\delta+1)}{2(n\delta^2+\mu)} \text{ and } p_F^\delta = p_H^\delta/\delta \tag{2}$$

The sales associated with these prices can be recovered from the respective demand curves in the two markets and these equal

$$x_H^\delta = \frac{n(\delta(n\delta-1)+2\mu)}{2(n\delta^2+\mu)} \text{ and } x_F^\delta = \frac{2n\delta^2-(n\delta-1)\mu}{2(n\delta^2+\mu)}$$

Provided the firm sells in both markets, global sales under the ERP constraint equal $x_G^\delta = x_H^\delta + x_F^\delta$. Using the above formulae, it is straightforward to show the following:

Lemma 1. *Provided the firm sells in both markets, the imposition of an ERP policy by the home country that leaves the firm with some room to price discriminate internationally (i.e. $\delta > 1$) but not complete freedom to do so (i.e. $\delta < \mu$) leads to lower global sales relative to international price discrimination:*

$$x_G^\delta - x_G^m = -\frac{n(\delta-1)(\mu-\delta)}{2(n\delta^2+\mu)} \leq 0.$$

Lemma 1 can be seen as a generalization of a central result in the literature on exhaustion of intellectual property rights that compares global sales under two extreme cases – one where the firm is completely free to price discriminate internationally (i.e. $\delta \geq \mu$) and another where it must set a common international price (i.e. $\delta = 1$).[12] This literature has shown that, under the assumptions of our model, global sales under the two types of pricing are the same. Observe from Lemma 1 that this result also holds in our model: when $\delta = 1$ total sales under the ERP constraint are indeed the same as those under price discrimination, i.e. $x_G^\delta = x_G^m$. However, for any positive level of price discrimination – i.e. for $\delta \in (1,\mu)$ – this result does not hold and the imposition of an ERP policy at home lowers total global sales relative to unconstrained price discrimination.

Using the prices p_H^δ and p_F^δ, the firm's global profit $\pi_G^\delta = \pi(p_H^\delta, p_F^\delta)$ when facing the ERP constraint is easily calculated

$$\pi_G^\delta = \pi_G\left(p_H^\delta, p_F^\delta\right) = \frac{\mu(n\delta+1)^2}{4(n\delta^2+\mu)} \tag{3}$$

As one might expect,

$$\frac{\partial \pi_G^\delta}{\partial \delta} > 0$$

[9] We should note here that ERP policies are typically implemented at the national level and therefore may apply to a wide range of patented products whereas our model is focused on a single product. Furthermore, while the foreign country has no incentive to use an ERP policy in our model, in the real world two countries can simultaneously belong to each other's reference baskets. Such an outcome can be rationalized via a generalized multi-product version of our model if demand elasticities for some products are higher at home than abroad with the opposite being true for other products. Alternatively, an Armington type assumption wherein consumers in both countries place a higher value on home products could also create a potential role for an ERP policy.

[10] It is worth pointing out here that our model embeds two frequently utilized market structures in international trade, i.e. those of perfect market integration and segmentation, with the former scenario corresponding to $\delta = 1$ and the latter to $\delta = \mu$.

[11] Within the context of our model, any foreign price that exceeds the choke off price abroad (i.e. $p_F \geq 1$) is tantamount to the firm selling only at home since no foreign consumers are willing to buy the good if $p_F \geq 1$.

[12] See Saggi (2016) for an extensive discussion of the relevant literature.

for $1 \leq \delta \leq \mu$, that is, the firm's global profit increases as home's ERP policy becomes looser.

Of course, the firm always has the option to escape the ERP constraint by eschewing exports altogether. If it does so, it collects the optimal monopoly profit π_H^m in the home market where

$$\pi_H^m = \frac{n}{\mu} p_H^m (\mu - p_H^m) = n\mu/4 \tag{4}$$

Since (*i*) $\partial\pi_G^\delta/\partial\delta > 0$; (*ii*) $\pi_G^\delta|_{\delta \geq \mu} = \pi^m > \pi_H^m$; and (*iii*) π_H^m is independent of δ, we can solve for the critical ERP policy above which the firm prefers to sell in both markets relative to selling only at home. We have:

$$\pi_G^\delta \geq \pi_H^m \Longleftrightarrow \delta \geq \delta^* \text{ where } \delta^* \equiv \frac{1}{2}\left(\mu - \frac{1}{n}\right) \tag{5}$$

We refer to δ^* as the *export inducing* ERP policy. Observe that the export inducing ERP policy δ^* is increasing in the two basic parameters of the model (i.e. μ and n) since an increase in either of these parameters makes the home market relatively more profitable for the firm thereby making it more reluctant to export under the ERP constraint. As a result, the more lucrative the home market, the greater the room to price discriminate that the firm requires in order to prefer selling in both markets to selling only at home.

The first main result can now be stated:

Proposition 1. *(i) When facing the ERP constraint the firm exports if and only if the ERP policy is less stringent than the export inducing ERP policy δ^* (i.e. $\delta \geq \delta^*$).*

(ii) Given that the firm sells in both markets when facing an ERP policy at home, the following hold:

(a) *The use of an ERP policy by home reduces the local price relative to the optimal monopoly price whereas it raises the foreign price: $p_H^\delta \leq p_H^m$ and $p_F^\delta \geq p_F^m$ with the inequalities binding at $\delta = \mu$.*
(b) *Home price and the firm's global profit increase in δ (i.e. $\partial p_H^\delta/\partial\delta > 0$ and $\partial\pi_G^\delta/\partial\delta > 0$) whereas foreign price decreases in it (i.e. $\partial p_F^\delta/\partial\delta < 0$).*
(c) *Prices in both markets increase if the home market gets larger i.e. ($\partial p_i^\delta/\partial n > 0$) or if home consumers start to value the product more (i.e. $\partial p_i^\delta/\partial\mu > 0$).*

Proof. See appendix. □

Part (*iia*) highlights that the introduction of an ERP policy at home moves prices in the two markets in opposite directions: it lowers the domestic price whereas it raises the foreign price. These price changes obviously imply that home's ERP policy makes domestic consumers better off at the expense of foreign consumers. It is worth noting that home's ERP policy induces the firm to raise its price *above* its optimal monopoly price p_F^m in the foreign market since it wants to avoid lowering the price in the more lucrative domestic market too much. Along the same lines, given that an ERP policy is in place at home and the firm exports, a decrease in the stringency of this policy (i.e. an increase in δ) makes foreign consumers better off. Thus, the use of an ERP policy by home generates a *negative international spillover* for foreign consumers, a theme to which we return below when analyzing the optimal ERP policy from a joint welfare perspective.[13]

Part (*iib*) also captures the conflicting effects of a tightening of home's ERP policy on the firm and domestic consumers – a trade-off that is at the heart of the welfare analysis that follows in Section 2.2. Part (*iic*) highlights the fact that the international price linkage created by home's ERP policy makes prices in *both* markets a function of the two key home demand parameters (i.e. μ and n) that determine the profitability of the domestic market relative to the foreign one.

2.2. Optimal ERP policy

Having understood the firm's pricing and export behavior, we are now in a position to derive home's optimal ERP policy. To do so, we assume that home's objective is to maximize its national welfare, i.e., the sum of local consumer surplus and total profit of the firm:

$$w_H(p_H, p_F) = cs_H(p_H) + \pi(p_H, p_F) \tag{6}$$

where $cs_H(p_H)$ denotes consumer surplus in the home market and it equals

$$cs_H(p_H) = \frac{n}{\mu}\int_{pH}^{\mu}(t - p_H)dt$$

Let $cs_H^\delta = cs_H(p_H^\delta)$. Since the firm exports iff $\delta \geq \delta^*$, domestic welfare as a function of the ERP policy can be written as:

$$w_H(\delta) = \begin{cases} w_H^m = \pi_H^m + cs_H^m & \text{if } \delta < \delta^* \\ w_H^\delta = \pi_G^\delta + cs_H^\delta & \text{if } \delta \geq \delta^* \end{cases}$$

The logic for why home welfare is discontinuous in its ERP policy is straightforward: for $\delta \geq \delta^*$, the firm exports and domestic welfare equals the sum of the firm's global profit π_G^δ and local consumer surplus cs_H^δ whereas for $\delta < \delta^*$ the firm only sells at home at its optimal monopoly price and domestic welfare equals $w_H^m = \pi_H^m + cs_H^m$.

An important feature of our model is that provided the firm exports, the tighter the ERP policy (i.e. the lower is δ), the higher is home welfare: i.e. $\partial w_H^\delta/\partial\delta \leq 0$ if $\delta \geq \delta^*$.[14] Thus, for all $\delta \geq \delta^*$, the home government has an incentive to reduce δ. But once $\delta = \delta^*$, any further reduction in δ leads the firm to eschew exports and home welfare drops from w_H^δ to w_H^m since the downward pressure on domestic price that is exerted by home's ERP policy disappears once the firm decides to sell only at home.[15]

We can directly state the main result:

Proposition 2. *Let $\mu^* \equiv 2 + 1/n$. Home's optimal ERP policy is δ^e where*

$$\delta^e = \begin{cases} 1 & \textit{if } \mu \leq \mu^* \\ \delta^* & \textit{otherwise} \end{cases}$$

Observe that for $\mu \leq \mu^*$ home's optimal ERP policy calls for the firm to set a common international price (i.e. $\delta^e = 1$) whereas for $\mu > \mu^*$, it permits some degree of international price discrimination (i.e. $\delta^e = \delta^* > 1$) on the part of the firm.[16] The logic behind this

[13] In an insightful survey of the relevant empirical literature, Goldberg (2010) notes that the use of ERP policies by developed countries could put developing countries in a situation where they end up facing prices in excess of local monopoly prices – something that emerges sharply in the equilibrium of our model.

[14] An explicit derivation of this welfare result is contained in the appendix.

[15] Indeed, for any ERP policy for which the firm does not export (i.e. for all $\delta < \delta^*$), home is strictly better off not imposing any ERP constraint on the firm at all (i.e. setting a δ higher than μ which allows the firm to charge its optimal monopoly prices in both markets); while the firm charges p_H^m at home both when $\delta < \delta^*$ and when $\delta \geq \mu$, it only exports when under the latter scenario where home's ERP policy is so lax that the firm's pricing behavior is completely unconstrained.

[16] It is worth noting here that Proposition 2 continues to describe the Nash equilibrium if the home country and the firm were to make their decisions simultaneously.

result is simple. In terms of home welfare, imposing an ERP policy that makes the firm abandon exporting is even worse than not having an ERP policy whatsoever – in both cases the firm makes monopoly profit π_H^m in the home market but only in the latter case does the firm collect monopoly profit π_F^m in the foreign market. The optimal ERP policy of the home government ensures that the firm does not refrain from exporting just so that it can charge its optimal monopoly price at home.[17] When $\mu \leq \mu^*$, the foreign market is fairly comparable to the domestic one and the firm does not drop it even if it has to charge the same price in both markets (i.e. $\delta^e = 1$) since its global profit under the ERP policy exceeds monopoly profit at home. But when $\mu > \mu^*$, the firm is only willing to export if it can engage in some price discrimination and the larger is μ, the more lax home's ERP policy needs to be in order to preserve the firm's export incentive. In general, the firm's export incentive is too weak relative to what is domestically optimal since the *firm cares only about its total profit and not where it comes from*. By contrast, the home government also cares about the *source* of that profit in the sense that any profit increase enjoyed by the firm that comes at the expense of domestic consumers does not increase total domestic welfare.

Given that home's ERP policy affects the firm's export incentive as well as the price it sets abroad, we now investigate the properties of the jointly optimal ERP policy.

2.3. Joint welfare

Let joint welfare be defined by:

$$w(p_H, p_F) \equiv w_H(p_H, p_F) + cs_F(p_F) \quad \text{where} \quad cs_F = \int_{pH}^{\mu} (t - p_F)dt$$

Joint welfare as a function of the home's ERP policy equals[18]

$$w(\delta) = \begin{cases} w_H^m & \text{if } \delta < \delta^* \\ w_H^\delta + cs_F^\delta & \text{if } \delta \geq \delta^* \end{cases}$$

Lemma 1 showed that an interior ERP policy (i.e. $\delta \in (1, \mu)$) lowers global sales relative to international price discrimination so that its imposition has two conflicting effects on world welfare: it reduces the international price differential across markets but also lowers total global sales relative to unrestricted price discrimination. What is the net effect? Lemma 2 provides the answer:

Lemma 2. *Given that the firm sells in both markets when facing an ERP policy at home, joint welfare increases as the home's ERP policy becomes tighter:*

$$\frac{\partial w}{\partial \delta} = -\frac{n\mu(\mu - \delta)(n\delta + 1)}{4(n\delta^2 + \mu)^2} < 0$$

[17] Suppose the home government attaches greater weight to the firm's profit relative to local consumer surplus home so that its ERP policy is chosen to maximize $\alpha\pi_H + cs_H$ where $\alpha \geq 1$. Under such a scenario, we can show that $\frac{\partial^2 w_H(\delta,\alpha)}{\partial\delta\partial\alpha} = \frac{n\mu(\mu-\delta)(n\delta+1)}{2(\mu+n\delta^2)^2} > 0$ – i.e. the marginal return from tightening the ERP policy (i.e. lowering δ) decreases in the weight given to the firm's profit. Alternatively, we can show that $\left.\frac{\partial w_H(\delta)}{\partial\delta}\right|_{\delta=\delta^*} > 0$ for all $\alpha > \widehat{\alpha} = \frac{3n^2\mu^2+8n\mu-3}{2(n\mu+1)^2}$ where $\widehat{\alpha} > 1$. Thus, if the home country were to put a sufficiently large weight on profits relative to consumer surplus (i.e. $\alpha > \widehat{\alpha}$) it would set a more lax ERP policy than the export inducing policy δ^*. Moreover, the optimal ERP policy is an increasing function of α and it converges to its upper-bound μ when α tends to infinity.

[18] Note that home welfare jumps from w_H^m to w_H^δ at $\delta = \delta^*$. It is straightforward to show that the size of this welfare jump is increasing in μ:

$$\left.\frac{\partial\left(w_H^\delta - w_H^m\right)}{\partial\mu}\right|_{\delta=\delta^*} > 0.$$

The literature on the exhaustion of intellectual property rights in the global economy has shown that the scenario of uniform pricing ($\delta = 1$) yields higher global welfare than international price discrimination ($\delta \geq \mu$) because it fully eliminates the price differential across countries that exists under price discrimination without lowering total global sales. What Lemma 2 shows is that home's ERP policy – regardless of its level – increases global welfare relative to unrestricted price discrimination. In other words, any degree of reduction in the international price discrimination is welfare-improving because it allocates sales away from low valuation (foreign consumers) to high valuation (home consumers).

The jointly optimal ERP policy maximizes

$$\max_{\delta} \; w(p_H, p_F) \text{ subject to } p_H \leq \delta p_F$$

We first state the key result and then explain its logic.[19]

Proposition 3. *Home's nationally optimal ERP policy δ^e maximizes joint welfare.*

Proposition 3 is rather surprising since it argues that home's (subgame perfect) Nash equilibrium ERP policy is efficient in the sense of maximizing aggregate welfare even though home chooses its policy *without* taking into account its effects on foreign consumers. We now explain the logic behind this result.

An efficient ERP policy has to balance two objectives. One, it has to lower the international price differential as much as possible since the existence of such a differential implies that the marginal consumer in the high-price country values the last unit sold more than the marginal consumer in the low-price country so reallocating sales towards the high-price country raises welfare. Two, the ERP policy must ensure that foreign consumers have access to the good. For $\mu \leq \mu^*$, the firm exports even when it must charge the same price in both markets so that it is socially optimal to fully eliminate the international price differential (i.e. set $\delta = 1$). For $\mu > \mu^*$, incentivizing the firm to export requires that it be given some leeway to price discriminate internationally.

To see why δ^* maximizes joint welfare when $\mu > \mu^*$, simply note that starting at δ^* lowering δ (i.e. making the ERP policy more stringent) reduces foreign welfare to zero since the firm does not export while it also reduces home welfare since domestic price increases from p_H^δ to p_H^m while the firm's profit remains unchanged (i.e. it equals π_H^m). Thus, implementing an ERP policy that is more stringent than δ^* results in a *Pareto-inferior outcome* relative to δ^*.

Now consider increasing δ above δ^*. At $\delta = \delta^*$ if the home's ERP policy is relaxed (i.e. δ is raised) the firm continues to export but increases its price at home while lowering it abroad. Thus, starting at δ^*, an increase in δ makes the foreign country better off while making home worse off. Indeed, from the foreign country's viewpoint it would be optimal to eliminate the ERP constraint since that yields the lowest possible price in its market (i.e. p_F^m). However, we know from Lemma 2 that joint welfare declines in δ for all $\delta > \delta^*$. Thus, it is jointly optimal to lower the international price differential as much as possible while simultaneously ensuring that foreign consumers do not lose access to the patented product. This is exactly what home's equilibrium ERP policy δ^e accomplishes.

Fig. 1 provides further intuition regarding Proposition 3. It illustrates why δ^* is jointly optimal for the case where $\mu > \mu^*$. For

[19] We should note here that the result stated in Proposition 3 rests on the assumption that the foreign country is policy inactive. Section 3.4 derives the jointly optimal ERP policy when the foreign country responds to home's ERP policy via a local price control. This jointly optimal ERP policy differs from the one chosen by home in equilibrium (see Proposition 4 and the ensuing discussion).

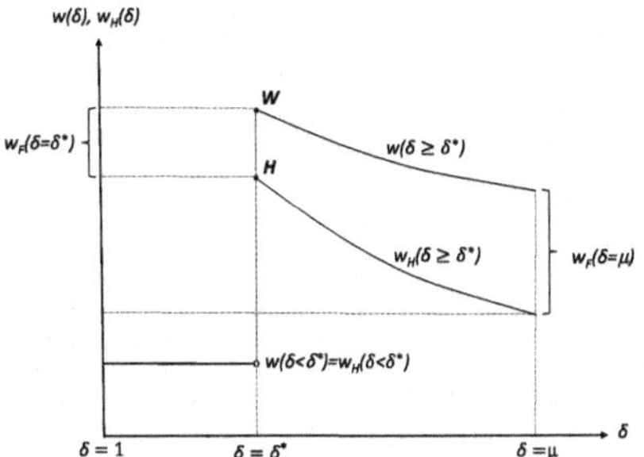

Fig. 1. Optimal ERP policy and joint welfare.

$\delta \in [1, \delta^*)$, the firm does not export and foreign welfare is zero so that joint welfare simply equals domestic welfare which does not depend on δ (when the firm only sells at home). The horizontal line shows that for $\delta < \delta^*$, $w = w_H$. If home's ERP policy is relaxed beyond δ^*, the firm starts to export and joint welfare w exceeds home welfare w_H by the amount w_F. However, as the figure shows, both home welfare and joint welfare decline with further increases in δ so that it is jointly optimal to not increase δ beyond δ^*.[20]

At the equilibrium ERP policy δ^* the price in the foreign market equals

$$p_F^* \equiv p_F^\delta(\delta^*) = \frac{n\mu}{1+n\mu} \tag{7}$$

Observe that since $n\mu \geq 1$, we have $p_F^* \geq p_F^m$ – i.e. the price in the foreign market under the equilibrium ERP policy δ^* implemented by home exceeds the price that the firm would have charged abroad in the absence of an ERP policy.

A well-known result in the existing literature is that for price discrimination to welfare dominate uniform pricing, a necessary (but not sufficient) condition is that the total output under discrimination be higher (Varian, 1985). As Lemma 1 notes, the total global output of the firm under price discrimination is indeed higher than that which it produces when facing an ERP constraint – i.e. the reduction in foreign sales caused by the ERP constraint exceeds the increase in home sales. However, it turns out that the positive effect of the ERP constraint on global welfare that arises due to a reduction in the international price differential dominates the negative effect of reduced global sales so that it is jointly optimal to restrain price discrimination to the lowest level that is necessary for ensuring that foreign consumers do not go unserved.[21]

While our benchmark model is useful for clarifying the mechanics of ERP policies, it does not address two important issues. First, it assumes that the foreign country's government is policy inactive. This is a potentially important shortcoming since the use of an ERP policy by home generates a negative price spillover for the foreign country, thereby creating an incentive for it to resort to a price control. Second, the benchmark model is silent on when and why a government would prefer to use an ERP policy over a standard price control. As we will show below, allowing the foreign government to directly control the price in its market not only allows us to understand the interaction between domestic ERP policy and the foreign price control but it also sheds light on the issue of when and why home prefers to use an ERP policy over a domestic price control.

3. ERP policy with a foreign price control

While price controls can take various forms, we model the foreign price control in the simplest possible manner: the foreign government directly sets the patented product's price ($\bar{p}_F$) in its market. Since the foreign country is a pure consumer of the patented good, its objective is to secure access to the good at the lowest possible price. If home does not impose an ERP policy, it is optimal for the foreign country to set the price control equal to the firm's marginal cost (i.e. $\bar{p}_F = 0$). In the absence of an ERP policy at home, the firm is willing to export for any foreign price greater than or equal to its marginal cost, and this allows the foreign country to impose its most desirable price control. Since the existence of an ERP policy at home causes the foreign price control to partly spill over to the home market thereby making the firm more reluctant to export, home's ERP policy *undermines* the effectiveness of the foreign price control.

To fully explore the nature of interaction between home's ERP policy and the foreign country's price control, we analyze the following three-stage game:[22] At the first stage, home chooses its ERP policy δ.[23] Next, foreign sets its local price control $\bar{p}_F$.[24] Finally, the firm chooses its domestic price p_H.

3.1. Pricing and export decision

As usual, we solve the game by backward induction. At the last stage, if the firm chooses to export, it sets p_H to maximize aggregate profit while being subject to an ERP policy at home and a price control abroad:

$$\max_{p_H \leq \delta\bar{p}_F} \frac{n}{\mu} p_H(\mu - p_H) + \bar{p}_F(1 - \bar{p}_F) \text{ where } \bar{p}_F \in [0, 1] \tag{8}$$

Assuming that the ERP constraint $p_H \leq \delta\bar{p}_F$ binds, the solution to the above problem requires the firm to set $p_H = \delta\bar{p}_F$ so that its total profit equals:[25]

$$\pi^\delta(\bar{p}_F) = \frac{n}{\mu}\delta\bar{p}_F(\mu - \delta\bar{p}_F) + \bar{p}_F(1 - \bar{p}_F) \tag{9}$$

In other words, when the firm faces an ERP policy at home and a price control abroad, it essentially has no freedom to choose prices if it opts to export: it charges $\bar{p}_F$ abroad and $\delta\bar{p}_F$ at home. If the firm chooses not to export, it charges its optimal monopoly price at home

[20] When $\mu \leq \mu^*$, the firm exports regardless of the ERP policy at home and in this case the discontinuity in Fig. 1 disappears: domestic welfare and total welfare both monotonically decline in δ so that it is socially optimal to set $\delta = 1$ (which is what the home country does in equilibrium).

[21] Under alternative assumptions regarding the structure of demand in the two markets, total output could very well be lower under price discrimination. Under such a situation, the ERP constraint is more likely to improve welfare since both effects (i.e. the reduction in the international price differential and the increase in global sales caused by it) would reinforce each other. See Schmalensee (1981).

[22] In Appendix A.1 we discuss the case where countries simultaneously choose their respective policies. As we show below, the simultaneous case is relatively tedious and our main insights emerge more sharply in the sequential policy game described above.

[23] In Section 4.1 we analyze a scenario where home chooses between a domestic price control and an ERP policy and describe circumstances under which each of the policies is preferable to the other – see Proposition 6.

[24] The foreign price control can also be thought of as the foreign government purchasing the good from the firm at the price $\bar{p}_F$ on behalf of local consumers. In Section 4.2 we extend this analysis to a situation where the firm and the foreign government bargain over price (as opposed to the foreign government having the power to determine it unilaterally).

[25] It will turn out that the ERP constraint necessarily binds in equilibrium.

and earns π_H^m. Thus, when facing a price control abroad and an ERP policy at home, the firm exports iff

$$\pi^{\delta}(\delta, \bar{p}_F) \geq \pi_H^m \tag{10}$$

Substituting the formulae for the two profit functions, this inequality binds at

$$\frac{n}{\mu}\delta\bar{p}_F(\mu - \delta\bar{p}_F) = \frac{n\mu}{4} - \bar{p}_F(1 - \bar{p}_F)$$

This equation can be solved for the *threshold ERP policy* (i.e. the ERP policy above which the firm exports) as a function of the foreign price control:[26]

$$\tilde{\delta}(\bar{p}_F) = \frac{\mu}{2\bar{p}_F} - \frac{1}{n\bar{p}_F}\sqrt{n\mu\bar{p}_F(1 - \bar{p}_F)} \tag{11}$$

Note that in the complete absence of policy intervention, the firm would charge its monopoly price p_F^m in the foreign market, which serves as the natural upper bound for $\bar{p}_F$ in the absence of an ERP policy at home. However, when an ERP policy is in place at home and it binds, the foreign price exceeds the monopoly level (*i.e.* $p_F^{\delta} \geq p_F^m$). Thus, in the presence of an ERP policy at home, the natural upper bound for the foreign price control is the choke-off price $\bar{p}_F = 1$.

Lemma 3. *The threshold ERP policy $\tilde{\delta}(\bar{p}_F)$ has the following properties:*

(i) $\partial\tilde{\delta}(\bar{p}_F)/\partial\bar{p}_F \leq 0$ *for* $0 < \bar{p}_F \leq p_F^*$ *with the equality binding at* $\bar{p}_F = p_F^*$.[27]
(ii) $\partial^2\tilde{\delta}(\bar{p}_F)/\partial\bar{p}_F^2 > 0$ *for* $0 < \bar{p}_F < 1$.
(iii) $\tilde{\delta}\,(\bar{p}_F = p_F^m) > \delta^*$.

Proof. See appendix. □

The first part of Lemma 3 says that if the foreign price control lies in the interval $0 \leq \bar{p}_F < p_F^*$ a tightening of the price control requires a relaxation of home's ERP policy if the firm is to continue to export. When $\bar{p}_F < p_F^*$, the foreign price control is below the firm's optimal price for the foreign market and a tightening of the price control lowers the firm's global profit under exporting, so the home's ERP policy has to be relaxed to offset the negative effect on the firm's incentive to export. This result is noteworthy since it shows that, over the range $0 \leq \bar{p}_F < p_F^*$, the foreign price control generates an international spillover by reducing the range of ERP policies that home can implement without undermining its firm's export incentive. Indeed, $\tilde{\delta}(\bar{p}_F)$ tends to infinity as $\bar{p}_F$ falls to zero: an extremely stringent price control ($\bar{p}_F \approx 0$) translates into a zero home price for any finite δ, so that there exists no feasible ERP policy that can provide the firm sufficient incentive to export.

The second part of Lemma 3 says that $\tilde{\delta}(\bar{p}_F)$ is convex in $\bar{p}_F$, indicating that the home's ERP policy must adjust to a larger extent as the price control abroad becomes stricter. This property of $\tilde{\delta}(\bar{p}_F)$ plays an important role in determining the jointly optimal pair of policies, an issue that we address in Section 3.4 below.

Part (*iii*) of Lemma 3 points out that even if the foreign price control is set at the firm's optimal monopoly price (i.e. $\bar{p}_F = p_F^m$) for that market, the export inducing ERP policy $\tilde{\delta}\,(p_F^m)$ is more lax than the policy that is chosen by home in the absence of a price control (δ^*). The intuition for this is that in the absence of a foreign price control, under the export inducing policy δ^* the foreign price actually exceeds the firm's optimal monopoly price abroad (i.e. $p_F^* > p_F^m$) so that a foreign price control set at p_F^m actually binds for the firm.

3.2. Foreign best response

Given the home's ERP policy, the foreign country picks the lowest possible price control that just induces the firm to export. For $\bar{p}_F \in [0, p_F^*]$ since the $\tilde{\delta}(\bar{p}_F)$ function is monotonically decreasing in $\bar{p}_F$, its inverse $\bar{p}_F(\delta)$ yields the best response of the foreign country to a given ERP policy of home. For $\bar{p}_F \in [p_F^*, 1]$ the $\tilde{\delta}(\bar{p}_F)$ function is increasing in $\bar{p}_F$ and there exist two possible price controls that yield the firm the same level of global profit for any given ERP policy. However, since it is optimal for foreign to pick the lower of these two price controls, the best response of foreign can never exceed p_F^*. Thus, foreign's best response curve coincides with the downward sloping part of the $\tilde{\delta}(\bar{p}_F)$ curve shown in Fig. 2.

3.3. Equilibrium ERP policy

Since home has the first move, it chooses its most preferred point on the downward sloping part of the $\tilde{\delta}(\bar{p}_F)$ curve in Fig. 2. For any ERP policy below this curve, the firm does not export so home welfare is at its lowest possible level whereas for any policy above the curve, home welfare can be increased by lowering δ: doing so lowers the home price without compromising the firm's export incentive. The following result is useful for understanding the equilibrium ERP policy chosen by home:

Lemma 4. *For all policy pairs that lie on the $\tilde{\delta}(\bar{p}_F)$ curve, changes in the foreign price control $\bar{p}_F$ affect the welfare of the two countries in the following manner:*

(i) *For all $\bar{p}_F \in (p_F^m, p_F^*]$ a reduction in $\bar{p}_F$ is Pareto-improving (i.e. makes both countries strictly better off).*
(ii) *For $\bar{p}_F \in (0, p_F^m]$, a reduction in $\bar{p}_F$ makes foreign better off at the expense of home.*

Fig. 2 is useful for explaining the logic of Lemma 4. The equilibrium policy pair in the absence of a foreign price control is given by point **E** in Fig. 2 the coordinates of which are (p_F^*, δ^*). To understand the intuition behind Lemma 4 first consider the case where $\bar{p}_F \in (p_F^m, p_F^*]$. Over this range, a reduction in the foreign price requires home to make its ERP policy less stringent ($\partial\tilde{\delta}(\bar{p}_F)/\partial\bar{p}_F < 0$)

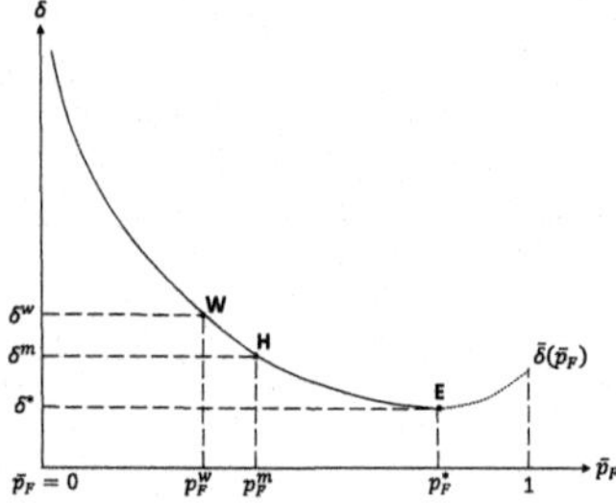

Fig. 2. Equilibrium policies.

[26] Observe that the ERP constraint necessarily binds so long as $p_H^m \geq \delta\bar{p}_F$ which is the same as $\delta \leq \delta^b(\bar{p}_F) \equiv p_H^m/\bar{p}_F$. Now observe that the ERP policy that induces the firm to export can be written as $\tilde{\delta}(\bar{p}_F) = p_H^m/\bar{p}_F - \gamma(\bar{p}_F)$ where $\gamma(\bar{p}_F) \equiv \sqrt{\mu n\bar{p}_F(1 - \bar{p}_F)}/(2n\bar{p}_F) \geq 0$. Therefore, $\tilde{\delta}(\bar{p}_F) \leq \delta^b(\bar{p}_F)$ which implies that the export inducing ERP policy necessarily binds. A detailed derivation of the expression for $\tilde{\delta}(\bar{p}_F)$ reported in Eq. (11) is contained in the appendix.

[27] *Note that* $\partial\delta(\bar{p}_F)/\partial\bar{p}_F \geq 0$ for $p_F^* \leq \bar{p}_F \leq 1$ but as we will show below, the equilibrium outcome never lies on this region of the $\delta(\bar{p}_F)$ *curve.*

to ensure that the firm's export incentive is preserved. But since $\left|\bar{\delta}(\bar{p}_F)/\partial\bar{p}_F\right|$ is relatively small in magnitude in this region, the direct decline in $\bar{p}_F$ dominates the increase in $\bar{\delta}(\bar{p}_F)$ so that $p_H^{\delta}(\bar{p}_F) = \bar{\delta}(\bar{p}_F)\bar{p}_F$ declines as $\bar{p}_F$ falls. Thus, *both countries gain from a tighter foreign price control* when $\bar{p}_F \in (p_F^m, p_F^*]$. Observe that home will not set an ERP policy tighter than $\delta\,(p_F^m)$, which we will denote simply by δ^m.

When $\bar{p}_F \in (0, p_F^m]$, any further reductions in the foreign price control require a sharp increase in the home's ERP policy in order to preserve the firm's export incentive. Here, a tightening of the foreign price control increases price at home (due to the sharp adjustment in its ERP policy) so that home loses while foreign gains from reducing $\bar{p}_F$. The following result is immediate:

Proposition 4. *In equilibrium, home implements the ERP policy* δ^m, *where*

$$\delta^m = \frac{1}{n}\left(n\mu - \sqrt{n\mu}\right).$$

This ERP policy is Pareto-efficient and it induces foreign to set its price control at the firm's optimal monopoly price (p_F^m) *for its market.*

The equilibrium policy pair (δ^m, p_F^m) is denoted by point **H** on Fig. 2. The reason point **H** is home's most preferred policy pair is that home price $p_H^{\delta}(\bar{p}_F) = \bar{\delta}(\bar{p}_F)\bar{p}_F$ declines in $\bar{p}_F$ when $\bar{p}_F \in (0, p_F^m]$ whereas it increases with it for $\bar{p}_F \in (p_F^m, p_F^*)$ so that, subject to the firm exporting, home price is minimized at point **H**. Intuitively, since the firm has the strongest incentive to export when its foreign price equals the optimal monopoly price p_F^m, by choosing to implement the policy δ^m home can induce foreign to pick the price control p_F^m. In the absence of a foreign price control, point **H** is unattainable for home since if it were to announce the policy δ^m the firm would export and its price abroad would equal $p_F^{\delta}(\delta = \delta^m) > p_F^m$ and its total profit would exceed π_H^m. But when the foreign price control exists and responds endogenously to home's ERP policy, home can implement δ^m knowing that foreign will impose the lowest price consistent with the firm exporting, which equals p_F^m. Thus, because it moves first, home is able to utilize the foreign price control to obtain a level of welfare that cannot be achieved in its absence.

Since the equilibrium foreign price equals p_F^m, from the viewpoint of foreign consumers the equilibrium outcome coincides with that which obtains when the firm is completely free to price discriminate across markets. Even though the firm charges its optimal monopoly price p_F^m abroad when home implements the policy δ^m, the ability of home to commit to an ERP policy makes foreign consumers *better off* relative to the case where there the foreign price control is absent because the foreign price under δ^* is strictly higher than that under δ^m (i.e. $p_F^* > p_F^m$).

Further note that as Fig. 2 shows $\delta^m > \delta^*$: i.e. home's most preferred ERP policy in the presence of a foreign price control is *more lax* than its ERP policy when there is no price control abroad. The intuition for this result is clear: absent the foreign price control, the firm raises its price abroad to p_F^* (which exceeds p_F^m) forcing home to set a stricter ERP policy to keep the domestic price low while preserving the firm's export incentive.

3.4. *Welfare: jointly optimal policies*

It is clear that a jointly optimal pair of policies must lie on the $\bar{\delta}(\bar{p}_F)$ curve in Fig. 2. Any combination of policies above this curve lowers welfare by widening the international price differential while any policy pair below the curve has the same effect by inducing the firm to not export. Furthermore, from Lemma 4 it is also clear that any jointly optimal price control has to lie in the range $(0, p_F^m]$. The jointly optimal pair of policies solves the following problem

$$\max_{\delta,\ \bar{p}_F} \; w(\delta\bar{p}_F, \bar{p}_F) \tag{12}$$

Substituting $\bar{\delta}(\bar{p}_F)$ into Eq. (12) and maximizing over $\bar{p}_F$ yields the jointly optimal price control:[28]

$$p_F^w = p_F^m(1 - \theta(n,\mu)) \tag{13}$$

where

$$\theta(n,\mu) = \frac{1}{\sqrt{1 + n\mu}} \tag{14}$$

Observe that

$$\frac{p_F^m - p_F^w}{p_F^m} = \theta(n,\mu) \tag{15}$$

Since $0 < \theta(n,\mu) \le 1$, the jointly optimal price control is strictly smaller than the firm's monopoly price for the foreign market (i.e. $p_F^w < p_F^m$). Indeed, $\theta(n,\mu)$ measures the percentage reduction in the firm's monopoly price abroad that is jointly optimal to impose. Since $\theta(n,\mu)$ is decreasing in n as well as μ, the more lucrative the firm's domestic market (i.e. the higher are n or μ), the less binding is the foreign price control. When either n or μ become arbitrarily large, $\theta(n,\mu)$ approaches 0 so that it becomes jointly optimal to let the firm charge its monopoly price in the foreign market. The jointly optimal ERP policy δ^w can be recovered by substituting $\bar{p}_F = p_F^w$ in Eq. (11). Since $p_F^w < p_F^m$ we must have $\delta^w > \delta^*$, i.e., the jointly optimal ERP policy in the presence of an optimally chosen foreign price control is *more lax* than when the foreign price control is absent. Thus, the foreign price control makes it possible to implement a more lax ERP policy provided the two countries coordinate their policies.

Finally, observe that home's equilibrium ERP policy δ^m is more stringent than the welfare maximizing policy δ^w (i.e. $\delta^w > \delta^m$) because it ignores the effect of its decision on foreign consumers. The welfare maximizing policy pair (p_F^w, δ^w) is denoted as point **W** in Fig. 2 and, for reasons explained above, it lies Northwest of the equilibrium point **H**.

4. Further analysis

In this section, we consider two important extensions of the policy game analyzed in Section 3. We first expand the menu of policies available to the home country by allowing it to choose between a direct price control and an ERP policy. Next, we extend the policy game to allow for a scenario where the foreign price is determined by bargaining between the firm and the foreign government as opposed to being set unilaterally by one party.

4.1. *An ERP policy or a price control?*

Thus far, our analysis has ignored the possibility that home might prefer a domestic price control to an ERP policy. We now extend the model to directly address this issue. Suppose at the first stage of the policy game home can choose between setting an ERP policy (δ) or a price control $\bar{p}_H$ with the rest of stages of the game remaining the

[28] It is easy to verify that the second-order condition holds at p_F^*.

same as in the three-stage policy game described at the beginning of Section 3.

We know from our previous analysis that if home uses an ERP policy then the equilibrium policy pair is (δ^m, p_F^m). Let home welfare under this policy pair be denoted by $w_H^m(\delta^m, p_F^m)$. Now consider the equilibrium outcome if home chooses a domestic price control. Unlike an ERP policy, a domestic price control does *not* affect the firm's foreign price and thus has *no bearing on its decision to export*. Therefore, in the second stage, foreign simply chooses the lowest price at which the firm is willing to sell in its market (i.e. it sets $\bar{p}_F = 0$ to maximize local consumer surplus). At the first stage of the game, home sets its price control to maximize its welfare knowing that the local price does not affect the firm's decision to export. Like foreign, home too finds its optimal to set the price control equal to the marginal cost of production (i.e. it sets $\bar{p}_H = 0$). Thus, when both countries use a price control, price equals marginal cost in each market and the firm makes zero profits. Let home welfare under $\bar{p}_H = 0 = \bar{p}_F$ be denoted by w_H^0 and firm profits in market i by π_i^0, $i = H$ or F.

From the perspective of home welfare, the trade-off between an ERP policy and a local price control boils down to the following: while a price control yields greater domestic surplus (defined as the sum of consumer surplus and firm's home profit), an ERP policy helps the firm earn greater profit abroad since the equilibrium price in the foreign market under the equilibrium ERP policy δ^m ends up being the optimal monopoly price p_F^m.

Let $\Delta\pi_F = \pi_F(\delta^m, p_F^m) - \pi_F^0$. Since $\pi_F^0 = 0$ we have $\Delta\pi_F = \pi_F(\delta^m, p_F^m)$. Similarly, $\Delta\pi_H = \pi_H(\delta^m, p_F^m) - \pi_H^0 = \pi_H(\delta^m, p_F^m)$. Furthermore, let Δcs_H be the amount by which consumer surplus at home under the ERP policy δ^m falls short of that under the price control $\bar{p}_H = 0$:

$$\Delta cs_H = -\frac{n}{\mu}\int_0^{\delta p_F^m}(t - \delta p_F^m)\,dt$$

Then, home prefers the ERP policy δ^m to the price control $\bar{p}_H = 0$ iff $\Delta w_H = w_H(\delta^m, p_F^m) - w_H^0 \geq 0$ which is the same as

$$\Delta\pi_F + \Delta\pi_H + \Delta cs_H \geq 0$$

where $\Delta\pi_H + \Delta cs_H \leq 0$ (i.e. the higher profit in the home market under its optimal ERP policy δ^m relative to the price control $\bar{p}_H = 0$ is more than offset by the accompanying loss in consumer surplus). Simplifying the the above inequality yields the following:

Proposition 5. *The home country prefers an ERP policy to a domestic price control (i.e.* $w_H(\delta^m, p_F^m) \geq w_H^0$*) iff* $\mu < \bar{\mu}(n)$ *where* $\bar{\mu}(n) = (2\sqrt{2} + 3)/n$.

This result sheds useful light on when and why a country might prefer an ERP policy to a domestic price control. If an ERP policy is in place at home, for all $p_F^\delta \leq p_F^m$ a stricter foreign price control translates into a lower home price (holding constant the ERP policy) and lower global profit for the home firm, something that tends to make exporting less attractive to the firm. Recognizing this link between prices in the two markets created by home's ERP policy, foreign is willing to push down its own price control only so far when home's price regulation takes the form of an ERP policy as opposed to a price control. In contrast, when home implements a price control rather than an ERP policy, there is no link between prices in the two markets and the foreign government is free to set its price control at marginal cost without affecting the firm's decision to export. While this outcome is desirable from the viewpoint of foreign consumers, it is not in the interest of the firm since it makes zero profits abroad when the foreign price control equals its marginal cost. An ERP policy can dominate a price control from the perspective of home welfare when the foreign market is not too different in size from the home own market so that the higher foreign profit ($\Delta\pi_F$) under an ERP policy dominates the loss in domestic surplus ($\Delta\pi_H + \Delta cs_H$) created by it relative to a price control. When $\mu > \bar{\mu}(n)$ the home market is significantly more lucrative for the firm than the foreign market and home's incentive to extract profit from foreign consumers is trumped by the loss in domestic surplus it suffers under an ERP policy relative to a local price control.[29]

It is worth noting that from home's perspective an ERP policy is dominated by a domestic price control when the firm does not face a price control abroad, i.e., $w_H(\delta^*, p_F^*) < w_H^0$. The logic for why the presence of a foreign price control makes it more attractive for home to use an ERP policy is as follows. First, recall that the firm is willing to export for all foreign price controls and ERP policy combinations that lie on the $\bar{\delta}(\bar{p}_F)$ curve. Second, in the presence of a foreign price control ($\bar{p}_F$), home can take advantage of the fact that the foreign government will set its price control $\bar{p}_F$ so as to ensure that the firm sells in its market. By contrast, in the absence of a foreign price control, home has to preserve the firm's export incentive entirely on its own. As a result, in the absence of the foreign price control, the only point on the $\bar{\delta}(\bar{p}_F)$ that is accessible to home is the pair (δ^*, p_F^*) whereas in the presence of an endogenously determined foreign price control, home can obtain any pair of policies on the $\bar{\delta}(\bar{p}_F)$ curve as an equilibrium outcome. This wider choice set allows home to pick its most preferred point on the $\bar{\delta}(\bar{p}_F)$ curve. Furthermore, we know from Lemma 3 (*i*) that home welfare strictly increases as we move along the $\bar{\delta}(\bar{p}_F)$ curve from point **E** towards point **H** (where it reaches its maximum value): as we move up the $\bar{\delta}(\bar{p}_F)$ curve from point **E** towards point **H**, the total profit of the home firm remains unchanged (equals π_H^m) whereas home price (p_H^δ) falls so that total domestic welfare increases.

4.2. Price bargaining

We now discuss the case where the foreign government and the firm bargain over price. The timing of moves is as follows. First, home chooses its ERP policy (δ). Next, the firm and the foreign government bargain over the firm's foreign price (p_F). We utilize the Nash bargaining solution as the outcome of the bargaining subgame. We first examine bargaining in the absence of side-payments and then consider the case where side-payments are possible between the two parties so that the price in the foreign market is chosen to maximize their joint surplus. We show that, from the perspective of home, an ERP policy can dominate a domestic price control under both scenarios.

4.2.1. Nash bargaining

It is clear that, given the ERP policy set by home, the range of prices over which the firm and the foreign government can find a mutually acceptable price is given by $[\bar{p}_F(\delta), p_F^\delta(\delta)]$ where the $\bar{p}_F(\delta)$ is the foreign government's most preferred price since it maximizes local consumer surplus $cs_F(p)$ (subject to the price being high enough to induce the firm to export) whereas $p_F^\delta(\delta)$ is that of the firm since it maximizes its global profit $\pi_G(p_F; \delta)$ where

$$\pi_G(p_F;\delta) = \pi_H(p_F;\delta) + \pi_F(p_F;\delta)$$
$$= \frac{n}{\mu}\delta p_F(\mu - \delta p_F) + p_F(1 - p_F)$$

[29] Observe that $\bar{\mu}(n)$ is decreasing in n. This makes intuitive sense: as the home market becomes larger relative to the foreign market (i.e. as n increases), the ERP policy becomes less attractive relative to a price control because domestic consumer surplus is proportional to n.

The price under Nash bargaining solves

$$\max_{p_F} \ \beta \ln[cs_F(p_F)] + (1-\beta)\ln\left[\pi_G(p_F;\delta) - \pi_H^m\right] \quad (16)$$

subject to $\pi_G(p_F;\delta) \geq \pi_H^m$. The parameter $\beta \in [0, 1]$ can be interpreted as the bargaining power of the foreign government relative to the firm. The first order condition for this problem is

$$\frac{\beta}{cs_F(p_F)}\frac{dcs_F(p_F)}{dp_F} + \frac{1-\beta}{\pi_G(p_F;\delta) - \pi_H^m}\frac{d\pi_G(p_F;\delta)}{dp_F} = 0$$

Using the relevant formulae, this first order condition can be rewritten as

$$\frac{2\beta}{1-p_F} = \frac{A(\delta,p_F)(1-\beta)}{p_F A(\delta,p_F) - n\mu/4}$$

where

$$A(\delta,p_F) \equiv \left[(n\delta+1) - [2(n\delta^2+\mu)]\frac{p_F}{\mu}\right]$$

It is straightforward to show that the solution to this equation is a price $p_F(\beta,\delta) \in [p_F(1,\delta), p_F(0,\delta)]$ where $\partial p_F(\delta,\beta)/\partial\beta < 0$.

Now consider home's ERP policy decision. Home sets its ERP policy taking into account the price $p_F(\delta,\beta)$ that emerges from the bargaining that follows its decision. When $\beta = 1$, the home's ERP policy is given by point **H** in Fig. 2. In this case, the firm has zero bargaining power and the foreign government effectively controls the price. As a result, home's most preferred policy ensures that the firm ends up charging its optimal monopoly price p_F^m abroad and therefore has the strongest incentive to export. When $\beta = 0$, the firm is free to pick any price abroad and home sets a much more stringent ERP policy with the equilibrium policy outcome being given by point **E** in Fig. 2. When bargaining power is split between the two parties, the firm earns strictly positive rents in the bargaining subgame and $p_F(\delta,\beta) > p_F^*$. At the first stage, home simply chooses its most preferred point on the $\bar{\delta}(\bar{p}_F)$ curve which will generally lie Northwest of point **E**.

Consider now the impact of bargaining on home's choice between an ERP policy and a local price control. We know from previous analysis that when $\beta = 0$ (i.e. when the home firm is free to set its foreign price) a domestic price control dominates an ERP policy whereas when $\beta = 1$ (i.e. foreign has all the bargaining power) an ERP policy dominates a price control if the countries are sufficiently alike (see Proposition 5). This suggests that the case for an ERP policy relative to a price control is likely to be stronger when the bargaining power of the domestic firm is lower. While analytical derivations are cumbersome, we have numerically confirmed this insight and illustrate in Table 1 below.[30] The last column of this table shows home's welfare gain (in percentage terms) from replacing the optimally chosen price control by the optimal ERP policy. The table illustrates that as the foreign government's bargaining power increases, the foreign price decreases and even though the home country relaxes its ERP policy, the price at home also falls. Furthermore, the higher the bargaining power of the foreign government, the smaller the amount by which domestic surplus under an ERP surplus falls short of he domestic surplus under a local price control and the higher the amount by which the firm's foreign profit under an ERP policy at home exceeds its foreign profit when it faces a price control at home. Perhaps most importantly, home prefers an ERP policy to a price control (i.e. $\Delta w_H > 0$) when its firm's bargaining position is weak relative to the foreign government (i.e. when β is higher).

[30] For the calculations presented in Table 1, we set $n = 1$ and $\mu = 4$.

Additional insight into the home country's choice between an ERP policy can be obtained by examining how this choice is affected by changes in μ– the key demand parameter that nails down the domestic monopoly price and therefore the relative profitability of the two markets from the firm's perspective. Table 2 shows that as μ increases, the loss in domestic surplus caused by an ERP policy relative to a price control increases whereas the gain in foreign profit experienced by the firm decreases.[31] As a result, the home country's welfare under an ERP policy exceeds that under a price control only when μ is not too large (i.e. foreign demand is relatively similar to domestic demand).

4.2.2. If side-payments are possible

Now consider the case where side payments are possible between the two parties so that the foreign price p_F is chosen to maximize their joint welfare.[32] In other words, given home's ERP policy δ, the foreign price is chosen to maximize the sum of the firm's global profit and consumer surplus in the foreign market:

$$\max_{p_F} \ S(p_F;\delta) \equiv \pi_G(p_F;\delta) + cs_F(p_F;\delta) \quad (17)$$

The solution to the above problem is described in the following lemma:

Lemma 5. *(i) Given home's ERP policy, the joint surplus $S(p_F;\delta)$ of the foreign government and the firm is maximized by setting $p_F = p_F^b(\delta)$ where*

$$p_F^b(\delta) = \frac{n\mu\delta}{\mu + 2n\delta^2} \quad (18)$$

(ii) $\partial p_F^b(\delta)/\partial n > 0$; $\partial p_F^b(\delta)/\partial\mu > 0$; and $\partial p_F^b(\delta)/\partial\delta > 0$ iff $\delta < \delta_B \equiv \sqrt{\mu/2n}$.

The jointly optimal price $p_F^b(\delta)$ has intuitive properties. As the home market becomes more lucrative for the firm (either due to an increase in n or μ), the two parties agree to set a higher price in the foreign market. The non-monotonicity of $p_F^b(\delta)$ in δ described in part (*ii*) of Lemma 5 can be understood as follows: when δ is small (i.e. near 1), the price in the home market is quite far from the firm's optimal home price p_H^m so that its global profit is well below its maximum value. Starting at $\delta \simeq 1$, the jointly optimal foreign price $p_F^b(\delta)$ increases in order to raise the firm's profit even though consumer surplus in the South declines. But once δ hits the threshold value of δ_B, the jointly optimal foreign price decreases with δ because the relatively lax ERP policy allows the firm to charge a fairly high price in the home market even though the foreign price is low. Note that $p_F^b(\delta)$ goes to zero as δ approaches infinity – i.e. if there is no ERP policy at home, the two parties agree to set price equal to marginal cost since doing so maximizes their joint surplus.

The firm's price at home equals $p_H^b(\delta) = \delta p_F^b(\delta)$. It is straightforward to show that

$$\frac{dp_H^b(\delta)}{d\delta} > 0$$

i.e. the price in home increases as home's ERP policy becomes more lax. Thus, a relaxation of the home's ERP policy makes domestic consumers worse off even when the foreign price maximizes the joint

[31] For the calculations presented in Table 2, we set $n = 1$ and $\beta = 0.8$.

[32] This would be the case if the two parties can make side-payments to each other to ensure that the jointly optimal price is charged in the foreign market. Of course, this does not maximize global welfare since neither party cares about consumer surplus at home.

D. Geng, K. Saggi / Journal of International Economics 109 (2017) 68–84 79

Table 1
ERP versus price control: the role of foreign bargaining power.

Foreign bargaining power (β)	δ^*	$\bar{p}_F(\delta^*)$	$p_H(\delta^*)$	$\Delta cs_H + \Delta\pi_H$	$\Delta\pi_F$	Δw_H	$\Delta w_H\%$
$\beta = 0.5$	1.867	0.652	1.218	−0.185	0.039	−0.146	−6.7%
$\beta = 0.6$	1.912	0.619	1.183	−0.175	0.076	−0.099	−4.6%
$\beta = 0.7$	1.948	0.586	1.142	−0.163	0.115	−0.048	−2.3%
$\beta = 0.8$	1.976	0.556	1.098	−0.151	0.157	0.006	0.3%
$\beta = 0.9$	1.993	0.527	1.050	−0.137	0.201	0.064	3.1%
$\beta = 1.0$	2.000	0.500	1.000	−0.125	0.250	0.125	6.3%

Table 2
ERP versus price control: the role of demand asymmetry.

Home demand	δ^*	$\bar{p}_F(\delta^*)$	$p_H(\delta^*)$	$\Delta cs_H + \Delta\pi_H$	$\Delta\pi_F$	Δw_H	$\Delta w_H\%$
$\mu = 3.0$	1.295	0.541	0.700	−0.081	0.158	0.077	4.8%
$\mu = 3.5$	1.634	0.548	0.897	−0.115	0.158	0.042	2.3%
$\mu = 4.0$	1.976	0.556	1.098	−0.151	0.157	0.006	0.3%
$\mu = 4.5$	2.318	0.562	1.302	−0.188	0.156	−0.032	−1.4%
$\mu = 5.0$	2.660	0.568	1.510	−0.228	0.155	−0.072	−2.8%
$\mu = 5.5$	3.001	0.573	1.721	−0.269	0.155	−0.115	−4.0%

welfare of the firm and the foreign government. Furthermore, we have

$$\frac{dS^b(\delta)}{d\delta} > 0$$

Since π_H^m is independent of δ, this implies that the joint surplus available to the firm and the foreign government from reaching agreement over the price $p_F^b(\delta)$ is higher when the home's ERP policy is looser. The intuition is straightforward: the firm's global profit as well as consumer surplus abroad increase when it has greater freedom to price discriminate internationally.

We assume that the bargaining process is such that the two parties agree to allocate the joint surplus created abroad at price $p_F^b(\delta)$ in the following manner: they first give each party a share of the total surplus that equals its payoff under disagreement and then share the remaining surplus between themselves with $\beta \in [0,1]$ denoting the share of the foreign government. Since the firm's profit under no agreement equals π_H^m, its payoff from reaching agreement with the foreign government under which it sells in the foreign market at price $p_F^b(\delta)$ equals

$$v^b(\delta) = \pi_H^m + (1-\beta)\left[S(p_F^b(\delta)) - \pi_H^m\right] \tag{19}$$

while that of the foreign government equals

$$w_F^b(\delta) = \beta\left[S\left(p_F^b(\delta)\right) - \pi_H^m\right]$$

Observe that for foreign sales to raise the total surplus available to the two parties and for the firm to prefer selling in both markets at price $p_F^b(\delta)$ to selling only at home at its optimal monopoly price p_H^m, we must have $S\left(p_F^b(\delta)\right) \geq \pi_H^m$. This inequality binds at $\delta = \delta^b$ i.e. we have:

$$S\left(p_F^b(\delta)\right) \geq \pi_H^m \Longleftrightarrow \delta \geq \delta^b = \frac{\sqrt{n\mu(n\mu-2)}}{2n} \tag{20}$$

i.e. if home's ERP policy is any tighter than δ^b then the firm is unwilling to sell abroad.[33]

The home government chooses its ERP policy δ to maximize local welfare taking into account the effect of its policy on the outcome of the bargaining process. It solves:

$$\max_{\delta} \; w_H^b(\delta) = \begin{cases} \pi_H^m + cs_H^m & \text{if } \delta < \delta^b \\ v^b(\delta) + cs_H^b(\delta) & \text{if } \delta \geq \delta^b \end{cases}$$

where $cs_H^b(\delta) = cs_H\left(p_F^b(\delta)\right)$. Since $v^b(\delta^b) > \pi_H^m$ and because $cs_H^b(\delta^b) > cs_H^m$ it follows that home will never set δ below δ^b. Furthermore, it is straightforward to show that

$$\frac{d(v^b(\delta) + cs_H^b(\delta))}{d\delta} < 0$$

i.e. given that the firm sells abroad at $p_F^b(\delta)$, home welfare declines in its ERP policy δ. Thus, in equilibrium, home sets its ERP policy at δ^b. We have:

Proposition 6. *Suppose the firm and the foreign government choose the foreign price p_F to maximize their joint welfare $S(p_F; \delta)$. Then, regardless of how the total surplus is split between the two parties, home's optimal ERP policy is δ^b at which the firm is indifferent between selling only at home (at its optimal monopoly price p_H^m) and selling in both markets while charging the price $p_F^b(\delta)$ abroad and $p_H^b(\delta) = \delta p_F^b(\delta)$ at home. Furthermore, the equilibrium ERP policy δ^b has the following properties: (i) $\partial\delta^b/\partial\mu > 0$; (ii) $\partial\delta^b/\partial n > 0$; and (iii) $\delta^b < \delta^m$.*

Several points are worth noting about the above result. First, since home moves first, it is able to extract all of the surplus created by bargaining between its firm and the foreign government by setting an ERP policy at which the total surplus available to the two parties at their jointly optimal price $p_F^b(\delta)$ equals the firm's profit from not exporting $\left(\text{i.e. } S(p^b(\delta)) = \pi_H^m\right)$. Second, home is able to implement a tighter ERP policy when negotiations between the firm and the foreign country yield the jointly efficient price $p_F^b(\delta)$ as opposed to the profit-maximizing price p_F^m $\left(\text{i.e. } \delta^b < \delta^m\right)$. Since total welfare is decreasing in δ (conditional on the firm exporting), price negotiations increase global welfare by resulting in a more stringent ERP policy even though they make the foreign country worse off relative to a situation where the price is chosen unilaterally by the firm. Intuitively, when price is not negotiated, home is limited in its ability to extract rent from the firm and the foreign country since, as argued earlier,

[33] Note that $\delta^b \geq 1$ only when $\mu \geq \mu^{**} = (1+\sqrt{4n^2+1})/n$, where $\mu^{**} > \mu^*$. In what follows, we focus on the case where $\mu \geq \mu^{**}$ is satisfied. When $\mu < \mu^{**}$, the efficient ERP policy is a corner solution (i.e. $\delta^b = 1$). We can show that even when $\delta^b = 1$ there exist parameter values for which home prefers an ERP policy to a local price control.

the bargained price in the absence of transfers must lie in the interval $[(\bar{p}_F(\delta), p_F^\delta(\delta)]$ over the $\bar{\delta}(\bar{p}_F)$ curve.

Finally, consider the comparison between an ERP policy and a domestic price control $\bar{p}_H$ when the firm and the foreign government choose the price to maximize their joint surplus. Given $\bar{p}_H$, the firm and the foreign government choose p_F to solve:

$$\max_{p_F} \; S_F(p_F) \equiv \pi_G(\bar{p}_H, p_F) + cs_F(p_F) \tag{21}$$

where

$$\pi_G(\bar{p}_H, p_F) = \pi_H(\bar{p}_H) + \pi_F(p_F)$$

Given that the firm's home profit $\pi_H(\bar{p}_H)$ is independent of the foreign price p_F, the solution to the problem in Eq. (21) is to set $p_F = 0$, i.e., when prices in the two markets are not linked – as is the case in the absence of an ERP policy at home – total surplus available to the two parties from the foreign market is maximized by setting price equal to marginal cost.

In the absence of an ERP policy, there is no link between prices in the two markets. As a result, when home uses a price control $\bar{p}_H$, the firm's payoff equals:

$$v^b(\bar{p}_H, p_F) = \pi_H(\bar{p}_H) + (1-\beta)[S_F(p_F) - \pi_H(\bar{p}_H)]$$

where $\pi_H(\bar{p}_H) = \bar{p}_H(n/\mu)(\mu - \bar{p}_H)$ is independent of p_F while $S_F(p_F)$ is independent of $\bar{p}_H$.

Let

$$S_F(0) \equiv S_F(p_F)\big|_{p_F=0}$$

and

$$v^b(\bar{p}_H, 0) = \pi_H(\bar{p}_H) + (1-\beta)[S_F(0) - \pi_H(\bar{p}_H)]$$

We are now ready to consider home's price control decision at the first stage of the game. It chooses its price control $\bar{p}_H$ to maximize

$$\max_{\bar{p}_H} \; w_H(\bar{p}_H) \equiv cs_H(\bar{p}_H) + v^b(\bar{p}_H, 0)$$

Since $S_F(0)$ is independent of $\bar{p}_H$, the above problem is the same as

$$\max_{\bar{p}_H} \; cs_H(\bar{p}_H) + \beta\pi_H(\bar{p}_H)$$

the solution to which is again $\bar{p}_H = 0$. Even though $\pi_H(\bar{p}_H)$ increases in $\bar{p}_H$ when $\bar{p}_H \leq p_H^m$, we know that $\beta \leq 1$ and welfare in the domestic market (i.e. $cs_H(\bar{p}_H) + \pi_H(\bar{p}_H)$) is maximized by setting domestic price equal to marginal cost.

Now we can compare home's equilibrium welfare under an ERP policy with that under a price control. It can be shown that[34]

$$w_H\left(\delta^b, p(\delta^b)\right) - w_H(\bar{p}_H)\big|_{\bar{p}_H=0} > 0 \;\text{ iff }\; \mu < \mu^b \;\text{ where}$$
$$\mu^b = \frac{2}{n}\left(\beta + \sqrt{\beta^2+1}\right). \tag{22}$$

[34] This welfare comparison applies for the case where the parameter values are such that the ERP policy δ^b is not at a corner solution (i.e. $\delta^b > 1$). As we noted earlier, this requires that $\mu \geq \mu^{**}$. Even when this condition fails (i.e. $\mu < \mu^{**}$ so that $\delta^b = 1$) we can show that home can still prefer the ERP policy δ^b to a domestic price control set at the firm's marginal cost ($\bar{p}_H = 0$).

In other words, once again, an ERP policy dominates price control when countries are similar enough, i.e. $\mu < \mu^b$. Note that μ^b is increasing in β, meaning that, once again, an ERP policy is more likely to dominate a price control when the foreign government's bargaining power is high.

5. Conclusion

This paper sheds light on the economics of external reference pricing (ERP) and how such a policy interacts with price controls abroad. We consider a model in which a single firm sells a patented product in potentially two markets (home and foreign) where, owing to differences in the structure of demand across countries, it has an incentive to price discriminate in favor of foreign consumers.

We model home's ERP policy as the degree to which the firm's foreign price is allowed to be lower than its domestic price and show that home's optimal policy is to tolerate a level of international price discrimination at which the firm is just willing to sell abroad. In other words, home balances the interests of local consumers against the export incentive of the firm. Intuitively, an ERP policy that is so stringent that it becomes profit maximizing for the firm to not sell abroad in order to charge its optimal monopoly price at home is never optimal for home. This result helps define the limits of ERP policies and it suggests that countries with large domestic markets (such as the USA or Germany) should use relatively less stringent ERP policies or else they can risk creating a situation where their firms choose to not sell abroad just so that they can charge high prices at home.

Almost by design, home's ERP policy generates a negative price spillover for foreign consumers in our model. However, quite surprisingly, we find that home's optimal ERP policy maximizes aggregate welfare even though it sets the policy not taking into account the interests of foreign consumers. Intuitively, since the home market is larger and its consumers have a greater willingness to pay for the firm's product, it is jointly optimal to reduce international price discrimination to the lowest possible level subject to the firm selling in both markets. This is exactly what home's nationally optimal ERP policy accomplishes in equilibrium. This result suggests that while ERP policies create international price spillovers, their use does not necessarily create an argument for international coordination. It is noteworthy in this regard that the TRIPS agreement of the WTO is silent on the subject of ERP policies for patented products and it also leaves member countries free to adopt exhaustion policies of their choosing, another type of policy that creates international price spillovers via the flow of parallel trade across countries.

Another insight provided by the model is that home's ERP policy reduces the effectiveness of the foreign price control since it increases the minimum price at which the home firm is willing to export. On the flip side, the presence of an ERP policy at home leads the foreign price control to generate an international spillover for home consumers although the nature of this spillover is not necessarily negative. Indeed, we demonstrate that there exist circumstances where a tighter foreign price control raises welfare in both countries. Furthermore, our welfare analysis shows that it is jointly optimal to restrict the firm's foreign price below its optimal monopoly price for that market while simultaneously granting it greater room to price discriminate internationally than home is willing to provide in the absence of a price control abroad.

While our model delivers several important insights, it does make certain specific assumptions (such as linear demand) in order to make sufficient analytical progress on key questions of interest. Nevertheless, we believe that the key driving force of the model – i.e. each country wants to secure access to the patented product at the lowest possible price taking the firm's incentives into account – is fairly general. Similarly, the insight that an ERP policy can be preferable to a local price control when the firm is subject to a foreign price control or is in a weak bargaining position abroad rests on a key aspect of an ERP policy that should continue to hold in a more general setting – i.e. unlike a local price control, an ERP policy links prices internationally and this can help the firm secure a more attractive price and therefore greater profit abroad.

Appendix A

A.1. Derivation of $\bar{\delta}(\bar{p}_F)$

Here we show that $\bar{\delta}(\bar{p}_F) = \frac{\mu}{2\bar{p}_F} - \frac{1}{n\bar{p}_F}\sqrt{\mu n \bar{p}_F(1-\bar{p}_F)}$. To simplify exposition, let $x = \bar{p}_F$ and $y = \delta$. The firm is indifferent between exporting and selling only at home whenever:

$$\frac{n}{\mu}xy(\mu - xy) + x(1-x) = \frac{n\mu}{4}$$

which can be rewritten as

$$\frac{nx^2y^2}{\mu} - nxy = x(1-x) - \frac{n\mu}{4}$$

Dividing both sides by nx^2/μ gives:

$$y^2 - \frac{\mu y}{x} = \frac{\mu(1-x)}{nx} - \frac{\mu^2}{4x^2}$$

This is a quadratic equation in y and the relevant solution is given by

$$y = \frac{1}{2x}\left(\mu - 2x\sqrt{\frac{\mu(1-x)}{nx}}\right)$$

which is the same as

$$y = \frac{\mu}{2x} - \sqrt{\frac{\mu(1-x)}{nx}}$$

which can be rewritten as

$$y = \frac{\mu}{2x} - \frac{1}{nx}\sqrt{\mu n x(1-x)}$$

which implies

$$\bar{\delta}(\bar{p}_F) = \frac{\mu}{2\bar{p}_F} - \frac{1}{n\bar{p}_F}\sqrt{\mu n \bar{p}_F(1-\bar{p}_F)}.$$

A.2. Alternative timing assumptions

Suppose the two countries set their respective policies simultaneously: home sets its ERP policy δ while foreign sets its price control $\bar{p}_F$. It is clear that given $\bar{p}_F$ the optimal ERP for home is the threshold policy $\bar{\delta}(\bar{p}_F)$. We now characterize foreign's optimal price control given home's ERP policy. If the firm does not export, foreign has no access to the good and its welfare equals zero. Moreover, conditional on the firm exporting, a more lax price control is counter-productive as it simply raises the local price. Hence, for a given ERP policy, foreign picks the lowest possible price control that just induces the firm to export. For $\bar{p}_F \in [0, p_F^*]$ since the $\bar{\delta}(\bar{p}_F)$ function is monotonically decreasing in $\bar{p}_F$, its inverse $\bar{p}_F(\delta)$ yields foreign's best response to a given ERP policy of home. For $\bar{p}_F \in [p_F^*, 1]$ since the $\bar{\delta}(\bar{p}_F)$ function is increasing in $\bar{p}_F$, it is optimal for foreign to pick the lowest price at which the firm is willing to export. Thus, foreign's best response curve coincides with the downward sloping part of the $\bar{\delta}(\bar{p}_F)$ curve. This implies that any point to left of p_F^* on the $\bar{\delta}(\bar{p}_F)$ curve (plotted in Fig. 2) is a Nash equilibrium. We can state the following:

Proposition 7. *Any pair of export inducing policies $(\bar{p}_F, \delta)$ where $\bar{p}_F \le p_F^*$ and $\delta \ge \delta^*$ constitutes a Nash equilibrium of the simultaneous move policy game. In all Nash equilibria, the firm's global profit equals π_H^m. For Nash equilibria in which $\bar{p}_F \in [0, p_F^*]$, the home price declines in the foreign price control (i.e. $\partial p_H^\delta(\bar{p}_F)/\partial \bar{p}_F = \partial[\bar{\delta}(\bar{p}_F)\bar{p}_F]/\partial \bar{p}_F < 0$) whereas for Nash equilibria in which $\bar{p}_F \in [p_F^m, p_F^*]$, it increases with it (i.e. $\partial p_H^\delta(\bar{p}_F)/\partial \bar{p}_F \ge 0$). Furthermore, $p_H^\delta(\bar{p}_F \to 0) = p_H^m$.*

Proposition 7 says that when the foreign price control is lax (i.e. $p_F^m < \bar{p}_F \le p_F^*$), a tightening of the foreign price control (i.e. a reduction in $\bar{p}_F$) lowers the home price through the adjustment of home's ERP policy whereas when the price control is relatively stringent ($\bar{p}_F \le p_F^m$), a further reduction in $\bar{p}_F$ raises the home price. The response of home's ERP policy to changes in the foreign price control (described in Lemma 3) is crucial to understanding the non-monotonicity of $p_H^\delta(\bar{p}_F)$. To see why, note that

$$\frac{\partial p_H^\delta(\bar{p}_F)}{\partial \bar{p}_F} = \bar{\delta}(\bar{p}_F) + \bar{p}_F\frac{\partial \bar{\delta}(\bar{p}_F)}{\partial \bar{p}_F} \tag{23}$$

so that if $\partial\bar{\delta}(\bar{p}_F)/\partial\bar{p}_F \ge 0$ then the home price would necessarily increase with the foreign price control since $\bar{\delta}(\bar{p}_F) > 0$. However, as Lemma 3 notes $\partial\bar{\delta}(\bar{p}_F)/\partial\bar{p}_F < 0$ whenever $0 < \bar{p}_F < p_F^*$, i.e., for this range of the foreign price control, home tightens its ERP policy as the foreign price control relaxes. This adjustment in the home's ERP policy tends to reduce the home price p_H^δ. Next, note that since $\partial^2\bar{\delta}(\bar{p}_F)/\partial\bar{p}_F^2 \ge 0$, the home's ERP policy adjusts to a larger extent when the foreign price control is stricter. Indeed, we can see this more directly by considering the elasticity of home's ERP policy with respect to the foreign price control, which is defined as

$$\varepsilon_\delta \equiv -\frac{\partial \bar{\delta}}{\partial \bar{p}_F}\frac{\bar{p}_F}{\bar{\delta}}$$

Observe that

$$\frac{\partial p_H^\delta(\bar{p}_F)}{\partial \bar{p}_F} \le 0 \Longleftrightarrow \varepsilon_\delta \ge 1 \tag{24}$$

It is straightforward to show that

$$\varepsilon_\delta \ge 1 \text{ iff } \bar{p}_F \le p_F^m \tag{25}$$

As a result, the home price declines in $\bar{p}_F$ for all $\bar{p}_F \in (0, p_F^m]$ whereas it increases with it for $\bar{p}_F \in (p_F^m, p_F^*)$.

The last statement of Proposition 7 says that as $\bar{p}_F \to 0$ the home price converges to the monopoly price p_H^m. This is because home has to completely drop its ERP policy (i.e. $\delta^*(\bar{p}_F)$ tends to $+\infty$) when $\bar{p}_F \to 0$ in order to maintain the firm's export incentive.

We have shown that when the two countries set their policies simultaneously there exist a continuum of Nash equilibria that constitute the downward sloping part of the $\bar{\delta}(\bar{p}_F)$ curve. Of course, as is clear from our analysis in Section 3, these equilibria have rather different welfare properties.[35] Furthermore, the firm's total profit

[35] In particular, note that there exist Nash equilibria where the foreign country's equilibrium price control lies above the optimal monopoly price for its market. Obviously, this happens when the home sets a very stringent ERP policy so that a high price in the foreign market is necessary to induce the firm to export.

does not play a role in determining the relative welfare ranking of these equilibria since in all Nash equilibria the firm's profit equals its monopoly profit under no exporting (π_H^m), i.e., the firm is indifferent between selling only at home and selling in both markets. From Lemma 4 we know that all Nash equilibria for which $\bar{p}_F \in (p_F^m, p_F^*]$ are *Pareto-dominated* by point **H** on the curve in Fig. 2 where home sets the policy δ^m and $\bar{p}_F = p_F^m$.

What if foreign selects its price control before home chooses its ERP policy? In such a scenario, foreign would set its price control equal to the marginal cost of production (i.e. $\bar{p}_F \simeq 0$) knowing that home will then impose no ERP policy on the firm in order to induce it to export. Price at home would then equal the optimal monopoly price p_F^m. Thus, the outcome when foreign chooses the price before home chooses its ERP policy coincides with that which obtains when home has no ERP policy in place at all.

A.3. Optimal reference basket in a three-country scenario

Suppose there are three countries: A, B and C and let $\mu_A \geq \mu_B \geq \mu_C = 1$. In what follows, we derive the optimal *reference basket* of country A. When setting its ERP policy, country A has four options: it can include only country B, only country C, both countries B and C, or none of them in its reference basket. We denote the alternative reference baskets by R where $R = \{B\}, \{C\}, \{B, C\}$, or $\{\Phi\}$. Country A's ERP policy requires that the firm's price in its local market be no higher than the lowest price it charges among all countries included in its reference basket. As will be shown below, country A's optimal reference basket depends on the firm's exporting decision, which in turn is affected by the degree of symmetry across the three markets as captured by μ_i.

When country A does not use any ERP policy (i.e. its policy is $\{\Phi\}$) the firm can charge a monopoly price in each country. We can write the firm's global profit in this case as the sum of its monopoly profits across countries: $\pi_G^m = \sum_i \pi_i^m$, $i = A, B$, or C. Each country's consumer surplus can be written as cs_i^m where $i = A, B, C$. Moreover, country A's welfare equals the sum of its consumer surplus and the firm's global profit: $w_A^m = cs_A^m + \pi_G^m$. World welfare is simply the sum of each country's welfare: $ww^m = \sum_i w_i^m$.

It is helpful to study country A's choice of its reference basket by analyzing three cases depending on the relationship between μ_A and μ_B. First, given that country A's reference basket is $\{B\}$, it can be shown that the firm exports to country B subject to the ERP iff $\mu_A \leq 3\mu_B$ and it only sells in country A if $\mu_A > 3\mu_B$. Second, when facing the ERP policy $\{C\}$, the firm exports to country C iff $\mu_A \leq 3$ and prefers to forego country C if $\mu_A > 3$. Thus the three cases we need to examine can be summarized as: (1) $\mu_A > 3\mu_B$; (2) $3 < \mu_A \leq 3\mu_B$ and (3) $\mu_A \leq 3$, where we have $\mu_A \geq \mu_B \geq \mu_C = 1$.

Also important to our analysis is the case where A's reference basket is $\{B, C\}$. In this case the firm can apply different pricing strategies depending on the relationship between the common price in countries A and C when it sells in both markets (denoted by $p(AC)$) and the monopoly price in country B (p_B^m). To see this, note that if $p(AC) \leq p_B^m$, then conditional on exporting, the firm can charge $p(AC)$ in country A and C and p_B^m in country B, which does not violate the ERP policy constraint of country A. Doing so gives the firm a higher global profit than charging a common price $p(ABC)$ in all countries. In contrast, if $p(AC) > p_B^m$ then the firm in principle has three options: (i) it can charge $p(ABC)$ in all countries or (ii) charge $p(AC)$ in country A and C while foregoing country B or (iii) charge $p(AB)$ in country A and B and forego country C. It can be shown that the second option is never chosen since it is less profitable for the firm than the first one. We can further calculate that $p(AC) \leq p_B^m$ iff (a) $\mu_B > 2$ or (b) $1 < \mu_B \leq 2$ and $\mu_A \leq \hat{\mu}_A \equiv \frac{\mu_B}{2-\mu_B}$ implying that $p(AC) > p_B^m$ iff $1 < \mu_B \leq 2$ and $\mu_A > \hat{\mu}_A$.

We are now ready to derive country A's optimal reference basket.

Case 1. $\mu_A > 3\mu_B$.

In this case, $\{B\}$ is dominated by $\{\Phi\}$. To see why, simply note that under $R = \{B\}$ the firm foregoes country B and charges monopoly prices in countries A and C, while under $\{\Phi\}$ it charges monopoly prices in all countries. Thus the firm's global profit is higher under $\{\Phi\}$, which also leads to higher welfare for country A. Analogously, it is easy to see that $\{C\}$ is also dominated by $\{\Phi\}$. Therefore, country A has to effectively choose between $\{\Phi\}$ and $\{B, C\}$. There are two sub-cases to be considered:

Sub-case 1.1: $p(AC) \leq p_B^m$.

Under $\{\Phi\}$, country A's welfare is w_A^m. Now consider the case where country A's reference basket is $\{B, C\}$. In this case, the firm has three options: (i) export to both foreign countries charging $p(AC)$ in countries A and C and p_B^m in country B or (ii) export to country B at price $p(AB)$ and forego country C or (iii) sell only at home at its optimal monopoly price. Since $\mu_A > 3\mu_B$, option (ii) is dominated by option (iii) from the firm's perspective. Moreover, it turns out that option (iii) also dominates option (i) when $\mu_A > 3\mu_B$. Therefore, $\mu_A > 3\mu_B$, the firm does not export to either market if country A sets its reference basket as $\{B, C\}$. It follows then that country A prefers $\{\Phi\}$ to $\{B, C\}$.

Sub-case 1.2: $p(AC) > p_B^m$.

In this case, if country A chooses $\{B, C\}$ the firm again has three options as in sub-case 1.1, except that its option (i) now becomes charging the price $p(ABC)$ in all countries. Given that option (ii) is dominated, we only need to compare the firm's global profit under options (i) and (iii). It is straightforward to show that the firm prefers option (i) to option (iii) iff $\mu_A < \tilde{\mu}_A \equiv 8\mu_B/(\mu_B + 1)$. Also note that country A's welfare is higher if the firm exports to country B and C since this helps lowers the price at home. Therefore, country A chooses the reference basket $\{B, C\}$ over $\{\Phi\}$ iff $\mu_A \leq \tilde{\mu}_A$.

Case 2. $3 < \mu_A \leq 3\mu_B$.

In this case, the firm exports to country B if country A's reference basket is $\{B\}$. Moreover, it is easy to see that from A's perspective $\{B\}$ always dominates $\{\Phi\}$ because it lowers price and improves consumer surplus at home. Thus, country A only has to decide between $\{B\}$ and $\{B, C\}$. To compare these choices, we need to consider two sub-cases.

Sub-case 2.1: $p(AC) \leq p_B^m$.

Under $\{B\}$ the firm charges the common price $p(AB)$ in countries A and B while charging its monopoly price p_C^m in country C. On the other hand, under $\{B, C\}$ the firm has three options: it can (i) export to both countries B and C charging $p(AC)$ in country A and C and p_B^m in country B or (ii) export to country B at price $p(AB)$ and forego country C or (iii) sell only at home at p_A^m. Since $\mu_A < 3\mu_B$ we know option (ii) dominates option (iii). Moreover, it can be shown that the firm prefers option (ii) to option (i) iff $\mu_A > \bar{\mu}_A \equiv \left(\mu_B\left(\mu_B + 1 + \sqrt{\mu_B^2 + 14\mu_B - 15}\right)\right)/2(3\mu_B - 4)$. Furthermore, if $\mu_A > \bar{\mu}_A$ then country A is better off under the reference basket $\{B\}$ since the firm still charges $p(AB)$ in country A and B but also exports to country C, hence making greater global profit.

Now consider the case where $\mu_A \leq \bar{\mu}_A$ so that the firm necessarily chooses option (i) under $\{B, C\}$. Comparing $\{B\}$ with $\{B, C\}$, it turns out that country A's welfare is higher under $\{B, C\}$. Hence country A prefers $\{B, C\}$ to $\{B\}$.

Sub-case 2.2: $p(AC) > p_B^m$.

When $p(AC) > p_B^m$, the option (i) under $\{B, C\}$ is to charge the common price $p(ABC)$ in all countries. Moreover, it can be shown that the firm always prefers option (i) to option (ii) under $\{B, C\}$. Comparing reference baskets $\{B\}$ and $\{B, C\}$, it is easy to show that country *A*'s welfare is higher under the latter.

Case 3. $1 \le \mu_A \le 3$.

In this case, it can be shown that country *A* prefers $\{C\}$ to $\{B\}$. The reason is that by referencing country *C* (as compared to *B*) an ERP policy can lead to a lower domestic price and thus higher consumer surplus in country *A*. To determine the optimal reference basket, country *A* needs to compare $\{C\}$ and $\{B, C\}$. As before, there are two sub-cases to consider.

Sub-case 3.1: $p(AC) \le p_B^m$.

As above under $\{B, C\}$ the firm can (i) export to both foreign countries charging $p(AC)$ in country *A* and *C* and p_B^m in country *B* or (ii) export to country *B* at price $p(AB)$ and forego country *C* or (iii) sell only at home (i.e. country *A*) at p_B^m. Given the set of permissible parameters for sub-case 3.1, the firm chooses option (i). Hence the reference baskets $\{C\}$ and $\{B, C\}$ are equivalent in the sense that they induce the same pricing strategy by the firm. As a result, country *A* is indifferent between $\{C\}$ and $\{B, C\}$.

Sub-case 3.2: $p(AC) > p_B^m$.

When $p(AC) > p_B^m$, under option (i) firm charges $p(ABC)$ in all countries under $\{B, C\}$ given it exports to both countries. Again, option (i) yields higher global profit to the firm than options (ii) and (iii). Moreover, country *A*'s welfare is higher under $\{B, C\}$ than $\{C\}$.

We can now state our main result:

Proposition 8. *Under an ERP policy set by country A that requires the firm's price in its market to be no higher than the lowest price it charges in the other markets in which it sells its product, country A's optimal reference basket is characterized as follows:*

(i) *When $\mu_A > 3\mu_B$ and $\mu_A > \tilde{\mu}_A$, country A's reference basket is empty (i.e. it is $\{\Phi\}$) and the firm is free to price discriminate internationally.*
(ii) *When $\mu_A \le 3\mu_B$ and $\mu_A > \bar{\mu}_A$, country A includes only country B in its reference basket and the firm is free to set its optimal monopoly price in country C.*
(iii) *When $\mu_A \le \tilde{\mu}_A$ and $\mu_A \le \bar{\mu}_A$, there are two possible outcomes: (a) if $\mu_A \le \widehat{\mu}_A$ and $\mu_A \le 3$ country A is indifferent between including only country C and including both countries B and C in its reference basket and (b) for all other parameter values, it prefers to include both countries B and C in its reference basket.*

Proposition 8 is illustrated in Fig. 3. As this figure shows, when μ_A is large relative to both μ_B and μ_C it is optimal for country *A* to not impose any ERP policy on its firm (i.e. its optimal reference basket is $\{\Phi\}$). When country μ_A and μ_B are similar in magnitude and both are large relative to μ_C, it is optimal for country *A* to include only country *B* in its reference basket. Finally, when both μ_B and μ_C are similar in magnitude to μ_A, it is optimal for country *A* to include both of them in its reference basket. Thus, the key insight of our two country model – i.e. the optimal ERP policy of the home country is more stringent when the markets of the two countries are relatively similar to each other – continues to hold in a three-country setting.

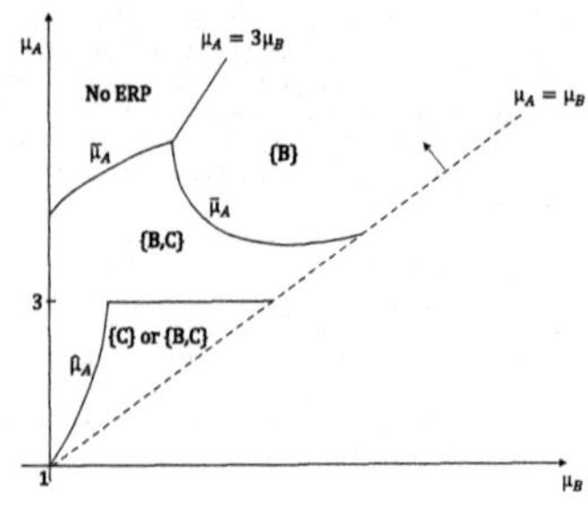

Fig. 3. Optimal reference basket of country A.

A.4. Proof of Proposition 1

(*ii*) It is straightforward to show that $p_H^\delta - p_H^m = \frac{\mu(\delta-\mu)}{2(n\delta^2+\mu)} \le 0$ iff $\delta \le \mu$. Also, we have $p_F^\delta - p_F^m = \frac{n\delta(\mu-\delta)}{2(n\delta^2+\mu)} \ge 0$ iff $\delta \le \mu$.

(*iii*) We have $\frac{\partial p_H^\delta}{\partial \delta} = \frac{\mu(2\mu n\delta - n\delta^2 + \mu)}{2(n\delta^2+\mu)^2}$. Observe that the sign of $\frac{\partial p_H^\delta}{\partial \delta}$ depends on the term $2\mu n\delta - n\delta^2 + \mu$, which is always positive when $\delta \ge \delta^*$. This implies $\frac{\partial p_H^\delta}{\partial \delta} > 0$.

We have

$$\frac{\partial p_F^\delta}{\partial \delta} = -\frac{\mu n(n\delta^2 + 2\delta - \mu)}{2(n\delta^2 + \mu)^2}$$

It follows from above that $\frac{\partial p_F^\delta}{\partial \delta} < 0$ whenever $\widehat{\delta} < \delta \le \mu$ where $\widehat{\delta} \equiv \frac{\sqrt{1+\mu n}-1}{n}$. Next, note that $\widehat{\delta} < 1$ whenever $\mu < n + 2$. But since we require $\delta \ge 1$, it follows immediately that whenever $\widehat{\delta} < 1$ we must have $\frac{\partial p_F^\delta}{\partial \delta} < 0$ for all permissible δ.

Now consider the case $\widehat{\delta} \ge 1$ (which holds whenever $\mu \ge n + 2$). In this case we also must have $\delta^* \ge 1$. This is because $\delta^* = \frac{1}{2}\left(\mu - \frac{1}{n}\right)$ is strictly increasing in μ and $\delta^*|_{\mu=n+2} \ge 1$ because $n \ge 1$. Furthermore, we have

$$\delta^* - \widehat{\delta} = \frac{\left(\sqrt{n\mu + 1} - 1\right)^2 - 1}{2n}.$$

from which it follows that $\delta^* \ge \widehat{\delta}$ if $\sqrt{n\mu + 1} \ge 2$, which requires $n\mu \ge 3$. But since $n \ge 1$ this condition necessarily holds whenever $\mu \ge n + 2$. Thus, whenever $\widehat{\delta} \ge 1$ we must have $\delta^* \ge \widehat{\delta}$. Since $\frac{\partial p_F^\delta}{\partial \delta} < 0$ for all $\widehat{\delta} < \delta$, it follows that $\frac{\partial p_F^\delta}{\partial \delta} < 0$ for all $\delta^* < \delta$.

Thus, we have shown that $\frac{\partial p_F^\delta}{\partial \delta} < 0$ for all $\delta^* < \delta \le \mu$.

(*iv*) We directly calculate $\frac{\partial p_H^\delta}{\partial n} = \frac{\mu\delta^2(\mu-\delta)}{2(n\delta^2+\mu)^2} > 0$, $\frac{\partial p_F^\delta}{\partial n} = \frac{\mu\delta(\mu-\delta)}{2(n\delta^2+\mu)^2} > 0$, $\frac{\partial p_H^\delta}{\partial \mu} = \frac{\mu\delta^3(n\delta+1)}{2(n\delta^2+\mu)^2} > 0$ and $\frac{\partial p_F^\delta}{\partial \mu} = \frac{\mu\delta^2(n\delta+1)}{2(n\delta^2+\mu)^2} > 0$. ■

A.5. Effects of ERP on domestic welfare

Straightforward calculations yield

$$\frac{\partial w_H^\delta}{\partial \delta} = -\frac{n\mu\delta\,(n^2\delta^3 + 3n\delta^2 - 3n\mu\delta + 2n\mu^2 + \mu)}{4(n\delta^2+\mu)^3}.$$

Since $n\mu\delta > 0$ and $4(n\delta^2+\mu)^3 > 0$, the sign of $\frac{\partial w_H^\delta}{\partial \delta}$ is determined by the term $g(\delta) \equiv n^2\delta^3 + 3n\delta^2 - 3n\mu\delta + 2n\mu^2 + \mu$. It suffices to show that $g(\delta) > 0$ for $\delta^* < \delta \leq \mu$. Now consider two cases depending on the value of μ.

First consider the case where $\mu > \mu^* = 2 + \frac{1}{n}$ (so that $\delta^* > 1$).

In this case, we have $g(\delta = \delta^*) = \frac{(n\mu+5)(n\mu+1)^2}{8n} > 0$. To show $g(\delta) > 0$ for $\delta^* < \delta \leq \mu$ it is sufficient to show $g(\delta)$ is increasing in δ over $\delta^* < \delta \leq \mu$. To see this, note that $\frac{\partial g}{\partial \delta} = 3n(n\delta^2 + 2\delta - \mu)$ so that $\frac{\partial g}{\partial \delta}|_{\delta=\delta^*} = \frac{3}{4}(n\mu+1)(n\mu-3) > 0$ whenever $\mu > 2 + \frac{1}{n}$. Moreover, we have $\frac{\partial^2 g}{\partial \delta^2} = 6n(n\delta+1) > 0$. This implies that $\frac{\partial g}{\partial \delta} > 0$ for all $\delta^* < \delta \leq \mu$. It follows that $g(\delta)$ is increasing in δ so that $g(\delta) > 0$ for all $\delta^* < \delta \leq \mu$.

Next consider the case where $\mu \leq \mu^* = 2 + \frac{1}{n}$ so that the firm sells abroad even when $\delta = 1$. In this case we need to show that $\frac{\partial w_H^\delta}{\partial \delta} < 0$ for all $1 < \delta \leq \mu$. Using similar logic above, it can be shown that $g(\delta = 1) = 2n\mu^2 + n^2 - 3n\mu + 3n + \mu > 0$ given $\mu \leq 2 + \frac{1}{n}$. Moreover, we have $\frac{\partial g}{\partial \delta} = 3n(n\delta^2 + 2\delta - \mu)$ and $\left.\frac{\partial g}{\partial \delta}\right|_{\delta=1} = 3n(n - \mu + 2) > 0$ given $\mu \leq 2 + \frac{1}{n}$. Since $\frac{\partial^2 g}{\partial \delta^2} > 0$ it must be that $\frac{\partial g}{\partial \delta} > 0$ for all $1 < \delta \leq \mu$ .It follows that $g(\delta)$ is increasing in δ and $g(\delta) > 0$ for all $1 < \delta \leq \mu$.

A.6. Proof of Lemma 3

(*i*) We have $\frac{\partial \bar{\delta}(\bar{p}_F)}{\partial \bar{p}_F} = \frac{\mu(\bar{p}_F - h(\bar{p}_F))}{2h(\bar{p}_F)\bar{p}_F^2}$, where $h(\bar{p}_F) \equiv \sqrt{n\mu\bar{p}_F(1-\bar{p}_F)}$. Observe that the sign of $\frac{\partial \bar{\delta}(\bar{p}_F)}{\partial \bar{p}_F}$ depends on the term $\bar{p}_F - h(\bar{p}_F)$. Solving $\bar{p}_F - h(\bar{p}_F) = 0$ for positive $\bar{p}_F$ we see it holds only when $\bar{p}_F = p_F^*$. It is also easy to check that $\bar{p}_F - h(\bar{p}_F) < 0$ when $0 < \bar{p}_F < p_F^*$. Therefore $\frac{\partial \bar{\delta}(\bar{p}_F)}{\partial \bar{p}_F} \leq 0$ for $0 < \bar{p}_F \leq p_F^*$ with the equality binding at $\bar{p}_F = p_F^*$.

(*ii*) We have $\frac{\partial^2 \bar{\delta}(\bar{p}_F)}{\partial \bar{p}_F^2} = \frac{\mu f(\bar{p}_F)}{4[h(\bar{p}_F)\bar{p}_F]^3}$ where $f(\bar{p}_F) \equiv n\mu\bar{p}_F^2(4\bar{p}_F - 3) + 4(h^3(\bar{p}_F))$. It follows that the sign of $\frac{\partial^2 \bar{\delta}(\bar{p}_F)}{\partial \bar{p}_F^2}$ depends on the sign of $f(\bar{p}_F)$. To establish the desirable result we need to show that $f(\bar{p}_F) > 0$ for $0 < \bar{p}_F < 1$. Note that $f(\bar{p}_F)|_{\bar{p}_F=0} = 0$ and $f(\bar{p}_F)|_{\bar{p}_F=1} = \eta\mu > 0$. Moreover, using

$$\frac{\partial f(\bar{p}_F)}{\partial \bar{p}_F} = 6n\mu(1 - 2p_c)[h(\bar{p}_F) - \bar{p}_F]$$

it is easy to see that there exist two inflection points for $f(\bar{p}_F)$ at $\bar{p}_F = \frac{1}{2}$ and $\bar{p}_F = p_F^* = \frac{n\mu}{n\mu+1}$. It can be shown that $f(\bar{p}_F) > 0$ at both these inflection points. Continuity of $f(\bar{p}_F)$ implies that we must have $f(\bar{p}_F) > 0$ and therefore $\frac{\partial^2 \bar{\delta}(\bar{p}_F)}{\partial \bar{p}_F^2} > 0$ for $0 < \bar{p}_F < 1$.

(*iii*) We have $\bar{\delta}(\bar{p}_F = p_F^m) - \delta^* = \frac{n\mu - 2\sqrt{n\mu} + 1}{2n} = \frac{(\sqrt{n\mu} - 1)^2}{2n} > 0$ given $\mu > 1$ or $n > 1$. ■

A.7. Further discussion of Proposition 4

(*i*) First consider the scenario where $\delta^m > 1$ which requires that $\mu > \mu_1(n) \equiv \left(2n + 1 + \sqrt{4n+1}\right)/2n$. Recall from Proposition 4 that in this case ERP dominates PC if $\mu < \bar{\mu}(n) \equiv (2\sqrt{2}+3)/n$. Thus, when $\mu > \mu_1(n)$, for the ERP policy to dominate a domestic price control we need $\mu_1(n) < \mu < \bar{\mu}(n)$ where $\bar{\mu}(n) > \mu_1(n)$ iff $n < \bar{n} \equiv 2 + \sqrt{2}$. As a result, when home's ERP policy is not a corner solution (i.e. $\delta^m > 1$) the ERP policy dominates a price control iff $\mu_1(n) < \mu < \bar{\mu}(n)$ and $n < \bar{n}$.

(*ii*) Now suppose $\delta^m = 1$ which happens whenever $\mu \leq \mu_1(n)$. In this case, it can be shown that from home's perspective an ERP policy dominates a price control iff $\mu < \tilde{\mu}(n) \equiv \sqrt{2} - n/2 + 2$. Combining the condition $\mu \leq \mu_1(n)$, we have that an ERP policy dominates a price control if $\mu \leq \mu_1(n)$ and $n < \bar{n}$ or $\mu < \tilde{\mu}(n)$ and $n > \bar{n}$.

References

Brekke, K.R., Holmas, T.H., Straume, O.R., 2011. Reference pricing, competition, and pharmaceutical expenditures: theory and evidence from a natural experiment. J. Public Econ. 95, 624–638.

Brekke, K.R., Ingrid, K., Straume, O.R., 2007. Reference pricing of pharmaceuticals. J. Health Econ. 26, 613–642.

Danzon, P.M., Epstein, A.J., 2012. Effects of regulation on drug launch and pricing in interdependent markets. Adv. Health Econ. Health Serv. Res. 23, 35–71.

Goldberg, P.K., 2010. Intellectual property rights protection in developing countries: the case of pharmaceuticals. J. Eur. Econ. Assoc. 8, 326–353.

Grossman, G.M., Lai, E., 2008. Parallel imports and price controls. Rand J. Econ. 39, 378–402.

Lanjouw, J.O., 2005. Patents, Price Controls and Access to New Drugs: How Policy Affects Global Market Entry. National Bureau of Economic Research Working Paper No. 11321.

Li, C., Maskus, K.E., 2006. The Impact of Parallel Imports on Investments in Cost-reducing Research and Development. J. Int. Econ. 68 (2), 443–455.

Malueg, D.A., Schwartz, M., 1994. Parallel imports, demand dispersion, and international price discrimination. J. Int. Econ. 37, 167–195.

Kyle, M., 2007. Pharmaceutical price controls and entry strategies. Rev. Econ. Stat. 89 (1), 88–99.

Miraldo, M., 2009. Reference pricing and firms' pricing strategies. J. Health Econ. 28, 176–197.

Richardson, M., 2002. An elementary proposition concerning parallel imports. J. Int. Econ. 56, 233–245.

Maskus, K.E., 2000. Parallel imports. World Econ. 23, 1269–1284.

Saggi, K., 2016. Trade, Intellectual Property Rights, and the World Trade Organization. In: K., Bagwell, R., Staiger, Chapter 18 of the Handbook of Commercial Policy. Elsevier.

Schmalensee, R., 1981. Output and welfare implications of monopolistic third-degree price discrimination. Am. Econ. Rev. 71, 242–247.

Roy, S., Saggi, K., 2012. Equilibrium parallel import policies and international market structure. J. Int. Econ. 87, 262–276.

Valletti, T.M., 2006. Differential pricing, parallel trade, and the incentive to invest. J. Int. Econ. 70, 314–324.

Varian, H., 1985. Price discrimination and social welfare. Am. Econ. Rev. 75, 870–875.

World Health Organization, 2013. Guideline on Country Pharmaceutical Pricing Policies. WHO, Geneva.

Chapter 18

Optimal price regulations in international pharmaceutical markets with generic competition[#]

Difei Geng*, Kamal Saggi

University of Arkansas-Fayetteville, 220 N Mcllroy Ave #422, Fayetteville, AR 72701, United States

ARTICLE INFO

Article history:
Received 17 April 2019
Received in revised form 25 February 2020
Accepted 4 March 2020
Available online xxx

JEL classification:
F10
F12
034
D42

Keywords:
External reference pricing policies
Price controls
Generic competition
Exporting
Welfare

ABSTRACT

In a two-country (home and foreign) model in which the home producer of a branded pharmaceutical product faces generic competition in each market, we analyze home's optimal policy choices regarding two major types of price regulations: external reference pricing (ERP) and direct price controls. Home's nationally optimal ERP policy lowers domestic price while maintaining the firm's export incentive. This ERP policy results in a negative international price spillover that the foreign country can (partly) offset via a local price control. Generic competition in either market reduces home's welfare gain from instituting an ERP policy. Weaker competition abroad or a greater weight on firm profits relative to consumer surplus in home's welfare function makes it more likely that home prefers an ERP policy to a price control. While international integration of national generic markets can improve welfare, such is not the case if it causes home to relax its ERP policy.

1. Introduction

The high prices charged by some pharmaceutical companies for their branded products are a serious health issue confronting consumers and policy-makers alike.[1] Governments concerned with limiting the adverse impact of such pricing behavior on consumers have a variety of price regulations at their disposal.[2] In addition to direct price controls, governments can utilize indirect price regulations such as *external reference pricing* (ERP) under which the price that a government permits a seller of a particular product to charge in its local market depends upon the seller's prices for the same product in a well-defined set of foreign markets.[3] Not only is such international referencing of prices practiced by a host of European countries, it has also been raised quite recently by President Trump

* Corresponding author.
E-mail addresses: dg017@uark.edu (D. Geng), k.saggi@vanderbilt.edu (K. Saggi).

[1] For example, see Howard et al. (2015) for a discussion of the rising prices of branded anti-cancer drugs.

[2] Ekelund and Persson (2003) show that the introductory prices of pharmaceuticals in Sweden have tended to fall over time due to the presence of intensive price regulations whereas they have tended to increase in the United States where such regulations have traditionally been quite weak.

[3] For example, Canada's ERP policy is based on prices in France, Germany, Italy, Sweden, Switzerland, the UK and the USA while that of France considers prices in Germany, Italy, Spain, and the UK. In a recent report, the World Health Organization (WHO) notes that 24 of 30 OECD countries and approximately 20 of 27 European Union countries use ERP (WHO, 2013).

[#] This chapter was originally appeared in *Journal of Health Economics* **71**, Article 102315.

as a possible means for lowering pharmaceutical prices in the United States (US).[4]

Of course, price regulations are not the only means for curtailing the market power of firms selling branded pharmaceuticals. Market competition from generics that possesses the same therapeutic qualities as branded products can potentially help achieve the same objective. The welfare gains resulting from generic competition have induced some countries to take measures aimed at increasing generic penetration rates in their markets. For example, in March 2015 France launched a national plan to promote the use of generics as part of the country's cost containment efforts. Furthermore, there seems to have been a decline in the market exclusivity periods enjoyed by branded drugs in some countries, mainly due to the more aggressive marketing strategies of generic manufacturers – see Dirnagl and Cocoli (2016).

Rules and regulations governing generics differ across countries but, generally speaking, generic producers are allowed to enter the market for a branded pharmaceutical product only after the patent underlying the branded product has expired or been successfully challenged in court. In the US, the Drug Price Competition and Patent Term Restoration Act of 1984, commonly known as the *Hatch-Waxman Act*, establishes the process via which firms can seek approval for producing generic molecules from the United States Food and Drug Administration (Lakdawalla, 2018). Provisions of this Act and analogous regulations in other countries give governments at least some ability to control the intensity of generic competition facing branded products in their markets. The duration of data exclusivity periods – during which generic producers are not permitted to use the safety and efficacy data generated by patent-holders – is one potential policy tool via which regulatory agencies such as the US FDA control the barriers to entry facing generic producers in their markets (Lakdawalla, 2018). For example, the Hatch-Waxman Act provides for a data exclusivity period of roughly 8 years in the US whereas the analogous period in Europe can be up to 11 years.

Our objective in this paper is to shed light on whether and how the presence of generic competition alters the welfare rationale behind two commonly used pricing regulations, i.e., ERP and direct price controls. Our analytical approach generalizes the two-country model of Geng and Saggi (2017) who examine cross-country policy linkages between ERP and price controls for patented products. There are two major modeling innovations of this paper relative to Geng and Saggi (2017). First, unlike Geng and Saggi (2017), the present paper allows for generic competition in each country's market. Second, this paper also derives the implications of allowing the home government to weigh firm profits differently than consumer surplus thereby providing a more general welfare analysis of ERP policies and price controls than Geng and Saggi (2017).

Incorporating generic competition in each market substantially generalizes the scope of Geng and Saggi (2017) since it makes their model applicable to pharmaceuticals that are under patent protection as well as those that are not (whereas the analysis of Geng and Saggi, 2017 applies only to patented products). This generalization is important since many countries (such as Austria, Portugal, and Slovenia to name a few) also apply ERP policies to branded pharmaceuticals that are no longer protected by patents. Moreover, an attractive feature of our modeling approach is that it captures the idea that the processes for the approval and marketing of generics differ across countries: an independent country-specific parameter measures the degree of therapeutic competition faced by the branded product in each market. This approach allows us to independently vary the intensity of generic competition in each country. For example, we can shut down generic competition in any market by setting the parameter measuring the degree of competition in just that market equal to zero.

Explicitly incorporating generic competition in the model in this way allows us to explore several real-world questions that are simply beyond the scope of Geng and Saggi (2017). More specifically, we address the following novel questions: How does a country's optimal ERP policy for a branded pharmaceutical depend upon the degree of generic competition faced by it? What type of international spillovers, if any, does local generic competition generate in the presence of an optimally chosen ERP policy? Does stronger generic competition enhance or reduce the welfare efficacy of an ERP policy? Do the welfare effects of generic competition depend upon whether such competition is national or international in scope?

In the model, a single firm produces a branded pharmaceutical product that it sells at home and potentially also in a foreign market. Since home consumers are assumed to value the product relatively more than foreign ones, the firm's optimal price at home is higher than that abroad. While the firm faces local generic competition in each market, it is free to price discriminate internationally since international arbitrage is assumed to be forbidden by the government of the high price market (i.e. home). As Lakdawalla (2018) notes, the international segmentation of markets created by such restrictions gives government some leverage over local pharmaceutical prices and motivates the use of various types of price regulations on their part. Before delving into an analysis of how policy choices of governments interact internationally, we first consider a scenario in which the foreign country is policy inactive and the only policy instrument available to the home country is an ERP policy that stipulates the maximum price ratio (δ) that the firm is permitted to sustain across countries (i.e. the foreign country serves as the reference country for home's ERP policy). We show that, given that the firm sells in both markets, home's ERP policy generates a negative international price spillover: it *raises* the price abroad just as it lowers it at home. Of course, the firm is subject to the ERP pricing constraint *only if it sells in both markets* and can therefore choose to evade this constraint altogether by electing to sell only at home.

When facing an ERP policy in its home market the firm weighs the incremental profit gain that accrues from sell-

[4] See "Trump Proposes to Lower Drug Prices by Basing Them on Other Countries' Costs,"New York Times, October 25, 2018. See also "How to Cut U.S. Drug Prices: Experts Weigh In"New York Times, December 10, 2018.

ing in the foreign market against the adverse impact that charging a lower price abroad has on its profit in the domestic market (due to the presence of an ERP policy at home). The home government, in turn, sets its ERP policy taking the firm's profit incentive into account. We show that, regardless of the degree of generic competition in each market, under home's optimally chosen ERP policy the firm (just) prefers serving both markets to selling only at home. Furthermore, the effect of generic competition on home's optimal ERP policy is determined by its location. Stronger generic competition at home lowers the firm's domestic profit and makes the foreign market relatively more appealing thereby increasing its incentive to export. This in turn allows the home government to *tighten* its ERP policy. On the other hand, stronger generic competition abroad makes the foreign market less attractive to the firm, which induces the home government to *relax* its ERP policy in order to maintain the firm's export incentive. Although the two types of generic competition have opposing effects on home's optimal ERP policy, the welfare gain enjoyed by the home country from instituting an optimally calculated ERP policy declines in the intensity of generic competition in *either* market. This welfare result implies that the ERP policies and generic competition act as *substitutes* so that the rise of generic competition in global markets should be expected to reduce the incentives that governments have to implement ERP policies and related price regulations.

An important insight of our model is that the presence of an ERP policy at home causes generic competition in one market to spill over to the other market. Moreover, whether this international spillover is positive or negative in nature depends crucially on the responsiveness of home's ERP policy to changes in the degree of generic competition as well as the location of such competition. Specifically, holding constant home's ERP policy, an increase in generic competition in either market lowers prices in *both* countries. But when home's ERP policy is endogenous, a strengthening of generic competition at home *lowers* the firm's price in the foreign country whereas a strengthening of generic competition in the foreign market *raises* price at home (because it forces the home government to relax its ERP policy to maintain the firm's export incentive). As one might expect, these price adjustments imply that the welfare effects of changes in generic market competition in the two countries are rather different in nature. In particular, while an increase in home generic competition raises welfare in both countries and is therefore Pareto-improving, an increase in foreign generic competition can actually hurt the home country and even lower joint welfare.

We build on our core ERP model by extending it to a three-stage policy game in which the foreign government is also policy active. In the first stage of this policy game, the home government chooses whether to impose a local price control ($\overline{p}_H$) or an ERP policy (δ) on its pharmaceutical producer. Next, the foreign government sets its local price control ($\overline{p}_F$).[5] Finally, the firm decides whether to export and then sets its price(s). Analysis of this policy game delivers several novel insights. First, in the presence of an endogenously chosen foreign price control, an increase in foreign generic competition *lowers* global welfare if the home country's market is relatively large compared to the foreign market. Second, the larger the size of the domestic market relative to the foreign one, the less likely it is that the home government prefers an ERP policy to a price control. This is because an increase in the relative size of the domestic market reduces the importance of safeguarding the firm's foreign profits (which we find to be the main advantage of an ERP policy over a price control). Third, domestic and foreign generic competition have rather different effects on home's choice between the two policy instruments: greater generic competition at home tilts the home government's choice in favor of an ERP policy whereas greater foreign competition has the opposite effect. Fourth, the higher the weight that the home country puts on firm profits relative to consumer surplus, the more likely it is that it prefers an ERP policy to a direct price control.

For the bulk of our analysis we assume that generic competition faced by the branded pharmaceutical product is local in nature. To determine how the scope of generic competition affects our main results, we also analyze the consequences of integrating the two national generic markets into a single global market. There are good practical reasons for addressing this question. For example, the European Union (EU) has been consistently pushing for a more integrated generic market for pharmaceuticals among its member states. There are multiple procedures within the EU through which a generic medicine can be approved simultaneously by more than one member state. Under the *centralized procedure* a generic medicine, once approved by any one member state, is automatically approved for sale in all the EU member states. Another approach relies on the principle of *mutual recognition* under which a generic drug approved by one country (called the "reference member state") is automatically cleared for sale in all other countries that recognize the first country's standard (called "concerned member states"). Both approaches can help integrate national generic markets that tend to be segmented due to international differences in regulations pertaining to the approval and sale of generics. We show that while the international integration of national generic markets can improve welfare, such is not the case if it results in a relaxation of home's ERP policy.

While we focus on reference pricing in an international context, reference pricing can also be internal and/or domestic in nature – under such policies drugs are grouped together according to some equivalence criteria (such as therapeutic quality) and a reference price within the same market is set for each group.[6] Brekke et al. (2007) provide an analysis of such internal reference pricing in a model in which two firms selling horizontally differentiated brand-name drugs compete against each other and a third firm selling a generic version, that like in our model, is perceived

[5] Since the firm's optimal foreign price is lower by assumption in our model, the foreign government can gain nothing from using an ERP policy and it is sufficient to focus only on its incentive to use a local price control.

[6] See Danzon and Ketcham (2004) for a description of the key prototypical systems of therapeutic reference pricing.

to be of lower quality by consumers. They compare the effects of generic and therapeutic reference pricing both with each other and with the complete absence of reference pricing.[7] One of their important findings is that therapeutic reference pricing generates lower prices than generic reference pricing.[8] Motivated by the Norwegian experience, Brekke et al. (2011) provide a comparison of price caps and reference pricing and show that whether or not reference pricing is based on market prices or an exogenous benchmark price matters a great deal since generic producers have an incentive to cut prices when facing an endogenous reference pricing policy, which in turn makes the policy preferable from the viewpoint of consumers.[9] Using a panel data set covering the 24 best selling off-patent molecules, Brekke et al. (2011) also examine the consequences of a 2003 policy experiment where a sub-sample of off-patent molecules was subjected to reference pricing, with the rest remaining under price caps. Their key finding is that prices of both brand names and generics declined due to the introduction of reference pricing while the market share of generics increased.

Our paper also contributes to the literature on the economics of exhaustion policies which determine whether or not holders of intellectual property rights (IPRs) are subject to competition from parallel imports which in turn determines their ability to engage in international price discrimination.[10] We add value to this literature in two important aspects. First, we focus on how ERP policies and price controls are possible means for controlling prices as opposed to potential competition from parallel imports. Second, while this literature focuses almost exclusively on patented products, our analysis focuses on branded products that face competition from generic producers.

[7] As Brekke et al. (2007) note, under generic reference pricing the cluster includes products that have the same active chemical ingredients whereas under therapeutic reference pricing the cluster includes products with chemically related active ingredients that are pharmacologically equivalent or have similar therapeutic effects. While generic reference pricing applies only to off-patent drugs, therapeutic reference pricing can also include on-patent drugs.

[8] Brekke et al. (2009) estimate the effects of a reform in Norwegian price regulation systems that replaced the price cap (PC) regulation with an internal reference pricing (RP) system. The authors find that RP is more effective than PC in lowering both branded and generic drug prices, with the effects being larger for branded drugs. Miraldo (2009) compares two different types of endogenous reference pricing policies in a two-period model of horizontal differentiation: one where the reference price is the minimum of the observed prices and another where it is a linear combination of them. In the model, the reference pricing policy is chosen in response to first period prices set by firms. The key result is that, in equilibrium, price competition between firms is less aggressive under the latter type of reference pricing policy.

[9] The Norwegian price cap regulation is an ERP policy where the reference basket is the following set of "comparable"countries: Austria, Belgium, Denmark, Finland, Germany, Ireland, the Netherlands, Sweden, and the UK. Unlike us, Brekke et al. (2011) focus on the domestic market and take foreign prices to be exogenously determined.

[10] See for example Malueg and Schwartz (1994), Maskus (2000), Richardson (2002), Li and Maskus (2006), Valletti (2006), Grossman and Lai (2008), and Roy and Saggi (2012).

2. How an ERP policy affects prices

Consider a world comprising two countries: home (H) and foreign (F). A single home firm sells a branded pharmaceutical product (x) whose quality is normalized to 1. The branded pharmaceutical product faces therapeutic competition from locally sold generics in each market.[11] For expositional ease, the unit production cost of both the branded product and the generic version are normalized to zero. Each country's generic market is assumed to be perfectly competitive so that, in equilibrium, the price of each generic equals marginal cost.[12] Let γ_i be the quality/effectiveness of country i's generic product as perceived by consumers, where $i = H, F$. We assume $0 \leq \gamma_i < 1$ so that, all else equal, consumers value generic products less than the branded version. This could either be because consumers are more loyal to the branded product or because they perceive the branded product to have higher quality than generics even though it may be no more effective in therapeutic terms than generics.[13]

Observe that the parameter γ_i also indirectly captures the intensity of competition faced by the branded product in market i: an increase in γ_i implies stiffer product market competition between the two types of products since, from the consumers' perspective, the two products become closer substitutes for one another. We let γ_i be a country-specific parameter because the perceived quality of generics can differ across countries, as can regulatory exclusivity due to differences in the scope of patent protection, the nature of procedures used for approving generics, and other types of market regulations that impact the ability of generic producers to compete with the branded product.

A consumer in country i buys at most 1 unit of the product regardless of its version. Let n_i denote the number of consumers in country i. If a consumer buys the original version her utility is given by $u_i = t - p_i$, where p_i is the price of the product and t measures the consumer's taste for quality. If a consumer buys the generic version her utility is given by $u_i = \gamma_i t$. Utility under no purchase equals zero. For simplicity, t is assumed to be uniformly distributed over the interval $[0, \mu_i]$ where $\mu_i \geq 1$. Given this preference structure, it is straightforward that consumers are partitioned into two groups depending on the taste parameter

[11] In the benchmark model we assume generic competition is *local*, i.e. each generic product is only sold in the domestic market. Later, in Section 5.1, we consider the case where generic products can be traded internationally.

[12] As Berndt and Newhouse (2012) note, it is indeed appropriate to model generic drug producers as price-takers operating in a perfectly competitive markets.

[13] One potential reason consumers may value the branded product more is because in many countries a person's ability to sue a drug manufacturer is limited to the branded company who created the label (i.e. generic producers do not face the same degree of product liability as firms producing branded products). For example, the US Supreme Court has ruled that people cannot bring design-defect claims against generic drug producers because such producers cannot redesign safer products while also complying with existing FDA regulations: redesigning a drug to make it safer effectively renders it a "new" drug as opposed to being a generic version of an existing branded product.

t: consumers in $[\tilde{t}_i, \mu_i]$ have a greater taste for quality and therefore buy the branded product whereas those in $[0, \tilde{t}_i]$ buy the generic where $\tilde{t}_i = p_i/(1-\gamma_i)$.

The two countries differ in three key aspects.[14] First, home consumers value quality relatively more, that is, $\mu_H = \mu \geq 1 = \mu_F$. Second, the home market is larger (i.e. has more consumers): $n_H = n \geq 1 = n_F$. Third, the degree of competition faced by the branded product can vary across countries i.e. γ_H needs not to equal γ_F.

The firm faces an external reference pricing (ERP) policy set by its home government which stipulates the maximum price ratio (δ) it can sustain across countries. Provided the firm sells in both markets, home's ERP policy imposes the following pricing constraint on the firm

$$p_H \leq \delta p_F, \tag{1}$$

where $\delta \geq 1$ represents the rigor of home's ERP policy; p_H and p_F are the firm's prices at home and abroad. Hence the firm's foreign price serves as a *reference* for its home price. A lower δ obviously implies a more stringent ERP policy because it gives the firm less room to price discriminate internationally. Note also that when $\delta = 1$ the firm does not have *any* room to price discriminate across markets. Since the general motivation behind ERP is to lower domestic prices, we focus on the case where $p_F \leq p_H$, that is, the home price of the branded product exceeds the foreign price.[15] It is straightforward to show that (see Appendix for details) the firm's optimal prices in the two markets when facing the ERP constraint given in (1) equal

$$p_H(\delta) = \frac{\mu\delta(n\delta+1)(1-\gamma_H)(1-\gamma_F)}{2[\mu(1-\gamma_H)+n\delta^2(1-\gamma_F)]} \text{ and } p_F(\delta) = p_H(\delta)/\delta \tag{2}$$

which can be used to calculate the firm's optimal global profit under the ERP policy δ:

$$\pi(\delta) \equiv \pi(p_H(\delta), p_F(\delta)) = \frac{\mu(n\delta+1)^2(1-\gamma_H)(1-\gamma_F)}{4[\mu(1-\gamma_H)+n\delta^2(1-\gamma_F)]}. \tag{3}$$

As one might expect, $\partial\pi(\delta)/\partial\delta > 0$, i.e. the firm's maximized global profit increases as home's ERP policy becomes less stringent.

It is useful to note that the firm's optimal market specific prices (in the absence of any ERP constraint) are given by

$$p_H^d = \frac{\mu}{2}(1-\gamma_H) \text{ and } p_F^d = \frac{1}{2}(1-\gamma_F). \tag{4}$$

As is clear, the use of an ERP policy can be an effective means for lowering the price at home only when $p_H^d > p_F^d$. Note that

$$p_H^d \geq p_F^d \Leftrightarrow \mu \geq \frac{1-\gamma_F}{1-\gamma_H}. \tag{5}$$

The above inequality shows that whether the domestic price exceeds the foreign price in the absence of an ERP policy depends on the degree of demand asymmetry across countries (as captured by μ) as well as differences in the intensity of generic competition in the two markets (captured by the ratio $(1-\gamma_F)/(1-\gamma_H)$). The higher is γ_F relative to γ_H, the stronger is the relative intensity of foreign generic competition and the higher is the relative price at home. Since $\mu \geq 1$, if generic competition at home is weaker (i.e. $\gamma_H \leq \gamma_F$), then the home price p_H^d necessarily exceeds the foreign price p_F^d. Condition (5) says that if $\gamma_H > \gamma_F$, for the home price to exceed the foreign price ($p_H^d \geq p_F^d$) we need the relatively higher demand pressure at home (captured by μ) on local price to dominate the relative downward pressure on prices exerted by generic competition in each market (captured by γ_i). In what follows, we will see that condition (5) is necessarily satisfied under all scenarios that are relevant for addressing the questions motivating our analysis. We can show the following:

Proposition 1. *If the firm sells in both markets when facing the ERP policy δ at home, the following hold:*

(i) The tighter the home's ERP policy (i.e. the smaller is δ), the lower the firm's home price and the higher its foreign price: i.e. $\partial p_H(\delta)/\partial\delta > 0$ and $\partial p_F(\delta)/\partial\delta < 0$.

(ii) Holding constant home's ERP policy, prices in both markets decrease with an increase in the intensity of generic competition in either market i.e. $\partial p_i(\delta)/\partial\gamma_i < 0$ and $\partial p_i(\delta)/\partial\gamma_j < 0$ where $i, j = H, F$, and $i \neq j$.

Part (*i*) of Proposition 1 says that a tighter ERP policy at home *lowers* the domestic price while simultaneously *raising* the foreign price. There is strong empirical support for these dual and opposing price effects of a country's ERP policy on local prices relative to foreign ones. For example, in their study of ERP policies in seven European countries for eleven pharmaceutical products, Kanavos et al. (2010) found that such policies lowered prices in those countries that based local prices on either the lowest (or the average) prices in their reference baskets. In our two-country model, owing to differences in demand across countries, the firm's foreign optimal price is lower than its home price but the basic idea is the same: a country instituting an ERP policy can lower the local price only if foreign prices are lower than the domestic price.

Kanavos et al. (2017a) note that when Croatia started to use the Czech Republic as a reference for its local pharmaceutical prices (as opposed to France where prices were relatively higher), local pharmaceutical prices in Croatia fell. In similar vein, Slovakia too experienced price reductions in 2009 when it started to base local pharmaceutical prices on average prices in the six lowest priced countries in Europe (Kaló et al., 2008; Leopold et al., 2012). Conversely, in the US – a country that does not use ERP policies or price controls of any type on pharmaceuticals – consumers find themselves paying significantly higher prices for branded pharmaceuticals relative to other parts of the world. For example, in their study of 79 drugs that accounted for 40% of all Medicare part D spending in the US, Kang et al. (2019) found that there was a wide gap between prices in the US and those in other countries: the ratio of US to foreign price for their sample of drugs ranged between 1.3 and 70.1. The authors conclude that the US could use ERP to signif-

[14] We later extend the model to allow for a foreign price control. As noted in the Introduction, price controls are highly prevalent in the pharmaceutical industry, which is where ERP policies occur most commonly.

[15] For example, drug prices in the UK tend to be lower than those in other EU countries and the UK does not use any ERP policy perhaps because higher foreign reference prices cannot help lower domestic prices.

icantly lower prices and improve local access to branded pharmaceuticals.

Consider now the slightly more subtle result that the domestic ERP policy causes a negative international spillover by raising the foreign price. As one might imagine, empirically identifying such international price spillovers is a rather challenging task. Yet, there is fairly convincing indirect evidence that such spillover effects indeed exist and are particularly worrisome for low and middle income countries who might find themselves at the receiving end of ERP policies implemented by richer countries (Goldberg, 2010). For example, in their study of orphan drugs spanning thirteen European countries, Young et al. (2017) note that while the use of ERP policies may have caused the absolute prices of such drugs to converge across countries, it also likely had the perverse effect of increasing net prices in poorer European countries that would have faced lower prices if ERP policies were not widely prevalent in Europe. The authors report that once buying power (via per capita national income) is taken into account, consumer access to such drugs in the lower income European countries such as Bulgaria, Romania, and Hungary was much worse than that in high income countries such as Norway, Sweden, France, and Germany because roughly similar prices of orphan drugs across these economically disparate countries implied a higher economic burden for consumers in countries with lower per capita incomes.

In a recent paper, Dubois et al. (2019) estimate a structural model of demand and supply for pharmaceuticals in the US and Canada to assess the potential role of ERP policies in the US. Their model accommodates the fact that Canadian prices are set via a bargaining process between firms and the Canadian government whereas US prices are unconstrained. The authors find that although the enactment of an ERP policy in the US would result in slightly lower prices locally, it would also impose large welfare losses on Canadian consumers because of the substantial increases in Canadian prices that would accompany such a policy change in the US. Thus, their study finds support for both local and international price effects highlighted by our analysis.

In our model, the reduction in domestic price of the branded product caused by the ERP policy lowers the market share of generics at home. Thus, the tighter the ERP policy enforced by the home country, the lower the market share of home generic producers. This result on the effect of home's ERP policy on the market share of generics fits well with the analysis of Danzon and Chao (2000) who note that market shares of generic producers competing with off-patent products are significantly higher in countries that permit (relatively) free pricing, such as the US, the United Kingdom, and Germany, relative to countries that have strict price or reimbursement regulations, such as France, Italy, and Japan. In their recent and detailed empirical study of generic drug markets in Europe and the US based on 2013 data on 200 off-patent active ingredients, Wouters et al. (2017) report a wide variation in the proportion of prescriptions filled with generics, from a low of 17% in Switzerland to a high of 83% in the US. No doubt this cross-country variation in the share of generics across countries partly reflects international differences in the processes by which generics are approved for sale. But it also stands to reason that by lowering prices of branded products, price regulations of various types make it harder for generics to capture market share. This perspective suggests that price regulations and generic competition substitute for one another to some degree, an issue we formally explore in Section 3.3 of the paper.

Part (*ii*) of Proposition 1 says that for any given ERP policy δ, an increase in generic competition in either market lowers prices in both markets. Thus, by linking prices across markets, home's ERP policy becomes a conduit for transmitting market conditions across countries. To the best of our knowledge, existing empirical studies have not (yet) examined how ERP policies can transmit market competition conditions across countries. However, the available evidence indicates that ERP policies do transmit price conditions internationally and whether price variations across countries are caused by market competition conditions or differences in demand owing to income differences is an interesting question for future empirical research to address.

3. Optimal ERP policy

The home government chooses its ERP policy to maximize national welfare. Provided the firm serves both markets, consumer surplus under the ERP policy in market i where $i = H, F$ is given by

$$cs_i(\delta) = \frac{n_i}{\mu_i}\int_0^{\tilde{t}_i(p_i(\delta))} \gamma_i t dt + \frac{n_i}{\mu_i}\int_{\tilde{t}_i(p_i(\delta))}^{\mu_i} (t - p_i(\delta))dt \tag{6}$$

where the first term captures the surplus enjoyed by consumers that buy the generic product while the second term measures the consumer surplus of those that buy the branded product. Total home welfare equals

$$w_H(\delta) = cs_H(\delta) + \pi(\delta) \tag{7}$$

whereas $w_F(\delta) = cs_F(\delta)$ and global welfare is defined as $w(\delta) \equiv w_H(\delta) + w_F(\delta)$. It is straightforward to show that

$$\frac{\partial w_H(\delta)}{\partial \delta} < 0 \tag{8}$$

i.e., domestic welfare declines as the ERP policy becomes less stringent. This happens because domestic price increases with δ and part of the increase in global profit experienced by the firm because of a greater ability to price discriminate internationally made possible by a more lax ERP policy comes at the expense of local consumers. While the firm cares only about its aggregate global profit, the home government takes into account the adverse effect of increasing local price on domestic consumers.

3.1. *Nature of optimal ERP policy*

In what follows, we first state our main result and then build intuition for it.

Proposition 2. *(i) The firm prefers serving both markets to selling only at home iff home's ERP policy is sufficiently lax: i.e.* $\pi(\delta) \geq \pi_H^d$ *iff* $\delta \geq \delta^*$ *where*

$$\delta^* = \frac{1}{2}\left[\frac{\mu(1-\gamma_H)}{1-\gamma_F} - \frac{1}{n}\right]. \tag{9}$$

(ii) Home welfare $w_H(\delta)$ is maximized by implementing the export-inducing ERP policy δ^*.

(iii) Home's optimal ERP policy δ^* is decreasing in the intensity of domestic generic competition ($\partial\delta^*/\partial\gamma_H < 0$) whereas it is increasing in the intensity of foreign generic competition ($\partial\delta^*/\partial\gamma_F > 0$).

(iv) Equilibrium prices in the two markets under this ERP policy are given by

$$p_F^* \equiv p_F(\delta = \delta^*) = \frac{n\mu(1-\gamma_H)(1-\gamma_F)}{1-\gamma_F+n\mu(1-\gamma_H)}$$

and

$$p_H^* \equiv \delta^* p_F^* = \frac{\mu}{2}\frac{(1-\gamma_H)(n\mu(1-\gamma_H)-(1-\gamma_F))}{1-\gamma_F+n\mu(1-\gamma_H)},$$

where $p_F^* > p_F^d$ whereas $p_H^* < p_H^d$.

Since the firm's maximized profit under the ERP constraint $\pi(\delta)$ when it sells in both markets is monotonically increasing in δ whereas its maximal domestic profit π_H^d is independent of it, there exists a unique ERP policy δ^* that solves $\pi(\delta) = \pi_H^d$. We call δ^* the *export-inducing ERP policy* since at $\delta = \delta^*$ the firm is indifferent between selling only at home and selling in both markets when facing the pricing constraint imposed by the ERP policy.[16] When $\delta > \delta^*$ we have $\pi(\delta) > \pi_H^d$ and the firm strictly prefers selling in both markets, whereas when $\delta < \delta^*$ we have $\pi(\delta) < \pi_H^d$ and the firm is better-off selling only at home. While setting its ERP policy, the government takes into account that the firm can escape the ERP constraint altogether by choosing to simply not sell in the foreign market and collecting π_H^d in the domestic market.

To understand the intuition behind why δ^* maximizes home welfare, suppose $\delta = \delta^*$ and consider how a reduction in δ affects domestic welfare. We know that for all $\delta < \delta^*$, the firm prefers to sell only at home at its optimal domestic price p_H^d. This implies that an ERP policy tighter than δ^* fails to exert *any* influence on the firm's price since under such a policy the firm does not export and there is no foreign price it has to take into account while setting its home price (making home's ERP policy irrelevant). Given that the firm charges p_H^d at home, for all $\delta < \delta^*$, domestic consumer surplus under the ERP policy δ exactly equals the level which obtains in the complete absence of an ERP policy (i.e. $cs_H(\delta) = cs_H^d$). However, since the firm does not export for all ERP policies tighter than δ^* and therefore earns no export profit, domestic welfare for all $\delta < \delta^*$ is *strictly lower* than w_H^d. Thus, an ERP policy tighter than δ^* can never be optimal from home's perspective: *home is better off eliminating the ERP policy altogether when $\delta < \delta^*$.*

Now consider why the home government has no incentive to raise δ above δ^*. We know that the firm continues to export if δ is raised above δ^* and in fact, its global profit strictly increases in δ (Proposition 1, part *iii*). However, total domestic welfare $w_H(\delta)$ is strictly declining in δ for all $\delta > \delta^*$ *since the loss in domestic consumer surplus from a higher local price dominates the firm's profit increase*. As a result, for all $\delta > \delta^*$, it is optimal for the home government to tighten its ERP policy all the way down to δ^*. Thus, the export inducing ERP policy δ^* maximizes home welfare.

As is clear, the firm's tendency to eschew the foreign market when it faces too strong an ERP policy at home is a crucial driver of our model. Considerable empirical evidence indicates that the presence of price regulations does induce firms to significantly delay (or completely avoid) the introduction of their products into new markets when they expect such foreign entry to have an adverse effect on their prices (and hence profitability) in their existing markets. For example, using launch data in 25 major markets, including 14 EU countries, of 85 new chemical entities (NCEs) launched between 1994 and 1998, Danzon et al. (2005) find that, controlling for per capita income and other country and firm characteristics, countries with lower expected prices or smaller expected market size have fewer launches and longer launch delays. They also note that these delays are noteworthy since companies have a strong financial incentive to launch early since patents have a limited duration. However, the risk of price spillovers makes companies more willing to delay launch or forego launch entirely in low-priced countries, particularly in countries with small markets.[17]

Using data from drug launches in 68 countries between 1982 and 2002, Lanjouw (2005) shows that price regulations and the use of ERP by industrialized countries contributes to launch delay in developing countries.[18] In similar vein, using data on 1444 drugs produced by 278 firms in 134 therapeutic classes from 1980 to 1999, Kyle (2007) finds that drugs invented by firms that have headquarters in countries that use price regulations are sold in fewer markets internationally and with longer delays than products that originate in countries that do not have such regulations. Danzon and Epstein (2012) uncover similar effects in their analysis of drug launches in 15 European countries over 12 different therapeutic classes during 1992–2003, i.e., the delay following a prior launch in a high-price EU country on a subsequent launch in a low-price EU country is stronger than the corresponding effect of a prior launch in a low-price EU country. Goldberg (2010) provides an insightful discussion of much of this evidence.

Our analysis suggests that optimally designed ERP policies should take export incentives of pharmaceutical companies into account. Of course, some degree of launch delay might simply be inevitable since governments cannot really fine tune ERP policies at the product level so that, when facing a common ERP policy that applies to a range of pharmaceutical products, only some producers are

[16] We break such indifference on the part of the firm in favor of exporting.

[17] In a recent paper, Maini and Pammolli (2019) develop and estimate a dynamic structural model to analyze the impact of ERP on launch delays using date on drug sales from Europe. They estimate that if ERP policies were removed then launch delays in eight low-income European countries would decline by as much as one year per drug.

[18] Lanjouw (2005) also reports a rather telling interview with a Bayer executive who states that Bayer chose not to introduce a patented antibiotic ciprofloxacin in India during the late 1980s because it was negotiating prices with several developed country markets at that time and it did not want those prices to be affected by its launch in India.

likely to find it optimal to forego foreign markets in order to preserve optimal prices in their relatively more important markets.

Observe from (9) that $\delta^* \geq 1$ iff $\mu \geq \mu^*$ where

$$\mu^* \equiv \frac{2n+1}{n}\frac{1-\gamma_F}{1-\gamma_H}. \tag{10}$$

In other words, the home government picks an interior ERP policy that gives the firm some room to price discriminate internationally (i.e. for $\delta^* > 1$) only when the domestic market is sufficiently larger than the foreign one (i.e. $\mu > \mu^*$). When the two markets are fairly similar, i.e. $\mu \leq \mu^*$, the firm is willing to sell abroad even under the strictest possible ERP policy (i.e. $\delta^* = 1$). Intuitively, when $\mu \leq \mu^*$ the foreign market is attractive enough to the firm that it is willing to sell there even when it has *no room* to price discriminate internationally. Thus, our model suggests that the ERP policies of countries with smaller markets are likely to be more stringent relative to those of larger countries.

While real-world ERP policies are more nuanced and complex than our analytical formulation, several pieces of indirect evidence indicate that the nature of observed ERP policies is quite consistent with our model. First, the *range* of pharmaceutical products subject to ERP policies seems to be larger in smaller countries in the sense that they are more likely to impose such policies on pharmaceuticals even when they are no longer protected by patents. For example, Rémuzat et al. (2015) and Kanavos et al. (2017b) note that it is more common for smaller countries to apply ERP to both on and off-patent drugs.[19] Similarly, it is more common for smaller countries (such as Belgium, Romania, Egypt, Jordan, UAE, and Turkey) to apply ERP to all drugs regardless of whether they are included in the national positive list (Kanavos et al., 2017a). Yet another piece of corroborating evidence is found in the *specification of the external price* that is used as a reference price by various European countries: Rémuzat et al. (2015) report that richer countries (such as Austria, Denmark, the Netherlands, and Switzerland) are more likely to use the mean price of their reference basket whereas poorer countries (such as Bulgaria, Romania, Hungary, and Slovenia) tend to use the lowest price. Clearly, basing the local price on the lowest price in the reference basket is a more stringent ERP policy. Evidence from outside Europe is also broadly consistent. For example, rich countries like Japan and Canada tend to use the average price in their reference baskets as the reference price whereas Turkey tends to use the lowest price in its reference basket. The final bit of evidence concerns the *composition* of the reference basket itself. It is well known that when setting their ERP policies, many countries typically tend to include only foreign countries with similar market sizes and per capita incomes in their reference baskets. For example, EU countries do not set ERP policies on the basis of prices in Asian or African developing countries. If lowering local prices were the sole motivation of ERP policies, European governments should be using the lowest available foreign prices while setting their ERP policies. The insight provided by our analysis is that setting too stringent an ERP policy can be counterproductive for a rich country since it can cause firms to forsake low-price markets abroad just so that they can sustain high prices in their relatively lucrative markets.

The intuition for part (*iii*) of Proposition 2 is as follows. More intense generic competition at home reduces the firm's local profit thereby making it more willing to export which in turn increases its tolerance for a tighter ERP policy at home. On the other hand, higher foreign competition renders the firm less willing to export so that the ERP policy needs to be looser to maintain the firm's incentive to export. As a result, home and foreign generic competition affect the export inducing ERP policy δ^* in opposite directions. Also, note that if $\gamma_H = \gamma_F$ then $\delta^* = \frac{1}{2}(\mu - \frac{1}{n})$ which is the same as the export inducing ERP policy in the *absence* of generic competition in either market. In other words, when generic competition is equally strong in both markets, although it lowers the absolute value of the firm's profit in each market, it does not affect its incentive to export since that depends upon its global profit under exporting *relative* to its domestic profit from selling only at home.

Since the corner case of $\delta^* = 1$ is relatively uninteresting, through-out the rest of the paper, we assume that the following inequality holds:

Assumption 1. $\mu \geq \mu^* \Leftrightarrow \delta^* \geq 1.$

Note that when Assumption 1 holds Condition (5) is automatically satisfied, i.e. $\mu \geq \mu^* \Rightarrow \mu \geq (1-\gamma_F)/(1-\gamma_H)$.

3.2. Price and welfare effects of generic competition

We now examine how generic competition affects prices when home's ERP policy adjusts endogenously in response to changes in market conditions:

Lemma 1. *(i)* $\partial p_H^*/\partial \gamma_H < 0$; *(ii)* $\partial p_F^*/\partial \gamma_H < 0$; *(iii)* $\partial p_H^*/\partial \gamma_F > 0$ *and (iv)* $\partial p_F^*/\partial \gamma_F < 0$.

As expected, an increase in home generic competition lowers domestic price. It is worth noting that this happens due to two reasons in our model. First, holding constant the ERP policy, competition directly lowers the market power of the firm. Second, the reduction in domestic profits makes exporting more attractive to the firm which in turn allows the home government to tighten its ERP policy. Both of these factors reinforce each other, leading to a decline in the firm's domestic price. The second part of Lemma 1 shows that changes in competition in the home market are transmitted abroad via home's ERP policy. On the one hand, an increase in generic competition at home pushes down the domestic price, which lowers the foreign price for a given level of ERP policy (since home price is simply a multiple of the foreign price, i.e. $p_H^* = \delta^* p_F^*$). On the other, an increase in domestic generic competition induces the home government to tighten its ERP policy (i.e. lower δ^*) and this tends to increase the foreign price (since $\partial p_F/\partial \delta < 0$). It turns out that the direct effect of an increase in local generic competition dominates the spillover effect created by the adjustment in home's ERP policy so that, on net, an increase in domestic generic competition lowers the foreign price. Part (*iii*)

[19] These countries include Austria, Bulgaria, Czech, Latvia, Poland, Portugal, Romania, Slovakia, Slovenia, Jordan, and Lebanon.

of Lemma 1 reports a counter-intuitive result: *a strengthening of generic competition in the foreign market raises the home price.* As is clear, competition from foreign generics makes exporting less attractive to the firm. As a result, home government has to relax its ERP policy to maintain the firm's export incentive and this tends to drive up the home price. On the other hand, foreign generic competition puts a downward pressure on the foreign price and this tends to lower the home price through the international price linkage created by home's ERP policy. Nevertheless, it turns out that the local effect created by the relaxation of home's ERP policy dominates the international spillover generated by the reduction in the foreign price so that the home price ends up increasing with a strengthening of foreign generic competition. The last part of Lemma 1 says that foreign generic competition serves to reduce price in the foreign market. For one thing, such competition lowers the firm's market power in the foreign market and forces it to lower its local price. For another, home's ERP policy *relaxes* in response to foreign competition and this further reduces the foreign price. Let $w_i^* = w_i(\delta = \delta^*)$ be country i's welfare under the equilibrium ERP policy δ^* so that $w^* = w_H^* + w_F^*$ denotes global welfare under δ^*. We can now describe the equilibrium welfare effects of changes in generic competition in the two markets:

Proposition 3. *In the presence of an optimally chosen ERP policy at home, an increase in generic competition at home raises welfare in both countries (i.e. $\partial w_H^*/\partial \gamma_H > 0$, $\partial w_F^*/\partial \gamma_H > 0$ and $\partial w^*/\partial \gamma_H > 0$), whereas an increase in generic competition abroad lowers home welfare, increases foreign welfare, and has no effect on global welfare (i.e. $\partial w_H^*/\partial \gamma_F < 0$, $\partial w_F^*/\partial \gamma_F > 0$ and $\partial w^*/\partial \gamma_F = 0$).*

Proposition 3 indicates that the welfare impacts of changes in the degree of generic competition in the two markets can be very different in nature due to the endogenous adjustment in home's ERP policy that accompanies such changes. As already shown, home generic competition lowers prices and raises consumer surplus in both markets. The associated reductions in the deadweight loss in both markets ensure that the welfare gains generated by increased competition dominate the loss in firm's global profit, so that global welfare increases. On the other hand, foreign competition lowers the foreign price (and therefore raises its welfare) whereas it raises home price (and therefore reduces home welfare). These two conflicting welfare effects end up perfectly offsetting each other so that changes in foreign generic competition do not affect aggregate global welfare. This perfect offsetting is surely an artifact of the specific structure of our model. However, the important point to note here is that changes in generic market competition that induce the firm to reduce its international price differential (due to a tightening of the ERP constraint faced by it) are necessarily welfare improving whereas increases in market competition that cause it to engage in a greater degree of international price discrimination generate a negative welfare effect that undermines the direct benefits of increased competition.

3.3. Generic competition and the welfare rationale for ERP

Since all government regulations are costly to implement in the real world, it is worth asking how the welfare gain delivered by an optimally chosen ERP policy depends upon the degree and scope of generic competition faced by the firm.[20] In other words, how does the marginal benefit of introducing an ERP policy at home depend upon the intensity of generic competition? Home's welfare gain from implementing an optimal ERP policy is measured by

$$\Delta w_H^* = w_H^* - w_H^d.$$

We can show the following:

Proposition 4. *An increase in generic competition in either market reduces home's welfare gain from implementing an ERP policy: $\partial \Delta w_H^*/\partial \gamma_i < 0$ for i = H, F.*

The intuition behind Proposition 4 is the following. Home generic competition lowers the potential gains for the home country from using an ERP policy because it helps reduce the domestic price of the branded product and makes further price containment less valuable. On the other hand, an increase in foreign generic competition reduces the effectiveness of home's ERP policy since it causes the home price to increase by inducing a relaxation in home's ERP policy, which in turn reduces home's welfare gain from introducing such a policy in the first place.

Proposition 4 has clear empirical implications: *all else equal, ERP policies should be more likely to be used by governments when generic competition is weaker.* This implication is consistent with the existing real-world evidence on the use of ERP policies: it is well known that developed countries use ERP policies to regulate prices of patented products much more frequently than they do for off-patent products (WHO, 2013). The insight provided by our model is that the presence of generic competition reduces the marginal benefit of instituting an ERP policy since part of the objective of lowering local prices via an ERP policy is already provided to some degree by generic competition. ERP policies provide a greater welfare kick when applied to patented products since such products typically do not face generic competition.

There is little direct empirical evidence on the role of ERP in the presence of generic competition, perhaps because this connection has not even been explored yet in any theoretical study. To the best of our knowledge, the only empirical paper that explores the joint impact of reference pricing and generic competition on prices is Koskinen et al. (2014). This study assesses the effects of internal reference pricing and the extension of generic substitution (a policy which essentially encourages generic production) on the market for antipsychotic drugs in Finland. An important aspect of this study is that it can identify the *marginal impact* of reference pricing in a market that already has

[20] For example, Espin et al. (2011) point out that the implementation of an ERP policy for pharmaceutical products requires considerable resources for the collection and analysis of price data from different countries.

generic competition because of the fact that reference pricing and generic substitution were implemented with a six year time gap between them. Thus, the results of the paper speak to the question addressed by Proposition 4. Koskinen et al. (2014) report three important findings, all of which are consistent with our analysis. First, reference pricing led to a substantial reduction in the daily cost of antipsychotic medication in Finland although the impact was not equally strong for all pharmaceuticals. Second, the additional cost reductions achieved due to the introduction of reference pricing after the adoption of generic substitution were comparatively minor since greater generic competition had already reduced prices – a finding that indicates that the two types of policies end up acting as substitutes for one another insofar as the goal is to lower prices. Third, the authors report that the drug for which the time gap between reference pricing and generic substitution was the smallest (so that the degree of generic competition was relatively weak when reference pricing was first introduced), reference pricing had the strongest effect on local prices. While Koskinen et al. (2014) focus on internal reference pricing based on close substitutes, as opposed to external reference pricing, their results are useful for understanding our analytical findings since both types of price regulations essentially serve to lower the prices of branded drugs.

4. ERP versus price controls

In our model, while only the home country can benefit from an ERP policy (since the firm's unconstrained price at home is higher, i.e., $p_H^d > p_F^d$), both countries have an incentive to impose a local price control on the firm since its price in each market exceeds marginal cost. Furthermore, as Proposition 1 notes, home's ERP policy raises the foreign price *above* that which prevails in its absence (i.e. $p_F^* > p_F^d$). This negative price spillover provides the foreign government an additional incentive to counter home's ERP policy via a local price control. Accordingly, we now build on our basic model by studying the following game:

Stage 1: Home government chooses between a local price control ($\overline{p}_H$) and an ERP policy (δ).

Stage 2: Foreign government sets its local price control $\overline{p}_F$.

Stage 3: Firm decides whether to export and sets its price(s).

Before proceeding further, we make two important observations. First, the home government cannot freely set both its local price $\overline{p}_H$ *and* its ERP policy δ since the latter indirectly determines the firm's local price (as a multiple δ of its foreign price). Thus, at the first stage of the game, it is sufficient to examine the home country's choice between the two policy instruments. Second, as noted earlier, the foreign government has nothing to gain from using an ERP policy since the firm's optimal foreign price is lower than the home price (i.e. $p_F^d < p_H^d$). Thus, allowing the foreign government to choose between a price control and an ERP policy would add nothing to our analysis and it is sufficient to consider only the foreign government's price control decision.

4.1. Firm's pricing and export decision

First note that the pricing and export decision of the firm when it faces price controls in both markets is trivial: it is willing to sell in country i so long as the price control $\overline{p}_i$ set by the local government is greater than or equal to its marginal cost.

Suppose now that at stage three of the game, the firm faces the ERP policy δ at home and the price control $\overline{p}_F$ abroad. When facing these policies, the firm is always free to collect maximal domestic profit π_H^d by choosing to sell only at home at its optimal home price p_H^d. To determine whether doing so is optimal, consider the firm's pricing decision if it sells in both markets. Since the ERP constraint $p_H \leq \delta\overline{p}_F$ binds in equilibrium, the firm's home price equals $p_H = \delta\overline{p}_F$ so that its total global profit is given by

$$\pi(\delta, \overline{p}_F) = \frac{n\delta\overline{p}_F}{\mu}\left(\mu - \frac{\delta\overline{p}_F}{1-\gamma_H}\right) + \overline{p}_F\left(1 - \frac{\overline{p}_F}{1-\gamma_F}\right). \quad (11)$$

Thus, when the firm faces an ERP policy at home and a price control abroad, it essentially has no freedom to set prices if it chooses to export: it charges $\overline{p}_F$ abroad and $\delta\overline{p}_F$ at home.

As before, the firm is indifferent between selling in both markets and selling only at home if and only if

$$\pi(\delta, \overline{p}_F) = \pi_H^d \quad (12)$$

The above equation implicitly defines the locus of policy pairs $(\delta, \overline{p}_F)$ along which the firm is indifferent between selling only at home and selling in both markets. Explicitly solving this equation for δ as a function of $\overline{p}_F$ yields a formula for the *export-inducing ERP policy* given any foreign price control $\overline{p}_F$:

$$\overline{\delta}(\overline{p}_F) = \frac{\mu}{2}\frac{(1-\gamma_H)}{\overline{p}_F} - \frac{\sqrt{n\mu\overline{p}_F(1-\gamma_H)(1-\gamma_F)(1-\gamma_F-\overline{p}_F)}}{n\overline{p}_F(1-\gamma_F)}. \quad (13)$$

Fig. 1 illustrates the $\overline{\delta}(\overline{p}_F)$ function in the $(\overline{p}_F, \delta)$ space.

Note from Fig. 1 that as the foreign price control tightens (i.e. $\overline{p}_F$ falls), the firm becomes less willing to export and home's ERP policy has to be relaxed to maintain its export incentive (i.e. to ensure that $\pi(\delta, \overline{p}_F) = \pi_H^d$ continues to hold). Conversely, if the foreign price control becomes more lax, the home country can implement a more stringent ERP policy without compromising the firm's export incentive. Note also that $\overline{\delta}(\overline{p}_F)$ is convex in $\overline{p}_F$, which implies that as the foreign price control gets tighter, home's ERP policy needs to adjust to an increasingly larger extent to keep the firm just willing to export. An increase in generic competition at home shifts the $\overline{\delta}(\overline{p}_F)$ curve down. Since home generic competition reduces the firm's profitability in the domestic market, for any given foreign price control $\overline{p}_F$, an increase in domestic generic competition requires a tighter ERP policy to keep the firm indifferent to exporting. Furthermore, an increase in generic competition abroad shifts the $\overline{\delta}(\overline{p}_F)$ curve up. This occurs since foreign generic competition lowers the firm's willingness to export. As a result, for a given level of foreign price control $\overline{p}_F$, the home coun-

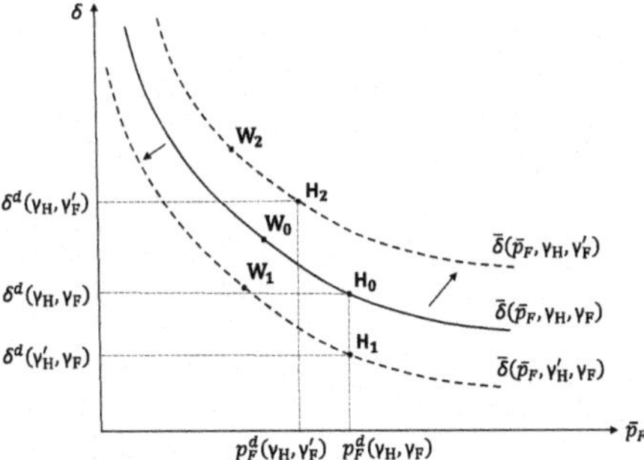

Fig. 1. Equilibrium policies ($\gamma'_H > \gamma_H$ and $\gamma'_F > \gamma_F$).

try's ERP policy needs to be looser to hold the firm's export incentive constant.

Next, consider the second stage of the game.

4.2. *Foreign government's best response*

Suppose home opts for a price control $\overline{p}_H$ at the first stage of the game and consider the foreign government's best response.

4.2.1. *If home opts for a price control*

Given the home price control $\overline{p}_H$, in the second stage, foreign simply chooses the lowest price at which the firm is willing to sell in its market. Thus, it sets $\overline{p}_F = 0$ to maximize local welfare. Given that, at the first stage of the game, home too finds its optimal to set its price control equal to the marginal cost of production (i.e. it sets $\overline{p}_H = 0$) since its price control has no bearing on the foreign price control and the export decision of the firm. Thus, when home chooses a price control as opposed to an ERP policy, equilibrium price in each market simply equals the firm's marginal cost and the firm makes zero profits in both markets.

Now consider the subgame starting at stage two given that the home country opts for an ERP policy at the first stage.

4.2.2. *If home opts for an ERP policy*

At the second stage of the game, given home's ERP policy δ, the foreign government chooses the level of its price control $\overline{p}_F$ taking into account the firm's pricing behavior as well as its export incentive. It is easy to see that it is optimal for the foreign country to pick the lowest price that just induces the firm to export. This is because, conditional on the firm exporting, foreign welfare is inversely related to local price. But if the firm does not export, then foreign consumers lose complete access to the good and foreign welfare drops to zero.

For $\overline{p}_F \in [0, p_F^*]$ since the $\overline{\delta}(\overline{p}_F)$ function is monotonically decreasing in $\overline{p}_F$, its inverse yields the best response of the foreign country to a given ERP policy of the home country. For $\overline{p}_F \in [p_F^*, 1]$ since the $\overline{\delta}(\overline{p}_F)$ function is increasing in $\overline{p}_F$, there exist two possible price controls that yield the firm the same level of global profit for any given ERP policy. However, since it is optimal for the foreign country to pick the lower of these two price controls, the best response of the foreign country can never exceed p_F*. Thus, foreign's best response as a function of the ERP policy implemented by home is simply (the downward sloping part of) the $\overline{\delta}(\overline{p}_F)$ curve in Fig. 1.

4.3. *Home's policy choice*

To determine the home government's optimal choice between the two policy instruments (i.e. δ and $\overline{p}_H$) at the first stage of the game, we need to compare home welfare under its optimal ERP policy with that under an optimally chosen price control. Proposition 5 below states the key result of this analysis.

4.3.1. *Nature of home's optimal ERP policy*

Deriving the welfare-maximizing ERP policy chosen by home taking into account the best response of the foreign government at stage two and the decisions of the firm at stage three yields:

Proposition 5. *(i) The home country's welfare-maximizing ERP policy is given by:*

$$\delta^d = \frac{1}{n(1-\gamma_F)}\left[n\mu(1-\gamma_H) - \sqrt{n\mu(1-\gamma_F)(1-\gamma_H)}\right].$$

(ii) This ERP policy is Pareto-efficient and the price control chosen in response by the foreign country equals the firm's optimal price p_F^d for the foreign market.

(iii) $\partial\delta^d/\partial\mu > 0$ and $\partial\delta^d/\partial n > 0$.

(iv) $\partial\delta^d/\partial\gamma_H < 0 < \partial\delta^d/\partial\gamma_F$.

The equilibrium policy pair (δ^d, p_F^d) is denoted by point $\mathbf{H_0}$ in Fig. 1. Since the firm has the strongest incentive to export when it can charge its optimal price p_F^d abroad, by choosing to implement the policy δ^d home can ensure that foreign indeed sets its local price exactly equal to p_F^d: if foreign were to set a tighter price control, the firm would not sell in its market and foreign welfare would drop to zero. It is worth noting that in the absence of a foreign price control, point $\mathbf{H}_0$ is *unattainable* for home since if it were to choose the policy δ^d the firm would export and its price abroad would equal $p_F(\delta = \delta^d) > p_F^d$ and its total profit would exceed π_H^d. But because of the foreign price control, home can implement δ^d *knowing* that foreign will impose the lowest price consistent with the firm selling in its market, which at the policy δ^d equals p_F^d. It is worth noting that, from the foreign country's perspective, although this outcome coincides with the complete absence of an ERP policy at home, its price control policy is still beneficial for local consumers since the foreign price under home's optimal ERP policy δ^* in the absence of a foreign price control is actually higher than that under δ^d (i.e. $p_F^* > p_F^d$).

The key to understanding why δ^d is Pareto-efficient is to note that for all $\overline{p}_F \in (p_F^d, p_F^*]$ a reduction in $\overline{p}_F$ benefits both home and foreign since prices fall in both countries without a change in the firm's global profits (which equal π_H^d all along the curve) whereas for $\overline{p}_F \in (0, p_F^d]$, a reduction in $\overline{p}_F$ makes the foreign country better off at the expense of home. Over the latter range, since $\partial^2\overline{\delta}/\partial^2\overline{p}_F \geq 0$ reductions in the foreign price control $\overline{p}_F$ necessitate a relatively sharp increase in the home's ERP policy in order to preserve the firm's export incentive. As a result for $\overline{p}_F \in (0, p_F^d]$, a tightening of the foreign price control *increases* price at home (due to the relatively sharp adjustment in its ERP policy) so that home loses while foreign gains from a reduction in $\overline{p}_F$. The intuition for why the equilibrium ERP policy δ^d increases in n and μ is the same as before: these changes make the home market more attractive to the firm who therefore needs to be granted greater leeway in international price discrimination in order for it to be willing to sell abroad. Part (*iv*) shows that the effects of generic competition on the ERP policy chosen by the home country as described in Proposition 2 are robust to the presence of a foreign price control. The intuition is also the same as before: generic competition at home makes the firm more willing to export whereas generic competition abroad makes it less willing to do so.

We are now ready to address the welfare effects of generic competition when home's ERP policy and the foreign price control are in place and adjust endogenously to any changes in such competition. We can show:

Proposition 6. *(i) An increase in the degree of generic competition at home raises domestic welfare while it does not affect foreign welfare: (i.e. $\partial w_H/\partial\gamma_H > 0$, $\partial w_F/\partial\gamma_H = 0$ and $\partial w/\partial\gamma_H > 0$).*

(ii) An increase in foreign generic competition lowers home's welfare ($\partial w_H/\partial\gamma_F < 0$) whereas it raises foreign welfare ($\partial w_F/\partial\gamma_F > 0$). It increases joint welfare ($\partial w/\partial\gamma_F > 0$) iff the following inequality holds:

$$n\mu(1 - \gamma_H) < 4(1 - \gamma_F). \tag{14}$$

It is useful to contrast Proposition 6 with Proposition 2, which reports the effects of generic competition in the two markets in the absence of a foreign price control. While domestic generic competition benefits the foreign country when it does not implement a price control, it has no bearing on foreign welfare when the foreign country imposes an optimal price control in response to home's ERP policy. The intuition for this is simply that the equilibrium price control is set at the firm's optimal price for the foreign market (p_F^d) which is independent of the degree of domestic generic competition. A comparison of Propositions 3 and 6 indicates that an increase in domestic generic competition is Pareto-improving *whether or not* a foreign price control is in existence.

Part (*ii*) of Proposition 6 obtains because an increase in foreign generic competition directly lowers p_F^d and therefore increases foreign welfare. Domestic welfare declines with γ_F because home is forced to relax its ERP policy when γ_F increases ($\partial\delta^d/\partial\gamma_F > 0$) and this raises the domestic price without affecting firm's global profit (which equals π_H^d in equilibrium). The question of how an increase in foreign generic competition affects global welfare turns on a comparison of its opposing welfare effects on the two countries. Inequality (14) indicates that the larger are n or μ, the less likely it is that global welfare increases due to an increase in γ_F: an increase in either parameter implies a larger welfare loss at home both due to the scale of the home market and due to the larger relaxation in its ERP policy necessitated by more intense foreign generic competition. Note also that an increase in γ_H makes it more likely that inequality (14) is satisfied whereas an increase in γ_F has the opposite effect. This tells us that when foreign generic competition is intense to begin with, the foreign welfare gain that results from a further increase in γ_F is fairly small.

4.3.2. Home's optimal price control

When the home country uses a price control, its welfare is maximized by setting the home price equal to marginal cost since this minimizes domestic deadweight loss without having any effect on the firm's export incentive which is determined completely by the foreign price control. The foreign country also sets the local price control equal to marginal cost while (just) maintaining the firm's incentive to export to its market. As a result, the firm makes zero profit in each market when both countries use price controls. Let $w_H(\overline{p}_i = 0)$ denote the home's equilibrium welfare when both countries use price controls.

4.3.3. Equilibrium policy choice: ERP versus price control

We are now ready to examine the home country's choice between an ERP policy and a price control at the first stage of the game. Recall that home's optimal ERP policy δ^d is such that it induces the foreign country to choose a price control equal to p_F^d. Thus the firm earns optimal monopoly profit in the foreign market. By contrast, when the home country opts for a price control, the firm makes zero profit abroad since the foreign government sets its price control equal to marginal cost. While implementing an ERP policy helps the home government preserve the firm's export profits, it also yields lower home consumer surplus than a price control since it does not push down domestic price all the way to marginal cost. Therefore, when choosing between the two types of price regulations, the home country essentially faces a trade-off between higher foreign profit earned by its firm (under its ERP policy) and greater domestic consumer surplus (delivered by the price control).

Straightforward calculations establish the following key result:

Proposition 7. *Home welfare under an ERP policy is higher than that under a local price control (i.e. $w_H(\delta^d, p_F^d) \geq w_H(\overline{p}_i = 0)$) if and only if the following inequality holds:*

$$n\mu \leq \widetilde{n\mu} \text{ where } \widetilde{n\mu} \equiv \frac{(1-\gamma_F)(2\sqrt{2}+3)}{(1-\gamma_H)}. \tag{15}$$

Thus, whether the home country opts for an ERP policy over a price control is determined by inequality (15). This simple inequality provides important insights into factors that determine a country's choice between an ERP policy and a price control. It indicates that the larger the relative size of the domestic market (i.e. the higher are n or μ), the less likely it is that the home government prefers an ERP policy to a price control. Intuitively, an increase in the relative size of the domestic market reduces the importance of maintaining the firm's foreign profits (which is the main advantage of the ERP policy over a price control). Although our model abstracts from innovation, it is worth noting that incentives for innovation typically respond positively to product market profits post innovation. This suggests that ERP policies might have an additional advantage over direct price controls to the extent that they do more to encourage innovation.[21]

Inequality (15) also clarifies that local and foreign generic competition have opposite effects on home's choice between the two policy instruments: greater local competition (i.e. higher γ_H) makes it more likely that home prefers an ERP policy to a price control whereas greater foreign competition (i.e. higher γ_F) makes it less likely that it does so.[22] Home competition increases the attractiveness of an ERP policy relative to a price control since it allows the home government to implement a tighter ERP policy (which is desirable from a welfare perspective) whereas an increase in foreign competition makes an ERP policy less attractive relative to a price control since such competition makes the optimal ERP policy more lax in nature.

5. Further analysis

In this section, we address two additional issues. First, we investigate the effects of integrating the two national generic markets into a single world market in which consumers are free to buy the generic product of either country. Second, we consider a situation where the welfare function of the home country does not weigh firm profits and consumer surplus equally. The latter analysis sheds light on how the presence of political economy motives – wherein the firm is more effective at lobbying the government than consumers – or considerations related to innovation – since innovation incentives can be driven by profitability – affect the nature of home's optimal ERP policy as well as its choice between an ERP policy and a direct control.

5.1. Integration of generic markets

As we noted earlier in the paper, regulatory divergences regarding national requirements for the approval and sale of generics tend to segment national markets and can have the effect of limiting international competition in generics (IGBA, 2015). Thus, it is reasonable to assume, as we do in our core model, that generic markets are segmented internationally (i.e. generic producers in each country can only sell their product in the local market). But international trade in generic products surely exists and has been growing, with India and China emerging as major international suppliers of generic products in world markets. Indeed, the Food and Drug Administration (FDA) of the United States has publicly argued in favor of lifting barriers to generic competition by implementing a single drug development program and utilizing common aspects of applications to facilitate filing for approval in multiple countries. Since the idea of facilitating international trade in generics has obvious intellectual and practical appeal, it is worth asking how the integration of national generic markets into a single world market affects the firm producing the branded product and consumers in both countries. We now address this issue.

When the perceived quality of generics differs across countries, an obvious argument in favor of such integration is that it makes it possible for consumers in both markets to purchase the higher quality generic. For example, if the home generic is seen by consumers as being superior to the foreign one (i.e. $\gamma_H > \gamma_F$) then integration of the generic market benefits foreign consumers who switch from buying their local generic to the one imported from the home country. However, the home firm loses from this switch on the part of foreign consumers since it ends up facing more intense competition in the foreign market. Such increased competition in the foreign market makes the firm more reluctant to export which in turn induces the home government to relax its ERP policy (Lemma 1). Furthermore, from Proposition 5 it immediately follows that this change in home's ERP policy reduces home welfare as well as global welfare when $n\mu(1-\gamma_H) \geq 4(1-\gamma_F)$. As we noted earlier, this inequality implies that if foreign generic competition is already quite intense (i.e. γ_F is high but smaller than γ_H), integrating the two generic markets can *lower* world welfare because integration does not substantially improve the quality of the generic product available to foreign consumers while it causes the home price to increase due to the relaxation in home's ERP policy caused by integration.

It should be clear from the above discussion that if consumers view the foreign generic to be superior to the home one ($\gamma_F > \gamma_H$), integration induces the home government to tighten its ERP policy and raises global welfare by lowering prices in both countries while also bringing them closer to each other. Finally, note from Proposition 7 that if the generic markets are globally integrated then the home country prefers ERP over a price control if and only if the two markets are of similar size, that is, $n\mu < 2\sqrt{2}+3$. Note that when generic markets are globally integrated, the

[21] We thank an anonymous referee for raising this point. The innovation effects of ERP policies relative to other types of price controls is surely a topic worthy of further research.

[22] It is important to be careful here: in an absolute sense, the presence of generic competition at home reduces the marginal benefit of both types of price regulations but its *relative* impact is larger for the case of a direct price control so that an ERP policy becomes *relatively more attractive* than a price control when domestic competition is stronger.

intensity of generic competition has no effect on home's ERP policy (and therefore on its choice between ERP and a price control) since the firm faces the same competition in each market. Under such a situation, an increase in generic competition in either market necessarily benefits consumers in both countries and increases aggregate welfare even as it hurts the firm.

5.2. A more general welfare function

Suppose the home country's welfare function takes the following form:

$$w_H(\delta;\alpha) = cs_H(\delta) + \alpha\pi(\delta) \tag{16}$$

where $\alpha \geq 0$. Obviously, the larger is α the greater the weight that the home country puts on profits relative to consumer surplus while making its policy choices. There are two important considerations that could induce the home government to weigh consumer surplus and firm profits unequally. The first perspective is that since we are considering pharmaceutical products, in certain markets (say HIV drugs) consumer interests maybe so dominant (in the sense that lack of adequate access can have catastrophic health consequences) that a government might be willing to discount firm profits heavily relative to consumer welfare – a scenario in which α would be much smaller than 1. The second perspective takes a more long-run view: since innovation is likely to be responsive to firm profits, a government might put greater weight on profits than consumer surplus since greater innovation is in the interest of both firms and consumers.[23] Both perspectives have a compelling argument so that, in what follows, we discuss both scenarios.

The main question we address is: how does the relative weight on profits (α) affect home's policy choices? To this end we analyze the three-stage game developed in Section 4 where home chooses between ERP and a price control taking into account the fact that the foreign government institutes a local price control to maximize local welfare. First note that when home implements an ERP policy, the value of α does not affect the equilibrium outcome (i.e. its optimal policy remains δ^d). This is because, in equilibrium, under the optimal ERP policy the firm's global profit is equal to its domestic monopoly profit π_H^d. Furthermore, the foreign country is better off by tightening its price control to extract any of the firm's profit beyond π_H^d without undermining the firm's incentive for selling in its market. It follows that the contribution of the firm's profit to home's welfare equals $\alpha\pi_H^d$. Since home cannot use ERP to increase its firm's equilibrium profit beyond π_H^d, it essentially chooses its optimal ERP policy to maximize local consumer surplus. This optimal level of ERP is exactly what we obtained under $\alpha = 1$.

Let us now consider home's choice of a price control when the government values consumer surplus more than firm profits so that $\alpha \in [0, 1)$. Since the foreign country chooses the tightest price control for which the firm is willing to serve its market, it sets the local price equal to marginal cost so that the firm's foreign profit equals zero. Home chooses its price control $\overline{p}_H$ to solve:

$$\max_{\overline{p}_H} w_H(\delta;\alpha) = \max_{\overline{p}_H} cs_H(\overline{p}_H) + \alpha\pi_H^d(\overline{p}_H) \tag{17}$$

Since we already know from previous analysis that home's optimal price control is zero for $\alpha = 1$, it must also be zero for all $\alpha < 1$ where home cares even more about consumer surplus.[24] Thus, the optimal foreign price control $\overline{p}_H^* = 0$ for all $\alpha \in [0, 1)$.

Proposition 8. *Suppose home welfare equals $w_H(\delta;\alpha) = cs_H(\delta) + \alpha\pi(\delta)$, where $\alpha \in [0, 1)$. Then, home prefers the optimal ERP policy δ^d to the optimal price control $\overline{p}_H^* = 0$ if and only if $\mu n \leq \tilde{\mu n}(\alpha)$ where*

$$\tilde{\mu n}(\alpha) = \frac{(1-\gamma_F)(2\sqrt{2(2-\alpha)} - 2\alpha + 5)}{(1-\gamma_H)(2\alpha - 3)^2} \tag{18}$$

Furthermore, we have $\frac{\partial \tilde{\mu n}}{\partial \alpha} > 0$; $\frac{\partial \tilde{\mu n}}{\partial \gamma_H} > 0$; and $\frac{\partial \tilde{\mu n}}{\partial \gamma_F} < 0$.

Proposition 8 implies that the message of Proposition 7 remains qualitatively unchanged when home has the more general welfare objective $w_H(\delta;\alpha)$. That is, home still prefers ERP to a price control provided market size is sufficiently similar across countries, i.e. $\mu n \leq \tilde{\mu n}(\alpha)$. The critical threshold $\tilde{\mu n}(\alpha)$, defined in (18), is increasing in α so that the higher the weight that home puts on firm profits relative to consumer surplus, the more likely it is to prefer an ERP policy to a price control. The comparative statics of the threshold $\tilde{\mu n}$ reported in Proposition 8 are similar to those reported in Proposition 7 so that the qualitative effects of generic competition on home's choice between ERP and price controls do not depend upon α: given any α, an increase in home generic competition makes ERP more attractive to the home country than a price control, while the opposite holds for generic competition in the foreign country.

Next suppose $\alpha \geq 1$. As noted above, this case is worth discussing since a government might value firm profits quite highly in order to incentivize innovation, something that we do not explicitly model in this paper. When $\alpha \geq 1$, we can solve the maximization problem in (17) for home's optimal price control $\overline{p}_H^*(\alpha)$:

$$\overline{p}_H^*(\alpha) = \frac{\mu(\alpha-1)(1-\gamma_H)}{2\alpha - 1} \tag{19}$$

Several observations about the optimal price control $\overline{p}_H^*(\alpha)$ are worth noting. First, it can be readily seen from (19) that $\overline{p}_H^*(\alpha)$ is positive whenever $\alpha > 1$ – i.e. if the home government values firm profits more than consumer surplus, it allows the firm to charge a positive mark-up. Second, it is easily checked that $\frac{\partial \overline{p}_H^*(\alpha)}{\partial \alpha} > 0$, implying that home's optimal price control increases with the weight attached to firm profits in the government's welfare function. Third, $\overline{p}_H^*(\alpha)$ converges to the monopoly price p_H^d from below as α gets larger – intuitively, the firm's domestic profit is maximized by at $\overline{p}_H^*(\alpha) = p_H^d$ and the more the

[23] We thank two external referees for raising these points.

[24] Of course, we rule out the uninteresting case where home can set a negative price control.

government cares about profits, the closer it sets the price control to the firm's optimal monopoly price. In general, home's optimal price control is always weakly lower than p_H^d and it equals p_H^d only when the relative weight on local consumer surplus is essentially zero (which is the case when α is arbitrarily large).

Plugging $\overline{p}_H^*(\alpha)$ into (17) we obtain home's optimal welfare under the price control. Denote this maximized welfare under the optimal price control $\overline{p}_H^*(\alpha)$ by $\overline{w}_H^*(\alpha)$. Then, comparing home's welfare under its optimal ERP policy with that under the optimal price control yields the following result for $\alpha \geq 1$:

$$w_H(\delta^d) \geq \overline{w}_H^*(\alpha) \text{ iff } \mu n \leq \hat{\mu n}(\alpha)$$

where

$$\hat{\mu n}(\alpha) \equiv \frac{(1-\gamma_F)(2\alpha-1)(2\sqrt{2\alpha(\alpha-1)}+4\alpha-1)}{1-\gamma_H}.$$

Thus, Proposition 8 continues to hold when $\alpha \geq 1$ with a minor modification: we simply need to replace $\tilde{\mu n}(\alpha)$ by $\hat{\mu n}(\alpha)$. Finally, it is easy to show that $\frac{\partial \hat{\mu n}}{\partial \alpha} > 0$; $\frac{\partial \hat{\mu n}}{\partial \gamma_H} > 0$; and $\frac{\partial \hat{\mu n}}{\partial \gamma_F} < 0$.

6. Conclusion

The market power of firms selling patented pharmaceutical products declines with the expiration of patents (after which generic competition becomes viable) but brand names can endow pharmaceutical companies with market power even in the absence of patents. This is presumably why governments attempt to lower prices of branded pharmaceutical products that are no longer protected by patents by using a variety of price regulations. In addition to such regulations, governments also have the ability to affect the degree of generic competition in their markets via the process by which they allow generic entry after the expiration of patents. Motivated by these observations, in this paper we have analyzed the effect that price regulations such as ERP and price controls have on consumers as well as firms that make pricing decisions taking such policies into account.

Our simple two-country model captures the trade-offs facing firms subject to price regulations as well as the incentives of the governments setting them. We show that generic competition has rather subtle effects on an optimally chosen ERP policy. When such competition is present in the market of the government setting the ERP policy, it allows the government to set a tighter ERP policy (i.e. one that restricts international price discrimination to a greater extent). However, a strengthening of generic competition in the foreign market induces the home government to relax its ERP policy, thereby leading to greater international price discrimination on the part of the firm. Such endogenous adjustment in home's ERP policy undermines the positive welfare effects of increased generic competition in the foreign market.

Since home's ERP policy imposes a negative price spillover on the foreign country, we allow the foreign government to impose a local price control in response to an ERP policy at home that can help limit its impact on foreign consumers. When both governments are policy active, we show that the equilibrium ERP policy of the home government is Pareto-efficient and it results in the foreign government allowing the home firm to charge its optimal price (p_F^d) in the foreign market. Though the foreign country is unable to lower the local price all the way to marginal cost, it still benefits from being able to use a price control since the price in its market when only the home government is policy active is actually higher than the firm's optimal foreign price (p_F^d).

We also examine the home government's choice between an ERP policy and a price control when the foreign government can respond to its policy decision by enacting a price control of its own. An important result here is that an ERP policy is more effective at preserving the firm's foreign profit than a price control so that the home country prefers to use an ERP policy when the foreign market is not too small relative to the domestic one. While our model abstracts from innovation, our analysis suggests that governments might have an incentive to prefer ERP policies to direct price controls if they expect innovation to respond positively to product market profits. We also show that stronger generic competition at home tilts the choice in favor of an ERP policy whereas stronger foreign generic competition has the opposite effect. Furthermore, due to the endogenous adjustment in home's ERP policy, global integration of the generic market does not necessarily improve welfare when home generics are superior in quality than foreign ones. Finally, we show that the greater the weight a government puts on firm profits relative to consumer surplus, the more likely it is to prefer an ERP policy to a price control.

In closing, we discuss the implications of our findings for the ongoing debate over the introduction of an ERP policy in the US. Overall, our theoretical findings coupled with existing evidence suggest that the implementation of an ERP policy by the US is likely to help curb local pharmaceutical prices but to be effective, the policy would need to be designed and implemented carefully. First, care must be taken when choosing the appropriate reference basket for the US. Our model indicates that the reference basket of the US should include countries that have relatively similar market demand conditions to it. This is because if the US reference basket were to include countries with very low market prices, US firms could simply choose to not sell in such markets thereby making its ERP policy rather ineffective. Second, to operationalize its ERP policy, the US would need to choose the appropriate prices to compare within its reference basket. In this regard, we suggest that an effective strategy for the US might be to operationalize its ERP policy via local ex-factory prices (i.e. prices listed by manufacturers) in its reference countries since these prices are controlled by manufacturers and are more likely to reflect their incentives to price discriminate internationally, something an ERP policy is designed to limit. Since ex-factory prices do not typically include markups charged by downstream sellers, taxes, or rebates/discounts they are relatively easy to observe and compare internationally thereby making them a useful benchmark for implementing ERP policies. Indeed, this is one potential reason that many countries base their ERP policies on ex-factory prices (WHO, 2013). Furthermore, since supply-chains of pharmaceuticals and channels of retail vary substantially across countries, prices set by manufacturers are more directly comparable across countries relative to retail prices.[25] The third major policy implication of our analysis is that generic competition acts as a substitute for ERP in containing the prices of branded drugs. As a result, the optimal ERP policy for the US would need to take account of the fact that local generic competition in the US is decidedly more robust than in other countries. Indeed, the gains from implementing an ERP policy for off-patent drugs in the US would appear rather limited and it would make eminent practical sense for the policy to be focused on only patented drugs. Finally, note that given that the US has a significant capacity for pharmaceutical innovation, it is crucial that its ERP policy should attempt to balance the objective of lowering domestic prices against maintaining the innovation incentives of firms. In the context of our model, this implies that it would be desirable for the US to put a relatively large weight on firm profits, something that would lead to a relatively lax ERP policy. To the extent the benefits of innovation spill across national boundaries, the rest of the world also has a substantial stake in how an ERP policy in the US affects incentives for innovation.

Author's contribution

Difei Geng and Kamal Saggi: Conceptualization, methodology, software, validation, formal analysis, writing – original draft, writing – review and editing, project administration.

Appendix A

For all of the proofs below, we maintain Assumption 1 which ensures that optimal ERP policy of the home country is an interior solution (i.e. $\delta^* > 1$).

A.1 Optimal pricing and profit maximization with and without ERP

If the firm faces no ERP constraint, it is free to charge its optimal local price in each market thereby extracting the maximum possible profit while facing local generic competition. More specifically, the firm solves

$$\max_{p_H, p_F} \pi(p_H, p_F; \gamma_H, \gamma_F) \equiv \frac{n}{\mu} p_H \left(\mu - \frac{p_H}{1-\gamma_H}\right) + p_F\left(1 - \frac{p_F}{1-\gamma_F}\right). \quad (20)$$

The solution to the above problem is given by

$$p_H^d = \frac{\mu}{2}(1-\gamma_H) \text{ and } p_F^d = \frac{1}{2}(1-\gamma_F)$$

As expected, p_i^d is decreasing in γ_i indicating that an increase in generic competition in market i lowers the firm's optimal price for that market. Sales in each market under international price discrimination equal $x_H^d = n/2$ and $x_F^d = 1/2$ while global sales equal $x^d = x_H^d + x_F^d = (n+1)/2$. Let the firm's global profit under optimal market specific prices be denoted by $\pi^d = \pi_H^d + \pi_F^d$, where $\pi_i^d = p_i^d x_i^d = n_i\mu_i(1-\gamma_i)/4$ and $i = H, F$.

Now suppose the home country implements the ERP constraint $p_H \le \delta p_F$. If the firm sells in both markets when facing this constraint its profit maximization problem is

$$\max \pi(p_i; \gamma_i) \text{ subject to } p_H \le \delta p_F.$$

Given that the ERP constraint is binding, we can solve for firm's optimal prices in the two markets as

$$p_H(\delta) = \frac{\mu\delta(n\delta+1)(1-\gamma_H)(1-\gamma_F)}{2[\mu(1-\gamma_H)+n\delta^2(1-\gamma_F)]} \text{ and } p_F(\delta) = p_H(\delta)/\delta. \quad (21)$$

The sales associated with these prices can be recovered from the respective demand curves in the two markets and these equal

$$x_H(\delta) = \frac{n[2\mu(1-\gamma_H)+\delta(n\delta-1)(1-\gamma_F)]}{2[\mu(1-\gamma_H)+n\delta^2(1-\gamma_F)]} \text{ and } x_F(\delta) = \frac{\mu(1-n\delta)(1-\gamma_H)+2n\delta^2(1-\gamma_F)}{2[\mu(1-\gamma_H)+n\delta^2(1-\gamma_F)]}. \quad (22)$$

Global sales under the ERP constraint equal $x(\delta) = x_H(\delta) + x_F(\delta)$.[26] The firm's optimal global profit under ERP policy δ can be calculated by substituting $p_H(\delta)$ and $p_F(\delta)$ into $\pi(p_H, p_F)$. We have

$$\pi(\delta) \equiv \pi(p_H(\delta), p_F(\delta)) = \frac{\mu(n\delta+1)^2(1-\gamma_H)(1-\gamma_F)}{4[\mu(1-\gamma_H)+n\delta^2(1-\gamma_F)]}. \quad (23)$$

Proof of Proposition 1. (i) We have

$$\frac{\partial p_H(\delta)}{\partial \delta} = A \cdot B_1$$

where

$$A = \frac{\mu(1-\gamma_H)(1-\gamma_F)}{2[\mu(1-\gamma_H)+n\delta^2(1-\gamma_F)]^2} \text{ and }$$

$$B_1 = [(2\delta\mu n + \mu)(1-\gamma_H) - n\delta^2(1-\gamma_F)]$$

[25] For useful introductions to the structure of pharmaceutical supply chains in some key foreign markets that are likely to be relevant for setting ERP policy in the US, see Vogler et al. (2012) who focus on major European countries and Paris and Docteur (2006) who study Canada.

[26] It can be calculated that $x(\delta) < x^d$, that is, global sales are lower under ERP than under discrimination for any levels of generic competition. However, as was shown earlier, joint welfare is higher under ERP. This is consistent with Schmalensee (1981) and Varian (1985) who establish that raising global output is only a necessary (but not sufficient) condition for price discrimination to yield higher welfare. In our model, the welfare enhancement from larger global output under discrimination is dominated by that from reducing the international price differential induced via ERP. As a result, joint welfare ends up being higher under ERP.

Since $A > 0$, we only need to show that $B_1 > 0$ for $\delta^* < \delta < \frac{\mu(1-\gamma_H)}{1-\gamma_F}$. It is easy to show that

$$\frac{\partial B_1}{\partial \delta} = 2n[\mu(1-\gamma_H) - \delta(1-\gamma_F)] > 0$$

for $\delta^* < \delta < \frac{\mu(1-\gamma_H)}{1-\gamma_F}$, so B_1 is increasing in δ for all relevant values of δ. Moreover, we have

$$B_1|_{\delta=\delta^*} = \frac{[\mu n(1-\gamma_H) + (1-\gamma_F)][3\mu n(1-\gamma_H) - (1-\gamma_F)]}{4n(1-\gamma_F)} > 0$$

It follows that $B_1 > 0$ for all $\delta^* < \delta < \frac{\mu(1-\gamma_H)}{1-\gamma_F}$.

Next, we have

$$\frac{\partial p_F(\delta)}{\partial \delta} = A \cdot B_2$$

where

$$B_2 = [\mu(1-\gamma_H) - \delta(n\delta + 2)(1-\gamma_F)].$$

It can be shown that

$$\frac{\partial B_2}{\partial \delta} = -2(n\delta + 1)(1-\gamma_F) < 0$$

so that B_2 is decreasing in δ for $\delta^* < \delta < \frac{\mu(1-\gamma_H)}{1-\gamma_F}$. Moreover, one can show that

$$B_2|_{\delta=\delta^*} = -\frac{[\mu n(1-\gamma_H) + (1-\gamma_F)][\mu n(1-\gamma_H) - 3(1-\gamma_F)]}{4n(1-\gamma_F)} < 0$$

for $\delta^* < \delta < \frac{\mu(1-\gamma_H)}{1-\gamma_F}$, which implies that $B_2 < 0$ for all relevant values of δ. Since $A > 0$, we have $\frac{\partial p_F(\delta)}{\partial \delta} < 0$ for all $\delta^* < \delta < \frac{\mu(1-\gamma_H)}{1-\gamma_F}$.

(ii) Direct calculations show that

$$\frac{\partial p_H(\delta)}{\partial \gamma_H} = -\frac{\mu n\delta^3(n\delta+1)(1-\gamma_F)^2}{2[\mu(1-\gamma_H) + n\delta^2(1-\gamma_F)]^2} < 0;$$

$$\frac{\partial p_F(\delta)}{\partial \gamma_F} = -\frac{\mu^2(n\delta+1)(1-\gamma_H)^2}{2[\mu(1-\gamma_H) + n\delta^2(1-\gamma_F)]^2} < 0;$$

$$\frac{\partial p_H(\delta)}{\partial \gamma_F} = -\frac{\mu^2\delta(n\delta+1)(1-\gamma_H)^2}{2[\mu(1-\gamma_H) + n\delta^2(1-\gamma_F)]^2} < 0$$

and

$$\frac{\partial p_F(\delta)}{\partial \gamma_H} = -\frac{\mu n\delta^2(n\delta+1)(1-\gamma_F)^2}{2[\mu(1-\gamma_H) + n\delta^2(1-\gamma_F)]^2} < 0.$$

Proof of Lemma 1. (i) We have

$$\frac{\partial p_H^*}{\partial \gamma_H} = -\frac{\mu B_3}{2[\mu n(1-\gamma_H) + (1-\gamma_F)]^2}$$

where

$$B_3 = \mu^2 n^2(1-\gamma_H)^2 + 2\mu n(1-\gamma_H)(1-\gamma_F) - (1-\gamma_F)^2.$$

Note that

$$\frac{\partial B_3}{\partial(\mu n)} = 2(1-\gamma_H)[\mu n(1-\gamma_H) + (1-\gamma_F)] > 0$$

so that B_3 is increasing in μn. Moreover, for $\mu > \frac{2n+1}{n}\frac{1-\gamma_F}{1-\gamma_H}$ we have $\mu n > (2n+1)\frac{1-\gamma_F}{1-\gamma_H} \geq \frac{3(1-\gamma_F)}{1-\gamma_H}$ as $n \geq 1$. But direct calculations show that

$$B_3|_{\mu n = \frac{3(1-\gamma_F)}{1-\gamma_H}} = 14(1-\gamma_F)^2 > 0.$$

This implies that $B_3 > 0$ and therefore $\partial p_H^*/\partial \gamma_H < 0$ for all $\mu > \frac{2n+1}{n}\frac{1-\gamma_F}{1-\gamma_H}$.

(ii) We have

$$\frac{\partial p_F^*}{\partial \gamma_H} = -\frac{\mu n(1-\gamma_F)^2}{[\mu n(1-\gamma_H) + (1-\gamma_F)]^2} < 0.$$

(iii) We have

$$\frac{\partial p_H^*}{\partial \gamma_F} = \frac{\mu^2 n(1-\gamma_H)^2}{[\mu n(1-\gamma_H) + (1-\gamma_F)]^2} > 0.$$

(iv) We have

$$\frac{\partial p_F^*}{\partial \gamma_F} = -\frac{\mu^2 n^2(1-\gamma_H)^2}{[\mu n(1-\gamma_H) + (1-\gamma_F)]^2} < 0.$$

Proof of Proposition 3. We first prove the effects of a change in γ_H. For home welfare we have

$$\frac{\partial w_H^*}{\partial \gamma_H} = \frac{\mu n[\mu n(1-\gamma_H) - (1-\gamma_F)]}{8[\mu n(1-\gamma_H) + (1-\gamma_F)]^3} B_4$$

where

$$B_4 = \mu^2 n^2(1-\gamma_H)^2 + 4\mu n(1-\gamma_H)(1-\gamma_F) + 7(1-\gamma_F)^2.$$

It is easy to check that $B_4 > B_3 > 0$ so that $\partial w_H^*/\partial \gamma_H > 0$. For foreign welfare, we have

$$\frac{\partial w_F^*}{\partial \gamma_H} = \frac{\mu n(1-\gamma_F)^3}{[\mu n(1-\gamma_H) + (1-\gamma_F)]^3} > 0.$$

Finally, direct calculations show that $\partial w^*/\partial \gamma_H = \frac{1}{8}\mu n > 0$.

Next we prove the effects of a change in γ_F. For home welfare it is easy to see that

$$\frac{\partial w_H^*}{\partial \gamma_F} = -\frac{\mu^2 n^2(1-\gamma_H)^2[\mu n(1-\gamma_H) + 3(1-\gamma_F)]}{2[\mu n(1-\gamma_H) + (1-\gamma_F)]^3} < 0.$$

Moreover, for foreign welfare we have

$$\frac{\partial w_F^*}{\partial \gamma_F} = \frac{\mu^2 n^2(1-\gamma_H)^2[\mu n(1-\gamma_H) + 3(1-\gamma_F)]}{2[\mu n(1-\gamma_H) + (1-\gamma_F)]^3} > 0.$$

It follows that

$$\frac{\partial w^*}{\partial \gamma_F} = \frac{\partial w_H^*}{\partial \gamma_F} + \frac{\partial w_F^*}{\partial \gamma_F} = 0.$$

Proof of Proposition 4. Direct calculations show that

$$\frac{\partial \Delta w_H^*}{\partial \gamma_H} = -\frac{\mu n(1-\gamma_F)^3}{[\mu n(1-\gamma_H)+(1-\gamma_F)]^3} < 0.$$

Next, we have

$$\frac{\partial \Delta w_H^*}{\partial \gamma_F} = -\frac{\mu n(1-\gamma_H)-(1-\gamma_F)}{4[\mu n(1-\gamma_H)+(1-\gamma_F)]^3} B_5$$

where

$$B_5 = \mu^2 n^2 (1-\gamma_H)^2 + 4\mu n(1-\gamma_H)(1-\gamma_F) + (1-\gamma_F)^2.$$

It is easy to check that $B_5 > B_3 > 0$ and thus $\partial \Delta w_H^* / \partial \gamma_F < 0$.

Proof of Proposition 5. (i) Home country's welfare maximizing ERP induces the foreign country to choose its local price at p_F^d. Thus δ^d is obtained by setting $\overline{p}_F = p_F^d$ in $\overline{\delta}(\overline{p}_F)$.

(ii) See the text.

(iii) We can calculate that

$$\frac{\partial \delta^d}{\partial \mu} = \frac{(1-\gamma_H)[2\sqrt{\mu n(1-\gamma_H)(1-\gamma_F)} - (1-\gamma_F)]}{2(1-\gamma_F)\sqrt{\mu n(1-\gamma_H)(1-\gamma_F)}}.$$

It can be checked that $2\sqrt{\mu n(1-\gamma_H)(1-\gamma_F)} - (1-\gamma_F) > 0$, which implies that $\partial \delta^d / \partial \mu > 0$. Besides, we have $\partial \delta^d / \partial n = \frac{\mu(1-\gamma_H)}{2n\sqrt{\mu n(1-\gamma_H)(1-\gamma_F)}} > 0$.

(iv) One can calculate that

$$\frac{\partial \delta^d}{\partial \gamma_H} = -\frac{\mu[2\sqrt{\mu n(1-\gamma_H)(1-\gamma_F)} - (1-\gamma_F)]}{2(1-\gamma_F)\sqrt{\mu n(1-\gamma_H)(1-\gamma_F)}} < 0$$

and

$$\frac{\partial \delta^d}{\partial \gamma_F} = \frac{\mu(1-\gamma_H)[2\sqrt{\mu n(1-\gamma_H)(1-\gamma_F)} - (1-\gamma_F)]}{2(1-\gamma_F)^3\sqrt{\mu n(1-\gamma_H)(1-\gamma_F)}} > 0.$$

Proof of Proposition 6. (i) First note that foreign welfare depends on the foreign price p_F only. In Nash equilibrium we have $p_F = p_F^d = \frac{1}{2}(1-\gamma_F)$ which does not depend on home's generic competition γ_H. Hence an increase in generic competition at home does not change foreign price and welfare. Next, one can show that

$$\frac{\partial w^d}{\partial \gamma_H} = \frac{\mu n[\sqrt{\mu n(1-\gamma_H)(1-\gamma_F)} - (1-\gamma_F)]}{8\sqrt{\mu n(1-\gamma_H)(1-\gamma_F)}} > 0,$$

implying higher generic competition at home raises world welfare. It follows that an increase in generic competition at home must raise domestic welfare.

(ii) Since in Nash equilibrium $p_F = p_F^d = \frac{1}{2}(1-\gamma_F)$, a higher γ_F lowers p_F and raises foreign welfare. Also one can show that

$$\frac{\partial p_H}{\partial \gamma_F} = \frac{\mu(1-\gamma_H)}{4\sqrt{\mu n(1-\gamma_H)(1-\gamma_F)}} > 0,$$

i.e. foreign generic competition raises domestic price and lowers domestic consumer surplus. Since the firm's equilibrium profit equals its domestic monopoly profit which does not change with γ_F, we know domestic welfare must fall. As for world welfare, we have

$$\frac{\partial w}{\partial \gamma_F} = \frac{2\sqrt{\mu n(1-\gamma_H)(1-\gamma_F)} - \mu n(1-\gamma_H)}{8\sqrt{\mu n(1-\gamma_H)(1-\gamma_F)}} > 0$$

$$\text{iff } \mu n > \frac{4(1-\gamma_F)}{(1-\gamma_H)}.$$

References

Berndt, E.R., Newhouse, J.P., 2012. Pricing and reimbursement in US pharmaceutical markets. In: Danzon, P.M., Nicholson, S. (Eds.), The Oxford Handbook of the Economics of the Biopharmaceutical Industry. Oxford University Press.

Brekke, K.R., Konigbauer, I., Straume, O.R., 2007. Reference pricing of pharmaceuticals. J. Health Econ. 26, 613–642.

Brekke, K.R., Holmas, T.H., Straume, O.R., 2011. Reference pricing, competition, and pharmaceutical expenditures: theory and evidence from a natural experiment. J. Public Econ. 95, 624–638.

Brekke, K.R., Grasdal, A.L., Holmas, T.H., 2009. Regulation and pricing of pharmaceuticals: reference pricing or price cap regulation? Eur. Econ. Rev. 53 (2), 170–185.

Danzon, P.M., Chao, L.-W., 2000. Does regulation drive out competition in pharmaceutical markets? J. Law Econ. 43 (2), 311–358.

Danzon, P.M., Epstein, A.J., 2012. Effects of regulation on drug launch and pricing in interdependent markets. Adv. Health Econ. Health Serv. Res. 23, 35–71.

Danzon, P.M., Ketcham, J.D., 2004. Reference pricing of pharmaceuticals for medicare: evidence from Germany, the Netherlands, and New Zealand. In: Cutler, D.M., Garber, M. (Eds.), Frontiers in Health Policy Research, vol. 7. MIT Press, Cambridge and London, pp. 1–54.

Danzon, P.M., Wang, Y.R., Wang, L., 2005. The impact of price regulation on the launch delay of new drugs – evidence from twenty-five major markets in the 1990. Health Econ. 14 (3), 269–292.

Dirnagl, A.J., Cocoli, M.A., 2016. Global Generic Pharmaceutical Industry Review. Bank of Tokyo-Mitsubishi, New York.

Dubois, P., Gandhi, A., Vasserman, S., 2019. Bargaining and International Reference Pricing in the Pharmaceutical Industry. Working Paper. Harvard University.

Ekelund, M., Persson, B., 2003. Pharmaceutical pricing in a regulated market. Rev. Econ. Stat. 85 (2), 298–306.

Espin, J., Rovira, J., de Labry, A.O., 2011. External Reference Pricing, Review Series on Pharmaceutical Pricing Policies and Interventions, Working Paper 1.

Geng, D., Saggi, K., 2017. International effects of national regulations: external reference pricing and price controls. J. Int. Econ. 109, 68–84.

Goldberg, P.K., 2010. Intellectual property rights protection in developing countries: the case of pharmaceuticals. J. Eur. Econ. Assoc. 8, 326–353.

Grossman, G.M., Lai, E., 2008. Parallel imports and price controls. Rand J. Econ. 39, 378–402.

Howard, D.H., Bach, P.B., Berndt, E.R., Conti, R.M., 2015. Pricing in the market for anticancer drugs. J. Econ. Perspect. 29 (1), 139–162.

International Generic and Biosimilar Medicines Association (IGBA), 2015. Fostering International Trade in Generic and Biosimilar Medicines. IGBA, Brussels.

Kaló, Z., Docteur, E., Moïse, P., 2008. Pharmaceutical Pricing and Reimbursement Policies in Slovakia, DELSA/HEA/WD/HWP(2008)1. OECD.

Kanavos, P., Nicod, E., Espin, J., Van Den Aardweg, S., 2010. Short- and Long-Term Effects of Value-Based Pricing vs. External Price Referencing. EMiNet.

Kanavos, P., Fontrier, A.-M., Gill, J., Efthymiadou, O., Boekstein, N., 2017a. The Impact of External Reference Pricing within and across Countries. London School of Economics, London, UK.

Kanavos, P., Fontrier, A.-M., Gill, J., Kyriopoulos, D., 2017b. The Implementation of External Reference Pricing within and across Country Borders. London School of Economics, London, UK.

Kang, S.-Y., DiStefano, M.J., Socal, M.P., Anderson, G.F., 2019. Using external reference pricing in Medicare Part D to reduce drug price differentials with other countries. Health Affairs 38 (5), 804–811.

Kyle, M., 2007. Pharmaceutical price controls and entry strategies. Rev. Econ. Stat. 89 (1), 88–99.

Koskinen, H., Elina, A., Leena, S.K., Hennamari, M., Jaana, M.E., 2014. The impact of reference pricing and extension of generic substitution on the daily cost of antipsychotic medication in Finland. Health Econ. Rev. 4 (9), 1–10.

Lakdawalla, D., 2018. Economics of the pharmaceutical industry. J. Econ. Lit. 56 (2), 397–449.

Lanjouw, J.O., 2005. Patents, Price Controls and Access to New Drugs: How Policy Affects Global Market Entry, National Bureau of Economic Research Working Paper No. 11321.

Li, C., Maskus, K.E., 2006. The impact of parallel imports on investments in cost-reducing research and development. J. Int. Econ. 68 (2), 443–455.

Leopold, C., Mantel-Teeuwisse, A.K., Seyfang, L., Vogler, S., de Joncheere, K., Laing, R.O., Leufkens, H., 2012. Impact of external price referencing on medicine prices – a price comparison among 14 European countries. South. Med Rev. 5 (2), 34–41.

Maini, L., Pammolli, F., 2019. Reference Pricing as a Deterrent to Entry: Evidence from the European Pharmaceutical Market, Working Paper.

Malueg, D.A., Schwartz, M., 1994. Parallel imports, demand dispersion, and international price discrimination. J. Int. Econ. 37, 167–195.

Maskus, K.E., 2000. Parallel imports. World Econ. 23, 1269–1284.

Miraldo, M., 2009. Reference pricing and firms' pricing strategies. J. Health Econ. 28, 176–197.

Paris, V., Docteur, E., 2006. Pharmaceutical Pricing and Reimbursement Policies in Canada, OECD Health Working Papers No. 24.

Rémuzat, C., Urbinati, D., Mzoughi, O., Hammi, E.E., Belgaied, W., Toumi, M., 2015. Overview of external reference pricing systems in Europe. J. Market Access Health Policy 3, 1.

Richardson, M., 2002. An elementary proposition concerning parallel imports. J. Int. Econ. 56, 233–245.

Roy, S., Saggi, K., 2012. Equilibrium parallel import policies and international market structure. J. Int. Econ. 87, 262–276.

Schmalensee, R., 1981. Output and welfare implications of monopolistic third-degree price discrimination. Am. Econ. Rev. 71, 242–247.

Valletti, T.M., 2006. Differential pricing, parallel trade, and the incentive to invest. J. Int. Econ. 70, 314–324.

Varian, H., 1985. Price discrimination and social welfare. Am. Econ. Rev. 75, 870–875.

Vogler, S., Zimmermann, N., Habl, C., Piessnegger, J., Bucsics, A., 2012. Discounts and rebates granted to public payers for medicines in European countries. South. Med Rev. 5 (1), 38–46.

World Health Organization, 2013. Guideline on Country Pharmaceutical Pricing Policies. WHO, Geneva.

Wouters, O.J., Kanavos, P.G., McKEE, M., 2017. Comparing generic drug markets in Europe and the United States: prices, volumes, and spending. Milbank Q. 95 (3), 554–601.

Young, K.E., Soussib, I., Toumi, M., 2017. The perverse impact of external reference pricing (ERP): a comparison of orphan drugs affordability in 12 European countries. A call for policy change. J. Market Access Health Policy 5 (1).

Part 5

Compulsory Licensing, Price Controls, and Global Welfare

Chapter 19

Compulsory licensing, price controls, and access to patented foreign products☆,#

Eric W. Bond [1], Kamal Saggi *

Department of Economics, Vanderbilt University, USA

ARTICLE INFO

Article history:
Received 21 November 2013
Received in revised form 26 March 2014
Accepted 1 April 2014
Available online 13 April 2014

Keywords:
Patented products
Compulsory licensing
Voluntary licensing
Price controls
Quality
Welfare

ABSTRACT

We analyze how a price control and the threat of compulsory licensing (CL) affect consumer access in a developing country (South) to a patented foreign product. In the model, the Southern government sets the level of the price control on a Northern patent-holder who chooses between entry and voluntary licensing (VL). While entry incurs a higher fixed cost, licensed production is of lower quality. If the patent-holder does not work its patent locally, the South is free to use CL. The threat of CL: ensures that consumers have access to (a lower quality version of) the patented good when the patent-holder chooses not to work its patent locally; improves the terms at which VL occurs; can cause the patent-holder to switch from VL to entry; and can delay consumer access when CL replaces VL or entry. We also show that a price control and CL are mutually reinforcing instruments.

1. Introduction

The use of price controls in the market for pharmaceuticals has a long history in developing countries. Consider, for example, the case of India. Price controls over drugs were first introduced by India in 1962 and have been essentially in effect ever since. Over the years, a series of price control orders have been issued by the central government of India, with the most recent one coming in 2013.[2] This price control order significantly expanded the list of drugs whose prices are subject to government control in India.[3] Based on the report of a specially appointed committee with the self-explanatory title of *The Committee on Price Negotiation for Patented Drugs*, the Indian government also circulated a draft proposal that discussed various options for regulating the local prices of patented medicines.[4] In its report, this committee noted that market prices for patented drugs were beyond the reach of the general masses of India and recommended several methodologies for lowering and/or directly controlling them. Of course, this concern is hardly unique to India and is, in fact, much more acute for countries whose local pharmaceutical industries are nowhere near as well developed as that of India.

As one might expect, regulation of prices in the pharmaceutical industry has important consequences for consumers. For example, in her structural study of 155 pharmaceutical products sold in India, of which 14 were under price control, Dutta (2011) finds that, if implemented, price deregulation would cause significant welfare losses for consumers.[5] According to her estimates, for some drugs, the negative effects of such deregulation could exceed even those of patent enforcement required by the WTO's Agreement on Trade Related Aspects of Intellectual Property (TRIPS).

Tempting as it is, a strategy of using price controls to improve consumer access can become counter-productive if foreign pharmaceutical companies refuse to sell their patented medicines in markets where such controls are too stringent. The existing empirical evidence on

☆ We thank co-editor Patrick Francois, two anonymous referees, Carsten Fink, Jay Pil Choi, and participants at the CES-Ifo conference on Applied Microeconomics, the 8th Annual Conference on Economic Growth and Development at the Indian Statistical Institute, and the World Intellectual Property Organization's seminar series on the Economics of Intellectual Property for helpful comments. Bond thanks the Leitner Center at Yale University for support.

* Corresponding author at: Department of Economics, Vanderbilt University, VU Station B# 351828, 2301 Vanderbilt Place, Nashville, TN 37235-1828, USA. Tel.: +1 615 322 3237.
E-mail addresses: eric.bond@Vanderbilt.Edu (E.W. Bond), k.saggi@Vanderbilt.Edu (K. Saggi).

[1] Tel.: +1 615 322 2388.

[2] Further details are available at http://pharmaceuticals.gov.in/.

[3] This policy announcement received wide press coverage both domestically and internationally. See, for example, "India Widens Price Control over Medicines" in *Wall Street Journal*, May 17, 2013 and "Government Notifies New Drug Price Control Order" in the *Indian Express*, May 17, 2013.

[4] This report is available online at http://spicyipindia.blogspot.com/2013/03/patents-vs-patients-department-of.html.

[5] Similarly, Chatterjee et al. (2013) find that the removal of price controls in the oral anti-diabetic segment of the Indian pharmaceutical market would have significant negative repercussions for Indian consumers.

This chapter was originally appeared in *Journal of Development Economics* **109**, 217–228. © 2014 Elsevier B.V.

drug launches indicates that the presence of price controls and related regulations indeed deters entry in pharmaceutical markets. For example, in her large sample study of 68 countries over the time period 1982–2002, Lanjouw (2005) found that price regulations delayed the introduction of new drugs. Similarly, in her study of the 28 largest pharmaceutical markets in the world, Kyle (2007) found that the presence of price controls and other such regulations delayed or reduced the probability of drug launch in countries that imposed them.

What options, if any, does a country have when a foreign patent-holder refuses to sell either due to the presence of price regulations or because it finds local sales unprofitable for other reasons? As per TRIPS rules, when faced with no or limited access to a patented foreign product, a country may choose to engage in compulsory licensing (CL), i.e., an authorization granted by a government to someone other than the patent-holder to produce the product without the patent-holder's consent.[6] Article 31 of TRIPS (which pertains to "use without authorization of the right holder") lays down the conditions that govern the use of CL of patented products. This Article requires that the entity (company or government) seeking a compulsory license should have been unable to obtain a voluntary license from the right holder on "reasonable" commercial terms and that "adequate remuneration" must be paid to the patent-holder in the event of CL.[7]

Motivated by common features of some recent cases of CL (discussed below) and WTO ground rules that govern the use of CL, this paper develops a North–South model to analyze the dual roles played by a price control and the threat of CL in determining consumer access in the South to a patented product sold by a Northern patent-holder. In the model, the Southern government sets the level of the price control while the patent-holder chooses between serving the Southern market by entering directly or by (voluntarily) licensing its technology to a local firm.[8] From the patent-holder's viewpoint, the trade-off between voluntary licensing (VL) and entry is that while the fixed costs incurred under licensing are relatively lower, so is the quality of production. To assess the value of CL to the South, we examine two scenarios: one where the Southern government can issue a CL to the local firm if the patent-holder fails to work the patent in the South and another where it cannot. The local firm's quality of production under CL is the same as that under VL (i.e. it is inferior to that under entry).

Our analysis addresses several inter-related questions: What factors determine the patent-holder's decision regarding its optimal entry mode? How does each instrument – i.e. a price control and CL – affect the patent-holder's decision? What is the relationship between the two instruments? What are their respective effects on Southern consumers, the patent-holder, and welfare? Does a price control obviate the need for CL?

In recent years, several countries have moved to issue compulsory licenses for patented drugs needed locally.[9] In a case that drew significant attention in the press, on January 2007 the government of Thailand issued a compulsory license for Kaletra, an AIDS drug, to the Government Pharmaceutical Organization (GPO) – a government owned Thai producer of medicines.[10] Regardless of one's views about the merits of CL, one aspect of the Thai experience that is worrisome for all concerned is that the quality of GPO's production was below world standards – an aspect of production under CL that is central to the model that we develop below. Indeed, the Global Fund to Fight HIV/AIDS had granted the GPO $133 million in 2003 so that it could upgrade its plant to meet international quality standards. Following in Thailand's footsteps, in May 2007 Brazil decided to issue a compulsory license for Efavirenz, another patented AIDS drug, after price negotiations with the patent-holder (Merck) had broken down. Brazil had previously used the threat of CL to pressure companies to lower prices of patented medicines, but Efavirenz was the first patented HIV medicine for which it actually issued a compulsory license.[11] It turned out that Farmanguinhos – the leading government owned pharmaceutical manufacturer in Brazil – struggled to manufacture Efavirenz since it lacked the technological know-how to do so (Daemmrich and Musacchio, 2011). It eventually took Farmanguinhos two years to be able to supply Efavirenz to the local market. In the meantime, Brazil had to resort to importing a generic version of the drug from India.

There are three common (and crucial) aspects of the experiences of Thailand and Brazil with CL. First, price considerations were a major factor in prompting the use of CL. Indeed, national governments seemed to have used their power to lower prices as well as the threat of CL for improving consumer access to patented foreign medicines. Second, in both Thailand and Brazil, there was essentially a single local producer that had the competence to produce the relevant drug. Third, in both instances, the local producer's technological capability was inferior to that of the original patent-holder. We believe that these features capture important ground realities confronting the potential use of CL in developing countries and the model that we develop puts them at center stage.

To isolate the roles of price controls and CL, we first analyze a scenario where the Southern government does not have the option to issue a CL. Due to the presence of mode-specific fixed costs, both entry and VL can be unprofitable for the patent-holder even in the absence of a price control. In such a situation, the product is simply not sold in the South and the price control policy of the government is irrelevant. When only one of the modes is profitable, it is optimal for the government to set the price control at a level that allows the patent-holder to break even (i.e. cover its fixed costs) under the profitable mode. However, when both modes are profitable and the break-even price under entry is relatively higher (i.e $\overline{p}_E \geq \overline{p}_L$), to be able to induce entry the government has to set a relatively lax price control that allows the patent-holder to earn some rents under entry. When $\overline{p}_E \geq \overline{p}_L$ setting the price control $\overline{p} = \overline{p}_E$ is not optimal since doing so induces the patent-holder to choose VL (under which it earns positive profits) which could be induced at $\overline{p}_L$. From the patent-holder's viewpoint, the scenario where $\overline{p}_E > \overline{p}_L$ is necessarily better but the government also prefers it if the quality of production under VL is quite low.

Our analysis shows that the option to use CL has the potential to increase Southern welfare due to three separate reasons. One, it lowers the licensing fee paid to the patent-holder under VL. Two, it can cause a switch from VL to entry thereby improving the quality of the product available to Southern consumers. Third, and perhaps most importantly, it can ensure that at least a lower quality version of the patented product is available locally if the patent-holder decides not to work its patent. However, these benefits of CL for the South are somewhat tempered by the fact that the possibility of CL can make it less likely that the

[6] Indeed, some observers have interpreted compulsory licensing as the "breaking of a patent" (Cahoy, 2011); what is broken is the right of a patent holder to exclude others.

[7] Article 5 of the Paris Convention for the Protection of Industrial Property (commonly known as the Paris Convention), originally adopted in 1883, allowed signatories to adopt legislative measures "for the grant of compulsory licenses to prevent the abuses which might result from the exercise of the exclusive rights conferred by the patent, for example, *failure to work*" (Pozen, 2008). Thus, even as early as 1883, the non-working of a patent (equivalent to not supplying a patented medicine to a particular country in our context) was seen as justifiable grounds for compulsory licensing.

[8] This aspect of our model is related to the literature that explores how the optimal entry strategy used by a firm to penetrate a foreign market depends upon the degree of IPR protection available in that market. See, for example, Ethier and Markusen (1996), Markusen (2001), and McCalman (2004).

[9] Of course, one of our key arguments is that for the option to invoke CL to matter, CL need not actually be observed: the threat to issue a compulsory license can affect the behavior of patent-holders to the advantage of developing countries thereby making its use unnecessary.

[10] The decision to issue a compulsory license was explained by Dr. Mongkol, the Thai Health Minister, as follows: "We ask for the understanding of pharmaceutical companies. Much of our affected population cannot afford your drugs and we want people to have access to the medicines that they need." He also noted that there would be no need for CL if pharmaceutical companies "would voluntarily reduce prices." (Baron, 2008).

[11] For example, prior to the negotiations with Merck, Brazil had threatened to issue a compulsory license for Kaletra but did not actually do so since Abbott Laboratories agreed to lower the price of Kaletra to $1380 per year through 2011.

patent-holder chooses to work its patent in the South. This is due to two reasons. One, since CL yields a royalty payment to the patent-holder its payoff from not working its patent in the South increases. Two, the threat of CL reduces the fee collected by the patent-holder under VL. When CL *replaces* VL or entry in this fashion, it can lower Southern welfare because it *delays* consumer access to the patented product. For example, when CL replaces VL the South can be made worse off if the welfare cost of delay (i.e. the consumer surplus foregone during the delay period) dominates the discounted value of the profit earned by the local firm net of the royalty fee paid to the patent-holder under CL.

The model also sheds light on the relationship between a price control and CL. We find that the two policy instruments can be complementary from the Southern perspective in two senses. First, by shifting the patent-holder's preference in favor of entry, the threat of CL makes it possible for the South to induce entry at a lower price. Second, CL gives the South the option of having the product produced locally at a price equal to the marginal cost of production, something that is not possible when CL is unavailable since the patent-holder has to make sufficient profit to cover its fixed cost of working the patent in the South. These results are consistent with the observed evidence that VL is rarely the outcome of episodes where CL has been brought up by governments negotiating prices with foreign patent-holders, and also resonate well with Goldberg (2010) who has argued that price regulations might need to be complemented by CL to ensure adequate access to medicines in developing countries.[12] However, we also note that in cases where the South government has the power to extract all surplus from the patent-holder in the absence of CL, the requirement of a royalty payment under CL raises the South's cost of obtaining access to the product.

2. Model

We consider the case of a Northern firm (referred to as the "patent-holder") that holds a patent over its product for T periods. There are a continuum of Southern consumers of measure 1, each of whom buys (at most) one unit of the product. If a consumer buys the product at price p, his utility is given by $U = \theta q - p$ where q measures quality and $\theta \geq 0$ is a taste parameter that captures the willingness to pay for quality. For simplicity, we assume that θ is uniformly distributed over the interval [0,1]. Assuming utility under no purchase equals zero, the per-period demand $d(p,q)$ for the product in the South is easily calculated: $d(p,q) = 1-\frac{p}{q}$.

If the patent-holder decides to enter the Southern market and produce the goods then its quality level equals q. To be able to undertake local production, the patent-holder has to incur the fixed entry cost φ.[13] The parameter φ plays an important role in our analysis and the economic basis for it deserves discussion. This parameter captures the costs of obtaining any necessary approval from local authorities as well as the costs of establishing an effective marketing and distribution network. As is well known, the pharmaceutical sector is heavily regulated in most countries and launching a drug in a new market is a costly endeavor. For example, the laws of Australia, Japan, the EU, and the USA all require that firms must secure drug approval from the relevant regulatory authority prior to introducing a new drug in the local market. This process can be fairly time consuming in some countries (such as Japan) and the profits foregone due to delay further increase the cost/benefit ratio of drug launch faced by patent-holders. While some small developing countries approve drugs conditional on prior approval in developed countries (Kremer, 2002), this is not the case for the larger developing countries such as Brazil and India. For example, in her extensive and insightful discussion of the likely effects of the introduction of pharmaceutical patents in India, Lanjouw (1998) notes that patent-holders sometimes deliberately chose to not introduce their new drugs in India because of the administrative costs involved: they are not only required to gain marketing approval from the Drugs Controller General but may also have to prove "utility", i.e., the new drug is needed in the Indian market. The exact interpretation of this utility requirement is unclear but there is little doubt that it presents yet another hurdle that a patent-holder wishing to market a new drug in India must confront.[14]

Regarding the role of marketing and distribution costs, recent work by Chaudhuri et al. (2006) demonstrates that the quality of a firm's marketing and distribution network can be an important factor determining consumer access to pharmaceuticals. In their study of a specific antibiotic segment of the Indian pharmaceutical market, they found that consumers generally preferred domestic suppliers when a given antibiotic was sold by both domestic and foreign sellers because the marketing and distribution networks of domestic firms were relatively superior.

In our model, the patent-holder can also sell in the South by licensing its patented technology to a local firm for the duration of the patent. We assume that there is only a single local firm with sufficient capability to be an effective licensee. While voluntary licensing (VL) also incurs the costs of securing drug approval and technology transfer, it offers the patent-holder the advantage of being able to use the local licensee's existing distribution and retail network. Thus, we assume that the fixed cost of VL is lower than that of direct entry and denote it by $\alpha\varphi$ where $0 < \alpha < 1$.[15] However, the disadvantage of VL is that the Southern firm has a lower level of technological capability than the patent-holder, and is thus unable to produce a product of equal quality (as was evidenced by the experience of Thailand and Brazil discussed previously). Accordingly, we assume that the quality of production under VL equals γq, where $\gamma < 1$ captures the quality disadvantage of VL.[16]

Normalizing the cost of production under VL to zero, the monopoly price for the licensee equals $p_L^* = \frac{\gamma q}{2}$. Let $\overline{p}$ denote the price control imposed by the government and $\beta \in [0,1]$ be the per period discount factor. Then the maximum gross profits accruing to the licensee over the life of the patent are:

$$v_L(\overline{p}, \gamma) = (1 + \Omega)\pi_L(\overline{p}, \gamma) \text{ where } \pi_L(\overline{p}, \gamma) \equiv \min[\overline{p}, p_L^*]\left(1 - \frac{\min[\overline{p}, p_L^*]}{\gamma q}\right) \quad (1)$$

where

$$\Omega = \sum_{t=1}^{T} \beta^t = \frac{\beta\left(1-\beta^T\right)}{1-\beta}$$

[12] From 1995–2011 there were 24 episodes where CL of a patented foreign medicine was publicly considered or implemented by a member country of the WTO (Beall and Kuhn, 2012). Half of these 24 episodes ended up with the issuance of a CL; a VL was the end result in only three of them. However, price reductions were achieved by local governments in almost all of the cases, suggesting a potential synergy between price controls and CL that we explore in this paper.

[13] We do not distinguish between the patent-holder entering the South via exporting or by establishing a foreign subsidiary. Either mode of entry would satisfy the condition for working the patent thereby preventing a compulsory license, and either would involve fixed entry costs. We assume the patent-holder chooses the entry mode that yields it higher profit.

[14] See also Maskus (2000) and Goldberg (2010) for a discussion of the wider literature pertaining to the role that rules and regulations play in determining consumer access to pharmaceuticals in developing countries.

[15] See Chatterjee et al. (2013) for a discussion of how Novartis decided to license vildagliptin (an anti-diabetic drug) to a local Indian firm called USV that had an established presence in the market. They note that the objective of Novartis in licensing the drug to USV was to "utilize USV's wider reach in the domestic market." A similar strategy was used by Merck to sell sitagliptin in India. These cases illustrate one advantage of VL from the viewpoint of foreign patent-holders selling in foreign markets that have local firms with well established marketing and distribution networks.

[16] The parameter γ may also reflect the frictions associated with arms length technology transfer relative to intra-firm technology transfer under entry, with more sophisticated products having a lower level of γ for the licensee.

converts future flow profits to present value. The distinction between first period returns and subsequent returns plays a role in the analysis of compulsory licensing in Section 4, since we interpret the first period as representing the delay required before a compulsory license can be imposed by the South if the local market is not served by the patent-holder.

Assuming that the marginal cost of production under entry is the same as that under VL, the unconstrained monopoly price under entry equals $p_E^* = \frac{q}{2}$ and the present value of the patent-holder's maximum gross profits under direct entry when facing the price control $\bar{p}$ equals

$$v_E(\bar{p}) = (1+\Omega)\pi_E(\bar{p}) \text{ where } \pi_E(\bar{p}) \equiv \min[\bar{p}, p_E^*]\left(1-\frac{\min[\bar{p}, p_E^*]}{q}\right). \quad (2)$$

Observe that since $p_E^* > p_L^*$, the *price control is more binding under entry* relative to VL and that the absence of a price control is equivalent to $\bar{p} = p_E^*$.

The per-period welfare of the South equals the sum of consumer surplus $S(p,q) = \frac{q}{2}\left(1-\frac{p}{q}\right)^2$ and the net profits of the local firm. Southern welfare under VL equals

$$W^L(\bar{p},\gamma) = (1+\Omega)\left[S(\min[\bar{p}, p_L^*], \gamma q) + \pi_L(\bar{p},\gamma)\right] - f \quad (3)$$

where f is the licensing fee paid to the patent-holder. Southern welfare under entry (W^E) consists solely of consumer surplus that accrues to the South over the life of the product:

$$W^E(\bar{p}) = (1+\Omega)S(\min[\bar{p}, p_E^*], q) \quad (4)$$

Thus, while licensing has the potential to provide the South some benefits in terms of the profits of the local firm (net of the license fee), these benefits come at the cost of having a lower quality product relative to entry.

In what follows, we begin with the benchmark case where the only instrument available to the South for improving consumer access is the price control $\bar{p}$. Then, we allow the South to use CL in the event the patent-holder does not work its patent in the South.

3. Benchmark case

We analyze the interaction between the patent-holder and the Southern government (referred to as simply "the government" from hereon) as a two stage game. In the first stage, the government chooses the domestic price control $\bar{p}$ to be imposed on the product. At the second stage of the game, taking the price control set by the government as given, the patent-holder decides whether to enter the market itself, to voluntarily license the product to the local firm, or to not sell the product at all in the South. This two stage game constitutes a benchmark scenario where the government does not have the option to use CL if the patent-holder refrains from selling locally. After analyzing this benchmark case, we introduce CL by adding a third stage to this game.

The government is assumed to know the fixed costs of both VL and entry, as well as the quality of the product that would be produced by the patent-holder or the licensee when making this decision. We also assume that once the price control has been set, the government is committed to it for the remainder of the game.[17]

We assume that the bargaining game for VL is one in which the patent-holder makes a take it or leave it offer to the Southern firm. If the offer is accepted then the Southern firm acts as a licensee and transfers the present value of its product market profit stream to the patent-holder as the licensing fee $f_L(\bar{p})$. If it rejects the patent-holder's offer of a VL, the Southern firm earns zero profits since it does not have the right to produce the patented product.

3.1. Patent-holder's decision

To determine how the patent-holder's choice between VL and entry depends upon the price control $\bar{p}$, first note that since $p_E^* > p_L^*$ a given price control either (i) fails to bind under both entry and VL (i.e. $\bar{p} = p_E^*$), (ii) binds only under entry (i.e. $p_L^* \le p < p_E^*$) or (iii) binds under both modes (i.e. $p < p_L^*$).

Denote the present value of the patent-holder's payoff under monopoly pricing by v_Z^* where $Z = L$ or E. Calculating the present value differential between the two modes allows us to write:

$$\Delta v(\bar{p}) \equiv v_E(\bar{p}) - v_L(\bar{p}) = \begin{cases} \Delta v^* = v_E^* - v_L^* = \dfrac{q(1+\Omega)(1-\gamma)}{4} & \bar{p} = p_E^* \\ \Delta v_1(\bar{p}) = (1+\Omega)\left[\bar{p}\left(1-\dfrac{\bar{p}}{q}\right) - \dfrac{\gamma q}{4}\right] & p_L^* \le p < p_E^* \\ \Delta v_2(\bar{p}) = (1+\Omega)\dfrac{\bar{p}^2}{q}\left(\dfrac{1-\gamma}{\gamma}\right) & p < p_L^* \end{cases} \quad (5)$$

We can utilize the expression for the present value differential in Eq. (5) to derive the patent-holder's optimal decision. We begin with the case where the price control is so lax that the patent-holder can charge its optimal monopoly price under direct entry and VL (i.e. $\bar{p} = p_E^*$). As is clear, this case also describes the market outcome when the government is unable or unwilling to use a price control, perhaps due to negative international repercussions.[18]

Both VL and entry are profitable modes of serving the market as long as the fixed costs are below their respective threshold levels:

$$\varphi \le \varphi_E \equiv v_E^* \text{ and } \varphi \le \varphi_L \equiv \frac{v_L^*}{\alpha}. \quad (6)$$

Since $v_L^* = \gamma v_E^*$, it follows from Eq. (6) that $\varphi_L > \varphi_E$ if $\gamma > \alpha$. This case is illustrated in Fig. 1, which shows the patent-holder's payoff (net of fixed costs) to VL and entry when there is no price control. Since $\gamma < 1$, the return to entry must exceed the return to VL when fixed costs are close to zero. We refer to this as the product quality effect, because the variable profits of the entrant exceed those of the licensee (i.e. $v_E^* > v_L^*$) due to the higher quality of production under entry. On the other hand, the payoff under entry is more steeply sloped than that under VL because entry involves a higher level of fixed costs. We refer to this as the fixed cost effect.

When $\gamma > \alpha$, the patent-holder prefers entry to VL for all $\varphi \le \tilde{\varphi}$ where[19]:

$$\tilde{\varphi} \equiv \frac{\Delta v^*}{1-\alpha}. \quad (7)$$

The product quality effect makes entry more profitable than VL when φ is below $\tilde{\varphi}$, but the fixed cost effect makes VL more attractive for $\varphi \in [\tilde{\varphi}, \varphi_L]$.

If $\gamma \le \alpha$, then $\varphi_L \ge \varphi_E$. In this case, the product quality advantage of entry dominates the fixed cost savings of VL to such an extent that the patent-holder always prefers entry to VL: if entry is unprofitable

[17] The government's concern about availability of the product at a reasonable price is reflected in our assumption that it can set a price control for sales in the local market. Since the patent-holder incurs a fixed cost of entry if it serves the market itself, there is a potential holdup problem if the government has the ability to alter the price control once the patent-holder has made its entry decision. To avoid this issue, we assume that the government is able to commit to the price control prior to the patent-holder's decision.

[18] For example, due to their weak protection of intellectual property rights many developing countries such as Brazil, China, and India have found themselves to be the target of US investigations under Section 301 of the U.S. Trade Act of 1974. This Act authorizes the US President to retaliate in response to a policy or practice of a foreign government that violates a trade agreement or is deemed to be detrimental to US commercial interests. Section 301 cases can not only be self-initiated by the United States Trade Representative (USTR) but also by a firm or industry group adversely affected by a foreign policy.

[19] We settle indifference on the patent-holder between entry and VL in favor of entry.

E.W. Bond, K. Saggi / Journal of Development Economics 109 (2014) 217–228 221

($\varphi > v_E^*$), so is VL and the patent-holder simply chooses to not sell in the South. Since the interesting scenario is the one where both entry and VL can arise in equilibrium, for the rest of the paper we make the following assumption [20]:

Assumption 1. $\gamma > \alpha$

We can now summarize the patent-holder's optimal choice in the absence of a price control:

Proposition 1. If the government's price control policy permits the patent-holder to charge optimal prices under entry and VL (i.e. $\overline{p} = p_E^*$) then $\tilde{\varphi} < \varphi_E < \varphi_L$ and the patent-holder chooses entry for all $\varphi \in [0, \tilde{\varphi}]$; VL for all $\varphi \in (\tilde{\varphi}, \varphi_L]$; and does not work its patent in the South if $\varphi > \varphi_L$.[21]

When both VL and entry are profitable ($\varphi \leq \varphi_E$) entry is chosen by the patent-holder only when fixed costs are sufficiently low, i.e., $\varphi \leq \tilde{\varphi}$. Observe that

$$\varphi \leq \tilde{\varphi} \Leftrightarrow \varphi \leq \frac{\varphi_E(1-\gamma)}{1-\alpha}.$$

Since $\frac{1-\gamma}{1-\alpha}$ is decreasing in γ and increasing in α, entry is less likely to be chosen when the quality disadvantage of VL is small and its fixed cost advantage is large.

We now turn to the case where the Southern government imposes a price control that is below the entry monopoly price p_E^*, and examine how the existence of such a price control affects the patent-holder's decision. Since variable profits are declining in $\overline{p}$ when the price control binds, a binding price control shifts the net profit loci in Fig. 1 downward and reduces the thresholds φ_E and φ_L. Under a binding price control, entry is the more profitable than VL if

$$\Delta v(\overline{p}) \geq (1-\alpha)\varphi. \tag{8}$$

It can be seen from Eq. (5) that $\Delta v(\overline{p})$ is increasing in $\overline{p}$, so the threshold level of fixed cost $\tilde{\varphi}$ at which entry is preferred to VL is increasing in $\overline{p}$. It is established in the proof of Proposition 2 that for all $\overline{p} > 0$, there exists a range of fixed costs $[0, \tilde{\varphi}(\overline{p})]$ over which the patent-holder chooses entry and a range of fixed costs $(\tilde{\varphi}(\overline{p}), \varphi_L(\overline{p})]$ over which it opts for VL. Thus, the patent-holder's pattern of serving the market identified in Proposition 1 continues to hold even in the presence of a binding price control.

To facilitate the discussion of the government's optimal price control below, it is useful to invert the threshold fixed cost relationships to obtain the break-even price for entry, $\overline{p}_E(\varphi) = \varphi_E^{-1}(\overline{p})$, and that for VL, $\overline{p}_L(\varphi) = \varphi_L^{-1}(\overline{p})$.[22] The properties of the threshold fixed costs above ensure that $\overline{p}_E(\varphi) > \overline{p}_L(\varphi)$ under Assumption 1. Similarly, we can define the entry-inducing price, $\tilde{p}(\varphi)$, as the price at which the patent-holder is indifferent between entry and VL. The entry inducing price $\tilde{p}$ is the solution to $\Delta v(p) - (1-\alpha)\varphi = 0$.[23]

The following result (proved in Appendix A) identifies the patent-holder's entry decision for a given level of fixed costs as a function of the price control chosen by the government:

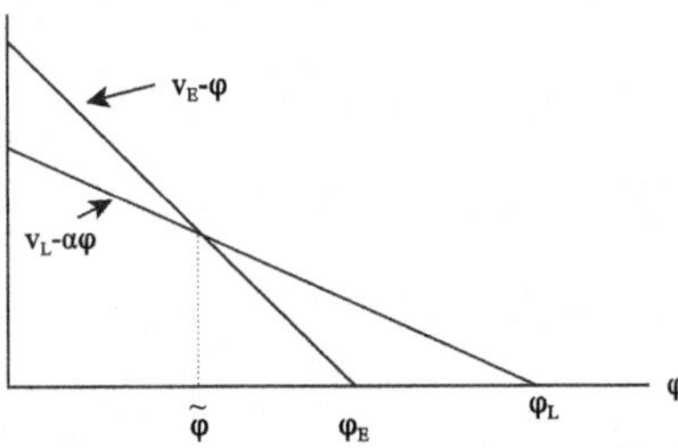

Fig. 1. Returns to licensing and entry with $\gamma > \alpha$.

Proposition 2. For $\overline{p} < p_E^*, \overline{p}_L(\varphi) < \overline{p}_E(\varphi) < \tilde{p}(\varphi)$: the patent-holder enters if $\overline{p} \geq \tilde{p}(\varphi)$, issues a VL if $\overline{p}_L(\varphi) \leq \overline{p} < \tilde{p}(\varphi)$; and does not serve the Southern market otherwise.

Fig. 2 illustrates the interplay between the level of the price control, the fixed cost parameter φ, and the patent-holder's decision for a specific example. The intuitive interpretation of this figure is as follows. For relatively low levels of the fixed cost parameter (i.e. $\varphi \in [0, \tilde{\varphi}]$), the patent-holder's optimal decision is to choose entry provided the price control exceeds the entry inducing price (i.e. $\overline{p} \geq \tilde{p}(\varphi)$), choose VL if the price control is in the intermediate range $\overline{p} \in [\overline{p}_L(\varphi), \tilde{p}(\varphi))$, and not serve the market if the price control is so stringent that even VL does not break even, i.e., if $\overline{p} < \overline{p}_L(\varphi)$. For intermediate values of the fixed cost parameter (i.e. $\varphi \in [\tilde{\varphi}, \varphi_L]$), entry does not arise at all and the patent-holder opts for VL so long as it is profitable (i.e. $\overline{p} \geq \overline{p}_L(\varphi)$). Finally, if fixed costs are sufficiently high, i.e. $\varphi > \varphi_L$, the patent-holder simply does not serve the Southern market.

3.2. Optimal price control

With the patent-holder's decision in hand, the government's optimal policy can now be derived. The government selects its price control to induce that mode of supply on the part of the patent-holder that maximizes local welfare. Since the patent-holder extracts all rents from the local firm under VL, local profits under both entry and VL equal zero. Therefore, the comparison between the two modes of supply rests squarely on consumer surplus. From the viewpoint of consumers, the trade-off between entry and VL is that while the quality of production under entry is higher, the price at which the patent-holder is willing to enter can also be higher.

It is obvious that if $\varphi > \varphi_L$ then the patent-holder finds neither entry nor VL worthwhile and Southern welfare equals zero. Furthermore, the price control is irrelevant under such a situation since the patent-holder stays out of the Southern market no matter what its level. As we will see below, this possibility creates a role for CL that is beyond the reach of a price control and helps highlight its value from the Southern perspective.

Next, note that if $\varphi_E \leq \varphi < \varphi_L$ then entry is unprofitable and the patent-holder prefers VL. Under such a situation, the optimal policy calls for the government to set the price control equal to the lowest price at which the patent-holder is willing to grant a VL, i.e., $\overline{p} = \overline{p}_L$. Here, since only VL is profitable, the optimal price control policy simply lowers the price at which the good is available without affecting the patent-holder's mode choice.

Now consider the scenario where both modes of supply are profitable for the patent-holder so that $\varphi < \varphi_E$. Since $\overline{p} > \overline{p}_L$ it is not possible for the government to induce entry by setting the price control at the break-even price $\overline{p}_E$. To see why, simply note that while entry breaks even at this price control, VL yields strictly positive profits. As a result,

[20] The case where $\gamma \leq \alpha$ was extensively discussed in an earlier version of this paper and is not considered here. Interested readers can contact the authors for the details of this case.

[21] It is interesting to note that Lanjouw (2005) finds that local technical capacity is a significant determinant of whether or not a new drug is launched in a country. This is consistent with our model since the ratio of licensing profits to fixed costs is larger when the technology disadvantage of the local firm is smaller.

[22] The break-even price function $\overline{p}_E(\varphi)$ is continuous and increasing on $[0, \varphi_E]$. Since there is no price at which the patent-holder can break even for $\varphi > \varphi_E$, we set $\overline{p}_E(\varphi) = \infty$ for $\varphi > \varphi_E$.

[23] If $\overline{p}_L(\varphi) < \overline{p}_E(\varphi)$ and $\varphi > \frac{\Delta v}{1-\alpha}$, no entry inducing price will exist. As with the break-even prices, we define $\tilde{p}(\varphi) = \infty$ in this case.

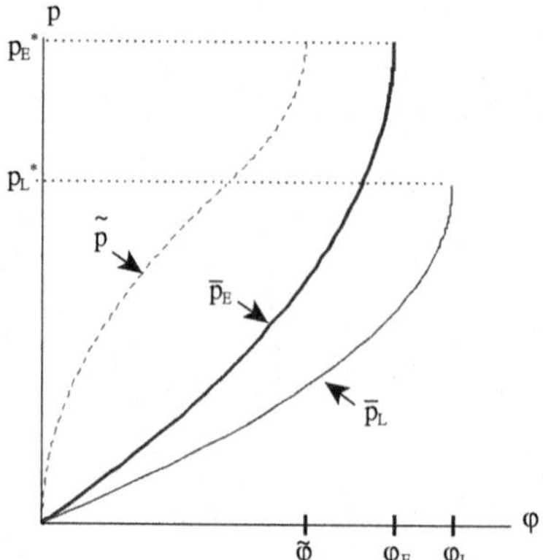

Fig. 2. Price controls, fixed cost, and mode of supply with $\gamma > \alpha$.

to be able to induce entry, the government has to set the price control at the entry inducing price $\tilde{p}$. Of course, setting $\overline{p} = \tilde{p}$ to induce entry is not the only option for the government. It could alternatively set the price control to $\overline{p}_L$ (the break-even price under VL) thereby inducing VL: the patent-holder prefers VL to entry at this price control since $\overline{p}_E > \overline{p}_L$. The trade-off between the government's two choices is then clear: entry offers a higher quality product but also requires a more lax price control. Thus, when $\overline{p}_E > \overline{p}_L$, the South prefers the price control $\tilde{p}$ to $\overline{p}_L$ iff

$$S(\tilde{p}, q) \geq S(\overline{p}_L, \gamma q). \tag{9}$$

We summarize the optimal price control policy below:

Proposition 3. The government's optimal price control policy is as follows:

(i) If $\varphi_E \leq \varphi < \varphi_L$ the government sets the price control equal to the break-even licensing price ($\overline{p}^* = \overline{p}_L$).

(ii) If $\varphi \leq \varphi_E$ it sets the price control at the entry inducing price ($\overline{p}^* = \tilde{p}$) if inequality (9) holds and at the break even licensing price ($\overline{p}^* = \overline{p}_L$) if it does not.

In accordance with the available case-study evidence (discussed in the Introduction), our analysis assumes that the Southern government sets a single price control that applies under both modes of supply (i.e. entry and VL). It is worth asking how our results are altered if the government has the ability to set *mode-specific* price controls. When the government has this flexibility, its optimal policy is actually quite simple. If only VL is profitable (i.e. $\varphi_E < \varphi \leq \varphi_L$), the optimal policy of the government is to set the price control equal to the break-even price $\overline{p}_L^C$. Thus, part (i) of Proposition 4 continues to hold.

Part (ii) of Proposition 4 is modified only slightly. If $\varphi \leq \varphi_E$ the government sets the price control at the break-even entry price ($\overline{p}^* = \overline{p}_E$) if $S(\overline{p}_E, q) \geq S(\overline{p}_L, \gamma q)$ holds and at the break-even licensing price ($\overline{p}^* = \overline{p}_L$) if it does not. Observe that if the government has access to only a single price control that applies to both modes, it has to offer the entry inducing price $\tilde{p}$ in order to ensure that the patent-holder prefers entry to VL. When two separate price controls can be used, the government no longer has to pay a premium to induce entry since it can always drive the patent-holder's net payoff under VL to zero by setting the VL price control at $\overline{p}_L$. An important implication of this is that *allowing for mode-specific price controls makes entry more desirable* from the Southern perspective since it can be induced at a lower price.

4. Incorporating CL

We now extend the benchmark model to allow for a third stage during which the government decides whether or not to issue a CL. If the product has not been sold in the market in the first period i.e. if the patent-holder neither enters nor grants a voluntary license to the local firm, the government can issue a compulsory license to the local firm who pays the per-period royalty R to the patent-holder for the duration of the patent. The structure of this extended game is intended to capture actual features of the TRIPS agreement and the concerns of developing countries as identified in the case studies. The TRIPS requirement that applicants for a compulsory license should have been unable to obtain a voluntary license is reflected in the assumption that the third stage of CL only arises if the patent-holder does not enter and there is no agreement on a voluntary license at the second stage.

The fee received by the patent-holder, R, is assumed to reflect the TRIPS requirement of a "adequate remuneration" to the patent-holder. As Scherer and Watal (2002) note: "since the purpose of virtually all known CL schemes is to increase competitive supply and reduce prices, the 'profits lost' test cannot logically be the standard to be met in determining compensation for CL." We interpret this as suggesting that in practice R may be quite low, which seems consistent with the payments observed in actual cases of CL.[24]

We analyze this three stage CL game using backward induction. In the next Section we present the analysis of stage three, at which the government decides whether or not to issue a compulsory license, given that the patent has not been worked by the patent-holder in the second stage. This analysis establishes the conditions under which CL represents a credible threat that affects the decision of the patent-holder at the second stage. We then examine the second stage decision of the patent-holder regarding whether to enter the market, negotiate a VL, or to not work the patent. The difference from the previous Section is that this decision is now taken under the shadow of a compulsory license if the patent is not worked. We refer to the second and third stages of this game, which treats the price of the product as exogenously given, as the CL subgame. In cases where the government does not have a price control available as a policy instrument or where the price control has been set exogenously by a different government agency, there will be no first stage to the entry game. If the government imposes a price control, the CL game is a proper sub-game of the three stage game, given the price control chosen at stage one. This approach allows us to highlight the value-added of CL as a policy instrument when a price control is already available. In addition, the stand-alone value of CL can be derived by considering the case where the government does not have a price control available as a policy tool.

4.1. The compulsory licensing decision

At stage three, the Southern government must decide whether or not to grant a compulsory license if the product has not been sold in the market in the first period. A compulsory license granted at stage three provides the licensee with the right to produce the good for $T - 1$ periods and delays the fixed cost by one period. We assume that under CL, the Southern firm faces the same price ceiling, produces the

[24] Tandon (1982) provides a model in which both the length of a patent as well as the royalty rate, given that the cost-reducing innovation is subject to compulsory licensing, are optimally determined. It should be noted that Tandon's definition of CL differs from that applied by the WTO, in that he allows compulsory licenses to be granted even if the patent is being worked by the patent-holder. With a perfectly elastic supply of potential licensees, this yields a perfectly competitive industry equilibrium in the product market.

same quality product, and incurs the same fixed cost that it would under the voluntary licensing agreement.[25] However, we allow the government to pay the local licensee a lump sum payment to compensate for any losses that it makes under the compulsory license. With these assumptions, the welfare of the South under a compulsory license equals:

$$W^{CL}(\overline{p}) = \Omega\left[S(\min\{\overline{p}, p_L^*\}, \gamma q) + \pi_L(\overline{p}, \gamma) - R\right] - \alpha\beta\varphi. \tag{10}$$

In order for CL to be a credible threat we need that $W^{CL}(\overline{p}) > 0$, a condition that is satisfied so long as the quality of licensed production is not so low that the total surplus generated for Southern consumers and the local licensee is insufficient to cover the royalty R paid to the patent-holder and the fixed cost incurred by the licensee.

We denote the maximum level of the fixed cost parameter φ below which CL is a credible threat as

$$\varphi_{CL}^{\max}(\overline{p}, R) = \frac{\Omega[S(\min\{\overline{p}, p_L^*\}, \gamma q) + \pi_L(\overline{p}, \gamma) - R]}{\alpha\beta}. \tag{11}$$

This threshold level of fixed cost $\varphi_{CL}^{\max}$ is decreasing in $\overline{p}$, since a lower price raises the sum of consumer surplus and producer profits. The threshold $\varphi_{CL}^{\max}$ is also decreasing in R.

Proposition 2 established that the largest fixed cost at which the Southern market is served for a given price control is $\frac{(1+\Omega)\pi_L(\overline{p}, \gamma)}{\alpha}$. Using Eq. (11), CL is a credible threat for all levels of fixed costs at which the patent-holder enters if $\Omega(S(\min\{\overline{p}, p_L^*\}, \gamma q) - R) > \beta^{T+1}\pi_L(\overline{p}, \gamma)$. This condition is more likely to be satisfied when the royalty under CL is not too large in comparison with consumer surplus and the duration of the compulsory license is sufficiently long relative to the delay before it can be imposed. For the following discussion, this condition is assumed to hold.

4.2. Patent-holder's payoffs

Given that CL is a credible threat, we now turn to stage where the patent-holder decides how to utilize its patent in the South. If the patent-holder enters the South, it earns a return of $v_E(\overline{p}) - \varphi$. If it chooses to license the product to the Southern firm, the patent-holder engages in a bargaining game with the local firm to determine the size of the license fee f_L^C that it receives, where the superscript C indicates that there is a credible threat of CL in period two if the patent is not worked in the first period. If it refrains from both entry and voluntary licensing in the first period, the Southern government issues a compulsory license to the local firm in the second period while paying the per period royalty R to the patent-holder, the present value of which equals ΩR.

As in the benchmark model, the patent-holder makes a take it or leave it offer to the Southern firm. If the offer is accepted then the Southern firm acts as a licensee and pays the fee f_L^C. If the offer is rejected and the patent-holder does not enter then the Southern firm's outside option is no longer zero profits since the government grants it a compulsory license in the next period. Therefore, the licensee earns a return under the compulsory license with a present value of max $[\Omega\pi_L(\overline{p}, \gamma) - \alpha\beta\varphi, 0]$. Defining the fixed cost level at which CL yields zero profits to the licensee as $\varphi_Z = \frac{\Omega\pi_L(\overline{p}, \gamma)}{\beta\alpha}$, a compulsory license yields positive profits for the licensee only if $\varphi < \varphi_Z$. The compulsory license is less attractive to the licensee than a voluntary license because the delay in issuance of a compulsory license shortens the period over which returns from the licensed product can be captured.[26]

The best that the patent-holder can do under VL is to make the Southern firm indifferent between agreeing to a voluntary license in the first period and waiting for a compulsory license in the next period, which yields the licensing fee under VL:

$$f_L^C(\varphi) = \begin{cases} \pi_L(\overline{p}, \gamma) - \alpha(1-\beta)\varphi & \varphi \leq \varphi_Z \\ v_L(\overline{p}, \gamma) - \alpha\varphi & \varphi > \varphi_Z \end{cases}. \tag{12}$$

When $\Omega\pi_L(\overline{p}, \gamma) - \beta\alpha\varphi > 0$, the licensee earns a strictly positive payoff under CL and the possibility of CL induces "profit-shifting" from the patent-holder to the local licensee since it reduces the fee that the licensee is willing to pay the patent-holder under VL. The effect of CL on the fee is illustrated in Fig. 3. The $v_L - \alpha\varphi$ line shows the licensing fee that drives the licensee to zero profits in the absence of a CL. The $\pi_L(\overline{p}, \gamma) - \alpha(1-\beta)\varphi$ is the net return to the licensee that is earned prior to the issuing of a compulsory license, which is the amount that a licensee forgoes by waiting for CL. For $\varphi > \varphi_Z$ a licensee does not earn any profit under CL so the license fee coincides with the no CL case. For $\varphi < \varphi_Z$, the patent-holder must leave the licensee with enough profit to cover what would have been earned under a CL. The vertical distance between v and $f_L^C(\varphi)$ to the left of φ_Z corresponds to the profit shifting effect of CL.

4.3. How CL affects the patent-holder's supply mode

Given these payoffs, the patent-holder's first period decision is to choose between entry with a return of $v_E(\overline{p}) - \varphi$, voluntary licensing with a return of f_L^C, and not work the patent in the South earning a payoff of ΩR under CL. Evaluating these payoffs using Eq. (12) yields the following threshold levels for the patent-holder's decision in the absence of a price control:

Lemma 1. Assume no price control (i.e. $\overline{p} \geq p_E^*$) and a credible threat of CL. Then the patent-holder prefers:

(i) Entry to not serving the market if $\varphi \leq \varphi_E^C \equiv v_E^* - \Omega R$.

(ii) VL to not serving the market if $\varphi \leq \varphi_L^C \equiv \min\left\{\frac{v_L^* - \Omega R}{\alpha}, \frac{\pi_L^* - \Omega R}{\alpha(1-\beta)}\right\}$.

(iii) Entry to VL when $\varphi \leq \tilde{\varphi}^C \equiv \max\left\{\frac{\Delta v^*}{1-\alpha}, \frac{\Delta v^* + \Omega\pi_L^*}{1-\alpha(1-\beta)}\right\}$.

The effects of CL on the patent-holder's decision can be seen by comparing the fixed cost thresholds in Lemma 1 with those when there is no threat of CL. First note that the maximum level of fixed cost at which entry is preferred to not serving the market is reduced due to the threat of CL from φ_E to φ_E^C, because the patent-holder can earn a return of ΩR if the compulsory license is issued. Indeed, $\varphi_E^C = \varphi_E - \Omega R$.

The level of fixed cost at which the patent-holder is indifferent between VL and staying out (recognizing that a compulsory license will be issued in the next period under which it earns ΩR) is the solution to $f_L^C(\varphi) = \Omega R$. In Fig. 3, this is the intersection of $f_L^C(\varphi)$ with a horizontal line at ΩR. The two terms in part (ii) of Lemma 1 represent the values at which the ΩR line intersects the $v_L - \alpha\varphi$ and $\pi_L(\overline{p}, \gamma) - \alpha(1-\beta)\varphi$ lines, respectively. As is clear from Fig. 3, the smaller of these two threshold values of φ is the relevant solution. In either case, the maximum level of fixed cost at which VL is preferred to staying out of the market falls from φ_L to φ_L^C due to the presence of the royalty R under CL. Intuitively, CL raises the patent-holder's return from staying out of the market thereby making it *less willing* to voluntarily license its patent.

[25] It is conceivable that the quality of production under CL is lower than that under VL since CL occurs without cooperation from the patent-holder. For simplicity, we ignore this possibility. In any case, allowing for the quality of production to differ across the two types of licensing modifies our analysis in a straightforward manner. It makes CL less attractive both to the patent-holder and the Southern government.

[26] Using the fact that $\Omega = \frac{\beta(1-\beta^T)}{1-\beta}$, we have $f_L^C(\varphi_Z^C) = \beta^T\pi_L(\overline{p}, \gamma) > 0$, i.e., if the CL just breaks even the patent-holder collects a strictly positive fee under VL. The intuition is that the compulsory licensee is driven to zero profits at a lower level of the fixed cost because it loses some of the returns over the patent's life because of the delay involved under CL (which vanishes as the patent life goes to infinity).

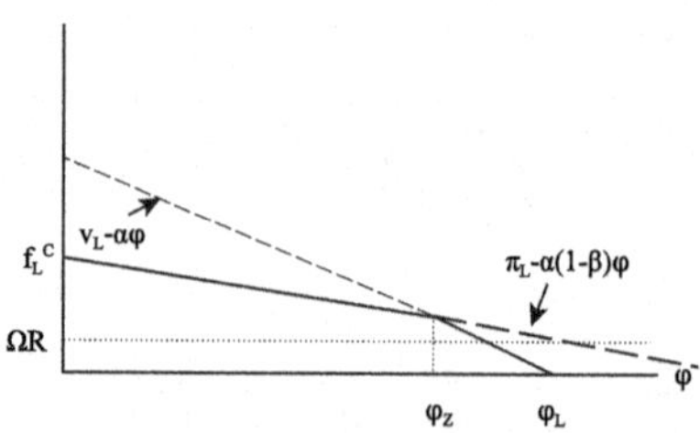

Fig. 3. How CL affects payoffs under VL.

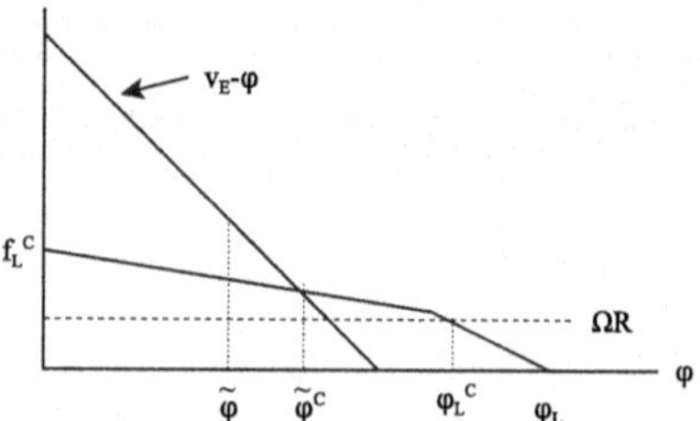

Fig. 4. Entry versus VL under the threat of a CL.

The threshold level of the fixed cost parameter φ that determines the patent-holder's choice between entry and VL is defined by where $f_L^C(\varphi) = v_E^* - \Omega R$. Recall that in the absence of CL, this threshold equals $\tilde{\varphi} = \frac{\Delta v^*}{1-\alpha}$. If $\varphi_Z < \tilde{\varphi}$, the return to VL at $\tilde{\varphi}$ is unaffected by the possibility of CL and the patent-holder's choice between entry and VL is unaffected. However, if $\varphi_Z > \tilde{\varphi}$, the patent-holder's return to VL due to the profit shifting effect and the threshold level of fixed cost determining the choice between entry and VL falls. The condition for $\varphi_Z > \tilde{\varphi}$ is that $\frac{\Delta v^* + \Omega \pi_L^*}{1-\alpha(1-\beta)} > \frac{\Delta v^*}{1-\alpha}$. To see which factors affect whether the threat of a CL raises the fixed cost threshold, note that as $\gamma \to 1$, we have $\frac{\Delta v^*}{1-\alpha} \to 0$ and $\pi_L^* \to \pi_E^*$. Thus, for sufficiently large values of γ the profit shifting under VL caused by the threat of a CL affects the entry margin so that $\tilde{\varphi}^C > \tilde{\varphi}$.

Fig. 4 illustrates the decision thresholds for the patent-holder in a case where $\varphi_Z > \tilde{\varphi}$. The patent-holder chooses the option that yields $\max\{v_E^* - \varphi, f_L^C(\varphi), \Omega R\}$. For $\Omega R < f_L^C$, as illustrated by the example in Fig. 4, the patent-holder's decision is to enter if $\varphi \in \left[0, \tilde{\varphi}^C\right]$, to negotiate a VL if $\varphi \in \left(\tilde{\varphi}^C, \varphi_L^C\right]$, and to allow a CL to be issued if $\varphi \in (\varphi_L^C, \varphi_{CL}^{max}]$. Note that as the royalty rate under CL increases, the range of fixed costs for which VL is chosen shrinks. This is due to the fact that the royalty represents a fixed opportunity cost for the patent-holder, whether the market is being served by VL or entry. Since the licensee produces a lower quality product and earns less revenues, this fixed cost falls more heavily on the VL option, which becomes relatively less attractive as R increases. For $\Omega R > f_L^C\left(\tilde{\varphi}^C\right)$, the royalty under CL is sufficiently large that VL will no longer be a viable option. The patent-holder's decision is to enter if $\varphi \in [0, \varphi_E^C]$ and to allow a compulsory license to be issued for $\varphi \in (\varphi_E^C, \varphi_{CL}^{max}]$.

The following result establishes that the relationship between royalty rates and the patent-holder's decision illustrated in the example in Fig. 4 are general properties of the model. In particular, we show that for a given α and R, there will exist a critical value of $A(\alpha,R)$ such that VL will not be a viable option if $\gamma < A(\alpha,R)$. For γ in this range, the profitability of VL is sufficiently low that the patent-holder will choose to enter or allow a CL to be issued. For $\gamma > A(\alpha,R)$, the patent-holder may either enter, negotiate a VL, or allow a CL depending on the level of fixed costs.

Proposition 4. Suppose there is no price control (i.e. $\overline{p} = p_E^*$) and $v_E^* > \Omega R$. Define

$$A(\alpha, R) \equiv \max\left\{\alpha\left(\frac{v_E^* - \Omega R}{v_E^*}\right) + \frac{\Omega R}{v_E^*}, \alpha(1-\beta)(1+\Omega)\left(\frac{v_E^* - R}{v_E^*}\right) + \left(\frac{R(1+\Omega)}{v_E^*}\right)\right\}$$

which is increasing in R with $A(\alpha,0) = \alpha$.

(i) If $\gamma \in (\alpha, A(\alpha, R)]$ the patent-holder chooses entry if $\varphi \in [0, \varphi_E^C]$. It does not work its patent otherwise and the government issues a CL in the second period for $\varphi \in [\varphi_E^C, \varphi_{CL}^{max}]$.

(ii) If $\gamma > A(\alpha, R)$ the patent-holder's optimal decision is to enter for $\varphi \in \left[0, \tilde{\varphi}^C\right]$ and to issue a voluntary license for $\varphi \in \left(\tilde{\varphi}^C, \varphi_L^C\right]$. The patent-holder does not work its patent and the South issues a CL for $\varphi \in (\varphi_L^C, \varphi_{CL}^{max}]$.

Note from part (i) that since $A(\alpha,R) > \alpha$ (so long as $R > 0$), *the threat of CL makes VL an unviable option* for the patent-holder for all $\gamma \in [\alpha, A(\alpha, R)]$. Indeed, for $\gamma \in [\alpha, A(\alpha, R)]$ the patent-holder never chooses VL: it either enters or stays out of the market depending upon whether or not $\varphi \le \varphi_E^C$.

We can compare the results of Proposition 4 with those of Proposition 1 to illustrate how the threat of CL affects the decision of the patent-holder. First consider the case when $\gamma \in [\alpha, A(\alpha, R)]$. The threshold levels of fixed costs in the absence of the threat of CL from Proposition 1 are illustrated in Fig. 5. The patent-holder chooses entry if $\varphi \in [0, \tilde{\varphi}]$; VL for all $\varphi \in (\tilde{\varphi}, \varphi_L]$; and does not work its patent in the South if $\varphi > \varphi_L$. Proposition 4(i) shows that entry occurs if $\varphi \in [0, \varphi_E^C]$, where $\varphi_E^C = v_E^* - \Omega R$. The threat of CL thus *reduces* the range of fixed costs for which entry occurs if $\varphi_E^C < \tilde{\varphi}$. Referring to Fig. 4, it can be seen that this could occur if R is sufficiently high. It is straightforward to show that the thresholds determining the entry decision under the two scenarios (i.e. with and without CL) can be ranked as follows:

$$\tilde{\varphi} \le \varphi_E^C \text{ iff } R \le R^* = \left[\frac{1+\Omega}{\Omega}\frac{\gamma-\alpha}{1-\alpha}\right]\frac{q}{4} > 0.$$

Intuitively, since VL is eliminated from the patent-holder's choice set, whether or not the threat of CL increases the likelihood of entry depends upon the royalty paid under CL. When the royalty under CL is relatively small (i.e. $R \le R^*$) we have $\tilde{\varphi} \le \varphi_E^C$ so that the threat of CL makes entry more likely by the patent-holder just as it eliminates VL. For $R \le R^*$, which is probably the empirically relevant case given that the royalties that have been observed in actual cases of CL have been relatively low, the possibility of CL results in two types of switches in the patent-holder's preferred mode of serving the market. Both of these switches occur due to the fact that CL reduces the licensing fee collected by the patent-holder under VL. Fig. 5 illustrates the threshold levels of fixed costs for the case where $\tilde{\varphi} \le \varphi_E^C$.

For $\varphi \in [\tilde{\varphi}, \varphi_E^C]$, the patent-holder switches from VL to entry whereas for $\varphi \in [\varphi_E^C, \varphi_L]$ it chooses not to engage in VL in order to collect royalty payments under the CL that is issued in the next period. Finally, note that for $\varphi \in (\varphi_L, \varphi_{CL}^{max}]$ CL results in the patent being worked locally whereas the South would not have been served in its absence.

Fig. 6 illustrates how the patent-holder's decision margins are affected by the threat of CL for the case where $\gamma > A(\alpha,R)$ and $\tilde{\varphi} < \tilde{\varphi}^C$. In this case there are three types of substitution that result from CL being an option for the South. For fixed costs in the interval $\left(\tilde{\varphi}, \tilde{\varphi}^C\right)$, the patent-holder substitutes entry for VL due to the improved threat point for the licensee. For fixed costs in the interval (φ_L^C, φ_L), the

E.W. Bond, K. Saggi / Journal of Development Economics 109 (2014) 217–228 225

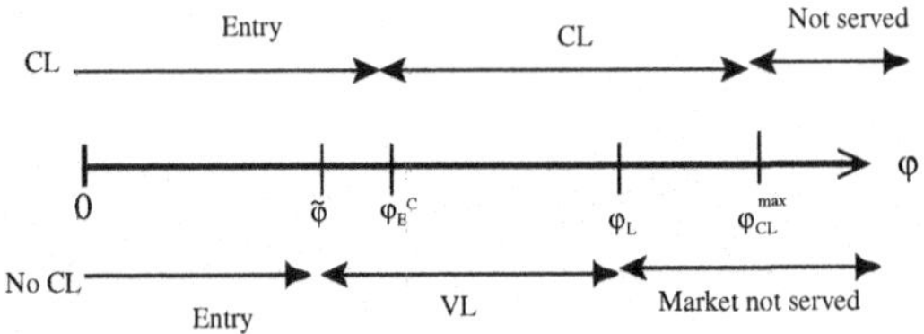

Fig. 5. Effects of the threat of a CL for $\alpha < \gamma < A(\alpha, R)$.

patent-holder switches from VL to not serving the market in order to obtain royalty payments under CL. Finally, for $\varphi \in (\varphi_L, \varphi_{CL}^{max}]$ a CL is issued by the government since the patent-holder does not find it profitable to serve the market when fixed costs are so high. Over this range, CL is necessary for providing local consumers access to the patented good.

Figs. 5 and 6 *illustrate that CL expands the range of parameters for which Southern consumers enjoy access to the patented good while it also reduces the range of fixed costs for which the patent-holder serves the market.* The figures also illustrate a substitution away from VL due to the improvement of the licensee's bargaining position under CL.

4.4. Welfare effects of CL

We now analyze the effect on CL on South welfare and patent-holder. To isolate the stand alone effects of CL, we divide the analysis into two scenarios. Under the first scenario, the Southern government has a credible threat of compulsory licensing, but chooses not to impose any price control on the patent-holder. Under the second scenario, the South chooses the welfare maximizing level of the price control given that it has the option to issue a compulsory license if its market goes unserved. The latter scenario highlights the interaction between the price control and CL. In what follows, we assume $R \leq R^*$.

4.4.1. Compulsory licensing without a price control

It is obvious that if $\varphi \in [0, \tilde{\varphi}]$, the threat of CL has no welfare effects since entry occurs with and without it. Thus, in what follows, we focus on the effects of CL when $\varphi > \tilde{\varphi}$. Following our previous analysis, it is convenient to separate the welfare effects of CL for the two parameter ranges identified in Proposition 4. We state the main result for the case where $\gamma \in (\alpha, A(\alpha, R)]$ and then discuss how its modified when $\gamma > A(\alpha, R)$.[27]

Proposition 5. Suppose $\gamma \in (\alpha, A(\alpha, R)]$. The welfare effects of CL are as follows:

(i) For $\varphi \in (\tilde{\varphi}, \varphi_E^C]$, the switch from VL to entry induced by the threat of CL benefits the South at the expense of the patent-holder and the effect on the joint welfare of the two parties is ambiguous.
(ii) For $\varphi \in (\varphi_E^C, \varphi_L]$, VL is replaced by CL and joint welfare declines.
(iii) For $\varphi \in (\varphi_L, \varphi_{CL}^{max}]$, CL makes both parties better off.

We now provide some intuition for parts (i) through (iii) of Proposition 5. Part (i) captures a situation where a switch from VL to entry arises due to the profit-shifting effect of the threat of CL. This switch necessarily benefits the South because the consumer surplus obtained from the higher quality product under entry exceeds that under VL, something the patent-holder does not take into account while choosing its mode of supply. The change in return to the patent-holder is $\Delta v^* - (1 - \alpha)\varphi$, which is non-positive for $\varphi \in [\tilde{\varphi}, \varphi_E^C]$. Here, the patent-holder loses because the increased bargaining power of the licensee induces it to switch to a less profitable mode of supply, something that the local government does not take into account during its decision-making. The effect of CL on joint welfare equals $[S(p_E^*) - S(p_L^*)](1 + \Omega) + \Delta v^* - (1 - \alpha)\varphi$. This expression must be positive for φ close to $\tilde{\varphi}$, since the losses of the patent-holder are sufficiently small that they are dominated by the gain in consumer surplus. However, for fixed costs in the neighborhood of φ_E^C it possible that the losses in profits of the patent-holder are larger than the gains in Southern consumer surplus. If the quality of the licensee's product approaches that under entry (i.e. $\gamma \to 1$), the gain in consumer surplus and Δv^* both approach zero so that the welfare change is negative when γ is sufficiently large and φ is close to φ_E^C. Under these circumstances, the profit shifting effect of the threat of CL leads the patent-holder to forego substantial savings in fixed costs under VL, which reduces joint welfare. The reasons a switch from VL to CL necessarily reduces joint welfare in part (ii) are easy to see: while the price and quality of the product are the same in either case, CL *delays access* to the product. Finally, for $\varphi \in (\varphi_L, \varphi_{CL}^{max}]$ the Southern market would not be served without a compulsory license so that the possibility of CL gives the South access to the product while also providing the patent-holder a per-period royalty R for the use of the patent.

Now consider the case where $\gamma > A(\alpha, R)$. A result analogous to part (i) of Proposition 5 holds when $\gamma > A(\alpha, R)$ except that the interval over which entry replaces VL is now given by $\varphi \in \left(\tilde{\varphi}, \tilde{\varphi}^C\right]$. The new consideration that arises when $\gamma > A(\alpha, R)$ is that for $\varphi \in (\tilde{\varphi}^C, \varphi_L^C]$ VL obtains with or without the threat of CL so that the joint welfare of the two parties remains unaffected. However, the patent-holder loses while the South gains if the threat of CL causes profit-shifting over this range, which it does if $\varphi < \varphi_z$. For $(\varphi_L^C, \varphi_L]$ VL is replaced by CL and joint welfare declines for reasons already explained. Finally, for $\varphi \in (\varphi_L, \varphi_{CL}^{max}]$, CL makes both parties better off: it ensures that the South obtains access to the product and the patent-holder receives some compensation for it.

4.4.2. CL under a price control

Proposition 3 established that in the absence of a CL, the optimal price control involves setting the price equal to the minimum value that ensures that the patent-holder chooses the South's preferred mode of supply. In the event that a compulsory license is actually issued, Southern welfare is maximized by choosing a price control equal to marginal cost, $\overline{p} = 0$. Thus, CL introduces an additional strategy for the South, which is to set the price control at $\overline{p} = 0$ which guarantees that the patent-holder stays out and a compulsory license is issued in the next period. This policy has the benefit of maximizing the surplus of the South given that the product is being provided by the licensee, although it has the cost of delaying access to the patented product.

Finding the optimal price control in the presence of CL involves a comparison of welfare under CL at $\overline{p} = 0$ with that obtained by choosing the minimum price consistent with obtaining the product via entry or VL. Consider first the case in which $\varphi > \varphi_E^C$, so that the South would issue a compulsory license in the case where a price control is not

[27] It is shown in Appendix A that these results extend to arbitrary price controls $\overline{p} \in (0, p_E^*)$.

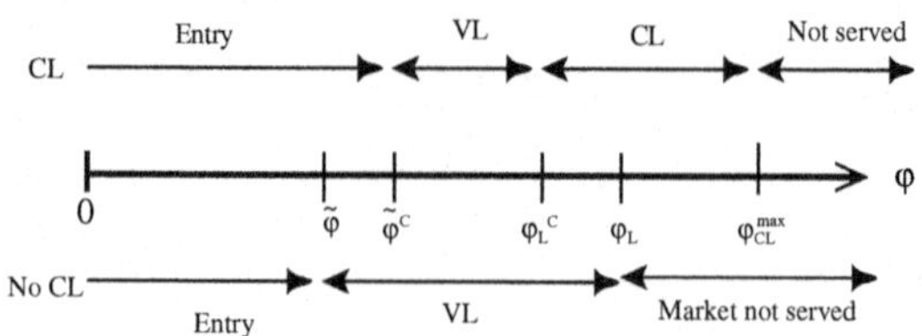

Fig. 6. Effects of the threat of a CL for $\gamma > A(\alpha,R)$.

used. Since entry does not occur for any price control for this range of fixed costs, the optimal policy for the South is to set $\overline{p} = 0$. Thus, the CL option creates *additional leverage* for the South in the sense that it allows the government to lower the local price to a greater degree thereby making the price control a more effective instrument for improving local welfare.

The price at which the patent-holder is indifferent between entering and not serving the market is given by $p_E^C(\varphi, R) = p_E(\varphi + \Omega R)$, which is greater than the break-even price without CL for $R > 0$. Similarly, the price at which the patent-holder is indifferent between VL and not serving the market, which we denote $p_L^C(\varphi, R)$, is the solution to $f_L^C = \Omega R$. Using Eq. (12), it can be seen that the break-even price for VL in the presence of CL satisfies $p_L^C(\varphi, R) > p_L(\varphi)$ for $R > 0$. The Southern market is not served by the patent-holder for $\overline{p} < \min\{p_L^C(\varphi, R), p_E^C(\varphi, R)\}$. If $p_L^C(\varphi, R) > p_E^C(\varphi, R)$, the patent-holder enters for $\overline{p} \geq p_E^C(\varphi, R)$ whereas when $p_L^C(\varphi, R) < p_E^C(\varphi, R)$, it enters if there exists a $p \leq p_E^*$ that satisfies

$$\Delta v(p) + \max\{\Omega\pi_L(p, \gamma) - \beta\alpha\varphi, 0\} = 0.$$

The solution to this equation is denoted by $\tilde{p}^C(\varphi)$, and it is the *entry-inducing price when CL is an available option.* Since $\Delta v(p)$ is increasing in $\overline{p}$ for $p < p_E^*$, we have

$$\tilde{p}^C(\varphi) \geq \tilde{p}(\varphi)$$

with strict inequality holding whenever CL is profitable for the local licensee (i.e. for $\Omega\pi_L(\tilde{p}, \gamma) - \beta\alpha\varphi > 0$).

In the case where $\overline{p}_E^C(\varphi, R) < p_E^* < p_L^C(\varphi, R)$, the South has to choose between the lowest price at which the patent-holder enters, i.e. $\overline{p} = \overline{p}_E^C(\varphi, R)$, or CL at $\overline{p} = 0$. Southern welfare under entry is $(1 + \Omega) S(p_E^C(\varphi, R))$ while that under CL is $W^{CL}(0) = \Omega[S(0, \gamma q) - R] - \alpha\beta\varphi$. The South is more likely to prefer entry when the cost of delay is large, which occurs for small Ω, or when the quality of the licensee's product is relatively low. Note that in the case where entry yields higher welfare, the option to issue a compulsory license makes the South worse off. The requirement that the South make a royalty payment under CL raises the price that the South must allow for the product in order to induce entry. This is a case where the South's ability to make a take it or leave it offer to the patent-holder allows it to extract all of the surplus from the patent-holder under entry, so the requirement of a royalty payment under CL actually *reduces* the ability of the South to extract surplus from the patent-holder. A similar issue arises if $\overline{p}_L^C(\varphi, R) < p_E^* < p_E^C(\varphi, R)$, since the existence of the royalty payment under CL raises the price that the South must permit if it prefers to have a voluntary license issued by the patent-holder to avoid the delay associated with the CL. The final case is one in which $p_E^* > \max\{\tilde{p}^C(\varphi), p_L^C(\varphi, R)\}$. Here, the patent-holder chooses among $\tilde{p}^C(\varphi)$, $p_L^C(\varphi, R)$, and a price of 0 under CL. If the South chooses the entry-inducing price, the existence of CL is beneficial since it reduces the price that the patent-holder is allowed to charge (i.e. $\tilde{p}^C(\varphi) \geq \tilde{p}(\varphi)$).

These results show that the threat of CL has two potentially favorable effects for a government that uses a price control for a patented product. One is the potential to obtain the product at a more efficient price when a CL is used, since marginal cost pricing can be imposed due to the ability of the government to subsidize the licensee. Second is the possibility that the profit shifting effect of the threat of CL reduces the amount of rent that must be paid to the patent-holder when it chooses $\overline{p} = \tilde{p}(\varphi)$. However, these two positive effects are counterbalanced by the potentially unfavorable effect that arises when the government chooses a price control that makes the patent-holder indifferent between serving the market or not. In this case, the patent-holder's option of obtaining a royalty payment under CL forces the government to permit a higher price to induce the patent-holder to serve the local market.

Finally, note that if the government has the ability to set two different price controls (one for entry and another for VL), then the menu of price options faced by the government effectively expands to three: 0, $\overline{p}_E^C(\varphi, R)$, and $\overline{p}_L^C(\varphi, R)$. As in the case where CL is not an option, the government does not have to pay a premium to induce entry since it can drive the patent-holder's net payoff under VL to zero by setting the price control under VL at $\overline{p}_L^C(\varphi, R)$.

5. Conclusion

High prices or outright unavailability of patented foreign products (such as pharmaceuticals) often prompt governments to undertake policies aimed at improving consumer access to such products. The two types of policies that have been used frequently in this context are price controls and CL. Given the human welfare cost at stake, it is imperative that our understanding of the feedback between these two policies be improved. Motivated by the rules specified in the TRIPS agreement and the actual experience of several developing countries with CL, we develop a model that sheds light on the stand alone effects of CL as well as its interaction with a price control.

The model is designed to capture actual WTO rules quite closely. In particular, the Southern government is allowed to use CL only if the Northern firm/patent-holder fails to work the patent locally. Our analysis shows that the option to use CL can benefit the South via three channels. First, CL ensures that local consumers have access to (a lower quality version of) the patented good when the patent-holder finds it unprofitable to sell locally. Second, the threat of CL improves the terms at which voluntary licensing occurs. Third, it can cause the patent-holder to switch from licensing to entry thereby leading to an improvement in the quality of the good available to local consumers. These benefits are somewhat offset by the possibility that CL delays access to the product when it replaces voluntary licensing or entry as the market outcome (while also lowering quality when it replaces entry).

We also show that the effects of a price control and CL are mutually reinforcing: the presence of a price control increases the need for and the use of CL while the threat of CL allows the South to use a more stringent price control policy thereby expanding consumer access. Our results not only point to some clear distinctions between the role the two instruments play in determining consumer access to patented foreign goods, they also expose their limits. For example, too stringent a price control on the part of a developing country can simply prompt the patent-holder to not work the patent at all. Similarly, if local production suffers from too large a quality gap, the threat of CL loses its bite.

The paper focusses on policy choices of the South and abstracts from the repercussions of those choices in other markets. For example, Grossman and Lai (2008) have shown how the Southern price control can affect Northern policy regarding the exhaustion of intellectual property rights which in turn determines prices and welfare in both regions. The interaction between CL and exhaustion policies deserves further study.

We also do not consider the dynamic consequences of CL for the South. In this context, Moser and Voena (2012) have shown that CL of nearly 130,000 German chemical inventions by the United States (US) after World War I under the Trading with the Enemy Act had a substantial positive effect on subsequent innovation by the US chemical industry. However, similar effects might not be as central to the types of CL considered in our model. This is due to two reasons. One, a few isolated cases of CL may not generate a substantial amount of knowledge transfer. Second, even if CL could be mobilized on a large scale, many developing countries lack the technological capability necessary for making effective use of licensed foreign technologies as an input into domestic innovation.

Even when CL does not result in significant knowledge transfer it has the potential to affect innovation incentives by affecting the profits collected by patent-holders. However, our model clarifies that the affect of CL on the patent-holder's payoff is not always negative. In particular, when the patent-holder does not find it profitable to itself serve the Southern market via entry or voluntary licensing, the issuance of a CL allows it to earn some royalties from the Southern market. On the other hand, the model also isolates circumstances where the conventional intuition (i.e. CL makes the patent-holder worse off) holds. When this is the case, innovation incentives of the patent-holder could certainly be reduced by CL.

All indications are that the use of CL as a tool for achieving general development goals is only likely to increase in the coming years. How the battle between improving consumer access to necessary medicines and preserving the intellectual property rights of patent-holders will play out globally is uncertain at this stage. But the importance of the issue and the need for further research seem clear.

Appendix A

Proof of Proposition 2. The break-even price for a licensee with quality γq and fixed costs $\alpha\varphi$ is the solution to $\pi(p, \gamma q)(1+\Omega) - \alpha\varphi = 0$, which yields

$$p_L(\varphi) = \frac{\gamma q}{2}\left(1-\left(1-\frac{\alpha\varphi}{v_L^*}\right)^{1/2}\right) \text{for} \varphi \in \left[0, \frac{v_L^*}{\alpha}\right] \tag{13}$$

where $v_L^* \equiv \frac{\gamma q(1+\Omega)}{4}$. We set $p_L(\varphi) = \infty$ for $\varphi > v_L^*$, since fixed costs exceed monopoly profits and the licensee cannot earn zero profits at any price.

$$p_E(\varphi) = \frac{q}{2}\left(1-\left(1-\frac{\varphi}{v_L^*}\right)^{1/2}\right) \text{for} \varphi \in [0, v_E^*] \tag{14}$$

where $v_E^* \equiv \frac{v_L^*}{\gamma}$ and $p_E(\varphi) = \infty$ for $\varphi > v_E^*$. It is straightforward to establish that the respective break-even prices are increasing and convex in φ, with $p_L(0) = p_E(0) = 0$.

Proposition 1 established that $\frac{\Delta v^*}{1-\alpha} < v_E^* < \frac{v_L^*}{\alpha}$ when $\gamma > \alpha$. To prove Proposition 2, we show that $p_E(\varphi) > p_L(\varphi)$ for all $\varphi \in (0, \frac{v_L^*}{\alpha}$ when $\gamma > \alpha$.

Since $\frac{v_L^*}{\alpha} > v_E^*$, we have $\left(1-\frac{\alpha\varphi}{v_L^*}\right)^{1/2} > \left(1-\frac{\varphi}{v_E^*}\right)^{1/2}$. Applying this inequality to Eqs. (13) and (14) and using the fact that $\gamma < 1$, we see that $p_L(\varphi) < p_E(\varphi)$ for all $\varphi \in [0, \frac{v_L^*}{\alpha}]$.

Proof of Lemma 1. Part (i) follows immediately from the fact that entry is preferred to not serving the market if $v_E^* - \varphi \geq \Omega R$. For (ii), note that the licensee's return from CL is positive for $\varphi < \frac{\Omega v_L^*}{\alpha\beta(1+\Omega)}$. Evaluating the patent-holder's return from VL at the licensee's break-even point for CL and using the definition of Ω yields $\pi_L^*(1-\beta^2)\beta^{T-2} > 0$. This implies that CL must be unprofitable in the neighborhood of $f_L^C = 0$. It then follows that the value of φ solving $f_L^C = \Omega R$ is $\min\left\{\frac{v_L^*-\Omega R}{\alpha}, \frac{v_L^*-\Omega R(1+\Omega)}{\alpha(1-\beta)(1+\Omega)}\right\}$. For (iii), CL affects the entry decision if it yields positive profits when evaluated at $\tilde{\varphi}$, which is satisfied if $[(1-\alpha)\gamma\Omega - \alpha\beta(1+\Omega)(1-\gamma)] \geq 0$. This condition must be satisfied for γ sufficiently close to 1 and α sufficiently close to 0. The maximum level of φ for VL to be preferred for entry is $\frac{v_L^*}{1-\alpha}$ if CL is unprofitable and $\frac{\Delta v^*+\Omega\pi_L^*}{1-\alpha(1-\beta)}$ if it is profitable, so that the threshold is $\min\left\{\frac{v_L^*}{1-\alpha}, \frac{\Delta v^*+\Omega\pi_L^*}{1-\alpha(1-\beta)}\right\}$.

Proof of Proposition 4. Using Lemma 2 and the fact that $v_L^* = \gamma v_E^*$, the requirement that $\varphi_L^C \geq \varphi_E^C$ can be expressed as

$$\min\left\{\frac{v_E^*(\gamma-\alpha)-\Omega(1-\alpha)R}{\alpha}, \frac{v_E^*(\gamma-\alpha(1-\beta)(1+\Omega))-\Omega R(1-\alpha(1-\beta))(1+\Omega)}{\alpha(1-\beta)(1+\Omega)}\right\} \geq 0.$$

The first term is non-negative for $\gamma \geq \alpha\left(\frac{v_E^*-\Omega R}{v_E^*}\right) + \frac{\Omega R}{v_E^*}$ and the second is non-negative for $\gamma \geq \alpha(1-\beta)(1+\Omega)\left(\frac{v_E^*-\Omega R}{v_E^*}\right) + \left(\frac{\Omega R(1+\Omega)}{v_E^*}\right)$. Combining these requirements yields $\gamma \geq A(\alpha, R)$ as defined in Proposition 4. The remaining parts follow using the same arguments as for Proposition 2.

Proof of Proposition 5. We assume $R < R^*$. Referring to Fig. 4, this case corresponds to one in which ΩR intersects the $v_E(\overline{p}) - \varphi$ line at a level of fixed costs between $\tilde{\varphi}$ and $\tilde{\varphi}^C$. The result is proven for an arbitrary price control $\overline{p} \in (0, p_E^*]$.

(i) A switch from VL to entry occurs for $\varphi \in \left[\frac{\Delta v(\overline{p})}{1+\alpha}, v_E(\overline{p}) - \Omega R\right]$. The change in the patent-holder's payoff is $\Delta v(\overline{p}) - (1-\alpha)\varphi$, which is non-positive for fixed costs in this interval. Since the Southern licensee receives zero profit under either VL or entry, the impact on Southern welfare is measured solely by the change in consumer surplus:

$$W^E(\overline{p}) - W^L(\overline{p}) = (1+\Omega)[S(\min\{\overline{p}, p_E^*\}, q) - S(\min\{\overline{p}, p_L^*\}, \gamma q)] > 0.$$

Thus, the South must benefit from gaining access to a higher quality product under entry with $\gamma < 1$.
The change in joint welfare of the two parties equals

$$(1+\Omega)[S(\min\{\overline{p}, p_E^*\}, q) - S(\min\{\overline{p}, p_L^*\}, \gamma q)] + \Delta v(\overline{p}) - (1-\alpha)\varphi.$$

This change must be positive at $\varphi = \frac{\Delta v(\overline{p})}{1-\alpha}$ since Southern consumer surplus increases while the patent-holder's payoff is unaffected. To show that joint welfare could be reduced, note that the change in joint welfare approaches $-(1-\alpha)\varphi$ as $\gamma \to 1$. This case is consistent with $\gamma < A(\alpha, R)$ for α sufficiently low and R sufficiently high.

(ii) A switch from VL to CL occurs for $\varphi \in \left[v_E(\overline{p}) - \Omega R, \frac{v_L(\overline{p})}{\alpha}\right]$. The change in the patent-holder's payoff is $\Omega R - v_L(\overline{p}) + \alpha\varphi$, which is increasing in φ. The patent-holder must gain for fixed costs in the neighborhood of $\frac{v_L(\overline{p})}{\alpha}$ and must lose at $\varphi = v_E(\overline{p}) - \Omega R$. The impact on Southern welfare is the sum of the consumer surplus foregone due to delayed serving of the market plus the gain in profit of the licensee caused by the profit-shifting effect of CL:

$$W^{CL}(\overline{p})-W^{L}(\overline{p}) = -S(\min\{\overline{p},p_L^*\},\gamma q) + \left[\frac{\Omega v_L(\overline{p})}{1+\Omega} - \alpha\beta\varphi - \Omega R\right].$$

No profit-shifting effect occurs for $\varphi \in \left[\frac{\Omega v_L(\overline{p})}{(1+\Omega)\beta\alpha}, \frac{v_L(\overline{p})}{\alpha}\right]$, so the second term is non-positive and the South must lose. However, the South might gain if the second term is positive and sufficiently large.

The effect on joint welfare is

$$-S(\min\{\overline{p},p_L^*\},\gamma q) - \left[v_L(\overline{p}) - \frac{\Omega v_L(\overline{p})}{1+\Omega} + \alpha(1-\beta)\varphi\right] < 0.$$

The second term must be negative because VL yields a higher return to the patent-holder than CL due to the delayed serving of the market under CL:

$$\frac{\Omega v_L(\overline{p})}{1+\Omega} - \alpha\beta\varphi = \beta\left[\frac{\left(1-\beta^T\right)v_L(\overline{p})}{\left(1-\beta^{T+1}\right)} - \alpha\varphi\right] < v_L(\overline{p}) - \alpha\varphi.$$

(iii) Each party receives a positive payoff under CL, whereas a zero payoff is received by each when the Southern market is not served by the patent-holder.

References

Baron, David, 2008. Compulsory Licensing, Thailand, and Abbott Laboratories. Stanford Graduate School of Business Case p. 66.

Beall, Reed, Kuhn, Randall, 2012. Trends in compulsory licensing of pharmaceuticals since the Doha Declaration: a database analysis. PLoS Med. 9 (1), 1–9.

Cahoy, Daniel R., 2011. Breaking patents. Mich. J. Int. Law 461–509 (Spring).

Chatterjee, Chirantan, Kobe, Kensuke, Pingali, Viswanath, 2013. The welfare implications of patent protection, pricing, and licensing in the Indian oral anti-diabetic drug market. Indian Institute of Management Working paper No. 408.

Chaudhuri, Shubham, Goldberg, Pinelopi K., Jia, Panle, 2006. Estimating the effects of global patent protection in pharmaceuticals: a case study of Quinolones in India. Am. Econ. Rev. 96, 1477–1514.

Daemmrich, Arthur A., Musacchio, Aldo, 2011. Brazil: Leading the BRICs. Harvard Business School Case (9-711-024).

Dutta, Antara, 2011. From free entry to patent protection: welfare implications for the Indian pharmaceutical industry. Rev. Econ. Stat. 93 (1), 160–178.

Ethier, Wilfred J., Markusen, James R., 1996. Multinational firms, technology diffusion and trade. J. Int. Econ. 41, 1–28.

Goldberg, Pinelopi K., 2010. Intellectual property rights protection in developing countries: the case of pharmaceuticals. J. Eur. Econ. Assoc. 8, 326–353.

Grossman, Gene M., Lai, Edwin, 2008. Parallel imports and price controls. RAND J. Econ. 39, 378–402.

Kremer, Michael, 2002. Pharmaceuticals and the developing world. J. Econ. Perspect. 16 (4), 67–90.

Kyle, Margaret, 2007. Pharmaceutical price controls and entry strategies. Rev. Econ. Stat. 89 (1), 88–99.

Lanjouw, Jean, 1998. The introduction of pharmaceutical product patents in India: heartless exploitation of the poor and suffering. NBER Working Paper 6366, Cambridge, MA.

Lanjouw, Jean, 2005. Patents, price controls and access to new drugs: how policy affects global market entry. NBER Working Paper 11321, Cambridge, MA.

Markusen, James R., 2001. Contracts, intellectual property rights, and multinational investment in developing countries. J. Int. Econ. 53, 189–204.

Maskus, Keith E., 2000. Intellectual Property Rights in the Global Economy. Institute of International Economics, Washington, D.C.

McCalman, Phillip, 2004. Foreign direct investment and intellectual property rights: evidence from Hollywood's global distribution of movies and videos. J. Int. Econ. 62, 107–123.

Moser, Petra, Voena, Alessandara, 2012. Compulsory licensing: evidence from the trading with the enemy act. Am. Econ. Rev. 102, 396–427.

Pozen, Robert C., 2008. Note on Compulsory Licensing. Harvard Business School Case (9-609-009).

Scherer, F.M., Watal, Jayashree, 2002. Post-TRIPS Options for access to patented medicines in developing nations. J. Int. Econ. Law 5 (4), 913–939.

Tandon, Pankaj, 1982. Optimal patents with compulsory licensing. J. Polit. Econ. 90, 470–486.

Chapter 20

Bargaining over Entry with a Compulsory License Deadline: Price Spillovers and Surplus Expansion[†,#]

By ERIC W. BOND AND KAMAL SAGGI*

We analyze bargaining between a developing country (South) and a multinational firm over the local price of its patented product. We use an alternating offers bargaining game in which the South can resort to compulsory licensing (CL) if the two parties fail to reach agreement by a certain deadline. The presence of international price spillovers introduces two novel features into the standard bargaining problem: the surplus from entry prior to the CL deadline may be negative, and CL can yield higher surplus than entry. We establish conditions under which equilibrium may exhibit immediate entry, preemptive entry just prior to the CL deadline, or the occurrence of CL. The South necessarily gains from the threat of CL if the joint payoff under entry is higher relative to CL but can lose if it is lower. (*JEL* D45, F11, F23, L24, L65, O34)

A crucial policy issue confronting low and middle income countries today is how to provide local consumers access to patented foreign medicines at affordable prices. Prior to the mid-90s, such countries could buy generic versions of these products from pharmaceutical companies in countries such as India and China that had fairly weak patent regimes. However, the ratification of the Agreement on Trade Related Aspects of Intellectual Property Rights (TRIPS) in 1995 by the World Trade Organization (WTO) essentially eliminated this option by requiring all WTO members to provide a minimum of 20 years of patent protection. As a result, governments across the world now need to rely primarily on negotiations with patent holders to obtain price reductions.

During such negotiations, pharmaceutical companies can be unwilling to cut prices of their patented products in developing countries, even when local profits could be made, because of the fear of undermining their ability to sustain higher prices in other countries. There are two reasons why a patent holder can be concerned about international price spillovers. First, international price discrimination can be undone by the flow of *parallel imports* from low price markets to high price ones. Second, governments of many countries resort to *external reference pricing*

*Bond: Department of Economics, Vanderbilt University, VU Station B #351819, 2301 Vanderbilt Place, Nashville, TN 37235 (e-mail: eric.bond@vanderbilt.edu); Saggi: Department of Economics, Vanderbilt University, VU Station B #351819, 2301 Vanderbilt Place, Nashville, TN 37235 (e-mail: k.saggi@vanderbilt.edu). We thank Giovanni Maggi, Larry Samuelson, and two anonymous referees for helpful comments. We have also benefited from comments of seminar participants at the Asia Pacific Trade Seminars, Drexel University, and Yale Trade Lunch. Bond thanks the Leitner Center on International Political Economy at Yale for support.

†Go to https://doi.org/10.1257/mic.20150031 to visit the article page for additional materials and author disclosure statement(s) or to comment in the online discussion forum.

This chapter was originally appeared in *American Economic Journal: Microeconomics* **9**, 31–62.

when bargaining over prices with pharmaceutical companies or setting their local price controls, a policy under which the prices that they are willing to permit locally depend on prices being charged by firms in *other* countries. This governmental practice can put firms in the awkward position of having to explain why they need to charge high prices in some countries when they find it profitable to sell at low prices in other countries.

Due to the possibility of international price spillovers, pharmaceutical companies may deliberately choose not to serve the local markets of many developing countries. What recourse does a developing country have when it finds itself in such a situation? As it turns out, WTO rules pertaining to intellectual property provide an escape route. When faced with limited or no access to a patented foreign product, a country may resort to *compulsory licensing*, i.e., an authorization granted to someone other than the patent holder to produce the patented product without the patent holder's consent.[1] Our goal in this paper is to analyze how the potential issuance of a compulsory license affects price negotiations between a patent holder and a developing country.

Motivated by WTO ground rules that govern the use of compulsory licensing (CL) and recent experience with CL (discussed in Section IB), we develop and analyze an alternating offers bargaining game between a multinational firm and the government of a developing country (called South). In our model, as the sole producer of a patented good, the multinational negotiates with the South over the terms of its entry into the local market. An agreement between the two parties consists of a price charged in the South for the duration of the patent and a lump sum transfer (which can be negative) paid by the multinational. We assume that the two parties have complete information about payoffs and analyze how the threat of CL affects the timing of entry by the multinational and the distribution of surplus between them. We model the WTO rules on CL as providing an exogenously given time at which the South can unilaterally terminate the bargaining problem by issuing a compulsory license, and analyze how this deadline affects the outcome of the bargaining game.

Two fundamental features of our bargaining problem distinguish it from the standard alternating offers bargaining game. The first concerns the amount of (per period) surplus generated by the entry of the multinational into the Southern market. The loss in profits suffered by the multinational in its home (North) market due to price spillovers from the South raises the possibility that the joint payoff resulting from the firm's entry into the South's market is actually negative. In such a scenario, there exists no price transfer pair that can make both parties better off if the multinational enters the South. The second crucial feature of our bargaining problem is the difference between the surplus under CL and entry. If the Southern licensee cannot produce a sufficiently high quality version of the patented product, the payoff generated under CL is lower than that under entry. However, it is also possible that the CL

[1] Parallel imports from another low price market would be an option but this would only work if the company does not choose to forsake that other market for the same reason. The freedom to allow parallel imports and the option to use compulsory licensing are widely seen as the two major *flexibilities* available under TRIPS to WTO member countries—see Maskus (2000a,b) for a detailed discussion of these flexibilities.

yields a *larger* payoff than entry. To see how this can happen, first note that WTO rules require that sales under a compulsory license should be restricted to the local market of the country issuing the license. Thus, to be compliant with WTO rules, the South has an incentive to discourage any arbitrage trade that can spill over to the multinational's home market. Similarly, any external reference pricing policy on the part of the North cannot reasonably hold the multinational accountable for the price of its product in the South under CL since production and pricing are no longer controlled by it. Thus, by *reducing* the degree of price spillovers between markets, the issuance of a compulsory license has the potential to increase the surplus available to the two parties.

In modeling the bargaining problem, we assume that the South cannot commit to not imposing a compulsory license if the two parties fail to reach agreement by the deadline. In the case where the joint payoff from CL is negative, this assumption prevents the multinational from making a cash transfer to the South in return for the latter agreeing to forgo the use of CL. We believe this assumption is realistic in the context of our model because a contract between the multinational and the South under which the latter agrees to forgo the use of CL would not be enforceable at the WTO. Furthermore, domestic political pressure would likely make it impossible for the Southern government to be able to deny local consumers access to a patented foreign product (such as a pharmaceutical) in return for a cash payment from the patent holder.

Our results show how the timing of the multinational's entry into the South and the split of the surplus between the two parties is determined by the two basic features of the bargaining problem discussed above. In the case where the surplus generated by entry is positive and exceeds that under a compulsory license, the threat of CL only redistributes surplus from the multinational to the South (provided the threat is credible). If the surplus generated by entry is negative, the multinational cannot pay the country not to issue a CL under our assumptions. Therefore, the firm may make a preemptive offer just prior to the deadline to prevent the imposition of a compulsory license. If this happens, the South benefits at the expense of the multinational because it obtains a high quality product that would otherwise not have been available to its consumers. In both cases, the payoff to the South is decreasing in the length of the delay period that must elapse before the South is free to issue a compulsory license. Furthermore, CL may be observed in equilibrium, even though it yields lower surplus than entry if the bargaining friction (defined as the time between offers) is sufficiently large.

We find that CL can also arise in equilibrium if it results in a higher payoff than entry *and* the required delay period before it can be implemented is not too long. The latter condition is important because even if the surplus under CL is higher than that under entry, it may not be worth delaying agreement too much to obtain that higher level of surplus. We also show that each party's equilibrium payoff in this case depends on the division of surplus under CL, leading to a variety of possible outcomes. In cases where a compulsory license is imposed in equilibrium, the payoff to the South is decreasing in the delay period before the license can be imposed. The multinational's payoff, on the other hand, can be either increasing or decreasing in the required delay period, depending on its share of total surplus under CL.

An interesting result of our paper is that it is possible for the South to receive a *lower* average payoff in equilibrium when there exists a credible threat of CL relative to what it receives in the absence of such a threat. This paradoxical outcome can only arise when CL yields a higher payoff than entry and the multinational's share of that higher surplus exceeds its share under bargaining (absent the threat of CL). The possibility of the multinational receiving a larger share of the surplus under CL arises if the license provides a substantial royalty payment to the multinational while also leading to an effective segmentation of the Southern market from the Northern one. Under these conditions, the threat of CL can lower the South's equilibrium payoff in one of two ways. First, even though the South earns a higher per period payoff under CL, the payoff starts to accrue only after the license goes into effect. It follows then that the South can be made worse off due to the threat of CL if the delay incurred before it can impose the license is sufficiently long.

The threat of CL can also lower the South's average payoff when the bargaining outcome results in immediate entry provided the two conditions isolated above—i.e., a larger surplus under CL relative to entry coupled with a larger share for the multinational—continue to hold. The South's loss in this case arises because the possibility of CL *weakens* its bargaining position. Even though the multinational cannot itself issue a compulsory license, it can delay agreement until the Southern government can do so. In such a situation, the South's ability to use CL actually shifts bargaining power in *favor* of the multinational. Indeed, when the multinational has an incentive to delay agreement until a compulsory license can be issued, the South would be better off if it could pre-commit to not issuing such a license.

Our analysis of price negotiations in the shadow of CL is related to the literature that examines bargaining under a deadline. One strand of this literature deals with the commitment effect of a deadline in a setting where a seller makes offers to a buyer with private information about his valuation of the object. According to the well-known Coase conjecture (e.g., Gul, Sonnenschein, and Wilson 1986), the inability of the seller to commit to future prices causes its profit to vanish as the time between offers goes to zero. Fuchs and Skrzypacz (2013) analyze the role of deadlines in a bargaining model by introducing an exogenously given deadline at which the players receive a payoff whose total can be no more than the buyer's valuation if no agreement has been reached.[2] They show that the seller's payoff converges to the present value of making a final offer at the deadline as the time between offers goes to zero. Thus, the deadline improves the seller's bargaining position by putting a bound on the extent to which the seller will cut price in the continuous time limit. Our analysis abstracts from this role of deadlines by assuming that parties have complete information about valuations. In our case, the payoff to the parties in the event of an agreement is the weighted average of the payoff that would be received if the compulsory license is imposed at the deadline and the payoff that would be received in the absence of a deadline.

A second focus of the literature on deadlines is the effect of deadlines on the timing of agreements. Fuchs and Skrzypacz (2013) show that the existence of a

[2]Their model is an extension of the Sobel and Takahashi (1987) model of multistage bargaining, which assumes that players receive zero payoffs if there is no agreement by the deadline.

deadline results in a mass of agreements being reached at the deadline, in order to avoid the shrinkage in payoff that arises if no agreement is reached. Spier (1992) considers the problem of pretrial negotiation, where a plaintiff makes offers to a defendant with private information about the size of damages. In her model, the two sides often fail to reach agreement and when settlement takes place, it usually does so quite close to the deadline. Introducing fixed costs of bargaining into the model delivers a U-shaped pattern of settlement, i.e., there is greater chance that the two parties reach agreement at the beginning or at the end of negotiations relative to the middle. Spier (1992) also considers the case in which the plaintiff has the option of choosing the time at which to go to trial, so that the deadline is endogenously determined.

In our model, the full information assumption means that if an agreement on entry is reached, it will either occur immediately or right before the deadline. The latter case arises if CL reduces the total payoff and bargaining frictions are sufficiently small. The possibility that the joint payoff increases under a compulsory license also means that it can be in the interest of both parties to have the license imposed, which can result in a delay in the serving of the Southern market relative to the case where a compulsory license cannot be issued.

The rest of the paper is organized as follows. In Section I, we provide a brief discussion of the empirical evidence that motivates our model. Section II presents our bargaining game and derives its equilibrium when CL is not an available option for the South. Section III introduces CL and analyzes how it affects equilibrium outcomes and welfare. Section IV contains some concluding remarks.

I. Empirical Relevance of the Model

This section discusses the key empirical facts motivating our model. First, we summarize the relevant findings of the empirical literature on international price spillovers arising from parallel imports and the governmental practice of external reference pricing. Next, we provide a brief discussion of the WTO rules on compulsory licensing and discuss some recent CL episodes to illustrate the role of CL in the bargaining process.

A. *International Price Spillovers*

A number of empirical studies have shown that new pharmaceutical products are not launched or experience substantial launch delays in markets where income levels are low and where there are price controls.[3] Not only do these factors lead to lower prices and profits in that particular market, they can also affect profitability in other markets. For example, Kyle (2007) studied drug launches in the 28 largest pharmaceutical markets from 1980–2000 and found that a country's use of price

[3] Danzon, Wang, and Wang (2005) studied launch data during 1994–1998 pertaining to 85 new chemical entities in 25 major markets and found that only about half of all potential launches actually occurred. Countries with lower prices or smaller markets size experienced fewer launches and longer launch delays. Danzon and Epstein (2008) studied drug launches in 15 countries during the period 1992–2003 and found that drug launch in low-price European Union (EU) countries was adversely affected by prior launch in high-price EU countries.

controls not only delays drug launches into its own market, but also lowers prices that *other* countries are willing to pay.[4]

An important channel of international spillovers is the policy of external reference pricing, under which a country uses the prices at which products are sold in other markets in setting the regulated prices for its own market. Ruggeri and Nolte (2013) report that 24 of 27 European countries use international price comparisons in negotiating prices with pharmaceutical companies, with the number of comparison countries ranging from 5 to 20. They also note that this policy is used by numerous countries outside Europe, including Brazil, South Africa, Australia, and Canada. Even in countries where reference pricing is not an explicit policy, the presence of low prices in other markets can generate public pressure for price reductions. For example, high prices of pharmaceuticals in the United States relative to the rest of the world frequently stirs up debate and discussion in the US press as well as in Congress.[5] As Goldberg (2010) notes, by delaying access to drugs or denying it altogether, reference pricing policies in high-price countries impose welfare costs on low-price countries and can potentially justify the use of CL on their part.

A second channel for price spillovers is the existence of parallel trade. The European Union (EU) allows free flow of parallel imports within its territory, which puts a limit on the extent to which firms can price discriminate between EU countries. By some estimates, such trade accounts for about 10 percent of the total EU market for pharmaceuticals.[6] As one might expect, parallel trade within the European Union generally flows from low price markets such as Greece and Spain to high price markets such as Germany, United Kingdom, the Netherlands, and the Scandinavian region. Ganslandt and Maskus (2004) found that after Sweden joined the European Union and opened its pharmaceutical market to parallel imports, prices of drugs that were subject to competition from parallel trade declined 12–19 percent.[7] Such trade is not legal between most developed and developing countries, but illegal trade still has the potential to arise if there are substantial price differences between markets. For example, it is well-known that the presence of price controls in Canada creates incentives for the illegal importation of pharmaceuticals into the United States from Canada.

B. *Price Negotiations and Compulsory Licensing*

Article 31 of TRIPS lays down rules that govern the use of CL by WTO member countries. In addition to the requirement that a compulsory license can be issued only if the patent is not worked locally, these rules require that CL "may only be permitted if, prior to such use, the proposed user has made efforts to obtain authorization from the right holder on reasonable commercial terms and conditions and

[4] Similar evidence emerges from Lanjouw's (2005) extensive study of drug launches in 69 countries of varying income levels during 1982–2002.

[5] A discussion of a few of these incidents is available in Pecorino (2002) and Roy and Saggi (2012). See also the recent report by the Office of the United States Trade Representative (2013).

[6] See "European drug groups fear parallel trade" *Financial Times*, June 7, 2010.

[7] Note that the mere possibility that such trade can arise puts limits on the ability of firms to engage in international price discrimination. This implies that the observed price declines and the volume of parallel trade are likely to underestimate the true impact of the possibility of parallel trade on the pricing behavior of firms.

that such efforts have not been successful within a reasonable period of time."[8] Article 31 also requires that "adequate remuneration in the circumstances of each case, taking into account the economic value of the authorization" must be paid to the patent holder and that the compulsory license "shall be authorized predominantly for the supply of the domestic market of the Member authorizing such use." The 2001 Fourth Ministerial Conference of the WTO expanded these powers by allowing compulsory licenses to be issued to producers in third countries in order to make CL accessible to those countries that lacked the capability to produce pharmaceuticals products domestically.

In addition to providing a means for countries to obtain access to a patented product when the local market is not being served, the TRIPS agreement also grants certain protections to patent holders. For example, countries issuing a compulsory license must provide a means for patent holders to have the ability to challenge a compulsory license. More importantly, Ho (2011, ch. 5) notes that, in the event of CL, the home country of the patent holder can challenge the compulsory license before the Dispute Settlement Body (DSB) of the WTO. Since the DSB has the potential to authorize trade sanctions as remedies against countries that fail to honor their WTO obligations, it provides an external enforcement mechanism that can help prevent violations of the various WTO clauses governing CL, such as providing compensation to patent holders and preventing export sales of products produced under CL.[9]

From the ratification of TRIPS in 1995 to 2011 there have been 24 international episodes where negotiations between developing countries and pharmaceutical companies proceeded to the point where CL was publicly considered or implemented. These episodes involved public officials and/or governments of 17 WTO members and covered 40 drug patents and 22 pharmaceuticals (Beall and Kuhn 2012). About half of these episodes ended up with the issuance of a compulsory license while nine of them resulted in significant price reductions and can be interpreted as a successful bargaining outcome between pharmaceutical companies and developing countries. In cases where compulsory licenses were issued, patent holders received royalties ranging from 0.5 percent of the generic price to 2 percent of revenues from the sale of the product.[10]

These cases illustrate the role CL plays in negotiations between multinationals and developing countries. In some cases, the threat of a compulsory license served as an effective means of negotiating a lower price for the product, while in others the result was the issuance of a compulsory license. Brazil's experience with negotiations over the price of AIDS drugs provides examples of both cases. Brazil's Health

[8] The WTO does not provide a minimum time required to pass before a compulsory license can be applied for. However, it does require that the standards of the Paris Convention on Industrial Property be adhered to. Article 5 of the Paris Convention specified a minimum time period of four years from the application for a patent or three years from the granting of a patent, whichever is greater.

[9] Although there have been no complaints to the DSB involving compulsory licenses so far, the TRIPS agreement as a whole has been cited in 34 complaints.

[10] The World Health Organization (2005) provides guidelines for calculating royalty rates for compulsory licenses. These royalty rates for CL are substantially below those from voluntary licenses, which typically average around 5 percent. This gap between the two types of royalties probably reflects the difference between the TRIPS mandated "adequate remuneration" that must be paid to the patent holder under a compulsory license and the "reasonable commercial terms" of a market-based voluntary license issued by the patent holder.

Minister threatened CL of nelfinavir (one of the 12 drugs used by the health ministry to combat HIV/AIDS) when price negotiations with Roche, the manufacturer of the drug, ran into difficulties. While price negotiations were ongoing, publicly visible efforts were made by Brazil to prepare Farmanguinhos—the leading government-owned pharmaceutical manufacturer—to initiate local production of the drug. In response, Roche agreed to reduce the price of nelfinavir by 40 percent, an offer that Brazil accepted. Similarly, Brazil threatened the CL of Kaletra, an HIV/AIDS medicine produced by Abbott but never actually implemented the threat since Abbott agreed to reduce the annual per patient cost of Kaletra by a substantial amount. Emboldened by its success with Abbott and Roche, Brazil negotiated fairly aggressively with Merck over the price of Efavirenz, another patented AIDS drug. Interestingly, do Nascimento (2010) notes that during these price negotiations the Brazilian government explicitly used external reference pricing as a strategy by noting that Merck was selling Efavirenz for relatively lower prices in some other middle income countries. These negotiations over Merck's price eventually broke down and ended with Brazil issuing a five-year compulsory license for Efavirenz, with Merck receiving a royalty of 1.5 percent on local sales of the drug.

These examples illustrate that in some cases the threat of CL results in a preemptive offer by the patent holder to deter the issuance of a compulsory license, while in other cases the patent holder prefers to allow a compulsory license to be issued rather than agree to further price reductions. Existing evidence also shows that the quality of the product provided by a potential licensee is a major concern in the implementation of CL, since it may take time to develop the technology to produce the product and generic versions may not be equivalent to the patented products.[11]

II. Model

We consider a multinational firm that has two markets for its patented product, North and South. The patent has a finite duration (T) during which the multinational has a monopoly over the product in both markets. Motivated by the empirical evidence discussed in the previous section, we examine the entry and pricing decisions of the multinational for the Southern market when there are spillovers between the two markets and the multinational negotiates the terms of its entry with the Southern government.

There is a continuum of Southern consumers, whose measure is normalized to one. Each consumer buys (at most) one unit of the product at each point in time. If a consumer buys the good at price p, utility is given by $U = \theta q - p$, where q measures quality and $\theta \geq 0$ is a taste parameter that captures the willingness to pay for quality. For simplicity, we assume that θ is uniformly distributed over the interval $[0, 1]$ in the South, which yields the demand function $d^S(p^S, q) = 1 - p^S/q$ for the patented good. Northern consumers value quality relatively more than Southern ones in that the preference parameter θ is uniformly distributed over the interval $[0, m]$, with $m > 1$. Assuming a mass of $n \geq 1$ consumers in the North, demand

[11] See Lybecker and Fowler (2009), Daemmrich and Musacchio (2011), and Harris (2014).

in the North is $d^N(p^N, q) = \frac{n}{m}(m - p^N/q)$. This specification of market demand allows for greater profitability of the Northern market in terms of the distribution of willingness to pay, as captured by m, as well as the scale of the market, n.

The multinational has a constant marginal cost for selling in each market, which we normalize to zero, yielding profits $\pi^j = p^j d^j(p^j, q)$ for market $j = N, S$. With perfect market segmentation and complete flexibility to price in each market, the multinational maximizes profits by charging a price $\hat{p}^S = q/2$ in the South and $\hat{p}^N = mq/2$ in the North. Profits in the respective markets with perfect market segmentation are $\hat{\pi}^S = q/4$ and $\hat{\pi}^N = mnq/4$.

We assume that the North follows a policy of national exhaustion under which parallel imports from the South are prohibited, but we allow for some degree of arbitrage between markets that prevent the multinational from engaging in perfect market segmentation. We assume that for all values of p^S at which there are sales in the South (i.e., $p^S < q$), the price in the North is subject to the no arbitrage constraint: $p^N \leq kp^S$. This no arbitrage condition would arise if the detection of parallel imports were to be imperfect, as is likely to be the case in the real world. If δ denotes the probability that a seller engaged in arbitrage is caught and has its products confiscated, then $k = \frac{1}{1-\delta}$ captures the degree to which the Southern price spills over to (or constrains) the price in the North. The no arbitrage condition will bind for $p^S < \min[mq/(2k), q]$, so we can express the multinational's global profits as follows:

$$(1)\quad \pi^G(p^S, q) = \begin{cases} \dfrac{knp^S}{m}\left(m - \dfrac{kp^S}{q}\right) + p^S\left(1 - \dfrac{p^S}{q}\right) & \text{if } p^S < \min\left[\dfrac{mq}{2k}, q\right] \\[2ex] \dfrac{mnq}{4} + p^S \max\left[\left(1 - \dfrac{p^S}{q}\right), 0\right] & \text{if } p^S \geq \min\left[\dfrac{mq}{2k}, q\right] \end{cases}.$$

The international pricing spillover exists as long as the Southern price is less than $mq/(2k)$, which is more likely to occur the lower the probability of detection of parallel trade and the greater the choke price in the North.

A similar specification of the global profit function arises if the North follows an external reference pricing policy for the patented product. Under the reference pricing interpretation, the parameter k is inversely related to the responsiveness of the North's pricing policy to changes in the Southern price. In this case, the spillover will exist as long as the Southern price is below a threshold level given by the North's reference pricing scheme.[12]

[12] Our treatment of reference pricing treats it as an exogenously given rule in the bargaining between the multinational and South. While it would be interesting to endogenize the reference pricing rule, we feel that it would require making marginal cost the private information of the multinational. One of our objectives in this paper is to illustrate that the structure of CL introduces some novel features into the bargaining problem even in the full information case. Endogenizing the reference pricing rule remains an issue for future work.

A. *The Bargaining Problem*

We assume that the multinational negotiates with the South over the terms of its entry into the local market, with an agreement consisting of a price $p^S \in [0, q)$ to be charged in the South for the duration of the patent and a lump sum transfer to be paid by the multinational (which could be negative).[13] An agreement yields a per period consumer surplus to the South of

$$S(p^S, q) = \frac{(q - p^S)^2}{2q} \tag{2}$$

and a per period global profit to the multinational of $\pi^G(p^S, q)$.

For $p^S \in [0, q)$, there are positive sales in the Southern market, and an agreement over entry generates a joint per period payoff of

$$v(p^S, q) = S(p^S, q) + \pi^G(p^S) \tag{3}$$

to the two parties. We treat time as continuous, so $v_E = \sup_{p^S<q} v(p^S, q)$ denotes the maximum flow of returns to the two parties created by an agreement over the multinational's entry into the South.

If no agreement is reached, the multinational stays out of the South. The multinational earns a disagreement flow payoff equal to the optimal monopoly profit, $\hat{\pi}^N$, in the Northern market, while the South gets nothing. We can then define the flow of joint surplus from an agreement, which is the difference between the maximum agreement payoff and the disagreement payoff, as

$$\gamma_E = v_E - \hat{\pi}^N. \tag{4}$$

It is straightforward to show that γ_E is decreasing in m and n when the arbitrage constraint binds, since the multinational's loss in profits in the North from entering the South is greater when the Northern market is more profitable. Similarly, a larger impact of a price reduction in the South on the Northern price (i.e., smaller value of k) reduces γ_E.

If the price spillover between markets is significant and the Northern market is sufficiently profitable, the price reduction required in the Northern market in order to sell in the South is so large that $\gamma_E < 0$. The following Lemma provides a characterization of the entry and pricing decisions that maximize the joint payoff under entry (proofs of results are in the Appendix).

[13] After the expiration of the patent, the good is assumed to be available at a competitive price in both markets so that an agreement between the two parties generates no additional surplus.

LEMMA 1: *There exists* $m^* \equiv \frac{1+\sqrt{1+(2nk)^2}}{n}$ *such that*

(*i*) *for* $m \leq m^*, \gamma_E \geq 0$ *and the joint payoff* $v(p^S, q)$ *is maximized by selling in the Southern market at a price*

$$\tilde{p} = \frac{mnqk}{2nk^2 + m}; \tag{5}$$

(*ii*) *for* $m > m^*, \gamma_E < 0$.

As a benchmark, we first examine the solution to the bargaining problem between the multinational and the South when CL is not an option. We assume that negotiations between the multinational and the South can be described by an alternating offers bargaining game, which has a finite horizon determined by the expiration of the patent at time T. Letting D denote the time between offers, period i of the bargaining game begins at calendar time iD. The magnitude of D can be interpreted as the amount of friction in the bargaining process.

Letting $N = T/D$ be the number of offers that occur before the patent expires, we have offers occurring at times $\{0, D, 2D, \ldots, (N-1)D\}$. Following Rubinstein (1982), we solve for the subgame perfect equilibrium in the bargaining game. The proposer in period $i \in \{0, \ldots, N-1\}$ makes an offer that makes the responder indifferent between accepting the offer and waiting to be the proposer in the next period. A delay in reaching an agreement for one period results in a loss of $\gamma_E(1 - e^{-rD})/r$. Using backward induction arguments, we obtain the standard result that an agreement is reached immediately if entry yields a nonnegative surplus. In light of our assumption of a finite horizon for the life of the patent, the exact split of the surplus between the two parties depends on which party moves first and which moves last. If $N = 1$ (i.e., $D = T$), the proposer captures all of the surplus by making a take it or leave it offer that makes the respondent indifferent between accepting and rejecting. As the time between offers (i.e., D) decreases, the order of moves becomes less important and payoffs approach an even split of the surplus between the two parties. Since we have no a priori reason to assume a particular order of moves, we report payoffs for the limiting case of $D \to 0$ in which payoffs are not sensitive to assumptions about the order and number of moves.[14] We can now state:

PROPOSITION 1: *The equilibrium of the alternating offers bargaining game has the following characteristics.*

(*i*) *If* $\gamma_E \geq 0$, *an agreement is reached in the first period and the multinational sells the product in the Southern market at price* $\tilde{p}$. *The multinational's average payoff in the limiting case as* $D \to 0$ *is* $\hat{\pi}^N + \frac{\gamma_E}{2}$, *while that of the South is* $\frac{\gamma_E}{2}$.

[14] This prevents us from having to present expressions for cases with both odd and even numbered periods, which differ due to our assumption of a finite horizon. This issue, as well as the first mover advantage, disappears as D becomes arbitrarily small.

(*ii*) *If* $\gamma_E < 0$, *no agreement is reached and the multinational does not sell in the South. In this case, the multinational obtains an average payoff of* $\hat{\pi}^N$, *while the South receives a payoff of zero.*

The alternating offers bargaining game yields an efficient outcome from the viewpoint of the total payoff of the two parties, since entry occurs only when it generates a joint surplus (i.e., $\gamma_E \geq 0$) and it occurs without delay. The efficient price is chosen because it is in the interest of both parties to maximize joint surplus given that a lump sum transfer is available to shift surplus between them. The limiting case eliminates any advantages derived from the order of moves, so the surplus is evenly split between the parties. Entry fails to occur when the Northern market is sufficiently profitable relative to the Southern one and/or the price spillover across markets is large. As we noted in Section II, there is strong support for this result in the relevant empirical literature.[15]

III. Bargaining under Threat of Compulsory Licensing

We now extend the model to allow for the possibility of CL. Suppose that if an agreement has not been reached by time $T_{CL} < T$, the South can impose a compulsory license in the next period. The time period T_{CL} captures the WTO rule that the patent holder must be given a reasonable period of time to work its patent before a government can issue a compulsory license to another entity.

Under CL, a domestic firm produces the patented product at marginal cost zero, but its quality q_{CL} is lower than that of the multinational ($q_{CL} \leq q$). Furthermore, the Southern government specifies the price at which the local firm must sell the product locally and it pays a per period royalty R to the multinational. We treat R as an exogenously given parameter reflecting the WTO specified obligation of providing reasonable compensation to the patent holder for the use of its patent.

Under CL, the Southern government chooses the local price to maximize the sum of consumer surplus and profits of the domestic firm:

$$\max_{p} S(p, q_{CL}) + \pi^S(p, q_{CL}).$$

Southern welfare under CL is maximized by setting price equal to marginal cost, which yields a per period payoff of

$$w_{CL}^S = \frac{q_{CL}}{2} - R. \quad (6)$$

[15]The assumption that the payoff in the North market is constant in all periods leads to the result that if entry occurs, it must occur in the first period. If the magnitude of the price spillover to the North market is declining over time, as might happen if there is entry of competing products, then entry might occur with delay if γ_E switches from a negative to a positive value over time.

The price under CL equals marginal cost because the South is not required to compensate the multinational for any lost profits in the Northern market. The flow payoff to the multinational under a compulsory license consists of the profits earned in the Northern market plus the royalty payment from the license:

$$w_{CL}^{M} = \frac{np_{CL}^{N}}{m}\left(m - \frac{p_{CL}^{N}}{q}\right) + R,$$

where p_{CL}^{N} is the price that the multinational is able to maintain in the Northern market when the compulsory license is granted. If pricing spillovers across markets are completely eliminated under CL, then we must have $p_{CL}^{N} = \hat{p}^{N}$. In general, we will have $p_{CL}^{N} \leq \hat{p}^{N}$. The sum of the two parties' flow payoffs under CL is

$$v_{CL} = w_{CL}^{S} + w_{CL}^{M}.$$

Denote the difference between the joint payoff under CL and the joint payoff under entry by $\gamma_{CL} \equiv v_{CL} - v_{E}$, which can be expressed as

$$(7) \quad \gamma_{CL} = \frac{1}{2}\left[q_{CL} - q\left(1 - \frac{\tilde{p}}{q}\right)\right] + \frac{n}{m}\left[\left(m - \frac{p_{CL}^{N}}{q}\right)p_{CL}^{N} - \left(m - \frac{k\tilde{p}}{q}\right)k\tilde{p}\right].$$

The first term in square brackets is the difference between the sum of profits and consumer surplus in the Southern market under CL and entry. This term shows that CL has two conflicting effects in the Southern market. It reduces the price at which the South obtains access to the product, but it also may result in a lower quality product being sold in the South. CL increases the sum of producer and consumer surplus in the South as long as the quality of the licensee's product satisfies

$$\frac{q_{CL}}{q} > \left(1 - \frac{\tilde{p}}{q}\right).$$

The above inequality is more likely to be satisfied the more profitable is the Northern market (as reflected in a higher bargained price under entry, $\tilde{p}$).

The second term in (7) measures the difference in profits in the Northern market between CL and entry. If the reduced price in the South market under CL lowers price in the Northern market, then the multinational's profit in the North market is reduced due to CL. The adverse impact of a compulsory license on North profits is mitigated if CL reduces the magnitude of the price spillover, and could even result in an increase in global profits earned by the multinational if it is able to sustain its monopoly price in the Northern market under CL. There is good reason to believe that the issuing of a compulsory license reduces the scope of international price spillovers. This is because WTO rules governing CL require that the output under a compulsory license be sold only in the domestic market. The existence of this geographical restriction, combined with the potential for a WTO dispute in case the restriction is violated, is likely to serve as a commitment mechanism that allows the South to make credible promises to restrict price spillovers to the Northern market.

Such promises may not be credible in the absence of WTO obligations. Similarly, a compulsory license is also likely to reduce the likelihood that the multinational is constrained by an external reference pricing policy on the part of the North since under CL it is the Southern government that controls the price and production of the good as opposed to the multinational. As a result, the local price in the South under CL is unlikely to be viewed as one at which the multinational voluntarily agreed to sell in the South. Indeed, as per WTO rules, a government is authorized to use CL precisely when a patent holder *refuses* to work its patent in the local market. If the quality of the licensee's product is very close to that of the multinational, and CL is effective in eliminating arbitrage, we must have $\gamma_{CL} > 0$, in which case CL increases the joint payoff relative to entry. Thus, in what follows, we allow γ_{CL} to be either positive or negative.

A. *Equilibrium Entry under Compulsory Licensing*

We begin our analysis of the alternating offers bargaining game by considering the decision of the South regarding whether to grant a compulsory license. We assume that the South can only issue a compulsory license when it is its turn to make a proposal. In any period after T_{CL} at which it is the South's turn to make an offer, it must decide whether to issue a compulsory license or to continue bargaining with the multinational. If the average payoff under CL, w_{CL}^S, exceeds the average payoff it can earn by continuing to bargain, then it will end the bargaining game and issue a compulsory license. Otherwise, it will continue to bargain.

We make two assumptions concerning the bargaining game with threat of a CL. The first simply limits attention to cases where the CL is a credible threat for the South.

ASSUMPTION 1 (Credible CL): *The payoff to the South under the compulsory license exceeds its payoff if it were to continue bargaining with the multinational at T_{CL}. In the limiting case as $D \to 0$, this assumption requires $w_{CL}^S > \max\left[\frac{\gamma_E}{2}, 0\right] \Leftrightarrow \frac{q_{CL}}{2} > R + \max\left\{\frac{\gamma_E}{2}, 0\right\}$.*

Compulsory licensing is a credible threat for the South if the quality of the licensee's product is not too low or the required royalty payment R to the multinational is not too high. Under Assumption 1, the bargaining game ends at the South's first opportunity to move after T_{CL}. Letting N_{CL} be the smallest integer greater than T_{CL}/D at which it is the South's turn to move, bargaining offers can be made at calendar times $\{0, D, 2D, \ldots, (N_{CL} - 1)D\}$ before the CL decision is made. If the South rejects the multinational's offer in period $N_{CL} - 1$, the game terminates with the issuance of a compulsory license. As in the benchmark bargaining game without CL, an offer consists of a price for the product and a net transfer to be paid to the multinational if it enters the Southern market.

Our second assumption is more substantive, in that it restricts the types of agreements that can be struck between the two parties.

ASSUMPTION 2 (No CL Buyout): *The South cannot give up its right to issue a compulsory license in return for a cash transfer from the multinational.*

We impose this assumption because we do not believe that an agreement that allows the multinational to "buy out" the South's right to issue a compulsory license can arise in the real world due to two reasons. First, it seems unlikely that a multinational firm would be able to enforce such an agreement if a developing country were to renege on its commitment once it had reached the time at which it can issue a compulsory license. Such an agreement between a multinational and a developing country government would be unenforceable at the WTO because WTO treaties are contracts between sovereign nations. Private agents (individuals or firms) have no standing at the WTO. Thus, any agreement between a multinational and a developing country over the latter agreeing to give up its right to issue a compulsory license cannot be interpreted as a WTO obligation. Furthermore, for obvious reasons, such an agreement would also be difficult to enforce in a domestic court of a developing country. A second reason as to why such an agreement between the two parties may be infeasible in the real world is that the government of a developing country would likely find it politically unpalatable to enter into an agreement under which it deliberately agrees to deny local consumers access to a patented product (such as an AIDS medication) in return for a cash transfer from a multinational. Furthermore, any transfers made to the government would be unlikely to reach those most in need of the patented product, making the agreement politically unpopular. In fact, governments in developing countries generally face significant public pressure from citizens, public interest watch groups, and nongovernmental organizations to improve local access to patented pharmaceuticals. Nevertheless, for the sake of completeness, in Section IIID we discuss the effects of relaxing Assumption 2.

In analyzing the bargaining game, we first identify the entry decision for periods $i = 0, \ldots, N_{CL} - 1$ that maximizes the total payoff to the two parties over the duration of the patent, given the threat of CL at $N_{CL} - 1$ if no agreement has been reached by that time. We then show that the solution to the bargaining problem results in the entry time that maximizes this total payoff.

The present value payoff to the two parties at time 0 if the multinational enters in period i equals

$$(8)\quad V_0^E(i) = \left[\hat{\pi}^N\left(1 - e^{-rDi}\right) + v_E\left(e^{-rDi} - e^{-rDN}\right)\right]/r, \quad i = 0, \ldots, N_{CL} - 1.$$

The payoff to entry at time i is the sum of the return from sales in the North market only for $i = 0, \ldots, i-1$ and sales in both markets from i until the end of the patent. Since $rV_0^E(i) - V_0^E(i-1) = -\gamma_E\left(e^{-rD(i-1)} - e^{-rDi}\right)/r$, the total payoff from entry will be maximized by entry at time 0 if $\gamma_E > 0$ and at time $N_{CL} - 1$ if $\gamma_E < 0$. The joint payoff to the two parties time 0 of waiting for a compulsory license is

$$(9)\quad V_0^{CL} = \left[\hat{\pi}^N\left(1 - e^{-rDN_{CL}}\right) + v_{CL}\left(e^{-rDN_{CL}} - e^{-rDN}\right)\right]/r.$$

The payoff from waiting for CL depends on both the flow payoffs under CL and the North market profits earned during the delay period preceding the compulsory license.

The payoff maximizing policy is obtained by comparison of $V_0^E(0)$ and V_0^{CL} if $\gamma_E > 0$ and a comparison of $V_0^E(N_{CL}-1)$ and V_0^{CL} if $\gamma_E < 0$. This yields the following result.

PROPOSITION 2: *The joint payoff maximizing regime, subject to the "no CL buy-out" assumption, takes the following form.*

(*i*) *For* $\gamma_{CL} < 0$ *and* $\gamma_E \geq 0$, *the multinational should enter at* $i = 0$.

(*ii*) *For* $\gamma_{CL} < 0$ *and* $\gamma_E < 0$, *entry should occur in period* $N_{CL} - 1$ *if*

$$r\left(V_0^E(N_{CL}-1) - V_0^{CL}\right) = \gamma_E\left(e^{-rD(N_{CL}-1)} - e^{-rDN_{CL}}\right) - \gamma_{CL}\left(e^{-rN_{CL}D} - e^{-rND}\right) \geq 0. \tag{10}$$

Otherwise a CL is issued. Equation (10) *must be satisfied for D sufficiently small.*

(*iii*) *For* $\gamma_{CL} \geq 0$ *and* $\gamma_E \geq 0$, *there exists a critical time* $\hat{T} \in [0, T]$ *such that the multinational should enter at* $i = 0$ *if* $DN_{CL} \geq \hat{T}$ *and wait for a compulsory license otherwise.* $\hat{T}$ *is the solution to*

$$\gamma_E\left(1 - e^{-r\hat{T}}\right) - \gamma_{CL}\left(e^{-r\hat{T}} - e^{-rND}\right) = 0. \tag{11}$$

(*iv*) *For* $\gamma_{CL} \geq 0$ *and* $\gamma_E < 0$, *a compulsory license should be issued.*

The question of whether entry or CL yields higher total payoff depends on a comparison of the discounted joint surplus from entry prior to the issuance of a CL and the flow payoff differential during the period when CL would be in effect. When γ_{CL} and γ_E have the opposite sign, the result is unambiguous because both comparisons favor the same regime. In (i), entry is preferred to both staying out and CL, so immediate entry must result. In part (iv), staying out dominates entry while CL is better than entry, making CL the surplus maximizing regime.

For the remaining cases where γ_E and γ_{CL} have the same sign, there are conflicting effects because one component favors CL while the other favors entry. Part (ii) is the case in which entry is less attractive than staying out but more attractive than CL. Entry by the multinational in the last possible period minimizes the losses resulting from the international price spillovers prior to the date at which a compulsory license is imposed, while avoiding the losses that would result in the imposition of a compulsory license during period N_{CL}. The losses from entry prior to T_{CL} shrink to 0 as $D \to 0$, so that preemptive *entry* maximizes total surplus, provided bargaining frictions are small enough that entry can occur arbitrarily close to the deadline for CL. Part (iii) is the case where entry is more attractive than staying out, but CL is more attractive than entry in terms of a per period payoff comparison. The question then becomes whether the delay prior to CL is sufficiently short so that it is worth waiting for it.

Recall that in the absence of the threat of CL, the solution to the bargaining problem results in entry by the multinational at the time that maximizes total surplus. We now show that this result also applies when the South can impose a compulsory license.

LEMMA 2: *In the alternating offers bargaining game with CL, the solution results in the first acceptable offer for entry being made at the surplus maximizing entry time identified in Proposition 2.*

This result is due to the fact that the proposer at any time i has an interest in choosing the decision that makes joint surplus as large as possible. Consider, for example, the decision at $N_{CL} - 1$, the last period before a CL would be imposed. The best acceptable offer by the multinational makes the South indifferent between accepting and waiting to impose a compulsory license at N_{CL}, which yields the multinational a payoff of

$$\left[v^E\left(1 - e^{-rD(N-N_{CL}+1)}\right) - w_{CL}^S\left(e^{-rD} - e^{-rD(N-N_{CL}+1)}\right)\right]/r.$$

If the multinational does not make an offer, its payoff is the return to waiting until a compulsory license is issued in the next period,

$$\left[\hat{\pi}^N\left(1 - e^{-rD}\right) + w_{CL}^M\left(e^{-rD} - e^{-rD(N-N_{CL}+1)}\right)\right]/r.$$

Entry is preferred to waiting for a compulsory license at $N_{CL} - 1$ if

$$\gamma_E\left(1 - e^{-rD}\right) - \gamma_{CL}\left(e^{-rD} - e^{-rD(N-N_{CL}+1)}\right) \geq 0. \tag{12}$$

It can be seen from (10) that this condition will be satisfied if and only if $V_0^E(N_{CL} - 1) - V_0^{CL} \geq 0$, so an offer is made at $N_{CL} - 1$ if and only if entry at $(N_{CL} - 1)$ yields a joint payoff that is at least as high as that obtained by waiting for a CL. The lemma then follows using induction arguments. Table 1 summarizes how the threat of CL affects the equilibrium of the bargaining game.

There are three possible reasons why a compulsory license can be issued in equilibrium. First, it can be issued when both CL and staying out dominate entry (i.e., $\gamma_{CL} > 0$ and $\gamma_E < 0$). In this case CL provides the South with access to a product that it would not have had otherwise. Second, CL can arise when it is preferred to entry ($\gamma_{CL} > 0$) but entry is preferred to staying out ($\gamma_E \geq 0$) and the delay period preceding CL is not too long. In this case, CL delays access to the product for the South because joint surplus is higher if the multinational stays out and reaps monopoly profits in the North market until the compulsory license is imposed. The third and final scenario where CL can arise is one where entry is preferred to CL ($\gamma_{CL} < 0$), staying out is preferred to entry ($\gamma_E < 0$), and bargaining frictions are sufficiently large. In this case as well, the threat of CL ensures that the South obtains access to the patented product that it would not have had otherwise, but the product is not provided by the most efficient means. Once the option of staying out is off the table, total surplus would be higher if the product were provided via entry as

TABLE 1—HOW THE THREAT OF CL AFFECTS THE EQUILIBRIUM

		CL is a credible threat	
	No threat of CL	$\gamma_{CL} < 0$	$\gamma_{CL} > 0$
$\gamma_E \geq 0$	enter at 0	enter at 0	CL at T_{CL} if $T_{CL} < \hat{T}$, otherwise immediate entry
$\gamma_E < 0$	no entry	entry at $T_{CL} - D$ if (10) holds CL at T_{CL} otherwise	CL at T_{CL}

opposed to CL. However, bargaining frictions prevent the multinational from making an acceptable offer to the South prior to the deadline for CL.

We now turn to the question of how the threat of CL affects the respective payoffs of the two parties.

B. *Equilibrium Payoffs with* $\gamma_{CL} < 0$

We begin with the case in which CL yields a lower joint payoff than entry, so that both parties have an interest in avoiding the imposition of a compulsory license. The length of the delay required before the South can issue a CL plays a critical role in determining the impact of the CL on the payoffs to the respective parties. Therefore, it is useful to define $\mu(T_{CL}) = \left(e^{-rT_{CL}} - e^{-rT}\right)/\left(1 - e^{-rT}\right)$ as a measure of the relative importance of payoffs received after the time at which a CL can be issued. If a party receives a constant payoff stream in the time interval $[0, T]$, then $\mu(T_{CL})$ is the share of the present value of that stream that is received after T_{CL}.

With this definition of $\mu(T_{CL})$, we can state the following proposition.

PROPOSITION 3: *In the bargaining game with a CL deadline of* T_{CL} *and* $\gamma_{CL} < 0$, *the equilibrium payoffs have the following properties.*

(*i*) *If* $\gamma_E \geq 0$, *entry occurs in the first period. The average payoff to the South in the limiting case as* $D \to 0$ *is*

$$\left(\frac{\gamma_E}{2}\right)(1 - \mu(T_{CL})) + w_{CL}^S \mu(T_{CL}) > \frac{\gamma_E}{2},$$

and the average payoff to the multinational is

$$\hat{\pi}^N + \frac{\gamma_E}{2} - \left(w_{CL}^S - \frac{\gamma_E}{2}\right)\mu(T_{CL}) < \hat{\pi}^N + \frac{\gamma_E}{2}.$$

(*ii*) *If* $\gamma_E < 0$, *and* (10) *holds, preemptive entry occurs at* T_{CL}. *The average payoff to the South in the limiting case as* $D \to 0$ *is*

$$w_{CL}^S \mu(T_{CL}) > 0,$$

and the average payoff to the multinational is

$$\hat{\pi}^N + \left(\gamma_E - w_{CL}^S\right)\mu(T_{CL}) < \hat{\pi}^N.$$

If $\gamma^E < 0$ and (10) is not satisfied, entry does not occur and each party receives the present value of its return from a compulsory license in period N_{CL}.

If $\gamma_E \geq 0$, the proposer has an incentive to make an offer in each period. The only difference between this bargaining problem and the one without CL is the terminal condition, which gives the South's payoff under a compulsory license at T_{CL}. The equilibrium payoff to the South with the threat of CL is a weighted average of its average payoff in the bargaining game without this threat, $\gamma_E/2$, and its average payoff that the South would receive if it were to impose a compulsory license, w_{CL}^S, where the weight placed on the payoff under the compulsory license is the effective fraction of the life of the patent that is captured under a compulsory license, $\mu(T_{CL})$. Since $\mu(T_{CL})$ is decreasing in T_{CL}, the South prefers a shorter deadline for the imposition of a license. The compulsory license has no effect on the timing of entry when $\gamma_E \geq 0$ and $\gamma_{CL} < 0$, but it redistributes surplus from the multinational to the South.

If $\gamma_E < 0$, entry occurs just prior to the time at which the compulsory license would be imposed if bargaining frictions are not too large. The average payoff to the South is its average payoff in the event that a compulsory license is imposed, weighted by the effective fraction of the life of the patent that is covered by the license. Since the South receives a payoff of zero in the absence of the threat of CL, the South benefits from the threat of CL in this case as well. The South also benefits in the case where D is sufficiently large that preemptive entry is not profitable, because a compulsory license provides a positive payoff to the South under Assumption 1. The difference from the previous case is that in addition to redistributing surplus, the threat of CL also changes the entry decision when $\gamma_E < 0$ and bargaining frictions are not too large.

To show the effect of the deadline for the case of $\gamma_E > 0 > \gamma_{CL}$, we provide a numerical example that is illustrated in Figure 1. The horizontal dotted line in Figure 1 at $\gamma_E/2 = 0.14$ represents the payoff to each party when there is no threat of CL. Parameter values are chosen such that the multinational (labeled M in Figure 1) produces a higher quality product than the licensee, but the payoff to the South (labeled S) under a compulsory license exceeds $\gamma_E/2$ due to the South's ability to price the product at marginal cost and pay a relatively low royalty to the multinational.[16] The vertical intercepts of the payoff loci for the respective parties in Figure 1 represent their respective payoffs under a compulsory license, since $T_{CL} = 0$ corresponds to immediate use of CL. In this example, the multinational receives a payoff that is less than its outside option payoff of $\hat{\pi}^N$ when T_{CL} is

[16]We assume $q = 1, n = 2$, and $m = 3.5$. These parameter values reflect a Northern market that has a larger scale (n) and a larger choke price (m) than the South, and result in a profit maximizing price of $7/4$ in the North and $1/2$ in the South. With a spillover parameter of $k = 2.5$, we obtain a price $\tilde{p} = 0.614$ that maximizes surplus and a gain from entry of $\gamma_E = 0.285$. While the Southern market is less profitable than the Northern market, the pricing spillover is sufficiently small that entry yields higher profits than staying out. We assume that the product has a useful life of $T = 20$, and that the discount factor $r = 0.05$. In the event of a compulsory license, it is assumed that the quality of the licensee's product is $q_{CL} = 0.8$ and that the multinational receives a royalty of $R = 0.025$, which is 10 percent of its monopoly profit. These assumptions give the South a payoff of $w_{CL}^S = 0.375$, which exceeds the payoff received under bargaining without the threat of CL.

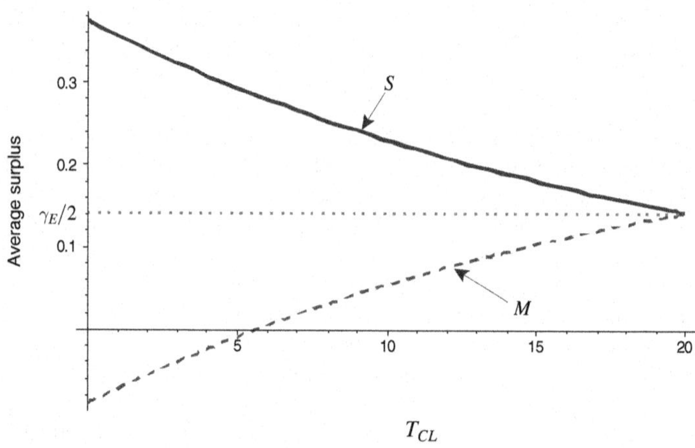

FIGURE 1. DIVISION OF SURPLUS WHEN $\gamma_{CL} < 0 < \gamma_E$

sufficiently low. The South is able to capture more than the surplus from entry in this case because it must be compensated for its threat to impose a CL. As T_{CL} increases, the value of CL as a threat point decreases and surplus is redistributed from the South toward the multinational. The payoff to each party converges to $\gamma_E/2$ as T_{CL} approaches $T = 20$, the duration of the patent.

It should be noted that the payoff to the multinational is independent of its payoff in the event that a compulsory license is issued, w_{CL}^M, as long as it continues to satisfy $\gamma_{CL} < 0$. This is due to the assumption that for all $D > 0$, the South is only able to impose the compulsory license at the first period after T_{CL} in which it is the proposer. The multinational always has the chance to make an offer in the last period before a compulsory license would be imposed, and at that point the multinational would make an offer that makes the South indifferent between accepting the offer and waiting for the compulsory license.[17]

C. *Equilibrium Payoffs with* $\gamma_{CL} \geq 0$

We now turn to the case in which the issuance of a compulsory license increases the flow surplus relative to entry. When CL has the potential to increase total surplus, we obtain a richer set of possible impacts on the average payoffs of the two parties. Indeed, we show below that when $\gamma_{CL} \geq 0$, the threat of CL can benefit the South at the expense of the multinational, benefit both parties, or somewhat paradoxically, benefit the multinational at the expense of the South.

[17] If we were to make the alternative assumption that the South makes the last offer before a compulsory license is imposed, it would choose an offer that makes the multinational indifferent between accepting the offer and receiving its payoff under the license. In that case, the multinational's payoff would depend on w_{CL}^M. But the conclusion that the South gains from the threat of CL would hold in this case as well.

PROPOSITION 4: *In the bargaining game with $\gamma_{CL} \geq 0$, the payoffs for the parties in the limit of the alternating offers bargaining game have the following properties.*

(i) *If $\gamma_E < 0$ or $\gamma_E \geq 0$ and $T_{CL} < \hat{T}$, the South issues a compulsory license at T_{CL}. The average payoff to the South is $w^S_{CL}\mu(T_{CL})$ and the average payoff to the multinational is $\hat{\pi}^N(1 - \mu(T_{CL})) + w^M_{CL}\mu(T_{CL})$.*

(ii) *If $\gamma_E \geq 0$ and $T_{CL} > \hat{T}$, entry occurs immediately. The average payoff to the South is*

$$\frac{\gamma_E(1 - e^{-r\tau})}{2(1 - e^{-rT})} + w^S_{CL}\mu(T_{CL}),$$

and the average payoff to the multinational is

$$\hat{\pi}^N(1 - \mu(T_{CL})) + \frac{\gamma_E(1 - e^{-r\tau})}{2(1 - e^{-rT})} + w^M_{CL}\mu(T_{CL})$$

where $\tau \in (\hat{T}, T_{CL})$ satisfies $\gamma_E(e^{-r\tau} - e^{-rT_{CL}}) - \gamma_{CL}(e^{-rT_{CL}} - e^{-rT}) = 0$.

Part (i) refers to cases in which the equilibrium results in the issuance of a compulsory license at T_{CL}. If $\gamma_E < 0$, the CL must make the South better off since it receives no payoff in its absence. The average payoff to the multinational is a weighted average of its payoff from the Northern market prior to the CL and its payoff under the CL. The multinational benefits from the CL if and only if

$$\pi_{CL} + R > \hat{\pi}^N.$$

We thus have the possibility that the CL leads to a Pareto improvement in this case.

If $\gamma_E \geq 0$ and $T_{CL} < \hat{T}$, the imposition of a compulsory license in equilibrium raises the payoff to the South above what it would obtain from multinational entry as long as $\gamma_E/2 \leq w^S_{CL}(e^{-rT_{CL}} - e^{-rT})/(1 - e^{-rT})$. As $T_{CL} \to 0$, this condition must hold as a result of Assumption 1. Note, however, that the payoff to a CL is declining in T_{CL} for $T_{CL} \in [0, \hat{T}]$ because of the increased delay in obtaining the product as T_{CL} increases. Therefore, the South benefits from a CL for all cases in (i) for $\gamma_E \geq 0$ if it benefits when $T_{CL} = \hat{T}$. Since $\hat{T}$ is defined by the condition that $\gamma_E(1 - e^{-r\hat{T}})/r = \gamma_{CL}(e^{-r\hat{T}} - e^{-rT})/r$, the South is at least as well off for $T_{CL} \in [0, \hat{T}]$ if

$$w^S_{CL} \geq \frac{\gamma_E + \gamma_{CL}}{2} = \frac{v_{CL} - \hat{\pi}^N}{2}. \tag{13}$$

Condition (13) shows that when $\gamma_{CL} > 0$ and $\gamma_E \geq 0$, the fact that the threat of CL is credible is *not* sufficient to ensure that the South benefits from it. Since the joint surplus from a CL is exactly equal to that from entry at $\hat{T}$, the South's share of the surplus from a CL must be at least as large as its share of the surplus from entry (i.e., $1/2$) in order for it to benefit from the CL.

Part (ii) considers the case where $\gamma_E \geq 0$ and $T_{CL} \in [\hat{T}, T]$, so that the deadline for imposing the compulsory license is sufficiently far off that the joint payoff is maximized by immediate entry. However, the fact that the CL yields higher per period surplus than entry means that there will exist some calendar time $\tau(T_{CL}) < T_{CL}$ at which the surplus from entry is exactly equal to that obtained by waiting for a CL. This results in an important change in the bargaining game, since no acceptable offers would be made at any $t > \tau$ because the surplus is larger if the parties wait for the CL. Thus, the relevant threat point for the bargaining game is the payoff to the proposer in the last period before time τ. The proposer in the last period before τ will receive a payoff equal to the difference between the payoff from entry and the payoff earned by the responder if it waits for the issuance of a CL in period N_{CL}. This last mover advantage disappears in the limit as $D \to 0$, because the calendar time at which the last offer is made will converge to τ. In the limiting case, the identify of the last mover does not matter because τ is defined to be the period at which the total surplus from entry exactly equals the total surplus from waiting for a CL. Each party will receive the value of its payoff under a CL, discounted to τ, if entry occurs at τ.

A comparison of the payoffs in (i) and (ii) illustrates that since $\tau(\hat{T}) = 0$, the payoffs will be continuous in T_{CL} at $T_{CL} = \hat{T}$. Differentiating the South's payoff with respect to T_{CL} (taking into account the dependence of τ on T_{CL}), it can be shown that the average payoff to the South is decreasing in T_{CL} for $T_{CL} > \hat{T}$ if and only if (13) holds. When (13) is satisfied, the payoff to the South from a compulsory license is sufficiently high that it serves as a valuable threat point for the South, so delaying the deadline for CL harms the South's interests. In this case, the payoff to the South will be monotonically decreasing on $[0, T]$. If (13) does not hold, the threat of CL is actually beneficial to the multinational, so the South benefits if the deadline for a compulsory license is delayed. Since the payoff to the South is less than $\frac{\gamma}{2}$ at $\hat{T}$ and equals $\frac{\gamma}{2}$ at T, the South is worse off from the threat of a CL on $[\hat{T}, T)$.

These observations yield the following relationship between the deadline and the value of CL for the South.

COROLLARY 1: *In the case where $\gamma_E \geq 0$ and $\gamma_{CL} > 0$, the following hold.*

(*i*) *If inequality* (13) *holds, the payoff to the South is non-increasing in T_{CL} and the threat of a CL cannot decrease the welfare of the South. The South is everywhere better off if the inequality is strict.*

(*ii*) *If* (13) *fails, the payoff to the South is decreasing in T_{CL} for $T_{CL} < \hat{T}$ and increasing in T_{CL} for $T_{CL} > \hat{T}$. The South is strictly worse off due to the threat of CL for all $T_{CL} \in [\hat{T}, T)$.*

We conclude by providing two numerical examples that illustrate each of the cases in the corollary. For each example, the payoffs under entry are identical to

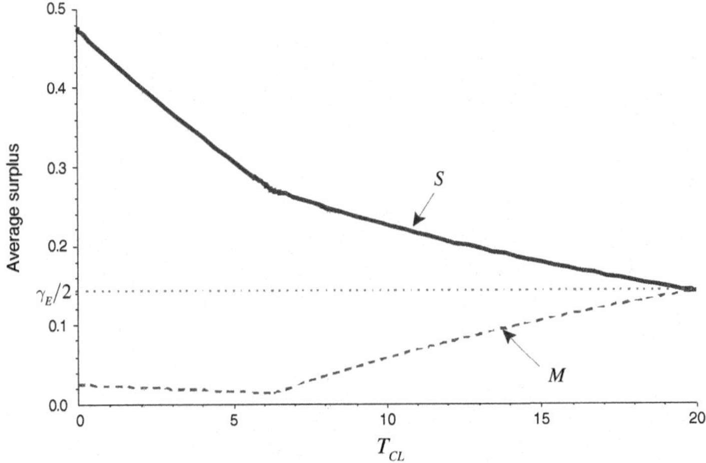

Figure 2. Division of Surplus When $\gamma_E, \gamma_{CL} > 0$ and (13) Holds

those in Figure 1, but the CL payoffs are chosen such that $\gamma_{CL} > 0$. Figure 2 illustrates the equilibrium payoffs to the parties as given by Proposition 4 for a case that is consistent with part (i) of the corollary. Here, the South captures most of the benefits of CL since the parameter values for this example imply that the South pays a royalty to the multinational that is only 10 percent of the profits that the multinational would have earned under entry; the licensee's product is of the same quality as that of the multinational; and CL eliminates the price spillover between markets.[18]

The vertical intercepts in Figure 2 reflect the average payoffs to the respective parties under a compulsory license, and show that the South captures virtually all of the surplus under the CL in this example. For $T_{CL} < \hat{T} = 6.34$, a compulsory license is the equilibrium outcome of the bargaining game, and each party receives the present value of the compulsory license payoff starting at time $\hat{T}$. The payoff to both parties is decreasing in T_{CL} in this region because delay in implementing the compulsory license reduces the period over which the license operates. For $T_{CL} > \hat{T}$, the delay for a compulsory license is sufficiently long that immediate entry is preferred. The sum of payoffs to the two parties is constant in this interval, so the effect of a change in T_{CL} is to redistribute surplus between the parties. The payoff to the South is decreasing in T_{CL} in this region, because delay weakens the use of the threat of CL for the South. The threat of CL benefits the South for all $T_{CL} < T$ in this case.

The second example illustrates part (ii) of Corollary 1, with the distribution of the surplus under CL favoring the multinational. The parameter values in this example differ in that the quality of the licensee's product is less than that of the multinational,

[18] Specifically, we assume that $q = q_{CL} = 1$ and $R = 0.025$. With these assumptions, $\gamma_{CL} = 0.215$ and $w_{CL}^S = 0.475 > (\gamma_E + \gamma_{CL})/2 = 0.25$ as required for (13) to be satisfied.

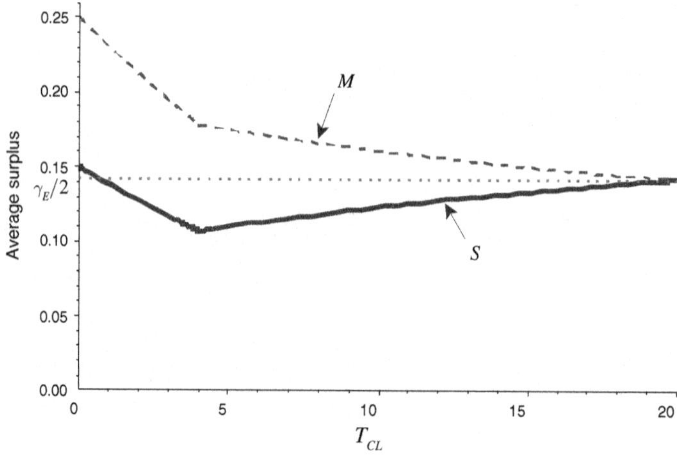

FIGURE 3. DIVISION OF SURPLUS WITH γ_E, $\gamma_{CL} > 0$ AND (13) DOES NOT HOLD

and the required royalty payment is equal to the profit the multinational would have earned if it entered the market and set the monopoly price. Both of these factors, i.e., a lower quality product and a higher royalty payment under CL, reduce the average CL payoff of the South compared with the previous case.[19] The average payoffs to the parties under a compulsory license are shown by the vertical intercepts in Figure 3, which illustrate that the multinational receives a higher absolute payoff under CL than the South. Note, however, that CL represents a credible threat for the South because its average payoff under CL exceeds that which it obtains by continuing to bargain: $w_{CL}^S = 0.15 > \gamma_E/2 = 0.14$.

A CL is issued for $T_{CL} < \hat{T} = 4$. Note that $\hat{T}$ is lower in this case relative to Figure 2, because the lower quality product of the licensee reduces γ_{CL}. For T_{CL} sufficiently close to 0, CL results in a Pareto improvement because both parties receive a payoff exceeding $\gamma_E/2$. The payoff to both parties is decreasing in T_{CL} for $T_{CL} < \hat{T}$, and the payoff to the South declines below that obtained without the threat of CL. For $T_{CL} > \hat{T}$, entry occurs at $t = 0$ and the sum of payoffs to the two parties is a constant. The difference with the previous example is that in this case, the payoff to the South increases with T_{CL}. This occurs because the South's surplus is sufficiently small under a compulsory license that the threat of CL actually favors the multinational.

The case where $\gamma_{CL} > 0$ requires that the WTO provides an enforcement mechanism that limits spillovers to the South from sales of the patented product under a compulsory license, and that the South's promise to limit such spillovers is not credible without the external enforcement provided by the WTO (say, via its dispute

[19] In this case, $q_{CL} = 0.8$ and $R = 0.25$. All other parameters remain the same as in the previous example. These parameter values result in $\gamma_{CL} = 0.1$. The payoff to the South under CL is $w_{CL}^S = 0.15 < (\gamma_E + \gamma_{CL})/2 = 0.2$, so (13) does not hold.

settlement process). We have shown that in such cases, the possibility of CL can *strengthen the bargaining position of the multinational* and hurt the South if the multinational's share of the surplus under a compulsory license is sufficiently large.

D. *Alternative Assumptions Regarding Permissible Agreements*

We conclude our analysis with a brief discussion of how our results would be affected under alternative assumptions regarding the types of agreements that are allowed. The first extension we consider is to allow agreements in which the multinational makes a transfer to the South in return for a promise on its part to not issue a compulsory license. The option of staying out yields a joint payoff of $V^N = \hat{\pi}^N(1 - e^{-rDN})/r$, so that the maximization of joint payoffs involves choosing the largest of $\{\max V^E(i), V^{CL}, V^N\}$. For $\gamma_E > 0$, V^N is dominated by $V_0^E(0)$, and the problem simplifies to choosing the largest of $\{V_0^E(0), V^{CL}\}$. Therefore, parts (i) and (iii) of Proposition 2 are unaffected by this extension. For $\gamma_E < 0$, staying out dominates entry so the maximum joint payoff is the largest of $\{V^{CL}, V^N\}$. The introduction of the option to stay out modifies parts (ii) and (iv) of Proposition 2 such that there will be no entry if $\gamma_E + \gamma_{CL} = v_{CL} - \hat{\pi}^N < 0$, and a compulsory license will be issued if $\gamma_E + \gamma_{CL} > 0$.

The main effect of allowing the multinational to offer a transfer to prevent the issuance of a compulsory license is that preemptive entry does not arise in equilibrium. A transfer to the South to avoid CL is a less costly way for the multinational to avoid CL relative to preemptive entry, so the multinational would choose that option if it is available. The cases with $\gamma_E > 0$ are unaffected, so the payoffs identified in Propositions 3 and 4 for the case with $\gamma_E \geq 0$ continue to apply.

A second extension is to consider the case where no transfers of any type are allowed in the bargaining game. In this case, the two parties bargain over price if the multinational enters. The prices from firm entry that are not Pareto dominated are $p \in [0, p_{\max}]$, where $p = 0$ reflects marginal cost pricing for the product, and $p_{\max} = \arg\max \pi^G(p, q)$ maximizes the multinational's global profits under entry. For the payoff functions defined in (1) and (2), we obtain a strictly concave payoff frontier for the bargaining game in the absence of transfers.

In the absence of CL, it can be shown that the multinational will enter as long as its maximum possible global profit from entry exceeds the profit from staying out, $\pi^G(p_{\max}, q) \geq \hat{\pi}^N$. This entry condition is more stringent than in the case with transfers because the South is unable to subsidize entry by making a transfer when the joint surplus is positive. It can also be shown that preemptive entry arises in the limiting case as $D \to 0$ if $\pi^G(p_{\max}, q) < \hat{\pi}^N$, and the joint payoffs under CL lie inside the payoff frontier under entry. This result is similar to that obtained in Proposition 2, part (ii), where the multinational enters at time $N_{CL} - 1$ if the losses from entry are smaller than those under CL and the bargaining friction D is not too large.

The above results illustrate two ways in which bargaining frictions affect the possibility of preemptive entry. The inability to use a lump sum transfer to prevent the issuance of a compulsory license, which represents a form of bargaining friction, is necessary for preemptive entry to arise. However, bargaining frictions in the form of delay between offers (i.e., $D > 0$) make it less likely that preemptive entry occurs because the losses resulting from preemptive entry prior to the CL deadline must be incurred for a longer period of time.

IV. Conclusion

During the last decade or so, developing countries have increasingly started to turn to CL as a tool for improving consumer access to patented foreign medicines. The available evidence indicates that in almost all cases of CL that have been observed since the ratification of TRIPS, price negotiations between multinational firms selling patented drugs and developing countries have tended to precede the actual issuance of a compulsory license. This observation lies at the heart of the model developed in this paper that considers bargaining between a multinational and a developing country that wishes to gain access to its patented product at as low a price as possible.

The model compares two scenarios: one where the two parties engage in bilateral price bargaining with no possibility of CL and another where the developing country has the authority to issue a compulsory license if negotiations between the two parties do not succeed by a certain time period. Each of the requirements specified in Article 31 of TRIPS that sanctions CL plays an important role in our model. While the "adequate remuneration" rule simply ensures that CL compensates the multinational to some degree, the effect of the other two rules is more subtle. For example, the requirement that CL can only be issued if the patent is not worked locally and price negotiations do not conclude successfully by a certain time period implies that, if it so chooses, the multinational can preempt the use of CL by the developing country government. Our model provides conditions under which the multinational finds it optimal to preempt CL as well as when it does not. In the former case, the credible threat of CL weakens its bargaining position and lowers its share of the total surplus.

Our model clarifies that the possibility of CL need not necessarily lead to an outcome where one party's gains come at the expense of the other. The logic for this is as follows. Since the government issuing a compulsory license has to ensure that the patented product is sold primarily in the local market, the possibility that international pricing spillovers undermine the multinational's profits in its other markets can be greatly reduced or eliminated altogether under CL. Similarly, the fact that the multinational does not control pricing and production under CL implies that the price at which the good is sold in a developing country issuing a compulsory license is less likely to run afoul of external reference pricing policies of other countries. Consequently, the low prices of drugs produced under CL are likely to have little or no bearing on high prices in rich countries.

It is clear that the enforcement of the "local consumption requirement" of the CL contract is quite valuable to the multinational. Our model shows that the proper enforcement of this requirement has the potential to expand the joint payoff shared between the multinational and the developing country. The implication of this result is that for the use of CL by developing countries to be more palatable to foreign patent holders, such countries need to ensure that there is no leakage of products produced under CL to markets in the rest of the world.

Although our analysis has focused on the case of compulsory licensing, our model would also apply to other bargaining problems where the payoff available to the two parties may increase at a prespecified deadline. Our results highlight the fact that in such situations, as the deadline approaches, the attractiveness of making an offer declines relative to waiting for the deadline. As a result, the ability to delay agreement until the deadline plays an important role in determining the payoffs to the parties.

Mathematical Appendix

PROOF OF LEMMA 1:

Suppose that $m > 2k$, so that the no arbitrage constraint binds for $p^S \in [0, q]$. In this case, $v(p^S)$ is strictly concave in p^S on $[0, q]$ by (1) and (2). For $m > 2nk^2/(nk - 1)$, $v(p^S)$ is strictly increasing on $[0, q]$. Since $v(q) = \pi^G(q)k$ and $kp^S < \hat{p}^N$ in this case, we have $v_E < \hat{\pi}^N$. For $m \leq 2nk^2/(nk - 1)$, $v(p^S)$ achieves a local maximum at

$$\tilde{p} = \frac{kmnq}{2nk^2 + m} \leq q,$$

yielding a joint payoff of

$$v_E = \frac{q}{2}\left(\frac{2nk^2 + m + n^2k^2m}{2nk^2 + m}\right).$$

Comparing this payoff with that obtained by selling only in the Northern market at $\hat{p}^N$, $mnq/4$, yields the condition $m < m^* \equiv \left(1 + \sqrt{1 + (2nk)^2}\right)/n$ for selling in the Southern market.

For $m < 2k$, $v(p^S)$ is strictly concave in p^S on $[0, mq/(2k)]$ and decreasing at $p^S = mq/(2k)$. The joint payoff is maximized by setting $p^S = \tilde{p}$. ∎

PROOF OF PROPOSITION 1:

Letting W_i^S be the payoff to S at a subgame starting in period i at which S is the proposer and $V_i^E = v_E\left(1 - e^{-rD(N-i)}\right)/r$ the current value of entry at i, we have

$$W_i^S = \max\left\{V_i^E - \hat{\pi}^N\left(1 - e^{-rD}\right)/r - e^{-rD}W_{i+1}^M, e^{-rD}W_{i+1}^S\right\}. \tag{A1}$$

The first term in brackets is the maximum return to S from making an acceptable offer to M, which is the difference between the joint payoff from entry and the payoff that M could earn by rejecting the offer and waiting to be proposer in the next period, $\hat{\pi}^N\left(1 - e^{-rD}\right)/r - e^{-rD}W_{i+1}^M$. The second term in brackets is the return to S from not making an offer. Since S earns nothing if M does not enter, the value of not making an offer is simply the discounted value of the payoff in the subgame beginning at $i + 1$. The payoff to M in a period j in which it is the proposer is

$$W_j^M = \max\left[V_j^E - e^{-rD}W_{j+1}^S, \hat{\pi}^N\left(1 - e^{-rD}\right)/r + e^{-rD}W_{j+1}^M\right]. \tag{A2}$$

Since $W_N^M = W_N^S = V_N^E = 0$, an acceptable offer will be made in period $N-1$ if and only if $\gamma_E \geq 0$. From (A1) and (A2), an acceptable offer will be made in period $i < N$ if

$$\text{(A3)} \qquad \gamma_E\left(1 - e^{-rD}\right) \geq re^{-rD}\left(W_{i+1}^S + W_{i+1}^M - V_{i+1}^E\right) \geq 0.$$

This condition is never satisfied for $\gamma_E < 0$, so M will not enter. If an offer is made in period $i+1$, the right side equals 0 and an offer will be made in period i if $\gamma_E \geq 0$. It then follows by induction that an acceptable offer will be made at $i = 0$ when $\gamma_E \geq 0$.

To solve for S's payoff when $\gamma_E \geq 0$, consider a period $i < N$ at which S is the proposer. Since S would make an acceptable offer at i and M would make an acceptable offer at $i+1$, we can substitute from (A2) into (A1):

$$\text{(A4)} \qquad W_i^S = \frac{\gamma_E\left(1 - e^{-rD}\right)}{r} + e^{-2rD}\, W_{i+2}^S.$$

Consider the case in which S moves first and M moves last. The patent expires at the beginning of period N, so $W_N^S = 0$. With this terminal condition, (A4) yields $rW_0^S = \gamma_E\left(1 - e^{-rD}\right)\sum_{i=0}^{N/2-1} e^{-2rDi} = \gamma_E\left(1 - e^{-rT}\right)/\left(1+e^{-rD}\right)$. Dividing by $\left(1 - e^{rT}\right)$ yields the average payoff of $\gamma_E/\left(1 + e^{-rD}\right)$ for S, which gives S a first mover advantage for $D > 0$. If M moves first and S moves last, the payoff to S is $rW_0^S = e^{-rD}\gamma_E\left(1 - e^{-rD}\right)\sum_{i=1}^{N/2} e^{-rD2(i-1)}$, yielding an average payoff of $e^{-rD}\gamma_E/\left(1 + e^{-rD}\right)$. In either case the S payoff converges to $\gamma_E/2$ as $D \to 0$. A similar result is obtained if one of the parties moves both first and last. ∎

PROOF OF PROPOSITION 2:

Entering at i dominates waiting for a CL if

$$\text{(A5)} \quad r\left(V_0^E(i) - V_0^{CL}\right) = \gamma_E\left(e^{-rDi} - e^{-rN_{CL}D}\right) - \gamma_{CL}\left(e^{-rN_{CL}D} - e^{-rT}\right) \geq 0.$$

If $\gamma_E \geq 0$, entering at $i = 0$ will dominate entering at any $i > 0$ so the comparison is between $V_0^E(0)$ and V_0^{CL}. If $\gamma_{CL} < 0$, (A5) must be satisfied at $i = 0$. If $\gamma_{CL} > 0$, there will exist some $\hat{T}$ such that (A5) will be satisfied at $i = 0$ only if $DN_{CL} \geq \hat{T}$. This establishes (i) and (iii).

For $\gamma_E < 0$, entering at $i = N_{CL} - 1$ dominates entering at any $i < N_{CL}$. Waiting for the CL must be preferred to entry at $N_{CL} - 1$ if $\gamma_{CL} \geq 0$, because (A5) must be negative. For $\gamma_{CL} < 0$, entry at $N_{CL} - 1$ is preferred to waiting for the CL if (10) is satisfied, which must hold for D sufficiently small since $\lim_{D\to 0, N_{CL}D \to T_{CL}} V_0^E(N_{CL} - 1) - V_0^{CL} = -\gamma_{CL}\left(e^{-rT_{CL}} - e^{-rT}\right)/r$. ∎

PROOF OF LEMMA 2:

(i) $\gamma_E \geq 0, \gamma_{CL} < 0$: Condition (12) is satisfied in this case, so an acceptable offer would be made at $N_{CL} - 1$. If an offer is made at $i + 1 < N_{CL} - 1$, the right-hand side of (A3) is 0 and the proposer will make an acceptable offer at i. It then follows by induction that an acceptable offer will be made at $i = 0$.

(ii) $\gamma_E < 0, \gamma_{CL} < 0$: If condition (12) fails, the proposer will not make an acceptable offer at $N_{CL} - 1$. Assuming no offer at $i + 1$, the right-hand side of (A3) will be positive and no offer will be made at i. It follows by induction that no offers will be made, and the CL is imposed at N_{CL}. If (12) is satisfied, an offer will be made at $N_{CL} - 1$. However, no offer will be made at $N_{CL} - 2$ because the right-hand side of (A3) is nonnegative. It then follows by the previous induction argument that no offer is made at $i < N_{CL} - 1$, so entry occurs at $N_{CL} - 1$. This case must apply as $D \to 0$ by the argument in Proposition 2, part (ii).

(iii) $\gamma_E \geq 0, \gamma_{CL} \geq 0$: For this case, it is useful to define the function

$$\text{(A6)} \qquad \Lambda(i, DN_{CL}, D) = \left[\left(1 - e^{-rD(N_{CL}-i)}\right)\gamma_E - e^{rDi}\left(e^{-rN_{CL}D} - e^{-rT}\right)\gamma_{CL}\right]/r,$$

which is the current value of the difference between the value of entering at period i and waiting until period N_{CL} for a compulsory license. $\Lambda(i, DN_{CL}, D)$ will be decreasing in i in this case, with $\Lambda(DN_{CL}, DN_{CL}, D) < 0$.

Suppose no acceptable offer has been made for any period with index greater than i, so that $W^S_{i_0+1} + W^M_{i_0+1} = e^{rDi}\left(e^{-rN_{CL}D} - e^{-rT}\right)v_{CL}$. Using (A3), the proposer in period i will make an acceptable offer if and only if $\Lambda(i, DN_{CL}, D) \geq 0$. If an acceptable offer is made in period i, then we can use the same induction argument as in (i) to show that an acceptable offer will be made for all periods $\{0, \ldots, i\}$. We then have two possibilities. If there exists a calendar time $\tau \in [0, DN_{CL})$ satisfying $\Lambda(\tau/D, DN_{CL}, D) = 0$, then acceptable offers will be made for all periods $i < \tau/D$ and M will enter at time 0. If $\Lambda(0, DN_{CL}, D) < 0$, then no proposer will make an acceptable offer and the equilibrium outcome will be a *CL*. Since $\Lambda(0, DN_{CL}, D)$ is increasing in DN_{CL} and $\Lambda\left(0, \hat{T}, D\right) = 0$, we have $\Lambda(0, DN_{CL}, D) < 0$ if and only if $DN_{CL} < \hat{T}$. This establishes (iii).

(iv) $\gamma_E < 0, \gamma_{CL} \geq 0$: Since (12) fails, the same induction argument as in (ii) yields no acceptable offers for $i < N_{CL}$. ∎

PROOF OF PROPOSITION 3:

(i) If $\gamma_E \geq 0$, then M enters at $i = 0$. If the bargaining game reaches period N_{CL}, then S will grant a compulsory license and receive a payoff of $W^S_{CL} = w^S_{CL}\left(1 - e^{-r(T-DN_{CL})}\right)/r$. We know from Lemma 2 that a proposer will be willing to make an acceptable offer for each period $i < N_{CL}$, so the payoff to S in a period in which S proposes will satisfy (A4) with the endpoint $W^S_{N_{CL}} = W^S_{CL}$. If N_{CL} is an even number, S moves first in period 0 and gets to make $N_{CL}/2$ offers before the CL deadline. The discounted payoff to S will be $\left[\gamma_E\left(\left(1 - e^{-rDN_{CL}}\right)/\left(1 + e^{rD}\right)\right) + w_{CL}^S\left(e^{-rDN_{CL}} - e^{-rT}\right)\right]/r$, which yields an average payoff of

$$\left[\gamma_E\left(\left(1 - e^{-rDN_{CL}}\right)/\left(1 + e^{rD}\right)\right) + w_{CL}^S\left(e^{-rDN_{CL}} - e^{-rT}\right)\right]/\left(1 - e^{-rT}\right).$$

The payoff to M is $W_0^M = V_0^E(0) - W_0^S$, so the average payoff is

$$\hat{\pi}^N + \left[\gamma_E e^{-rD}\left(1 - e^{-rDN_{CL}}\right)/\left(1 + e^{-rD}\right)\right.$$
$$\left. + \left(\gamma_E - w_{CL}^S\right)\left(e^{-rDN_{CL}} - e^{-rT}\right)\right]/\left(1 - e^{-rT}\right).$$

Taking the limit as $D \to 0$ yields the limiting average payoffs for the respective parties in the proposition. As in the proof of Proposition 1, the same limiting payoff is obtained in the case where N_{CL} is an odd number and M makes the first offer.

(ii) If $\gamma_E < 0$ and D is sufficiently small, M enters at $N_{CL} - 1$ with an offer that makes S indifferent between accepting and obtaining a compulsory license. The present value of this payoff to S is $W_0^S = e^{-rDN_{CL}} W_{CL}^S$, which yields an average payoff of $w_{CL}^S\left(e^{-rDN_{CL}} - e^{-rT}\right)/\left(1 - e^{-rT}\right)$. The present value of the total payoff to the two parties is the sum of M's profit in the North from time 0 to $D(N_{CL} - 1)$, $\hat{\pi}^N\left(1 - e^{-rD(N_{CL}-1)}\right)/r$, and the payoff to the two parties from time $D(N_{CL} - 1)$ to the expiration of the patent, $v_E\left(e^{-rD(N_{CL}-1)} - e^{-rT}\right)/r$. Converting this to an average payoff and subtracting the average payoff to S gives an average payoff to M of

$$\hat{\pi}^N + \left[\left(\gamma_E - w_{CL}^S\right)\left(e^{-rDN_{CL}} - e^{-r(T-DN_{CL})}\right)\right.$$
$$\left. + \gamma_E\left(e^{-rD(N_{CL}-1)} - e^{-rDN_{CL}}\right)\right]/\left(1 - e^{-rT}\right).$$

Taking the limit as $D \to 0$ yields the result. ∎

PROOF OF PROPOSITION 4:

(i) It follows from Proposition 2 and Lemma 2 that a CL will be issued if either $\gamma_E < 0$ or if $\gamma_E \geq 0$ and $N_{CL} < \hat{T}/D$. S's payoff under CL is $W_0^S = e^{-rDN_{CL}} W_{CL}^S$, and M's payoff is $W_0^M = \hat{\pi}^N\left(1 - e^{-rDN_{CL}}\right)/r + e^{-rDN_{CL}} W_{CL}^M$, where $W_{CL}^i = w_{CL}^i\left(1 - e^{-r(T-DN_{CL})}\right)/r$ for $i = S, M$. The average payoffs as $D \to 0$ will be $w_{CL}^S\left(e^{-rT_{CL}} - e^{-rT}\right)/\left(1 - e^{-rT}\right)$ for S and $\left(\hat{\pi}^N\left(1 - e^{-rT_{CL}}\right) + w_{CL}^M\left(e^{-rT_{CL}} - e^{-rT}\right)\right)/\left(1 - e^{-rT}\right)$ for M.

(ii) The proof of Lemma 2, part (iii) showed that if $N_{CL} \geq \hat{T}/D$, then there will exist a time $\tau \in [0, DN_{CL})$ such that an acceptable offer will be made in period i if and only if $i \leq \tau/D$. Defining i_τ to be the largest integer less than or equal to τ/D, the proposer in period i_τ would make an offer that makes the respondent indifferent between accepting the offer and waiting for a compulsory license. If M makes the last offer, the payoffs to the respective parties from an offer in period i_τ will be

$$\text{(A7)} \quad W_{i_\tau}^S = e^{-rD(N_{CL}-i_\tau)} W_{CL}^S; \; W_{i_\tau}^M = \frac{v_E\left(1 - e^{-rD(N-i_\tau)}\right)}{r} - e^{-rD(N_{CL}-i_\tau)} W_{CL}^S.$$

The payoff to S from this bargaining game is the payoff to an alternating offers bargaining game in which S is the first mover: $W_0^S = \gamma_E\left(1 - e^{-rD}\right) \times \sum_{i=0}^{i_\tau} e^{-2rDi} + e^{-rDN_{CL}} W_{CL}^S$. As $D \to 0$, we have $i_\tau D \to \tau, N_{CL}D \to T_{CL}$, which yields $W_0^S \to \gamma_E(1 - e^{-r\tau})/(2r) + e^{-rT_{CL}} W_{CL}^S$. The average payoff is then $\left(\gamma_E(1 - e^{-r\tau})/2 + w_{CL}^S\left(e^{-rT_{CL}} - e^{-rT}\right)\right)/\left(1 - e^{-rT}\right)$. The average payoff to M is $v_E - \left(\gamma_E(1 - e^{-r\tau})/2 + w_{CL}^S\left(e^{-rT_{CL}} - e^{-rT}\right)\right)/\left(1 - e^{-rT}\right)$.
If instead S makes the last offer at i_τ, the payoffs are

$$\text{(A8)} \quad W_{i_\tau}^S = \frac{v_E\left(1 - e^{-rD(N-i_\tau)}\right)}{r} - e^{-rD(N_{CL}-i_\tau)} W_{CL}^M; \; W_{i_\tau}^M = e^{-rD(N_{CL}-i_\tau)} W_{CL}^M.$$

Note that as $D \to 0$, both (A7) and (A8) converge to $W_{i_\tau}^j = e^{-r(T_{CL}-\tau)} W_{CL}^j$ for $j = M, S$. For $i_\tau < \tau/D$, the last mover is able to capture the excess of the return from entry over waiting for a compulsory license. However, this last mover advantage disappears as $Di_\tau \to \tau$. ∎

PROOF OF COROLLARY 1:

Differentiation of the average payoff to S for $T_{CL} > \hat{T}$ yields

$$\text{(A9)} \qquad \frac{r}{1 - e^{-rT}}\left(\frac{\gamma_E e^{-r\tau}}{2}\frac{d\tau}{dT_C} - w_{CL}^S e^{-rT_{CL}}\right).$$

From the definition of τ, $d\tau/dT_{CL} = (\gamma_E + \gamma_{CL})e^{-r(T_{CL}-\tau)}/\gamma_E$. Substituting this result into (A9) yields the result that the average payoff is nondecreasing in T_{CL} if and only if (13) is satisfied. ∎

REFERENCES

►**Beall, Reed, and Randall Kuhn.** 2012. "Trends in Compulsory Licensing of Pharmaceuticals Since the Doha Declaration: A Database Analysis." *PLoS Medicine* 9 (1): e1001154.

Daemmrich, Arthur A., and Aldo Musacchio. 2011. "Brazil: Leading the BRICs." Harvard Business School Case 711-024.

Danzon, Patricia M., and Andrew J. Epstein. 2008. "Effects of Regulation on Drug Launch and Pricing in Interdependent Markets." National Bureau of Economic Research (NBER) Working Paper 14041.

►**Danzon, Patricia M., Y. Richard Wang, and Liang Wang.** 2005. "The impact of price regulation on the launch delay of new drugs—Evidence from twenty-five major markets in the 1990s." *Health Economics* 14 (3): 269–92.

do Nascimento, J. M., Jr. 2010. "Compulsory Licensing of Efavirenz in Brazil." Presentation, Access to Pharmaceuticals 2010 Meeting, Rio de Janeiro, Brazil, February 23, 2010. http://www.accesstopharmaceuticals.org/case-studies-in-global-health/efavirenz-brazil/.

▶**Fuchs, William, and Andrzej Skrzypacz.** 2013. "Bargaining with Deadlines and Private Information." *American Economic Journal: Microeconomics* 5 (4): 219–43.

▶**Ganslandt, Mattias, and Keith E. Maskus.** 2004. "Parallel imports and the pricing of pharmaceutical products: Evidence from the European Union." *Journal of Health Economics* 23 (5): 1035–57.

▶**Gul, Faruk, Hugo Sonnenschein, and Robert Wilson.** 1986. "Foundations of Dynamic Monopoly and the Coase Conjecture." *Journal of Economic Theory* 39 (1): 155–90.

▶**Goldberg, Pinelopi Koujianou.** 2010. "Intellectual Property Rights Protection in Developing Countries: The Case of Pharmaceuticals." *Journal of the European Economic Association* 8 (2–3): 326–53.

Harris, Gardiner. 2014. "Medicines Made in India Set Off Safety Worries," *New York Times*, Feb 15, A1.

Ho, Cynthia M. 2011. *Access to Medicines in the Global Economy: International Agreements on Patents and Related Rights*. Oxford: Oxford University Press.

▶**Kyle, Margaret K.** 2007. "Pharmaceutical Price Controls and Entry Strategies." *Review of Economics and Statistics* 89 (1): 88–99.

Lanjouw, Jean O. 2005. "Patents, Price Controls, and Access to New Drugs: How Policy Affects Global Market Entry." National Bureau of Economic Research (NBER) Working Paper 11321.

▶**Lybecker, Kristina M., and Elisabeth Fowler.** 2009. "Compulsory Licensing in Canada and Thailand: Comparing Regimes to Ensure Legitimate Use of the WTO Rules." *Journal of Law, Medicine & Ethics* 37 (2): 222–39.

Maskus, Keith E. 2000a. *Intellectual Property Rights in the Global Economy*. Washington, DC: Institute of International Economics.

▶**Maskus, Keith E.** 2000b. "Parallel Imports." *World Economy* 23 (9): 1269–84.

Office of the United States Trade Representative. 2013. *2013 Special 301 Report*. Executive Office of the President of the United States. Washington, DC, May.

▶**Pecorino, Paul.** 2002. "Should the US allow prescription drug reimports from Canada?" *Journal of Health Economics* 21 (4): 699–708.

▶**Roy, Santanu, and Kamal Saggi.** 2012. "Equilibrium parallel import policies and international market structure." *Journal of International Economics* 87 (2): 262–76.

▶**Rubinstein, Ariel.** 1982. "Perfect Equilibrium in a Bargaining Model." *Econometrica* 50 (1): 97–109.

Ruggeri, Kai, and Ellen Nolte. 2013. *Pharmaceutical pricing: The use of external reference pricing*. Cambridge, UK: RAND Europe.

▶**Sobel, Joel, and Ichiro Takahashi.** 1983. "A Multistage Model of Bargaining." *Review of Economic Studies* 50 (3): 411–26.

▶**Spier, Kathryn E.** 1992. "The Dynamics of Pretrial Negotiation." *Review of Economic Studies* 59 (1): 93–108.

World Health Organization. 2005. "Remuneration guidelines for non-voluntary use of a patent on medical technologies." Health Economics and Drugs TCM Series Paper 18.

Chapter 21

COMPULSORY LICENSING AND PATENT PROTECTION: A NORTH-SOUTH PERSPECTIVE*,#

Eric W. Bond and Kamal Saggi

In a stylised model involving a developing country (called South) and a foreign patent holder, we analyse whether and how the incidence and social value of compulsory licensing (CL) depends upon the South's patent protection policy. If South is free to deny patent protection, CL fails to arise in equilibrium and the option to use it makes both parties worse off. If South is obliged to offer patent protection, CL can occur and even yield a Pareto improvement. The ability to control price increases the South's incentive for patent protection as well as the likelihood of CL.

The ratification of the Agreement on Trade Related Aspects of Intellectual Property Rights (TRIPS) by the World Trade Organisation (WTO) in 1995 was a watershed event in the history of the multilateral trading system. Post-TRIPS, international violations of intellectual property rights (IPRs) became subject to the potent dispute settlement mechanism of the WTO.[1] It is no secret that, prior to TRIPS, pervasive imitation and piracy in many developing countries of a wide range of products protected in the West by copyrights, trademarks and patents – such as DVDs, designer consumer items, software and pharmaceuticals – was a major source of friction between the developed and the developing world.

The text of the TRIPS agreement that eventually emerged out of the contentious and protracted negotiations of the Uruguay Round embodies the clashing views of developing and developed countries over IPR protection. On the one hand, TRIPS obliges all WTO members to offer and enforce certain minimum standards of IPR protection (such as twenty years for patents).[2] On the other hand, TRIPS contains some important flexibilities that allow national governments some degree of discretion in the implementation and enforcement of IPRs within their territories. Perhaps the most important such flexibility is contained in Article 31 of TRIPS that provides conditions under which WTO members can permit the 'use of the subject matter of a patent without the authorisation of the right holder, including use by the government

* Corresponding author: Kamal Saggi, Department of Economics, Vanderbilt University, VU Station PMB #351828, 2301 Vanderbilt Place, Nashville, Tennessee 37325-1828, USA. Email: k.saggi@vanderbilt.edu.

For helpful comments and discussions, we thank two anonymous referees and seminar audiences at the following venues: 2nd InsTED Workshop at the University of Oregon, 8th Biennial Conference of the Hong Kong Economics Association (Shandong University), CESifo workshop on the WTO and Economic Development (Venice), Delhi School of Economics, Fudan University, Hitotsubashi University, Heinz School of Public Policy (Carnegie Mellon University), Indian Insititute of Management at Bangalore, Indian Statistical Institute (New Delhi), SMU and Vanderbilt University. All errors are our own.

[1] See Maskus (2000, 2012) for comprehensive overviews of the economics of IPRs in a global setting.

[2] In accordance with the notion of special and differential treatment that exists in other parts of the WTO contract, developing countries were given fairly long-time horizons within which they had to make their IPR regimes TRIPS compliant, with the greatest accommodation being made for the least developed countries.

This chapter was originally appeared in *The Economic Journal* **128**, 1157–1179.

or third parties', or what is commonly referred to as the compulsory licensing (CL) of a patent.[3] Article 31 requires the following:

(*i*) the entity (company or government) applying for a compulsory licence should have been unable to obtain a voluntary licence from the right-holder on 'reasonable' commercial terms;
(*ii*) if a compulsory licence is issued, adequate remuneration must be paid to the patent holder; and
(*iii*) a compulsory licence must be granted mainly to supply the domestic market.[4]

In this article, we develop a simple model to evaluate the costs and benefits of CL as well as those of strengthening patent protection in developing countries. Our stylised model involves two parties: a developing country (called South) and a Northern firm (called patent holder) whose patent over its product lasts for T periods. The order of decision making is as follows. At the beginning of the first period, the South decides whether or not to protect the patent holder's patent in its local market. Next, the patent holder decides whether or not to enter the Southern market. If the South provides patent protection and the patent holder does not enter in the first period, the South has the option of issuing a compulsory licence to a domestic firm that authorises it to produce (its own version of) the patented product for sale in the local market. In the event the South chooses not to implement patent protection, a competitive local industry producing an imitated version of the patented product comes into existence, regardless of whether the patent holder enters or not. Due to the South's limited technological capacity, the quality of production under imitation is assumed to be lower than that of the patent holder.

Our modelling of CL follows the relevant WTO rules quite closely. We require that the South allow the patent holder a reasonable amount of time (assumed to be one period) for serving the local market prior to the issuance of the licence. Furthermore, in the event of CL, the South is required to pay (an exogenously given) per-period royalty to the patent holder. We make the reasonable assumption that the quality of production under CL is the same as that under imitation.[5]

We use our model to analyse the effect of introducing the option of CL under two alternative scenarios: a 'pre-TRIPS' world wherein the South is free to choose whether or not to offer patent protection and a 'post-TRIPS' world under which patent protection is mandatory. We show that if CL is not permissible then the South ends up granting patent protection in the pre-TRIPS world iff such protection is necessary to induce the patent holder to enter its market and the quality of local production under

[3] The other major TRIPS flexibility (that we do not analyse here) is specified in Article 6 which states that 'nothing in this Agreement shall be used to address the issue of the exhaustion of intellectual property rights'. For economic analyses of exhaustion policies, see Malueg and Schwartz (1994), Gansland and Maskus (2004), Valleti (2006), Grossman and Lai (2008) and Roy and Saggi (2012).

[4] While TRIPS mentions national emergencies, other circumstances of extreme urgency and anti-competitive practices as possible grounds for compulsory licensing, a WTO member has the right to issue a compulsory licence even when none of these conditions are met.

[5] The available case-study evidence shows that even countries such as Brazil and Thailand have found it difficult to produce world class products under CL: see Baron (2008) and Daemmrich and Musacchio (2011).

imitation is sufficiently low.[6] We then show that the option of CL reduces the South's willingness to offer patent protection, i.e. there exist parameter regions under which the South offers patent protection only if it cannot resort to CL. The intuition for this result follows from a two-step logic. First, the royalties involved under CL increase the patent holder's payoff from not entering the South (and letting CL occur). Second, imitation dominates CL from the Southern viewpoint since it does not incur royalties and also avoids the (one-period) delay involved under CL. As a result, whenever the patent holder prefers CL to entry, the South chooses not to offer patent protection since it prefers imitation to CL.[7]

We also consider the impact of CL in the post-TRIPS world where the South is required to provide patent protection. As expected, such forced patent protection benefits the patent holder at the expense of the South. However, more interestingly, CL now emerges as an equilibrium outcome. This result formally confirms the insight that with imitation becoming difficult, developing countries have an incentive to turn towards CL as a means for accessing patented foreign products at low prices. Furthermore, we identify circumstances under which joint welfare decreases (as well as when it increases) due to the shutting down of Southern imitation. We also find that, given patent protection, the option to use CL can even make both parties better off.

Since prices of patented products are often negotiated between governments of developing countries and patent holders, we extend our model to incorporate price negotiations between the two parties. We compare equilibrium outcomes under two contrasting scenarios: in the first scenario, consistent with our core model, the patent holder makes a take-it-or-leave it price offer the South; in the second scenario, the South makes it to the patent holder. This comparison is conducted for both when CL is an option as well as when it is not. The analysis yields several new insights. First, given that CL is not possible, having the ability to dictate price via a take-it-or leave it offer makes the South more inclined to offer patent protection. This happens because the patent holder is willing to sell at a lower price when it does not face competition from imitators relative to when it does.[8] Second, the possibility of CL allows the South to secure the product at a more favourable price even if the patent holder makes a take-it-or-leave it offer. This is because CL raises the South's disagreement payoff by making it possible for it to provide local consumers access to (at least) the lower quality version of the patented product. Third, by increasing the disagreement payoffs of both parties, the possibility of CL reduces the payoff of the party that makes the take-it-or-leave-it

[6] Our model suggests a non-monotonic relationship between a country's level of development and its degree of patent protection. Evidence of a U-shaped relationship between per capita GDP and the strength of intellectual property rights, as suggested by our results, is reported by Maskus (2000) and Chen and Puttitanun (2005).

[7] Thus, our analysis shows that developing countries may have had little use for CL when they were free to imitate foreign products that were protected by IPRs in other countries. In this context, it is worth noting that while CL was explicitly recognised in the Paris Convention for the Protection of Industrial Property of 1883, actual incidents of CL in the international context have started to emerge only during the post-TRIPS era. According to Beall and Kuhn (2012), during 1995–2011 there were 24 episodes where CL was explicitly and publicly discussed between government officials and foreign patent holders. By contrast, during the pre-TRIPS era, we observed very little, if any, such international episodes of CL.

[8] This result implies that the strengthening of patent protection should make it possible for developing countries to tighten their price controls on foreign patent holders as opposed to having to weaken them.

offer. In other words, the option of CL benefits the party with the weaker bargaining power during price negotiations.

Our study contributes to the large and influential literature exploring the effects of IPR protection in a North-South setting.[9] Grossman and Lai (2004) develop a model of optimal patent protection and endogenous innovation and show that the international harmonisation of IPR protection is neither necessary nor sufficient for efficiency. In a recent article, Mukherjee and Sinha (2013) consider the effects of strengthening Southern IPR protection in a duopoly model with market segmentation. They argue that by increasing the Southern firm's incentive for innovation, the strengthening of Southern IPR protection can actually make the Northern firm worse off; whether or not the welfare of each country (and that of the world as a whole) increases as a result of stronger IPR protection in the South turns out to depend upon the efficiency of Southern innovation.

Our benchmark case is similar to Saggi (2013) where the option to use CL does not exist. By endogenising the South's decision regarding patent protection, we significantly expand the analysis of Bond and Saggi (2014) who examine the effects of CL under the assumption that the South necessarily offers patent protection. Thus, the model developed in the present article sheds light on two major issues that are outside the scope of Bond and Saggi (2014). One, it allows us to evaluate how the possibility of CL affects Southern incentives for patent protection. Two, we can assess whether and how the role of CL as a tool for gaining access to patented products has been modified due to the strengthening of patent protection in developing countries required under TRIPS.[10]

The rest of the article is organised as follows. Section 1 presents our core model and its main results both with and without the option of CL. Next, in Section 2, we consider the consequences of forcing the South to offer patent protection. This analysis sheds light on the welfare implications of TRIPS. Section 3 incorporates price negotiations into the model while Section 4 concludes.

1. Model

We study the entry decision of a patent holder into a developing country (South) where its technology is potentially subject to imitation. Our benchmark model is a two stage game between the patent holder and the South. In the first stage, the South chooses whether or not to allow imitation (denoted by subscript I), where imitation generates local competition for the patent holder. Next, the patent holder decides whether to enter the South by incurring the fixed cost φ.[11]

[9] For an in-depth survey of this literature, see Saggi (2017).

[10] Bond and Saggi (2014) explicitly consider voluntary licensing (VL) in the context of CL. Here, to facilitate the analysis of patent protection, we abstract from the possibility of VL and focus on entry as the means via which the patent holder can sell its product locally. Sinha (2006) develops a two-period oligopoly model in which a Northern firm chooses between licensing, direct entry, or exports and the degree of IPR enforcement in the South affects the firm's choice between these three supply modes as well as its investment in R&D. Yang and Maskus (2009) explore related questions in an oligopolistic setting while also considering the effect of Southern IPR protection on technology transfer and Southern exports.

[11] Any fixed costs involved under local production (either via CL or imitation) are normalised to zero. The parameter φ should be interpreted as the additional fixed costs that are faced by the patent holder relative to local producers. Such additional costs could arise from not just production activities but also from having to secure approval from the local government prior to selling locally and/or from having to establish a local marketing and distribution network.

1.1. *Demand and Payoffs*

There is a continuum of Southern consumers of measure 1, each of whom buys (at most) one unit of the product. If a consumer buys the product at price p, his utility is given by $U = \theta q - p$, where q measures quality and $\theta \geq 0$ is a taste parameter that captures the willingness to pay for quality. For simplicity, we assume that θ is uniformly distributed over the interval [0, 1].

The patent holder's patent lasts for T periods provided it is protected by the South. Let $\beta \in [0, 1)$ be the per period discount factor and let the marginal cost of production equal zero. Normalising utility under no purchase to zero, the per-period demand $d(p, q)$ in the South for the patented product in the absence of imitation equals $d(p, q) = 1 - p/q$. In each period the patent holder chooses its price p to maximise:

$$\max \pi_E(p) = p(1 - p/q). \tag{1}$$

The present value of the patent holder's entry profits (gross of fixed costs) as a function of its price p equals:

$$v_E(p) = (1 + \Omega)\pi_E(p) \quad \text{where} \quad \Omega = \sum_{t=1}^{T} \beta^t. \tag{2}$$

The per-period consumer surplus that accrues to the South from purchasing the patented product at price p equals:

$$s_E(p) = \int_{p/q}^{1} (q\theta - p)\mathrm{d}\theta = \frac{(p - q)^2}{2q}, \tag{3}$$

which implies that Southern welfare over the duration of the patent under entry at price p equals:

$$w_E^S(p) = (1 + \Omega)s_E(p). \tag{4}$$

Solving the problem in (1) yields the patent holder's optimal monopoly price $p^m = q/2$. Thus, the maximised payoff from entry to the patent holder when its patent is protected equals:

$$v_E(p^m) = (1 + \Omega)p^m(1 - p^m/q), \tag{5}$$

while that to the South equals:

$$w_E^S(p^m) = (1 + \Omega)s_E(p^m). \tag{6}$$

When the South does not protect the patent holder's patent, imitation results in the emergence of a competitive industry that produces a lower quality version of the patented product. Let γq denote the quality of Southern imitation where $0 < \gamma \leq 1$.[12]

Competition within the Southern industry ensures that the imitated good is sold at marginal cost. When two different qualities are available for purchase at prices p (high

[12] In the context of the pharmaceutical industry, the imitated product is probably best viewed as a generic that can only be sold in the South.

quality) and 0 (low quality), Southern consumers can be partitioned into two groups: those in the range $[0,\ \theta_h(p;\ \gamma)]$ buy the low quality whereas those in $[\theta_h(p;\ \gamma),\ 1]$ buy the high quality where:

$$\theta_h(p;\gamma) = \frac{p}{q(1-\gamma)}.$$

When facing competition from imitation, the patent holder chooses its price p to maximise:

$$\max \pi_I(p;\gamma) = p[1-\theta_h(p;\gamma)],$$

with the associated value $v_I(p) = (1+\Omega)\pi_I(p)$. The patent holder's profit maximising price when facing competition from the imitative industry equals:

$$p_I^m(\gamma) = q(1-\gamma)/2 = (1-\gamma)p^m.$$

Observe that $p_I^m \le p^m$ since $0 < \gamma \le 1$. Thus, competition from imitation lowers the patent holder's gross entry payoff to:

$$v_I(p_I^m;\gamma) = (1+\Omega)(1-\gamma)\pi^m = (1-\gamma)v_E(p^m), \tag{7}$$

where $\gamma \le 1$.

If the South permits imitation and the patent holder does not enter then local consumers obtain access (only) to the lower quality imitated good at a price equal to marginal cost (set to zero). Under this scenario, Southern welfare equals:

$$w_N^S(\gamma) = (1+\Omega)s_N(\gamma) \text{ where } s_N(\gamma) = \int_0^1 \gamma q\theta \,\mathrm{d}\theta. \tag{8}$$

However, if the patent holder enters the Southern market despite imitation, Southern welfare equals:

$$w_I^S(p_I^m;\gamma) = (1+\Omega)s_I(p_I^m;\gamma) \quad \text{where} \quad s_I(p_I^m;\gamma) = \int_0^{1/2} \gamma q\theta \,\mathrm{d}\theta + \int_{1/2}^1 (q\theta - p_I^m)\,\mathrm{d}\theta. \tag{9}$$

It is straightforward to show that $w_I^S(p_I^m;\ \gamma) > w_E^S(p^m)$. Thus, provided the patent holder enters, Southern welfare increases due to imitation. When the South permits imitation, those Southern consumers that are unwilling to pay the price for the higher quality product sold by the patent holder gain access to a lower quality version that sells at a lower price. This variety enhancing effect of imitation is one reason the South benefits from imitation. The second reason, of course, is that the imitated product competes with the patented product and this competition lowers the price of the high quality.

In the absence of competition from imitation, only half of the market in the South is covered since $\theta_h(p^m) = p^m/q = 1/2$ in equilibrium. By contrast, when imitation occurs, all those consumers that buy the high quality in the absence of imitation continue to do so although they now pay a lower price for it. In addition, all consumer in the range $[0,\ 1/2]$ end up buying the low quality imitative good so that the entire Southern market ends up being covered.

1.2. *Equilibrium*

The patent holder's entry decision at the second stage depends upon the patent protection policy implemented by the South at the first stage. Given patent protection, the patent holder sells in the South iff:

$$v_E(p^m) - \varphi \geq 0 \Leftrightarrow \varphi \leq \varphi_E \equiv v_E(p^m). \tag{10}$$

Similarly, when facing imitation, the patent holder chooses to enter iff:

$$v_I(p_I^m;\gamma) - \varphi \geq 0 \Leftrightarrow \varphi \leq \varphi_I \equiv v_I(p_I^m;\gamma). \tag{11}$$

Since $\varphi_I \leq \varphi_E$, the lack of patent protection makes the patent holder less willing to sell in the South.

Anticipating the patent holder's entry decision, the South's optimal patent protection policy is as follows:

PROPOSITION 1. *In the benchmark model (where compulsory licensing is not possible), the South offers patent protection if and only if*

(*i*) $\varphi_I < \varphi \leq \varphi_E$ *and*
(*ii*) $\gamma \leq \gamma^S \equiv 1/4$.

Figure 1 illustrates Proposition 1. In this Figure, the equilibrium outcome is denoted by a pair (X, Y) where $X = I$ or P denotes the South's patent protection policy and $Y = E$ or N denotes the patent holder's entry decision. In region **A**, where $\varphi < \varphi_I$, the patent holder enters even if it faces imitation in the South. Given entry by the patent

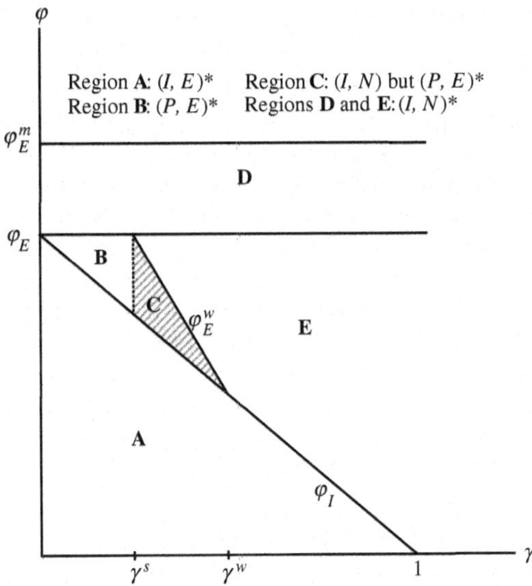

Fig. 1. *Efficiency of Equilibrium Outcomes*

holder, South has no incentive to offer patent protection since doing so lowers local consumer surplus by eliminating the imitated (low quality) product from the market. As a result, the equilibrium outcome over region **A** is (*I*, *E*). In region **D**, where $\varphi > \varphi_E$, the South once again has no incentive to grant patent protection since the Patent holder does not sell in the South even if its patent is protected. Here, the equilibrium outcome is (*I*, *N*). When $\varphi_I < \varphi \leq \varphi_E$, the patent holder enters iff the South offers patent protection. Under such a situation, the South faces a trade-off: imitation provides consumers access to the low quality product while simultaneously denying access to the high quality. As a result, the South's decision is determined by the quality gap $(1/\gamma)$ between the two products. When this gap is large, as illustrated by region **B** where $\gamma \leq \gamma^S$, the South offers patent protection and the outcome is (*P*, *E*). For the remaining areas, **C** and **E**, the quality of the imitated product is sufficiently high that the South prefers it over the patented product at monopoly price so that the equilibrium outcome is (*I*, *N*).

The main insight behind Proposition 1 is that the South grants patent protection iff such protection is necessary to induce the patent holder to sell locally and the quality of local production under imitation is sufficiently low that shutting down imitation to obtain access to the high quality patented product raises local welfare.

It is also useful to compare the South's decision on whether to grant patent protection with the decision that would maximise joint welfare. Defining joint welfare as the sum of their individual welfare levels, joint welfare in the case where the South offers patent protection becomes:

$$w_E(p^m) = (1+\Omega)s_E(p^m) + v_E(p^m) - \varphi.$$

Given patent protection, if the patent holder does not enter (which it does not whenever $\varphi > \varphi_E$), the welfare of each party equals zero. Therefore, entry is jointly optimal iff:

$$w_E(p^m) \geq 0 \Leftrightarrow \varphi \leq \varphi_E^m,$$

where $\varphi_E^m > \varphi_E$ which reflects the fact that the Patent holder ignores local consumer surplus. Throughout the article, we assume that $\varphi < \varphi_E^m$.

The Southern government's decision regarding patent protection does not take into account the welfare of the patent holder. As a result, the South's incentive for patent protection is weaker than what joint optimality requires, as shown in the following result:

PROPOSITION 2. *Given that the patent holder makes the profit-maximising entry decision, joint welfare is maximised by having the South offer patent protection over the following parameter regions:*

(*i*) $\gamma \leq \gamma^S \equiv 1/4$ *and* $\varphi_I < \varphi \leq \varphi_E$ *and*
(*ii*) $\varphi \in [\varphi_I, \varphi_E^w]$ *and* $\gamma \in [\gamma^S, \gamma^w]$, *where* $\varphi_E^w \equiv q(3-4\gamma)(1+\Omega)/8$ *and* $\gamma^w = 1/2$.

For all other parameter values, joint welfare is maximised by allowing imitation in the South.

Proposition 2 can be illustrated using Figure 1. The jointly efficient outcome in this Figure over each particular region is denoted by an asterisk superscript, i.e. as $(X, Y)^*$, where $X = I$ or P and $Y = E$ or N. The South's decision to deny patent protection is jointly optimal for all $\varphi \in [0, \varphi_I]$ (region **A** in Figure 1) as well as for $\varphi > \varphi_E$

(region **D**). For parameters in region **A**, the outcome is socially optimal because the patent holder enters even though the South does not offer patent protection; for parameters in region **D**, the patent holder would not enter even if its patent were protected which makes it socially optimal to not protect it. For region **B**, we have $\varphi \in [\varphi_I, \varphi_E]$ and $\gamma < \gamma^S$ so that patent protection is socially optimal and the South chooses to offer it. Here, even though the patent holder acts as a monopolist, its quality advantage over Southern imitators (if allowed to operate) is so large that it is optimal to restrict competition from imitation.

For region **C** in Figure 1, we have $\varphi \in [\varphi_I, \varphi_E^w]$ and $\gamma \in [\gamma^S, \gamma^w]$. In this region the equilibrium outcome is for the South to allow imitation and the patent holder not to enter, i.e. (I, N), while joint welfare is maximised under (P, E), wherein the South offers patent protection and the patent holder enters. From the South's perspective, the technological superiority of the patent holder is outweighed by the cost to the Southern consumers of allowing it monopoly power in this region. But taking account of the profits earned by the patent holder (which the South ignores) tips the balance in favour of patent protection. In region **E** in Figure 1, we have $\max\{\varphi_I, \varphi_E^w\} < \varphi < \varphi_E$ and the South's decision to deny patent protection is again optimal. Here, the quality of the imitated product is high enough to render monopoly pricing for the patented product socially suboptimal and the costs of entry are low enough that the patent holder enters despite imitation.

1.3. *Model with Compulsory Licensing*

We now extend the model to include a third stage where the South decides whether or not to grant a compulsory licence. If the product has not been sold in the market in the first period, the South can issue a compulsory licence to a local firm who pays the per-period royalty R to the patent holder for the duration of the patent. The royalty R reflects the TRIPS requirement of 'adequate remuneration' being paid to the patent holder in the event of CL. With these assumptions, the welfare of the South under a compulsory licence equals:

$$w_{CL}^S(\gamma, R) = \Omega[s_N(\gamma) - R]. \tag{12}$$

CL is a credible threat for $w_{CL}^S(\gamma, R) \geq 0 \Leftrightarrow \gamma \geq \gamma_m = R/p^m$. Thus, CL is a credible threat so long as the quality of licensed production is not so low that the total surplus generated for Southern consumers is insufficient to cover the royalty R paid to the patent holder.

When making its entry decision, the patent holder takes the possibility of CL into account. If given patent protection by the South, the patent holder has to decide whether to:

(*i*) incur the fixed cost φ and collect the payoff $v_E(p^m)$ or
(*ii*) to not enter and wait for CL to occur in the next period under which its payoff is ΩR.

The patent holder prefers entry to CL iff:

$$v_E(p^m) - \varphi \geq \Omega R \Leftrightarrow \varphi \leq \varphi_E(R) \equiv v_E(p^m) - \Omega R. \tag{13}$$

Thus, the patent holder chooses entry for all $\varphi \leq \varphi_E(R)$, whereas it waits for CL if $\varphi > \varphi_E(R)$. Observe that $\varphi_E(R) = \varphi_E - \Omega R$, i.e. the possibility of CL makes the patent holder less willing to enter by allowing it to collect royalty payments from the Southern market for the duration of the compulsory licence if it chooses to stay out.[13]

As before, if imitation is allowed by the South, the patent holder's payoff from entry falls to $(1-\gamma)v_E(p^m) - \varphi$. Observe that $\varphi_E(R) = \varphi_I \Leftrightarrow v_E(p^m) - \Omega R = (1-\gamma) \times v_E(p^m)$ which holds when $\gamma v_E(p^m) = \Omega R$. Since imitation precludes CL, the patent holder's decision in the face of imitation is trivial: it prefers entry to staying out iff $\varphi \leq \varphi_I$. Foreseeing the patent-holder's decision, the South sets the following patent protection policy:

PROPOSITION 3. *When compulsory licensing is an available option, the South chooses to grant patent protection iff:*

(*i*) $\varphi_I < \varphi \leq \varphi_E(R)$ *and*
(*ii*) $\gamma \leq \gamma^S$.

Observe that for $R > 0$, $\varphi_E(R) < \varphi_E$: given that CL yields a strictly positive royalty payment to the patent holder, the South is less willing to offer patent protection when it has the option to use CL. More specifically, over the parameter region $\max\{\varphi_E(R), \varphi_I\} < \varphi < \varphi_E$ (region **B1** in Figure 2) the option to use CL leads the South to not offer patent protection since, over this set of parameter values, the patent holder would prefer to stay out to collect royalties under CL even if it is protected from imitation. It is important to note that though CL does not arise in equilibrium, by raising the patent holder's payoff from staying out the possibility of CL increases the likelihood that the South denies patent protection.

1.4. *Welfare Effects of CL*

How does the option of CL affect the two parties? The result here is surprising and clear:

PROPOSITION 4. *Given that the South is free to allow imitation, not only does CL fail to arise in equilibrium but the option to use CL makes both parties worse off.*[14]

The intuition for this result is as follows. We noted above that when $\max\{\varphi_E(R), \varphi_I\} < \varphi < \varphi_E$ and $\gamma \leq \gamma^S$ the possibility of CL induces the South to not offer patent protection since, for this set of parameter values, the patent holder prefers to stay out of the South in order to collect royalty payments under CL if its patent is protected. This, in turn, makes patent protection counter-productive for the South:

[13] In formulating this problem, we simplify the analysis by ruling out the possibility of the patent holder delaying entry until a later period. Delayed entry has the potential to affect the South's decision regarding compulsory licensing since the patent holder could enter and compete with the licensee after the South has granted a CL or it could enter as a monopolist if the South chooses not to issue a CL in period two. Introducing these possibilities into the model substantially complicates the analysis without affecting the qualitative nature of our main results.

[14] Both parties strictly lose when $\max\{\varphi_E(R), \varphi_I\} < \varphi < \varphi_E$ and $\gamma \leq \gamma^S$ whereas they are unaffected otherwise.

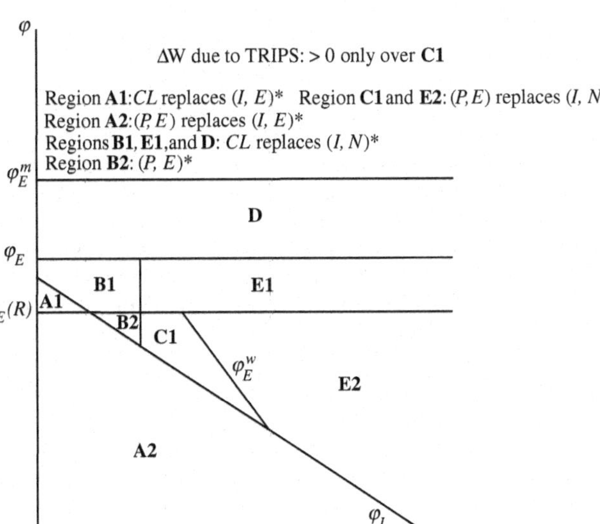

Fig. 2. *How TRIPS Affects Equilibrium and Welfare*

since Southern welfare under imitation dominates that under CL (due to the delay involved and the royalties incurred under CL), the South is better off permitting imitation to preclude CL.

The important point is that for this set of parameter values, the South would actually be better off if only the patented product were to be sold in its market since the local industry's product is of fairly low quality ($\gamma \leq \gamma^S$). Similarly, the patent holder would be strictly better off under entry since $v_E(p^m) > \varphi$ for $\varphi < \varphi_E$. It follows then that if imitation is possible then a credible commitment on the part of the South to not use CL would make both parties better off when $\max\{\varphi_E(R), \varphi_I\} < \varphi < \varphi_E$ and $\gamma \leq \gamma^S$. As we show below, the option to use CL can never make both parties worse off if the South cannot allow local imitation.

2. If South must Offer Patent Protection

What are the consequences of forcing the South to offer patent protection, say due to an international agreement such as TRIPS? Figure 2 proves useful in addressing this question.

When imitation is not permitted, the patent holder chooses entry for all $\varphi \leq \varphi_E(R)$ whereas it waits for CL to occur when $\varphi > \varphi_E(R)$. If $\varphi > \max\{\varphi_E(R), \varphi_I\}$, (regions **B1**, **E1**, and **D** in Figure 2) in the absence of TRIPS, the South permits imitation whereas the patent holder stays out. Shutting down imitation converts the market outcome from one where a competitive local industry supplies the low quality product to one where the same product is supplied by the local licensee (at price equal to marginal cost) under CL. While the price and quality under CL and imitation are the same, CL occurs with delay since, as per WTO rules, the South is required to give the patent holder a chance to work its patent. Furthermore, the South has to pay royalties under CL whereas it does not compensate the patent holder under imitation. Both the delay involved under CL and the compensation paid to the patent holder make the South worse off. The patent holder obviously benefits: absent CL, it stays out and collects no profit from the Southern market.

Next consider the parameter range where $\varphi_E(R)<\varphi<\varphi_I$ (region **A1** in Figure 2). Over this range, in the absence of TRIPS, the patent holder enters the South despite the fact that South permits imitation. With TRIPS in place, the patent holder chooses to stay out and wait for CL to occur since the value of royalty payments under CL exceeds its payoff under entry (even though entry is profitable in an absolute sense). When this happens, the South loses because the high quality product is eliminated from the market (i.e. both competition and variety decline). It is worth noting here that for $\varphi_E(R)<\varphi<\varphi_I$ it is patent protection that induces the patent holder to stay out of the Southern market, as opposed to the lack of such protection. This happens because the payoff under CL to the patent holder exceeds that under entry even though it chooses to enter when patent protection is missing.

Over the range $\varphi_I<\varphi<\varphi_E(R)$ the consequences of requiring South to extend patent protection depend upon whether or not $\gamma\leq\gamma^S$. When this inequality holds (i.e. region **B2** in Figure 2), local production suffers from a large enough quality gap that the South willingly offers patent protection to induce the patent holder to sell locally. Thus, the South is coerced to offer patent protection only when $\gamma>\gamma^S$ (i.e. regions **C1** and **E2** in Figure 4). Suppose this inequality holds. Then, forcing the South to implement patent protection converts the local market from a competitive imitative industry selling the low quality product to one where the patent holder sells the high quality at its optimal monopoly price. This switch benefits the patent holder at the expense of the South (which does not find it worthwhile to offer such protection due to the relatively small quality gap between the patented and the imitated product). Furthermore, this switch also increases joint welfare for $\varphi\in[\varphi_I,\varphi_E^w]$ and $\gamma\in[\gamma^S,\gamma^w]$ (region **C1** in Figure 2). But for parameters outside these ranges (i.e. in region **E2** in Figure 2) this change reduces joint welfare.

Finally, over the range where $\varphi<\min\{\varphi_I,\varphi_E(R)\}$ (i.e. region **A2** in Figure 2) the patent holder enters the South regardless of whether or not its patent is protected. Under such a scenario, shutting down local imitation hurts the South because it reduces competition as well variety in the local market. For the same reasons, joint welfare declines.

We summarise this discussion below:

PROPOSITION 5. *Requiring the South to offer patent protection benefits the patent holder at the expense of the South. In addition, it has the following effects:*

(*i*) *If* $\varphi>\max\{\varphi_E(R),\varphi_I\}$, *imitation is replaced by CL and joint welfare declines.*
(*ii*) *If* $\varphi_E(R)<\varphi<\varphi_I$, *CL replaces a market structure where the patent holder competes with the imitative industry and joint welfare declines.*

(*iii*) *Over the range* $\varphi_I < \varphi < \varphi_E(R)$, *when* $\gamma > \gamma^S$, *the low quality Southern imitative industry is replaced by the high quality patent holder and joint welfare increases iff* $\varphi \in [\varphi_I, \varphi_E^w]$ *and* $\gamma \in [\gamma^S, \gamma^w]$.[15]

(*iv*) *For* $\varphi < \min\{\varphi_E(R), \varphi_I\}$, *joint welfare declines because competition from the imitative industry is eliminated.*

An important insight provided by Proposition 5 is that, when forced to offer patent protection, the South turns towards CL as a means for securing the product at a low price. Recall that when imitation is possible, CL does not even arise in equilibrium since, from the Southern viewpoint, it is dominated by imitation. Thus, even though CL predates the TRIPS agreement, our model shows that one should expect it to be observed more frequently during the post-TRIPS era during which member countries of the WTO have had to clamp down on imitation.

In light of Proposition 5, it is worth asking how the option to use CL affects the two parties when the South can no longer avail of imitation. For $\varphi \leq \varphi_E(R)$, the patent holder enters with and without CL so neither party is affected. For $\varphi \in (\varphi_E(R), \varphi_E]$ the possibility of CL induces the patent holder to stay out of the market in order to collect royalties under CL. While the patent holder necessarily gains from this switch, the South benefits from it iff:

$$(1+\Omega)s_E(p^m) \leq \Omega[s_N(\gamma) - R],$$

which is the same as:

$$\gamma \geq \gamma_{CL} \equiv (1 + 1/\Omega)\gamma^S + R/p^m. \tag{14}$$

Note that the minimum value at which the South prefers CL to entry, γ_{CL}, exceeds the minimum value at which imitation is preferred to entry, γ^S, because CL involves delay in obtaining the product as well as royalty payments. The term $1 + 1/\Omega$ captures the importance of the delay relative to the overall life of the product while the term R/p^m reflects the importance of the royalty payment. Of course, for $\gamma \geq \gamma_{CL}$, the South is actually better off under CL but the patent holder pre-empts it by entering. We can now state:

PROPOSITION 6. *Given that the South must grant patent protection, the option of using CL has the following effects:*

(*i*) *For* $\varphi \leq \varphi_E(R)$, *entry occurs whether or not the South can use CL. However, for* $\gamma \geq \gamma_{CL}$ *the South is better off with CL but the patent holder pre-empts it via entry.*

(*ii*) *When* $\varphi \in (\varphi_E(R), \varphi_E]$, *the patent holder chooses to stay out and wait for CL. If* $\gamma < \gamma_{CL}$ *the patent holder gains while the South loses; otherwise, both parties gain.*

(*iii*) *For* $\varphi > \varphi_E$, *the option of CL benefits both parties.*

In part (*i*), when $\gamma \geq \gamma_{CL}$ the South has sufficient technological capability that it is better off producing the product under CL but the patent holder's entry costs are low

[15] The two parties are unaffected if $\gamma \leq \gamma^S$ since the South willingly offers patent protection and the patent holder chooses to enter.

enough that it chooses to enter thereby precluding CL. In part (*ii*), the possibility of CL can hurt the South when its technological capability is relatively weak (i.e. $\gamma < \gamma_{CL}$) but the costs of entry are high enough for the patent holder to prefer royalty payments under CL to entry.[16]

Our analysis has shown that the desirability of the CL option hinges very much on whether or not the South is free to deny patent protection. When the South can do so, CL is essentially counter-productive – not only does it not arise in equilibrium but the option to use it makes both parties worse off; when South must offer patent protection, CL can play a much more useful role and can even make both parties better off.

Thus far we have assumed that the patent holder is free to charge its optimal monopoly price p^m when selling in the South. We now extend our model to incorporate price negotiations between the two parties.

3. Entry with Price Negotiations

Since the South may not equate the availability of the patented product at monopoly price to having access to it at 'reasonable commercial terms', it is worthwhile extending the model to allow for price negotiations between the South and the patent holder. Rather than assuming a specific bargaining protocol for price negotiations, we illustrate the impact of these negotiations by comparing the case where the patent holder achieves its most preferred price outcome with that when the South achieves its best outcome.[17]

3.1. *Price Negotiations without CL*

For the case where the South does not have the option of issuing a compulsory licence, we analyse a two-stage game in which the South chooses whether or not to offer patent protection in the first stage and then negotiates with the patent holder over price in the second stage. We consider two different scenarios at the second stage: one where the patent holder makes a take-it-or-leave it price offer and another where the South does so.

If the South has granted patent protection at the first stage, the maximum price that it is willing to accept is q, since it receives a payoff of zero if the patent holder does not enter. The patent holder's disagreement payoff is also zero because it cannot enter the market if the two parties fail to reach agreement. The minimum price that the patent holder would accept is the solution to $v_E(p) = \varphi$ which yields:

$$p_E^{\min}(\varphi) = p^m\left[1 - \left(1 - \frac{4\varphi}{q(1+\Omega)}\right)^{1/2}\right]. \tag{15}$$

[16] Since the interests of the two parties can conflict, it is worth asking when CL yields higher joint welfare than entry. We can show that $w_{CL}^S(\gamma, R) > w_E(p^m)$ iff $\varphi > \varphi_{CL} = q[3(1+\Omega) - 4\Omega\gamma]/8$ and that $\varphi_{CL} > \varphi_E$ iff $\gamma < \gamma_{CL}^w = (1+\Omega)/4\Omega$.

[17] In Bond and Saggi (2017), we analyse a finite-horizon alternating offers game in which the patent holder bargains with the South over the local price of its patented good. The focus of that article is on how the presence of international price spillovers (between the South and the patent holder's home market) and the threat of CL alter the equilibrium of the bargaining game.

Any price above the monopoly price p^m is Pareto dominated by p^m, so the interval $[p_E^{\min}(\varphi),\, p^m]$ is the set of prices that are individually rational and not Pareto dominated. The set of feasible prices, $[p_E^{\min}(\varphi),\, p^m]$, is non-empty for $\varphi \leq \varphi_E$.

If the South had chosen not to provide patent protection in the first stage, the minimum price that the patent holder is willing to accept is the price at which it earns zero profits when facing competition from imitators, which equals:

$$p_I^{\min}(\varphi,\gamma) = p_I^m\left[1-\left(1-\frac{4\varphi}{q(1-\gamma)(1+\Omega)}\right)^{1/2}\right]. \tag{16}$$

where p_I^m is the maximum price that the patent holder would ever charge and $p_I^m = (1-\gamma)p^m$. The set of feasible prices $[p_I^{\min}(\varphi),\, p_I^m]$ is non-empty for $\varphi \leq \varphi_I$.

If the patent holder makes a take-it-or-leave-it offer, it offers the price p^m if the South implements patent protection and the price p_I^m if it does not. The analysis in this case is identical to the case without price bargaining, so the South's choice of patent policy in the absence of CL is identical to that reported in Proposition 1.

If the South makes a take-it-or-leave-it offer, it offers the price $p_E^{\min}(\varphi)$ under patent protection and the price $p_I^{\min}(\varphi)$ in its absence. The following Proposition, proven in Appendix A, derives the range of parameter values for which the South provides patent protection when it has all of the bargaining power:

PROPOSITION 7. *Suppose that the South makes a take-it-or-leave-it price offer for the patented product and compulsory licensing is not an option.*

(*i*) *In region* **A** *of Figure 3, the South provides patent production and the patent holder enters at price* $p_E^{\min}(\varphi)$.

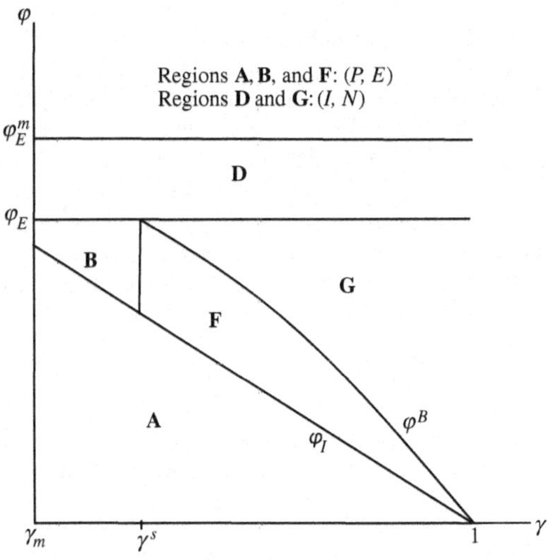

Fig. 3. *Equilibrium with Price Bargaining and w/o CL*

(*ii*) *In regions* **B** *and* **F**, *the South provides patent protection and the patent holder enters at price* $p_E^{\min}(\varphi)$ *where region* **F** *is determined by conditions* (*a*) $\gamma \geq \gamma^S$ *and* (*b*) $\varphi \in [\varphi_I, \varphi^B]$ *where:*

$$\varphi^B(\gamma) \equiv q(\sqrt{\gamma} - \gamma)(1 + \Omega).$$

(*iii*) *In regions* **G** *and* **D**, *the South does not grant patent protection and the patent holder chooses not to enter.*

In region **A**, $\varphi \leq \varphi_I$ and the patent holder can earn positive profits regardless of whether it receives patent protection. If the South does not offer patent protection, it gets the product at a price $p_I^{\min}(\varphi) < p_I^m$ when it has all of the bargaining power. Note however, the South's power is limited by the fact that the patent holder sells fewer units at any given price when there is imitation (with $\gamma > 0$). As a result, the patent holder requires a higher minimum price to enter in the absence of patent protection: i.e. $p_I^{\min}(\varphi, \gamma) > p_E^{\min}(\varphi)$ for $\gamma > 0$. The trade-off for the South is that if the South offers patent protection, it loses the product variety benefit of having the lower quality product available to consumer but it is able to obtain the high quality product at a lower price. It is shown in Appendix A that the latter effect dominates, so that the South will provide patent protection in region *A*.

For regions **B**, **F**, and **G**, the patent holder enters only if it obtains patent protection. It is in the interest of the South to provide patent protection if the consumer surplus from the patented product, $s_E[p_E^{\min}(\varphi)]$, is greater than the surplus obtained from consuming only the imitated product, $s_N(\gamma)$. The critical value $\varphi^B(\gamma)$ that separates regions **F** and **G** is the level of fixed cost for which these payoffs are equal to each other. The South obtains a price for the patented product that is sufficiently low in regions **B** and **F** that it is willing to offer patent protection but such is not the case in region **G**. Observe that $\varphi^B(\gamma)$ is decreasing in γ, because an increase in the quality of the imitated product reduces the maximum price that the South is willing to pay for the patented product.

A comparison of Propositions 1 and 7 illustrates that the South's ability to drive the patent holder to its minimum acceptable price significantly expands the parameter region over which it chooses to provide patent protection. In regions **A** (i.e. $\varphi \leq \varphi_I$) and region **F** ($\gamma > \gamma^S$ and $\varphi < \varphi^B(\gamma)$), the South offers patent protection when it has all of the bargaining power but does not offer patent protection when the patent holder has all of the bargaining power. In addition, the South obtains the patented product at a more favourable price in region **B** when it has all of the bargaining power.[18]

3.2. *CL, Bargaining, and Patent Protection*

We now examine price negotiations when the South has the option of issuing a compulsory licence if no agreement is reached after the first period. Since patent

[18] Note that the result that price negotiations expand the range of γ for which the South prefers patent protection holds for any degree of bargaining power for the South that yields a price below the monopoly price.

protection is a prerequisite for CL, we assume that the South provides patent protection throughout this subsection.

The option of CL alters the South's disagreement point from a payoff of 0 to present value of consumer surplus under CL, which equals $[s_N(\gamma) - R](1 + \Omega)$. For the patent holder, the fact that the South would issue a compulsory licence in the absence of an agreement raises its disagreement payoff from zero to the present value of royalty payments it would obtain under CL, which equals ΩR. We show below that this change in the disagreement payoffs of the two parties due to the option of CL narrows the range of fixed costs for which an agreement can be reached while also altering the price that is negotiated in the event that the patent holder enters.

We first consider the effects of CL on the subgame in which the South provides patent protection. From (15), due to existence of royalty payments under CL, the minimum price the patent holder is willing to accept is $p_E^{\min}(\varphi + \Omega R)$. Since $p_E^{\min}(\varphi + \Omega R)$ is increasing in R, the possibility of CL raises the minimum price that the South must pay to induce entry.

The existence of CL can also affect the maximum price that the South is willing to pay. To see why, first note that the price that makes the South indifferent between entry and CL solves the following equation:

$$(1+\Omega)s_E(p) = \Omega[s_N(\gamma) - R] \Leftrightarrow \int_{p/q}^{1} (q\theta - p)\, \mathrm{d}\theta = \frac{\Omega}{1+\Omega}\left(\int_0^1 \gamma q\theta\, \mathrm{d}\theta - R\right),$$

which yields:

$$p_E^{\max}(\gamma, R) = q\left[1 - \left(\frac{(\gamma q - 2R)\Omega}{q(1+\Omega)}\right)^{1/2}\right]. \tag{17}$$

Observe that $p_E^{\max}(\gamma, R)$ is decreasing in γ and increasing in R, because CL is more attractive to the South the greater is the quality of the imitated product and the lower is the royalty rate under CL. The possibility of CL reduces the maximum price the South is willing to pay only when $p_E^{\max}(\gamma, R) < p^m$, which is satisfied only if the imitative capacity of the South is such that it prefers CL to entry at the monopoly price, i.e. $\gamma \geq \gamma_{CL}$ as defined in (14). In the core model without price negotiations, the South does not have the ability to deny entry by the patent holder because it was assumed that entry by the patent holder pre-empted the South's right to issue a compulsory licence.

When CL is an available option, the patent holder and the South negotiate over prices that lie in the interval $[p_E^{\min}(\varphi + \Omega R), \min\{p_E^{\max}(\gamma, R), p^m\}]$. An agreement is reached for all levels of fixed costs for which this interval is non-empty. For $\gamma < \gamma_{CL}$, CL is not a credible threat for the South and an agreement is reached for $\varphi \leq \varphi_E(R)$. For $\gamma \geq \gamma_{CL}$, this interval is non-empty for $\varphi \leq \varphi_{CL}^B(\gamma, R)$, where $\varphi_{CL}^B(\gamma, R)$ is the solution to $p_E^{\min}(\varphi + \Omega R) = p_E^{\max}(\gamma, R)$. Since $p_E^{\max}(\gamma, R) < p^m$ for $\gamma > \gamma_{CL}$, we have $\varphi_{CL}^B(\gamma, R) < \varphi_E(R)$.

We can now determine how the possibility of CL affects the equilibrium outcome. When CL is not an option, the patent holder enters for $\varphi \leq \varphi_E$ and does not sell the product otherwise. When CL is an option, the patent holder enters in the first period for $\varphi < \min[\varphi_E(R), \varphi^B_{CL}(\gamma, R)]$ and waits for CL to issued in the next period otherwise. This results in a switch from entry to CL for $\varphi \in [\min\{\varphi_E(R), \varphi^B_{CL}(\gamma, R)\}, \varphi_E]$, which is shown by regions **V**, **W**, and **X** in Figure 4.

In region **D**, the option to use CL causes a switch from the product not being sold in the South to Southern consumers having access to it via the issuance of a compulsory licence. The option of using CL expands consumer access to the product in the South, but it also reduces the range of fixed costs for which the patent holder is willing to enter. Note that the interval over which entry occurs depends on the imitative ability of the South and the required royalty payment but is independent of the relative bargaining power of the two parties.

Comparing Figures 2 and 4, it can be seen that CL replaces entry for a larger range of parameter values when the patent holder and the South negotiate over the entry price than when there is no negotiation. For fixed costs in region **X** in Figure 4, the option to issue a compulsory licence results in a switch from entry to CL when price is negotiated between the two parties. In contrast, the patent holder enters with or without CL in region **X** when there are no price negotiations. In region **X**, the South's ability to imitate is sufficiently high that it prefers to deny entry at the patent holder's preferred price to obtain the product under CL when it is able to negotiate with the patent holder.

A second important effect of CL is to influence the price that is negotiated between the two parties. If the patent holder has all of the bargaining power, it sells at the maximum price in the range of feasible prices. Referring to Figure 4, the patent holder makes a take or leave it offer of p^m to the left of the vertical line line at γ_{CL} for $\varphi \leq \varphi_E(R)$. For $\gamma > \gamma_{CL}$, the patent holder makes an offer of $p_E^{\max} < p^m$ for $\varphi \leq \varphi^B_{CL}(\gamma, R)$. The ability of the South to deny entry by the patent holder benefits

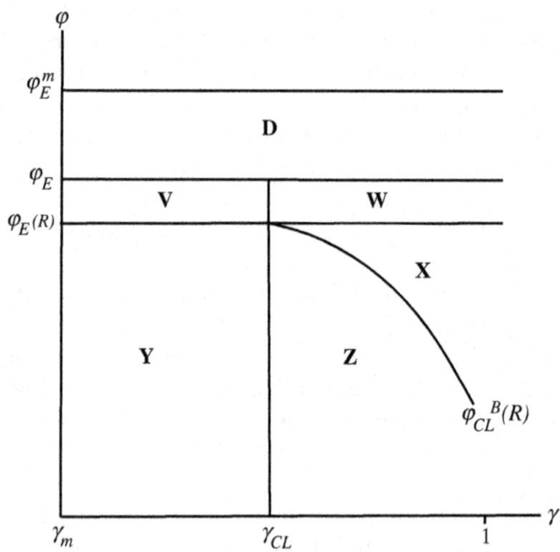

Fig. 4. *Effects of CL with Price Negotiations*

the South by reducing the price from p^m to $p_E^{\max}$ when CL is a credible threat. On the other hand, when the South makes a take or leave it offer, it offers the lowest price in the range of feasible prices for $\varphi < \min\{\varphi_E(R), \varphi_{CL}^B(\gamma, R)\}$. The price at which the South obtains the product increases from $p_E(\varphi)$ to $p_E(\varphi + \Omega R)$ due to the option of CL, because the South must compensate the patent holder for the royalty it would receive under a compulsory licence.

Combining the effect of CL on the region over which the patent holder enters and the impact on the negotiated price under entry, we obtain the following result (proven in Appendix A) regarding the impact of the threat of CL on both parties:

PROPOSITION 8. *Suppose that the South offers patent protection.*

(*i*) *If the patent holder has all of the bargaining power, the threat of CL benefits the South in regions* **D**, **W**, **X**, *and* **Z** *in Figure* 4 *whereas it harms the South in region* **V**. *The patent holder benefits from the possibility of CL in regions* **D**, **V** *and* **W** *whereas it loses in regions* **X** *and* **Z**. *Neither party is affected in region* **Y**.

(*ii*) *If the South has all of the bargaining power, the threat of CL benefits the patent-holder in all regions in Figure* 4. *The South also gains in region* **D** *and over portions of regions* **W** *and* **X** *for which* $p_E^{\max}(\gamma, R) < p_E^{\min}(\varphi)$.

Proposition 8 illustrates that the South's ability to deny entry by the patent holder under price negotiations benefits the South. This can be seen by comparing the result of Proposition 8(*i*) with the effect of allowing CL in the absence of price negotiations. The South gains from the option of CL for parameter values in region **X** when price is negotiated but loses when it is not. For parameter values in region **X** the imitative ability of the South is sufficiently high that it prefers CL to entry at the monopoly price and price negotiations make it possible for it to deny entry.

An important insight contained in Proposition 8 is that the South's ability to impose CL primarily benefits the party whose bargaining power is weaker. The option of CL raises the disagreement payoff of each party and the party making a take-it-or-leave-it offer has to account for the other party's higher disagreement payoff. This effect benefits the South in regions **X** and **Z** when the patent holder has all of the bargaining power and CL is a credible threat. For the patent holder, the existence of a positive royalty payment under CL provides a benefit that must be compensated for all parameter values for which it would be willing to enter at the monopoly price. Finally, Proposition 8 highlights the role of the South's imitative ability in determining the effects of CL since the threat of CL is credible only when $\gamma > \gamma_{CL}$.

4. Conclusion

TRIPS flexibilities such as compulsory licensing are intended to provide member countries of the WTO with a safety valve when domestic considerations make it imperative to opt out of TRIPS obligations. While CL predates TRIPS, developing countries had little use for it when they were free to deny patent protection to foreign firms. During the pre-TRIPS era, imitation and reverse-engineering allowed developing countries with adequate technological capability to obtain cheap access to pharmaceuticals that were patented in the rest of the world. Even those developing countries that lacked the ability to produce pharmaceuticals domestically were able to import them from countries such as India and China. But with the ratification of TRIPS, developing countries have come under increasing pressure to offer and enforce patent protection at a level that is on par with the Western world. As a result, during the post-TRIPS era CL has the potential to become an important policy tool using which developing countries can provide local consumers access to patented pharmaceuticals at reasonable prices provided its use is not met with serious resistance from developed countries.

We construct a stylised model in which a developing country (South) chooses its patent protection policy taking into account the effect of its policy on the incentive of a patent holder to sell in its market. As per TRIPS rules, we assume that the South has the option of issuing a compulsory licence to a local firm only if the patent holder chooses not to work its patent locally. Our analysis provides several interesting insights. First, we find that the South has an incentive to offer patent protection if and only if it is necessary for inducing the patent holder to serve its market and the quality of the imitated local product is sufficiently low. Second, from the Southern perspective, TRIPS consistent CL is an imperfect substitute for imitation: not only does it involve a waiting period (during which the patent holder is given an opportunity to work its patent), it also requires royalties to be paid to the patent holder. Third, from the perspective of joint welfare, the desirability of CL hinges very much on whether or not the South has the freedom to deny patent protection. When the South has such policy freedom, CL is essentially counter-productive: not only does it not arise in equilibrium but the option of using it results in a Pareto inferior outcome. On the other hand, when the South has no choice but to offer patent protection (as is basically true today for all members of the WTO), CL plays a much more useful role: not only does it arise in equilibrium, it can even generate a Pareto improving outcome. This result argues in favour of Article 31 of TRIPS under which CL is sanctioned by the WTO.

We also extend the basic model to the case where the patent holder and the South bargain over the price. We show that patent protection becomes more likely when the South can negotiate a price below the optimal monopoly price. This effect arises in two ways. First, if the patent holder would not enter in the absence of patent protection, the ability to obtain the higher quality product at a lower price makes entry more attractive to the South than relying on the low quality imitated product. Second, when the South makes a take-it-or-leave-it offer to the patent holder, it has an incentive to provide patent protection even if the patent holder is willing to enter without it. This is because the price needed to induce entry is higher under imitation since competition from imitators reduces the patent holder's sales in the South. This adverse effect of imitation on the price required to induce entry dominates the benefit of making the low quality product available to local consumers.

Appendix A. Proofs

A.1. *Proof of Proposition* 2

(*i*) We need to show $w_I(p_I^m;\gamma) \geq w_E(p^m)$. Using:

$$w_I(p_I^m;\gamma) = (1+\Omega)s_I(p_I^m) + v_I(p_I^m) - \varphi \tag{A.1}$$

and

$$w_E(p^m) = (1+\Omega)s_E(p_I^m) + v_E(p^m) - \varphi, \tag{A.2}$$

we have:

$$w_I(p_I^m;\gamma) - w_E(p^m) = q\gamma(1+\Omega)/8 \geq 0.$$

(*ii*) We need to show that $w_I(p_I^m;\gamma) \geq w_N(\gamma)$ iff $\varphi \leq \varphi_I^w$. Using:

$$w_N(\gamma) = (1+\Omega)s_N(\gamma), \tag{A.3}$$

and (A.1) we have:

$$w_I(p_I^m;\gamma) \geq w_N(\gamma) \text{ iff } \varphi \leq \varphi_I^w = 3q(1-\gamma)(1+\Omega)/8,$$

i.e. given imitation, entry raises joint welfare iff $\varphi \leq \varphi_I^w$.

(*iii*) We need to show that $w_E(p^m) \geq w_N(\gamma)$ iff $\varphi \leq \varphi_E^w$. Using (A.2) and (A.3) we have:

$$w_E(p^m) \geq w_N(\gamma) \text{ iff } \varphi \leq \varphi_E^w = q(3-4\gamma)(1+\Omega)/8.$$

A.2. *Proof of Proposition* 7

(*i*) For $\varphi \leq \varphi_I$, the South offers patent protection iff:

$$s_E[p_E^{\min}(\varphi)] \geq s_I[p_I^{\min}(\varphi,\gamma)],$$

which is the same as:

$$\int_{p_E^{\min}(\varphi)/q}^{1} [q\theta - p_E^{\min}(\varphi)]\,\mathrm{d}\theta \geq \int_0^{\theta_I^{\min}} \gamma q\theta \mathrm{d}\theta + \int_{\theta_I^{\min}}^{1} [q\theta - p_I^{\min}(\varphi,\gamma)]\,\mathrm{d}\theta,$$

where $\theta_I^{\min} = p_I^{\min}(\varphi,\gamma)/q(1-\gamma)$. Substituting for $\theta_I^{\min}$, $p_E^{\min}(\varphi)$ and $p_I^{\min}(\varphi,\gamma)$ allows us to rewrite the above inequality as:

$$G(\gamma) \geq 0 \quad \text{where} \quad G(\gamma) = \left[q\left(q - \frac{4\phi}{1+\Omega}\right)\right]^{1/2} - q\gamma - \left[q(1-\gamma)\left(q(1-\gamma) - \frac{4\phi}{1+\Omega}\right)\right]^{1/2} \geq 0.$$

Straightforward differentiation shows that for all $\varphi < \varphi_I$, we have $G'(\gamma) > 0$ and $G(\gamma)_{\gamma=0} = 0$ so that it must be that $G(\gamma) \geq 0$ for all γ when $\varphi < \varphi_I$.

(*ii*) For $\varphi \in [\varphi_I, \varphi_E)$, patent protection is preferred by the South iff:

$$s_E[p_E^{\min}(\varphi)] \geq s_N(\gamma) \Longleftrightarrow \int_{p_E^{\min}(\varphi)/q}^{1} [q\theta - p_E^{\min}(\varphi)]\, \mathrm{d}\theta \geq \int_0^1 \gamma q \theta\, \mathrm{d}\theta,$$

which is the same as:

$$p_E^{\min}(\varphi) \leq q(1 - \sqrt{\gamma}). \tag{A.4}$$

Using (15), the South is indifferent between patent protection at $p_E^{\min}(\varphi)$ and no patent protection for fixed costs satisfying the following inequality:

$$\varphi \leq \varphi^B(\gamma) \equiv q(\sqrt{\gamma} - \gamma)(1 + \Omega), \tag{A.5}$$

where $\varphi^B(\gamma) \geq \varphi_E^m$ iff $\gamma \geq \gamma^S$.

(*iii*) For $\varphi > \varphi_E$, the patent holder will not enter with patent protection. The South does not offer patent protection.

A.3. *Proof of Proposition* 8

In region **D** we have $\varphi > \varphi_E$, so entry would not have occurred without CL and both players receive 0. When the option of CL exists, the South obtains the product under CL and both parties receive a positive payoff. Thus, both parties gain from CL.

In regions **Y** and **Z**, $\varphi < \min\{\varphi_E(R), \varphi_B^{CL}(\gamma, R)\} < \varphi_E$, so entry occurs with or without the threat of CL. If the patent holder has all of the bargaining power, it enters at a price of p^m if there is no option of CL. The threat of CL is not credible in **Y**, since $\gamma < \gamma_{CL}$, so it has no effect on the payoffs. For region **Z** with $\gamma > \gamma_{CL}$, CL is a credible threat and the patent holder enters at a price $p_E^{\max} < p^m$. This benefits the South and harms the patent holder. If the South has all of the bargaining power, the patent holder enters at a price of $p_E^{\min}(\varphi)$ when the option of CL does not exist and a price of $p_E^{\min}(\varphi + \Omega R)$ when it does. The South is harmed by the increase in price caused by the option of CL whereas the patent holder benefits.

It remains to consider regions **V**, **W**, and **X**, where the threat of CL results in a switch from entry to the issuance of a compulsory licence. Let p^B denote the price determined by the bargain if the patent holder enters when there is no threat of CL. The South gains from a switch from entry to CL if $(1 + \Omega)s_E(p^B) > \Omega s_N(\gamma)$, which is equivalent to $p^B > p_E^{\max}(\gamma, R)$.

The patent-holder gains from a switch from entry to CL if $v_E(p^B) < \varphi + \Omega R$, which is equivalent to $p^B < p_E^{\min}(\varphi + \Omega R)$. In the case where the patent-holder has all of the bargaining power, the bargained price under entry equals the monopoly price ($p^B = p^m$) and the South benefits from the threat of CL if $p_E^{\max}(\gamma, R) < p^m$. This condition is satisfied iff $\gamma > \gamma_{CL}$, so the South benefits in regions **W** and **X** whereas it loses in region **V**. In regions **V** and **W**, the patent-holder benefits from the switch from entry to CL because $v_E(p^m) < \varphi + \Omega R$.

In the case where the South has all of the bargaining power, in the absence of the threat of CL we have $p^B = p_E^{\min}(\varphi) < p_E^{\min}(\varphi + \Omega R)$. Since the patent-holder is driven to zero profits under bargaining, the patent-holder must gain from the switch to CL for all $R > 0$. For the South, welfare is increased by this switch for all parameter values such that $p_E^{\min}(\varphi) > p_E^{\max}(\gamma, R)$. In region **V** where $\gamma < \gamma_{CL}$ and $\varphi \leq \varphi_E$, the South cannot gain because $p_E^{\max}(\gamma, R) \geq p^m \geq p_E^{\min}(\varphi)$. The South gains for the set of $\{\gamma, \varphi\}$ in regions **W** and **X** such that $p_E^{\min}(\varphi) > p_E^{\max}(\gamma, R)$, is a non-empty set if $p_E^{\min}(\varphi) > p_E^{\max}(1, R)$.

Vanderbilt University

Submitted: 3 August 2015
Accepted: 5 September 2016

References

Baron, D. (2008). 'Compulsory licensing, Thailand, and Abbott Laboratories', Stanford Graduate School of Business Case P-66.

Beall, R. and Kuhn, R. (2012). 'Trends in compulsory licensing of pharmaceuticals since the Doha declaration: a database analysis', *PLos Medicine*, vol. 9(1), pp. 1–9.

Bond, E.W. and Saggi, K. (2014). 'Compulsory licensing, price controls, and access to patented foreign products', *Journal of Development Economics*, vol. 109, pp. 217–28.

Bond, E.W. and Saggi, K. (2017). 'Bargaining over entry with a compulsory license deadline: price spillovers and surplus expansion', *American Economic Journal: Microeconomics*, forthcoming.

Chen, Y. and Puttitanun, T. (2005). 'Intellectual property rights and innovation in developing countries', *Journal of Development Economics*, vol. 78(2), pp. 474–93.

Daemmrich, A. and Musacchio, A. (2011). 'Brazil: leading the BRICs', Harvard Business School Case 9-711-024.

Gansland, M. and Maskus, K.E. (2004). 'Parallel imports and the pricing of pharmaceutical products: evidence from the European Union', *Journal of Health Economics*, vol. 23, pp. 1035–57.

Grossman, G.M. and Lai, E.L.-C. (2004). 'International protection of intellectual property', *American Economic Review*, vol. 94(5), pp. 1635–53.

Grossman, G.M. and Lai, E.L.-C. (2008). 'Parallel imports and price controls', *Rand Journal of Economics*, vol. 39(2), pp. 378–402.

Malueg, D.A. and Schwartz, M. (1994). 'Parallel imports, demand dispersion, and international price discrimination', *Journal of International Economics*, vol. 37, pp. 167–95.

Maskus, K.E. (2000). *Intellectual Property Rights in the Global Economy*, Washington, DC: Peterson Institute for International Economics.

Maskus K.E. (2012). *Private Rights and Public Problems: The Global Economics of Intellectual Property in the 21st Century*, Washington, DC: Peterson Institute for International Economics.

Mukherjee, A. and Sinha, U.B. (2013). 'Patent protection, Southern innovation and welfare in an North-South model', *Economica*, vol. 80(318), pp. 248–73.

Roy, S. and Saggi, K. (2012). 'Equilibrium parallel import policies and international market structure', *Journal of International Economics*, vol. 87(2), pp. 262–76.

Saggi, K. (2013). 'Market power in the global economy: the exhaustion and protection of intellectual property', ECONOMIC JOURNAL, vol. 123(567), pp. 131–61.

Saggi, K. (2017). 'Trade, intellectual property rights, and the WTO', in (K. Bagwell and R.W. Staiger, eds.), *The Handbook of Commercial Policy*. Amsterdam: Elsevier.

Sinha, U.B. (2006). 'Patent enforcement, innovation, and welfare', *Journal of Economics*, vol. 88(3), pp. 211–41.

Valleti, T.M. (2006). 'Differential pricing, parallel trade, and the incentive to invest', *Journal of International Economics*, vol. 70, pp. 314–24.

Yang, L. and Maskus K.E. (2009). 'Intellectual property rights, technology transfer and exports in developing countries', *Journal of Development Economics*, vol. 90(2), pp. 231–6.

Chapter 22

Full length articles

Patent protection in developing countries and global welfare: WTO obligations versus flexibilities[#]

Eric W. Bond, Kamal Saggi *

Department of Economics, Vanderbilt University, USA

ARTICLE INFO

Article history:
Received 4 March 2019
Received in revised form 15 November 2019
Accepted 18 November 2019
Available online 6 December 2019

JEL classifications:
O34
O38
F12
F13
F23

Keywords:
Patent protection
Compulsory licensing
Exhaustion policies
Imitation
TRIPS
Quality
Welfare
WTO

ABSTRACT

This paper develops a North-South model to evaluate the South's incentive for patent protection when a Northern firm's investment in quality-enhancing research and development (R&D) is affected by its patent policy. The model is used to (a) evaluate the impact of requiring the South to fulfill its key WTO *obligation* of instituting patent protection and (b) to address the role of two major *flexibilities* that WTO members enjoy with respect to their patent policies: the freedom to implement exhaustion policies of their choosing and the right to use compulsory licensing (CL) subject to certain stipulations. Two forces drive the model: how much the firm invests in R&D and whether or not selling in the South maximizes its global profit. CL improves consumer access in the South and can even raise innovation and global welfare. Provided the South implements patent protection, innovation and welfare are higher if the North follows national as opposed to international exhaustion. However, the South's incentive for patent protection is not necessarily stronger under national exhaustion. Not only is CL more likely to be used under international exhaustion, the welfare gain resulting from its application is also higher relative to that under national exhaustion.

1. Introduction

The Agreement on Trade Related Aspects of Intellectual Property Rights (TRIPS) *obligates* member countries of the World Trade Organization (WTO) members to offer and enforce certain minimum standards of protection for virtually all major types of intellectual property rights (IPRs). At the same time, TRIPS contains two major *flexibilities* that grant national governments some discretion in the design and enforcement of their respective IPR policies: the right to use compulsory licensing (CL) to ease consumer access to patented products and the freedom to implement exhaustion policies of their choosing. This paper analyzes how these two key flexibilities available under TRIPS interact with its central obligation, both from the viewpoint of developing countries and global welfare.

Before describing our analytical approach in detail, we discuss the economically relevant institutional aspects of the two TRIPS flexibilities motivating this paper. Consider CL first. As per TRIPS rules, when a country is faced with no or limited access to a patented foreign product, it has the right to issue a compulsory license to someone other than the patent-holder to produce the product.[1] Article 31 of TRIPS provides conditions under which WTO members can resort to CL of a patent. In particular, this Article stipulates that " the right holder shall be paid adequate remuneration in the circumstances of each case, taking into account the economic value of the authorization" and that "any such use shall be authorized predominantly for the supply of the domestic market of the Member authorizing such use".[2] Our model incorporates both these key features of Article 31 of TRIPS.

Now consider the policy flexibility available to WTO members with respect to exhaustion of IPRs. Article 6 of TRIPS explicitly states that "nothing in this Agreement shall be used to address the issue of the exhaustion of intellectual property rights". Exhaustion policies determine

* Corresponding author.
E-mail addresses: eric.bond@Vanderbilt.Edu (E.W. Bond), k.saggi@Vanderbilt.Edu (K. Saggi).

[1] The word 'compulsory' reflects the fact that the country issuing the license does not have to obtain the patent-holder's consent (who has no choice but to comply).

[2] The latter requirement was loosened in 2003 to allow a country to import a patented product via CL if it lacks the technological capability to produce it locally and also fails to secure it from the patent-holder directly. Clearly, exports under CL to those markets that are already served by the patent-holder (including its home market) are not permitted under TRIPS.

[#] This chapter was originally appeared in *Journal of International Economics* **122**, Article 103281.

the legality of *parallel trade* – i.e. the type of trade that occurs when a product protected by an IPR offered for sale by the right holder in one country is re-sold in another country without the right holder's permission. As is clear, the incentive to engage in such trade naturally arises in the presence of significant international price differences. Furthermore, since parallel trade flows from low-price markets to high-price ones, the exhaustion policies of high-price markets are more consequential than those of low-price ones.[3] Accordingly, in our North-South framework we consider the effects of alternative exhaustion policies on the part of the North.[4] We examine *national* and *international* exhaustion: under the former policy, the North prohibits parallel imports into its market whereas under the latter policy, it permits them. A key difference between the two exhaustion policies is that under national exhaustion the firm can charge its optimal price in each market whereas under international exhaustion it faces a trade-off: it can either sell only in the North at its optimal price for that market or sell in both markets at a common international price (so as to eliminate the flow of parallel imports into the more lucrative Northern market). As a result, the firm is less inclined to sell in the South when the North implements international exhaustion.

In practice, the two TRIPS flexibilities studied by our model are of special concern to the pharmaceutical industry. First consider CL. A country's ability to operationalize CL is likely to depend not just on its technological capability, but also on the nature of the product. One would expect that the issuance of a compulsory license is facilitated when the product is protected by a single (or just a few patents), as opposed to a large number of them. In this sense, the pharmaceutical industry is a natural candidate for CL since most patented drugs are typically protected by a single patent, unlike say, the smartphone industry where a single phone can contain literally hundreds of patents.[5] Furthermore, imitation in the pharmaceutical industry is remarkably cheap relative to innovation, thereby making patent protection especially valuable for firms. With regard to exhaustion policy, the cost of shipping patented drugs internationally is often fairly miniscule relative to their value so that the incentive for arbitrage-induced parallel imports is strong in this industry. This implies that both the main TRIPS obligation of providing IPR protection as well as its two key flexibilities – CL and exhaustion policy – are especially relevant to the pharmaceutical industry.

Our stylized North-South model involves two parties: the Southern government and a Northern firm that sells a product that is protected by a patent (that lasts for T periods) in its local market. The timing of decision making is as follows. In the first period, the South decides whether or not to institute patent protection in its market while the firm chooses its investment in quality-enhancing research and development (R&D) and decides whether or not to incur the fixed cost of entry necessary for selling its product in the South. As in related literature, our model assumes that if the South does not implement patent protection then the firm's technology diffuses locally and a competitive local industry producing an imitated version of the firm's product comes into existence. Due to the limited technological capability of the South, the quality of the imitated product is assumed to be (weakly) lower than that of the original.

Our core model assumes that the North follows national exhaustion and it delivers three main results. First, the South chooses to institute patent protection iff such protection is necessary and sufficient to induce entry by the firm and the quality disadvantage suffered by local imitators is sufficiently large. This finding clarifies how a balancing of the competing welfare effects of its patent policy – on local consumers on the one hand and foreign innovation incentives on the other – can induce a developing country to voluntarily institute patent protection even though it itself lacks the ability to innovate. Our second key finding is that the introduction of patent protection in the South increases the firm's R&D investment as well as its incentive to enter the Southern market. The beneficial effect of Southern patent protection on R&D has consequences for not just the firm but also Northern consumers. The third major result delivered by the core model is that even if the firm is willing to sell in the South in the absence of local patent protection, providing such protection increases global welfare since the South's incentive for patent protection is too weak relative to what is jointly optimal. This last result provides a potential rationale for the strengthening of patent protection in developing countries required under TRIPS. However, we also find that if the firm has no incentive to sell in the South even when it's granted patent protection, then forcing the South to offer such protection lowers global welfare. The intuition here is that if the Southern market does not factor into the firm's global profit then the South's patent policy has no affect on the firm's R&D incentive. Under such a situation, denying Southern consumers access to the imitated product inflicts a welfare loss on them without generating *any* gains for the firm or Northern consumers.

As the above discussion clarifies, an important driver of the welfare consequences of Southern patent protection in our model is its effect on the firm's entry decision. How relevant is this channel empirically? A well-developed empirical literature has demonstrated beyond doubt that this channel is very much operative in the real world. For example, using export data at the 3-digit ISIC level from 1962 to 2000, Ivus (2010) investigates the impact of TRIPS induced IPR reforms in developing countries on the exports of developed countries to their markets and finds that the strengthening of IPR protection undertaken by 18 non-colonies (in her set of 53 developing countries) increased the annual value of developed country exports to their markets in patent-sensitive industries by about \$35 million (or about 8.6%). She also shows that the increases in the value of imports was driven largely by changes in quantities as opposed to prices.[6] Using data on launches of 642 new drugs in 76 countries during 1983–2002, Cockburn et al. (2016) estimate that, controlling for a variety of economic and demographic factors, starting from the complete lack of patent protection, the introduction of product patents (lasting 18 years) increases the per-period hazard of drug launch in a country by about 55%. This finding is of vital importance since new drugs are launched only in a handful of rich countries and usually become available in other parts of the world with significant delay. For example, in their entire sample of 642 new drugs, 39% were launched in ten or fewer countries and only 41% were launched in more than 25 countries.[7]

We extend the core model to analyze the role of two key TRIPS flexibilities: the South's right to use CL licensing and the North's right to implement the exhaustion policy of its choosing. Consistent with TRIPS rules, our model incorporates CL as follows: given that the South offers patent protection and the firm chooses not to enter in the first period, for the remaining duration ($T-1$ periods) of the patent the South has the authority to issue a compulsory license to a local producer who is required to set price equal to marginal cost. In the event of CL, the South

[3] See Maskus (2000) for a useful but slightly dated discussion of the observed variation in exhaustion policies across countries. For more recent accounts see Ghosh (2013) and Ghosh and Calboli (2018).

[4] In our model, the exhaustion policy of the South is immaterial since equilibrium price is always (weakly) higher in the Northern market.

[5] Beall and Kuhn (2012) report that during 1995–2011 there were 24 cases of CL of patented pharmaceuticals in 17 countries. These 24 episodes collectively involved 22 products and only 40 patents. As noted above, the low number of patents involved surely facilitated CL. Furthermore, the level of CL activity occurring in the least developed and low-income countries was fairly limited (accounting for only a third of the 24 cases). Factors that help explain the low incidence of CL in such countries include the low level of their technological capabilities, legislative difficulties confronting the approval and implementation of CL, and the limited capacity of their healthcare systems (Beall and Kuhn, 2012).

[6] In a follow up paper, using data at the 10-digit HMS level, Ivus (2015) investigates the effects of stronger IPR protection on US exports to 64 developing countries. She finds that changes in the IPR regimes of developing countries induced by TRIPS increased the annual value of US exports in industries that rely heavily on patent protection (such as pharmaceuticals) by roughly 16% and that almost the entire increase in exports was driven by an expansion in product variety.

[7] Similar findings are reported by Kyle and Qian (2014).

pays a per-period royalty to the Northern firm. This royalty captures the adequate remuneration requirement of Article 31 of TRIPS. The one-period waiting period before CL can be activated by the South captures the TRIPS requirement that a patent-holder must be granted a "reasonable" amount of time to work its patent in a market before the local government can issue a compulsory license.

Our analysis shows that the effects of CL on innovation incentives are more nuanced than previously understood. In our model, making CL available to the South has an adverse effect on the firm's R&D incentive only when the possibility of CL induces the firm to forsake entry in order to collect royalty payments under CL. On the other hand, when the firm has no intention of selling in the South in the absence of CL, making CL available allows the firm to collect royalties from the Southern market that are proportional to the quality of its product and this tends to increase its R&D investment.[8] We also identify circumstances where CL is preferable to entry from a joint welfare perspective as well as when it is not. When CL encourages R&D, it welfare dominates entry since it also economizes on the fixed cost of entry. A welfare trade-off between the two modes only arises when CL dampens R&D incentives and delivers a lower quality product to consumers. When such is the case, entry is preferable from a global welfare perspective whenever the fixed cost of entry is low and the technological disadvantage under CL is large.

In Section 4 of the paper, we examine how the firm and consumers in the two region fare if the North were to implement international exhaustion as opposed to national exhaustion. As in related literature, we find that holding constant the South's patent protection policy, the firm is more willing to sell in the South under national exhaustion. Furthermore, the South is better off under national exhaustion due to two separate reasons: first, holding constant the quality of the product across the two exhaustion regimes, price in the South is lower under national exhaustion. Second, the Northern firm invest more in R&D and therefore delivers a higher quality product under national exhaustion. From the North's viewpoint, these two forces work against each other: price is higher under national exhaustion but quality is also higher. All in all, national exhaustion delivers higher joint welfare than international exhaustion provided the firm sells in both markets. This result fits well with the traditional argument that parallel trade reduces innovation incentives by undermining the ability of IPR holders to profit from their R&D investments.[9]

How do Southern incentives for patent protection depend upon North's exhaustion policy? As in the case of national exhaustion, the South chooses to provide patent protection under international exhaustion only when its imitative ability is low and patent protection is necessary to induce entry by the firm although the relevant thresholds are not the same under the two scenarios. Interestingly, the fact that profits from entry are lower under international exhaustion results in an ambiguous relationship between North's exhaustion policy and Southern patent protection. Relative to national exhaustion, both the maximum level of the fixed entry cost below which the South is willing to offer patent protection *and* the minimum level of fixed entry cost above which patent protection is desirable for the South are lower under international exhaustion. As a result, the relationship between North's exhaustion policy and South's incentive for patent protection is generally ambiguous. This ambiguity implies that Northern R&D could be either higher or lower under national exhaustion once the induced effect of the South's patent policy on R&D is taken into account.[10] Finally, we examine the interaction between CL in the South and the nature of Northern exhaustion policy and show that not only is CL more likely to arise in equilibrium under international exhaustion, it is also more likely to be socially efficient relative to entry.

This paper makes several novel contributions to the literature.[11] First, it brings together two important but separate strands of related literature: the rather well-developed literature exploring the economics of alternative exhaustion policies and the emerging literature on the effects of CL.[12] While these two TRIPS flexibilities have been studied separately, there exists no model that analyzes them jointly. Second, we provide a model of CL in which both innovation *and* the South's patent protection policy are endogenous. Although there exist several models of exhaustion that allow for endogenous innovation – such as Valleti (2006) and Grossman and Lai (2008) – these models consider neither CL nor the South's incentive for patent protection. Furthermore, existing models of CL – such as Bond and Saggi (2014, 2017, 2018) – abstract from innovation and therefore cannot address the effects of CL on innovation incentives.

The model developed in this paper significantly generalizes the analysis of CL developed by Bond and Saggi (2018) in two key dimensions: first, it incorporates endogenous innovation into their model and, second, it sheds light on how the North's exhaustion policy affects the firm's R&D as well as the South's incentive for patent protection. Bond and Saggi (2018) provide a useful starting point for our analysis since, like the model developed here, Southern patent protection policy and the Northern firm's decision to sell in the South are endogenously determined in their model. However, the results reported in the present paper on the linkages between innovation and the two key TRIPS flexibilities are simply beyond the scope of Bond and Saggi (2018) since not only does their model abstract from innovation, it also assumes that the royalty payment under CL is fixed and therefore unresponsive to the quality of the product. While a fixed royalty payment is a reasonable assumption in their model since it does not consider innovation, it nevertheless is limiting in nature since it implies that the return to the firm from licensing its product is unlinked to its economic value – a feature that does not correspond well with existing TRIPS rules on CL.

2. Model

We consider a world economy comprising two regions: North (N) and South (S) denoted by subscript i where $i = N, S$. A single Northern firm sells a patented product (x) with quality level q (endogenously determined). While the firm's technology is protected in the North via the enforcement of intellectual property rights (IPRs), it is potentially subject to imitation in the South.

Our core model is a simple game between the firm and the Southern government. In the first stage, the South chooses whether or not to offer patent protection in its market. Next, the firm invests in R&D that

[8] In this context, it is interesting to note that Baten et al. (2017) find that the compulsory licensing of German chemical patents by the United States at the end of World War I was associated with a 30% increase in invention by German firms whose inventions were licensed.

[9] We should note, however that several papers have shown that the traditional argument against parallel trade need not always hold. See, for example, Li and Maskus (2006), Li and Robles (2007), and Grossman and Lai (2008). In a model similar to us, assuming that the monopolist necessarily serves all markets, Valleti (2006) has shown that whether national exhaustion delivers more R&D than international exhaustion depends upon the underlying reason for international price discrimination on the part of the monopolist. He shows that when such discrimination is demand-based (as is the case in our model) then incentives for quality improvement are lower when parallel trade can occur but the opposite is true when discrimination arises because the monopolist faces different costs of accessing markets. See also Valletti and Szymanski (2006).

[10] In Grossman and Lai (2008), the South is assumed to provide patent protection but has the ability to impose a price control on patented products whereas we abstract from price controls but allow the South to control its patent policy. Grossman and Lai (2008) argue that there is a presumption that the induced change in the price control due to a switch from national to international exhaustion results in an increase in R&D since the South has an incentive to allow for a higher local price under international exhaustion to ensure that its market is served. By contrast, in our model the South's patent protection policy under international exhaustion is not necessarily more favorable to the firm relative to that under national exhaustion.

[11] For an in-depth survey of the literature on TRIPS and trade, see Saggi (2016).

[12] Major contributions to the literature on exhaustion of IPRs include Malueg and Schwartz (1994), Scherer and Watal (2002), Li and Maskus (2006), Valleti (2006), Gansland and Maskus (2004), Grossman and Lai (2008), Roy and Saggi (2012), and Saggi (2013). By contrast, the formal literature on CL is fairly nascent and recent contributions to it are Bond and Saggi (2014, 2017, 2018).

determines the quality of its product while also deciding whether or not to enter the South by incurring the fixed cost φ.[13]

2.1. Demand and payoffs

Each consumer in region i buys at most 1 unit of the good at the local price p_i, where $i = N, S$. The number of consumers in region i equals n_i. If a consumer buys the good, her utility is given by $u_i = q\theta - p_i$, where θ measures the consumer's taste for quality. Utility under no purchase equals zero. For simplicity, θ is assumed to be uniformly distributed over the interval $[0,\mu_i]$ where $\mu_i \geq 1$.

Demand structures in the two regions differ in two ways. First, Northern consumers value quality relatively more, that is, $\mu_N = \mu \geq 1 = \mu_S$. Second, the Northern market is larger: $n_N = n \geq 1 = n_S$. As one might expect, given these differences in demand, the firm has an incentive to price discriminate internationally. We assume that the North practices national exhaustion of IPRs so that the firm is free to set a market specific price in each region to maximize its global profit.[14] Let the firm's marginal cost of production equal zero. The firm's monopoly in the North lasts for the entire life of the product (which equals T periods). In the South, it enjoys monopoly status only if the South offers patent protection.

If the South does not offer patent protection, the firm's technology is imitated locally and imitation leads to the emergence of a competitive industry that produces a lower quality version of the firm's product. Let the quality of the Southern imitation be denoted by γq where $0 < \gamma \leq 1$.[15] Observe that when $\gamma = 0$, the South is incapable of imitation so that its patent protection policy becomes moot.

2.1.1. Pricing and profits

If the South offers patent protection to the firm and the firm chooses to sell there, it sets its market-specific price in each period to solve:

$$\max_{p_N} \pi_N(p_N) \equiv np_N(1-p_N/\mu q) \text{ and } \max_{p_S} \pi_S(p_S) \equiv p_S(1-p_S/q) \quad (1)$$

It is straightforward to show that the firm's optimal prices in the two markets are: $p_N^*(q) = \mu q/2$ and $p_S^*(q) = q/2$. The associated sales in each market equal $x_N^* = n/2$ and $x_S^* = 1/2$. Denote the firm's maximized profit in region i when the South offers patent protection by $\pi_i^*(p_i^*(q))$, where $\pi_N^* = n\mu q/4$ and $\pi_S^* = q/4$.

In the absence of Southern patent protection, competition within the Southern imitative industry ensures that the imitated good is sold at marginal cost in the local market.[16] Given our assumptions on consumer preferences, when two different qualities are available for purchase at prices p_S (high quality) and 0 (low quality), Southern consumers can be partitioned into two groups: those in the range $[0, \theta(p_S; \gamma)$ buy the low quality whereas those in $[\theta(p_S; \gamma), 1]$ buy the high quality where

$$\theta(p_S; \gamma) = \frac{p_S}{q(1-\gamma)} \quad (2)$$

When facing competition from imitation in the Southern market, the patent-holder chooses its Southern price p_S to maximize

$$\max_{p_S} \pi_S(p_S; \gamma) = p_S[1 - \theta(p_S; \gamma)]$$

The firm's profit maximizing price in the face of imitation equals $p_S^I = q(1-\gamma)/2 = (1-\gamma)p_S^*$, where the superscript I indicates the presence of competition between the patent-holder and the imitative industry. Observe that $p_S^I \leq p_S^*$ since $0 < \gamma \leq 1$.

Let $\beta \in [0, 1)$ be the per period discount factor so that the present value of the firm's profits from region i equals

$$(1+\Omega)\pi_i^*(q) \text{ where } \Omega = \sum_{t=1}^{T} \beta^t \quad (3)$$

Competition from imitation lowers the firm's gross payoff from entering the Southern market to

$$v_S^I(q; \gamma) = (1+\Omega)(1-\gamma)\pi_S^*(q) = (1-\gamma)v_S^*(q) \quad (4)$$

The per-period consumer surplus that accrues to region in i from purchasing the product at price p_i equals

$$cs_i = n_i \int_{p_i/q}^{\mu_i} \frac{(q\theta - p_i)}{\mu_i} d\theta = \frac{n_i(\mu_i q - p_i)^2}{2q\mu_i} \quad (5)$$

2.1.2. R&D and entry

While conducting its R&D, the firm makes a forward looking decision that takes into account both the fixed cost of selling in the South and the policies of the two governments. We require that the firm's R&D investment be time-consistent with its eventual decision regarding entry into the Southern market. For simplicity, we assume that the cost function for R&D is $c(q) = tq^2/2$ where $t > 0$.

Given patent protection, the firm's optimal R&D investment when it intends to sell in both markets solves

$$\max_q (1+\Omega)\sum_i \pi_i^*(q) - c(q)$$

Let the solution to this problem be denoted by q^* and let

$$v^*(q^*) = (1+\Omega)\sum_i \pi_i^*(q^*) - c(q^*)$$

If the firm intends to sell only in the Northern market, it solves

$$\max_q (1+\Omega)\pi_N^*(q) - c(q)$$

Denote the firm's optimal R&D investment when it sells only in the North by q^N and let

$$v^N(q^N) = (1+\Omega)\pi_N^*(q^N) - c(q^N)$$

It is easy to show that $q^N < q^*$ – i.e. the firm invests more in R&D when it sells in both markets relative to when it sells only at home since the marginal benefit of R&D is strictly higher in the former case.

Given these optimal R&D investments, the firm prefers selling in both markets to selling only at home iff

$$v^*(q^*) - \varphi \geq v^N(q^N)$$

Let

$$\varphi^* \equiv v^*(q^*) - v^N(q^N)$$

define the threshold value of the fixed cost φ below which the firm prefers selling in both markets to selling only at home. We can show that $\partial\varphi^*/\partial n > 0$ and $\partial\varphi^*/\partial\mu > 0$: when there is patent protection in the South, there is a *positive* link between the relative size and profitability of the Northern market (as captured by n and μ) and the incentive to sell

[13] It is straightforward to show that, in our model, this two stage game is equivalent to a three stage game where the firm's R&D decision *precedes* its entry decision (see Appendix).

[14] In Section 4, we consider a scenario where the Northern policy is international exhaustion under which the firm ends up setting a common international price to eliminate possible competition from parallel imports.

[15] In the context of the pharmaceutical industry the imitated product is probably best viewed as a generic that can only be sold in the South.

[16] We assume that due to enforcement of IPRs in the North, the imitated product can only be sold in the South.

in the South since the firm's R&D investment is based on the global market. A larger or more profitable Northern market increases the firm's incentive to invest in R&D which, ex post, also makes it more attractive for it to sell in the South.

The firm's maximized payoff function under patent protection equals

$$\begin{cases} v^*(q^*) - \varphi \text{ if } \varphi \le \varphi^* \\ v^N(q^N) \text{ if } \varphi > \varphi^* \end{cases}$$

The firm's R&D decision in the absence of patent protection in the South is analogous to above. Let

$$q^I = \arg\max_q (1+\Omega)[(1-\gamma)\pi_S^*(q) + \pi_N^*(q)] - c(q)$$

and let

$$v^I(q^I) = (1+\Omega)[(1-\gamma)\pi_S^*(q^I) + \pi_N^*(q^I)] - c(q^I)$$

Since imitated products are not sold in the North, the firm's R&D investment if it sells only in the North continues to equal q^N. Given this, when facing competition from imitated products in the South, the firm prefers selling in both markets to selling only at home iff

$$\varphi \le \varphi^I \text{ where } \varphi^I \equiv v^I(q^I) - v^N(q^N)$$

We can show that $\partial\varphi^I/\partial n > 0$ and $\partial\varphi^I/\partial\mu > 0$. As before, these comparative statics arise from the fact that increases in n or μ induce the firm to invest more in R&D (i.e. $\partial q^*/\partial n > 0$ and $\partial q^*/\partial\mu > 0$) so that the profit that accrues to the firm from the Southern market increases thereby making it more willing to enter. Furthermore, as one might expect, $\partial\varphi^I/\partial\gamma < 0$; $\partial^2\varphi^I/\partial^2\gamma > 0$; and if $\gamma = 0$ we have $\varphi^I = \varphi^*$. Finally, note that $\varphi^I = 0$ when $\gamma = 1$ – i.e. if Southern imitation suffers from no quality disadvantage relative to the patented product then the firm is unwilling to enter the South even when such entry entails no fixed costs since price competition eliminates all rents in such a situation.

The firm's maximized payoff in the absence of Southern protection equals

$$\begin{cases} v^I(q^I) - \varphi \text{ if } \varphi \le \varphi^I \\ v^N(q^N) \text{ if } \varphi > \varphi^I \end{cases}$$

We can show the following:

Proposition 1. The lack of patent protection in the South reduces the firm's R&D investment (i.e. $q^I \le q^*$) as well as its incentive to enter the Southern market (i.e. $\varphi^I \le \varphi^*$). Furthermore, changes in the pattern of Northern demand (such as increases in μ or n) that increase the firm's R&D investment (q^*) strengthen its incentive to sell in the South (i.e. $\partial\varphi^*/\partial n > 0$ and $\partial\varphi^*/\partial\mu > 0$). Finally, the stronger the intensity of imitative competition in the South, the lower the firm's investment in R&D (i.e. $\partial q^I/\partial\gamma < 0$) and the weaker its incentive to sell in the South (i.e. $\partial\varphi^I/\partial\gamma < 0$).

2.2. Southern patent protection

The South sets its patent protection policy anticipating the patentholder's R&D and entry decisions. We assume that the objective of the South is to maximize local consumer welfare over the life of the product. As we explain below, Southern consumer surplus depends upon not just its patent protection policy but also on the R&D and entry decisions of the firm.

Southern welfare under patent protection equals

$$\begin{cases} w_S^*(q^*) = (1+\Omega)cs_S(p_S^*(q^*)) \text{ if } \varphi \le \varphi^* \\ 0 \text{ if } \varphi > \varphi^* \end{cases}$$

Note that when $\varphi > \varphi^*$, the firm does not sell in the South even if its patent is protected and Southern consumers have no access to its product so that $w_S = 0$.

If the South permits imitation and the firm sells only in the Northern market, then Southern consumers have access to only the low quality imitated product and per-period consumer surplus equals

$$cs_S^L(\gamma q_N) = \int_0^1 \gamma q_N \theta d\theta \tag{6}$$

whereas if the firm sells in both markets then per-period consumers surplus in the South equals

$$cs_S(p_S^I(q^I);\gamma) = \int_0^{1/2} \gamma q^I \theta d\theta + \int_{1/2}^1 [q^I\theta - p_S^I(q^I)] d\theta$$

Thus, the Southern welfare function in the absence of patent protection equals

$$\begin{cases} w_S^I(q^I) = (1+\Omega)cs_S(p_S^I(q^I);\gamma) \text{ if } \varphi \le \varphi^I \\ w_S^L(\gamma q^N) = (1+\Omega)cs_S^L(\gamma q^N) \text{ if } \varphi > \varphi^I \end{cases}$$

When $\varphi > \varphi^I$, the firm does not enter the Southern market and local consumers obtain access (only) to the lower quality imitated good at a price equal to marginal cost (set to zero) and Southern welfare equals $w_S^L(q^N;\gamma)$ where the superscript L indicates that Southern consumers have access to only the low-quality imitated product. However, if the firm enters the Southern market despite imitation (which it does when $\varphi \le \varphi^I$), Southern welfare equals $w_S^I(q^I;\gamma)$. Observe that since the firm does greater R&D when it sells in both markets, the quality of the product that Southern consumers obtain access to via imitation is lower when the firm sells only in the Northern market (i.e. $q^I \ge q^N$).

It is straightforward to show the following:

Lemma 1. The following hold: (i) $w_S^I \ge \max\{w_S^*, w_S^L\}$ and (ii) there exists γ^* such that $w_S^* \ge w_S^L$ iff $\gamma \le \gamma^*$ where $\partial\gamma^*/\partial n < 0$ and $\partial\gamma^*/\partial\mu < 0$.

Lemma 1 says that the South's most preferred outcome is one where it allows imitation and the firm enters its market despite the competition it faces from imitators. The reason $w_S^I \ge w_S^L$ is easy to see: not only do local consumers have access to both products when the firm enters despite imitation, the quality of the two products is also higher since the R&D investment of the firm is higher when it sells in both markets ($q^I \ge q^N$).

Given that the firm is willing to sell in the South even without patent protection, Southern consumers value imitation due to two reasons. First, imitation increases variety in the local market and those Southern consumers that are unwilling to pay the price for the high quality patented product gain access to the low quality imitated version that sells at a lower price. Second, competition from the imitated product lowers the price of the high quality patented product. However, these two positive effects of imitation are counterbalanced by the fact that offering patent protection induces the firm to invest more in R&D so that the quality of the patented product is higher under patent protection ($q^* > q^I$). It turns out that, from the South's perspective, the two positive effects of imitation on consumer welfare dominate the negative effect that results from the reduction in the firm's R&D investment. As a result, given that the firm sells in its market, the South is better off without patent protection.

Finally, when the firm sells in the South only if its patent is protected, the South faces the following trade-off: it can either provide local consumers with the high quality patented product at the firm's optimal monopoly price or the low quality imitated product at the competitive price (i.e. at marginal cost). In such a scenario, the South is better off with patent protection only when the quality disadvantage suffered by local imitators is sufficiently large (i.e. $\gamma \le \gamma^*$). An important point to note here is that the larger or more profitable the Northern market is, the less likely the South is to offer patent protection (i.e. $\partial\gamma^*/\partial n < 0$ and $\partial\gamma^*/\partial\mu < 0$) because Southern protection is relatively less important for incentivizing R&D when n and/or μ are large.

We can now state the following:

Proposition 2. In equilibrium, the South offers patent protection to the firm iff such protection is necessary and sufficient to induce entry by the firm (i.e. $\varphi \in [\varphi^I, \varphi^*]$) and the quality disadvantage suffered by local imitators is sufficiently large (i.e. $\gamma \le \gamma^*$).

The CL model of Bond and Saggi (2018) reports a finding similar to the one above. However, since that model abstracts from innovation, the critical thresholds for the fixed cost parameter φ as well as the technological capability parameter γ differ across the two scenarios. A comparison of the two models provides a confirmation of the intuition that the South has a stronger incentive to institute patent protection in the presence of Northern innovation that responds to its patent policy. Indeed, we can show that $\gamma^* - \gamma_N^* = 1/(4n\mu)$ where γ_N^* is the critical level of technological capability above which the South implements patent protection in the absence of Northern innovation in the CL model of Bond and Saggi (2014). Note also that as either of the two parameters (μ and n) determining the relative profitability of the Northern market increase, the two thresholds converge (i.e. γ^* approaches γ_N^*) since the Southern market becomes a less important driver of Northern innovation.

2.3. Global welfare and TRIPS

Northern welfare when the South implements patent protection equals

$$\begin{cases} w_N^*(q^*) - \varphi \text{ where } w_N^*(q^*) = (1+\Omega)cs_N(p_N^*(q^*)) + v^*(q^*) \text{ if } \varphi \le \varphi^* \\ w_N^N(q^N) = (1+\Omega)cs_N(p_N^*(q^N)) + v^N(q^N) \text{ if } \varphi > \varphi^* \end{cases}$$

whereas Northern welfare in the absence of patent protection equals

$$\begin{cases} w_N^I(q^I) - \varphi \text{ where } w_N^I(q^I) = (1+\Omega)cs_N(p_N^I(q^I)) + v^I(q^I) \text{ if } \varphi \le \varphi^I \\ w_N^N(q^N) = (1+\Omega)cs_N^N(p_N^*(q^N)) + v^N(q^N) \text{ if } \varphi > \varphi^I \end{cases}$$

It is obvious that the firm is better off when the South offers patent protection relative to when it does not. A slightly more subtle observation is that Southern patent protection is also in the interest of Northern consumers since, given that the firm sells in both markets, the firm invests more in R&D when its patent is protected relative to when it is not – i.e. the quality of the product sold in the North is higher if the South implements patent protection (i.e. $q^* > q^I$) when the firm sells in the South. A related point is that, all else equal, Northern consumers benefit if the firms sells in the South since it invests more in R&D when it serves both markets relative to when it sells only at home (i.e. $q^* > q^N$ and $q^I > q^N$). Of course, both the firm and the Southern government ignore the impact of their respective decisions on Northern consumers.

Global welfare under Southern patent protection equals

$$\begin{cases} w^*(q^*) - \varphi \text{ where } w^*(q^*) = w_N^*(q^*) + w_S^*(q^*) \text{ if } \varphi \le \varphi^* \\ w^N(q^N) = w_N^N(q^N) \text{ if } \varphi > \varphi^* \end{cases}$$

whereas in the absence of patent protection it equals

$$\begin{cases} w^I(q^I) - \varphi \text{ where } w^I(q^I) = w_S^I(q^I) + w_N(q^I) \text{ if } \varphi \le \varphi^I \\ w^L(q^N;\gamma) = w_S^L(\gamma q^N) + w_N^N(q^N) \text{ if } \varphi > \varphi^I \end{cases}$$

We have:

Proposition 3. (i) Even if the firm is willing to sell in the South in the absence of patent protection (i.e. $\varphi \le \varphi^I$), providing such protection increases world welfare: $w^I(q^I) < w^*(q^*)$.

(ii) If patent protection is necessary to induce the firm to sell in the South (i.e. $\varphi^I < \varphi < \varphi^*$), it is jointly optimal to provide such protection iff $\varphi < \varphi^w$ where $\varphi^w \equiv w^*(q^*) - w^L(q^N;\gamma)$ where (a) $\partial\varphi^w/\partial\gamma < 0$, $\partial\varphi^w/\partial n > 0$, and $\partial\varphi^w/\partial\mu > 0$, and (b) $\varphi^w \ge \varphi^*$ iff $\gamma \ge \gamma^w$ where (a) $\gamma^w > \gamma^*$, (b) $\partial\gamma^w/\partial n < 0$ and $\partial\gamma^w/\partial\mu < 0$.[17]

(iii) If the firm does not sell in the South even if its granted patent protection (i.e. $\varphi > \varphi^*$), then offering such protection lowers welfare: $w^L(q^N;\gamma) > w^N(q^N)$.

Fig. 1 illustrates the South's optimal patent policy as well as the firm's equilibrium decision and it proves useful for assessing the welfare effects of TRIPS.

In this figure, the equilibrium outcome is denoted by pair (X,Y) where $X = P$ or I where P denotes the existence of patent protection in the South and I denotes imitation (or, equivalently, the absence of patent protection) and $Y = E$ or N denotes the firm's equilibrium choice, with E denoting entry and N its decision to stay out of the Southern market. Furthermore, the joint welfare maximizing outcome is denoted by an asterisk. Furthermore, $\varphi^m = w^*(q^*)$ denotes the maximum level of fixed cost below which entry is socially desirable given that the South offers patent protection.

Fig. 1 shows that the South chooses to offer patent protection in only region **B**: over this region, the South's technological disadvantage is large (i.e. $\gamma \le \gamma^*$) *and* patent protection is necessary to induce the firm to enter its market (i.e. $\varphi^I < \varphi < \varphi^*$). For all other parameter values, the South chooses to deny patent protection to the firm. Whereas South offers patent protection only over region **B** in Fig. 1, it is jointly optimal to offer it over regions **A**, **B**, and **C**. While setting its patent policy, though the South accounts for the effects of R&D on local consumers, it ignores not just the profit effects of R&D but also the benefits enjoyed by Northern consumers.

Fig. 1 shows that once the effects of Southern patent policy on all parties are accounted for, it is generally optimal to institute patent protection in the South whenever the firm is willing to enter given protection (i.e. $\varphi \le \varphi^*$) except for when γ is high and φ is close to or exceeds φ^* (i.e. in region **D1**). In region **D1**, $\varphi \approx \varphi^*$, the Southern market yields very little to the firm in the way of rents and is therefore not particularly consequential for incentivizing innovation on its part and the negative spillover on Northern consumers caused by the lack of patent protection in the South is rather small. Furthermore, since γ is near 1 in region **D1**, the imitative capacity of the South is high (and the local product is fairly close in quality to the Northern product). Under such circumstances, offering patent protection to induce entry by the firm is especially damaging to Southern consumers since the patented product is sold at monopoly price whereas the local imitated product is available at price equal to marginal cost. When $\varphi > \varphi^*$ (i.e. in region **D2**) the Southern market has absolutely no effect on innovation since the firm has no interest in selling there even if its patent is protected. As a result, in region **D2**, Southern imitation does not affect the firm (or Northern consumers) while offering large welfare gains to Southern consumers, thereby making the lack of patent protection in the South socially optimal.

[17] The three statements of Lemma 1 together imply that joint welfare is maximized by having the South offer patent protection whenever $\varphi \le \min\{\varphi^*, \varphi^w\}$.

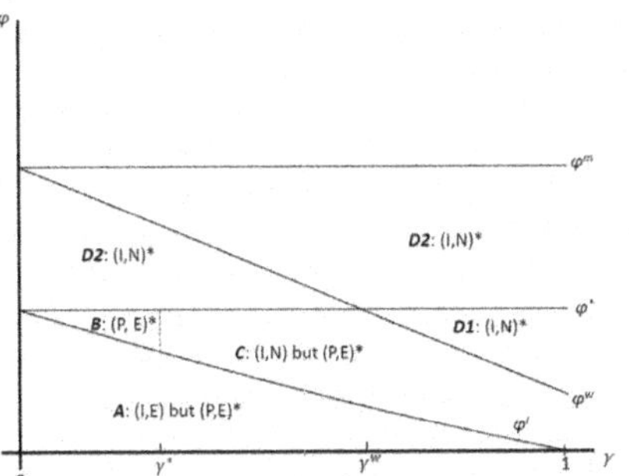

Fig. 1. Equilibrium outcomes and efficiency.

What are the implications of shutting down Southern imitation (i.e. TRIPS)? As Fig. 1 shows, such a policy change raises welfare in regions **A** and **C** whereas it lowers it in region **D1** and **D2**. In region **A**, although the firm sells the South even in the absence of patent protection, TRIPS raises welfare by increasing the firm's R&D investment. In region **C**, patent protection in the South is also socially optimal since the loss to the South from eliminating the imitated product is trumped by the gains enjoyed by the firm and consumers worldwide due to an increase in R&D. For $\varphi > \varphi^*$ (i.e. region **D2**), the firm continues to stay out of the South even when its granted patent protection. As a result, its R&D incentive is unchanged due to TRIPS, and shutting down imitation makes the South lose access to the imitated product without conferring any welfare gain on the North. Thus, for all $\varphi > \varphi^*$, enforcing patent protection in the South reduces welfare. Finally, as explained above, over region **D1**, while the North loses from lack of patent protection, its loss is dominated by South's gain due to its strong ability to imitate.

To better understand the consequences of requiring the South to offer patent protection, it is useful to consider the globally optimal level of R&D investment. Assuming the South implements patent protection and the firm sells in both markets, the globally optimal R&D is given by

$$q_w \equiv \arg\max w_N^*(q) + w_S^*(q)$$

where we can show that $q_w > q^*$ – i.e. the firm under-invests in R&D since it does not take into account the additional consumer surplus generated by its R&D investment. Similarly, the optimal R&D investment for when the firm sells only in the North is defined by $q_w^N \equiv \arg\max w_N^*(q)$ where $q_w^N > q^N$.[18] Thus, in our model, patent protection is attractive whenever it helps nudge the firm's R&D investment in the right direction.

3. Compulsory licensing and exhaustion policy

We first extend our model to allow for the possibility of compulsory licensing and then examine the robustness of our key conclusions for the case where the North practices international exhaustion of IPRs.

3.1. Incorporating compulsory licensing

As noted above, forcing the South to offer patent protection can lead to a situation where the imitated product is eliminated from its market but the firm still does not enter. If this happens, patent enforcement hurts the South without offering any benefit to the North. In such a situation, we now allow the South the option of issuing a compulsory license to a local producer who is granted the authority to produce the patented product for the local market.

Consistent with WTO rules, we assume that the South can issue a compulsory license to a local firm *only if* the patented product is not sold in the South in the first period. The length of the first period captures the time-period that is available under TRIPS to a patent-holder to work its patent in a country before the local government is authorized to issue a compulsory license. Under the Berne Convention, this "reasonable" time period is interpreted to be 3 years long.

As per Article 31 of TRIPS, we require that in the event of CL the South provide remuneration to the firm for utilizing its patent locally. According to recommendations of the World Health Organization (WHO), royalty rates under a compulsory license should be specified as a percentage of the wholesale price. We model this by assuming that the per-period royalty rate r under CL is a fraction $\alpha \in (0,1)$ of the price that the licensee would charge as a monopoly supplier, i.e., we set $r = \alpha p^L$ where $p^L = \gamma^R q/2$, where $\gamma^R q$ denotes the quality of the product under CL. Since, the firm may provide some technical assistance to the local licensee under CL, we assume that the technological capability of the licensee is at least as high as that of an imitator: i.e. $\gamma^R \geq \gamma$. However, since the firm's incentive for sharing knowledge with the licensee is limited (because it can only extract part of the surplus earned by the licensee), we assume $\gamma^R < 1$ so that we have $\gamma \leq \gamma^R < 1$.

Given that the objective of CL is to improve consumer access, we posit that the Southern government requires the licensee to sell the licensed product locally at price equal to marginal cost (inclusive of the royalty payment r). This implies that the price in the South under CL equals $r = \alpha p^L = \alpha\gamma^R q/2$ with the associated sales of $x^{CL} = 1 - p^L = 1 - \alpha/2$.

3.2. CL versus entry: the firm's perspective

The per-period royalty payment $R(q)$ collected by the firm under CL for the remaining duration of the patent ($T - 1$ periods) equals

$$R(q) = rx^{CL} = \frac{(2-\alpha)\alpha\gamma^R q}{4} \tag{7}$$

Observe that an increase in the technological capability of the licensee (γ^R) increases the royalty payment $R(q)$ while lowering the quality adjusted price faced by Southern consumers.

Given that consumers in the South pay a price of $r = \alpha p^L$ in the event of CL, Southern welfare under CL equals:

$$w_S^{CL}(q) = \Omega\left[\frac{(\gamma^R q - r)^2}{2\gamma^R q}\right] = \Omega\left[\frac{\gamma^R(2-\alpha)^2 q}{8}\right] \tag{8}$$

The $w_S^{CL}(q)$ function is decreasing in α and increasing in $\gamma^R q$. A larger value of α reduces Southern welfare because it raises the royalty payment made to the firm, while an increase in the quality of the licensee's product raises consumer surplus. Since Southern welfare in the absence of any local sales equals zero, the South issues a compulsory license if the firm does not enter in the first period and the licensee has at least some technological capability to produce the product (i.e. $\gamma^R \neq 0$). Thus, for all $\gamma^R > 0$, CL is a credible threat for the South.

The firm takes the possibility of CL into account when making its R&D decision. The firm foresees two options for selling in the South: (a) incur the fixed cost φ and enter or (b) stay out of the South in the first period and wait for CL in the next period. If a compulsory license is issued, the firm's profits over the life of the patent equal the discounted value of its profits in the Northern market and the stream

[18] Note that we could also discuss the socially optimal entry thresholds if R&D is done at the socially optimal level.

of royalty payments collected the South, i.e.

$$v^{CL}(q) = (1+\Omega)\pi_N^*(q) + \Omega R(q) - c(q). \tag{9}$$

The firm's optimal quality under CL maximizes $v^{CL}(q)$ and it is given by

$$q^{CL} = q^N + \frac{\Omega\alpha\gamma^R(2-\alpha)}{4t} < q^* \text{ where } q^* = q^N + \frac{1+\Omega}{4t} \tag{10}$$

Observe that $q^{CL} > q^N$: this is because the royalty payments under CL provide the firm with a stronger incentive to improve product quality relative to a scenario where it only sells in the North. Furthermore, q^{CL} is increasing in α and γ^R, since each of these parameters increases the marginal return to quality from royalty payments collected under CL. However, $q^{CL} < q^*$ since the firm's incentive for R&D under CL is less than that under entry due to the lower return per unit sold ($\gamma^R < 1$ and $\alpha \le 1$) and the one-period delay involved under CL.

Although the firm earns higher product market profits under entry relative to CL, entry also incurs the fixed cost φ. Thus, the firm prefers entry to CL iff

$$v^*(q^*) - \varphi \ge v^{CL}(q^{CL}) \Leftrightarrow \varphi \le \varphi^{CL}(\alpha, \gamma^R) \equiv v^*(q^*) - v^{CL}(q^{CL}) \tag{11}$$

Since the per-period royalty payment under CL is increasing in α for $\alpha \in [0, 1)$, we have $\partial\varphi^{CL}/\partial\alpha < 0$. Similarly, $\partial\varphi^{CL}/\partial\gamma^R < 0$ because a greater ability on the part of the licensee raises the royalties under CL. Observe that since $v^{CL}(q^{CL}) \ge v^N(q^N)$, we have $\varphi^{CL} \le \varphi^*$. In other words, the possibility of CL makes the firm *less willing to enter* the South because it can earn a positive return from royalty payments under CL (which necessarily occurs in the second period if the firm stays out), so that the preceding two inequalities are strict provided $\alpha > 0$ and $\gamma^R > 0$.

The impact of CL on R&D thus depends on how the firm's entry decision is affected by the possibility of CL. For $\varphi > \varphi^*$, there are no sales in the South if CL is not an option, so the availability of CL raises the equilibrium quality of the firm's product. On the other hand, for $\varphi \in \varphi[\varphi_{CL}, \varphi^*)$, the existence of CL undermines the firm's R&D incentive because the firm would have entered had CL not been possible. Finally, for $\varphi < \varphi^{CL}(\alpha, \gamma^R)$ there is no effect on product quality because the firm enters with or without the CL option. We can now state:

Proposition 4. When the South can avail of CL, the firm enters if its fixed cost φ is less than the threshold level $\varphi^{CL}(\alpha, \gamma^R)$, which is decreasing in α and γ^R. Furthermore, the following hold:

(i) For $\varphi > \varphi^*$, the option of CL gives the South a product of quality $\gamma^R q^{CL}$ whereas no product would have been available in the South in its absence.

(ii) For $\varphi \in [\varphi^{CL}(\alpha, \gamma^R), \varphi^*)$, which is a non-empty interval if $\alpha, \gamma^R > 0$, the option of CL causes the firm to switch from entry in the first period to waiting for CL in the second period.

(iii) For $\varphi < \varphi^{CL}$, the firm enters whether or not the South can utilize CL.

How does the option of CL affect Southern welfare? We now address this key question.

3.3. *CL versus entry from South's perspective*

From Proposition 4 it follows that for $\varphi > \varphi^*$ the South is better off due to the CL option since it obtains access to the locally produced version of the patented product under CL whereas it is unaffected for $\varphi < \varphi^{CL}$ since the firm enters whether or not CL is permissible. For $\varphi \in (\varphi^{CL}, \varphi^*]$ the comparison is ambiguous because the possibility of CL induces the firm to switch from entry in the first period to CL in the second. Relative to entry, the price paid by Southern consumers is lower under CL ($\alpha\gamma^R q^{CL}/2 < q^*/2$) but the quality of the product is also lower ($\gamma^R q^{CL} < q^*$) and the product becomes available after a delay of one-period.

Evaluating (8) at q^{CL} yields welfare of the South under CL:

$$w_S^{CL}(\alpha, \gamma^R) = \Omega\left[\frac{\gamma^R(2-\alpha)^2 q^{CL}(\alpha, \gamma^R)}{8}\right] \tag{12}$$

Lemma 2. Southern welfare $w_S^{CL}(\alpha, \gamma^R)$ under CL has the following properties:

(i) w_S^{CL} is convex and increasing in γ^R.

(ii) A sufficient condition for w_S^{CL} to be decreasing in α is $\frac{1+\Omega}{\Omega}\mu n > 2\gamma^R$.

(iii) If $\gamma^R > \gamma_m^R \equiv \frac{(1+\mu n)(1+\Omega)}{4\mu n\Omega}$, the South prefers CL to entry for $\varphi \in [\varphi^{CL}, \varphi^*)$ and for α sufficiently low.

The royalty parameters α and γ^R have a direct effect on Southern consumer surplus (for a given q) and an indirect effect through their impact on the quality of the product created by the firm (q^{CL}). For an increase in γ^R both of these effects work in the same direction. An increase in γ^R increases the quality of the licensee's product (for a given q) and it increases the firm's R&D investment in quality improvement since its payoff from CL increases with γ^R. For an increase in α, on the other hand, the direct and indirect effect work in opposite directions. A higher α reduces Southern consumer surplus by raising the royalty paid to the firm, but it also simultaneously increases the firm's R&D investment in quality improvement. A sufficient condition for an increase in α to harm the South is that the Northern market be sufficiently large relative to the South, since in such a situation the Southern market has a limited impact on the firm's R&D incentive. Similarly, the South must lose in the neighborhood of $\alpha = 1$ since an increase in α has minimal impact on the firm's R&D.

Part (iii) of Lemma 2 shows that the South prefers CL to entry at $\alpha = 0$ provided the licensee's technological capability γ^R is sufficiently high (i.e. $\gamma^R > \gamma_m^R$). The critical threshold γ_m^R is decreasing in Ω since a longer duration of the patent implies that the one-period delay involved in CL is a relatively minor concern for the South. The threshold γ_m^R is also decreasing in n and μ, since a larger or more lucrative Northern market reduces the relative importance of the Southern market in determining the firm's overall R&D incentive.

For the North, welfare under CL is simply the sum of firm's total payoff under CL and consumer surplus:

$$w_N^{CL}(\alpha, \gamma^R) = v^{CL}(q^{CL}) + (1+\Omega)cs_N^N(p_N^*(q^{CL}))$$

The impact of CL on Northern welfare depends on the firm's choices regarding entry as well as R&D. For $\varphi > \varphi^*$, the option of CL creates royalties for the firm and increases product quality, so both the firm and North consumers benefit from it. For $\varphi \in (\varphi^{CL}, \varphi^*]$, the option of CL increases the firm's profits but it reduces product quality relative to entry. The North necessarily prefers entry to CL at $\varphi = \varphi^{CL}$, since at that point the firm is indifferent between entry and CL but Northern consumers lose from the lower quality product under CL. Whether the North prefers entry to CL at φ^* depends on the values of the two key parameters under CL: α and γ^R. The North is more likely to prefer CL to entry when royalty payments are sufficiently high and the negative impact of CL on product quality is small. For $\varphi < \varphi^{CL}$, the firm enters regardless of the availability of the CL, so Northern welfare is unaffected.

3.4. CL and global welfare

From a global welfare perspective, entry is preferable to CL iff

$$w_S^*(q^*) + w_N^*(q^*) - \varphi \geq w_S^{CL}(\alpha, \gamma^R) + w_N^{CL}$$

For $\varphi > \varphi^*$, world welfare must necessarily increase from the option of CL since, as noted above, welfare in both regions is higher if CL is available. It is also clear that the CL option has no effect on world welfare for $\varphi < \varphi^{CL}$ since, over this region, the firm chooses to enter whether or not CL is possible.

For $\varphi \in (\varphi^{CL}, \varphi^*]$, there are two conflicting effects that together determine whether or not the option to use CL is welfare-improving. Over this parameter range, the firm switches from entry to CL and although this switch economizes on the fixed entry cost φ, it also reduces consumer surplus due to the the reduction in R&D (recall $q^* > q^{CL}$). Entry yields higher joint welfare than CL iff $\varphi \leq \varphi_W^{CL}$ where

$$\varphi_W^{CL} \equiv w_S^*(q^*) + w_N^*(q^*) - w_S^{CL}(\alpha, \gamma^R) - w_N^{CL} \tag{13}$$

We can establish the following properties of the threshold value of fixed cost φ_W^{CL} at which world welfare under CL equals that under entry:

Lemma 3. The threshold level of the fixed entry cost $\varphi_W^{CL}(\alpha, \gamma^R)$ below which entry in the first period yields higher global welfare than CL in the second has the following properties:

(i) $\varphi^* < \varphi_W^{CL}(\alpha, 0)$.

(ii) $\frac{\partial \varphi_W^{CL}}{\partial \gamma^R} < \frac{\partial \varphi^*}{\partial \gamma^R} < 0$.

(iii) If $\Omega > 1$, then $\varphi_W^{CL}(\alpha, 1) - \varphi^*$ is decreasing in μ and n.

(iv) $\varphi^{CL}(1,1) < \varphi_W^{CL}(1,1)$.

When $\gamma^R = 0$, the product is unavailable in the South and it incurs no royalty payments. Part (i) of Lemma 3 reflects the fact that the firm ignores the gains in consumer surplus in *both* regions that result from its entry into the South, so its threshold for entering the Southern market is lower than the socially optimal threshold $\varphi_W^{CL}(\alpha, 0)$ because the welfare gains to the world from the firm's entry into the South exceed those to the firm. The firm's failure to internalize the consumer surplus effects of the innovation induced by entering the South also explain part (ii). Increases in γ^R raise firm profits and consumer surplus in both markets under CL, so the threshold for entry for the firm declines more slowly with γ^R because the firm does not consider the effect of its decisions on consumer surplus.

When $\gamma^R = 1$ the licensee is able to produce the same quality product as the firm. Lemma 3 (iii) shows that the differential between $\varphi_W^{CL}(\alpha, 1)$ and φ^* declines more rapidly the larger is the Northern market relative to the South. This indicates that if the delay involved under CL is not too long, increased effective market size in the North causes world welfare under CL to increase more rapidly relative to the firm's profits under CL. Part (iv) establishes that when the royalty rate is set to capture the entire monopoly profit (i.e. $\alpha = 1$) and the licensee is as efficient as the patent holder (i.e. $\gamma^R = 1$), the firm is too willing to wait for CL relative to the social optimum.

Fig. 2 uses the results of Lemma 3 to illustrate how the option of CL affects world welfare for the case where the royalty rate is sufficiently low that $\varphi_W^{CL} < \varphi^{CL}$ at $\gamma^R = 1$. In regions **A** and **B** the firm has no incentive to enter the South (since $\varphi > \varphi^*$) so the option of CL provides South consumers access to the product while simultaneously providing the firm with royalty payments which in turn increase its incentive to produce a higher quality product. Therefore, the option of CL increases world welfare in regions **A** and **B**. Note, however, that in region **A**, the quality of the product under CL is sufficiently low that world welfare would be higher if the firm could be induced to choose entry.

In regions **C** and **D**, where $\varphi \in (\varphi^{CL}, \varphi^*)$, the option of CL results in a switch from entry to CL. In region **D**, which lies below the φ_W^{CL} locus, this switch reduces world welfare due to the lower quality of the product produced by the licensee. In region **C**, the quality of the licensee's product is sufficiently high that world welfare rises from the switch from entry to CL. In regions **E** and **F**, which lie below the φ^{CL} locus, the existence of the CL has no effect on the equilibrium outcome. However, the ability of the licensee is sufficiently high in Region **F** that world welfare would be higher if CL were to occur as opposed to entry.[19]

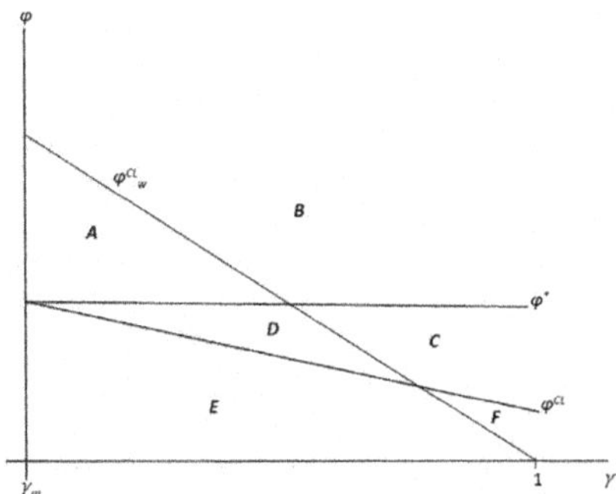

Fig. 2. CL versus Entry and joint welfare.

Finally, we note that world welfare is increasing in α at $\alpha = 0$ whereas it is decreasing in α at $\alpha = 1$. In the neighborhood of $\alpha = 0$, an increase in the royalty rate raises welfare by encouraging additional R&D on the part of the firm. In the neighborhood of $\alpha = 1$, on the other hand, the increase in product quality obtained by raising the royalty rate is sufficiently small that it is dominated by the loss in consumer surplus in the South. Therefore, world welfare is optimized by setting a royalty rate that is positive but less than the monopoly price for the licensee's product.

Next, we analyze our model for the case where the North practices international exhaustion of IPRs as opposed to national exhaustion.

4. International exhaustion of IPRs

We begin by describing product market outcomes under international exhaustion.

4.1. Product market

When the North implements international exhaustion of IPRs, when selling in both markets it is optimal for the firm to set a common global price to eliminate any possible competition from parallel imports. This global price p solves:

$$\max_p \pi(p) \equiv np(1 - p/\mu q) + p(1 - p/q)$$

which yields the optimal global price

$$p^G = \frac{\mu q}{2} \frac{n+1}{n+\mu} \tag{14}$$

It is straightforward to show that $p_S^* < p^G < p_N^*$ – i.e. the firm's common international price under international exhaustion is bound by its optimal discriminatory prices for the two markets. Let the firm's

[19] Two other cases are possible. If $\varphi^* > \varphi_W^{CL} > \varphi^{CL}$ at $\gamma = 1$, region **F** does not exist. If $\varphi_W^{CL} > \varphi^*$ at $\gamma = 1$, neither region **C** nor region **F** exist.

maximized per-period profit under international exhaustion be denoted by $\pi^G = \pi(p^G) = p^G(n+1)/2$.

If the firm faces competition from imitators in the South then its optimal price under international exhaustion equals

$$p^{IG} = \frac{\mu q}{2} \frac{(n+1)(1-\gamma)}{n(1-\gamma)+\mu} \tag{15}$$

which can be rewritten as

$$p^{IG} = \sigma(\gamma)p_N^*$$

where $0 \le \sigma(\gamma) < 1$. Furthermore, p^{IG} is increasing in m and n whereas it is decreasing in γ – i.e. competition from imitation partly spills over to the Northern market under international exhaustion. Furthermore, as one might expect, we have $p^{IG} > p_S^*$. It is worth noting that $p^{IG} > (1-\gamma)p^G$. In other words, since the firm sets a common international price under international exhaustion, the price reduction that the South enjoys due to imitation is relatively smaller when the firm sets a common international price relative to when the firm price discriminates internationally (as it does when North practices national exhaustion of IPRs). We have $\pi^{IG}(q) = p^{IG}(n+1)/2$.

4.2. R&D under international exhaustion

Let $q^G =$ arg max $(1+\Omega)\pi^G(q) - c(q)$ be the optimal R&D investment of the firm in the presence of patent protection in the South. Similarly, let $q^{IG} =$ arg max $(1+\Omega)\pi^{IG}(q) - c(q)$ be its R&D investment in the absence of patent protection. As before, let $v^G = (1+\Omega)\pi^G(q^G) - c(q^G)$ and $v^{IG} = (1+\Omega)\pi^{IG}(q^{IG}) - c(q^G)$.

The firm's maximized payoff under international exhaustion when its patent is protected in the South equals

$$\begin{cases} v^G - \varphi \text{ if } \varphi \le \varphi^G = v^G - v_N^* \\ v_N^* \text{ if } \varphi > \varphi^G \end{cases}$$

Similarly, the firm's payoff under international exhaustion in the absence of patent protection equals

$$\begin{cases} v^{IG} - \varphi \text{ if } \varphi \le \varphi^{IG} = v^{IG} - v_N^* \\ v_N^* \text{ if } \varphi > \varphi^{IG} \end{cases}$$

We can use these conditions to obtain the following result on the threshold values at which the firm will enter the South market under international exhaustion.

Lemma 4. (i) $\varphi^G \ge 0$ iff $\mu \le \mu^* \equiv 2 + 1/n$.

(ii) $\partial\varphi^G/\partial\mu|_{\mu=1} > 0$ whereas $\partial\varphi^G/\partial\mu|_{\mu=\mu^*} < 0$.

(iii) $\varphi^{IG} \ge 0$ iff $\mu \le (1-\gamma)\mu^*$.

Part (i) of Lemma 4 says that when $\mu > \mu^*$, the firm prefers to sell only in the North even when the fixed cost of selling in the South equals zero and its patent is protected there. Part (iii) establishes a similar (and more stringent) condition for the firm to be willing to sell in the South in the absence of patent protection. These conditions show that when the willingness to pay is sufficiently higher in the North market, preserving profit in the Northern market is so important that the firm is willing to forsake the Southern market to charge its optimal price in the North. The condition is more stringent without patent protection because the firm faces competition from imitators. In contrast, the firm is willing to enter the South when fixed costs are zero under national exhaustion for all values of μ because there is no negative spillover from its price in the Southern market on its profits in the North.

Part (ii) of Lemma 4 highlights the fact that the fixed cost threshold φ^G below which the firm is willing to sell in the South is a non-linear function of μ. When $\mu \approx 1$, consumer preferences in the two regions are very similar and an increase in the willingness to pay on the part of Northern consumers makes the firm more willing to sell in the North whereas the opposite is true $\mu \approx \mu^*$. This result reflects two conflicting effects. As μ increases, the firm's R&D investment q^G goes up and this makes selling in the South more profitable. On the other hand, the larger is μ the greater the loss the firm suffers in terms of reduced profitability in the Northern market from having to set a common international price under international exhaustion. For μ small, the R&D effect dominates whereas for μ large, the loss in Northern profits implied by uniform pricing drives the firm's entry decision. We can show the following:

Proposition 5. (i) Even when the North practices international exhaustion, the lack of patent protection in the South reduces the firm's R&D investment (i.e. $q^{IG} \le q^G$) as well as its incentive to enter the Southern market (i.e. $\varphi^{IG} \le \varphi^G$). Furthermore, the stronger the intensity of imitative competition in the South, the lower the firm's investment in R&D (i.e. $\partial q^{IG}/\partial\gamma < 0$) and the weaker its incentive to sell in the South (i.e. $\partial\varphi^{IG}/\partial\gamma < 0$).

(ii) For a given South patent policy, the firm is more willing to sell in the South under national exhaustion ($\varphi^G < \varphi^*$ and $\varphi^{IG} < \varphi^I$) and chooses a higher level of R&D under national exhaustion ($q^G \le q^*$ and $q^{IG} \le q^I$).

(iii) There exists $\gamma^f \ge 0$ such that $\varphi^I > \varphi^G$ iff $\gamma \le \gamma^f$ where (a) $\partial\gamma^f/\partial n > 0$; (b) $\partial\gamma^f/\partial\mu > 0$; and (c) at $\mu = \mu^*$, $\gamma^f = 1$.

(iv) $q^I \ge q^G$ iff $\gamma \le \gamma^f$.

Part (i) of this Proposition establishes that the threshold level of fixed costs for entry with international exhaustion is lower when the South does not provide patent protection, which is similar to the result obtained in Proposition 1 for the case of national exhaustion. Part (ii) is easy to understand: having to set a common international price under international exhaustion makes the firm more reluctant to sell in the South because of the resulting loss in profits in the North market. Furthermore, the fact that profits from entering the South market are higher with national exhaustion means that there is a greater incentive to improve the quality of the product by investing in R&D.

Parts (iii) addresses the relative impact of the loss of patent protection and the inability to price discriminate on the profitability of entry in the South. The profit from entry without patent protection is decreasing in the South's imitative ability, so there is a critical value γ^f at which the firm earns the same level of profits with price discrimination and no patent protection as it does with no price discrimination and patent protection. This threshold level of the South's imitative ability is increasing in μ and n because the inability to price discriminate is more damaging to firm profits when the North market is more profitable. Interestingly, part (iv) shows that the marginal profit from improving product quality is also equalized between the cases of national exhaustion without patent protection and international exhaustion with patent protection when $\gamma = \gamma^f$ so $q^I(\gamma^f) = q^G$. Since q^I is decreasing in the imitative ability in the South, $q^I(\gamma) > q^G$ for $\gamma > \gamma^f$ if the firm enters under both regimes.

4.3. South's patent protection policy

Having derived the firm's payoffs, we are now ready to derive the South's equilibrium patent policy. Southern welfare under patent protection equals

$$\begin{cases} w_S^G = (1+\Omega)cs_S(p^G(q^G)) \text{ if } \varphi \le \varphi^G \\ 0 \text{ if } \varphi > \varphi^G \end{cases}$$

whereas that in the absence of patent protection equals

$$\begin{cases} w_S^{IG} = (1+\Omega)cs_S(p^{IG}(q^{IG});\gamma) \text{ if } \varphi \le \varphi^{IG} \\ w_S^I = (1+\Omega)cs_S^I(\gamma q^N) \text{ if } \varphi > \varphi^{IG} \end{cases}$$

We are now ready to state the following:

Lemma 5. The following hold regarding Southern welfare under various outcomes:

(i) $w_S^{IG} \geq \max\{w_S^G, w_S^I\}$ for $\mu \leq (1-\gamma)\mu^*$.

(ii) There exists γ^G such that $w_S^G \geq w_S^I$ iff $\gamma \leq \gamma^G$ where $\partial\gamma^G/\partial n < 0$ and $\partial\gamma^G/\partial\mu < 0$.

(iii) $\gamma^G < \gamma^*$.

(iv) $w_S^G \leq w_S^*$ for $\mu < \mu^*$.

Part (i) establishes that the best outcome for the South occurs if the firm's entry costs are sufficiently low that it enters without patent protection. The fact that entry is desirable when there is no patent protection is immediate, since it increases product variety and leads to a higher quality level. Compared to entry with patent protection, the South gets lower prices and greater variety without protection but a lower product quality. As in the case of national exhaustion, the former effects dominate and the South is better off if the firm enters without patent protection. Part (ii) shows that Southern consumers are better-off having access to (only) the patented product relative to consuming when the South's imitative ability is below a threshold level. Part (iii) says that the maximum level of imitative ability for preferring patent protection is lower under international exhaustion than under national exhaustion because the price of the patented product is higher under international exhaustion.

Parts (iv) of Lemma 5 says that, given that it implements patent protection, the South is better off under national exhaustion. This is due to two reasons. First, holding constant the quality of the product across the two exhaustion regimes, price in the Southern market is lower under national exhaustion (i.e. $p_S^* < p^G$). Second, the firm invest more in R&D and therefore delivers a higher quality product under national exhaustion. From the South's viewpoint, both forces reinforce each other thereby making national exhaustion clearly preferable to international exhaustion.[20] Using Lemma 3, we can now state the South's optimal patent protection policy when the North implements international exhaustion:

Proposition 6. Suppose the Northern policy is international exhaustion and compulsory licensing is not an option. Then, the South's equilibrium patent protection policy is as follows: (i) If $\mu < (1-\gamma)\mu^*$, the South offers patent protection to the firm iff $\varphi \in [\varphi^{IG}, \varphi^G]$ and $\gamma \leq \gamma^G$; (ii) If $\mu \in [(1-\gamma)\mu^*, \mu^*]$ the South offers patent protection iff $\varphi \in [0, \varphi^G]$ and $\gamma \leq \gamma^G$; and (iii) if $\mu > \mu^*$ the South does not offer patent protection regardless of its local technological capability (γ) or the fixed costs of entry (φ).

The basic message of Proposition 6 is that the South only provides patent protection in cases where the level of φ is such that the firm is willing to enter only if it receives patent protection and the level of γ is sufficiently low. This result is is analogous to Proposition 2, which established the corresponding range of parameter values for which the South provides patent protection when North pursues a policy of national exhaustion. The important point to note is that North's exhaustion policy alters the parameter values for which the South is willing to provide patent protection. For parameter values at which the South chooses to provide patent protection under national exhaustion, patent protection may no longer be sufficient to induce entry under international exhaustion because entry in the South is less attractive to the firm since it has to charge a common international price. For these parameter values, imitation becomes relatively more attractive to the South. Observe, however, that for parameter values at which the firm enters without patent protection under national exhaustion, the firm may no longer be willing to enter without patent protection under international exhaustion. Thus, for $\varphi \in [\varphi^{IG}, \varphi^I)$, providing patent protection for the South becomes relatively more attractive under international exhaustion when imitators are of relatively low quality because it can be used to induce entry by the firm.

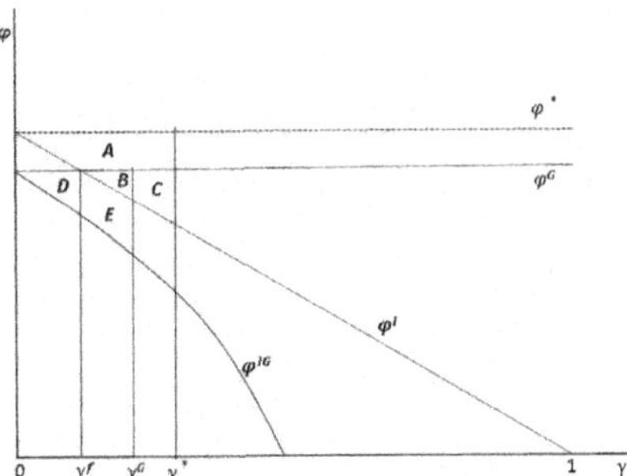

Fig. 3. Equilibrium outcomes with International Exhaustion.

The impact of the North's exhaustion policy on the South's patent decision is illustrated in Fig. 3, which compares the entry thresholds under international exhaustion, φ^G and φ^{IG}, with those under national exhaustion, φ^* and φ^I for a case where $\mu < \mu^*$. For the values of μ and n used in Fig. 3, the horizontal intercept of the φ^{IG} line occurs at $\gamma = 1 - \mu/\mu^* > \gamma^G$.

The set of values of $\{\varphi, \gamma\}$ for which the South offers patent protection under international exhaustion is illustrated by the triangular area made up of regions **B**, **D**, and **E** in Fig. 3, as that area satisfies part (i) of Proposition 6. This area can be compared with the triangular area made up of regions **A**, **B**, and **C**, which is the set of values of $\{\varphi, \gamma\}$ for which the South offered patent protection under national exhaustion. The fact that the price the South faces when the firm enters under international exhaustion is higher than that under national exhaustion means that the threshold quality at which the South prefers imitated goods is lower under international exhaustion, as established in Lemma 3(iii). Furthermore, the fact that the firm earns less profit from the South market under international exhaustion means that the threshold levels of fixed costs for entry, φ^G and φ^{IG}, are lower than their corresponding values under national exhaustion as established in Proposition 5.[21]

When $\mu > \mu^*$, the firm does not sell in the South even when its patent is protected and the fixed cost of entry equals zero since it wants to preserve its profit in the Northern market. When such is the case, the South has no incentive to offer patent protection under international exhaustion since doing so eliminates the low quality imitated product from the local market without eliciting entry by the firm. By contrast, under national exhaustion, even when $\mu > \mu^*$ the South is willing to offer patent protection so long as it is necessary and sufficient to induce entry by the firm and $\gamma \leq \gamma^*$.

For a given patent policy in the South, international exhaustion results in lower innovation that national exhaustion. The negative effect of international exhaustion on R&D is reinforced if the South has a weaker incentive to offer patent protection under international exhaustion. On the other hand, a more stringent patent policy in the South under international exhaustion has a conflicting effect on firm R&D. Fig. 3 can also be used to illustrate how the policy reaction of the South affects R&D incentives under national exhaustion relative to international exhaustion.

[20] From the North's viewpoint, the two effects work in opposite directions because $p_N^* > p^G$ whereas $q^G < q^*$ – i.e. international exhaustion helps lower the price in the North but it also lowers the firm's incentive to invest in R&D.

[21] If $1 - \mu/\mu^* < \gamma^G$, the horizontal intersection of the φ^{IG} locus occurs to the left of γ^G. In that case part (*i*) of the proposition applies for $\gamma \in [0, 1 - \mu/\mu^*]$ and part (*ii*) applies for $\gamma \in (1 - \mu/\mu^*, \gamma^G]$.

In regions **A** and **C**, a switch from national to international exhaustion causes the South to drop its patent protection. The elimination of patent protection in the South further reduces the incentive of the firm to do R&D, so a switch to international exhaustion must unambiguously reduce the quality of the product in regions **A** and **C**. In regions **D** and **E**, the switch from national to international exhaustion causes the South to introduce patent protection. In these two areas, the change in South patent policy tends to raise the firm's innovation incentive while the North's policy change to international exhaustion tends to reduce it. Applying Proposition 5(iv), the firm's innovation is lower under international exhaustion in region **D** (since $\gamma < \gamma^I$) while it is greater under international exhaustion in Region **E**.

In summary, innovation is higher under international exhaustion relative to national exhaustion only in cases where the Southern market is sufficiently profitable relative to the Northern one ($\gamma^I < \gamma^G$) and only for entry costs satisfying $\varphi \in [\varphi^{IG}, \varphi^I]$. For all other areas of the parameter space where the firm would enter with national exhaustion, innovation is lower under international exhaustion. Our results on the effect of international exhaustion on R&D can be compared with those of Grossman and Lai (2008), who consider the case where the South provides patent protection but also imposes price controls on the Northern producers. In their model, the South chooses a more liberal price control under international exhaustion, leading to a presumption that Northern firms engage in more R&D under international exhaustion. In contrast, we find that when the South's only policy instrument is patent protection, the induced policy change in the South under international exhaustion may either increase or decrease R&D incentives. The South has an incentive to drop patent protection under international exhaustion in cases where such protection is needed to induce entry under national exhaustion. However, the South may choose to adopt patent protection to induce entry under international exhaustion in cases where the firm is willing to enter without patent protection under national exhaustion.

4.4. Welfare under international exhaustion

Let global welfare under international exhaustion when the firm sells in both markets under patent protection be given by w^G where

$$w^G = w_S^G + w_N^G - \varphi$$

and $w_N^G \equiv (1+\Omega)cs_N(p^G(q^G)) + v^G$. Similarly define

$$w^{IG} = w_S^{IG} + w_N^{IG} - \varphi$$

where $w_N^{IG} \equiv (1+\Omega)cs_N(p^{IG}(q^{IG})) + v^{IG}$. We can show the following:

Proposition 7. The following inequalities hold regarding global welfare (gross of fixed costs of entry) under different policy regimes:

(i) $w^{IG} \leq w^G$ and $w^I \leq w^*$.
(ii) $w^G \leq w^*$ and $w^{IG} \leq w^I$.
(iii) $w^I \leq w^G$ iff $\gamma > \gamma^I$.

Part (i) of Proposition 7 says that, provided the firm sells in both markets regardless of the global policy environment faced by it, total welfare is higher if the South offers patent protection relative to when it does not. In other words, the introduction of patent protection in the South raises global welfare under both national and international exhaustion provided the firm sells in both markets under all possible policy configurations. Part (ii) of Proposition 7 informs us that, provided the firm sells in both markets, national exhaustion delivers higher joint welfare than international exhaustion when the South's patent protection policy is held constant across the two regimes.

It is well known that in a model with linear demands in both regions and no innovation, international exhaustion is preferable to national exhaustion provided there is patent protection in the South and the firm sells in both markets. When quality is fixed, the firm's total output turns out to be equal under national and international exhaustion, but it is more efficiently allocated globally under international exhaustion because price is equalized across markets. Our result shows that when quality is endogenously determined by the firm's R&D investment and the South's patent policy is held constant, the welfare gain arising from a higher level of innovation under national exhaustion dominates the efficiency gains from price equalization across markets that obtains under international exhaustion.

Part (iii) of Proposition 7 shows that world welfare could be higher under international exhaustion if it leads the South to adopt patent protection. If $\gamma = \gamma^I$, the switch from national exhaustion in the North coupled with no patent protection in the South to international exhaustion with patent protection leaves world welfare unaffected because firm profits and consumer surplus are unaffected. For $\gamma > \gamma^I$, however, the increased innovation resulting from a switch to international exhaustion in the North together with patent protection in the South results in higher world welfare. Thus, for parameter values in region **E** in Fig. 3, world welfare is higher under international exhaustion than under national exhaustion since the South's patent protection policy is not the same under the two regimes. For the other parameter values at which the firm is willing to enter with national exhaustion, world welfare is lower under international exhaustion.

4.5. CL and exhaustion policy

Finally, we consider the effect of allowing CL under international exhaustion. Observe that under a compulsory license, the licensee is prevented from exporting the product to the North.[22] This constraint effectively segments the two markets, so the firm is able to charge its monopoly price in the North when CL occurs in the South. We maintain the assumption that the royalty rate under CL is a fraction α of the monopoly price $p^L = \gamma^R q/2$ that would be charged by the licensee, i.e. $r = \alpha p^L = \alpha\gamma^R q/2$, so that the global profit of the firm under CL under international exhaustion is the same as that under national exhaustion which equals $v^{CL}(q) = (1+\Omega)\pi_N^*(q) + \Omega R(q) - c(q)$.

As in the case of national exhaustion, the South enjoys a positive surplus under CL for all $\gamma^R > 0$, so that the imposition of CL is a credible threat if the firm does not enter in the first period. The fact that prices and firm profits under CL are unaffected by the exhaustion regime means the welfare of the two regions and the firm's payoff does not depend on the exhaustion policy of the North. However, the North's exhaustion policy does affect the desirability of CL relative to entry from the perspective of both regions.

First consider the firm's incentives. Given that the Northern policy is international exhaustion, the firm prefers entry to CL iff $v^G(q^G) - \varphi \geq v^{CL}(q^{CL}) \Leftrightarrow \varphi \leq \varphi_{CL}^G \equiv v^G(q^G) - v^{CL}(q^{CL})$. It immediately follows from the properties of $v^{CL}(q^{CL})$ that $\varphi_{CL}^G \leq \varphi^G$ with strict inequality for $\alpha, \gamma > 0$. If $\varphi > \varphi^G$, the option of CL increases the firm's R&D incentive since its royalty payments from CL increase with R&D. For $\varphi \in (\varphi_{CL}^G, \varphi^G]$, the option of CL results in the firm switching from entry in the first period to waiting for CL in the second. In contrast to the case of national exhaustion, the possibility of CL has an ambiguous effect on product quality under international exhaustion. This ambiguity arises due to the lower level of profits (and hence R&D) under international exhaustion.

Since $\varphi_{CL}^G < \varphi^{CL}$, the region of the parameter space where CL is used is larger under international exhaustion than under international exhaustion. For $\varphi > \varphi^G$, the option of CL provides the South with access to the patented product, while also benefiting Northern consumers and the firm (i.e. it is Pareto-improving). For $\varphi \in (\varphi_{CL}^G, \varphi^G]$, the option of CL raises firm profits but, as noted above, has an ambiguous effect on product quality. Since world welfare is higher under national exhaustion than

[22] Indeed, as noted earlier, TRIPS rules and the 2003 waiver decision of the WTO explicitly state that production under CL should be sold predominantly in the domestic market or exported to a third country that itself lacks the technological capability to produce the product and cannot obtain it from the patent-holder.

under international exhaustion and world welfare under CL is independent of the exhaustion regime, CL provides a larger welfare gain under international exhaustion.

We can now state the following:

Proposition 8. Not only is compulsory licensing more likely to arise in equilibrium under international exhaustion compared to national exhaustion, its usage also generates a relatively larger welfare gain.

5. Conclusion

The TRIPS agreement of the WTO forced many developing countries to strengthen their IPR regimes. However, at the same time it left WTO members unconstrained in two key respects: they could avail of compulsory licensing to provide local consumers greater access to patented products and were free to implement exhaustion policies of their choice. This paper provides a unified analysis of the key TRIPS obligation calling for harmonized patent protection across all member states and the two main policy flexibilities it granted them. In so doing, the paper integrates several strands of existing literature that explore various aspects of the multi-faceted relationship between IPR protection and international trade.

Our analysis is couched in a simple North-South model where the two regions differ in terms of their demand structure as well as their innovative capacity (with all of the R&D being done by a Northern firm). We show that the South's unilateral incentive for patent protection is too weak relative to what is jointly optimal. However, this does not imply that forcing the South to offer patent protection is *always* welfare improving. The welfare effects of TRIPS in our model are driven by two forces: how much the firm invests in research and development (R&D) and whether or not it finds it profit-maximizing to sell in the South.

We show that if the Northern firm is unwilling to sell in the South even when it is granted patent protection, forcing the South to implement patent protection makes it worse off without making the North better off. Luckily, however, by including the possibility of CL the TRIPS agreement provides developing countries with an important flexibility that allows them to secure access to foreign patented products when local patent protection fails to induce patent-holders to sell their products in their markets. We show that CL has the potential to make both regions better off and can even increase the firm's R&D investment when it finds it unprofitable to enter the Southern market – in such a situation, CL provides Southern consumers access to its product while allowing the firm to benefit from royalty payments that increase with the quality of its product. However, if the firm chooses to forsake entry in order to take advantage of CL (since its relative payoff under entry is lower), its R&D investment as well as global welfare can decline due to CL.

Finally, we examine how the exhaustion policy of the North affects the two regions as well as the likelihood of CL arising in equilibrium. We show that, provided the South offers patent protection to the firm, global welfare and innovation are higher if the North follows national exhaustion as opposed to international exhaustion. However, there are circumstances where the South is more willing to offer patent protection under international exhaustion and when this is the case, international exhaustion yields greater welfare. Finally, we examine the interplay between the two flexibilities and show that CL is more likely to arise in equilibrium under international exhaustion because the firm is less willing to sell in both markets when it has to set a common international price. Furthermore, the incidence of CL is more likely to be welfare-improving socially under international exhaustion relative to national exhaustion.

Acknowledgements

For helpful comments, we thank the editor, two anonymous referees, and seminar audiences at the following venues: Asia Pacific Trade Seminar 2018, Huazhong University of Science and Technology, Indiana University, Jadavpur University, National University of Singapore, the Southern Economic Association 2018 Conference, and the Western Economics Association 2019 Conference.

Appendix

Here we provide supporting calculations for results reported in the paper.

If quality is chosen before entry

We examine the case where the firm has the option of a CL. The case without a CL is similar.

Suppose that the firm choose the quality q of its product before making its entry decision. Then, given q, the maximum value of the fixed cost φ below which the firm is willing to enter is

$$\varphi^M(q) = v^{CL}(q) - v^*(q) = \frac{q}{4}(1 + \Omega(1 - 2\alpha\gamma + \alpha^2\gamma)) \tag{A.1}$$

Evaluating φ^M at the respective qualities yields

$$\varphi^M(q^{CL}) < \varphi^{CL} < \varphi^M(q^*) \tag{A.2}$$

Suppose $\varphi < \varphi^{CL}$ and the firm has chosen to produce a product of quality q^*. Then, as inequality (A.2) notes, at the time of the entry decision the firm's fixed cost is below the threshold for entry, $\varphi < \varphi^M(q^*)$, so that it is indeed optimal for the firm to enter. Similarly, suppose $\varphi > \varphi^{CL}$ and the firm has chosen to produce a product of quality q^{CL}. Again, inequality (17) implies that at the time of the entry decision, the fixed cost facing the firm is above the threshold for entry, $\varphi > \varphi^M(q^{CL})$ so that staying out is optimal for the firm. Thus, the cutoff rule used by the firm in our two-stage game – i.e. if $\varphi < \varphi^{CL}$ do R&D that yields quality q^* and enter in the first period; otherwise, do R&D that delivers quality q^{CL} and wait for CL in the second period – is subgame perfect.

Proof of Proposition 1

It is straightforward to show that

$$q^I = \frac{(1 + \Omega)(n\mu + 1 - \gamma)}{4t} \tag{A.3}$$

where

$$q^* = q^I|_{\gamma=0} \tag{A.4}$$

Observe that $\partial q^I/\partial\gamma < 0$. It follows then that $q^* > q^I$ for all $\gamma \in 0, 1)$.

Next, note that

$$\varphi^* = \frac{(1 + \Omega)^2(2n\mu + 1)}{32t} \tag{A.5}$$

It is obvious that φ^* is increasing in n and μ.

We have

$$\varphi^I = \frac{(1 + \Omega)^2(1 - \gamma)(2n\mu + 1 - \gamma)}{32t} \tag{A.6}$$

so that

$$\frac{\partial\varphi^I}{\partial\gamma} = -\frac{(1 + \Omega)^2(n\mu + 1 - \gamma)}{16t} < 0$$

Proof of Lemma 1

Direct calculations show that

$$W_S^*-W_S^L=\frac{(1+\Omega)^2(n\mu+1-4\gamma n\mu)}{32t}$$

from which it immediately follows that

$$W_S^* \geq W_S^L \text{ iff } \gamma \leq \gamma^* \equiv \frac{n\mu+1}{4n\mu} \tag{A.7}$$

It is obvious that γ^* is decreasing in n and μ.

Proof of Proposition 3

(i) We have

$$w^*-w^l=\frac{(1+\Omega)^2\gamma^2}{16t}\geq 0 \tag{A.8}$$

(ii) Direct calculations show that

$$\varphi^w=w^*-w^L=\frac{(1+\Omega)^2(2n\mu(1-\gamma)+1)}{16t} \tag{A.9}$$

from which it directly follows that $\partial\varphi^w/\partial\gamma<0$; $\partial\varphi^w/\partial\mu<0$; and $\partial\varphi^w/\partial n<0$. Also, we have

$$\varphi^w-\varphi^*=\frac{(1+\Omega)^2}{32}\frac{2n\mu+1-4n\gamma\mu}{t}$$

From this expression, it immediately follows that $\varphi^w\geq\varphi^*$ iff $\gamma\geq\gamma^w$ where

$$\gamma^w=\frac{2n\mu+1}{4n\mu} \tag{A.10}$$

Note that $\partial\gamma^w/\partial\mu<0$ and $\partial\gamma^w/\partial n<0$.

Proof of Proposition 4

(i) Evaluating (11) yields $\varphi^{CL}(\alpha,\gamma^R)=\frac{A^2+A2\mu n(1+\Omega)}{32t}$, where $A=1+\Omega-(2-\alpha)\alpha\gamma^R\Omega$ is decreasing in α and γ^R. Using (A.5),

$$\varphi^*-\varphi^{CL}=\frac{(2-\alpha)\alpha\gamma^R\Omega((2-\alpha)\alpha\gamma^R\Omega+2\mu n(1+\Omega))}{32t}\geq 0 \tag{A.11}$$

The above expression is strictly positive for $\gamma^R>0$ and $\alpha>0$, and is increasing in γ^R and α.

Proof of Lemma 2

Evaluating (8) using (10) yields the equilibrium payoff to the South under CL:

$$W_S^{CL}(\alpha,\gamma^R)=\frac{(2-\alpha)^2\Omega\gamma^R((1+\Omega)\mu n+\Omega\alpha\gamma^R(2-\alpha))}{32t} \tag{A.12}$$

Differentiating with respect to γ^R yields

$$\frac{\partial W_S^{CL}}{\partial\gamma^R}=\frac{(2-\alpha)^2\Omega[(1+\Omega)\mu n+(5\alpha-2(2-\alpha))\alpha\Omega\gamma^R]}{32t}>0, \tag{A.13}$$

so W_S^{CL} is convex and increasing in γ^R.

Differentiating $W_S^{CL}(\alpha,\gamma^R)$ with respect to α yields

$$\frac{\partial W_S^{CL}}{\partial\alpha}=\frac{-(2-\alpha)\Omega\gamma^R[(1+\Omega)\mu n+(5\alpha-2(1+\alpha^2))\Omega\gamma^R]}{16t} \tag{A.14}$$

Since $5\alpha-2(1+\alpha^2)$ is increasing in α, a sufficient condition for $\frac{\partial W_S^{CL}}{\partial\alpha}<0$ is that the bracketed expression be positive at $\alpha=0$. Evaluating at $\alpha=0$ yields the condition in the Lemma.

Evaluating the difference between Southern welfare under entry with that under CL at $\alpha=0$, we have

$$W_S^*-W_S^{CL}(0,\gamma^R)=\frac{(1+\mu n)(1+\Omega)^2-4\mu n\gamma^R\Omega(1+\Omega)}{32t} \tag{A.15}$$

The welfare gain from entry over CL is decreasing in γ^R, so solving for the value of γ^R such that (A.15) equals zero yields the threshold γ_m^R. Since W_S^{CL} is continuous in α, CL is preferable to entry for α sufficiently close to 0 if $\gamma^R>\gamma_m^R$.

Proof of Lemma 3

Solving (13) yields

$$\varphi_W^{CL}(\alpha,\gamma^R)=\frac{(2\mu n+1)(1+\Omega)^2-\alpha((2-\alpha)\Omega\gamma^R)^2-(2+\alpha-\alpha^2)\Omega(1+\Omega)\mu n\gamma^R)}{16t} \tag{A.16}$$

Evaluating this expression yields $\varphi_W^{CL}(\alpha,0)=\frac{(1+\Omega)^2(1+2\mu n)}{16t}=2\varphi^*$ and $\frac{\partial\varphi_W^{CL}}{\partial\gamma^R}<0$. We also have

$$\varphi_W^{CL}(\alpha,\gamma^R)-\varphi^{CL}(\alpha,\gamma^R)=\frac{(2\mu n+1)(1+\Omega)^2-2(2-\alpha)\Omega(1+\Omega)\mu n\gamma^R-\alpha(2-\alpha)^3(\Omega\gamma^R)^2}{32t} \tag{A.17}$$

Evaluating the above difference in the two cost thresholds at $\alpha=1$ and $\gamma^R=1$ yields $\varphi_W^{CL}(1,1)-\varphi^{CL}(1,1)=\frac{2\mu n(1+\Omega)+1+2\Omega}{32t}>0$.

Proof of Lemma 4

(i) We have

$$\varphi^G=\frac{\mu^2(2n^2+2n+1+n\mu)(2n+1-n\mu)(1+\Omega)^2}{32t(n+\mu)^2} \tag{A.18}$$

from which it directly follows that $\varphi^G\geq 0$ iff $\mu\leq\mu^*=2+1/n$.

(ii) We have

$$\partial\varphi^G/\partial\mu|_{\mu=1}=\frac{(1+\Omega)^2}{16}\frac{n}{t}>0$$

and

$$\partial\varphi^G/\partial\mu|_{\mu=\mu^*}=-\frac{n(1+\Omega)^2}{16}\frac{(2n+1)^2}{t(n+1)^2}<0$$

(*iii*) We have

$$\varphi^{JG}=\frac{(1+\Omega)^2\mu^2[(2n^2+2n+1)(1-\gamma)+n\mu)][(2n+1)(1-\gamma)-n\mu]}{32t(n(1-\gamma)+\mu)^2} \tag{A.19}$$

Observe that $\varphi^{JG}\geq 0$ iff $(2n+1)(1-\gamma)-n\mu\geq 0$ or $\mu\leq(1-\gamma)\mu^*$. Also note that

$$\frac{\partial\varphi^{JG}}{\partial\gamma}=-\frac{(1+\Omega)^2\mu^3(n+1)^4(1-\gamma)}{16t(n(1-\gamma)+\mu)^3}\leq 0$$

Proof of Proposition 5

(i) We have

$$q^{IG} = \frac{(1-\gamma)(1+\Omega)\mu(n+1)^2}{4t(n(1-\gamma)+\mu)} \tag{A.20}$$

where

$$q^G = q^{IG}\big|_{\gamma=0} = \frac{(1+\Omega)\mu(n+1)^2}{4t(n+\mu)} \tag{A.21}$$

We have

$$\partial q^I/\partial\gamma = -\frac{(1+\Omega)\mu^2(n+1)^2}{4t(n(1-\gamma)+\mu)^2}<0$$

It follows then that $q^G > q^{IG}$ for all $\gamma \in [0, 1)$.

(ii) We have

$$\varphi^I - \varphi^{IG} = \frac{(1+\Omega)^2 n^2(\gamma+\mu-1)^2\left(2\mu n^2(1-\gamma)+n(\mu+1-\gamma)^2-\gamma\mu\right)}{32t(n(1-\gamma)+\mu)^2} \geq 0$$

This implies $\varphi^* - \varphi^G \geq 0$. Similarly,

$$q^I - q^{IG} = \frac{(1+\Omega)n(\gamma+\mu-1)^2}{4t(n(1-\gamma)+\mu)} \geq 0,$$

which implies $q^* - q^G \geq 0$.

(iii) Using the definitions of φ^I and φ^G we have:

$$\varphi^I \geq \varphi^G \text{ iff } \gamma \leq \gamma^I = \frac{n(\mu-1)^2}{n+\mu} \tag{A.22}$$

using which the stated properties of γ^I can be established immediately.

(iv) If follows from (A.3) and (A.21) that $q^I - q^G$ is decreasing in γ, and is equal to 0 at γ^I.

Proof of Lemma 4

(i) $w_S^{IG} > w_S^I$ follows immediately from the fact that $q^{IG} \geq q^N$ and that consumers have an additional option to purchased the imitated product when the firm enters without patent protection. To establish that the South's payoff under entry without patent protection exceeds that from entry with patent protection, we can write the difference in payoffs as:

$$w_S^{IG} - w_S^G = A(\mu, n, \gamma)B(\mu, n, \gamma), \tag{A.23}$$

where

$$A(\mu, n, \gamma) = \frac{\gamma(\Gamma\mu(1+n))^2}{32(\mu+n)^3 t(\mu+n(1-\gamma))^3} \geq 0$$

and

$$\begin{aligned} B(\mu, n, \gamma) = {} & (1-\gamma)^2(\mu n^5 + (10\mu-4)n^4) - (2(2-\gamma)\mu^4 + (5-13\gamma+4\gamma^2)\mu^3)n \\ & -(3(1-\gamma)\mu^3 - 12(2-3\gamma+\gamma^2)\mu^2 + 7(1-\gamma)\mu)n^3 \\ & -((2-\gamma)\mu^4 - 2(9-9\gamma+2\gamma^2)\mu^3 + 4\gamma(3-2\gamma)\mu^2)n^2 \end{aligned}$$

The differential (A.23) is non-negative if $B(m, n, \gamma)$ is non-negative on the region of the parameter space where the firm would enter without patent protection, which is the set $F = \{(\mu, n, \gamma) | \mu \in [1, \mu^*(1-\gamma)], n \geq 1, \gamma \in [0, 1-\frac{1}{\mu^*}]\}$.

The proof (available online) shows that for given (m, n),the function B is (a) strictly convex in γ for , $\gamma \in [0, 1-\frac{1}{\mu^*}]$, (b) positive and decreasing in γ at $\gamma = 0$, and (c) positive and decreasing in γ at $\gamma = \frac{1}{\mu^*}$. As a result, $B > 0$ for $\gamma \in [0, 1-\frac{1}{\mu^*}]$.

(ii) The critical value of γ at which welfare under patented entry is equal to that under imitation without entry is the solution to $w_S^G = w_S^I$,which yields

$$\gamma^G \equiv \frac{1}{4}\frac{(n+1)^2[n(\mu-2)-\mu]^2}{n(n+\mu)^3}. \tag{A.24}$$

The fact that γ^G is decreasing in n and μ follows by differentiation of (A.24).

(iii) From the definitions of the two thresholds, we have $\gamma^* - \gamma^G = (\mu-1)[\mu^2(\mu+1) + (5\mu+1)\mu n + (7\mu-1)n^2 + (3-\mu)\mu n^3]/(4\mu(\mu+n)^3)$, which must be non-negative for $\mu \leq \mu^* \leq 3$.

(iv) With patent protection, the quality of the good is higher under national exhaustion,

$$q^* - q^G = \frac{(1+\Omega)n(\mu-1)^2}{4t(n+\mu)} \geq 0$$

and the price per unit quality in the South is lower

$$\frac{p^*}{q^*} = \frac{1}{2} \leq \frac{p^G}{q^G} = \frac{\mu(n+1)}{2(\mu+n)}$$

Therefore, welfare in the South is higher with patent protection when the North follows a policy of national exhaustion.

Proof of Proposition 7

(i) We have

$$w^* - w^I = \frac{(1+\Omega)^2\gamma^2}{16t} \geq 0$$

Furthermore, we have

$$\frac{\partial w^G}{\partial\gamma} = -\frac{(1+\Omega)^2(n+1)^2\mu^2 F(m, n, \gamma)}{8t(n(1-\gamma)+m)^3}$$

where

$$F(m, n, \gamma) = \gamma(2mn + m - n) + n(m-1)^2$$

Observe that $\frac{\partial w^G}{\partial\gamma} \leq 0$ iff $F(m, n, \gamma) \geq 0$.

Next, note that

$$\frac{\partial F(.)}{\partial\gamma} = (2m-1)n + m > 0$$

and that $F(m, n, \gamma)|_{\gamma=0} = n(m-1)^2 > 0$. This means that $F(m, n, \gamma) > 0$ for all γ. Thus, we must have

$$\frac{\partial w^G}{\partial\gamma} < 0$$

which implies that $w^G > w^{IG}$ since $w^G = w^{IG}|_{\gamma=0}$.

(ii) We can show that

$$w^{*}-w^{G}=\frac{(1+\Omega)^{2}n^{2}(\mu-1)^{4}}{16t(n+\mu)^{2}}\geq 0 \tag{A.25}$$

Next note that

$$w^{J}-w^{JG}=\frac{(1+\Omega)^{2}n^{2}(\mu+\gamma-1)^{2}G(m,n,\gamma)}{16t(n(1-\gamma)+\mu)^{2}}$$

where

$$G(m,n,\gamma)=2m\gamma(n+1)+n(m-1)^{2}-\gamma^{2}n$$

Observe that $w^{J}-w^{JG}\geq 0$ iff $G(m,n,\gamma)\geq 0$. Next, note that

$$\frac{\partial G(.)}{\partial\gamma}=2n(m-\gamma)+2m>0$$

and that $G(m,n,\gamma)|_{\gamma=0}=n(m-1)^{2}>0$. This means that $G(m,n,\gamma)>0$ for all γ. Thus, we must have

$$w^{J}\geq w^{JG}$$

(iii) Taking the difference of (A.8) and (A.25) yields

$$w^{J}-w^{G}=\frac{n^{2}(\mu-1)^{4}-(\mu+n)^{2}\gamma^{2}}{16(\mu+n)^{2}t},$$

which is decreasing and strictly concave in γ, positive at $\gamma=0$, and equal to 0 at $\gamma=\gamma^{J}$.

References

Baten, J., Bianchi, N., Moser, P., 2017. Compulsory licensing and innovation – historical evidence from German patents after WWI. J. Dev. Econ. 126, 231–242.

Beall, R., Kuhn, R., 2012. Trends in compulsory licensing of pharmaceuticals since the Doha declaration: a database analysis. PLoS Med. 9 (1), 1–9.

Bond, E.W., Saggi, K., 2014. Compulsory licensing, price controls, and access to patented foreign products. J. Dev. Econ. 109, 217–228.

Bond, E.W., Saggi, K., 2017. Bargaining over entry with a compulsory license deadline: price spillovers and surplus expansion. Am. Econ. J. Microeconomics 9 (1), 31–62.

Bond, E.W., Saggi, K., 2018. Compulsory licensing and patent protection: a north-south perspective. Econ. J. 128 (610), 1157–1179.

Cockburn, I.M., Lanjouw, J.O., Schankerman, M., 2016. Patents and the global diffusion of new drugs. Am. Econ. Rev. 106 (1), 136–164.

Gansland, M., Maskus, K.E., 2004. Parallel imports and the pricing of pharmaceutical products: evidence from the European Union. J. Health Econ. 23, 1035–1057.

Ghosh, S., 2013. The implementation of exhaustion policies: lessons from national experiences. International Centre for Trade and Sustainable Development, Issue Paper No. 40.

Ghosh, S., Calboli, I., 2018. Exhausting Intellectual Property Rights: A Comparative Law and Policy Analysis. Cambridge University Press, Cambridge, UK.

Grossman, G.M., Lai, Edwin L.-C., 2008. Parallel imports and price controls. RAND J. Econ. 39 (2), 378–402.

Ivus, O., 2010. Do stronger patent rights raise high-tech exports to the developing world? J. Int. Econ. 81 (1), 38–47.

Ivus, O., 2015. Does stronger patent protection increase export variety? Evidence from U.S. product-level data. J. Int. Bus. Stud. 46 (6), 724–731.

Kyle, M., Qian, Y., 2014. Intellectual property rights and access to innovation: evidence from TRIPS. N.B.E.R. Working Paper 20799.

Li, C., Maskus, K.E., 2006. The impact of parallel imports on investments in cost-reducing research and development. J. Int. Econ. 68 (2), 443–455.

Li, C., Robles, J., 2007. Product innovation and parallel trade. Int. J. Ind. Organ. 25 (2), 417–429.

Malueg, D.A., Schwartz, M., 1994. Parallel imports, demand dispersion, and international price discrimination. J. Int. Econ. 37, 167–195.

Maskus, K.E., 2000. Parallel imports. World Econ. 23 (9), 1269–1284.

Roy, S., Saggi, K., 2012. Equilibrium parallel import policies and international market structure. J. Int. Econ. 87 (2), 262–276.

Saggi, K., 2013. Market power in the global economy: the exhaustion and protection of intellectual property. Econ. J. 123 (567), 131–161.

Saggi, K., 2016. Trade, intellectual property rights, and the WTO. In: Bagwell, Kyle, Staiger, Robert W. (Eds.), Chapter 18 of the Handbook of Commercial Policy. Elsevier edited by.

Scherer, F.M., Watal, J., 2002. Post-TRIPS options for access to patented medicines in developing nations. J. Int. Econ. Law 5 (4), 913–939.

Valleti, T.M., 2006. Differential pricing, parallel trade, and the incentive to invest. J. Int. Econ. 70, 314–324.

Valletti, T., Szymanski, S., 2006. Parallel trade, international exhaustion and intellectual property rights: a welfare analysis. J. Ind. Econ. 54 (4), 499–526.

Part 6

Trade, FDI, and Industrial Policies

Chapter 23

Endogenous trade policy under foreign direct investment[#]

Hideo Konishi, Kamal Saggi*, Shlomo Weber

Department of Economics, Southern Methodist University, Dallas, TX 75275-0496, USA

Received 29 October 1996; received in revised form 5 August 1998; accepted 26 August 1998

Abstract

Using Bernheim and Whinston (1986) common agency game, we endogenize trade policy in a duopoly composed of a domestic firm and a foreign firm, where both firms influence the domestic government's trade policy via their contributions. The foreign firm can jump over trade restrictions by undertaking foreign direct investment (FDI) in the domestic market. The government prefers a voluntary export restraint (VER) to a tariff for two reasons. First, a VER leads to higher contributions from the foreign firm than a tariff. Second, a VER provides a higher level of protection to the domestic firm without generating FDI by the foreign firm.

Keywords: Trade policy; Tariff; VER; Lobbying; Foreign direct investment

JEL classification: F12; F13; F23

1. Introduction

Economists are puzzled by the prevalence of voluntary export restraints (VERs) since tariffs can provide protection to domestic firms without transferring tariff revenue to foreign firms. Our goal in this paper is to provide an explanation for the common use of VERs instead of tariffs. We construct a political economy model in which a domestic firm and a foreign firm influence the domestic government's trade policy (a tariff or a VER) through their campaign contributions (as in

*Corresponding author. Tel.: +1-214-768-3274; fax: +1-214-768-1821.
E-mail address: ksaggi@mail.smu.edu (K. Saggi)

[#] This chapter was originally appeared in *Journal of International Economics* **49**, 289–308. © 1999 Elsevier Science B.V.

Grossman and Helpman, 1994).[1] As in Hillman and Ursprung (1993), the VER is voluntary in our model because the foreign firm participates in the formation of domestic trade policy. After the domestic government chooses its trade policy, the foreign firm may avoid trade restrictions by switching from exporting to foreign direct investment (FDI) as the means of serving the domestic market. Thus, the foreign firm can use FDI as a threat to influence trade policy.

We characterize equilibrium contributions of the two firms and show that the domestic government prefers a VER to a tariff for two reasons. First, if the government weighs dollar contributions relatively more than domestic surplus (perhaps due to the greater flexibility it enjoys in using contributions relative to domestic surplus), it prefers a VER over a tariff since a VER generates greater contributions. We call this motive the political economy motive for a VER. The second advantage of a VER is its ability to discourage the foreign firm from undertaking FDI. Since FDI results in free competition between the two firms, the domestic firm benefits from preventing FDI. The foreign firm refrains from FDI only if exporting yields profits at least as high as FDI. We show in the paper that the protection enjoyed by the domestic firm is higher under the VER that just deters FDI by the foreign firm than under the tariff that just deters FDI. Why? Unlike a VER, a tariff increases the foreign firm's marginal cost of selling in the domestic market. Consequently, what the foreign firm loses under the FDI deterring tariff in higher costs must be compensated by higher revenues for it to collect its FDI level of profits. In effect, the possibility of FDI by the foreign firm implies that a VER allows the domestic government to implement protection levels not feasible under a tariff. Therefore, there exists an FDI-deterring motive for a VER.[2]

The idea that the enactment of protectionist trade policies can induce FDI by foreign firms has existed in the literature for a long time. Bhagwati et al. (1987, 1992) argued that the mere threat of future trade restrictions may lead to anticipatory investment (termed 'quid pro quo' investment) by foreign firms.[3] Recently, Grossman and Helpman (1996) further develop the notion of 'quid pro

[1]Grossman and Helpman (1994) were the first to apply the common agency game developed by Bernheim and Whinston (1986) to trade policy formation. In their model, faced with a menu of contingent contributions from different lobby groups, the government commits to its trade policy. For other political economy models, see Mayer and Riezman (1987) and Hillman and Ursprung (1993).

[2]If FDI is not an option for the foreign firm, then the domestic firm can influence the government to choose a prohibitive trade policy and monopolize the market. Since monopoly profits are certainly higher than the sum of duopoly profits, given the same efficiency of production, the government can expect higher contributions from the domestic firm through a completely protectionist policy (see Lemma 3). It will choose such a policy as long as it does not value consumer welfare too heavily. The possibility of FDI by the foreign firm prevents the government (and the domestic firm) from achieving this outcome.

[3]See Takemori and Tsumagari (1997) for an approach that allows the foreign government, instead of foreign firms, to select levels of investment recognizing that protectionist trade polices abroad enhance the returns to such investments.

quo' investment in a model where the host country government chooses protection in response to policy-contingent campaign contributions by domestic firms. While our model shares some common features with theirs, there are some important differences. First, our main focus is on the government's choice between alternative instruments of trade policy. Second, as in (Hillman and Ursprung, 1988, Hillman and Ursprung, 1993) and unlike Grossman and Helpman, we allow the foreign firm to lobby the domestic government just as the domestic firm. We argue that the possibility of FDI not only limits the level of trade protection that the domestic government can implement but also influences its choice between alternative policy instruments. The threat of FDI affects the contribution schemes chosen by the two firms, and consequently the resulting trade policy.[4]

The choice between a VER and a tariff was first examined by Hillman and Ursprung (1988). In their model, the dominance of a VER over a tariff stems mainly from the presence of multiple foreign firms. One key element our paper shares with Hillman and Ursprung is that the higher profits under a VER are reflected in higher contributions. Consequently, the government prefers this outcome because it prefers contributions to tariff revenues (the political economy motive).[5] Rosendorff (1996a,b) shows that a government chooses a VER instead of a tariff if it weighs the domestic firm's profits more than consumer surplus. In his model, the foreign firm makes an offer to restrict its exports voluntarily if the domestic government reduces its tariff level. The reduction in the tariff level compensates the foreign firm for its restricted sales under a VER.

Finally, a VER can emerge as an equilibrium policy by generating a collusive outcome (see Harris, 1985; Krishna, 1989). Levinsohn (1989) has argued that if foreign firms can undertake FDI, the quota's role as a collusive device disappears. Our model complements Levinsohn's analysis by suggesting another channel through which FDI influences trade policy. In our model, the possibility of FDI generates a non-equivalence between a VER and a tariff.[6]

The rest of the paper is organized as follows. Section 2 describes a simple model of duopoly competition between a domestic and a foreign firm where the two firms exert political influence on domestic trade policy. Section 3 presents preliminary analysis of Cournot equilibrium under trade policy restrictions. Section 4 describes the common agency game where firms offer contributions contingent on trade policy. Section 5 explains the two motives for the use of a

[4] As the referee has pointed out, the FDI deterring motive depends crucially upon the assumption that the foreign firm cannot make a credible commitment to restrain from FDI. As the referee also noted, if the foreign firm can make a credible commitment regarding its FDI decision, then its FDI decision and the government trade's policy are simultaneously determined and the FDI deterring effect vanishes.

[5] In fact, in Hillman and Ursprung (1988), the candidates put no weight on tariff revenue.

[6] A closely related literature deals with the strategic issues that arise under alternative trade policies in imperfectly competitive models (see Itoh and Ono, 1982, 1984).

VER instead of a tariff. Section 6 concludes. All lemmas are proved in Appendix A.

2. The model

Consider an industry composed of two firms: a domestic firm (denoted by A) and a foreign firm (denoted by J). The foreign firm currently exports to the domestic market. Our model is a four stage game (see Fig. 1). In the first stage, the two firms simultaneously choose contribution levels contingent on the government's trade policy.[7] In the second stage, the government chooses its trade policy. In the third stage, the foreign firm chooses whether to continue with exporting or to establish a new plant in the domestic market through FDI. In the fourth stage, the two firms choose their quantities of production.

The marginal cost of producing a unit of the homogenous good in either country is set to zero for simplicity. Denote the (inverse) demand function in the domestic market by $p(q)$ where q denotes the aggregate output in the industry. We assume that $p(q)$ is twice continuously differentiable and $p'(q)<0$.

We model the political interaction between the two firms and the government as a common agency game, studied by Bernheim and Whinston (1986). In this game, the two firms (principals) attempt to influence the domestic government's (agent) trade policy choice by offering contributions to the government contingent on its trade policy. Each firm's strategy is a menu of contributions $C_i(a)$, where $C_i(a) \geq 0$ and a denotes the government's trade policy. The government chooses between a tariff t or a VER $\bar{q}_J$. Denote the government's choice set by $V=[0, t^M] \cup [0, q^D]$ where t^M denotes the prohibitive tariff and q^D denotes the foreign firm's output under free trade.[8]

Given the contribution schedules of the two firms, the government chooses its trade policy a to maximize its objective function, a weighted sum of total contributions and domestic social welfare:

$$U_G(a) = C_A(a) + C_J(a) + \alpha[CS(a) + T(a) + \pi_A(a)], \tag{1}$$

where $CS(a)$, $T(a)$, and $\pi_A(a)$ denote consumer surplus, tariff revenue, and profits of the domestic firm respectively. The parameter $\alpha \geq 0$ represents the weight the government places on total domestic surplus relative to contributions. For example, $\alpha<1$ implies that the government values a dollar collected as a contribution from the firms more than a dollar equivalent of domestic welfare.

[7] All discussion of the government should be understood to refer to the domestic government, as the foreign government is assumed inactive.

[8] Note that any tariff level higher than t^M has exactly the same effect as t^M. Similarly, any VER bigger than q^D results in free trade and need not be considered.

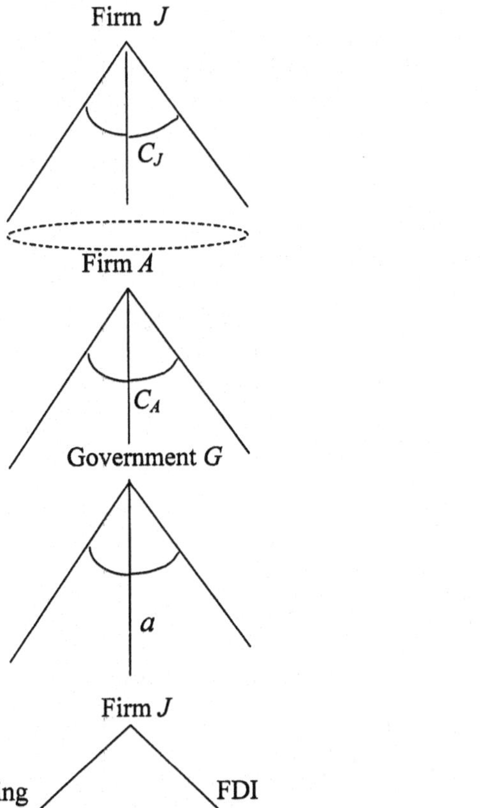

Fig. 1. The structure of the game.

Such a preference for contribution money may reflect the greater discretion enjoyed by the government in using its lobbying contributions relative to domestic surplus.

After the government chooses its trade policy, the foreign firm may jump over any trade restrictions by switching from exporting to FDI. Thus, FDI by the foreign firm makes trade policy inconsequential and the standard Cournot equilibrium occurs in the fourth stage. We assume that FDI involves a fixed cost

$F>0$. Since the cost of production is same in both markets, FDI has no direct efficiency gains in our model.

If the foreign firm continues with exporting, however, the chosen trade policy affects its profits and behavior. Under a VER, the foreign firm can produce at most $\bar{q}_J$ while under a tariff the two firms play an asymmetric Cournot game where the domestic firm's marginal cost equals 0 and the foreign firm's equals the tariff t.

3. Product market

In this section, we describe the product market interaction between the firms first under free trade and then under trade restrictions. Then, working backwards, we consider the common agency game in the next section.

3.1. Free trade equilibrium

Recall that $q=q_A+q_J$ denotes total industry output and the marginal cost of production is assumed to be zero. In the absence of any trade policy restrictions, firm i's profit function is given by:

$$\pi_i(q_i, q_j)=p(q)q_i\,, \tag{2}$$

where $i, j=A, J$. Profit maximization requires

$$\frac{\partial \pi_i(q_i, q_j)}{\partial q_i}=p'(q)q_i+p(q)=0\,. \tag{3}$$

We assume that the second order condition holds

$$\frac{\partial^2 \pi_i(q_i, q_j)}{\partial q_i^2}=p''(q)q_i+2p'(q)<0\,. \tag{4}$$

Furthermore, we also assume that the two firm's choice variables are *strategic substitutes*: q_j decreases if q_i increases for any $i, j=A, J$ (see Bulow et al., 1985). From the first order condition (3) we have:

$$\frac{\mathrm{d}q_j}{\mathrm{d}q_i}=\frac{p''(q)q_i+p'(q)}{-(p''(q)q_i+2p'(q))}\,. \tag{5}$$

Thus, given the second order condition, q_i and q_j are strategic substitutes if and only if the following condition holds:

$$p''(q)q_i+p'(q)<0\,. \tag{6}$$

Note that this condition implies the second order condition in Eq. (4). Finally, consider the effect of an increase in q_i on total industry output:

$$\frac{dq}{dq_i} = \frac{-p'(q)}{-(p''(q)q_i + 2p'(q))} > 0 . \tag{7}$$

Thus, total industry output increases when the output of any one firm increases. We assume that the Cournot equilibrium (defined by the solution to the first order conditions of the two firms) is unique. Since the two firms are symmetric, the unique equilibrium is also symmetric and we denote this equilibrium by (q^D, q^D).

Both under free trade and FDI, each firm's equilibrium output equals q^D. Let π^D denote each firm's profits in the free trade equilibrium (q^D, q^D). Clearly, the domestic firm is indifferent between free trade and FDI while the foreign firm strictly prefers free trade to FDI since FDI incurs a fixed cost F.

3.2. Trade restrictions

Ethier (1989) has noted that a VER does not alter the best response function of the domestic firm since it reacts to a *given* level of foreign sales, regardless of how such sales are determined. Therefore, the domestic firm is indifferent among all policies that result in equal output on the foreign firm's part. Under a VER that limits the foreign firm's output to $\bar{q}_J$, the equilibrium outputs of the two firms are denoted by $(q_A(\bar{q}_J), q_J(\bar{q}_J))$. We first show that the VER constraint binds.

Lemma 1. *For any VER level $\bar{q}_J \in [0, q^D]$, the foreign firm produces $\bar{q}_J$ and the domestic firm's output increases as the VER becomes more severe (as $\bar{q}_J$ decreases). The foreign firm's profits decrease whereas the domestic firm's profits as well as total industry profits increase as the VER becomes more severe.*

The next lemma discusses the product market equilibrium under a tariff. Let the equilibrium outputs of the two firms under a tariff t be given by $(\tilde{q}_A(t), \tilde{q}_J(t))$ and let $\tilde{q}(t) = \tilde{q}_A(t) + \tilde{q}_J(t)$ denote the total industry output.

Lemma 2. *For any tariff $t \in (0, t^M)$, an increase in the tariff level t causes the domestic firm's output to rise, the foreign firm's output to fall, and total industry output to fall. Moreover, the foreign firm's profits decrease and the domestic firm's increase with an increase in the tariff level t.*

Now that we have described the consequences of a tariff and a VER on the product market equilibrium, we are ready to determine the political equilibrium.

4. Common agency game

In this section, we analyze the first stage of our game. We use the common agency game developed by Bernheim and Whinston (1986) to model the political process underlying the formation of trade policy. The two firms (principals) offer menus of contributions ($C_i(a)$ where C_i: $V \to \Re_+$) to the government (agent), and then the government chooses its trade policy $a \in V$. The profits for the two firms, gross of any contributions and fixed costs of FDI, are denoted by $\Pi_i(a)$ where $i = A, J$. The government's utility from its action $a \in V$ (excluding contributions) equals domestic welfare: $\Pi_G(a) = \alpha[CS(a) + T(a) + \Pi_A(a)]$, where $CS(a)$ and $T(a)$ are the resulting consumer surplus and the tariff revenue as in Eq. (1). Since the above game admits multiple Nash equilibria, we restrict attention to coalition-proof Nash equilibria, as in Bernheim and Whinston (1986) and Bernheim et al. (1987). Let (C_A^*, C_J^*, a^*) denote a coalition-proof Nash equilibrium of the policy game. Then, the resulting payoff structure for the three players is

$$u_A \equiv \Pi_A(a^*) - C_A^*(a^*),$$

$$u_J \equiv \Pi_J(a^*) - C_J^*(a^*),$$

and

$$u_G \equiv C_A^*(a^*) + C_J^*(a^*) + \Pi_G(a^*)$$

Bernheim and Whinston (1986) characterization result of the payoff structures of a coalition proof Nash equilibrium in a common agency game translates into the following result in our context.[9]

Proposition 1. *(*Bernheim and Whinston, 1986, *Theorems 2 and 3): In every coalition proof Nash equilibrium*

$$(C_A^*, C_J^*, a^*),\ a^* \in \arg\max_{a \in V}(\Pi_A(a) + \Pi_J(a) + \Pi_G(a))$$

and the two firms' equilibrium payoffs are an efficient vector (u_A^*, u_J^*) *among the vectors that satisfy the following conditions:*

$$\text{(i) } u_A + u_J \leq \max_{a \in V}(\Pi_A(a) + \Pi_J(a) + \Pi_G(a)) - \max_{a \in V}(\Pi_G(a)),$$

$$\text{(ii) } u_A \leq \max_{a \in V}(\Pi_A(a) + \Pi_J(a) + \Pi_G(a)) - \max_{a \in V}(\Pi_J(a) + \Pi_G(a)),$$

$$\text{(iii) } u_J \leq \max_{a \in V}(\Pi_A(a) + \Pi_J(a) + \Pi_G(a)) - \max_{a \in V}(\Pi_A(a) + \Pi_G(a)).$$

Moreover, any efficient vector that satisfies the above conditions can be supported by a coalition proof Nash equilibrium.

The first statement of proposition 1 says that in a coalition proof Nash

[9]For other applications of common agency games to international trade theory, see Grossman and Helpman (1994, 1996) and Tsumagari and Yanagawa (1997).

equilibrium, the government selects an action that maximizes the joint utility of the three players. This implies that

$$u_A^* + u_J^* + u_G^* = \max_{a \in V} [\Pi_A(a) + \Pi_J(a) + \Pi_G(a)].$$

As for the three conditions in the second statement, condition (i) says that the government's utility exceeds the reservation level $\max_{a \in V[} \Pi_G(a)]$, so that the firms are limited in their ability to extract surplus from the government. Conditions (ii) and (iii) say that each firm is limited in its ability to extract surplus from the other firm and the government. For example, condition (ii) says that the domestic firm's equilibrium utility can be no higher than the difference between the maximized total surplus and the maximum payoff a coalition of the foreign firm and the government can ensure for themselves. If condition (i) fails to bind at an efficient vector, then the government gets more than its reservation level of utility.[10] On the other hand, if condition (i) binds, many equilibria exist that result in the same policy action and generate the same total contributions even though the contribution shares of the two firms may differ. If condition (i) binds, then the government's payoff equals its reservation utility level.

5. Equilibrium analysis

In this section we demonstrate that the dominance of a VER over a tariff obtains because of two separate reasons: a political economy motive (applicable for $\alpha < 1$) and a FDI deterring motive (illustrated for $\alpha = 1$). Then, we present a decomposition formula of the total surplus, which nicely illustrates the joint interaction of the two motives.

5.1. Political economy motive for a VER

Let $\mathcal{W}_\alpha: V \rightarrow \mathfrak{R}_+$ be the total surplus function given $\alpha \geq 0$: i.e.,

$$\mathcal{W}_\alpha(a) = \Pi_G(a) + \Pi_A(a) + \Pi_J(a)$$

$$= \alpha[CS(a) + \Pi_A(a) + T(a)] + \Pi_A(a) + \Pi_J(a).$$

Recall that $V \equiv [0, t_M] \cup [0, q^D]$, and $a \in V$ denotes the government's trade policy. Note that by the first part of proposition 1, the equilibrium trade policy maximizes $\mathcal{W}_\alpha(a)$. The political economy motive is best understood by considering the case where the foreign firm cannot switch from exporting to FDI.

[10]Under this scenario, the agent extracts a positive rent from this game. Laussel and Le Breton (1995) give general conditions under which the 'no rent property' is violated.

Proposition 2. *Suppose $\alpha<1$. Then, by selecting a VER $\tilde{q}_J(t)$ instead of a tariff t, the government can ensure the domestic firm the same level of profits as the tariff t while increasing the foreign firm's profits, the total surplus for the three players, and the total contribution of the two firms.*

Proof. Under the Cournot-Nash assumption, as long as two alternative trade policies result in the same level of output for the foreign firm, the domestic firm's profits under the two policies are equal: $\Pi_A(t)=\Pi_A(\tilde{q}_J(t))$ where $\tilde{q}_J(t)$ is a VER that results in the foreign firm producing the same output as the tariff t (see Section 3.2). Since part of the foreign firm's total revenue under the tariff t accrues to the government as tariff revenue, we have $\Pi_J(\tilde{q}_J)(t)=T(t)+\Pi_J(t)$. Thus (i) is straightforward. As for (ii), since the total industry output is unaffected by the choice between t and $\tilde{q}_J(t)$, we must have $CS(\tilde{q}_J(t))=CS(t)$. By manipulating the definition of total surplus under t, we obtain:

$$\mathcal{W}_\alpha(t)=\alpha[CS(t)+\Pi_A(t)+T(t)]+\Pi_A(t)+\Pi_J(t)$$

$$=\alpha[CS(t)+\Pi_A(t)+T(t)+\Pi_J(t)]+\Pi_A(t)+(1-\alpha)\Pi_J(t)$$

Since $\Pi_A(t)=\Pi_A(\tilde{q}_J(t))$ and $\Pi_J(\tilde{q}_J(t))=T(t)+\Pi_J(t)$ we have

$$\mathcal{W}_\alpha(t)=\alpha[CS(\tilde{q}_J(t))+\Pi_A(\tilde{q}_J(t))+\Pi_J(\tilde{q}_J(t))]+\Pi_A(\tilde{q}_J(t))+(1-\alpha)[\Pi_J(\tilde{q}_J(t))-T(t)]$$

$$=\alpha[CS(\tilde{q}_J(t))+\Pi_A(\tilde{q}_J(t))]+\Pi_A(\tilde{q}_J(t))+\Pi_J(\tilde{q}_J(t))-(1-\alpha)T(t)$$

$$=\mathcal{W}_\alpha(\tilde{q}_J(t))-(1-\alpha)T(t)$$

Therefore, as long as $\alpha<1$, we obtain $\mathcal{W}_\alpha(t)<\mathcal{W}_\alpha(\tilde{q}_J(t))$. This proves (ii).

As for (iii), since the foreign firm gets higher profits under a VER, it is willing to make a higher contribution for a VER than for a tariff. Clearly, the domestic firm is indifferent among the two policies. As a result, total contributions are higher under a VER than under a tariff. ■

Each firm's output under the tariff t is equal to its output under the VER $\tilde{q}_J(t)$. Thus, the only difference between these two trade policies is that the VER transfers tariff revenue to the foreign firm in terms of higher profits which find their way into contributions. The condition $\alpha<1$ means that the government values one dollar contribution more than one dollar in tariff revenue (perhaps due to the greater flexibility it enjoys in using contributions relative to domestic surplus) and hence prefers a VER to a tariff. The government can expect the foreign firm to transfer the tariff revenue in its contribution since the government can threaten to institute a tariff instead of a VER. Note that only result (ii) is affected if $\alpha<1$ does not hold. Result (iii) holds even if $\alpha>1$. However, the government prefers tariff revenue to the foreign firm's contribution when $\alpha>1$ and the political economy motive works in the opposite direction.

5.2. FDI deterring motive for a VER

Suppose now that the foreign firm can switch from exporting to FDI. Since the possibility of FDI constrains the government's choice set, we first define the maximum protection levels the government can implement under the two instruments. Let q^F be the VER level that satisfies

$$\Pi_J(q^F)\equiv\pi^D-F$$

We call q^F the FDI deterring VER since a VER slightly stricter than q^F induces FDI by the foreign firm. Similarly, we define the FDI deterring tariff by the following equation

$$\Pi_J(t^F)\equiv\pi^D-F$$

We have seen in Section 5.1 that the magnitude of α affects the government's preferences over a tariff and a VER. To suppress the political economy motive, assume $\alpha=1$ to make a tariff and a VER perfectly equivalent in the absence of FDI possibilities. Let $\mathcal{W}_1(t)$ denote $\mathcal{W}_\alpha(t)$ when $\alpha=1$. Note that $\mathcal{W}_1(t)=\mathcal{W}_1(\tilde{q}_J(t))$ (see the proof of Proposition 3).[11] Note that when $\alpha=1$, the government is indifferent between a dollar collected in contributions and an increase in domestic surplus worth a dollar. In order to ease the exposition of the FDI deterring motive, we introduce a hypothetical total surplus function $W(q_J)$ where W: $[0, q^D]\to\mathfrak{R}_+$. This function denotes the total surplus in the common agency game (i.e. sum of the three players utilities) under two assumptions. First, in order to neutralize the political economy motive it assumes $\alpha=1$. Second, it ignores the possibility of FDI by the foreign firm. This function helps us characterize the $\mathcal{W}_1$ function in the following way: (i) $\mathcal{W}_1(q_J)\equiv W(q_J)$ if $q_J\geq q^F$, (ii) $\mathcal{W}_1(\tilde{q}_J(t))\equiv W(\tilde{q}_J(t))$ if $t\leq t^F$, and (iii) $\mathcal{W}_1(q_J)\equiv W(q^D)$-$F$ if $q_J<q^F$ or $t>t^F$. Under cases (i) and (ii) trade restrictions do not induce FDI by the foreign firm and the W function gives the total s/urplus as a function of the foreign firm's output. In case (iii) trade policies are restrictive enough to induce FDI by the foreign firm. As a result of FDI, total surplus drops below the free trade level by the amount F (the fixed cost of FDI). The next lemma states an important property of the function $W(q_J)$.

Lemma 3. *If $\alpha=1$, then $W(q_J)$ is decreasing in the foreign firm's output q_J.*

An immediate implication is that the FDI deterring VER q^F maximizes total

[11] We thank the referee for this suggestion, which significantly improved the readability of the paper.

surplus among all VERs. Similarly, the FDI deterring tariff t^F also maximizes total surplus among all tariffs. Further, from Proposition 1, an equilibrium trade policy maximizes total surplus. Thus, to derive the equilibrium trade policy we need only compare total surplus under the two FDI deterring policies: the VER q^F and the tariff t^F.

Proposition 3. *If* $\alpha = 1$, *then the government implements the FDI deterring VER* q^F.

Proof. From Lemma 3, $W(q_J)$ is decreasing in q_J. In order to show that $W(q^F) > W(\tilde{q}_J(t^F))$, it is sufficient to show that $q^F < \tilde{q}_J(t^F)$. Note that:

$$\begin{aligned}\Pi_J(t^F) &= [p(q_A(\tilde{q}_J(t^F)) + \tilde{q}_J(t^F)) - t^F]\tilde{q}_J(t^F)\\ &< p(q_A(\tilde{q}_J(t^F)) + \tilde{q}_J(t^F))\tilde{q}_J(t^F)\\ &= \Pi_J(\tilde{q}_J(t^F)).\end{aligned}$$

Since $\Pi_J(t^F) = \Pi_J(q^F) = \pi^D$, we obtain $\Pi_J(q^F) < \Pi_J(\tilde{q}_J(t^F))$. From Lemma 2, we know Π_J is increasing in q_J. Therefore, $q^F < \tilde{q}_J(t^F)$. ■

Fig. 2 shows the intuition behind the result by utilizing the function $W(q_J)$. The function $W(q_J)$ shows the negative relationship between the total surplus of the three players and the foreign firm's output level q_J (Lemma 3). If the VER $\bar{q}_J \in V$ restricts the foreign firm's output below q^F, the foreign firm switches from exporting to FDI and total surplus drops to $\mathcal{W}_1(\bar{q}_J) = W(q^D) - F$, the free trade level of surplus minus the fixed cost F. Thus, the VER q^F yields the highest total surplus among the set of all feasible VERs $\mathcal{W}_1(q^F) = W(q^F)$. Note further that the foreign firm produces the same level of output under VER $\tilde{q}_J(t^F)$ as it does under the tariff t^F. Since $W(q_J)$ is strictly decreasing in q_J, the VER $\tilde{q}_J(t^F)$ must yield the same total surplus as the FDI deterring tariff t^F: $\mathcal{W}_1(t^F) = W(\tilde{q}(t^F))$. However, what distinguishes the two instruments is that, unlike the VER $\tilde{q}_J(t^F)$, the tariff t^F increases the foreign firm's marginal cost. Consequently, the foreign firm captures a higher share of the domestic market under the tariff t^F relative to the VER q^F. What the foreign firm loses in increased costs under the tariff relative to the VER, it must make up through increased sales to refrain from doing FDI. This increased market share of the foreign firm under the tariff t^F translates into a milder protection (lower market share) for the domestic firm. In other words, the VER allows the government to attain the highest total surplus $\mathcal{W}_1(q^F) = W(q^F)$ by implementing protection levels in the range $(\tilde{q}_J(t^F), q^F)$, which is not possible under a tariff.

Before turning to a more general result, we briefly note that it is easy to calculate the two firms' contributions explicitly: $C_A = F - (\Pi_G(q^F) - \Pi_G(q^D))$ and

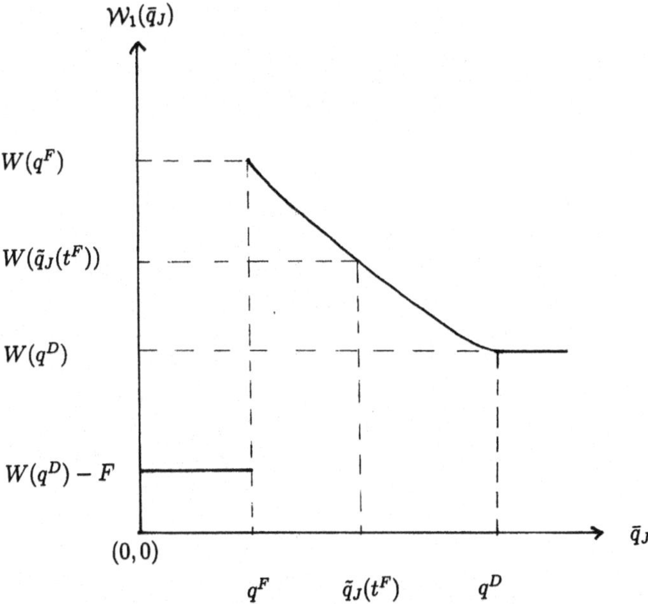

Fig. 2. The optimal VER policy and the FDI deterring motive.

$C_J = 0$ as q^F and q^D maximize $\Pi_A + \Pi_G$ and $\Pi_J + \Pi_G$ respectively, and condition (i) in Proposition 1 is not binding.

5.3. A general result

Now, we investigate the equilibrium trade policy for any arbitrary α. First, we define a function which helps us construct an intuitive decomposition formula of the total surplus function. From the previous section, we know the relevant policy choices are those that do not induce FDI and these lie in the set $[q^F, q^D] \cup [0, t^F]$. Let $Q_J: [q^F, q^D] \cup [0, t^F] \to [q^F, q^D]$ be such that $Q_J(a) = a$ if $a \in [q^F, q^D]$, and $Q_J(a) = \tilde{q}_J(a)$ if $a \in [0, t^F]$. When the government's trade policy a is a tariff, this function simply translates the tariff to an equivalent VER, in the sense that the foreign firm's output is equal under the two policies. On the other hand, when the trade policy a is a VER, this function is simply the VER level. Since we assume Cournot competition on the product market, the domestic firm's output q_A as well as profits Π_A depend only on q_J: as long as two different trade policies result in the same level of output by the foreign firm, the domestic firm is indifferent among them.

Lemma 4. *The total surplus function* $\mathcal{W}_\alpha$: $V \to \Re^+$ *satisfies the following properties*:

(i) *for any* $a \notin [q^F, q^D] \cup [0, t^F]$, $\mathcal{W}_\alpha(a) = \mathcal{W}_\alpha(q^D) - F$, *and*
(ii) *for any* $a \in [q^F, q^D] \cup [0, t^F]$,

$$\mathcal{W}_\alpha(a) = \alpha W(Q_J(a)) + (1 - \alpha)[\Pi_A(Q_J(a)) + \Pi_J(Q_J(a)) - T(a)]. \tag{8}$$

Since once FDI happens, trade policy becomes ineffectual, we restrict attention to only those policies that do not solicit FDI (case (ii) above). As we have seen in Section 5.2, the first term of $W_\alpha(a)$ captures the FDI deterring motive for a VER. The contents of the second term in brackets describe the profits of the two firms. Note that $\Pi_J(t) = \Pi_J(Q(t)) - T(t)$, and $\Pi_J(Q(t)) = \Pi_J(Q(t)) - T(Q(t))$ since $T(Q(t)) = 0$. Since the government can extract higher contributions from the firms by increasing their profits, the second term captures the political economy motive for a VER. When $\alpha = 1$, only the first term remains whereas when $\alpha \neq 1$ both motives are present.[12] We have already isolated the two motives for a VER and explained the intuition behind each of them in Section 5.1 Section 5.2. The only remaining issue is how the two motives interact with one another. Proposition 4 below argues that when $\alpha \leq 1$, the two motives reinforce each other and the government implements the VER q^F.

Proposition 4. *If* $\alpha \leq 1$, *then, the government implements the FDI deterring VER* q^F.

Proof. Since $\alpha \leq 1$, by the political economy motive, we know that a tariff will never be implemented in equilibrium. In fact, the second term of Eq. (8) is maximized by setting the term $T(a) = 0$ for each $Q_J(a)$. Thus, we can confine our attention to VERs that belong to the interval $[q^F, q^D]$ since $T(a) =$ for any VER. We know that the first term, $\alpha W(q_J)$, is maximized at $q_J = q^F$ (Lemma 3). We now show that the second term is also maximized at $q_J = q^F$. Since $1 - \alpha \geq 0$, it suffices to show that $\Pi_A(q_J) + \Pi_J(q_J)$ is maximized at q^F. However, from Lemma 1, we know that industry profits are strictly decreasing in $\bar{q}_J$, and that in equilibrium, the VER constraint binds so that $q_J = \bar{q}_J$. Thus, $\bar{q}_J = q^F$ maximizes $\Pi_A(\bar{q}_J) + \Pi_J(\bar{q}_J)$ over $[q^F, q^D]$. This completes the proof. ■

Proposition 4 shows that for $\alpha \leq 1$ both the political economy motive and the FDI deterring motive lead to the dominance of a VER over a tariff. As before, it is

[12] Note that when the trade policy action is a VER, the government collects no tariff revenue so that $T(a)$ equals 0.

easy to show that the contributions of the two firms are as follows: $C_A = F - (\Pi_G(q^F) - \Pi_G(q^D))$ and $C_J = 0$. This is because q^F and q^D maximize $\Pi_A + \Pi_G$ and $\Pi_J + \Pi_G$ respectively and condition (i) in proposition 1 is not binding.

What happens when $\alpha > 1$? No definite answer can be found here. When $\alpha > 1$, government prefers tariff revenues to contributions and the two motives clash (the two terms in Eq. (8)). While the tariff is attractive because it yields revenues at the expense of contributions, it is not as effective a tool for deterring FDI as a VER and if FDI realizes, tariff revenues disappear completely. Thus when α is close to 1, it is likely that the government the will still adopt the VER q^F – in this situation, the government views contributions and tariff revenue relatively similarly and the FDI deterring motive dominates. However, if α is significantly larger than 1, a tariff may be selected as an equilibrium trade policy. We should note that such a reversal is unlikely since the government is always free to donate its contributions to domestic consumers.

6. Conclusion

In this paper, we endogenize the formation of trade policy in a duopoly comprised of a foreign firm and a domestic firm by employing a common agency game. The two firms make contributions to the domestic government contingent on its trade policy actions. We show that the government institutes a VER instead of a tariff due to two separate reasons. First, if the government weighs dollar contributions relatively more than domestic surplus, then it prefers a VER to a tariff because the former results in a higher level of industry contributions (political economy motive for a VER). Second, the VER proves more effective in deterring FDI than a tariff. For any given tariff level, the government can find a VER that increases the foreign firm's exporting profits without altering the domestic firm's profits, so that the foreign firm is less inclined to do FDI. Therefore, FDI plays a critical role in determining not only the level of trade protection (as has been recognized), but also the choice between alternative trade policy instruments (the contribution here). This role suggests that trade policy results derived under the assumption of no possibility of FDI need reconsideration.

We have restricted attention to the choice between a tariff and a VER. Of course, one may also consider the case where the government has a wider selection of policy tools at its disposal. In our framework, these possibilities are redundant. Consider the case of an import quota. A quota is a quantitative restriction like a VER but the government sells the right to import foreign goods (import licenses) to local agents. Thus, the foreign firm loses profits under a quota relative to a VER. Consequently, a switch from a VER to a quota creates an incentive for FDI, and also transfers the sales revenue of import licenses from the contribution account to the revenue account much the way a tariff does.

Acknowledgements

We thank Bill Ethier, Ron Jones, Pravin Krishna, Peter Rosendorff, Shumpei Takemori, and seminar participants at Kobe University, SMU, and the Midwest International Economics meetings, Fall 1996 for useful comments. Insightful comments from an anonymous referee, Amy Glass, and associate editor Raquel Fernandez were particularly helpful.

Appendix 1

Proofs of Lemmas

Proof of Lemma 1

Suppose the foreign firm faces a VER $\bar{q}_J < q^D$ on its exports. We will show that the foreign firm will produce the amount $\bar{q}_J$ in a Cournot–Nash equilibrium. Suppose, to the contrary, that there is an equilibrium (q'_J, q'_A) with $q'_J < \bar{q}_J < q^D$. Since the VER constraint is not binding, (q'_J, q'_A) must be an equilibrium for the original economy. This contradicts the assumption that the equilibrium in the original economy is unique. Therefore, it must be that $q_J = \bar{q}_J$. Differentiating $\Pi_A(\bar{q}_J)$ with respect to $\bar{q}_J$, we obtain:

$$\frac{\mathrm{d}\Pi_A}{\mathrm{d}\bar{q}_J} = p' q_A \frac{\mathrm{d}q}{\mathrm{d}\bar{q}_J} + p \frac{\mathrm{d}q_A}{\mathrm{d}\bar{q}_J}$$

$$= \frac{-(p')^2 q_A - p(-p'' q_J - p)}{-(p'' q_J + 2p')} < 0$$

where we made use of Eqs. (5) and (7). Similarly, differentiating $\Pi_J(\bar{q}_J)$ with respect to $\bar{q}_J$, we obtain:

$$\frac{\mathrm{d}\Pi_J}{\mathrm{d}\bar{q}_J} = \frac{-(p')^2 q_J}{-(p'' q_J + 2p')} + p > 0 .$$

Finally, we investigate the effect of an increase in $\bar{q}_J$ on the joint profits.

$$\frac{\mathrm{d}\Pi_A}{\mathrm{d}\bar{q}_J} + \frac{\mathrm{d}\Pi_J}{\mathrm{d}\bar{q}_J} = \frac{-(p')^2 q_A - p(-p'' q_J - p') - (p')^2 q_J - p(p'' q_J + 2p')}{-(p'' q_J + 2p')}$$

$$= \frac{-(p')^2 q - p(-p')}{-(p'' q_J + 2p')} = \frac{-(p')(p' q + p)}{-(p'' q_J + 2p')} \leq 0 .$$

The last inequality follows since q is greater than a monopolist's output level (if

$\bar{q}_J=0$, then q is a monopolist's output level, and q is increasing in $\bar{q}_j$), and $p'q+p=0$ is the optimization condition for a monopolist. ■

Proof of Lemma 2

Totally differentiating the first order conditions yields the following system:

$$\begin{pmatrix} 2p'+p''\tilde{q}_J & p'+p''\tilde{q}_J \\ p'+p''\tilde{q}_A & 2p'+p''\tilde{q}_A \end{pmatrix}\begin{pmatrix} \mathrm{d}\tilde{q}_J \\ \mathrm{d}j\tilde{q}_A \end{pmatrix}=\begin{pmatrix} 1 \\ 0 \end{pmatrix}\mathrm{d}t\,.$$

Let the 2×2 matrix on the LHS be D. The determinant of D, $|D|$, is calculated as follows:

$$|D|=(2p'+p''\tilde{q}_J)(2p'+p''\tilde{q}_A)-(p'+p''\tilde{q}_J)(p'+p''\tilde{q}_A)$$

$$=p'[(p'+p''\tilde{q}_J)+(p'+p''\tilde{q}_A)+p']>0\,.$$

where we used the assumption of strategic substitutability to determine the sign of $|D|$. Applying Cramer's rule, we have:

$$\frac{\mathrm{d}\tilde{q}_J}{\mathrm{d}t}=\frac{2p'+p''\tilde{q}_A}{|D|}<0\,,$$

$$\frac{\mathrm{d}\tilde{q}_A}{\mathrm{d}t}=\frac{-(p'+p''\tilde{q})}{|D|}>0\,,$$

$$\frac{\mathrm{d}\tilde{q}}{\mathrm{d}t}=\frac{p'}{|D|}<0\,.$$

Let $\Pi_J(t)=(p(\tilde{q}(t))-t)\tilde{q}_J$, and $\Pi_A(t)=p(\tilde{q}(t))\tilde{q}_J$. Differentiating the foreign firm's profits with respect to t we have:

$$\frac{\mathrm{d}\Pi_J}{\mathrm{d}t}=(p-t)\frac{\mathrm{d}\tilde{q}_J}{\mathrm{d}t}-\tilde{q}_J+\tilde{q}_Jp'\frac{d\tilde{q}}{dt}$$

$$=\frac{(p-t)(2p'+p''\tilde{q}_A)}{|D|}-\tilde{q}_J+\frac{\tilde{q}_J(p')^2}{|D|}$$

$$=\frac{-p'\tilde{q}_J(p'+p''\tilde{q}_A)+\tilde{q}_J(p')^2}{|D|}-\tilde{q}_J$$

$$=\frac{-p'\tilde{q}-J(p'+p''\tilde{q}_A)}{|D|}-\tilde{q}_J<0\,.$$

where we make use of the first order condition for the foreign firm to obtain the expression in the third line. Similarly,

$$\frac{d\Pi_A}{dt} = p\frac{d\tilde{q}_A}{dt} + \tilde{q}_A p'\frac{d\tilde{q}}{dt}$$

$$= -p\tilde{q}_A\frac{d\tilde{q}_A}{dt} + \tilde{q}_A p'\frac{d\tilde{q}}{dt}$$

$$= p'\tilde{q}_A\left(\frac{d\tilde{q}}{dt} - \frac{d\tilde{q}_A}{dt}\right) = p'\tilde{q}_A \times \frac{d\tilde{q}_J}{dt} > 0 .$$

Again, we make use of the first order condition for the domestic firm. ■

Proof of Lemma 3

First note that domestic welfare $\Pi_G(a) = CS(a) + \Pi_A(a) + T(a)$ when $\alpha = 1$. Thus, regardless of the choice of the trade policy instrument the sum of $\Pi_G(a)$ and $\Pi_J(a)$ is equivalent to $S(q_J) = \int_0^{q(q_J)} p(q')dq'$, where $q(q_J)$ is the total industry output given the foreign firm produces q_J. Thus, we have $W(q_J) = \Pi_A(q_J) + \Pi_J(q_J) + \Pi_G(q_J) = \Pi_A(q_J) + S(q_J)$, so that we simply need to calculate the following:

$$\frac{dW}{dq_J} = \frac{d\Pi_A}{dq_J} + \frac{dS}{dq_J}$$

$$= \left(p'\frac{dq}{dq_J}q_A + p\frac{dq_A}{dq_J}\right) + p\frac{dq}{dq_J}$$

$$= \frac{-(p')^2 q_A - p(-p''q_J - p')}{-(p''q_J + 2p')} + \frac{-pp'}{-(p''q_J + 2p')}$$

$$= \frac{-(p')^2 q_A + pp''q_J}{-(p''q_J + 2p')} .$$

To move from the first line to the second line, we used (9) as well as the final equation in the proof of Lemma 1. Now, from the first order condition for the domestic firm's profit maximization, we have: $p'q_A + p = 0$. Substituting $p'q_A = -p$ into the above formula gives:

$$\frac{dW}{dq_J} = \frac{p(p' + p''q_J)}{-(p''q_J + 2p')} < 0 .$$

where the last inequality follows from the assumption of strategic substitutes. ■

Proof of Lemma 4

If $a \notin [q^F, q^D] \cup [0, t^F]$, the foreign firm does FDI. Once FDI takes place the total surplus is equivalent to that under free trade minus the fixed cost of FDI: i.e., $\mathcal{W}_\alpha(a) = \mathcal{W}_\alpha(q^D) - F$ (under $a = q^D$, a free trade allocation is attained). On the other hand, if $a \in [q^F, q^D] \cup [0, t^F]$ we can use the result derived in the previous subsection to write:

$$\mathcal{W}_\alpha(a) = \alpha[CS(a) + \Pi_A(a) + T(a)] + \Pi_A(a) + \Pi_J(a)$$

$$= \alpha[CS(a) + \Pi_A(a) + T(a) + \Pi_J(a)] + \alpha\Pi_A(a)$$

$$+ (1 - \alpha)[\Pi_A(a) + \Pi_J(a)]$$

$$= \alpha W(Q_J(a)) + (1 - \alpha)[\Pi_A(Q_J(a)) + \Pi_J(Q_J(a)) - T(a)]\,. \qquad \blacksquare$$

References

Bernheim, B.D., Peleg, B., Whinston, M.D., 1987. Coalition-Proof Nash equilibria I, concepts. Journal of Economic Theory 42, 1–12.

Bernheim, B.D., Whinston, M.D., 1986. Menu auctions, resource allocation, and economic influence. Quarterly Journal of Economics 101, 1–31.

Bhagwati, J.N., Brecher, R.A., Dinopoulos, E., Srinivisan, T.N., 1987. Quid pro quo foreign investment and welfare: A political-economy-theoretic model. Journal of Development Economics 27, 127–138.

Bhagwati, J.N., Dinopoulos, E., Wong, K.-Y., 1992. Quid pro quo foreign investment. American Economic Review 82, 186–190.

Bulow, J., Geanakoplos, J., Klemperer, P., 1985. Multimarket oligopoly, strategic substitutes and complements. Journal of Political Economy 93, 488–511.

Ethier, W.J., 1989. Voluntary export restraints. In: Takayama, A., Ohyama, M., Ohta, H. (Eds.), Trade, Policy, and International Adjustment, Academic Press, San Diego.

Grossman, G.M., Helpman, E., 1994. Protection for sale. American Economic Review 84, 833–850.

Grossman, G.M., Helpman, E., 1996. Foreign investment with endogenous protection. In: Feenstra, R.C., Grossman, G.M., Irwin, D.A. (Eds.), The Political Economy of Trade Policy, Papers in Honor of Jagdish Bhagwati, The MIT Press, Cambridge.

Harris, R., 1985. Why voluntary export restraints are voluntary. Canadian Journal of Economics 18, 799–809.

Hillman, A.L., Ursprung, H.W., 1988. Domestic politics, foreign interests and international trade policy. American Economic Review 51, 59–79.

Hillman, A.L., Ursprung, H.W., 1993. Multinational firms, political competition, and international trade policy. International Economic Review 34, 347–363.

Itoh, M., Ono, Y., 1982. Tariffs, quotas, and market structure. Quarterly Journal of Economics 97, 295–305.

Itoh, M., Ono, Y., 1984. Tariffs versus quotas under duopoly of heterogenous goods. Journal of International Economics 17, 359–373.

Krishna, K., 1989. Trade restrictions as facilitating practices. Journal of International Economics 26, 251–270.

Laussel, D., Le Breton, M., 1995. The structure of equilibrium payoffs in common agency, mimeo.

Levinsohn, J.A., 1989. Strategic trade policy when firms can invest abroad: when are tariffs and quotas equivalent?. Journal of International Economics 27, 129–146.

Mayer, W., Riezman, R.G., 1987. Endogenous choice of trade policy instruments. Journal of International Economics 23, 377–381.

Rosendorff, B.P., 1996a. Voluntary export restraints, antidumping procedure, and domestic politics. American Economic Review 86, 544–561.

Rosendorff, B.P., 1996b. Endogenous trade restrictions and domestic political pressure In: Feenstra, R.C., Grossman, G.M., Irwin, D.A. (Eds.), The Political Economy of Trade Policy, Papers in Honor of Jagdish Bhagwati, The MIT Press, Cambridge.

Takemori, S., Tsumagari, M., 1997. A political economy theory of foreign investment, an alternative approach, Keio University and Boston University, mimeo.

Tsumagari, M., Yanagawa, N., 1997. Political decision of trade policies and the cost for lobbying. Boston University and the University of Tokyo.

Chapter 24

FDI policies under shared factor markets[#]

Amy Jocelyn Glass[a], Kamal Saggi[b,*]

[a]*Department of Economics, Ohio State University, 1945 North High Street, Columbus, OH 43210-1172, USA*

[b]*Department of Economics, Southern Methodist University, Dallas, TX 75275-0496, USA*

Received 20 May 1997; received in revised form 21 May 1998; accepted 2 July 1998

Abstract

We examine the consequences of foreign direct investment (FDI) policies in a general equilibrium setting with several oligopolistic industries. By shifting labor demand across countries, FDI raises the wage in the host country and lowers the wage in the source country, thereby raising profits of source country firms at the expense of host country firms. The extent of cross-ownership of firms, the relative number of firms and the relative supply of skilled labor alter the impact of FDI policy on national welfare. The tension between profits and wages determines whether the optimal policy is designed to encourage FDI.

Keywords: Foreign direct investment; Strategic trade policy; Oligopoly; Tax; Subsidy

JEL classification: F12; F13; F23

1. Introduction

The global sales by foreign affiliates of multinational firms now exceed worldwide exports of goods and services (see the United Nations *World Investment Report* 1995 and 1996 (United Nations, 1995 United Nations, 1996)). Many firms are choosing to serve foreign markets through establishing foreign production subsidiaries rather than producing domestically and exporting. In addition, many

*Corresponding author. Tel.: +1 214 7683274; fax: +1 214 7681821.
E-mail address: ksaggi@mail.smu.edu (K. Saggi)

[#] This chapter was originally appeared in *Journal of International Economics* **49**, 309–332. © 1999 Elsevier Science B.V.

potential host countries actively pursue multinationals, offering incentives to establish production subsidiaries, while many source countries seem to fear the erosion of their production base as production is shifted abroad. How does FDI affect profits and factor earnings in host and source countries? What is the optimal policy toward FDI for host and source countries?

Despite the increasing importance of FDI, the impact of FDI policies on the countries involved has received relatively little attention in the trade literature. Most of the existing literature examining the welfare impact of capital flows assumes perfectly competitive markets (see Ruffin, 1984 for survey) even though multinational firms operate mostly in oligopolistic industries (Markusen, 1995; Brainard, 1997). Furthermore, we are interested more in the consequences of production shifting involved under FDI.

Our paper shares with Levinsohn (1989) a view of FDI as moving production abroad and also shares the point that introducing FDI into strategic trade models can lead to fundamentally new conclusions. Levinsohn (1989) showed that if FDI by foreign firms is possible, a tariff and a quota are equivalent instruments even in a model of imperfect competition. This equivalence arises as the possibility of FDI eliminates the asymmetric foreign supply response under the two policy instruments obtained in the absence of FDI. We demonstrate that a strategic rationale for FDI policies arises from the production shifting effects of FDI in the presence of oligopolistic competition.[1]

In this paper, we explore the welfare consequences of FDI where firms operate in oligopolistic markets. These firms establish production facilities abroad due to lower costs there (inclusive of any tax or subsidy to FDI). Factor prices and the extent of FDI are determined in general equilibrium. As in Dixit and Grossman (1986), many high technology industries use a factor (skilled labor) available in fixed supply and firms compete in quantities. We add FDI, so firms shift production to the low wage country until wage equalization (net of any tax or subsidy) removes further incentives for FDI.[2] We derive the optimal policies (tax or subsidy) toward FDI from both the host and the source country perspective.

Our model captures the tension that FDI creates between the interests of the workers and local firms. Inward FDI generates increased labor demand, which benefits workers through raising wages in the host country but consequently damages the profits of host firms. The reverse implications hold for the source

[1]Rodríguez-Clare (1996) argues that multinationals benefit the host country when they generate linkage effects beyond those generated by the local firms that they displace. Multinationals may even benefit local producers by expanding the set of intermediate goods. Haddad and Harrison (1993) reject the hypothesis of spillovers from FDI to the productivity of local firms in Morocco. In our paper, multinationals and local firms always have opposing interests since the presence of multinationals raises rather than lowers the costs of local firms.

[2]Lucas (1993) shows high costs in the source country create a push while Coughlin et al. (1991) shows lower wages in the host country (state) create a pull in generating incentives for FDI.

country: profits rise but wages fall. This tension between wages and profits implies that government policies toward FDI benefit one group at the expense of the other.

The view that shifting production abroad raises host wages at the expense of source wages is widely held. To mention a few examples, in March 1996, General Motors employees in Dayton, Ohio went on strike to protest G.M. shifting production to low wage countries. In October 1995, Boeing employees in Kansas, Washington, and Oregon went on strike to protest Boeing shifting production to China. More formal empirical evidence supports the view that the entry of multinationals raises wages in host countries (see Harrison, 1994 and Aitken et al., 1996).[3]

This detrimental effect of FDI on the source wage is countered by the increased profitability of source firms (hence G.M. and Boeing's desire to shift production abroad). In oligopolistic markets, the increased profitability of source firms comes at the expense of host firms. Thus host firms are hurt due to FDI not only because competition increases (partial equilibrium effect) but also due to higher factor prices (general equilibrium effect).

Brander and Spencer (1985) demonstrated that trade policies can shift profits across countries under imperfect competition. We confirm that policies designed to influence FDI have the ability to shift profits across countries as well. FDI raises the costs of host firms and simultaneously lowers the costs of source firms by transferring demand for the fixed factor across countries. While the rational for export subsidies is sensitive to a number of assumptions, we demonstrate that the rational for strategic FDI subsidies is robust.

Dixit and Grossman (1986) argued that if several symmetric oligopolies all use a factor in fixed supply, uniform export subsidies may fail to improve source welfare. Instead of promoting source firms, export subsidies bid up the wage of the factor in fixed supply, offsetting the effect of export subsidies on market shares and thus profits. We show, however, that the problem Dixit and Grossman describe does not arise when subsidizing FDI. *The increase in output that results from a subsidy raises costs at home under exporting whereas it raises costs abroad under FDI.*

Even if a source country were to subsidize exports, as long as firms have the option of FDI, the original Brander-Spencer argument survives the Dixit-Grossman criticism. The point is that a subsidy which causes firms to expand their output raises the source wage thereby creating an incentive for FDI. The increased labor demand in the host country raises the costs of host firms thereby shifting rents to host firms. Thus, the important point is not that policies explicitly target FDI but rather that firms have the option of undertaking FDI in response to wage conditions.

[3]In what follows, for the sake of brevity, we refer to the source country as just source and the host country as just host.

The Brander and Spencer result is also sensitive to firm behavior, the number of firms, and cross-ownership of firms. Eaton and Grossman (1986) argued that export taxes are required if firms behave as Bertrand/price-setting rather than Cournot/quantity-setting oligopolists. Dixit (1984) argued that export taxes are required if the number of firms is large. Lee (1990); Miyagiwa (1992) and Dick (1993) argued international cross shareholding reduces the magnitude of optimal export subsidies substantially.[4] We also consider more than one firm in each country (in the base model), cross-ownership of firms (in an extension) and Bertrand behavior (in the appendix). We find that the basic nature of our argument is robust to these preceding criticisms of the Brander-Spencer argument.

As mentioned above, a subsidy to FDI raises wages abroad while lowering wages at home. The adjustment in wages lowers the costs of source firms and consequently shifts profits in their direction. Given the trade-off between wages and profits, the optimal source policy depends upon the parameters in an intuitive fashion. When the ratio of domestic to host firms is not large relative to the ratio of domestic to host skilled labor supply, the optimal source policy is a subsidy to outward FDI. Under this scenario, the extent of outward FDI is small (since autarkic wages are approximately the same in the two countries), so the subsidy payments needed to achieve a gain in source profits at the expense of host firms are relatively small. However, when the extent of FDI is large because the autarkic source wage is high (due to high demand for and low supply of skilled labor), the total subsidy payments required will exceed the benefits obtained by shifting profits from rivals. The optimal source policy is then a tax on outward FDI.

Our investigation of the optimal host country policy toward FDI in the base model reveals that the host can raise welfare by taxing FDI. Government policies in many countries such as Japan, South Korea, and Brazil (historically or currently), have actively discriminated against FDI to encourage the development of local firms. Many emerging markets in South-East Asia (Malaysia, Philippines and Thailand) and India still do not allow free entry of multinational firms in order to protect local firms. FDI in Japan is negligible, with McDonalds and General Electric the key exceptions; Japan maintains practices that discourage foreign investors (*The Economist* March 1, 1997). The policies adopted may not literally be taxes but such policies act like taxes in discouraging FDI.

On the other hand, many less developed countries (LDCs) now appear eager to attract FDI (although historically many of them did shut out FDI).[5] Economic reform in many formerly communist countries has added to the list of countries vying for FDI (United Nations *World Investment Report*, (United Nations, 1995)).

[4]See also Markusen and Venables (1988); Harris (1989) and Qiu (1994, 1995) for entry, retaliation, asymmetric information, uncertainty and related concerns.

[5]Incidentally, tax treatment of multinationals also varies within an economy. For an analysis of the impact of inter-state variation in tax treatment of multinationals and flows of FDI within the U.S., see Hines (1996).

Frank (1997) provides details of recent policy changes in favor of FDI in the Eastern European countries. Ford, enticed by tax incentives, recently opened an assembly plant in Belarus; the picture accompanying one article (The Economist July 26, 1997) is quite telling: a farmer hauling a wagon-load of hay with two horses is labelled "Ford's competition takes a test drive". Even Japan, known as a hostile environment for FDI, is contemplating encouraging FDI in Okinawa, a southern island with little local manufacturing (*The Economist* July 19, 1997). The Belarus and Okinawa (and other LDC-like) scenarios involve *government objectives that are more concerned with improving local factor earnings than the negative impact higher factor prices would have on local producers.*

We believe the explanation for this cross-country variation in FDI policies involves variation in the state of development of the local industries or in the extent of foreign ownership of local firms. LDCs usually have small or non-existent local firms in industries that are dominated by multinationals since brand names, R&D, and reputation are of central importance in such industries (Markusen, 1995 Brainard, 1997). Furthermore, in many small open economies, a substantial fraction of the ownership of firms may belong to other countries. China illustrates the dividing line nicely as its local industries are developing to the point where they are pressuring the Chinese government to remove its FDI incentives (*The Economist* March 1, 1997).

If the economic environment of a country is such that profits of local firms are unimportant either (because local industries are extremely underdeveloped so that national income comprises mostly of wage earnings or because local profits do not accrue to domestic agents), the country has an incentive to subsidize inward FDI. The loss in profits incurred due to the increased entry of multinationals is small relative to the gain accruing to workers. We demonstrate that if the host country owns a small enough share of local oligopolists, subsidies to inward FDI by the host country do indeed raise host country welfare. Such subsidies may also benefit the source if part of the ownership of host country firms lies with a third country. Of course, such policies improve source and host welfare at the expense of the third country.

Since substantial cross-ownership of firms exists across developed countries, we extend our model to consider the consequences of cross-ownership of firms. The presence of cross-ownership lowers the optimal outward FDI subsidy. As in the case of substantial third country ownership of its firms, under sufficient cross-ownership, the host country can raise its welfare (net of subsidy payments) by subsidizing inward FDI. However, the presence of cross-ownership reduces the profit-shifting effects: the damage to host firms is partially offset by the benefit to source firms. The key difference from the case of third country ownership of host firms is that with cross-ownership, the interests of the source and the host must conflict.

Section 2 finds a Cournot oligopoly equilibrium when a common factor is available in fixed supply and examines the impact of various FDI policies on the key endogenous variables. Section 3 determines the welfare effects of FDI policies for each country. Section 4 presents extensions of our base model involving cross-ownership and third country ownership of firms. Section 5 concludes. The Appendix provides the details for Bertrand behavior.

2. Model

Our model closely parallels the model developed in Dixit and Grossman (1986) but introduces the potential for FDI. All goods are produced using only skilled labor, which is available in fixed supply in each country. The economy is composed of $n \geq 1$ industries indexed by $j = 1, 2, \ldots, n$.[6] One unit of good j is produced using one unit of skilled labor. The market for skilled labor is competitive; enough different industries hire skilled labor that each firm views the wage as given.

Dixit and Grossman (1986) include a low-technology sector where a numeraire good is produced by unskilled workers in a perfectly competitive market. The unit labor requirement for unskilled workers in the low-technology industry is normalized to one. Since the price of the low-technology good is normalized to one, the wage for unskilled workers is one, regardless of export subsidies. Any identical unit labor requirement for unskilled workers across high-technology industries, combined with otherwise symmetric industries, makes uniform export subsidies ineffective in raising domestic welfare. We set the unit labor requirement for unskilled workers in high-technology industries to zero, but a positive value that is identical across industries would not alter our results.

For the bulk of their model, Dixit and Grossman (1986) assume the host wage is exogenous: the host does not face a common factor market in the high-technology sector.[7] However, since we consider shifting labor demand abroad through FDI, we consider the general equilibrium consequences on the host as well. Adding a host resource constraint causes the host wage to rise as the source wage falls in response to FDI from the source to the host.

We expand the Cournot duopoly case to consider the implications of the number of firms in the industry along the lines of Dixit (1984). Since the allocation of labor demand across countries plays an important role, not only the total number of firms in each industry but the number that are source and the number that are host play important roles as well. In each industry, m identical source firms and M identical host firms produce a homogeneous good for sale to consumers in another

[6] The number of industries plays no important role but n being large does help to justify the assumption that firms take the wage as given.

[7] They do perform an extension introducing a foreign skilled labor constraint that appears to further weaken the profit-shifting role for export subsidies.

location. In a symmetric equilibrium with FDI, each of the m source firms in each industry will be a multinational producing in both countries.

2.1. Output market

Let y_j denote the output of a representative source firm in industry j (so total industry output of source firms is my_j). Let capital letters denote the host analogues of each variable: in particular, the output of a representative host firm in industry j is Y_j (so total industry output of host firms is MY_j). Total output in industry j is $Q_j \equiv my_j + MY_j$, the sum of source and host production by firms in industry j. Let the demand function in some third country be given by $P_j = p_j(Q_j)$ where $p_j'(Q_j) < 0$ and $p_j''(Q_j) \leq 0$.[8]

Each source firm decides whether to produce each unit at home or abroad. Let α_j denote the share of skilled labor demanded abroad by a source firm in industry j, which provides a measure of the extent of FDI. Host firms do not undertake FDI in the source country. FDI seeks lower production costs, so in equilibrium FDI occurs in only one direction.[9]

Suppose source firms in industry j are offered a subsidy σ_j for each unit of output that they produce in the host country.[10] If $\sigma_j > 0$, the subsidy acts like a reduction in the host wage for skilled labor hired by source firms. Note that we do not require $\sigma_j > 0$: negative values are taxes.

The wage for skilled labor in the source country is z and in the host country is Z. The net marginal cost of a source firm in industry j is $c_j \equiv (1 - \alpha_j)z + \alpha_j(Z - \sigma_j)$ and the marginal cost of a host firm is $C \equiv Z$. All firms take the source and host wage for skilled labor as given.

If the source wage is less than the host wage minus the subsidy $z < Z - \sigma_j$, then all production by source firms remains in the source $\alpha_j = 0$. If the source wage is greater than the host wage minus the subsidy $z > Z - \sigma_j$, then all production by source firms occurs in the host $\alpha_j = 1$. Hence, the source wage must equal the host wage minus the subsidy

$$z = Z - \sigma_j \tag{1}$$

for production by source firms to be split across countries $0 < \alpha_j < 1$. The FDI

[8]For the symmetric case and under quasilinear preferences (the standard assumption in this literature), the location of consumption is irrelevant since the resource constraint fixes the price by fixing output in each industry. In the presence of local consumption, welfare would be our welfare measures plus some constant consumer surplus.

[9]Two-way FDI is commonly observed but not addressed in our model, which explains the net flow of FDI.

[10]At the moment, who pays the subsidy is immaterial; we address this issue later.

subsidy places a wedge between the source and host wages.[11] We are interested in how FDI subsidies encourage a greater extent of FDI, which shifts production across countries. We focus on the case where some but not all production is shifted abroad in equilibrium.

As Cournot oligopolists, each firm picks its quantity to maximize its profits, given the quantity chosen by the other firms. The profits of a source firm equal $\pi_j=[p_j-c_j]y_j$ while the profits of a host firm equal $\Pi_j=[p_j-Z]Y_j$. The first order conditions (simplified using $z=Z-\sigma_j$) are[12]

$$\frac{\partial \pi_j}{\partial y_j}=p_j+y_jp_j'-c_j=p_j+y_jp_j'-z=0 \tag{2}$$

$$\frac{\partial \Pi_j}{\partial Y_j}=p_j+Y_jp_j'-Z=0 \tag{3}$$

To completely describe an equilibrium, we also need to specify how the wage in each country is determined. In what follows, we restrict attention to a symmetric equilibrium where all industries are identical and thus source firms split production across countries to the same extent regardless of industry. We examine how FDI policies affect that split.[13]

2.2. Labor market

Only a fixed supply k of skilled labor per industry is available in the source country, so the wage must adjust to equate the demand for skilled labor with the supply of skilled labor.[14] The source labor constraint is

$$(1-\alpha)my=k \tag{4}$$

The source labor constraint relates production of each source firm to the extent of FDI and implicitly the source wage. Similarly, only a fixed supply K of skilled labor per industry is available in the host country. The host labor constraint is

$$\alpha my+MY=K \tag{5}$$

[11] Skilled labor is measured in efficiency units (one skilled worker produces one unit of high-technology output), so the model can be consistent with higher observed source wages (in the absence of any FDI policy) if observed wages are not measured in efficiency units and host skilled labor is less productive than source skilled labor.

[12] All second order conditions are easily verified.

[13] Industries do differ substantially in their extent of FDI. The industries here should be viewed as all being high-tech industries, the kind of industries where FDI is prevalent. Thus, our analysis should capture the impact on a representative high-tech firm.

[14] We keep the number of industries n fixed throughout our analysis so there is no loss of generality in working with the supply of skilled labor per industry.

Adding the source and host labor constraints dictates that the total production of each industry is constant.

$$Q \equiv my + MY = k + K \tag{6}$$

With symmetric industries, the fixed availability of skilled labor in each country *fixes total output* in each industry. This aspect of the model greatly simplifies the analysis since, in equilibrium, price and total output in each industry are unaffected by government policy – only FDI responds to policy and thus FDI affects the equilibrium through the changes in wages induced by FDI.

2.3. General equilibrium

An equilibrium must specify the output of a representative source firm y, the output of a representative host firm Y, the source wage z, the host wage Z, and the extent of FDI α of a representative source firm. Let $\{y^*, Y^*, z^*, Z^*, \alpha^*\}$ denote the solution to the system of equations: the FDI equilibrium condition Eq. (1), the first order conditions Eqs. (2) and (3), and the labor constraints Eqs. (4) and (5). The key parameters are the source skilled labor supply per industry k, the host skilled labor supply per industry K, the number of source firms in each industry m, and the number of host firms in each industry M.

Let $f \equiv m/M$ denote the ratio of source firms to host firms in each industry and $r \equiv k/K$ denote the ratio of skilled labor in the source relative to the host. Abbreviate p for $p(Q^*)$ and p' for the slope of the demand function at the equilibrium industry output Q^* given by Eq. (6), where $p'<0$. Further let $\psi \equiv -p'>0$.

Solving the system of equations gives the equilibrium extent of FDI

$$\alpha^* = \frac{\psi K(f-r) + \sigma f M}{[\sigma M + \psi K(r+1)]f} \tag{7}$$

source wage

$$z^* = \frac{[(f+1)pM - (r+1)\psi K] - \sigma M}{(f+1)M} \tag{8}$$

host wage

$$Z^* = \frac{[(f+1)pM - (r+1)\psi K] + \sigma f M}{(f+1)M} \tag{9}$$

representative source firm output

$$y^* = \frac{\psi K(r+1) + \sigma M}{\psi(f+1)M} \tag{10}$$

and representative host firm output.

$$Y^* = \frac{\psi K(r+1) - \sigma f M}{\psi (f+1) M} \tag{11}$$

Next we investigate the properties of the above equilibrium and then the welfare consequences of FDI policies.

2.4. Equilibrium analysis

FDI exists between asymmetric countries even in the absence of subsidies since autarkic wages would differ, providing the firms facing higher wages an incentive to shift production to the low wage country. Substituting $\sigma=0$ in Eq. (7) gives the initial equilibrium extent of FDI

$$\alpha_0^* = \frac{f-r}{f(r+1)} > 0 \Leftrightarrow f > r \tag{12}$$

Therefore, in the absence of any subsidy to FDI, FDI occurs $\alpha_0^* > 0$ iff $f > r$, when host skilled labor (measured in efficiency units) per firm is higher abroad than at home.

Since we are interested in equilibria in which FDI occurs from the source to the host, we assume $f > r$ (satisfied trivially by labeling the countries accordingly). In the absence of FDI, the host wage would be lower than the source wage due to lower demand for skilled labor relative to the fixed supply. Since an incentive for FDI exists as long as wages abroad are lower, FDI equalizes wages across the two countries in the absence of any taxes or subsidies to FDI.

The extent of FDI, Eq. (7), increases with the number of source firms relative to host firms. The greater source labor demand due to the increased number of source firms puts upward pressure on the source wage, which encourages source firms to engage in more FDI. Since part of the increase in labor demand is shifted abroad through FDI, host wages increase. Thus source wages Eq. (8) as well as host wages Eq. (9) increase with the relative number of source firms. An increase in the relative number of source firms reduces the output of each firm, Eqs. (10) and (11). As noted in Eq. (6), total production of each country is fixed by the world supply of skilled labor per industry, regardless of the number of firms in each industry. Thus, as the number of firms expands, industry output must be spread across more firms. The impact of relative source resources is exactly opposite that of the relative number of source firms.

Proposition 1. *An increase in the number of source relative to host firms increases both the source and the host wage, decreases both source and host output of each firm, and increases the extent of FDI. An increase in source relative to host skilled labor supply decreases both the source and the host wage, increases both source and host output of each firm, and decreases the extent of FDI.*

What are the consequences of FDI subsidies? A subsidy to FDI directly increases the incentive for source firms to shift production to the host country. This production shifting transfers labor demand from the source to the host thereby raising host wages and lowering source wages. This movement of wages implies that the source firms enjoy a lower cost of production relative to host firms and therefore gain market share and enjoy higher profits.

Proposition 2. *A subsidy to FDI leads to a greater extent of FDI, a lower source wage, a higher host wage, larger output by each source firm and smaller output by each host firm.*

The effect of a subsidy to FDI on the equilibrium follows immediately from simple differentiation of the equilibrium values. A wage differential arises between the two countries (host wage exceeds source wage) that exactly equals the magnitude of the subsidy. According to Eq. (6), the increase in the source output exactly offsets the decrease in the host output, leaving total output of each industry unchanged.

Note that the subsidy cannot become too large or else host firm output would fall to zero.

$$\sigma \leq \bar{\sigma} \equiv \frac{\psi K(1+r)}{fM} \Leftrightarrow Y^* \geq 0 \tag{13}$$

Also, the subsidy cannot become too low (the tax cannot become too large) or else the extent of FDI would fall to zero.

$$\sigma \geq \underline{\sigma} \equiv -\frac{\psi K(f-r)}{fM} \Leftrightarrow \alpha^* \geq 0 \tag{14}$$

We determine the optimal FDI policies within this interval $\sigma[\underline{\sigma}, \bar{\sigma}]$.

3. FDI policies with complete ownership

We have established that a subsidy to FDI increases the extent of FDI and increases the share of source firm production in total production. FDI subsidies lower the costs of source firms and effectively promote these firms, even if all industries are identical and share a common factor available in fixed supply. Under what circumstances are such subsidies optimal?

3.1. Optimal source policy

Define source welfare as the sum of the profits of source firms and the earnings of source skilled labor minus any subsidy payments $s \equiv \sigma\alpha my$.

$$w \equiv m\pi + zk - s \tag{15}$$

For a subsidy to raise source welfare, the profits of source firms net of the subsidy must rise by more than the reduction in the earnings of source skilled labor. Differentiating total source welfare with respect to the subsidy level

$$\frac{dw}{d\sigma} = \frac{f[\psi K(2r-(1-f)) - 2\sigma Mf]}{\psi(f+1)^2} \tag{16}$$

Solving the first order condition yields the optimal subsidy

$$\sigma^* \equiv \frac{\psi K(2r+1-f)}{2fM} > 0 \Leftrightarrow f < 1 + 2r \tag{17}$$

The source subsidizes FDI iff $\sigma^* > 0$. In particular, if the two countries have the same number of firms $M = m$, then $f = 1$ and $\sigma^* > 0$. The optimal policy remains a subsidy even when the number of source firms is somewhat greater than the number of host firms, provided $f < 1 + 2r$. The properties of the optimal policy follow from simple differentiation of Eq. (17).

Proposition 3. *The optimal source policy toward outward FDI is a subsidy iff the relative number of source firms is sufficiently small $f < 2r + 1$. The optimal subsidy decreases in the number of source relative to host firms and increases in the source relative to host skilled labor supply.*

When $f < 2r + 1$, the ratio of domestic firms to host firms is not that large relative to the ratio of domestic to host supply of skilled labor. From Eq. (7), under this scenario, the extent of outward FDI is small, so, the subsidy payments that have to be made to achieve a gain in profits at the expense of the host rivals are relatively small. However, when $f > 2r + 1$, the extent of FDI is large since autarkic source wage is high (due to high demand and limited supply of skilled labor) so that the total subsidy payment required exceeds the benefits obtained by shifting profits from rivals. Subsidy payments are high because both the number of firms and the extent of FDI are large. Alternatively, when the relative number of firms f is big compared to relative skilled labor supply r, a small tax on FDI can lead to a large increase in labor demand at home so that the losses incurred through reduced firm profits are dominated by increase in wage earnings, making a tax on outward FDI an optimal policy.

A subsidy to outward FDI depresses the source wage and shifts profits toward the source firm in each industry, but increased outward FDI also increases the wage abroad. How does the source subsidy to outward FDI affect aggregate host welfare? Define host welfare as the sum of the profits of host firms and the earnings of host skilled labor.

$$W \equiv M\Pi + ZK \tag{18}$$

Profits shifted toward source firms due to a FDI subsidy come at the expense of the profits of host firms. However, host wages rise due the increased demand for host skilled labor.

For a subsidy paid by the source to reduce host welfare, the profits of host firms must fall by more than the improvement in host skilled labor earnings. As might be expected, the benefits to source welfare are achieved at the expense of host welfare. Differentiating host welfare with respect to the level of the subsidy, host welfare falls by the magnitude that source welfare rises $(\mathrm{d}W/\mathrm{d}\sigma) = -(\mathrm{d}w/\mathrm{d}\sigma)$. Host welfare is minimized at the optimal FDI policy chosen by the source. Intuitively, whenever the source prefers a subsidy, the host prefers to restrict FDI because FDI raises the host wage and shifts profits away from host firms. Total world welfare $w+W=(r+1)Kp=Qp$ is independent of any taxes or subsidies to FDI. Thus, an outward FDI subsidy by the source country increases source welfare at the expense of host welfare. We turn next the optimal host policy toward inward FDI.

3.2. Optimal host policy

Let $\tilde{\sigma}$ now denote the subsidy implemented by the host, given that the source institutes no policy toward outward FDI. The trade-off facing the host government is clear: inward FDI benefits workers at the expense of firms. Can the host government intervene to raise host welfare? Welfare in the host equals

$$\tilde{W} = M\Pi + ZK - S \tag{19}$$

where $S \equiv \sigma\alpha m y$ denotes the magnitude of any subsidy payments. Differentiating host welfare with respect to the subsidy level gives

$$\frac{\mathrm{d}\tilde{W}}{\mathrm{d}\tilde{\sigma}} = -\frac{\psi K(2f + rf - r) + 2\tilde{\sigma}fM}{\psi(f+1)^2} < 0 \tag{20}$$

which is negative since $f > r$ (by labeling of countries). Thus host welfare is strictly decreasing in the host subsidy to inward FDI: the host can increase its welfare by *taxing* inward FDI.

Such a tax discourages the inflow of FDI. Therefore, the optimal host policy must respect the constraint that the extent of FDI be non-negative as in Eq. (14).[15]

$$\tilde{\sigma}^* = \underline{\sigma} \equiv -\frac{\psi K(f-r)}{fM} < 0 \tag{21}$$

The minimum subsidy is negative since $f > r$ by labeling of the host and source countries so the optimal policy is a tax on inward FDI.

[15]The value of the tax that solves the first order condition is greater than the value defined in Eq. (14), so the constraint always binds.

Proposition 4. *The optimal host policy toward inward FDI is the prohibitive tax. The optimal tax increases with the relative number of source firms and decreases with the relative source skilled labor supply.*

The above result illustrates that when the host values profits as well as wages, it taxes inward FDI. Properties of the optimal tax Eq. (21) are easily established by differentiation. Intuition for these properties is simple: as the number of source firms increases, the wage in the source country increases making FDI more attractive, which forces the host to increase its tax to continue blocking FDI. Similarly, a high source labor supply implies a low relative wage in the source country. This low wage makes FDI less attractive so that a smaller tax can prohibit FDI.

4. FDI policies with incomplete ownership

Many countries do implement measures to attract FDI yet our base model suggests potential host countries should only discourage FDI. How can our model explain FDI promotion policies? Next, we discuss two different extensions that accomplish this objective.

The first variant assumes that the host weighs profits less than wages because a substantial portion of the ownership of its firms lies with a third country. This scenario provides some insight into whether small less developed economies that have few local firms of their own have an incentive to subsidize inward FDI.

The second extension introduces cross-ownership of firms among the two countries (portfolio investment). Since substantial cross-ownership of firms exists among developed countries, this second model applies to FDI between two developed economies. Both these models are capable of generating subsidies to inward FDI as optimal host policies.

4.1. Optimal host policy with external ownership

Suppose the host firms are not fully host-owned but partially owned by some third country. Let $1-\beta$ represent the host country's ownership share of host firms where β belongs to the rest of the world (ROW) with $0\leq\beta\leq1$. Host welfare with some external ownership of source firms is

$$W_e=(1-\beta)M\Pi+ZK-S \tag{22}$$

which differs from Eq. (18) by weighting source firm profits by $1-\beta$ instead of one. What is the optimal host policy toward FDI? Maximizing host welfare with respect to the subsidy yields the optimal host subsidy

$$\sigma_e^* \equiv \frac{\psi K[2\beta f(r+1) - r(f-1) - 2f]}{2fM(\beta f + 1)} \tag{23}$$

Above a critical threshold level of external ownership of host firms,

$$\beta > \bar{\beta}_e \equiv \frac{2f + r(f-1)}{2f(1+r)} \Leftrightarrow \sigma_e^* > 0 \tag{24}$$

the host chooses to subsidize inward FDI.[16] Differentiating Eq. (23) with respect to β reveals that the optimal host subsidy is increasing in the external ownership of host firms.

Proposition 5. *The host subsidizes inward FDI iff a sufficiently large share of host firms are owned by some third country* $\beta > \bar{\beta}_e$. *The optimal host subsidy increases in the share of host firms owned by other countries.*

How does the subsidy to inward FDI affect source welfare? Unlike the base model where the host and source country's interests were always in conflict, subsidizing inward FDI here can raise source as well as host welfare. In the absence of a source FDI policy, source welfare Eq. (15) simplifies to

$$w_e = m\pi + zk \tag{25}$$

Differentiating source welfare over the FDI subsidy (implemented by the host country) gives

$$\frac{dw_e}{d\sigma_e} = \frac{\psi K(2f + rf - r) + 2\sigma_e fM]}{\psi(f+1)^2} > 0 \tag{26}$$

Thus, source welfare is strictly increasing in the inward FDI subsidy offered by the host: source profits rise more than source wage earnings fall. The FDI policy adopted by the host improves source welfare whenever the host FDI policy is a subsidy $\beta > \bar{\beta}_e \leftrightarrow \sigma_e^* > 0$.

Proposition 6. *The optimal host policy improves welfare in both countries when it subsidizes inward FDI, whereas it improves only host welfare when it taxes inward FDI.*

How can welfare improve in both countries? Recall that some third country owns some share of host firms. Whenever, the extent of this ownership is large, interests of the source and the host coincide. In fact, the source and the host can

[16]This result applies even when ownership of host firms lies with the source country; however, the results regarding the impact on source welfare in this section are derived based on the external ownership of host firms belonging to some third country.

cooperate to increase joint welfare at the expense of the third country; cooperating would entail implementing a subsidy even higher than the one chosen by the host alone since, when acting alone, the host ignores the benefits that accrue to the source as a result of its policy.

4.2. Optimal source policy with cross-ownership

Suppose now that some share of firms in each country are owned by the other country. Let β represent the source ownership share of host firms and γ represent the source ownership share of source firms with $0 \leq \gamma \leq 1$. When all firms are owned within the source and host, strategic FDI subsidies have a beggar-thy-neighbor character since total world welfare is independent of such policies. This trait holds in the base model where $\beta=0$ and $\gamma=1$ and continues to hold under general cross-ownership here.

We examine how the presence of cross-ownership alters the incentives for governments to offer subsidies to FDI. From the viewpoint of the source country, not all of the increased profits of source firms due to a subsidy to outward FDI accrue to the source country under cross-ownership. Additionally, some of the decreased profits of host firms now accrue to the source. Thus, cross-ownership weakens the incentive for subsidizing outward FDI.

Source welfare with cross-ownership is

$$w_c = \gamma m \pi + \beta M \Pi + zk - s \tag{27}$$

Under $\beta=0$ and $\gamma=1$, source welfare reduces to Eq. (15). Differentiating source welfare with respect to the subsidy level and solving for the optimal outward FDI subsidy yields

$$\sigma_c^* = \frac{\psi K[2(r+1)(\gamma - \beta) - (f+1)]}{2M[1 - \gamma + (1 - \beta)f]} > 0 \Leftrightarrow \gamma - \beta > \frac{1}{2}\left(\frac{f+1}{r+1}\right) \tag{28}$$

In a fully symmetric model, $r=f=1$ so the above inequality requires that $\gamma - \beta > 1/2$. The source government wants to subsidize outward FDI iff the source share of its own profits exceeds its share of host profits by a wide enough margin. Subsidizing FDI increases profitability of source firms at the expense of host firms; if a large share of the profits of host profits are owned by the source, such a subsidy to FDI would be counterproductive.

Furthermore, when $\gamma=\beta$, the optimal source policy is a tax: when the source has equal ownership in the profits of all firms, it prefers to discourage outward FDI because it can gain from the increased host profits from restricting FDI, but it receives no benefit from raising wages abroad. The outputs of all firms remain positive under the policy σ_c^* iff $\beta < \beta_c \equiv (2r+1)/(2r+2)$ where β_c is found by substituting $\tilde{\sigma}_c^*$ from Eq. (28) into y^* from Eq. (10) and solving $y^* > 0$ for β.

Cross-ownership shares are typically not that large: Dick (1993) provides measures of cross-ownership for the U.S. that correspond to $\beta = 3.36\%$ and

$\gamma = 86\%$. Note well that $3.36\% \ll \bar{\beta}_c$ as $\beta < 1/2$ is sufficient for any $0 < r < \infty$ and only $\beta < 3/4$ is required for $r = 1$. Thus we proceed under the assumption that $\beta < \bar{\beta}_c$.

How does the existence of cross-ownership affect the optimal source subsidy to outward FDI? From Eqs. (17) and (28), the optimal source subsidy under cross-ownership is lower than the optimal subsidy under no cross-ownership.

$$\sigma_c^* - \sigma^* = -\frac{\psi K(f+1)[(2r+1)(1-\gamma)+\beta f]}{2fM[1-\gamma+(1-\beta)f]} < 0 \tag{29}$$

Therefore, cross-ownership shrinks the level of the optimal outward FDI subsidy.

How does the optimal subsidy vary with the extent of cross-ownership? As the source share of source firms rises, the optimal subsidy increases

$$\frac{\partial \sigma_c^*}{\partial \gamma} = \frac{\psi K(f+1)[2r+1-2\beta(r+1)]}{2M[1-\gamma+(1-\beta)f]^2} > 0 \tag{30}$$

as the last term in the numerator is positive due to the assumption that source ownership of host firms is not too large $\beta < \bar{\beta}_c$. Thus a source subsidy to outward FDI increases in the source share of source profits. Similarly, as the source share of host profits rises, the optimal subsidy decreases

$$\frac{\partial \sigma_c^*}{\partial \beta} = -\frac{\psi K(f+1)[2(r+1)(1-\gamma)+f]}{2M[1-\gamma+(1-\beta)f]^2} < 0 \tag{31}$$

Since a source subsidy to FDI shifts profits away from host firms, the incentive for such a subsidy declines as source ownership of host firms increases.

Proposition 7. *The optimal source subsidy to outward FDI under cross-ownership is smaller than the optimal subsidy under no cross-ownership. The optimal source subsidy increases with the source share of source profits* (γ) *and decreases with source share of host profits* (β).

4.3. Optimal host policy with cross-ownership

Suppose the source government does not subsidize outward FDI, and the host government considers whether subsidizing inward FDI would improve host welfare. Foreign welfare with cross-ownership is

$$\tilde{W}_c = (1-\beta)M\Pi + (1-\gamma)m\pi + ZK - S \tag{32}$$

Under $\beta = 0$ and $\gamma = 1$, host welfare reduces to Eq. (19). How is the analysis altered relative to the case of no cross-ownership? Differentiating host welfare with respect to the subsidy level and solving for the optimal inward FDI subsidy gives

$$\tilde{\sigma}_c^* \equiv \frac{\psi K[2f(\beta-\gamma)(r+1)+r(f+1)]}{2fM(\gamma+\beta f)} > 0 \Leftrightarrow \gamma-\beta < \frac{1}{2}\left(\frac{r}{f}\right)\left(\frac{f+1}{r+1}\right) \tag{33}$$

Under what conditions is the above inequality satisfied? The host has an incentive to subsidize inward FDI whenever β is not too small relative to γ (whenever source ownership of host firms is not too small relative to source ownership of source firms). If β is not too small, then the losses incurred by host firms due to inward FDI subsidies do not affect host welfare substantially whereas all of the increase in labor earnings are captured by the host. When $\beta=\gamma$ (so that the source has equal ownership in both countries), the above condition clearly holds and the host prefers to subsidize inward FDI.

The optimal subsidy $\tilde{\sigma}_c^*$ is consistent with positive output levels of all firms iff $\gamma>\underline{\gamma}_c\equiv(1/2)(r/(r+1))$ where $\underline{\gamma}_c$ is found by solving $\tilde{\sigma}_c^*<\bar{\sigma}$ from Eqs. (33) and (13) for γ (equivalent to substituting $\tilde{\sigma}_c^*$ into Y^* and solving $Y^*>0$ for γ). As before, we impose this assumption. In this case, γ being sufficiently large is the range where host ownership of source firms is sufficiently small, consistent with extents of cross-ownership that are not too large.

We next explore the properties of the optimal inward FDI subsidy under cross-ownership. The optimal inward subsidy increases with the source share of host firms

$$\frac{\partial\tilde{\sigma}_c^*}{\partial\beta} = \frac{\psi K(f+1)[(2\gamma(r+1)-r]}{2M(\gamma+f\beta)^2} > 0 \tag{34}$$

since $\gamma>\underline{\gamma}_c$. This finding accords well with intuition: a bigger β means that profits of host firms matter less to the host. Thus, the bigger β is, the stronger the incentive for the host to increase labor earnings by promoting FDI. Further, the optimal inward subsidy decreases with the source share of source firms.

$$\frac{\partial\tilde{\sigma}_c^*}{\partial\gamma} = -\frac{\psi K(f+1)[(2f\beta(r+1)+r]}{2fM(\gamma+f\beta)^2} < 0$$

The larger the source ownership in source firms, the smaller the benefit of increasing source profits to the host.

Proposition 8. *Under cross-ownership, the host can increase welfare by subsidizing inward FDI. The optimal subsidy to inward FDI decreases with source ownership of source firms* (γ) *and increases with the source ownership of host firms* (β).

Just as in the no cross-ownership case, world welfare is independent of subsidy levels so the root of the mutual conflict is clear: a subsidy by the host government always hurts source welfare. From Eqs. (28) and (33), if $r=f$, then the region over which the source country prefers a subsidy is exactly the region over which the host country prefers a tax to inward FDI.

5. Conclusion

We construct a model that examines the welfare consequences of FDI across countries. We argue that by shifting labor demand across countries and raising the wage in the host at the expense of the wage in the source, FDI not only benefits host workers at the expense of source workers, it also reduces profits of host firms by raising wages abroad. Thus, a tension arises between worker interests and firm profits in the two countries. In the base model, the source subsidy to outward FDI always hurts host welfare. Similarly, the host tax on inward FDI always hurts source welfare.

However, if a substantial share of the ownership of host firms lies with a third country, a subsidy to inward FDI by the host may also benefit the source since increased FDI lowers the costs of source firms (both due to the subsidy and due to the reduction in source wage that results from shifting production abroad). Further, since part of the ownership of host firms now lies with the third country, such policies improve host welfare at the expense of the third country.

We also examine the case of cross-ownership of firms. In the presence of cross-ownership of firms, subsidies to inward FDI can raise host welfare. By encouraging the shifting production into its economy, the host government raises host wages while hurting host profits. However, cross-ownership reduces the loss in profits thereby allowing the wage effect to dominate.

Ultimately, this paper has provided *an argument for strategic FDI policies* that persists in situations where shared factor markets impinge on the effectiveness of export subsidies. While shared factor markets work against the efforts of export subsidies designed to make source oligopolists more aggressive in competing against host firms, shared factor markets facilitate the effects of FDI subsidies.

Ever since Eaton and Grossman (1986), it is widely recognized that the nature of the optimal policy is quite sensitive to the assumptions related to market conduct. How would our results change if firms competed in prices rather than quantities? In the presence of resource constraints, our FDI policies function under Bertrand behavior (with imperfect substitutes to maintain profits) in essentially the same manner as for Cournot behavior. Thus our results regarding strategic FDI policy are not only robust to the presence of multiple symmetric industries that share a common factor but also to the behavior of firms.

In companion papers, we pursue the interrelations between multiple country groupings. This work emphasizes the crowding out effects of FDI from one source on FDI from another source into the same host and also the effects of FDI into one host contracting FDI from the same source into another host. This analysis provides insights into the competition between similar countries for FDI, a prevalent phenomenon.

Acknowledgements

We thank Patrick Conway, Ping Lin, Devashish Mitra, Nikos Vettas, participants at the Midwest International Economics and Southeast International Trade Conferences, and an anonymous referee for extremely helpful comments.

Appendix 1

Our key results go through even when firms behave as Bertrand competitors.

Bertrand equilibrium analysis

To ease exposition, we derive our results for the case of n duopolies, each facing the demand functions

$$p_S = a - q_S - sq_H$$

$$p_H = a - sq_S - q_H$$

where q_i is the output and p_i the price of firm i, $i \in \{S, H\}$ for source and host respectively. The parameter $s \in [0, 1]$ represents the substitutability of the products: the two products are homogeneous if $s=1$ and completely unrelated if $s=0$. As noted in Dixit (1979), the above demand system can be derived from utility maximization when the representative consumer's utility is given by

$$U = a(q_H + q_S) - \frac{q_H^2 + q_S^2 + sq_Hq_S}{2} + x$$

where x is some numeraire good. Rewrite the demand system in terms of quantities as

$$q_S = \frac{a}{1+s} - \frac{1}{1-s^2}\, p_S + \frac{s}{1-s^2}\, p_H$$

$$q_H = \frac{a}{1+s} + \frac{s}{1-s^2}\, p_S - \frac{1}{1-s^2}\, p_H$$

According to the Bertrand assumption, each firm i chooses its price p_i to maximize its profits

$$\pi_i = [p_i - c_i]\left[\frac{a}{1+s} - \frac{1}{1-s^2}\, p_i + \frac{s}{1-s^2}\, p_j\right]$$

given the price of the other firm p_j, where the marginal costs of production are $c_S \equiv \alpha z + (1-\alpha)(Z-\sigma) = z$ and $c_H \equiv Z$. Solving the above problem yields the following first order condition:

$$p_i = \frac{a(1-s) + c_i + sp_j}{2}$$

Solving for the equilibrium prices yields

$$p_i = \frac{a(1-s) + c_i}{2-s}$$

As in the Cournot case, imposing the resource constraints (in per industry terms) $(1-\alpha)y_S = k$ and $\alpha y_S + y_H = K$ and the FDI equilibrium condition $z = Z - \sigma$ gives the equilibrium extent of FDI

$$\alpha^* = \frac{K(1-r)(1-s)(2+s) + \sigma}{K(1+r)(1-s)(2+s) + \sigma}$$

the source wage

$$z^* = a - \frac{1}{2}\,[K(1+r)(2-s)(1+s) + \sigma]$$

and the host wage

$$Z^* = a - \frac{1}{2}\,[K(1+r)(2-s)(1+s) - \sigma]$$

In the absence of any subsidies to FDI, $\alpha_0 = (1-r)/(1+r)$ so we require $r < 1$ by the labeling of the countries as host and source. This condition is the same as required for the Cournot case (but $f = 1$ here so $f > r \Leftrightarrow r < 1$). Now we can consider optimal FDI policies: we discuss each scenario in turn, pointing out the underlying similarity between the two cases.

Optimal source policy

Maximizing source welfare yields the optimal source policy

$$\sigma^* = \frac{K(1-s)(2+s)(sr + r - 1)}{3+s}$$

The source subsidizes outward FDI iff

$$r > \frac{1}{1+s}$$

Recall that $0<r<1$ and $0<s<1$. When s is small, each producer is essentially a monopolist since the products are highly differentiated. Consequently, the incentive for profit shifting is slight so that the incentive to raise domestic wages by taxing outward FDI dominates. The price level is now affected by the subsidy so world welfare is not exogenous. Hence, source welfare gains do not arise entirely from host welfare losses.

Optimal host policy

Maximizing host welfare yields the optimal host policy

$$\tau^* = \frac{Ks(1-s)(2+s)(1-r+s)}{s+3} > 0$$

As under the Cournot case, the host taxes inward FDI. The difference is that now the host may impose its optimal tax since the tax that shuts down FDI completely may be bigger than τ^*. It is easy to show that this maximum tax is $\tau_{max} = K(1-s)(2+s)(1-r) > 0$.

Optimal host policy with external ownership

The optimal host policy when β of its profits belong to a third country is

$$\sigma_E = -\frac{K(1-s)(2+s)[1+s-r-\beta(1+r)(1+s)]}{2+(1+\beta)(1+s)}$$

The host chooses to subsidize inward FDI iff a substantial enough share of its firms are owned by the third country.

$$\beta > \beta_E \equiv \frac{1+s-r}{(1+r)(1+s)}$$

For s small, the host subsidizes inward FDI even when β is small. When s is small, profit shifting incentive disappears (firms are almost monopolies) and the wage incentive dominates.

Optimal source policy with cross-ownership

The optimal source policy with cross-ownership is

$$\sigma_C^* = \frac{K(1-s)(2+s)[2+s+(1+r)(1+s)(\beta-\gamma)]}{(\beta+\gamma)(1+s)-2(2+s)}$$

The source country subsidizes outward FDI iff source ownership of host firms is sufficiently slight

$$\beta < \beta_C \equiv \gamma - \frac{2+s}{(1+r)(1+s)}$$

Once again we obtain a condition quite analogous to the one obtained for the Cournot case. The properties of the optimal policy with respect to the extent of cross-ownership remain the same $(d\sigma_C^*)/(d\gamma)>0$ and $(d\sigma_C^*)(d\beta)<0$.

Optimal source policy with cross-ownership

The optimal host policy with cross-ownership is

$$\tilde{\sigma}_C = \frac{K(1-s)(2+s)[r(2+s)+(1+r)(1+s)(\beta-\gamma)]}{2+(\gamma+\beta)(1+s)}$$

The host subsidizes inward FDI iff source ownership of host firms is substantial enough

$$\beta > \tilde{\beta}_C \equiv \gamma - \frac{r(2+s)}{(1+r)(1+s)}$$

Again the result corresponds quite well to the Cournot case. The optimal policy has the same sensible properties with respect to the extent of cross-ownership: $(d\tilde{\sigma}_C^*)/(d\gamma)<0$ and $(d\tilde{\sigma}_C^*)/(d\beta)>0$.

References

Aitken, B., Harrison, A., Lipsey, R.E., 1996. Wages and foreign ownership: A comparative study of Mexico, Venezuela, and the United States. Journal of International Economics 40, 345–371.

Brainard, S.L., 1997. An empirical assessment of the proximity-concentration trade-off between multinational sales and trade. American Economic Review 87, 520–544.

Brander, J.A., Spencer, B.J., 1985. Export subsidies and international market share rivalry. Journal of International Economics 18, 83–100.

Coughlin, C.C., Terza, J.V., Arromdee, V., 1991. State characteristics and the location of foreign direct investment within the United States. Review of Economics and Statistics 73, 675–683.

Dick, A.R., 1993. Strategic trade policy and welfare: The empirical consequences of cross-ownership. Journal of International Economics 35, 227–249.

Dixit, A., 1979. A model of duopoly suggesting a theory of entry barriers. Bell Journal of Economics. 10, 20–32.

Dixit, A., 1984. International trade policy for oligopolistic industries. Economic Journal 94, 1–16.

Dixit, A.K., Grossman, G.M., 1986. Targeted export promotion with several oligopolistic industries. Journal of International Economics 21, 233–249.

Eaton, J., Grossman, G.M., 1986. Optimal trade and industrial policy under oligopoly. Quarterly Journal of Economics 101, 383–406.

Frank, R., 1997. Czechs join rivalry in Eastern Europe to lure host firms with incentives. Wall Street Journal, September 22, A18.

Haddad, M., Harrison, A., 1993. Are there spillovers from direct foreign investment? Evidence from panel data for Morocco. Journal of Development Economics 42, 51–74.

Harris, R.G., 1989. The new protectionism revisited. Canadian Journal of Economics 22, 751–778.

Harrison, A., 1994. The role of multinationals in economic development: the benefits of FDI. Columbia Journal of World Business 29, 6–11.

Hines, Jr. J.R., 1996. Altered states: taxes and the location of foreign direct investment in America. American Economic Review 86, 1076–1094.

Lee, S., 1990. International equity markets and trade policy. Journal of International Economics 29, 173–184.

Levinsohn, J.A., 1989. Strategic trade policy when firms can invest abroad: when are tariffs and quotas equivalent?. Journal of International Economics 27, 129–146.

Lucas, R.E.B., 1993. On the determinants of direct foreign investment: evidence from East and Southeast Asia. World Development 21, 391–406.

Markusen, J.R., 1995. The boundaries of multinational enterprises and the theory of international trade. Journal of Economic Perspectives 9, 169–189.

Markusen, J.R., Venables, A.J., 1988. Trade policy with increasing returns and imperfect competition: contradictory results from competing assumptions. Journal of International Economics 24, 299–316.

Miyagiwa, K., 1992. International shareholdings and strategic export policy. International Economic Journal 6, 37–42.

Qiu, L.D., 1994. Optimal strategic trade policy under asymmetric information. Journal of International Economics 36, 333–354.

Qiu, L.D., 1995. Strategic trade policy under uncertainty. Review of International Economics 3, 75–85.

Rodríguez-Clare, A., 1996. Multinationals, linkages and economic development. American Economic Review 86, 852–873.

Ruffin, R.J., 1984. International factor movements. In: Jones, R.W., Kenen, P.B. (Eds.), Handbook of International Economics, Vol. 1. North Holland, Amsterdam, pp. 237–288.

United Nations, 1995. World Investment Report: Transnational Corporations and Competitiveness. United Nations, New York.

United Nations, 1996. World Investment Report: Investment Trade and International Policy Arrangements. United Nations, New York.

The Economist, 1997. Not quite so sparkling China and Japan's appeal (March 1, 1997), Okinawa's rethink (July 19, 1997), and Hell on wheels (July 26, 1997).

Chapter 25

Mode of foreign entry, technology transfer, and FDI policy[#]

Aaditya Mattoo[a,1], Marcelo Olarreaga[a,b,*], Kamal Saggi[c,2]

[a] *The World Bank, 1818 H Street, N.W., Washington, DC 20433, USA*
[b] *CEPR, London, UK*
[c] *Department of Economics, Southern Methodist University, Dallas, TX 75275-0496, USA*

Received 1 April 2001; accepted 1 August 2003

Abstract

Foreign direct investment (FDI) can take place either through the direct entry of foreign firms or the acquisition of existing domestic firms. The preferences of a foreign firm and a welfare-maximizing host country government over these two modes of FDI are examined in the presence of costly technology transfer. The trade-off between technology transfer and market competition emerges as a key determinant of preferences. The clash between the foreign firm's equilibrium choice and the local government's ranking of the two modes of entry can provide a rationale for some frequently observed FDI restrictions.

JEL classification: F13; F23; O32
Keywords: Foreign direct investment; Technology transfer; Investment policies

1. Introduction

Host countries often associate inflows of foreign direct investment (FDI) with a wide variety of benefits, the most common of which are transfers of modern

* Corresponding author. The World Bank, 1818 H Street, N.W., Washington, DC 20433, USA. Tel.: +1-202-458-8021; fax: +1-202-522-1159.

E-mail addresses: amattoo@worldbank.org (A. Mattoo), molarreaga@worldbank.org (M. Olarreaga), ksaggi@mail.smu.edu (K. Saggi).

[1] Tel.: +1-202-458-7611; fax: +1-202-522-1159.

[2] Tel.: +1-214-768-3274; fax: +1-214-768-1821.

[#] This chapter was originally appeared in *Journal of Development Economics* **75**, 95–111. © 2004 Elsevier B.V.

technologies and more competitive product markets. The extent to which a host country can secure these benefits of FDI is likely to depend upon the mode of entry of foreign firms. The goal of this paper is to shed light on the relationships between mode of entry, technology transfer, and market structure. To this end, we develop a simple model where a foreign firm can choose between two modes of entry: *direct entry* where in it establishes a new wholly owned subsidiary, or it can opt for *acquisition* of one of the existing domestic firms.[3]

In the model, the degree of technology transfer and the intensity of market competition depend upon the mode of entry chosen by the foreign firm. The competition enhancing effect of FDI is greater under direct entry. However, one mode does not unambiguously dominate the other in terms of the extent of technology transfer. On the one hand, the relatively larger market share that the foreign firm enjoys under acquisition increases its incentive for transferring costly technology (scale effect). On the other hand, strategic incentives to transfer technology in order to wrest market share away from domestic rivals can be stronger in more competitive environments (strategic effect).

Our results show that divergence between the foreign firm's choice and the welfare interest of the domestic economy can create a basis for policy intervention. More specifically, it is shown that for high costs of technology transfer, domestic welfare is generally higher under acquisition relative to direct entry, whereas the foreign firm chooses direct entry. Thus, restricting direct entry in order to induce acquisition can improve welfare, even in highly concentrated markets. On the other hand, if the cost of technology transfer is low then domestic welfare is higher under direct entry relative to acquisition whereas the foreign firm prefers acquisition to direct entry. As a result, a restriction on the acquisition of a domestic firm can help improve host country welfare by inducing direct entry by the foreign firm. Finally, for intermediate costs of technology transfer, both the government and the foreign firm prefer acquisition to direct entry.

Thus, according to our analysis the objective of frequently observed restrictions on FDI may not be to limit inflows of FDI, but rather to induce foreign firms to adopt the socially preferred mode of entry in the host country. More specifically, it is shown that restrictions on the degree of foreign ownership, even when applied symmetrically to both modes of entry (acquisition and direct entry), can induce the foreign firm to adopt the host country's preferred mode of entry.

Some of the issues addressed here have been studied separately before, but we know of no analytical study of the relationship between technology transfer and mode of entry by foreign firms (as in direct entry versus acquisition). The literature has tended to focus on licensing and direct entry where the foreign firm seeks to prevent the dissipation of its technological advantage (see Ethier and Markusen, 1996; Markusen, 2001; Saggi, 1996, 1999). Yu and Tang (1992) discuss several potential motivations for international acquisition of firms. These include the following: cost

[3] Our model is most relevant to situations where cross-border delivery is either infeasible or not the most efficient mode of supply. For example, in many services, ranging from construction to local telecommunications, commercial presence of foreign firms via FDI is required in the host country.

reduction, risk sharing, and competition reduction (also a consideration in our framework).[4]

Lee and Shy (1992) demonstrate that restrictions on foreign ownership may adversely affect the quality of technology transferred by the foreign firm. However, they do not allow for direct entry.[5] In a duopoly model, Roy et al. (1999) identify the degree of cost asymmetry between the foreign and local firm and market structure as the crucial determinants of optimal domestic policy. However, they assume technology transfer be costless and do not examine the differing incentive to transfer technology under alternative market structures.

The literature on mergers and acquisitions in both the domestic and international context is also relevant to our paper. This literature implies that when firms are symmetric, a firm will always prefer direct entry to acquisition of an existing firm when there is more than one target firm in the market (see Salant et al., 1983; Kamien and Zang, 1990).[6] It turns out that this result does not hold in the presence of technology transfer, as shown later in this paper.[7] On the international side, there exists a large literature that is concerned with the relationships between trade and competition policy and the international effects of purely national mergers. For example, Head and Ries (1997) study incentives for national and supra-national merger regulations to authorize mergers in the presence of international trade whereas Horn and Levinsohn (2001) focus on the substitutability between trade policy and competition policy.[8] Neither of these papers is concerned with technology transfer.

The remainder of the paper is organized as follows. Section 2 presents the theoretical setup and describes the foreign firm's decisions regarding its mode of entry (acquisition versus direct entry) into the host country where the extent of technology transfer depends upon the entry mode. Section 3 focuses on welfare analysis and draws its implications for the host government incentives for policy intervention. Section 4 concludes.

2. Model

There are two goods (z and y) and preferences in the domestic economy over these two goods are quasi-linear: $U(z,y)=u(z)+y$. Good y serves as a numeraire good and it is produced under perfect competition with constant returns to scale technology. Let $p(q)$ be

[4] Svejnar and Smith (1984) focus on the interaction between transfer pricing and local policy in an international joint venture whereas Al-Saadon and Das (1996) construct a model of in which the ownership shares of joint venture partners are endogenously determined as the outcome of a bargaining game. Neither of these papers allow for technology transfer and direct entry.

[5] Mutinelli and Piscitello (1998) argue that foreign firms may prefer joint ventures rather than full ownership in uncertain environments and provide evidence for Italian firms investing abroad.

[6] Although the formal games these papers analyze differ significantly from ours, the mechanism underlying this result also exists in our model.

[7] See also Perry and Porter (1985) where, at any given average cost, a merged firm can produce more output than either of the two independent firms because of the intangible asset it acquires from its two partners.

[8] Other models of mergers that deal with international issues include Barros and Cabral (1994), Cowan (1989), Das and Sengupta (2001), and Richardson (1999).

the inverse demand function for good z generated by consumer maximization, where q is total consumption of good z. For simplicity, assume that $u(z)$ is quadratic so that $p(q)=a-q$.

There are $n-1$ denote domestic firms that can produce good z at constant marginal cost c. A foreign firm has two options for entering the domestic market. It can either acquire a domestic firm or it can set up a wholly owned subsidiary that directly competes with domestic firms. Thus, under acquisition the total number of firms in the market equals $n-1$ whereas under direct entry it equals n.

The game proceeds as follows. In the first stage, the foreign firm chooses its mode of entry (E denotes direct entry and A denotes acquisition).[9] If it wants to acquire a domestic firm, it makes a take-it-or-leave-it offer to the target firm which specifies a fixed transaction price (v). If the target firm accepts the offer, they form a new firm that is owned by the foreign firm. If the foreign firm's offer is refused by the domestic firm, the foreign firm can enter the market by establishing its own subsidiary or by acquiring some other domestic firm.

After selecting its mode of entry, the foreign firm chooses the quality of technology it wishes to transfer to its subsidiary. Technology transfer lowers the marginal cost of production but is a costly process. By incurring the cost $C(x)$, the foreign firm can lower the cost of production of its subsidiary in the domestic economy to $c-x$. In other words, if it opts to transfer no technology, the marginal cost of its subsidiary equals that of the domestic firm. In the last stage, firms compete in a Cournot–Nash fashion. The perfect equilibrium of this game is found by solving backwards.

2.1. Product market

In the last stage of the game, domestic and foreign firms simultaneously choose their output levels. Firm i's profit function at the output stage is given by:

$$\pi_i(q_i, q_{-i}) = (p(q) - c_i)q_i = (a - q_{-i} - q_i - c_i)q_i \tag{1}$$

where $c_h=c$ is the marginal cost of a typical home firm (h), $c_f=c-x$ the marginal cost of the foreign firm (f), q_{-i} is the sum of outputs of all firms other than firm i, and q is total output (or domestic consumption).

Let the cost function for technology transfer be $C(x)=\tau x^2/2$ where $\tau=\partial^2 C/\partial x^2$ determines the convexity of this function. As τ increases, the cost function for technology transfer shifts up while at the same time incremental technology transfer also becomes more costly. Thus, with an increase in τ, both the total cost and the marginal cost of technology transfer increase.

Solving for the optimal output levels under Cournot competition is straightforward. These are given in the appendix for domestic and foreign firms under both entry and acquisition (see Appendix A.1).

[9] Later in the paper, when analyzing local policy we allow for a partial acquisition on the part of the foreign firm. In the absence of any policy restrictions, full acquisition is optimal from the foreign firm's perspective.

2.2. Technology transfer

In the second stage of the game, given the mode of entry, the foreign firm chooses the level of technology transfer. Here, we describe the foreign firm's incentives for technology transfer under the two modes of entry.

Under direct entry, the foreign firm's first-order condition for technology transfer can be written as

$$\frac{\partial \pi_f^E}{\partial q_f}\frac{\mathrm{d}q_f^E}{\mathrm{d}x} + (n-1)\frac{\partial \pi_f^E}{\partial q_h}\frac{\mathrm{d}q_h^E}{\mathrm{d}x} + \frac{\partial \pi_f^E}{\partial x} - \frac{\mathrm{d}C(x)}{\mathrm{d}x} = 0 \tag{2}$$

where q_h^E denotes the output of a typical domestic competitor and is reported in Appendix A.1.

The above equation is interpreted as follows. From the first-order condition at the output stage, the first term of the above equation equals zero (i.e. $\partial \pi_f^E/\partial_f = 0$). The second term captures the *strategic effect* of technology transfer: an increase in x lowers the output of the domestic firms thereby increasing the foreign firm's profits (see Brander and Spencer, 1983). The third term captures the stand-alone incentive for technology transfer. We call this the *scale effect* because the higher the output of the foreign firm, the stronger its incentive for technology transfer. The last term simply denotes the marginal cost of technology transfer. Using Eq. (1) to obtain the derivatives of profits with respect to their arguments, we can rewrite Eq. (2) as:

$$(n-1)(-q_f^E)\frac{\mathrm{d}q_h^E}{\mathrm{d}x} + q_f^E - \tau x = 0 \text{ where } \frac{\mathrm{d}q_h^E}{\mathrm{d}x} = -\frac{1}{n+1} < 0. \tag{3}$$

It is straightforward to show that under acquisition Eq. (3) becomes:[10]

$$\frac{n-2}{n} q_f^A + q_f^A - \tau x = 0 \tag{4}$$

as there are only $n-2$ domestic firms in the market.

Replacing q_f^A and q_f^E from Appendix A.1 into the first terms in Eqs. (3) and (4), it is easy to show that the strategic effect is concave in n: it increases with n if $n < n^c$ and decreases with n if $n > n^c$.[11] In other words, the strategic effect increases with the number of existing domestic firms only if the domestic market is not too competitive. By contrast, in a relatively competitive market, the presence of an extra firm in the domestic market actually decreases the strategic incentive to transfer technology. The intuition for this is that as the market gets more competitive, the scope for strategic interactions among firms decreases and the foreign firm's choice regarding technology transfer has a small impact on their

[10] Here we report the case of full acquisition of the domestic firm, as in equilibrium the foreign firm does not choose partial acquisition (see Section 2.3).

[11] We show in the appendix that

$$n^c = \frac{\tau - 2 + \sqrt{2}\sqrt{(\tau-2)(2\tau-1)}}{\tau - 2}.$$

output levels. Since the number of firms in the market is greater under direct entry (n) than under acquisition ($n-1$), for $n<n^c$, the strategic incentive for technology transfer is higher under direct entry than under acquisition and vice versa. This result helps explain why in environments that are not very competitive one may observe greater technology transfer under direct entry.

Solving Eqs. (3) and (4) for x yields the extent of technology transferred to the subsidiary under the two modes:

$$x^E = \frac{2n(a-c)}{(\tau-2)n^2+(2n+1)\tau} \text{ and } x^A = \frac{2(n-1)(a-c)}{(4n-2)+(\tau-2)n^2} \tag{5}$$

The equilibrium technology transfers have reasonable properties: under both direct entry and acquisition, technology transfer diminishes with n as well as with the cost parameter τ.

Proposition 1. *The foreign firm transfers less technology under acquisition than under direct entry iff* $\tau<\tau_t(n)$ *where*

$$\tau_t(n) = \frac{2n(n-1)}{n^2-n-1} \tag{6}$$

Furthermore, τt(n) is decreasing in n and it approaches 2 as n approaches infinity.

Thus, direct entry may yield more technology transfer if τ and n are sufficiently small. In general, the strategic effect is strong when τ is small because it is proportional to the foreign firm's output and that declines with τ. Furthermore, as was noted above, the strategic effect is concave in n. As a result, for small n, the strategic effect is stronger under direct entry than under acquisition whereas for large n, both the scale effect and the strategic effect are stronger under acquisition. The fact that $\tau_t(n)$ approaches 2 when n approaches infinity implies that when the domestic market is extremely competitive, acquisition necessarily delivers greater technology transfer (τ cannot be less than 2 for the second-order condition in the choice of technology transfer to hold).

2.3. Foreign firm's preferred mode of entry

In the first stage of the game, the foreign firm chooses whether to enter through acquisition or direct entry. Since the foreign firm has all the bargaining power under acquisition, we must have $v=\pi_h^A(x^A)$. In other words, a target domestic firm accepts an offer that leaves it with a payoff equal to that it makes as a competitor when some other domestic firm is acquired. The foreign firm opts for acquisition iff it is more profitable than direct entry:

$$\Delta\Pi \equiv \pi_f^A(x^A) - C(x^A) - \pi_h^A(x^A) - \left[\pi_f^E(x^E) - C(x^E)\right] > 0$$

As might be expected, the expression for $\Delta\Pi$ is quite cumbersome and non-linear in τ and n (see Appendix A.3). However, dividing $\Delta\Pi$ by $(a-c)^2$ permits us a convenient graphical analysis in the (n,τ) space. Fig. 1 plots the contours of three different functions in the (n,τ) space. The *TT* curve is the contour of the function $\Delta X/(a-c)^2$ where $\Delta X \equiv$

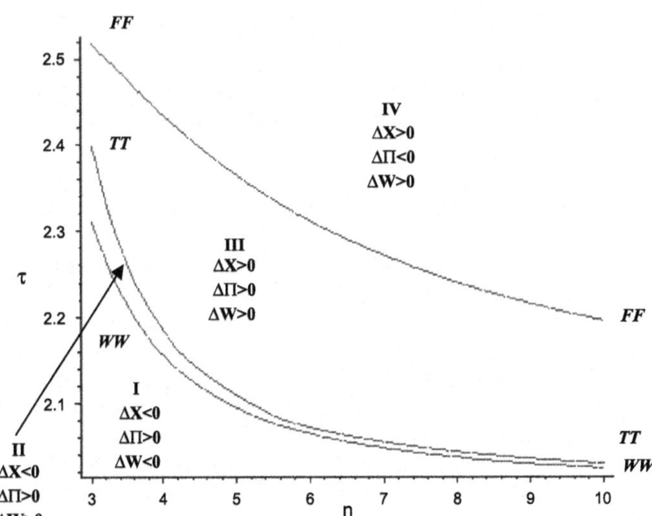

Fig. 1. Mode of entry, technology transfer and policy intervention.

$x^A - x^E = 0$. Along this function (given by Eq. (6)), acquisition and direct entry deliver the same amount of technology transfer. The *FF* curve is the contour of the $\Delta\Pi/(a-c)^2=0$ function along which the foreign firm is indifferent between acquisition and direct entry; the *WW* curve is the contour of the function $\Delta W/(a-c)^2=0$, where $\Delta W=(W^A - W^E)$ and W^j denotes aggregate domestic welfare under mode $j=A,E$. Along the *WW* curve, aggregate domestic welfare under the two modes is the same (see the next subsection for greater details on domestic welfare). To focus on the equilibrium mode of entry chosen by the foreign firm, restrict attention to the *TT* and *FF* curves.

The parameter space in Fig. 1 can be divided into four regions: I, II, III, and IV. In regions I and II, direct entry leads to more technology transfer whereas the foreign firm prefers acquisition. In region III, acquisition leads to more technology transfer and is indeed preferred by the foreign firm. Finally, in region IV, direct entry is chosen by the foreign firm whereas acquisition leads to more technology transfer.

To see the intuition behind the equilibrium mode choice, consider region IV. In this region, τ is large and technology transfer is of marginal importance (due to its high cost). As a result, the buy-out price of the local firm $(\pi_h^A(x^A))$ is relatively high. Under this scenario, the considerations studied in Salant et al. (1983) and Kamien and Zang (1990) become important, making acquisition less profitable than direct entry.[12] In all other regions, the foreign firm prefers acquisition over direct entry. The reason for this is as follows. Acquisition lowers the degree of competition in the market relative to direct entry but the foreign firm has to buy-out a local firm to achieve that competition reduction.

[12] See Mattoo et al. (2001) for a demonstration of the Kamien and Zang (1990) result in our model without technology transfer.

Thus, the foreign firm has to weigh the price at which acquisition occurs (i.e. $\pi_h^A(x^A)$) against the gain competition reduction brings. As long as the *absolute* level of technology transfer under acquisition is sufficiently high (even though it may be lower than under direct entry), the buy-out price $\pi_h^A(x^A)$ is small and acquisition is more attractive to the foreign firm relative to direct entry.

It is worth emphasizing the crucial role technology transfer plays in our model. If technology transfer were infeasible, all firms would be symmetric in the model. In such a situation, the existing literature (Salant et al., 1983; Kamien and Zang, 1990) has shown that acquisition cannot occur in equilibrium when there are more than two firms in the market. Briefly put, the argument is as follows. An acquiring firm has to offer the target firm a payoff equal to what it collects if it is not acquired. If firms are symmetric, this condition fails to hold because the profits of a single firm with $n-2$ competitors are lower than the *total* profits of two independent firms with $n-1$ firms in the market. As noted above, the foreign firm may find acquisition more profitable than direct entry if it transfers sufficient technology to the new enterprise.[13] This result relates well to Perry and Porter's (1985) model of mergers where a merged unit has a greater stock of an indivisible asset relative to other firms in the industry (thereby creating asymmetry between merging firms and others).

3. Host country welfare

We prove the following result in Appendix A.4:

Proposition 2. *In the host country, consumers are better off under direct entry than under acquisition ($p^E < p^A$) whereas a typical domestic producer is better off under acquisition ($\pi_h^A > \pi_h^E$).*[14]

Thus, we have a conflict between the interests of domestic producers and consumers. Given this conflict, the main question is whether total domestic welfare (defined as the sum of consumer surplus and producer surplus) is higher under direct entry or acquisition. It is straightforward to show that:

$$\Delta W \equiv W^A - W^E = \left[a - \frac{p^E + p^A}{2}\right]\left[p^E - p^A\right] + (n-1)\left[\pi_h^A - \pi_h^E\right] \tag{7}$$

As noted earlier, the WW curve in Fig. 1 plots the contours of the $\Delta W/(a-c)^2$ function in the (n,τ) space. In each of the regions in Fig. 1, the preferences in terms of the mode of entry of the government and the foreign firm are denoted by indicating whether ΔW is larger or smaller than zero in the different regions.

In region IV, the foreign firm prefers direct entry whereas the government prefers acquisition (and the extent of technology transfer is higher under full acquisition). In

[13] We thank an anonymous referee for helping us improve the exposition of this result.

[14] The difference between prices under full acquisition and direct entry declines as the number of firms increases. At the limit, when n approaches infinity, this difference tends to zero.

region I, for low levels of τ, the opposite is true whereas in region III for intermediate values of τ, both the government and the foreign firm prefer full acquisition to direct entry. Finally, in region II, the firm prefers acquisition while welfare is higher under acquisition even though there is more technology transfer under direct entry.

The logic for these results is as follows. From Proposition 2, we know that consumers always prefer direct entry whereas local firms always prefer acquisition since direct entry has a stronger profit shifting effect. For domestic welfare to be higher under direct entry relative to acquisition, it is necessary that direct entry leads to more technology transfer than acquisition but it is not sufficient. In region I, welfare is higher under direct entry because it leads to sufficiently more technology transfer than acquisition. By contrast, in the vicinity of the *TT* locus, the government prefers acquisition even though it leads to less technology transfer because direct entry hurts local profits too much and the level of technology transfer under the two modes is not significantly different. In regions III and IV, technology transfer under direct entry is lower than that under acquisition so that direct entry is never preferred from a welfare perspective.

In general, in regions I and IV there is room for government intervention. In region I, policy measures that induce direct entry and/or discourage full acquisition can improve domestic welfare. Similarly, in region IV, restricting direct entry and/or encouraging acquisition by the foreign firm can improve domestic welfare. Finally, in regions II and III, there is harmony between local welfare and the equilibrium entry mode chosen by the foreign firm: acquisition is the preferred mode from both points of view.

Introducing political economy considerations into the analysis does not change the qualitative results in any significant way. From Proposition 2 we know that domestic firms prefer acquisition to direct entry. Thus, if domestic firms could influence local policy they would want to lobby for restrictions on direct foreign entry. Further, if under lobbying pressure the government puts a higher weight to domestic firms' profits than on consumer welfare, then the *WW* curve in Fig. 1 will shift downwards thereby making it more likely that the government prefers acquisition to direct entry. This in turn implies that the likelihood of observing restrictions on acquisition of domestic firms would be lower. On the other hand, the incentives to restrict entry when this is the preferred mode by the foreign firm would remain the same (i.e. region IV does not change) despite lobbying by domestic firms.

Finally, it is possible that under direct entry, sunk costs are higher than under acquisition (e.g. cost of hiring new qualified employees). In this case, the *FF* locus will shift outwards towards the northeast. This will obviously make direct entry relatively less attractive and therefore will reduce the likelihood of observing restrictions on direct entry (i.e. region IV becomes smaller).

3.1. Equity restrictions on foreign ownership

Thus far we have allowed full foreign ownership and noted that local welfare considerations might motivate FDI restrictions on acquisition and/or direct entry by foreign firms. However, FDI restrictions frequently limit the degree of foreign ownership. In this section, we analyze such restrictions and show that they can be used to induce a foreign firm to adopt the socially preferred mode of entry.

An equity restriction on the degree of foreign ownership can be implemented in one of two ways. First, it might be applied *symmetrically* in that policy restricts the degree of foreign ownership of both an acquired firm as well as that of a newly established subsidiary of the foreign firm. Alternatively, it might be *asymmetric* in nature wherein policy restricts the degree of foreign ownership of an acquired firm but not that of a newly established foreign subsidiary. There are numerous examples of symmetric restrictions: e.g. in life insurance services, India limits foreign ownership in existing and new firms to 26% and China to 50%; in basic telecommunications, both countries have imposed limits of 49%. Asymmetric restrictions are less frequently observed, but there are some prominent examples: in Japan and Korea, foreign ownership of incumbent telecommunications companies was limited (to 20% in NTT and KDD in Japan, and 20% in Korea Telecom) but there were either no or much weaker restrictions on foreign equity in new firms. The quite common presence of public monopolies in the service sector, which make acquisition by foreign firms a complex political decision, also tends to lead to a de facto discrimination between foreign equity participation in existing domestic firms (public firms) and new firms in the sector (when these are allowed). In what follows, we show that both symmetric and asymmetric equity restrictions may be used to induce foreign firms to adopt a different mode of entry into the host country.

First consider an asymmetric equity restriction that limits the degree of foreign ownership of an existing domestic firm to $\theta \leq 1$ but not that of a newly established subsidiary. How does such a restriction affect the foreign firm's choice between the two modes of entry? We first show that, under an acquisition *the foreign firm chooses the maximum permitted degree of ownership* (i.e. $\theta^* = \bar{\theta}$). Let the pair (θ,v) denote an arbitrary offer by the foreign firm to a target domestic firm under the restriction $\bar{\theta}$ where v denotes the transaction price offered in return for the equity share θ. Since there is one foreign firm and several domestic firms, we assume that a domestic firm is willing to accept any offer that leaves it with a net payoff equal to that which it makes if some other domestic firm is acquired.[15] Thus, any offer (θ,v) that satisfies the following constraint is acceptable to any domestic firm:

$$(1-\theta)\pi_f^A(x^A(\theta)) + v \geq \pi_h^A(x^A) \tag{8}$$

where $\pi_h^A(x^A)$ denotes the profits of a non-acquired domestic firm under acquisition and $x^A(\theta) \equiv \arg\max \theta\pi_f^A(x) - C(x)$ denotes technology transfer when the foreign firm's equity share equals θ (the expression for $x^A(\theta)$ is reported in Appendix A.5). Since the foreign firm has all the bargaining power, the above constraint binds in equilibrium so that $v = \pi_h^A(x^A) - (1-\theta)\pi_f^A(x(\theta))$. As a result, the problem facing the foreign firm becomes:

$$\max_{\theta} \pi_f^A(x^A(\theta)) - C(x^A(\theta)) - \pi_h^A(x^A(\theta)) \text{ subject to } \theta \leq \bar{\theta}$$

[15] A second reasonable candidate for the acquisition price is $\pi_h^E(x^E)$: the profits of a typical domestic firm under direct entry. The advantage of using $\pi_h^A(x^A)$ is that a domestic firm that agrees to sell out to the foreign firm fares no worse than those that compete with the new enterprise. In any case, our qualitative results do not depend upon which acquisition price is used.

Differentiating the objective function above gives:

$$\left[\frac{\partial \pi_f^A}{\partial x} - \frac{\partial C}{\partial x} - \frac{\partial \pi_h^A(x^A)}{\partial x}\right]\frac{\mathrm{d}x^A(\theta)}{\mathrm{d}\theta} \tag{9}$$

Since x^A is chosen by the foreign firm to maximize $\theta\pi_f^A(x^A) - C(x^A)$, the following first-order condition must hold:

$$\theta\frac{\partial \pi_f^A}{\partial x} = \frac{\partial C}{\partial x}$$

Using the above equation, the first-order condition in Eq. (9) can be rewritten as:

$$\left[(1-\theta)\frac{\partial \pi_f^A}{\partial x} - \frac{\partial \pi_h^A(x^A)}{\partial x}\right]\frac{\mathrm{d}x^A(\theta)}{\mathrm{d}\theta} > 0 \tag{10}$$

The above first-order condition with respect to θ is always positive (note that $\partial\pi_h^A(x^A)/\partial x<0$), implying that the foreign firm chooses the maximum permitted degree of ownership, i.e. $\theta^* = \bar{\theta}$.

Eq. (10) shows that there are two reasons why the foreign firm opts for full acquisition. First, since x is chosen optimally at a later date by the foreign firm, $\pi_f^A(\cdot)$ is strictly increasing in θ and the foreign firm fully acquires the domestic firm to internalize the benefits of technology transfer. Second, $\pi_h^A(x^A(\theta))$ is decreasing in θ: the higher the degree of technology transfer the lower the profits of a non-acquired firm. As a result, through its choice of technology transfer, the foreign firm can make it less attractive for a domestic firm to be a competitor thereby lowering the price at which acquisition occurs.

How does an asymmetric restriction θ affect the foreign firm's choice between acquisition and direct entry? First note that such a restriction has no first-order effect on the payoff of the foreign firm. The reason is as follows. Under an asymmetric equity restriction θ, the transaction price v offered by the foreign firm under a (partial) acquisition equals $v = \pi_h^A(x^A(\bar{\theta})) - (1-\bar{\theta})\pi_f^A(x^A(\bar{\theta}))$. At this acquisition price, the foreign firm's payoff equals $\pi_f^A(x^A(\bar{\theta}) - C(x^A(\bar{\theta}))$ whereas under no equity restrictions it equals $\pi_f^A(x^A - C(x^A)$. In other words, since the foreign firm can lower the transaction price offered to the local firm to offset the payoff the latter receives via the equity restriction (which is $(1-\bar{\theta})\pi_f^A(x^A(\bar{\theta})))$, the equity restriction affects the foreign firm's profits only because $x^A(\theta)$ increases in θ (so that $x^A(\bar{\theta}) < x^A$ and $\pi_f^A(x^A(\bar{\theta}) - C(x^A(\bar{\theta})) < \pi_f^A(x^A) - C(x^A))$.[16] Thus, an asymmetric equity restriction makes acquisition less attractive to the foreign firm because it hampers its incentives for technology transfer. As a result, relative to the case of no restrictions, an asymmetric equity restriction makes direct entry relatively more attractive to the foreign firm and a sufficiently stringent equity restriction (i.e. $\bar{\theta}$ small enough) can induce direct entry by the foreign firm. On the other hand, if the restriction is relatively lax, i.e. $\bar{\theta}$ is

[16] It is straightforward to show that the extent of technology transfer $x^A(\theta)$ increases with θ; see Appendix A.5.

close to 1, the foreign firm still prefers (partial) acquisition to direct entry and the only effect of the restriction is that it results in less technology transfer to the local economy.

Now consider a symmetric equity restriction $\bar{\theta} \leq 1$ that applies to both entry modes. When facing a symmetric equity restriction, under direct entry the foreign firm forms a new enterprise and collects θ of its total profit (with the rest accruing to the domestic economy). There are two points worth noting about a symmetric equity restriction. First, such an equity restriction makes direct entry less attractive to the foreign firm even though it applies to both modes of entry. The reason is that the foreign firm suffers a first-order loss in profits only under direct entry where it essentially pays a fee of $(1-\bar{\theta})\pi_f^E(x^E(\bar{\theta}))$ to enter the market. As noted above, under a (partial) acquisition, the foreign firm can ensure itself a payoff of $\pi_f^A(x^A(\bar{\theta}) - C(x^A(\bar{\theta}))$ by manipulating the transaction price v. Second, despite the fact that the equity restriction applies across both modes, the level of technology transfer differs across modes because market structure depends upon the mode of entry (see Appendix A.5). However, the first-order effect of a symmetric restriction makes direct entry less attractive to the foreign firm. The following proposition summarizes the results of this section.

Proposition 3. *While an asymmetric equity restriction makes acquisition less attractive to the foreign firm, a symmetric equity restriction makes direct entry less attractive.*

Thus, in terms of Fig. 1, the introduction of an asymmetric equity restriction shifts the foreign firm's *FF* contour outwards, whereas a symmetric equity restriction shifts it inwards.

One final point is worth noting: equity restrictions are not the only means of inducing the foreign firm to adopt a different mode of entry. Fiscal and financial incentives (such as the frequently witnessed tax breaks and subsidies to FDI) can also be used to induce direct entry. Of course, such concessions impose budgetary costs on the government that equity restrictions do not.

4. Conclusion and discussion

This paper has explored a foreign firm's choice between acquisition and direct entry when the degree of technology transfer is endogenously determined. Our analysis indicates that a foreign firm can find acquisition of an existing domestic firm profitable under oligopoly when it is accompanied by technology transfer and that conflict between the foreign firm's objective and the preferences of a welfare maximizing government can serve a basis for policy intervention in such markets. Existing literature has noted that national security concerns the appropriation of domestic rents by foreigners, and purely nationalistic views over domestic ownership as potential explanations behind the existence of FDI restrictions (see, for example, Neven and Siotis, 1996). This paper shows that a purely welfare-maximizing government might use FDI restrictions in order to influence the foreign firm's choice between different modes of entry.

The costs of technology transfer play a major role in our analysis. While the modeling of factors that determine the magnitude of such costs is beyond the scope of this paper, it is useful to reflect on our results in light of existing empirical evidence. For example, several micro-level studies have shown that costs of technology transfer for FDI projects stem from knowledge gaps between the parties involved.[17] At the aggregate level, technology differentials between countries can be proxied by national differences in stocks of R&D expenditures (see, for example, Coe and Helpman, 1995). Following this interpretation, a prominent stylized fact regarding the global patterns of FDI fits well with our results. For example, during 1994–1999, on average about 93% of the total FDI inflows to OECD countries took the form of mergers and acquisitions. Given that OECD countries are unlikely to be far behind the technology frontier even in industries in which they host FDI, costs of technology transfer involved in FDI into such countries are likely to be low, making mergers and acquisitions more attractive relative to direct entry. In contrast, costs of technology transfer to developing countries are likely to be high, making direct entry the preferred mode for firms, whereas social welfare is likely to be higher with acquisition. It is therefore not surprising that where policy restrictions still exist in developing countries, they typically take the form of restrictions on new entry (e.g. in financial services in countries ranging from Brazil to Malaysia) and symmetric equity restrictions, which make direct entry less attractive (Proposition 3).

Several other stylized facts deserve mention. First, the rapid increase in the relative importance of worldwide acquisitions in the late 1990s has coincided with the development of new information and communication technologies. Such technological change should, in principle, have lowered the cost for cross-border technology transfer. Furthermore, while the share of foreign acquisitions in total FDI flows was constant between 1988 and 1993, it doubled by the year 1999 (see OECD, 2001, p. 47). Thus, firm preferences over modes of entry into foreign markets seem to have shifted towards acquisition with a decline in the cost of cross-border technology transfer. Second, a recent OECD (2001) study finds that foreign acquisitions are more likely to occur in host countries with low levels of competition. This fact is also consistent with our theoretical results.

The policy implications of our analysis should, nevertheless, be treated with caution. We have developed our results in a simple model under some special assumptions. For example, our analysis does not extend to a monopolistic competitive setting, where rents are dissipated by domestic or foreign entry into the host country. In such a setup, the case for policy intervention vanishes as, in the long-run equilibrium, the foreign firm and the government would be indifferent between the two modes of entry.[18] One may be tempted to further note that indeed FDI restrictions are more common in services (telecommunications, utilities, banking, etc.) than in manufacturing, where barriers to entry are generally lower, and for which most countries offer incentives to FDI, rather than try to restrict it.

[17] For example, Teece (1977) and Ramachandran (1993) have shown that variables such as the age of the technology, the number of previous applications of the technology and the experience of the transferee all affect the costs of technology transfer in an expected manner.

[18] As a referee noted, this implies that FDI restrictions should be more commonly observed in markets where there are high barriers to entry.

Acknowledgements

We are grateful to Eric Bond, Mary Hallward-Driemeier, Michael Nicholson, Maurice Schiff, Beata Smarzynska, two anonymous referees and participants at seminars at the World Bank, the AEA meetings in January 2002, and the EEA meetings in August 2002 for very helpful comments and suggestions. The views expressed here are those of the authors and do not necessarily correspond to those of the institutions with which they are affiliated.

Appendix A

Here, we provide all analytical derivations that underlie the results contained in the body of the paper.

A.1. Cournot competition

We directly report the output levels of all firms:

$$q^A = \frac{a+(n-1)x-c}{n} \quad \text{and} \quad q_h^A = \frac{a-c-x}{n} \quad \text{for } h = 1 \ldots n-2.$$

Similarly, in case of direct entry, we have

$$q_f^E = \frac{a+nx-c}{n+1} \quad \text{and} \quad q_h^E = \frac{a-c-x}{n+1} \quad \text{for } h = 1 \ldots n-1.$$

A.2. The strategic incentive for technology transfer

The strategic incentive for technology transfer is given by

$$S(n,\tau) \equiv -(n-1)q_f^E \frac{\mathrm{d}q_h^E}{\mathrm{d}x}$$

It is easy to show that $S(n,\tau)$ decreases with τ:

$$\frac{\mathrm{d}S(n,\tau)}{\mathrm{d}\tau} = \frac{-2(n-1)(a-c)n^2}{(-2n^2+\tau n^2+2\tau n+\tau)^2} < 0$$

Furthermore,

$$\frac{dS(n,\tau)}{dn} = \frac{-(a-c)(-2n^2+\tau n^2-2\tau n-3\tau+4n)\tau}{(-2n^2+\tau n^2+2\tau n+\tau)^2}$$

which implies that

$$n^c(\tau) = \frac{\tau-2+\sqrt{2}\sqrt{(\tau-2)(2\tau-1)}}{\tau-2}$$

A.3. Mode of entry

Profit levels gross of costs of technology transfer and the buy-out price under acquisition are

$$\pi_f^A = \frac{(a-c)^2}{2n(2-n)+\tau n^2} \quad and \quad \pi_h^A = \left[\frac{(a-c)(\tau n+2-2n)}{2n(2-n)+\tau n^2}\right]^2. \tag{11}$$

Under direct entry, we have:

$$\pi_f^E = \frac{(a-c)^2\tau}{2n(\tau-n)+\tau(n^2+1)} \quad and \quad \pi_h^E = \left[\frac{(a-c)(n\tau-2n+\tau)}{2n(\tau-n)+\tau(n^2+1)}\right]^2 \tag{12}$$

A.4. Proof of Proposition 2

We have

$$P^A - P^E = \frac{(a-c)\left[n^2(\tau-2)^2+n(\tau^2-4)+4\tau\right]}{((\tau-2)n^2+\tau(2n+1))((\tau-2)n^2+2(2n-1))} \tag{13}$$

Since $\tau>2$, the above expression is positive. Domestic firms prefer acquisition to direct entry iff $\pi_h^A>\pi_h^E$. Using Eqs. (11) and (12), we have:

$$\begin{aligned}\pi_h^A - \pi_h^E &= (a-c)^2 n(n\tau+\tau+2-2n)(2n\tau+\tau-4n+2)\\ &\quad\times(4n^2-4n^2\tau+n^2\tau^2+n\tau^2-4n+4\tau)/(n^2\tau-2n^2+2n\tau+\tau)^2\\ &\quad\times(4n-2n^2-2+n^2\tau)^2\end{aligned} \tag{14}$$

Again, since $\tau>2$, the above expression is also positive.

A.5. Symmetric equity restriction

It is easy to solve for the level of technology transfer under the two entry modes:

$$x^A(\theta) = \frac{2\theta(n-1)(a-c)}{(4n-2)+(\tau-2\theta)n^2} \quad \text{and} \quad x^E(\theta) = \frac{2\theta n(a-c)}{\tau(2n+1)+(\tau-2\theta)n^2}. \tag{15}$$

It follows from above that

$$x^A(\theta) - x^E(\theta) = \frac{2\theta(a-c)[(\tau-2\theta)+2\theta n-\tau n-\tau]}{[((\tau-2\theta)n^2+2\theta(2n-1))(\tau-2\theta)n^2+2\tau(n+1)]}$$

which implies that under a symmetric equity restriction, direct entry results in more technology transfer than acquisition iff

$$\tau < \frac{2\theta n(n-1)}{(n^2-n-1)}$$

Note that technology transfer under both modes is increasing in the foreign firm's equity share:

$$\frac{dx^A(\theta)}{d\theta} = \frac{\tau n^2\left[x^A(\theta)\right]^2}{2(a-c)(n-1)\theta^2} > 0$$

and

$$\frac{dx^E(\theta)}{d\theta} = \frac{\tau(n+1)^2\left[x^E(\theta)\right]^2}{2(a-c)n\theta^2} > 0.$$

References

Al-Saadon, Y., Das, S.P., 1996. Host-country policy, transfer pricing and ownership distribution in international joint ventures: a theoretical analysis. International Journal of Industrial Organization 14, 345–364.

Barros, P., Cabral, L., 1994. Merger policies in open economies. European Economic Review 38, 1041–1055.

Brander, J., Spencer, B., 1983. Strategic commitment with R&D: the symmetric case. Rand Journal of Economics 14, 225–235.

Coe, D.T., Helpman, E., 1995. International R&D spillovers. European Economic Review 39, 859–887.

Cowan, S., 1989. Trade and competition policies for oligopolies. Weltwirtschaftliches Archiv 125, 464–483.

Das, S., Sengupta, S., 2001. Asymmetric information and international mergers. Journal of Economics and Management Strategy 10, 565–590.

Ethier, W.J., Markusen, J.R., 1996. Multinational firms, technology diffusion and trade. Journal of International Economics 41, 1–28.

Head, K., Ries, J., 1997. International mergers and welfare under decentralized competition policy. Canadian Journal of Economics 30, 1104–1123.

Horn, H., Levinsohn, J., 2001. Merger policies and trade liberalization. Economic Journal 111, 244–276.

Kamien, M.I., Zang, I., 1990. The limits of monopolization through acquisition. Quarterly Journal of Economics 105, 465–499.

Lee, F.C., Shy, O., 1992. A welfare evaluation of technology transfer to joint ventures in the developing countries. International Trade Journal 2, 205–220.

Markusen, J.R., 2001. Contracts, intellectual property rights, and multinational investment in developing countries. Journal of International Economics 53, 189–204.

Mattoo, A., Olarreaga, M., Saggi, K., 2001. Mode of foreign entry, technology transfer and FDI policy, Policy Research Working Paper #2737, The World Bank.

Mutinelli, M., Piscitello, L., 1998. The entry mode choice of MNE: an evolutionary approach. Research Policy 27, 491–506.

Neven, D., Siotis, G., 1996. Technology sourcing and FDI in the EC: an empirical evaluation. International Journal of Industrial Organization 14, 543–560.

OECD, G., 2001. New Patterns of Industrial Organization: Cross-border Mergers and Acquisitions and Strategic Alliances, Paris. OECD, Paris.

Perry, M.K., Porter, R.H., 1985. Oligopoly and the incentive for horizontal merger. American Economic Review 75, 219–227.

Ramachandran, V., 1993. Technology transfer, firm ownership, and investment in human capital. Review of Economics and Statistics 75, 664–670.

Richardson, M., 1999. Trade and competition policies: concordia discors? Oxford Economic Papers 51, 649–664.

Roy, P., Kabiraj, T., Mukherjee, A., 1999. Technology transfer, merger, and joint venture: a comparative welfare analysis. Journal of Economic Integration 14, 442–466.

Saggi, K., 1996. Entry into a foreign market: foreign direct investment versus licensing. Review of International Economics 4, 99–104.

Saggi, K., 1999. Foreign direct investment, licensing, and incentives for innovation. Review of International Economics 7, 699–714.

Salant, S.W., Switzer, S., Reynolds, R.J., 1983. Losses from horizontal merger: the effects of an exogenous change in industry structure on Cournot–Nash equilibrium. Quarterly Journal of Economics 98, 185–199.

Svejnar, J., Smith, S., 1984. The economics of joint ventures in less developed countries. The Quarterly Journal of Economics 99, 149–168.

Teece, D.J., 1977. Technology transfer by multinational firms: the resource cost of transferring technological know-how. Economic Journal 87, 242–261.

Yu, C.-M., Tang, M.-J., 1992. International joint ventures: theoretical considerations. Managerial and Decision Economics 13, 331–342.

Chapter 26

Is There a Case for Industrial Policy? A Critical Survey*

Howard Pack • Kamal Saggi

What are the underlying rationales for industrial policy? Does empirical evidence support the use of industrial policy for correcting market failures that plague the process of industrialization? This article addresses these questions through a critical survey of the analytical literature on industrial policy. It also reviews some recent industry successes and argues that public interventions have played only a limited role. Moreover, the recent ascendance and dominance of international production networks in the sectors in which developing countries once had considerable success implies a further limitation on the potential role of industrial policies as traditionally understood. Overall, there appears to be little empirical support for an activist government policy even though market failures exist that can, in principle, justify the use of industrial policy.

Many countries in recent years have encountered great disappointment with the results of pursuing the conventional economic policies that John Williamson (1990) crystallized and named the Washington Consensus. Although few countries ever followed the pristine form of this consensus, some countries in East Asia adhered to many (but hardly all) of its components and experienced extraordinarily rapid growth for three decades or more. Although there was a brief and sharp recession in some of these countries during the 1997–99 financial crisis, most have rebounded, with the exception of Indonesia. Yet other countries that have gotten their macroeconomic and trade regimes much closer to the idealized consensus than the Asian countries did have failed to experience comparable growth. In many Latin American countries and in some African countries, there is an understandable search for a magic solution, and many policymakers have expressed interest in some form of industrial policy.

Few phrases elicit such strong reactions from economists and policymakers as *industrial policy*. As Evenett (2003) notes, industrial policy means different things to different people. This article defines industrial policy as any type of selective

* This chapter was originally appeared in *World Bank Research Observer* **21**, 267–297.

government intervention or policy that attempts to alter the structure of production in favor of sectors that are expected to offer better prospects for economic growth in a way that would not occur in the absence of such intervention in the market equilibrium. It is not surprising that those who believe strongly in the efficient working of markets view any argument in favor of industrial policy as fiction or, worse, an invitation to rent seeking, whereas those who believe that market failures are pervasive think that economic development requires a liberal dose of industrial policy.

This article addresses arguments for and against industrial policy and asks whether empirical evidence helps to settle the debate. Although there are cases where government intervention coexists with success, there are many instances where industrial policy has failed to yield any gains. The most difficult issue is that relevant counterfactuals are not available. Consider the argument that Japan's industrial policy was crucial for its success. Because we do not know how Japan would have fared under laissez-faire policies, it is difficult to attribute its success to its industrial policy. It might have done still better in the absence of industrial policy—or much worse. Given this basic difficulty, only indirect evidence can be obtained regarding the efficacy of industrial policy. Direct evidence that can "hold constant" all the required variables (as would be done in a well-specified econometric exercise) does not exist and likely never will.

The following section analyzes the main conceptual arguments in favor of industrial policy. Because the infant industry argument for trade protection anticipates most of the rationales for industrial policy, this argument is discussed extensively. Next, India's successful software industry is examined in the context of industrial policy. The following section examines how the expansion of international production networks has altered the case for industrial policy. The final section considers the issue of policy space.

Why Industrial Policy?

At a general level there is room for government intervention when there are market distortions (such as externalities or market power) or when markets are incomplete (for example, future markets for many goods simply do not exist). As is known from a basic theorem of welfare economics, under such market failures a competitive market system does not yield the socially efficient outcome. Any argument for industrial policy is a special case of this general argument.

Three specific arguments for industrial policy have received the most attention. One is derived from the presence of knowledge spillovers and dynamic scale economies, a second from the presence of coordination failures and a third from informational externalities. Before discussing these arguments in detail, it is useful to begin with the infant industry argument for trade protection because it is a precursor of modern arguments for industrial policy.

The Infant Industry Argument: A Precursor of Modern Industrial Policy

The infant industry argument is one of the oldest arguments for trade protection and perhaps the only such argument that is not dismissed out of hand by economists. The most popular (and the simplest) version of the argument runs as follows. Production costs may initially be higher for newly established domestic industries than for well-established foreign competitors, which have more experience. Over time, however, domestic producers can reduce costs as they learn by doing (they enjoy dynamic scale economies), and they can eventually attain the production efficiency of their foreign rivals. However, if the fledgling domestic industry is not initially protected from foreign competition, it may never takeoff. Furthermore, if dynamic scale economies are strong enough, temporary protection of the domestic industry can be in the national interest.

A stronger version of the argument states that the domestic industry might even be capable of attaining production costs below its foreign rivals if it is given sufficient protection. In this version of the argument, true comparative advantage lies with the domestic industry, and temporary protection can be in the global interest, because consumers in the rest of the world also benefit from the eventual lower production cost of the domestic industry.

In an influential paper, Baldwin (1969, p. 297) provided an incisive criticism of the infant industry argument, contending that "if after the learning period, unit costs in an industry are sufficiently lower than those during its early production stages to yield a discounted surplus of revenues over costs (and therefore indicate a comparative advantage for the country in the particular line), it would be possible for firms in the industry to raise sufficient funds in the capital market to cover their initial excess of outlays over receipts." If future returns indeed outweigh initial losses, capital markets would finance the necessary investment needed by the domestic industry. It is obvious, but worth stressing, that if future returns fall short of initial losses, the industry should not be established in the first place.

A frequently cited counter to Baldwin (and one that he acknowledged) is that capital market imperfections might prevent the infant industry from obtaining the required financing. For example, because of informational asymmetries investors, unlike producers, may not know that the industry will be profitable in the long run and therefore fail to provide the capital needed to cover the initial costs. However, such an argument defies credibility because it requires one to believe that firms that have not even begun production know more about their prospects than investors whose main objective is to find profitable uses for their excess capital and have previously analyzed and financed similar projects. And even if one grants the presence of asymmetric information, what prevents potential producers from conveying such information to likely investors? After all, entrepreneurs seeking funds for new businesses overcome this problem on a routine basis.

While the infant industry argument assumes that it is known with certainty that the industry in question will eventually be profitable, it seems more likely that the prospects for most new industries are uncertain and that *no one* really knows whether a particular infant industry will be profitable in the future. Under such circumstances capital markets would require compensation for the risks involved, and the resultant interest rates required might make the investment unprofitable. But efficiency requires that those bearing risks should be compensated, and there is no market failure if the underlying problem is that investors do not provide the necessary capital because they perceive the rewards not to be commensurate with the risks they are asked to bear.

Nevertheless, the assumption of omniscient financial intermediaries should be viewed with some skepticism. From early bubbles such as the tulip mania of the seventeenth century to the Internet bubble of the late 1990s, it is clear that financial actors are often deficient. In the Asian countries that suppressed the financial sector and directed loans to specific industries and firms as a part of industrial policy, the banking sector was itself in need of substantial improvement in operating procedures, much as industrial firms were. Thus, the belief that if there were opportunities investors would exploit them might be somewhat of a weak link in Baldwin's argument. On the contrary, it also implies that any selective economic policies would have to simultaneously address the weakness of the financial sector along with that of goods and other services. Indeed there might be an argument for initially strengthening the banking sector, perhaps by allowing foreign financial intermediaries into the country, before pursuing targeted sectoral policies. In any case, as Baldwin notes, if there is a problem with capital markets, policy ought to narrowly target that problem rather than resort to trade protection.

In today's world of global capital markets the simple version of the infant industry argument runs into another difficulty: Investors ought to be able to determine the prospects for the domestic infant industry from the experience of foreign producers. If domestic investors lack such information, surely foreign investors ought to have it. Why cannot the borrowing be international rather than local? One answer to this question may be that investors believe that an industry that has succeeded abroad will not necessarily succeed at home. But this explanation can be consistent with the very hypotheses underlying the infant industry argument only if investors are not fully rational.

What light has formal analysis shed on the infant industry argument? A seminal paper by Bardhan (1971, p. 1) noted that the infant industry argument is dynamic and that "any elaboration of this idea involves explicitly dynamic analysis, and it has hardly been integrated into the main corpus of trade theory which is mostly comparative-static in nature." Bardhan provides the first dynamic model of learning by doing in an open economy and derives the optimum extent and time path of protection to the learning industry. His model has two goods, c and m, and two factors of production, capital and labor, with constant returns to scale in production of both goods. The learning effect is assumed to depend on the cumulated volume of industry output in good m, and it shifts out the production function for the good in a Hicks neutral fashion.[1]

Bardhan models learning by doing as a classic Marshallian externality: The higher the cumulative output of the industry, the more productive is the technology of each individual firm. When learning is unbounded, Bardhan shows that it is socially optimal to subsidize the infant industry and that the time profile of the optimal subsidy depends on initial conditions. However, his framework does not capture the idea that international spillovers may partially substitute for domestic learning because the learning effect function contains the stock of domestic and foreign outputs as separate arguments, and the relationship between the two is not really considered.[2]

Succar (1987) extends Bardhan (1971) analysis to allow the learning in one sector to generate spillovers for both sectors, thereby providing an interindustry spillover rationale for the infant industry argument. However, the presence of such economies is not sufficient to justify intervention. As Succar notes, the discounted stream of productivity gains generated by learning by doing in the infant industry should outweigh the discounted stream of subsidies or else intervention is socially undesirable.[3] The intuitive idea underlying Succar's model is that the production of capital goods can enhance growth by acting as an "informal learning center where technical skills are required" thereby contributing to a country's technical infrastructure (p. 523).[4] Such improvements in the skill base of workers complement investments in human capital and can advance industrialization in developing countries.

The distinction between firm- and industry-level learning by doing becomes quite important because firms are heterogeneous. Suppose that some firms are more efficient at learning than others. Optimal subsidies would have to be nonuniform, and the government is unlikely to possess the information needed to implement an optimal subsidy program. It might thus make sense for the government to adopt a uniform policy even though that might not be the first-best policy. While in theory, mechanisms could be designed that induce firms to reveal their learning capabilities, the practical relevance of such mechanisms is far from clear.

As might be expected, there is more to the infant industry argument than the simple version formalized by Bardhan and Succar. As Baldwin notes, there are four more nuanced versions of the infant industry argument. First, acquisition of knowledge involves costs, but knowledge may not be appropriable by an individual firm. This is the standard argument for subsidizing research and development (R&D). Second, firms may provide costly on-the-job training but may be unable to prevent the diffusion of such knowledge as workers move to other companies (a free-rider problem in worker training). While firm-specific training involves no potential externality, general training can lead to externalities that would justify subsidies. Third, static positive externalities in the production of a good may justify trade protection. And fourth, determining the profitability of a new industry might require a costly investment, and the results could become freely available to potential competitors. In other words, investment in new industries might result in informational externalities that make it difficult for investors to earn a rate of return high enough to justify the initial investment. This argument has been formalized by Hausmann and Rodrik (2003), who call it the process of self-discovery, of determining what a company can produce profitably at world prices.

The infant industry argument does not really specify how learning occurs. It just assumes that dynamic scale economies will somehow be realized by the infant industry. Of course, learning is rarely exogenous, and it usually requires considerable effort and investment by firms (Pack and Westphal 1986). If such investments are made, firms need to be able to appropriate the benefits of the knowledge gained. Knowledge is a nonrival good and, once created, any number of agents can use it simultaneously. If firms cannot prevent the leakage of knowledge that is costly to create, they will have little incentive to create such knowledge. If property rights over knowledge are not enforceable, this can create a rationale for government intervention.

As Baldwin (1969) notes, many types of knowledge acquisition are not subject to the externality described above because entrepreneurs can often prevent the leakage of their knowledge to potential competitors. Similarly, if there are only a few firms in the industry, interfirm negotiations should help offset the externality problem (Coase 1960). But what if many rival firms benefit from the investment undertaken by a knowledge acquiring firm, and the firm can do nothing to prevent such diffusion? Is government intervention justified?

Trade protection is certainly not called for. A tariff does nothing to solve the basic externality problem and may well worsen it. A production subsidy to the entire sector will also fail to remedy the externality. What is needed are subsidies to initial entrants into the industry that help create new knowledge and discover better production technologies. As with R&D subsidies governments should target the marginal rather than inframarginal research. In the case of new firms it takes time to discover whether a new idea or technology is socially valuable, and the adoption of a novel technology by others is the strongest proof of its social value. Thus, a policy of rewarding early entrants requires an accurate forecast of the social value of their inventions and discoveries—a process that can be fraught with failure. Not only that, given the uncertainty associated with new technologies, a delayed pattern of adoption might even be socially optimal.

Knowledge Spillovers, Dynamic Scale Economies, and Industrial Targeting

Ever since David Ricardo, it has been well known that under free trade a country can increase its national income (and welfare) by moving resources into sectors in which its opportunity cost of production is lower than that of its trading partners. But is this prescription sufficient to generate economic growth? Perhaps not. Allocating resources according to comparative advantage can only ensure static efficiency and in no way guarantees dynamic efficiency. Succar (1987, pp. 533–34) argues that "the comparative advantage theory is a static construct that ignores [that] forward linkages exist between present choices and future production possibilities. Therefore it cannot guide the pattern of international specialization when there are asymmetric learning opportunities associated with the production of different goods, use of certain techniques, or both. Promotion of industries which generate substantial learning by doing economies should be an integral part of a strategy of human capital formation in [developing countries]." In other words, Succar argues for some sort of industrial targeting, although her model does not explicitly deal with this issue.

Even if one accepts the premise that certain industries are more likely to generate spillovers (based on knowledge diffusion or other factors), can policy be designed to encourage the "right" industries? The ideal but rarely attained goal of industrial policy is the development of a general-purpose technology. The Defense Advanced Research Projects Agency (DARPA), a small unit within the U.S. Department of Defense that generated and financed a portfolio of projects, is widely credited with having been the key contributor to the development of the Internet, in response to the need to maintain communications during an assault on the United States. This instance of success addressed a market failure, in that the social benefits of the research were much larger than the anticipated private benefits. Moreover, DARPA foresaw a potential need that private firms might not have. While the Internet was a main technological breakthrough and suggests the potential gains from such activity, it is useful to remember that the discovery of such general purpose technologies is a rare event and less likely in low innovation-intensity developing countries than in research-rich industrial countries.

The informational constraints facing policymakers pursuing industrial policy are severe and any realistic model of industrial targeting needs to account for them. In a recent paper Klimenko (2004) models industrial targeting as an optimal experimentation strategy for a government that lacks information about the set of industries in which the economy has a comparative advantage. He examines the set of industries in which a country will specialize as a result of such policy. In his model, for any set of targeted industries, it is possible to know with positive or zero probability whether a country will specialize in this set. He shows that an optimally designed industrial policy can lead a country to specialize in sectors in which it does *not* have comparative advantage. Depending on the beliefs of the policymaker, a country can end up abandoning the industries in which it has "true" comparative advantage.

Furthermore, Klimenko argues that policymakers may stop looking for better targets when the favored industries perform well enough. He interprets this outcome as a failure of industrial targeting policy even though it may not appear to be. He goes on to show that despite the existence of market failures, the outcome of the learning process through private experimentation (without any assistance from the government) can yield outcomes that are closer to the full information social optimum. Klimenko's rigorous analysis underscores the intuitive argument that the relevant counterfactuals are unavailable, and what may appear to be a successful industrial policy may not be the first-best outcome from a country's perspective. Merely doing something well need not imply that one might not be better at something else.

Coordination Failures as a Rationale for Industrial Policy

The idea behind the coordination failure argument for industrial policy is that many projects require simultaneous investments to be viable, and if these investments are made by independent agents, there is little guarantee that each agent, acting in its own self-interest, would choose to invest.[5] As Scitovsky (1954) noted, reciprocal pecuniary externalities in the presence of increasing returns can lead to market failure, because the coordination of investment decisions requires a signaling device to transmit information about present plans and future conditions, and the pricing system is not capable of playing this role.

Pack and Westphal (1986) argue that such pecuniary externalities related to investments in technology are pervasive during industrialization. They provide an example of two infant industries, where industry A produces an intermediate that is required in industry B and neither industry is profitable if it is established alone. However, if both industries are established together, both are profitable, implying that it is socially optimal to establish both. Of course, the problem is that without explicit coordination of investment decisions, this outcome would not be obtained.

Okuno-Fujiwara (1988) presents a formal model of such interdependence between industries and the coordination failure that can result. He considers an economy with three goods, x, y, and z, where good z serves as a numeraire and is produced under perfect competition with constant returns to scale. Good x is produced by a competitive industry and requires good y as an intermediate. The technology for good y exhibits large economies of scale, and the industry is assumed to be oligopolistic with the number of firms endogenously determined to ensure zero profits in equilibrium.

A coordination problem arises in the industry because the derived demand for the intermediate good y depends on its price, which in turn determines incentives for entry into the intermediate sector. If y producers anticipate low demand for their good, given the fixed costs of entry, few new producers would want to enter, implying a higher price for the intermediate. This could make industry x unsustainable. The key assumption here is that the intermediate good y must be locally supplied. On the contrary, if y producers are certain of high demand for their product, more would enter, lowering its price and allowing the high demand for the intermediate to be sustained.[6] Okuno-Fujiwara (1988) shows that there is no unique equilibrium in a small open economy with the above production structure. In the bad equilibrium the economy ends up specializing in good z whereas in the good equilibrium it produces both goods x and y and exports good x to the rest of the world (where the good equilibrium is welfare superior to the bad).

Turning to policy analysis, Okuno-Fujiwara (1988) suggests that three types of traditional government intervention can help ensure that the good equilibrium is realized: The government can provide a production subsidy to industry x or industry y or both, causing the two sectors to expand; it can provide an export subsidy to industry x; or it can shutoff international trade. However, he notes that trade protection can be effective only if the autarkic equilibrium production of good x is sufficiently large—something that is less likely to be true of small developing countries. In addition to traditional industrial policies (the first two options), Okuno-Fujiwara (1988) also suggests that the government can play a coordinating role between x and y producers by facilitating information exchange.[7] However, he argues that only repeated information exchanges can resolve the coordination failure. It is difficult to believe that policymakers can effectively execute such information exchanges between industries about whose day-to-day business they likely know little. Furthermore, this policy prescription suggests a massive role for government intervention in industrialization. Okuno-Fujiwara himself is skeptical of whether the mechanisms captured by his model and the policy prescriptions that emerge from his analysis had any practical analog in the Japanese experience.

In a paper along the lines of Okuno-Fujiwara (1988), Rodrik (1996) argues that for coordination failures to exist between upstream and downstream industries there must be some type of scale economies in production and imperfect tradability must hold across national borders for some of the goods, services, or technologies associated with manufacturing. In his model the intermediate good sector is characterized by monopolistic competition rather than oligopoly. He suggests that the non-tradable intermediate goods sector should be viewed as representing different categories of specialized skill labor. The idea is that a worker's decision to acquire a skill depends on demand for that skill and that it is costly or simply infeasible to import labor services should certain skills be in short supply locally. Like Okuno-Fujiwara (1988), Rodrik (1996) is hesitant to offer strong policy recommendations based on his analysis and concludes that government intervention designed to resolve such coordination failures is a risky strategy. The World Bank's (1993) well-known report on the East Asian miracle argues that East Asian efforts to coordinate investment decisions led to a number of inefficient industries.

While the theoretical rationale for redressing coordination failure appears to be sound, the argument rests on certain key assumptions, particularly that the organization of production activity is exogenously given. Why would industries whose profitability is so intimately intertwined not find ways to help coordinate decisions, as is the case in the many international supply networks (Sturgeon and Lester 2002, 2003; Gereffi and Memedovic 2003)? For example, vertical integration between intermediate and final goods producers can help resolve some coordination problems, although there are clearly limits to the extent to which organizations can adjust their scale and scope to solve coordination problems. At some point all firms have to interact with others in the market. But long-term contracts between firms have been used to solve problems of relation-specific investments in many industries. It is not clear why contracts could not play the same role for coordination failures.

Perhaps the biggest problem with the coordination failure argument is that it relies heavily on the assumption of nontradable intermediate inputs, partly reflecting the fact that much of the early literature was based on the example of the steel and automobile industries of the 1960s rather than products for which transportation costs for intermediates are likely to be low. Virtually all the models make this assumption although most international trade is in intermediate goods. Thus, the coordination failure argument runs up against the central fact about which much of the "new" trade theory has been built (see, for example, Ethier 1982).

This is no small contradiction, and if the coordination failure story is to be rescued, it needs to appeal to nontradable services as in Rodriguez-Clare (1996b). But the problem then is that the case for industrial policy on the basis of coordination failures is quite thin if inward foreign direct investment (FDI) is feasible. If local firms do not produce sufficient intermediates because of coordination failures, why could intermediates not be produced by foreign multinationals that are surely not dependent on the production structure of any one economy? In small developing countries a large-scale investment by a multinational can create sufficient demand for intermediates and easily resolve the coordination problem. This is partly what the literature on the backward linkage effects of FDI argues (Rodriguez-Clare 1996a; Markusen and Venables 1999).

It is unlikely that multinational firms would experience the type of coordination problems that confront small producers in developing countries. Indeed, the huge growth in international supply chains established by multinational firms has become one of the most visible features of industrial growth in the last decade (Sturgeon and Lester 2002). The role of multinational firms in determining the overall case for industrial policy is discussed in more detail below.

Informational Externalities

In a recent paper Rodrik (2004) argues that the traditional view of industrial policy (based on technological and pecuniary externalities) does not capture the complexities of industrialization. He argues that industrial policy is more about eliciting information from the private sector than it is about addressing distortions through first-best instruments. He envisions industrial policy as a strategic collaboration between the private and the public sectors with the primary goal of determining the areas in which a country has comparative advantage. The fundamental departure of this viewpoint from classical trade theory is that entrepreneurs may lack information about where a country's comparative advantage lies. Or more to the point, at the microlevel, entrepreneurs may simply not know what is profitable and what is not.

In the presence of informational externalities, a free-rider problem arises between initial and subsequent investors. Suppose no one knows whether activity x is profitable and that the uncertainty can be resolved only by making a sunk investment. By definition the investment cannot be recovered if the outcome turns out to be unfavorable. If there is free entry ex post, no entrepreneur may be willing to make the required investment ex ante: If the activity indeed turns out to be profitable, other entrepreneurs will be attracted to it, thereby eliminating all rents.

It is worth noting that Baldwin's (1969, p. 302) classic paper anticipates Rodrik's argument almost exactly: "suppose, for example, that a potential entrant into a new industry, if he could provide potential investors with a detailed market analysis of the industry, could borrow funds from investors at a rate that would make the project socially profitable. However, should this information become freely available to other investors and potential competitors, the initial firm might not be able to recoup the cost of making the market study....under these circumstances the firm will not finance the cost of the study, and a socially beneficial industry will not be established." Similarly in the context of the adoption of high yielding varieties of crops by farmers in developing countries, Besley and Case (1993, p. 399) note that late adopters may learn from early adopters: "[when] a technology is of uncertain profitability, some potential adopters may wait until they observe whether others have fared well by using it" and that such "externalities are potentially important in agricultural technology adoption."

Given the importance of this argument for the debate on industrial policy, it is useful to examine the framework presented in Hausmann and Rodrik (2003) in some detail. They consider a small open economy with two sectors, traditional and modern. The production technology in the traditional sector is constant returns to scale, and the presence of a fixed factor generates diminishing returns. In the modern sector, which consists of many goods, there are constant returns to scale in production, but the cost of production of a good depends on an unobserved productivity parameter, θ_i, that becomes known only when the production of a good is attempted. This requires a time period in which resources must be used but no production takes place—what Baldwin called a "market study." Entrepreneurs lack information about the profitability of production of various goods in the modern sector, and this information can be obtained only by undertaking a sunk investment.

After uncertainty regarding θ_i is resolved, entrepreneurs compare their production costs with world prices and produce goods for which they make monopoly profits, which accrue for length of time *T*—call this the monopolization period. Of course, once information becomes public, which it does in period three when the monopolization period has elapsed, there is further entry into goods that yield positive profits until all profits are competed away to zero.

Hausmann and Rodrik (2003) analyze the laissez-faire equilibrium of the above model and compare it with the social planner's problem to derive the market failures that result from the presence of informational externalities. They argue that the market equilibrium is deficient in two respects. First, the level of investment and entrepreneurship delivered by the market does not coincide with the social optimum, because the entrepreneurs care only about profits and not about the economy-wide benefits of their investment. If the monopolization period is long, the market economy can actually deliver too much investment in the modern sector rather than too little. This suggests that in economies where firms face substantial entry barriers, the underinvestment problem noted by Hausmann and Rodrik (2003) is not likely to be serious. For example, the industrial licensing regime pursued by India during the first 40 or so years after independence made it difficult for firms to enter new markets. And the recent literature on the business climate emphasizes other factors that discourage investment in the modern sector, such as the time to obtain business permits, telephone lines, and other utility hookups (World Bank 2006). Such barriers should have helped protect rents for those that did manage to enter profitable markets.

The second market failure identified by Hausmann and Rodrik (2003) is that the market equilibrium yields too little specialization—all activities that turn out to be profitable are sustained whereas optimality requires that only the one activity with the highest return be pursued. In other words, while it is optimal in their model for the small open economy to produce only the good for which the profit margin is the highest, the market solution allows all those that make positive profits to stay in business during monopolization period.

This result reflects the general equilibrium nature of their model and the fact that they consider a small open economy. To see this, first note that the modern sector draws resources out of the traditional sector and that optimality requires that these resources be used where they generate the largest profits, which happens to be in the modern good for which the productivity parameter (θ_i) is the highest. Second, because the country's output of a good does not affect the world price, one can never have a situation where the markups across different goods are equalized. Clearly, if world prices changed with a country's exports or output, complete concentration in the modern sector need not obtain. A more likely scenario would be that a country should produce higher quantities of modern goods for which it has a more favorable productivity draw and lower quantities of other goods.

Hoff (1997) argues that if initial producers benefit subsequent producers, the case for subsidizing initial producers hinges much on the assumption that the externalities operate in a deterministic fashion (do not involve any uncertainty). She constructs a model in which initial entrants provide information that is socially valuable by reducing uncertainty for potential followers regarding production conditions. In her model factors that increase the informational barrier to entry can actually imply a lower optimal subsidy for the infant industry. By contrast in most models the externalities are assumed to remove all uncertainty rather than simply reducing it. Because Hoff's model is clearly more realistic, it is notable that her results weaken the case for subsidizing an infant industry.

The International Dimension: Role of Exports and FDI

For small developing countries the case for industrial policy is rarely a purely domestic one. International considerations are fundamental, and the role of exports (on the part of domestic firms) and inward FDI has received considerable attention. A potential rationale for industrial policy in the context of exports arises when product quality is unknown to foreign consumers. The information asymmetry can lead to market failure that can then potentially justify some form of intervention. Adding an explicit process of reputation acquisition may be an objective of policy. Grossman and Horn (1988) focus on reputation acquisition at the firm level, whereas Mayer (1984) focuses on the country level. In the view of Grossman and Horn, Toyota can affect only its own reputation in foreign markets whereas in Mayer's model, experience with Toyota also influences how foreign consumers view other Japanese companies, such as Honda. The difference matters because returns to reputation acquisition are appropriable in the Grossman and Horn model whereas they are not in the Mayer model.[8]

Policy intervention with respect to FDI has a long history. The rationale has frequently been the effects of FDI on the productivity of local firms through technology transfer and linkage effects. The literature on FDI, technology transfer, and linkages is extensively surveyed by Saggi (2002). The review here is limited to aspects of FDI that relate intimately to local industrial development and its linkage effects, because these correspond quite well to the coordination failure rationale for industrial policy.

There is a voluminous informal as well as empirical literature on backward linkages. For example, the *World Investment Report 2001* (UNCTAD 2001) was devoted entirely to the effects of FDI on backward linkages in host countries. However, analytical models that explore the relationship between multinationals and backward linkages in the host country are hard to come by. Two examples of such models are Markusen and Venables (1999) and Rodriguez-Clare (1996a). Both models emphasize the demand-creating effects of FDI on the host economy: Multinationals generate derived demand for intermediate goods, thereby promoting industrial development of the intermediate goods sector in the host country.[9] As noted, a common problem with analytical models in this area is the assumption that intermediates are nontradable. These models assume no trade in intermediates and then use FDI as the channel that provides some intermediates or increases demand for local intermediate goods producers. As a result, the models are likely to overstate the impact of multinationals on industrial development.

Mexico's experience in the automobile industry is illustrative of how FDI can contribute to industrial development in the host country (Laderman, Maloney, and Serven 2003). Initial investments by U.S. car manufactures into Mexico were followed by investments by Japanese and European car manufacturers and automobile parts and component manufacturers. As a result, competition in the automobile industry increased at multiple stages of production, efficiency improved, and Mexican automobile industry exports boomed. The pattern of FDI behavior in Mexico—investment by one firm followed by investment by others—probably reflects strategic considerations involved in FDI decisions. Most multinational firms compete in concentrated markets and are highly responsive to each other's decisions. An important implication of this interdependence among competing multinationals is that a host country may be able to unleash a sequence of investments by successfully inducing FDI from one or two important firms. However, the concentration of inward FDI into a handful of developing countries suggests that only a few countries can benefit from this process—Egypt and Tanzania are not China.

A recent case study of the effects of Intel's investment in Costa Rica by Larrain, Lopez-Calva, and Rodriguez-Clare (2000) finds evidence that local suppliers benefited substantially from Intel's investment. Similar evidence exists for other sectors and countries and is discussed in Moran (1998, 2001). For example, in the electronics sector in Malaysia, Moran (2001) notes that foreign investors helped their local subcontractors keep pace with modern technologies by assigning technicians to the suppliers' plants to help set up and supervise large volume automated production and testing procedures. In a broader study Batra and Tan (2002) use data from Malaysia's manufacturing sector to study the effect of multinationals on interfirm linkages and productivity growth during 1985–95. Their results show that not only are foreign firms more involved in interfirm linkages than domestic firms but also that such linkages are associated with technology transfer to local suppliers. Such technology transfers were found to have occurred through worker training and the transmission of knowledge that helped local suppliers improve the quality and timeliness of supply.

Javorcik (2004) examines backward linkages and technology spillovers using data from the Lithuanian manufacturing sector during 1996–2000. She finds that firm productivity is positively affected by a sector's intensity of contacts with multinational customers but not by the presence of multinationals in the same industry. Thus, her results support vertical spillovers from FDI but not horizontal spillovers.

Furthermore, she finds that vertical spillovers occur only when the technological gap between domestic and foreign firms is moderate. Blalock (2001) uses a panel data set from Indonesian manufacturing establishments to check for the same effects. He finds strong evidence of a positive impact of FDI on productivity growth of local suppliers, showing that technology transfer does take place from multinationals. He also plausibly suggests that because multinationals tend to source inputs that require relatively simple technologies relative to the final products they produce, local firms that manufacture such intermediates may be in a better position to learn from multinationals than those that compete with them.

If one accepts the optimistic view of the effects of FDI—and some of the evidence discussed above suggests reasonable grounds for doing so—does this have implications for industrial policy? The answer is a qualified yes. Basic economic theory tells us that it is optimal to subsidize an activity if it generates positive externalities—if the activity benefits agents other than those directly involved in the activity. The potential surely exists for positive externalities from FDI, and evidence exists that this potential is often realized. Incentives to attract FDI may be justified on the grounds of such externalities from inward FDI, but the magnitude of some of the incentives being used seems difficult to justify (Moran 1998), and such policies are not typically what proponents of industrial policy have in mind. Indeed, the thrust of such arguments is typically in favor of encouraging the development of indigenous firms. Investment incentives and tax breaks to multinational investors work against their local competitors. Thus, if there are local firms that could potentially compete with multinationals, the adverse effect on such firms of tax incentives to multinationals needs to be taken into account. The efficacy of investment incentives is also unclear—such policies could easily end up transferring rents to foreign investors without affecting their investment decisions.

Government Knowledge Requirements

This review of arguments for industrial policy suggests the enormous difficulties of implementing industrial policies quite apart from the possibilities for rent-seeking. The range and depth of knowledge that policymakers would have to master to implement successful policy is extraordinary. They would have to be accurately informed about an enormous range of complex questions, understand their relevance, and be able to accurately evaluate subtle differences. Some of the issues on which policymakers would have to be knowledgeable derived from the preceding discussion include:

- The firms and industries that generate knowledge spillovers.
- The firms and industries that benefit from dynamic scale economies—the precise path of such learning and the magnitude of the cost disadvantage at each stage of the learning process.

- The sectors that have a long-term comparative advantage.
- The size of scale economies of different firms and sectors, to facilitate investment coordination.
- An ability superior to that of individual firms to learn about their potential competitiveness.
- The nature and extent of capital market failures.
- The magnitude and direction of interindustry spillovers.
- The relative amount of learning by individual firms from others and from their own experience.
- The extent to which early entrants generate benefits for future entrants.
- The extent of heterogeneity of firms' learning abilities.
- Whether consumers learn the quality of a good after consuming rather than by inspecting it.
- Whether firms that are trying to reduce production costs also begin a simultaneous effort to improve their product's quality to obtain a better reputation.
- The potential effects of FDI or international trade on coordination problems, including a detailed knowledge of which of tens of thousands of intermediates are tradable.
- A forecast of which firms can create new knowledge and discover better production methods.
- The spillover effects of FDI and the likely intensity of foreign purchase of domestic intermediates.

It is possible that government officials might be this omniscient, but the performance of the portfolio managers in industrial country stock markets suggests that few of the well-trained (and remunerated) equity analysts can evaluate even much more certain and grosser characteristics of existing firms and industries with long track records. Nor do industrial firms themselves have the ability to successfully forecast such developments. Acknowledging that a first-best policy would argue for the government to address such market failures or externalities, the task is daunting. Quite apart from the dangers of optimal policy being subverted by industries and firms that would benefit, the sheer knowledge and skill requirements would exceed that possessed by almost any institution, including the best consulting firms. On a far more circumscribed set of tasks, measuring and explaining the sources of lower total factor productivity for a small number of sectors in Brazil and the Republic of Korea relative to the United States, McKinsey & Co., a preeminent consulting firm, spent several years and employed dozens of people with qualifications exceeding those of officials in most developing countries (McKinsey Global Institute 1998a,b).

No study has attempted to assess whether governments have mastered these 15 areas (or others that can be derived from the discussion here) that have to be addressed. The efficacy of industrial policy has to be evaluated on the basis of the realized results of the firms or industries that have been encouraged. The underlying market failures or externalities that contributed to the decision to foster a firm or sector cannot be identified from the policy (such as subsidized directed credit). Only the effects of the policy can be assessed. This task is taken up next.

Does Industrial Policy Work?

As noted, it is impossible to offer a single agreed counterfactual to evaluate the success of industrial policy targeted to individual industries. Thus there have been a number of research strategies to provide an empirical evaluation of industrial policy. These are reviewed in Noland and Pack (2003). Among other issues, researchers have examined the impact of trade protection, subsidies to R&D, general subsidies, and preferential lending rates on the evolution of productivity, capital accumulation, and sectoral structure. Few of the empirical analyses find that sectoral targeting has been particularly effective.

Consider some of the evidence. In Japan more than 80 percent of on-line budget subsidies were devoted to agriculture, forestry, and fisheries in 1955–80, the peak of Japan's industrial policy efforts.[10] Implicit tax subsidies for investment were highest in the mining sector and low in the high technology sectors. Government subsidies to R&D were also small. Unless elasticities of investment and R&D with respect to subsidies were implausibly high, their effect was limited. Industries that were encouraged did not experience significantly faster rates of total factor productivity growth than others, and R&D subsidies were largely ineffective.

Beason and Weinstein (1996) examine the connection between industrial policy and sectoral total factor productivity growth in Japan. Working with a 13-sector sample for 1955–90, they fail to uncover evidence that preferential policies (measured by the effective rates of protection, taxes, or subsidies) targeted sectors with increasing returns to scale or contributed to the rate of capital accumulation in targeted sectors or to their total factor productivity growth. They do find some evidence that before the first oil shock, industrial policy targeted sectors with high labor usage. Employing a slightly different data set, Lawrence and Weinstein (2001) extend this research and find that differential corporate tax rates had an impact on sectoral total factor productivity growth, whereas direct subsidies and subsidized loans did not. Moreover, they find the paradoxical result that the effective rate of protection was negatively associated with sectoral total factor productivity growth and that imports, not exports, were positively associated with total factor productivity growth.

There are at least two channels through which imports could contribute to increasing productivity. First, imports allow domestic producers to use new, improved, or specialized intermediate inputs to which they would not otherwise have access. Second, imports compete with domestic products, and their availability acts as a constant spur to domestic producers to cut costs and improve quality. Lawrence and Weinstein (2001) divide imports into "competitive" and "noncompetitive" and find evidence for Japan to support this second channel. From this they conclude that Japan's growth would have been even faster if it had cut tariffs and exposed a greater share of its domestic producers to foreign competition.[11]

Following a method broadly similar to that of Beason and Weinstein (1996), Lee (1996) finds a similar lack of impact of Korean industrial policies on sectoral capital accumulation or total factor productivity growth. Pack (2000) follows a different strategy, assuming that total factor productivity increased in favored manufacturing sectors in both Japan and the Republic of Korea and estimates how much of an impact even an *assumed* successful policy could have had on the growth of gross domestic product. The most favorable estimate is a roughly 0.5 percentage point increase in total gross domestic product growth rate of roughly 10 percent over the relevant periods. While this is significant, it is hardly the magic key to accelerated growth.

It is possible that the impact of industrial policy is manifest largely in sectors that purchased inputs from the promoted sectors, even if the promoted sectors did not themselves benefit. However, Pack (2000) finds that sectors that were encouraged in Japan and the Republic of Korea had few linkages with nonfavored sectors through input–output relations, and there is little evidence of labor flowing from favored to neglected sectors, a likely mechanism for the transmission of knowledge.

Nevertheless, as noted at the beginning of this article, the difficulty of constructing a single agreed on counterfactual precludes a robust conclusion. Moreover, all the empirical analysis examines the contemporaneous impact of policies—for example, did Korean industries that were encouraged experience greater total factor productivity growth in the period when main promotion occurred, 1973–85? Someone doubting these results could point to the performance of Korean firms such as Samsung and LG in the following two decades in such diverse product lines as plasma televisions, RAM chips, and cellular phones and attribute these later successes to the earlier stimulation the firms received for other product lines. These more recent successful efforts by the firms could be attributed, in this interpretation, to their earlier growth in other product categories. In this view learning to perform R&D on microwaves had future carryover effects on plasma televisions. Fully resolving divergent views is impossible, but detailed firm histories by Kim (1997) or Hobday (1995) do not suggest such carryover.

Even if it could be shown that the success of a few firms is attributable to earlier encouragement by the government, the aggregate effects cited above suggest there was not a major impact at the national level during the main period of growth acceleration. And any such effects would have to be weighed against the negative long-run impacts in the financial sector cited by those skeptical of industrial policy. For example, the Asian financial crises of the late 1990s and Japan's stagnation since 1990 can be interpreted as partly the result of earlier government directed lending that minimized the need for banks to learn modern techniques of evaluating individual projects and managing the riskiness of their overall portfolio.

New Industrial Policy

Recent discussion of "new" industrial policy including the desirability of fostering learning and obtaining benefits from agglomeration economies offered by industrial clusters has received little systematic empirical evaluation. Rodriguez-Clare (2004a,b) provides an extensive discussion and a formal treatment of clusters. Humphrey and Schmitz (2002) provide an extensive survey of the empirical literature on clusters and discuss whether they offer a locally controlled alternative to participation in networks.

Export Processing Zones and Other Clusters

In principle, the development of clusters could boost productivity through the provision of overhead services by the organizers plus the interaction of the firms entering the cluster. Clusters could offer an alternative to dependence on either buyer- or manufacturer-led networks.

The benefit of clusters may arise from face-to-face interactions that are productivity enhancing (interactions between software writers and chip manufacturers, for example), a pool of workers with the relevant skills, or reduced transportation costs. Individual market agents may not be aware of the externality they generate for others, and this provides an additional market failure that could in principle be addressed by public intervention. The main example usually cited is that of Silicon Valley in California, which most accounts suggest arose spontaneously. Similarly, the rapid development of the software industry in Bangalore and other cities in India, discussed below, appears to be the outcome of the combination of a large group of well-educated English-speaking students, the entrepreneurial abilities of a small group of residents, and the activities of a large Indian expatriate community, particularly in Silicon Valley. While publicly financed education institutions generated the fundamental resource, educated workers, there was no explicit effort to galvanize the agglomeration economies that developed. Texas Instruments financed a critical communications satellite. Positive government efforts followed the takeoff of the sector.

There are interesting descriptions of a number of clusters in high-income countries, but few normative evaluations of their success employing social cost-benefit analyses or even grosser measures such as growth of exports relative to firms outside the cluster but in the same sector. However, some insights can be obtained about whether recent success stories in Asia conform to the contours of the new industrial policy.

Development of the Indian software sector reflected a complex set of interactions between domestic and foreign responses to perceived opportunities. The evolution of the Indian software industry centered in Bangalore is explained in detail in the following section. Many of the same patterns, with different details, can be documented for other success stories, such as the Hsinchu Science Park in Taiwan, China (Saxenian 1999, 2001), the special economic zones in China (Rosen 1999; Huang 2003), and Bangladesh's rise as a clothing exporter (Rhee 1990). In the Indian software sector and the Bangladesh garment sector, the initiating force was private, with the government playing almost no role except for the fundamental one in India of providing good education.

The establishment of a science park in Taiwan, China, and legislation in China to allow special economic zones to attract FDI resulted from an initial government stimulus. A critical input for success was foreign participation that dealt with some of the roles cited above as components of industrial policy (source of new technology, facilitation of learning, source of new product ideas, centralized marketing allowing economies of scope, and coordination of entry of complementary firms). In China, the special economic zones mimicked the effects of a free trade policy, neutralizing adverse public policies. The zones did not discriminate among sectors. The decision by Taiwan, China, to foster a science park comes closer to a proactive industrial policy, but the experience at Hsinchu has not been systematically evaluated.

Many countries have attempted to use export-processing zones to attract FDI and perhaps generate agglomeration economies. Evaluation suggests that while potentially useful, they have had indifferent results (for references, see World Bank 2005). There have been a few success stories, such as the Republic of Korea and Taiwan, China, in the 1950s and early 1960s and the special economic zones of China. But there have been more than a thousand such efforts. There are few clues in the existing literature about why some export processing zones have been successful, while most have failed (for a review and an evaluation of the Philippine experience, see Calanog 2006).

The Indian Software Industry

In India a precondition for the development of the software industry was high-quality education in junior colleges and universities financed by the government. University graduates went abroad for further training, remained as expatriates in the high-technology sector, and later returned home or interacted intensively with newer Indian firms. The lamented brain drain became, with a lag, a source of strength and a critical catalytic input to development of the Indian software industry.

Large numbers of English-trained programming graduates. In the 1980s there were a growing number of programming graduates at levels ranging from postsecondary technical schools to those trained at the Indian Institutes of Technology, and many were underemployed. Almost all of them had been educated in English. The government's continuing investments in education had resulted in more than 1,800 educational institutions and polytechnics producing 70,000 to 85,000 computer science graduates every year (James 2000).[12] Many Indian graduates also had a second university degree or postgraduate degree from schools in the United States or the United Kingdom, often in computer technology (Deshmukh 1993). Other Indian software programmers received training in private software institutes to keep abreast of developments in the industry and acquired a breadth of software skills. Hence, many were familiar with main computer hardware systems (Lakha 1990), computer-aided software engineering tools, object-oriented programming, graphical user interface, and client networking (Lekshman and Lal 1998).

Series of serendipitous events. The main impetus to demand came from abroad from of a series of serendipitous events. In the 1990s the ratio of world prices for programming services relative to those in India rose because of a global shortage of programmers and the demands for solutions to the anticipated Y2K problem. Enterprising businesses in India capitalized on this opportunity by setting up firms that were essentially employment agencies. Indian software programmers were hired on behalf of clients in the United States on short-term contracts to provide onsite services. "Bodyshopping," as this practice was called, became the predominant mode of Indian software exports. The development work was performed on the client's premises, saving software firms the high costs of acquiring computer hardware. The National Association of Software and Service Companies, the software trade association, reported that the software sector earned $2.5 billion from Y2K billing from 1996 to 1999, a critical period in the growth of the industry (Software & Information Industry Association 2001). As late as 1988 software exports had been less than $200 million. By 1998 they were $3.6 billion, accounting for more than 10 percent of total Indian exports.

Indian software firms also benefited from another fortuitous event, the European Union's move to the euro. Many Indian software professionals were involved in adapting computer systems and databases to accommodate the euro. Between 2000 and 2002 India earned an estimated $3 billion in revenues from euro-related information technology projects. A contributing factor was the level of programming costs in India, which conferred a Ricardian comparative advantage in some subsectors of software. As late as 1995, after substantial wage increases because of a rising demand for Indian software services, the annual wages of Indian software professionals were only 14–59 percent those of their counterparts in Canada, Switzerland, the United Kingdom, and the United States. This combination of skills and cost savings led firms in some industrial countries to outsource their software development requirements to India.

Thus random events—the Y2K problem and the shift to the euro—exerted positive feedback and generated a succession of mutually reinforcing benefits. As for industrial policy, of whatever form, it seems unlikely that any government could have foreseen and acted on these serendipitous demands.

The foreign role. A main contributor to development of the Indian software industry was the large number of expatriate Indian information technology professionals in Silicon Valley. In 1998, 774 (9 percent) of the high-technology firms were led by Indian chief executive officers (CEOs) (James 2000). Many Indian expatriates helped to convince large firms such as Oracle, Novell, and Bay Networks to establish operations in India (Saxenian 1999). Aware of the obstacles some Indians faced in raising capital for their software start-ups in India, they actively raised venture capital from U.S. investment firms and organized conferences in the United States to heighten awareness of the potential of India's software industry (Kripalani 2000). Finally, some of these expatriates lobbied the Indian government to revamp its telecommunication policies and other regulations that had impeded growth of the Indian software industry (Kripalani 2000).

FDI accounted for a large share of early investment in the sector—70 percent in Bangalore in 1996, for example (*The Economist* 1996). And this contribution understates the true impact. Texas Instruments, the first foreign firm to establish an offshore software facility in Bangalore in 1984, augmented Bangalore's inadequate land-based telecommunication infrastructure by investing in its own satellite communications network. Some of its lines were later leased to other software firms, enabling them to expand their India-based operations instead of relying solely on onsite services abroad. Until the government built software technology parks in the 1990s linked to earth stations and other telecommunications infrastructure, Texas Instrument's satellite network remained an important driving force behind the offshore development of software exports.

Once U.S.-based firms became interested in India, Bangalore's reputation for technical excellence and its abundant supply of information technology graduates made it a natural choice for foreign companies to locate their software business there (Stremlau 1996). With FDI came much of the infrastructure and international knowledge that allowed Indian firms to exploit international opening. Indian software firms also benefited from foreign joint ventures and partnerships, which created markets for Indian software exports. Partnerships with foreign firms added to the credibility of Indian firms, serving as an endorsement of its quality and reliability without government encouragement. Thus, other foreign firms looking to outsource their software development would invariably choose a software firm with a proven track record with another foreign company. And for small Indian firms attempting to move out of the low-end of the software business by venturing into software packaging, having foreign partners gave them access to an established distribution network and knowledge of recent trends in the software market (because of proximity to demand in the United States). It also significantly lowered marketing costs. Because marketing costs account for as much as 70–80 percent of the final price of a software package (Lakha 1994), small Indian firms without a known brand, an extensive sales network, or sufficient revenue found it more profitable to sell their packages through a foreign collaborator.

The Indian software industry and the new industrial policy. How does this experience of a successful sector square with the many strands of new industrial policy? All of it was privately initiated. Governments at various levels became involved only after the success of the sector was evident, ratifying the success rather than catalyzing it. The industry expanded on the basis of comparative advantage and never needed any protection. Indeed, one advantage of the software sector was that its inputs, largely downloads from satellites, and its output, uploaded to satellites, could not be easily taxed by the Indian authorities. A symbiosis of foreign and domestic firms was critical. Although there was clearly an agglomeration of firms in Bangalore, this was achieved spontaneously without government direction. Foreign contracts rather than government subsidies provided the basis for international exploration of markets. There is no evidence of government initiation or preference.

Is Industrial Policy Still Relevant?

From Hamilton and List to contemporary discussions of industrial policy, the implicit framework has been that of a firm producing tradable goods at an initial cost disadvantage because of the limited industrial history of the country, learning to become more efficient, and then competing with imports in the local market or successfully exporting. Marketing of the efficiently manufactured product was implicitly assumed to be routine. Reduction of production costs, whether through internal learning by doing or through spillovers within industrial clusters, was viewed as paramount. In discussions of postwar Asian experience, some attention was given to the catalytic role of Japanese, Korean, and Taiwanese trading companies in assembling large quantities of goods and achieving scale economies in marketing, but this activity was not given center stage (Lall and Keesing 1992). Even if countries today could pursue the export-oriented policies of the Republic of Korea and Taiwan, China, of four decades ago, it is not clear that they would be efficacious, given the changed nature of both retailing and production networks.

In the last two decades there has been a shift in the institutional mechanism of international trade, as two types of organization have evolved. One is international production networks in which a producing firm organizes large numbers of suppliers in several locations. The other is buyer-led networks, in which large retail chains provide specifications for the desired final product and encourage suppliers in developing countries to organize their own production system, which most often include large numbers of local subcontractors.[13] These networks have become increasingly important and are dominant in clothing and electronics and are growing in importance in products such as automotive components. In East Asia, in recent years, components "constitute at least a fifth of manufacturing exports and ... have typically grown 4–5 percent faster than overall trade in East Asia" (Yusuf and others 2003, p. 272).

One effect of the growing importance of international product networks is their efficiency at organizing production and continuously reducing costs so that the global price that nonmember firms must compete with shifts down rapidly. Infant firms undergoing learning face other hurdles: rapidly improving quality, changing characteristics of products, and an array of new goods that compete with existing ones (Ernst 2002). For firms attempting to enter export markets, it cannot be assumed that simply achieving low cost is sufficient to realize foreign sales. There is no guarantee that lead firms will be able to identify one or two firms in a small African country. The existence of supply networks imposes a significant challenge for developing-country firms that are not embedded in such a network, because the lead firms usually succeed in generating higher performance in design, engineering, effective use of information and communication technology, and ability to coordinate production in several locations (Yusuf and others 2003).

Further militating against the classical view of infant industries is the change in the nature of retailing. Consider a mundane product such as socks that can be produced efficiently with relatively labor-intensive technology. Huge retailers such as Wal-Mart and Target buy socks in quantities that exceed the production capacity of small (by international standards) companies. The special economic zones in China have become a series of clusters that produce enormous quantities of socks, ties, and other clothing. Retailers and wholesalers place large orders that are well beyond the production capacities of smaller firms, even if they have quickly learned to become cost-competitive in relatively small quantities. "These days buyers from New York to Tokyo want to be able to buy 500,000 pairs of socks all at once, or 300,000 neckties, 100,000 children's jackets" (Barboza 2004, section D, p. 1). European firms buy smaller, more varied products but expect local suppliers to provide "in-house design and sample making capabilities that would allow them to translate and adapt the design from Europe" (Sturgeon and Lester 2002, p. 49).

In textiles, clothing, electronics, automotive parts, and other sectors being part of an international product network is critical to exporting and quality upgrading. Firms that are not part of such networks may not succeed even if they are as efficient as members in production costs. Local participants in the network must "label, track, respond to product orders in real time on the basis of style, color, fabric, and size; exchange information on an ... electronic basis, provide goods to a retailer's distribution center that can be efficiently moved to stores ... including containers with bar codes concerning contents" (Yusuf and others 2003, p. 283). These requirements, now fairly standard in many product areas, suggest that successful penetration of high-income markets will become increasingly difficult for countries that have not yet industrialized.

In electronics, an important labor-intensive growth sector in the past for many Asian countries, much of the production is now carried out by contract manufacturers that have grown enormously in the last decade. The activities of firms such as Solectron and Flextronics, formerly undertaken by main industrial country firms, are now outsourced. Sturgeon and Lester (2002) examined the location of several activities of Solectron—headquarters, manufacturing, materials purchasing and management, new production introduction centers, and after sales repair centers—and found that most of these activities take place in industrial countries or in the more advanced semi-industrial countries contiguous to them, such as Mexico, Puerto Rico, Romania, and Turkey. Ernst (2002, p. 24) confirms these results and points out that specialized clusters in countries such as the Nordic countries, France, Germany, and the United States are main sources as are Hungary, Israel, the Republic of Korea, Singapore, and Taiwan, China. Poorer countries even if they have a potential cost advantage after a long learning period will have trouble breaking into these existing networks.

Moreover, China and India present formidable competitors, as demonstrated by the concern over the termination of the Multifiber Arrangement and the Agreement on Textiles and Clothing and the potential losses incurred by countries that formerly had guaranteed access to Organisation for Economic Co-operation and Development markets. While it might be argued that the two giant countries will encounter rising wages and thus will enter more capital- and technology-intensive sectors, making room for new countries, both still have hundreds of millions of workers, largely in the rural sector, who remain poor and will keep a lid on real wages faced by industrialists over the next decades, implying a continuing supply of low-cost products in many sectors. While in principle poorer countries can find niches in which they have a comparative advantage, finding them is likely to require skills that are best nurtured by membership in a production network or direct interaction with large retailers.

What does the growing importance of production networks imply for potential government interventions? The Republic of Korea and Taiwan, China, had numerous trading companies that aggregated the orders of local manufacturers, following the Japanese model of the *shosha soga*. Most of these arose spontaneously from private efforts. Governments could encourage the development of trading companies where there are market failures—setup costs may be high whereas the marginal costs of adding firms to the network may be small. Such trading firms would operate across clusters of manufacturing firms. Again, this assumes that there are capital market failures that preclude a nascent trading firm from obtaining finance.

Other policy questions arise. Will government-sponsored clusters be as effective in generating continuing improvements in product development, quality upgrading, and efficiency to sustain competition on the world market or will firms within clusters improve faster by becoming part of networks? There is some anecdotal evidence that international networks attempt to limit the extent of upgrading, especially in higher value-added segments of design. If so, the question once again is whether to promote specific activities within the entire production nexus, but this is beyond the capacity of all but the most competent of governments (Humphrey and Schmitz 2002). Taiwan, China's experience in the Hsinchu Science Park may be an exception, but it is so far unconfirmed by systematic evidence.

Concluding Remarks

Does the current policy landscape of the multilateral trading system even permit developing countries to pursue industrial policy? Should it? Developing countries have to contend with several multilateral agreements that were not in existence when the rich countries of today were developing. Have the constraints and disciplines imposed by World Trade Organization (WTO) agreements such as Trade-Related Aspects of Intellectual Property Rights, and Trade-Related Investment Measures become too restrictive to allow developing countries to chart their preferred course to economic development? This is a difficult question, but it cannot be dismissed out of hand. Certainly, the international policy environment today imposes constraints on the use of national policies that were absent even 15 years ago, and the constraints are backed by the potent dispute settlement procedure of the WTO (Noland and Pack 2003, chapter 5).

The experience in several countries in the last two decades suggests that private firms have often been successful in pursuing learning strategies that earlier analysts had advocated. The growth of the Indian software sector, Bangladesh's clothing industry, and China's special economic zones was driven primarily by private-sector agents (often from abroad). In Bangladesh and India the main role of the government was benign neglect, whereas China imitated the earlier success of Singapore by enabling the location of foreign investment in enclaves that were well provided with infrastructure. Much of the earlier investments came from overseas Chinese.

In none of these cases was there a government policy that singled out individual firms or industries with high learning potential and likely spillovers. In Bangladesh and China foreign firms brought standard technology but important extensive marketing networks. Standard comparative advantage can explain the pattern of sector choice. Compared with the exceptionally complex process of either picking sectors (or firms) or allowing firms to identify their own competitive advantage, it seems much more efficient in the current state of intensifying world competition and the growing importance of extensive and complex supply networks to allow foreign firms to facilitate cost reduction in the host economy.

This suggests a change in focus from even the new industrial policy to one that focuses on negotiation with multinational firms on issues ranging from environmental regulation and taxes to efforts to ensure local learning. The difficulty with this approach is the limited amount of FDI going to developing countries—many countries in Africa, the Middle East, and Latin America continue to receive little. This may be because of their weak overall economic prospects given their poor policies. But in these economies hewing to some of the main tenets of the Washington Consensus (while recognizing some of its weaknesses) might prove a better investment of limited government competence and legitimacy than the extraordinarily complex strategies required by either the new or the old industrial policy.

Notes

Howard Pack is a professor of business and public policy, economics, and management in the Wharton School at the University of Pennsylvania, Philadelphia; his e-mail address is packh@wharton.upenn.edu. Kamal Saggi is a professor of economics in the Department of Economics at the Southern Methodist University; his e-mail address is ksaggi@smu.edu. The authors acknowledge support from the U.K. Department for International Development project "Global Trade Architecture and Development." Wenying Choy provided superb research assistance.

1. Bardhan's model is in the spirit of the original learning by doing model of Arrow, which posited learning that occurred in the machine-producing sector. Some of the endogenous growth literature also posits such effects. However, the literature on technological innovation summarized in Evenson and Westphal (1995) and Ruttan (2001) shows that learning can occur in all sectors, a fact that would enormously complicate the results of much of the literature.

2. Pack and Saggi (2001) explore the implications of the provision of free technology by the purchasers of a firm's exports, a further complication.

3. It is not likely that this criterion has been satisfied by the European Airbus effort, widely considered a main example of a successful industrial policy. Furthermore, one also needs to account for the cost of distortions that are generated by the taxes needed to finance the subsidies.

4. Succar's emphasis on the capital goods sector is similar in spirit to Arrow's learning by doing model and endogenous growth models such as Romer's (1986), which employed it as a building block.

5. Rodriguez-Clare (1996a) has shown that coordination failures can lead to "development traps."

6. As will be discussed below, good x could be produced by multinationals that establish local production, thus obviating the coordination problem.

7. Much of the effort of the Ministry of International Trade and Industry and the Ministry of Finance in Japan can be described as the interchange of information among firms and interaction with the government to reduce any obstacles to the realization of consistent plans. The same is true of French indicative planning of the 1950s and 1960s. As noted earlier, it is difficult to assess whether such sector-specific targeting was successful. For an extensive review of the empirical evidence on Japan, see Noland and Pack (2003).

8. The complexity of these issues is underlined by the fact that Bagwell and Staiger (1989) reach still other conclusions. They argue that if asymmetric information blocks the entry of high-quality firms,

export subsidies can improve welfare by breaking the entry barrier facing high-quality firms. Thus, whether an export subsidy is desirable hinges on the nature of the distortion that is caused by the presence of asymmetric information.

9. It is worth nothing that if production is intended primarily for a protected domestic market, local suppliers, especially if there are local content requirements, may have costs above world prices, raising the possibility that greater linkages may lower the value of domestic output.

10. The following paragraphs are based on Noland and Pack (2003, chapter 2).

11. Japan's Ministry of Finance apparently agrees. In a June 2002 report issued by its Policy Research Institute, it maintains that "the Japanese model was not the source of Japanese competitiveness but the cause of our failure" and specifically argues that sectors sheltered by Ministry of International Trade and Industry became bloated and inefficient, whereas those exposed to international competition tended to be more market-aware, efficient, and profitable (Morita 2002).

12. Some observers feel this was an incorrect allocation of education funds and that the returns would have been greater to more extensive and higher quality primary and secondary education. The success of the software industry does not disprove this view. For example, the favorable effect of the adoption of the green revolution package on the income of Indian farmers of elementary school education is well established.

13. A good description of these alternatives and evidence on their quantitative importance is given in Gereffi (1999); see also Yusuf and others (2003, chapter 7). UNCTAD (2001) and Sturgeon and Lester (2002) provide evidence on the empirical importance of the international production networks.

References

Bagwell, Kyle, and Robert W. Staiger. 1989. "The Role of Export Subsidies When Product Quality is Unknown." *Journal of International Economics* 27(1–2):69–89.

Baldwin, Robert E. 1969. "The Case against Infant Industry Protection." *Journal of Political Economy* 77(3):295–305.

Barboza, David. 2004. "In Roaring China, Sweaters Are West of Socks City." *New York Times*. December 24.

Bardhan, Pranab. 1971. "On Optimum Subsidy to a Learning Industry: An Aspect of the Theory of Infant-Industry Protection." *International Economic Review* 12(1):54–70.

Batra, Geeta, and Hong W. Tan. 2002. *"Inter-Firm Linkages and Productivity Growth in Malaysian Manufacturing."* International Finance Corporation, Washington, D.C.

Beason, Richard, and David E. Weinstein. 1996. "Growth, Economies of Scale, and Targeting in Japan (1955–1990)." *Review of Economics and Statistics* 78(2):286–95.

Besley, Timothy, and Anne Case. 1993. "Modeling Technology Adoption in Developing Countries." *American Economic Review* 83(2):396–402.

Blalock, Garrick. 2001. "Technology from Foreign Direct Investment: Strategic Transfer Through Supply Chains." Cornell University, Department of Applied Economics and Management, Ithaca, N.Y.

Calanog, Victor. 2006. "Essays on the Economics of Development Strategies." Ph.D. diss. The Wharton School, University of Pennsylvania, Philadelphia.

Coase, Ronald. 1960. "The Problem of Social Cost." *Journal of Law and Economics* 3:1–44.

Deshmukh, Vikas. 1993. "Bangalore: India's Hi-Tech Birthplace." *Economic Reform Today* 3.

The Economist. 1996. "Software in India: Bangalore Bytes." *The Economist*. March 23.

Ernst, Dieter. 2002. "Global Production Networks in East Asia's Electronics Industry." East-West Center, Honolulu, Hawaii.

Ethier, Wilfred J. 1982. "National and International Returns to Scale in the Modern Theory of International Trade." *American Economic Review* 72(3):389–405.

Evenett, Simon. 2003. "Study on Issues Related to a Possible Multilateral Framework on Competition Policy." WT/WGTCP/W228. World Trade Organization, Geneva.

Evenson, Robert E., and Larry E. Westphal. 1995. "Technological Change and Technology Strategy." In Jere Behrman and T. N. Srinivasan, eds., *Handbook of Development Economics 3a*. Amsterdam: North Holland.

Gereffi, Gary. 1999. "International Trade and Industrial Upgrading in the Apparel Commodity Chain." *Journal of International Economics* 48(1):37–70.

Gereffi, Gary, and Olga Memedovic. 2003. "The Global Apparel Value Chain: What Prospects for Upgrading by Developing Countries?" Sectoral Studies Series 12770. United Nations Industrial Development Organization, Vienna.

Grossman, Gene, and Henrik Horn. 1988. "Infant Industry Protection Reconsidered: The Case of Informational Barriers to Entry." *Quarterly Journal of Economics* 103(4):767–87.

Hausmann, Ricardo, and Dani Rodrik. 2003. "Economic Development as Self-Discovery." *Journal of Development Economics* 72(2):603–33.

Hobday, Mike. 1995. *Innovation in East Asia: The Challenge to Japan*. London: Edward Elgar.

Hoff, Karla. 1997. "Bayesian Learning in an Infant Industry Model." *Journal of International Economics* 43(3–4):409–36.

Huang, Yasheng. 2003. *Selling China*. Cambridge: Cambridge University Press.

Humphrey, John, and Hubert Schmitz, 2002. "Governance and Upgrading: Linking Industrial Cluster and Global Value Change Research." Working Paper 120. University of Sussex, Institute for Development Studies, Brighton, United Kingdom.

James, David. 2000. "India Starts Up." *Upside Magazine* 12(4):265–69.

Javorcik, Beata S. 2004. "Does Foreign Direct Investment Increase the Productivity of Domestic Firms? In Search of Spillovers through Backward Linkages." *American Economic Review* 94(3):605–27.

Kim, Linsu. 1997. *Imitation to Innovation: The Dynamics of Korea's Technological Learning*. Boston: Harvard Business School Press.

Klimenko, Mikhail. 2004. "Industrial Targeting, Experimentation and Long-run Specialization." *Journal of Development Economics* 73(1):75–105.

Kripalani, Manjeet. 2000. "A Typhoon of Venture Capital?" *Business Week*. January 31.

Laderman, Daniel, William F. Maloney, and Luis Serven. 2003. *Lessons from NAFTA for Latin American and Caribbean Countries*. Washington, D.C.: World Bank.

Lakha, Salim. 1990. "Growth of the Computer Software Industry." *Economic and Political Weekly*, January 6:49–56.

———. 1994. "The New International Division of Labour and the Indian Computer Software Industry." *Modern Asian Studies* 28(2):381–408.

Lall, Sanjaya, and Donald Keesing. 1992. "Marketing Manufactured Exports from Developing Countries: Learning Sequences and Public Support." In G. Helleiner, ed., *Trade Policy, Industrialization, and Development: New Perspectives*. Oxford: Clarendon Press.

Larrain B., Felipe, Luis F. Lopez-Calva, and Andres Rodriguez-Clare. 2000. "Intel: A Case Study of FDI in Central America." CID Working Paper 58. Harvard University, Center for International Development, Cambridge, Mass.

Lawrence, Robert Z., and David E. Weinstein. 2001. "Trade and Growth: Import Led or Export Led? Evidence from Japan and Korea." In Joseph E. Stiglitz and Shahid Yusuf, eds., *Rethinking the East Asian Miracle*. Oxford: Oxford University Press.

Lekshman, Pai, and Uday Lal. 1998. "A Major Exporter Turns Inward." *Computerworld* 32(14). April 6.

Lee, Jong-wha. 1996. "Government Interventions and Productivity Growth in Korean Manufacturing Industries." *Journal of Economic Growth* 1(3):391–414.

Markusen, James R., and Anthony Venables. 1999. "Foreign Direct Investment as a Catalyst for Industrial Development." *European Economic Review* 43(2):335–56.

Mayer, Wolfgang. 1984. "The Infant-Export Industry Argument." *Canadian Journal of Economics* 17(2):249–69.

McKinsey Global Institute. 1998a. *Productivity—The Key to an Accelerated Development Path for Brazil.* Washington, D.C., and Sao Paulo: McKinsey & Co.

———. 1998b. *Productivity Led Growth in Korea.* Washington, D.C. and Seoul: McKinsey & Co.

Moran, Theodore. 1998. *Foreign Direct Investment and Development.* Washington, D.C.: Institute for International Economics.

———. 2001. *Parental Supervision: The New Paradigm for Foreign Direct Investment and Development.* Washington, D.C.: Institute for International Economics.

Morita, Issei. 2002. *Financial Times.* June 27.

Noland, Marcus, and Howard Pack. 2003. *Industrial Policy in an Era of Globalization: Lessons from Asia.* Washington, D.C.: Institute for International Economics.

Okuno-Fujiwara, Masahiro. 1988. "Interdependence of Industries, Coordination Failure, and Strategic Promotion of an Industry." *Journal of International Economics* 25(1/2):25–43.

Pack, Howard. 2000. "Industrial Policy: Growth Elixir or Poison?" *World Bank Research Observer* 15(1):47–68.

Pack, Howard, and Larry Westphal. 1986. "Industrial Strategy and Technological Change: Theory versus Reality." *Journal of Development Economics* 22(1):87–128.

Pack, Howard, and Kamal Saggi. 2001. "Vertical Technology Transfer via International Outsourcing." *Journal of Development Economics* 65(2):389–415.

Rhee, Yung W. 1990. "The Catalyst Model of Development: Lessons from Bangladesh's Success with Garment Exports." *World Development* 18(2):333–46.

Rodriguez-Clare, Andres. 1996a. "The Division of Labor and Economic Development." *Journal of Development Economics* 49(1):3–32.

———. 1996b. "Multinationals, Linkages, and Economic Development." *American Economic Review* 86(4):852–73.

———. 2004a. "Clusters and Comparative Advantage: Implications for Industrial Policy." Research Department Working Paper 523. Inter-American Development Bank, Washington, D.C.

———. 2004b. "Microeconomic Interventions After the Washington Consensus." Research Department Working Paper 524. Inter-American Development Bank, Washington, D.C.

Rodrik, Dani. 1996. "Coordination Failures and Government Policy: A Model with Applications to East Asia and Eastern Europe." *Journal of International Economics* 40(1–2):1–22.

———. 2004. "Industrial Policy for the Twenty-First Century." CEPR discussion Paper 4767. Centre for Economic Policy Research, London.

Romer, Paul M. 1986. "Increasing Returns and Long Run Growth." *Journal of Political Economy* 94(5):1002–37.

Rosen, Daniel H. 1999. *Behind the Open Door: Foreign Enterprises in the Chinese Marketplace.* Washington, D.C.: Institute for International Economics.

Ruttan, Vernon. 2001. *Technology, Growth, and Development: An Induced Innovation Perspective.* New York: Oxford University Press.

Saggi, Kamal. 2002. "Trade, Foreign Direct Investment, and International Technology Transfer: A Survey." *World Bank Research Observer* 17(2):191–235.

Saxenian, AnnaLee. 1999. *Silicon Valley's New Immigrant Entrepreneurs*. San Francisco: Public Policy Institute of California.

———. 2001. "Taiwan's Hsinchu Region: Imitator and Partner for Silicon Valley." Policy Paper 00–44. Stanford Institute for Economic Policy Research, Stanford, Calif.

Scitovsky, Tibor. 1954. "Two Concepts of External Economies." *Journal of Political Economy* 62(2):143–51.

Software & Information Industry Association. 2001. "Submission of the Software & Information Industry Association to the U.S. Trade Representatives: 2000 Special 301 Recommendations, February 18, 2000." (March 18, 2001). Washington, D.C.

Stremlau, John. 1996. "Dateline Bangalore: Third World Technopolis." *Foreign Policy* 102:152–59.

Sturgeon, Timothy, and Richard Lester. 2002. "Upgrading East Asian Industries: New Challenges for Local Suppliers." Massachusetts Institute of Technology, Industrial Performance Center, Cambridge, Mass.

Sturgeon, Timothy, and Richard Lester. 2003. "The New Global Supply-Base: New Challenges for Local Suppliers in East Asia." Working Paper 03-001. Massachusetts Institute of Technology, Industrial Performance Center, Cambridge, Mass.

Succar, Patricia. 1987. "The Need for Industrial Policy in LDCs—A Restatement of the Infant Industry Argument." *International Economic Review* 28(2):521–34.

UNCTAD (United Nations Conference on Trade and Development). 2001. *World Investment Report: Promoting Linkages*. New York.

Williamson, John. 1990. "What Washington Means by Policy Reform." In John Williamson, ed., *Latin American Adjustment: How Much Has Happened?* Washington, D.C.: Institute for International Economics.

World Bank. 1993. *The East Asian Miracle*. Washington, D.C.: The World Bank.

———. 2005. *World Development Report 2005: A Better Investment Climate for Everyone*. Washington, D.C.: World Bank and Oxford University Press.

———. 2006. *Doing Business in 2006*. Washington, D.C.: World Bank.

Yusuf, Shahid, M. Anjum Altaf, Barry Eichengreen, Sudarshan Gooptu, Kaoru Nabeshima, Charles Kenny, Dwight H. Perkins, and Marc Shotten. 2003. *Innovative East Asia: The Future of Growth*. Washington, D.C.: World Bank and Oxford University Press.

Chapter 27

Tariff barriers and the protection of intellectual property in the global economy#

Difei Geng[a,*], Kamal Saggi[b]

[a] *Department of Economics, University of Arkansas-Fayetteville, Fayetteville, AR 72701, United States of America*
[b] *Department of Economics, Vanderbilt University, Nashville, TN 37235, United States of America*

ARTICLE INFO

JEL classification:
F12
F13
F23

Keywords:
International patent protection
Import tariffs
National treatment
R&D
Welfare

ABSTRACT

This paper develops a simple two-country model of quality-improving innovation to study the role tariff barriers play in shaping the welfare impact of global patent protection. We show that international patent policy coordination via national treatment is desirable only if tariff barriers between countries are sufficiently low. Furthermore, if countries are free to impose their optimal tariffs on one another, requiring national treatment in patent protection unambiguously lowers world welfare. Hence, constraining tariffs helps pave the way for international coordination over patent protection. This insight provides a potential rationale for the historical sequencing of policy reforms observed in the global trading system: multilateral rules on intellectual property were adopted only after decades of trade negotiations had succeeded in substantially reducing global tariffs.

1. Introduction

During the past seventy years or so, the multilateral trading system has been remarkably successful in reducing traditional policy barriers to international trade. From 1947–95, eight rounds of multilateral trade negotiations were conducted under the auspices of the General Agreement on Tariffs and Trade (GATT), a multilateral treaty focused on international trade in goods. These eight GATT rounds delivered substantial multilateral trade liberalization, eventually reducing the average ad-valorem tariff on industrial goods to under four percent (Bagwell et al., 2016). The last major GATT round – i.e. the Uruguay round – led to the formation of the World Trade Organization (WTO) in 1995, an organization that today includes not just GATT but also the Agreement on Trade Related Aspects of Intellectual Property (TRIPS) – the key multilateral treaty that now governs rules and regulations pertaining to the protection of intellectual property in the global economy. The inclusion of TRIPS in the WTO raises a key question: what role do tariff barriers play in determining the welfare impact of national patent policies?[1] We address this question by focusing on a core TRIPS obligation, i.e., the *national treatment* clause which calls for WTO member countries to offer foreign firms the same level of patent protection that they provide their domestic firms.[2] We show that trade liberalization is a *prerequisite* for national treatment

* Corresponding author.
E-mail addresses: dg017@uark.edu (D. Geng), k.saggi@vanderbilt.edu (K. Saggi).

[1] Existing literature has argued persuasively that IPRs are *trade-related*, i.e., the IPR policies of trading countries affect the pattern and volume of trade — see, for example, Maskus and Penubarti (1995) and Ivus (2010, 2015). But the welfare question we address here has not received much attention in this literature — see Saggi (2016) for a survey.

[2] To be sure, the notion of national treatment did not originate with TRIPS. Indeed, national treatment is specified as an obligation even under the Paris Convention of 1883. But TRIPS obligations are backed by the WTO's potent dispute settlement process that allows an aggrieved country to file a case with the WTO (and potentially retaliate) in case the IPRs of its nationals have been violated by another member country. Access to the WTO's dispute settlement procedures gives TRIPS a level of bite that earlier IPR treaties such as the Paris Convention lacked.

in patent protection to be welfare-improving. This result suggests that the liberalization of trade in goods that occurred under the GATT/WTO system eventually helped pave the way for TRIPS by making its welfare impact relatively more palatable.

To address the key issues motivating the paper, we build a tractable two-country model of trade and innovation. Each country has one firm that sells its product in both markets. For simplicity, the products of the two firms are assumed to be unrelated to each other (i.e. each firm is a monopolist in its own product market). Prior to production and sales, firms invest in R&D which determines the quality of their respective products. Countries have multiple policy instruments at their disposal that affect innovation and trade. First, each country chooses whether or not to offer patent protection to firms. If a firm receives patent protection in a market, it enjoys monopoly status there. When such protection is absent, it faces competition from the imitated product. Second, each country chooses its ad-valorem import tariff. Finally, we consider a scenario where countries can also utilize R&D subsidies to incentivize innovation.

Our benchmark model focuses on the interaction between import tariffs and patent protection in a symmetric setting. We show that the lower the import tariff of a country, the less likely is the *other* country to grant patent protection to its own firm since greater profitability abroad makes domestic patent protection less crucial for incentivizing innovation. Interestingly, it turns out that there is a non-monotonic relationship between a country's import tariff and the impact that granting patent protection to the foreign firm has on its welfare (which is *negative* if the foreign firm receives patent protection from its own government). Specifically, a reduction in a country's tariff has two opposing effects on its incentive for granting patent protection to the foreign firm. First, a reduction in a country's import tariff makes its patent protection more effective in incentivizing the foreign firm's R&D by increasing its product market profits (a *complementary effect*). Second, a reduction in a country's import tariff makes its patent protection toward the foreign firm less salient for incentivizing R&D on its part (i.e. the tariff reduction partly *substitutes* for foreign patent protection). It turns out that the complementary effect dominates when the initial tariff is high whereas the opposite holds when the initial tariff level is low. This finding suggests that there may be diminishing returns in the innovation dividends that can be expected from trade liberalization: i.e. all else equal, the innovation incentive effects of reducing tariff barriers in countries where such barriers are still relatively high (such as Egypt or India) are likely to exceed those that can be obtained from further liberalizing trade in economies that are already quite open (such as the United States or Germany).

Holding tariffs constant, we find that national patent protection levels are *substitutes across countries*. In particular, a country is *less likely* to protect a firm (regardless of whether it is domestic or foreign) if that firm receives patent protection from the other country. An important implication of this finding is that countries have incentives to free ride on each other, so that the Nash equilibrium features insufficient patent protection. Such strategic substitutability and the under-provision of patent protection also arise in trade models of variety-expanding R&D (Grossman and Lai, 2004; Geng and Saggi, 2015). The present paper complements this literature by revealing that strategic incentives underlying national patent policies do not depend on the nature of innovation being considered.

An important result of this paper is that, in Nash equilibrium, each country grants patent protection to its own firm while denying such protection to the foreign firm. Such a pattern of discriminatory equilibrium patent policies is consistent with anecdotal evidence as well as the formal empirical literature on the subject – i.e. countries indeed tend to discriminate against foreign firms in the enforcement of intellectual property rights (IPRs).[3] In our model, countries discriminate against foreign firms primarily due to profit considerations: when a country grants patent protection to a foreign firm, the resulting increase in firm's monopoly profits accrues entirely to the foreign country and therefore does not contribute to its welfare.

A natural question that follows is whether the lack of patent protection for foreign firms can ever be justified on welfare grounds. To answer this question, we examine international patent coordination that requires each country to follow national treatment by extending patent protection to each other's firms. One practical example of such type of coordination is the Patent Cooperation Treaty (PCT) which allows innovators to file patent applications simultaneously in multiple countries that are signatories of the treaty. As de Rassenfosse et al. (2019) show, the PCT helps reduce discrimination in national patent policies by making them better aligned with national treatment. We show that the impact of such patent coordination depends critically on the level of tariffs imposed by countries. In particular, requiring a country to follow national treatment in patent protection lowers world welfare when its tariff is high whereas it raises welfare when it is low. The intuition for this unexpected finding is as follows. When a country's import tariff is high, its patent policy toward the foreign firm does not play a major role in determining the firm's R&D incentive since its export profits are small and this, in turn, weakens the rationale for protecting the foreign firm. In the limit, when a country's tariff is almost prohibitive, it has virtually nothing to gain from protecting the foreign firm since doing so simply eliminates the imitated version of the product from the local market without providing *any* offsetting benefit to local consumers.[4] This result shows that the degree of trade liberalization in the global economy is a major determinant of the desirability of providing stronger patent protection to foreign innovators.

Do these results hold when tariffs are endogenously determined? To address this question, we derive equilibrium patent policies when countries impose nationally optimal tariffs on one another. The key conclusion is that allowing for endogenous tariffs does not affect the incentives that countries have to deny patent protection to foreign firms. More importantly, in the presence of nationally

[3] For empirical studies examining the actual implementation of national treatment in patent policy see Kotabe (1992), Liegsalz and Wagner (2013), Azagra-Caro and Tur (2014), Webster et al. (2014), de Rassenfosse and Raiteri (2016), de Rassenfosse et al. (2019), and Mai and Stoyanov (2019).

[4] This result fits well with the argument that stronger patent protection in developing countries will fail to raise local and global welfare if patent-holders simply choose to stay out of their markets despite such protection because they either do not find market conditions to be particularly attractive (Bond and Saggi, 2018) or are concerned about international price spillovers arising from parallel trade and/or the presence of external reference pricing policies that undercut their profits in larger markets.

optimal tariffs, requiring countries to follow national treatment in patent protection necessarily *lowers* world welfare. When tariffs are endogenous, strengthening patent protection toward the foreign firm induces a country to raise its import tariff. The intuition for this result is that when the foreign firm is freed from imitative competition, its profit margin increases which, in turn, increases the importing country's incentive to extract rent from it. The tariff increase that results from the strengthening of patent protection granted to the foreign firm dampens its innovation incentive and therefore reduces welfare. Interestingly, these findings echo the widely held concern that stronger patent protection in the global economy could lower welfare (see, for example, Boldrin and Levine, 2013). Our analysis identifies a plausible scenario where this concern is borne out: i.e. extending patent protection to foreign firms when import tariffs are completely unconstrained is unambiguously welfare-reducing.

We also investigate how trade policy coordination affects the efficiency implications of national treatment in patent protection. First, since tariffs are efficiency reducing in our model, countries choose to eliminate tariffs if trade policies are chosen to maximize joint welfare. The move to national treatment in patent protection in the presence of trade coordination is socially desirable in our model since strengthening foreign patent protection under free trade necessarily raises world welfare. Hence, trade policy coordination is sufficient for countries to benefit from instituting national treatment in international patent protection. An important policy implication of this result is that trade policy coordination produces not only direct welfare gains through liberalizing trade but also indirect gains by facilitating coordination over behind-the-border policy instruments such as patent protection.

Finally, we consider two important extensions of the benchmark model. First, we examine the implications of market asymmetry across countries so as to capture a key difference between developed and developing countries. While our main conclusions remain qualitatively unchanged, we show that the under-protection of patents tends to be more severe in countries with smaller markets. As a consequence, patent coordination between asymmetric countries may need to focus on the tightening of patent standards in smaller or less developed countries, a finding consistent with the provisions of many real-world trade agreements, both preferential trade agreements such as the North American Free Trade Agreement (NAFTA) and multilateral agreements such as TRIPS. Our analysis also yields an interesting auxiliary result: countries with larger markets tend to impose lower tariffs because they benefit more from foreign R&D. This finding is in line with the evidence found in Naito (2019), and it provides a novel insight: i.e. the observed negative correlation between market size and tariff rates may partly be driven by innovation considerations.

In our second extension, we allow countries to subsidize R&D. This is an empirically relevant case as R&D subsidies are widely used and are indeed permitted by the WTO. In addition, it is well-known that patent protection is not necessarily the most effective means for incentivizing innovation as it increases monopoly power and can also give rise to various other problems that tend to reduce efficiency (Boldrin and Levine, 2013). We show that, as expected, R&D subsidies are more efficient in promoting innovation than patent protection. As a result, coordination over R&D subsidies can lead to a superior welfare outcome than international patent coordination. This insight offers a potential explanation for why R&D subsidies are not banned under the WTO and also suggests that there might be a fruitful role for international coordination over such subsidies.

To the best of our knowledge, only two other theoretical papers examine the interaction between tariff and patent policies.[5] The first is Geng and Saggi (2015) who also analyze the impact of tariff reductions on global patent protection. However, there are important differences between that paper and the present one. First, the two papers examine innovations of different nature: innovation expands varieties in Geng and Saggi (2015) but improves quality in the present model. Second and perhaps more importantly, Geng and Saggi (2015) assume tariff barriers to be exogenous so that their analysis cannot answer the central question addressed in our paper, which is the welfare impact of requiring national treatment in patent policy when countries are free to set their optimal tariffs on one another.

Mandelman and Waddle (2020) also identify linkages between one country's tariff policy and its trading partner's patent policy. Their analysis differs from ours in several aspects. First, Mandelman and Waddle assume both tariffs and patent protection as exogenous policy variables whereas we endogenize both. Second, they do not consider policy coordination - a central focus of this paper. Third, Mandelman and Waddle consider a macro type model of monopolistic competition which allows them to study transitional dynamics of policy changes. By contrast, we develop a micro model of vertical quality differentiation and focus on its comparative statics.

Finally, our paper also relates to a small number of theoretical studies on the linkages between tariffs and national treatment in internal measures other than patent protection. Some of these studies examine corporate taxes (Horn, 2006) while others look at product standards (Geng, 2021). A common insight yielded by this literature is that tariff liberalization is conducive to the welfare impact of requiring national treatment in internal measures.[6]

The paper proceeds as follows. In Section 2 we develop the benchmark model. Section 3 uses this model to analyze the interaction between national trade and patent policies. Section 4 considers various extensions of the benchmark model and Section 5 concludes.

2. Model

Consider a world economy comprising two countries: i and j. A single firm in each country produces a distinct good. Consumers in both countries consume both goods so that country i exports good i to country j while importing good j from it. Each consumer buys at most one unit of each good. If a consumer buys one unit of good k where $k = i$ or j, her utility is given by $u_k = q_k\theta - p_k$,

[5] There also exists a theoretical literature that examines strategic patent policy in an open economy (Lai and Qiu, 2003; Grossman and Lai, 2004; Lai and Yan, 2013). However, all these papers assume free trade (i.e. do not consider tariff policies).

[6] Our paper also relates to a burgeoning literature on the economics of deep integration which focuses on coordination over behind-the-border measures (for example Bagwell and Staiger, 2001; Ederington, 2001; Grossman et al., 2021). See Maggi and Ossa (2020) for a recent review of this literature.

where q_k measures the quality of good k and θ measures the consumer's taste for quality. Utility under no purchase is normalized to zero. For simplicity, we assume that θ is uniformly distributed over the interval $[0, m_k]$ in country k where $m_k \geq 1$. It follows that the average willingness of consumers to pay for quality in country k is $m_k/2$.[7] The total utility of a consumer in country k is additively separable over the two goods such that $u_k = u_{ki} + u_{kj}$. The number of consumers in country k is given by $n_k > 0$. Let $\mu_k = m_k n_k$ measure the effective size of country k's market demand.

The quality of good k is endogenously determined by firm k's R&D investment. Let the R&D cost function for firm k be given by $C_k(q_k) = \delta_k q_k^2/2$ where $\delta_k > 0$ measures the firm's R&D productivity. Each country may choose to grant a R&D subsidy to its firm which is denoted with $s_k \geq 0$. To facilitate exposition, we initially assume $s_k = 0$ and discuss the case where $s_k > 0$ in Section 4.2. The marginal cost of production of each firm is normalized to zero.[8] Markets are segmented so that firms can freely set market-specific prices to maximize their global profits.

Government in each country imposes an ad-valorem import tariff on the foreign firm. Let τ_k denote country k's import tariff on firm $\tilde{k}$, where $0 \leq \tau_k < 1$ and $\tilde{k}$ stands for not k. Each country also needs to choose its patent policies toward the domestic and the foreign firms. Let $\boldsymbol{\Omega}_k = \{\Omega_{kk}, \Omega_{k\tilde{k}}\}$ be country k's patent policy profile where Ω_{kk} and $\Omega_{k\tilde{k}}$ represent its patent protection for the domestic and the foreign firm. In our simple formulation, the variable Ω either equals P (protection) or I (no protection). In particular, when a firm is granted patent protection by country k, it acts as a monopoly in the country's market.

If a firm receives no patent protection in a country, its technology is imitated locally and imitation leads to the emergence of a competitive industry that produces a lower quality version of the firm's product. Let $\gamma_{kk} q_k$ and $\gamma_{k\tilde{k}} q_{\tilde{k}}$ denote the quality of country k's imitation of the domestic and the foreign good, with γ_{kk} and $\gamma_{k\tilde{k}} \in [0, 1)$ representing country k's imitation capacity for the two goods respectively.[9] We allow $\gamma_{kk} \neq \gamma_{k\tilde{k}}$ so that a country's imitation capacity can be different for domestic and foreign goods. This is true, for example, when it is more difficult to imitate the foreign good due to factors such as information frictions, in which case we have $\gamma_{k\tilde{k}} < \gamma_{kk}$. Observe that when a country is incapable of imitating a firm's product (i.e. γ_{kk} or $\gamma_{k\tilde{k}}$ equals 0), its patent policy toward the firm becomes irrelevant. Finally, all imitated products are assumed to be sold locally.[10]

The timing of decision making is as follows. In the first stage, countries choose their respective patent and tariff policies (and possibly R&D subsidies). Then, given the policies set by countries, each firm chooses its investment in R&D that determines the quality of its product. Finally, international trade and consumption take place. We use backward induction to solve this game.

Before proceeding with formal analysis, it is useful to highlight the empirical relevance of our modeling approach. The central real-world motivation behind our model's key features is the structure of the pharmaceutical industry and its reliance on patent protection. First, as is well known, the R&D/sales ratios in the pharmaceutical industry is much higher (almost 5 times as much) as that for the manufacturing sector at large (Scherer, 2010). Second, patent protection plays an outsized, almost unique role in the pharmaceutical industry. A dated but influential survey by Levin et al. (1987) of 650 corporate R&D managers found that patents were perceived to be a highly effective means for encouraging innovation in the pharmaceutical industry.[11] Third, and somewhat crucially so, not only are substantive R&D investments required for successful drug discovery, the costs of imitating successful drugs are rather small, sometimes trivially so. By contrast, for example, while the aircraft industry also has to invest large amounts in R&D to come up with successful innovations (such as a new commercial jet engine or plane), the costs of imitating a commercially successful product in this industry are roughly the same order of magnitude as inventing a new one. It seems clear then that patents are most effective for incentivizing innovation when high costs of innovation co-exist with low costs of imitation, as they do in the pharmaceutical industry. This juxtaposition of high innovation costs on the one hand and low imitation costs on the other is captured sharply in our model by assuming costly R&D and essentially free imitation (provided local patent protection policy permits it).

The ease with which pharmaceuticals can be imitated together with the existence of weak IPR regimes is primarily what allowed several major developing countries (such as India and Brazil) to develop significant pharmaceutical industries of their own. For example, prior to 2005, India did not even recognize product patents for pharmaceuticals; only process patents were protected. This meant that if a local Indian firm could reverse-engineer a patented foreign pharmaceutical product (i.e. make it with its own process), it was free to produce and sell the drug locally as well in any other country that followed a similar patent regime. This patent policy created conditions suitable for the development of a robust pharmaceutical industry in India that has now become a

[7] Without loss of generality, we have implicitly assumed that the distributions of θ for the two goods are identical within each country, although they can be different across countries when $m_i \neq m_j$. Such heterogeneity in preferences for quality across countries is commonly observed in the sense that consumers in rich countries tend to have a higher willingness to pay for quality than that those in poor countries.

[8] For simplicity, we abstract from global supply chains which involve production and trade of intermediate goods. Doing so allows us to tractably characterize the inter-relationship between incentives for patent protection and tariff barriers. The role of intermediate goods trade has drawn increasing attention from recent studies (Buera and Oberfeld, 2020; Cai et al., 2020; Mandelman and Waddle, 2020). One important effect of intermediate goods trade is that it may facilitate technology diffusion from multinational parents to their foreign subsidiaries. This channel is not present in our model as we focus on imitation of the final good in the absence of patent protection as the sole channel of technology diffusion. If the good subject to imitation/diffusion were an intermediate good then patent protection or the lack of it would impact producers at multiple stages. Incorporating such vertical linkages into the analysis of tariff and patent policies is an important direction for future research.

[9] Modeling patent protection as a binary decision variable is without loss of generality. The key insights yielded by our analysis carry over when patent protection is continuous, e.g. when countries can choose the degree of imitation (γ_i) facing firms.

[10] This could be due to countries enforcing different patent policies. For example, an imitated product in one country may not be allowed for sale in another if the latter's patent protection for the product remains effective. Moreover, even when patent protection for a product is globally absent, an imitated product may only be sold locally if quality standards for it differ across countries. See Difei and Saggi (2019) for a discussion of trade of generic drugs as an example of this scenario.

[11] Related findings were reported by Mansfield (1986) wherein R&D executives of pharmaceutical firms reported that almost 60% of their commercialized innovations between 1981–83 would not have been developed in the absence of patent protection.

key producer of generics for the global market, and is often referred to as the "pharmacy of the world".[12] Watal (2001) provides a fascinating account of the role that the US pharmaceutical industry played in pushing for IPR reforms in countries such as Brazil and India and how the industry's proposals helped shape the eventual form and content of the TRIPS agreement. She also notes how developing countries were successful in pushing for incorporating compulsory licensing into TRIPS in situations where a country had a national emergency or could not gain access to key patented pharmaceuticals. This latter point dovetails nicely with our central argument: if patent protection does not improve access in developing countries to patented pharmaceuticals because trade barriers are high, it is difficult to see how the TRIPS-mandated strengthening of patent protection in developing countries under such conditions could be welfare-improving.

2.1. Pricing and trade

We begin by analyzing the final stage of the game where firms choose their prices across markets to maximize their global profits, treating as given the quality levels of their products as well as government's patent and trade policies. Without loss of generality, let us focus on firm i's profit maximization problem as firm j's problem can be formulated and solved analogously. Given tariff τ_j, firm i chooses its market-specific prices to maximize the sum of its profit in each market

$$\max_{p_{ii},\, p_{ij}} \pi_{ii}^{R}(p_{ii}) + (1-\tau_j)\pi_{ij}^{R}(p_{ij}) \tag{1}$$

where the superscript $R = P$ or I denotes whether the firm receives patent protection from a country or not. Since markets are segmented, the firm's problem is the same as separately maximizing its profit in each market

$$\max_{p_{ii}} \pi_{ii}^{R}(p_{ii}) \text{ and } \max_{p_{ij}} (1-\tau_j)\pi_{ij}^{R}(p_{ij}) \tag{2}$$

Note that firm i's profit in country k depends upon the patent policy of only that country. When receiving patent protection in country k, firm i becomes the monopoly seller of the good in the country. It is easy to show that given the firm's price p_{ik}, country k's consumers are partitioned into two groups: those in the range $[p_{ik}/q_i, m_k]$ buy good i and those in $[0, p_{ik}/q_i]$ do not buy. Thus firm i's pre-tariff profit earned in country k is given by

$$\pi_{ik}^{P}(p_{ik}) = \frac{n_k}{m_k} p_{ik}\left(m_k - \frac{p_{ik}}{q_i}\right) \quad \text{for } k = i, j \tag{3}$$

It can be shown that firm i's optimal price in country k is $p_{ik}^{*}(q_i) = m_k q_i/2$. The associated sales and profits equal $x_{ik}^{*} = n_k/2$ and $\pi_{ik}^{*} = \mu_k q_i/4$ respectively.

When firm i does not receive patent protection in country k, competition within the imitative industry ensures that the imitated good (of lower quality) is sold in the local market at marginal cost. When two different qualities are available for purchase in country k at prices p_{ik} (high quality) and 0 (low quality), consumers can be partitioned into two groups: those in the range $[0, p_{ik}/q_i(1-\gamma_{ki})]$ buy the low quality whereas those in $[p_{ik}/q_i(1-\gamma_{ki}), m_k]$ buy the high quality. Hence firm i's pre-tariff profit in country k is

$$\pi_{ik}^{I}(p_{ik};\gamma_{ki}) = \frac{n_k}{m_k} p_{ik}\left[m_k - \frac{p_{ik}}{q_i(1-\gamma_{ki})}\right] \quad \text{for } k = i, j \tag{4}$$

It follows that the firm's optimal price when facing competition from the imitative industry equals $\hat{p}_{ik} = m_k q_i(1-\gamma_{ki})/2$. Observe that $\hat{p}_{ik} = (1-\gamma_{ki})p_{ij}^{*}$ so that $\hat{p}_{ik} \le p_{ik}^{*}$ for $\gamma_{ki} \in [0,1)$. This indicates that each firm charges a lower price when facing competition from imitation. Finally, it is easily shown that firm i's maximized profits under imitation satisfy the following conditions

$$\hat{\pi}_{ik} = (1-\gamma_{ki})\pi_{ik}^{*} \quad \text{for } k = i, j \tag{5}$$

which implies that $\hat{\pi}_{ik} \le \pi_{ik}^{*}$, i.e., imitation lowers the firm's profits.

2.2. R&D

Next consider the second stage of the game where firms decide on their R&D investments. Each firm's R&D incentives depend on its expected global profit which further hinges on the patent protections it receives in the two countries. When given no patent protection in either country, firm i's optimal R&D investment solves

$$\max_{q_i} \pi_{ii}^{I}(q_i) + (1-\tau_j)\pi_{ij}^{I}(q_i) - C_i(q_i) \tag{6}$$

Let the solution to this problem be denoted by q_i^{I}. It is easy to show that

$$q_i^{I}(\gamma_{ii}, \gamma_{ji}) = \frac{(1-\gamma_{ii})\mu_i + (1-\tau_j)(1-\gamma_{ji})\mu_j}{4\delta_i}. \tag{7}$$

[12] It is worth noting that this technological capacity has been crucial for making it possible for India to produce the Oxford/AstraZeneca COVID-19 vaccine at a large scale. If this had not been possible, much of India's population may have had very limited access to a protective vaccine. Although India's pharmaceutical industry has not yet become a true global innovator, it might cross this threshold one day in part due to cumulative learning by doing and the extensive international collaboration that is occurring in this industry today.

Observe that q_i^I is decreasing in γ_{ki} and τ_j but increasing in μ_k. Intuitively, competition from either imitation (e.g. higher γ_{ki}) or foreign tariff (e.g. higher τ_j) dampens firm i's R&D incentives by reducing its expected global profit, whereas greater market demand (e.g. higher μ_k) raises the firm's profits and thus its R&D incentives.[13] Hence we can state the following:

Lemma 1. *(i) A firm's R&D investment is decreasing in the intensity of competition it faces from the imitated product in either country (i.e. $\partial q_k^I/\partial \gamma_{lk} < 0$ for $k, l = i, j$) as well as in the degree of foreign tariff barriers (i.e. $\partial q_k^I/\partial \tau_{\tilde{k}} < 0$ for $k = i, j$).*
(ii) A firm's R&D investment increases with market demand in either country (i.e. $\partial q_k^I/\partial \mu_l > 0$ for $k, l = i, j$).

We use q_i^{Ik} to denote firm i's optimal R&D investment when it faces imitation in country k only. In particular, $q_i^{Ik} = q_i^I(\gamma_{\tilde{k}i} = 0)$. Also, let q_i^* be firm i's R&D investment when receiving patent protection in both countries so that $q_i^* = q_i^I(\gamma_{ii} = 0, \gamma_{ji} = 0)$.

2.3. Welfare

When firm k does not receive patent protection either country, aggregate consumer surplus in country i over good k can be calculated as

$$cs_{ik}(\gamma_{ik},\gamma_{jk}) = \frac{n_i}{m_i}\int_0^{p_{ki}/q_k^I(\gamma_{ik},\gamma_{jk})(1-\gamma_{ik})} \gamma_i q_k^I(\gamma_{ik},\gamma_{jk})\theta d\theta + \frac{n_i}{m_i}\int_{p_{ki}/q_k^I(\gamma_{ik},\gamma_{jk})(1-\gamma_{ik})}^{m_i} \left[q_k^I(\gamma_{ik},\gamma_{jk})\theta - p_{ki}\right] d\theta \quad \text{for } k = i, j \tag{8}$$

where the first and the second terms represent the welfare of consumers who buy the imitated and the original good respectively. Note that $cs_{ik}(\gamma_{ik},\gamma_{jk})$ also depends on the patent protection firm k receives in country j since it affects the firm's choice of quality q_k^I. When country i extends patent protection to firm k, its consumer surplus over good k is $cs_{ik}|_{\gamma_{ik}=0}$. Similarly, when both countries protect firm k, country i's consumer surplus over good k becomes $cs_{ik}|_{\gamma_{ik}=\gamma_{jk}=0}$.

Country i's national welfare is defined as the sum of its consumer surplus over the two goods, its firm's global profit and its tariff revenue

$$w_i = \sum_k cs_{ik} + \pi_i + TR_i \quad \text{for } k = i, j \tag{9}$$

It is useful to write w_i as

$$w_i = w_{ii} + w_{ij} \tag{10}$$

where w_{ii} and w_{ij} are country i's welfare derived from good i and j respectively, where

$$w_{ii} = cs_{ii} + \pi_i \text{ and } w_{ij} = cs_{ij} + TR_i \tag{11}$$

with $TR_i = \tau_i \pi_{ji}$ being country i's tariff revenue collected from firm j. The expression of w_{ii} indicates that country i's welfare over good i arises from two sources: its consumer surplus derived from good i and firm i's global profit. Similarly, country i's welfare over good j has two components: its consumer surplus derived from good j and the tariff revenue it collects from firm j.

Let world welfare be the sum of each country's national welfare

$$WW = w_i + w_j. \tag{12}$$

Note that world welfare can also be decomposed as

$$WW = WW_i + WW_j \tag{13}$$

where WW_i and WW_j represent the components of world welfare associated with good i and j respectively, where

$$WW_i = w_{ii} + w_{ji} \text{ and } WW_j = w_{ij} + w_{jj}. \tag{14}$$

Notably, since there is no strategic interaction between firms, WW_k depends on the quality of good k but not that of good $\tilde{k}$. An important consequence is that WW_i and WW_j are independent of each other in the sense that they are determined by two independent sets of policy instruments. In particular, WW_k is affected by each country's patent protection toward firm k (Ω_{ik} and Ω_{jk}) as well as the tariff firm k faces when exporting to country $\tilde{k}$ ($\tau_{\tilde{k}}$). Thus to analyze how government policy impacts world welfare we can examine changes in WW_i and WW_j separately.

[13] Our model abstracts from heterogeneity in imitation quality or R&D effectiveness across industries. While a complete analysis of this issue is beyond the scope of this paper, our model does yield some relevant insights. For example, it can be shown that the welfare gains from national treatment under free trade increase with the quality of imitation (γ). This suggests that the case for national treatment may be stronger in industries where imitation poses a greater threat for innovation incentives (e.g. the pharmaceutical industry). The bottom line is that a one-size-fits-all patent policy that is prevalent today is unlikely to be economically optimal even though it maybe administratively efficient.

Before proceeding further, it is useful to solve for the socially optimal level of R&D. To this end, differentiating world welfare over good k (WW_k) with respect to firm k's quality (q_k) and solving the obtained first-order condition yield:

$$q_k^w(\gamma_{kk}, \gamma_{\tilde{k}k}) = \frac{\mu_k(\gamma_{kk} + 3) + \mu_{\tilde{k}}(\gamma_{\tilde{k}k} + 3)}{8\delta_k} \quad \text{for } k = i, j$$

Comparing q_k^w with the profit-maximizing level of R&D q_k^I establishes the following result:

Lemma 2. *Firms underinvest in R&D relative to the socially optimal level q_k^w, i.e. $q_k^I < q_k^w$ for $k = i, j$.*

The intuition for Lemma 2 is clear: when choosing their R&D investments, firms only consider their profits and do not take into account the positive effects of their R&D on consumers.

3. Benchmark case: symmetric countries

In this section we analyze the benchmark model with symmetric countries. Focusing on the symmetric case makes it easier to identify the fundamental channels through which patent and trade policies take effect.[14] Particularly, we make the following assumption:

Assumption 1 (*Symmetry*). $m_k = m$; $n_k = n$; $\mu_k = \mu$; $\gamma_{kk} = \gamma_d$; $\gamma_{\tilde{k}\tilde{k}} = \gamma_f$; $\delta_k = \delta$ for $k = i, j$.

Note that Assumption 1 implies that countries have identical imitation capacities for copying the products of their own firms (i.e. γ_d) as well as foreign firms (i.e. γ_f). This assumption does not drive our results and is made primarily for expositional ease.

3.1. *Patent protection with exogenous tariffs*

We begin by assuming exogenous tariff barriers and characterizing each country's unilateral incentives for patent protection. First consider each country's decision regarding its national patent protection Ω_{kk}. Recall that country k's own patent protection Ω_{kk} only affects its national welfare derived from good k, w_{kk}. Let

$$\Delta w_{kk} = w_{kk}(\Omega_{kk} = P, \Omega_{\tilde{k}k} = I) - w_{kk}(\Omega_{kk} = I, \Omega_{\tilde{k}k} = I) \tag{15}$$

denote country k's welfare change from extending patent protection to its own firm, given that the firm does not receive patent protection abroad. Then, it can be shown that

$$\Delta w_{kk} > 0 \text{ if and only if } \gamma_d > \hat{\gamma}_d = \frac{(1 - \gamma_f)(1 - \tau_{\tilde{k}})}{2} \tag{16}$$

Hence, country k chooses to protect its own firm if and only if the technological capacity for imitation in its market is sufficiently large. The trade-off underlying this policy is as follows. On one hand, offering the firm patent protection benefits local consumers since it incentivizes the firm to invest more R&D which raises the quality of its product. On the other hand, by shutting down production of the imitated version of the local firm's product, patent protection hurts consumers in two ways. One, it reduces variety and those consumers that prefer the imitated product to the original (because they find it to be a better deal in terms of quality adjusted price) lose access to their preferred product. Two, the lack of competition from the imitated product allows the firm to charge a higher price for the original product.[15] It follows that when γ_d is high enough, the benefit of own patent protection outweighs its costs, making it optimal for a country to grant patent protection to its firm.[16]

How do country k's incentives for protecting its own firm depend on country $\tilde{k}$'s patent protection policy with respect to the firm? It is straightforward to show that

$$\frac{\partial \hat{\gamma}_d}{\partial \gamma_f} < 0 \tag{17}$$

that is, a rise in country $\tilde{k}$'s imitation capacity with respect to firm k lowers $\hat{\gamma}_d$ above which country k extends own patent protection. This indicates that a country is *more likely* to protect its own firm that does not receive patent protection from the foreign country. An important implication of this result is that patent protection from abroad serves as a *strategic substitute* for domestic protection.

Next consider the impact of foreign tariff barriers on country k's incentives for protecting its firm. It is easily checked that

$$\frac{\partial \hat{\gamma}_d}{\partial \tau_{\tilde{k}}} < 0 \tag{18}$$

i.e., an increase in country $\tilde{k}$'s import tariff lowers $\hat{\gamma}_d$ thereby making it more attractive for country k to implement own patent protection. Intuitively, a higher foreign tariff undermines domestic firm's R&D incentives by reducing its overseas profit. This in turn increases the marginal benefit of a country's own patent protection since it becomes more important for stimulating R&D. We can now state the following:

[14] We discuss the case of asymmetric countries in Section 4.1.

[15] Thus, our model features the classic trade-off between the dynamic benefits and static costs of patent protection (Nordhaus, 1969).

[16] We provide supporting calculations in the appendix for this and other results established in the paper.

Lemma 3. *(i) A country has a unilateral incentive to implement own patent protection iff the local capacity for imitation is sufficiently strong, i.e.* $\Delta w_{kk} > 0$ *iff* $\gamma_d > \hat{\gamma}_d$.

(ii) An increase in the intensity of imitative competition facing its firm in the foreign market raises a country's incentive to extend patent protection to its firm (i.e. $\partial\hat{\gamma}_d/\partial\gamma_f < 0$*).*

(iii) An increase in foreign tariff barriers makes a country more likely to protect its own firm (i.e. $\partial\hat{\gamma}_d/\partial\tau_{\tilde{k}} < 0$*).*

Now consider country k's incentives for protecting the foreign firm. Note that this policy decision affects country k's welfare only over good $\tilde{k}$, i.e. $w_{k\tilde{k}}$. Let

$$\Delta w_{k\tilde{k}} = w_{k\tilde{k}}(\Omega_{k\tilde{k}} = P, \Omega_{\tilde{k}\tilde{k}} = I) - w_{k\tilde{k}}(\Omega_{k\tilde{k}} = I, \Omega_{\tilde{k}\tilde{k}} = I) \tag{19}$$

be country k's welfare change from extending patent protection to the foreign firm, assuming the firm receives no patent protection from its own country. It can then be shown that

$$\Delta w_{k\tilde{k}} > 0 \text{ if and only if } \gamma_f > \hat{\gamma}_f = \frac{4\tau_k^2 + 2\gamma_d\tau_k - 8\tau_k - 3\gamma_d + 5}{(1-\tau_k)(3-2\tau_k)} \tag{20}$$

In other words, a country chooses to offer patent protection to the foreign firm if its technological capacity to imitate the foreign product is high enough. The intuition behind this result is the following. Protecting the foreign firm benefits a country through two channels. First, it benefits domestic consumers by increasing the foreign firm's R&D that improves the quality of its product.[17] Second, it raises the tariff revenue paid by the foreign firm due to its higher sales in the importing country. This is a novel gain from patent protection which does not arise under free trade. On the other hand, protecting the foreign firm also incurs two types of costs on domestic consumers. One, it eliminates their access to the imitated foreign good. Two, it allows the foreign firm to raise its price in the domestic market. For sufficiently high γ_f, the benefits of extending patent protection to the foreign firm dominate its costs, making it optimal to offer such protection.

It can be further calculated that

$$\frac{\partial\hat{\gamma}_f}{\partial\gamma_d} < 0 \tag{21}$$

i.e. the threshold value of γ_f above which country k protects firm $\tilde{k}$ falls with the other country's imitation capacity with respect to its own firm's product. Thus a country is less likely to protect the foreign firm if it receives patent protection in its own country. This implies that each country's own patent protection is a *strategic substitute* for the other country's foreign protection.

How does a country's import tariff affect its incentives for protecting the foreign firm? It is straightforward to show the following

$$\frac{\partial\hat{\gamma}_f}{\partial\tau_k} > 0 \text{ if and only if } \tau_k > \hat{\tau}_k = \frac{3\gamma_d + 1 - \sqrt{2(1-\gamma_d)}}{2(\gamma_d+1)} \tag{22}$$

that is, a tariff reduction by country k increases its incentive to protect the foreign firm if and only if the initial tariff level is high. It follows that the impact of country k's tariff on its incentives for extending foreign patent protection is non-monotonic (it has an inverted U-shape). To gain some intuition, note that a reduction in a country's import tariff has two conflicting effects on its incentive for extending patent protection to the foreign firm. On the one hand, it improves the profitability of the country's market to the foreign firm, which increases the effectiveness of the country's patent protection in enhancing the foreign firm's incentive for R&D. This tends to make a country more willing to protect the foreign firm (a complementary effect). On the other, a reduction in tariff barriers *per se* increases the foreign firm's R&D incentives and this tends to lower the marginal benefit of foreign patent protection. This makes the country less willing to protect the foreign firm (a substitution effect). When country k's import tariff τ_k is high, a reduction in τ_k implies a stronger innovation stimulating effect of its foreign patent protection so that the complementary effect dominates, and country k is more likely to grant foreign patent protection. We summarize as follows:

Lemma 4. *(i) A country provides foreign patent protection if and only if its capacity to imitate the foreign firm is sufficiently high, i.e.* $\Delta w_{k\tilde{k}} > 0$ *if and only if* $\gamma_f > \hat{\gamma}_f$.

(ii) An increase in the intensity of imitative competition facing the foreign firm in its local market raises a country's incentive to extend patent protection to the foreign firm (i.e. $\partial\hat{\gamma}_f/\partial\gamma_d < 0$*).*

(iii) A reduction in its import tariff increases a country's incentive to extend patent protection to the foreign firm if its initial tariff is high whereas it decreases it when the initial tariff is low, i.e. $\partial\hat{\gamma}_f/\partial\tau_k > 0$ *if and only if* $\tau_k > \hat{\tau}_k$.

Lemma 4 yields a novel insight about the interaction between a country's tariff and non-tariff barriers. In our model, weaker patent protection works much like a non-tariff barrier that reduces a firm's profitability in a foreign market. The result above suggests that non-tariff barriers may rise in response to tariff reductions only if tariffs fall from already low levels. Interestingly, this finding seems consistent with the increasing concern about the growing prevalence of non-tariff barriers since that is more likely to happen in an environment where tariffs are low (as they indeed are today relative to historical levels).

[17] Note that protecting the foreign firm also raises its profit in the home market. But when setting its patent policy, the home country does not take this into account since the foreign firm's profits do not contribute to its welfare.

As mentioned, parts (*i*) of Lemmas 3 and 4 together indicate that patent protection levels of individual countries for the same firm are strategic substitutes for one another. A direct implication is that countries have an incentive to free ride on each other's patent protection. The strategic substitutability between national patent policies also arises in models of variety-expanding innovation such as Grossman and Lai (2004).[18] Our analysis shows that such a pattern of strategic interaction in patent policies holds regardless of whether innovation is horizontal or vertical in nature.

Before proceeding, we establish a useful result that follows readily from Lemma 4:

Corollary 1. $\frac{\partial \hat{\gamma}_f}{\partial \tau_k}|_{\gamma_d=0} > 0$ *for all* $0 \leq \tau_k < 1$

Corollary 1 says that provided a firm receives patent protection in its own country, a tariff reduction by the other country makes it more willing to protect the firm. When a firm receives patent protection in its own market, the other country's tariff policy is less important for determining its overall R&D incentive. As a result, the substitution effect of a tariff reduction on a country's benefit from foreign patent protection is dominated by its complementary effect, so that it is more willing to protect the foreign firm when its own tariff is lower.

3.2. Equilibrium patent policies

We now derive equilibrium patent policies. It is useful to start by analyzing each country's decision about extending foreign patent protection assuming it necessarily protects its own firm. Specifically, we have $\gamma_d = 0$ for both countries when domestic patent protection is enforced. Applying Lemma 4 it is easy to see that countries extend foreign patent protection to each other if and only if $\gamma_f > \hat{\gamma}_f|_{\gamma_d=0} > 1$. Since this is impossible given $\gamma_f < 1$, we can state the following result:

Proposition 1. *Assume that each country grants patent protection to its own firm. Then, in Nash equilibrium, each country denies patent protection to the foreign firm, i.e.*

$$(\Omega_i^*, \Omega_j^*) = (\{P, I\}, \{P, I\})$$

Proposition 1 says that countries have no incentives to protect foreign firms if they *already* receive patent protection in their own countries. Note that this is true regardless of a country's tariff barriers (τ_k) and its imitation capacity with respect to the foreign firm (γ_f). This result is driven by profit considerations: when a country grants patent protection to the foreign firm, it does not benefit from the increased profit earned by that firm which accrues solely to the foreign country. As a result, the total benefit of extending foreign patent protection is not sufficient for covering its cost and it proves optimal to deny protection to the foreign firm.[19]

Note that Proposition 1 also implies that *discriminatory* patent policies arise in equilibrium since, given that domestic firms are protected in both countries, foreign firms are not. Empirical evidence indicates that discriminatory patent policies indeed arise in the real world. For example, de Rassenfosse et al. (2019) and Webster et al. (2014) examine patent granting in five major countries (i.e. U.S., Japan, EU, Korea, and China) which together account for about 80 percent of global patenting activity and find that patent offices in these countries are more likely to grant patents to domestic firms relative to foreign firms. Mai and Stoyanov (2019) examine data on Canadian IP rights cases and find that Canadian firms are more likely to protect their IP rights relative to non-Canadian firms. Furthermore, they demonstrate that such ruling decisions by Canadian courts are aligned with national welfare maximization principles.

We now analyze the case where countries choose both domestic and foreign patent protections. Recall from Lemma 3 that when countries do not protect each other's firms, they choose to protect their own firms if and only if $\gamma_d > \hat{\gamma}_d$. Then, Proposition 1 implies that for all $\gamma_d > \hat{\gamma}_d$ the Nash equilibrium must be such that each country only implements own patent protection. Now consider $\gamma_d < \hat{\gamma}_d$. In this case the damage that imitation causes to firm profits is minor so that countries do not protect their own firms regardless of foreign patent policy. Another way of stating this result is that some degree of imitative competition is welfare-improving even when R&D incentives are taken into account. Moreover, it is easy to see that countries do not grant foreign protection as well, as the incentives to protect foreign firms are even weaker than that for domestic firms. Thus, we obtain the Nash equilibrium outcome as follows:

Proposition 2. *Suppose countries are free to choose their domestic and foreign patent protection policies. Then, in equilibrium, if* $\gamma_d > \hat{\gamma}_d$ *both countries provide patent protection to only their local firms whereas when* $\gamma_d \leq \hat{\gamma}_d$ *they protect neither firm.*

Proposition 2 has two interesting implications. First, it indicates that the lack of foreign patent protection can be a robust equilibrium outcome. That is, countries choose to not extend protection to foreign firms even if they can optimize over both foreign and domestic patent protection. Note that since such an equilibrium outcome arises for all levels of tariffs, an important policy

[18] It is worth noting that Grossman and Lai consider a CES aggregate innovation function with labor and human capital as inputs. In their model, patent protections across countries are strategic substitutes only when $\beta \leq 0$ where β represents the substitutability between labor and human capital in the innovation process. But they argue that this case should be most realistic, as when $\beta \leq 0$ patent protection exhibits diminishing returns, i.e. innovation rises at a lower rate as patent protection continues to increase.

[19] It is worth noting that the incentive to deny patent protection to foreign firms is also a feature of models with variety-expanding innovation (Geng and Saggi, 2015).

implication is that a shallow trade agreement that only involves the exchange of tariff concessions between countries would not be effective in inducing them to strengthen their patent protection toward each other. In this case, provided more protection for foreign firms is socially desirable, a trade agreement such as TRIPS that *directly* coordinates patent policies across countries would be necessary. The second key implication of Proposition 2 is that although tariff reductions cannot prevent discriminatory patent policies when $\gamma_d > \hat{\gamma}_d$, they do help temper countries' incentives for engaging in such discrimination. To see this, note that as τ_k falls $\hat{\gamma}_d$ rises, implying that countries facing lower foreign tariffs are less likely to make use of own patent protection. This in turn reduces the gap between a country's domestic and foreign patent protection, i.e. it lowers the degree of discrimination in the country's patent policy.

3.3. Requiring international patent protection

We have seen that a salient feature of Nash equilibrium policies is the lack of patent protection extended to foreign innovators. In this section, we ask if this outcome is inefficient and whether it can be remedied by following *national treatment* in international patent protection, a policy regime under which both countries must extend the same patent protection to foreign firms that they do to local firms. Such a policy regime is empirically relevant and can be considered, for example, as capturing the Patent Cooperation Treaty which has been shown to help reduce discrimination in national patent policy de Rassenfosse et al. (2019). To this end, we assume parameter values are such that countries have a unilateral incentive to provide patent protection to their own firms (i.e. $\gamma_d > \hat{\gamma}_d$).[20] The key question, therefore, is whether asking them to also protect foreign firms raises welfare.

Recall that world welfare WW is additively separable in the two goods, i.e. $WW = WW_i + WW_j$. Moreover, since countries are symmetric and country k's extending patent protection to firm $\tilde{k}$ affects $WW_{\tilde{k}}$ but not WW_k, it is sufficient to focus on the coordination that requires country k to grant patent protection to firm $\tilde{k}$. Let

$$\Delta WW_{\tilde{k}} = WW_{\tilde{k}}(\Omega_{k\tilde{k}} = P, \Omega_{\tilde{k}\tilde{k}} = P) - WW_{\tilde{k}}(\Omega_{k\tilde{k}} = I, \Omega_{\tilde{k}\tilde{k}} = P) \quad (23)$$

denote the change in world welfare over good $\tilde{k}$ due to country k's granting of patent protection to firm $\tilde{k}$. Then it can be shown that

$$\Delta WW_{\tilde{k}} > 0 \text{ if and only if } \gamma_f > \overline{\gamma}_f \quad (24)$$

i.e. the granting of patent protection by country $\tilde{k}$ to the foreign firm improves world welfare if and only if country $\tilde{k}$'s imitation capacity with respect to that firm is sufficiently high. The intuition for this result is the following. On one hand, requiring a country to protect the foreign firm necessarily lowers its own welfare because, left to its own devices, it prefers not to do so in equilibrium. On the other, granting patent protection to the foreign firm creates two positive externalities for the foreign country. One, it raises the foreign firm's global profit by eliminating imitation of its good. Two, it increases foreign consumer surplus by incentivizing the foreign firm to invest more in quality improving R&D. For sufficiently high γ_f, a firm's R&D investment becomes too low when it faces imitation in the other country. When this is the case, extending patent protection to foreign firms is socially optimal.

We next examine the role of tariff barriers in shaping the welfare impact of international patent protection. First, it can be readily shown that $\overline{\gamma}_f < 0$ if and only if $\tau_k < 1/2$. Since $\gamma_f > 0$ by assumption, we have $\gamma_f > \overline{\gamma}_f$ for all γ_f. It follows that when each country's tariff is sufficiently low, extending patent protection to the foreign firm necessarily improves world welfare. On the other hand, we have $\overline{\gamma}_f > 1$ if and only if $\tau_k > \sqrt{3} - 1$. Since $\gamma_f < 1$ this implies that $\gamma_f < \overline{\gamma}_f$ for all γ_f. Thus, mandating national treatment in international patent protection necessarily lowers world welfare when each country's tariff is high. Thus we can state the following:

Proposition 3. *The welfare effects of implementing national treatment in international patent protection, i.e. a policy under which countries extend the same patent protection to foreign firms that they do to domestic firms, depend on tariff levels. In particular, when tariffs are low, i.e. $\tau_k < 1/2$, national treatment in international patent protection increases global welfare whereas when tariffs are sufficiently high, i.e. $\tau_k > \sqrt{3} - 1$, it lowers it.*[21]

Importantly, Proposition 3 highlights the key role tariff barriers play in shaping the welfare impact of national treatment in international patent protection. The intuition for this finding is by now crystal clear. Lower tariff barriers make foreign markets more profitable so that R&D incentives of firms become more responsive to changes in patent protection abroad. This increases the effectiveness of foreign patent protection in incentivizing innovation. In addition, lower tariffs raise the domestic consumer surplus derived from the purchase of foreign goods, thus reducing the static cost of foreign patent protection. Both of these forces reinforce each other and increase the welfare gains delivered by foreign patent protection, making its implementation more socially desirable. Interestingly, Proposition 3 is consistent with the observation that the world's major multilateral IP agreement (i.e. TRIPS) was successfully negotiated only *after* average tariffs in the world had been reduced substantially via several successful rounds of multilateral trade negotiations since the formation of GATT in 1947. Moreover, it also helps explain why TRIPS incorporates the

[20] The analysis for the case where $\gamma_d < \hat{\gamma}_d$ is analogous but a bit more tedious. Note that when domestic patent protection is absent, extending foreign protection leads countries to discriminate against their own firms. While such an outcome is consistent with the principle of national treatment (which requires foreign firms to be treated *no worse* than domestic ones), we do not think it is of great practical interest.

[21] When tariffs are of intermediate magnitude, i.e. $1/2 < \tau_k < \sqrt{3} - 1$, (24) shows that protecting foreign firms raises world welfare when the intensity of competition generated by foreign imitation is high, i.e. $\gamma_f > \overline{\gamma}_f$; but reduces it when $\gamma_f < \overline{\gamma}_f$.

clause of national treatment as a core principle: such an institutional arrangement is more likely to be justified on welfare grounds when member countries impose low tariffs on each other.

Proposition 3 also suggests that Nash equilibrium patent protection may be too weak from a social welfare perspective. To see this, simply note that, left to their own devices, countries *never* protect foreign firms (Proposition 2) whereas extending such protection can be socially optimal for low tariff barriers. Intuitively, such under-protection occurs because of the positive externalities a country's patent protection generates on its trading partner. Since countries do not take such cross-border spillovers into account when acting non-cooperatively, they end up providing insufficient patent protection to foreign firms.[22]

3.4. *If tariffs are optimally chosen*

The previous section explains how exogenously given tariff barriers affect the desirability of national treatment in international patent protection. We next allow countries to choose their import tariffs along with their patent policies. In particular, we consider two scenarios depending on whether countries coordinate their tariffs. In the first scenario, countries non-cooperatively choose their tariffs to maximize their national welfare. In the second case, countries coordinate their tariffs to maximize global welfare. A central question of interest is how tariff coordination may affect the welfare implications of national treatment in international patent protection.[23]

To begin, note that each country's import tariff only affects its welfare over the foreign good. In light of welfare being additively separable over the two goods, this implies that tariffs chosen by the two countries are independent of each other. Hence we can analyze each country's optimal tariff separately.

Consider the first scenario where tariffs are determined non-cooperatively. Given the equilibrium patent protection described in Proposition 2, each country chooses its import tariff to maximize its national welfare

$$\max_{\tau_k} w_{k\tilde{k}}(\tau_k) \tag{25}$$

It is easy to show that there exists a unique optimal level of tariff that maximizes country k's welfare

$$\tau_k^{na} = \frac{3-5\gamma_f}{4(1-\gamma_f)} \tag{26}$$

Note that $\tau_k^{na} \geq 0$ if and only if $\gamma_f \leq 3/5$, i.e. each country's optimal trade policy is an import tariff if $\gamma_f \leq 3/5$ and is an import subsidy otherwise. To restrict our attention to import tariffs we focus on the case where $\gamma_f \leq 3/5$.

The intuition underlying the determination of the nationally optimal tariff τ_k^{na} is as follows. Each country faces both a benefit and a cost when raising its import tariff. The benefit is the tariff revenue the country collects from the foreign firm, while the cost is the fall in domestic consumer surplus that results from the reduction in the foreign firm's R&D.[24] When a country's capacity to imitate the foreign product is weak (i.e. $\gamma_f < 3/5$), the benefit of tariff protection dominates the cost so that it is optimal for the country to choose a strictly positive import tariff. It is also readily checked that

$$\frac{\partial \tau_k^{na}}{\partial \gamma_f} < 0 \tag{27}$$

i.e. each country's optimal tariff decreases in its imitation capacity with respect to the foreign product. Intuitively, a higher γ_f dampens the foreign firm's R&D incentives and lowers the quality of its product. As a result, each country's import volume as well as tariff revenue fall. This in turn reduces the nationally optimal tariff.

Now consider each country's incentive for extending patent protection to the foreign firm when it charges its optimal import tariff. It is easy to see that when a country chooses to protect the foreign firm from local imitation, its equilibrium tariff becomes $\tau_k^{na}|_{\gamma_f=0} = 3/4$. Plugging $\tau_k^{na}|_{\gamma_f=0}$ and τ_k^{na} into country k's welfare over good $\tilde{k}$ we can show that

$$w_{k\tilde{k}}(P, P, \tau_k^{na}|_{\gamma_f=0}) - w_{k\tilde{k}}(P, I, \tau_k^{na}) < 0 \tag{28}$$

i.e. granting foreign patent protection necessarily *lowers* country k's welfare when it sets its tariff optimally. It follows that countries do not extend patent protection to each other even when they are free to use their optimal tariffs.

A natural question, then, is whether mandating the provision of foreign protection is socially desirable under Nash equilibrium tariffs. To see the answer, simply substitute $\tau_k^{na}|_{\gamma_f=0}$ and τ_k^{na} into the world welfare functions to obtain

$$WW_{\tilde{k}}(P, P, \tau_k^{na}|_{\gamma_f=0}) - WW_{\tilde{k}}(P, I, \tau_k^{na}) < 0 \tag{29}$$

[22] It is worth noting that the result that Nash equilibrium policies induce insufficient patent protection may depend on the institutional rule that is in place. For example, while it has been shown that under-protection of patents may occur in the absence of any institutional constraints as well as under national treatment (Grossman and Lai, 2004; Geng and Saggi, 2015), Geng and Saggi (2020) argue that under the principle of *mutual recognition*, Nash equilibrium policies can lead to *over-protection* of patents.

[23] For simplicity, we maintain our assumption that countries always protect their own firms, although the argument remains qualitatively the same even when this assumption is relaxed.

[24] In particular, since there is no strategic interaction between firms, tariffs do not have any profit-shifting effects in our model. Moreover, an import tariff does not affect domestic consumers through the price channel since it is absorbed by the foreign firm.

that is, extending foreign patent protection necessarily *lowers* world welfare under nationally optimal tariffs.[25] Thus, we can state the following:

Proposition 4. *Suppose countries choose tariffs non-cooperatively. Then, in Nash equilibrium, (i) each country grants patent protection to only its local firm and (ii) requiring national treatment in international patent protection unambiguously lowers world welfare.*

Part (*i*) of Proposition 4 indicates that the lack of foreign patent protection in Nash equilibrium arises regardless of whether tariffs are exogenously given or endogenously determined. Part (*ii*) of the proposition implies that countries have no incentive to coordinate their patent policy by extending patent protection to each other's firm. This is an important result; it clarifies that if tariff policies are non-cooperatively set, requiring national treatment in international patent protection is actually counterproductive. Hence, this result captures a plausible scenario under which the TRIPS agreement harms global welfare, a concern that has been raised by many policy-makers and researchers (see, for example, Boldrin and Levine, 2013).

It is worth explaining the intuition behind Proposition 4. In particular, we already know from Proposition 3 that requiring national treatment increases welfare when import tariffs are low and exogenously fixed. So why does welfare necessarily fall when tariffs are endogenous? The reason is that countries *raise* their optimal tariffs if they have to extend patent protection to each other — see Eq. (27). This tariff increase results in a *reduction* in the foreign firm's R&D as opposed to an increase that one might expect from a strengthening of patent protection that it faces. In fact, it is easy to calculate that firm $\widetilde{k}$'s choice of quality under country k's optimal tariff τ_k^{na} is given by

$$q_{\widetilde{k}}(\tau_k^{na}(\gamma_f);\gamma_f) = \frac{\mu(\gamma_f - 2\gamma_d + 5)}{16\delta_{\widetilde{k}}}$$

Observe that $q_{\widetilde{k}}$ *increases* in γ_f. Since R&D is already under-provided by firms (see Lemma 2), the decline in R&D caused by the increase in tariff protection that accompanies national treatment in patent protection lowers global welfare. Thus, the indirect negative effect of the tariff increase on R&D incentives caused by extending patent protection to the foreign firm turns out to dominate the direct positive effect of such protection. As a result, requiring national treatment in international patent protection reduces world welfare when tariff policies of countries are unconstrained so that they end up imposing optimal tariffs on one another. This result underscores the crucial role that restraints on trade policy play in creating a meaningful role for international patent protection.

Next, we show that trade policy coordination between countries that eliminates internal tariffs is sufficient for national treatment in international patent protection to be welfare improving. To see this, suppose that countries coordinate their tariffs so as to maximize their joint welfare. Then simply differentiating $WW_{\widetilde{k}}$ with respect to τ_k to obtain

$$\frac{\partial WW_{\widetilde{k}}}{\partial \tau_k} < 0 \text{ for all } 0 \le \tau_k, \gamma_f < 1 \tag{30}$$

that is, the marginal social value of raising a country's import tariff is negative regardless of the level of the tariff and the status of patent protection. Notably, this finding is consistent with the well-known efficiency-reducing properties of import tariffs. However, the channel through which import tariffs work against efficiency is different in our context. More specifically, an import tariff is inefficient in our model because it reduces the foreign firm's R&D investment, which in turn hurts consumers in both countries.[26]

Given that tariffs are welfare-reducing, tariff coordination calls for the elimination of tariffs regardless of patent policies. Comparing this outcome with the Nash equilibrium, we see that nationally optimal tariffs are too high relative to the social optimum. Intuitively, an increase in a country's import tariff hurts the foreign country in two ways. One, it lowers the foreign firm's profit. Two, it discourages the foreign firm's R&D investment, which in turn lowers the foreign product's quality and the surplus enjoyed by foreign consumers. Since countries do not take these negative cross-border spillovers into account, they end up choosing inefficiently high import tariffs.

Next consider the determination of patent policies under free trade. From Proposition 1 we know that the removal of tariff barriers does not change the Nash equilibrium patent policies since countries do not grant patent protection to foreign firms regardless of the levels of their tariffs. Nevertheless, Proposition 3 implies that trade coordination that removes the tariff barriers indeed makes it jointly optimal for countries to extend patent protection to each other's firm. Hence we have the following proposition:

Proposition 5. *If countries coordinate both trade and patent policies they eliminate tariffs and follow national treatment in patent protection. Such a policy outcome yields strictly higher welfare than when international coordination occurs only over tariffs or patent protection (but not both).*

[25] In fact, the result is even stronger in the sense that when tariffs are optimally chosen a *marginal* decrease in the intensity of imitation reduces global welfare, i.e. $\partial WW_{\widetilde{k}}(\tau_k^{na})/\partial\gamma_f > 0$.

[26] In our model, an import tariff is completely borne by the foreign firm, thus leading to a lump-sum transfer of profit from the foreign firm to the importing country. Although this might appear to be a somewhat peculiar feature of our model, we regard it as an advantage because it allows us to identify the welfare-reducing effect of tariffs through their impact on innovation while controlling for other well-understood efficiency implications of tariffs. It is worth noting that empirical studies reveal that tariff pass through could occur and can be asymmetric between countries (Feenstra, 1989; Cavallo et al., 2021). Incorporating these features into the analysis of tariff and patent policies is an interesting direction for future research.

Proposition 5 says that tariff coordination can help ensure that a regime of national treatment in international patent protection is welfare superior to one where countries only protect their own firms. This is an important result as it indicates that trade coordination yields welfare gains not just by liberalizing world trade, but can also lead to additional welfare improvement by potentially inducing international coordination over patent policies. At a broad level, Proposition 5 makes a case for the tenet that shallow integration targeting border policies (e.g. import tariffs) can facilitate deeper integration involving behind-the-border policies (e.g. patent protection). In this way, Proposition 5 helps explain why TRIPS was negotiated after the GATT/WTO system had succeeded in substantially lowering global tariff barriers, i.e. the success of traditional trade liberalization efforts under the GATT/WTO system may have contributed to the ratification of TRIPS.[27]

4. Further analysis

This section examines two extensions of our benchmark model. First, we relax the assumption that markets are symmetric across countries and consider the case where one country has a larger market demand than the other. This extension is important given the fact that there is great tension between developed and developing countries over the protection of IPRs. Second, we incorporate R&D subsidies into the analysis. This extension is of policy relevance as the WTO allows countries to subsidize R&D. Our main goal is to analyze how these empirically relevant features affect incentives for patent protection, both with and without national treatment. For ease of exposition, we maintain the assumption that countries always enforce own patent protection (i.e. $\gamma_d = 0$) and focus on their decisions about protecting foreign firms. Our results remain qualitatively unchanged when countries are free to deny patent protection to local firms.

4.1. *Market size asymmetry*

In this section we incorporate market asymmetry between countries into the benchmark model. Specifically, we assume one country (e.g. country i) has a larger market demand for both goods than the other (e.g. country j), which implies that $\mu_i > \mu_j$. In this way, the extended model can be considered as a North–South one where country i (j) is the North (South).[28] To identify the fundamental channels of interest, we abstract from R&D subsidies and focus on each country's incentives for setting its foreign patent protection.

The first interesting observation we can make is that relative market size shapes the effect of tariff reductions on a country's incentives for extending foreign patent protection (e.g. $\Delta w_{k\tilde{k}}$). Recall that part (*iii*) of Lemma 4 shows that under symmetry, tariff reductions are first complementary and then substitutable for increasing foreign patent protection, with the tariff cutoff for the two opposing effects being $\hat{\tau}_k$. Given asymmetric countries, $\hat{\tau}_k$ becomes a function of μ_k and $\mu_{\tilde{k}}$ so that one can show

$$\frac{\partial \hat{\tau}_k}{\partial \mu_k} > 0 \tag{31}$$

Importantly, condition (31) says that a larger country is *less likely* to see tariff reductions as complementary for its foreign protection. In fact, as μ_k becomes sufficiently high, $\hat{\tau}_k$ can be greater than one so that tariff reductions always yield the substitution effect. This is because for a larger country the foreign (smaller) market is not highly profitable, so a fall in the foreign tariff does not create much additional incentives for the larger country to protect the foreign firm. The reverse of this logic is also true, that is, a smaller country is more likely to see tariff reductions as complementary for its foreign patent protection as the foreign market is relatively more profitable. In fact, it is easy to show that $\hat{\tau}_k$ falls below zero as μ_k becomes sufficiently low.

Next, it can be shown that

$$\Delta w_{k\tilde{k}} > 0 \text{ if and only if } \gamma_{k\tilde{k}} > \gamma_{k\tilde{k}}^{na} = \frac{4\mu_k\tau_k^2 - 6\mu_k\tau_k - 2\mu_{\tilde{k}}\tau_k + 2\mu_k + 3\mu_{\tilde{k}}}{\mu_k(1-\tau_k)(3-2\tau_k)} \tag{32}$$

that is, each country extends its foreign patent protection if and only if its imitation capacity with respect to the foreign firm is sufficiently large. Moreover, we can calculate that

$$\frac{\partial \gamma_{k\tilde{k}}^{na}}{\partial \mu_k} < 0 \tag{33}$$

and

$$\frac{\partial \gamma_{k\tilde{k}}^{na}}{\partial \mu_{\tilde{k}}} > 0 \tag{34}$$

[27] Both Propositions 4 and 5 would remain qualitatively unchanged under continuous patent policy such that each country chooses the level of its imitation intensity γ_f. First note that under non-cooperative tariffs, it is easy to show that world welfare derived from either good is strictly increasing in γ_f. This implies that strengthening foreign patent protection as required by national treatment necessarily reduces world welfare. On the other hand, under free trade, world welfare derived from either good is strictly decreasing in γ_f. Hence, under free trade, social optimality requires each country to enforce maximum level of foreign patent protection, i.e. $\gamma_f = 0$ so that national treatment necessarily improves welfare.

[28] One could also allow for supply side asymmetry by assuming R&D effectiveness δ to be different across countries. This will not change our results given that δ proportionally affects the cost and the benefit of patent protection and therefore drops out in the equations. That being said, if there exists a fixed cost of enforcing patent protection that is weakly lower in the North, which is likely the case, then it is straightforward to show that the North has a stronger incentive to protect patents, the same result that obtains under market size asymmetry.

Importantly, (33) and (34) say that each country's tendency to offer foreign patent protection increases in domestic demand but decreases in foreign demand. On one hand, larger domestic demand has two opposing effects on a country's gain from offering foreign patent protection. It increases the foreign firm's R&D incentives and reduces the gain for the country to protect the firm's patent. Meanwhile, it also implies a greater benefit for domestic consumers from improvement in the quality of the foreign good, which increases the gain from protecting the foreign firm. The second positive effect turns out to dominate so that a country is more likely to protect the foreign firm when its domestic market is larger. On the other hand, larger foreign demand raises the foreign firm's R&D incentives and this reduces the gain for the home country from further extending patent protection to the foreign firm.

An important implication of the above observations is that as market size becomes more asymmetric across countries, the national incentives for patent protection diverge. In particular, the country with the larger market is more likely to protect the foreign firm whereas the opposite is true for the smaller country. Recall that when countries are identical they deny patent protection to each other in equilibrium. It follows that in an asymmetric equilibrium, the smaller country never chooses to protect the foreign firm as its incentive for doing so become is weaker relative to the symmetric case. By contrast, the larger country may choose to offer foreign patent protection if its market is sufficiently bigger.

The above findings also suggest that patent coordination between asymmetric countries should focus on the strengthening of patent protection in small countries. To see this, first note that

$$\Delta WW_{\tilde{k}} > 0 \text{ if and only if } \gamma_{k\tilde{k}} > \gamma^{so}_{k\tilde{k}} = \frac{\tau_k(2\mu_k\tau_k - 2\mu_k + \mu_{\tilde{k}})}{\mu_k(1-\tau_k)(2-\tau_k)} \tag{35}$$

that is, it is socially optimal for country k to protect the foreign firm if and only if its imitation capacity with respect to the foreign firm is sufficiently large. Moreover, direct calculations show that

$$\gamma^{na}_{k\tilde{k}} - \gamma^{so}_{k\tilde{k}} > 0 \tag{36}$$

i.e. the socially optimal threshold of $\gamma^{so}_{k\tilde{k}}$ is lower. It follows that each country's equilibrium foreign protection is too weak relative to the social optimum. As discussed before, this occurs because countries do not take into account the positive externalities of their patent policies on each other. We can further define $d^{\gamma}_k = \gamma^{na}_{k\tilde{k}} - \gamma^{so}_{k\tilde{k}}$ as a measure of the degree of under-protection in equilibrium, with a larger d^{γ}_k indicating more severe under-protection and a greater need for patent coordination. It can then be shown that

$$\frac{\partial d^{\gamma}_k}{\partial \mu_k} < 0 < \frac{\partial d^{\gamma}_k}{\partial \mu_{\tilde{k}}} \tag{37}$$

that is, the value of implementing national treatment declines with the market size of the larger country but rises in that of its trading partner. Intuitively, as a country's market gets larger it is more willing to protect the foreign firm and this is aligned with socially optimality. On the other hand, when the foreign market expands both individual and social incentives for protecting the foreign firm fall. But individual incentives decline faster so that the gap between nationally and socially optimal foreign protection increases. It follows that d^{γ}_k decreases in country k's relative market demand, indicating that there is a greater need for smaller countries to strengthen their foreign patent protection.

Now suppose countries non-cooperatively choose their import tariffs. In this case, country k's optimal import tariff is given by

$$\tau^{na}_k = \frac{\mu_k + 2\mu_{\tilde{k}} - 5\mu_k\gamma_{k\tilde{k}}}{4\mu_k(1-\gamma_{k\tilde{k}})} \tag{38}$$

It is easily shown that

$$\frac{\partial \tau^{na}_k}{\partial \mu_k} < 0 \tag{39}$$

Hence a country's optimal import tariff *decreases* in its market size, which implies that smaller countries tend to impose higher import tariffs than larger ones. Interestingly, this result is consistent with the evidence that richer countries tend to implement lower tariff rates, as provided in Naito (2019). Naito further develops a Ricardian model to show that the observed pattern of tariff rates may be due to richer countries caring more about the negative growth effect of tariffs. Here, we offer an alternative explanation that is more relevant when R&D activity is relevant: richer countries may prefer lower tariffs because they derive more welfare gains from foreign innovations.

As mentioned, a country with smaller domestic market benefits less from innovation so that it has weaker incentives to encourage foreign R&D by setting lower tariff barriers. Substituting τ^{na}_k and $\tau^{na}_k|_{\gamma_{k\tilde{k}}=0}$ into $\Delta WW_{\tilde{k}}$ we obtain that

$$\Delta WW_{\tilde{k}} < 0 \tag{40}$$

Hence, requiring asymmetric countries to extend patent protection to each other necessarily reduces world welfare if Nash tariffs are in place. This suggests that trade coordination is needed for patent coordination to be potentially socially optimal. To see this is indeed the case, note that (30) also holds when countries are asymmetric, which implies that trade policy coordination would lead to zero tariffs between countries. Then it is straightforward to show that

$$\Delta WW_{\tilde{k}}|_{\tau_k=0} > 0 \tag{41}$$

so that patent coordination improves welfare under free trade. This implies that our results under country symmetry remain qualitatively unchanged when countries differ with respect to market size.[29]

4.2. R&D subsidies

In this section we allow each country to subsidize its own firm's R&D investment. Our goal is to examine the interactions between R&D and patent policies, as well as the implications of such interaction for national treatment in patent protection. To highlight the role of R&D subsidies, in what follows we assume tariffs are zero (although our analysis applies to any exogenous levels of import tariffs). The analysis below delivers three key messages: one, allowing countries to use R&D subsidies reduces the gains from patent protection; two, coordination over R&D subsidies eliminates the need for patent protection; three, world welfare tends to be higher with R&D subsidies since they are more effective in incentivizing innovation than patent protection.

We begin by examining the implications of exogenous R&D subsidies for patent policies. First consider the Nash equilibrium where countries non-cooperatively choose their patent policies. In this case, country k's R&D subsidy s_k affects firm k's R&D decision, which in turn impacts both countries' incentives for extending patent protection to firm k. We can show that

$$\frac{\partial \Delta w_{kk}}{\partial s_k} < 0 \text{ and } \frac{\partial \Delta w_{\bar{k}k}}{\partial s_k} < 0 \tag{42}$$

i.e. an increase in country k's R&D subsidy reduces the welfare gains for both countries from granting patent protection to firm k. Thus, as expected, from each country's point of view a R&D subsidy works as a substitute for patent protection. It follows that the use of R&D subsidy by one country makes both countries less likely to enforce patent protection. Importantly, this implies that the presence of R&D subsidies does not change each country's equilibrium patent policy toward the foreign firm: since countries do not extend patent protection to each other in the absence of R&D subsides, they would continue to follow the same policy even when R&D subsidies are available.[30]

How do (exogenous) R&D subsidies affect the desirability of strengthening patent protection given to foreign firms? It can be shown that

$$\Delta WW_k > 0 \text{ if and only if } \gamma_f > \overline{\gamma}_f = \frac{6s_k}{\mu} \tag{43}$$

i.e. coordination improves world welfare if and only if γ_f is sufficiently high. Further note that $\partial \overline{\gamma}_f / \partial s_k > 0$ so that higher R&D subsidies raise the threshold of γ_f above which national treatment is socially optimal. Therefore, the presence of R&D subsidies reduces the incentives for countries to offer patent protection to foreign firms. The intuition for this result is clear: when R&D subsidies can be used to fund innovation, patent protection becomes less important for achieving the same objective. A direct implication is that when coordination of international patent protection is not ensured, the availability of R&D subsidies can help improve global innovation and welfare. This insight offers a potential explanation for why R&D subsidies are not prohibited under the WTO even though they may distort trade and undermine competition: given the prevalent failure to adequately protect foreign innovators' patent rights, allowing countries room to employ R&D subsidies is conducive to fostering innovation incentives.

Next consider endogenous R&D subsidies. We examine two scenarios depending on whether R&D subsidy coordination is present: in the first countries non-cooperatively choose their R&D subsidies while in the second they coordinate their R&D subsidies to maximize joint welfare. In the absence of coordination over R&D subsidy, it can be shown that the R&D subsidy s_k that maximizes country k's welfare is given by

$$s_k^{na} = \frac{\mu_k}{8} \tag{44}$$

Thus it is optimal for each country to use a strictly positive R&D subsidy. Intuitively, firms do not take account of the positive externality of their R&D on domestic consumers. Therefore, a R&D subsidy is needed to address the loss in domestic consumer surplus due to inadequate innovation undertaken by its firm.[31] Also note that $\partial s_k^{na} / \partial \mu_k > 0$ so that the optimal R&D subsidy of a country is increasing in its market size. The intuition is that a larger domestic market implies greater gains in domestic consumer surplus from innovation, making it is optimal for the country to set a higher R&D subsidy. Substituting s_k^{na} into $\overline{\gamma}_f$, we see that under nationally optimal R&D subsidies countries benefit from national treatment in patent protection if $\gamma_f > 3/4$. Therefore, even though patent protection becomes less important in the presence of R&D subsidies, the under-protection of patents remains when R&D subsidies are unilaterally determined.

[29] Our analysis has been focused on demand side asymmetry. It is worth noting how asymmetry in the supply side such as imitative capability (i.e. $\gamma_{ij} \neq \gamma_{ji}$) may affect countries' choices of tariff and patent policies. First, (27) indicates that a country's optimal tariff decreases in its imitation capacity for the foreign good, so that countries with better imitation capacity tend to impose lower tariffs. This is because a country's greater imitation capacity lowers the R&D incentives of foreign innovators. As a result, the country needs to reduce its tariff to incentivize foreign innovation. The same logic indicates that countries with stronger imitative capabilities also have a stronger incentive to enforce patent protection (see also part (*ii*) of Lemma 4). In addition, our welfare results remain quantitatively unchanged when countries have asymmetric imitative capability. Assume symmetric market size without loss of generality. Then, we can show that $WW_k^{\tau}(P, P, \tau_k^{na}|_{\gamma_{\bar{k}k}=0}) - WW_k^{\tau}(P, I, \tau_k^{na}) < 0$ for $k, = i, j$. Thus, national treatment under Nash tariffs remains welfare-reducing when imitation capacity varies between countries. Moreover, the calculations in Section 4.1 (as in the appendix) also show that national treatment is welfare-improving under free trade when imitative capacity differs across countries.

[30] We can show that R&D subsidies also make countries less likely to protect their own firms.

[31] This explains why s_k depends only on the market characteristics of country k but not that of the foreign country.

Now suppose countries coordinate their R&D subsidies to maximize joint welfare. Differentiating world welfare with respect to s_k and solving the associated first order condition yields the socially optimal R&D subsidy:

$$s_k^{so} = \frac{\mu_k(3\gamma_f + 1) + \mu_{\bar{k}}}{8} \tag{45}$$

It is easy to see that $s_k^{so} > s_k^{na}$, i.e. nationally optimal R&D subsidies are too low from the social point of view. This is because each country, when acting non-cooperatively, does not take into account the positive externality of its R&D subsidy on foreign consumers. Substituting s_k^{so} into $\bar{\gamma}_f$ we know that national treatment in patent protection increases world welfare iff $\gamma_f > 9\gamma_f/4 + 3/2$, which can never hold. This implies that under coordinated R&D subsidies, the Nash equilibrium policy outcome (featuring no foreign patent protection) is indeed socially optimal. The reason is simply that R&D subsidies are more effective than patent protection in stimulating innovation since they strengthen R&D incentives without enhancing monopoly power. As a result, coordination over R&D policy allows countries to achieve optimality without resorting to patent protection. In fact, it can be shown that world welfare is always higher under R&D policy coordination than under patent coordination in the absence of R&D subsidies. Therefore, coordination over R&D subsidies can be a more desirable substitute for patent coordination.[32]

5. Conclusion

This paper investigates the implications of tariff barriers for international patent protection. To this end, we develop a simple model of trade and quality-upgrading innovation. Our analysis highlights the key role that tariff barriers play in determining the welfare implications of requiring national treatment in patent protection, a policy regime wherein foreign firms are granted the same level of patent protection as domestic ones. We show that tariff barriers affect incentives for patent protection in non-obvious ways. For example, the lower the import tariff of a country, the weaker the incentive of the *other* country to grant patent protection to its own firm since the ability to earn higher profits abroad makes its patent policy a less crucial determinant of its firm's R&D incentive.

As in past literature, we find that national patent protection policies tend to act as strategic substitutes and that countries have an incentive to under-protect foreign firms relative to domestic ones. However, this does not necessarily imply that implementing national treatment in international patent protection is welfare-improving. More specifically, we find that requiring a country to follow national treatment in patent protection raises welfare only if its import tariff is low. Furthermore, if countries are free to impose optimal tariffs on each other, national treatment in patent protection actually *lowers* welfare. This key result establishes the importance of negotiating down tariff barriers *prior* to imposing disciplines on national patent policies. The fact that the actual historical experience of countries is consistent with this finding is rather reassuring: after all, multilateral disciplines on intellectual property policies (as captured by the TRIPS agreement) came into existence only after decades of trade liberalization had been undertaken by the GATT/WTO system. Our analysis shows why such a particular sequencing of policy reforms – i.e. multilateral trade liberalization followed by international patent coordination — makes sense from an economic welfare perspective.

Appendix

We provide proofs and supporting calculations for the results reported in the paper.

Proof of Lemma 1.

(*i*) It is straightforward to calculate that

$$\frac{\partial q_k^I}{\partial \gamma_{kk}} = -\frac{\mu_k}{4\delta_k} < 0$$

$$\frac{\partial q_k^I}{\partial \gamma_{\bar{k}k}} = -\frac{\mu_{\bar{k}}(1-\tau_{\bar{k}})}{4\delta_k} < 0$$

$$\frac{\partial q_k^I}{\partial \tau_{\bar{k}}} = -\frac{\mu_{\bar{k}}(1-\gamma_{\bar{k}k})}{4\delta_k} < 0$$

(*ii*) We calculate that

$$\frac{\partial q_k^I}{\partial \mu_k} = \frac{1-\gamma_{kk}}{4\delta_k} > 0$$

$$\frac{\partial q_k^I}{\partial \mu_{\bar{k}}} = \frac{(1-\gamma_{\bar{k}k})(1-\tau_{\bar{k}})}{4\delta_k} > 0$$

[32] One could also allow countries to subsidize imports instead of R&D. It can be shown that import subsidies, like R&D subsidies, are more effective than patent protection in incentivizing innovation as they do not give firms greater monopoly power.

Proof of Lemma 3.

(*i*) We have

$$\Delta w_{kk} = \frac{\mu^2 \gamma_d A_1(\gamma_d, \gamma_f, \tau_{\tilde{k}})}{32\delta}$$

where $A_1(\gamma_d, \gamma_f, \tau_{\tilde{k}}) = (1-\gamma_f)\tau_{\tilde{k}} + 2\gamma_d + \gamma_f - 1$. It is easy to check that $\Delta w_{kk} = 0$ iff

$$\gamma_d = \hat{\gamma}_d = \frac{(1-\gamma_f)(1-\tau_{\tilde{k}})}{2}$$

Note that the sign of Δw_{kk} is the same as that of $A_1(\gamma_d, \gamma_f, \tau_{\tilde{k}})$. Hence, to show that $\Delta w_{kk} > 0$ iff $\hat{\gamma}_d < \gamma_d < 1$ we only need to show $A_1(\gamma_d, \gamma_f, \tau_{\tilde{k}}) > 0$ iff $\hat{\gamma}_d < \gamma_d < 1$. To this end, note that $\partial A(\gamma_d, \gamma_f, \tau_{\tilde{k}})/\partial \gamma_d = 2 > 0$ so that $A_1(\gamma_d, \gamma_f, \tau_{\tilde{k}})$ is increasing in γ_d. Given $A_1(\gamma_d, \gamma_f, \tau_{\tilde{k}}) = 0$ it must be the case that $A_1(\gamma_d, \gamma_f, \tau_{\tilde{k}}) > 0$ iff $\hat{\gamma}_d < \gamma_d < 1$. It follows that $\Delta w_{kk} > 0$ iff $\gamma_d > \hat{\gamma}_d$.

(*ii*) It is straightforward to check that

$$\frac{\partial \hat{\gamma}_d}{\partial \gamma_f} = -\frac{1}{2}(1-\tau_{\tilde{k}}) < 0$$

(*iii*) It is straightforward to check that

$$\frac{\partial \hat{\gamma}_d}{\partial \tau_{\tilde{k}}} = -\frac{1}{2}(1-\gamma_f) < 0$$

Proof of Lemma 4.

(*i*) We have

$$\Delta w_{k\tilde{k}} = \frac{\mu^2 \gamma_f A_2(\gamma_d, \gamma_f, \tau_k)}{32\delta}$$

where $A_2(\gamma_d, \gamma_f, \tau_k) = 2(\gamma_f - 2)\tau_k^2 - (2\gamma_d + 5\gamma_f - 8)\tau_k + 3\gamma_d + 3\gamma_f - 5$. It can be calculated that $\Delta w_{k\tilde{k}} = 0$ iff

$$\gamma_f = \hat{\gamma}_f = \frac{4\tau_k^2 + 2(\gamma_d - 4)\tau_k - 3\gamma_d + 5}{(1-\tau_k)(3-2\tau_k)}$$

Since the sign of $\Delta w_{k\tilde{k}}$ is the same as that of $A_2(\gamma_d, \gamma_f, \tau_k)$, it is sufficient to show $A_2(\gamma_d, \gamma_f, \tau_k) > 0$ iff $\hat{\gamma}_f < \gamma_f < 1$. To this end, we can calculate that $\partial A_2(\gamma_d, \gamma_f, \tau_k)/\partial \gamma_f = (1-\tau_k)(3-2\tau_k) > 0$ so that $A_2(\gamma_d, \gamma_f, \tau_k)$ is increasing in γ_f. By $A_2(\gamma_d, \gamma_f, \tau_k) = 0$ at $\gamma_f = \hat{\gamma}_f$, we must have $A_2(\gamma_d, \gamma_f, \tau_k) > 0$ iff $\hat{\gamma}_f < \gamma_f < 1$. It follows that $\Delta w_{k\tilde{k}} > 0$ iff $\gamma_f > \hat{\gamma}_f$.

(*ii*) It is straightforward to check that

$$\frac{\partial \hat{\gamma}_f}{\partial \gamma_d} = -\frac{1}{1-\tau_i} < 0$$

(*iii*) We can calculate that

$$\frac{\partial \hat{\gamma}_f}{\partial \tau_k} = -\frac{A_3(\gamma_d, \tau_k)}{(1-\tau_k)^2(3-2\tau_k)^3}$$

where $A_3(\gamma_d, \tau_k) = 4(\gamma_d +)\tau_k^2 - (12\gamma_d + 4)\tau_k + 9\gamma_d - 1$. Solving $\frac{\partial \hat{\gamma}_f}{\partial \tau_k} = 0$ yields two solutions: $\tau_k = (3\gamma_d + 1 + \sqrt{2(1-\gamma_d)})/(2(\gamma_d + 1))$ and $\tau_k = (3\gamma_d + 1 - \sqrt{2(1-\gamma_d)})/(2(\gamma_d + 1))$. But $\tau_k > 1$ cannot be a solution given $0 \leq \tau_k < 1$, so the only feasible solution for $\partial \hat{\gamma}_f/\partial \tau_k = 0$ is τ_k. To show $\partial \hat{\gamma}_f/\partial \tau_k > 0$ iff $\hat{\tau}_k < \tau_k < 1$, we only need to show $A(\tau_k) < 0$ iff $\hat{\tau}_k < \tau_k < 1$. To this end, note that $\partial A(\tau_k)/\partial \tau_k = 0$ iff $\tau_k = (3\gamma_d + 1)/(2(\gamma_d + 1))$ and $\partial^2 A(\tau_k)/\partial \tau_k^2 = 8(\gamma_d + 1) > 0$. This implies that $\partial A(\tau_k)/\partial \tau_k > 0$ iff $\tau_k > (3\gamma_d + 1)/(2(\gamma_d + 1))$. Moreover, we have $(3\gamma_d + 1 + \sqrt{2(1-\gamma_d)})/(2(\gamma_d + 1)) < (3\gamma_d + 1)/(2(\gamma_d + 1))$, indicating that $A(\tau_k)$ first decreases and then increases for $\hat{\tau}_k < \tau_k < 1$. It is easy to show that $\lim_{\tau_k \to 1} A(\tau_k) = \gamma_d - 1 < 0$, which together with $A(\tau_k) = 0$ at τ_k imply that $A(\tau_k) < 0$ for $\hat{\tau}_k < \tau_k < 1$. Hence $\partial \hat{\gamma}_f/\partial \tau_k > 0$ for $\hat{\tau}_k < \tau_k < 1$. As a final step, let us show $\partial \hat{\gamma}_f/\partial \tau_k < 0$ for $0 < \tau_k < \hat{\tau}_k$. But this must be the case given that $A(\tau_k)$ is decreasing to 0 over $0 < \tau_k < \hat{\tau}_k$ so that $A(\tau_k) > 0$ for $0 < \tau_k < \hat{\tau}_k$.

Proof of Corollary 1.

Direct calculations show $(\partial \hat{\gamma}_f/\partial \tau_k)|_{\gamma_d=0} = (1 + 4\tau_k - 4\tau_k^2)/((1-\tau_k)^2(3-2\tau_k)^2) > 0$ for all $0 \leq \tau_k < 1$.

Proof of Proposition 1.

Given countries enforce own patent protection, firms face no imitation domestically. This implies that $\hat{\gamma}_f|_{\gamma_d=0} = (4\tau_k^2 - 8\tau_k + 5)/((1-\tau_k)(3-2\tau_k)) > 1$. Hence it is impossible to have $\gamma_f > \hat{\gamma}_f|_{\gamma_d=0}$, which implies that countries would not protect the foreign firms given they already enforce own patent protection.

Proof of Proposition 4.

Direct calculations show how foreign patent protection affects national welfare under endogenous tariffs

$$w_{k\tilde{k}}(\tau_k^N|_{\gamma_f=0}) - w_{k\tilde{k}}(\tau_k^N) = -\frac{\mu^2 \gamma_f (10 + \gamma_f)}{256\delta} < 0$$

Moreover, one can calculate how foreign patent protection affects national welfare under endogenous tariffs

$$WW_{\tilde{k}}(\tau_k^N|_{\gamma_f=0}) - WW_{\tilde{k}}(\tau_k^N) = -\frac{\mu^2\gamma_f(3\gamma_f+34)}{512\delta} < 0$$

Calculations about the effects of import tariffs on world welfare.

Direct calculations show that

$$\frac{\partial WW_{\tilde{k}}}{\partial \tau_k} = -\frac{\mu^2(1-\gamma_f)[2(1-\gamma_f)\tau_k + 3(\gamma_d+\gamma_f)+2]}{32\delta} < 0$$

whenever $\tau_k > 0$.

Calculations in Section 4.1

We have

$$\gamma_{k\tilde{k}}^{na} - \gamma_{k\tilde{k}}^{so} = \frac{2(2\mu_k + 3\mu_{\tilde{k}} - 2\mu_k\tau_k - 2\mu_{\tilde{k}}\tau_k)}{\mu_k(2-\tau_k)(3-\tau_k)} > 0$$

Defining $d_k^\gamma = \gamma_{k\tilde{k}}^{na} - \gamma_{k\tilde{k}}^{so}$, we calculate

$$\frac{\partial d_k^\gamma}{\partial \mu_k} = \frac{2\mu_{\tilde{k}}}{\mu_k(2-\tau_k)} < 0$$

$$\frac{\partial d_k^\gamma}{\partial \mu_{\tilde{k}}} = \frac{2}{\mu_k(2-\tau_k)} > 0$$

Under Nash tariffs, we have

$$\frac{\partial \tau_k^{na}}{\partial \mu_k} = -\frac{\mu_{\tilde{k}}}{2\mu_k^2(1-\gamma_{k\tilde{k}})} < 0$$

When country k extends foreign patent protection to conform to national treatment, the changes in world welfare under Nash tariffs and free trade are calculated respectively as

$$\Delta WW_{\tilde{k}}|_{\tau_k=\tau_k^{na}} = -\frac{\mu_k\gamma_{k\tilde{k}}(3\mu_k\gamma_{k\tilde{k}} + 18\mu_k + 16\mu_{\tilde{k}})}{512} < 0$$

and

$$\Delta WW_{\tilde{k}}|_{\tau_k=0} = \frac{1}{16}\mu_k^2\gamma_{k\tilde{k}}^2 > 0$$

Calculations in Section 4.2

Regarding the effects of R&D subsidy on the welfare gains from patent protection, we have

$$\frac{\partial \Delta w_{kk}}{\partial s_k} = -\frac{3\mu\gamma_d}{8\delta} < 0$$

and

$$\frac{\partial \Delta w_{\tilde{k}k}}{\partial s_k} = -\frac{\mu\gamma_f(3-2\tau_{\tilde{k}})}{8\delta} < 0$$

References

Azagra-Caro, Joaquín M., Tur, Elena M., 2014. Differences between examiner and applicant citations in the European patent office: A first approach. In: Paper Presented At the 19th International Conference on Science and Technology Indicators, Leiden, September 3-5.

Bagwell, Kyle, Chad, Bown, Staiger, Robert W., 2016. Is the WTO passé? J. Econ. Lit. 54 (4), 1125–1231.

Bagwell, Kyle, Staiger, Robert W., 2001. Domestic policies, national sovereignty and international economic institutions. Q. J. Econ. 116 (2), 519–562.

Boldrin, Michele, Levine, David K., 2013. The case against patents. J. Econ. Perspect. 27 (1), 3–22.

Bond, Eric W., Saggi, Kamal, 2018. Compulsory licensing and patent protection: A north-south perspective. Econom. J. 128 (610), 1157–1179.

Buera, Francisco J., Obereld, Ezra, 2020. The global diffusion of ideas. Econometrica 88 (1), 83–114.

Cai, Jie, Santacreu, Ana Maria, Li, Nan, 2020. Knowledge diffusion, trade and innovation across countries and sectors, forthcoming. Am. Econ. J. Macroecon.

Cavallo, Alberto, Gita, Gopinath, Brent, Neiman, Jenny, Tang, 2021. Tariff pass-through at the border and at the store: Evidence from US trade policy. Am. Econ. Rev. Insights 3 (1), 19–34.

de Rassenfosse, Gaétan, Jensen, Paul H., Julius, T'Mir, Palangkaraya, Alfons, Webster, Elizabeth, 2019. Are foreigners treated equally under the trade-related aspects of intellectual property rights agreement? J. Law Econ. 62 (4), 663–685.

de Rassenfosse, Gaétan, Raiteri, Emilio, 2016. Technology Protectionism and the Patent System: Strategic Technologies in China. Swiss Federal Institute of Technology, Lausanne, Unpublished manuscript.

Difei, Geng., Saggi, Kamal., 2019. Optimal price regulations in international pharmaceutical markets with generic competition. J. Health Econ. 71, 102315.

Ederington, Josh, 2001. International coordination of trade and domestic policies. Amer. Econ. Rev. 91 (5), 1580–1593.

Feenstra, Robert, 1989. Symmetric pass-through of tariffs and exchange rates under imperfect competition: An empirical test. J. Int. Econ. 27 (1–2), 25–45.

Geng, Difei, 2021. Tariff Liberalization and the Welfare Impact of National Treatment in Product Standards. Working paper, University of Arkansas-Fayetteville.

Geng, Difei, Saggi, Kamal, 2015. Is there a case for non-discrimination in the international protection of intellectual property? J. Int. Econ. 97 (1), 14–28.

Geng, Difei, Saggi, Kamal, 2020. Mutual Recognition in International Patent Protection. Working paper, University of Arkansas-Fayetteville.

Grossman, Gene M., Lai, Edwin L.-C., 2004. International protection of intellectual property. Amer. Econ. Rev. 94 (5), 1635–1653.
Grossman, Gene M., McCalman, Phillip, Staiger, Robert W., 2021. The 'new' economics of trade agreements: From trade liberalization to regulatory convergence? Econometrica 89 (1), 215–249.
Horn, Henrik, 2006. National treatment in the GATT. Amer. Econ. Rev. 96 (1), 394–404.
Ivus, Olena, 2010. Do stronger patent rights raise high-tech exports to the developing world? J. Int. Econ. 81 (1), 38–47.
Ivus, Olena, 2015. Does stronger patent protection increase export variety? Evidence from U.S. product-level data. J. Int. Bus. Stud. 46 (6), 724–731.
Kotabe, Masaaki, 1992. The impact of foreign patents on national economy: A case of the United States, Japan, Germany, and britain. Appl. Econ. 24, 1335–1343.
Lai, Edwin L.-C., Qiu, Larry D., 2003. The north's intellectual property rights standard for the south? J. Int. Econ. 59, 183–209.
Lai, Edwin L.-C., Yan, Isabel K.M., 2013. Would global patent protection be too weak without international coordination? J. Int. Econ. 89 (1), 42–54.
Levin, Richard C., Klevorick, Alvin K., Nelson, Richard, Winter, Sidney, 1987. Appropriating the returns from industrial research and development. Brook. Pap. Econ. Act. 18 (3), 783–832.
Liegsalz, Johannes, Wagner, Stefan, 2013. Patent examination at the state intellectual property office in China. Res. Policy 42, 552–563.
Maggi, Giovanni, Ossa, Ralph, 2020. The Political Economy of Deep Integration. NBER Working Paper 28190.
Mai, Joseph, Stoyanov, Andrey, 2019. Anti-foreign bias in the court: Welfare explanation and evidence from Canadian intellectual property litigation. J. Int. Econ. 117, 21–36.
Mandelman, Federico S., Waddle, Andrea, 2020. Intellectual property, tariffs, and international trade dynamics. J. Monetary Econ. 109, 86–103.
Mansfield, Edwin, 1986. Patents and innovation: An empirical study. Manage. Sci. 32 (2), 173–181.
Maskus, Keith E., Penubarti, Mohan, 1995. How trade-related are intellectual property rights? J. Int. Econ. 39 (3–4), 227–248.
Naito, Takumi, 2019. A larger country sets a lower optimal tariff. Rev. Int. Econ. 27 (2), 643–665.
Nordhaus, William, 1969. An economic theory of technological change. Amer. Econ. Rev. 59 (2), 18–28.
Saggi, Kamal, 2016. Trade, intellectual property rights, and the world trade organization. Chapter 18 of the Handbook of Commercial Policy. Elsevier,
Scherer, Frederic M., 2010. Pharmaceutical innovation, pages 539-576. In: Hall, Bronwyn H., Rosenberg, Nathan (Eds.), Economics of Innovation. Vol. 1. North-Holland, Amsterdam.
Watal, Jayashree, 2001. Intellectual Property Rights in the WTO and Developing Countries. Kluwer Law International, The Hague.
Webster, Elizabeth, Jensen, Paul H., Palangkaraya, Alfons, 2014. Patent examination outcomes and the national treatment principle. Rand J. Econ. 45 (2), 449–469.

Part 7

Oligopolistic Competition: R&D and Vertical Contracts

Chapter 28

Leasing versus selling and firm efficiency in oligopoly[#]

Kamal Saggi[a,*], Nikolaos Vettas[b,c]

[a]*Department of Economics, Southern Methodist University, Dallas, TX 75275-0496, USA*
[b]*The Fuqua School of Business, Duke University, Durham, NC 27708-0120, USA*
[c]*CEPR, London, UK*

Received 5 April 1999; accepted 24 September 1999

Abstract

We examine sales and leasing of a durable good in an asymmetric duopoly. We show that the inefficient firm leases more than the efficient firm, and that an increase in unit costs implies a higher ratio of leased units to sales.

Keywords: Durable goods; Leasing; Dynamic oligopoly

JEL classification: L13; D43

---

1. Introduction

Leasing has been viewed as a possible solution to the "durable goods monopoly" problem, since it allows the monopolist to maintain ownership of the units, making the "promise" to not overproduce in future periods credible (see Bulow, 1982).[1] In reality, durable goods markets are primarily oligopolistic rather than monopolistic, and firms sell as well as lease goods.[2] This note focuses on strategic considerations that determine the choice between leasing and selling. That this choice has strategic implications is already known from Bucovetsky and Chilton (1986) and Bulow (1986). They show that a monopolist facing the threat of entry chooses to sell part of the units supplied (or,

*Corresponding author. Tel.: +1-214-768-3274; fax: +1-214-768-1821.
E-mail address: ksaggi@mail.smu.edu (K. Saggi)

[1]It is well known that a durable good monopolist faces a time inconsistency problem which leads to lower profit relative to the profit the monopolist can earn by committing to selling the good only once (see e.g. Tirole (1988), pp. 79–87 and references therein).

[2]Examples include automobiles, house appliances, computers, copy machines, and machinery equipment.

[#] This chapter was originally appeared in *Economics Letters* **66**, 361–368.

equivalently, increase the durability of its product).[3] Bulow (1986) also shows that in a two-period oligopoly, firms use a mixture of sales and leasing (in the first period). We further explore these ideas in a dynamic asymmetric duopoly. By allowing costs of production to vary across firms, we offer new insights with respect to the strategic implications of leasing and selling.

We study a three-period quantity-setting duopoly.[4] Each firm chooses its volume of leasing and sales in each period. By keeping the model as simple as possible, we obtain analytic solutions. The main implication is that inefficient (high-cost) firms tend to lease more. In particular, while the low-cost firm sells more than the high-cost firm in every period, the high-cost firm leases more (in each of the first two periods). Further, an increase in the unit cost of a given firm (holding constant the other firm's cost) implies a higher ratio of leased units to sales. Similarly, when the costs are equal, this ratio increases with cost. We abstract from other factors that may influence the lease versus sell choice, such as informational asymmetries, to show how strategic incentives may differ solely because of cost differences. Based on our analysis, an empirical investigation of whether high-cost firms lease more may help determine whether the lease versus sell choice is driven by strategic considerations, or is primarily influenced by other factors.

While leasing helps solve the durable goods problem, in the presence of competition leasing becomes less attractive. Sales allow a firm to capture part of the market whereas leasing may result in loss of future market share to a rival since both firms can compete anew for consumers that leased in the past. Also note that future profit levels are affected not only by current sales (because demand is lower) but also by current leasing volumes because units leased in the past return to the firm and can be supplied again at no additional cost. In other words, in each period the marginal cost of supplying units previously leased is zero.[5] With respect to cost differences, in a quantity-setting dynamic game with only sales, the low-cost firm sells more. When both leasing and sales contracts are possible, we find that while the low-cost firm still sells more, it is the high-cost firm that leases more. The intuition is that the high-cost firm has a strategic disadvantage in competing directly with its low-cost rival and leasing allows it to capture part of the demand in a more indirect way. For comparison purposes, the paper also considers the case where costs decrease significantly over time (as with new products). We discuss why in this case the incentives are reversed and it is the efficient firm that leases more.

2. The model

The market lasts for three periods. There is a durable good which is perfectly homogeneous. In each of the three periods, the demand for the services of the good is

$$p_t = a - bQ_t, \tag{1}$$

[3]More precisely, in a two-period model where Cournot competition takes place in the second period, a monopolist in the first period sells the good in order to capture some of the second-period demand.

[4]Three periods is the minimum length needed to explore the dynamics. The analysis of a two-period model leads to similar conclusions but is restrictive in the sense that it does not allow us to consider a period of leasing followed by another period where firms face a lease versus sell decision.

[5]In this sense, our analysis is linked to the literature on capacity expansion (see e.g. Dixit, 1980). Here we examine a durable good and in every period firms decide how much to produce, as well as the volumes of sales and leasing.

$t = 1, 2, 3$, with $a, b > 0$, and where p_t is the one-period leasing price and Q_t is the total stock of the good available. Note that Q_t includes units sold by the firms, units previously sold, and units currently leased.[6] There are two firms, A and B, with a constant unit cost of production, c^i, for each firm $i = A, B$. We assume that $c^A \leq c^B$ so that A is the "efficient" and B the "inefficient" firm. The two firms and the consumers have one-period discount factor $\delta \in [0, 1]$.

In every period, the two firms choose their sales and leasing volumes. The units sold by firm i in period t are denoted s_t^i and the units leased are denoted l_t^i, where $i = A, B, t = 1, 2, 3$. In the last period, leasing and selling are equivalent and we write $l_3^i = 0$. The good is assumed perfectly durable: it does not depreciate, so that consumers view units previously sold and units just produced as identical. To calculate the total production cost of firm i in period t (which we denote TC_t^i) the unit cost c_t^i has to be multiplied by the number of units *produced in that period*.[7] The units produced in period t equal the difference between the units supplied (sold or leased) in that period and the units leased in the previous period, assuming that this difference is non-negative. To keep the analysis simple, we focus on the case where this difference is non-negative in every period. Direct calculations show that this condition is guaranteed if demand, as parameterized by a, is high enough.[8]

From the leasing prices, p_t, we can derive the sale prices, which we denote $\hat{p}_t$. It is easy to see that we should have

$$\hat{p}_1 = p_1 + \delta\hat{p}_2 \quad \text{and} \quad \hat{p}_2 = p_2 + \delta\hat{p}_3. \tag{2}$$

These conditions reflect no-arbitrage requirements.[9] We assume that firms maximize the present value of their profits. In period t each firm i chooses s_t^i and l_t^i taking the other firm's choices as given. We look for a subgame perfect equilibrium.

3. Analysis

The usual parameter restrictions that guarantee smoothness of solutions in Cournot games are assumed to hold. We start from the last period, $t = 3$. Firm i, $i = A, B$, solves

$$\max_{s_3^i} p_3 s_3^i - TC_3^i \tag{3}$$

where

[6]Consumers have preferences over the services of the good and the fundamental relation is the flow demand in each period, while the demand for *purchasing* the good can be derived. Note that the *residual* demand curve in every period (the portion of the demand curve to the right of the current stock of units sold) captures the demand for the services of the good by consumers who have not yet purchased the good.

[7]Also, from the viewpoint of firms, a unit previously leased can be brought to the market without incurring any additional cost.

[8]This is because, if demand is not too low, firms find it profitable to supply additional units to the market in each period. If the difference mentioned above is negative, the analysis needs to be modified in a straightforward way.

[9]A consumer should be indifferent, for example, between paying p_2 to lease the good for the second period, and paying $\hat{p}_2$ to purchase the good at the beginning of the second period and selling it for $\hat{p}_3$ at the end of the second period.

$$p_3 = \hat{p}_3 = a - b\left(\sum_{t=1}^{2} \sum_{k=A,B} s_t^k + s_3^A + s_3^B\right) \tag{4}$$

and

$$TC_3^i = c^i(s_3^i - l_2^i). \tag{5}$$

As discussed above, this expression for TC_3^i is valid when $s_3^i \geq l_2^i$ and $s_2^i + l_2^i \geq l_1^i$, which hold in equilibrium for a high enough.[10] In the third period, we derive each firm's sales as a function of the history. For compactness, let h_t denote the history of the game up to the beginning of period t. So h_3 represents $\{s_t^i, l_t^i\}$, $i = A, B$, $t = 1,2$. Then the equilibrium in the third period generates $s_3^i(h_3)$, $i = A, B$ from which we can also calculate the price $\hat{p}_3^*(h_3)$ as well as $\Pi_3^{i*}(h_3)$, the third-period profit for firm i.

At $t = 2$, taking as given the history of selling and leasing in period one, firm i solves

$$\max_{s_2^i, l_2^i} p_2 l_2^i + \hat{p}_2 s_2^i - TC_2^i + \delta \Pi_3^{i*}(h_3) \tag{6}$$

where

$$p_2 = a - b\left(\sum_{k=A,B} s_1^k + s_2^A + s_2^B + l_2^A + l_2^B\right), \quad \hat{p}_2 = p_2 + \delta \hat{p}_3^*(h_3), \tag{7}$$

and

$$TC_2^i = c^i(s_2^i + l_2^i - l_1^i). \tag{8}$$

Note that now each firm chooses two variables, one for leasing and one for sales.[11] Again we derive $s_2^{i*}(h_2)$, $l_2^{i*}(h_2)$, $\hat{p}_2^*(h_2)$ and $\Pi_2^{i*}(h_2)$.[12]

Finally, at $t = 1$, firm i solves

$$\max_{s_1^i, l_1^i} p_1 l_1^i + \hat{p}_1 s_1^i - TC_1^i + \delta \Pi_2^{i*}(h_2) \tag{9}$$

where

$$p_1 = a - b(s_1^A + s_1^B + l_1^A + l_1^B), \quad \hat{p}_1 = p_1 + \delta \hat{p}_2^*(h_2), \tag{10}$$

and

$$TC_1^i = c^i(s_1^i + l_1^i). \tag{11}$$

[10] See the discussion below for precise parameter restrictions. If written explicitly over its entire domain, the cost function for firm i would have a "kink" at l_2^i. The marginal cost is equal to zero for supplying each of the first l_2^i units and equal to c^i for any additional units.

[11] Again, we assume that $s_2^i + l_2^i \geq l_1^i$.

[12] Π_2^{i*} represents the equilibrium profit for the last two periods, since it is defined as the value of the problem of maximizing profit from period two onwards.

Once we derive the equilibrium levels s_1^i* and l_1^i*, we proceed to the appropriate substitutions and obtain the equilibrium path of leasing and sales. Clearly, there is a unique subgame perfect equilibrium. As these calculations are standard, we only report here the results:

$$s_1^A* = \frac{c^B(250+35\delta-39\delta^2) - c^A(375+30\delta-87\delta^2) + (125+120\delta+27\delta^2)a}{b(125+63\delta)(5+3\delta)}, \tag{12}$$

$$l_1^A* = \frac{-c^B(125+40\delta+384\delta^2+189\delta^3) - c^A(125+40\delta-741\delta^2-378\delta^3) + (250+330\delta+108\delta^2)a}{3b(125+63\delta)(5+3\delta)} \tag{13}$$

$$s_2^A* = s_3^A* = \frac{c^B(55+22\delta) - c^A(70+41\delta) + (15+9\delta)a}{b(125+63\delta)}, \tag{14}$$

$$l_2^A* = \frac{-c^B(5+48\delta+21\delta^2) + c^A(-5+77\delta+42\delta^2) + (10+6\delta)a}{b(125+63\delta)}. \tag{15}$$

Clearly, the expressions for the quantities supplied by firm B can be found by exchanging c^A and c^B.[13]

4. Main results

Our first result is that while A, the efficient firm, sells more in every period, B, the inefficient firm, leases more (in each of the two first periods):[14]

Proposition 1. *If* $c^A < c^B$, *in equilibrium we have* $s_t^A > s_t^B$, $t = 1, 2, 3$ *and* $l_t^A < l_t^B$, $t = 1, 2$.

Proof. This can be shown using the expressions for the leasing and sales levels derived above. Direct calculations show that $l_1^A - l_1^B = 3(c^A - c^B)\delta^2/b(3\delta+5) < 0$, $l_2^A - l_2^B = (c^A - c^B)\delta/b < 0$, $s_1^A - s_1^B = (2\delta - 5)(c^A - c^B)/b(3\delta+5) > 0$, and $s_2^A - s_2^B = s_3^A - s_3^B = (c^B - c^A)/b > 0$. □

Note that, if a firm has such a great cost advantage that it is de facto a monopolist, we know from past work that it would choose to only lease. When the cost difference, however, is not too great, so that strategic considerations are important, our analysis shows that the less efficient firm is expected to lease more.[15] In addition to Proposition 1, there is another sense in which "inefficient firms lease more." As the unit production cost of a given firm increases, its ratio of leasing to sales increases:

[13] The fact that $s_2^A* = s_3^A*$ comes from the linearity of the problem in the last two periods.

[14] The aggregate quantity supplied, including both leasing and sales, is higher for the efficient firm. This can be shown with direct calculations: $(s_1^A + l_1^A) - (s_1^B + l_1^B) = (s_2^A + l_2^A) - (s_2^B + l_2^B) = (\delta - 1)(c^A - c^B)(3\delta^2 + 2\delta - 5)/b > 0$, since the quadratic term is negative for $\delta \in (0, 1)$.

[15] We can also check how sales and leasing evolve over time for the same firm. Direct calculations show that $s_1^i > s_2^i$ and $l_1^i > l_2^i$ as long as a is not too low.

Proposition 2. *In equilibrium, an increase in c^A (while keeping c^B fixed) or a decrease in c^B (while keeping c^A fixed), leads to a decrease in s_t^A, $t = 1, 2, 3$, to an increase in l_t^A, $t = 1,2$, (as long as δ is not too low) and to an increase in the (l_t^A / s_t^A) ratios, $t = 1, 2$.*

Proof. From (12) and (14) it is easy to see that an increase in c^A (or a decrease in c^B) leads to a decrease in s_t^A for $t = 1, 2, 3$. With respect to leasing, simple calculations involving the coefficients of the relevant parameters show the following. An increase in c^A increases l_1^A at least as long as $\delta > 0.4$, and a decrease in c^B increases l_1^A for all δ. An increase in c^A leads to a higher l_2^B at least as long as $\delta > 0.1$ and a decrease in c^B increases l_2^A for all δ. Similarly, it is possible to show that an increase in c^A or a decrease in c^B always leads to a higher ratio l_t^A / s_t^A, $t = 1,2$. □

A related question of interest is what happens when the two firms are equally efficient and their unit cost increases.

Proposition 3. *Suppose that $c^A = c^B = c$. Then a higher c leads to higher (l_t / s_t) ratios, $t = 1,2$.*

Proof. Substituting $c^A = c^B = c$ into (12)–(15) and collecting common factors gives the following leasing to sales ratio for each of the two firms: $l_1 / s_1 = [c(-50 + 14\delta + 63\delta^2) + (50 + 36\delta)a]/ [3(c(-25 + 16\delta) + (25 + 9\delta)a)]$ and $l_2 / s_2 = [c(-10 + 29\delta + 21\delta^2) + (10 + 6\delta)a]/[c(-15 - 19\delta) + (15 + 9\delta)a]$. Differentiation with respect to c delivers the results. □

Since we have derived explicit expressions, we can easily calculate numerical examples. For illustration, suppose that $a = 80$, $b = 2$, $c^A = 7$, $c^B = 8$, and $\delta = 0.8$. Then, we find $s_1^A* = 7.20$, $s_2^A* = s_3^A* = 4.67$, $l_1^A* = 5.94$ and $l_2^A* = 3.74$. Similarly, for the inefficient firm $s_1^B* = 6.97$, $s_2^B* = s_3^B* = 4.17$, $l_1^B* = 6.07$ and $l_2^B* = 4.14$. Using these sales and leasing volumes, we calculate that firm A's total profit approximately equals 579 while that of firm B equals 552. It is useful to compare these numbers with the equilibrium levels of sales when leasing is not possible. In other words, we solve the model again when the two firms compete only in sales in every period. With sales only, in equilibrium, firm A sells 11.22, 4.48, and 2.02 in periods one, two, and three respectively, while the levels for firm B are 11.00, 4.25, and 1.52. Total profit in this case is 366 for firm A and 340 for firm B. Additional examples suggest that this is a typical pattern. In particular, the ability to lease increases the equilibrium profit of both firms and, as illustrated by a comparison of the ratio of profits, it is the high cost firm that benefits relatively more from the ability to lease. This is consistent with our result that the high cost firm chooses to lease relatively more.[16]

5. Discussion and conclusion

The analysis is presented under the assumption that there is (positive) production in every period. As mentioned above this assumption holds for a high enough. Let us now examine more carefully this

[16] As these observations are only based on numerical results, they are only suggestive. Analytic expressions at this point become too complicated to allow us to derive a general result.

parameter restriction. Four inequalities need to be satisfied, $s_2^i + l_2^i \geq l_1^i$ and $s_3^i \geq l_2^i$ for $i = A, B$. Using the equilibrium expressions from the above analysis, it can be shown that both the first and the second constraints are more binding for the inefficient firm than for the efficient firm and, furthermore, that the second constraint is more binding than the first.[17] It is then easy to derive an explicit lower bound for the demand intercept: all four of the required inequalities are satisfied if and only if a is not lower than $[c^B(42\delta^2 + 118\delta + 65) - c^A(21\delta^2 + 70\delta + 60)]/(5 + 3\delta)$. We can further show that this parameter restriction is very mild when the cost asymmetry is small, and that it becomes more severe the larger the asymmetry between the firms and the larger the discount factor. Of course, as a becomes low (below the critical value given above) and when the cost asymmetry is large, the inefficient firm's total supply (that is, sales) in period three becomes low. In this case, the inefficient firm's period three sales volume may be lower than its leasing volume in period two. At the margin, this would create an incentive to decrease the leasing volume in period two (given that it is no longer true that all the leased units can be brought again to the market after period two) and part of this decrease would be translated as an increase in sales. However, we expect our main results to remain qualitatively valid at least for intermediate values of the parameters.

Since cost comparisons are central in our analysis, it is also important to check that the results do not change qualitatively with alternative specifications of the production technology. In particular, we can show that the results remain valid under an alternative formulation (Bulow, 1986) where the present value of unit costs is proportional to the number of periods the product is being used in: $c_1^i = 3c^i$, $c_2^i = 2c^i/\delta$, and $c_3^i = c^i/\delta^2$, $i = A, B$.[18]

Finally, we consider markets where the unit production cost decreases significantly over time. The above analysis is relevant for "mature" industries with costs that are roughly constant. In other markets, there are substantive cost decreases over time, especially when introducing new products. To investigate the implications for our problem, we examine a simple example where for every firm and in every period the unit cost is half of its previous period level: $c_1^i = 4c^i$, $c_2^i = 2c^i$, and $c_3^i = c^i$, $i = A$, B. Then it can be shown that the low-cost firm sells more as well as leases more in every period. In addition, the low-cost firm leases relatively more in the first period $(s_1^A - l_1^A < s_1^B - l_1^B)$ but relatively less in the second period $(s_2^A - l_2^A > s_2^B - l_2^B)$.[19] The intuition is as follows. When costs decrease over time, producing in early periods is less attractive relative to later periods. While both firms prefer to sell a relatively higher volume in later periods (compared to the constant cost case), the efficient firm has a greater incentive to "preserve" the market, because it will have stronger strategic position and

[17] This is not surprising since residual demand and thus firms' supply levels are lower from period to period and because firm B sells less but leases more than firm A. We require demand to be large enough that firm B' total supply in period three is not less than that firm's leasing volume in period two.

[18] In this case we find $l_1^A - l_1^B = (3\delta + 8)(1 - \delta)(c^A - c^B)/\delta b(3\delta + 5) < 0$, $l_2^A - l_2^B = (1 - \delta)(c^A - c^B)/\delta^2 b < 0$, $s_1^A - s_1^B = 8(c^B - c^A)/\delta b(3\delta + 5) > 0$, and $s_2^A - s_2^B = s_3^A - s_3^B = (c^B - c^A)/\delta^2 b > 0$. Note that the cost formulation in the main analysis follows Bucovetsky and Chilton (1986). In reality, costs may be in between the two bounds considered here. The continuity of the solutions implies that our qualitative results hold for such other in-between cases and are not crucially dependent on how this aspect of the game is formulated.

[19] We have $l_1^A - l_1^B = 2(\delta + 1)(3\delta - 5)(c^A - c^B)/b(5 + 3\delta) > 0$, $l_2^A - l_2^B = (\delta - 1)(c^A - c^B)/b > 0$, $s_1^A - s_1^B = (2\delta - 10)(c^A - c^B)/b(5 + 3\delta) > 0$, and $s_2^A - s_2^B = s_3^A - s_3^B = (c^B - c^A)/b > 0$. Also $(s_1^A - l_1^A) - (s_1^B - l_1^B) = 6\delta(1 - \delta)(c^A - c^B)/b(5 + 3\delta) < 0$ and $(s_2^A - l_2^A) - (s_2^B - l_2^B) = -\delta(c^A - c^B)/b > 0$.

thus enjoy greater profit. Due to its greater concern to preserve the market, the efficient firm sells relatively less early on.[20]

The main result in this paper is that, when the choice between sales and leasing is driven primarily by strategic considerations, we should expect inefficient firms to lease more (while efficient firms sell more). Of course, additional factors may also affect the choice between leasing and sales. Also, our results have been obtained within a parametric (although standard) formulation. However, the simplicity of the model allows us to identify some key implications of strategic behavior in this context.

References

Bucovetsky, S., Chilton, J., 1986. Concurrent renting and selling in a durable-goods monopoly under threat of entry. Rand Journal of Economics 17, 261–275.

Bulow, J., 1982. Durable goods monopolists. Journal of Political Economy 90, 314–332.

Bulow, J., 1986. An economic theory of planned obsolescence. Quarterly Journal of Economics 51, 729–749.

Dixit, A.K., 1980. The role of investment in entry deterrence. Economic Journal 90, 95–106.

Tirole, J., 1988. Theory of Industrial Organization, MIT Press.

[20]Continuity implies that, as we vary the rate at which costs decrease over time, there is a critical rate below which the inefficient firm leases more whereas above which the pattern is reversed.

Chapter 29

Product differentiation, process R&D, and the nature of market competition[#]

Ping Lin[a,*], Kamal Saggi[b]

[a]*Department of Economics, Lingnan University, Tuen Mun, Hong Kong*
[b]*Department of Economics, Southern Methodist University, Dallas, TX 75275-0496, USA*

Received 1 February 1999; accepted 1 May 2000

Abstract

We investigate the relationship between process and product R&D and compare the incentives for both types of R&D under different modes of market competition (Bertrand versus Cournot). It is shown that: (i) process R&D investments increase with the degree of product differentiation and firms invest more in product R&D when they can do process R&D than when they cannot; (ii) Bertrand firms have a stronger incentive for product R&D whereas Cournot firms invest more in process R&D; and (iii) cooperation in product R&D promotes both types of R&D relative to competition whereas cooperation in both types of R&D discourages R&D relative to cooperation in just product R&D.

JEL classification: L13; O32

Keywords: Product R&D; Process R&D; Complementarity

1. Introduction

Most of the rather large theoretical literature on R&D focuses on process innovation. However, this focus is striking given the fact that approximately three-fourths of R&D investments by firms in the United States are devoted to

* Corresponding author. Tel.: + 852-2616-7203; fax: + 852-2891-7940.
E-mail address: plin@ln.edu.hk (P. Lin).

[#] This chapter was originally appeared in *European Economic Review* **46**, 201–211. © 2002 Elsevier Science B.V.

product R&D (Scherer and Ross, 1990). In contrast to the theoretical literature, product R&D and its relationship to process R&D have drawn considerable attention in empirical studies. For example, Mansfield (1981), Scherer (1991), and Cohen and Klepper (1996) analyze how market concentration and firm size influence the choice between product and process R&D. Our goal in this paper is to contribute to the theoretical development of this line of research. In particular, we explore the linkages between the two types of R&D and shed light on the dependence of these linkages on the nature of product market competition.

Building upon previous work by Dixit (1979) and Singh and Vives (1984), we construct a duopoly model comprised of three stages. In the first stage, firms choose their investments in product R&D. These product R&D investments determine the degree of differentiation between their products. In the second stage, they choose their investments in process R&D. Product market competition takes place in the final stage.[1] In our model, both product and process R&D affect firm profitability through the price–cost margin. While process R&D enlarges the price–cost margin by reducing the marginal cost of production, product R&D allows firms to charge higher prices by increasing consumer willingness to pay for their products. Since total profit equals output times the price–cost margin, the larger a firm's output, the more attractive is either form of R&D to the firm. This *output effect* leads to a two-way complementarity between the two types of R&D. First, product R&D increases demand for the products of both firms. This increased demand raises the equilibrium output levels and thus enhances their returns from process R&D (see also Athey and Schmutzler, 1995). Second, process R&D also increases equilibrium output levels by lowering costs of production and therefore makes product R&D more attractive.

Using this complementarity property, we obtain the following results. First, the equilibrium level of process R&D investment increases with the degree of product differentiation. Second, firms invest more in product R&D when they can do process R&D than when they cannot. Third, while cooperation in product R&D increases investments in both types of R&D, cooperation in process R&D discourages both types of R&D. Consequently, cooperation in product R&D enhances social welfare relative to competition whereas cooperation in both types of R&D lowers welfare relative to cooperation in just product R&D.

We also find that Bertrand firms invest more in product R&D than Cournot firms. This result complements the existing finding that, given the extent of product differentiation, the incentive for process R&D is stronger under

[1] Our assumption regarding the sequential pattern of R&D (product R&D followed by process R&D) formalizes a stylized view of the life cycle of a typical product: After establishing their products in the market, firms then invest in process R&D to lower production costs. Empirical evidence supports such a formulation (see Klepper, 1996; Utterback and Abernathy, 1983).

Cournot competition than under Bertrand competition.[2] The reason this ranking is reversed under product R&D is as follows. While the strategic incentive for process R&D is positive for Cournot firms and negative for Bertrand firms, the strategic incentive for product R&D is actually negative for Cournot firms and positive for Bertrand firms. Thus, our results show that the *type* of R&D interacts in a non-obvious way with the *nature* of product market competition.

In a related paper, Rosenkranz (1996) develops a model where firms make *simultaneous* decisions regarding product and process innovations. The focus of her paper is on the optimal division of investment between the two types of R&D. Unlike us, Rosenkranz (1996) does not examine the interaction between process and product R&D. In fact, a sequential model may be better suited for studying this interaction. Furthermore, we also consider Bertrand competition, whereas Rosenkranz considers only Cournot competition. Using a linear demand system similar to the one employed in this paper, Vives (1990) analyzes a two-stage game where two duopolists first invest in improving their competitive position, and then compete in the product market.[3] In Vives' model, first-stage investments can be interpreted as either product or process R&D. However, Vives did not examine the interaction between the two types of R&D.[4]

2. Product differentiation only

Consider two firms that produce differentiated goods. The representative consumer's utility is a function of the consumption of the two differentiated goods and the numeraire good m and is given by

$$u(q_1, q_2, m) = a(q_1 + q_2) - (q_1^2 + q_2^2)/2 - sq_1q_2 + m, \quad 0 \leq s \leq 1. \tag{1}$$

Utility maximization gives rise to the following demand system:

$$p_1 = a - q_1 - sq_2 \quad \text{and} \quad p_2 = a - sq_1 - q_2, \tag{2}$$

where q_i is the output of firm i and p_i its price. The parameter s represents the degree of substitutability between the two products: Products are homogeneous

[2] This finding was reported by Qiu (1997), who considered process R&D only (see also Bester and Petrakis, 1993).

[3] In Vives (1990), product differentiation by a firm enhances the demand for its product but, unlike our model, it does not affect the demand for its rival's product.

[4] More recently, Bonanno and Haworth (1998) study incentives for product and process R&D under different modes of competition in a model of vertical (as opposed to horizontal) product differentiation. Firms are not allowed to conduct both types of R&D in their model.

if $s = 1$ and unrelated if $s = 0$. Note that an increase in the degree of product differentiation (a decline in s) shifts the demand curves for *both* firms outward.

The firms' investments in product R&D, denoted by d_i, determine the extent of product differentiation as follows: $s = \bar{s} - (d_1 + d_2)$, where $\bar{s}$ is the initial level of product substitutability and $0 \leq d_i \leq \bar{s}/2$. The cost of product R&D is given by $F(d_i)$, $F' > 0$, $F'' > 0$. To obtain interior solutions, we assume that $F'(0) = 0$ and $F'(\bar{s}/2)$ is very large. After simultaneously choosing their product R&D investments, firms compete in the product market. The marginal cost of production is constant and equals $c > 0$. Denote firm i's profit function as a Cournot competitor by $\pi_i^{\mathrm{C}}(s, q_i(s), q_j(s))$ where $q_i(s)$ and $q_j(s)$ represent the two firms' output levels. At the product R&D stage, firm i chooses d_i, taking d_j, $q_i(.)$, and $q_j(.)$ as given. By the envelope theorem, we have

$$\frac{\mathrm{d}\pi_i^{\mathrm{C}}}{\mathrm{d}d_i} = -\frac{\partial \pi_i^{\mathrm{C}}}{\partial s} - \frac{\partial \pi_i^{\mathrm{C}}}{\partial q_j}\frac{\mathrm{d}q_j}{\mathrm{d}s}. \tag{3}$$

An increase in d_i has two conflicting effects on firm i's profits. The direct effect (captured by the first term of Eq. (3)) is positive because an increase in the degree of product differentiation (i.e., a decline in s) shifts its own demand curve outward. However, the strategic effect (the second term of Eq. (3)) is negative because the demand curve facing firm j also shifts outward and the resulting increase in firm j's output hurts firm i.

Similarly, denote the profit function for Bertrand firms by $\pi_i^{\mathrm{B}}(s, p_i(s), p_j(s))$. We have

$$\frac{\mathrm{d}\pi_i^{\mathrm{B}}}{\mathrm{d}d_i} = -\frac{\partial \pi_i^{\mathrm{B}}}{\partial s} - \frac{\partial \pi_i^{\mathrm{B}}}{\partial p_j}\frac{\mathrm{d}p_j}{\mathrm{d}s}. \tag{4}$$

Under Bertrand competition, the strategic effect of an increase in d_i is positive: As firm i differentiates its product more, firm j raises its price and this price increase *benefits* firm i. Consequently, one expects Bertrand firms to invest more in product R&D than Cournot firms. For the demand system in (2), it is straightforward to show that the equilibrium profits for Cournot and Bertrand firms, respectively, are

$$\pi_i^{\mathrm{C}}(s) = \left(\frac{a-c}{2+s}\right)^2 \quad \text{and} \quad \pi_i^{\mathrm{B}}(s) = \frac{(1-s)}{(1+s)}\left(\frac{a-c}{2-s}\right)^2.$$

In the product R&D stage, firm i chooses d_i to maximize $\pi_i^k(s) - F(d_i)$, where, $k = \mathrm{C}, \mathrm{B}$. The first-order conditions for Cournot and Bertrand firms, respectively, are

$$\frac{2(a-c)^2}{(2+s)^3} = F'(d) \quad \text{and} \quad \frac{2(s^2-s+1)(a-c)^2}{(1+s)^2(2-s)^3} = F'(d), \tag{5}$$

where $s = \bar{s} - 2d$. Since $(s^2 - s + 1)(2 + s)^3 > (1 + s)^2(2 - s)^3$ for all $s \in (0, 1)$, it follows that the marginal benefit of product R&D is higher under Bertrand competition than under Cournot competition. We thus have the following result:

Proposition 1. The equilibrium level of product differentiation is higher under Bertrand competition than under Cournot competition.

3. Interaction between process and product R&D

In this section, we examine how the presence of process R&D alters the two firms' incentives for product R&D. To do this, we study a three-stage game. After choosing their product R&D investments, firms conduct process R&D and then compete in the product market. Process R&D investment by firm i, denoted by x_i, lowers its marginal cost from c to $c - x_i$. The cost function for process R&D is $\gamma(x_i)^2/2$, $\gamma > 0$. We assume that $\gamma \geq 8/9$ in order to guarantee that the second order condition for process R&D holds.[5]

First consider how process R&D investments depend on the degree of product substitutability s. For the demand system in Eq. (2), it is easy to derive the equilibrium levels of process R&D for Bertrand and Cournot firms (see footnote 5):

$$x^{\mathrm{B}}(s) = \frac{2(a-c)}{\gamma(1+s)(2+s)(2-s)^2/(2-s^2) - 2} \quad \text{and}$$

$$x^{\mathrm{C}}(s) = \frac{4(a-c)}{\gamma(2+s)^2(2-s) - 4}. \tag{6}$$

Proposition 2. (i) *Equilibrium process R&D investment under Bertrand competition strictly decreases with s, whereas under Cournot competition it decreases with s when $s < 2/3$ and increases when $s > 2/3$.* (ii) *Equilibrium process R&D investment is higher under Cournot competition ($x^{\mathrm{B}} < x^{\mathrm{C}}$ for all s).*

Part (i) of the above proposition highlights one side of the two-way complementarity between product and process R&D. Increased product differentiation shifts the demand curves of both firms outwards, thereby increasing their

[5] The corresponding second-order condition is $8/(4 - s^2)^2 \leq \gamma$ for Cournot firms, which holds for all s if $\gamma \geq 8/9$, and is $2(2 - s^2)^2/(1 - s^2(4 - s^2)^2 \leq \gamma$ for Bertrand firms, which holds for $0 < s < 0.8$ if $\gamma \geq 8/9$. These derivations and the proof of Proposition 2 can be found in Lin and Saggi (1999).

output levels and making cost-reducing R&D more attractive. As a result, equilibrium process R&D investments increase with the degree of product differentiation.[6]

Part (ii) of Proposition 2 can be understood in terms of the strategic effect of process R&D. Firm i's profits in the product market, as a Cournot competitor, can be written as $\pi_i^C(s, x_i, x_j, q_i, q_j)$. We have

$$\frac{d\pi_i^C}{dx_i} = \frac{\partial \pi_i^C}{\partial x_i} + \frac{\partial \pi_i^C}{\partial q_j}\frac{\partial q_j}{\partial x_i} \quad \text{for all } s. \tag{7}$$

An increase in x_i affects firm i's profits in two reinforcing ways. The direct effect (the first term of Eq. (7)) is positive because an increase in x_i lowers firm i's marginal cost. The strategic effect (the second term of Eq. (7)) is also positive because a reduction in its marginal cost enables firm i to steal market share from its rival. In contrast to Cournot firms, the strategic effect is actually negative for Bertrand firms and works against the direct effect. A reduction in firm i's marginal cost induces it to lower its price which in turn forces firm j to also lower its price. The price reduction by firm j undermines firm i's incentive for process R&D. As a result, Bertrand firms invest less in process R&D than Cournot firms (for any given s).[7]

Next, consider the product R&D stage. Let $x^*(s)$ denote the symmetric equilibrium level of process R&D derived in Proposition 2. Further, for Cournot firms, let $\prod_i(s, x_i, x_j) = \pi_i^C(s, x^*(s), x^*(s), q_i(.), q_j(.))$. For Bertrand firms, $\prod_i$ is defined as a function of equilibrium prices instead of quantities. Obviously, $\prod_i$ increases with x_i and decreases with both s and x_j.

Firm i chooses d_i to maximize $\prod_i(s, x^*(s), x^*(s)) - (\gamma/2)(x^*(s))^2 - F(d_i)$, where $s = \bar{s} - d_1 - d_2$. Since x_i is chosen optimally, the envelope theorem implies that the equilibrium level of product differentiation is determined by

$$-\frac{\partial \prod_i(s, x^*(s), x^*(s))}{\partial s} + \frac{\partial \prod_i(s, x^*(s), x^*(s))}{\partial x_j}\frac{dx^*(s)}{ds}(-1) = F'(d). \tag{8}$$

The first term of the above equation says that an increase in d_i raises firm i's profits (the direct effect). However, the second term of the above equation captures an indirect negative effect: an increase in d_i induces firm j to invest more in process R&D, hurting firm i in the product market. This negative effect

[6] If $s > 2/3$, process R&D increases with s for Cournot firms. This is because the strategic effect of process R&D, which is positive under Cournot competition, gets stronger for larger s. For a general oligopoly, it can be shown that the range over which process R&D increases with s shrinks as the number of firms increases.

[7] Note that this statement may not hold when s is chosen *endogenously*. This is because Bertrand firms invest more in product R&D which leads to more process R&D.

is absent if firms cannot do process R&D. However, the presence of process R&D strengthens the direct effect of product R&D.[8] For the linear demand system given in Eq. (2), we prove in the appendix that the direct positive effect outweighs the indirect negative effect so that the presence of process R&D strengthens the incentives for product R&D.

Proposition 3. Under both Bertrand and Cournot competition, firms invest more in product R&D when they can do process R&D than when they cannot.

4. R&D cooperation and welfare

We consider two scenarios in this section: Semi-cooperation whereby firms cooperate only in product R&D and full cooperation under which firms co-operate in both types of R&D. Thus, under either scenario, at the product R&D stage, firms choose a common investment level d to maximize the profit of each firm:

$$\max\left[\prod_i (s, x^*(s), x^*(s)) - \frac{\gamma}{2}(x^*(s))^2 - F(d)\right], \tag{9}$$

where $s = \bar{s} - 2d$. Under semi-cooperation, process R&D investments are the same as under competition, whereas under full cooperation these are chosen jointly.[9]

A positive externality exists between firms at the product R&D stage: Product differentiation by one firm also enhances demand for the other firm's product. Semi-cooperation internalizes this externality and thus increases product R&D relative to competition. By the complementarity property, process R&D increases as well. Under full cooperation, however, the well-known negative externality at the process R&D stage is also internalized. Thus, full cooperation lowers process R&D for all s. Less process R&D in turn implies less product R&D. We, therefore, have the following result:

---

[8] The first term of (8) is bigger when evaluated at $x_i = x^*(s) > 0$ (i.e., under optimal process R&D) than when evaluated at $x_i = 0$ (i.e., in the absence of process R&D).

[9] It is straightforward to show that the cooperative level of process R&D for Cournot firms is $x^{CC} = 2(a-c)/(\gamma(2+s)^2 - 2)$ and for Bertrand firms is

$$x^{BC} = \frac{2(a-c)}{\gamma(1+s)(2-s)^2/(1-s) - 2}.$$

These investments are smaller than their counterparts under R&D competition (see Lin and Saggi (1999) for details).

Proposition 4. Semi-cooperation promotes both types of R&D relative to competition. Full cooperation discourages both types of R&D relative to semi-cooperation.[10]

Another way of understanding the result regarding full cooperation is as follows. Let $\pi_f(s)$ denote the profit per firm at the product R&D stage under full cooperation and $\pi_s(s)$ under semi-cooperation. Two observations follow immediately. First, $\pi_f(s) > \pi_s(s)$ for all s because cooperation in process R&D necessarily raises profits. Second, the difference $\pi_f(s) - \pi_s(s)$ increases with s: The more similar the products, the stronger the magnitude of the negative externality at the process R&D stage, and thus larger the gain from R&D cooperation. Given that the derivative of $\pi_f(s) - \pi_s(s)$ is positive, we have $-(\mathrm{d}/\mathrm{d}s)\pi_f(s) < -(\mathrm{d}/\mathrm{d}s)\pi_s(s)$. Therefore, the marginal benefit of product R&D is lower under full cooperation than under semi-cooperation.

We next examine the welfare effects of R&D cooperation, starting with the case of semi-cooperation. We focus on Cournot competition (where cleaner results are possible) and comment on the Bertrand case whenever appropriate. In the symmetric equilibrium, consumer utility as given in Eq. (1) simplifies to $u = u(q, q, I - pq - pq) = (1 + s)q^2 + I$, where I is the consumer's endowment of the numeraire good. Under Cournot competition, we have $u = (1 + s)((a - c + x_C)/(2 + s))^2 + I$ which, by Eq. (6), is proportional to the market size parameter $(a - c)^2$. Thus, only the process R&D cost parameter, γ, determines how consumer surplus varies with s. Since algebraic complexity did not permit analytical derivations, we conducted numerical simulations to investigate the dependence of consumer welfare on s and γ. Table 1 contains representative results from our various simulations. It reports how consumer surplus (multiplied by $100/(a - c)^2$) varies with γ and s.

When $\gamma = 1$, consumer surplus initially decreases and then increases with s (for $s > 0.8$). Similarly, for $\gamma = 2$, simulations show that consumer surplus reaches a minimum at $s = 0.97$. However, when γ is larger ($\gamma = 3, 4$ in Table 1), consumer surplus *always* declines with s. In fact, our simulation results show that consumer surplus decreases with s for all $\gamma > 2.23$. We can, thus, conclude that semi-cooperation improves welfare for $\gamma > 2.23$: Semi-cooperation necessarily benefits firms and since it lowers s, it also makes consumers better off.[11] The relationship between consumer surplus and s (as reported in Table 1) can be understood as follows. First note that in the absence of process R&D ($x_C = 0$), consumer welfare always decreases with s under Cournot competition. Despite

[10] Since full cooperation internalizes both externalities, its total effect on R&D depends upon the relative magnitudes of the two externalities. In general, relative to competition, full cooperation may either promote or hamper R&D.

[11] If products are initially not very similar (if $\bar{s} < 0.8$), or if product R&D cost is low (so that the equilibrium s is very small), semi-cooperation improves welfare even for small γ.

Table 1
Consumer surplus under Cournot competition

	$s=0.1$	$s=0.2$	$s=0.3$	$s=0.4$	$s=0.5$	$s=0.6$	$s=0.7$	$s=0.8$	$s=0.9$
$\gamma=1$	91.3	84.8	79.7	75.9	73.0	71.0	69.8	69.5	70.1
$\gamma=2$	43.0	41.8	40.6	39.6	38.8	38.1	37.5	37.0	36.8
$\gamma=3$	35.3	34.6	33.9	33.2	32.6	32.1	31.6	31.1	30.8
$\gamma=4$	32.1	31.6	31.1	30.6	30.1	29.6	29.1	28.7	28.4

increased prices, consumers benefit from a decrease in s because they value product differentiation and because output of both firms increases as s falls. Why does the presence of process R&D raise the possibility that consumers lose from an increase in product differentiation, especially when s is large and γ is small? From Section 3, we know that the strategic effect of process R&D under Cournot competition is quite strong when s is large. Hence, if s is large and if process R&D is not costly (i.e., γ is not big), an increase in s induces firms to invest a lot more in R&D, significantly lowering prices and thus raising consumer welfare. When γ is large, however, the increase in process R&D caused by an increase in s is insufficient to counter the decline in consumer surplus that results from the reduction in the degree of product differentiation.[12] Consequently, consumer welfare always decreases with s when γ is large.[13]

How does full cooperation affect social welfare? The fact that consumer surplus decreases with s (for $\gamma > 2.23$) implies that under semi-cooperation there is under-investment in product R&D relative to the social optimum. Since product R&D is further reduced if firms also cooperate in process R&D, social welfare declines under full cooperation relative to semi-cooperation if $\gamma > 2.23$.[14]

The above results have an interesting policy implication. When product R&D and process R&D are complementary, cooperation in one type of R&D promotes the other type of R&D if and only if it enhances incentives for the first type of R&D. Therefore, in assessing the desirability of cooperation in one type of R&D, analysis should not be confined to that type of R&D alone. The costs

[12] For example, when $\gamma = 1$, process R&D as a percentage of market size $(a - c)$ is quite large (76.2% when $s = 0.9$) whereas for $\gamma = 3$ it is quite small (only 16.8% for $s = 0.9$).

[13] Under Bertrand competition, product differentiation is not as desirable for consumers as it is under Cournot competition because prices approach marginal cost as products become more similar. In fact, simulations reveal that consumer surplus under Bertrand competition increases with s even if γ is large. As a result, semi-cooperation is less beneficial to consumers and is less likely to improve welfare under Bertrand competition than under Cournot competition.

[14] It can be shown that, given s, cooperation in process R&D lowers welfare. Thus, in addition to the above welfare loss due to reduced product R&D, full cooperation also hampers welfare by lowering process R&D.

and benefits of cooperation may spill over to the other type of R&D and such interaction should be taken into account when designing R&D policy.

5. Concluding remarks

Using a model in which increased product differentiation enhances demand, we find that product and process R&D are mutually reinforcing. As a result, firms invest more in product R&D in the presence of process R&D than in its absence. Cooperation in the two types of R&D affects R&D incentives in different ways. While cooperation in product R&D encourages both types of R&D, cooperation in process R&D has the opposite effect.

We expect our results to hold in more general settings provided that product R&D increases output (via its effect on demand). However, product R&D may sometimes result in the introduction of completely new products.[15] In these cases, product R&D by a firm may lower the demand for all existing products. If so, product R&D and process R&D may fail to be complements and product R&D decisions may be subject to a negative, rather than a positive externality. The interaction of product and process R&D under such a scenario deserves future research.

Acknowledgements

We thank editor Xavier Vives and two anonymous referees for their comments and suggestions which greatly improved the quality of this paper. Of course, we alone are responsible for any errors.

Appendix

Proof of Proposition 3. Under Cournot competition, firm i chooses d_i to maximize $[(a-c+x^{\mathrm{C}})(2+s)]^2 - \gamma/2x^{\mathrm{C}2} - F(d_i)$. The marginal benefit of product R&D is, thus,

$$\frac{2(a-c+x^{\mathrm{C}})^2}{(2+s)^3} + \frac{2s(2-s)(a-c+x^{\mathrm{C}})}{(4-s^2)^2}\frac{\mathrm{d}x^{\mathrm{C}}}{\mathrm{d}s}, \tag{A.1}$$

which, by noting (5), is greater than that in the absence of process R&D if and only if

$$\frac{x^{\mathrm{C}2}}{(2+s)^3} + \frac{2(a-c)x^{\mathrm{C}}}{(2+s)^3} + \frac{s(2-s)(a-c+x^{\mathrm{C}})}{(4-s^2)^2}\frac{\mathrm{d}x^{\mathrm{C}}}{\mathrm{d}s} > 0. \tag{A.2}$$

[15] We are grateful to an anonymous referee for raising this point.

Since $x^C = 4(a-c)/(\gamma H - 4)$, where $H = (2+s)^2(2-s)$, (A.2) becomes

$$x^C + 2(a-c) + \frac{(a-c+x^C)s(2+s)}{(2-s)}\frac{(-\gamma)H'(s)}{\gamma H - 4} > 0,$$

which holds if

$$1 > \frac{s(2+s)}{(2-s)}\frac{H'(s)}{H-4/\gamma} = \frac{s(2+s)}{(2-s)}\frac{(2+s)(2-3s)}{(2+s)^2(2-s)-4/\gamma}. \quad \text{(A.3)}$$

Using Maple, we plotted the right-hand side of (A.3) and found that it is less than 1 when $\gamma = 8/9$. So (A.3) holds for all $\gamma \geq 8/9$. This proves the proposition for Cournot firms. The result for Bertrand case can be similarly proved. □

References

Athey, S., Schmutzler, A., 1995. Product and process flexibility in an innovative environment. Rand Journal of Economics 26, 557–574.

Bester, H., Petrakis, E., 1993. The incentives for cost reduction in a differentiated industry. International Journal of Industrial Organization 11, 519–534.

Bonanno, G., Haworth, B., 1998. Intensity of competition and the choice between product and process innovation. International Journal of Industrial Organization 16, 495–510.

Cohen, W.M., Klepper, S., 1996. Firm size and the nature of innovation within industries: The case of process and product R&D. Review of Economics and Statistics 78, 232–243.

Dixit, A., 1979. A model of duopoly suggesting a theory of entry barriers. Bell Journal of Economics 10, 20–32.

Klepper, S., 1996. Entry, exit, growth, and innovation over the product life cycle. American Economic Review 86, 562–583.

Lin, P., Saggi, K., 1999. Notes on product differentiation, process R&D, and the nature of product market competition, Mimeo.

Mansfield, E., 1981. Composition of R&D expenditures: Relationship to size of firm, concentration, and innovative output. Review of Economics and Statistics 63, 610–615.

Qiu, L., 1997. On the dynamic efficiency of Bertrand and Cournot equilibria. Journal of Economic Theory 75, 213–229.

Rosenkranz, S., 1996. Simultaneous choice of process and product innovation. Discussion paper no. 1321, CEPR, London.

Scherer, F.M., 1991. Changing perspectives on the firm size problem. In: Zoltan, J.A., David, B.A. (Eds.), Innovation and Technological Change: An International Comparison. Harvester Wheatsheaf, New York.

Scherer, F.M., Ross, D., 1990. Industrial Market Structure and Economics Performance. Houghton Mifflin, Boston, MA.

Singh, N., Vives, X., 1984. Price and quantity competition in a differentiated duopoly. Rand Journal of Economics 15, 546–554.

Utterback, J.M., Abernathy, W.J., 1983. A dynamic model of process and product innovation. Omega 3 (6), 639–656.

Vives, X., 1990. Information and competitive advantage. International Journal of Industrial Organization 8, 17–35.

Chapter 30

On intrabrand and interbrand competition: The strategic role of fees and royalties[#]

Kamal Saggi[a], Nikolaos Vettas[b,c,d,*]

[a]*Department of Economics, Southern Methodist University, Dallas, TX 75275-0496, USA*
[b]*The Fuqua School of Business, Duke University, Durham, NC 27708-0120, USA*
[c]*Department of Economics, University of Athens, Athens 10559, Greece*
[d]*Centre for Economic Policy Research, London, UK*

Received 1 April 1999; accepted 1 April 2000

Abstract

We examine oligopolistic markets with both intrabrand and interbrand competition. We characterize equilibrium contracts involving a royalty (or wholesale price) and a fee when each upstream firm contracts with multiple downstream firms. Royalties control competition between own downstream firms at the expense of making them passive against rivals. When the number of downstream firms is endogenous, each upstream firm chooses to have only *one* downstream firm. This result is in sharp contrast to previous literature where competitors benefit by having a larger number of independent downstream firms under only fixed fee payments. We discuss why allowing upstream firms to charge per-unit payments in addition to fixed fees dramatically alters their strategic incentives.

JEL classification: L13; L14; L22; L42

Keywords: Intrabrand competition; Strategic contracting; Two-part tariffs; Royalties

1. Introduction

In a large number of market transactions, firms do not sell their products directly to final consumers but instead contract with independent downstream

* Corresponding author. Tel.: + 1-919-660-7756; fax: + 1-919-684-2818.
E-mail addresses: ksaggi@mail.smu.edu (K. Saggi), nikos.vettas@duke.edu (N. Vettas).

[#] This chapter was originally appeared in *European Economic Review* **46**, 189–200. © 2002 Elsevier Science B.V.

firms who act as final sellers. Vertical market relations include franchising, retailing, licensing of technology, and supply of intermediate products. Since such relations are pervasive, it is important to understand the forces that govern vertical contracts. In this paper we explore how strategic considerations shape vertical contracts in oligopolistic markets. We focus on two key strategic decisions of 'upstream' firms: The number of independent 'downstream' firms and the terms of vertical contracts. We consider two-part tariffs, contracts that specify a fixed fee and a per-unit payment which we call royalty.[1] The main result is that, when each upstream firm commits to its number of downstream firms prior to signing a fee-and-royalty contract with each of them, each upstream firm chooses to be represented by a single downstream firm.

We allow oligopolistic competition to be both intrabrand and interbrand. Specifically, we first characterize fee-and-royalty contracts when each upstream firm is associated with an arbitrary number of downstream firms. Past work has developed important insights for the case of a monopolist contracting with multiple downstream firms and for upstream oligopolists each contracting with a single downstream firm. Our analysis nests these two situations as special cases.[2] When choosing royalty rates, an upstream firm has to balance two opposing incentives. On the one hand, it prefers its downstream firms to be more *passive* against one another. On the other hand, it would like them to be committed to more *aggressive* behavior against rival downstream firms. In equilibrium, the larger the number of its own downstream firms relative to that of rival firms and the higher the degree of differentiation between products, the higher will be the royalty rate.[3]

The central result of this paper is obtained by endogenizing the number of downstream firms. We consider a three-stage game with upstream firms choosing the number of their independent (i.e. maximizing own profit) downstream firms and then choosing their royalty rates (and fees). In the last stage, downstream firms compete in quantities. We find that each upstream firm prefers to *minimize* the number of its independent downstream firms so that, in equilibrium, each upstream firm chooses only one downstream firm. This result is in sharp contrast to previous work showing that upstream firms prefer to have a *higher* number of downstream firms for strategic reasons. In particular, Baye et al. (1996), Corchón (1991), and Polasky (1992) have shown that, in a two-stage game where the choice of the number of downstream divisions by upstream firms is followed by quantity competition in the product market, upstream firms have an incentive to increase the number of downstream divisions since this

[1] Such payment schemes are widely prevalent in vertical relations. In our framework, the per-unit payment can be also viewed as a wholesale price.

[2] Bonanno and Vickers (1988, p. 264), refer to the first of these two cases as $(1, n)$ and the second as $(m, 1)$. Our analysis contributes to the understanding of the (m, n) case.

[3] When taking the number of downstream firms as given, our analysis is related to Dixit (1984), who explores aspects of trade policy in oligopolistic markets.

practice represents a commitment to more aggressive downstream behavior, a 'divide and conquer' strategy.[4] This insight is often offered as a rationale for 'divisionalization' policies of firms. However, we show that allowing upstream firms to charge both fees and per-unit payments, as opposed to only fees, dramatically alters their strategic incentives: A larger number of downstream firms implies that, for any royalty rate, the rival has a stronger incentive to behave strategically when selecting royalties.[5] This change in strategic incentives completely overturns the existing result. Since per-unit payments are very often used in addition to fees, our analysis implies that the existing argument in support of the 'divide and conquer' strategy requires important qualifications.

Finally, we demonstrate how the equilibria that arise depend critically upon the order in which firms make decisions. In particular, if the number of downstream firms is chosen simultaneously with (or subsequently to) the terms of contracts, upstream firms may then have incentives to contract with many downstream firms, thereby reversing our main result. Similarly, the main result may not hold if only a single instrument (either a fee only or a royalty only) can be utilized in the contract.[6]

2. The model

We consider two upstream firms, A and B, each of which may contract with multiple downstream firms. The number of downstream firms associated with upstream firm i is $n_i \geq 1, i = A, B$. We assume that production cost is zero, both at the upstream and the downstream stages.[7] Market demand is given by

$$p_i = a - Q_i - sQ_j, \quad i,j = A, B, \tag{1}$$

where $Q_i = \sum_{k=1}^{n_i} q_i^k$ denotes the aggregate output of all downstream firms selling product i, $i = A, B$; q_i^k, $k = 1, \ldots, n_i$, denotes the output of each downstream firm contracting with upstream firm i; and p_i denotes the market price. The parameter $s \in [0, 1]$ measures the degree of substitution between the two

---

[4] This point is related to the idea that, for strategic reasons, horizontal mergers may be unprofitable (see e.g. Salant et al., 1983).

[5] That it may be desirable for an upstream firm to restrict the number of its downstream is also a feature of some previous work including Kamien and Tauman (1986) and Katz and Shapiro (1986) on licencing an innovation. However, they consider a single upstream firm whereas upstream competition is critical for our results.

[6] Rey and Stiglitz (1995) consider exclusive territories which, like picking a single downstream firm, eliminate downstream competition. However, unlike us they do not examine oligopolistic intrabrand competition and compare perfect competition and exclusive territories under price competition. In addition, they consider downstream price competition and the strategic incentives are different in their model. See also Gal-Or (1991) for downstream price competition (with each upstream firm contracting with one downstream).

[7] As long as unit costs are constant, this assumption is without loss of generality.

products. Clearly, when $s = 1$ the two products are perfect substitutes whereas when $s = 0$ they are perfectly differentiated.

We study a three-stage game. In the first stage, the two upstream firms simultaneously choose the number of their own downstream firms, $n_i \geq 1$, $i = A, B$. Next, the two upstream firms (simultaneously) make a take-it-or-leave-it offer to each of their downstream firms that specifies a pair (f_i, r_i), where f_i is a fixed fee and r_i is a royalty rate per unit sold.[8] Thus, the total payment to an upstream firm from a downstream firm that produces q units equals $f_i + r_i q$. The outside option of each downstream firm is normalized to zero. We assume that the same contract is offered to all downstream firms associated with a given upstream firm.[9] Finally, in the third stage of the game, firms that accept the offer (f_i, r_i) compete in quantities in the downstream market. We consider the subgame perfect equilibrium of this game.

Note that the timing adopted here (the choice of number of downstream firms precedes the choice of royalties) reflects a situation where it is costlier to change the number of downstream firms than to change royalties. Later in the paper we discuss the implications of alternative timing assumptions. Also note that we assume quantity competition in the downstream market.[10] As known from the strategic contracting literature, it matters whether the strategic variables in the downstream market are prices or quantities, since the slopes of downstream reaction functions depend upon the strategic variable. In our framework, quantity competition is attractive because it allows us to capture the idea that a firm may want its downstream firms to be more passive against its own firms but more aggressive against rivals. Moreover, assuming quantity competition facilitates comparison of our results to previous work on the strategic choice of downstream divisions (discussed above) which also employs this assumption.

3. Analysis: Competition with given numbers of downstream firms

We first take the number of downstream firms (n_A and n_B) as given and analyze the choice of contracts and downstream quantity competition. This is, of course, a necessary first step before we can consider the choice of the number of downstream firms. Moreover, the analysis of competition with a given number of downstream firms is of independent interest.

[8] Placing all the bargaining power in the hands of upstream firms corresponds to having a competitive supply of potential downstream firms. This assumption is standard in this class of models.

[9] In reality, there is indeed uniformity regarding contracts of the same firm (see, for example, Lafontaine and Slade, 1997, pp. 15–16). Often, legal restrictions also contribute to this wholesale-price uniformity.

[10] With respect to this modelling choice, both the usual criticism of quantity competition models ('firms choose prices') as well at its usual defences (including capacity precommitment) apply.

3.1. Equilibrium royalties and quantities

Suppose that downstream firms have accepted contracts that involve royalty rates r_i. The fixed fees specified in the contracts clearly do not affect output decisions, as long as downstream firms have an incentive to operate. Profit (net of royalty payments) for a downstream firm m that accepts a contract involving a royalty rate $r_i, i = A, B$, equals

$$(a - Q_i - sQ_j - r_i)q_i^m, \quad i,j = A, B. \tag{2}$$

Taking the output levels of other firms as given, the reaction function of downstream firm m is $q_i^m(Q_{i,-m}, Q_j; r_i) = (a - Q_{i,-m} - sQ_j - r_i)/2$, where $Q_{i,-m} \equiv \sum_{k=1,k\neq m}^{n_i} q_i^k$ is the aggregate quantity produced by all other downstream firms contracting with firm i except firm m. We then solve the system of downstream reaction functions for equilibrium output levels as functions of the number of firms and royalty rates:

$$q_i = \frac{a - r_i - n_j(a(s-1) + r_i - sr_j)}{1 + n_i + n_j + n_i n_j(1 - s^2)}. \tag{3}$$

Next, we determine equilibrium royalty rates. Substituting the above output levels into (2), we obtain downstream profits. Since upstream firms have all the bargaining power, they extract the entire residual profit of downstream firms by choosing a fee equal to their after-royalty profit. Therefore, taking as given the royalty rate of firm j, the objective of upstream firm i is to choose its royalty rate r_i to maximize the aggregate profit of its downstream firms $\pi^i(r_i, r_j; n_i, n_j) = n_i p_i q_i$, where per-firm quantities are given by (3) and prices by (1). This optimization generates the royalty reaction functions of upstream firms:

$$r_i(r_j; n_i, n_j) = \frac{[n_j((s^2 - 1)n_i + 1) - n_i + 1][n_j(a(s-1) - sr_j) - a]}{2(n_j + 1)[(1 - s^2)n_j + 1]n_i},$$

$$i,j = A, B. \tag{4}$$

Solving the system of the two royalty reaction functions we obtain:

Proposition 1. With two upstream firms, each contracting with n_i, $i = A, B$, downstream firms, the equilibrium royalty rates are

$$r_i^* = r(n_i, n_j) = \frac{a[2 - s + n_i(2 - s^2 - s)][n_i - 1 - n_j(s^2 n_i - n_i + 1)]}{n_i[n_i n_j(s^4 - 5s^2 + 4) + (n_i + n_j)(4 - 3s^2) + 4 - s^2]},$$

$$i,j = A, B. \tag{5}$$

This expression appears somewhat complicated – a discussion and intuition are provided below. The equilibrium royalty captures a central tension in our analysis. From the viewpoint of an upstream firm, charging a positive royalty makes downstream firms more passive and has two conflicting effects. On the one hand, passive behavior is desirable in order to control competition with other downstream firms contracting with the *same* upstream firm. On the other hand, passive behavior is undesirable from the point of view of competing with firms contracting with a different upstream firm.[11]

3.2. Analysis of the equilibrium contracts

There are three critical parameters that determine equilibrium royalty rates (5): n_A, n_B, and s. To isolate the role of each parameter, consider first the case where products of the two upstream firms are perfectly differentiated ($s = 0$). In this case of *pure intrabrand competition*, we have

$$r_i^*(s = 0) = a(n_i - 1)/2n_i, \quad i = A, B. \tag{6}$$

Thus, an upstream monopolist charges a positive royalty if and only if the number of downstream firms exceeds one. A positive royalty serves to effectively raise the downstream firms' marginal cost and makes them internalize the horizontal externality that exists among them. It is easy to check that the optimal contract for the upstream firm drives the downstream market to the monopoly level (with price $a/2$) and allows the upstream firm to obtain exactly the monopoly profit ($a^2/4$).[12] It is also easy to see that the optimal royalty decreases in the number of downstream firms. In the extreme case with only one downstream firm, the upstream firm charges no royalties: Extracting a per-unit payment from a downstream monopolist simply leads to 'double marginalization'.

In the other extreme case, *pure interbrand competition*, each upstream firm signs a contract with a single downstream firm: $n_i = n_j = 1$. To focus the discussion, assume no differentiation ($s = 1$). In this case, Eq. (5) yields[13]

$$r_i^*(n_i = n_j = 1;\ s = 1) = -\,a/5, \quad i = A, B. \tag{7}$$

[11] One could define the 'aggregate' or 'brand' reaction function of upstream firm i, indicating the aggregate output of all of firm i's downstream firms given the output of all of firm j's downstream firms. Then, when firm i chooses r_i, and taking r_j as given, firm i acts as a Stackelberg leader along firm j's 'brand' reaction function. This reasoning delivers the expressions we have derived above (see Saggi and Vettas, 1999).

[12] This intuition is central in Dixit (1983), Mathewson and Winter (1984), and other work that examines 'minimally sufficient instruments' to replicate vertical integration outcomes. See Katz (1989, pp. 678–679) for downstream price competition as a negative externality.

[13] More generally, when $n_i = n_j = 1$ and $s \in [0, 1]$, we have $r_i = s^2 a/(s^2 - 2s - 4)$.

This represents a standard result in the strategic contracting and delegation literature.[14] In this case, the upstream firms subsidize their downstream firms per unit of output sold. Note that, since in this model there is an analogy between royalties and wholesale prices, a subsidy simply means charging wholesale prices below upstream cost. If negative royalties (that is, subsidies) are not possible, the equilibrium involves zero royalties (and fees equal to the per-firm Cournot profit). The basic intuition is that, by charging a lower royalty rate, an upstream firm reduces the unit cost of its own downstream firm, thereby allowing it to obtain a stronger strategic position against its rival.

Next consider how the number of downstream firms matters. In the case of homogenous products ($s = 1$), we obtain

$$r_i^*(s = 1) = a(n_i - n_j - 1)/n_i(n_A + n_B + 3), \quad i,j = A, B, \tag{8}$$

so that firm A employs a positive royalty if and only if $n_A > n_B + 1$. Further, when $n_A > n_B + 1$ firm B does not employ a positive royalty. The intuition is that a positive royalty is used only when the incentive to soften downstream competition among *own* contracting firms is stronger than the incentive to give them a stronger strategic position against rival downstream firms.[15]

Next, to isolate the role played by the degree of product differentiation (s), suppose $n_A = n_B = n$. Then, from (5) we obtain

$$r^*(n_A = n_B = n) = a[n^2(1 - s^2) - 1]/n[n(2 + s - s^2) + (s + 2)]. \tag{9}$$

Thus $r^* > 0$ if and only if $n^2(1 - s^2) > 1$. As s increases, n must also increase for the royalty rate to be positive. In other words, more similar the downstream products (i.e., the higher is s), stronger must be the competitive externality between firms that contract with a single upstream firm for the latter to charge a positive royalty. In the limit when products become perfectly homogenous ($s \to 1$), optimal royalties are never positive.

Finally, we note an important property of the optimal royalty rates:

Remark 1. The equilibrium royalty of firm i decreases as the number of rival downstream firms (n_j) increases (regardless of the magnitude of s).

This relation underlies a key strategic incentive when we endogenize the number of downstream divisions in the following analysis. An upstream firm

[14] See, for example, Brander and Spencer (1985) in the context of international trade policy, and Bonanno and Vickers (1988), Fershtman and Judd (1987), McGuire and Staelin (1983), Sklivas (1987) and Vickers (1985) on delegation and managerial incentives. The central insight is that competing principals may have a (unilateral) incentive to make their agents commit to more aggressive behavior.

[15] This analysis suggests an empirically testable implication: Dominant upstream firms (in the sense of having a higher number of downstream firms) are likely to charge relatively higher royalty rates and lower fixed fees than their smaller competitors.

recognizes that, if it chooses a larger number of downstream divisions, it induces its rival to become more aggressive in terms of royalties.[16]

4. Equilibrium number of downstream firms

Firm i, $i = A, B$, chooses its number of downstream firms to solve

$$\max_{n_i} \{n_i p_i(r_i^*(n_i, n_j), r_j^*(n_i, n_j)) q_i(r_i^*(n_i, n_j), r_j^*(n_i, n_j))\}.$$

Substitution of the equilibrium royalty rates and differentiation with respect to n_i yields

$$\frac{\partial \pi^i(n_i, n_j)}{\partial n_i} = -\frac{2s^3 a^2(n_j + 1)[(2 - s^2 - s)n_j + 2 - s][1 + (1 - s^2)n_j][(2 - s^2 - s)n_i + 2 - s]}{[n_i n_j(4 + s^4 - 5s^2) + (n_i + n_j)(4 - 3s^2) + 4 - s^2]^3} < 0 \tag{10}$$

for all $0 < s \leq 1$.[17] It follows that each upstream firm wants to minimize the number of its own downstream firms, regardless of the number of firms chosen by its rival. Thus, we have:

Proposition 2. If $s > 0$, in equilibrium, $n_A^* = n_B^* = 1$, so that each upstream firm chooses to have only one downstream firm. Moreover, it is strictly optimal for firm i to have only one downstream firm, regardless of the number of downstream firms chosen by firm j.

The intuition is as follows. In our framework, a commitment to more aggressive behavior in the downstream market can be achieved by either having a higher number of downstream firms or choosing a lower royalty rate. So why is it preferable to choose low royalties instead of (also) choosing a larger number of firms? When choosing its number of downstream firms, while an upstream firm takes the rival number of downstream firms as given, *it does consider the effect of its choice of number of firms on the rival's royalty rate.* In particular, a larger number of downstream firms implies that, for any royalty rate, an

---

[16] Differentiating r_i^* from (5) with respect to n_j delivers the result:

$$\frac{\partial r_i^*}{\partial n_j} = \frac{-2as^2(n_i + 1)[(s^2 + s - 2)n_i + s - 2][(s^2 - 1)n_i - 1]}{n_i[(s^4 - 5s^2 + 4)n_i n_j - (3s^2 - 4)(n_i + n_j) - s^2 + 4]^2} < 0.$$

[17] Since $0 < s \leq 1$, the following hold: (i) $2 - s > 2 - s^2 - s \geq 0$; (ii) $4 + s^4 - 5s^2 \geq 0$ and (iii) $4 - s^2 > 4 - 3s^2 > 0$. It is easy to show that these inequalities imply that $\partial \pi^i(n_i, n_j)/\partial n_i < 0$.

upstream firm's brand reaction function becomes steeper and, as a result, the rival has a stronger incentive to behave strategically (by choosing a lower royalty rate). Since it is desirable to have higher rival royalty rates, each firm has an incentive to lower its number of downstream firms.[18]

Using the terminology of Fudenberg and Tirole (1984), the incentives of upstream firms to employ 'top-dog' strategies (be strong to look aggressive), as a result of the downstream quantity competition, are replaced by 'puppy-dog' behavior (be weak to look inoffensive) when the number of downstream firms is selected prior to the terms of contracts. The choice of royalties in the second stage corresponds to 'top-dog' behavior, while the prior commitment to the number of downstream firms corresponds to 'puppy-dog' behavior.

To illustrate the effect of increasing the number of downstream firms consider the following example. Suppose $s = 1$, $n_B = 1$, and that n_A increases from 1 to 2. It is easy to calculate the relevant royalties, quantities, prices, and profits from the expressions given above. As n_A increases, firm A's royalty increases (from $-a/5$ to zero) and B's royalty decreases (from $-a/5$ to $-a/3$). The total output of firm A's downstream firms decreases from $2a/5$ to $a/3$ and that of B's increases from $2a/5$ to $a/2$. The price decreases from $a/5$ to $a/6$. Finally, firm A's profit decreases from $2a^2/25$ to $a^2/18$ while that of B increases from $2a^2/25$ to $a^2/12$. Thus (when $n_B = 1$) firm A would not like to increase its number of firms.

5. Alternative formulations and comparison

To further clarify the interaction between royalties and the number of downstream competitors, we consider a number of alternative structures below. We show that the equilibria depend critically on the sequence in which firms make decisions and on the type of contracts that upstream firms can utilize.

Consider first the *fees-only* case. In the absence of royalties, the only strategic choice facing upstream firms is the number of downstream firms. As the literature (e.g. Baye et al., 1996; Corchón, 1991; Polasky, 1992) shows, when

[18] One may ask if upstream firms prefer to become vertically integrated. While both firms are better-off under vertical integration, they do not have a *unilateral* incentive to vertically integrate. In particular, it is a dominant strategy for each firm to choose delegation (and so this situation is a 'prisoners' dilemma'). Formally, we can enlarge the game so that firms first choose to either become vertically integrated (VI) or not (N). Assuming $s = 1$, for simplicity, we obtain the following profits. If both choose VI, firms' profits are $\pi(\mathrm{VI},\mathrm{VI}) = a^2/9$ (this expression follows from our analysis when royalties equal zero and is, of course, equal to Cournot profit with two firms). Further, $\pi(\mathrm{N},\mathrm{N}) = 2a^2/25$ (this corresponds to the equilibrium where each firm contracts with only one downstream firm and sets royalties equal to $-a/5$). Finally, it is easy to check that $\pi(\mathrm{VI},\mathrm{N}) = a^2/16$ and $\pi(\mathrm{N},\mathrm{VI}) = a^2/8$ (the firm that does not integrate vertically sets its royalty equal to $-a/4$). We see that $\pi(\mathrm{N},\mathrm{VI}) > \pi(\mathrm{VI},\mathrm{VI})$ and $\pi(\mathrm{N},\mathrm{N}) > \pi(\mathrm{VI},\mathrm{N})$, thus, vertical separation is a dominant strategy for each firm.

contracts can specify only fees, each upstream firm has a strict incentive to have a *higher* number of downstream firms than its rival.[19] If in the simple example discussed above (with $s = 1$ and $n_B = 1$) only fees can be used, increasing n_A from 1 to 2 causes the total output of firm A's downstream firms to increase from $a/3$ to $a/2$, whereas that produced by B's downstream firms increases from $a/3$ to $a/4$. The price decreases from $a/3$ to $a/4$. Firm A's profit increases from $a^2/9$ to $a^2/8$ and, thus, firm A has an incentive to increase its number of firms from 1 to 2.

In the case of *royalty-only* contracts, each upstream firm prefers to increase its number of downstream firms, as long as the rival number of firms are not too large (see Saggi and Vettas, 1999). When fees are infeasible, the incentive to assume a more aggressive posture against the rival can be *reinforced* by the incentive to induce competitive behavior in the downstream market.[20] If in the example above ($s = 1$, $n_B = 1$) fees are infeasible, both firms' royalty rates decrease with an increase in n_A from 1 to 2 (in contrast to the fee-and-royalty case). Firm A's royalty decreases from $a/3$ to $7a/22$ and B's from $a/3$ to $3a/11$). The total output of firm A's downstream firms increases from $2a/9$ to $7a/22$ and that of B's decreases from $2a/9$ to $9a/44$. Firm A's profit increases from $2a^2/27$ to $49a^2/484$ and thus, in this case, firm A would increase the number of its firms from 1 to 2.

Finally, the assumption that the number of downstream firms is chosen *before* the contracts is crucial for our main result. If the number of firms is chosen at the same time as (or after) the terms of the contracts, both firms have an incentive to increase the number of downstream firms. In particular, *for given royalty rates* that are not too low, each firm has an incentive to have a larger number of downstream firms than its rival.[21] The intuition should be clear from the preceding analysis: The strategic incentive of a firm to decrease the number of its downstream divisions is present only if a choice of a rival's royalty rate follows.

6. Conclusion

This paper examines strategic interactions in vertically related markets where both intrabrand and interbrand competition may be present. We focus on contracts that specify a fixed fee and a per-unit payment (royalty). We characterize equilibrium contracts when each upstream firm contracts with multiple

[19] Our analysis provides one important qualification to this result; it holds only when $s = 1$. In Saggi and Vettas (1999), we show that for $0 < s < 1$ (i.e., when products are differentiated), each firm chooses to have $n^* > 1$ downstream firms, where $n^* = 1/\sqrt{1 - s^2}$.

[20] For example, when $s = 1$, if one upstream firm were to choose a small number of downstream firms (say one), the other upstream firm's best response is to have an *infinite* number of downstream firms.

[21] See Saggi and Vettas (1999) for details.

downstream and show how strategic interactions affect the design of these contracts. The basic tension is that higher royalties help control competition among own downstream firms while making them less aggressive against rival downstream firms.

Our main contribution lies in using the analysis of contracts as a building block to endogenize the number of downstream firms. Thus, the present paper creates a link between the work on strategic contracting and the work exploring the choice of downstream divisions. In contrast to previous literature that has emphasized the strategic benefit of having a large number of downstream firms (when contracts specify only a fixed fee), we show that the strategic incentives are reversed when upstream firms can also choose per-unit payments. In particular, under such contracts, each firm prefers to minimize the number of its downstream firms.[22] Our analysis is not purely of theoretical interest: contracts that specify both fees and royalties are frequently used in the real world.

Like most work in this area, our model assumes that upstream firms commit to their contracts and that these contracts are observable. Further, to highlight the strategic motives and to facilitate comparison with the literature, we have kept the model as simple as possible. Of course, we omit a number of factors that play an important role in vertical contracts, such as uncertainty. Encompassing such factors in our model could modify our results.

Acknowledgements

We wish to thank Xavier Vives (the editor) and two anonynous referees, Jim Anton, Jack Hughes, Ping Lin, Margaret Slade, and Juuso Välimäki for helpful comments and discussions, and Wen Zhou for excellent research assistance. All errors are ours.

References

Baye, M.R., Crocker, K., Ju, J., 1996. Divisionalization, franchising, and divestiture incentives in oligopoly. American Economic Review 86, 223–236.

Bonanno, G., Vickers, J., 1988. Vertical separation. Journal of Industrial Economics 36, 257–266.

Brander, J.A., Spencer, B.J., 1985. Export subsidies and international market share rivalry. Journal of International Economics 18, 83–100.

Corchón, L.C., 1991. Oligopolistic competition among groups. Economics Letters 36, 1–3.

[22] Kühn (1997) considers fully nonlinear wholesale schedules and finds that, with constant marginal costs, the number of downstream firms is irrelevant for strategic contracting. His result differs from ours because with fully nonlinear contracts upstream firms control not only the position but also the slope of the downstream firms' reaction functions. In general, the class of contracts that can be written should depend on the informational structure. See Rey and Tirole (1986) for informational assumptions underlying two-part tarrifs.

Dixit, A., 1983. Vertical integration in a monopolistically competitive industry. International Journal of Industrial Organization 1, 63–78.

Dixit, A., 1984. International trade policy for oligopolistic industries. Economic Journal 94, 1–16.

Fershtman, C., Judd, K., 1987. Equilibrium incentives in oligopoly. American Economic Review 77, 927–940.

Fudenberg, D., Tirole, J., 1984. The fat-cat effect, the puppy-dog ploy, and the lean and hungry look. American Economic Review 74, 361–366.

Gal-Or, E., 1991. Duopolistic vertical restraints. European Economic Review 35, 1237–1253.

Kamien, M., Tauman, Y., 1986. Fees versus royalties and the private value of a patent. Quarterly Journal of Economics 101, 471–491.

Katz, M.L., 1989. Vertical contractual relations. In: Schmalensee, R., Willig, R. (Eds.), Handbook of Industrial Organization, Vol. 1, North-Holland, Amsterdam (Chapter 11).

Katz, M.L., Shapiro, C., 1986. How to license intangible property. Quarterly Journal of Economics 101, 567–589.

Kühn, K., 1997. Nonlinear pricing in vertically related duopolies. Rand Journal of Economics 28, 37–62.

Lafontaine, F., Slade, M., 1997. Retail contracting: Theory and practice. Journal of Industrial Economics 45, 1–25.

Mathewson, G.F., Winter, R., 1984. An economic theory of vertical restraints. Rand Journal of Economics 15, 27–38.

McGuire, T.W., Staelin, R., 1983. An industry equilibrium analysis of down-stream vertical integration. Marketing Science 2, 161–191.

Polasky, S., 1992. Divide and conquer: On the profitability of forming independent rival divisions. Economic Letters 40, 365–371.

Rey, P., Stiglitz, J., 1995. The role of exclusive territories in producers' competition. Rand Journal of Economics 26, 431–451.

Rey, P., Tirole, J., 1986. The logic of vertical restraints. American Economic Review 76, 921–939.

Saggi, K., Vettas, N., 1999. On intrabrand and interbrand competition: The strategic role of fees and royalties. Working paper no. 2110, CEPR, London.

Salant, S.W., Switzer, S., Reynolds, R., 1983. Losses from horizontal merger: The effects of an exogenous change in industry structure on Cournot–Nash equilibrium. Quarterly Journal of Economics 48, 185–199.

Sklivas, S., 1987. The strategic choice of managerial incentives. Rand Journal of Economics 18, 452–458.

Vickers, J., 1985. Delegation and the theory of the firm. Economic Journal (suppl.) 95, 138–147.

Printed in the United States
by Baker & Taylor Publisher Services